UNGER'S

GUIDE
TO THE
BIBLE

UNGER'S

Preceding page: Mount Sinai—where Moses and Israel met God (EPA)
Left: Barren hills enfold the Dead Sea. (EPA)
Right: Rugged heights of historic Mount Sinai (EPA)
Opposite: John the Baptist stirred these Jordan waters. (R.B.)

Merrill F. Unger

GUIDE TO THE BIBLE

TYNDALE HOUSE PUBLISHERS, Inc.
Wheaton, Illinois

Library of Congress Catalog Card Number 74-79606. ISBN 8423-7790-5
Copyright © 1974 by Tyndale House Publishers, Inc., Wheaton, Illinois. All rights reserved.
Fourth printing, November 1978. Printed in the United States of America.

CONTENTS

Part Two: BIBLE DICTIONARY/*423*

*Animals, Customs, People, Places, and Scriptural Teachings of Zion—A to Z
Descriptions of Bible Life*

Part Three: BIBLE CONCORDANCE/*621*

PREFACE

The Bible is one of God's greatest gifts to mankind. Its revelation of truth concerning God and human redemption constitutes a priceless treasure. Its spiritual ministry to the race places it in a category of incomparable uniqueness and importance.

No small part of the unique importance of the Bible is the relevance of its spiritual message today. Yet it sprang out of a time and a culture far removed from our modern world. All of its content is separated from today's scene by many centuries, some parts of it by more than three millennia.

Does this fact make the Bible incomprehensible to modern man? No. The great truths of the Bible are omnitemporal. They transcend the centuries and the cultures out of which they rose.

Yet much of the Bible suffers from neglect and misunderstanding because its historical, geographical, social, and political backgrounds are obscure. Further, the message of the Bible often is interpreted without the light of the manners and customs of peoples in ancient Bible lands.

The first feature (Part One) of this *Guide to the Bible* is a survey, beginning with introductory insights concerning facts about the Bible, principles of interpretation, and the teachings of the Bible as a whole. Background studies in this section also include an evaluation of extra-biblical writings and an historical-archaeological review of the biblical period. Then follows a careful book-by-book survey of each Bible book, with emphasis on the main themes and the difficulties of proper interpretation.

Part Two consists of dictionary descriptions and illustrations enlightening the Bible student as to the meaning and significance of places, objects, people, and doctrines of the Bible. In both the survey and the dictionary, a simplified system of transliteration of the Hebrew is used in which the length of vowels is not indicated except in the case of an occasional long vowel.

Part Three is a handy concordance for ascertaining the location of particular words and verses in the Scriptures. This may be used to pursue study of a theme or a topic throughout the Bible.

Part Four presents colorful maps to orient the reader to Bible locations and topography. A knowledge of Bible geography greatly enhances the student's understanding of Bible events.

Unger's Guide to the Bible is sent forth with an earnest prayer that it will be a useful tool in unfolding the eternal truths of God's Word.

—*Merrill F. Unger*

Acknowledgments

Photograph sources are listed with each photo caption according to the following abbreviations:

EPA — Editorial Photocolor Archives, New York
HPS — Historical Pictures Service, Chicago
IGTO — Israel Government Tourist Office, Chicago
MPS — Matson Photo Service, Alhambra, Cal.
OI-UC — Oriental Institute, University of Chicago
RTHPL — Radio Times Hulton Picture Library, London
R.B. — Russ Busby, Billy Graham Evangelistic Association, Atlanta
UMP — University Museum, University of Pennsylvania, Philadelphia

The concordance is used by special arrangement with Zondervan Publishing House, Grand Rapids, Mich. All rights reserved.

The chronology chart on page 158 is reproduced by courtesy of Eerdmans Publishing Co., Grand Rapids, from Edwin R. Thiele's *The Mysterious Numbers of the Hebrew Kings.*

Upper: Cultures intersect in Israel's capital. (EPA)
Lower: Jewish farm boys in Judean hills (EPA)

Upper: A young carpenter toils in Nazareth. (R.B.)

Center left: St. Stephen's Gate opens Jerusalem's northeast wall. (R.B.)

Center right: Yemenite carries burden in Jerusalem street. (EPA)

Lower left: Fishermen still reap the Sea of Galilee. (R.B.)

Lower right: Shepherds tend their flock outside Bethlehem. (R.B.)

Clockwise from lower left:
In the Garden—of Gethsemane (R.B.)

God-garbed lilies of the field (R.B.)

Modern Haifa links Mount Carmel
  with Mediterranean Sea. (R.B.)

Akko (Acre) is ancient port on Bay of
  Haifa. (EPA)

Hebrew University library in
  Jerusalem (EPA)

Churches and mosques dot
  Bethlehem. (R.B.)

Beautiful for situation, the joy of the whole earth

...'s Mount Zion, the city of the great King.—Psalm 48:2

Upper left: Statues of the gods surveyed Athens from the Parthenon. (R.B.)

Upper right: Arch in Rome commemorates Titus' conquest of Jerusalem. (R.B.)

Lower: Zeus' forsaken temple in Athens (R.B.)

Upper: First-century aqueduct brought fresh water to Caesarea. (EPA)

Lower: Sphinx and pyramid perpetuate shadows of the pharaohs near Cairo. (R.B.)

Part One

BIBLE SURVEY

INTRODUCTORY INSIGHTS

What the Bible Is

The Bible is the revelation of God to fallen and sinful mankind. Preserved for us in written form, the Bible consists of 39 books of the Old Testament and 27 books of the New Testament. These 66 books together actually form one book, the Bible. This word is derived from the Latin word *biblia,* meaning "book" and stresses the unity of the theme and purpose of the Holy Scriptures.

Theme of the Bible

The Bible reveals the divine plan and purpose for the redemption of fallen man. Although it gives fleeting glimpses into eternity past, these matters are secondary. They serve mainly as background material to the central theme of the Bible — *the redemption of lost mankind.*

The Bible thus begins not with eternity but with time. The opening chapter of Genesis describes the renovation of a chaotic earth for the latecomer, man, God's last created order of beings. Sinless man's tragic response to the temptation of the Edenic serpent, the tool of Satan (Gen. 3:1-12), quickly sets the stage for the unfolding of the drama of human redemption.

The first pronouncement of the gospel in "the seed of the woman" (Gen. 3:15) anticipated the virgin-born Son of God (Isa. 7:14; Matt. 1:18-25; Luke 1:35; Gal. 4:4, 5). The Eternal Son, the Word, who was "with God and was God" (John 1:1), became incarnate in the Person of Jesus Christ (John 1:14). As God and man united in one

A devout Jew bows in prayer as an Israeli guard looks on at the Temple "Wailing Wall" recaptured from the Arabs. *(IGTO photo)*

Person, God became man to take away man's sin and to restore man to fellowship with himself (Heb. 1:1-3).

As the result of his sinless life, vicarious death, and bodily resurrection, Jesus Christ effected man's salvation from the curse of sin. The eventual result will be a sinless, blissful eternity enjoyed by unfallen angels and redeemed, glorified men (Heb. 12:22-24; Rev. 21:1-27). Satan, fallen angels, and Christ-rejecting men will be quarantined in eternal hell (Rev. 20:11-15), never to pollute God's sinless universe again.

Purpose of the Bible

The Bible was given 1) *to reveal God and his plan of salvation for fallen man,* so that man might trust Christ and be saved; 2) *to warn the unsaved of eternal hell,* the penalty of breaking God's moral law and rejecting Christ as the Redeemer (Gen. 2:17; Matt. 25:41; Rev. 20:11-15; and 3) *to reveal the total authority of the eternal moral law of God.* Both unsaved and saved mankind will be judged for their deeds, that is, the degree of response of each human being to the moral law.

The Bible thus reveals that there will be different degrees of punishment in hell (Rev. 20:11-15) as well as different degrees of reward in heaven.

Although the Bible has a message of salvation for all mankind and specific warnings for the unsaved, it is directed mainly to the saved, to inculcate in them Christian truths and principles of godly living and to reprove and correct in the case of error and sin, "that the man of God may be perfect (complete), throughly furnished unto all good works" (2 Tim. 3:17).

A portion of Isaiah from a ninth-century copy of the Septuagint translation (© *MPS*)

Importance of the Bible

In revealing God's saving grace in Christ to fallen mankind, and in warning the impenitent of the consequences of unbelief, the Bible is forever stamped as the most important and practical Book in the world. As God's inspired and authoritative revelation to man, the Bible stands in a category that is completely unique.

Other books are written by men; *God* is the Author of the Bible (2 Tim. 3:16). Other books contain man's wisdom; the Bible is a record of *God's* wisdom. Other books may *expound* God's revelation; the Bible *is* God's revelation. Viewing the Scriptures as the moral and spiritual guide of the human race, Abraham Lincoln aptly described the Bible as "the best gift that God has given to man."

Any book that tells a man how to know God and fellowship with him is a book of supreme importance. But the significance of the Bible goes beyond this. The Holy Scriptures open up man's destiny beyond the grave and set forth the status of each man in eternity (Rev. 20:11 – 22:21).

Languages of the Bible

Hebrew is the language of the Old Testament, except for a few small portions written in Aramaic (Dan. 2:4 – 7:28; Ezra 4:8 – 6:18; 7: 12-26; Jer. 10:11). Both Hebrew and Aramaic belong to the Semitic group of languages, spoken by the descendants of Noah's son Shem (Gen. 10:22).

Greek is the language of the New Testament – not the formal classical Greek of the intellectuals but the common or "koine" Greek, the universal speech that came into the Greco-Roman world following the conquests of Alexander the Great. This wonderfully expressive cosmopolitan tongue, widely spoken from 300 B.C. to A.D. 330, was the current speech of the common people and a providentially prepared vehicle for the New Testament revelation.

Christianity came with a message of hope for the poor, the uneducated, and the oppressed. The gospel of Christ was to be heralded to the masses. Thus God recorded the great revealed truths of human redemption in the simple language of the common people.

Origin of the Bible

The Bible came into existence as God revealed himself to human agents in such a manner that they recorded accurately and free from human error whatever was divinely disclosed to them (2 Tim. 3:15, 16; 2 Pet. 1:20, 21). This process, called *inspiration,* means that God breathed his Word into the minds of the human authors. They, in turn, under the Spirit's control wrote down for posterity what was given to them as a result of the divine inbreathing.

The result of inspiration is *a written revelation once for all given and thoroughly accredited.* Miracles, fulfilled prophecy, and redemptive power in human experience all attest the fact of the inspiration of Scripture. The written revelation, unique in its origin and preservation as inspired Scripture, constitutes the 39 books of the Old Testament and the 27 books of the New Testament. This divine library of 66 books is at the same time *one* book, with God as its one Author. Its one theme is Christ the Redeemer, and its one purpose is the record of human redemption.

The Old Testament came into being during the thousand-year period from 1400 B.C. (the time of Moses) to 400 B.C. (the time of Malachi). From the time of Malachi until the writing of the New Testament books, revelation and inspiration that produced canonical Scripture were in abeyance. The New Testament was produced during the last two-thirds of the first century, from about A.D. 33 to A.D. 100.

Thus the entire Bible was produced over a period of about a millennium and a half, from 1400 B.C. to A.D. 100. Each book had from its beginning the stamp of divine inspiration and authority, and each one was recognized by the faithful, even though their canonization in the familiar form we know today took centuries and is veiled in obscurity. (The canonicity of some Old Testament books, as Song of Solomon, Ecclesiastes, Esther, and Proverbs was questioned by some rabbis as late as the second century A.D.)

By A.D. 200 the New Testament books generally recognized as canonical were the same as we acknowledge today. However, not until around A.D. 400 in the West and A.D. 500 in the East were all questions of canonicity finally settled.

Inspiration and Authority of the Bible

A sound position on inspiration, which subscribes to the testimony of Scripture on this question, holds what is called the *plenary verbal* view. Such a view—that *"all* scripture" (that is, in the original copies or autographs) is "inspired by God" or "God-breathed" (2 Tim. 3:15) in its very words as well as its thoughts, and equally in all its parts—results in a *fully authoritative* Bible in and through which God himself speaks.

Authority accordingly resides in the divinely inspired Word itself interpreted by God's Spirit operating through Spirit-taught human agents. Orthodox Protestantism claims no authority other than canonical Scripture as the voice of the Holy Spirit. In contrast, the Church of Rome sets ecclesiastical tradition alongside the Holy Scriptures (including some extra-canonical Old Testament books) as the source of authority in matters of faith and morals.

Neo-orthodox and liberal segments of Protestantism deny final authority to Scripture as inerrant and infallible. Substituted is some other source of authority, such as conscience, experience, Christ speaking through the Holy Spirit, etc. The question of authority is of primary concern in today's religious world.

The Bible and Non-Christian Sacred Writings

Other religions also have their holy writings. Brahmanism, for example, is based on a collection of sacred writings known as the Veda, the holy Scriptures of the ancient Hindus. Taoism, one of the principal forms of Chinese religion, is founded on the writings of Lao-tse, a teacher of the sixth century B.C. Confucianism is a system of moral philosophy based on the writings of the Chinese teacher Confucius, of the fifth century B.C. The Koran is the holy book of Islam, claimed by millions of Muslims to contain the revelations of Allah (God) to Mohammed (died A.D. 632).

One question of supreme importance is the relation of the Christian Scriptures to the holy writings of non-Christian faiths. Is the Bible just another holy writing, or is it *uniquely the Word of God, divinely inspired and fully authoritative* in a sense different from all other literature (including the sacred literature of non-Christian religions), so that it is *the standard of truth by which all other faiths are to be measured and evaluated?* Negative, destructive, unbelieving "scholarship," employing many specious but unsound arguments, denies the Bible its unique inspiration and authority in the moral and spiritual realm and makes it merely one sacred book among several sacred books of the world.

This denial is a serious error because it undermines the foundations of revealed truth and opens the door to every heresy and false teaching instigated by demonic spirits (1 Tim. 4:1, 2; 1 John 4:1-3). It also fails to see the sublime superiority of divinely revealed truths over the treatment (if any) of these majestic themes in non-Christian holy writings. (The Hebrew Scriptures are regarded as an integral part of Christian Scripture, since they intrinsically form the foundation upon which the Christian revelation was given.)

This denial of the Bible's authority reduces Christianity to the status of "just another religion," robbing it of its uniqueness. For only the Bible shows lost humanity the one way of salvation through the vicarious death and glorious bodily resurrection of Jesus the Christ, the Savior of the world. Thus this denial nullifies the Christian gospel and the believer's hope of eternal life and glorification of the body through Christ's conquest of sin, death, and hell.

All of this means that by the denial of the full inspiration and authority of the Christian Scriptures, Christianity would become a religion originated and propagated by "spirits not of God" (1 John 4:1, 2) instead of by the Spirit of truth (John 16:12, 13), and would become, like non-Christian religions, a system of "doctrines of demons," that is, doctrines instigated by demon spirits (1 Tim. 4:1, 2).

Authenticity of the Bible Text

OLD TESTAMENT AUTHENTICITY

EXTERNAL EVIDENCE. The reception of the Hebrew Scriptures from the earliest times as the inspired Word of God and their early inclusion in the Sacred Canon are attestations of their authenticity. Added to this is the fact that the revelation of truth and the historical narrative they contain have been validated by Old Testament believers and by the unanimous witness of the Jewish nation.

The authenticity of the Old Testament has been further attested by the New Testament. The foundation of revelation established in the Old Testament supports the superstructure of truth revealed in the New Testament; likewise, the types and prophecies enumerated in the Old Testament are realized and fulfilled in the New Testament. The New Testament truly forms the capstone of the Old Testament revelation.

The Old Testament has been remarkably authenticated by the Jewish historian Flavius Josephus (A.D. 37-95) and by other extrabiblical writers, so that it may truly be said that secular history accredits the authenticity of the Old Testament.

Archeology, the handmaid of history, also adds its voice. Modern archeological research in Bible lands has had a truly phenomenal ministry not only in exploding the radical, negative, critical theories of destructive critics but in attesting, illustrating, and supplementing the biblical record and in verifying its accuracy in historical and general matters.

Archeology has in hundreds of cases shown the Old Testament to be correct, even in instances where the gravest critical doubts and denials had previously existed. Of course, this does not mean that archeology will necessarily solve every difficulty or remove every problem. In some cases it creates new problems instead of solving old ones. We must recognize that faith will always be a necessary prerequisite to *everyone* who approaches God's Word to drink of the water of salvation it offers. But it can truly be said that no archeological evidence, objectively and impartially interpreted, has ever proved the Scripture record to be in error. In the realm of authentic local color — in physical and geographical allusions, in social customs and religions, in political and linguistic affiliations — scientific research has demonstrated the accuracy of the Old Testament.

INTERNAL EVIDENCE. The theology of the Old Testament authenticates it as the Word of God. This is demonstrated in its *lofty doctrine of God,* who is presented as Creator and Redeemer, infinite in holiness, wisdom, and power; in its *realistic view of man,* showing him to be fallen, sinful, lost, separated from God, and under the sentence of death; in its *gospel of saving grace,* which offers redemption by the shed blood of the Lamb of God, the world's Savior to come; and in its *hope of life after death,* which looks forward to a redeemed humanity, a restored earth, and a regained paradise in a sin-cleansed eternal state. Its theology and theme are totally unique and incomparably superior to those of other pre-New Testament holy writings of the non-Christian religions of the world.

NEW TESTAMENT AUTHENTICITY

EXTERNAL EVIDENCE

Christian testimony. All during the first three centuries of Christianity, Christian writers residing in all parts of the civilized world testified to the life, death, resurrection, and ascension of Christ and the resulting gospel of grace.

Non-Christian testimony. The *Annals* of Tacitus, the *Biographies* of Seutonius, and the *Letters* of Pliny all attest the life and death of Jesus Christ under Pontius Pilate, the remarkable spread of the Christian gospel throughout the Roman world, and the vast numbers of converts who worshiped Christ as God and thereby suffered cruel persecution.

Archeological testimony. Evidence from the excavation of buried cities — coins, inscriptions, letters, papyri, etc. — all bear evidence of the truthfulness of the New Testament in general and of the historical narratives of Luke in the Book of Acts in particular. Allusions to such varied places as Antioch in Syria, Antioch in Pisidia, Cyprus, Iconium, Thessalonica, Philippi, Athens, Corinth, and Rome are found to be thoroughly correct. References to such details as imperial and senatorial provinces, Roman procurators and proconsuls, Greek "politarchs" and Asiatic aediles, and natives of pagan districts such as Lycaonia and the island of Malta invariably prove authentic. Even where critics have alleged discrepancies, mounting evidence continues to support the New Testament. Difficulties that persist await solution by future discoveries. Meanwhile the New Testament merits trust in its integrity, based upon its past record of vindication by archeological discovery.

INTERNAL EVIDENCE. The theology of the New Testament builds upon and combines with the theology of the Old Testament to authenticate the whole Bible as the Word of God. No other sacred literature in the world presents the doctrine of God, man's lost condition, the gospel of redemptive grace, the position and glorious destiny of those redeemed by Christ, and the fate of the unregenerate as does the New Testament in harmony with the Old Testament. In this realm the Bible is absolutely unique. No other literature can compare with it. It is God's revelation to fallen men—the *one and only* true revelation that shows lost man how to be saved. The efficacy of the New Testament as a regenerative dynamic attests it as the Word of God—God's way of salvation for fallen man.

Integrity of the Bible Text

THE OLD TESTAMENT HEBREW TEXT

EARLIEST EXTANT HEBREW MANUSCRIPTS. Before the sensational discovery of the Dead Sea Scrolls in 1947, the oldest available Hebrew manuscripts did not date much before A.D. 900, if even this early. The Leningrad Codex of the Prophets is dated A.D. 916. An undated British Museum document of the Pentateuch is possibly somewhat earlier, as well as a manuscript in the Cambridge University Library. The earliest manuscript of the complete Hebrew Bible does not date earlier than the eleventh century.

THE MASORETIC TEXT OF THE HEBREW SCRIPTURES. These pre-Dead Sea Scroll manuscripts and fragments represent the traditionally transmitted Hebrew text of the Bible as it emerged from the Masoretic period (about A.D. 500-900). The Masoretes were learned rabbis who adhered rigidly to the traditional Hebrew text. They standardized and "froze" the text to give it the form it had had for many centuries. This same form has remained with us all through the era of early and modern printing. The task of the Masoretes or "traditionalists" was to determine the exact text transmitted to them from all available sources and to solidify it in an unalterable form, so that it might be passed on to future generations without change. One feature of this text is that it contains vowel signs and accentual marks intended to standardize pronunciation of the Old Testament Hebrew language.

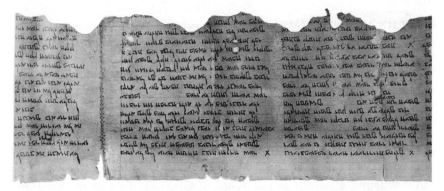

A portion of the famed Dead Sea Scrolls in an Israeli museum (*Russ Busby photo*)

THE DEAD SEA SCROLLS AND THE HEBREW TEXT. The discovery of these manuscripts revolutionized scholarly approach to the text of the Old Testament. These scrolls are handwritten manuscripts that date 800 years before the Masoretic apparatus and approximately a thousand years before the oldest previously available documents! Consequently they cast a dramatically different light on the critical allegation that all divergent texts had been suppressed about A.D. 100. But the greatest significance of the Dead Sea manuscripts is that they controvert the former critical contention that the original form of the ancient autographs was irretrievably lost. Instead, they provide remarkable confirmation of the reliability of the transmission of the currently accepted text. The Isaiah Scroll from Qumran, for example, contains scribal phenomena peculiar to an early period, but wording strikingly in accord with the much later standard Masoretic text, the text of modern Hebrew Bibles.

The new manuscript discoveries from Qumran vindicate the reverential attitude of the Jews toward their Holy Scriptures and their meticulous care in transmitting them accurately. As the ancient Jewish historian Josephus said, "We have given practical proof of our reverence for our Scriptures. For, although such long ages have now passed, no one has ventured either to add, or to remove, or to alter a syllable; and it is an instinct with every Jew, from the day of his birth, to regard them as the decrees of God, to abide by them, and, if need be, cheerfully to die for them" (*Against Apion I,* pp. 179-180, Loeb Edition.)

THE SAMARITAN PENTATEUCH. This valuable witness to the reliability of the text of the Old Testament dates from the fifth century B.C. and represents a form of the books of Genesis, Exodus, Leviticus, Numbers, and Deuteronomy that was transmitted by the separatist Samaritan religious sect at Mount Gerizim (near ancient Shechem) in complete independence from the Hebrew text of the Jews. When the first copy of the Samaritan Pentateuch came to the attention of modern scholars in 1616, great contributions to textual criticism were expected of it. Long and careful study by scholars, however, has resulted in one basic conclusion: this independent text strikingly attests the textual authenticity of the Pentateuch. The text does contain numerous variations in spelling and grammar, but these are apparently due to the preservation of North Israelite dialectal peculiarities and actually form a valuable witness to the substantial purity of the Hebrew text as preserved in the Masorete tradition.

THE GREEK SEPTUAGINT. Sometimes called "the Version of the Seventy," the Septuagint is a translation of the Hebrew Old Testament into Greek, the common language of the civilized world of the day. It was executed about 250 to 150 B.C. and represents, so far as we know, the oldest translation not only of the Scriptures but of any book into any other language. Despite variations between the Septuagint and the Hebrew text, especially in some of the prophetic books and the writings (Psalms, Proverbs, Job, Song of Solomon, Ruth, Lamentations, Ecclesiastes, Esther, Daniel, Ezra, Nehemiah, and Chronicles), there is substantial agreement overall, thereby attesting the careful and accurate transmission of the Hebrew text.

Important manuscripts of the Greek version of the Old Testament are written in large, separate capital letters called *uncials* (from the Latin *uncia,* "an inch," and *uncialis,* "large") in distinction to later *cursives* (from the Latin *curro,* "run, flow") written in small "flowing" script (and less valuable critically). About 170 uncial manuscripts have been discovered. The oldest and most important of these are *Codex*

Vaticanus (B), dating about A.D. 325 to 350, *Codex Alexandrinus* (A), dating about A.D. 450, *Codex Sinaiticus* (Aleph), belonging to the late fourth century, and *Codex Ephraemi Rescriptus* (C), from the fifth century.

THE TARGUMS. Like the Septuagint, the Targums were rendered from the original Hebrew texts. However, unlike the Septuagint, the Targums are not strict translations. They are free paraphrastic renderings of the Hebrew Bible into the Aramaic language (which from the time of Ezra began to supplant Hebrew as the common tongue of the people—see Neh. 8:8). The *Targum of Onkelos* (Aquila) is the oldest and best Targum of the Pentateuch and attests the reliability of the Hebrew text. The *Targum of Jonathan* on the Prophets is more paraphrastic and free. The *Targums on the Hagiographa* (the third section of the Hebrew Scriptures) are late and have less value than the Targums of Onkelos and Jonathan. There is one Targum of Psalms, Job, and Proverbs, another of the rolls (Song of Solomon, Ruth, Lamentations, Ecclesiastes, and Esther), another of Chronicles, and another of Esther. In elucidating the meaning of the language in the original Hebrew text, the Targums constitute a valuable witness to the authentic nature of the text.

THE NEW TESTAMENT GREEK TEXT

General evidence for the text of the New Testament comes from four sources: manuscripts, lectionaries, patristic quotations, and ancient versions.

MANUSCRIPTS. Manuscripts of all or part of the New Testament constitute the most important source for establishing the text of the New Testament. These are of such antiquity and quality that it can be said that no work handed down to us from classical writers has a better attested text than the Greek New Testament. Several manuscripts of the Roman poet Virgil (70 to 19 B.C.) claim an antiquity as high as the fourth or fifth century, but in general the available manuscripts of the secular classics date from the ninth to the fifteenth centuries.

As in the case of the Greek version of the Old Testament, the earliest manuscripts of the New Testament are uncials, written in large letters on fine vellum (the highly prepared skins of calves or kids). The uncials date earlier than the ninth century while the cursives date from the ninth century to the fifteenth century. After the fifteenth century, printing became the dominant method of transmitting Scripture.

Of uncial manuscripts of the New Testament, somewhat more than a hundred are known, while of cursives some 2,533 have now been cataloged. While generally less important than uncials, cursive manuscripts may possess high value if they happened to be copied from an early uncial manuscript. The mass of manuscript evidence available for the New Testament is truly overwhelming. This becomes all the more striking when we remember that ten or twelve manuscripts, usually modern, are all that exist for determining the text of most classical authors!

Of the 241 uncials that appear in the latest official lists, the following are the most important: 1) *Codex Sinaiticus* (Aleph), fourth century; discovered by Count Tischendorf in 1859 at Saint Catherine's Convent on Mount Sinai. The New Testament is complete, the Old Testament incomplete; 2) *Codex Alexandrinus* (A), fifth century; donated to Charles I in 1627 and now in the British Museum. Neither the Old Testament nor the New Testament is complete. Of the latter are missing Matthew 1:1-25; 6:1-34; John 6:50 — 8:52; 2 Corinthians 4:13 — 12:6; 3) *Codex Vaticanus* (B) fourth century; lacks 1 and 2 Timothy, Titus, and Philemon. Hebrews 9:14 to the end of Revelation have been supplied by a much later hand (fifteenth century). In the Old Testament it offers on the whole the best text of the Septuagint; 4) *Codex Ephraemi Rescriptus* (C), fifth century; in addition to fragments of the Septuagint it contains about three-fifths of the New Testament. It is a palimpsest; the original writing was erased in the twelfth century and Greek translations of Ephraem Syrus' works were written over it; 5) *Codex Bezae* (D), sixth century; discovered by Theodore Beza (1519-1605), the French theologian and textual scholar, in the Monastery of Saint Irenaeus at Lyons in 1562, and presented by him to the University of Cambridge. For the text of the Gospels and the Acts this manuscript in both Greek and Latin is of fundamental significance; 6) *Codex Claromontanus* (D^p), sixth century; contains all the Pauline Epistles in Greek and Latin and is in the Paris Library; 7) *Codex Laudianus*, (E^a), sixth century; contains the Acts in Greek and Latin; finally fell into the hands of Archbishop Lau, who presented it to the Bodleian Library, Oxford, in 1636; 8) *Codex Coislinianus* (H^p), sixth century; consists of 43 leaves of Paul's Epistles, scattered among a number of libraries in France, Russia, Italy, etc.; 9) *Codex Cyprius* (K), ninth century; one of the most important of late uncials. It contains the Gospels (except Matt. 4:22 — 5:14; 28:17-20; Mark 10:16-20;

John 21:15-25). It agrees remarkably with the quotations found in Origen and with Codex Vaticanus.

LECTIONARIES. The lectionaries are the service books that contain the lessons to be read on every day of the calendar year and of the church year. Selections were made from the Gospels and from the Epistles. The number of lectionaries that are now included in the official catalog of manuscripts is 1,838. They date from the fourth to the seventeenth century. Recent scholarship has established the value of the lectionaries in the study of the history of the transmission of the text, and these sources will in the future play an ever-increasing role of importance in textual research of the New Testament.

PATRISTIC QUOTATIONS. Quotations of the New Testament by the Church Fathers are important for the study of the text because the time and place of their writing can be definitely established. The *Index Patristicus* compiled by J. W. Burgon and housed in the British Museum contains 86,489 quotations. But even this is incomplete. Moreover, the problem of loose or paraphrastic quotation complicates the usefulness of this source of information. Quotations are of value only from a critical edition and when supported by other good evidence.

Ancient Versions of the Bible

The most significant versions for the study of the text of the New Testament are those which were executed before the year 1000 and which are *direct* translations from the Greek. The most important of these are in a) *Latin* (Old Latin and the Vulgate), b) *Syriac* (Old Syriac, Peshitta, Philoxenian, and Palestinian), c) *Coptic* (Sahidic and Bohairic), d) *Armenian*, e) *Old Georgian*, f) *Old Slavic*, and g) *Gothic*.

OLD TESTAMENT VERSIONS

THE SEPTUAGINT. The Greek term *septuaginta*, meaning "seventy," refers to the seventy elders who are said to have translated the Torah (the Pentateuch) into Greek. Later the name was applied to the whole Old Testament as it was gradually translated into Greek (about 250-150 B.C.). The Septuagint is also known as the *Alexandrian Version* because it was made at Alexandria, Egypt, for use by the large Jewish population there. The Septuagint is the oldest and most important translation of the Hebrew Old Testament. The Pentateuch, which was translated first, is carefully and literally executed; the Prophets are somewhat less literally translated, and the Writings are the least literal of all.

In the course of centuries the Septuagint became corrupt through repeated copyings and required revision. A notable revision was undertaken by Origen in the third century A.D. The earliest Septuagint documents (Codex Sinaiticus, Codex Alexandrinus, Codex Vaticanus, and Codex Ephraemi Rescriptus) antedate the pre-Dead Sea Scroll Hebrew manuscripts (early tenth century A.D.) by more than a half-century. Despite the exciting biblical manuscript discoveries made since 1947, the Septuagint still remains the earliest available witness to the original Old Testament text (except for the Samaritan text of the Pentateuch). However, for a number of reasons the Septuagint's critical value in determining the pure Hebrew text is somewhat limited.

AQUILA'S VERSION. Made about A.D. 130, this was a slavishly literal Greek translation intended to substitute for the Septuagint for Greek-speaking Jews. Although making the text almost incomprehensible, the extreme literalness of the version does give it value for textual criticism. Aquila had become a Jewish proselyte and had received a thorough training under the noted Rabbi Akiba, thus enabling him to accomplish the translation.

THEODOTIAN'S VERSION. Early in the second century, at about the time Aquila made his version, Theodotian, an Ebionite or Judaizing Christian, revised the Septuagint to bring it into harmony with the Hebrew text. He was not a disciple of Rabbi Akiba nor a slavish literalist. His version became popular among Christians and his rendering of Daniel prevailed over the weak Septuagint version.

SYMMACHUS' VERSION. This was a revision of Aquila's version in reaction against the frequent incomprehensibly literal renderings of that translation. It was executed with the aid of the Septuagint and Theodotian and was aimed at the sense rather than the letter.

ORIGEN'S VERSION. Origen (A.D. 185-254) undertook to purify the text of the Septuagint, which had become woefully corrupt in his day. He accomplished this in a six-column textual apparatus called the *Hexapla* ("sixfold"). The first column was Hebrew. The other five columns were Greek, as follows: Hebrew rendered in Greek letters, Aquila's Version, Symmachus' Version, revised Septuagint, and Theodotian's Version. The important fifth column (Origen's revised Septuagint) was recopied repeatedly, but when it became separated from the footnotes and textual apparatus it lost its critical value. However, a valuable Syriac translation of part of the fifth column with critical notes, called the Syro-Hexaplaric Version, has survived in fragments.

VERSIONS OF THE WHOLE BIBLE

THE SYRIAC VERSION. Evidently produced in the second century, this version enjoyed wide circulation, becoming known by the ninth century as the *Peshitta,* that is, the "simple" or "plain" version. The translators were well acquainted with Hebrew, a sister Semitic tongue of Syriac. Despite the influence of the Septuagint, the books of the Old and New Testament are rendered with precision. At the beginning of the seventh century the Syriac New Testament was revised by Thomas of Harkel. The resulting *Harcleian Syriac,* like Aquila's Greek Version, is marked by extreme literality.

THE PALESTINIAN SYRIAC. This was another Syriac version apparently made for "Hebrew" Christians in distinction to Hellenists (Greek-speaking Jews—Acts 6:1). It survives only in fragments in a tongue resembling Aramaic.

THE OLD LATIN VERSIONS. Apparently several of these existed to accommodate Latin-speaking Christians, especially in North Africa, where the Church was Latin-speaking from the outset. Another Old Latin Version appeared in Europe and was superseded by a revised text known as the *Italian.* In the Old Testament these versions were made from the then-current unrevised Septuagint text.

THE LATIN VULGATE. The Old Latin (Italian) version was succeeded by the Vulgate. This important version was executed by Eusebius Hieronymus, better known as Jerome, who mastered both Hebrew and Greek in order to translate the Bible into the language of the day. Jerome's Latin Bible in its completed form was a composite work. It consisted of the following: the Old Testament, except the Psalms, from the *original* Hebrew; the Psalms in the Old Latin revised with the aid of Origen's Hexaplaric text of the Septuagint; the Gospels, consisting of the Old Latin revised from the original Greek; and finally, the rest of the New Testament more superficially revised. The Apocrypha were added, but they were not considered a part of the Canon.

A path of Paul, the Appian Way, into Rome *(Russ Busby photo)*

The Latin Vulgate was executed between A.D. 383 and 405. From A.D. 500 to 1500, when Latin held sway as the *lingua franca* of Western Europe, Jerome's translation was *the* Bible of the Western World. In the thirteenth century it became known as "the Vulgate," i.e. "the Common Version" of the people. In 1228 it was divided into chapters, and in 1455, after the printing press was invented, it was the *first* book ever printed in movable type. It was revised during 1590 to 1592 for use as the standard text of the Roman Catholic Church. In 1907 work on a modern critical edition was begun, with various books appearing since 1926.

OTHER VERSIONS. Besides the Syriac and the Latin, many other versions were made at different times and in various lands. These include the Gothic, the Armenian, the Arabic, the Ethiopic, and the Coptic (Egyptian). These are for the most part independent testimonies and not mere copies of some one common original, as their verbal differences demonstrate. However, their complete agreement in all essential points attests the care with which the Sacred Scriptures have been prepared and transmitted. More important, these ancient versions establish the integrity of the Bible more satisfactorily than that of any other ancient book.

Modern Translations of the Bible

ANGLO-SAXON VERSIONS

Aldhelm, Bishop of Sherborne (eighth century), is said to have translated the Psalter into Anglo-Saxon verse. In the tenth century Alfred the Great reputedly did the same. The famous Vespasian Psalter appeared about A.D. 900. Aelfric at the end of the tenth century produced a version of the Pentateuch and Joshua in West Saxon, and the West Saxon version of the Gospels appeared A.D. 1000. Anglo-Saxon Homilies give evidence of a native version of the Scriptures prior to the Norman Conquest.

ENGLISH VERSIONS

Wycliffe's Bible, a translation into English from the Latin Vulgate, appeared in 1382.

The style, tone, and to a large extent the wording of the English Bible were settled permanently by William Tyndale. *Tyndale's New*

Testament appeared in 1525 and Tyndale's Pentateuch in 1530. His last revision (the true primary version of the English New Testament) appeared during 1534 to 1535.

The first printed version of the entire English Bible was the *Coverdale Bible* (1535), translated by Miles Coverdale from Luther's Bible and the Vulgate.

Next in order of importance after Tyndale's publication was *Matthew's Bible* (1537), giving the results of Tyndale's latest work. It consisted of Tyndale's translation to the end of 2 Chronicles and Tyndale's New Testament of 1534 and 1535. All the rest was taken from Coverdale's Bible of 1535 and was actually the first "Authorized Version," being published by Grafton and Whitchurch of London with the king's license.

The Great Bible (1539) was a revision of the Coverdale Bible of 1535.

The Whittingham New Testament (1557) was the first English testament divided into verses.

The Geneva Bible (1560) was printed in Geneva, Switzerland, and was the first complete Bible divided into verses.

The Bishop's Bible (1568) was a revision of the Great Bible of 1539, named after the nine bishops and scholars who produced it at the suggestion of Archbishop Parker. Its text as printed in the 1602 edition was taken as the basis of the Authorized Version of 1611.

The Rheims Version of the New Testament (1582), an accurate and literal translation of the Vulgate made at Rheims, exerted a very powerful influence on the King James Version of 1611.

The King James Version (1611), commonly called the *Authorized Version* and which became *the* English Bible for the past three-and-one-half centuries, was never actually officially authorized by either King James or the church. It was simply appointed to be read in the churches in the place of the Bishop's Bible.

The Revised Version (1881-85) was a revision of the Authorized Version of 1611 based on a literal translation of the Hebrew and Greek texts by 65 English scholars. It did not capture public fancy.

The American Standard Version (1901) was issued by a group of American scholars as a revision of the Revised Version of 1885, including preferred readings and format changes. It never supplanted the Authorized Version for popular use, but it was used fairly widely in scholarly circles.

The New Testament in Modern Speech (1903), by Richard F. Weymouth, was one of the first translations rendered in truly modern

English. The work enjoyed a fair measure of popularity for several years. It has been revised by others since its original publication.

The New Testament: A Translation in the language of the People (1937), by Charles B. Williams, is generally well regarded by scholars but has achieved only moderate acceptance with the reading public.

The Revised Standard Version (1952; New Testament only, 1946) was a revision of the *American Standard Version* by mostly liberal scholars. This work was intended to become the standard text for public and personal use. Despite certain excellencies of translation it never achieved this goal, though it has been fairly popular among certain ecclesiastical groups.

The New Testament in Modern English (1958), by J. B. Phillips, was actually a loose translation or paraphrase, and had great appeal to the reading public.

The Holy Bible: The Berkeley Version in Modern English (1959) has been revised and renamed *The Modern Language Bible*. Originally the work of Gerrit Verkuyl in the New Testament and twenty conservative American scholars in the Old Testament, the work has been revised carefully to provide uniformity of style. It is now generally regarded as fairly readable without being excessively paraphrastic and reasonably accurate without being overly literal.

The New Testament—An Expanded Translation (1961), by Kenneth S. Wuest, was designed as a precise translation of the Greek. The work uses as many English words as the translator deemed necessary to convey the meaning of the original. Though rather wordy for this reason, the translation has become moderately popular with serious Bible students.

The Amplified Bible (1965; New Testament only, 1958) was undertaken by a group of unspecified translators headed by Frances Siewert. This version seeks to clarify the meaning of the original languages by including explanatory words and phrases in the immediate text of the translation. The translation has enjoyed widespread popularity.

Good News for Modern Man: The New Testament in Today's English Version (1966) is a semi-paraphrase translated by Robert G. Bratcher and sponsored by the American Bible Society. It has been one of the most widely distributed of all modern versions of the New Testament.

The New English Bible (1970; New Testament only, 1961) was prepared as a totally new translation by a group of British scholars under the direction of C. H. Dodd. This translation, like the earlier

Revised Standard Version, was intended to dominate public and private use of the Bible. While it did not reach this goal, it is enjoying a steadily widening distribution.

The New American Standard Bible (1971; New Testament only, 1960-63) is a careful revision of the American Standard Version (1901) by a group of 58 unnamed conservative scholars. It is a fairly literal translation, with up-to-date diction, and is becoming recognized as a valuable study version.

The Living Bible (1971; portions published earlier) is a thoroughly evangelical paraphrase produced by Kenneth N. Taylor and reviewed by various scholars. It has become established as one of the most popular versions of recent times.

Principles of Interpreting the Bible

The Bible is to be interpreted as the divine-human book it is. As a *divine* book it is to be recognized as a God-given revelation, inspired in its thoughts and in its words by God's Spirit, imbued with intrinsic authority as God's voice, and understood only by complete dependence of the regenerated expositor upon the tuition of the Holy Spirit himself (John 16:12, 13). As a *human* book the Bible is to be interpreted like any other piece of literature, using the rules of grammar, the facts of history, and the principles of sound logic.

The Bible is to be interpreted as a coherent and coordinated body of revealed truth. Although it consists of 66 books, these must be seen not as disconnected entities but as *one* book comprising *a unified whole with a definite theme and consummation,* just like any other orderly and well-written narrative. The theme of Scripture is *human redemption.* The principal character is *the world's Redeemer,* Jesus Christ, God incarnate. Everything in the Old Testament that precedes his incarnation points to this grand event and its outworking in human redemption. The culmination of the Bible's story of redemption is *a sinless universe* peopled with unfallen angels and redeemed and glorified humanity. The only isolation ward is Gehenna, the lake of fire (Rev. 20:11-15), reserved for fallen angels, demons, and unregenerate men (Matt. 25:41). Thus the Bible has a *definite plan* and a *clear purpose,* which must be ascertained for correct interpretation.

The Bible is to be interpreted in the light of its overall plan and purpose. The Bible's plan and purpose must be determined by inductive logic (reasoning from the particulars to the generalizations) and not by *deductive* logic (reasoning from generalizations to the particulars). Thus it is the business of the interpreter to allow the Spirit of God to say freely through the human author exactly what he intends to convey rather than what the interpreter thinks he ought to say. This is another way of saying that *every biblical text must be interpreted in its context*—both in its immediate connection with the chapter and book in which it occurs and also in its general connection with the overall plan and purpose of the Bible.

The Bible is to be interpreted literally as the inspired Word of God. The literal method seeks to arrive at the precise meaning of the language of each of the Bible writers as is required by the laws of grammar, the facts of history, and the common-sense logic used in communication between rational creatures. This means of arriving at the normal, original meaning of each Bible text does not entail a wooden literalism that disregards figurative language or symbology, nor does it preclude spiritual applications of the literal interpretation of the passage.

The literal interpreter takes the Scriptures at face value. He honors the Word by treating it honestly, as one would treat any piece of literature. He realizes that Scripture is its own best illustrator, and so constantly compares Scripture with Scripture, seeking the *one* true interpretation of each passage, following the rule of thumb that the simplest interpretation is to be preferred when there is a choice.

The Bible is to be expounded under one consistent method of interpretation. The literal method must be applied to the *entire* Bible—to the prophetic as well as to the nonprophetic portions. Premillennial interpretation is consistent in applying inductive logic in the literal interpretation of all Scripture. It allows the details to dictate the generalizations.

Time-Periods of the Bible

NECESSITY OF TIME DISTINCTIONS

The biblical story of human redemption, like any other story of quality, has plot, plan, and purpose, and hence has necessary time distinctions to suit these. A simple illustration will demonstrate this. Suppose a biography is written about a particular person, depicting his life as a boy, as a married man with a family, and then as a widower, deprived of his wife and children by their sudden and tragic death. In quoting and interpreting what this man said and did, his words and deeds must obviously be placed in *the time-period* to which they belong. To ignore such time-periods and to quote his words and deeds without relationship to the time context and circumstances under which they were uttered would violate common-sense principles of correct interpretation and would result in biographical havoc.

May not the story of human redemption be expected to have time periods similar to any other logically written story? Can it be correctly interpreted apart from the time context of its texts? Can its various eras be denied or ignored without violating its message, distorting its meaning, and dissipating its deserved respect? Yet this is exactly how the story of redemption is treated by many who attempt to interpret the Bible!

THE COVENANTS AND ADMINISTRATIONS OF SCRIPTURE

A time-period in the story of human redemption is called an *era, economy, dispensation,* or *administration.* During each such period man is given a specific revelation of God's will for him in a relationship of responsibility called a *covenant.* God monitors man's response to his divinely-revealed covenant for the duration of each such time-period. God has seen fit to make several important covenants with man, each of which relates to man's moral and spiritual history on the earth. Each covenant introduces a new administration having a time element and expiring at a certain period. The administrations which correspond to nine important covenants of Scripture can be arranged as follows.

THE EDENIC COVENANT AND THE ADMINISTRATION OF INNOCENCE. This covenant was given to Adam and Eve in Eden, before the fall of man, and inaugurated the Administration of Innocence (Gen. 1:28-30; 2:15-17). The conditions of this covenant were 1) *to populate the earth* with an unfallen race; 2) *to subdue the earth to man's needs* by learning to control the forces of nature; 3) *to have dominion over the animals* (Psa. 8:3-9); 4) *to live on a vegetable diet;* 5) *to till the Garden* (seen as delightful light work); 6) *to abstain from eating of the tree of the knowledge of good and evil.* Man was innocent, not knowing what sin was. Had he obeyed God, he would have remained forever free of sin. Instead, he disobeyed, broke the Covenant, and learned what sin was; 7) *to avoid death.* The punishment of disobedience and loss of innocence was *threefold death* (Gen. 2:17): *immediate spiritual death* (estrangement from God and loss of fellowship with

God); *gradual physical death* (note that Adam lingered on for 930 years); and *eventual eternal death* in everlasting separation from God in Gehenna. Adam was delivered from eternal death by God's grace in view of Christ's redemptive work (Gen. 3:21).

Had God not intervened and instituted a new covenant, Adam and Eve would have met with instant physical death as well as irrevocable spiritual and eternal death as the penalty of their disobedience. Thus the Edenic Covenant was abrogated completely and the Administration of Innocence ended.

THE ADAMIC COVENANT AND THE ADMINISTRATION OF CONSCIENCE AND MORAL RESPONSIBILITY. This covenant was given to Adam and Eve in their fallen state, and included the whole fallen race descended from them (Gen. 3:14-19). It introduced the Administration of Conscience and Moral Responsibility. Although man had lost his innocence and had become a sinner, God remained unchangeably holy and thus required his creatures, though fallen, to honor their Creator by keeping his moral law written in man's heart and conscience. Man, in token of his inability to do this in the degree necessary to satisfy God's holiness, was required to approach God by animal sacrifice, showing that he appealed to God's grace (eventually to be manifested in Christ's atoning death – see Genesis 3:21; 4:4, 5). Hence, the Adamic Covenant governs the fallen race and is operative upon all unglorified men, whether redeemed or unredeemed, as long as they are on the earth. Thus the Administration of Conscience and Moral Responsibility *overlaps and spans all succeeding administrations.* As a specific period of testing, it ended in the Noahic flood, God's divine judgment on man's thorough immorality.

The Adamic Covenant embodied a fourfold "curse," involving the serpent, the woman, the man, and the earth, and operative throughout the entire Administration of Conscience and Moral Responsibility.

The Serpent. Satan's agent in the temptation was changed from a beautiful, upright, intelligent creature to a loathsome, crawling reptile.

The Woman. Her state was altered in three particulars: *multiplied conception* would occasion a population explosion, as the young race became very productive to "fill" the earth; *sorrowful motherhood* would occasion the peril, pain, and anguish of childbirth; *the headship of man* would entail the loss of equality which woman had by creation, because she caused man's fall (see 1 Tim. 2:12-15).

The Man. The earth was cursed because of his disobedience. In contrast to the delight it had been to cultivate the Garden, now man must wrest a living from the soil by sweat and toil, which would exhaust him and finally eventuate in his physical death.

The Earth. From the moment man disobeyed God and became a sinner, the ground was cursed with "thorns" and "thistles." Weeds, blight, drought, and everything that would make food-getting and livelihood difficult would appear in an earth under the curse of man's sin.

The Promise. The Adamic Covenant was without conditions, and embodied a *promise* to offset the *curse*. This promise was the glorious prediction that "the seed of the woman" (the virgin-born Christ) would bruise "the serpent's head" (Satan) and redeem fallen mankind from Satan's power and from sin, death, and hell (Gen. 3:15).

THE NOAHIC COVENANT AND THE ADMINISTRATION OF HUMAN GOVERNMENT. This Covenant was enacted with Noah. As the Adamic Covenant extends to the entire fallen race in Adam, so the Noahic Covenant extends to the entire race descended from Noah (Gen. 8:20 – 9:17). The Administration of Human Government which it initiated governs antediluvian man, and, like the Administration of Conscience and Moral Responsibility which it overlaps, is operative so long as fallen, unglorified mankind exists on the earth. Hence it too spans *all* succeeding ages in time, till the creation of the new heaven and new earth (2 Pet. 3:7-13; Rev. 21:1 – 22:5). However, as a *specific period of testing*, this administration ended in the judgment upon sinful man's first attempt to establish a world state in opposition to the divine rule. This judgment took the form of the confusion of languages at Babel (Gen. 11:1-9) and God's abandonment of mankind at large, "giving them up" to universal idolatry (Rom. 1:24, 26, 28).

The fact that the Noahic Covenant is coterminous with the Adamic Covenant shows that the administrations, although successive, are *not* necessarily mutually exclusive. Rather, they overlap other administrations in a number of cases. This is true because the particular covenant which governs a certain administration still continues in force despite the fact that another covenant, introducing a new administration, may be instituted. Failure to see this has produced much of the present hostility against scriptural time-distinctions.

The Noahic Covenant, in force till the establishment of the new heaven and new earth, contains the following provisions. 1) *Protection of the earth from another universal catastrophe* such as the flood (Gen. 8:21; 9:11). This will be operative until the renovation of the earth by fire (2 Pet. 3:10-13) in preparation for eternity (Rev. 21:1). The sign of the covenant is the rainbow (Gen. 9:12-16), the symbol of the orderly ongoing of nature (Gen. 8:22). This sign intimates that the deluge was a *supernatural* catastrophe, never to be repeated in time (Gen. 8:22). 2) *Institution of human government.* Since the threat of divine judgment in the form of another flood had been removed, the Noahic Covenant instituted the principle of human government to check the rise of lawlessness. Man was made responsible to protect the sanctity of human life, even to the extent of administering capital punishment (Gen. 9:5, 6; cf. Rom. 13:1-7). 3) *Reaffirmation of the conditions of life of fallen man as contained in the Adamic Covenant.* This is to be expected, since the two covenants overlap each other and are coterminous. Noah and his descendants were to multiply and fill the earth (Gen. 9:1) and to dominate the animal creation (Gen. 9:2). Animal food, however, was added to man's diet in the Noahic Covenant (Gen. 9:3, 4). Apparently this had been restricted from man's previous vegetable diet.

THE ABRAHAMIC COVENANT AND THE ADMINISTRATION OF PROMISE. This covenant was originally made with Abraham (Gen. 12:1-3) and was confirmed to Isaac (Gen. 26:1-5) and Jacob (Gen. 28:10-15). Until the call of Abraham, the race had been a unit. There was neither Jew nor Gentile. By Abraham's time, however (about 2000 B.C.), the race had become wholly idolatrous. To purge off a pure remnant to be a witness to the worship of the one true God, God called a descendant of Shem to form a separated people. Israel was to become a witness to all other nations of the blessing of serving the one true God and looking for his promised Redeemer.

The Abrahamic Covenant introduced the Administration of Promise. The promise of the Redeemer, given to the entire race in Adam (Gen. 3:15) but utterly lost sight of through idolatry, was now revived. Abraham and his descendants became heirs of the promise of redemption. *As a specific period of testing* the Administration of Promise ended with the Israelites' acceptance of the Law and Mosaic Covenant at Sinai (Exod. 19:8). However, the conditions of this covenant span all succeeding ages, like those of the previous Administrations of Moral Responsibility and Human Government. Although the covenant centers in the nation of Israel, its blessings reach out to all mankind.

The Abrahamic Covenant, in force till the new heaven and earth, contains the following promises, all of which are *unconditional.* 1) *Blessings through Abraham's posterity. The nation Israel* is privileged to provide the Messiah-Redeemer and to inherit a specific territory forever (Gen. 12:2; 15:18-21; 17:7, 8). *The Church* becomes the heir of salvation, promised to all who believe (Gal. 3:16, 28, 29). *The Gentile nations* will be recipients of Christ's salvation in the coming age when Israel accepts the Messiah at the second advent (Gen. 12:3; Deut. 28: 8-14; Isa. 60:3-5). 2) *Blessing to those who bless Abraham's descendants and a curse upon those who curse them* (Gen. 12:3; Matt. 25:31-46). This promise coupled with warning was particularly evident during the specific period of testing of the Administration of Promise. It is seen working on individuals (Gen. 12:17; 20:3, 17) and nations (especially Egypt — see Gen. 47 — 50, Exod. 1 — 15), but appears throughout the entire span of this administration. The sign of this covenant was circumcision (Gen. 17:9-14).

THE MOSAIC COVENANT AND THE ADMINISTRATION OF LAW. This covenant was made with the nation Israel through Moses. It was never made with Gentiles. The legal economy which it introduced consequently comprehended only the nation Israel. During this era Israel as an *elect* people through Abraham and as a people redeemed out of Egypt (Exod. 15:13) were placed on exhibition before all the nations of the world. They were to be witnesses to the fact that a) the infinitely holy God could save fallen mankind only by the atoning death of the Savior to come (prefigured by Israel's sacrificial system and priesthood), and that b) a redeemed people can glorify God only by keeping his eternal moral law, summarized in the Decalogue from Sinai.

The Mosaic Covenant was in force from Sinai to Calvary (Matt. 27:50, 51). It was conditioned on a) faith in God's grace to save sinners by blood sacrifice and b) obedience to the moral law of God as a means of exemplifying the efficacy of God's redeeming power. Hence it consists of three parts: 1) *the moral law* (Exod. 20:1-17), summarizing the requirements of the infinitely holy God of his redeemed people; 2) *the civil law,* conditioning the social life of Israel (Exod. 21:1 — 24:11). 3) *The ceremonial law,* governing the religious life of Israel (Exod. 24:12 — 31:18). The ceremonial law was abolished when Christ died and fulfilled its prescriptions, which pointed to him.

The moral law of God was adapted to the Mosaic Covenant at Sinai. As a reflection of the eternal character of God it was binding upon *all* men from the beginning. It condemned fallen man and showed him his lost condition and his need of God's redemptive grace. It disclosed to redeemed man how he ought to live in order to glorify his Creator-Redeemer. The moral law of God, accordingly, far transcends its form in the Ten Commandments. It extends to *all* administrations and underlies *all* the covenants. *All* men, both saved and unsaved, of every era will be judged by their response to it. This means that there will be degrees of punishment in Gehenna for the lost (Rev. 20:11-15) as well as degrees of reward in the future sin-cleansed universe for the saved (2 Cor. 5:10).

The Sabbath was the *sign* of the Mosaic Covenant. The fourth commandment (Exod. 20:8-11) constituted the one unique feature of the Moral Law *in its Mosaic dress*. The Sabbath as such was never imposed upon *fallen* man, but only upon unfallen man (Gen. 2:2, 3). When man fell, *God's Sabbath rest in creation was broken*. God then began *working* in redemption (John 5:17; Gen. 3:15, 21). Later God imposed the Sabbath upon *the redeemed nation Israel* (Exod. 20:8-11; 31:12-17). This was in token that his creation rest would one day be restored by that nation. Restoration will transpire when Christ redeems Israel at the second advent and through Israel mediates this redemption to all the nations of the earth during the kingdom age (Isa. 11:1-16; 60:1-22).

For this reason Sabbath-keeping is not Christian but Mosaic. It is legalistic, the badge of the Mosaic Covenant. The commandment of Sabbath-keeping represents the moral law of God only as it was adapted to the requirements of the Mosaic Covenant and the elect nation Israel. It has no direct relevance to the Church or Christianity.

THE NEW COVENANT AND THE ADMINISTRATION OF THE CHURCH. The New Covenant was secured by Christ's blood (Luke 22:20), which purchased the Church of God (Acts 20:28), the Body of Christ (1 Cor. 12:12, 13). The Apostle calls the Church "the mystery . . . which in other ages was not made known" (Eph. 3:3-6), being "hid in God" from "the beginning of the world" (Eph. 3:9). The Administration of the Church comes between Israel's rejection because of unbelief and the nation's restoration at the second advent. During the interval God is visiting the Gentiles to take out of them "a people for his name" (Acts 15:14). During this era the divine purpose comprehends a wholly new entity, the Church, composed of regenerated Gentiles and Jews baptized by the Holy Spirit into vital union with each other in Christ. This is the mystery which welds together believing Jews and Gentiles in a completely new entity, the Church, through the blood of the New Covenant shed at Calvary.

This age is often called "the Dispensation of the Holy Spirit" because the Spirit has been especially manifested by his formation and indwelling of the Church (John 16:7, 8, 13). The age will be consummated by his completion and glorification of the Church (2 Thess. 1:7,

10). This age is also often called "the Dispensation of Grace." Although God's grace operates in every dispensation, the present period is nevertheless a special era of grace. This appears in the vast multitude of Gentile sinners saved in it. God's purpose is that "in the ages to come he might show the exceeding riches of his grace in his kindness toward *us* through Christ Jesus" (Eph. 2:7). In this age God's grace is on display *now* as well as for the ages to come.

THE DAVIDIC COVENANT AND THE ADMINISTRATION OF THE KINGDOM. This covenant was made with King David (2 Sam. 7:4-17). It spans from David's time through the era of the Church, but finds its special fulfillment in Christ (Luke 1:30-33) and the coming kingdom over Israel. It secures three paramount advantages to Israel through the Davidic house. 1) *An everlasting throne.* David's kingdom is in abeyance now, but will be restored someday. Since the Babylonian exile, only one king of the Davidic family has been crowned—and he with thorns (Matt. 27:29). But the Davidic Covenant provides that this thorn-crowned one shall receive the kingdom when the time comes to restore it to David's Son and Lord (Psa. 2:1-12; 110:1; Luke 1:30-33). 2) *An everlasting kingdom.* David's Son and Lord is guaranteed an earthly sphere of rule that will extend over the entire millennial earth. He will have dominion "from sea to sea, and from the river to the ends of the earth" (Psa. 72:1-20). 3) *An everlasting King.* This will be realized in the second advent of Christ as King par excellence and Lord par excellence (Rev. 19:16).

THE PALESTINIAN COVENANT AND THE MESSIANIC ADMINISTRATION. This covenant discloses what the Lord will yet do in regathering, restoring, and blessing Israel to and in her own land (Deut. 30:1-10). It takes the place of the Mosaic Covenant, which came to an end with the crucifixion of Christ, the destruction of Jerusalem, and the dispersion of the Jewish nation in A.D. 70. This covenant ushers in the millennial age and, like the Davidic Covenant, finds its fulfillment in kingdom blessing.

THE NEW COVENANT AND THE ADMINISTRATION OF THE FULLNESS OF TIMES. The New Covenant, based on the redemptive work of Christ, has application not only to the Church in this age but also to the restored nation Israel in the age to come (Jer. 31:31-34; Heb. 8:6-13). In its application to the Church the covenant is "new" in the sense that it is the basis for the outcalling of the new people of God, the Church. In Israel's case it is "new" in that it supersedes the Mosaic Covenant, which Israel broke. On the other hand, it does not alter or conflict with the Palestinian, the Abrahamic, or the Davidic Covenants. Its blessings, yet future, and assured by God's faithfulness, include spiritual regeneration and fellowship with God as a result of *forgiveness,* that is, the complete removal of sin (Jer. 31:33, 34). Guaranteeing eternal salvation, this covenant will cover the kingdom age and the perfect age of the new heaven and new earth that follows, in which righteousness shall dwell and all sin will be removed (Rev. 21:1–22:5). It is called "the dispensation of the fullness of times" (Eph. 1:10). This perfect age is the prelude to eternity, when Christ will surrender his perfect kingdom to the Father, "that God may be all in all" (1 Cor. 15:28).

The ancient Scriptures still live in modern Jerusalem. *(Russ Busby photo)*

Major Themes of the Bible

Side by side with its presentation of the grand theme of human redemption, the Bible sets forth numerous other vital teachings that are essential to the exposition of its main subject of salvation. Chief among these are the following corollary themes.

THE BIBLE AS THE WORD OF GOD

Internal and external evidence, as well as the witness of the Holy Spirit, combine to authenticate the Bible as the fully inspired and authoritative Word of God. The Bible throughout assumes this fact in hundreds of passages (e.g. Psa. 12:6; Isa. 55:10, 11; Rom. 10:17) and directly declares it in Second Timothy 3:15, 16. Externally, the nature of the Bible, its subject matter, and its regenerative ministry among men support this truth.

THE UNITY AND TRINITY OF THE GODHEAD

Elohim, Jehovah, Adonai.

The Old Testament emphasizes the unity of God (Deut. 6:4; Exod. 20:3) but also intimates a triune relationship (Gen. 1:26; 3:22; 11:7; Isa. 9:6; Psa. 2:7). The New Testament emphasizes the trinity (Matt. 28:19; John 14:16) and intimates the unity (John 10:30; 14:9; Col. 1:15). The primary Old Testament names of God (Elohim, Jehovah, Adonai) suggest unity in trinity, as do the various attributes of God.

GOD THE FATHER

THE FATHER OF CHRIST THE SON. The Father begot the Son (Psa. 2:7; John 1:14, 18; 3:16; John 9:35). This was acknowledged by the Son (Matt. 11:27; 26:63, 64; John 17:1; 8:29) and by men (Matt. 16:16; John 1:34). Even the demons recognized this relationship between the Father and the Son (Matt. 8:29).

THE FATHER OF THOSE WHO BELIEVE ON CHRIST THE SON. This truth is taught in Matthew 5:44, 45; John 1:12; Romans 8:14-17; Second Corinthians 6:16-18; and Galatians 4:4-7. The unregenerate are children of the Wicked One (Matt. 13:38; John 8:44; Eph. 2:2, 3).

GOD THE SON

His preexistence is taught in Isaiah 9:6, 7; Micah 5:2; John 8:58 and 17:5; and Hebrews 1:2, 3 and 13:8.

His incarnation is described in John 1:14, 18; Philippians 2:6-8; and First Timothy 3:16.

His substitutionary death is seen in Isaiah 53:4-6; Romans 3:24, 25; John 1:29; Second Corinthians 5:21; and many other passages.

His resurrection is intimated in Genesis 22:1-18; Psalm 16:10; Isaiah 26:19 and 53:10-12; it is clearly expounded in First Corinthians 15:3-8, 12-20; First Timothy 6:14-16; and Second Timothy 1:10.

His ascension is intimated in Leviticus 16:1-34 and taught in Hebrews 9:24, 25; John 20:17; Acts 1:9-11; and First Timothy 3:16.

His priestly ministry is explained in First John 1:9 and 2:1; Hebrews 7:22-27; 8:1, 2; 9:11, 12, 24; and Romans 8:34.

His second advent is referred to in dozens of Scripture passages. First he comes *for* his own, as shown in Philippians 3:20, 21; First Thessalonians 4:13-18; and First John 3:1, 2. Later he comes *with* his own to establish his everlasting kingdom, as seen in Colossians 3:4; First Thessalonians 3:13; and Jude 1:14, 15.

GOD THE HOLY SPIRIT

HIS PERSONALITY. John 14:16, 17 and 16:7-15 show that the Holy Spirit is an actual personage and not merely an "influence for good."

HIS ADVENT. He was present in the world before his advent at Pentecost (Gen. 1:2; 41:38; Exod. 31:3; Psa. 139:7; Zech. 4:6), though it was at Pentecost that he took up residence in the Church (John 14: 16, 17; 16:7; Eph. 2:18-22).

HIS DEPARTURE. He will leave the earth when the Church is completed (2 Thess. 2:7) in the special sense in which he came to institute the Church's formation at Pentecost (Acts 1:5; 11:15, 16). He will then resume his pre-Pentecost ministry in the tribulation period and will inaugurate a special ministry during the kingdom age (Isa. 11:1-3; Joel 2:28, 29).

HIS MINISTRY. He restrains lawlessness and sin (2 Thess. 2:7). He convicts sinners of 1) the sin of disbelief in the Savior, of 2) God's justifying righteousness provided in Christ, and of 3) divine judgment to come upon all who reject Christ's atonement (John 16:7-11). He regenerates the believing sinner (John 3:5), baptizing him into vital union with Christ and with all other believers (1 Cor. 12:13; Rom. 6:3, 4; Gal. 3:27). The Holy Spirit also indwells him (1 Cor. 6:19), anoints him (2 Cor. 1:22; Eph. 1:13; 4:30), and fills him for power and service (Acts 2:4; 4:8; Eph. 5:18).

THE ANGELS

As a special order of creation, angels are incorporeal persons or spirits, having a heavenly position above the earthly sphere of man but infinitely below that of God (Psa. 8:5; Heb. 2:7). They consist of two categories: unfallen and fallen. The unfallen angels are ministering spirits for believers (Heb. 1:14) and are called "holy" (Matt. 25:31). The fallen angels (Satan and the demons) primevally rebelled against God (Isa. 14:12-14; Ezek. 28:11-19). Some of the demons are free and are at work in the world today (1 Tim. 4:1; 1 John 4:1, 2; cf. Mark 5:6-13; Luke 8:30). Others are bound in the abyss (Rev. 9:1-12; 2 Pet. 2:4).

SATAN

Satan is an angelic personality originally created holy and sinless who fell through pride and introduced sin into an originally sinless universe (Ezek. 28:11-19; Isa. 14:12-17). He reigns as king over the realm of darkness comprising the fallen angels and demons (Matt. 12:26). Satan works through man's fallen nature and the evil world system to keep men from Christ's salvation and from obedience to and fellowship with God (Eph. 2:2; 6:10-20; 2 Cor. 4:3, 4; 1 Pet. 5:8; 1 John 5:19; 1 Tim. 4:1). His destiny is Gehenna (Rev. 20:10), the lake of fire prepared for him and his angels (Matt. 25:41).

MAN

Man is a special order of God's creation, lower than the angels but higher than the animals. God created man, permitted his temptation and fall, and planned his redemption through the sacrificial death of the incarnate Word. The result will be not only man's glorification but earth's deliverance from the curse of sin (Eph. 1:13, 14; Rev. 21:1, 2; Rom. 8:20-23). Unbelieving mankind will suffer the fate of Satan and the fallen angels in Gehenna (Matt. 25:41). Eternity will realize a sin-cleansed universe.

SIN

Sin is a terrible reality and "exceedingly sinful" (Rom. 7:13). Going far deeper than human speculation, Scripture presents sin as any lack of conformity to the infinitely holy character of God (Isa. 6:1-5). Fallen man is found to be totally unacceptable to God in the face of the infinite purity of Deity. Man is helplessly cast upon the divine grace revealed in Christ's redemption (Rom. 3:9-31).

IMPUTED SIN. Adam's sin is imputed (reckoned or attributed) to the fallen race. This forms the basis of the doctrine of original sin (Rom. 5:12-18). Man's sin is in turn imputed to Christ, forming the basis of the doctrine of salvation. God's righteousness is imputed to those who believe in Christ, forming the basis of the doctrine of justification.

SIN NATURE. Every descendant of Adam is born with a fallen nature constantly prone to sin. Though this evil disposition was judged by Christ on the cross (Rom. 6:10), it is never said to be removed in this life. But for the believer, overcoming power is provided through the indwelling Spirit (Rom. 8:4; Gal. 5:16, 22-25).

THE SINFUL AND LOST STATE OF THE RACE. Fallen humanity is regarded by God as "under sin" (Rom. 3:9; Gal. 3:22; Rom. 11:32). God looks upon all mankind as totally lacking in merit which might contribute to salvation, so that every sinner is totally confined to God's grace in Christ (Eph. 2:8, 9).

PERSONAL SIN. Everything in the daily life of the individual that fails to conform to God's character is included under this category.

GOD'S REMEDY FOR SIN. The cross of Christ, whether in prospect (Lev. 1:4; Acts 17:30; Rom. 3:25) or retrospect (John 3:16; 1 Pet. 2:24) is the divine remedy for sin. Only faith in Christ's atoning death removes the penalty of sin, eternal death. The unsaved will answer for their sin by punishment both here and eternally in Gehenna. The saved will also answer by loss of blessing now and forfeiture of reward in heaven (1 Cor. 3:9-15; 2 Cor. 5:10).

SALVATION

This term represents the whole work of God, in which he rescues man from the ruin of sin, bestows on him eternal life now, and grants him eternal glory hereafter in accordance with the riches of his grace. Salvation is in every respect an undertaking of God in behalf of man (Jonah 2:9). In no sense is it an activity of man in behalf of God.

THE THREE TENSES OF SALVATION. In the *past tense* the believer became saved when he believed on Christ (Luke 7:50; 1 Cor. 1: 18; 2 Cor. 2:15; Eph. 2:5-8). In the *present tense* the believer *is being delivered* from the power of sin by counting on what he is in union with Christ (Rom. 6:11; Gal. 2:19, 20; 2 Cor. 3:18). In the *future tense* the believer *will yet be saved* into full conformity to Christ (Rom. 8:29; 13:11; 1 Pet. 3:2; 1 John 3:2).

THE TWO ASPECTS OF SALVATION. *The final work of Christ* must be distinguished from *the saving work of God*. The first has been completed to infinite perfection for *all* mankind (John 3:16; 19:30; Heb. 10:14) and provides the ground on which God in his infinite holiness can save guilty sinners, including the worst of them. The second of these—the saving work of God—is accomplished the moment the sinner believes; it includes redemption, reconciliation, propitiation, forgiveness, regeneration, justification, sanctification, and glorification (1 Cor. 1:30; 2 Cor. 5:21; John 1:12; 2 Cor. 5:17; Col. 2:10; Rom. 8:29).

THE ONE CONDITION OF SALVATION. Actual personal faith in the finished work of Christ on the cross is the one and only requisite for salvation (Acts 16:31; Eph. 2:8-10; John 3:16, 36; 5:24; Rom. 1: 16; 5:1). Confessing Christ, confessing sin, praying, making restitution, etc. ought to and do *accompany* genuine salvation experience, but are not *conditions* of salvation.

SANCTIFICATION

Sanctification is an integral part of salvation. It is the setting apart of the saved person for God's worship and service. As presented in Scripture, sanctification is in three aspects: past, present, and future.

PAST ASPECT. This is the position which *all* believers have from the moment they exercise saving faith in Christ the Redeemer (1 Cor. 1:2, 30). It represents the sphere in which God sees them "in Christ." It is static and unalterable, resting securely on the finished work of Christ.

PRESENT ASPECT. This represents the experience which all believers enjoy as they depend upon what they are in Christ (Rom. 6:11). It is progressive and changeable, depending upon the believer's yieldedness to God's Word (Rom. 6:13) and conformity to God's will (Rom. 12:2).

FUTURE ASPECT. This represents the final phase of sanctification, when we see the Lord and are made like him (1 Cor. 15:54; 1 John 3: 2). It is eternal, and will be our destiny in glory (Phil. 3:21; Rom. 8:29; 1 Cor. 15:49).

SECURITY

Scripture reveals that those whom Christ saves he saves eternally. The positive doctrine of security rests upon no less than twelve unchangeable facts about God's grace and its accomplishments in behalf of the believer.

GOD'S ETERNAL PURPOSE. This is realized and assured through sovereign grace, totally apart from human merit or work (Rom. 8:29, 30; John 5:24; 6:37; 10:38), through the new covenant of redemption (Heb. 8:6-13).

GOD'S POWER. The Bible declares that God, being free from every barrier to forgive sin, is able to preserve all who are redeemed by Christ (John 10:29; Rom. 4:21; 8:31, 38, 39; Jude 1:24).

GOD'S LOVE. His love for his own can never fail. If he loved men enough to give his Son to die for them when they were sinners and enemies, he will love them much more "now that they are reconciled to him" (John 3:16; Rom. 5:8-11).

CHRIST'S PRAYER. While on earth Christ prayed that those whom the Father had given him should be kept (John 17:9-12, 15, 20, 21). This prayer, which commenced on earth, is continued in heaven (Rom. 8:34; Heb. 7:25).

CHRIST'S DEATH. The efficacious, substitutionary death of Christ is the sufficient remedy for the condemning power of sin (Rom. 8:34). Christ bore *all* the sins of the believer—past, present, and future—so that salvation and safekeeping depend only on the sacrifice and merit of Christ. Thus all condemnation is removed forever (John 3:18; 5:24).

CHRIST'S RESURRECTION. Christ's resurrection makes possible God's gift of eternal life (John 3:16; 10:28). Since this life is the life of the resurrected Christ (Col. 2:12; 3:1-4), it is as eternal as he is eternal, as incapable of dissolution as is the risen Christ. Moreover, by union with the resurrected Christ, by baptism with the Spirit, and by impartation of eternal life, the believer is made a part of the new creation (2 Cor. 5:17; Gal. 6:15). Taken out of his place under the federal headship of the first Adam, he is placed "in Christ" under the federal headship of the Last Adam (1 Cor. 15:20-22, 45-48). Since the Last Adam (the risen Christ) cannot fall, it is impossible for the weakest saint united to him to fall. The infinitely Holy God regards *every* saint as "in Christ" now and forever.

CHRIST'S INTERCESSION. In this present ministry in glory Christ prays for his own who are in the world, having in view their weakness, ignorance, and immaturity (Luke 22:31, 32; John 17:9, 15, 20; Rom. 8:34). His heavenly intercession guarantees that they will be kept saved forever (John 14:19; Rom. 5:10; Heb. 7:25).

CHRIST'S ADVOCACY. Christ's present ministry as Advocate concerns the believer's sin. Since God is infinitely holy, the believer's sin in every case merits eternal condemnation. Moreover, that judgment would of necessity be executed if Christ as Advocate did not continually plead the saving efficacy of his own blood before the throne of God (1 John 2:1, 2; Rom. 8:34; Heb. 9:24).

THE SPIRIT'S REGENERATING WORK. The Spirit regenerates the child of God (John 1:13; 3:3-6; Tit. 3:4-6; 1 Pet. 1:23). By this operation the believer is constituted a son and joint-heir of God with Christ (Rom. 8:16, 17). Being born of God, he partakes of the divine nature, which is never removed or annulled.

THE SPIRIT'S BAPTIZING WORK. The moment the sinner believes, the Spirit baptizes him into the Body of Christ, the Church (1 Cor. 12:13) and into Christ, the Head of the Body (1 Cor. 12:12; Rom. 6:3, 4; Gal. 3:27). The believer is then in union with Christ and with all other believers. His new position "in Christ" is a vital and permanent one because God himself has personally placed him there. The believer is "accepted in the beloved" forever (Eph. 1:6).

THE SPIRIT'S INDWELLING. The Spirit now indwells *every* believer (John 7:37-39; Rom. 5:5; 8:9; 1 Cor. 2:12; 6:19; 1 John 3:24). He never leaves the believer (John 14:16). The Spirit may be *grieved* by unconfessed sin (Eph. 4:30) or *quenched* (suppressed) (1 Thess. 5:19), but as the divine Presence in the heart he is never removed. God's own remain his forever.

THE SPIRIT'S SEALING. All believers are sealed with the Spirit unto the day of full redemption or glorification (Eph. 4:30; 2 Cor. 1:22; Eph. 1:13). The Holy Spirit himself is the seal. He is God's stamp of the security of *all* who are saved.

ASSURANCE

Assurance is personal confidence in a present salvation. It rests upon two lines of evidence: a) an experience of genuine salvation through Christ and b) the truth of God's revealed Word.

CHRISTIAN EXPERIENCE. The impartation of new life from God is sure to be manifested in the believer. This new life is Christ himself indwelling the believer (Col. 1:27; 1 John 5:11, 12). On the basis of this fact the believer is to judge himself as to whether he is in the faith (2 Cor. 13:5). Normal manifestations of the indwelling Christ include the knowledge of God as Father (Matt. 11:27; John 17:3; 1 John 1:3), new ability to understand God's Word (John 16:12-15; 1 John 2:27), a new sense of the sinfulness of sin (Rom. 7:18), a new love for both the unsaved (2 Cor. 5:14; Rom. 9:1-3; 10:1) and the saved (John 13:34, 35; 1 John 3:14), a new concept of prayer (Rom. 8:26, 27; 1 Tim. 2:1, 2; Eph. 6:18, 19), a manifestation of Christ-likeness (John 13:34, 35; 15: 11, 12; 2 Cor. 3:18; Gal. 5:22, 23), and a consciousness of salvation through faith in Christ (Rom. 8:16; 2 Tim. 1:12).

THE VERACITY OF GOD'S WORD. Above and beyond Christian experience, which is at best tarnished by carnality, lies the sure foundation of the Word of God, upon which all experience is to be based and evaluated. Assurance springs from believing the Word (1 John 5: 13). The promises of Scripture are a title deed upon which faith can rest in confident assurance (John 6:37; 5:24; Rom. 1:16; 3:22, 24; 10:13).

THE CHURCH

THE LOCAL CHURCH. As employed in the New Testament, the word "church" denotes any called-out or assembled company of people. In its theological usage it refers to a local gathering of professing Christians who meet together for group worship and service.

THE MYSTICAL CHURCH. In its primary theological usage in the New Testament the word "church" denotes a company of people called out of the old creation into the new (1 Cor. 12:12, 13; Rom. 6:3, 4; Eph. 1:20-23). The Church (often capitalized to distinguish this mystical church from the local assembly) is composed of the total number of redeemed persons from Pentecost (Acts 1:5; 2:4; 11:14-16) to Christ's return to receive his own (1 Thess. 4:13-18; 1 Cor. 15:52). All members of the Church are united to Christ and to one another by the baptism with the Holy Spirit (Gal. 3:27; 1 Cor. 12:12, 13). Believing Jews and Gentiles in this manner become united in "the Church of God" (1 Cor. 10:32). The Church thus represents *all* the saved people of this age. God's purpose in this age is to call out his elect body principally from the Gentiles, but also from the Jews (Acts 15:14).

The mission of the Church is to represent Christ to an unsaved world as "ambassadors for Christ," beseeching men to be "reconciled to God" (2 Cor. 5:20) by believing the gospel of salvation (1 Cor. 15:2-4).

THE SABBATH

THE INSTITUTION OF THE SABBATH. God instituted the Sabbath to memorialize the finished work of the old creation (Gen. 2: 2, 3). It commemorated God's rest from the work of refashioning the earth for the latecomer man (Gen. 1:1-31). God could rest because everything he had made, including man, was "very good" (Gen. 1:31). It was upon *unfallen* man that God imposed the Sabbath—*not* upon fallen man. When man fell, God's creation rest was broken by man's sin. It was then that God began working in redemption (John 5:17). No longer could he rest in a "very good" creation, for creation had now been made "very bad" by sin.

THE SABBATH AND SINAI. Mankind from Adam to Moses was thus no longer under the law of Sabbath observance (despite the fact that the fallen race during this interval attempted to perpetuate the practice, as archeology shows). This fact explains the silence of Scripture about the Sabbath during this period. But with startling suddenness the Sabbath was revived in the fourth commandment of the Decalogue (Exod. 20:8-11). It was not merely one small part of the Mosaic Covenant but was one of its unique and dominant features (Exod. 31: 12-18). The severest penalty possible—death—was attached to its infraction (Num. 15:32-36). This was a warning to every Israelite that they were *God's* people, elect to be an example to all other peoples. God intended to show them that his plan to restore through Christ his creation rest in man and the earth centered in *them* as his chosen nation. The Sabbath was the sign that this was Israel's messianic calling.

THE SABBATH AND THE CHURCH. The Sabbath as the sign of the Mosaic Covenant was the peculiar stamp of the Jew. It was never imposed upon the Church, nor upon any other segment of the fallen race beside the nation Israel. Christians, who observe the first day of the week in honor of Christ's resurrection, are not only free from the obligation of the Sabbath but are actually *warned against* Sabbath-keeping as a form of grace-denying legalism (Col. 2:16, 17; Gal. 4:9, 10). While Christians are not under the Law of Moses, *they are under the eternal moral law of God as reflected in the Ten Commandments.* The fourth commandment enjoining Sabbath-keeping is the *one* and only exception. While all the other commandments are binding upon all ages and all peoples in all times, the Sabbath is strictly Jewish. It is the sign to all mankind that through his elect messianic nation, Israel, God will restore his creation rest destroyed by the fall and man's sin. The new heavens and the new earth will usher in an eternal Sabbath of rest (Rev. 21:1 – 22:6).

THE LORD'S DAY

THE OBSERVANCE OF THE LORD'S DAY. While the Sabbath (seventh day) is nowhere imposed upon the Church, abundant reasons support the observance of the *first* day of the week.

A new day was predicted and appointed under grace. The crucified Christ was the Stone rejected by Israel. Through his resurrection, however, he has been made the Headstone of the Corner (Psa. 118:22-24; Acts 4:10, 11). This marvelous event was God's doing, and the time of its accomplishment was divinely appointed as a day of rejoicing. Hence Christ's salutation to his own on the morning of his resurrection was "All hail!" or, literally, "O Joy!" (Matt. 28:9). It was indeed "the day which the Lord had made" and was thus aptly designated "the Lord's Day" (Rev. 1:10).

The New Testament supports the observance of the Lord's Day. This is true despite the fact that no command is given to keep the day, nor is any manner of its observance prescribed. This liberty is in accordance with the grace of God manifested in the finished redemption which it commemorates. It is to be observed willingly and from the heart. It preserves the concept that one-seventh of our time is to be devoted to God as a token that *all* of our time actually belongs to him. A day of rest under the Mosaic Law belonged to a people related to God by works which were to be accomplished. In the Church a day of ceaseless worship and service is the portion of a people who are related to God through the finished work of Christ.

Observance of the First Day is indicated by various events. On that day Christ arose (Matt. 28:1), he first met with his disciples (John 20:19), instructed them (Luke 24:13-45), and ascended to heaven as "the firstfruits" (John 20:17). It was on the *first* day of the week that the Spirit came at Pentecost (Acts 2:1-4) and that believers assembled for communion (Acts 20:7) and brought their offerings (1 Cor. 16:2).

THE LORD'S DAY AND THE NEW CREATION. As the Sabbath celebrated the old creation (Exod. 20:10, 11), so the Lord's Day celebrates the new creation. The latter began with the resurrection of Christ and consists of the called-out company of the redeemed (Acts 15:13-18) from Pentecost to the glorification of the Church. These are baptized by the Spirit into union with the risen and glorified Christ in heaven (Rom. 6:3, 4; Col. 2:12, 13; 3:1-4). The Body of Christ, the Church united to Christ its Head (Eph. 1:22; 4:15; Col. 1:18), forms the new creation (2 Cor. 5:17).

THE LOVE OF GOD

GOD'S ESSENTIAL NATURE. "God is love" (1 John 4:8). He is not only the *source* of love but he *is* love. Love is at the essence of his being. He is what he is in large measure because of his love. His love is everlasting and changeless (Jer. 31:3; John 13:1; 15:9) because it is a vital and inseparable part of his being. It is ceaseless in its activity (Rom. 5:8; 1 John 3:16). It is infinite in its purity (1 Pet. 1:22). It is inexhaustible in its benevolence (John 15:13; Tit. 3:4, 5). It is limitless in its intensity (Rom. 5:8-10; 8:35-39).

THE MANIFESTATION OF THE NEW NATURE. God's love is manifested not only *to* his own but *through* them. The impartation of the divine nature (2 Pet. 1:4) enables redeemed men to love as Christ loved (John 13:34, 35). This is the badge of regeneration (1 John 3:14) and one of the prime manifestations of the Spirit (Gal. 5:22). The supernatural character of God's love operating through the believer is described in First Corinthians 13:1-8.

PRAYER TO GOD

Prayer, whether petition, praise, or thanksgiving, assumes an important place in Scripture. It is the direct communion of man with God, and appears in various aspects.

PRAYER IN THE OLD TESTAMENT. Unfallen man had free and full communion with the Lord God (Gen. 3:8). Fallen man, however, could approach the infinite holiness only through the covering of sacrificial blood, which pointed to the coming Redeemer (Gen. 3:21; 4:3-5; 8:20). The basis of prayer consisted in pleading the covenants of the Lord (1 Kings 8:22-26; Dan. 9:4; Neh. 9:32), the holy character of God (Gen. 18:25; Exod. 32:11-14), and the shedding of sacrificial blood (Heb. 9:7).

PRAYER FOR THE KINGDOM. Both John the forerunner and Christ the Messiah at the outset of their ministries preached the messianic kingdom which had been promised to Israel in the Old Testament (Matt. 3:3; 4:17; cf. Dan. 2:44; 4:25, 32). During the early days of his preaching, before the kingdom was rejected, Christ taught his disciples to pray for this kingdom (Matt. 6:9-13). The prayer he gave them is adapted particularly to kingdom expectations, as are the prayer instructions found in Matthew 7:7-11 and Luke 11:2-13.

PRAYER IN THE CHURCH. Anticipating his death and resurrection, as well as the giving of the Spirit and the founding of the Church, Christ in the upper room discourse revealed the new dimensions which prayer would have in the economy soon to be inaugurated (John 14:12-14; 15:7; 16:23, 24). In the new age the believers, having been baptized by the Spirit into vital union with Christ and being indwelt continually by the Spirit (John 14:16, 17), would enjoy unique new privileges and blessings in prayer.

As a result of union with Christ, prayer was to become *a partnership of the believer with his Lord.* It is because his own would soon become a living part of him (Eph. 5:30) and share both his service and his glory that Jesus said, "Greater works than these shall he (the believer) do" (John 14:12). The believer would do these "greater works" through prayer. "And whatsoever ye ask in my name, that will I do, that the Father may be glorified in the Son. If ye shall ask anything in my name, I will do it" (John 14:13, 14). True prayer "in Christ's name" can be offered only by believers linked with Christ in a partnership of life and destiny.

As a result of union with Christ, *prayer was to become unlimited in its potential* within the will of God. "If ye abide in me" (depend upon your union with me) "and my words abide in you" (submit to my word and my will), "ye shall ask what ye will, and it shall be done unto you" (John 15:7).

As a result of union with Christ, *prayer was to be offered in his name.* Conversely, union with Christ would be the *prerequisite* for prayer in his name. Praying "in his name" is praying a prayer that Christ might pray; hence it is sure of an answer. This is what Jesus meant when he declared, "Whatever ye shall ask the Father in my name, he will give it you. Hitherto have ye asked nothing in my name" (John 16:23, 24). They had not yet prayed "in his name" because he had not yet died, risen, and given the Holy Spirit to baptize them into vital union with himself.

As a result of union with Christ *prayer was to be directed to the Father.* This is stated in Jesus' words, "In that day ye shall ask me nothing. Verily, verily, I say unto you, whatsoever ye shall ask the Father in my name, he will give it you" (John 16:23). At Pentecost the Holy Spirit baptized believers into union with Christ, so that they could pray in his name *to the Father*. The order of prayer, then, is *to the Father, in the name of Christ, by the power of the Holy Spirit* (Jude 1:20).

SERVICE

Service is any work performed for the benefit of another. In the case of God's people, service is to be first rendered to God and then to one's fellow man. If we love our Creator-Redeemer we will necessarily love his creatures as well (Exod. 20:1-17; Matt. 22:34-40).

SERVICE FOR GOD. *Service for God is a ministry of sacrifice.* It is the act of presenting our redeemed bodies "a living sacrifice to God" (Rom. 12:1). In the New Testament such priestly service in sacrifice toward God includes the dedication of self (Rom. 12:1), the sacrifice of the life in ceaseless praise (Heb. 13:15), and the sacrifice of material possessions in giving to God (Heb. 13:16).

The priest of the Old Testament typifies the believer's service of sacrifice. As he was born into the priestly family, likewise the believer is set apart by being born into God's family. As he was ceremonially cleansed by a once-for-all bathing at the beginning of his ministry (Exod. 29:4), so the believer is cleansed wholly and once-for-all at the moment he is saved (Tit. 3:5; 1 Cor. 6:11). This once-for-all bathing was followed, however, by a *partial* bathing at the bronze laver before any priestly service was undertaken. The New Testament believer, too, though wholly cleansed and forgiven when he becomes saved, is at all times to confess any known sin in order to be qualified for spiritual service and fellowship with God.

Service for God is a ministry of worship. Worship is basic to service in all ages. Acceptable service can only spring out of spiritual worship. Old Testament priests were governed in their worship by two prohibitions. No "strange" (unauthorized) incense was to be burned (speaking symbolically of man-devised religion and mere formality in worship—Exod. 30:9). Also, no "strange" fire was to be kindled (symbolizing the substitution of fleshly emotion for true spiritual zeal—Lev. 10:1; Col. 2:23).

Service for God is a ministry of intercession. The New Testament priest-believer has unhindered access to God on the basis of the blood of Christ continually presented in intercession before God (Rom. 8:26,

27; Heb. 10:19). Although the Mosaic priests represented the people before God, only the high priest himself could enter the Holiest Place, and this only once a year, and always with sacrificial blood. This prefigures Christ, who opened the way for all believers to draw near to God in intercession for others.

SERVICE FOR MAN. *Service for man is the inevitable result of service for God.* Dedication to God's will brings consecration, and with consecration spiritual anointing to serve man (Rom. 12:1, 2).

Service for man entails the exercise of spiritual gifts (Rom. 12:3-8). A gift is administered by the indwelling Spirit. The Spirit himself performs the service, employing the Christian as an instrument (1 Cor. 12:7-11). Normally the Spirit-filled life is active in service. Occasionally, however, it is God's will for all activity to cease and for the believer to "come apart . . . and rest awhile" (Mark 6:31).

STEWARDSHIP

A steward is someone who is entrusted with the management of the property of another. Christians are stewards because all that they are or have is given as a trust from God and is to be used for his glory. Stewardship is the use we make of all that God entrusts to us in the form of life, health, talents, and material possessions.

THE STEWARDSHIP OF LIFE. The believer belongs to God by creation and re-creation; hence he is to give *his whole being* to God *first*—before he attempts to give anything else (2 Cor. 8:5). This giving of oneself is concretely performed by presenting one's body to the Lord (Rom. 12:1), since in reality it already belongs to him anyway (1 Cor. 6:19, 20). This means one's time and energy are to be given to God.

THE STEWARDSHIP OF TALENT. Both natural endowments and spiritual gifts are to be freely and wholly given over to God to glorify him in service to man (Rom. 12:1-3).

THE STEWARDSHIP OF POSSESSIONS. This includes acquiring, possessing, and distributing material possessions for God's glory and man's benefit. For a Christian, *acquiring* money is to be actuated by the principle of doing everything "to the glory of God" (1 Cor. 10:31). *Possessing money* is to be guided by the principle that all a believer possesses, whether little or much, is a trust from God, held only as he directs, and always subject to his control. *Distributing money* is to be guided by Christ's example (2 Cor. 8:9), by yieldedness to God's will

(2 Cor. 8:2), by the principle of cheerful liberality (2 Cor. 9:7), and by the giving of oneself (2 Cor. 8:5). It is to be done in a systematic manner (1 Cor. 16:2), relying on God to graciously sustain the giver (2 Cor. 9:8-10). The believer realizes that true wealth is spiritual rather than material (Mark 8:36, 37).

OLD TESTAMENT PROPHECY

The pre-announcement by God of a certain thing he intends to do is called *prophecy*. Thus prophecy is actually history foretold. It forms a large part of divine revelation: nearly one-fourth of Holy Scripture was predictive when it was penned. The large number of biblical predictions that have now been literally and precisely fulfilled furnish a solid basis for deducing that all remaining prophecies will be as literally realized. Major themes of Old Testament prophecy include the following.

PROPHECY OF MESSIAH'S ADVENT. So completely was the present age of the outcalling of the Church hidden in the counsels of God that the Old Testament prophets saw the two advents as one. They were unable to determine how the two lines of prediction, one centering in his first advent and the other in his second advent, could be fulfilled *time*-wise (cf. 1 Pet. 1:10, 11). Jesus' quotation of Isaiah 61:1, 2 illustrates this. He ceased abruptly when he had finished reading about the features predicted for the first advent (Luke 4:16-21), making no mention of the remaining features to be fulfilled at his second advent. The angel Gabriel, too, when announcing the ministry of Christ, combined the undertakings which belong to both advents (Luke 1:31-33). Old Testament seers envisioned the Coming One as both an unresisting sacrificial Lamb (Isa. 52:13 – 53:12) and a glorious, conquering Lion (Jer. 23:5, 6).

Prophecy stipulated that the Messiah would be of the tribe of Judah (Gen. 49:10) and of the house of David (Isa. 11:1, 2; Jer. 33:20, 21); that he would be virgin-born (Gen. 3:15; Isa. 7:14) in Bethlehem of Judea (Mic. 5:2); that he would die an atoning death (Isa. 53:1-12) by crucifixion (Psa. 22:1-21; Zech. 12:10); that he would rise from the dead (Heb. 11:17-19; Psa. 16:8-11; Isa. 53:10-12); and that he would return to earth a second time (Deut. 30:3) in glory and power (Dan. 7:13, 14).

PROPHECY OF THE MESSIANIC KINGDOM. This is a very extensive forecast of Israel's restoration from worldwide dispersion to her own land, conversion at the second advent, and marvelous blessing as head of the nations (Deut. 28:13) in the kingdom age to come (Deut. 30:3-10; Isa. 11:1-16; 12:1-6; 35:1-10; 54:1 – 55:13; Jer. 23:3-8; Ezek. 36:32-38).

PROPHECY CONCERNING THE DAY OF THE LORD. The day of the Lord encompasses the prolonged period extending from the second advent and its accompanying earth judgments to the end of the kingdom age (Isa. 2:10-22; Zech. 12:1 – 14:21). Because the day of the Lord is closely associated with the second advent and the kingdom, Scripture prophecies regarding this "day" are very extensive.

PROPHECY CONCERNING THE TRIBULATION. The Tribulation is the time of unprecedented trouble in the earth preceding Christ's second advent (Deut. 4:29, 30; Psa. 2:5; Isa. 24:16-20; Jer. 30: 4-7; Dan. 12:1). It centers in Israel's end-time woes previous to her restoration and is distinctively "the time of Jacob's trouble" (Jer. 30:4-7), the period of chastisement for Israel's national sins.

PROPHECY CONCERNING THE NATIONS. Predictions about the nations begin with the descendants of Noah (Gen. 9:25-27). The various nations contiguous to Israel, such as Egypt, Babylon, Assyria, Chaldea, Moab, Ammon, Philistia, etc. form the subject of a large body of predictions. Daniel had visions of monarchies that would rule the world from his own time (about 600 B.C.) until the second advent of Christ (Dan. 2:37-45; 7:1-14). This entire period is called "the times of the Gentiles" (Luke 21:24) and encompasses the years during which Israel will be in servitude to foreign powers or in dispersion among the nations. The judgment of the nations (Joel 3:2-16; Zeph. 3: 8) and the eventual blessing of the Gentiles in the kingdom age are also subjects of prediction (Isa. 11:10; 42:1, 6; 49:6, 22; 60:3; 62:2).

PROPHECY CONCERNING ISRAEL. All Scripture from the Abrahamic Covenant (Gen. 12:1-3) to the end of Malachi relates directly or indirectly to God's elect people, Israel. To them has been granted a national entity (Jer. 31:36), a land (Gen. 13:15), a king (Jer. 33:21), a kingdom (Dan. 7:14), and a throne (2 Sam. 7:16; Psa. 89:36). These blessings may be interrupted by sin and divine chastisement, but they can never be abrogated; their fulfillment is certain.

PROPHECY OF ISRAEL'S DISPERSION AND RESTORATION. God prophesied that his people would be scattered because of sin (Lev. 26:14-39; Deut. 28:15-68; Jer. 18:15-17), but that they would also be regathered, converted, and blessed with every covenant promise made to them (Deut. 30:1-10; Jer. 23:3-8; Ezek. 37:21-28).

Worshipers and tourists mass at the Western (Wailing) Wall near Herod's ancient Temple site. *(IGTO photo)*

NEW TESTAMENT PROPHECY

The New Testament records the fulfillment of prophecies concerning the first advent of Christ and advances and broadens the message of prophecy contained in the Old Testament. This is particularly true in respect to Israel's sin and present worldwide dispersion, her regathering and suffering during the great tribulation (Matt. 24:4-51; Rev. 6:1 – 18:24), and her establishment in kingdom blessing (Rom.

11:25-36; Rev. 20:1-9). However, the new age and the new divine purpose, together with the judgment of believers and unbelievers and the eternal state of the saved and lost, constitute lines of truth which are confined solely to the New Testament.

THE NEW AGE. This period between the first and second advents is unrevealed in the Old Testament but constitutes a major New Testament prediction (Matt. 13:1-50; John 14:1 − 16:33; Rom. 9:1 − 11:36; 2 Tim. 3:1-9; Rev. 2:1 − 3:22).

THE NEW DIVINE PURPOSE. The Church, composed of saved Jews and Gentiles (1 Cor. 10:32) comprehends the new people of God (Acts 15:14-18). Its position is outlined and its earthly career and heavenly destiny are foreseen in Matthew 16:18; John 14:1-3, Philippians 3:20, 21; and First Thessalonians 4:13-17.

JUDGMENT OF THE BELIEVER'S WORKS

In dealing with judgment as it affects the believer, the doctrine of salvation must be clearly distinguished from the doctrine of rewards. The judgment of the believer's works *in no case* involves the issue of salvation, but simply that of rewards. Rewards depend on the quality of life and service *after* salvation.

THE DOCTRINE OF SALVATION. The judgment of the believer's sins at the cross (John 12:31) resulted in the death of Christ and the justification of the believer, who can now never again be faced with the penalty of sin, eternity in Gehenna (John 3:18; 5:24; Rom. 5: 1; 8:1; 1 Cor. 11:32). Salvation is by faith and is a gift, totally separate from works (Eph. 2:8, 9), and must never be confused with the issue of service.

THE DOCTRINE OF REWARDS. Although all the believer's sins have been atoned for and the penalty fully remitted (Heb. 10:17), every work must nevertheless come into judgment (2 Cor. 5:10; Rom. 14:10; Eph. 6:8; Col. 3:24, 25). The result is either bestowal or forfeiture of rewards (1 Cor. 3:11-15). This judgment occurs immediately following the coming of Christ to receive his glorified Church (1 Cor. 4:5; 2 Tim. 4:8; Rev. 22:12). Sinning saints who are unproductive in spiritual service will not only forfeit future rewards in eternity but will also be chastised in this life so that they may not be condemned with the unsaved (1 Cor. 11:32).

JUDGMENT OF THE WICKED

THE BASIS OF JUDGMENT. *All* of God's intelligent creatures, angels as well as men, will face judgment for their works. This includes redeemed man, as noted in the preceding section, as well as unredeemed man. Although Gehenna, also called "the lake of fire," was prepared for the Devil and his fallen angels rather than for human beings (Matt. 25:41; Rev. 20:10), unbelieving men must go there (Rev. 20:15). This fact is true not because the unsaved have been good or bad by human standards, but because they have rejected the knowledge of God through his creation and the conviction of sin through the Holy Spirit (Rom. 1:18-20; 2:14, 15). Men go to hell, therefore, because they fail to seek forgiveness and cleansing from the infinitely holy God on the basis of the righteousness of Christ (Rom. 3:23-26). Thus many "very good" or "highly moral" people (judged by human standards) will go to hell.

DEGREES OF PUNISHMENT. Just as there will be bestowal or forfeiture of rewards for the saved in an eventual sin-cleansed universe, so there will be degrees of punishment in the one isolation ward of eternity for sin and all sinners. This place is called Gehenna or "the lake of fire" (Rev. 20:11-15). This is the inescapable meaning of judgment according to works. No human being can keep the moral law of God to God's satisfaction. This is why God provided salvation through faith in Christ. Nevertheless, men are held accountable to keep the moral law of God *in degree*. This will not admit them to heaven, however, because sinful man can never meet the standard of infinite, divine holiness. But to the extent that men keep the moral laws of God their punishment in hell will be lessened. An unsaved man may not be able to refrain from hating his neighbor, but he can avoid killing him (Exod. 20:13). He may not be able to curb his petty stealing, but he had better not commit grand larceny (Exod. 20:15)!

THE RESURRECTIONS. There are two resurrections. The first embraces the redeemed (1 Cor. 15:22, 23; 1 Thess. 4:14-17). It is in stages and is *almost* entirely before the thousand years of the kingdom age. However, the end of it is coterminous with the second resurrection of the unredeemed at the end of the kingdom age (Rev. 20:5) since millennial saints will die and must of necessity be judged with the wicked. This is why "the book of life" is opened with "the books" in which the works of the unsaved are recorded (Rev. 20:12, 15). The white throne judgment, however, is predominantly a judgment of condemnation because it comprises the vast multitudes of the lost and the wicked from Adam to the end of time.

ETERNAL STATE OF THE REDEEMED

A SIN-CLEANSED UNIVERSE. God is working through Christ to effect a sin-cleansed universe. This will be accomplished by the resurrection and glorification of all the redeemed of all ages and the creation of new heavens and a new earth, "in which dwelleth righteousness" (2 Pet. 3:13; Rev. 21:1—22:5). All evil and evildoers will be rigidly isolated in Gehenna, the one quarantine ward in a sinless universe (Rev. 20:14, 15). This is the culmination toward which God's redemptive program for man is moving.

Heaven as the abode of God is only part of this sin-cleansed universe. To be sure, the unfallen angels and redeemed saints will have access to heaven, when "God shall be all in all" (1 Cor. 15:28). But the new heavens and the new earth will also be the habitation of the redeemed.

THE NEW JERUSALEM. This city is not heaven per se, since it descends "from God out of heaven" (Rev. 21:2). Yet together with heaven it is the eternal abode and destiny of the redeemed of all the ages. The inhabitants of the city will be God the Father, glorified Old Testament saints (Heb. 11:40), New Testament saints, myriads of holy angels, and our blessed Redeemer himself (Heb. 12:22, 23; Rev. 21:11-21). Both Israel and the Church appear prominently in the city (Rev. 21:12, 14). The great, high wall of the city denotes the security of its inhabitants, bathed in God's radiant and unveiled glory (1 Cor. 15:28).

BACKGROUND STUDIES

Extrabiblical Writings

Diana, the love goddess, bewitched the Ephesians. *(Russ Busby photo)*

THE APOCRYPHA

Introduction

DEFINITION. The Old Testament Apocrypha consist of fourteen books which came into existence largely between 200 B.C. and A.D. 200.

THE OLD TESTAMENT APOCRYPHA		
Order in English Versions	*Classification*	*Subject*
1. First Esdras	Historical (621-539 B.C.)	Parallel to Chronicles, Ezra-Nehemiah
2. Second Esdras	Apocalyptic	Apocalyptic visions
3. Tobit	Didactic; fictional romance	Trials of a godly man and his vindication
4. Judith	Didactic; fictional romance	Exploits of a godly woman
5. Additions to Esther	Legendary additions to Esther	Hand of God in Esther
6. The Wisdom of Solomon	Wisdom literature	Antidote against idolatry
7. Ecclesiasticus	Wisdom literature	Everyday morality
8. Baruch (with Jeremiah's Letter)	Prophetic additions to Jeremiah	Confessions, promises, warning against idolatry
9. Azariah's Prayer and the Song of the Three	Legendary additions to the Book of Daniel	Prayer and praise for deliverance
10. Susanna		Defense of virtue
11. Bel and the Dragon		Exposé of idolatry
12. The Prayer of Manasseh	Legendary addition to 2 Chronicles	Manasseh's repentance in exile
13. First Maccabees	Historical (175-135 B.C.)	Struggle of Judaism against Hellenism
14. Second Maccabees	Historical (175-160 B.C.)	Panegyric of the Maccabean revolt

CONNECTION WITH THE OLD TESTAMENT. The Apocrypha formed part of the sacred literaure of the Jews in Alexandria, Egypt. With the exception of Second Esdras, these writings are found interspersed among the canonical Old Testament books in the ancient copies of the Septuagint (the first Greek version of the Old Testament). From the Septuagint they passed into the Latin Vulgate (translated about A.D. 400) and into early English translations. However, since 1629 they have been omitted in some editions. Since 1827 they have been omitted from practically all Protestant editions of the Bible.

QUESTION OF CANONICAL AUTHORITY. In its early years the Christian Church used as its Old Testament the Septuagint with the Apocrypha rather than the Hebrew Old Testament. For this reason both the Eastern and Western Church began to accept the Apocrypha as canonical, despite strong scholarly warning to the contrary. (It is important to note that the Hebrew Old Testament never contained any of the apocryphal books.) The Roman Church recognized eleven of the fourteen apocryphal books as canonical, rejecting only First and Second Esdras and the Prayer of Manasseh. (These were placed in an appendix at the end of the New Testament.)

At the advent of the Reformation, Protestant scholars renewed their commitment to the sole authority of God-inspired Scripture and in consequence rejected the Apocrypha, accepting instead only the books of the ancient Hebrew Canon.

The First Book of Esdras

First Esdras consists of an independent and somewhat free version of portions of Second Chronicles and Ezra-Nehemiah. The account extends from Josiah's Passover (2 Chron. 35, 621 B.C.) to Cyrus' Decree after the Exile (Ezra 1:1-3) in 539 B.C. The interesting thing about First Esdras is that it contains a section (3:1—5:6) that has no parallel in the Hebrew Bible. This is the account of a competition between three Jewish pages at Darius' court intended to determine the meaning of true wisdom. Zerubbabel, who was to become the governor of the restored community, won the contest. The prize was permission of the Jews to return to Palestine. The work ends with the reading of the Law by Ezra (9:36-55), as in Nehemiah 7:38—8:12.

The purpose of the unknown author of First Esdras was to emphasize the contributions of Josiah, Zerubbabel, and Ezra in reforming Israelite worship. The book is commonly dated toward the end of the second century B.C.

The Second Book of Esdras

Second Esdras differs from the other books of the Apocrypha in being an apocalypse, that is, an "unveiling" of the future. Like the book of Daniel and the Revelation, which are also apocalypses, Second Esdras contains numerous symbols involving mysterious numbers, strange beasts, and the disclosure of hidden truths through angelic visitants. The original and main part of the book (Chapters 3—14) was written by an unknown Jew toward the end of the first century A.D. It consists of a series of seven revelations—3:1—5:20; 5:21—6:34; 6:35—9:25; 9:38—10:59; 11:1—12:51; 13:1-58; and 14:1-48. In these disclosures the seer is instructed by the angel Uriel. Second Esdras wrestles with the problem of theodicy, that is, the reconciliation of

God's justice, goodness, and power with the many evils that beset mankind. Chapters 1 and 2 and chapters 15 and 16 are later Christian additions to the original Jewish apocalypse.

Tobit

This religious fictionalized romance concerns Tobit, a devout Jew of Thisbe in Naphtali of Galilee. With his wife, Hannah, and their son Tobias, Tobit was carried away captive to Nineveh in the reign of the Assyrian emperor Shalmaneser IV (782-772 B.C.). In Nineveh he continued his good deeds, especially the giving of alms and the providing of proper burial to those of his own race cruelly slain by Sennacherib (705-681 B.C.). When the Emperor heard of this practice, Tobit was forced to flee Nineveh. But when Sennacherib's son, Esarhaddon (681-669 B.C.), came to the throne, Tobit was enabled to return to the capital through the influence of his nephew, Ahikar, who became the chief minister of the new king.

Improved fortune, however, was not unmixed with tragedy. Tobit was required to sleep outdoors in the courtyard because his continued practice of providing decent burial for his murdered countrymen rendered him ceremonially "unclean." One night as he slept, the droppings of sparrows fell into his eyes and cost him his sight. After four years of incurable blindness, he called upon God in utter despair.

At this very moment in Ecbatana, the capital of Media (in Persia), one Sarah was uttering a prayer for deliverance from her own plight. Sarah's condition was as tragic as Tobit's. Her seven husbands had been slain one by one in the bridal chamber by the jealous demon Asmodaeus. But now the prayers of both Tobit and Sarah were being heard. God was sending the angel Raphael ("God heals"), disguised as a man, to help them.

Tobit, believing that the time of his death was drawing near, made plans to send Tobias to Rages in Media, not far from Ecbatana, to recover from a kinsman, Gabael, a sum of money (ten talents of silver, about $20,000) which had been deposited for safekeeping with him years before. Raphael, posing as a dependable kinsman who knew the way, was engaged to conduct Tobias on the trip. In bidding them goodby, Tobit unwittingly implored God that his angel attend them.

As the travelers camped at the Tigris River, a large fish literally leaped at Tobias from the water, furnishing them a good meal. At Raphael's suggestion the heart, liver, and gall of the fish were saved for future use.

Before they arrived at Ecbatana, Raphael proceeded to tell young Tobias about Sarah, the attractive daughter of Raguel. He pointed out that by reason of kinship Tobias was the only eligible husband left for her. Before he was through with the matter, Raphael had persuaded Tobias to marry Sarah, instructing him to exorcize the husband-killing demon, Asmodaeus, by burning the heart and liver of the fish on the incense fire in the bridal chamber.

After the arrival, exchange of greetings, and consummation of the marriage, Tobias carried out Raphael's instruction, and the smoke and smell of the burned heart and liver of the fish drove Asmodaeus away into upper Egypt, the traditional home of magic and witchcraft (cf. Exod. 7:11), where Raphael quickly followed and fettered him. In the meantime, fearing the worst, Sarah's father had had a grave dug during the night. The next morning, however, he was overjoyed to find his new son-in-law alive. At Raguel's insistence a fourteen-day wedding celebration was carried on. During this time Raphael went on alone to Rages and obtained the money from Gabael.

Back in Nineveh, Tobit and Hannah were in despair at their son's long absence. What a rejoicing took place when Tobias returned with his new wife and Raphael! Then Tobias took the gall of the fish, whose heart and liver had already brought such wonderful deliverance, and with it anointed his father's eyes, according to Raphael's directions. Immediately Tobit's sight was restored.

Gratitude overwhelmed the family, and they offered Raphael half the fortune. But at this point the angel revealed his true identity. He bade them thank God for his mercies and vanished. Tobit thereupon uttered a beautiful prayer of thanksgiving (chap. 13). The book ends happily with instructions of Tobit to Tobias and with predictions of mercy and blessing for God's people (chap. 14).

Judith

Judith, like Tobit, belongs to the category of religious fiction. It has both a patriotic and a didactic purpose. It relates the exciting story of how a small Jewish town, inspired by the example of a devout woman, withstood the overwhelming power of a pagan army. The first part of the book (chapters 1—7) describes in somewhat tedious detail how Nebuchadnezzar's general, Holofernes, invaded the west and at length laid siege to the Jewish town of Bethulia. Situated strategically in relation to the plain of Esdraelon and the central mountain ridge of

Palestine, this fortress city barred access to the road leading to Jerusalem.

Amazed that the Jews should offer such audacious resistance, Holofernes called the chieftains of the Ammonites and Moabites to inquire about this strange people. Achior the Ammonite gave Holofernes a full account of the history of the Jews, declaring that the secret of their success was their faith in God. Since they were invincible as long as they did not sin against their God, Achior urged Holofernes to find out if there were any defection among them regarding the Lord. He advised the proud pagan general to refrain from attacking them if no unfaithfulness were found (1:1—5:19).

Holofernes replied to Achior, "Who is God except Nebuchadnezzar?" and ordered Achior bound and delivered to the foot of the steep hill on which Bethulia stood, to share the fate of the doomed city. The Jews, finding him, took him into the city. Meanwhile an immense army of 182,000 troops besieged the city for thirty-four days, making every effort to force its capitulation by hunger and thirst. When the cisterns of the city became empty, Ozias, the mayor of Bethulia, and his chief advisers decided to capitulate should no relief arrive within five days (5:20—7:32).

Judith, a beautiful and pious widow, is introduced in chapter 8. She was grieved by the decision to surrender. Such a course of action would open the road to Jerusalem and mean the destruction of the Temple and the nation. So Judith announced a bold plan. She declared that she would leave the city with her maid, hinting that God through her would accomplish Bethulia's deliverance. After first humbling herself before God in sackcloth and ashes, she put on her finest attire and proceeded from her beleaguered city to the camp of the pagan armies with her maid, who carried a bag of ceremonially clean food in her hand (8:1—10:5).

The Assyrian guards, smitten by Judith's beauty, conducted her at her request to Holofernes. She assured the general that Achior had told him the truth, that no harm could come to the Jews unless they would sin against their God. But the general need not despair, she assured him, since sin had already overtaken them in their plans to eat consecrated food to relieve their hunger. They would capitulate, she said, because their God-given resistance would vanish.

Delighted, Holofernes invited Judith to be his guest for three days. She accepted on the condition that she be allowed to eat only the clean food she had brought with her, and that she be allowed to go each night to the fountain of Bethulia to perform her ceremonial washings. On the fourth night Holofernes invited Judith to a banquet in his tent. Her beauty, wit, and finery made her the center of attention. After the subaltern officers left and Holofernes was alone with Judith, he fell asleep, overcome by the many toasts he had drunk to Judith's beauty.

Fortified by prayer, Judith quickly seized Holofernes' scimitar. With two quick blows she severed the general's head and handed it to her maid, who deposited it in her food bag. Both women left the camp without suspicion. However, this time Judith bypassed the spring and returned to Bethulia with her trophy.

The citizens of Bethulia were electrified with joy and courage. At daybreak they fell on the sleeping and leaderless army, which became easy prey to them. The huge host was cut to pieces in the ensuing confusion and the survivors were pursued in flight beyond Damascus. A great thanksgiving took place and Judith sang a psalm of praise to the Lord (10:6 – 16:25).

Written in Hebrew in the latter part of the second century B.C., the story has been transmitted to us today in three Greek and two Latin versions, as well as in a Syriac Version and later Hebrew recensions. It has inspired numerous works of painting, sculpture, and literature.

Additions to Esther

Apocryphal Esther consists of six passages (105 verses) which are not found in the Hebrew text of the canonical book. These additions were interspersed throughout the Greek translation in the Septuagint. They were apparently penned about 100 B.C. by an Alexandrian Jew who was eager to inject a more pronounced religious note into the canonical story and heighten its anti-Gentile character. The additions frequently refer to God, emphasize his choice of Israel, and highlight prayer. Jerome, when making the Latin Vulgate in the fourth century A.D., removed all the additions and put them in an appendix at the end of Esther, leaving only the original Hebrew as the text.

Some of the additions had evidently been introduced by Lysimachus, an Alexandrian Jew who resided at Jerusalem and translated the canonical book about 100 B.C. Other additions appear to have been inserted some years later.

The Wisdom of Solomon

This important apocryphal book of nineteen chapters belongs to the category of wisdom literature. As in the case of its sister apocry-

Underground "Solomon's stables," built by Crusaders over earlier stalls (*Russ Busby photo*)

phal book of Ecclesiasticus and the canonical book of Ecclesiastes, the Wisdom of Solomon (second century B.C.) expounds practical righteous living through fellowship with God and obedience to the moral law of God. The author, unknown but probably Jewish, personifies wisdom as a divine attribute of God (7:25-27). This contrasts with the canonical book of Proverbs (Prov. 8:22-36), where wisdom is more than the personification of an attribute of God or of the will of God, and is instead a distinct foreshadowing of the coming Messiah. Certain peculiar conceptions of the Logos and the Holy Spirit are also prominent features of the book (cf. John 1:1 and Heb. 1:1, 2 with Wisdom 7:26). Wisdom 9:17 combines God, wisdom, and the Holy Spirit in a manner that suggests the Christian doctrine of the Trinity.

The book falls into three sections. The first section (chaps. 1—5) is eschatological, portraying in vivid contrast the fate of the righteous and the ungodly. The second section (chaps. 6—10) is a noble poem extolling goodness and praising wisdom (which gives its names to the book). The third section (chaps. 11—19) is a theological interpretation of history, broken by a dissertation on the origin and evils of idolatry (chaps. 13—15). Chapters 11, 12, 16, 17, 18, and 19 contrast the lot of Israel in the wilderness with that of the Egyptians during the plagues. The writer seeks to prove two propositions: first, that "by what things a man sins, by these he is punished" (11:16); second, that by what things Israel's foes were punished, by these the Lord's people "in their need were benefited" (11:5).

Ecclesiasticus

Like the Wisdom of Solomon of the apocryphal books and like Job, certain Psalms, Proverbs, and Ecclesiastes of the canonical books, Ecclesiasticus belongs to the wisdom literature of the Hebrews. Called also "The Wisdom of Jesus, Son of Sirach," Ecclesiasticus (Latin "The Church Book") is a long and valuable ethical treatise (51 chapters) and contains a wide range of instructions in general morality and practical godliness. It is patterned after the model of Proverbs, Ecclesiastes, and Job, and has been popular in the Roman Catholic Church, where it is accorded canonical status.

Ecclesiasticus was composed originally in Hebrew by Ben Sira at about 180 B.C. and was later translated into Greek, in 132 B.C. Jerome knew the Hebrew text. In 1896 fragments of it turned up in the Cairo Geniza and also in the caves at Qumran. About two-thirds of the Hebrew text has been found.

Baruch

This book of five chapters purports to be the work of Jeremiah's secretary, Baruch (Jer. 32:12; 36:4), written during the exile in Babylon and sent to Jerusalem to be read on festal occasions as a confession of sins (1:14). Part one, in prose, consists of an introduction (1:1-14) and a confession of Israel's guilt (1:15—3:8). Part two is composed of two poems. One extols wisdom as the Lord's special gift to Israel (3:9—4:4). The other is occupied with the subject of comfort and restoration (4:5—5:9).

The book was originally written in Hebrew but exists today only in Greek, from which a number of ancient versions had been made. The date when the several component parts of the book were brought together is commonly placed between 150 and 60 B.C.

The Letter of Jeremiah

The so-called Letter of Jeremiah purports to be the copy of an epistle dispatched by Jeremiah to the Jews who were about to be deported to Babylon in 597 B.C. The letter warns against the peril of idolatry, so rampant in the country to which they were being taken. The author elaborates on Jeremiah 10:11: "Thus shall ye say to them: The gods who did not make the heavens and the earth shall perish from the earth and from under the heavens." The author also draws upon Jeremiah 10:3-9, Jeremiah 14, and Psalm 115:4-8 and echoes the anti-idol sentiment of Isaiah 40:18-20 and 41:6, 7. The refrain "this shows that there are no gods" runs through the discourse (verses 16, 23, 40, 44, 52, 56, 65, and 69).

The letter is commonly dated in the second century B.C. The oldest manuscript remains of the book are a tiny fragment of Greek papyrus containing a part of verses 43 and 44. These were discovered in Cave Seven at Qumran and date from about 100 B.C. Though the book has usually been attached to Baruch, the Revised Standard Version prints it as a separate book, since it actually has nothing to do with Baruch.

Azariah's Prayer and the Song of the Three

This is one of three important apocryphal additions to the canonical book of Daniel. The other two are Susanna and Bel and the Dragon. At chapter 3, verse 23 The Prayer and Song follow the account of the fiery furnace into which three Jewish captives were thrown for refusing to worship the golden image which Nebuchadnezzar had set up. The interpolation is in three parts: 1) Azariah's prayer (vv. 1-22) (Azariah being the Hebrew name for Abednego, his pagan name— Dan. 1:7); 2) description of the fiery furnace (vv. 23-27); and 3) The Song of the Three (vv. 28-68).

The refrains "Blessed art thou, O Lord . . . Blessed art thou . . . Bless the Lord" run through the entire song (vv. 26-28), endowing it with a deep solemnity and majestic rhythm. The unknown poet in the second or first century B.C. derived much of his inspiration from the antiphonal liturgies which appear in Psalms 136 and 148.

The History of Susanna

Of the three additions to Daniel, this tale of the triumph of virtue over villainy constitutes one of the finest short stories in world literature. The tale runs as follows.

Susanna, the lovely and virtuous wife of Joakim, a wealthy and honorable Jew of Babylon, becomes the object of the lust of two unscrupulous elders who had been made judges in the Jewish community. One morning they discovered each other near Joakim's garden, where Susanna walked, and acknowledged their mutual passion for the woman. They agreed to accost Susanna, but were repulsed with scorn. To protect themselves they accuse their victim. They betake themselves to the city and issue a summons to Susanna. Appearing with her household, she is ordered to be unveiled, while the elders appear as witnesses against her before the assembled people. They declare that they saw her commit adultery in her husband's garden with a youth who had escaped. The testimony of the elders leads the whole synagogue to condemn Susanna.

As Susanna is on the way to be executed in accordance with Mosaic Law, a youth (Daniel) questions the verdict and reopens the trial. He cross-examines the two witnesses. The one asserts the crime was enacted under "a mastic tree," the other under "an evergreen oak" (RSV). The discrepancy condemns both as false witnesses. Susanna ("lily") is exonerated, Daniel ("God is my Judge") is lauded, and the two elders are gagged, cast in a ravine, and devoured by fire from heaven (Deut. 19:16-21).

The position of this addition to canonical Daniel varies. In the Septuagint and the Latin Vulgate it follows chapter 12, being numbered chapter 13. In other ancient versions, such as Theodotian, Old Latin, Coptic, and Arabic it is prefixed to chapter 1 (cf. Susanna 1:45). The date of *all* the additions to Daniel is evidently the second or first century B.C. Hebrew (or Aramaic) was apparently the original language in which they were written.

Bel and the Dragon

This addition to the book of Daniel consists of two popular tales, both designed to satirize the folly of idolatry and expose the snare of pagan priestcraft. The first story concerns Bel or Marduk, the patron deity of Babylon. Bel's idol is represented as devouring huge quantities of food and drink every night. By this means the image was thought to prove itself a living god. But Daniel ridiculed the king's credulousness. In anger Cyrus, who became king in 538 B.C., challenged the seventy priests of Baal to tell him who was eating these provisions or die. If Bel were really eating them, then Daniel would die.

Playing the role of a clever detective, Daniel had a light coating of ash dust scattered on the floor after the king had personally placed the provisions in the temple and sealed all the doors with his own signet. Next morning as he and the king went to see what had transpired, they found the food gone and the seals unbroken. Gleefully Daniel interrupted the king's praise of Bel by pointing out to the king the footprints of the seventy priests with their wives and families on the ash-strewn floor. Then the king was enraged. He seized the priests and their wives and children. When they showed him the secret doors through which they were accustomed to enter and devour what was on the table, he "put them to death and gave Bel over to Daniel, who destroyed it and its temple" (1:22).

The dragon story concerns a serpent worshiped as a deity (cf. Num. 21:8, 9; 2 Kings 18:4). Daniel refuses to prostrate himself before the serpent. Instead he challenges the king. If permission is granted him, he will destroy the creature alleged to be a god. Granted his request, Daniel prepares a mixture of pitch, fat, and hair in cake form. When fed to the dragon, the concoction causes the dragon to burst open. Infuriated, the Babylonians accuse the king of destroying their gods and becoming a Jew. They thereupon demand that Daniel be handed over to them.

Hard-pressed to save his own life, the king releases Daniel to them. They promptly throw him to the hungry lions (making a second time that Daniel was put into the lions' den—see Daniel 6:16-24). On the sixth day, while Habakkuk in Judea is carrying lunch to the reapers, the angel of the Lord appears to him and directs him to take the food to Daniel in the lions' den in Babylon. When the prophet pleads his inability to comply, the angel takes him by the hair and sets him down in Babylon "right over the den" (v. 36).

Daniel gets up and eats the lunch and the angel of the Lord returns Habakkuk to Judea. On the seventh day, when the king comes to mourn Daniel, he finds him hale and hearty among the lions. Glorifying Daniel's God, he pulls Daniel out and throws Daniel's enemies in. They are devoured immediately before Daniel's eyes (v. 42).

In the Septuagint, Bel and the Dragon is appended to chapter 12 of Daniel. In the Latin Vulgate it appears as chapter 14, Susanna constituting chapter 13. Along with the other Danielic additions, it belongs to the second or first century B.C..

The Prayer of Manasseh

This classic of penitential devotion is attributed to Manasseh ("Manasses" in Greek), the idolatrous king of Judah. It is thought to follow Second Chronicles 33:18, 19, which outlines the king's wicked reign and his repentance when carried away prisoner by the Assyrians. It is known from archeology that Esarhaddon (681-669 B.C.) rebuilt Babylon and that he summoned Manasseh to Nineveh to see his new palace. The prayer is divided into fifteen verses. This division is generally followed and appears in the Revised Standard Version of the Apocrypha.

The prayer itself is constructed in accord with the best liturgical forms and breathes throughout a deep note of genuine contrition and profound religious feeling. The date of composition is hard to determine with precision. Most scholars date it sometime in the last two centuries B.C. It is not known whether it was composed originally in Hebrew, Aramaic, or Greek. It has survived in Greek, Latin, Syriac, Armenian, and Ethiopic.

The First Book of Maccabees

This is a first-class historical work, consisting of sixteen chapters. It narrates the heroic struggle of the Jews for religious liberty and political independence during the years 175 to 135 B.C., featuring in particular the exploits of Judas Maccabeus, who is regarded as the central figure in Jewish resistance against encroaching Hellenism.

The book sketches the conquests of Alexander the Great and the division of his empire, giving the background of the origin of Greek rule in the East (1:1-9). Then the author outlines briefly the causes of the Maccabean revolt against the Seleucid king Antiochus Epiphanes (1:10-64). The beginning of the struggle under Mattathias, the aged priest of Modin, is highlighted (2:1-70). Then are portrayed at length the political and military careers of Mattathias' heroic sons Judas (3: 1−9:22), Jonathan (9:23−12:53), and Simon (13:1−16:17). The book ends with a short notice of the rule of Simon's son, John Hyrcanus (134-104 B.C.).

The book presents the continual providence of God over his people during the Greek era and may be dated about 110 B.C. It was most certainly written in Hebrew, as Jerome distinctly avers. Though the original Hebrew was lost at an early period, the work has been preserved in Greek and Latin as well as in several versions based on the Greek.

The Second Book of Maccabees

This historical work of fifteen chapters claims to be a condensation of a five-volume history (now lost) authored by a Hellenistic Jew, Jason of Cyrene (2:23). Second Maccabees itself is anonymous. It covers part of the same period as First Maccabees (175-160 B.C.) and is primarily concerned with the history of Judas Maccabeus. The book opens with two letters from the Jews of Judea to their colleagues in Egypt (1:1-9; 1:10—2:18). Both epistles are concerned with the observance of the Feast of Dedication, which celebrated the reconsecration of the sanctuary after it had been profaned by Antiochus Epiphanes. After a prologue describing the nature of the book as a condensation of the history of the period written by Jason of Cyrene (2:19-32), the epitome proper follows 3:1—15:36); the book ends with a brief epilogue (15:37-39).

The epitome is a theological interpretation of the patriotic revolt against the paganistic encroachments led by Judas. The following main headings constitute a general summary: 1) Divine blessing upon Jerusalem in the protection of the Temple from desecration by Heliodorus during the devout administration of the high priest Onias under Seleucus IV, 187-175 B.C. (chapter 3); 2) Divine punishment of Jerusalem under Antiochus IV Epiphanes (175-163 B.C.), with profanation of the Temple and proscription of Judaism (chapters 4—7); 3) Divine deliverance and reconsecration of the Temple as a result of the heroism of Judas and his men (8:1—10:9); and 4) Divine help for Judas and his men in their victories during the reign of Demetrius I, 162-150 B.C. (14:1—15:36).

THE PSEUDEPIGRAPHA

The Pseudepigrapha constitute another body of religious literature beside the Apocrypha that came into being in the general period of 200 B.C. to A.D. 200. Although these books have many affinities with the Apocrypha, they never vied for canonical status or were considered canonical in any sense by either Jews or Christians. They are commonly called Pseudepigrapha ("false writings") because, though attributed to worthies of a much earlier age, such as Adam, Enoch, Noah, Moses, Elijah, Isaiah, etc., they were actually penned by men in the first two centuries B.C. and A.D. These works are largely apocalyptic, legendary, and didactic, frequently using history to propagate the issue of Judaism versus Hellenism. Some of the more important pseudepigraphical works are described below.

The Book of Jubilees

This is one of the longest and most important books of the pseudepigraphical literature. It is a revised version of the book of Genesis and the first twelve chapters of Exodus, rewritten from the point of view of later Judaism. The utmost importance is placed on the Mosaic Law, and the writer of Jubilees traces the origin of its various enactments to the patriarchal age. Strict separation between Jew and Gentile is taught, so much so that intermarriage is prohibited under penalty of death. Circumcision and the Sabbath are emphasized as distinctive marks of Judaism. The book takes its name from the author's chronology. He divides history into jubilees or fifty-year periods (Lev. 25:8-12). The treatise was written in the period 135 to 115 B.C., evidently by a Pharisaic Jew who sympathized with the Maccabean movement and favored strict separation from the demoralizing influences of Greek customs.

The Book of Enoch

This apocalypse is not a single book but is rather a library of at least five volumes penned by various authors at different periods in the last two centuries of the pre-Christian era. The following table describes the contents of the book.

The Book of Enoch has undoubtedly had a large influence on New Testament theology, particularly in its messianic conceptions. It is in the Book of Enoch that the term "Christ" first appears in Jewish literature as the designation of the coming messianic king. "The Son of Man" (cf. Dan. 7), "the Righteous One," and "the Elect One" (Acts 3:14; 7:52) are other messianic designations in Enoch that are prominent in the New Testament, as well as the concept of Messiah as Judge (cf. John 5:22). Messiah is also depicted as "preexisting" and as "sitting on the throne of his glory" (cf. John 1:1, 18; Matt. 25:31).

THE BOOK OF ENOCH

Book and Date	Contents
Book 1 (Chaps. 1−36) Before 170 B.C.	Deals with problem of evil. Origin of evil is placed not in Adam's fall but in fallen angels of Gen. 6:1-8. Demons are the result of angelic cohabitation with women. Millennium is a time of sensuous enjoyment.
Book 2 (Chaps. 37−70) 94-79 B.C.	"The Similitudes." Denounces later Maccabean princes and their allies, the Sadducees. Solution of problem of evil is given as the advent of Messiah.
Book 3 (Chaps. 71−82)	"Book of Celestial Physics." Attempts to establish a Hebrew calendar to offset pagan calendars then in vogue.
Book 4 (Chaps. 83−90) 166-161 B.C.	Evil laid to failure of 70 shepherds (angels) to whom God entrusted Israel. Israel will be restored through a righteous family (Judas Maccabeus).
Book 5 (Chaps. 91−104) 134-95 B.C.	Author a Pharisee. He finds the solution to the problem of evil in neither an earthly messianic kingdom nor the advent of a great deliverer, but instead in the future life. Righteous will be raised as spirits. Wicked doomed to eternal punishment in hell.

The Ascension of Isaiah

This apocalypse is in three parts.

The Martyrdom (1:1-3; 5:2-14; first century B.C.) recounts Isaiah's death by being "sawn asunder with a wooden saw" under wicked King Manasseh. It is a Jewish sacred legend.

The Testament of Hezekiah (3:13b−4:18) is a Christian apocalypse showing how Isaiah's prophecy of Christ's second advent will be fulfilled.

The Vision of Isaiah (chaps. 6−11) is also Christian rather than Jewish, dating from the second century A.D. It depicts Isaiah's journey through the seven heavens to God's throne. There the voice of the Most High is heard speaking to his Son ("The Beloved"), bidding him to descend through the heavens to the world. The Son ("The Beloved") does this by means of the incarnation and the virgin birth. The Beloved's life, death, resurrection, and ascension are described, as well as his return to the seventh heaven and his placement at the right hand of the "Great Glory." (Note that these concepts were obviously taken from the New Testament Scriptures.)

The Testaments of the Twelve Patriarchs

Consisting of twelve small pamphlets, this work purports to contain the last utterances of Jacob's twelve sons. Each of these men is represented as calling his children around him on his deathbed and giving them words of counsel with regard to life, after the manner of Genesis 49. The work is apparently Jewish in origin (109-107 B.C.), with later Jewish and Christian interpolations. The Jewish origin of the original is suggested by the recovery of Aramaic fragments of the Testament of Levi from the Cairo Genizah and at Qumran.

Scholars maintain that there is no Jewish document that has had a greater influence on the New Testament, particularly upon the thinking of Paul. The work also represents a high-water mark in the ethical teaching of Judaism, especially upon the subject of forgiveness. Another important feature of the book is its exceptionally broad outlook, broader than any other document of the period. The book teaches, for example, that the Law was given "to illuminate every man" (not merely the Jew) and envisions worldwide salvation for Gentiles.

The Sibylline Oracles

Between the second century B.C. and the fifth century A.D. both Jews and Christians composed verses which they published under the name and authority of the ancient Sibyls (pagan seeresses). Of the fifteen ancient Jewish and Christian Oracles three books (numbers 9, 10, and 15) are lost, and some of the others exist only in fragments. The Jewish books (numbers 3, 4, and 5) are apocalyptic and predict the destruction of pagan kingdoms and the ultimate triumph of the Jew in the messianic kingdom (3:702-704; 5:418-427). The Sibylline Oracles share with other apocalyptic writings a deep dissatisfaction with present conditions, as well as an assurance that divine intervention in history will right human wrongs and vindicate the faith of God's elect.

The Books of Adam and Eve

Written in Aramaic during the first century A.D. by a Jew, this is a legendary amplification of the Genesis story of Adam and Eve which has survived in Latin and Greek manuscripts. Christian interpolations have been added to the original Jewish work. Legends are interwoven around the expulsion from paradise, Cain's murder of Abel, and Seth's birth. On his deathbed Adam is portrayed blessing his sixty-three children. In answer to the prayers of angels, Adam is pardoned and his soul consigned to the angels, who bury his body near the earthly paradise but carry his soul to the heavenly paradise to await the resurrection.

The author envisions a period of lawlessness and wickedness before the golden age of divinely manifested power on earth. Future judgment is emphasized. In contrast to the judgment of water at the flood, the final judgment is seen to be by fire. The "body" of Adam is said to be placed in "paradise in the third heaven," suggesting a heavenly counterpart to the physical body buried on earth.

The Psalms of Solomon

These are eighteen Psalms apparently written as a result of the destruction of Jerusalem by the Roman general Pompey in 63 B.C., called "the sinner," "the lawless one," and "the adversary." The invader breaks down Jerusalem's wall, enters the Temple, pollutes the altar, massacres many, and sends many others into exile. Retribution, however, overtakes the conqueror for his profanity. He is assassinated in Egypt and his unclaimed body tossed on the waves of the sea.

The psalms were written by several Pharisees. They stress the chief tenets of Pharisaism as a corrective to the erroneous teachings of Sadduceeism. They particularly emphasize 1) *the belief in theocracy.* In the face of Roman domination their slogan was "The Lord is King"; 2) *the belief in the Mosaic Law.* This was the divine ideal. True righteousness consists of meticulously observing its ordinances and avoiding any violation of ceremonial purity. But the Pharisaism reflected here is on a much higher plane than that which Jesus encountered almost a century later. Much more stress is laid on the inner spiritual life of repentance, faith, and prayer; 3) *the belief in the future life.* The righteous will rise to life eternal, the wicked to eternal death. However, physical resurrection, a common tenet of Pharisaism, does not appear clearly in these Psalms, although the idea is not excluded.

The most noteworthy feature of the Psalms is the messianic prediction of Psalm 17:17-51. The prophesied Messiah, raised up by God to deliver the people from the Roman yoke, is purely human, in striking contrast to inspired Scripture's prophecy of him.

The Third Book of Maccabees

This work is historical fiction, the scene of which is laid in the reign of Ptolemy IV (222-204 B.C.). The book has no connection with

First and Second Maccabees, nor with the Maccabean age. It does, however, recount the story of God's faithfulness and the fidelity of the Jewish people in times of persecution. This is apparently the only point it has in common with the other books of Maccabees. It stresses the value of prayer and the working of "the unconquerable Providence." This is seen in the sudden paralysis which Ptolemy IV experienced when he attempted to enter the Temple at Jerusalem. It is seen, too, in the futility of his attempt to slaughter the Jews of Alexandria by having them trampled to death in the hippodrome by intoxicated elephants. In both instances the prayers of the godly priest brought about providential deliverance.

The Fourth Book of Maccabees

This is a hortatory address of fourteen chapters urging a life of faithfulness to God and self-control toward men. Dated probably between 50 B.C. and A.D. 50, this work portrays heroic events of the Maccabean age as illustrations of its religious and philosophical principles. Hence, unlike Third Maccabees, it *does* have a valid reason for its title. The writer's thesis and method of proof may be summarized in his own words. "I might prove to you from many other considerations that pious reason is the sole master of the passions, but I shall prove it most effectually from the fortitude of Eleazar, and of the seven brothers and their mother; for all these proved by their contempt of torture and death that reason has command over the passions" (1:7-9). But the author stipulates a limitation. Although reason is master over the passions, it is not master of its own affections, and so cannot control thoughts and motives.

Fourth Maccabees is of great value for the student of the New Testament, particularly in studies of the life of Paul. The stoic Pharisaism of the writer was essentially that of the Apostle before his conversion. It was only when Paul realized that the Law did not enable him to keep the commandment "Thou shalt not covet," and that it gave no power to rule the inner realm of the spirit, that the crisis came which proved to be the turning-point in the Apostle's spiritual life. This limitation, which the writer of Fourth Maccabees recognizes so acutely, gave Paul no peace till he found it in the gospel of Christ.

Important also to New Testament study is the prominence given to the concept of "propitiation" in the book. The idea presented is that the blood of the martyrs atones for the sins of the people (2 Mac. 17: 22). Paul, of course, also features propitiation. But in his inspired teaching it is the blood of Christ alone that atones for sin! (See Romans 3:25).

The Testament of Job

A legendary expansion of the canonical book of Job, this Aramaic Midrash stems from the first century B.C. Its fanciful tales were intended to comfort the godly in separatist Judaism in times of bitter persecution by inspiring them in the hope of the resurrection. It was also slanted to shield the faithful against the encroachments of Hellenism.

The unknown author weaves his legends around Job's wife, who is named Sitidos. She is pictured as supporting her husband when he is reduced to direst sickness and poverty. She lived to see her husband vindicated, but died before his fortunes were restored. On the day of her death, however, Job showed her that her children killed in the ruins of their house were safe in heaven. Bidding her and Job's three friends (who had given Job's wife no comfort in her children's safety) to turn their eyes toward the East, they saw the children wearing celestial crowns. Comforted in the truth of the resurrection and bliss in heaven, Sitidos died.

The Letter of Aristeas

Apparently written at Alexandria around 100 B.C., this pseudepigraphical Epistle of 322 verses claims to have been penned by an officer in the court of Ptolemy II Philadelphus (285-245 B.C.) to his brother Philocrates. It alleges to be an account of the translation of the Hebrew Pentateuch into Greek. Demetrius the librarian at Alexandria is represented as urging the king to send to Jerusalem to ask the high priest Eleazer to send six scholars from each of the twelve tribes. The request was complied with. The Jewish scholar worked for seventy-two days on the island of Pharos to produce the Greek Pentateuch, called the Septuagint ("the Seventy"), in memory of the seventy-two translators.

Scholars are hesitant to accept the historical reliability of the Letter. Perhaps it does preserve the germinal truth of the Septuagint's origin and does illustrate how Hellenistic Jews sought to bridge the gap between Hebrew and Greek thought.

The Lives of the Prophets

This work, written in Hebrew during the first century A.D., consists of a collection of extrabiblical traditions concerning the prophets.

The text deals with the four major prophets (Isaiah, Jeremiah, Ezekiel, and Daniel), the minor prophets, and, in addition, Nathan, Ahijah, Joed (Neh. 11:7; 2 Chron. 9:24), Azariah (2 Chron. 15:1-15), Zechariah (2 Chron. 24:20-22), Elijah, and Elisha.

Qumran—these desolate caves yielded the Dead Sea Scrolls, the oldest copies of the Hebrew Scriptures ever discovered. (© *MPS*)

THE DEAD SEA SCROLLS

In 1947 the ancient library of a monastic Jewish community with headquarters in the Wadi Qumran, northwest of the Dead Sea, was accidentally discovered. Eleven caves in the area yielded manuscripts of practically all of the Old Testament books as well as the apocryphal and pseudepigraphical works of Tobit, Ecclesiasticus, Enoch, Jubilees, and the Testament of Levi. The Qumran library also contained an important body of sectarian literature describing the life and distinctive doctrines of the religious community located not far from the caves where the manuscripts were discovered. The community flourished from its apparent founding at about 110 B.C. until the great earthquake of 31 B.C. It was rebuilt after Herod the Great's death in 4 B.C. and again flourished until destroyed by the Romans in A.D. 68. But the valuable library escaped destruction by the Romans because it had been removed to the nearby caves.

The Manual of Discipline

This document, dating about 70 B.C., presents the rules and liturgy of the community (1:1 – 3:12), its doctrines (3:13 – 4:26), its regulations concerning admission and punishment of crimes, and its description of the holy life to be cultivated in an evil world (5:1 – 9:26). The Manual supplies valuable insight into ceremonial Jewish legalism as practiced by an Essene sect during the time of Christ. Ritual washings were performed to remove uncleanness when transgressions of the code defiled the community. By contrast, Jesus' teachings plainly demonstrated that righteousness is a condition of the heart rather than a matter of external conformity to legal minutiae (Matt. 16:10, 11). The teaching of the Manual concerning two contrasts – light and darkness, truth and error – finds parallels in the New Testament (John 3: 19; Rom. 13:12; 2 Cor. 6:14; 1 John 1:5). The Qumranian, like the Christian, was taught to turn from darkness to walk in the light.

The communal life at Qumran is also paralleled by the practice of the early Christian Church (Acts 4:32). The appendix of the Manual refers to a sacred meal which served as a foretaste of the future messianic banquet. Like the Christian communion supper, this meal was founded on the Jewish ceremonial custom of breaking bread and drinking wine at the beginning of each meal. Jesus took this traditional Jewish blessing and interpreted it in the light of his impending death, which would open the way for fellowship with his disciples at a future banquet in the kingdom of God (Mark 14:25).

The Damascus Document

This document represents the convictions of a Jewish sectarian group that fled to the desert northwest of the Dead Sea to escape persecution and to await deliverance from their foes and vindication of the principles for which they suffered. The full title of the work is "The Document of the New Covenant in the Land of Damascus." Whether the term "Damascus" is a prophetic name for the Qumran area or is a literal designation of the ancient city in the Anti-Lebanon district where the sect may have sojourned during the period that Qumran was abandoned (31-4 B.C.) is not known.

The Damascus Document consists of 1) an introductory exhortation and 2) a collection of ordinances. Rigid conformity to the ordinances based on the Mosaic Law was enjoined upon this sect of Judaism, which held the Hebrew Scriptures in high regard. The teachings of the Document have much in common with the tenets of the Pharisees. It inculcates the doctrine of the future life and affirms the existence of angels and spirits. It directs hope to the advent of a messianic deliverer. The Lord's people are exhorted to prepare themselves for his coming.

The people of the Damascus Document identified themselves with the priest Zadok (1 Chron. 24:3). The first fragments of the Damascus Document discovered in 1896-97 in a manuscript storeroom (*genizah*) in Old Cairo were entitled *Fragments of a Zadokite Work.* Because they placed proper emphasis on Old Testament prophecy, the Zadokites were naturally predisposed to accept Christ and doubtless formed part at least of the "great company of the priests" that became "obedient to the faith" (Acts 6:7).

The Thanksgiving Scroll

The Thanksgiving Scroll (*Hodayot*) is the hymn and praise book of the Qumran Community. The present copy, recovered from Caves One and Four, contains some gaps. These songs reflect fierce persecution and conflict (4:8, 9). Although couched in personal terms, the songs reflect the group experiences of the Qumran Community. The formula "I will praise thee, my Lord" occurs in many of the hymns, and faith in God's delivering and preserving power is emphasized. Messianic expectation imbues the poet. However, he envisions a severe trial that will first try men (3:26-36) as the prelude to God's intervention. Yet even in the present state of sin and persecution the pious community is considered a segment of "paradise" (8:5-7).

The Genesis Apocryphon

Made of four leather sheets sewed together, this is a document of 22 columns of Aramaic text. This scroll, unlike other Cave One documents from Qumran, was not stored in a jar. As a result it was severely damaged, and was published in 1956 only as the result of the most painstaking ingenuity.

The Apocryphon is a paraphrase of the book of Genesis, freely embellished with fictional details. The embellished text is sectioned into four parts: 1) The Story of Lamech (1–5); 2) The Story of Noah (6–15); 3) The Table of Nations (16, 17); and 4) The Story of Abraham (18–22). The Apocryphon was intended to encourage the persecuted numbers of the Community to remain true to their faith in view of the coming messianic age.

The War Scroll

More fully entitled "War of the Sons of Light with the Sons of Darkness," this document was recovered from Cave One at Qumran in 1947. It consists of 18½ columns of text, with from 16 to 18 lines on each column. It was written anonymously sometime after 63 B.C. Columns 1 through 9 deal with the rules for equipment and the tactics of battle. Columns 10 through 19 set forth exhortations and prayers. The sons of light (true Israel) are encouraged to fight in the light of God's promises and faithfulness to Israel in the past. Israel's enemies (the Kittim) are doomed to eventual defeat.

Although the Scroll deals with an eschatological war (reminiscent of biblical Armageddon – Rev. 16:12-16), the contest suggests a perennial spiritual struggle between light and darkness, as in John's Gospel and First Epistle. The Scroll also gives a realistic description of military operations of the first century B.C. as seen through Jewish eyes.

The Habakkuk Commentary

This commentary from Cave One expounds chapters 1 and 2 of Habakkuk in the light of the history of the Qumran community. It mentions the "Teacher of Righteousness," who broke with the Jerusalem priesthood and led a number of priests and laymen to Qumran to establish a settlement of the true Israel. It also deals with the foe of the Teacher of Righteousness, known as the "Wicked Priest." The commentator interprets the Chaldeans (Hab. 1:6) as the "Kittim" (Romans), who will devastate the nation and bring judgment upon the wicked priests at Jerusalem.

The precise date of the Habakkuk Commentary is not known and the identification of the Teacher of Righteousness and his wicked antagonist is uncertain. Fragments of other commentaries on Micah, Zephaniah, and the Psalms were found in Cave One. Cave Four yielded four commentaries on Hosea, two on the Psalms, and one on Nahum (all in fragmentary form). The Nahum Commentary clearly connects with the despotic rule of Alexander Jannaeus (103-76 B.C.).

This bas-relief sculpture found at Capernaum represents the Ark of the Covenant. (© *MPS*)

Historical-Archeological Backgrounds

The Bible as the revelation of God's plan of redemption for the lost human race is not history in the commonly accepted use of the term (the systematic record of events of the past). Even those parts of Scripture that are more closely associated with history, such as the books of Joshua, Judges, Kings, Chronicles, Ezra, and Nehemiah in the Old Testament, and the book of the Acts in the New Testament, are history only in a very specialized sense – the sense that they portray the story of human redemption.

In the strictest sense these books constitute a *philosophy* of history, for they interpret only highly selected events in the story of redemption. In the Old Testament these events focus first on the promised line through which the world's Redeemer was to come, then on the nation Israel and her relation to the Lord, and finally on God's redemptive program for the entire world. In the New Testament, after the nation Israel rejects the Messiah, God's new people, the Church, enter the stage of history.

THE BIBLE AND HISTORY

THE NATURE OF BIBLICAL HISTORY. Besides being a highly specialized and interpretive account of significant events in the story of human redemption, biblical history is always grounded in God-ordained morality. It realistically catalogs the evil as well as the good. Yet it never condones evil. Instead it warns against sin, presenting it as a dishonor to God, a violation of God's eternal moral laws, and the legitimate object of God's divine punishment. Biblical history is, therefore, eminently instructive. It teaches lessons in right living and admonishes against wrong conduct by both precept and example. The moral and spiritual tone of Old Testament history gives it timeless relevance and universal usefulness. This is why the books of Joshua, Judges, Samuel, and Kings (listed among the historical books in the English order) constitute the former *prophets* in the Hebrew Bible.

But the "historical" portions of the Old Testament are more than a specialized history of redemption or a philosophy of that history which emphasizes ethical and spiritual values. Redemptive history contains the *predictive* element in addition to the moral and ethical emphasis. Prediction of the Messiah by promise, type, and symbol is so thoroughly woven into the fabric of Old Testament redemptive history that it cannot be separated from it. The Old Testament must be seen as Messiah-centered history wedded to Messiah-centered prophecy in preparation for the advent of the Redeemer.

In the New Testament the book of the Acts as the account of the formation of the Church and the spread of Christianity is more like conventional history. However, the four Gospels are neither histories nor biographies of the life of Christ. Instead, they are *portraits* of Christ, presenting four different poses of the *one* unique personality. Yet each Gospel writer, while turning the spotlight on one feature of his Person, maintains his full-orbed character. Together they present four pictures that portray in wonderful fullness and clarity the one and same unique Person, the King of Israel, the Servant of the Lord, the God-Man, the Redeemer of humanity.

THE GOAL OF BIBLICAL HISTORY. While the Bible is accurate when it touches secular history, it is in no sense a secular account of events or of the lives of people. Its aim is strictly religious and redemptive. Hence, it begins with the earth when it was recreated for the latecomer man (Gen. 1:1-31), and not with the original creation of the universe. It traces man's creation upon the earth, his innocence, his fall, and the story of his redemption.

The goal of biblical history is to portray God's plan and purpose for the ages. It looks forward to a sin-cleansed universe in eternity, including a new heaven and a new earth (Rev. 20, 21). It envisions only one isolation ward for all sinners, angelic and human. As it moves through the arena of human history it includes only those things that relate to the unfolding of the divine plan for man's salvation.

THE BIBLE AND ARCHEOLOGY

THE SCIENCE OF BIBLICAL ARCHEOLOGY. Biblical archeology is concerned with the excavation, decipherment, and critical evaluation of those ancient records of the past that touch directly or indirectly on the Bible. Modern archeology had its beginnings in the early nineteenth century, when the antiquities of Egypt were opened up to scientific study by Napoleon's expedition. The treasuries of Assyria-Babylonia came to light toward the middle and latter part of the same century. Interest in Palestinian antiquities was given great impetus as a result of the discovery of the Moabite Stone in 1868.

However, the greatest discoveries of biblical archeology have been made in the twentieth century. During this period biblical archeology has become an exact science and has made remarkable contributions to the understanding of biblical history.

ARCHEOLOGY AND BIBLICAL HISTORY. Archeology has been called "the handmaid of history." As such it expands and clarifies historical backgrounds. In no sphere is this ministry more clearly illustrated than in the case of the Bible, particularly the Old Testament. Before the advent of the science of biblical archeology very little was known about the historical backgrounds of the Old Testament. As the result of archeological research in Bible lands, the Old Testament has now been authenticated in innumerable instances on the historical plane. In addition, its vastly broadened historical background has furnished a very effective setting for illustrating its manners, customs, and general narrative. Archeology has literally caused the Old Testament to come alive historically.

As far as the New Testament is concerned, the contributions of biblical archeology have not been nearly so dramatic as in the case of the Old Testament. Greek and Roman historians had supplied a great mass of background material. However, archeology has had a notable career in clearing up many historical difficulties, particularly validating Luke's accuracy as a historian in his Gospel and the Acts.

ARCHEOLOGICAL SURVEY OF OLD TESTAMENT HISTORY

THE PRIMEVAL PERIOD (10,000 to 2000 B.C.) The original earth, created in the dateless past, experienced various geologic ages and prehistoric stone ages before undergoing a gigantic catastrophe somewhere in the undated past. Much later it was refashioned for the latecomer man (somewhere between 6000 and 10,000 B.C., or possibly somewhat earlier).

The Creation Account in Archeology (Genesis 1 & 2). Polytheistic accounts of creation are found in *Enuma Elish,* the Babylonian flood story written in cuneiform script on seven clay tablets. Although the bulk of the creation epic was recovered from Ashurbanipal's library at Nineveh (late seventh century B.C.), it was composed much earlier, in the time of Hammurabi the Great (1728-1686 B.C.). However, the story goes back several millennia to the Sumerians, who entered the plain of Shinar in lower Babylonia as early as 4000 B.C. Their account comes down from the original event, preserved in the memory of the human race, and reflects the actual event described by inspiration in Genesis 1.

The Location of Eden (Genesis 2 & 3). Archeology has established the lower Tigris-Euphrates Valley as the general location of Eden and the earliest human civilization. The Hiddekel was the Tigris River.

The Fall (Genesis 3). The Myth of Adapa is not actually a parallel to the fall of Genesis 3, but it does deal with the perplexing problem of why mankind must suffer and die. However, elements in the legend correspond to Genesis. The "food of life" corresponds to "the fruit" of "the tree of life" (Gen. 3:3, 22).

Earliest Civilization (Genesis 4). Man's civilization began in farming and cattle raising, the occupations of Cain and Abel. The rise of urban life and the beginning of arts, crafts, and music (Gen. 4:16-24) are illustrated in the lowest levels of excavated cities in Mesopotamia, such as Nineveh, Tell Obeid, and Tepe Gawra. Tell Obeid, northwest of Ur, reveals the earliest clearly defined culture in lower Babylonia, showing that around 4000 B.C. the marshlands of that area were drained and occupied.

Long Life before the Flood (Genesis 5). Genesis 5 indicates that the pre-flood span of human life was as much as 969 years (Methuselah). Archeology has recovered a very ancient Sumerian king list that enumerates eight pre-flood rulers who reigned in Lower Mesopotamia for a total of 241,200 years, with the shortest reign set at 18,600 years. Such a parallel at least puts the comparatively modest figures of Gene-

Babylonian ruins — once the pride of King Nebuchadnezzar, now a monument to idolatry and divine judgment (© *MPS*)

sis in a different light and corroborates the biblical description of longevity before the flood.

The Noahic Flood (Genesis 6-9). The historicity of this event as a worldwide cataclysm (Gen. 6:19-24; cf. 2 Pet. 3:6) has been hotly debated. But attempts to make it local and connect it with C. L. Woolley's flood stratum at Ur or S. Langdon's at Kish are futile. Those who deny the historicity of the event as a worldwide catastrophe face the evidence of archeology. The flood tablets (both Sumerian and later Babylonian) unearthed at Nineveh (1853) furnish the most amazing and detailed extrabiblical parallel to any biblical event. If such a world-engulfing deluge never took place, how did the extrabiblical traditions and the biblical account arise?

The Ethnic Complexion of the Post-Flood World (Genesis 9:24 — 10:32). Genesis 9:24-27 presents a remarkable forecast of the moral and spiritual history of the nations after they descended from Noah's three sons. The purpose of this prophecy is to show the origin of the Canaanites and the source of their moral pollution, which centuries later was to lead to the loss of their land to Israel. Shem's blessing was religious.

All divine revelation was to be given through the Semitic line, from which Christ, humanly speaking, was born. From Japheth would rise the enlarged nations that would "dwell in the tents of Shem," that is, eventually share in the blessings of Shem's spiritual heritage.

Noah's prediction of the moral and spiritual history of the nations (Gen. 9:24-27) constitutes an indispensable introduction to the great prophecy of the ethnographical constitution of the postdiluvial world contained in Genesis 10. This so-called "Table of the Nations" displays a remarkable perception of the ethnic and linguistic complexion of the descendants of Noah. What is most amazing is that archeological research in the last century and a half has substantiated the accuracy of this remarkable document and illuminated virtually all of the names and places it contains.

The Tower of Babel (Genesis 11:1-9). The scene here depicted evidently belongs to a period not more than a century and a half after the flood (about 4800 B.C.). The tower was apparently the first tower attempted, and represented the symbol of man's revolt against God and his determination to promote and glorify himself. The polytheistic temple towers ("ziggurats") of later centuries were doubtless copied after it. More than two dozen such ziggurats are now known in Mesopotamia. They were gigantic artificial mountains of sun-dried bricks painted various colors. The oldest existing ziggurat is that at Uruk (biblical Erech; Gen. 10:10), dating from the fourth millennium B.C. Ruins of other famous ziggurats are found at Ur, Babylon, and Borsippa.

The Confusion of Languages (Genesis 11:1-9). This judgment took place about 4800 B.C. in connection with the pride of the Babel builders. The race was scattered over the ancient biblical world as a result. City-states arose in Babylonia. Archeology traces Halafian culture (about 4500 B.C.) at Tell Halaf, east of Carchemish. Obeidan culture (about 3600 B.C.) can be traced at Tell Obeid, near Ur. Warka (Erech, Uruk) flourished at about 3200 B.C., giving birth to the earliest writing and the first cylinder seals. Jemdet Nasr culture, near Babylon, developed about 3000 B.C. Various languages were spoken by different peoples.

Civilization developed early on the Nile River. The union of Lower and Upper Egypt took place at about 2900 B.C., with the first and second dynasties extending from 2900 to 2700 B.C. The Old Kingdom with its pyramids flourished between 2700 and 2200 B.C. Contemporaneous was the Sumerian period in Babylonia. The empire of Sargon I spread over much of the ancient Near East in the period from 2360 to 2180 B.C.

THE PATRIARCHAL PERIOD (2000 TO 1871 B.C.)

Terah's Home and Religion (Genesis 11:25-32). Abraham's father, Terah, was a native of Ur (modern Tell el-Muqayyar in lower Babylonia). C. L. Woolley has traced the history of this site from the Tell Obeid period (about 3600 B.C.) until it was abandoned about 300 B.C. The principal deity worshiped was Nannar, the moon god, whom Terah evidently adored (cf. Josh. 24:2). The famous temple tower or ziggurat built by Ur-Nammu, the founder of the prosperous third Dynasty at Ur (about 2150-2050 B.C.) dominated the city of the moon god. On its uppermost stage was the shrine of Nannar. In front of the temple tower were twin temples of the moon god and his consort, Nin-gal.

Ur of the Chaldees—this was a flourishing city when God called Abram away to the Promised Land in Canaan. (© *MPS*)

Abraham and Ur (Genesis 11:28). Abraham was born at Ur about 2161 B.C., as the city was rising to the height of its power under the powerful third dynasty of Sumerian kings. Archeological excavations have made Ur a very well-known city. It is possible that Terah was one of the prosperous wool merchants of the town. Houses such as he and his son lived in have come to light through the spade of the archeologist.

Abraham at Haran (Genesis 11:28). As early as Abraham's time, Haran (Assyrian *harranu*, "main road") was an important link in the great east-west trade route linking Nineveh, Carchemish, and Damascus. The city is known from cuneiform sources from the nineteenth and eighteenth centuries B.C. Excavations since 1951 show that it was occupied from at least the third millennium B.C. Terah evidently settled there because he was a devotee of the moon god, who had temples both there and at Ur (cf. Gen. 11:31, 32).

Abraham in Canaan (Genesis 12-17). At about 2086 B.C. Abraham entered Canaan, according to the underlying chronology of the Hebrew Bible. The patriarchal period, then, extends from 2086 B.C. to 1871 B.C. (Gen. 12:4, 5). The highland ridge was then sparsely populated, with ample room for the movement of seminomadic people like Abraham and Lot. Cities such as Shechem, Dothan, Bethel, Gerar, and Jerusalem are archeologically attested for this early period. Abraham's visit to Egypt (Gen. 12:10-20) evidently occurred in the early years of the Middle Kingdom (about 1989 B.C.).

The Invasion of the Mesopotamian Kings (Genesis 14). While the actual kings have not as yet been satisfactorily identified, their line of march on the King's Highway is substantiated, as well as such place names as Ashtaroth-karnaim and Ham.

Sodom and Gomorrah (Genesis 19). The cities of the Plain ("Circle") of the Jordan are proved to have existed during Abraham's period; they were situated at the southern end of the Dead Sea. The valley of Siddim was overwhelmed by a conflagration, probably caused by an earthquake in which the salt and sulfur of the region exploded and the waters of the Dead Sea inundated the burned-out region of oil and asphalt.

Jebel Usdum ("Mountain of Sodom") is a great salt mass at the southwestern end of the Dead Sea, recalling the fact that Lot's wife was turned into a pillar of salt in this general region.

Patriarchal Customs. Such patriarchal customs as marriage, adoption, the right of the firstborn, and the possession of teraphim (household deities) are mentioned not only in Scriptures (Gen. 12 – 50), but are substantiated by the inscribed tablets recovered from Nuzu (a site near Kirkuk) as well as by the Mari Letters from Tell el Hariri on the Middle Euphrates. In Abraham's time Mari was one of the most flourishing cities of the Mesopotamian world.

Hebrew Residence in Padan-Aram. Terah died in Haran (Gen. 11:31), a town still in existence 60 miles west of Tell Halaf. The city of Nahor, Rebekah's home (Gen. 24:10), occurs often in the Mari Letters (18th century B.C.). Evidence of Hebrew residence in this region also appears in the names of Abraham's forefathers – Serug and Terah.

THE EGYPTIAN PERIOD (1871 TO 1441 B.C.)

The Egyptian Sojourn (Exodus 1 — 6). According to the biblical chronology preserved in the Hebrew Bible, Isaac is to be dated about 1950 B.C., Jacob about 1900 B.C., and the emigration into Egypt about 1871 B.C. (under the Twelfth Egyptian Dynasty of the strong Middle Kingdom, which ruled from 1989 to 1776 B.C. and was headed by Amenemes I-IV and Senwosret I-III). It was apparently under Amenemes I or II that Israel entered Egypt. Elsewhere during this period Hammurabi the Great (1728-1686 B.C.) ruled over the First Dynasty of Babylon (1850-1550 B.C.) Mari was a powerful city-state on the Middle Euphrates during this time.

The Hyksos Invasion (Exodus 1 — 4). The Hyksos were foreign invaders who lodged themselves in the Delta and dominated Lower Egypt in the period of confusion that followed the dissolution of the Twelfth Dynasty. During the Hyksos rule, about 1730-1570 B.C., Israel lived in the Delta and was controlled by these "rulers of foreign countries," as the term Hyksos means. Kamose, the last Egyptian ruler of Dynasty XVII at Thebes in Upper Egypt, began the expulsion of the Hyksos, which was completed by the first ruler of Dynasty XVIII, Ahmose (about 1570-1545 B.C.). Under this famous line of kings Moses was born (about 1520 B.C.). Under this new regime the Israelites were enslaved, perhaps as a reaction against the Hyksos.

The Career of Moses (Exodus 2 — 12). The Egyptian princess who found Moses in the ark of papyrus was perhaps the famous Hatshepsut (1504-1482 B.C). The name "Moses" is apparently nothing more than Egyptian *Mase,* pronounced *Mose* after the twelfth century B.C. and meaning simply "the child." The interpretation by the sacred writer, however, is connected with Hebrew root *masha,* "to draw out," because Pharaoh's daughter drew the infant out of the water (Exod. 2:10).

The Egyptian Plagues (Exodus 7 — 11). The entire Egyptian sojourn abounds in authentic local color. The miracles consist of events that were natural to Egypt. The supernatural element is seen in the vast increase of their intensity. No phenomena were imported.

The Exodus. The underlying chronology of the Hebrew Bible would indicate that Thutmose III (1490-1445 B.C.) was Israel's oppressor, and that Amenhotep II (1445-1425 B.C.) was the Pharaoh of the Exodus (about 1441 B.C.). Israel was in the desert during the reign of Thutmose IV (1425-1412 B.C.).

THE PERIOD OF THE CONQUEST (1401 TO 1361 B.C.)

The Fall of Jericho (Joshua 6). According to the biblical chronology the fall of Jericho occurred about 1401 B.C. Professor John Garstang, the British excavator of Jericho, agreed with this view. Supporting this position are the chronological notices in Judges 11:26 and First Kings 6:1, as well as the whole time-scheme underlying the body of history from Genesis to Second Kings. In addition, this interpretation has the distinct advantage of allowing at least a partial equation of the Habiru of the Amarna Letters with the Hebrews. These famous letters from Tell el-Amarna in Egypt, discovered in 1887, parallel the period of the Conquest. The Amarna period covers the reign of Amenhotep III (about 1412-1359 B.C.). The letters describe a situation in Palestine that in many respects remarkably coincides with the invasion of the Hebrews. The letters give a first-hand picture of conditions in Canaan. The country was nominally subject to Egypt, but Egyptian control had completely broken down. This condition was ideal for Joshua's invasion and conquest of the land.

The Conquest of Ai (Joshua 8). Identification of Ai with et-Tell is obviously erroneous and has produced confusion. Ai was evidently quite small but nevertheless strategically important as a military outpost (Josh. 7:3). It may have been nothing more than a fort protecting Bethel. Only further archeological research can clear up the situation and vindicate the early date of the conquest.

The Conquest of the Canaanites (Joshua 1−11). Archeological evidence from Lachish, Debir, and Hazor supposedly also contradicts the fourteenth century date of the conquest. But the thirteenth-century destruction of these towns should not be connected with Joshua's wars, but rather with the strife and invasions of the later lawless period of the judges.

God's command to exterminate the Canaanites is demonstrated by archeology to be a moral necessity rather than an impugnment of God's justice and goodness, as many rationalistic critics contend. The religious epic literature recovered from Ras Shamra (the ancient Canaanite city of Ugarit in North Syria) since 1929 has revealed the moral viciousness of the Canaanite cults. These documents attest that Canaanite religion revolved around war, violence, and sexual immorality. Depraved male and female deities were worshiped with foul rites that "filled up" the iniquity of the land (cf. Gen. 15:16) by the time of Joshua and the Israelite invasion.

THE PERIOD OF THE JUDGES (1375 TO 1075 B.C.)

The Period and Archeology. Archeology has helped to place the events of this extended period in the framework of contemporary Egyptian,

Aramean, Assyrian, Phoenician, and Hurrian history. Excavations at Megiddo, Bethshan, Lachish, Debir, and Hazor will one day, we believe, vindicate the biblical chronology of this era against the late-date theories of the Exodus that telescope the "dark ages" of Israel's history. *The Judges and the Contemporary Scene.* For the chronology of the period see under the Book of Judges. During the reign of the boy king Tutankhamun (1359-1350 B.C.) and Harmhab (1350-1299 B.C.), when Egyptian influence over Palestine was slight, the Aramean Cushan-Rishathaim invaded Israel. It was at this time that Othniel delivered God's people (about 1361-1313 B.C.; Judg. 3:7-10). Eglon of Moab oppressed Israel 18 years (about 1313-1295 B.C.), until Ehud delivered the nation. Peace followed for eighty years (1295-1215 B.C.; Judg. 3:12-30). This long period of security was made possible by a strong Egypt under Rameses II (1295-1223 B.C.), who ruled all southern Syria after the battle of Kadesh (about 1286 B.C.) and his treaty with the Hittites. His son and successor, Merenptah, alludes to Israel in Palestine on his victory stele (about 1224 B.C.).

Jabin, king of Hazor, overran Israel (1215-1195 B.C.) under the weak pharaohs that followed Merenptah (Judg. 4:1-24). Hazor was a Canaanite kingdom of North Palestine near Lake Huleh. Deliverance by Deborah and a forty-year peace (1195-1155 B.C.) was possible because of a new dynasty in Egypt with the strong Pharaoh Rameses III (1198-1167 B.C.), who was able to maintain order in Asia.

Oppression by the Midianites for seven years (about 1155-1148 B.C.) was due to the decline in Egyptian power under the weak Rameses IV and V, who followed Rameses III (Judg. 6, 7). Under Gideon, however (1148-1108 B.C.), peace prevailed despite decline in Egyptian power, fostering Israel's growing desire for their own king. This resulted in Abimelech's unhappy reign at Shechem for three years (about 1108-1105 B.C.; Judg. 9).

Oppression by the Ammonites (Judg. 10) and Jephthah's judgeship took place about 1105 to 1099 B.C. Coeval with this was the Philistine rise (about 1099-1059 B.C.) and Samson's twenty-year judgeship (about 1085-1065 B.C.) (Judg. 13 – 16). Decline in Hittite, Assyrian, and Egyptian imperial power made possible the rise of the Hebrew monarchy but brought with it also the Philistine threat to Israel.

THE PERIOD OF SAUL (1040 TO 1010 B.C.)

Saul's Initial Exploits. Saul repulsed not only the encroaching Ammonites but the Philistines as well (1 Sam. 11:1-14; 14:1-46). In doing so he was popularized as a hero and became the natural choice for the kingship, which the threat of the times seemed to necessitate. His early victories over the Philistines weakened the iron-refining monopoly held by this people (1 Sam. 13:19-21). When Saul and David broke the power of the Philistines, the iron-smelting formula became public property, and the stage was set for an economic and political revolution in Israel.

Saul's Fortress at Gibeah. Saul's fortress-palace at Tell el-Ful, about four miles north of Jerusalem, has been excavated. It was more like a dungeon than a royal residence and displays Saul as a rustic chieftain in reference to architecture and other amenities of life. His self-will and disobedience to divine direction through Samuel landed him in occultism and cost him his life and kingdom (1 Sam. 13:13, 14; 15:1-35; 28:3-25).

THE PERIOD OF DAVID AND SOLOMON (1010 TO 971 B.C.)

David's Activity as King. David's magnanimity toward the house of Saul, his brilliant diplomacy with surrounding nations, and his courageous conquests of avowed foes soon won him a strong kingdom. His capture of Jerusalem from the Jebusites (2 Sam. 5:8), making it the religious and governmental capital of the kingdom, was a masterly exploit. Archeology has fully clarified the location of "the city of David" (2 Sam. 5:7) on the eastern hill above the Gihon spring. Though it consisted of a walled space not exceeding eight acres, the city of David was of immense political importance. It became the hub of the united kingdom and, when David moved the ark to Jerusalem (2 Sam. 6:12-15), it became the center of Jewish worship as well.

Archeology has shed a great deal of light on the tabernacle, its ritual, and its sacred music. Now it is quite clear that there is nothing incongruous in the biblical representation of David as the patron saint of Jewish hymnology and the organizer of Temple music. In fact, his skill as a diplomat and prowess as a conqueror combined with his religious zeal to gain him a strong kingdom. His allocation of Levitical cities and cities of refuge cemented his conquests together on a religious basis and helped root out divisions and local feuds. He began the religious and political organization that his son Solomon was to develop so effectively.

Solomon's Power and Splendor. The period of Solomon's reign (971-931 B.C.) was favorable for the Israelite empire because the great powers of the times—Egypt, Hatti, and Assyria—were all in eclipse or abeyance. Solomon used diplomacy on a grand scale to forestall problems in foreign policy. He married the daughter of the then-reigning

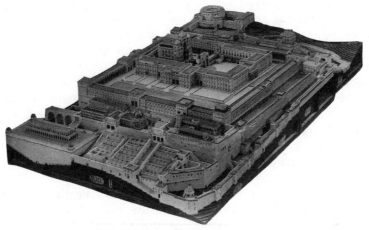

An opulent model of Solomon's Temple (© *MPS*)

Pharaoh (1 Kings 3:1, 2) and followed the general policy of royal marriages (1 Kings 11:1-8) and implemented other ties of amity that prevented war (but led to other evils). Solomon's domestic policy was also designed to foster peace and prosperity. He organized his realm into twelve administrative districts (1 Kings 4:7-20) and initiated various public works and building projects, including the Temple at Jerusalem.

Solomon's industrial expansion was remarkable. He controlled the caravan trade of Syria-Palestine and cultivated the horse-and-chariot commerce between Egypt and Kue (Cilicia) (1 Kings 10:28, 29, RSV), which brought him enormous revenues. He built a fleet of ships at Ezion-geber on the Red Sea (1 Kings 9:26-28) and exploited the copper-rich Arabah in his refinery at Ezion-geber (modern Tell el-Keleifeh, excavated in 1938-40). All of these commercial ventures have been verified and illustrated by modern archeological research, including the magnificent Temple he constructed at Jerusalem. Both the plan and furnishings of the latter are much better understood in the light of recent Near Eastern excavations.

THE DIVIDED MONARCHY (931 TO 722 B.C.)

Rehoboam and Shishak's Invasion. The folly of Rehoboam (about 931-913 B.C.) led to the division of the kingdom. In addition to being weakened by wars between Rehoboam and Jeroboam I (1 Kings 14:30; 15: 6), Judah was invaded by Shishak (Sheshonq I of Egypt, founder of the twenty-second dynasty; 1 Kings 14:25-28). The gold-masked mummy of this pharaoh was discovered in his burial chamber at Tanis in 1938. His triumphal inscription at Karnak (ancient Thebes) includes conquests in both Judah and Israel, despite his previous friendship for Jeroboam (1 Kings 11:40).

Jeroboam and His Idolatry. To strengthen his kingdom and wean his subjects away from the Jerusalem Temple, Jeroboam set up gold calves (bulls) at Dan and Bethel (1 Kings 12:25-53). These were apparently thought to represent the invisible deity enthroned or standing on a bull's back. Ancient Near Eastern iconography shows pagan gods like Baal represented in the form of a bolt of lightning on a bull's back.

Israel and Aram In Conflict. After Solomon's death the Aramean power which was centered in Damascus became a threat to the Northern Kingdom from about 900 B.C. till the fall of Damascus in 732 B.C. In 1940 the inscribed Stele of Benhadad I was discovered in North Syria. It attests "Benhadad, son of Tabrimmon, the son of Hezion, king of Aram" (1 Kings 15:18). This was evidently Benhadad I (about 900-842 B.C.), the foe of Ahab, who was succeeded by the usurper Hazael (2 Kings 8:7-15). Assyrian records declare that "Hazael, son of nobody, seized the throne" after Benhadad's death.

Hazael was a powerful ruler who was God's scourge to Israel during the reigns of Jehu (841-814 B.C.) and Jehoahaz (814-798 B.C.). Benhadad II (about 798-770 B.C.), the son of Hazael, continued his father's oppression of Israel into the reign of Joash (798-782 B.C.). Joash then recouped Israelite fortunes and was able to repel Benhadad. Benhadad II is mentioned in the contemporary stele of Zakir, discovered in 1903. He is represented as heading a coalition of kings against Zakir because of the latter's alliance with Luash. This move upset the balance of power in Syria and precipitated war.

Joash's successes were continued by his son Jeroboam II (782-753 B.C.), who restored Israel to full power and made Damascus a practical vassal of Israel (2 Kings 14:25-28). The resurgence of Assyrian power upon the rise of the great conqueror Tiglathpileser III (745-727 B.C.) gave Ahaz of Judah a chance to pit the Assyrian against Aram and Israel. This resulted in the overthrow of Damascus in 732 B.C. and the death of the last Aramean king, Rezin (750-732 B.C.). These events appear prominently in Assyrian monuments recovered by archeological research.

The Omride Dynasty and Archeology. Omri and Ahab of Israel and Mesha of Moab figure prominently in the famous Moabite Stone set up at Dibon about 840 B.C. and discovered in 1868. Omri's capital of Samaria has been unearthed by extensive excavations at the site by G. A. Reisner, D. G. Lyon, and C. S. Fisher (1908-1910) and J. W. Crowfoot, Kathleen Kenyon, and E. L. Sukenik (*The Buildings of Samaria,* 1942).

From Omri's time onward Israel appears in cuneiform records as Bit-Humri ("House of Omri"), and Israelite kings were dubbed *mar-Humri* ("son of Omri" in the sense of "royal successor of Omri"). Omri's son and successor, Ahab, is mentioned in Assyrian annals in connection with a western coalition that fought the advance of Assyria at Karkar in 854 B.C. Ahab is said to have supported the alliance against Assyria with 2000 chariots and 10,000 men that fought against the armies of Shalmaneser III (859-824 B.C.).

Jehu and the Advance of Assyria. Jehu (about 841-814 B.C.), the extirpator of the house of Ahab and the cult of Baal from Israel, submitted to Shalmaneser III. The Black Obelisk shows Jehu actually prostrating himself before the Assyrian monarch. The inscription reads, "Tribute of Iaua [Jehu] son of Omri. Silver, gold, a golden bowl, a golden beaker, golden goblets, pitchers of gold, lead, staves for the hand of the king, javelins I received from him."

The Last Years of the Northern Kingdom. Just at the time of Jeroboam II's death and the assassination of his son shortly thereafter, the powerful Tiglathpileser III (745-727 B.C.) resurrected the moribund Assyrian Empire and advanced westward. Under his popular name, Pul (Pulu), he placed Menahem (about 752-742 B.C.) under heavy tribute (1 Kings 15:19). The same event is recorded in the Assyrian annals. "As for Menahem, terror overwhelmed him; like a bird, alone he fled and submitted to me . . . I received . . . his tribute."

Hoshea, the last king of the Northern Kingdom (732-722 B.C.), was an Assyrian vassal whom Tiglathpileser set over Israel. In the delusive hope of receiving aid from Egypt Hoshea ceased paying tribute to Assyria. Shalmaneser V (726-722 B.C.) thereupon advanced against him. Although Hoshea sought to placate his overlord, his belated overtures of submission did not save him from imprisonment (2 Kings 17:3, 4), and his capital was placed under siege by the Assyrians.

The Fall of Samaria. After a stubborn, three-year resistance, Samaria finally fell to Assyria. Before the overthrow had been accomplished, however, Shalmaneser V had been succeeded by Sharrukin II (721-705 B.C.), who assumed the ancient name of Sargon. In the Khorsabad annals of his reign, the monarch lists the fall of Samaria as the chief event of his first regnal year. He claims to have deported 27,290 of the capital's inhabitants, set his officers over the city, and exacted tribute. This was probably in the opening months of 721 B.C.

Judah and the Assyrian Menace. The flood of Assyrian power that carried Israel to destruction caused untold anguish to Judah. There is evidence of a Palestinian coalition against Assyria as early as Azariah (791-740 B.C). Tiglathpileser III makes clear reference in his annals to *Azriyau of Yaudu* (Azariah of Judah) in connection with what is obviously such a coalition. Azariah's son Jotham (740-736 B.C.) apparently continued an anti-Assyrian policy. However, Jotham's son Ahaz, an idolatrous apostate, refused to join Pekah of Israel and Rezin of Syria in an alliance to stem Assyrian advance. The result was that Pekah and Rezin invaded Judah, precipitating the Syro-Ephraimite War (about 734 B.C.). Ahaz, hard-pressed, appealed to Assyria for help and introduced a century of vassalage for Judah.

THE KINGDOM OF JUDAH (722 TO 586 B.C.)

Hezekiah and Sennacherib. Hezekiah (716-687 B.C.) inherited the Assyrian menace and did all he could to prepare for an eventual showdown with Assyria. He cleansed out the idolatrous contaminations his father had introduced, strengthened Jerusalem's defenses, and safeguarded the city's water supply by building the Siloam tunnel (2 Kings 20:20).

In 701 B.C. Sennacherib invaded Judah. His account on the Taylor prism represents Hezekiah as the ringleader of the Western revolt. Sennacherib claims to have taken forty-six fortified towns and to have shut up Hezekiah "like a caged bird in Jerusalem, his royal city." Though the Lord intervened to destroy the Assyrian army (2 Kings 19:35-36), Judah suffered a paralyzing blow.

Manasseh and the Assyrians. Manasseh was co-ruler with his father Hezekiah from 696 to 687 B.C. and was the sole ruler from 687 to 642 B.C. His reign witnessed a paganizing movement caused by fear of Assyria and fascination for her cults (2 Kings 21:1-15). The result was an absorption of both Baalism (a cult of Astarte at the "high places") and occult-oriented religionism centering in astrology and star worship. Manasseh's anti-Jehovistic reign was long and cruel.

The name "Manasseh, king of Judah" occurs on the Prism of Esarhaddon and on the Prism of Ashurbanipal, along with twenty-one other tributaries of Assyria. Second Chronicles alludes to Manasseh's deportation to Babylon, his repentance, and his release (2 Chron. 33: 10-13). It is known that a revolt against Assyria took place during

Manasseh's reign, in support of the viceroy of Babylon. Manasseh may well have been involved in it. Necho I of Egypt was captured and subsequently released by Ashurbanipal, as is known from the Rassam Cylinder. (This offers an interesting parallel to the Chronicler's claim concerning Manasseh's deportation to Babylon.) His wicked son, Amon (642-640 B.C.), swept away the superficial reform his father inaugurated before his death.

Josiah and Religious Reform. Josiah (640-609 B.C.) is known as a great and good king who inaugurated a religious reformation in Judah (2 Kings 22, 23; 2 Chron. 34, 35). The climax of this movement was reached in the eighteenth year of Josiah (621 B.C.), when "the book of the Law" was discovered in the Temple. But idolatry had laid such a hold upon the people during the wicked reign of Manasseh that the effects of Josiah's purge were superficial. After Josiah's untimely death in battle with Pharaoh Necho (608 B.C.), the nation reverted to its evil ways and plunged headlong into national ruin.

Jeremiah's prophecies (chaps. 2−6) belong to this period. The Lachish Letters (recovered from the town of Lachish or Tell ed-Duweir in southeastern Palestine) bring to life Jeremiah's era, especially just before Nebuchadnezzar's invasion (588-586 B.C.).

The Last Days of Judah. Jehoahaz, Josiah's son, succeeded his father. He reigned only three months before being deposed by Pharaoh Necho, who placed Jehoahaz' brother Jehoiakim (609-597 B.C.) on the throne. But Jehoiakim's evil reign ended in disgrace and death. He was succeeded by his son Jehoiachin, who was carried to Babylon after he ruled for only three months and ten days (2 Chron. 36:9; cf. 2 Kings 25:8-16).

In Babylon Jehoiachin was treated as a royal hostage. His name occurs in Babylonian tablets dated between 595 and 570 B.C. as "Yaukin, king of the land of Yahud." Evil-Merodach, Nebuchadnezzar's successor, set him free from prison in 561 B.C. (2 Kings 25:27-30).

Zedekiah, Josiah's youngest son, was the last king of Judah (597-586 B.C.). Nebuchadnezzar seated him as king and changed his name to Mattaniah as a mark of vassalage. But he rebelled against Nebuchadnezzar and precipitated the siege of Jerusalem. After holding out for 18 months, the city fell in July, 586 B.C. during conditions of horrible famine. Zedekiah and a remnant of his army managed to escape by night from the doomed city. However, they were pursued and captured near Jericho. The king's eyes were put out and he was deported to Babylon. The city and Temple were destroyed. The Chaldeans and the Kingdom of Judah collapsed (2 Kings 24:18−25:7).

THE PERIOD OF THE EXILE (586 TO 538 B.C.)

The Chaldean Empire (605 to 539 B.C.). Short-lived but powerful, this kingdom was divinely raised up to chastise God's sinful people; its existence was coterminous with Judah's captivity. Nabopolassar (625-605 B.C.), the governor of Babylon and father of Nebuchadnezzar, threw off the Assyrian yoke. He became an imperial figure with the fall of Nineveh (612 B.C.) and Haran (609 B.C.).

Nebuchadnezzar II (605 to 552 B.C.). His first deportation of Judah (Dan. 1:2) included Daniel; his second, in 597 B.C., included Ezekiel; and the third, in 586 B.C.., resulted in the destruction of Jerusalem and the kingdom of Judah. He ruthlessly conquered the West, desolating Moab, Ammon, Edom, and Lebanon. His siege of Tyre (585-573 B.C) furnishes an example of his tenacity. He invaded Egypt in 568, but little is known of the last thirty years of his reign.

Nebuchadnezzar was a great builder of temples and shrines at Babylon, Sippar, Marad, and Borsippa. He made Babylon the wonder city of the world with the Ishtar Gate, the ziggurat, the processional way, the defense walls, and the canal network. He was very religious, providing regular offerings and garments for the sacred statues. This accords well with the episode of the golden image (Dan. 3).

Evil-Merodach ("The Man Is Marduk") (562-560 B.C.) succeeded his father to the throne. He was the king who released Jehoiachin of Judah from imprisonment (Jer. 52:31; 2 Kings 25:27-30). He was killed by Neriglissar ("Nergal protect the king"), who was apparently an army general married to Nebuchadnezzar's daughter (Jer. 39:3, 13).

Neriglissar (560 to 556 B.C.) reigned only four years. His son Labashi-Marduk was assassinated after a reign of only four months.

Nabonidus (556 to 539 B.C.) was a Babylonian noble who usurped the throne to become the last king of the Neo-Babylonian Empire. His son Belshazzar was coregent with him from the third year of his reign. The very existence of Belshazzar (Dan. 5:1-31; 7:1; 8:1) was doubted until cuneiform accounts chronicling his reign were recovered. Records of both Nabonidus and Belshazzar, however, are fragmentary. Authentication and clarification of the precise details of the fall of Babylon and Belshazzar's death as mentioned in Daniel await further discoveries.

THE POST-EXILIC PERIOD (539 TO 400 B.C.)

The Persian Empire Founded. Cyrus II the Great came to the throne of Anshan around 559 B.C. He soon won supremacy over the Medes and began a career of conquest that founded the Persian Empire. In 546 Lydia was conquered and in 539 Babylon, under crown prince Belshazzar (Dan. 5), fell to him. Unlike most ancient rulers, however, Cyrus was a humane conqueror. Instead of destroying Babylon he won its people over by mercy. He even allowed the Jews to return to their homeland (Ezra 1:1-4).

The spirit of Cyrus' decree of release which is alluded to in the Old Testament (2 Chron. 36:23; Ezra 1:2-4) is confirmed by the Cyrus cylinder. The king records how he permitted the captives of his conquered realms to return to their own lands and rebuild their temples.

Cyrus was slain in battle in 530 B.C. His son Cambyses II (530-522) succeeded him. After conquering Egypt and adding it to the Empire, Cambyses went mad and committed suicide, plunging the empire into revolt.

Darius I and Haggai and Zechariah. Darius I (522-486 B.C.) saved the Empire. He, too, proved to be a very humane administrator. Religiously, Darius I was an ardent Zoroastrian and worshiper of Ahura Mazda, as were later Persian kings Xerxes and Artaxerxes. The beginning of both Haggai's and Zechariah's ministry is dated in the second year of Darius (Hag. 1:1; Zech. 1:1). Likewise, the completion of the restoration Temple is dated in the sixth year of Darius, i.e. 515 B.C. (Ezra 6:15). Darius I's rock-hewn tomb at Naqsh-I-Rustam (a few miles northeast of Persepolis) bears a trilingual inscription relating his character and achievements. Similar tombs were cut from the cliff for the three successors of Darius — Xerxes, Artaxerxes I, and Darius II.

Darius I and the Behistun Inscription. Carved on a cliff 500 feet above the plain of Karmanshah near the small village of Behistun, the relief depicts and records Darius' victory over the rebellion that inaugurated his reign and his salvation of the Empire. Composed in three languages, Old Persian, Elamite, and Akkadian, the inscription became the key that unlocked Akkadian cuneiform, much as the Rosetta Stone had opened up Egyptian hieroglyphics.

Xerxes and the Book of Esther. Darius I was followed on the Persian throne by his son Xerxes (486-465 B.C.). He is no doubt the Ahasuerus mentioned between Darius and Artaxerxes (Ezra 4:6), the husband of Esther. (Ahasuerus is the Hebrew form of the Persian name Khshayarsha, of which the Greek form is Xerxes.) His invading armies were defeated by the Greeks at Thermopylae and Salamis in 480 B.C.

Artaxerxes I and Nehemiah. The successor of Xerxes was Artaxerxes I Longimanus (465-423 B.C.). Nehemiah's request to visit Jerusalem, according to Nehemiah 2:1, was made in the month Nisan in Artaxerxes' twentieth year. The reference is very likely to Artaxerxes I. The date indicated is therefore Nisan (April-May), 445 B.C.

Archeology confirms generally that Nehemiah had lived at about this time. The Elephantine Papyri, discovered in 1903 on the island of Elephantine at the First Cataract in Egypt and dating from the end of the fifth century B.C., mention two persons connected with Nehemiah in the Old Testament. The first is Sanballat, whose two sons are referred to as governors of Samaria in 408 B.C. Doubtless their father was the leading opponent of Nehemiah (Neh. 2:19, etc.). The second person is Johanan, who was high priest in Jerusalem in 408 B.C., according to the papyri. Nehemiah is said to have been in Jerusalem when Johanan's father, Eliashib, was high priest (Neh. 3:1; 12:23). This also agrees well with the date of 445 B.C. for Nehemiah.

Artaxerxes I and Ezra. It is stated that Ezra the scribe came to Jerusalem in the seventh year of Artaxerxes (Ezra 7:1, 8). This reference is certainly to Artaxerxes I and the date is therefore 458 B.C. This would mean that Ezra preceded Nehemiah. Since Johanan, the son of Eliashib, is mentioned in connection with the work of Ezra (Ezra 10:6), some scholars think that Ezra's mission may have followed Nehemiah's, under Artaxerxes II.

Artaxerxes II and Malachi. Following Artaxerxes I, the Persian throne was occupied by Darius II (423-404 B.C.), Artaxerxes II Mnemon (404-359), Artaxerxes III Ochus (359-338), Arses (338-335), and Darius III (335-331). Malachi's ministry and the close of the Old Testament period took place under either Darius II or Artaxerxes II.

Intertestamental History

THE INTERTESTAMENTAL PERIOD

The era of approximately four centuries between Malachi and John the Baptist (and Jesus) is commonly known as the interbiblical or intertestamental period. Sometimes it is referred to as "the four hundred silent years." During this interval, revelation and inspiration (in the special sense in which this divine operation produced canonical Scripture) was in abeyance.

Unsound higher critical theories deny this position, tending to place books like Esther, Daniel, Chronicles, and even some of the Psalms, during this period, sometimes quite late in the period. However, sound critical scholarship cannot accept these views. Instead, conservative scholarship substantially agrees with Josephus, a prominent Jewish historian of the first century A.D. According to Josephus

Gigantic Temple of El-Khazne (treasure) in Edom's rock-bound Petra (© *MPS*)

the completion of the Hebrew Canon took place in the reign of Artaxerxes I (465-414 B.C.). (This fact does not mean that other religious
literature was not produced. The Apocrypha, Pseudepigrapha, and
other religious writings such as those retrieved from the Dead Sea
Caves came into being during this general period.)

THE PERSIAN EMPIRE (400 TO 323 B.C.)

THE JEWS UNDER PERSIAN RULE. Malachi, the last Old Testament prophet (about 400 B.C.), ministered under the reign of Darius II
(423-404 B.C.), or early in the reign of Artaxerxes II (404-358 B.C.).
During the heyday of Persian power Palestine was a tiny province in a

mighty Empire that stretched from Asia Minor to India and from Ethiopia to the mountains of Armenia. Palestine fell within the bounds of the Fifth Persian Satrapy. From his capital at Damascus or Samaria the Persian governor (satrap) ruled and administered justice.

Artaxerxes II was succeeded by Artaxerxes III (358-338 B.C.), Arse (338-336 B.C.), and Darius III (336-331 B.C.). During this extended period the Jews enjoyed comparative peace and prosperity under their Persian overlords. Persian power radiated from both Shushan (Susa), the winter capital, located about a hundred miles east of the Tigris River in Anshan, and Achmetha (Ecbatana), the summer capital, located about two hundred miles northeast of Susa in Media. Another center of Persian power was Persepolis, twenty-five miles southwest of Pasargadae, to which Darius I transferred the main capital of Persia. These great capitals with their wealth and splendor were destined to be looted by Alexander the Great.

THE RISE OF MACEDON. Philip II (359-336 B.C.), a military genius, organized Macedonia, the mountainous territory north of Greece, into a strong state. At Chaeronea in 338 he defeated the Greeks and at Corinth in 337 he united them behind himself to fight Persia. He forged the weapons with which his twenty-year-old son, Alexander, was able to conquer the world.

ALEXANDER THE GREAT (336-323 B.C.). In 334 Alexander crossed the Hellespont and defeated the Persian army at Granicus in Asia Minor. His victory at Issus over a huge army of Darius III in 333 opened up Syria, Palestine, and Egypt to his victorious forces. Tyre resisted, but was taken after a seven-month siege in July 332. Gaza, at the entrance to Egypt, fell before him. In Egypt he founded the brilliant city of Alexandria. His contacts with the Jews at this time were amicable.

Alexander advanced eastward, and on October 1, 331 B.C. he clashed with an immense Persian army at Gaugamela, not far from the ruins of Nineveh. Darius III was defeated and fled eastward, only to be treacherously murdered by his own cousin, the satrap of Bactria. Persian power collapsed. Alexander became king of Babylon, looting and destroying the Persian palaces at Susa, Ecbatana, and Persepolis. In 327 he crossed the Indus River into the Punjab, extending his sway to the Hydaspes River, southeast of Taxila. He planned to unite East and West in a world brotherhood predominantly Greek in culture.

Intoxicated by his seemingly limitless power, the youthful world conqueror lived like an Oriental Sultan. But his dissolute life, combined with a fever he could not overcome, led to his premature death in Babylon in June, 323 B.C. at the age of 32. His conquests were divided among his generals. Eventually, after the battle of Ipsus in 301, Macedonia fell to Cassander, Asia Minor to Lysimachus, Syria to Seleucus, and Egypt to Ptolemy.

PALESTINE UNDER THE PTOLEMIES
(323 TO 198 B.C.)

PTOLEMAIC PALESTINE AND THE JEWISH DIASPORA. Ptolemy I Soter claimed Palestine along with Egypt at Alexander's death. However, Antigonus, one of Alexander's generals, contested the claim and ravaged Jerusalem, causing thousands of Jews to flee to Egypt. After the victory of Ptolemy I Soter (323-285 B.C.) over Antigonus at Gaza in 312 B.C., 100,000 Jews were deported to Egypt. Alexandria became the greatest center of the Jewish diaspora. (Alexander himself had brought many Jews to his newly founded city.) Within a century after Alexander there were more than a million Jews in Egypt from migrations that took place under Ptolemy II Philadelphus (285-246 B.C.), and Ptolemy III Euergetes (246-221 B.C.). But Ptolemy IV Philopator (221-203 B.C.) was a weakling, and in 198 B.C. Palestine came under Seleucid rule.

Under the Ptolemies the Jews had fared well both in Palestine and Egypt. It is during this period that tradition (preserved in The Letter of Aristeas) places the beginning of the translation of the Old Testament into Greek (the Septuagint). The process of Hellenizing the Jews at Alexandria and in the diaspora all over the Hellenistic world also continued during this period (2 Kings 15:29; 17:6; 24:15; 25:7; 1 Chron. 5:26). The New Testament indicates the importance of the worldwide Jewish diaspora (John 7:35; Acts 2:5-11).

THE RISE OF THE TARGUMS, THE SYNAGOGUE, AND THE SANHEDRIN. During this period Aramaic, the universal language of the time, had begun to supplant Hebrew. Aramaic paraphrases of the Hebrew Scriptures, called Targums, began to be produced for the people. At about 200 B.C. the Phoenician alphabet which had been used in preceding centuries was discarded in favor of the square Aramaic characters found in the Dead Sea biblical manuscripts and in later Hebrew Bibles. This era also witnessed the development of the synagogue and of the Sanhedrin. The former had its origin as a house gathering (Greek *sunagoge*, "an assembly") in homes in Babylonia (cf. Ezek. 8:1;

20:1-3). After the exile the synagogue gradually developed into formal assemblies for public worship and instruction by *sopherim,* or scribes learned in the Hebrew Scriptures. The synagogue became a necessity for Jews in the far-flung diaspora and for those in Palestine who resided at too great a distance from the Temple for regular Sabbath worship. They also became schools and petty law courts.

The Sanhedrin (Aramaized form of Greek *sunedrion,* "a sitting together" or "assembly") was a seventy-member civil and judicial body which came into being during this era and was presided over by the high priest.

PALESTINE UNDER THE SELEUCIDS (198-168 B.C.)

ANTIOCHUS III THE GREAT AND THE MASTERY OF PALESTINE. Because it lay between the Ptolemaic and Seleucid empires, Palestine played the role of a helpless pawn in the incessant intrigues and wars that engulfed the two rival powers on its borders. This era of confusion and turmoil was predicted in detail by the prophet Daniel (Dan. 11:1-35). When Ptolemaic power began to wane under Ptolemy IV and V after 221 B.C., Antiochus III the Great (223-187 B.C.) finally gained control of Palestine in 198 B.C. (Dan. 11:16). He then married his daughter to Ptolemy V (Dan. 11:17). His dreams of further greatness were shattered, however, by his defeat by the Romans at Magnesia (190 B.C.) and his death in 187 B.C. (Dan. 11:18, 19).

His successor, Seleucus IV Philopator (187-175 B.C.), represented a decrease in power from Antiochus III but foreshadowed approaching trouble for the Jews when he attempted to rob the Temple (Dan. 11: 20). At his death his brother Antiochus IV Epiphanes usurped the throne (175 B.C.).

THE JEWISH FAITH AND THE THREAT OF HELLENIZATION. Hellenism, because of its purely humanistic outlook on life, clashed head-on with the theocentric faith and austere moral life of Judaism. The broad-minded liberalism of Greek thought, which fostered a relativistic philosophy (Acts 17:21; 1 Cor. 1:21, 22), presented as serious a threat to Israel's faith as had Baalism and the debauched religion of the Canaanites in a previous era.

While a certain degree of Hellenization was inevitable, the agony of the Hasidim or "pious" was rendered all the more acute by the compromise and capitulation on the part of the Jerusalem aristocracy in order to secure governmental favor. Joseph of the Tobiad family became a leader of this worldly party under Ptolemy IV. Simon, son of Joseph, aided Seleucus IV in his attempt to plunder the Temple. With the accession of Antiochus IV Epiphanes in 175 B.C., the Greek party became more openly active (1 Macc. 1:11-15). In the diaspora the process of Hellenization proceeded further than in Palestine.

THE MACCABEAN UPRISING (168 to 143 B.C.).

ANTIOCHUS IV EPIPHANES AND ENFORCED HELLENIZATION. Repulsed from conquering Egypt by Rome in 168 B.C., Antiochus IV in anger determined to unite his empire under Hellenism (Dan. 11:30). He was opposed by the Jews but retaliated by slaughtering the Hasidim in Jerusalem and erecting an altar to Zeus in the Jewish Temple in December, 168 B.C. He outlawed all Jewish customs, including sacrifice, circumcision, Sabbath-keeping, and the dietary laws. To possess a copy of the Law was made a capital offense. Many Jews capitulated (Dan. 11:32), while others fled (1 Macc. 1:62-64; 2 Macc. 7).

THE MACCABEAN REVOLT. Mattathias, an aged priest of the Hasmonean family at Modin, rejected the pagan sacrifices and killed a fellow Jew who had capitulated to this practice. He accompanied this bold act with a ringing declaration of war: "Whoever is zealous for the law, and maintaineth the covenant, let him come forth after me" (1 Macc. 2:27). Mattathias aroused the Hasidim to guerrilla attacks against the Syrians and apostate Jews. He appointed his son Judas to be his successor after his death in 167 B.C.

JUDAS MACCABEUS (167 TO 161 B.C.). By courage, strategy, and divine help Judas won four great victories in 166 and 165 B.C. (Dan. 8: 25; Zech. 9:13-17). By December, 165 B.C. he was able to cleanse the Temple and reestablish the daily sacrifice. This great event came to be celebrated annually as "The Feast of Dedication" or "The Feast of Lights" (John 10:22). Antiochus Epiphanes died in 164 B.C., opening up the way for Judas to conquer Idumea, Transjordan, and Philistia (1 Macc. 5).

Despite the defeat of Judas at Bethzacharias in 163 B.C. by young Antiochus V, revolt at Antioch compelled the Seleucid invaders to withdraw, and Judea was granted religious liberty. In 162 B.C. Demetrius I (162-150 B.C.) murdered his cousin Antiochus V and seized the throne of Syria. He appointed Alcimus, a corrupt Hellenizer, as high priest. Judas not only drove out Alcimus but destroyed a Syrian army at Adasa in March, 161 B.C. However, the next month Judas died heroically in battle at Elasa (1 Macc. 9:1-22) in the face of a large invading force of Syrians.

JONATHAN AND SIMON MACCABEUS AND POLITICAL INDEPENDENCE. The brothers of Judas now fought for political liberty. Jonathan (161-143 B.C.) carried on Judas' role as a guerrilla leader and a foe of Hellenizing Jews (1 Macc. 9:58-73). In the struggle among rival claimants for the Seleucid throne, Alexander I, another son of Antiochus IV, appointed Jonathan as high priest in order to gain his favor. Alexander I also defeated and killed Demetrius I in 150 B.C. Demetrius II, the son of Demetrius I, was able with the help of Ptolemy VII to defeat and kill Alexander in 145 B.C. He bestowed upon Jonathan the districts of Samaria to court his favor.

Intrigue, however, continued in the struggle for the Syrian throne, and an infant son of Alexander was now brought forward as Antiochus VI by a general named Tryphon. But the general not only put Antiochus VI to death and arrogated the crown to himself, but treacherously murdered Jonathan as well. However, Tryphon's rival, Demetrius II, granted to Simon Maccabeus (143-135 B.C.) the long-fought-for political independence of Judea (143 B.C.; 1 Macc. 13:36-43).

THE HASMONEAN PRIEST-KINGS (143 to 37 B.C.)

SIMON (143 TO 135 B.C.). Simon was confirmed in the position of King-Priest by the Romans (1 Macc. 14:16-24). While the rivals for the Syrian throne, Demetrius II and Tryphon, fought one another, Simon was able to strengthen Judea and expel the last Syrian garrison from Jerusalem. When Antiochus VII, the brother of Demetrius II, came into power, Simon defeated his attempt to reimpose the Seleucid yoke on Judea (1 Macc. 16:8-10). Simon stabilized the Jewish kingdom until he was treacherously murdered by his son-in-law, Ptolemy, in 135 B.C.

JOHN HYRCANUS I (135 TO 105 B.C.). As the sole surviving son of Simon, John Hyrcanus came to power and drove out Ptolemy. But he was dominated by Antiochus VII (139-129). After the latter's death in 129 B.C. and the ensuing struggle for power in Syria between Demetrius II (who was released by the Parthians) and Alexander II, John Hyrcanus was free to expand his realm, especially since his position had become strengthened by a strong treaty with the Romans. He conquered Idumea, Transjordan, and Samaria. In 128 B.C. he destroyed the Samaritan Temple on Mount Gerizim. He occupied Jezreel in 109 B.C. when he repulsed Antiochus IX.

ARISTOBULUS I (105 TO 104 B.C.). Aristobulus shared the rule with his brother Antigonus I initially, but murdered him as soon as opportunity allowed, thereafter assuming the kingship himself. He was opposed by strict Jews for his cruelties and for his Hellenistic leanings. But he ruled reasonably well nevertheless, and added Galilee to his realm.

ALEXANDER JANNAEUS (104 TO 78 B.C.). A brother of Aristobulus, Alexander Jannaeus, was designated king by Aristobulus' widow, Alexandra, whom he married. He was able to enlarge his kingdom considerably, partly because of the continuing struggle in Syria of rival claimants for the Seleucid throne. However, the rise of Nabataean power under Aretas III put an end to his conquests in 85 B.C.

ALEXANDER (78 TO 69 B.C.) AND THE RISE OF JEWISH PARTIES. Alexander Jannaeus' widow succeeded her husband as regent, though their son Hyrcanus II was high priest. In reality, however, the rule passed into the hands of the Sanhedrin, dominated by the Pharisees. Members of this latter sect were apparently the successors of the Hasidim who had been God's "loyal ones" in the Maccabean era and who had stood true to Judaism against the pressures of Hellenism. They were separatists and strict legalists who stressed prayer, repentance, and charitable giving. They believed in foreordination, immortality, resurrection, angels, judgment, and eternal rewards (Acts 23:8).

The Sadducees were the Zadokite priests and their partisans (1 Kings 2:35). They were principally composed of the aristocratic, worldly-minded priests. They maintained the Temple ritual but were actually more interested in politics than in religion. As worldly followers of the later Hasmoneans they had Hellenistic sympathies. They were the religious rationalists of the day and opposed the traditions of the Pharisees. They laid emphasis on human ability, and denied immortality, the existence of angels, the resurrection, and future retribution. Their religion was anthropocentric (man-centered).

The Essenes were ascetics who withdrew from normal life into monastic colonies in the desert. Their faith was apocalyptic and their morality very severe. Their customs are seen in the Dead Sea Scrolls, especially The Manual of Discipline and the Damascus Document from the Qumran Caves.

ARISTOBULUS II, HYRCANUS II, AND ROMAN SUBJECTION (69 TO 37 B.C.). The sons of Jannaeus, Aristobulus II (69-63 B.C.) and Hyrcanus II (63-40 B.C.), vied with each other for the throne. Both appealed to Rome for help, which furnished the ideal situation for a Roman takeover. By 64 B.C. Pompey, the Roman general, had already made Syria a Roman province with headquarters in Damascus. When Aristobulus lost the confidence of the Romans and his supporters entrenched themselves in the Temple, Pompey besieged Jerusalem. In 63 B.C. the city surrendered, after three months' siege. Pompey outraged the Jews by entering the Holy of Holies.

Aristobulus II was taken prisoner to Rome. His older brother, Hyrcanus II, was appointed high priest and ethnarch under the Romans. Hasmonean independence came to an end. From that time on the Jews were subject to Rome.

Survey of New Testament History

PALESTINE IN CHRIST'S DAY (4 B.C. to A.D. 30).

THE RISE OF THE ROMAN EMPIRE. After a long period of conquest and expansion from about 500 B.C. Rome entered a period of civil war, beginning with Pompey's conquest of Palestine in 63 B.C. The First Triumvirate (60 B.C.) consisted of Pompey, Crassus, and Julius Caesar. Pompey attacked Caesar, but was defeated at Pharsalus in 48 B.C. and was killed by Ptolemy XIV. Crassus was killed in a campaign against the Parthians (53 B.C.). Caesar's assassination in 44 B.C. opened the way for the Second Triumvirate, consisting of Mark Antony, Octavian, and Lepidus in 43 B.C. These vied for control of the Empire against opposition led by Brutus and Cassius. The republican forces under Brutus and Cassius were crushed at Philippi (42 B.C.). The final clash between Octavian and Mark Antony eventuated in the defeat of the latter and the emergence of the Roman Empire under Octavian ("Augustus Caesar"), who reigned as sole ruler from 31 B.C. to A.D. 14.

THE RISE OF HEROD THE GREAT (37 TO 4 B.C.). Herod was the son of Antipater, the native governor of Idumea under Alexander Jannaeus and the power behind Hyrcanus II (63-40 B.C.). After Pharsalus (48 B.C.), Antipater was awarded the official procuratorship of Judea (47-43 B.C.) for assisting Julius Caesar. Antipater then appointed

Model of Herod's Temple, by Shick (© *MPS*)

his son Phasael as governor of Jerusalem and his son Herod as governor of Galilee. After Antipater's death by poisoning, both Phasael and Herod gained the favor of Mark Antony and were made tetrarchs over Palestine.

When Antigonus II (40-37 B.C.) took Jerusalem with Parthian help and deposed Hyrcanus II, Phasael committed suicide. Herod, however, fled to Rome, ostensibly to promote the cause of the last of the Hasmonean princes, young Aristobulus III (36-35 B.C.). Instead, he was himself made king of Judea by grant of the Roman Senate. He then married Mariamne, the Hasmonean princess and sister of Aristobulus III, to help strengthen his new position of power.

HEROD'S ADMINISTRATION. Herod had a long and energetic rule. But he was hated by his subjects as an Idumaean or "half Jew" and as a fawning friend of the Romans. In character he was a jealous, crafty monster. No one was safe from his cruelty and suspicion. His slaughter of the male children at Bethlehem (Matt. 2:13, 16) is consistent with his reputation for murder. On the merest suspicion he slew members of his own immediate family, putting to death his favorite wife, Mariamne, and also her brothers, Aristobulus and Alexander. Just five days before he died he ordered the death of his son Antipater. No wonder Augustus said, "It is better to be Herod's hog than to be his son!"

However, Herod ruled fairly well overall, and peace and prosperity

resulted. He loved Hellenic culture and architecture and had numerous temples, palaces, theaters, and baths constructed throughout his
realm. At the site of ancient Samaria he built Sebaste in honor of
Emperor Augustus. On the coast he built the brilliant Hellenistic city
of Caesarea, which was to become the capital of the country.

Herod's most magnificent building enterprise was the splendid
Temple at Jerusalem begun in 20 B.C. It was constructed in strict conformity with Jewish principles. Herod himself refrained from going
into the inner sanctuary, the precinct of the priests. The edifice proper
was finished in only one year and six months, though other construction continued for as long as forty years. Only about seven years after
its final completion the entire Temple was destroyed in the razing of
Jerusalem in A.D. 70.

THE SONS OF HEROD. Of the sons of Herod's ten legal marriages,
several had perished in intrigues or had been executed by their father.
Thus three younger sons were destined to inherit the kingdom.

Herod Antipas (4 B.C. to A.D. 39). He was the younger son of Malthace
and became tetrarch of Galilee and Perea. His capital was built on the
western shore of the Sea of Galilee and was called Tiberias in honor
of the then-reigning emperor, Tiberius Caesar (A.D. 22). Antipas divorced his first wife, the daughter of King Aretas IV of Nabatea, to
marry Herodias, the wife of his half-brother, Herod Philip. John the
Baptist was imprisoned and executed by Antipas (Mark 6:14-28) because he denounced this second marriage as unlawful. Jesus once described Antipas as "that fox" (Luke 13:31-33). He also had a brief
encounter with Jesus when the latter was sent to him by Pilate for
judgment (Luke 23:6-12). Aretas IV avenged Herod's insult in A.D. 36
by defeating him in war. Antipas ended up in banishment in Gaul
when deposed from his tetrarchy by Emperor Caligula.

Archelaus (4 B.C. to A.D. 6). He was the older son of Herod by Malthace and received the principal part of Herod's kingdom, comprising
Judea, Samaria, and Idumea. His father intended him to have the title
of king, but he was actually made only an ethnarch. He was a violent,
cruel, and incompetent administrator and was consequently banished
to Vienne in Gaul in A.D. 6. When Joseph took Mary and the infant
Jesus from Egypt to return to the land of Israel, Joseph was afraid to
go into Judea because Archelaus was on the throne. (Joseph withdrew to Galilee instead—see Matthew 2:22, 23).

Herod Philip (4 B.C. to A.D. 34). He was Herod the Great's son by
Cleopatra and became tetrarch of regions north and east of the Sea of

Galilee (Gaulonitis, Trachonitis Batanea, and Ulatha). He ruled well for thirty years, and, like his father, was a builder. At the sources of the Jordan he rebuilt the city of Panias, calling it Caesarea in honor of the emperor. Its full name was Caesarea Philippi (Matt. 16:13; Mark 8:27) to distinguish it from Caesarea the capital of Judea, on the Mediterranean coast. He also enlarged and adorned Bethsaida near the spot where the Jordan River enters the Lake of Galilee. He called it Bethsaida Julias after Augustus Caesar's daughter Julia.

LOCAL RULE OF THE JEWISH PARTIES. Five prominent parties in Judaism vied with Roman authority for a voice of power in affairs in Judea in the days of Jesus. The *Sadducees* dominated the priesthood (Acts 5:17) and had a disproportionately large voice in the governing council, the Sanhedrin (Acts 4:1). Influential *Pharisees* also tried to control this supreme legislative body. They opposed the Herods, but were willing to co-exist peaceably with the Romans (John 11: 48). Christ condemned their hypocrisy and self-righteous legalism (Matt. 23:13-36). Infuriated, they plotted his death under the pretense of loyalty to Caesar (John 19:12-15).

The *Herodians* were partisans of Rome and supporters of Rome's puppets, the Herods, and of Hellenism (Mark 3:6; 8:15). The *Zealots* were those Jews fired with messianic hope and hatred of Rome. They were ready to make Christ a revolutionary leader (John 6:15). From the *Essene movement,* illustrated from the discoveries at Qumran, may have come John the Baptist (Luke 3:1-4, 15, 16). Rigid separation and call to reformation constituted the battle cry of this group. Each of these sects had a part in preparing for Christ's advent and ministry. Yet all of these parties became off-balance and extremist. Only in Christ could their central truth find complete fulfillment.

JUDEA UNDER ROMAN PROCURATORS (A.D. 4 TO 66). When Herod's son Archelaus was banished in A.D. 6, his territory became a Roman province ruled directly by the Emperor through a governor of the equestrian order called a *procurator.* This governor could receive help from the legate who governed the imperial province of Syria. His residence was at Caesarea, but he could occupy quarters at Jerusalem when special need arose. From A.D. 6 till the Jewish war with Rome (with the exception of the period A.D. 41-44, when Agrippa I was a Jewish king) Judea and Samaria were governed by a series of Roman procurators.

THE PROCURATORS OF CHRIST'S DAY. Of the Roman procurators of Christ's day by far the most important from the standpoint of Christ's life was Pontius Pilate (A.D. 26-36). In A.D. 26 Tiberius Caesar appointed him to be the fifth procurator of Judea. In accordance with a recent reversal in the policy of the Roman Senate (A.D. 21), Pilate took his wife with him (Matt. 27:19). As procurator he had full control in the province, being in charge of detachments of cavalry and infantry stationed at Caesarea and in the fortress of Antonia at Jerusalem. He had jurisdiction over life and death and could reverse capital sentences passed by the Sanhedrin, which had to be submitted to him for ratification. He also named the high priests and controlled the temple and its funds. At the festivals the procurator took up residence in Jerusalem and brought in additional troops to maintain order.

Pilate had a reputation for giving offense to the Jews. An example of his cruelty is the otherwise unknown act of violence referred to in Luke 13:1, in which he mingled the blood of certain Galileans with that of their animal sacrifices. He took money from the Temple treasury to build an aqueduct to Jerusalem and mercilessly beat down the crowds protesting this act. Later he put inscribed shields in Herod's palace. These were taken down only when the Jews appealed to Tiberius Caesar. His atrocities against the Samaritans led to complaint to Vitellius, the legate of Syria, and ultimately resulted in his replacement.

THE PERIOD OF THE EARLY CHURCH
(A.D. 30 to 65).

THE BIRTH OF THE CHURCH. The death and resurrection of Christ resulted in the gift of the Spirit at Pentecost in A.D. 30 and the formation of the Church. Although the Church was at first composed only of regenerated Jews (Acts 1 – 7), it soon began to include racially mixed Samaritans (Acts 8) and eventually included even Gentiles (Acts 10). The settled order of the new age was established when Jew and Gentile were made one in a new entity that exemplified God's purpose: "to visit the Gentiles to take out of them a people for his name" (Acts 15:14, 15). The Church spread rapidly because it had a vital redemptive message for *all* mankind through the sacrificial death of Jesus Christ, God incarnate.

THE CHURCH AND JEWISH PERSECUTION. The unbelieving part of the Jewish nation rejected and persecuted Christ's Church much as it had rejected and persecuted Christ himself. Judea was the scene of fierce persecutions of the early followers of Jesus (Acts 4 – 7).

These trials, however, served to scatter Christian witnesses far and wide and were an important factor in the Church's growth throughout the Empire.

A bust of Tiberius Caesar, as he may have appeared on the penny handed Jesus *(Russ Busby photo)*

THE CHURCH AND THE ROMAN EMPERORS. Tiberius (A.D. 14-37) was succeeded by his nephew Caligula (A.D. 37-41), who was appointed emperor by the Praetorian guards. A cruel, insane tyrant, he alienated everyone and was eventually murdered by the guards. Claudius (A.D. 41-54), Caligula's uncle and successor, is mentioned in the New Testament. He banished the Jews from Rome (Acts 18:2), but later restored them. During his reign there was a severe and widespread famine (Acts 11:28). Claudius was murdered by his niece, the mother of Nero. Nero (A.D. 54-68) was Claudius' adopted son and, like Caligula, was appointed to the imperial power by the Praetorian guards.

Nero was educated by the famous philosopher Seneca. Yet despite this fact he became a profligate monster. Among his atrocities was a fearful persecution of Christians, whom he accused of burning Rome in A.D. 64. Numerous Christians suffered martyrdom at this time, including the Apostle Peter and the Apostle Paul. Deserted by the Praetorian guards, Nero took his own life.

Civil war followed Nero's death. The army took control, appointing in succession several military figures to supreme power — Galba of

Spain, Otho of the Praetorians, and Vitellius of the Rhine (A.D. 68-69). None of these proved long-lasting. Vespasian (A.D. 69-79), commander of the Syrian legions, left his son Titus in the East to put down the Jewish uprising in Palestine. He himself hastened to Rome to make a bid for the emperorship. He was successful, founding the Flavian dynasty and establishing a stable and just administration.

THE CHURCH AND THE LATER HERODS. Herod's sons, Archelaus, Herod Antipas, and Herod Philip, figure prominently in the background of the lives of Jesus and John the Baptist. The later Herods, Herod Agrippa I and Herod Agrippa II, color the history of the early Church.

Herod Agrippa I, King of Judea (A.D. *41 to 44*). He was a grandson of Herod the Great and was sent to Rome to be educated in the family of emperor Tiberius. His extravagant living reduced him to poverty, and he was compelled to return to Judea. His sister Herodias secured him employment with Herod Antipas. But he quarreled with both Antipas and Flaccus, the legate of Syria. Eventually he returned to Rome to become a personal friend of Caligula and to support the latter's rise to power.

Tiberius had replaced Pilate as Procurator of Judea with Marcellus (A.D. 36-37). When Caligula became emperor, he appointed Marullus (A.D. 37-41) to the procuratorship of Judea and rewarded Agrippa with the tetrarchy of Trachonitis, giving him the title of king (A.D. 37). Herodias, the wife of Herod Antipas, in envy prevailed upon her husband to also seek the kingly title over Galilee. Agrippa, anticipating this rivalry, used his influence with Caligula to have Antipas banished to Gaul, and he himself received Galilee (A.D. 39). Being in Rome at the time Caligula was murdered, he urged Claudius to assume the emperorship. As a result Claudius awarded him Judea and Samaria. He was now king of all the territory once held by Herod the Great.

Herod Agrippa I skillfully placated the Jews. This policy involved him in the murder of the Apostle James, the brother of John, and the attempted murder of the Apostle Peter (Acts 12:1-19). He came under the severe judgment of God for accepting divine honors (Acts 12:20-23).

Herod Agrippa II. He was the son of Herod Agrippa I and was in line for the kingship. However, this was precluded by his youth, as he was only seventeen years of age. As a result the procuratorship was reinstituted. In A.D. 48, after his uncle Herod's death, Claudius gave him the kingdom of Chalcis in Lebanon. In A.D. 50 Agrippa II was given Trachonitis and parts of Galilee, with the accompanying title of king. In this way Agrippa became Agrippa II, the last of the Herodian line.

Agrippa II's sister, Drusilla, married the procurator Felix (A.D. 52-60). Felix heard Paul's case, expecting a bribe (Acts 24:1-26). Festus (A.D. 60-62), the most just of the procurators, also heard Paul's defense, together with Agrippa II and Berenice, the latter's corrupt sister-mistress (Acts 25:13—26:32). This event shows the deference Rome was prepared to pay to a puppet king, who was a typical Herod of the better sort—regal, intelligent, and pro-Roman but sympathetically understanding toward Judaism, which he saw as the key to the history of his land. With Agrippa II ended the line of the Herods, whose adroit pro-Roman policy went far to postpone the inevitable clash between Rome and the Jews. As a result peace was maintained in the crucial formative years of the Christian Church in Palestine.

THE JEWISH-ROMAN WAR (A.D. 66 to 70).

THE INEVITABLE CLASH WITH ROME. The rejection and crucifixion of Jesus Christ displayed the moral and spiritual deterioration to which the Jewish people had sunk. It was this spiritual decay which led the Jews to their national ruin. Although their Roman overlords were frequently oppressive and corrupt, the real cause for the impending clash with Rome was the inability of the Jews themselves to preserve tranquility, the one thing upon which Rome insisted.

Unrest mounted dangerously under the latter procurators. Extreme zealots called "Sicarii" murdered innocent people, including the high priest, Jonathan, for his policy of moderation. A fanatical Egyptian who claimed to be Messiah led a mob of Sicarii out of Jerusalem (Acts 21:38). Felix killed or captured most of these, but the leader escaped. Severe Jewish-Gentile riots in Caesarea led to the recall of Felix. Even under a good procurator such as Festus (A.D. 60-62), the threat of the Sicarii increased. Albinus (A.D. 62-64) unscrupulously encouraged lawlessness for self-enrichment.

Ananus, the Sadducean high priest, had James the brother of Christ executed in A.D. 62. Gessius Florus (A.D. 61-66), the last procurator, was unprincipled, and precipitated a hopeless situation. Race riots were rampant. Florus demanded money from the Temple treasury. The Jews refused. When soldiers attempted to seize the money, the Jews drove them back. The war was underway.

THE EARLY CAMPAIGNS OF THE WAR. Cestius Gallus, the

Syrian legate, sent Agrippa II to mediate the quarrel. The Zealots, however, would not listen to reason. But the Pharisees wanted to avoid all-out war and so appealed to Agrippa for troops. His forces captured part of Jerusalem, but were unable to take the Temple and eventually deserted or surrendered. Cestius Gallus brought a force against Jerusalem but was thoroughly repulsed in A.D. 66. The Sanhedrin then appointed Flavius Josephus, an educated Pharisee, as governor of Galilee.

Rome undertook to quell the Jewish revolt by sending one of its best generals, Vespasian, and his son Titus. Josephus was forced to yield to Rome in A.D. 67 as a result of heavy sieges and disloyalty of Zealots within the Jewish ranks.

THE DESTRUCTION OF JERUSALEM (A.D. 70). Vespasian in A.D. 68 proceeded to subdue all Judea. Jerusalem, however, held out, despite the fact that within the city rival zealot factions fought each other. For five months the city was besieged against fanatical resistance fanned by popular expectation of messianic intervention. In August, A.D. 70, Titus, the son of Vespasian, took the city. Roman legionary standards were set up in the Temple, and the victorious soldiers presented sacrifices to them. The Temple and the city were destroyed and the Jews were slaughtered in great numbers. With the fall of Jerusalem the Jewish nation came to an end, and the Jew began his weary worldwide exile that has lasted till the modern revival of the Jewish state in 1948.

BOOK-BY-BOOK SURVEY

Summary of Old Testament Books

ORDER OF BOOKS IN THE HEBREW BIBLE

The Jews arranged their sacred books in a threefold division:

The Law (Torah), comprising Genesis, Exodus, Leviticus, Numbers, and Deuteronomy — the five books of Moses.

The Prophets (Nebhiim), comprising Joshua, Judges, First and Second Samuel, First and Second Kings, Isaiah, Jeremiah, Ezekiel, and the twelve Minor Prophets.

The Writings (Kethubim), consisting of 1) Psalms, Proverbs, and Job; 2) Song of Solomon, Ruth, Lamentations, Ecclesiastes, and Esther; and 3) Daniel, Ezra, Nehemiah, and First and Second Chronicles.

BASIS OF THE HEBREW ARRANGEMENT

Although a number of factors led to the threefold division of the Hebrew Scriptures, the main reason is probably to be found in *liturgical usage*. The Torah or Pentateuch held a special place in the minds and hearts of the Jewish people because it had been divinely given through Moses, the great lawgiver and founder of the Hebrew theocracy. The Torah was also considered the basis of the Jewish state and the foundation of everything written in the Prophets and the Writings. For these reasons it was placed first in the Hebrew Canon. The Torah was divided into fifty-four sections called *Parashioth,* which were read on consecutive Sabbaths throughout the Jewish year.

The Prophets were likewise subdivided into consecutive Sabbath

Michelangelo's Moses, in a church in Rome *(Russ Busby photo)*

readings. These were called *Haphtaroth* or "dismissals" because they were read immediately before the close of each public service. In the ninth century A.D. these were further subdivided by the Massoretes into verses. Chapter divisions, ascribed to Stephen Langton, Archbishop of Canterbury, came into use in the thirteenth century. The Massoretic division into verses was then combined with the chapter divisions and passed from the Latin Vulgate into English through the Geneva Bible in 1560.

The Writings were read less frequently than the Torah and the Prophets. The devotional books were used in the synagogue services, the Psalms and Proverbs weekly, and Job at most of the great fasts.

The Scrolls (the so-called "Five Rolls" — Song of Solomon, Ruth, Lamentations, Ecclesiastes, and Esther) were read at special festivals. The remaining books (Daniel, Ezra, Nehemiah, and Chronicles), formed a sort of appendix, read upon various special occasions.

ORDER OF BOOKS IN THE ENGLISH BIBLE

The books are conveniently arranged according to their subject matter.

The Pentateuch — the five books of Moses, Genesis to Deuteronomy.

The Historical Books — Joshua to Esther.

The Poetic and Wisdom Books — Job to Song of Solomon.

The Prophetic Books — Isaiah to Malachi.

The Pentateuch

TITLE

The term *Pentateuch* is the Greek name given to the first five books of the Old Testament. The word means "the five-volume Book." The Pentateuch apparently existed originally as one book in scroll form. If this was the case, its fivefold division became necessary in the course of history for liturgical reasons, to facilitate the reading of the Law (Torah) in the synagogue service. This was because ancient "books" were in the form of scrolls. The Jews employed the standard-size rolls, about thirty feet long, sufficient to accommodate the unvocalized text of Genesis or Deuteronomy. They did not use the huge scrolls employed by the Egyptians, sometimes over four times this length, as in the case of the Book of the Dead and the Papyrus Harris.

The Pentateuch has also been referred to by various other terms descriptive of its contents. These include "the law" (Josh. 1:7; Matt. 5:17), "the book of the law" (Josh. 8:34), "the book of the law of Moses" (Josh. 8:31), "the book of the law of God" (Josh. 24:26), "the law of the Lord" (Luke 2:23), and "the law of Moses" (Luke 2:22).

AUTHORSHIP

The traditional view is that the Pentateuch is the product of one author, Moses. This position was universally held by the ancient Jewish synagogue, the inspired New Testament writers, the early Christian Church, and virtually all commentators until comparatively recent times.

Modern critical theory, however, contends that the Pentateuch was pieced together from a number of documents written by various authors several centuries after the time of Moses, though containing Mosaic traditions. The so-called "Yahwist document," designated "J," is dated in the ninth century B.C., the "Elohist document" (E) in the eighth century B.C., and the combining of these two documents in the seventh century B.C. Deuteronomy is dated 621 B.C. and the addition of the Priestly Code (P) around 500 B.C. These documents were allegedly pieced together by "redactors" or editors who gave the Pentateuch the order and arrangement it now has.

Several lines of evidence converge to refute this unsound theory.

The Pentateuch itself bears explicit witness to its Mosaic authorship. The legal codes (Exod. 24:4; 25:1; Lev. 1:1; 4:1; Num. 1:1; Deut. 31:9, 24-26) as well as the narrative sections (Exod. 17:14; Num. 33:2) claim to be written by Israel's great lawgiver.

The remainder of the Old Testament also testifies to Mosaic authorship of the Pentateuch (Josh. 1:7; 8:32; 22:5; Judg. 3:4; 1 Chron 15:15; 1 Kings 2:3; 2 Kings 18:12; 23:25; Dan. 9:11, 13; Ezra 3:2; 6: 18; Neh. 1:7, 8; Mal. 4:4).

The New Testament likewise attests Mosaic authorship of the Pentateuch (Mark 12:26; Matt. 8:4; 19:7; Mark 1:44; 10:31; Luke 5: 14; John 1:17; 5:46, 47; 7:19; 2 Cor. 3:15; Acts 15:21).

Tradition also confirms the same view. The Samaritan Pentateuch (fifth century B.C.) proves that both Jews and Samaritans had believed for many years that Moses wrote this portion of the Bible. The apocryphal book of Ecclesiasticus (45:5) as well as Second Maccabees (7:30) attest the same view, as do Philo (*Life of Moses* 3:39) and Josephus (*Antiquities* IV:8, 48), and all the early lists of canonical books.

Internal evidence and local color also confirm Mosaic authorship. The Pentateuch was written in the desert (Deut. 12:1-10) by an eyewitness-author who knew Egypt intimately (Deut. 11:10; Exod. 5:1-14). By certain archaic expressions of thought and by the elemental nature of its doctrinal teachings the Pentateuch bears witness that it belongs to an early period in God's progressive revelation to man.

IMPORTANCE

The Pentateuch's intrinsic worth as divinely-inspired Scripture is enhanced by its antiquity and its position of primacy in both the Jewish and Christian Canons of Scripture. *Doctrinally* it is the seed plot for every other teaching of Scripture, forming the foundation for all divinely revealed truth. *Cosmically* it presents God as the Creator of the heavens and the earth and of all plant, animal, and human life, in sublime contrast to the naive polytheistic creation stories of antiquity. In presenting the universe as the creative act of one God, the Pentateuch sets forth a concept which is totally beyond the grasp of unaided human thought. *Historically* the Pentateuch provides the foundation for every accurate appraisal of the human race and for every realistic account of its progress. It outlines the essentials of redemptive history, incorporating human events only as they are necessary for this purpose. In this respect it is absolutely unique in all the literature of the world.

MOSAIC UNITY

The conservative scholar upholds the Mosaic unity of the Pentateuch, that is, 1) that this portion of Scripture is historical and originates from the time of Moses; 2) that Moses was its only human author; and 3) that though it may have been revised and edited by later inspired writers, these revisions and/or additions are just as fully inspired of God as are the other portions (see Deut. 34:5-12; Exod. 11:3; Num. 12:3). The documentary theory denies without adequate evidence the Mosaic unity and hence the historicity and reliability of this foundational portion of divine revelation.

Genesis

TITLE

Genesis is a word derived from the Septuagint (the Greek version of the Old Testament) and means "origin" or "beginning." This is indeed a most appropriate title for this first book of the Bible, for it is in a most distinctive sense the *book of beginnings*. Important beginnings described are 1) the beginning of the earth as man's habitation (Gen. 1:1 – 2:3); 2) the beginning of the human race (Gen. 2:7-25); 3) the beginning of human sin (Gen. 3:1-8); 4) the beginning of redemptive revelation (Gen. 3:9-24); 5) the beginning of the human family (Gen. 4:1-15); 6) the beginning of civilization (Gen. 4:16 – 9:29); 7) the beginning of nations (Gen. 10:1-32); 8) the beginning of human languages (Gen. 11:1-9); and 9) the beginning of the Hebrew race (Gen. 11:10 – 50:26).

IMPORTANCE

As the "book of beginnings" Genesis constitutes an indispensable introduction to the entire Bible. It forms the foundation of all revealed truth. For this reason and because of its antiquity, no historical work in existence can be compared with it.

The three primary names of deity (*Elohim, Jehovah,* and *Adonai*) and the five most important compound names of God occur in Genesis as part of the progressive self-revelation of God to man.

Of the eight great covenants which regulate human life on earth and outline man's salvation, four of these – the Edenic, Adamic, Noahic, and Abrahamic – are found in Genesis.

OUTLINE

A. The Early History of Man (chapters 1 – 11)
  1. The creation (chapters 1, 2)
  2. The fall to the flood (chapters 3 – 5)
  3. The flood (chapters 6 – 9)
  4. The flood to Abraham (chapters 10, 11)
B. The Patriarchal History of Israel (chapters 12 – 50)
  1. Abraham (12:1 – 25:10)
  2. Isaac (25:11 – 28:9)
  3. Jacob (28:10 – 36:43)
  4. Joseph (37:1 – 50:26)

KEY WORD

The key word of Genesis is *election* Divine electing grace pervades the book. Genesis records a number of family histories in which God personally chooses individuals through whom he will work out his redemptive plan for the fallen race. Of Adam's posterity, Cain drops out and Seth is chosen instead. Of Noah's progeny, Ham and Japheth are passed over and Shem is selected. Of Terah's family, Nahor and Haran drop out and Abram is called. Of Abram's sons, Ishmael is rejected and Isaac is chosen. Of Isaac's sons, Esau is bypassed and Jacob comes into the line of blessing. Of Jacob's sons, Judah is selected to perpetuate the line of Messiah (Gen. 49:9, 10). Underlying the divine plan of redemption in its progressive unfolding is eternal election (Eph. 1:4).

PROBLEMS

Among the difficulties presented by Genesis are the date of creation and the age of the earth, the antiquity of man, the fall of man, and the historicity of the flood.

THE DATE OF CREATION AND THE AGE OF THE EARTH.
Many conservative scholars have held that Genesis 1:1-31 describes the original creation of the universe alluded to in Job 38:1-6, John 1:3, and Colossians 1:16. Yet this position is an interpretation rather than an exegetical necessity. It actually fails to explain certain crucial facts, such as the vast age of the earth, the origin of sin and Satan (Gen. 3), the existence of chaos (Gen. 1:2), and the six apparently literal days of creation (often interpreted as geological ages).

The interpretation that sees in these verses not the original creation of the universe but the re-creation of a judgment-ridden earth for the latecomer man is exegetically sound and solves many of the scientific and theological problems of the passage. It recognizes the fact that Genesis does not date the creation of the earth or the universe. It also recognizes that long before the creation of man the earth was inhabited by Lucifer and other angelic beings (Isa. 14:12-14; Ezek. 28:12-15). These denizens of the earth rebelled against God, thereby introducing sin into a universe that was originally sinless as it came from its Creator's hand (Job 38:4-7; Isa. 45:18; John 1:3; Col. 1:16).

THE ANTIQUITY OF MAN. Both science and the Genesis account agree that man is a latecomer on the earth. The only disagreement is *how late?* The Bible permits a date of probably no earlier than 10,000 B.C., and gives the lie to the very much earlier datings of the evolutionist.

However, the re-creation of the earth and the creation of man (Gen. 1:1 — 2:25) cannot be dated at about 4004 B.C., as did Archbishop Ussher by using the genealogies of Genesis chapters 5 and 11. These lists, which trace human descent from Adam to Abraham, are abbreviated and skeletal, as is now generally recognized by conservative scholarship. Symmetry and beauty are aimed at, rather than unbroken succession of father to son. Evidently *extreme brevity* characterizes these two short lists, for they apparently cover as many as eight or ten millennia between Adam and Abraham.

The terms "beget," "bear," "father," and "son" are employed in Semitic languages to mean not only a direct father-to-son relationship but also a more distant relationship of great-grandfather to great-grandson, etc. For example, Jacob's offspring were known as "the sons of Jacob" centuries after the death of the patriarch (Mal. 3:6). Usage extends to tribes and countries (Gen. 10:2-32) and even (in the case of royalty) to non-blood descendants. On the Black Obelisk of Shalmaneser III Jehu is styled "son of Omri" by the Assyrians even though he was actually the founder of a new dynasty in Israel, with no blood relationship whatever with the house of Omri.

The standard genealogical formula of Genesis 5 and 11 reads as follows: "A lived ____ years and begat B. And A lived after he begat B ____ years and begat sons and daughters." B might not have been the literal son of A at all, but rather a distant descendant. If so, the age of A was his age at the birth of the child from whom B was descended. *Centuries may therefore have intervened between A and B.* In addition, great longevity was characteristic of pre-flood humanity (Gen. 5:5, 8, 14, 17, 25), a fact amply illustrated by archeology, which demonstrates that traditions of primeval longevity were widespread in antiquity. According to the Weld-Blundell Prism, eight pre-flood kings ruled in lower Mesopotamian cities, the *shortest* of whose reign was 18,600 years. This is obviously a corrupted tradition of the actual historical facts as preserved in the long-lived patriarchs of Genesis 5.

A "tower of Babel" in Babylonia (© *MPS*)

THE FALL OF MAN. If Genesis 1:1, 2 describes the original creation of a *sinless* universe, how can the chaos of Genesis 1:2 be explained? How can the presence of Satan's tool, the serpent, and the existence of evil be accounted for in chapter 3, as well as the fallen angels in chapter 6? How can man's fall, calling forth God's redemptive plan in Christ, be established if Genesis omits any allusion to the origin of Satan and sin in its opening chapters? The fact is that Genesis does not *omit* these matters but *presupposes* them. It begins with a re-created earth and a new creature — man. Through man God would undo the effects of sin *not only on the earth but also in the universe.* Thus in a certain sense the fall of man in Genesis 3 was a necessity to God's plan and purpose for the ages. This is why Genesis 3 is of such immense theological significance.

THE HISTORICITY OF THE FLOOD. The date of the flood, like the date of the creation of man, can be determined only very approximately, for the genealogical table from Shem to Abraham (Gen. 11:10-30) contains extensive gaps. This is demonstrated by the fact that these tables if taken literally allow only about 4000 years from the creation of man to the birth of Christ. Modern archeology, on the other hand, clearly traces highly developed sedentary pottery cultures, such as the Halafian, well before 4000 B.C. If the Genesis genealogies are used in dating, the Noahic flood would be placed at 2348 B.C., an archeological impossibility. The deluge certainly took place long before 4000 B.C.

Moreover, the flood was a worldwide cataclysm. Theories of a local flood clash with explicit declarations of Scripture (Gen. 6:13; 7:20, 23; 8:21) and are concessions to the false, naturalistic theory of uniformity. The Bible clearly teaches supernatural catastrophism, as shown in the judgmental chaos visited on the earth after the fall of Lucifer and his angels (Isa. 14:12-15; Ezek. 28:13-17) and by the Noahic flood (2 Pet. 3:6).

Geological uniformitarianism, like the naturalistic theory of evolution, is based on false presuppositions. Until geology recognizes supernatural catastrophism, manifested in the destruction and reconstruction of the earth and in the Noahic flood, it will continue to ignore part of the evidence that tells the *complete* story of the earth's crust. It will also continue to deny that such a worldwide flood ever took place. In doing so it utterly fails to explain both the biblical and the extrabiblical evidence of this global event. Significant among the extrabiblical evidences of the worldwide flood are the Sumerian and Babylonian flood epics. Of all ancient traditions that have close affiliation with the Old Testament, none is more striking than the Babylonian-Assyrian flood story, constituting the eleventh book of the Epic of Gilgamesh. If the flood never took place, how can the universal deluge of both the Sumerian and Babylonian accounts be explained, as well as flood traditions of other peoples of antiquity?

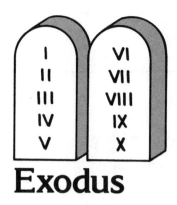

Exodus

TITLE

The name *Exodus* originated from the Greek word employed in the Septuagint Version. It signifies "exit" or "departure," as in Hebrews 11:22. The book narrates the *going out* or *departure* of the Israelites from bondage in Egypt to freedom in the Promised Land. The key word in the book is *redemption*. Man's ruin and God's electing love in Genesis are followed by redemption in Exodus. The need of redemption is seen in the people's condition (Exod. 1, 2). The way of redemption is by blood (Exod. 12) and by God's manifested power (Exod. 14). The law of redemption is the divine will set forth in the Decalogue (Exod. 20) and the Book of the Covenant (Exod. 21 – 24). The means of redemption is pictured in the tabernacle and priesthood (Exod. 25 – 40), which point to Christ (Heb. 8:1 – 10:18).

OUTLINE

A. Subjection: Israel in Egypt (1:1 – 12:36)
  1. Bondage in Egypt (chapter 1)
  2. Preparation of the deliverer (chapters 2 – 4)
  3. Contest with the oppressor (chapters 5 – 11)
  4. Deliverance by the Passover (12:1-36)
B. Emancipation: Israel from Egypt to Sinai (12:37 – 18:27)
  1. Conduct to the Red Sea (12:37 – 14:14)
  2. Deliverance through the Red Sea (14:15 – 15:21)
  3. Leading from the Red Sea (15:22 – 18:27)
C. Revelation: Israel at Sinai (chapters 19 – 40)

1. The will of God made known (chapters 19—31)
    (a) In the Law (chapters 19—24)
    (b) In the Tabernacle (chapters 25—27)
    (c) In the priesthood (chapters 28, 29)
    (d) In the service (chapters 30, 31)
2. The will of God flouted (chapters 32—34)
    (a) The great sin (32:1-6)
    (b) The divine anger (32:7—33:23)
    (c) The renewal of the Covenant (chapter 34)
3. The will of God fulfilled (chapters 35—40)
    (a) The Tabernacle commenced (35:1—39:31)
    (b) The Tabernacle completed (39:32—40:33)
    (c) The Tabernacle consecrated (40:34-38)

PORTRAYAL OF THE REDEEMER IN EXODUS

IN MOSES. As a prefigurement of Christ, Moses illustrates how re-demption is centered in a man, the man Christ Jesus. Like Christ, he was born under the dire threat of death but was divinely chosen and preserved (Exod. 3:7-10; Acts 7:25). Rejected by Israel, he turned to the Gentiles (Exod. 2:11-15). During the period of rejection he took a Gentile bride (Exod. 2:16-21; Matt. 12:14-21). Later he appeared again as Israel's deliverer and was accepted (Exod. 4:29-31; Rom. 11:24-25).

IN THE PASSOVER LAMB (EXOD. 12:1-28; JOHN 1:29; 1 COR. 5:6, 7; 1 PET. 1:18, 19). The Lamb was *without defect* (Exod. 12:5; John 8:46) and was *slain* (Exod. 12:6; Heb. 9:22). The applied *blood* shielded from judgment (Exod. 12:13; Heb. 9:11-14). The Passover feast speaks of Christ, the Bread of Life (Matt. 26:26-28; 1 Cor. 11:23-26).

IN THE TABERNACLE. The life of the nation was conducted in direct relationship to the tabernacle, every part of which speaks of Christ, the true gathering place of his redeemed (Matt. 18:20). The ark of acacia wood overlaid with gold points to Christ as both human and divine (Exod. 25:10-22). It held a pot of manna, envisioning Christ as Life-Sustainer; the Ten Commandments, portraying Christ as Cher-isher of God's law; and Aaron's rod that budded, pointing to Christ as resurrected Redeemer (Num. 17:10). The mercy seat pictures Christ as the way of access to God. The veil between the holy of holies and the holy place symbolizes Christ's human body (Matt. 27:51; Heb. 10:20). The table of showbread typifies Christ as the Bread of Life (John 6:32-

58). The golden lampstand typifies Christ as our Light (Exod. 25:31-40). The golden altar of incense presents Christ in his intercession (Exod. 30:1-10; John 17:1-26; Heb. 7:25). The laver comprehends Christ cleansing his people from defilement (Exod. 30:18-21; John 13:2-10; Eph. 5:25-27). The brazen altar prefigures Christ enduring the wrath of God in the place of his redeemed (Exod. 27:1-8; Heb. 9:14).

IN THE PRIESTHOOD. Aaron, the high priest, typifies Christ in the exercise of his office after the Aaronic pattern, the holy garments for "glory and beauty" representing Christ's glory and beauty as our High Priest (Exod. 28:1-5). The breastplate of precious stones engraved with the names of Israel's tribes illustrates Christ's continual intercession, in which he bears his saints on his heart in God's presence (Exod. 28:15-29). The robe of the ephod of blue portrays the present heavenly priesthood of Christ (Exod. 28:31-35). The golden headplate inscribed with "Holy to the Lord" (RSV) is a reminder of the unsullied purity of Christ's priestly ministry (Exod. 28:36-38).

Aaron's consecration by washing (Exod. 29:1-4) symbolized regeneration, in which Aaron took part because he was a sinner and required cleansing. Our Lord as the spotless Lamb of God (Heb. 7:26-28) did not need cleansing, yet nonetheless yielded to John's baptism in order to identify himself with sinners, thus fulfilling the Aaronic pattern (Matt. 3:13-17). Aaron's clothing and anointing are symbolic of Christ's glory and anointing with the Spirit (Matt. 3:16). Aaron, prefiguring the sinless Christ, was anointed *before* the blood was shed (Exod. 29:5-25).

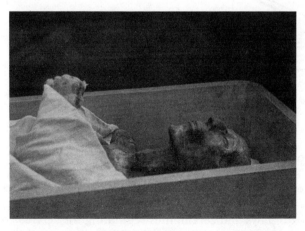

Mummy of Rameses II, possibly the pharaoh of the exodus (*Russ Busby photo*)

It should be noted that while only two chapters are occupied with the story of creation, fourteen chapters are devoted to the tabernacle. This shows the importance which God places on the work of redemption and on Christ as the center and object of the Holy Spirit's revelation.

CHRONOLOGY

Explicit scriptural statements require the date of the Exodus to be about 1441 B.C., since it occurred 480 years (1 Kings 6:1) before the fourth year of Solomon's reign (about 961 B.C., according to conservative scholarship). In this case 1871 B.C. becomes the year in which Israel entered Egypt, since the sojourn lasted 430 years (Exod. 12:40, 41). Present-day theories that argue for the date of the Exodus a century and a half later (1290 B.C., W. F. Albright) or over two centuries later (1225 B.C., H. H. Rowley) reject not only the specific biblical statements but also the whole chronological arrangement underlying the books of Joshua and Judges. This is done as the result of inferences from inconclusive archeological evidence.

Leviticus

TITLE

The book of Leviticus gets its name from the Septuagint and the Latin Vulgate, where the titles *Leueitikon* and *Leviticus* are used. These mean "relating to the Levites." The aptness of the title "Leviticus" is borne out by the contents of the book, for Leviticus is essentially a handbook of laws and ceremonies regulating the services of the Tabernacle by members of the sacred tribe of Levi, who were divinely appointed as substitutes for the natural priests (the firstborn male of every tribe).

BACKGROUND

Man's ruin and God's electing love in Genesis, opening the way for redemption in Exodus, is followed by communion in Leviticus.

COMPARISON OF EXODUS AND LEVITICUS	
Exodus	*Leviticus*
God's approach to us	Our approach to God
Begins with sinners	Begins with saints
People brought near to God	People kept near to God
The fact of atonement	The doctrine of atonement
Christ presented as Savior	Christ operative as sanctifier
Guilt removed	Defilement cleansed
God as love	God as holiness and light
Brought into union with him	Introduced to communion with him
Offers pardon	Calls to purity
Delivered from world, flesh, and Satan	Separated and dedicated to God
God speaks out of the mountain	God speaks out of the tabernacle
Unsaved man condemned by the moral law of God	Saved man enabled to keep God's law
Keynote: redemption	Keynote: separation, communion
The way of salvation	Provisions for holy living

OUTLINE

A. Access to God (chapters 1 – 10)
  1. By knowledge of Christ's sacrifice (1:1 – 6:7)
     (a) The burnt offering – Christ perfect in death Godward (chapter 1)
     (b) The meal offering – Christ perfect in life manward (chapter 2)
     (c) The peace offering – Christ the Bestower of peace (ch. 3)
     (d) The sin offering – Christ removing guilt Godward (ch. 4)
     (e) The trespass offering – Christ atoning for the injury of sin (5:1 – 6:7)
  2. By appropriation of Christ's sacrifice (6:8 – 7:38)
     (a) The burnt offering (6:8-13)
     (b) The meal offering (6:14-23)
     (c) The sin offering (6:24-30)
     (d) The trespass offering (7:1-10)

(e) The peace offering (7:11-38)

3. By appropriation of Christ's mediation (chapters 8 – 10)

    (a) As typified in the consecration of the priests (chapter 8)

    (b) As typified in the ministry of the priests (chapter 9)

    (c) As typified in the regulation of the priests (chapter 10)

B. Communion with God (chapters 11 – 27)

1. By separation from uncleanness (chapters 11 – 15)

    (a) Instructions regarding food (11:1-23)

    (b) Instructions regarding personal cleanliness (11:24 – 12:8)

    (c) Instructions regarding leprosy (chapters 13, 14)

    (d) Instructions regarding personal defilement (chapter 15)

2. By cleansing through atonement (chapter 16)

3. By sanctification in holiness of life (chapters 17 – 27)

    (a) In food (chapter 17)

    (b) In social conduct (chapters 18 – 20)

    (c) In priestly relations (chapters 21, 22)

    (d) In public worship (chapter 23)

    (e) In one's whole life (chapter 24)

    (f) In economic affairs (chapter 25)

    (g) In recognition of God's covenant claims (chapter 26)

    (h) In performing vows (chapter 27)

THE OFFERINGS AND THE PERSON OF CHRIST	
Offering	*Typical Significance*
Burnt Offering	Christ offering himself spotless to God (Heb. 9:11-14; 10:5-7). The ox (Phil. 2:5-8), sheep (Isa. 53:7; John 1:29), and dove (Isa. 38:14; Heb. 7:26) portray the yieldedness and innocence of Christ in death. Fire (God's holiness) wholly consumes this offering (2 Cor. 5:21).
Meal Offering	Christ's sinless humanity (fine flour) anointed with the Holy Spirit (oil – Luke 3:21, 22) was fragrant Godward (frankincense). Baking speaks of Christ's testings and sufferings.
Peace Offering	Christ's atonement procuring peace – God propitiated, the sinner reconciled (Eph. 2:14, 17; Col. 1:20; Rom. 5:1).
Sin Offering	Christ bearing the sins of his people (2 Cor. 5:21), thus vindicating the claims of the Law through substitutionary atonement.
Trespass Offering	Christ atoning for injury of sins committed against God or man.

THE PRIESTHOOD AND CHRIST'S MEDIATION	
Person	*Symbolism*
The High Priest	Christ as High Priest effecting redemption, thereby opening communion with God. Two features distinguish the High Priest (Christ) from ordinary priests (prefiguring believers). 1) He was anointed *before* the consecration sacrifices were slain, thus picturing the sinlessness of Christ. 2) Only upon him was the anointing oil poured (John 3:34; Heb. 1:9).
Ordinary Priests	They were first washed, symbolizing regeneration (Tit. 3:5; Exod. 29:1-4; Lev. 8:6), for they were sinners. Then they were clothed, symbolizing Christ's righteousness. Next they were anointed with oil (the Spirit). All believers are priests with direct access to God because of their relation to Christ, as Aaron's sons were related to Aaron.

PROVISIONS FOR HOLY LIVING

Leviticus is a manual for holy living. Leviticus says "Get right with God" (the message of the five offerings; Lev. 1—7), "Enjoy communion with God" (the provision of priesthood; Lev. 8—10), and "Walk with God in holiness of life" (the call of Lev. 11—27). Leviticus is the book of *holiness*. This keynote is sounded 87 times. "Be ye holy, as I am holy" is God's command in Leviticus 11:44, 45; 19:2; 20:7, 26.

A walk with God is based on holiness, which is achieved by sacrifice (Lev. 1—7), priestly communion (Lev. 8—10), separation from sin and defilement (Lev. 11—15), accomplished atonement (Lev. 16), and a dedication to God that results in virtuous living (Lev. 17—27).

THE FEASTS AND UNFULFILLED PROPHECY	
The Feast (Leviticus 23)	*The Prophetic Symbolism*
The Sabbath	Not actually one of the seven feasts of Leviticus 23:4-44, but basic to the entire festival cycle and covenant relationship (Exod. 31:12-17).
The Passover	Redemption from Egypt (Exod. 12:1-13; 1 Cor. 5:7; 1 Pet. 1:19). First feast, basic to all the rest. Spiritual blessing rests on Christ's redemption of sinful man (Hebrew *Pesah*, "a passing over").

Unleavened Bread	Redemption is to be followed by a holy life and walk (1 Cor. 5:7, 8; 2 Cor. 7:1; Gal. 5:7-9). Communing with Christ, the unleavened Bread, will result in separation from evil (leaven).
Firstfruits	The resurrected Christ (the firstfruits) and the saints who will be resurrected at his coming (1 Cor. 15:23).
Pentecost	Advent of the Spirit at Pentecost (Acts 2) to unite the "two loaves" of the Jew (Acts 2) and Gentile (Acts 10) in the Church, the new meal offering (1 Cor. 12:13). Leaven is included because the Church is seen unglorified.
Trumpets	Picture of Israel's end-of-the-age regathering to her homeland after her worldwide dispersion between the advents (Matt. 24:31; Ezek. 37:12-14; Rom. 11:25-36).
Day of Atonement	Repentance and conversion of Israel at Christ's second advent (Lev. 16:1-34; Zech. 12:10−13:1). Spiritual highlight of cycle.
Tabernacles	Israel's kingdom rest after regathering and conversion. Commemorates redemption out of Egypt and is prophetic of the restoration of the kingdom.

Numbers

TITLE

The book receives its name from the Septuagint *Arithmoi,* "Numbers," and the Latin *Liber Numeri,* "Book of Numbers." These "Numberings" refer to the dual census of the Hebrew people (Num. 1−3, 26).

BACKGROUND

The book of Numbers continues the history of Israel as a "kingdom of priests and a holy nation" where Exodus leaves off. As Genesis is the book of election, Exodus the book of redemption, and Leviticus the book of worship and communion, Numbers is the book of the service and walk of God's redeemed people.

IMPORTANCE

Numbers narrates the continuation of the journey begun in Exodus, commencing with the events of the second month of the second year (Num. 10:11) and concluding with the eleventh month of the fortieth year (Deut. 1:3). The interval of 38 years and 9 months records the disobedience and failure of God's people under testing. In spite of every provision for their welfare and speedy entrance into their promised inheritance, the people failed miserably at Kadesh-Barnea (Num. 14). Their punishment by defeat and death in the desert (Num. 20:1 — 33:49) presents a warning to God's people of every age of the peril of unbelief and disobedience to God's Word. The wanderings of a rebellious people are to be contrasted with the journeyings of a people yielded to the will of God. The book of Numbers presents this contrast.

OUTLINE

A. Preparations for Departure (1:1 — 10:10)
   1. The numbering of the people (chapter 1)
   2. The arrangement of the camp (chapter 2)
   3. The instruction of the priests and Levites (chapters 3, 4)
   4. The provision for cleansing from defilement (chapter 5)
   5. The law of the Nazarite (chapter 6)
   6. The gifts of the princes (chapter 7)
   7. The lighting of the lamps (8:1-4)
   8. The cleansing of the Levites (8:5-26)
   9. The observance of the Passover (9:1-14)
   10. The guidance for the journey (9:15-23)
   11. The signals for action (10:1-10)
B. Mount Sinai to Moab (10:11 — 21:35)
   1. Traveling in unbelief (10:11 — 14:45)
   2. Wandering in discipline (chapters 15 — 19)

THE CENSUS

The two numberings of the people (Num. 1:1 − 2:34; 26:1-65) had several purposes. The Sinai count of 603,550 males 20 years of age and over and the Moab count of 601,730 males of the same age illustrates the order God's people are to have. The two registrations indicated not only God's promises of blessing and increase but also his warnings of chastisement for disobedience. Of the more than two million Israelites in the desert only Joshua and Caleb entered the land. These records also facilitated the assignment of territory to the various tribes as they entered Palestine. In addition they made it possible for later generations to trace the genealogy of the coming Redeemer.

Liberal critics reject the biblical figures as grossly exaggerated. They maintain that it would be impossible for a company of two million or more to exist in the desert without continuous miraculous intervention by God. Conservatives accept the figures on this very basis in accordance with the claims of Scripture, as no flaws in the numbers themselves can be proved.

THE ARRANGING OF THE CAMP

The camp of God's people was divinely arranged and ordered. In the center was the tabernacle, demonstrating that the worship and service of God were to be first in importance. Each tribe had its particular location around the tabernacle (Num. 2:1-34). Priests, illustrating believers in priestly capacity, ministered in the tabernacle before the Lord (Num. 3:1-4). The Levites, portraying believers watching over the precious things of the faith (Jude 1:3), were assigned to guard and transport the holy things of the Lord through the wilderness (Num. 3: 5 − 4:49). Everyone was to be at his post and perform his divinely assigned task. Compare the New Testament figure of the body and its members (1 Cor. 12:12-27).

Absolutely essential to the camp was separation from sinful defilement, typified by leprosy, physical secretions, and death (Num. 5:1-4). This illustrates the necessity of thoroughly judging sin in order to be free to serve the living God (Heb. 9:14). Injunctions covering restitution for wrongdoing (Num. 5:5-10) and avoidance of adultery (Num. 5: 11-31) further show how necessary it is for God's people to keep themselves morally clean. The need for a holy walk is emphasized by the Nazarite. This was a person who voluntarily dedicated himself to the Lord. The Nazarite became a visible token among the people that those who serve the Holy God must themselves be holy (Num. 6:1-27). Such separation from evil and devotion to God are beautifully portrayed

THE CENTRAL PLACE OF THE TABERNACLE
Christ To Be Accorded First Place

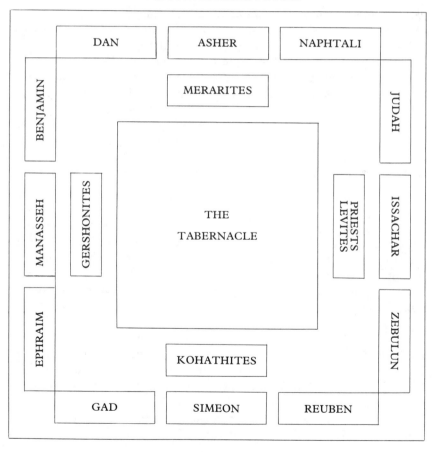

by the gifts of the princes (Num. 7:1-89) and the consecration of the Levites (Num. 8:1-26) based on Passover redemption (Num. 9:1-14). Resulting guidance for the redeemed is seen in the blowing of the silver trumpets and the orderly movement of the camp from Sinai (Num. 10:1-36).

UNBELIEF AND FAILURE OF GOD'S PEOPLE

The book of Numbers emphasizes the truth that although people may have faith to apply redemptive blood (Exod. 12:28) and quit Egypt (the world), they may still lack faith to enter Canaan rest (Heb. 3:1 – 4: 16). The first intimation of defection was the murmuring at Taberah (Num. 11:1-3) and the rejection of the manna (Num. 11:4-9). God sent quail, but punished the lusting people with a plague (Num. 11:31-35). Miriam and Aaron's criticism of Moses (Num. 12:1-16) was still another evidence of sin in the camp. Sin showed itself again in the adverse report of the spies sent to explore Canaan (Num. 13:1-33) and the rebellion of the people at Kadesh-Barnea (Num. 14:1-45).

What an illustration of many believers! They have faith to trust God to save them from the penalty of sin, but refuse to trust him for deliverance from the power of sin. They wander fruitlessly in the desert of murmuring and defeat under the control of the old, sinful nature. They reject Canaan victory and rest because of imaginary difficulties. As a result they die in defeat like the whole generation of Israelites who disbelieved Caleb and Joshua at Kadesh-Barnea.

THE REBELLION OF KORAH

The sin of Korah and his followers (Num. 16) was the rejection of Moses' authority as God's mouthpiece and the flagrant intrusion into the authority of the priesthood, an honor which no one was to assume except "he that is called by God, as was Aaron" (Heb. 5:4). The insurgents tried to create a priestly order without divine sanction (Heb. 5: 10). The punishment (Num. 16:20-50) was so extremely severe because the Levitical priesthood was instituted to bear the iniquity of the people (Num. 18:1-7), and Korah's rebellion threatened the spiritual security of the entire nation. If it were not for the priestly service, all Israel would have been destroyed by the wrath of God. Similarly Christ, our Great High Priest, always lives to make intercession for us in order to guarantee our salvation (Heb. 7:25). Ecclesiastical priestism that denies or encroaches upon the priesthood of every believer is a modern analogy of Korah's sin.

The budding of Aaron's rod was the divine attestation of the Levitical priesthood (Num. 17), for only in Aaron's rod did God cause life to spring up. Thus Aaron became a picture of Christ, who through resurrection was exalted as High Priest (Heb. 4:14; 5:4-10).

THE ORDINANCE OF THE RED HEIFER

This symbolism (Num. 19) beautifully illustrates Christ's sacrifice as the basis of the cleansing of the believer from sinful defilement contracted in his earthly walk (John 13:3-10; 1 John 1:7—2:2). The choice of the blemish-free heifer (Num. 19:2) portrays Christ's sinlessness (Heb. 9:13, 14). The choice of the yoke-free heifer (Num. 19:2) bespeaks Christ's total freedom from compulsion in undergoing the sufferings involved in redemption (Psa. 40:7, 8; Heb. 10:5-9). The heifer killed "outside the camp" (Num. 19:3) looks forward to the one who suffered "outside the gate" (Heb. 13:12). The blood sprinkled seven times toward the tabernacle (Num. 19:4) speaks of full atonement. The ashes of the heifer (Num. 19:9) were the memorial of an accepted sacrifice. Death (Num. 19:11-22) typifies the polluting effect of sin as it renders the conscience of the saint defiled and unworthy to serve the living God (Heb. 9:14).

THE BRONZE SERPENT

The bronze serpent (Num. 21:1-9) portrays sin judged in the cross of Christ (John 3:14, 15; 2 Cor. 5:21). (The serpent as Satan's tool in the fall of man became God's illustration in nature of the effects of sin.) Bronze suggests judgment—in the bronze altar of divine judgment and in the bronze laver of self-judgment. Looking at the serpent of bronze for healing from the snake bite (Num. 21:8, 9) speaks of believing in the Christ of Calvary for spiritual healing from the venom of sin.

BALAAM'S PROPHETIC PARABLES

Four in number, these magnificent prophecies envision Israel as God's eternally elect nation, destined for unforfeitable blessing, and incapable of being cursed (Num. 23:1 — 24:25). The reason for the certainty of Israel's blessings is that she had an immutable standing before God as a redeemed people despite her morally reprehensible condition. God chastised his people for their sins but could not call down curses upon them (Num. 23:1-30; Rom. 11:29). God remained *for* Israel and *against* Balak (Num. 23:23; Rom. 8:31). Balaam's allusion to blessing upon those who bless Israel and cursing upon those who curse her recalls the Abrahamic Covenant (Gen. 12:3).

The fourth parable contains a splendid messianic prophecy. The "Scepter out of Israel" and the "Star out of Jacob" (Num. 24:17; Gen. 49:10) looks beyond David to David's Lord, who at his second advent restores the kingdom to Israel (Acts 1:6; Isa. 11:6-16).

Deuteronomy

TITLE

The name "Deuteronomy" is derived from the Septuagint translation of Deuteronomy 17:18: "And he shall write for himself this *repetition* of the Law." The Hebrew actually means "and he shall write out for himself a *copy* of the Law." However, the inaccuracy upon which the English title rests is not serious. Deuteronomy is in a very true sense a *repetition* of the Law to the new generation about to enter Canaan.

AUTHOR

The book itself *most explicitly* declares its authorship by Moses (Deut. 31:9, 24-26, 30). This Mosaic authorship is also sustained by Deuteronomy's close similarity to the other books of the Pentateuch and by evidence of early authorship (about 1410 B.C.) indicated in other books of the Old Testament. The critical theory that postulates Deuteronomy's origin during Josiah's reign (about 621 B.C.—2 Kings 22) makes the book nothing more than a pious fraud. Such a hypothesis, built upon specious presuppositions, is utterly at odds with internal evidence and the whole fabric of revealed truth and cannot be supported by sound scholarship.

Reputed Mount Sinai (also Horeb) towers over shepherd and sheep. (© *MPS*)

IMPORTANCE

As the last of the five books of the Pentateuch, Deuteronomy was called the "five fifths of the Law" by the Jews. The book has been a target of critical attack, which attempts to date it late and label it a forgery. No critical questions, however, can lessen the moral and spiritual value of this great book, with its words of Moses in the Plains of Moab. It has been aptly categorized as "literature of power," and is one of the most spiritual books of the Old Testament.

In its relation to the other four books of the Pentateuch, Deuteronomy has been likened to the relation of John to the Synoptic Gospels, for both John and Deuteronomy interpret spiritually the historical facts of the books which precede them. The dominating notes of the preceding books are all here—the *choice* of Genesis, the *deliverance* of Exodus, the *holiness* of Leviticus, and the *guidance* of Numbers.

Taken as a whole, Deuteronomy is an exposition of the first and greatest commandment, "Thou shalt love the Lord thy God with all thy heart, and with all thy soul, and with all thy might." It was from this book that our Lord summarized the whole of the Mosaic Covenant in a single sentence (Matt. 22:37; Deut. 6:5). From it he drew his weapons to rout the tempter (Matt. 4:4, 7, 10; Deut. 8:3; 6:16; 6:13).

OUTLINE

A. Moses' First Address: Historical (1:1—4:43)
   1. Introduction (1:1-5)
   2. Review of travels (1:6—3:29)
   3. Appeal to keep the Law (4:1-40)
   4. Note on cities of refuge (4:41-43)
B. Moses' Second Address: Legal (4:44—26:19)
   1. Superscription (4:44-49)
   2. Exposition of the Decalogue (chapters 5-11)
   3. Exposition of the special laws (chapters 12-26)
C. Moses' Third Address: Prophetic (chapters 27-30)
   1. The distant future of Israel (chapters 27, 28)
   2. The near future of Israel (chapters 29, 30)
D. Historical Appendices (chapters 31—34)
   1. Final exhortations (chapter 31)
   2. The song of Moses (32:1-47)
   3. Final events (32:48—34:12)

THEMES

The great central truth that underlies Deuteronomy is the uniqueness of the Lord and his relationship to his uniquely chosen people

(Deut. 6:4). Israel's one God is to be worshiped at one central sanctuary (Deut. 12:1-32). The motto of the book may be said to be "one God, one sanctuary."

THE LORD, THE UNIQUE GOD. The Lord (Yahweh) is the only God. "There is none beside him" (Deut. 4:35, 39; 6:4; 32:39). He is the absolute and peerless Lord and God (Deut. 10:17). He is the one *living* God (Deut. 5:26), all other "deities" being imaginary or "dead." He is "the faithful God who keeps the Covenant" (Deut. 7:9). To him idolatry in any form is an insult (Deut. 7:25, 26; 12:31; 13:13-15; 18: 12). He is Creator and Possessor of the universe (Deut. 10:14), Ruler of nations (Deut. 7:19), with a fatherly relation to Israel (Deut 32:6). Being the *only* God, he is justly outraged by would-be rivals (Deut. 7: 4; 29:24-26; 31:16, 17). Idolatry must be rooted out and the pagan worship of the Canaanites completely exterminated (Deut. 7:1-5; 12:2, 3; 20:16-18).

ISRAEL, A UNIQUE PEOPLE. God's chosen people were elected in Genesis, redeemed in Exodus, set apart in Leviticus, led in God's way in Numbers, and instructed in the blessings of obedience in Deuteronomy. An elect people, they were redeemed to be a chosen nation at Horeb (Exod. 19:6). The new Israel born in the desert were to inherit the blessings promised their fathers (Deut. 4:31; 7:12; 8:18; 26:16-19; 29:1). Even though the nation would apostatize and go into captivity, Israel would be regathered from Babylon and from her final worldwide dispersion to be reinstated in kingdom blessing under Messiah (Deut. 30:1-10), through whom the nation would become a medium of salvation to all nations and the means of the redemption and restoration of the earth itself to a sinless eternal state.

THE LORD AND ISRAEL IN A UNIQUE RELATIONSHIP. Israel was chosen as a nation in order to be an example to all the other nations of the value of serving the one true God (Exod. 19:5-7). Other nations *feared* their phony deities. Israel was expected to adhere to her Lord out of *love* as well as respect (Deut. 6:5; 10:12; 11:1; 30:6). Israel was given the highest possible privileges through her covenant blessings. All other peoples were to be considered strangers and foreigners, to be admitted only by special permission (23:1-8).

PROPHETIC ELEMENTS

Deuteronomy contains some of the most striking predictions in the Pentateuch.

CONCERNING CHRIST. Deuteronomy forecasts the coming of the unique Prophet, greater than Moses, yet like him (Deut. 18:15-10). That this allusion is to our Lord is attested by the New Testament (John 1:21, 45; 6:14; Acts 3:22, 23; 7:37).

CONCERNING THE ELECT NATION ISRAEL. The Palestinian Covenant (Deut. 30:1-10) predicts dispersion as a punishment for disobedience (Deut. 30:1; cf. Deut. 28:63-68), the future repentance of Israel in dispersion (Deut. 30:2), the return of the Lord (Deut. 30:3; cf. Amos 9:9-15; Acts 15:14-17), restoration to the land (Deut. 30:5; cf. Hos. 2:14-16), the judgment of Israel's foes (Deut. 30:7; cf. Isa. 14:1, 2; Joel 3:1-8; Matt. 25:31-46), and national prosperity, (Deut. 30:9; cf. Amos 9:11-15).

No passage of Scripture is more remarkable in its prophetic scope or in its confirmation of prophecy in the events of history than Deuteronomy chapters 28 to 30. From A.D. 70 onward the Jewish nation has been dispersed worldwide because of disobedience and rejection of Christ, experiencing exactly the punishments foretold by Moses. In the present century initial steps toward the prophesied restoration of the exiled people to Palestine have been witnessed. The punishment and blessing of Israel have followed precisely the predictions of Moses in these three remarkable chapters.

The Historical Books

THE ENGLISH ORDER

In English Bibles the order of the historical books is as follows: Joshua, Judges, Ruth, First and Second Samuel, First and Second Kings, First and Second Chronicles, Ezra, Nehemiah, and Esther. This order is entirely different from the Hebrew arrangement, having been influenced by the Septuagint and other ancient versions and by the content of the books themselves. The period covered by these books extends from the death of Moses (about 1400 B.C.) to the end of Old Testament history (about 400 B.C.), a period of approximately a millennium.

The long period covered by the historical books falls into three main divisions: 1) from the death of Moses to the accession of Saul (1400-1020 B.C.); 2) from the accession of Saul to the fall of Judah

(1020-586 B.C.); 3) from the fall of Judah to the end of Old Testament history (586-400 B.C.)

THE NATURE OF OLD TESTAMENT HISTORY

The Old Testament historical narrative is history with a religious purpose. This purpose determines inclusion or omission of facts and is true of the Pentateuch as well as the historical books. The millennium covered by the historical books was a period of mighty empires, great conflicts, and stirring events. Yet this whole fascinating story has no place in the Bible record except as these powers and persons interact with God's elect nation, Israel. Even much of the history of Israel itself is passed over briefly, including many events which the secular historian would consider historically important. On the other hand, events which at first glance seem relatively unimportant are recorded at length. The reason for this is that the purpose of Old Testament history is not journalistic. As the account of God's self-revelation for the redemption of the human race, Bible history is *moral and spiritual. All omissions and inclusions must be evaluated in this light.*

Herodotus (fifth century B.C.) is known as the father of history. Yet the Hebrews wrote history a millennium before Herodotus was born! The historical portions of the Old Testament were penned by different authors who wrote in different places and at various times. They nevertheless present a coherent and constructive account of many centuries of history. Divine inspiration was at work, even as the Scriptures themselves declare (2 Tim. 3:16).

Joshua

TITLE

The name Joshua means "The Lord is deliverance (salvation)." The Greek form of this name is "Jesus" (Acts 7:45; Heb. 4:8). The book takes its title from the great leader whose exploits it recounts.

AUTHOR

The title would not necessarily prove that the book was personally written by Joshua. Yet internal evidence indicates that the book was written either by Joshua himself or by someone who lived during or shortly after Joshua's time. Thus the history it contains is authentic. Some of these internal evidences are as follows: 1) Large parts of the book were apparently written by an eyewitness (Josh. 1–10); 2) Numerous evidences in the narrative show that it was written very early (Josh. 6:25; 15:63; 16:10; etc.).

BACKGROUND

Critics commonly deny that the book is a literary unit, distinct in authorship from the Pentateuch. They place it in a so-called "Hexateuch," alleging that it originated from the same late and unreliable literary sources as the Pentateuch. That the term Hexateuch, however, is a pure critical invention is demonstrated by the following considerations: 1) It is part of the entire unsound documentary theory of the Pentateuch and is based on the same false literary, historical, religious, and philosophical presuppositions; 2) Evidence that Joshua was ever considered by the ancients as belonging to the Pentateuch is nonexistent; 3) Certain distinct linguistic peculiarities found in the Pentateuch are absent from the book of Joshua.

OUTLINE

A. The Conquest of the Land (chapters 1 – 12)
    1. The commissioning of the leader (1:1-9)
    2. The preparation for the crossing (1:10 – 2:24)
    3. The crossing of the Jordan (chapters 3, 4)
    4. The circumcision of the people (chapter 5)
    5. The conquest of Jericho (6:1 – 8:29)
    6. The erection of the altar (8:30-35)
    7. The reception of the Gibeonites (chapter 9)
    8. The conquest of the south (chapter 10)
    9. The conquest of the north (11:1-15)
   10. The summary of the conquest (11:16 – 12:24)
B. The Apportionment of the Land (chapters 13 – 22)
    1. The instruction of Joshua (13:1-7)
    2. The assignment of the eastern tribes (13:8-33)
    3. The assignment of the western tribes (chapters 14 – 19)
    4. The provision of the cities of refuge (chapter 20)
    5. The allotment of Levitical towns (chapter 21)
    6. The dismissal of the eastern tribes (chapter 22)
C. The Last Words of Joshua (chapters 23, 24)

MIRACLES

The miraculous element is conspicuous in Joshua, as is also true of the Pentateuch. This is to be expected, since as redemptive history the book continues those events that illustrate God's salvation of the human soul (1 Cor. 10:11). The detailed redemptive typology of the Pentateuch, recording Israel's deliverance out of Egypt, is expanded in Joshua to include the consummation of redemption into the Promised Land, the sphere of victory and blessing. In a sense Joshua is to the Old Testament what Ephesians is to the New Testament. Canaan was to the Israelite what "the heavenly places" (Eph. 1:3) are to the Christian – not a figure of heaven, but an experience here and now of conflict and victory through God's manifested power (Eph. 6: 10-20).

Rationalistic critics, who have never experienced redemption, quite naturally regard the large number of miracles in the book (and in the Pentateuch as well) as legends and seek to explain them away by the documentary theory of late and historically unreliable sources. The Christian scholar, however, has every reason to believe in miracles, since he has already experienced the greatest miracle of all — new birth through Christ Jesus.

THE MEANING OF "THE SUN STOOD STILL"

The miracle that has caused the most controversy in the book is that recorded in chapter 10, verses 12 to 14. The common interpretation has been that God prolonged daylight for from ten to twelve (or more) hours, "about a whole day" (Josh. 10:13). God in his omnipotence could, of course, have performed such a stupendous miracle, involving the entire solar system. However, the pertinent question is whether this is truly the correct interpretation.

That the miracle performed in answer to Joshua's prayer (Josh. 10:12) involved not *more* light and heat but rather alleviation from it is shown from the following considerations.

There is no word of such an extended day in ancient history or astronomy — a completely inconceivable fact had the event actually occurred.

There is no *clear* reference to such an extended day in the rest of the Bible (Habakkuk 3:11 is inconclusive), a remarkable silence if the event had taken place, since it would have involved a more stupendous miracle than the crossing of the Red Sea or the Jordan River, events celebrated as climactic of the manifestation of God's power in the Old Testament.

God has established an orderly universe. He does not display his miraculous powers wastefully, but only in sufficient measure to bring bona fide honor to himself.

What Joshua needed and prayed for was not more *sunshine* with its intense midsummer heat (it was about July 22), but rather *shielding* of his men, already taxed by 17 hours of forced march from Gilgal. For the sun to cease in the rainless season would be miracle enough. But God also answered by a cooling storm that not only refreshed Joshua's army but crushed and delayed his enemies with hailstones. The idea that the sun "stood still" — in other words, that the earth temporarily ceased rotating on its axis — has arisen from the unfortunate rendering of the Hebrew *dom* as "stand thou still" (Josh. 10:12). The word means basically "to be dumb, silent, or still" and secondarily "to cease or desist" (from usual activity), as in Job 30:27; 31:34; Psalm 27:7; Lamentations 2:18. Thus in *poetical* language the sun is said to be "dumb" when not emitting light (its words or speech being its world-wide shining and universal heat—Psalm 19:2-6). Hence the root *dm* in Babylonian astronomical texts has the connotation "to be darkened."

Likewise the synonym *ᶜamad,* translated "stayed" and "stood still" (Josh. 10:13) frequently has the meaning "to cease" (Gen. 30:9; 2 Kings 4:6; Jonah 1:15). So Joshua's request may be rendered "O sun, be dumb (darkened) at Gibeon, and thou moon, in the Valley of Ajalon. And the sun was dumb (darkened) and the moon ceased (to shine), until the nation took vengeance on its enemies—is it not written in the Book of Jasher—for the sun ceased (to shine) in the midst of the day, *and yet* it did not hasten to set about a whole day."

The violent storm obscured the scorching sun at high noon and sent darkness and death upon Israel's enemies. The clause "and (the sun) did not hasten to go down about a whole day" is adversative in Hebrew. Instead of declaring that the sun and moon "stood still," this clause declares *exactly the opposite.* The sun ceased (to shine) at high noon, "*but* (yet) it did *not* hasten to set." That is, it went on its *normal* course from its rising at that time of the year (about 5 A.M.) till its setting at 7 P.M. But the Lord nevertheless darkened it and made it stop shining in order to refresh his people, so that they could exterminate their foe completely.

Judges

TITLE

The book of Judges takes its name from the charismatic military leaders who rescued Israel from invading foes and ruled over her tribes in her national youth. The Hebrew word "to judge" (*shafat*) includes the thought of "settling a dispute by maintaining justice" as well as the idea of delivering or liberating. The Hebrew judges consequently discharged a twofold task. First, when the nation was only a loose confederacy, lacking a stable central government and subject to enemy incursion, the judges delivered their people from foreign oppression. Second, they ruled over the tribes and dispensed justice. In their governing function they were like the *Shufetim* of Phoenicia and the *Sufetes* of Carthage, who in turn resembled Roman Consuls.

AUTHOR

Rationalistic higher criticism regards the book as a compilation of old hero tales taken from two independent sources. These two sources were supposedly combined in the seventh century B.C. and infused with religious teachings by a "Deuteronomist" in the sixth century B.C. This theory is to be rejected because it is founded upon the same unsound presuppositions as the partition theory of the Pentateuch and Joshua.

The book was probably written by Samuel or a member of the prophetic school around 1020 B.C. The book displays the unity of a single author-editor. The religious motif is no doubt due partly to the influence of the book of Deuteronomy, written 400 years earlier. It is obvious, however, that the author was in large measure a compiler, since the events extended over several centuries. His use of the early poetic "Song of Deborah" in chapter 5 after the prose account of chapter 4 illustrates this. He emphasized the stories of Gideon, Jephthah, and Samson because of their valuable spiritual lessons.

The book contains evidence of belonging to the time of Saul at the beginning of the monarchy. The time was clearly before the reign of David, who captured Jerusalem (Judg. 1:21; 2 Sam. 5:6-8) and before Israel had a king (Judg. 17:6; 18:1; 19:1; 21:25).

IMPORTANCE

The preeminent interest of the author is spiritual edification and admonition. He recounts the history of the Lord's chosen people from the time of Joshua (about 1375 B.C.) to the time of Samuel (about 1075 B.C.). However, the account is not a record of Israel's past for its own sake. The avowed purpose is to use the events and experiences of adversity as a text from which to inculcate religious warning and instruction. The author demonstrates that unbelief and apostasy could lead only to anarchy, for "every man did that which was right in his own eyes" (Judg. 17:6; 21:25). The result of this state of lawlessness was servitude and punishment. Repentance alone could bring deliverance and restoration.

The events included in the narrative illustrate this spiritual principle. The Jews were therefore correct in including this book among the prophetic writings, for it is a book of prophecy as much as a book of history. It displays and reinforces lessons that are useful to all generations of men, teaching the righteousness, justice, and love of God as well as the hopelessness of man apart from God.

OUTLINE

A. Introduction (1:1 — 2:5)
    1. Existing political situation (chapter 1)
    2. Existing religious situation (2:1-5)
B. The Administration of the Judges (2:6 — 16:31)
    1. Description of the people (2:6 — 3:6)
    2. Description of the judges (3:7 — 16:31)
        (a) Othniel (3:7-11)
        (b) Ehud (3:12-30)
        (c) Shamgar (3:31)
        (d) Deborah and Barak (chapters 4, 5)
        (e) Gideon and Abimelech (chapters 6 — 9)
        (f) Tola (10:1, 2)
        (g) Jair (10:3-5)
        (h) Jephthah (10:6 — 12:7)
        (i) Ibzan (12:8-10)
        (j) Elon (12:11, 12)
        (k) Abdon (12:13-15)
        (l) Samson (chapters 13 — 16)
C. Postlude (chapters 17 — 21)
    1. Idolatry of Micah (chapters 17, 18)
    2. Crime at Gibeah (chapters 19 — 21)

CAUSE OF ISRAEL'S SUFFERING

The failure of the Israelites to drive out the Canaanites (Judg. 1) and their refusal to separate themselves from these people with their vile worship (Judg. 2:1 — 3:4) constituted the source of the sadness,

THE OPPRESSORS AND THE JUDGES				
Oppressing Nation	Duration of Oppression	Delivering Judge	Duration of Deliverance	Approximate Dates
Mesopotamians	8 years	Othniel	40 years	1300 B.C.
Moabites Ammonites Midianites	18 years	Ehud	80 years	1280-1182 B.C.
Canaanites	20 years	Deborah Barak	40 years	1182-1122 B.C.
Midianites	7 years	Gideon Abimelech Tola Jair	40 years 3 years 23 years 22 years	1122-1075 B.C. 1075-1072 B.C. {same general period
Ammonites	18 years	Jephthah Ibzan Elon Abdon	6 years 7 years 10 years 8 years	1110-1086 B.C. {same general period
Philistines	40 years	Samson	20 years	1100-1075 B.C.

bondage, and defeat that characterize the book of Judges and make it such a contrast to the book of Joshua. The book begins in compromise, is filled with confusion, and ends in anarchy. It stands as a perpetual warning of the snare of unbelief and the peril of complicity with evil.

Instead of enjoying the freedom, prosperity, and blessing which the Promised Land offered them in obedience to God's Word and Covenant, the Israelites entered the dark ages of their national existence. They forsook the Lord (Judg. 2:13) and the Lord forsook them (Judg. 2:23).

At Bochim the Lord appeared in angelic form to enjoin complete separation from the Canaanites (Judg. 2:1-5), but the nation disobeyed. Consequently the Lord warned Israel that he would not drive out her foes, but that they would instead become a snare to Israel and a thorn in her side. Israel wept but did not repent, thus forfeiting national prosperity and blessing.

THE PROBLEM OF CHRONOLOGY

Critics who hold the late date of the Exodus (1290 B.C. under Rameses II) are compelled to compress the period of the Judges into less than 175 years. In doing so they must reject the time notice given in First Kings 6:1 and the whole chronological scheme underlying Joshua and Judges. Those who adopt the early date of the Exodus under Amenhotep II (1440 B.C.) place the period of the book of Judges from Joshua's death, about 1375 B.C., to Saul's accession, about 1020 B.C., a span of about 355 years. This allows ample time for the events of the period. (The chronological references in the Book of Judges at first reading seem to indicate a total of 410 years during which Israel was alternately oppressed and ruled in peace by the various judges. But this apparent discrepancy is easily explained by the fact that some of the judgeships, such as Jephthah's and Samson's, were contemporaneous.) The chronological notice in Judges 11:26, specifying an interval of 300 years from Israel's sojourn at Heshbon (Num. 21:25) to Jephthah's judgeship, tallies well with the longer chronology generally accepted by conservatives but contradicts the compressed time scheme proposed by higher criticism.

THE PROBLEM OF JEPHTHAH'S VOW

Did Jephthah, the eighth judge, actually offer as a human sacrifice his only child, an unmarried daughter (Judg. 11:29-40)? On the eve of battle with the Ammonites the warrior had made a vow that whoever was the first to come forth from his house to meet him on his victorious return would be the Lord's, and he would offer him up for a burnt offering. This apparently involved an actual human sacrifice. 1) It fitted in with the lawless spirit rampant in the era of the Judges (Judg. 17:6; 21:25). 2) It was in line with the half-pagan background of Jephthah, who would have been following a pagan custom and would not have known or been deterred by the Mosaic Law forbidding such a practice, especially since his daughter concurred in the decision. 3) Jephthah's excessive grief (Judg. 11:35) bears witness that the sacrifice actually took place. 4) There is no suggestion in the story that his conduct was sanctioned by the Lord. 5) The daughter asked for time to "lament" her virginity (Judg. 11:37), because no greater misfortune could befall a Hebrew woman than to die childless. 6) The notion that her perpetual virginity was a fulfillment of the vow seems to fall short of the scope of the passage.

Ruth

TITLE

This lovely pastoral story takes its name from its chief character, the Moabite woman, Ruth. It is one of only two books of the Bible that bear the name of a woman (the other book being Esther).

AUTHOR

The author is unknown. The book was apparently written during the reign of David, about 1000 B.C. The period of the Judges was past (Ruth 1:1), and the genealogy was terminated at David (Ruth 4:17, 22). Had the book been written after David's death, Solomon's name would be expected. The approximate date of 1000 B.C. is also supported by writing style, vocabulary, and mention of local customs.

BACKGROUND

The book of Ruth appears in the Hebrew text among the five scrolls (Megilloth) in the third part of the Canon—"The Writings" (Hagiographa). The book was removed from this position by the Greek translators and placed after Judges because it describes events contemporaneous with that period. This sequence was adopted in the Latin Vulgate and has since then passed into all modern Bibles.

IMPORTANCE

Ruth is the tale of a friendship between two women. Ruth's avowal of love for her mother-in-law, Naomi, is as eloquent a passage as can be found in the whole range of world literature (Ruth 1:16, 17).

The events of the book took place in the period of the judges. But what a contrast the story offers to the sad defeat and tragic lawlessness of the Book of Judges! In Ruth, instead of unfaithfulness we find loyalty; instead of immorality, purity. Instead of battlefields appear harvest fields; instead of the warrior's shout, the harvester's song.

The book is much more than a pastoral tale of love. It has a rich underlying typology that links the romance it narrates with the divine plan of redemption which it unfolds. The story presents in figure our Lord as the great Kinsman-Redeemer, especially in his role of future Redeemer of his people Israel. It also presents an important link in the messianic family, from which the Promised One came some eleven centuries later.

SYMBOLOGY OF REDEMPTION IN RUTH	
Person	*Symbolism*
Naomi	Naomi, the "Pleasant One," portrays Israel, the chosen people, married to Elimelech ("My God is King") and prosperous in the land. Famine pictures spiritual failure. Migration to Moab illustrates Israel's worldwide dispersion and woe. Return to Bethlehem prefigures restoration of the nation in unbelief.
Orpah	Unbelieving mass of Israel electing to remain among the nations.
Ruth	Believing remnant will return and find the Kinsman-Redeemer.
Boaz	Christ as Kinsman-Redeemer (2:20), Lord of Harvest (2:3), Dispenser of Bread (3:15), and Giver of Rest (3:1). Marriage to Ruth represents redemption of both land and people.
Nearer Kinsman	Illustrative of the Law, which could do nothing for the poor foreigner, but instead shut her out as a Gentile (Deut 23:3). Hence Ruth was "Lo-Ammi," "Not My People," until Boaz' redemption.

OUTLINE

A. Deciding by Faith (chapter 1)
   1. Naomi's misfortunes (1:1-5)
   2. Ruth's decision of faith (1:6-13)

      3. Naomi and Ruth in Bethlehem (1:19-22)
- B. Serving in Grace (chapter 2)
    1. Gleaning in the fields (2:1-17)
    2. Learning about Boaz (2:18-23)
- C. Abiding in Fellowship (chapter 3)
    1. The obedience of fellowship (3:1-13)
    2. The expectation of fellowship (3:14-18)
- D. Resting in Redemption (chapter 4)
    1. Renunciation by nearest kinsman (4:1-8)
    2. Redemption by Boaz (4:9-17)
    3. Messianic genealogy (4:18-22)

1 and 2 Samuel

TITLE

These books are so named not because Samuel was the author but because that prophet is the most prominent person in the opening portion and the human agent in the founding of the Hebrew monarchy.

AUTHOR

Critics who hold to the documentary theory of the Pentateuch and Joshua usually postulate two principal sources for the books of Samuel—"J," about the tenth century B.C., and "E," about the eighth century B.C. These documents, supposedly similar but not identical to the Pentateuchal documents, are said to have been combined in the seventh century and to thus account for the problems and difficulties of the books. This critical theory is to be rejected because 1) it is at variance with the evident unity of the books; 2) it requires the compiler or editor to be an incompetent blunderer; 3) it accepts the erroneous theory that differences of point of view are evidences of variety of authorship; and 4) it employs inconclusive evidence based on supposed differences of style.

Although the author of First and Second Samuel is unknown, the writer-compiler was most likely a prophet under the kings and used earlier documents left by Samuel, Gad, Nathan, and others (1 Chron. 29:29). The date of composition was in all likelihood not later than the end of David's reign, with which period the books end.

BACKGROUND

First and Second Samuel are essentially a single work. They are so regarded in the Hebrew Canon. However, the Septuagint translators divided the Book of Samuel and the Book of Kings into four books. They named these the *Books of the Kingdoms*. This fourfold division was followed by the Latin Vulgate under the name *Books of the Kings*. Under Jerome's influence the first two Books of Kings became known as First and Second Samuel. This designation remains with us today.

IMPORTANCE

First and Second Samuel span the period from the closing years of the administration of the judges until the establishment of the kingdom under David. Samuel's career as the last of the judges and first of the prophets (Acts 13:20) is described, including the use of the prophetic office alongside the kingly office. Samuel established the schools of the prophets (1 Sam. 19:20; 2 Kings 2:3-5; 4:38) and anointed Saul and later David, but died before God's chosen king came to the throne. David's reign is one of the prime subjects of the books of Samuel.

OUTLINE

A. Judge Samuel (1 Samuel chapters 1—7)
    1. Samuel's boyhood (1:1—2:10)
    2. Samuel's call (2:11—3:21)
    3. Israel's folly (4:1—7:2)
    4. Samuel's ministry (7:3-17)

B. King Saul (1 Samuel chapters 8—31; 2 Samuel chapter 1)
1. Israel demands a king (chapter 8)
2. God selects Saul for Israel (chapters 9—11)
3. Samuel addresses the people (chapter 12)
4. Saul fights the Philistines (chapters 13, 14)
5. Saul disobeys God (chapter 15)
6. Samuel anoints David (chapter 16)
7. David kills Goliath (chapters 17—23)
8. David flees for his life (chapters 24—30)
9. Saul dies in battle (chapter 31)
10. David laments Saul's death (2 Samuel chapter 1)
C. King David (2 Samuel chapters 2—24)
1. The coronation of the king (chapters 2—6)
2. The covenant of God to David (chapter 7)
3. The wars of David (chapters 8—10)
4. The sin of David (chapters 11, 12)
5. The crimes of Absalom (chapters 13, 14)
6. The rebellion of Absalom (15:1—19:8)
7. The resurgence of David (19:9—20:26)
8. The revenge of the Gibeonites (21:1-14)
9. The war with the Philistines (21:15-22)
10. The song of David (22:1—23:7)
11. The heroes of David (23:8-39)
12. The census of David (chapter 24)

PROBLEMS

Numerous problems are found in the books of Samuel, but all of these can be resolved by careful study and spiritually discerning interpretation of the text. The problems are not (as negative criticism maintains) the result of contradictions, duplications, and differences in point of view contained in supposedly unreliable early documents cleverly combined to form the present books.

Who slew Goliath? Second Samuel 21:19 apparently reports that "Elhanan . . . slew Goliath" while Second Samuel 17:50, 19:5, and 21:9 assert that David did so. Moreover, First Chronicles 20:5 reports that "Elhanan the son of Jairi slew Lahmi the brother of Goliath the Gittite." It is quite obvious to the student of the Hebrew text that the solution of this apparent contradiction is purely textual. The text of Samuel is in a poorer state of preservation than that of any other part of the Old Testament, with the possible exception of Ezekiel and Hosea. Evidence furnished by a study of the original text suggests that the reading in Samuel and Chronicles was originally either "And Elhanan, the son of Jairi, slew Lahmi the brother of Goliath" or "And Elhanan, the son of Jairi the Bethlehemite, slew the brother of Goliath." The obvious original text of both passages indicates that David slew Goliath and Elhanan slew Goliath's brother.

Are there diametrically opposed attitudes about the monarchy in the Book? Negative critics assert that this is the case, using First Samuel 9:1-10, 16 and First Samuel 7:2 — 8:22 as evidence. They attribute the supposed divergency of viewpoint to a multiplicity of authors. What the critics fail to understand is God's capacity to condemn Israel for their lack of faith in demanding a king and yet to accede to their demand to the point of blessing the king which he reluctantly chose for them.

Was Saul twice deposed from the throne and yet continued to rule, his legitimacy being unchallenged to the day of his death? Critics assert that this is so, as described by a duplicate account in the narrative (1 Sam. 13:14; 15:26-29). But Saul in the first instance was simply told that his kingdom would not be "established . . . upon Israel forever" (1 Sam. 13:13). In his second and more serious offence he himself was divinely rejected. Instead of remaining unchallenged to the day of his death he continued in office apart from the divine presence — adequate proof of his rejection.

MESSIANIC FLASHES

Hannah's prophetic prayer (1 Sam. 2:1-10), which bears a resemblance to Mary's song ("the Magnificat" — Luke 1:46-55), contains a prediction of Christ as King: "The Lord shall judge the ends of the earth; and he shall give strength unto his king, and exalt the horn of his anointed" (1 Sam. 2:10; cf. Psa. 2:1-9).

The Davidic Covenant (2 Sam. 7:8-17) envisions the future kingdom of Christ as belonging to "the seed of David" (Rom. 1:3). It assures to the posterity of the Davidic house a throne and a kingdom rule on earth. The Davidic Covenant given to David by the oath of the Lord and confirmed to Mary by the Angel Gabriel (Luke 1:31-33) is immutable (Psa. 89:20-37). To him who was thorn-crowned at his first advent God will give the throne of David at his second advent (Acts 2: 29-32; 15:14-17).

PRINCIPAL PERSONALITIES OF FIRST AND SECOND SAMUEL	
Person	*Description*
Samuel	Last of judges, first of prophets. Founded schools of the prophets. Anointed both Saul and David. Reprover of Saul.
Saul	First king of Israel. Displayed serious defect of character in presumptuously intruding into priests' office (1 Sam. 13), disobeying divine orders (1 Sam. 15), treacherously massacring Gibeonites (2 Sam. 21:1-9), and visiting spirit medium at Endor (1 Sam. 28).
David	Born leader, magnanimous, tactful, a man after God's heart. Conquered Jebusite stronghold and founded Jerusalem as central capital city and political and spiritual center. United nation and raised it to a significant power. Had a weak side to his character, shown in adultery with Bathsheba and murder of Uriah. Example of a sinning and chastened saint.
Jonathan	Noble son of an ignoble father. His selfless love for David reveals him as one of the finest characters in the Bible.
Joab	Captain of David's army. Crafty and ruthless. Treacherously killed Abner after the latter transferred allegiance to David. Murdered his rival, Amasa. Yet a man of great valor who did many exploits.
Abner	Cousin of King Saul and commander of Saul's army. Supported Ishbosheth, but later went over to David.

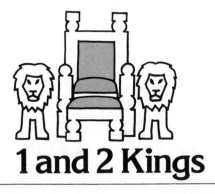

1 and 2 Kings

TITLE

First and Second Kings are entitled the Third and Fourth Books

Hezekiah's tunnel, 500 yards long, brought water into Jerusalem. *(Russ Busby photo)*

of Kingdoms in the Greek Version and the Third and Fourth Books of Kings in the Latin and in Hebrew Bibles since the sixteenth century.

IMPORTANCE

Originally one book, they narrate the history of the undivided kingdom from David's death (971 B.C.) through Solomon's reign (971-931 B.C.) till the divided Kingdom under Rehoboam (931 B.C.). Then the book traces the fortunes of the dual kingdom from 931 B.C. till the demise of the Northern Kingdom in 722 B.C. and the fall of the Southern Kingdom in 586 B.C.

The historian made use of available sources (1 Kings 11:41; 14:19; 2 Kings 24:5). He wrote with a strictly spiritual purpose, evaluating each king according to his loyalty to the Lord and the Covenant relationship, especially as set forth in the book of Deuteronomy. Tradition names the prophet Jeremiah as the author. He could well have been the author, since the scriptural attitude toward idolatry and apostasy emphasized in First and Second Kings coincides with Jeremiah's views as expressed in his life and preaching.

FIRST AND SECOND KINGS AS A WARNING AGAINST APOSTASY

First Kings	Second Kings
Begins with King David	Ends with king of Babylon
Opens with Solomon's glory	Closes with Jehoiachin's shame
Begins with the blessings of obedience	Ends with the curse of disobedience
Opens with the building of the Temple	Closes with the burning of the Temple
Traces the progress of apostasy	Shows the consequences of apostasy
Describes failure to work for God	Records forfeiture of right to rule
Displays the longsuffering of the Lord	Shows the inevitable punishment of sin

THE KINGDOM PERIOD (1010-586 B.C.)
DAVID (1010-971) SOLOMON (971-931) DIVISION (931)

Judah			Israel		
King	Period	Co-Regency	King	Period	Co-Regency
Rehoboam	931-913		1 {Jeroboam	931-913	
Abijam	913-911		{Nadab	910-909	
Asa	911-870		2 {Baasha	909-886	
			{Elah	886-885	
			3 {Zimri	885	
			{Tibni	885-880	
			{Omri	880-874	
Jehoshaphat	873-848	873-870	{Ahab	874-853	
Jehoram	853-841	853-848	4 {Ahaziah	853-852	
Ahaziah	841		{Joram	852-841	
Athaliah	841-835		{Jehu	841-814	
Joash	835-796		{Jehoahaz	814-798	
Amaziah	796-767		{Joash	798-782	
Azariah	767-740	791-767	5 {Jeroboam II	782-753	793-782
(Uzziah)			{Zachariah	753-752	
			6 Shallum	752	
			7 {Menahem	752-742	
			{Pekahiah	742-740	
Jotham	740-732	750-740	8 Pekah	740-732	
Ahaz	732-716		9 Hoshea	732-722	
			Fall of	722	
			Samaria		
Hezekiah	716-687	729-716			
Manasseh	687-642	696-687	Chronology is that of		
Amon	642-640		Edwin R. Thiele, *The*		
Josiah	640-608		*Mysterious Numbers of*		
Jehoahaz	608		*the Hebrew Kings* (Grand		
Jehoiakim	608-597		Rapids: Eerdmans,		
Jehoiachin	597		revised edition, 1965).		
Zedekiah	597-586		Used by permission.		

CAPSULE HISTORY OF JUDAH AND ISRAEL (931-722 B.C.)			
Judah		*Israel*	
King	Important Events	King	Important Events
Rehoboam (931-913)	Division of Kingdom. Invasion of Shishak of Egypt (Sheshonq I) in 924 B.C.	Jeroboam I (931-913)	Shrines established at Dan and Bethel, precipitating religious anarchy.
Abijam (913-911)	Weak, unworthy three-year reign.	Nadab (910-909)	Unworthy rule of two years.
Asa (911-870)	Good king. Bribed Benhadad I of Syria to attack Israel. Rooted out idolatry.	Baasha (909-886)	Fought with Asa. Cursed because of idolatry and sin.
		Elah (886-885)	Drunkard; reigned 2 years.
		Zimri (885)	7-day reign.
		Tibni (885-880)	Succumbed to rival, Omri.
		Omri (880-874)	Founded new and powerful dynasty. Capital Samaria.
Jehoshaphat (873-848)	Generally godly but made alliance with the godless house of Ahab.	Ahab (874-853)	Sagacious, wicked; married the pagan Jezebel. War with Syria. Conflict with Elijah on Carmel.
Jehoram (853-841)	Married wicked Athaliah.	Ahaziah (853-852) Joram (852-841)	Weak sons of Ahab. Dynasty rooted out by Jehu.
Ahaziah (841)	Slain by Jehu.		
Athaliah (841-835)	Seized the throne.	Jehu (841-814)	Destroyed Baalism.
Joash (835-796)	Hidden in Temple and ruled under the High Priest Jehoiada. Later turned evil and slew Zechariah, son of Jehoiada.	Jehoahaz (814-798)	Weak; Israel reduced by Hazael of Syria.
Amaziah (796-767)	Conquered Edomites and defeated by Israel. Murdered.	Joash (798-782)	Victorious against Syria and Judah. Made Israel a power.

Judah		Israel	
King	*Important Events*	*King*	*Important Events*
Azariah (767-740)	Defeated external foes and brought Judah to great power. Became a leper.	Jeroboam II (782-753)	Victorious over Syria. Lifted Israel to zenith of power.
		Zachariah (753-752)	Last of Jehu Dynasty.
		Shallem (752)	Usurper. Reigned only 6 months.
		Menahem (752-742)	Paid tribute to Assyria.
		Pekahiah (742-740)	Lasted only 2 years.
Jotham (740-732)	Good and powerful king. Builder.	Pekah (740-732)	Assyrian advance.
Ahaz (732-716)	Judah judged by Israel and Aram. Alliance with Assyria. Wicked apostate.	Hoshea (732-722)	Vassal of Assyria. Last king of Israel.
			Fall of Samaria, 722.

THE MIRACLE CONNECTED WITH AHAZ' SUNDIAL

Like the miracle of Joshua's so-called "long day" (Josh. 10:12-14) the return of the shadow ten degrees on the dial of Ahaz in answer to Isaiah's prayer (2 Kings 20:8-11) has occasioned much controversy. In the case of both Joshua and Isaiah, supernatural, divine intervention is unquestioned by believers. The only point of issue is the *extent and scope* of the miracles involved. Those who hold that the sun stood still in one case and went back ten degrees in the other, i.e., that the earth ceased to rotate in the case of Joshua and reversed its rotation in the case of Isaiah, rightly rely on divine omnipotence but fail to take historical and astronomical evidence into consideration.

Since the narrative does not tell us *how* the divinely wrought sign was effected in answer to Isaiah's plea, it is arbitrary to insist that the sun had to back up in its trajectory to satisfy the scope of the passage. That the miracle evidently consisted of *the refraction of the sun's rays* out of the ordinary course of nature is shown from the following considerations.

Having created an orderly universe with consistent natural laws, God is careful to transcend those laws only when it is essential to do so. He does not need to upset the universe to show his power. No testimony in ancient history or astronomy attests such an enormous and far-reaching disturbance in the machinery of the heavens. Moreover, Second Chronicles 32:31 apparently restricts the phenomenon to Palestine.

CAPSULE HISTORY OF JUDAH
AFTER FOREIGN CONQUEST OF ISRAEL
PERIOD COVERED: 722-586 B.C.

King	Important Events	Prophets
Hezekiah (716-687)	Wicked Ahaz was still reigning when Samaria fell, but his son Hezekiah was associated with him in rule from 729. Hezekiah cleansed the Temple of idolatry, celebrated the Passover. Withstood Sennacherib's invasion (701). God granted him 15 years extension of life. Embassies sent from Merodach-Baladin, king of Babylon (721-710, 704).	Isaiah — warns against foreign alliances. Micah
Manasseh (687-642)	Became a fanatical idolater. Built altars to Baal, made a symbol of Asherah, worshiped the stars, cultivated occultism, offered his son to Moloch. Was carried to Babylon by the King of Assyria but later restored to his throne. Repented and tried to undo the evil he did.	Isaiah — according to tradition was put to death by Manasseh.
Amon (642-640)	Evil son of Manasseh; slain by officials of his court.	Nahum
Josiah (640-608)	Crowned king at age of 8. Rapid decline of Assyria after death of Ashurbanipal (669-633). Fall of Nineveh in 612 B.C. Finding of Mosaic Law in Temple (622) led to great revival. Josiah killed at Megiddo in effort to stop Pharaoh Necho (609-595) from aiding Assyria. Rise of Chaldeans under Nabopolassar (625-606).	Zephaniah, Jeremiah
Jehoahaz (608)	Third son of Josiah; deposed and taken to Egypt in chains by Pharaoh Necho after 3-month reign.	Jeremiah
Jehoiakim (608-597)	Second son of Josiah; made king by Pharaoh Necho. Oppressive and thoroughly godless. Died in dishonor and was buried in disgrace (Jer. 22:19).	Jeremiah persecuted by Jehoiakim
Jehoiachin (597)	Son of Jehoiakim. Reigned evilly 3 months, then was carried to Babylon by Nebuchadnezzar (605-561), where he spent the rest of his life.	Daniel
Zedekiah (597-586)	Last king of Judah; son of Josiah; set up by Nebuchadnezzar in place of Jehoiachin. Evil ruler. Rebelled against Nebuchadnezzar. Sons killed before his eyes; blinded and carried to Babylon.	Ezekiel

It is not said that the *sun* went back, but that the *shadow* went back (2 Kings 20:10). Isaiah's statement that "the sun returned ten degrees (steps)" (Isa. 38:8) is a perfectly natural idiom employed even today. Ahaz' dial, as the Hebrew indicates, was a series of steps, either circular or running east and west. As the sun sank, the shadow would descend the steps, visible to Hezekiah from his sickroom. The ten "degrees" were ten steps of the stairway.

The theory of J. L. Butler is that the miracle was a "supernatural superior mirage of the sun" (*Journal of the American Scientific Affiliation*, Dec. 1951, p. 13). Some attribute the phenomenon to an eclipse, but it is difficult to see how this could satisfy the scope of the passage. However accomplished, the miracle was proof of divine power to heal Hezekiah's sickness and rescue him from death.

1 and 2 Chronicles

TITLE

In the Hebrew these two books were originally one great historical work. The twofold division made by the Septuagint was not introduced into Hebrew Bibles until the sixteenth century. The name "Chronicles" comes from Jerome (A.D. 400). He suggested that the Hebrew title *Divre Hayyamim*, "Events or Annals of the Times" (1 Chron. 27:24) might better be called "A Chronicle."

AUTHOR

The work was undoubtedly written by Ezra (400 B.C.) and placed last in the third part of the Hebrew Bible. It was put after First and Second Kings in Latin and English versions, following the arrangement of books in the Septuagint.

BACKGROUND

The books of Samuel and Kings are pre-exilic. The books of Chronicles are post-exilic. The former are written from the prophetic outlook and the latter from the priestly viewpoint, emphasizing the implications of true worship and witness. Thus the blessing of God's grace toward David as the establisher of the kingdom (1 Chron. 11–21) and the Temple ritual (1 Chron. 22–29) is emphasized in First Chronicles. In Second Chronicles Solomon's reign is spotlighted, since this monarch was second only to David in connection with the Temple and its service (2 Chron. 1–9).

Although the narrative of Second Chronicles treats both the Northern and Southern Kingdoms, most of the attention is centered on the Southern Kingdom (Judah). The Northern Kingdom is regarded as unrepresentative of true Israel and hence unworthy of major notice in the historical record. Judah was also guilty of gross departures from the true faith, especially in her later years, but God's immutable promises to David, as well as the godly reigns of such kings as Asa, Jehoshaphat, Hezekiah, and Josiah (2 Chron. 10–36), retained for the kingdom of Judah a privileged position in the sight of God.

IMPORTANCE

Chronicles was penned for the post-exilic community, to instruct it in the spiritual heritage of the nation and to inspire it in its messianic hope, its Levitical priesthood and sacrificial system, and its fidelity to the Mosaic Covenant.

Chronicles is therefore an interpretive history of the Jerusalem priesthood and its growth and development under the royal line of David. The writer gives prominence only to those aspects of history that illustrate the cultivation of the Mosaic ritual and the observance of the Mosaic Covenant as a medium of spiritual blessing and prosperity in the kingdom.

OUTLINE

A. Genealogies: Adam to David (chapters 1–9)
   1. Adam to Jacob (1:1–2:2)
   2. Jacob's posterity (2:3–9:44)
B. King David (chapters 10–29)
   1. The death of Saul (chapter 10)

    2. The capture of Zion (chapters 11, 12)
    3. The reign of David (13:1 – 22:1)
    4. The religion of David (22:2 – 29:30)
C. King Solomon (2 Chronicles chapters 1 – 9)
    1. His wealth and wisdom (chapter 1)
    2. His temple-building program (chapters 2 – 7)
    3. His fame and influence (chapters 8, 9)
D. Kings of Judah (2 Chronicles chapters 10 – 36)
    1. Rehoboam to Zedekiah (10:1 – 36:21)
    2. Cyrus' edict (36:22, 23)

RELIABILITY AND AUTHENTICITY

Since Chronicles evidently represents Ezra's crusade to bring post-exilic Judah back into conformity with the Law of Moses (Ezra 7: 10), many modern critics reject the work as Levitical propaganda, a fiction of "what ought to have happened" (*Interpreter's Bible,* Vol. III, p. 341) rather than what actually took place. Liberal writers, however, with their prior repudiation of the Mosaic origin of Old Testament religion, have rendered themselves incapable of objective evaluation of the work. The repeated validation of the Pentateuchal priesthood and sacrificial system leaves them no alternative but to deny the historicity of First and Second Chronicles.

Yet the religious epic literature recovered from Ugarit, a Canaanite city of Moses' day, amply attests the existence of such contemporary religious practices. Moreover, the reliability of many of the historical statements that are found exclusively in Chronicles has been established by recent archeological discoveries. The fact that the chronicler was interested in those men, institutions, and events which were to be the basis for rebuilding a shattered nation is insufficient reason to reject him as an authentic historian. The writer had a right to highlight the positive virtues of David and Solomon and the succeeding kings of the Davidic line rather than rehearsing their sins. He is not to be demeaned because he magnifies acts of faith, obedience to God's law, and consequent triumphs. As inspired Scripture the books of Chronicles can be expected not only to hold their own in the light of developing research but also to thoroughly vindicate both their historical reliability and their high spiritual value.

Ezra

TITLE

The book takes its name from its principal character. In both the Hebrew Bible and the Greek Septuagint Ezra and Nehemiah were originally combined into one book, "The Book of Ezra." Around A.D. 400 this book was divided by Jerome into two portions in the Latin Vulgate. Not until the fifteenth century, however, was the division into two books introduced into the Hebrew Bible.

AUTHOR

The book may also get its name from Ezra because of his authorship. Jewish tradition maintains that Ezra was indeed the author. The fact that chapters 7 through 10 are penned in the first person singular while events in which he did not participate are narrated in the third person supports this view. Most contemporary critics, however, hold that an unknown chronicler compiled and edited Chronicles, Ezra, and Nehemiah as one large work between 400 and 300 B.C. Ezra's ministry is to be placed during the reign of Artaxerxes I (465-424 B.C.).

IMPORTANCE

The book of Ezra continues the narrative where Chronicles leaves off. It tells the story of the return from Babylon and the building of the Temple. The author's aim is to show how God fulfilled his promise to restore his people to their homeland. He tells how God raised up such men as Zerubbabel, Haggai, and Zechariah to build the Temple and led Ezra to reestablish the ancient modes of worship and put a stop to compromise with paganism. Whatever does not contribute to this purpose he stringently excludes.

OUTLINE

A. The First Return—Under Zerubbabel (chapters 1, 2)
    1. The edict of Cyrus (chapter 1)
    2. The enumeration of the exiles (chapter 2)
B. The Building of the Temple (chapters 3—6)
    1. The construction (3:1—6:15)
    2. The dedication (6:16-22)
C. The Second Return—Under Ezra (chapters 7, 8)
D. The Reinstatement of Separation (chapters 9, 10)

CHRONOLOGY OF THE RETURN (ALL DATES B.C.)	
605-536	General period of the Exile
605-597	Deportation of leading citizens, including Daniel and Ezekiel
586	Destruction of Jerusalem and dissolution of kingdom of Judah
538	Edict of Cyrus sanctioning the return
536	Return of 49,897 Jews to Jerusalem
536	Rebuilding of altar, re-institution of sacrifice
535	Initiation of Temple construction
535-520	Economic difficulty, political struggle
520	Call of Haggai to complete the Temple
520-515	Ministry of Zechariah
515	Completion of Temple
458	Return of Ezra
445	Reconstruction of walls under Nehemiah

RISE OF PERSIA	
549	Union of Persia and Media under Cyrus
546	Conquest of Lydia by Cyrus
539	Conquest of Babylon by Cyrus
539-331	Height of Persian Empire
530	Death of Cyrus
530-522	Reign of Cambyses
522-486	Permission for Temple reconstruction
490	Defeat of Darius I
486-464	Epic of Esther and Xerxes I
480	Defeat of Persians by Greeks
464-424	Careers of Ezra and Nehemiah

Nehemiah

TITLE

The book takes its name from its main character and traditional author. The introductory preface is "The words of Nehemiah the son of Hachaliah" (Neh. 1:1).

AUTHOR

The book claims to be "the words of Nehemiah." There is no valid reason to deny authorship to him. Nehemiah 1:1 to 7:5 consists of an excerpt from the author's memoirs, as the first person narrative indicates. Other such passages are Nehemiah 11:1, 2; 12:27-43; and 13:4-31. The book is to be dated in the reign of Darius Nothus (424-395 B.C.; Neh. 12:22). It is possible that some of the genealogies were amplified by a later scribe (Neh. 12:22).

OUTLINE

A. Nehemiah's Restoration of the Walls (chapters 1–7)
    1. Preceding providential events (chapters 1–2)
    2. The rebuilding of the walls (chapters 3–6)
    3. Watchmen set and a census taken (chapter 7)
B. Ezra and Nehemiah's Religious Reforms (chapters 8–13)
    1. Revival and renewal of the Covenant (8:1–10:39)
    2. Lists of princes, priests, and dedication of walls (11:1–13:3)
    3. Reforms of Nehemiah's second governorship (13:4–31)

Esther

TITLE

The book is named from its chief character, Esther. Her Hebrew name, meaning "Myrtle," was changed to a Persian name meaning "star." It is from this Persian word that we derive the name "Esther." In the Hebrew Scriptures the book occurs in the third section among the Five Scrolls (Megilloth) which were read at the great feasts. Esther was read at the Feast of Purim (Lots). Due to a rearrangement of books in the Septuagint and Latin Vulgate, Esther is found among the historical books in English Bibles. Although the name of God does not occur in the book, nor is there any allusion to the story in the New Testament, yet in no other part of the Bible is God's providential care of his people more conspicuous. This divine care is the central theme of the book.

BACKGROUND

There is no valid reason to deny the historicity of the narrative despite the fact that Vashti, Esther, and Mordecai have not as yet come to light in secular history (in the reign of Xerxes I, 485-465 B.C., when the story evidently took place). But it must be remembered that Esther did not become queen till the seventh year of Xerxes' reign (478 B.C.), after his return from defeat by the Greeks at Thermopylae and Salamis (Esth. 2:16). At that time Herodotus records that the king paid attention to his harem (IX:108). Although Herodotus declares that Amestris was the queen, an important monarch like Xerxes must certainly have had a large harem, with many wives and concubines (Esth. 2:14).

Ahasuerus is the Hebrew equivalent of the Persian name, which in the Greek is Xerxes. The portrayal of the Persian king in Esther corresponds with the character of Xerxes as known from history. The author of Esther clearly intended his words as history (Esth. 10:2). He certainly possessed accurate knowledge of Persian life and customs. Even negative critics, who deny the essential historicity of the story, confess that the storyteller knew something of the administration of the Persian kingdom, especially of the palace at Shushan or Susa. Susa was situated in southwestern Iran on the Ulai Canal (Dan. 8:2, 16), which connected the Kerkha and Abdizful rivers. The city and its palaces are well known from archeological research.

OUTLINE

A. God's People in Peril (chapters 1 – 3)
    1. Esther's rise to royalty (chapters 1, 2)
    2. Haman's conspiracy to kill (chapter 3)
B. Epic of Divine Deliverance (chapters 4 – 10)
    1. The courage of the queen (chapters 4 – 7)
    2. The Jewish revenge (8:1 – 9:19)
    3. The Feast of Purim (9:20-32)
    4. The exaltation of Mordecai (chapter 10)

The Poetic Books

THE ENGLISH ORDER

The poetical and wisdom books are Job, Psalms, Proverbs, Ecclesiastes, and Song of Solomon. In the English order these follow the Pentateuch and the historical Books. In the Hebrew, however, the sequence is entirely different. All of these books belong to the third and final part of the Hebrew Bible, the Writings. These are comprised of Psalms, Proverbs, Job and the Scrolls, including (among others) the poetical books of Song of Solomon and Ecclesiastes. The Hebrew order was dictated by liturgical convenience and other criteria that did not have special relevance to non-Jews. The translators of the Septuagint therefore rearranged the order into the sequence that has prevailed in non-Jewish versions.

Besides the books classified as poetical, large sections of poetry are found elsewhere in the Old Testament, as in Exodus 15, Deuteronomy 32, Judges 5, and extensive portions of the prophetic writings.

THE NATURE OF HEBREW POETRY

Parallelism of thought is the basis of Hebrew poetry. Rhythm is not attained by similarity of sound, as in rhymed verse, or by metrical accent, as in blank verse, but principally by the repetition, contrast, and elaboration of ideas. This is called *parallelism.* When the thoughts are essentially the same, the parallelism is *synonymous:*

He that sitteth in the heavens shall laugh,
The Lord shall have them in derision (Psa. 2:4).

When the thoughts are contrasting, the parallelism is *antithetic:*

The young lions do lack, and suffer hunger,
But they that seek the Lord shall not want any good thing (Psa. 34:10).

When the primary idea is developed and enriched, the parallelism is *synthetic:*

And he shall be like a tree planted by the rivers of water,
That bringeth forth fruit in its season,
Whose leaf also shall not wither;
And whatsoever he doeth shall prosper (Psa. 1:3).

By no means does all Hebrew poetry fit precisely into these basic categories. The matching and developing of concepts displays a wide variety and broad adaptation of parallelism that makes Hebrew poetry pleasing to the ear and instructive to the mind. Hebrew words are extremely vivid, and Old Testament poetry abounds in such figures of speech as simile, metaphor, alliteration, hyperbole, and personification. Scholars are also discovering in certain passages of Scripture such structural devices as rythmic beat, stanzas, refrains, and acrostics.

THE NATURE OF WISDOM LITERATURE

This literary style, common not only to the Bible but to the ancient Near East as well, gives instructions for successful living and often deals with the perplexities of human existence. Three of the poetical books—Job, Proverbs, and Ecclesiastes—as well as certain Psalms, such as 1, 10, 14, 19, 37, and 90, furnish excellent examples of wisdom literature. Proverbs deals especially with the practical problems of life, as does Psalm 1. Ecclesiastes grapples with such questions as fatalism, pessimism, and materialism. Psalm 37 wrestles with the tantalizing problem of the prosperity of the wicked, while the book of Job deals with the vexing question of the suffering of the righteous.

Wisdom literature is clearly distinct from speculative philosophy. It is characterized by clear-sighted practicality. It instructs man to have his feet on the ground but his head in the clouds, in communion with the one true God. The emphasis on God's wisdom (Prov. 8) in this body of literature helped prepare for the coming of Christ (John 1:1-3; 1 Cor. 1:24; Col. 2:3), who is made unto us the wisdom of God (1 Cor. 1:30).

Job

TITLE

The book gets its title from its main character. The name "Job" is found extrabiblically as early as the nineteenth century B.C. in the Berlin execration texts. Job is pictured as a prince of the land of Damascus. In the Amarna Age (fourteenth century B.C.) the name occurs as a prince of Pella (modern Fahil). The biblical Job was a godly man who lived in the steppes eastward or southeastward of Canaan in a region called Uz.

BACKGROUND

Job was a real, historical character, and the events related in the book actually took place. The references in Ezekiel 14:14, 20 and James 5:11 attest this fact. Moreover, there is nothing in the poem itself, in names, places, or circumstances, to suggest that the book narrates anything less than a literal, historical story.

Job is one of mankind's most magnificent dramatic poems. The sublimity of its theme, the grandeur of its thought patterns, and the masterliness of its literary sweep place it in the forefront of the great literature of the world. The value of the book is quite independent of time and its great message is dateless. No doubt this is why it is practically impossible to place it in time or surmise its human author. So little is there in the poem to pinpoint the age in which Job lived that opinions concerning the date of the book vary by as much as a thousand years and more. Yet this uncertainty does not in the least detract from the vibrant, omnitemporal ministry and appeal of the great dramatic poem.

IMPORTANCE

Job deals with the problem of suffering, especially on the part of the righteous and in the light of the providential and ethical government of God. Neither Job, who justified himself, nor his three friends, who charged him with sin, had the answer to this problem. Elihu, who saw Job's suffering as an instance of the divine chastening for the purpose of experiential sanctification, came nearer the truth. The full answer did not come, however, until God himself spoke in his majestic power (Job 38 — 41). Then only did Job, turning from his own goodness, cry out the real answer: "I abhor myself, and repent in dust and ashes" (Job 42:6). It was only then that Job saw himself in true perspective before the infinitely holy God and realized that what he was *personally* was more evil than anything he had ever done. After learning this lesson Job emerged from his suffering into blessing and restoration.

OUTLINE

The Prologue: Job's Testing (chapters 1, 2)
The Drama: Why Do the Righteous Suffer? (3:1 — 42:6)
    Act 1 — The Unsatisfactory Answer: The Righteous Suffer Because of Sin (chapters 3 — 31)
        (a) Job laments, showing need for character development (chapter 3)
        (b) Job philosophizes, but finds no satisfaction (chapters 4 — 31)
    Act 2 — The Partial Answer: The Righteous Suffer to be Refined in Righteousness (chapters 32 — 37)
        (a) Elihu speaks — "God instructs through affliction" (chapters 32, 33)

(b) Elihu speaks again—"God is infinitely just and prudent" (chapter 34)

(c) Elihu speaks a third time—"Piety has advantages despite suffering" (chapter 35)

(d) Elihu speaks a fourth time—"God's greatness shows man's ignorance" (chapters 36, 37)

Act 3—The Ultimate Answer: The Righteous Suffer to Fulfil the Perfect Purposes of God (38:1—42:6)

(a) God speaks—"Creation proclaims God's omnipotence" (38:1—40:2)

(b) Job answers—"I am vile; what shall I answer?" (40:3-5)

(c) God speaks again—"God's power infinitely overwhelms human frailty" (40:6—41:34)

(d) Job answers—"I abhor myself, and repent in dust and ashes" (42:1-6)

The Epilogue: Job's Restoration (42:7-17)

AUTHENTICITY

Critics commonly deny that the prose prologue and epilogue and the speeches of Elihu belong to the original poem. But there is no valid reason for ascribing the prologue (Job 1, 2) and the epilogue (Job 42:7-17) to a later author. It is extremely unlikely that the dialogue had an independent existence, for it presupposes the description of Job's illness (Job 8:4; 29:5) as given in the narrative.

Without the epilogue it would have appeared that Satan had been victorious and that God had abandoned Job. In any case the combination of prose narrative and poetic dialogue is not unusual, having parallels in Egyptian literature.

Because Elihu is not introduced in the prologue or named in the epilogue, and because his speeches are deemed wordy and inferior in style, they are regarded by some critics as ungenuine. But it is purely arbitrary to assume that he had to appear in the prologue. He is not included in the epilogue because he spoke the truth and made a real contribution to the solution of the problem of suffering; thus he needed no rebuke. Far from parroting the words of Job's three friends, he spoke to correct their error (Job 32:3-5). He contributes the important truth that the affliction of the righteous is disciplinary, corrective, and refining (Job 33:16-18; 36:10-12). Elihu's speeches answer Job's problem in part and prepare him for the full answer of the Lord.

Psalms

TITLE

Spiritual experience is the keynote of the Psalter, which the ancient Jews called *Sepher Tehillim,* "Book of Praises." Our English word "Psalms," from the Septuagint *Psalmoi,* means "songs" or "songs accompanied by string music."

AUTHOR

According to the titles of the Psalms the authors were as follows: David, 73 Psalms (37 in Book 1, 18 in Book 2, 1 in Book 3, 2 in Book 4, and 15 in Book 5); Asaph, 12 Psalms (Psa. 50, 73–83); the Korahites, 12 Psalms (Psa. 42–49, 84, 87, 88); Solomon, 2 Psalms (Psa. 72, 127); Moses, 1 Psalm (Psa. 90); and Ethan, 1 Psalm (Psa. 89).

That David was one of the principal authors of the Psalms is supported by the following facts: 1) he had unusual gifts as a musician and poet (1 Sam. 16:16-18; 18:10; Amos 6:5); 2) he was Spirit-endued (2 Sam. 23:1); 3) his name is connected with the composition and publication of liturgical song (1 Chron. 16:4; 2 Chron. 7:6; 29:30); and 4) the Psalter attests his influence by both the titles and content of many of the Psalms (Psa. 23, 51, 57); his authorship is claimed for 73 of the 150 Psalms.

The great song period of Israel's history was the three centuries from David to Hezekiah. The Psalter contains songs which predate and antedate this era, but the majority are to be placed within these limits. Evidence from the epic religious poetry retrieved from Ras Shamra (Ugarit), stemming from the fourteenth century B.C., demonstrates the antiquity of many of the Psalms. This evidence shows the fallacy of dating the Psalter in post-exilic and Maccabean times, as higher critics have commonly done.

A kind shepherd pours refreshing oil. (© *MPS*)

IMPORTANCE

The Psalms constitute the great devotional treasury of God's ancient people, the Jews. Because they express the experiences of the Lord's people in every age, the Psalms have a universal appeal which make them the hymnbook of God's people even today.

In the English order the Psalms are placed in the poetical and wisdom division after the historical books. But in the Hebrew Bible the Psalter heads the whole third section (the Writings), coming after the Major and Minor Prophets. The importance of the Book of Psalms is attested by the fact that in New Testament times it could represent the entire third part of the Hebrew Canon (Luke 24:44).

Two principal themes dominate the Psalms:

THE SPIRITUAL STRUGGLES AND TRIUMPHS OF SAINTS IN THE PRE-CHRISTIAN ERA. These experiences constitute the basic subject. However, they echo the conflicts of the Lord's people in every age.

THE PROPHETIC ELEMENT. This strand forms the warp and woof of the book, as New Testament allusions and quotations show. Great predictions center in the following: 1) the Messiah (Luke 24:44). This includes his first advent, embracing his incarnation, death, burial, resurrection, ascension, exaltation, and present session (Psa. 2, 8, 16, 22, 45, 69, 72, 89, 110, 118, 132); 2) the nation Israel. Particularly emphasized are the sorrows and sufferings of the believing portion of Israel in the nation's coming time of trouble and the subsequent deliverance and restoration to kingdom glory (Psa. 46, 52, 58, 59, 109, 140); 3) the earth and the nations. Israel's future glories of restoration are stressed, as well as the participation of the nations in these blessings (Psa. 72, 110, 148).

PROBLEMS

More than twenty of the Psalms (e.g. Psa. 35, 69, 109, 139) call down curses upon the godless and pray for the overthrow of the wicked. Such imprecations cause many Christians to wonder how these Psalms ever found a place in the Bible and how they can be reconciled with Christian morality and love. In considering the difficulty the following observations must be made. First, such prayers are uttered by the godly, who identify themselves so closely with God and his cause that they pray with his glory alone in view, totally apart from the human or the personal element. In such a state of identification they realize that God's love can never be separated from his holiness. They must love what God loves and hate what God hates. They must hate sin because God hates it. They must hate sin in the sinner, though not the sinner himself. God loves the sinner, and his love is extended to make the sinner holy. When the sinner rejects God's love and persists in sin, then God's glory can only be realized in the judgment of the wicked and the consequent vindication of his holiness. Imprecatory prayers are uttered upon those who have rejected God's love, for they have become the objects of God's offended holiness and judgment (Psa. 139:21, 22).

Second, we must use the imprecatory Psalms in the light of our Lord's teaching about loving our enemies (Matt. 5:44, 45). We must, like him, hate the sin but love the sinner. Only as the sinner rejects God's love and offends God's holiness to such an extent that divine judgment must fall does God's Spirit impel the godly to pray with imprecations. When human wickedness in the coming period of Israel's trouble reaches its fullness, the godly Israelite remnant, whom the imprecatory Psalms envision, will utter such prayers, for the day of divine wrath and vengeance will have arrived (2 Thess. 2:8-10; Rev. 6: 10, 17).

Proverbs

TITLE

A proverb is a short, pithy saying centering in a comparison or antithesis that strikes the ear and arrests the attention.

AUTHOR

The witness of the book itself concerning its contents attests that it is a compilation principally, but not entirely, of Solomonic proverbs (Prov. 1:1; 10:1). Solomon uttered "three thousand proverbs," in which much of his famous wisdom was enshrined (1 Kings 4:32). However, the collection as we have it today could not have been completed before Hezekiah's time (716-687 B.C.), since many of the Solomonic proverbs were written out and added at that time (Prov. 25:1 – 29:27). The words of Agur (Prov. 30:1-33) and of Lemuel (Prov. 31:1-

9) and the acrostic poem of the virtuous wife (Prov. 31:10-31) were apparently added even later.

IMPORTANCE

Springing out of monotheistic faith and conduct, the Proverbs inculcate practical virtues for successful living and belong to the wisdom literature of the Old Testament (see introduction to the poetical and wisdom books). The sententious sayings that constitute the book of Proverbs are a distillation of the wisdom of the age of the Hebrew monarchy. Mere human wisdom is, however, not the only subject of the book. Divine wisdom — God revealed as the Creator and Goal of all things — is anticipated as well (Prov. 8:22-31). Apart from divinely revealed grace and power, fallen man cannot please God or live a virtuous life. The book of Proverbs shows that in all ages God requires men to live a righteous life.

PROVERBS AND NONBIBLICAL WISDOM LITERATURE

The proverb as a literary style is not confined to the Bible, but is common also to other ancient near Eastern nations beside Israel, notably Egypt. One of the oldest of these wisdom pieces is the *Instruction of Ptah-Hotep,* about 2450 B.C. Important also are the *Instruction of Ani* and the *Wisdom of Amenemope.* In addition the *Story of Ahikar,* (7th cent. B.C.), a tale from Mesopotamia, is embellished with many proverbs that were evidently influenced by the canonical book. Some scholars have tried to prove that the biblical book borrowed from the nonbiblical books. But broad parallels may be expected in any general moral instructions, for they are not the heritage of any one nation.

PROVERBS AND THE NEW TESTAMENT

Our Lord fulfilled not only the Law and the Prophets (Matt. 5:17), but also the wisdom writings. He did so by revealing the fullness of God's wisdom (Matt. 12:42; 1 Cor. 1:24, 30; Col. 2:3; Prov. 8:22-31). But the book of Proverbs has also left its stamp on the New Testament by a number of quotations. (Compare Prov. 3:7 with Rom. 12:16; Prov. 3:11, 12 with Heb. 12:5, 6; Prov. 3:34 with James 4:6 and 1 Pet. 5:5; Prov. 4:26 with Heb. 12:13; Prov. 10:12 with 1 Pet. 4:8; Prov. 25:21, 22 with Rom. 12:20; and Prov. 26:11 with 2 Pet. 2:22). A number of indirect allusions to the book of Proverbs also occur in the New Testament. (Col. 2:3 refers to Prov. 2:4; Luke 2:52 refers to Prov. 3:1-4; Matt. 7:24-27 refers to Prov. 12:7.)

Ecclesiastes

TITLE AND ORDER IN THE CANON

The book of Ecclesiastes takes its name from the Greek version, in which it bears the title *ekklesiastes,* meaning "assembly." The Hebrew title is *Koheleth.* This term has been taken to mean either "one who collects" wise sayings (Eccl. 12:9, 10) or "one who addresses an assembly," that is, a "speaker" or "preacher." The correct interpretation is evidently "one who assembles a group for the purpose of addressing it." In the Hebrew Bible Ecclesiastes appears in the third section of the Canon after Psalms, Job, and Proverbs, among the so-called Five Scrolls (Ruth, Song of Solomon, Lamentations, Ecclesiastes, and Esther). The order in English Bibles follows that of the Septuagint.

AUTHOR

The preacher is distinctly represented as Solomon, "son of David, king in Jerusalem" (Eccl. 1:1), excelling all his predecessors in wealth and wisdom (Eccl. 1:16; 2:7, 9). The book may be regarded either as a writing of Solomon himself in his old age or as words which, though not actually uttered by Solomon, accurately sum up his completed experience. Today most scholars hold that Solomon himself was not the author. Many date it after the Exile. They usually agree, however, that the central figure of the book is Solomon, whom the unknown writer (perhaps himself of the royal line of David) employed as a literary device to convey his message forcefully and dramatically. Those who hold this position insist that there was no intent to deceive and that no one was in fact deceived.

IMPORTANCE

The primary goal of the author is to attest from personal experience that all earthly ambitions and attainments, when pursued as ends in themselves, wind up in emptiness and dissatisfaction. His thematic term is "vanity of vanities" (Eccl. 1:2), a Hebraism denoting "supreme vanity" or "unrelieved emptiness." The man "under the sun" is the secular, unspiritual man, who concerns himself solely with his present life on earth. The author's reasonings and philosophy lay no claim to be revealed truth, but are recorded by inspiration for our instruction, to show us that only God can satisfy the deepest hunger of the human heart, and that living for him in the light of eternity imparts the only true meaning to life.

The sadness and pessimism of the author resulted from unbelief. But after tasting its bitter fruits he returned in faith to God (Eccl. 12: 13, 14). This important theme of the emptiness of life apart from God should be compared with what the Apostle Paul declares about the vanity of the world (Rom. 8:20-25, 28).

OUTLINE

A. The Preacher's Theme: Life without God Is Vain (1:1-3)
B. The Preacher's Proof (1:4 – 3:22)
    1. Everything is transitory (1:4-11).
    2. Evil is everywhere (1:12-18)
    3. Pleasure, wealth, and work are unsatisfying (chapter 2)
    4. Death is inevitable (chapter 3)
C. The Preacher's Elaboration (4:1 – 12:8)
    1. Life is inequitable and oppressive (chapter 4)
    2. Wealth is transitory and unsatisfying (chapter 5)
    3. Death destroys all of life's gains (chapter 6)
    4. Wickedness permeates righteousness (chapter 7)
    5. God's providence overrules all (chapters 8, 9)
    6. Life abounds with disorder (chapter 10)
    7. Without God life is truly empty (11:1 – 12:8)
D. The Preacher's Conclusion: Vanity Can Be Overcome (12:9-14)
    1. Follow the truth (12:9-12)

2. Live for God (12:13)
3. Consider future judgment (12:14)

CANONICITY

The startling nature of some of the statements of Ecclesiastes led certain Jews to question its right to a place among the inspired books. By A.D. 90, however, its right to remain in the Canon was universally accorded. Those who question the book's canonicity forget that the reasonings of a secularist apart from divine revelation are set down by inspiration much as are the words of Satan (compare Eccl. 9:2 with Gen. 3:4, 5 and Job 1:9-11; 2:4, 5). The New Testament contains no direct quotation from the book or unequivocal allusion to it.

Song of Solomon

TITLE AND ORDER IN THE CANON

The designation "Song of Songs" is a literalizing of the Hebrew idiomatic name, denoting the superlative degree, that is, "the best or most exquisite Song." The designation "Song of Solomon" is taken from the data of 1:1. In the Hebrew Bible, the Song of Solomon, like Ecclesiastes, constitutes one of the five *Megilloth* or Scrolls, which were brief enough to be read on festal occasions. The Song heads the list because it was used at the Passover, the first and greatest feast of the year. The English order follows the Septuagint and all later translations.

AUTHOR

The opening verse of the book attributes the Song to Solomon.

The king was as famous for his songs as for his proverbs (1 Kings 4: 32). The Song of Songs was the crowning jewel of his romantic compositions. The Solomonic authorship is attested by internal evidence and local color, though some of the phraseology may have been altered at a later date. This would account for several Persian and Greek words. Since Solomonic commerce was incredibly widespread, there was an inevitable influx of foreign words, which may explain the Aramaic influence.

BACKGROUND

The Song is a unified lyrical poem with the dramatic form of dialogue. Critics who regard it as an anthology of loosely connected love lyrics do not justify its inclusion in the Canon. But they fail to account for the presence of identical imagery and local color in all parts of the Song, the occurrence of the same refrain, and the appearance of the same persons in all parts.

There are three common interpretations of the Song of Solomon.

THE LITERAL INTERPRETATION. This method construes the poem as a representation of chaste marital love without any other meaning. Some who adopt this view justify its place in the Canon by making it a reminder that God, "who has placed love in the human heart, is Himself pure" (E. J. Young, *Introduction to the Old Testament*, 1949, p. 237). Most scholars who hold this interpretation attempt to justify canonicity by resorting to the shepherd hypothesis. Under this supposition a shepherd-lover of the bride is introduced, whom Solomon, villain-like, tries to seduce from her lover. The poem is thus construed as the triumph of pure love over lust. Unfortunately, the shepherd has no tangible existence. He is nothing more than a shadow cast by the person of Solomon.

THE ALLEGORICAL INTERPRETATION. To the Jews the poem represents the Lord's love for Israel. To the Christian it represents Christ's love for his church. The objections to this treatment are mainly that it unnecessarily rules out the actual historicity of the events and lends itself to extravagant, far-fetched interpretations.

THE TYPICAL INTERPRETATION. This is a mediating view between the literal and allegorical views. It avoids the secularity of the literal view and the extravagances of the allegorical view. Since types normally prefigure their antitypes in only a few salient points, the typical view discourages fantastic interpretations of details and recognizes the historical nature of the story. It does not deny that the book is primarily the expression of pure marital love as ordained by God in creation. However, it sees that the secondary and larger interpretation is of Christ and his heavenly Bride, the Church (2 Cor. 11:2; Eph. 5:23-32; Rom. 7:4; Rev. 19:6-8).

The story itself goes somewhat as follows: King Solomon owned a vineyard at Baal-Haman (unknown) and let it out to keepers (Song 8: 11), consisting of a mother (1:6), sons (1:6), and two daughters—the Shulamite (6:13) and a little sister (8:8). The Shulamite was the "Cinderella" (1:5), naturally beautiful but unnoticed. Her brothers made her a slave in the vineyard (1:8; 2:5), and so she had little time to care for her personal appearance (1:6). Being so much in the open, she became very sunburned (1:5).

One day a handsome stranger came to the vineyard. It was Solomon in disguise. He took notice of her, and she became embarrassed about her personal appearance (1:6). She thought he was a shepherd, and inquired about his flocks (1:7). He replied evasively, but spoke loving words to her (1:8-10), promising rich gifts for the future (1:11). He won her love and departed with the promise that he would return. She dreamed of him at night and felt him near (3:1). Finally he did come back in all his royal grandeur to take her as his bride (3:6, 7). All this typifies Christ, who first appeared as a humble Shepherd to woo his Bride. Later he will come again as King of Kings, and then the marriage of the Lamb will be consummated.

OUTLINE

A. Rhapsody of Love (1:1 — 3:5)
   1. Palace musings (1:1-17)
   2. Romance in full bloom (2:1 — 3:5)
B. Invitation and Acceptance (3:6 — 5:1)
   1. Bridegroom and bride at Jerusalem (3:6-11)
   2. Bridegroom's delight in the bride (4:1-15)
   3. Bridegroom's anticipation of marital joy (4:16 — 5:1)
C. Separation and Restoration (5:2 — 6:3)
   1. Dream of separation (5:2-8)
   2. Reality of restoration (5:9 — 6:3)
D. Love's Fellowship (6:4 — 8:14)
   1. Love's laudation (6:4-10)
   2. Love's desire (6:11-13)
   3. Love's devotion (7:1 — 8:14)

The Prophetic Books

NAMES AND HEBREW AND ENGLISH ORDER

In the Hebrew Bible the prophetic books (except Daniel) occur in the second division of the Canon, called the Nebhiim (Prophets). These follow the Pentateuch and consist of the *Former Prophets* (Joshua, Judges, Samuel, and Kings) and the *Latter Prophets* (Isaiah, Jeremiah, and the twelve Minor Prophets). Ruth is joined to Judges and Lamentations to Jeremiah. Following the order in the Septuagint, the English Bible closes with the prophetic books, ending with Malachi. In contrast, the Hebrew Bible closes with the poetical and wisdom books (Psalms, Job, and Proverbs), followed by the Five Rolls (Song of Solomon, Ruth, Lamentations, Ecclesiastes, and Esther) and Daniel, Ezra, Nehemiah, and Chronicles. The Greek-English order is based on logical arrangement of content. The Hebrew arrangement is founded on artificial criteria of limited relevance, including liturgical usage.

NATURE OF THE OLD TESTAMENT PROPHET

Prophets were men raised up by God in times of declension and apostasy to call Israel back to God. They were primarily revivalists and patriots. They were God's spokesmen to the heart and conscience of the nation. But the political and social aspects of the prophets' messages were always secondary. First and foremost the prophet's message was spiritual. He announced the will of God to men. He called for complete obedience to the Word of God. He spoke under inspiration and with divine authority. "Thus saith the Lord" was the theme of his pronouncements as God's spokesman.

The Hebrew terms used to designate a prophet furnish an indication of the nature of the prophet's ministry. He was called a *ro'eh*, "one who sees" (1 Sam. 9:9), a *hozeh*, "one who sees supernaturally" (2 Sam. 24:11), and a *nabbhi*, "one who announces" (1 Sam. 9:9). Usually the "seeing" and "announcing" functions of the prophet pertained to the Word and will of God as they affected the everyday lives of God's people. Sometimes, however, they embraced the future and became predictive.

THE PREDICTIVE ELEMENT IN PROPHECY

Foretelling played a legitimate role in prophecy, but this role was not that of prediction for its own sake. The foretelling of the future was usually not even employed to establish the genuineness of the prophet, although occasionally this was the case, as in Deuteronomy 18:22. Prediction was rather a preview of the future arising from the spiritual circumstances of the present. The purpose was always practical, warning the unfaithful of judgment and encouraging the faithful to persevere in well-doing.

The two great themes of predictive prophecy are the first and second advents of Christ. Associated with the first advent is a suffering Messiah (e.g. Isa. 53:1-9) and with the second advent a reigning Messiah (Isa. 11:1-16). This duality of suffering and glory, weakness and power, and cross and crown presented a mystery which perplexed the prophets (1 Pet. 1:10-12; Luke 24:26, 27). They saw both advents in one blended view. This was the case because the interval between the

THE PROPHETS AND THEIR MESSAGE		
Prophet	*Message*	*Audience and Period*
Jonah	God calls Gentiles (Nineveh) to repent.	To Israel before the Northern Kingdom fell (722 B.C.)
Amos	God will punish persistent sin.	
Hosea	God loves his chosen people, Israel.	
Joel	The day of the Lord and the judgment of the nations.	To Judah in her increasing apostasy (750-650 B.C.)
Obadiah	Edom's judgment.	
Isaiah	The two advents of the world's Savior and Israel's King.	
Micah	The Bethlehem-born King and his kingdom.	
Nahum	Nineveh and Assyria will be destroyed.	To Judah in the last 64 years before her exile (650-586 B.C.)
Habakkuk	The Lord's kingdom will triumph.	
Zephaniah	A remnant will be preserved for blessing.	
Jeremiah	The coming Messiah and the New Covenant.	
Ezekiel	Restoration of Israel and the land.	To the exiles in Babylon (606-538 B.C.)
Daniel	The times of the Gentiles and Israel's kingdom.	
Haggai	Restoration of the Temple and future kingdom.	To the restored remnant (538-400 B.C.)
Zechariah	Establishment of the kingdom with Messiah-King-Priest.	
Malachi	Second advent of Christ, the Sun of Righteousness	

advents, revealed in the mysteries of the kingdom (Matt. 13:1-50), had not been made known to them. The formation of the New Testament Church following the rejection of the Messiah was also unknown to the Old Testament prophets. These and other events were "mysteries hid in God" (Eph. 3:1-10), to be revealed through our Lord and the New Testament prophets.

Broadly speaking, Old Testament predictive prophecy is occupied with the fulfillment of the covenants made with Israel, especially 1) the Palestinian Covenant of restoration and conversion of the nation (Deut. 30:1-9), 2) the Davidic Covenant of messianic kingship (2 Sam. 7:8-17), and 3) the Abrahamic Covenant that promises salvation to all mankind (Gen. 12:1-3). Old Testament prophecy therefore centers in Israel. Only the distinctive prophecies of Daniel deal directly with world history. This is because Daniel is the prophet of "the times of the Gentiles."

Isaiah

AUTHOR

The author is Isaiah, the son of Amoz (Isa. 1:1). He is the fore-most messianic prophet of the Old Testament. For beauty of style and profundity of prophetic vision he is unequalled among the prophetic writers.

OUTLINE

A. Predictions of Punishment and Blessing (chapters 1—35)
   1. Regarding Judah and Jerusalem (chapters 1—12)
   2. Regarding foreign nations (chapters 13—23)

3. Regarding the future kingdom (chapters 24–27)
4. Regarding Judah and Assyria (chapters 28–35)
B. Ties With the Past and the Future (chapters 36–39)
1. The invasion of Sennacherib (chapters 36, 37)
2. The sickness and recovery of Hezekiah (chapter 38)
3. The imprudence of Hezekiah (chapter 39)
C. The Exile and the Glories to Come (chapters 40–66)
1. The coming restoration (chapters 40–48)
2. The coming Redeemer (chapters 49–57)
3. The coming glories (chapters 58–66)

THE MESSIAH IN THE BOOK OF ISAIAH	
Characteristic of Messiah	*Description and Reference*
Deity	"A Son is given" (9:6)
Eternity	"Everlasting Father" or "Father of Eternity" (9:6) means "Eternal One"
Omnipresence	40:22
Omnipotence	"The Mighty God" (9:6); see also 40:12
Omniscience	40:12-14
Holiness	"Holy, holy, holy" (6:3) means infinitely holy; "Holy One of Israel" mentioned 22 times
Glory	6:1—compare John 12:41; see also 60:1, 2
Creatorship	40:26; 42:5; 43:1; 45:11, 18
Uniqueness	40:12-18, 25
Humble Service	42:1; 53:1-3
Incarnation	7:14 shows both humanity (virgin birth) and deity (name "Immanuel" means "God with us")
Youth	7:15; 11:1; 53:2
Mildness	42:2; no shouting or other demagogic tactics
Tenderness	42:3; compare Matthew 12:18-20
Obedience	11:2, 3; 42:1-7; 52:13; 53:7
Saviorhood	53:5-7, 11, 12; 60:16
Kingship	9:7; 32:1, 43:15
Exaltation	9:6, 7; 53:12
Peacefulness	2:4; 9:6, 7; 11:6-9
Justifying Power	53:11
Anointing	11:2; 42:1; 61:1; see also John 3:34
Message	61:1, 2
Sufferings	50:6; 52:14; 53:4-7, 10-12
Rejection	53:3-6; compare 49:7
Vicarious Death	53:4-6, 8, 10-12; burial 53:9
Resurrection	53:10-12
Second Advent	9:6, 7; 11:4-16; 42:1-4; 52:13-15; 61:1-6
Judgeship	11:1-5
Spiritual Progeny	53:10, 11

GREAT MESSIANIC PROPHECIES

Isaiah is the messianic prophet of the Old Testament *par excellence*. To him more than to any other Old Testament seer was granted clear and far-reaching foreviews of Messiah. Christ's first coming to redeem and second coming to reign were seen by this prince of Old Testament prophets with a fullness of glory not found in any other book, with the possible exception of some of the great prophetic Psalms and certain passages of Zechariah.

PROPHECIES OF ISAIAH YET TO BE FULFILLED	
Designation	*Reference and Description*
The Day of the Lord	Period of apocalyptic judgments preceding the second advent and establishment of the kingdom (2:10-22; 4:1; 13:9-13; 24:1-23; 63:1-6).
The Restoration of Israel to Palestine	11:10-12; 14:1, 2; 27:12, 13; 35:10; 43:5, 6; 66:20.
The Restoration of Palestine Itself	30:23-26; 35:1-10.
Jerusalem as the Capital of the Earth	1:25-27; 2:3; 52:1-9; 60:1-22; 62:1-7.
The Conversion of the Jewish Remnant	12:1-6; 25:1-12; 26:1-19; 35:10; 44:21-24; 54:1-17.
The Conversion of the Nations	11:10-12; 25:6-9; 60:1-12.
The New Heaven and the New Earth	Isaiah dimly saw the eternal state, but it was blended with millennial conditions (65:17; 66:22).

ISAIAH 53 AND THE QUESTION "IS HEALING IN THE ATONEMENT?"

This great prophecy of Christ's atoning work is frequently taken to teach that physical healing is guaranteed by the atonement. According to Isaiah 53:4, 5, it is claimed, Christ died for all the ills of the body just as he did for all the sins of the soul. On this assumption it is taught that a regenerated believer can by faith in Christ's finished sacrifice expect his body to be healed of sickness just as surely as he experienced the spiritual healing of his soul.

But this kind of healing is not in the atonement. The true healing of the atonement is spiritual, accompanied by the glorification of the body at the rapture and first resurrection. Our present bodies, although redeemed, remain subject to sin, the old nature, infirmity, sickness, pain, and death. These physical impediments *will not be removed* until our redeemed mortal bodies are glorified and made immortal at the first resurrection.

Isaiah's prophecy that Christ would bear our sicknesses and carry our infirmities (Isa. 53:4) was fulfilled in our Lord's ministry of physical healing (Matt. 8:17) and not in his atoning death on the cross. Christ's miracles of healing served to certify him as the Redeemer. They were signs of the greater spiritual healing which he came to bring. They were also pledges of the ultimate full deliverance of the redeemed from all the consequences of sin, physical sickness included. It was in this sense that Isaiah prophesied that Christ would atone for our physical ills.

DOES ISAIAH PREDICT THE VIRGIN BIRTH OF CHRIST?

Many critics contend that he does not. But the validity of the virgin-birth prophecy (Isa. 7:14, 15) is proved by the following considerations: 1) The sign foretelling this event was *divinely* given: "The Lord himself" (emphatic) gave it. 2) It was given to the Davidic royal house (not to Ahaz—"to you" is plural in Hebrew). 3) It clearly involved a stupendous miracle, for the sign was "deep as Sheol" or "high as heaven" (Isa. 7:11, RSV). 4) It envisioned the preservation of the Davidic house till the sign should be realized. 5) It necessitates a "virgin" (*calmah*) to satisfy the context and to square with the declarations of inspired Scripture (Matt. 1:22, 23, *parthenos*). The Septuagint translators used this same specific Greek word in their rendering of Isaiah 7:14. Arguments declaring that *calmah* cannot mean "virgin" not only ignore the emphasis on miraculous intervention in this passage but also overlook the probable meaning of "virgin" for this word in Genesis 24:43, Exodus 2:8, Psalm 68:25, Song of Solomon 1:3, and Proverbs 30:19. 6) The very name "Immanuel," meaning *"with us is God,"* requires the incarnation of Christ, the greatest miracle of the ages. 7) Although the child who was born would be fully divine, he would also be truly human, growing to maturity like other children (Isa. 7:14, 15; Luke 2:52).

The reluctance to accept the virgin-birth prophecy of this passage is sometimes caused by failure to understand that *Isaiah had with him in his arms his own infant son, Shearjashib (Isa. 7:3).* This babe was to constitute the *immediate* sign to unbelieving Ahaz. Verse 16 refers to *this* infant rather than to the messianic child to be born seven centuries later. "Before the child" (the child which Ahaz could see in the prophet's arms) "shall know how to refuse the evil, and choose the good, the land before whose two kings thou art in deadly fear shall be rid of them" (literal rendering). This portion of the prophecy was fulfilled when Tiglath-pileser took Damascus in 732 B.C. and slew Rezin (2 Kings 16:9). Pekah was also slain about two years after this remarkable prophecy.

PROBLEMS

Critics commonly deny that the prophet Isaiah wrote all 66 chapters of the book, despite the fact that the Hebrew Bible attributes them to him. Most of the first part of the book (Isa. 1–39) is attributed by the critics to Isaiah. The second section (Isa. 40–66), however, is ascribed by them to an unknown author (or authors) who lived after 550 B.C., toward the close of the exile in Babylon. Critics argue that differences in literary style and theological concepts support their contention that these two sections of the book were authored by different persons.

A favorite line of reasoning is that the historic function of prophecy is violated by attributing chapters 40 to 66 to Isaiah. (The prophet, according to this reasoning, is supposed to predict the future only from the historical context of his own age.) But the prophet Ezekiel was transferred (Ezek. 40:2) to the idealistic future standpoint of the millennium to see the Temple and the restored nation Israel in the land during the kingdom age (Ezek. 40–48). Why deny Isaiah the possibility of doing the same? Indeed, the essential notion of prophecy—the direct operation of the Spirit of God upon the faculties of man—cannot be circumscribed by time or space or even understood at all apart from the supernatural.

The New Testament witnesses positively to the unity of authorship of the entire book (Matt. 3:3; 8:17; Rom. 9:27-33; 10:16-21). The Dead Sea manuscript of Isaiah indicates no evidence of a "second Isaiah" in the second century B.C. Nor do Jewish or Christian traditions allow room for this theory. The "second Isaiah" is an invention of modern negative criticism.

Jeremiah

AUTHOR

Authorship by Jeremiah is supported by both internal and external evidence. Chapter 36 relates how the prophet dictated his message to his secretary, Baruch. This material, reaching to the fourth year of Jehoiakim, was destroyed by the king (Jer. 36:23). But these prophecies were rewritten with many additions (Jer. 36:32). Then other, later prophecies were added. Chapter 52 was perhaps added by Jeremiah from Second Kings 24:18–25:30, with which it is practically identical.

BACKGROUND

Jeremiah was one of the greatest Hebrew prophets. His birthplace was Anathoth, a town of the tribe of Benjamin located about three miles northeast of Jerusalem. He was a member of a priestly family, his father being Hilkiah (Jer. 1:1). Because of the autobiographical nature of his book, Jeremiah's life and times are better understood than those of any other Hebrew seer. He was called to his career in the thirteenth year of Josiah (626 B.C.). This was five years after the great revival of religion described in Second Kings 23.

Isaiah had prophesied in the heyday of Assyrian power. Jeremiah began his ministry when Assyria was tottering on the brink of ruin. Babylon and Egypt were in a struggle to take over world control. The prophet warned of Babylon's victory and the futility of relying upon Egypt. But when the effects of Josiah's revival wore off, the nation plunged on in unbelief. The prophet was called to warn of impending judgment, particularly during the last two-thirds of his forty-year ministry. The fate of the apostate nation predicted in Deuteronomy 28—30 became inevitable. Judah would be conquered by Babylon. Jeremiah warned that it would be wise to surrender and thus save the city of Jerusalem and many lives in Judah.

This message, coming to men whose desperate nationalism was all they had to cling to, was completely rejected. Jeremiah was looked upon as a meddler and a traitor. He was persecuted by the king and his courtiers, as well as by the people. Jeremiah's immense sorrow at the impenitence of the people gave him the title of "the weeping prophet."

POLITICAL SITUATION DURING JEREMIAH'S MINISTRY	
King	*Political Situation*
Manasseh (696-642 B.C.)	Jeremiah born toward end of reign of this apostate.
Amon (642-640 B.C.)	Wicked son of Manasseh. Murdered.
Josiah (640-608 B.C.)	Godly son of Amon whose 31-year reign temporarily arrested the avalanche of apostasy and ruin. Reforms begun in 627 B.C. and Josiah's great revival instituted in 621 B.C. Scythian invasion, 620 B.C. Rise of Neo-Babylonia and rule of Nabopolassar, 625-605 B.C. Fall of Nineveh, 612 B.C. Fall of Haran, 609 B.C. Josiah killed by Pharaoh-Necho in 608 B.C.
Jehoahaz (608 B.C.)	Deposed by Necho after 3-month reign.
Jehoiakim (608-597 B.C.)	Blatant idolater. Nebuchadnezzar II's rise, 605-562 B.C.
Jehoiachin (597 B.C.)	Exiled by Nebuchadnezzar after 3-month reign.
Zedekiah (597-586 B.C.)	Last king of Judah (Jer. 34—37). Blinded and carried to Babylon, where he died.
Gedaliah (Governor after 586 B.C.)	Jeremiah treated kindly by captors, allowed to remain in Judah. Gedaliah made puppet governor. When Gedaliah was assassinated, the Jews fled to Egypt, compelling Jeremiah to accompany them. There he died an old man.

OUTLINE

A. Introduction: God Commissions the Prophet (chapter 1)
B. God Deals with Judah and Jerusalem (chapters 2—45)
    1. During Josiah and Jehoiakim (chapters 2—20)
        (a) Sermon 1—The Ingratitude of the Nation (2:1—3:5)
        (b) Sermon 2—The Judgment from the North (3:6—6:30)
        (c) Sermon 3—The Warning of Exile (chapters 7—10)

    (d) Sermon 4 – The Breaking of the Covenant (chapters 11 – 13)

    (e) Sermon 5 – The Meaning of the Drought, the Sign of the Unmarried Prophet, and the Warning about the Sabbath (chapters 14 – 19)

    (f) Sermon 6 – The Sign of the Potter's House (chapters 18 – 20)

2. During other periods (chapters 21 – 39)

    (a) Zedekiah's punishment (chapters 21 – 29)

    (b) Kingdom predictions (chapters 30 – 33)

    (c) Zedekiah's disobedience versus Rechabites' obedience (chapters 34, 35)

    (d) Jehoiakim's sacrilege (chapter 36)

    (e) Jeremiah's experiences (chapters 37 – 39)

3. After Jerusalem's defeat (chapters 40 – 45)

    (a) The ministry of Jeremiah to the remnant (chapters 40 – 42)

    (b) The ministry of Jeremiah in Egypt (chapters 43, 44)

    (c) The message of Jeremiah to Baruch (chapter 45)

C. God Deals with the Nations (chapters 46 – 51)

1. Egypt (chapter 46)
2. Philistia (chapter 47)
3. Moab (chapter 48)
4. Ammon (49:1-6)
5. Edom (49:7-22)
6. Damascus (49:23-27)
7. Arabia (49:28-33)
8. Elam (49:34-39)
9. Babylon (chapters 50, 51)

D. Postscript (chapter 52)

1. Defeat and captivity of Judah (52:1-30)
2. Release and reinstatement of Jehoiachin (52:31-34)

AUTHENTICITY

The Old Testament contains explicit references to the prophecy of Jeremiah. Daniel refers to Jeremiah's prediction of the 70-year captivity (Dan. 9:2; Jer. 25:11-14; 29:10). The prophecy is confirmed by Second Chronicles 36:21 and Ezra 1:1. The Apocrypha and Josephus confirm the book, as does the New Testament. Jeremiah 31:15 is quoted in Matthew 2:17, 18. Jeremiah 7:11 is quoted in Matthew 21:13, Mark 11:17, and Luke 19:46. Jeremiah 31:31-34 is quoted in Hebrews 8:8-12.

PROPHECIES OF JEREMIAH YET TO BE FULFILLED	
Designation	*Reference and Description*
The Regathering of Israel	Future regathering from worldwide dispersion "to dwell in their own land" (23:7, 8; 30:10).
The Great Tribulation	Future time of "Jacob's trouble," worldwide in scope but centering upon the Jew regathered to Palestine (30:5–8).
The Conversion of Israel	The nation will be "saved" at the second advent by faith in "the Lord our Righteousness" (23:6; 30:10).
The New Covenant with Israel	Benefits of Christ's redemption (Matt. 26:27, 28) as applied to believing Israel at the second advent. It will assure regeneration, forgiveness of sins, and inner heart experience of salvation (31:31-34).
Christ's Kingdom Reign	The "Righteous Branch," the "King," will execute "justice in the earth" (23:5). He is "the Branch of righteousness to grow up unto David" (33:15).

ARCHEOLOGY

The Lachish Letters discovered in 1935 and 1938 at Lachish (Tell ed-Duweir) illustrate Jeremiah's age at the time of Nebuchadnezzar's invasion of Judah in 588-586 B.C. Jehoiachin's exile in Babylon (2 Kings 25:27-30) is confirmed by Babylonian records. "Yaukin of the land of Yahud" ("Jehoiachin of Judah") is listed as one of the recipients of royal rations in Babylon. This text was published in 1940. Jeremiah thrice calls Jehoiachin "Coniah" (Jer. 22:24, 28; 37:1).

TRUE SPIRITUAL RELIGION

God's prophet unfolds the depths of human sin and predicts the interposition of divine grace. He foresees that someday a new and better covenant would replace the old Mosaic one. In that day God's law will be written on men's hearts, bringing them inner spiritual reality (Jer. 31:31-34). God will then bestow "a heart to know him" (Jer. 24:7) upon his renewed people. Jeremiah's confessions (Jer. 10:23, 24; 20:7-18) display the prophet's penetrating comprehension of both his own heart and the hearts of the people around him. His preaching and weeping (Jer. 9:1; 13:17; Lam. 1:16) demonstrate his emphasis on the inner spiritual character of true religion.

Lamentations

TITLE AND ORDER IN THE BIBLE

The full title of this book is *The Lamentations of Jeremiah*. It follows the book of Jeremiah in the English order as the result of the arrangement adopted in the Septuagint and Latin Vulgate. The Hebrew Bible, however, places the work among the five scrolls in the third part of the Canon among the Writings, where it is entitled *ᶜekah* ("How!"), from the initial word of the book. The Septuagint renamed the book *Threnoi* ("Elegies"), followed by both the Latin (*Threni*, "Lamentations") and by the English translations.

AUTHOR

That the book is the work of Jeremiah has been the universal belief of both Jews and Christians from earliest times. The Septuagint, the earliest extant translation of the Old Testament, specifically ascribes the book to Jeremiah in a note prefixed to the first chapter. "And it came to pass after Israel was taken captive and Jerusalem made desolate, Jeremiah sat weeping, and lamented with this lamentation over Jerusalem, and said. . . ." That the book could not have been written long after the fall of the city is clear from the vivid eyewitness account of the horrors of the siege. Critics who deny Jeremiah's authorship can present no satisfactory alternative.

NEW TESTAMENT ALLUSION

The Apostle Paul refers to Lamentations 3:45: "Thou hast made us as the offscouring and refuse in the midst of the people." He applies the passage to the despised condition of himself and his fellow apostles in First Corinthians 4:13: "We are made as the filth of the world, and are the offscouring of all things unto this day."

CONTENT AND FORM OF LAMENTATIONS		
Division	*Poetical Form*	*Subject*
First Dirge (Chapter 1)	Acrostic; each verse begins with next succeeding letter of Hebrew alphabet and has three parts (22 verses total).	Desolation and grief of the city.
Second Dirge (Chapter 2)	Acrostic with same form as first dirge (22 verses).	Jerusalem's destruction the result of sin.
Third Dirge (Chapter 3)	Acrostic; stanzas begin with successive letters of Hebrew alphabet, each stanza having 3 verses (66 verses total).	God's chastening but merciful hand traced in the people's sufferings.
Fourth Dirge (Chapter 4)	Same general form as dirges 1 and 2 (22 verses).	Horrors of the siege and fall of the city.
Fifth Dirge (Chapter 5)	Not an acrostic but contains 22 verses.	Prayer for deliverance.

Ezekiel

BACKGROUND

Ezekiel was *the* prophet of the Exile, as Jeremiah was *the* prophet of the closing years of the Kingdom of Judah. Ezekiel had the tastes and interests of the priest that he was, condemning ritual offenses side by side with moral offenses (Ezek. 22:8-12). The climax of his prophecy is reached in the prediction of the reinstated Temple worship in the restored nation during the kingdom age (Ezek. 40–48). He was the champion of established religion. It was his conviction that the best way to promote true worship was to conserve and purify the Temple ritual. His name means "God strengthens."

Ezekiel was carried to Babylon in 597 B.C. with King Jehoiachin. He began his ministry in Jehoiachin's fifth year of exile (Ezek. 1:1, 2) in 593 B.C., continuing until at least April, 571 B.C. (Ezek. 29:17), the year of his last dated prophecy. The prophet lived in the town of Tel-Abib on the Chebar, a canal connecting the Tigris and Euphrates Rivers and running through the city of Nippur.

IMPORTANCE

While Jeremiah was warning the Jews in Palestine of the imminent fall of Jerusalem, Ezekiel was forecasting the same fate to the exiles in Babylonia (Ezek. 1–24). However, Ezekiel had a dominant note of comfort to the discouraged captives. He showed them that the Lord was justified in sending his people into captivity (Ezek. 8:1–33:20). The complaint of the disconsolate exiles was that "the way of the Lord is not equal (right or just)" (Ezek. 18:25, 29; 33:17, 20).

Ezekiel's response from the Lord was, "Hear now, O house of Israel, is not my way equal? are not your ways unequal?" (Ezek. 18:25). The prophet showed that instead of blotting his people out, as God had done with other nations who had committed similar abominations, his dealings with his own people were preventive and corrective. His object was to teach them to "know that he was God." The surrounding nations, who were jubilant over Israel's fall, would also be judged (Ezek. 25:1–32:32). Israel, on the other hand, would finally be restored to the land with all foes conquered and the Temple worship restored under messianic and kingdom blessing (Ezek. 33:1–48:35).

OUTLINE

A. Introduction – Call of Ezekiel (chapters 1–3)
B. Condemnation of Judah and Jerusalem (chapters 4–24)
   1. Signs, symbols, and prophecies (chapters 4–7)
   2. Visions of sin and punishment (chapters 8–11)
   3. Inevitability of punishment (chapters 12–19)
   4. Final warning (chapters 20–24)

C. Judgment of Surrounding Nations (chapters 25 – 32)
    1. Ammon (25:1-7)
    2. Moab (25:8-11)
    3. Edom (25:12-14)
    4. Philistia (25:15-17)
    5. Tyre (26:1 – 28:19)
    6. Sidon (28:20-26)
    7. Egypt (chapters 29 – 32)
D. Restoration of Israel (chapters 33 – 48)
    1. The preparation for restoration (chapters 33 – 39)
      (a) The warning of the wicked (chapter 33)
      (b) The promise of the true Shepherd (chapters 34, 35)
      (c) The repossession of the land (chapters 36, 37)
      (d) The judgment of the aggressors (38:1 – 39:24)
      (e) The vision of restoration (39:25-29)
    2. The glory of restoration (chapters 40 – 48)
      (a) The restored Temple (chapters 40 – 43)
      (b) The restored worship (chapters 44 – 46)
      (c) The restored land (chapters 47, 48)

THE REALITY OF ISRAEL'S RESTORATION

Many liberal critics deny that chapters 34 through 48 are authentic to Ezekiel and therefore give little authority or credence to their prophetic teachings. Some conservative scholars defend the authenticity of these chapters but deny their literal application to Israel. That the actual nation of Israel is the subject of these chapters and that these prophecies are yet to be fulfilled literally is necessitated by several important considerations.

The details of these prophecies go far beyond any previous fulfillment.

For example, Ezekiel 34:23-30 predicts a restoration in which Israel shall "no more be a prey to the nations." Neither the remnant which returned from Babylon nor their descendants could have fulfilled this prophecy, for they were under continuous Gentile yoke until A.D. 70, when they were driven out from the land entirely. Nor can Ezekiel's description of the Temple be made to fit Solomon's, Zerubbabel's, or Herod's edifices.

Ezekiel's prophecies were not uttered in a vacuum, but dovetail with the covenants and promises made to the nation and with the great kingdom predictions of all the Old Testament prophets.

EZEKIEL'S PROPHECIES OF ISRAEL'S RESTORATION

Prophecy	Description
The Judgment of the Nations (34:1–19)	The Lord (the Good Shepherd) will gather the flock and judge between the sheep (the saved Israelite remnant) and the rams and goats (the nations who have abused Israel).
Israel under Messiah, the True Shepherd (34:20-31)	Fulfilled not in Zerubbabel at restoration from Babylon, nor in David raised from the dead at the second advent, but in Messiah, David's name used typically (Jer. 23:5, 6; Hos. 3:5; Isa. 9:6, 7; 55:3, 4).
Israel Restored to the Land (chapter 36)	Assurance of restoration by sovereign "I will" (18 times). Land to be restored and cleansed because Israel is to be regathered and regenerated (chaps. 22 – 29).
Israel Reinstated to Spiritual Blessing (chapter 37)	Vision of the dry bones sets forth Israel's national and spiritual restoration in kingdom blessing. The bones represent the exiles; the valley, their dispersion; and the graves, their national death.
The Destruction of Israel's Last Foes (chapters 38, 39)	Last-day Northern Confederacy headed by Russia in "the uttermost parts of the north" (38:6). Attack on Israel yet future (38:7-23). Defeat is by God and is complete.
Restored Israel in the Land (39:25-29)	Remarkable vision of restored Israel in Palestine during the coming kingdom age.
The Restored Temple (chapters 40 – 43)	A literal future sanctuary to be erected in Palestine during the kingdom age. Details of arrangement are given (chap. 41). The purposes are to demonstrate God's holiness (42:1-20), to provide a dwelling place for the divine glory (43:1-7) and a center for the divine government (43:8-17), and to perpetuate the memorial of sacrifice (43:18-27).
Worship in the Kingdom (chapters 44 – 46)	Ezekiel sees the temporal aspect of the kingdom rather than the eternal, sinless aspect into which it finally emerges (1 Cor. 15:24-28). Hence "the prince" is a mortal man.
Palestine in the Kingdom (chapters 47, 48)	A literal river results from topographical changes. The boundaries and tribal apportionment of the land are given. Jerusalem's status in the kingdom age is described (not its eternal status, as seen by John in Revelation 21:10-27).

See "Time-Periods of the Bible" under "Bible Survey" for the covenants and promises made to Israel (Rom. 9:4, 5). Ezekiel's theme of Israel's restoration is a dominant theme of virtually all the prophets.

If these prophecies are denied literal fulfillment in the nation Israel, there is no other interpretation of them that squares with the facts. A consistent literal hermeneutic applied to the rest of the Bible must be abandoned in the case of prophecy for an arbitrary, mystical interpretation. Such an interpretation attempts to "explain away" the details but does not actually explain them at all.

History is beginning to authenticate the prophecy of Israel's restoration. The incipient return of the Jews to Palestine, the establishment of the state of Israel, and the role of the Israelis in the world today evidence the eventual setting of the stage for the events predicted by Ezekiel.

IS EZEKIEL'S TEMPLE TO BE CONSTRUED AS A LITERAL EDIFICE TO BE ERECTED IN THE KINGDOM AGE?

The answer to this question must be affirmative. The Temple vision is part and parcel of the reality of Israel's restoration. If the restoration is to be taken literally, the Temple must also be construed in the same way. Non-literal views are inadequate in this regard. They clash with details of the prophecy and violate the context of the entire last third of the book of Ezekiel.

PROBLEMS CONNECTED WITH A LITERAL TEMPLE

These difficulties are significant, but can be adequately resolved. Objections based upon them do not constitute valid grounds for rejecting a literal, futuristic interpretation of Ezekiel's Temple and ritual. The chief charge is that *such a literal Temple, entailing a restoration of Judaistic ritual and animal sacrifice, is at variance with New Testament teaching, particularly the Epistle to the Hebrews.* But this objection fails to reckon with the biblical distinction between the elect nation of Israel and the Christian Church, as well as the time period and divine dealing peculiar to each. The Epistle to the Hebrews and the other New Testament epistles govern the Church in the era between Christ's rejection by Israel at his first advent and his acceptance by Israel at the second advent. When Israel as a nation is saved and brought back into God's favor, the priesthood and kingship will be reinstated. Without doing violence to the Epistle to the Hebrews, the civil and ceremonial Law of Moses will then unfold its spiritual depth and meaning in the worship and constitution of the thousand-year reign under the promises of the Palestinian and New Covenants.

The sacrifices will of course no longer be prospective, as before Christ's finished redemption, but *purely retrospective and commemorative,* like the Lord's Supper in the Church age. Like other Old Testament prophets, Ezekiel envisions a spiritually restored Judaism in the coming kingdom age, with the Sabbath day as its unique sign. Israel will be blessed directly by God, while the kingdom nations will be blessed mediately and indirectly—a situation quite different from that of present-day Christianity.

Another objection against the literal and futuristic interpretation of Ezekiel's Temple and ritual is that it supposedly requires geographical impossibilities and untenable supernatural features. For example, the objection is made that the marvelous river issuing from the Temple could not be an earthly river, but must be interpreted figuratively. From this incorrect premise it is concluded that neither the Temple, the ritual, nor the division of the land can be regarded as literal.

That the river is a literal stream and that the mount of the Temple will be exalted on a high eminence as the result of an earthquake and vast physical changes in the topography of Palestine is foretold by others beside Ezekiel. Zechariah in particular emphasizes this point (Zech. 14:4, 5). God can and will do all that is necessary to make Palestine a suitable scene and focal point for all the glorious events of the kingdom age.

Daniel

TITLE

The historical-prophetical book of Daniel takes its name from its principal character and author. Daniel ("God's judge") was carried away with other promising youths as a hostage by Nebuchadnezzar II (604-562 B.C.). Early in the period of exile he became renowned for godliness and wisdom (Ezek. 14:14, 20).

AUTHOR

Because of its remarkable events and prophecies, the book of Daniel is a battleground between faith and unbelief. The author, date, historicity, and authenticity of the book are frequently disputed by liberal critics. In fact, modern criticism views the establishment of a Maccabean date (about 167 B.C.) as one of its assured achievements. These allegations, however, are based upon fallacious reasoning.

The chief charge is that the author of Daniel makes erroneous statements about historical information belonging to the sixth century B.C. When these alleged inaccuracies are analyzed, however, they usually turn out to be erroneous assumptions based upon arguments from silence or upon faulty presuppositions. When the problems are faced objectively, apart from critical bias, the book stands unimpugned by any testimony that can be produced from any reliable source of information. This does not mean that every difficulty has already been cleared up. Some persist because of lack of pertinent historical or archeological information. Thus in certain details the book can as yet be neither vindicated nor impugned. Meanwhile, faith must take the work at its face value, granting it the authenticity and historical reliability it deserves in the absence of objective proof to the contrary.

It must be said, however, that in numerous instances historical and archeological research has cleared up difficulties that were once employed to deride Daniel's authenticity. The most notable case is that of Belshazzar, whose existence was once denied and his designation as "king" and "son of Nebuchadnezzar" (Dan. 5:1, 2, 11, 18, 22) scoffed at. Archeology has not only attested Belshazzar's existence but has clarified his kingship (it was entrusted to him by his father Nabonidus) and confirmed his relationship to Nebuchadnezzar as a royal "son." (Semitic idiom sometimes uses the word "son" to designate a successor rather than a son by immediate birth.)

It is also sometimes alleged that the literary features of Daniel prove that it was written long after the sixth century B.C. Critics list some fifteen or more Persian words in the book. But certainly it is not far-fetched to expect Daniel to have displayed Persian influence in his book if he wrote it after the Persian conquest of Babylon, particularly

A statue marks the area of Daniel's encounter with caged lions in Babylon. (© *MPS*)

in designating offices, institutions, and the like. Nor does the presence of a few Greek words in chapter 3 prove a late date. Mounting evidence indicates that Greek culture penetrated into the Near East at a much earlier date than had previously been supposed.

The fact that the book is written in two languages (Dan. 2:4 – 7: 28 in Aramaic and the remainder in Hebrew) has also been used as an argument for a late date. The simple explanation for the two languages is that Daniel intentionally employed the two tongues. Since Daniel was the primary prophet of "the times of the Gentiles" (Luke

GREAT PROPHECIES OF THE BOOK OF DANIEL	
The Vision	*The Meaning*
The Colossus Vision (2:31-45)	The colossus itself symbolizes the times of the Gentiles from Nebuchadnezzar (605 B.C.) to the second advent of Christ. The Smiting Stone (2:34, 35), who will destroy the Gentile world system, is Christ. The four metals are four empires — Babylon (head of gold), Medo-Persia (chest and arms of silver), the Roman Empire (legs of iron), and the Roman Empire revived at the end time (feet of iron and clay). Rome is envisioned panoramically, first as it would exist in ancient imperial glory and then as divided in East and West Empires (A.D. 364), as symbolized by the two legs. These two divisions will enjoy a last-day revival, a 10-kingdom European United States composed of dictatorships (iron) and democracies (tile). Then the Smiting Stone will strike and become a mountain (the kingdom restored to Israel — Isa. 2:2; Acts 1:6) which fills the earth. After this temporal kingdom runs its course it will merge into the eternal kingdom (1 Cor. 15:24-28; Rev. 20:4, 5).
The Vision of the Four Beasts (7:1-8)	These trace the same four world empires as the colossus of 2:31-45. The colossus, however, presents the *outward* power and splendor of "the times of the Gentiles" while the four beasts depict the *inner* rapacious and warlike character of the Gentile world governments of the period — Babylon (lion), Medo-Persia (bear), Greece (leopard), and Rome (nondescript iron beast). The ten horns (kings) correspond to the ten toes of 2:40-44. The "little horn" is the last-day Antichrist, the final terrible ruler of the times of the Gentiles. He will be destroyed by Messiah at his advent and kingdom.
The Vision of Messiah's Second Advent (7:9-28)	The "Ancient of Days" is God. "One like the Son of Man" is Christ invested with the kingdom and returning in glory (Rev. 19:16). Messiah's investiture with the kingdom takes place in heaven (7:13, 14) but occurs before his coming (7:9-12). Destruction of the "little horn" is fulfilled at the second advent. "The saints of the Most High," who "possess the kingdom" (7:18, 22, 25, 27), are the saved Jewish remnant. The kingdom will be eternal (7:18), the mediatorial and temporal aspects of it (the thousand years — Rev. 20:4-7) merging into the eternal state when Christ delivers the kingdom to God the Father (1 Cor. 15:24-28). The fourth beast with the ten-kingdom confederation is last-day revived Rome.
The Vision of the Ram, the He-Goat, and the little Horn (8:1-27)	The ram with the two horns (Media and Persia) is the Medo-Persian Empire (539-531 B.C.). The "he-goat" is Macedonian Greece seen in the rapid conquests of Alexander the Great, the "conspicuous horn" of the goat (8:1-7). Four horns (8:8) represent the division of Alexander's empire among his four generals. Out of one division, Syria, came Antiochus Epiphanes (175-163 B.C.), the "little horn" (8:9-14), a foreshadowing of the Antichrist (8:24, 25) and the great tribulation, "the time of the end" (8:17), "the last end of the indignation" (8:19).

The Vision	The Meaning
The Vision of the Seventy Weeks (9:24-27)	The seventy weeks (heptads of 7 years each) equal 490 years. These are divided into a) *7 weeks* (49 years) beginning with the decree of Artaxerxes I to rebuild Jerusalem's walls (Mar.-Apr., 445 B.C.); b) *62 weeks* (434 years), at the end of which "Messiah-Prince" was to be cut off in death and have nothing (no kingdom which was rightly his as king); c) *An unreckoned period* during which the Romans, "the people of the prince that shall come," would destroy the city and the sanctuary" (A.D. 70); since then the Jews have been scattered; d) *A final week* of 7 years as the climax of Jewish history. During the first half of the week the "prince" or "little horn" of 7:8 makes a covenant with the Jews in Palestine, who have by then resumed Temple worship. In the middle of the week the covenant is broken, the Temple worship ceases, and the great tribulation breaks. Christ's second advent consummates this period of desolation, bringing everlasting righteousness to Israel and judgment upon the "desolator," the prince and his armies (Rev. 19:20).
The Vision of the Wars of the Ptolemies and Seleucids (11:1-35)	History has verified the precise fulfillment of these prophecies by the Persian kings (11:12), Alexander the Great (11:3, 4), the Ptolemies of Egypt ("kings of the south"), and the Seleucids ("kings of the north") (11:6-35). The Romans (11:30), Antiochus Epiphanes (prefiguring the Antichrist of the last day), and the Maccabees also had their part in the fulfillment of these prophecies.
The Vision of the End-Time: The Man of Sin (11:36-40a) and The King of the North (Russia) (11:40b-45)	The "wilful king" is the Antichrist, the "man of sin" of 2 Thess. 2:3, 4 and Rev. 13:1 – 10. The King of the North is Russia, and vv. 40b-45 are parallel to Ezek. 38 and 39, and describe the Russian invasion of Palestine at the end-time.
The Great Tribulation and Israel's Deliverance (12:1)	This terrible period of Jacob's trouble is also mentioned in Jer. 30:5-7 and described in Rev. 12 – 18. It takes place in the last half of Daniel's 70th week (Dan. 9:27) and is climaxed by Christ's second advent. "Thy people" are Daniel's people, the Jews, who are to be delivered from physical death and regenerated to enjoy kingdom blessing.
The Resurrection of Israel (12:2, 3)	Physical resurrection of the saved Israel into kingdom blessing in fulfillment of Matt. 8:11 and 19:28 and other Old Testament predictions.
The Final Consummation (12:4-13)	The period between Daniel's time and the second advent, especially the latter years (12:4, 9). But the prophecy was to be "sealed up" (not understood) until the end time (12:4). Verses 11 and 12 describe the time of the erection of the image of the Antichrist (9:27) and the duration of great wrath.

21:24), the Spirit of God directed him to use the language then spoken by non-Jews to pen those great prophetic portions that deal primarily with the history of Gentiles.

BACKGROUND

As mentioned previously, Daniel is the prophet of "the times of the Gentiles" (Luke 21:24). This period extends from the captivity of Judah under Nebuchadnezzar to the second advent of Christ and the establishment of the messianic earthly kingdom. During this long era the nations have predominated, and Israel has been an outright vassal of Gentile world powers or has been scattered among them, or has at best been mercilessly exposed to their hatred. The scope of Daniel's descriptions of this long interval makes his visions an indispensable introduction to the study of New Testament prophecy. Daniel's dominant themes are the great tribulation, the revelation of the Antichrist, the second advent of Christ, the resurrections, and the establishment of the millennial kingdom. These are also great New Testament prophetic disclosures. Daniel's prophecies particularly link up with our Lord's Olivet discourse (Matt. 24:15) and the book of the Revelation.

IMPORTANCE

The book of Daniel is *the key to all biblical prophecy.* Our Lord's Olivet Discourse (Matt. 24, 25; Mark 13; Luke 21), as well as the prophecies in Second Thessalonians 2 and the entire book of the Revelation can be understood only through a correct comprehension of Daniel's predictions. The prophetic sweep and import of the book is doubtless a prime reason for the relentless critical attack leveled against it. Conservative scholars, who recognize the strategic place which the prophecy holds in unfolding the divine plan of the ages, realize that it is necessary both to defend the authenticity of the book against negative criticism and to master the prophetic sweep of its predictions.

OUTLINE

A. Early History and Visions (chapters 1—6)
    1. Daniel's stand for God (chapter 1)
    2. Nebuchadnezzar's vision of the image (chapter 2)
    3. Daniel's three friends' deliverance from the furnace (chapter 3)
    4. Nebuchadnezzar's vision of the tree (chapter 4)
    5. Belshazzar's feast (chapter 5)

6. Daniel's deliverance from the lions (chapter 6)
B. Later History and Visions (chapters 7—12)
   1. The vision of the four beasts (chapter 7)
   2. The vision of the ram and goat (chapter 8)
   3. The vision of the seventy weeks (chapter 9)
   4. The vision of the glory of God (chapter 10)
   5. The vision of the end times (chapters 11, 12)

SPIRITUAL EMPHASES OF THE MINOR PROPHETS		
Prophet	*Period*	*Spiritual Emphasis*
Hosea	755-715 B.C.	God unfailingly loves Israel
Joel	835-796 B.C.	Israel will enjoy latter-day revival
Amos	765-750 B.C.	God's justice must judge sin
Obadiah	850-840 B.C.	Merciless pride must be judged
Jonah	780-750 B.C.	God's grace embraces the world
Micah	740-690 B.C.	Bethlehem-born Messiah will be deliverer
Nahum	630-612 B.C.	Nineveh's sin is to be judged
Habakkuk	615 B.C.	Justification is by faith
Zephaniah	625-610 B.C.	The day of the Lord precedes the kingdom
Haggai	520 B.C.	The Lord deserves top priority
Zechariah (Chaps.	520-515 B.C.	The Lord remembers Israel
9—14)	after 500 B.C.	The second advent of Christ
Malachi	430-400 B.C.	The wicked will be judged

Hosea

BACKGROUND

Hosea ("salvation") has been styled "the Jeremiah of the Northern Kingdom." Like Jeremiah, he was called to weep and suffer for a decadent nation that was ripening for ruin. His ministry began in the closing years of Jeroboam II's prosperous and morally declining reign and extended on beyond the fall of Samaria (722 B.C.) into the reign of Hezekiah of Judah (Hos. 1:10). Hosea was thus a contemporary of Amos, Isaiah, and Micah.

IMPORTANCE

Hosea is the herald of God's unchanging love for Israel. During his ministry the nation had sunk to the lowest depths of idolatrous immorality. Despite the fact that the people gave every evidence that *they did not love the Lord,* Hosea labored with suffering and tears to show the people that *God still loved them.* Throughout the fourfold theme—the nation's idolatry, wickedness, captivity, and final restoration—God's enduring love for his people is interwoven with a tender strain of sadness.

Israel is portrayed as the Lord's adulterous wife. That Hosea might know the poignancy of God's unrequited love for his own, and that he might be a sign to the unfaithful nation, he was instructed to marry a woman who would prove unfaithful. The children of this marriage were given names symbolic of Hosea's principal predictions. The son's name, Jezreel ("the Lord sows or scatters"), points to judgment on the Jehu dynasty (1 Kings 19:15-17; 2 Kings 10:1-14) as well as to Israel's future restoration (Hos. 2:21-23). Lo-ruhamah ("unpitied"), a girl, would be a living reminder that Israel would no longer be pitied because of her harlotry. Lo-ammi ("not my people"), another boy, would be a living reminder of *why* the Lord would no longer pity—he was temporarily setting aside Israel as his elect people.

OUTLINE

A. Hosea's Home Life Portrays God's Relation to Israel (chapters 1–3)
   1. The children portray the Lord's impending punishment (chapter 1)
   2. The wife portrays the nation's shocking infidelity (chapter 2)
   3. The husband portrays the Lord's undying love (chapter 3)
B. Hosea's Homeland Portrays God's Judgment and Mercy (chapters 4–14)
   1. The guilt of the sinful kingdom (chapters 4–8)
   2. The punishment of the sinful kingdom (chapters 9–13)
   3. The restoration of the repentant people (chapter 14)

THE MORAL PROBLEM OF HOSEA

Did the Lord command Hosea to marry a harlot, or did she become a harlot after his marriage? Or is the incident only an allegory? For centuries commentators have struggled with the difficulty involved. To construe the incident as an allegory is a patent makeshift that dodges rather than deals with the problem. To insist that God commanded Hosea to marry a woman who was already a harlot would be to attribute an unworthy act to an infinitely holy God. To Hosea, too, would be ascribed an act unworthy of a prophet of God.

The best solution to the problem is the interpretation that Gomer became a woman of loose morals sometime after her marriage to Hosea, her future infidelity being foreknown to God. If Hosea delivered his message in later years, he may well have looked back upon his own domestic tragedy as a divinely permitted picture of the sin of God's chosen people. Hence the Lord's initial leading to marry Gomer would have been tantamount to a command.

PROPHECY OF ISRAEL'S FUTURE IN HOSEA

ISRAEL'S PRESENT-DAY CONDITION (HOS. 3:4). Israel is seen deprived of her ceremonial and civil institutions during a period of divine disciplinary actions. The ephod speaks of priesthood, the teraphim of insight into the future, and the king of millennial blessing. All of these the Lord withdrew from Israel, as well as his own personal presence (Hos. 5:15—6:3). Her interim affliction will continue until Messiah returns at his second advent (Hos. 5:15). The "two days" (representing a long period of chastisement) will end in "the third day" (Hos. 6:2, 3), the period of regeneration and millennial blessing (Joel 2:28, 29).

THE FUTURE BELIEVING REMNANT (HOS. 6:1-3). The heart-cry of the repentant Israelites of the last days is recorded in Hosea 6:1-3. See also Isaiah 1:9 and Romans 11:5.

THE FUTURE RESURRECTION OF ISRAEL (HOS. 13:14). This is a promise of physical resurrection (1 Cor. 15:55) of saved Israelites preceding the kingdom (Dan. 12:2). This is a sure event (Hos. 13:14).

THE FUTURE RESTORATION OF ISRAEL (HOS. 1:10, 11; ROM. 9:23-26). Lo-ammi ("not my people") prefigures Israel temporarily set aside (Rom. 11:1-5). Ultimately she will be restored and called Ammi ("my people"). Then she will own the Lord as Ishi ("my husband") (Hos. 2:14-23). The full kingdom restoration is predicted in Hosea 14:1-9. Israel as the "lily" and the "olive tree" (Rom. 11:16-24) will flourish in the beauty of holiness.

NEW TESTAMENT QUOTATION

Our Lord quotes Hosea 6:6, "I will have mercy and not sacrifice" (Matt. 9:13), and alludes to the striking metaphor "They shall say to the mountains, Cover us, and to the hills, Fall on us" (Hos. 10:8) in Luke 23:30, as does also John (Rev. 6:16; 9:6). Hosea 11:1 is quoted in Matthew 2:15 and Hosea 2:23 is quoted in Romans 9:25

Joel

AUTHOR

Joel ("The Lord is God") is distinguished from others of the same name only by the name of his father. The precise time of his prophetic career is unknown, for no king or foreign nation that might aid in dating is mentioned in the book. Conservative scholars tend to date Joel either early, during the reign of Joash (835-796 B.C.), or somewhat later, during the reign of Uzziah, Jotham, Ahaz, or Hezekiah.

IMPORTANCE

Joel is the prophet of the day of the Lord, the end-time apocalyptic period preceding the establishment of the kingdom over Israel. During this era the Lord will manifest his power in crushing his (and Israel's) enemies in order to deliver his covenant people for millennial blessing promised them throughout the Old Testament. The locust plague (Joel 1:1-20) is a symbol of this future apocalyptic period (Isa. 2:12-22; 4:1-6; Ezek. 30:3; Rev. 6:1 – 19:21).

OUTLINE

A. Symbols of the Day of the Lord (chapter 1)
   1. Plague and drought (1:1-14)
   2. Starvation and fire (1:15-20)
B. Events of the Day of the Lord (chapters 2, 3)
   1. The army from the north (2:1-10)
   2. The army of the Lord (2:11)
   3. The remnant's repentance (2:12-17)
   4. The remnant's acceptance (2:18-27)
   5. The remnant's blessing (2:28-32)
   6. The restoration of Israel (3:1)
   7. The judgment of the nations (3:2-16)
   8. The establishment of the kingdom (3:17-21)

JOEL'S PROPHECY OF THE DAY OF THE LORD

THE LAST-DAY INVASION OF PALESTINE (JOEL 2:1-10). The terrible destructiveness of the invading host from the North is described. "My holy mountain" (Joel 2:1; see also Psa. 2:6) is Moriah, the Temple hill. The invasion is preparatory to Armageddon (Rev. 16: 13-16).

THE SECOND ADVENT OF CHRIST (JOEL 2:11). The divine intervention of Christ is signaled by the appearance of the Lord's army (Rev. 19:11-16) in the climactic phase of the titanic struggle at Armageddon.

THE OUTCALLING OF THE ISRAELITE REMNANT (JOEL 2:12-27). The Lord calls upon the remnant in Palestine to repent and receive his deliverance (Joel 2:12-14). He promises his fiery jealousy for them instead of his decimating wrath against them, as well as prosperity, military deliverance, joy, and kingdom blessing.

THE OUTPOURED SPIRIT (JOEL 2:28-32). This spiritual revival will inaugurate the kingdom age. Peter used this prophecy at Pentecost (Acts 2:16-21) to illustrate that the effusion taking place then was merely a sample of what the Jews could expect when the kingdom was introduced at the second advent. The kingdom outpouring is to be universal (Joel 2:28, 29) and is the climactic phase of the day of the Lord. It will be preceded by signs portending the doom of the wicked enemies of Israel.

ISRAEL'S END-TIME RESTORATION (JOEL 3:1). This great event of the day of the Lord (Isa. 11:10-12; Jer. 23:5-8; Ezek. 37:1-28) is preceded by the judgment of the nations that persecuted Israel.

THE JUDGMENT OF THE NATIONS (JOEL 3:2-16). The basis of this judgment will be the treatment of Israel, illustrated historically by the Phoenicians and Philistines, among others. This judgment connects with Armageddon (Isa. 29:1-8; Jer. 25:13-17; Zech. 1:14, 15; Matt. 25:31-46).

FULL KINGDOM BLESSING (JOEL 3:17-21). Israel finally accepts her Messiah, her rightful King. This is a common prophetic theme, toward which all Old Testament prophets gravitate (Zech. 14:20, 21).

Amos

AUTHOR

Practically all critics concede the substantial integrity of the book. Only a few passages are seriously disputed: the notable messianic passage (Amos 9:11-15), three doxologies (Amos 4:13; 5:8; 9:5, 6), and Amos 1:9-12 and 2:4, 5. These verses are viewed as later glosses on unwarranted theories of Israel's religious development. Objectively considered, however, no proof exists for assigning any part of the prophecy to any author beside Amos.

BACKGROUND

Amos was a fiery and fearless prophet who warned of impending judgment upon a rapidly apostatizing nation. His ministry was conducted in the latter part of the reign of Jeroboam II (782-753 B.C.). This was a period of economic prosperity and luxurious living, with rampant immorality and idolatry. Amos was a simple herdsman and fruit picker (Amos 7:14) from Tekoa, a hill-country hamlet some ten miles south of Jerusalem.

Although Amos was called to be a prophet to the whole house of Jacob (Amos 3:1, 13), his recorded ministry was directed chiefly to the Northern Kingdom (7:14, 15) at the main sanctuary in Bethel (Amos 7:10). There Amos collided with the easy-going, compromising religion of the day, represented by the high priest, Amaziah. Not to be intimidated by Amaziah's threats or the king's displeasure, the prophet continued to thunder forth his warning of approaching judgment.

OUTLINE

A. Indictment of Gentiles and Jews (chapters 1, 2)
  1. Indictment of six Gentile nations (1:1 – 2:3)
  2. Indictment of Judah and Israel (2:4-16)
B. Judgment of the Twelve Tribes (chapters 3 – 8)
  1. Three messages of condemnation (chapters 3 – 6)
  2. Five visions of punishment (chapters 7, 8)
C. Restoration of All Israel (chapter 9)
  1. A rebuilt Tabernacle (9:11, 12)
  2. A revitalized land (9:13)
  3. A reinstated people (9:14, 15)

AMOS'S PROPHECY OF THE FINAL RESTORATION OF ISRAEL (9:11-15)

Amos's theme of impending judgment upon sin thunders in unabated fury throughout the book. Only at the end does judgment melt

Tuthmosis III ruled the entire Near East as well as Joseph's descendants in Egypt. (© *MPS*)

into mercy, like a calm sunset after a tempest. Then Amos's great prediction of future blessing describes 1) the restoration of the Davidic dynasty (Amos 9:11); 2) the conversion of the nations (Amos 9:12); 3) the revival of the land of Palestine (Amos 9:13); 4) Israel's return from worldwide captivity (Amos 9:14); 5) the rebuilding of desolated cities (Amos 9:14); and 6) Israel's permanent settlement in the land (Amos 9:15).

James quoted this great prophecy at the first council of the Christian Church (Acts 15:15-17). On that momentous occasion the Holy Spirit employed it to unfold the divine program for the future *after* the present age of the outcalling of the Church. Then the Lord will return, as Amos foresaw, to reestablish the Davidic dynasty in Christ (Amos 9:11, 12). Millennial prosperity (Amos 9:13) will characterize restored Israel (Amos 9:14, 15).

Obadiah

AUTHOR

Obadiah is completely unknown apart from the meaning of his name ("servant of the Lord"). The date is equally unknown, although a period before Jeremiah seems most likely.

BACKGROUND

The book has the form of a dirge of doom. Its single theme is judgment upon Edom, the nation sprung from Esau. In Obadiah's time Sela (later called Petra) was Edom's capital. The ruins of this ancient city were discovered in 1812. Hewn out of rose-colored cliffs, the remains of Edom's power in the arid region south of the Dead Sea stand as a silent witness to the fulfillment of Obadiah's prophecy.

OUTLINE

A. The Destruction of Edom (1:1-14)
    1. Description of the destruction (1:1-9)
    2. Reason for the destruction (1:10-14)
B. The Day of the Lord (1:15-21)
    1. The judgment of Edom and the nations (1:15, 16)
    2. The exaltation of Jacob and all Israel (1:17-20)
    3. The supremacy of Jehovah as King (1:21)

ISRAEL'S FUTURE

The final verse of the prophecy (Obad. 1:21) is clearly messianic.

Brief as his prophecy is, Obadiah envisions the promise of future deliverance for Israel in the kingdom, as do so many of the other prophets. The "saviors" are deliverers on the earth, as in Judges 3:9, 15. They will serve under the Messiah, the King of kings (Rev. 19:16; 20:4).

Like so many of the prophets, Obadiah also had a vision of the day of the Lord, when all nations, including revived Edom (Obad. 1:18; Isa. 11:14), will be judged for their treatment of Israel (Obad. 1:15, 16, 18). Edom's cruelty to Israel (Obad. 1:10-14) foreshadows the cruelty of the nations to Israel in the great tribulation which precedes the kingdom.

Messiah's deliverance of Israel at the second advent, as well as the nation's regeneration (Rom. 11:26), will result in a holy people and a holy kingdom (Obad. 1:21). Only the Holy One of Israel will be able to set up such a kingdom. Unholy man by himself can never establish it.

Jonah

AUTHOR

Under the view that Jonah is predictive and typical *history* rather than mere fiction or allegory, there is no compelling reason to deny that Jonah himself was the narrator. The miracles of the book, the presence of some Aramaic forms, and a few alleged historical problems are commonly cited as evidence of a date much later than the era of Jonah. But none of these arguments is decisive against traditional authorship by Jonah.

Significantly, the period in which Jonah lived witnessed conditions in Nineveh that were favorable for the prophet's ministry there. Under Semiramis, the queen regent, and her son Adad-nirari III (810-

782 B.C.) there was an approach to monotheism under the worship of the god Nebo. It was either in the latter years of this reign or early in the reign of Assurdan III (771-754 B.C.) that Jonah appeared at Nineveh.

BACKGROUND

Jonah, meaning "dove" in Hebrew, was an actual, historical person and not a fictional character, as some higher critics would suggest. He was the son of Amittai (Jonah 1:1). His home was in Gath-hepher of Zebulun, a few miles northeast of Nazareth in Galilee. He occupies a unique place as the first foreign missionary in the Bible. His ministry reflects Israel's God-ordained mission to the nations. His theme is God's love for mankind and the extension of divine mercy to all peoples. Jonah prophesied under Jeroboam II (782-755 B.C.) that Israel would regain its ancient boundaries (2 Kings 14:25).

The historicity of Jonah is further attested by Christ, who compared Jonah's fish experience and his preaching to his own burial and resurrection (Matt. 12:38-42).

IMPORTANCE

Not only was Jonah himself a historical person, but his book is likewise a narration of actual events. It is neither myth, legend, parable, prophetic allegory, nor fiction, as is sometimes alleged. Both Jewish and Christian traditions maintain that the book is a masterpiece of condensed history. None of the events of the story, including the miracle of the great fish, is incredible to enlightened faith.

Although the book is historical, it is more than mere history. If it were only the recital of events, without a higher moral and spiritual meaning, it would have no proper place among the minor prophets. But the book possesses not only this higher moral and spiritual quality, but also the additional motif of predictive or typical history. It is thus of far-reaching prophetic and typical value.

In one aspect of his ministry Jonah reflects Christ as the One who was sent by the Father, suffered entombment, rose from the dead, and carried salvation to the Gentiles (Matt. 12:39-41; Luke 11:29-32). In another aspect of his mission Jonah foreshadows the nation Israel—a serious trouble to the Gentiles outside its own land, yet meanwhile witnessing to them. Cast out by the nations but miraculously preserved in the future tribulation at the end of the age (Dan. 12:1), Israel finally calls upon Jehovah, finding salvation and deliverance (Rom. 11: 25, 26). The Israelites then become missionaries to the Gentiles in the future earthly Davidic Kingdom (Zech. 8:7-23).

OUTLINE

A. Jonah Disobeys His First Commission (chapters 1, 2)
  1. Disobedience (1:1-3)
  2. Chastisement (1:4-7)
  3. Acknowledgement (1:8-12)
  4. Repentance (1:13-17)
  5. Restoration (2:1-10)
B. Jonah Obeys His Second Commission (chapters 3, 4)
  1. Jonah's preaching (3:1-4)
  2. Nineveh's repentance (3:5-9)
  3. Nineveh's preservation (3:10)
  4. Jonah's anger (4:1-4)
  5. God's reproof (4:5-11)

THE MIRACLE OF THE GREAT FISH

The book has frequently been labeled as allegory or fiction in order to avoid the supposed problem of the swallowing and disgorgement of Jonah by a large marine animal. The story of Jonah and the so-called "whale" has elicited much derision and has for many people negated the important message of the book. In defense of the genuineness of the miracle the following observations are made. The animal in question is described by Scripture not as a whale but a "great fish" (Jonah 1:17). The Greek word *ketos*, translated "whale" in the King James Version of Matthew 12:40, means a huge fish or marine animal, possibly the whale shark or rhinodon. This is the largest of all fish, sometimes attaining a length of seventy feet. Such a sea monster was "prepared" ("appointed" or "ordered") by the Lord to swallow Jonah. We know that there are creatures capable of swallowing a fully grown man, for there are authenticated cases of men who, like Jonah, have been swallowed and disgorged alive. The real miracle is not so much the swallowing as the fact that Jonah was alive when he was vomited by the great fish so many hours later.

Although skepticism has magnified this episode out of all proportion with the other marvels recounted in the book (the storm, the gourd, the conversion of the Ninevites), it is not one whit greater than those which honeycomb all of Scripture: the exodus, the manna from heaven, the water from the rock, or the resurrection of Christ. It is significant that Christ specifies Jonah's fish experience as a prefigurement of his own resurrection (see Matt. 12:39-41; Luke 11:29-32).

Micah

AUTHOR

The name *mikah* is apparently abbreviated from *mikayahu*, "Who is like the Lord?" Micah was a native of the village of Moresheth (Mic. 1:1, 14), located about 20 miles southwest of Jerusalem. Micah was a contemporary of Isaiah and ministered under the reigns of Jotham, Ahaz, and Hezekiah (Jer. 26:18).

BACKGROUND

In Micah's day the Assyrian power was a great threat. The prophet foretold the fall of Samaria (Mic. 1:5-7) and the inevitable desolation of Judah (Mic. 1:9-16), against which his warnings were especially directed. Micah's emphasis was upon personal and social righteousness. His twofold theme was judgment and the coming kingdom.

OUTLINE

A. The Coming Judgment (chapters 1, 2)
   1. Judgment of Samaria (1:1-8)
   2. Judgment of Judah (1:9-16)
   3. Judgment of oppressors (2:1-11)
   4. Blessing of the remnant (2:12, 13)

B. The Coming Kingdom (chapters 3 – 5)
  1. Preparatory judgments (3:1-12)
  2. Nature of the kingdom (4:1-5)
  3. Establishment of the kingdom (4:6-13)
  4. Rejection of the king (5:1, 2)
  5. Interval between advents (5:3)
  6. Return of the king (5:4-15)
C. The Final Controversy (chapters 6, 7)
  1. The sin of the people (6:1 – 7:6)
  2. The intercession of the prophet (7:7-20)

GREAT PREDICTIONS OF MICAH	
Prediction	*Description*
Christ's First Advent and Rejection	The Smitten Judge (5:1) who was struck upon the cheek as the height of insult (1 Kings 22:24) is the Bethlehem-born yet preexistent and eternal One (5:2) of the Davidic line. Ephrath was an early suburb of Bethlehem (Gen. 35:19), David's home.
Israel's Condition Between the Advents	Israel is to be set aside because of rejection of the Messiah. "She who travails" is Israel in tribulation, travailing to bring forth a last-day believing remnant (the remnant of Christ's brethren; 5:3; Matthew 25:31-46).
Christ's Second Advent and Acceptance	The rejected one becomes the Shepherd of Israel (5:4) and the peace of Israel (Isa. 9:7) when he dispenses the peace he has purchased for his restored people (Eph. 2:14, 15). He also attains peace by defeating the northern invader of the end-time (5:6).
The Remnant's Blessing	The remnant dwells securely (5:4) as a witness (5:7) and avenger of wrongs (5:8, 9) in the administration of the kingdom at the second advent.
The Establishment of Christ's Kingdom	Jerusalem is to be the capital of the restored Davidic kingdom (4:1-3; Isa. 2:2-4). The kingdom is to be characterized by justice, peace, security, and loyalty to the Lord (4:3-5). Israel is to be gathered into the kingdom (4:6-8). The intervening Babylonian exile typifies the final regathering (4:9, 10).
Christ's Kingdom Rule	Armageddon is the prelude to the kingdom (4:11-13; Rev. 16:13-16). Jerusalem's victory is assured as she threshes the sheaves (the hostile nations gathered against her). Christ's kingdom rule as supreme King and Lord (Rev. 19:16) is denoted by "the Lord of the whole earth." It is his by virtue of both creation and redemption (Zech. 4:14; 6:5; Rev. 4:11).

Nahum

AUTHOR

Nahum's prophecy is a literary classic. Its poetic descriptions of God's majestic holiness and Nineveh's fall constitute some of the finest poetry of the Old Testament. Critics sometimes deny 1:2 – 2:2 to Nahum, viewing it essentially as a post-exilic, acrostic poem later prefixed to Nahum's poem. But such a view is arbitrary, being based on the theory that the poem had been drastically altered. Even if the acrostic arrangement could be proved, there is no valid reason for robbing Nahum of the credit for it.

BACKGROUND

Nahum (*comfort*) gave consolation to Judah by his prophecy of the fall of Nineveh, the capital of the Assyrian Empire. The destruction of the "bloody city" (Nah. 3:1) meant the fall of the "giant among the Semites," whose tyrannical cruelty periodically scourged the ancient world from 850 B.C. until its fall in 612 B.C. Nahum uttered his oracles between the conquest of No-Amon (Thebes) in Egypt (Nah. 3: 8) in 661 B.C. and the fall of Nineveh in 612 B.C. Nineveh's destruction constituted the vindication of God's holiness, for the infinitely holy God of Israel could not allow such a cruel and bloody nation as Assyria to go unpunished for its crimes and atrocities against humanity.

OUTLINE

A. The Majesty of God (1:1 – 2:2)

      1. Superscription (1:1)
      2. The fury of the Lord (1:2-11)
      3. The mercy of the Lord (1:12—2:2)
  B. The Fall of the City (2:3—3:19)
      1. Description of destruction (2:3-13)
      2. Explanation of destruction (3:1-19)

Habakkuk

AUTHOR

Little is known of Habakkuk. He lived, it may be inferred, during the rise of the Neo-Babylonian Empire, about 625-605 B.C. The Chaldeans became a serious threat to Judah after the battle of Carchemish in 605 B.C. Thus Habakkuk probably ministered during the reign of Jehoiakim (608-597 B.C.). His work shows that he, like Nahum and Isaiah, was a great poet. (Chapter 3 constitutes a magnificent lyric ode. It describes a theophany and looks forward to the second advent. See Second Thessalonians 1:7-10.)

IMPORTANCE

Habakkuk deals with a question that has troubled many thoughtful people. How can God's patient tolerance of the wicked be reconciled with his holiness? The answer the prophet gives is valid for all times. God is sovereign. He is holy as well as loving, and both of these attributes must be satisfied. He will therefore deal with evil-doers in his own time and way. Meanwhile the Lord's people must keep in mind that proud sinners like the Chaldeans have no faith, in contrast to God's people, who live by faith. "Behold, his soul which is lifted up is not upright in him but the just (righteous) shall live by his faith" (Hab. 2:4).

Habakkuk therefore announces the great spiritual principle that separates fallen mankind into two categories. Those who exercise faith for their salvation are called "the righteous" and are redeemed by God's grace, while those who rely on their own self-sufficiency for their salvation are regarded by God as unrighteous, and do not obtain eternal life. The proud, overweening Chaldeans were used as an example of the unrighteous. Lacking faith in God, they possessed neither spiritual life (fellowship with God) nor eternal life (escape from eternal death in Gehenna—Rev. 20:11-14).

Habakkuk deals with a question that has troubled many thoughtful people. How can God's patient tolerance of the wicked be reconciled with his holiness? The answer the prophet gives is valid for all times. God is sovereign. He is holy as well as loving, and both of these attributes must be satisfied. He will therefore deal with evil-doers in his own time and way. Meanwhile the Lord's people must keep in mind that proud sinners like the Chaldeans have no faith, in contrast to God's people, who live by faith. "Behold, his soul which is lifted up is not upright in him; but the just (righteous) shall live by his faith" (Hab. 2:4).

Although Habakkuk declared this great truth in reference to the historical situation which he and God's people faced at the time, it is also very correctly used by the Apostle Paul to express the fact of salvation by grace through faith in our time (Rom. 1:17; Gal. 3:11; Heb. 10:38). The essential basis of salvation remains the same through every era of human history.

OUTLINE

A. The Prophet's Perplexity (chapters 1, 2)
  1. The first perplexity (1:1-11)
     (a) Question: Why is Israel's sin unjudged? (1:2-4)
     (b) Answer: The Chaldeans will judge the sin! (1:5-11)
  2. The second perplexity (1:12 — 2:20)
     (a) Question: How can the wicked Chaldeans render judgment? (1:12 — 2:1)
     (b) Answer: The Chaldeans will also be judged for their own sin! (2:2-20)
B. The Prophet's Prayer (chapter 3)
  1. The petition for mercy (3:1, 2)
  2. The vision of God (3:3-15)
  3. The joy of the Lord (3:16-19)

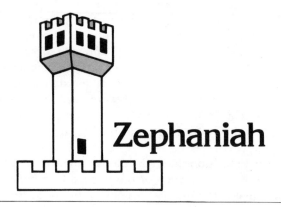

AUTHOR

Zephaniah ("the Lord hides or protects") was apparently a great-grandson of Hezekiah (Zeph. 1:1). If this is not the case, it is difficult to explain the prophet's departure from the normal custom of mentioning only the father in the superscription. The prophet ministered in the reign of Josiah (640-608 B.C.) and was doubtless instrumental in the revival of 621 B.C. Nahum and Jeremiah were contemporaries.

IMPORTANCE

Zephaniah's message was a warning of impending judgment upon Judah and Jerusalem. The coming invasion of the Chaldeans is treated as a prefigurement of the apocalyptic day of the Lord, in which all earth judgments culminate (Isa. 2:10-22; Joel 1, 2; Rev. 4:1 – 19:16). Israel's restoration to the kingdom is treated in 3:9-20. The establishment of the kingdom is preceded by the judgment of the nations (Zeph. 3:8-13) and the revelation of Israel's Messiah-King (3:14-20).

OUTLINE

A. The Day of the Lord (1:1 – 3:7)
   1. Judgment of Judah (1:1 – 2:3)
   2. Judgment of the Gentiles (2:4-15)
   3. Judgment of the Jewish leaders (3:1-7)
B. The King and the Kingdom (3:8-20)
   1. Judgment of the Gentiles (3:8-13)
   2. Manifestation of the Messiah (3:14-20)

PROPHETIC EMPHASES

THE DAY OF THE LORD IN FIGURE (ZEPH. 1:1–3:7). The scope of this passage encompasses a worldwide judgment of the end-time tribulation. The Chaldean advance under Nebuchadnezzar foreshadows the time of Jacob's trouble (Jer. 30:5-7) which precedes Messiah's second advent (Zeph. 1:14-18).

THE OUTCALLING OF A REMNANT (ZEPH. 3:10-13). "The shameless nation," apostate Israel, is called to repent (Zeph. 2:1-3), prefiguring a call to the Jewish remnant of the end time to separate from the sinful nation.

THE JUDGMENT OF THE NATIONS (ZEPH. 3:8). This event, prefigured by judgment upon surrounding nations (Zeph. 2:4-15), is a necessary prelude to Israel's establishment in kingdom blessing.

CONVERSION OF THE NATIONS (ZEPH. 3:9). The Lord will "turn to the peoples a pure language." This indicates a spiritual transformation of the Gentiles, manifested in their purified speech.

ISRAEL'S RESTORATION (ZEPH. 3:14-20). The call to ecstatic joy envisions the termination of Israel's judgments, her triumph over her foes, and the enthronement of her King-Messiah in her midst (Zeph. 3:15, 17). Regathered, healed, restored, and blessed (Zeph. 3: 19, 20), Israel finds the fulfillment of her predicted destiny as stated in Deuteronomy 26:19.

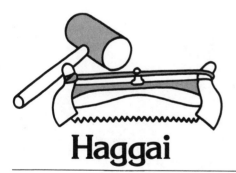

Haggai

AUTHOR

Haggai labored with Zechariah to encourage the returned exiles to finish building the temple. This project had been begun in the second year of Cyrus (535 B.C.), but had been abandoned in despair because of economic difficulties and opposition.

In Darius I's second year (520 B.C.) Haggai delivered four prophetic messages. Parts of these form the present book. The first message (Hag. 1:1-15) was delivered in August-September, the second (Hag. 2:1-9) in September-October, the third (Hag. 2:10-19) in November-December, and the fourth (Hag. 2:20-23) in November-December.

BACKGROUND

Haggai, Zechariah, and Malachi belong to the post-exilic period.

BACKGROUND OF HAGGAI	
Date	*Events*
549-539 B.C.	Cyrus the Great unites Persia and Media. Conquers Lydia and Babylon. Death of Belshazzar and fall of Babylon.
538 B.C.	Edict of Cyrus.
536 B.C.	Jews return to Jerusalem.
536-534 B.C.	Altar laid. Economic depression.
530-522 B.C.	Cambyses extends Persian Empire. Egypt conquered.
522-486 B.C.	Darius I ascends throne of Persia.
520 B.C.	Haggai ministers.
520-515 B.C.	Zechariah ministers. Temple completed.

OUTLINE

A. A Message of Rebuke (chapter 1)
   1. The neglect of the Temple (1:1-11)
   2. The response of the people (1:12-15)
B. A Message of Encouragement (2:1-9)
   1. "Build the present Temple" (2:1-5)
   2. "Anticipate the millennial Temple" (2:6-9)
C. A Message of Promise (2:10-19)
   1. "Past disobedience brought judgment" (2:10-14)
   2. "Present obedience will bring blessing" (2:15-19)
D. A Message of Prophecy (2:20-23)
   1. Judgment of the Gentile nations (2:20-22)
   2. Establishment of the messianic kingdom (2:23)

PROPHETIC EMPHASES

THE GREAT TRIBULATION. Haggai refers to the period of end-time trouble (Jer. 30:5-7; Dan. 12:1) as "the shaking of all nations" (Hag. 2:7) and "the shaking of the heavens and the earth" (Hag. 2:6, 21). It is preliminary to the restoration of the Davidic kingdom. It is also described as the overthrow of the "throne of kingdoms of the nations" (Hag. 2:22), so that the kingdom of Messiah may be set up. Christ is the "Stone" that smites the image (Gentile world power) and destroys it (Dan. 2:44, 45).

THE SECOND ADVENT. The text of Haggai 2:7 reads, "the desire of all nations shall come." This is an apt prophetic designation of him who is objectively the Desire of all nations. Through him alone can the nations be blessed with that righteousness and peace for which they really yearn.

MESSIAH'S KINGDOM RULE. Zerubbabel the governor was of the Davidic line (Matt. 1:12; Luke 3:27) and typifies Christ as David's son. In the kingdom Christ will receive his Davidic throne and will wear his royal signet ring. The prophecy envisions Christ invested with all rule and authority. Zerubbabel will no doubt himself participate as one of Christ's prime ministers in the kingdom (Dan. 12:2; Matt. 19:28).

THE BUILDING OF THE MILLENNIAL TEMPLE. That the temple ("house") referred to in Haggai 2:7 is not Zerubbabel's but the future kingdom temple is obvious from the context describing the preliminary end-time worldwide tribulation. The Septuagint reads, "The desirable things of all nations shall come," a reference to the costly treasures collected to adorn the millennial temple. "The future glory of this house (the millennial temple) shall be greater than the former" (Solomon's temple—Hag. 2:9). Peace will be bestowed through the Prince of Peace (Isa. 9:6, 7; Mic. 5:5) in that future kingdom of peace (Isa. 11:5-10).

Zechariah

AUTHOR

Zechariah, the son of Berechiah, the son of Iddo (Zech. 1:1) had, like Haggai, a ministry of encouragement for the remnant who had returned from Babylon. His name, meaning "the Lord remembers," suggests his divinely bestowed task of impressing upon the people that in their hardships and testings God had not forgotten them, for they were his elect nation. He would bless them in every way and enable them to complete the temple. He would give them far-reaching assurances of the coming of the Messiah, both as Savior and Redeemer in his first advent and as deliverer-king in his second advent.

Zechariah began his prophetic ministry two months after Haggai, in November, 520 B.C. Their combined preaching brought about the completion of the temple at the beginning of 515 B.C. Haggai's total recorded ministry lasted four months and Zechariah's about two years. His last dated prophecy was given in December, 518 B.C. (Zech. 7:1). Little question exists that Zechariah is the author of chapters 1 through 8.

Chapters 9 through 14 are undated and therefore frequently ascribed to another author. Although they are to be dated much later than the previous chapters of the book (probably after 480 B.C. in the light of the reference to Javan or Greece), there is no decisive reason to reject Zecharian authorship. Zechariah evidently had a long ministry, lasting perhaps fifty years.

OUTLINE

Introduction: The Call to Repentance (1:1-6)

A. The Hope of the Future (1:7—8:23)
    1. Visions of comfort and judgment (1:7—6:8)
        (a) The man among the myrtles (1:7-17)
        (b) The four horns and craftsmen (1:18-21)
        (c) The man with the measuring line (chapter 2)
        (d) The cleansing of the high priest (chapter 3)
        (e) The lampstand and the olive trees (chapter 4)
        (f) The flying scroll (5:1-4)
        (g) The woman in the ephah (5:5-11)
        (h) The four chariots (6:1-8)
    2. Symbolic crowning of Joshua (6:9-15)
    3. Religion: the true and the false (chapters 7, 8)
B. The Burdens of the Future (chapters 9—14)
    1. Messiah's first advent and rejection (chapters 9—11)
    2. Messiah's second advent and acceptance (chapters 12—14)

CHARACTER OF THE BOOK

Zechariah is by far the most messianic and apocalyptic of all the Minor Prophets. His prophecy contains more prophetic allusions to the person, work, and future glory of Christ than all the Minor Prophets combined. He ranks with Isaiah and Ezekiel in abundance of detail regarding the second advent of Christ and the establishment of the future messianic kingdom.

GREAT PROPHECIES OF ZECHARIAH 9-14

THE FIRST ADVENT OF CHRIST. In contrast to Alexander, the proud world-conqueror (Zech. 9:1-8), the Messiah is lowly, riding upon a humble beast of burden, and righteous, thus validating his Saviorhood (Zech. 9:9).

THE REJECTION OF CHRIST, THE GOOD SHEPHERD. Zechariah performs a symbolic act of prophecy in order to portray "the flock destined for butchery." The nation's abusive treatment of Zechariah prefigures its future treatment of Messiah himself (Zech. 11:4-6). The two rods, "Graciousness" and "Unity" (Zech. 11:7, 8), are broken to picture the cessation of national unity after the rejection of Messiah (Zech. 11:9-11) and his betrayal for "thirty pieces of silver" (Zech. 11:12).

THE ACCEPTANCE OF ANTICHRIST, THE BAD SHEPHERD.
The prophet performs a second symbolic act in order to foreshadow
this tragedy which precedes the second advent. He describes Antichrist's vicious character and doom (Zech. 11:15-17; John 5:43).

ISRAEL'S END-TIME REGATHERING. The presence of Christ is
promised to the remnant, guaranteeing their triumph (Zech. 10:5-7).
Israel will be gathered together to Palestine out of her present worldwide dispersion. Every impediment to her blessing will be removed
(Zech. 10:8-12).

MESSIANIC IMPLICATIONS OF THE EIGHT NIGHT VISIONS

Vision	Interpretation
The Man among the Myrtles (1:7-17)	Hope for scattered Israel, symbolized by the myrtle trees in the deep glen. These express Israel's depressed condition in the world during the times of the Gentiles (605 B.C. to the second advent). The Red-Horse Rider (1:8) is Christ in theophanic form as Redeemer and delivering Warrior. The patrol scouts (angelic agents) ascertain the condition of the earth as it affects Israel's restoration (Hag. 2:21, 22), which was not imminent (1:9-12) because the earth was "quiet."
The Four Horns and Craftsmen (1:18-21)	Israel finally triumphant over her foes. The four horns represent the four great world powers of the times of the Gentiles (Babylon, Persia, Greece, and Rome, the latter to be revived at the end time Dan. 2:37-45; 7:7, 8, 20; Rev. 13:1). The four craftsmen symbolize kingdoms the Lord employs to cast down the persecutors of his covenant people. Three of these (Persia, Greece, and Rome) were horns, which in turn become craftsmen. The fourth horn is Messiah's millennial kingdom, which destroys revived Rome (Rev. 19:15; Dan. 2:44).
The Survey-or (chapter 2)	Jerusalem in kingdom glory. Surveyor is probably the same divine Person as the Red-Horse Rider of vision 1. His measuring activities point to the prosperity of Jerusalem both then and in the kingdom age, as the promises of 2:4-13 demonstrate.
Joshua's Cleansing (chapter 3)	Restoration of Israel as a high-priestly nation. The high priest, Joshua, represents the self-righteous, Christ-rejecting nation (Rom. 10:1-4). The angel (the Lord) effectually rebuffs Satan on the ground of God's sovereign election of Israel. The nation is saved at the second advent (3:4, 5) by accepting the Redeemer-Messiah, the Branch (3:8-10; Isa. 53:1-10; Phil. 2:6-8). He will be the "Stone," a precious carved gem, when Israel receives him at his glorious second advent (Zech. 12:10).

ISRAEL'S CONVERSION. The vision of the crucified Messiah, the Pierced One (Zech. 12:10; Rev. 1:7) results in national conversion and a copious outpouring of the Spirit, fulfilling Joel 2:28-32 and Ezekiel 39:29. Acts 2:16-21 is used as an *illustration* of the Pentecostal effusion that will be fulfilled in the Millennium.

ISRAEL'S NATIONAL CLEANSING. The basis of cleansing is the "fountain" (Zech. 13:1), namely Calvary. Idolatry, occultism, and false prophecy will be removed by Christ (Zech. 13:1-6). The provision for cleansing is Messiah, introduced with dramatic suddenness (Zech. 13:

Vision	Interpretation
The Gold Lampstand (chapter 4)	Israel as the light of the world in fellowship with Christ, the true Light (John 8:12). The lampstand in the midst of Israel (Exod. 25:31-40; John 8:12) portrays Christ in his deity (pure gold). The plenitude of the sevenfold Spirit (Heb. 1:9; Rev. 1:4) is prefigured by the seven lamps (fullness of testimony). "The Lord of the whole earth" (Gen. 14:19; Mic. 4:13; Zech. 6:5; Rev. 11:3, 4) is the kingdom name of the victorious King-Priest, who will combine the civil and priestly offices (the two olive trees).
The Flying Scroll (5:1-4)	Messiah's rigid rule in the kingdom. The scroll, illustrating the enforcement of the divine moral law, represents the curse of God against sinners (Deut. 28-30; Gal. 3:10-14). The flying motion denotes the worldwide extent of the curse against all offenders (Psa. 2:9; Rev. 2:27; 12:5; 19:15).
The Woman in Ephah (5:5-11)	Removal of commercial and ecclesiastical wickedness from the millennial earth. The ephah, a Hebrew dry measure (1.05 bushels) represents godless business, the commercial aspects of Babylon (Rev. 18). The talent is also associated with commerce of the Satanic world system. The woman, the personification of wickedness (Matt. 13:33; Rev. 2:20; 17:3-7), represents the religious aspects of Babylon (Rev. 17). Her position in the ephah suggests her complicity with godless business, which ultimately works her undoing (Prov. 5:22).
The Four Chariots (6:1-8)	The judgment of the nations prior to Messiah's kingdom. "The two mountains" (Olivet and Zion) are the locations from which divine judgment goes forth in the horsed chariots. The *red* horses portray blood and war (Rev. 6:4); the *black*, starvation (Rev. 6:5, 6); the *white,* conquest (Rev. 6:2); the *grizzled and bay,* death (Rev. 6:8). The four spirits (angelic ministers) are the celestial agents of judgment who will dislodge the wicked for possession by "the Lord of the whole earth" (6:5).
Finale: Coronation of the High Priest (6:9-15)	*All* eight night visions point to the kingdom restored to Israel under Messiah as the King-Priest (Heb. 7:1-3; Psa. 110:4). The significance of the coronation is that the crown was to be placed *not* upon the head of the civil ruler but upon the head of the high priest, pointing to the kingdom role of Christ as King-Priest.

6). Both his death and deity are described in Zechariah 13:7, where God ("the Lord of hosts" refers to the Messiah as "the man my equal," a strong intimation of the unique divine-human nature of Christ. The prelude to Israel's national conversion is her world wide scattering (Zech. 13:7) and last-day tribulation, resulting in a delivered remnant (Zech. 13:8, 9) that appropriates Christ's redemption (Zech. 13:9).

ISRAEL'S END-TIME DELIVERANCE. Deliverance of the converted remnant will occur at Armageddon and in the future siege of Jerusalem (Zech. 12:1-9; 14:1-3). The enemy is cut down by God at the moment of apparent triumph.

ISRAEL'S NATIONAL HOPE. This centers in the returning Messiah, the "Prince of Peace" (Isa. 9:6). He will bring peace (Zech. 9:10). In prospect of suffering Israel is encouraged (Zech. 9:11, 12). The Maccabean conflict with paganism (175-130 B.C.) was envisioned as an illustration of Israel's final conflict and deliverance (Zech. 9:16 – 10:1).

PERSONAL ADVENT OF MESSIAH. He will come to the Mount of Olives, causing a gigantic earthquake which will produce vast topographical changes (Zech. 14:4). He will come with his angels and saints (glorified men) to deliver his people and destroy their foes (2 Thess. 1:7-10; Jude 1:14, 15).

ESTABLISHMENT OF THE KINGDOM OVER ISRAEL. It is at this time that the restoration of the kingdom which the disciples inquired about in Acts 1:6 will be fulfilled. Because of the absolute lordship of the King (Zech. 14:9), all the blessings of the kingdom center in Jerusalem, his capital of the millennial earth (Zech. 14:10, 11, 16-19). With a retrospective glance Zechariah reviews the destruction of Israel's enemies (Zech. 14:12-15), then climaxes his prophecy with a description of Israel's holiness as a high priestly nation (Zech. 14:20, 21).

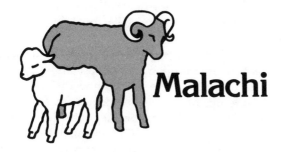

Malachi

AUTHOR

Malachi means "my messenger." This is the prophet's personal name—not an appellation based on Malachi 3:1, as some critics hold. As the last prophetic voice of the Old Testament, Malachi must be placed considerably later than Haggai and Zechariah, including the later portion of Zechariah. The book evidently belongs to a period some time after Ezra's and Nehemiah's reforms, for spiritual decline had set in again. A date between 435 and 400 B.C. would be reasonable.

BACKGROUND

THE WORLD OF MALACHI	
Date	*Event*
522-486 B.C.	Reign of Darius I
520 B.C.	Ministry of Haggai and Zechariah
515 B.C.	Completion of Temple
490 B.C.	Defeat of Darius I at Marathon by Greeks
486-465 B.C.	Reign of Xerxes I (Ahasuerus, Esther's husband)
485-425 B.C.	Life and works of Herodotus, "father of history"
475 B.C.	Later ministry of Zechariah (Zechariah 9-14)
470-399 B.C.	Life and works of Socrates
465-424 B.C.	Reign of Artaxerxes I; "Golden Age" of Pericles
458 B.C.	Return from exile under Ezra
445 B.C.	Rebuilding of walls under Nehemiah
435-400 B.C.	Ministry of Malachi; final message of Old Testament

IMPORTANCE

Malachi rebukes formalism and hypocritical religionism for its total contradiction of God's grace and electing love. In doing this the prophet deals with the sins of the priests of his day. But his emphasis extends far beyond the priestly sins, for these serve only as the background for his prophecies of judgment upon the whole nation. At that coming day of the Lord the wicked will be judged and the righteous will be delivered into the blessings of the restored kingdom. Prerequisite to this climactic event is the coming of the Messiah's forerunner and the Messiah himself at the first advent. This expanded foreview thus includes most of the major themes of Old Testament prophecy.

OUTLINE

A. God's Love for His People (1:1-5)
  1. Disbelieved by Israel (1:1-3)
  2. Demonstrated by Jehovah (1:4, 5)
B. Israel's Sins against God (1:6–2:17)
  1. The sins of the priests (1:6–2:9)
  2. The sins of the people (2:10-17)
C. God's Warning of Judgment (3:1–4:6)
  1. God will send a forerunner (3:1-6)
  2. The people have robbed God (3:7-15)
  3. God will spare a remnant (3:16-18)
  4. Judgment is coming (4:1-4)
  5. God will send Elijah (4:5, 6)

GREAT PROPHETIC THEMES

THE PREDICTION OF MESSIAH'S FORERUNNER. "My messenger" is John the Baptist (Matt. 11:10; Mark 1:2; Luke 7:27). His mission of preparing the way for Christ at his first advent is foretold (Mal. 3:1).

THE SECOND ADVENT OF MESSIAH IN JUDGMENT. He is "the messenger of the covenant," particularly in his second advent to judge (Mal. 3:2-5; Rev. 19:11) in reply to the taunt "Where is the God of Judgment?" (Mal. 2:17). The covenant is the Palestinian Covenant (Deut. 29, 30; esp. 30:3-10).

THE GODLY JEWISH REMNANT. These are the believing Jews

of the end-time, who will be rewarded for their fidelity in times of gross apostasy (Mal. 3:16-18) and be the Lord's peculiar treasure in the day when the Lord separates the righteous from the wicked, previous to the establishment of the kingdom.

THE DAY OF THE LORD. Judgment will be visited upon both the wicked nations and apostate Israel. Evildoers will be purged out by the returning Christ before he sets up his righteous regime (Mal. 4:1).

THE SECOND ADVENT OF MESSIAH IN BLESSING. To the believing remnant who fears his name he will appear as "the Sun of righteousness with healing in his wings." As the "righteousness of God" (1 Cor. 1:30) he will bring to those who believe on him salvation instead of condemnation. As "the Lord our righteousness" (Jer. 23:6) he will bring them healing instead of destruction, blessing and empowering them so that they will be able to tread down their wicked foes.

THE COMING OF ELIJAH. "Elijah" will appear before the onset of "the great and terrible day of the Lord" (Mal. 4:5, 6), when sinners will be punished. He will call out a godly remnant, lest the returning Christ smite the earth with a curse because of its wicked inhabitants (Mal. 4:6).

WHO IS THE ELIJAH OF MALACHI 4:5, 6?

This vexing problem has caused much confusion and called forth many erratic interpretations. That Elijah will not be the Old Testament prophet Elijah returned to earth from heaven but an unglorified member of the godly Jewish remnant in the period of judgment preceding Messiah's second advent is suggested by the following considerations. Our Lord applied the name Elijah to John the Baptist (Matt. 11:14) in his official capacity as a prophet. John was an Elijah in spirit (Luke 1:16, 17), but obviously not the literal Elijah (John 1:21). Preceding Messiah's second advent will be another "Elijah," a man with a preparatory ministry similar to that of John the Baptist. Christ declared that this Elijah (perhaps Elijah will be his real name) will "restore all things" (Matt. 17:3, 11), attesting Malachi's prediction that a prophet would arise in the period of judgment preceding the second advent (Acts 3:21).

That the Elijah predicted by both Malachi and our Lord (Matt. 17:11) is one of the two witnesses of Revelation 11:3-13 seems inescapable. Since both of these two witnesses are first killed for their testimony and then resurrected by God, the Elijah of the Old Testament could not be one of them, for he had long previously been translated to heaven and thus made immune to physical death.

Summary of New Testament Books

RELATION TO THE OLD TESTAMENT BOOKS

The books of the New Testament constitute the capstone of the Old Testament revelation. They also have counterparts in the Old Testament books. Thus the four Gospels correspond to the Pentateuch in showing the need for the Savior and foreshadowing his coming in type and prophecy. The Acts of the Apostles present the early history of God's redeemed people, the Church. They thus correspond to the historical books of the Old Testament (especially Joshua and Judges), since these catalog the story of God's Old Covenant people, Israel.

The twenty-one epistles of the New Testament expound the meaning of Christ's redemption in Christian life. In this way they correspond to the Old Testament prophetic writings, which established the principles of Pentateuchal Covenant and Law that governed God's ancient people. The Book of the Revelation previsions the future of the Church, of Israel, and of the Gentiles and thus corresponds in part to the books of Daniel and Zechariah and the last thirteen chapters of Ezekiel.

DIVISIONS OF THE NEW TESTAMENT

The books of the New Testament may be arranged in the following order:

BIOGRAPHICAL – THE FOUR GOSPELS. These are historical and theological portraits of the person and work of Jesus Christ. Two were written by apostles (Matthew and John) and two by close friends of apostles (Mark and Luke).

HISTORICAL – THE ACTS OF THE APOSTLES. This book is a record of the results of Christ's redemptive work seen in the formation and early experiences of the Christian Church. It forms the link between the biographical and doctrinal portions.

The Golden Gate in the Jerusalem Wall, viewed from the Church Of All Nations (*Russ Busby photo*)

INSTRUCTIVE—THE PAULINE EPISTLES. These epistles unfold the full ramifications of the redemptive work of Christ. They fall into three general categories:

Doctrinal, addressed to churches. These epistles include Romans, Corinthians, Galatians, Ephesians, Philippians, Colossians, and Thessalonians.

Pastoral, addressed to young men with a pastoral gift. These include the epistles to Timothy and Titus.

Special, addressed to an individual (Philemon).

INSTRUCTIVE—THE GENERAL EPISTLES. These are the "non-Pauline" epistles (with the possible exception of Hebrews). They include Hebrews and James (addressed especially to Christians of Jewish background) and the epistles by Peter, John, and Jude (addressed to the Church at large).

PROPHETIC AND APOCALYPTIC—THE REVELATION. The "Revelation of Jesus Christ" (1:1) is the grand consummation of all inspired prophecy.

The Four Gospels

THE DESIGNATION "GOSPEL"

As applied to the four inspired biographies that open the New Testament, the term "gospel" signifies the good news of salvation for lost humanity provided through the life, death, and resurrection of Jesus Christ, the God-Man. The word "gospel" is the Old English rendering of the Greek word *evaggelion,* the Latin *evangelium,* and the English *evangel.* The term is a contraction of "Godspel" and means "news about God." Wycliffe's translation of the Bible (1382) popularized the use of the term. The four Gospels constitute the basis for the gospel message as presented doctrinally in the Pauline Epistles, "that Christ died for our sins according to the Scriptures, and that he was buried, and that he rose again the third day according to the Scriptures" (1 Cor. 15:3, 4). The Apostle shows that the fact of personal salvation is predicated solely upon *faith in what Christ did for the believer* rather than upon anything the believer can do for Christ (Eph. 2:8, 9).

WHY FOUR GOSPELS?

There are four Gospel accounts because a single narrative could never adequately present the glory of the person and work of him who was King of Israel (Matthew), Servant of the Lord (Mark), Son of Man (Luke), and Son of God (John). One pose by a renowned painter could hardly do justice to a great man who was at the same time an educator, a general, a president, and a legislator. How much less could one biographical portrait set forth him who was at the same time a Prophet, Priest, and King and who also combined God and man in one Person!

Neither could a single Gospel narrative adequately meet the varied needs of fallen and lost humanity. Matthew, the Gospel of the "King of Israel," was written for the unregenerate religious man, represented by the nation Israel. Mark, the Gospel of the "Servant of God" — the Gospel of action and miracle — was written for the unregenerate strong man, represented by the world-ruling Roman of Christ's day. Luke, the Gospel of the "Son of Man," was written for the unregenerate thinking man, represented by the intellectual Greek of Christ's day. John, the Gospel of the "Son of God," was written for the unregenerate and insignificant man, represented by the underprivileged Oriental races of Christ's day. These various classes comprise humanity in general in every age.

Matthew

AUTHOR AND DATE

No portion of Scripture displays a clearer impress of divine inspiration than the four Gospels. The Holy Spirit is their obvious Author. Yet each also had, of course, a human agent. The first Gospel is the work of Matthew, a Hebrew, whose preconversion name was Levi. Matthew was a "publican" or collector of tolls and customs imposed on persons and goods crossing the Lake of Gennesaret at Capernaum (Matt. 9:9). He made a great feast at his house in honor of Jesus on the occasion of his call (Luke 5:29). He was among those who waited in the upper room for the promised Spirit just before Pentecost (Acts 1: 13). After this we hear no more of him.

The early Church unanimously ascribed this Gospel to the Apostle Matthew. External evidence abundantly testifies to the early existence and use of the Gospel of Matthew (the *Didache,* the *Epistle of Barnabas,* and many other early sources). Papias, Irenaeus, and Origen comprise a uniform second-century attestation of the genuineness of Matthew's Gospel. Internal evidence also authenticates the Gospel. Since Matthew was not conspicuous among the apostles it would have been strange for tradition to assign the Gospel to him if he had not actually written it.

Conservative scholars date Matthew's Gospel at about A.D. 50.

ORDER AMONG THE GOSPELS

For the following reasons it is appropriate that Matthew stands first in order among the four Gospels: 1) It has historically been considered the earliest Gospel, designed to meet the needs of the earliest Christian converts, who were Jews. 2) Its author was an apostle. 3) The Gospel fulfills the Old Testament in a remarkable way. 4) It bridges the gap between the Old and New Testaments and, like the Book of Hebrews, shows the relationship of Christianity to Judaism and the Law of Moses to the teachings of Christ. For these reasons it is fitting that the Gospel of Matthew not only heads the list of Gospels but also serves as an introduction to the entire New Testament.

PURPOSE

Matthew wrote to supply an account of the life of Christ that would encourage and confirm the earliest Christian converts in their new-found faith. These believers were Jews who turned to the crucified and risen Messiah in the period between Christ's ascension and the outreach of the gospel of grace to the Gentiles (Acts 1-10). In this era, as Peter's sermons in the first part of Acts indicate, the gospel was enunciated primarily in the sphere of the Law, the Prophets, and the

Snows of Mount Hermon (Mount of Transfiguration) to the north furnish water for Sea of Galilee and Tiberias. (© *MPS*)

Psalms, since all believers at this time were either Jews or Jewish proselytes.

While encouraging and confirming these persecuted Jewish believers in their Christian faith, Matthew at the same time undertook to confute their persecutors and to show that in Christ's death and resurrection the promises made to Abraham and David were being fulfilled. A clear presentation of the nature of Christ's person and mission was needed to refute the objections of unbelieving Jews.

PLAN OF MATTHEW'S GOSPEL

The author undertook to achieve his purpose by presenting proof that Jesus was truly the divine-human Messiah and King of Israel prophesied in the Old Testament. Matthew shows that the kingdom he offered, as well as the words he spoke and the works he performed, were those predicted of Israel's Messiah-King. Both the King and his proffered kingdom were rejected by Israel. Israel was consequently rejected by the King. During the time of the nation's rejection the kingdom will assume a new form, existing in concealment during this present age, the outcalling of the Church (13:1-58; 16:16-18). The nation through its leaders murdered the Messiah-King, but his death was nevertheless a ransom for many through resurrection and ascension to heaven. Christ will shortly return to reward his own and set up his kingdom (chaps. 24, 25). Meanwhile his followers are commissioned to carry the gospel to all nations.

OUTLINE

A. Introduction of the King (chapters 1–4)
   1. Qualifications and birth (chapter 1)
   2. Recognition as King-Messiah (chapter 2)
   3. Preparation for ministry (chapters 3, 4)
B. Presentation of the Kingdom (chapters 5–7)
   1. Spiritual principles (5:1–7:27)
   2. Anticipated rejection (7:28, 29)
C. Manifestation and Rejection of the King (chapters 8–12)
   1. The response of Israel's leaders (chapters 8, 9)
   2. The King's messengers to Israel (chapter 10)
   3. The King's rejection by Israel (chapter 11)
   4. The nations rejection by the King (chapter 12)
D. Prophecies of the King (chapter 13)
E. Ministry of the King (chapters 14–23)
   1. Previews of world outreach (chapters 14, 15)
   2. Predictions of death and the church (chapter 16)
   3. Glimpses of the future kingdom (chapter 17)
   4. Descriptions of the kingdom's subjects (chapter 18)
   5. Earthly relationships and the kingdom (chapter 19)
   6. Service and awards in the kingdom (chapter 20)
   7. Final appearances of the King (chapters 21, 22)
   8. Pronouncements of doom (chapter 23)
F. Further Prophecies of the King (chapters 24, 25)

1. The destruction of the Temple (24:1-3)
2. The end-time Tribulation (24:4-51)
3. The testing of Jewish profession (25:1-13)
4. The testing of service (25:14-30)
5. The testing of individual Gentiles (25:31-46)

G. Death and Resurrection of the King (chapters 26 — 28)
   1. The betrayal and denial of the King (chapter 26)
   2. The crucifixion and death of the King (chapter 27)
   3. The resurrection of the King (28:1-9)
   4. The commissioning of the disciples (28:10-20)

THE CONCEPT OF THE KINGDOM

Being the Gospel directed to the Jew, Matthew naturally deals with the King and the kingdom. The King is, of course, the Messiah-King so extensively foretold in the Old Testament, and the kingdom is the one described in such detail by the Hebrew prophets. In Matthew the term "kingdom of heaven" occurs thirty-three times; it is peculiar to this Gospel. The expression derives from its use in Daniel (Dan. 2: 44; 4:25, 32) and refers to the rule of the God of heaven over the earth.

The term "kingdom of heaven" is employed in a threefold sense by Matthew. Understanding of this triple usage is essential to the correct comprehension of this important Gospel.

First, the kingdom of heaven is revealed as "at hand," offered in the person of the King (of whom John the Baptist was the forerunner—3:1-3; 4:17). The biblical expression "at hand" (literally "drawn near") means that the King was then present and that a bona fide offer of the kingdom was being made to Israel on the sole condition of her repentance. The failure of the nation to repent and her rejection of both the King and the kingdom were included in the overall plan of God in order to demonstrate the exceeding sinfulness of sin. This necessitated the King's atoning death as a prerequisite for the future establishment of the kingdom at his second advent. The kingdom offered was the Davidic, earthly, theocratic kingdom promised so glowingly in the Old Testament (2 Sam. 7:4-17; Isa. 11:1 — 12:6; and many other passages).

Second, the kingdom of heaven in Matthew is revealed in its "mystery" form during the long interval when the King and the kingdom are rejected by Israel (Matt. 13). It is designated a "mystery" (Matt. 13:11, 17) because so far as the Old Testament was concerned it was locked up in the secret counsels of God (Eph. 3:3-12). It was to be announced only after the kingdom per se had been rejected by the nation (Matt. 12:1-45). This phase of the rule of God on the earth includes the worldwide preaching of the cross and the outcalling of the Church (Acts 15:14, 15) during the interval between the two advents.

Third, the kingdom of heaven in Matthew is revealed in its future aspect, fulfilled after the second advent of Christ. This is the kingdom offered to Israel by John the Baptist and Jesus but rejected by the nation as a whole. It will be realized as the future millennial kingdom predicted by Daniel (Dan. 2:34-36, 44, 45) and covenanted to David (2 Sam. 7:12-16). It is to be established after the return of the King in glory (Matt. 24:29−25:46) and the national conversion of Israel (Zech. 12:1−14:21; Acts 15:14-17; Rom. 11:26-36; Rev. 20:4-6).

Matthew does employ the term "kingdom of God" four times. But since he was writing to Jews he usually employed the term "kingdom of heaven" because of its special relevance to the kingdom covenanted to David and the divine plan to be realized through the nation Israel. The kingdom of heaven is similar in many respects to the kingdom of God and is therefore often used synonymously with it in the other Gospels, where the divine rule embraces the larger context of the Church, the nations, and the angels.

GENTILE CONCERN

Despite the fact that Matthew is distinctly addressed to the Jew — presenting Christ as Israel's King and quoting or alluding to the Old Testament no less than sixty-five times — the Gospel also reveals a distinct concern for the Gentiles. This is demonstrated by the following considerations.

Matthew mentions two Gentile women (Rahab and Ruth) in Christ's genealogy (1:5). He includes the story of the Magi (2:1-12). He includes Christ's declaration that many from the east and west will sit down in the kingdom of heaven, while the "sons of the kingdom" (its rightful heirs, the Jews) will be cast out (8:11, 12). He quotes the prophecy that Messiah would proclaim judgment to the Gentiles and that the Gentiles would hope in him (12:18, 21). He includes Christ's disclosure that the mystery form of the kingdom would comprehend Gentiles (13:1-58), that the ministry of the King in rejection and death would bring salvation to the whole world (chaps. 14, 15), and that the Gentiles would enter the kingdom after divine judgment (25:31-46). Matthew also includes the resurrected King's commission to disciple "all nations" (28:19, 20).

Mark

AUTHOR AND DATE

The second Gospel is the work of John Mark. Mark's mother was the Mary whose house in Jerusalem was used as a meeting place for Christian believers (Acts 12:12-17). Mark was apparently Peter's convert (1 Pet. 5:13). In any case Peter was well acquainted with Mark's mother. It was to her home that he went after being miraculously released from prison (Acts 12:12). It seems that Mark assisted Peter, Paul, and Barnabas in their missionary work at one time or another (Acts 12:25; 15:36-39).

Mark labored with Paul at Rome (Col. 4:10; Philem. 1:24), apparently having reconciled the differences that separated them on Paul's second missionary tour (Acts 15:38, 39). In his last epistle Paul urges Timothy to come to him in Rome and bring Mark with him, adding that "he is useful to me for ministering" (2 Tim. 4:11). Mark thus appears to have been a servant rather than a preaching minister, a circumstance admirably in line with his delineation of Jesus Christ as the Servant of the Lord.

That Mark wrote the second Gospel is amply supported by the testimony of early Church Fathers, including Papias, Justin Martyr, Irenaeus, Clement of Alexandria, Tertullian, Origen, and Eusebius. Since Mark was not an especially prominent church leader, there would have been no reason to assign his name to this Gospel if he had not actually written it.

Mark himself was not one of the Twelve. His Gospel, however, has all the earmarks of a firsthand witness. This witness, according to numerous early accounts, was none other than Simon Peter, from

Marker of Tenth Roman Legion, stationed in Jerusalem during Christ's crucifixion (*Russ Busby photo*)

whom Mark is said to have obtained his information.

Strong evidence points to the fact that Mark's Gospel was written at Rome between A.D 65 and 70, shortly before the fall of Jerusalem. Mark explains Jewish customs because he is writing to Gentiles. He also employs ten Latin words, some of which do not occur elsewhere in the New Testament, thus furnishing additional evidence that he wrote from Rome to Romans.

ORDER AMONG THE GOSPELS

Modern criticism tends to assign to Mark priority in both time and importance. Because Mark has so little material that is peculiar to him, most present-day scholars favor the theory that his Gospel was written first and was employed by Matthew and Luke when they wrote their accounts of Christ's life. It is assumed that the freshness and vividness of Mark's language also suggest that it was written first.

But those who hold to the full inspiration and authority of Scripture and discern the Holy Spirit's obvious superintendence in the four Gospels cannot help being suspicious of such a theory. Why should

Matthew and Luke be so dependent on Mark if the Holy Spirit really led them? Why, too, should Mark be assigned priority in time and importance when it was never placed first in ancient Greek manuscripts and lists or in the writings of the Church Fathers, but was invariably placed second, third, or fourth? Why in the early Church did the Gospel of Mark receive the least attention of any of the four Gospels, if it had priority over the others?

Whatever the exact reasons, the position of Mark after Matthew in the present-day order of the New Testament books is certainly providential. Matthew's thoroughly Jewish emphasis makes it a far more suitable bridge between the Old and New Testaments.

PURPOSE

Mark wrote to supply an account of the life of Christ that would meet the need of the Roman, as Matthew had met the need of the Jew. Thus, while Matthew depicts the Messiah as King of the Jews, Mark delineates him as the Servant of the Lord. This unique Servant displayed a remarkable blending of submission and strength that achieved victory through apparent defeat. Such a portrayal of Christ had a special fascination for Roman Christians.

PLAN OF MARK'S GOSPEL

In presenting Christ as the faithful and obedient Servant, the Holy Spirit through Mark especially fulfills two prophecies by Isaiah: "Behold, my servant . . ." (Isa. 42:1-3) and "Who is blind, but my servant? or deaf as my messenger that I sent? Who is blind as he that is perfect, and blind as the Lord's servant?" (Isa. 42:19).

Mark by the Spirit presents Christ as blind to every object but God's glory and deaf to every call but the voice of God—truly the ultimate example of the perfect Servant! His service, as portrayed by Mark, is distinguished by many beautiful and significant details. For example, his service was undertaken in secret prayer (1:35) and was rendered promptly. Ten times in the opening chapter and forty times in the Gospel we find the Greek word which is translated *immediately,* *straightway,* or *forthwith,* indicating a rapidity of action which befits an energetically obedient servant (1:12, 21; 2:8; etc.). As if there were scarcely a pause in our Lord's wonderful ministry from first to last, the word "and" occurs over and over in the course of the story of Christ's obedient, unfaltering zeal.

OUTLINE

A. Introduction of the Servant (1:1-13)
    1. The forerunner (1:1-8)
    2. The baptism (1:9-11)
    3. The temptation (1:12, 13)
B. Ministry of the Servant (1:14 − 13:37)
    1. In eastern Galilee (1:14 − 7:23)
    2. In northern Galilee (7:24 − 9:50)
    3. In Perea (10:1-31)
    4. In Jerusalem (10:32 − 13:37)
C. Redemptive Work of the Servant (chapters 14, 15)
    1. Plottings to kill (chapter 14)
    2. Crucifixion and death (chapter 15)
D. Authentication of the Redemption (chapter 16)
    1. Resurrection (16:1-8)
    2. Appearances (16:9-14)★
    3. Commission (16:15-18)★
    4. Ascension (16:19)★
    5. Postlude (16:20)★

★Note: These verses are absent from some of the oldest and best manuscripts. Many scholars view them as later additions, assuming that the original ending of Mark was lost at a very early date.

OTHER CHARACTERISTICS

Mark is the shortest of the four Gospels, most of its contents being found in the other two Synoptic Gospels (Matthew and Luke). Christ's death and resurrection receive special emphasis, with over a third of the book devoted to the climactic last week of Christ's earthly career (chaps. 11 − 16). As the Gospel of the Servant of the Lord, Mark is a narrative of action and deeds. Neither a genealogy nor an account of Christ's birth or early years is given since these are not essential to the description of a servant. Although Mark depicts Christ primarily in the servant role, he also mentions his kingly characteristics (11:10; 14:62; 15:2). In contrast, Matthew highlights Christ as King, but also refers to him as a Servant (Matt. 12:18-21). Mark's treatment is concise, straightforward, and chronological throughout, in contrast to Matthew's Gospel, in which chapters 1 − 4 are chronological, 5 − 13 are topical, and 14 − 28 are again chronological.

Luke

AUTHOR AND DATE

The third Gospel is the work of Luke, "the beloved physician" (Col. 4:14; 2 Tim. 4:11; Philem. 1:24). Luke was a Gentile, since he is distinguished from "those of the circumcision" (Col. 4:10, 11). However, it is quite possible that he may have been a Jewish proselyte (a Gentile convert to Judaism). Tradition regards him as a native of Syrian Antioch, in which he displayed a special interest (Acts 6:5; 11:19-27; 13:1-3; 14:26-28; 15:1, 2, 22, 30-40; 18:22, 23). He apparently also lived in Philippi, as the "we" sections of Acts seem to indicate (16:10-17; 20:5-15), and probably studied at the medical school there. He must have been a person of winsome character to have earned the Apostle Paul's adjective "beloved" (Col. 4:14).

The authenticity of Luke's Gospel is well established. Clement apparently alludes to it about A.D. 95. References to it are frequent in the second century (Polycarp, Papias, Marcion, etc.). It is listed as the work of Luke by the Muratorian fragment (A.D. 170) and by Irenaeus (A.D. 180). Such attestation continues into the third century, with Clement of Alexandria, Tertullian, and Origen adding their witness.

The Gospel was probably written about A.D. 58, while Luke was in Caesarea—the city in which Paul was imprisoned (Acts 24, 25, 26). Both the time and the place would have been appropriate for the research which Luke mentions he conducted in order to write his Gospel. Since Luke wrote his Gospel before he wrote the Book of Acts in approximately A.D. 61 (see Acts 1:1 for order of books), it is highly likely that Luke's stay in Caesarea served as his ideal opportunity to pen this Gospel account.

ORDER AMONG THE GOSPELS

The position in our English versions is found in nearly all the Greek and Syrian manuscripts; it was popularized by Eusebius and Jerome. Origen was acquainted with it, though he frequently cites the Gospels in the order Matthew, Luke, and Mark. Occasionally Luke is found in second or fourth place, but never in the first position.

PURPOSE

Luke states plainly that he wrote his Gospel so that Theophilus "might know the certainty" of the things in which he had been instructed (1:4). Theophilus was undoubtedly a Gentile and a person of rank. He was probably a recent convert, perhaps acting as a sponsor for the production of the book.

But a second and far wider purpose for the Gospel was to supply an account of the life and work of Christ that would meet the needs of people at large, especially the Greek-speaking world opened up to Christianity by Paul's missionary tours.

PLAN OF LUKE'S GOSPEL

While Matthew presents Christ as King of the Jews and Mark as Servant of the Lord to the Romans, Luke portrays him as Son of Man to the Greeks. Luke places emphasis upon the perfect humanity of Christ, portraying him as the human-divine Savior, the virgin-born God-Man. Hence Luke lays great stress upon Christ's sinless conception, his genealogy being traced from Mary to Adam. Luke alone tells of Christ's boyhood; he delineates more fully than the other Gospel writers the wonderful prayer life of the pattern Man. He strives to set forth the perfections of the Son of Man as the Friend and Redeemer of men, the Savior of all who will trust in him (1:68; 2:38; 21:28; 24:21).

The term "Son of Man" is a key phrase. Luke 19:10 is commonly designated as the key verse: "For the Son of man is come to seek and to save that which was lost." While beautifully highlighting the humanity of the Divine One, Luke also carefully guards Christ's deity and kingship (Luke 1:32-35). Luke's Gospel is a marvelous exposition of Zechariah's prophecy of "the man whose name is the Branch" (Zech. 6:12). His gospel is emphatically "good tidings of great joy to all people" (2:10), for he tells us how God became man to save a lost and ruined race.

OUTLINE

Introduction (1:1-4)
A. The Son of Man Humanly Related (1:5 — 4:13)
   1. To John the Baptist and Mary and Joseph (1:5 — 2:52)
   2. To John's ministry, the human race, and testing (3:1 — 4:13)
B. The Son of Man in Ministry (4:14 — 21:38)
   1. As Prophet-King in Galilee (4:14 — 9:50)
   2. From Galilee to Jerusalem (9:51 — 21:38)
C. The Son of Man in Rejection and Death (chapters 22, 23)
D. The Son of Man in Resurrection and Ascension (chapter 24)

OTHER CHARACTERISTICS

In this Gospel of Christ's perfect manhood, our Lord is shown in his human development, feelings, sympathies, and powers. The evangelist describes Christ's birth, childhood, growth, and social life. In Luke Jesus is seen rejoicing (10:21), weeping (19:41), praying in agony (22:44), eating with ordinary men (7:36-50), fellowshiping with Mary and Martha (10:38-42), lodging with Zacchaeus (19:1-10), and eating with his disciples after the resurrection (24:41-45).

Glimpses of Christ's sympathy and concern for lost and suffering humanity appear throughout the Gospel. The story of the widow of Nain and her son (7:11-15), the account of the raising of Jairus' daughter (8:41, 42, 49-56), and the parable of the Good Samaritan (10:30-37) all illustrate the tenderness of Christ.

Praise and thanksgiving are also featured in Luke. Often it is said that men "glorified God" (2:20; 5:25, 26; 7:16; 13:13; 17:15; 18:43). Outbursts of praise are found in the book, such as the Ave Maria (1:28), the Magnificat (1:46-55), the Benedictus (1:68-79), the Gloria in Excelsis (2:14), and the Nunc Dimittis (2:29-32).

Luke is the longest, the most literary, and the most beautiful of the four Gospels. Its classic introduction (1:1-4) recalls the works of Herodotus and Thucydides. Its general vocabulary and diction show that the author was an educated man. Luke's medical background appears in his many medical terms and in his special interest in the ill and their illnesses. Evidencing his careful research (1:1-4), Luke displays high accuracy in the recording of events, as shown by W. M. Ramsay's work on the archeological backgrounds of the Gospel and the Acts. Luke was truly a historian of the highest rank.

John

AUTHOR AND DATE

The fourth Gospel is the work of John, "the disciple whom Jesus loved . . . who also leaned on his breast at supper" (John 21:20, 24). That this was the Apostle John is evidenced by external and internal evidence as substantial as that for any book of the New Testament. The existence of the Gospel is attested in Egypt before A.D. 150 by the Rylands Papyrus 457, the earliest known fragment of a New Testament manuscript. The use of John as an authoritative Gospel along with the other three Gospels is likewise attested by the Egerton Papyrus 2, also dated before A.D. 150. Tatian also evidences the use of John in the *Diatessaron*, and there are traces of Johannine language in Ignatius (A.D. 115) and Justin (A.D. 150-160). The Gospel was also known and used in heretical Gnostic circles around A.D. 150.

Since 1947 the Dead Sea Scrolls, particularly the *Manual of Discipline* and other Essene materials from the last century-and-a-half preceding Jesus' ministry, demonstrate that "there is no reason to date the Gospel after A.D. 90; and it may be earlier" (W. F. Albright, "The Bible after Twenty Years of Archeology," *Religion in Life*, 21:4:152: 550). Remarkably close parallels to the concepts of John's Gospel are found in the Essenic literature; these parallels support the genuineness of John's Gospel as a true product of a Jew living in Jesus' day rather than a forger from a second-century Gnostic environment.

Irenaeus declares that John, the Lord's disciple, published the Gospel at Ephesus. This tradition is reinforced by Clement of Alexandria (A.D. 200). The Muratorian Canon (A.D. 190) espouses authorship by the Apostle John. Some opposition to the apostolic authorship of

Entrance to the Garden Tomb, possible burial—and resurrection!—site of Jesus Christ
(*Russ Busby photo*)

John developed at the beginning of the third century, apparently because the Gospel had been misused by the Gnostics.

Internal evidence for apostolic authorship by John has received its
classic formulation from B. F. Westcott and J. B. Lightfoot (*Biblical
Essays*, 1893, pp. 1-198) on the well-founded basis that the Gospel was
written by a Palestinian Jew and an eyewitness of the events recorded.
Critical attempts to discount this evidence have been futile, especially
the attempts to prove geographical and historical inaccuracies. The
most recent archeology has attested John's geographical accuracy in a
remarkable manner (R. D. Potter, "Topography and Archeology in the
Fourth Gospel," *Studia Evangelica*, pp. 329-337). The allegation that
John was incapable of writing such a masterful treatise because he was
an uneducated man (Acts 4:13) ignores the fact of divine inspiration.

The date of the fourth Gospel is to be assigned between A.D 85
and 95. This is commonly accepted, especially if early tradition that
connects John with Ephesus and Asia Minor is given credence. A later
date, beyond the limits of the apostolic age, is now untenable in the
face of recent manuscript finds.

ORDER AMONG THE GOSPELS

As noted in the preceding Synoptic Gospels, the present order of the four Gospels was established by early tradition. John was usually placed last because it was thought to have been written last. However, John occasionally appears in all four possible positions. During the third and fourth centuries it sometimes occurred first (in Chrysostom, Tertullian, and Latin Codex k). Codex Bezae (D) and other Western documents generally follow the order Matthew, John, Luke, and Mark, assigning first place to the apostles. But the order based on date of writing generally prevailed.

PURPOSE

The author of the fourth Gospel states his purpose in the most explicit terms in John 20:30, 31. He undertakes to set forth the Messiahship and deity-humanity of Jesus (1:1, 14) as the world's Savior-Redeemer (3:16) by presenting irrefutable proofs of these from Christ's miraculous signs. He does this with the avowed evangelistic aim of persuading men to trust in Christ as their Savior and Redeemer (20:31).

This Gospel was penned for the benefit of all sin-cursed and lost mankind. The aim was that the Jew might be convinced that the historical Jesus was indeed "the Christ" and that the Gentile might accept this same Jesus as "the Son of God," the Savior of mankind. The Gospel of John is thus the "Gospel of Belief" and is directed to all men everywhere — Jew, Roman, Greek, and "whosoever believeth" (3: 15, 16; 4:13, 14; 12:46).

Although John's primary purpose in writing the Gospel was evangelistic, he also had instructive and corrective goals in view. He enunciates clearly the true nature of Christ and shows how the perfections of Christ provide a thoroughly adequate basis for human redemption. Through this positive presentation he refutes wrong views of Christ's person held by unbelieving Jews and Gentile gnostics.

PLAN OF JOHN'S GOSPEL

In accordance with his stated purpose of presenting Christ as the Son of God (20:30, 31), John selects eight of our Lord's miracles, six of which are peculiar to this Gospel. All of these reveal Christ's divine-human nature and the life he came to impart.

Miracle one, turning the water to wine (2:1-11), shows the omnipotence of the Son of God and the exhilarating nature of eternal life. Miracle two, the healing of the nobleman's son (4:46-54), reveals faith as the condition for receiving eternal life. Miracle three, healing the cripple at Bethesda (5:1-9), demonstrates the power available to live the new life. Miracle four, the feeding of the five thousand (6:1-14), discloses the Son of God as the Sustainer of eternal life. Miracle five, walking on the sea (6:15-21), illustrates the miraculous nature of eternal life. Miracle six, the restoration of sight (9:1-41), portrays the Son of God as the Light of life. Miracle seven, the raising of Lazarus from the dead (11:1-44), presents the Son of God as the Resurrection and the Life, displaying the victory of life over death. Miracle eight, the supernatural catch of fish (21:1-14), shows the resurrected Son of God as the ideal Guide, supplying full fellowship in the life he imparts by faith.

OUTLINE

A. The Son of God Revealed to the World (chapters 1 – 12)
    1. Prologue: God the Word becomes incarnate (1:1 – 1:14)
    2. John's witness concerning him (1:15-34)
    3. His witness in public ministry (1:35 – 12:50)
        (a) By his miracles (eight throughout the Gospel)
        (b) By his discourses (eleven throughout the Gospel)
B. The Son of God Revealed to His Own (chapters 13 – 17)
    1. As Savior-Sanctifier (chapter 13)
    2. As Bestower of the Spirit (chapters 14, 16)
    3. As Basis of the believer's union with God (chapter 15)
    4. As Intercessor for his own (chapter 17)
C. The Son of God Glorified (chapters 18 – 21)
    1. By his suffering and death (chapters 18, 19)
    2. By his resurrection (chapter 20)
    3. By his post-resurrection commission (chapter 21)

OTHER CHARACTERISTICS

Christ's birth, genealogy, youth, baptism, temptation, transfiguration, and ascension are omitted from John's Gospel because of the strong emphasis on Christ's deity. By contrast, Luke's Gospel contains all of these important human events. Christ's deity is indicated in many other ways in John's Gospel, notably by the many different titles applied to him, such as the Word, the Only-Begotten, the Lamb of

God, the Son of God, the True Bread, the Life, the Resurrection, and the Vine. Many of these are prefixed by the formula "I am," emphasizing Christ's preexistent and eternal deity.

John's Gospel gloriously presents the good news of grace, by which sinners find regeneration and new life in Christ (3:16; 10:10; 20:30, 31). The evangel which Paul expounds theologically in his epistles is anticipated and illustrated in John's Gospel, with special emphasis on the death and resurrection of incarnate deity.

John's Gospel wonderfully predicts the Spirit's advent and the new people of God to be brought into being at Pentecost (chaps. 13 – 17). Although the word "church" does not occur in the Gospel, it is prefigured in the new vine and branches, which are to replace the old vine (the earthly people Israel). Jesus himself is the stem from whom life flows to the branches, enabling them to bear fruit (chap. 15). This union of vine and branches was to be effected by the Holy Spirit when he came to unite true believers with Christ and with each other (14:16-20; 16:7, 8, 13). The Holy Spirit was also to personally indwell these believers (14:16, 17). All of this finds historical fulfillment in Acts (1:5; 2:4; 11:14-16) and doctrinal exposition in the epistles (1 Cor. 12:12, 13; Rom. 6:3, 4; etc.). Christ's revelation of himself to his own in John chapters 13 – 17 is thus one of the most sublime passages in all of Holy Scripture.

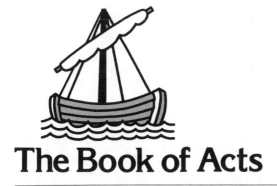

The Book of Acts

TITLE

The title "Acts" or "Acts of the Apostles" is found even in very early manuscripts and refers to the activities of the apostles. Actually only the activities of two apostles are described in any detail—Peter's ministries in chapters 1 – 12 and Paul's evangelization of the Roman Empire in chapters 13 – 28. Acts is therefore not a history of all the apostles but rather a narrative of selected experiences of a few of them. These experiences were selected to show the birth and growth of the Church during the first several decades of Christianity. The title "Acts of the Holy Spirit" has been suggested as an appropriate title for the book, for it is actually the story of the Holy Spirit given as our Lord's ascension gift and working in men to "continue to do and teach" what Jesus merely began (Acts 1:1, 2).

AUTHOR AND DATE

The Book of Acts is the work of Luke, the author of the Gospel of Luke (Luke 1:3, 4; Acts 1:1). The "former treatise" addressed to Theophilus (Acts 1:1; Luke 1:3) is Luke's Gospel. See the biographical sketch of Luke under "Authorship of Luke's Gospel." Luke was a participant in some of the events recorded, indicated by the three "we" passages (16:10-17; 20:5 – 21:18; 27:1 – 28:16).

The evidence for the recognition of Acts as a canonical book does not appear as early or as frequently as the evidence for the Gospels and Paul's epistles, yet sufficient data is available to demonstrate that Acts was early recognized as an authoritative book. The Muratorian Canon, Clement of Alexandria, Tertullian, and Irenaeus all attest the work, and by the time of Eusebius the book was generally acknowledged as part of the Canon.

Internal evidence over and above that given in the discussion of Luke's Gospel is strong for Lukan authorship. The "we" sections in Acts (see above) indicate that the author was one of Paul's companions on his journeys. Similarity of style indicates that the "we" passages were authored by the same person who wrote the rest of Acts. Under no rational hypothesis could these sections in the first person plural be interpolations from some author or source beside Luke. Too, the writer's interest in sickness and the sick and his use of medical language evidence the fact that he was a physician (Col. 4:14).

Scholars date the book either 1) in the decade before the fall of Jerusalem (A.D. 70) or 2) late in the first century or early in the second century. The most probable date is around A.D. 61, soon after the events recorded in Acts 28:30, covering Paul's two-year custody in Rome. The optimistic note on which Acts ends, with Paul being allowed to preach freely in Rome, suggests a period before the outbreak of persecution there in A.D. 64. Scholars who date the book after A.D.

93 surmise dependence of the author upon Josephus. But such dependence is very improbable. If the identification of Theophilus (1:1) were possible, a more precise date for the book could be determined.

PURPOSE

The purpose of the author is first and foremost *historical*. In the Book of Acts Luke continues the account of the origin of Christianity which he began in his Gospel, showing how certain events led to the birth and growth of the Christian Church. Such historical material was needed to show how the life, death, and resurrection of Christ as presented in the Gospels became a vibrant reality in the lives of Christ's followers. This narrative also gives important historical orientation to the New Testament Epistles.

But the historical purpose of Luke is also inseparably connected with a *theological* goal. His history is accurate, even in minute details, but it is not history simply for history's sake. It is the unique history of human and divine interaction, the Holy Spirit working in men through signs and miracles, continuing "to do and teach" what Jesus merely began (1:1). Luke is thus interested in authenticating Christianity as a supernatural regenerating force in a new age in which Christ as Lord operates in and through his people by the Holy Spirit.

In the Book of Acts Luke therefore records the ascension of Christ and his promise to return (chap. 1) as well as the advent of the Spirit and the first historical baptism of the Spirit (chap. 2; see also 1: 5; 11:16). He also records Peter's use of the keys of the kingdom of heaven (see Matt. 16:18, 19) in order to open gospel opportunity to Jews (Acts 2, esp. v. 14), Samaritans (chap. 8, esp. vv. 14-17), and Gentiles (chap. 10, esp. vv. 44-48). Luke traces the spread of the gospel from Jerusalem, Judea, and Samaria to "the uttermost part of the earth" (Acts 1:8).

The purpose of the Acts is also *apologetic*. It supplies proof that the Christian movement was one, whether the believers were Jews, proselytes, Samaritans, Gentiles, or former adherents of John the Baptist. All believed *one* gospel and were baptized by *one* Spirit "into one body" (1 Cor. 12:13), having their oneness *in Christ* (1 Cor. 12:12). Acts likewise presents Paul in the right perspective—not as a renegade and apostate (as his enemies charged), but as God-called and God-approved in his missionary labors. At the same time Acts authenticates the whole Christian movement (Heb. 2:4), connecting it with the redemptive work of the risen and ascended Christ. The author also

Paul ascended Mars Hill to preach the gospel. *(Russ Busby photo)*

shows that Christianity, far from being a menace to imperial law and order, was a peaceful and law-abiding movement. Riots and civil disturbances occurred only when uninformed or prejudiced people (usually unbelieving Jews) stirred up opposition.

OUTLINE

A. Birth of the Church at Jerusalem (chapters 1 – 12)
    1. The birth of the Church promised (chapter 1)
    2. The birth of the Church effected (chapter 2)
    3. The power of the Church manifested (chapters 3 – 5)
    4. The persecution of the Church climaxed (chapters 6, 7)
    5. The extension of the Church to Samaritans (chapter 8)
    6. The conversion of the Church's greatest leader (chapter 9)
    7. The extension of the Church to Gentiles (chapters 10 – 12)
B. Extension of the Church from Antioch (chapters 13 – 28)
    1. Through Paul's first missionary tour (chapters 13, 14)
    2. Through the decisions of the first Church council (15:1-35)
    3. Through Paul's second missionary tour (15:36 – 18:22)
    4. Through Paul's third missionary tour (18:23 – 21:36)
    5. Through Paul's arrest and imprisonment (21:37 – 28:31)

ARCHEOLOGY

Luke's trustworthiness as a historian has been amply attested by modern archeological research. The author's theological and apologetic interests do not detract from his detailed historical accuracy. These theological and apologetic interests do, however, control his selection and presentation of facts. Luke places his account of Christian origins in the framework of contemporary history. His narrative is replete with references to provincial governors, client kings, city magistrates, etc. These allusions constantly turn out to be correct for the time and place in question. True local color, even of widely differing localities, is reflected in his story. A. T. Robertson has concisely reviewed the evidence for the modern reader in *Luke the Historian in the Light of Research* (New York: Scribner's, 1930), following pioneer work by Sir W. M. Ramsay, the Scottish historian and archeologist, in *St. Paul the Traveller and Roman Citizen* (1895).

THE BAPTISM OF THE SPIRIT

Although the working of the Holy Spirit in the early Christians is a dominating theme in the Acts, the book is *not* a doctrinal treatise on the Holy Spirit, but rather a historical account of the Spirit's operation. That the baptism of the Spirit, *prophetic* in the Gospels (Matt. 3:11; Mark 1:8; Luke 3:16; John 1:33), became *historical* in Acts on the day of Pentecost (compare Acts 1:5 and 2:4 with 11:14-16) is generally recognized. But what is often forgotten is that the doctrine of the baptism of the Spirit must be formulated *not from the historical account of its occurrence in Acts but from its doctrinal exposition in the Epistles.* There it is revealed to be not an experience but *a position in Christ accomplished by the Spirit for all believers.* It is shown to be an inseparable part of Christ's "so great salvation" (Heb. 2:3), effected upon all believers at the moment they are saved (1 Cor. 12:13; Rom. 6:3, 4; Gal. 3:27).

The baptism of the Spirit was effected on Jewish believers when they were given the gift of the Spirit and introduced to Christ's salvation in Acts 2, upon racially mongrel Samaritans when they were admitted into the same gospel privilege (Acts 8), and upon Gentiles when the gospel opportunity of the new age was extended to them (Acts 10). For each of these ethnic groups the Holy Spirit's baptism was accompanied by his work of regeneration, sealing, and indwelling, at the same time granting each believer the privilege of continual infilling. The infilling, although available to every believer, was to be experienced only by those who comprehend what they are in Christ and act in faith upon that position.

THE CHURCH

Pentecost marked the beginning of the Church, since it occasioned the first historical occurrence of the baptism of the Spirit (Acts 1:5; 2:4; 11:14-16). Only by this operation could the Church be formed, as the Epistles of Paul reveal (1 Cor. 12:12, 13; Rom. 6:3, 4; Gal. 3:27). The Church at first included only believing Jews (Acts 2). Then believing Samaritans were added (Acts 8). When Gentiles were eventually admitted (Acts 10), the normal course of the age was attained. Then Jew and Gentile were constituted *one* in Christ, losing their racial identity (Eph. 3:1-10), and the divine purpose for the age was revealed at the first Church council. God's plan was to visit principally the Gentiles, in order to take out of them the new people of God, the Church; then he would again take up Israel in the kingdom age which followed (Acts 15:14-16).

CHARISMATIC LANGUAGES

Three instances of supernatural utterance of genuine languages unfamiliar to the speaker occur in Acts (2:4; 10:46; 19:6). In each case the miraculous demonstration of the Spirit constituted a sign to the Jews (1 Cor. 1:22). Together with the wind and fire (Acts 2:2, 3), the supernatural languages at Pentecost evidenced to the Jews that the Mosaic age under which they had lived for 1500 years had passed away and that the new age of the Church was dawning. At Caesarea, when Gentiles were admitted to gospel privilege and brought into the benefits of the gift of the Spirit outpoured at Pentecost, the supernatural languages were once again a sign to Peter and the Jews that the Gentiles had not received an inferior salvation to the Jews, but an *identical* gift (Acts 11:17).

The disciples of John the Baptist, who knew only his preparatory baptism in water (Acts 18:25) and nothing at all of the baptism of the Spirit effected by Christ's death and resurrection (Matt. 3:11; Mark 1:8; Luke 3:16; John 1:33), spoke in supernatural languages as a sign to Jews that John's message and baptism had become antiquated. Now that Christ had died, ascended, and given the Holy Spirit from heaven to work out his great salvation in each believer, the Jews must understand that their spiritual heritage included being baptized into union with Christ and with every other believer the moment they believed (1 Cor. 12:12, 13; Rom. 6:3, 4; Gal. 3:27).

IMPORTANCE OF THE BOOK OF ACTS

Acts is a great historical and missionary document and is one of the most indispensable books of the New Testament. It is conceivable that we might get along without one of the Gospels or Epistles. But to be deprived of the Acts would entail irreparable loss. The historical continuity of the Gospels would be broken, the provision of the outpoured Spirit would be largely unknown, the story of the birth and early growth of the Christian church would be an enigma, and the Epistles, especially those of Paul, would exist in an almost total vacuum. In particular, Paul's doctrine of the Holy Spirit would be largely bereft of historical and experiential illustration.

These facts become all the more striking when we remember that the Book of Acts supplies the background for ten of Paul's Epistles (First and Second Thessalonians, First and Second Corinthians, Galatians, Romans, Colossians, Philemon, Ephesians, and Philippians). The book has also blessed the Church with inspiration for missionary and evangelistic fervor, imparting zeal to carry out the great commission of world evangelization and furnishing living illustrations of this outreach in action.

The Epistles of Paul

BACKGROUND

The thirteen letters of Paul and the eight letters by other New Testament writers form a unique collection among the sacred books of the world. Other "Holy Books" — the Vedas, the Zend-Avesta, the Koran, and the writings of Confucius — contain no letters at all. Instead they consist of philosophical discourses, poems, and legendary histories. When Christianity arose in the Greco-Roman world, communication by letters was common in all walks of life. The Apostles thus found an excellent existing means of communicating with the churches they had established.

FORM AND NATURE

Certain features characterize the epistolary form, especially as it was employed by the Apostle Paul: 1) *a salutation or greeting* which identified the author and expressed his well wishes; 2) *an expression of thanksgiving or commendation* for some grace manifested by the specific church addressed; 3) *a main doctrinal section* dealing with some special doctrine or doctrines needing exposition or correction; 4) *a practical instructive section* developed out of the doctrinal portion; 5) *a personal section* containing greetings and brief messages to individuals; and finally 6) *a concise autographic conclusion* authenticating the letter.

CHRONOLOGICAL ORDER

In most versions of the Bible, Paul's thirteen letters are arranged in nonchronological order. The Roman and Corinthian Epistles are usually placed first, apparently because of the size and importance of the cities of Rome and Corinth and because of the length of these Epistles and the significance of their subject matter. But these Epistles were by no means the first written by the Apostle. The probable chronological order of the Pauline Epistles is indicated in the following table:

Epistle	General Period	Approximate Date (A.D.)	Place of Writing
1 Thessalonians	Second Missionary Tour	50	Corinth
2 Thessalonians		51	Corinth
1 Corinthians	Third Missionary Tour	54	Ephesus
2 Corinthians		54	Macedonia
Galatians		55	Corinth
Romans		56	Corinth
Colossians	During the First	61	Rome
Ephesians	Imprisonment	61	Rome
Philemon		61	Rome
Philippians		62	Rome
1 Timothy	After the First	64-66	Macedonia
Titus	Imprisonment	64-66	Uncertain
2 Timothy	During the Second Imprisonment	66-68	Rome

DISTINCTIVES

Two great distinctives characterize the Pauline Epistles. The first of these is the Church's calling, hope, and destiny. The second is the doctrinal exposition of the redemptive work of Christ. The four Gospels describe the one basis of these two distinctive lines of truth—Christ in his flawless person and finished work. The Book of the Acts sketches the results of these historical events in the birth and growth of the Church. The Pauline Epistles expound the doctrinal meaning and theological importance of these events in great detail.

In the parables of the kingdom of heaven in Matthew 13 Christ gave a preliminary revelation about the nature of the era between his rejection at his first advent and his return in glory. However, the union of Jew and Gentile in one new entity, the Church, was not revealed at this time. Instead, it was revealed several years later to the Apostle Paul (Eph. 3:8, 9). In Matthew 16:18 our Lord had preannounced the core of the divine plan regarding the Church, but it was reserved for Paul to expound the position and relationship of the new people of God. Although salvation by grace through faith had always been God's only method of saving fallen men, Paul for the first time expounded this truth in the light of the redemption which Christ had completed on the cross. For the first time in biblical history God's gospel of grace was fully defined by such doctrines as justification, sanctification, and glorification. Paul's Epistles clarify the specific relationship of these doctrines to all believers (Rom. 1−8), to Jews (Rom. 9−11), and to the Law of Moses (Gal. 1−6).

SKETCH OF PAUL'S LIFE

EARLY YEARS (A.D. 5-45). Paul was born at Tarsus (Acts 22:3) about A.D. 5; was educated in Pharisaic Judaism about A.D. 15-25; began his career as a zealous, Christian-hating persecutor about A.D. 25-37; consented to Stephen's death (Acts 7:58) about A.D. 35; was converted near Damascus (Acts 9:3-18) about A.D. 37; resided in Arabia (Gal. 1:17) about A.D. 37-39; visited Jerusalem (Acts 9:26-29) about A.D. 39; returned to Tarsus (Acts 9:30) in A.D. 39; and ministered at Antioch (Acts 11:25, 26) during A.D. 43-45.

FIRST MISSIONARY TOUR (A.D. 46-47). In A.D. 46 Paul toured both Cyprus (Acts 13:4-12) and Asia Minor—Perga, Pisidian Antioch, Iconium, Lystra, and Derbe (Acts 13:13−14:25). He returned to Syrian Antioch (Acts 14:26-28) in A.D. 47 and attended the Jerusalem Council (Acts 15) in A.D. 48.

SECOND MISSIONARY TOUR (A.D. 48-51). Left Antioch by land for Syria and Cilicia (Acts 15:41); revisited Derbe and Lystra (Acts 16:1-5); evangelized Phrygia, Galatia, Troas, Samothrace, Neapolis, and Philippi (Acts 16:6-40). Proceeded to Thessalonica, Berea, Athens, and Corinth (Acts 17:1 – 18:17). *Wrote First and Second Thessalonians.* Ministered at Ephesus and went on to Caesarea and Jerusalem (Acts 18:18-22), then returned to Antioch (Acts 18:22).

THIRD MISSIONARY TOUR (A.D. 54-58). Revisited and strengthened the churches in Galatia and Phrygia (Acts 18:23) in A.D. 54 and ministered extensively in Ephesus during A.D. 54-57. *Wrote First and Second Corinthians, Galatians, and Romans.* Visited Macedonia, Achaia, Troas, and Miletus (Acts 20:1-38) in A.D. 57. Went on to Jerusalem, where he was arrested (Acts 21:1-36) in A.D. 58.

IMPRISONMENT AND MARTYRDOM (A.D. 58-68). Paul was a prisoner of Rome at Caesarea (Acts 23:23 – 26:32) during A.D. 58-60. The trip to Rome by sea took place in A.D. 60. He was imprisoned in Rome during A.D. 61-63, where he wrote the Prison Epistles: *Colossians, Ephesians, Philemon, and Philippians.* He was apparently released sometime during A.D. 64-67, after which he wrote *First Timothy and Titus.* May have visited Spain, Crete (Tit. 1:5), Asia (2 Tim. 4:13), Macedonia (1 Tim. 1:3), and Greece (2 Tim. 4:20). May have been arrested for a second time in A.D. 67. In any case wrote *Second Timothy* at about this time. Laid down his life for Christ as a martyr in approximately A.D. 68.

Weeds grow in the ruins of the once elegant Roman Forum. (*Russ Busby photo*)

UNGER'S GUID

Romans

AUTHOR

The Epistle to the Romans is the work of Paul, the great Apostle to the Gentiles (Rom. 1:1, 7). Internal evidence is strong for Pauline authorship (11:13; 15:15-21). Style, theology, subject matter, and many other factors add their attestation. External evidence is also very abundant, including such witnesses as Clement of Rome, Ignatius, Justin Martyr, Polycarp, Marcion, the Muratorian Canon, and the Old Latin and Syriac Versions. From the time of Irenaeus onward practically all orthodox scholars attest the Epistle as both Pauline and canonical.

BACKGROUND AND DATE

Paul penned the Roman Epistle about A.D. 56, apparently from Corinth during his three-month stay there (Acts 20:2, 3; cf. 1 Cor. 16: 5-7) and near the end of his third missionary tour. The Apostle expressed regret that he had not as yet had the opportunity to visit the believers in the Imperial City (1:10-13; 15:22, 23; cf. Acts 19:21). He reminds the Roman Christians that he must first visit Jerusalem with the money raised for the needy of Judea (Acts 15:25-27). After visiting Rome the Apostle planned a trip to Spain, for which he hoped to enlist the approval and support of the Roman believers (15:24, 28).

IMPORTANCE AND PURPOSE

The Epistle to the Romans heads the thirteen letters of Paul not because it was written first but because it covers the broadest scope of

Christian doctrine. The Roman Epistle can truly be called "The Constitution of Christianity," since it lays the broad foundation upon which the Christian gospel rests. Its subject material, its logical reasoning, its vigorous style, and its relevance to human need accord it a foremost place in divine revelation. In one sense it is a book of great simplicity and clarity and in another sense it is a book of vast profundity. So deep is it, in fact, that it has challenged some of the greatest intellects of the world, men like Augustine, Luther, and Calvin.

"The gospel of God" (1:1) is the subject of the Epistle. This is the good news of the divine redemption of God in Jesus Christ. The gospel of God is the theological exposition of the finished work of Christ. In its broadest sense the term describes the whole body of redemptive truth. Paul designates it "the good news of God" because with God there is no respect of persons (Acts 10:34; Rom. 2:11). He is not the God of the Jews only but of the Gentiles also (3:29). "All the world" is found guilty (3:19), and the salvation presented is as available as the worldwide need. The only human response required in order to obtain this salvation is faith in the finished work of Christ.

Paul's immediate purpose in presenting the gospel of God was to teach the believers at Rome (and throughout the world) the fundamental doctrines of salvation, so that they might be fortified against legalistic perversions of the truths of justification, sanctification, and glorification (chaps. 1 – 8). A further objective in the Apostle's presentation was to explain the unbelief of the majority of Jews and to indicate the nature, extent, and duration of their rejection by God. He shows that the gospel of God does *not* abolish the covenant promises to Israel, but that these will positively be fulfilled after God has completed his Church and has once again reinstated his people Israel (chaps. 9 – 11).

In the light of the glorious provisions of the gospel of God Paul also purposed to urge his readers to appropriate in daily experience the full blessing of the Christian life. This they were to do by surrendering completely to God (chap. 12), by being subject to existing governmental powers and by loving one another (chap. 13), and by exercising forbearance toward the weak (chaps. 14, 15). Paul also had in mind commending Phoebe, the deaconess, to the church at Rome (16:1-4) as well as conveying greetings to many of the friends he had acquired in his evangelistic travels throughout the Empire.

OUTLINE

A. The Gospel of God Expounded (chapters 1 – 8)

THE SAVED AND THE LOST

Are the heathen lost if they have never heard the gospel? Is it possible for good, moral, and religious people, either in pagan or Christian lands, to be lost? If so, what is the basis of being saved or lost? The Book of Romans, as an exposition of the gospel of grace, necessarily deals with these crucial questions. It declares that *all* members of Adam's fallen race are lost sinners, are alienated from God, and are totally unable to save themselves or to stand before God's infinitely holy presence (1:18 – 3:20). They are *all* shown to be under his wrath (the eternal and unchangeable antagonism of God against sin) and under the curse of threefold death – spiritual death (severed fellowship with God), physical death (inevitable death of the body), and eternal death (separation from God for all eternity) (1:18-32). This is true of moral and good-living pagans as well as immoral ones (2:1-29). It is equally true of unbelieving Jews, moral as well as immoral (3:1-8). God's verdict is that *the whole world* of unregenerate mankind stands guilty and condemned before him (3:9-20).

The Book of Romans teaches that *no one* will attain eternal life except persons who have been justified (declared righteous) by God himself (3:21 – 5:11). Such a declaration results not from possessing some supposed personal righteousness based on self-effort or good deeds, but from having God's own righteousness imputed to the believing sinner who puts his entire trust in Christ's completed work of redemption. Before the cross this reckoning was made on the basis of what God's grace *would do* for the sinner through Christ (Gen. 15:6). After the cross the reckoning is made on the basis of what God's grace *has done* for the sinner through the death and resurrection of Christ (3: 24-26).

Accordingly, Romans reveals that *only* those who have God's righteousness actually reckoned to their account are justified by him and possess eternal life (1:17). Conversely, *all* who are so justified are at the same time sanctified (5:12 − 7:25) and guaranteed glorification (8:30). This constitutes the great dividing line between heaven and hell and the saved and unsaved. Men are placed on either side *solely on the basis of their faith in Christ as God's provision for human sin.*

In the light of these revealed truths, are men really lost? The Epistle to the Romans answers with an emphatic *Yes.* Men are lost not because they are "good" or "bad" by human standards but because they have failed to receive God's perfect righteousness made available to them by faith in Christ.

Are the lost without excuse? This Epistle, as the grand unfolding of the gospel of God, deals with this vexing question. It reveals not only that all unbelievers are lost, but that they are *without excuse* as well. This is true of the unsaved in Christian lands as well as the lost in pagan lands, including those who have never had any chance to hear the gospel. This fact raises serious moral and ethical questions in the minds of finite, fallible men and causes them to question the justice and love of a perfect God. To aid us in grappling with this facet of revealed truth, the Epistle presents the following facts that disclose *why* the lost are without excuse.

The lost are without excuse because they have the revelation of the created universe all around them. The heathen may not have the gospel and the Word of God brought by the missionary, but they have the revelation of the power and deity of God in the book of creation. In this book "that which is known about God is evident" to the pagans and it is "made plain in their inner consciousness, because God (Himself) has shown it to them. For ever since the creation of the world His invisible nature and attributes, that is, His eternal power and divinity, have been made intelligible and clearly discernible in and through the things that have been made—His handiworks. So (men) are without excuse—altogether without any defense or justification" (1:19, 20, *Amplified Bible*).

If pagans read the wide-open book of creation, they will find that "the heavens declare the glory of God, and the firmament shows and proclaims His handiwork. Day after day pours forth speech, and night after night shows forth knowledge. There is no speech nor spoken word (from the stars); their voice is not heard. Yet their voice (in evidence) goes out through all the earth, their sayings to the end of the world" (Psa. 19:1-4, *Amplified Bible*).

If men will read and believe the testimony of God's book of creation and walk in the light which it sheds on their path, God will grant them added light by sending them his book of revelation and redemption through the missionary. If he does not, he will judge each man according to the light with which that man has been favored.

The lost are without excuse because they do not follow the light they have been given in the created universe. Like the ancient heathen, the present-day pagan rejects the testimony of nature. "Because when they" (the heathen who apprehend God through the revelation of creation) "knew and recognized Him as God" (1:19), "they did not honor and glorify Him as God, or give Him thanks . . ." (1:21), *Amplified Bible*). As a result they gradually sank into idolatry. Paganism itself constitutes a witness that God had implanted in the human mind the concept of deity by means of creation, for the concept of a single supreme being appears at the root of all the varied forms of paganistic worship. But instead of receiving the full light of creation, man chose to withdraw his heart and will from it, thereby quenching truth instead of developing it and thus sinking into ever-increasing darkness.

The lost are without excuse because they deliberately and knowingly choose the course of lawlessness and rejection of God. They are guilty because they persist in idolatry and sin and methodically banish the knowledge of God from their thinking (1:28). Despite their realization of the judgment of God upon evildoers, they approve and applaud them (1:32). For this reason God gives them up (1:24, 26, 28) to follow their own sinful course of action to its disastrous end.

The lost are without excuse because they stifle the voice of conscience. The creator has endowed all his creatures with a conscience, that God-implanted inner monitor that tells a man right from wrong. In youth conscience is tender and supple. It responds to truth and light, including God's revelation of himself in his creation. However, when this light is rejected the conscience becomes seared and insensitive. Paul writes that the conscience of the heathen "bears witness" to their actions, "their thoughts the meanwhile accusing or excusing them" (2:15).

Is God unjust and unloving in reprobating the lost? How about those who have never had the opportunity to hear the gospel of saving grace? Is God unjust in condemning these? The answer from the Roman Epistle is *No!* God is not unfair or unloving in condemning *any* lost soul. The Epistle gives the following reasons:

God is not unjust or unloving in reprobating the lost because they are all guilty and without excuse before him. They have no grounds for defense or self-justification because they have rejected the light given to them — that of creation and conscience (see preceding two sections).

God is not unjust or unloving in reprobating the lost because in his sovereign will and long-range purpose he is unimpugnable by finite and erring creatures. He is infinitely holy, just, and impartial as well as infinitely compassionate. "His judgment is according to truth" (2:2). "There is no respect of persons with him" (2:11). He is "faithful, true, and righteous" (3:3-5). He is loving, commending "his love toward us . . . while we were yet sinners" (5:8). He is merciful, yet his mercy is guided by his sovereign will (9:14-24). "He has mercy on whomever He wills (chooses) and He hardens — makes stubborn and unyielding the heart of — whomever He wills" (9:18, *Amplified Bible*).

This manifestation of mercy on the basis of sovereign will appears unreasonable, if not unjust, to sin-blinded men, but only because they cannot discern the full sweep of God's purpose in the case of both saved and the lost. Thus their criticism of God is "Why then does He still find fault and blame us (for sinning)? For who can resist and withstand His will?" (9:19, *Amplified Bible*).

To this objection the Apostle Paul shows that God, being infinitely sovereign and all-wise, is absolutely above the carping criticism of his finite creatures. "But who are you, a mere man, to criticize and contradict and answer back to God? Will what is formed say to him that formed it, 'Why have you made me thus?' " (9:20, *Amplified Bible;* cf. Isa. 29:16; 45:9).

The divine Potter has the absolute right to make of the clay whatever vessel he wishes for whatever purpose he plans. In the final analysis his plan will redound to his eternal glory in the case of both the saved (the vessels unto honor) and the unsaved (the vessels unto dishonor) (9:21). In the case of the saved he will advertise "the riches of the glory" of his love and grace in "vessels of mercy" prepared for glory (9:23). In the case of the unsaved ("the vessels of wrath fitted for destruction"), he will vindicate his holiness and wrath against sin and will reveal his power (9:22).

God is not unjust or unloving in reprobating the lost because he is not obligated to save any, much less all. All members of Adam's fallen race "have sinned and come short of the glory of God" (3:23). Even the best fall short of the divine standard of holiness and hence cannot claim to merit salvation (3:10-23). All of the unsaved are entirely bereft of any righteousness of their own (3:11) and are thus "concluded under sin" (3:9), that is, are completely under sin's dominion and condemnation and are entirely cut off from the love and mercy of God because of his holiness. Only as God freed his love and mercy to act in behalf of fallen men in accord with his holiness could God save *any* of the ruined race. This he did through Christ. Now he can manifest his mercy and grace to save some, in accord with his sovereign will and unimpugnable choice.

God is not unjust or unloving in reprobating the lost because he will judge them and all men on the basis of their works. This must be so, and is revealed to be so, because he is a just, impartial, and fair Judge (2:2, 11; 3:3-5). "For He will render to every man according to his works – justly, as his deeds deserve" (2:6, *Amplified Bible*). God's principles of judgment are outlined (2:1-16). "To those (the saved) who by patience in well-doing seek for glory and honor and immortality, he will give eternal life" (2:7, RSV). They will be rewarded for fidelity in service at the judgment seat of Christ (14:10-12; 2 Cor. 5:10).

"But for those who are factious and do not obey the truth, but obey wickedness (the unsaved), there will be wrath and fury" (2:8, RSV; cf. Rev. 20:11-15). What the sinner does with God's grace revealed in Christ will determine his eternal destiny in heaven (the sin-cleansed universe) or in hell (the one eternal isolation ward for fallen angels and unregenerate men).

God is not unjust or unloving in reprobating the lost because this divine act, like all the divine actions, is regulated by moral law. This moral law, reflected in the Decalogue given to Israel from Sinai (Exod. 20:1-17), is as eternal and unchangeable as God himself, for it is a reflection of his divine being and character. This law, far from saving sinners, shows them their lost and helpless condition (3:19, 20) and drives them to God's grace in Christ so that they can be saved by faith. Nevertheless, even though God's moral law was never meant to be a means of salvation, it is binding upon every human being, both saved and the unsaved, as a way of life.

Man's response to this moral law conditions his actions. Although the unsaved cannot keep the moral law inwardly and vitally, as the saved can, they are nevertheless expected to keep it outwardly in living decent, law-abiding lives. The degree to which they keep this law outwardly determines their degree of punishment in eternal hell. Correspondingly, the degree to which the saved keep this law determines the degree of their reward in heaven.

THE ROMAN EPISTLE, A CRITERION TO DETECT DOCTRINAL ERROR

As a masterful exposition of the salvation purchased by Jesus Christ on the cross, Romans furnishes the criterion by which all basic teachings about the Christian faith are to be tested. Doctrinal subjects which frequently require such examination include the gospel, salvation, justification, sanctification, security, and Christian liberty. These are discussed in the following paragraphs.

THE GOSPEL. The gospel is frequently misrepresented as *something that man does for God*. But in Romans Paul presents the gospel as *everything that God has done for man through Christ*—to be accepted wholly by faith plus nothing (3:24). Another perversion of the gospel is to view it as a matter of *faith plus works*. But Paul shows that works which God can accept follow *salvation*—springing out of it—and never produce it in any degree.

Man often presents only the gospel for the sinner: "Christ died for me." Romans presents the gospel for the saint as well: "I died in Christ and was buried, raised, ascended, and seated with him in the heavenlies" (Rom. 6:1-10). Reckoning on this fact, that is, believing it to be true (Rom. 6:11), enables the believer to obtain daily victory over sin and to enjoy all that has been given to him through Christ (Rom. 8:1-39).

SALVATION. This term includes everything that Christ accomplished on the cross for the sinner (1:16). It is derived from the Greek word *soteria*, meaning "safety," "soundness," or "security," and includes such elements as justification, regeneration, sanctification, glorification, redemption, propitiation, forgiveness, and eternal life. Salvation is a gift received by faith and is totally disconnected from acts of supposed merit on the part of the recipient (1:17; 3:20-24). The gift of salvation contains all of the aforementioned elements and can never be forfeited, either in whole or in part. As a gift from God the salvation of the individual rests securely on the eternal faithfulness of God and cannot be conditioned by human failure.

JUSTIFICATION. Justification is an official act by which God renders a guilty sinner righteous because the condemned one has trusted Christ as his sin-bearer. The individual is not only acquitted of all charges but is pronounced positively righteous (3:22, 24-28; 4:5-8, 22-25; 5:1, 9, 16-21). This foundational element of salvation finds its fullest and grandest exposition in all of Scripture in Romans 3:21—5:21. This vital truth became the clarion call of the Protestant Reformation under Martin Luther.

SANCTIFICATION AND GLORIFICATION. Both of these result from union with Christ by the Spirit's baptizing work in salvation. These too receive their fullest and grandest exposition in Scripture in Romans, in chapters 6—8. This Epistle is the great corrective of common errors on sanctification, presenting this truth in its three aspects—past, present, and future—and inseparably connecting the future aspect with glorification.

SECURITY AND ASSURANCE. Both of these important themes also have their grandest and fullest treatment in Romans, which again serves as the great corrective against popular errors that cluster around these two vital, interrelated themes.

THE FUTURE OF ISRAEL. That God has a future for the nation of Israel in the age to come is most clearly and emphatically taught in this Epistle (chaps. 9—11). This too serves as a corrective for popular errors that deny such a future to the Jewish nation. In dealing with Israel's rejection in the light of Gentile salvation, the Apostle sets forth not only the justice (9:1-29), cause (9:30—10:21), and extent (11:1-10) of that rejection, but its duration as well (11:11-24). He shows that when "the times of the Gentiles" have run their course, the kingdom will be established over Israel (11:25-36).

CHRISTIAN LIBERTY. The entire Epistle to the Romans is an antidote against the poison of legalism which Judaizing teachers were always eager to inject into the grace and truth which Christ had introduced by his salvation. The Christians at Rome and elsewhere were also in danger of becoming enslaved to legalistic issues of conscience and conduct. So the Apostle applies the principles of grace to matters of everyday living: avoid judging fellow believers (14:1-12), discontinue any practice that would offend a brother in Christ (14:13-23), and follow the initiative of love which Christ exemplified (15:1-13).

1 Corinthians

AUTHOR

That Paul wrote First Corinthians is abundantly attested by internal evidence (1:1; 3:4, 6, 22; 16:21) and by the manner in which the book reflects the historical notices of Acts 18:1-18. External evidence of Pauline authorship is also abundant from the first century onward. Clement of Rome, Ignatius, Polycarp, Justin Martyr, and many others attest the genuineness of the Epistle. Clement of Alexandria and Tertullian especially quote extensively from this Epistle.

BACKGROUND AND DATE

In Acts 18:1-11 Luke recounts the circumstances of the founding of the church at Corinth. This metropolis was the most splendid commercial city of Greece, strategically situated just south of the narrow isthmus connecting central Greece with the Peloponnesus. The city was the mecca of trade between the East and West. Its eastern port was Cenchrea (Rom. 16:1) and its western emporium was Lechaeum. The city derived rich income from the transport of cargoes across the narrow isthmus (which was not successfully bridged by a canal until 1881-1893).

As a port city Corinth was both wealthy and immoral. So dissolute was the city that the term "to Corinthianize" was coined to denote the very practice of immorality. If ever the gospel had a place to prove its power (Rom. 1:16, 17), it was at Corinth. It was therefore especially encouraging that "many of the Corinthians, hearing, believed and were baptized" (Acts 18:8). In a night vision the Lord assured Paul that he had "much people in this city" (Acts 18:10). So successful was the gospel outreach at Corinth that the Apostle remained there a year-and-a-half, "teaching the word of God" (Acts 18:11).

Paul probably penned this first letter to the Corinthians about A.D. 54, although a slightly later date is possible. See the discussion under "The Date of First Corinthians and Its Relevance to the Question of Spiritual Gifts."

Revelry is ended and life silenced in Old Corinth. (*Russ Busby photo*)

IMPORTANCE AND PURPOSE

The immediate occasion of the letter was an inquiry from Corinth about marriage and several other matters (7:1). But Paul also used this opportunity to deal with several other problems that were troubling the Corinthian church at this time. What makes the Epistle so vital is that these same problems have vexed local churches in every age, including our own. The following chart lists these problems and the Apostle's directives.

Problem	Inspired Solution
Factions and Divisions (1:10—4:21)	Stop following human leaders and follow Christ instead. Count on him for unity with all believers (1:10-17). Stop relying on human wisdom and rely upon Christ, God's wisdom (1:18—2:16). Avoid carnality (3:1-4); regard service as rendered to God and rewarded by God (3:5-23); regard God's servant as judged by God (4:1-8). Follow only godly apostolic example (4:9-21).
Gross Immorality Accompanied by Indifference (5:1-13)	Offender to be excommunicated and formally delivered to Satan and physical death as the ultimate in chastisement (5:5-13).
Litigation in Pagan Courts (6:1-8)	For a Christian to sue another Christian was shameful enough (6:7), but to take the case to pagan courts was even more shameful. Christians will judge angels and are competent to judge such cases (6:1-6).
General Immorality (6:9-20)	Immorality is totally at variance with the standards of God's kingdom and rewards (6:9, 10) as well as with the believer's position of justification and cleansing (6:11). Temperance and chastity are mandatory because the body is destined for glorification (6:12-14), is joined to Christ (6:15-17), belongs to God as the temple of the Spirit (6:18, 19), and is the vehicle with which God is to be glorified (6:20).
Misunderstanding of Marriage and Celibacy (7:1-9, 25-29)	Celibacy is good (7:1) if one has a special gift from God (7:7), has self-control to avoid sin, and is not inflamed with passion (7:8). If this is not the case, marriage is advocated, but it is to be strictly monogamous and "in the Lord" (7:7, 39, 40). Married couples are not to deny one another intercourse, except for a time and only by mutual consent for prayer (7:3-5). To marry or to remain single is a matter for individual determination before God (7:25). Marriage entails economic responsibilities and worldly troubles (7:26-31). The unmarried state permits a person to serve God without distraction (7:32-35). But marriage is a necessity for those who cannot control their passions (7:36-38).
Misuse of Divorce (7:10-17)	A Christian wife should not separate from her husband. If she does she must either be reconciled or remain unmarried. The husband should not divorce his wife. But if he must, whether or not he has a right to remarry is *not* specified.

Problem	Inspired Solution
Misuse of Christian Liberty (8:1 – 11:1)	Example: partaking of food offered to idols is in itself harmless, but it becomes a sin if it offends a weaker brother. Hence the practice is to be avoided if it offends (8:1-13). Example: receiving remuneration for Christian ministry is proper and right. Yet Paul would gladly forego this right rather than hinder the effectiveness of his ministry (9:1-14) or be a stumblingblock (9:15-23) or fall in the Christian race (9:24-27). Self-indulgence is to be avoided (10:1-13) as well as all complicity with idol (demon) worship (10:14-22). The law of love is to guide in the exercise of Christian liberty (10:23-33).
Violation of the Order of the Sexes (11:2-16)	The woman is subordinate to the man, denoted by her headdress, as the man in turn is subordinate to Christ (11:2-6). As a token of this a woman should not pray or prophesy with her head unveiled or uncovered. By the same token a man should not pray or prophesy with his head covered or wear long hair like a woman (11:7-16).
Irreverent Participation in the Lord's Supper (11:17-34)	No one is worthy to partake of this ordinance except those who are redeemed. Yet those who are redeemed may partake in an unworthy manner because of unconfessed sin. The penalty is divine chastening of the sinning saint, possibly even to the point of physical death, so that he might not be lost with the world.
Misuse of Spiritual Gifts (12:1 – 14:40)	Spiritual gifts are given and controlled by the Holy Spirit (12:1-7). Nine such gifts were operative in the apostolic Church (12:8-11). The body of Christ is formed by the baptism of the Spirit and is composed of all believers (12:12-31). The gifts as operative in people are listed in 12:28-31. To be of value these must be exercised in love (13:1-8), which, along with faith and hope, will remain throughout the Church age (13:13). However, three gifts were to be in operation only until the New Testament was completed (13:8-13). These include directly inspired prophecies, knowledge, and supernatural languages (13:8). When the New Testament would be completed and God's full revelation available, these sources of truth would no longer be needed. However, their regulation in the early Church, in which they *were* needed, is indicated in Chapter 14.
Denial of Physical Resurrection (15:1-58)	The denial (15:12) does not take into account the fact (15:1-11) or the necessity of bodily resurrection (15:12-19). Christ's resurrection assures physical resurrection for all who are "in Christ" (15:20-23). The "first resurrection" will be in stages (15:23): 1) Christ's resurrection; 2) later those that are Christ's at his coming (1 Thess. 4:13-18); 3) "the end" (15:24), that is, *the end of the first resurrection.* This is coterminous with the second resurrection of the unsaved (Rev. 20:11-15), after the Millennium. It will involve believers who die during the kingdom age. Paul expounds the logic of the resurrection (15:29-34) and the nature of the resurrection body (15:35-50). The hope of the resurrection forms the secret of Christian confidence (15:51-58).

THE DATE OF FIRST CORINTHIANS
AND ITS RELEVANCE TO THE QUESTION
OF SPIRITUAL GIFTS

First Corinthians was apparently written from Ephesus (1 Cor. 16:8, 9) during the latter period of Paul's three-year ministry in that city (Acts 20:31; cf. 19:8-22). The spring of A.D. 54 is the most plausible date, though some scholars would date it as late as A.D. 59. It is important to remember that when First Corinthians was written there was practically no New Testament in existence (except the Book of James, addressed to Hebrew Christians, and First and Second Thessalonians). Even these had very limited circulation.

Only in the light of these facts can Paul's instructions on the permanent versus the impermanent gifts of the Spirit in chapter 13 be understood. Love is permanent and all-essential (13:1-8a) and is contrasted with certain gifts that were impermanent and would eventually be superseded. These temporary gifts included direct inspirational prophecy, direct inspirational knowledge, and supernatural languages. Before the New Testament was written and became readily available by circulation, groups of Christians had only the Old Testament to preach and expound when they gathered together for worship and instruction.

Dependence for New Testament truth therefore had to be placed almost completely on the direct ministry of the Spirit through the inspired prophet, rather than on the expositor of Scripture, as is done today. The inspired teacher endowed with the gift of wisdom and knowledge would receive spontaneous revelations from the Holy Spirit during the course of the church service, and would immediately convey the message to the congregation. Often the directly inspired prophet or teacher would present the message supernaturally in a foreign language, which was afterwards translated into the vernacular by someone endowed with the gift of interpretation.

The Apostle envisioned the time when the New Testament Scriptures would be completed. The partial revelation so essential in his time would give way to "that which is perfect" (literally "the complete and final *thing*" — v. 10), meaning the completed Canon of Scripture, as the context shows. Paul then illustrates the early period of the Church, when it had to depend on partial, spontaneous revelation through special gifts. He employs the figures of a child growing to maturity (v. 11) and an indistinct image in a metal mirror. This was the doctrinal situation before the true mirror of the New Testament became available. "Now I know in part," Paul declares of that early period, "but then I shall know even as I am known" — by the Lord himself as revealed in his Word, the New Testament Scriptures.

2 Corinthians

AUTHOR

The intensely personal and autobiographical nature of this Epistle, as well as its distinctive theology and eschatology, plainly stamp it as genuinely Pauline. External evidence for the existence and early use of the letter (especially second-century evidence) is virtually unchallenged.

BACKGROUND AND DATE

Sometime after Paul had sent his first letter to the Corinthians, news apparently reached him of discord perpetrated at Corinth by the Judaizing party (11:4, 5, 12, 13, 20-23). An immediate visit showed that the reports were true, for Paul had apparently been openly flouted by the Corinthian assembly. Returning to Ephesus, he penned a severe epistle (2:3, 4, 9; 7:8, 12) and sent it to Corinth (probably by Titus — 7: 6-8) with the instruction to return with news from Corinth. This severe epistle has not survived, although some scholars imagine that it is preserved in chapters 10 — 13 of Second Corinthians.

Eventually Paul met Titus in Macedonia (2:12, 13). His news was good. The crisis had passed, and the church had been reconciled to Paul. With deep emotion Paul wrote the letter now known as Second Corinthians. It was penned not long after First Corinthians, possibly as early as autumn, A.D. 54, or conceivably a year or so later. Shortly thereafter Paul traveled to Corinth and spent three months there (Acts 20:1-3), during which time he wrote to the Romans.

IMPORTANCE AND PURPOSE

Paul wrote Second Corinthians for at least the following reasons: 1) to explain how God's comfort sustained him abundantly in his trials in Asia (1:3-11); 2) to explain why he changed his plans to return to Corinth (1:12 − 2:4); 3) to give further instructions about the treatment of the offender of First Corinthians (2 Cor. 2:5-11; 1 Cor. 5:1-8); 4) to express his joy at the good news from the Corinthians (2:12, 13); 5) to demonstrate the superiority of the gospel ministry to the Law ministry (2:14 − 6:10); 6) to issue a call for separation from evil and for reconciliation with him (6:11 − 7:16); 7) to urge the Corinthians to consummate the offering for the poor (chaps. 8, 9); and 8) to establish his authority as an apostle (chaps. 10 − 13).

OUTLINE

A. The Glory of the Christian Ministry (chapters 1 − 7)
  1. Concerned for the salvation and welfare of others (1:1 − 2:4).
  2. Concerned for the restoration of offenders (2:5-11).
  3. Concerned for the well-being of churches (2:11-13).
  4. Glorious in service under the New Covenant (2:14 − 7:16).
    (a) Triumphant (2:14-17).
    (b) Accredited (3:1-5).
    (c) Spiritual and non-legal (3:6-18).
    (d) Honest and dynamic (4:1-18).
    (e) Noble in its ambition (5:1-10).
    (f) Exalted in its motives (5:11-21).
    (g) Supernatural in its results (6:1-10).
    (h) Sublime in its appeal for separation from sin (6:11 − 7:1).
    (i) Zealous in its call for true repentance (7:2-16).
B. The Grace of Christian Giving (chapters 8, 9)
  1. Christians first giving themselves (8:1-6).
  2. Christians following Christ's example (8:7-15).
  3. Christians providing for legitimate needs (8:16-24).
  4. Christians realizing no one can outgive God (9:1-15).
C. Paul's Defense of His Ministry (chapters 10 − 13)
  1. Divinely authenticated (10:1-18).
  2. Characterized by godly jealousy (11:1, 2).

3. Fruitful in its warning against false teachers (11:3-15).
4. Free of empty boasting (11:16-33).
5. Authenticated by visions and revelations (12:1-6).
6. Tested by severe physical sufferings (12:7-10).
7. Possessed apostolic credentials (12:11-18).
8. Faithful in exhortation against evil (12:19 – 13:14).

PAUL'S "THORN IN THE FLESH"

In describing the glory of the Christian ministry and defending his apostolic authority against enemy attack, Paul refers to the visions and revelations which the Lord granted him. He tells how he was caught up to "the third heaven," to paradise, the place of God's abode and manifested glory (12:1-6). Alongside such experiences of God's glory he relates experiences of his testing and chastening, including his "thorn in the flesh." This was some painful affliction in his physical body that had mental, psychological, and emotional repercussions.

The vehicle of suffering is specified only as an "angel" or "messenger" of Satan to buffet him. It was apparently some physical weakness caused by Satanic or demonic power and permitted by God, but not removable by prayer or faith (12:7-10). It had the specific divine purpose of keeping the Apostle humble in the face of all the visions and revelations accorded him. It was also intended to show him that God's grace is completely adequate for his tested servants and that his strength is fully realized only in human weakness. God's servants are therefore to glory in human weakness, so that divine power may rest upon them. They are to remember that when they are weak in themselves they are strong in Christ.

GENERAL CHARACTERISTICS OF THE EPISTLE

Second Corinthians has been aptly described as the Apostle Paul's defense of his life. It contains some teaching, but it is not doctrinal or instructive in the strictest sense of the term. As the most autobiographical of all of Paul's Epistles, Second Corinthians lays bare the heart and soul of one of God's greatest servants. The Apostle here presents the most magnificent portrait of the glory of the Christian ministry to be found anywhere in the Scriptures. The Epistle illustrates the effectiveness of personal integrity and testimony in service for Christ. In alluding to the offering taken for the poor saints of Judea, the Epistle also contains the most extended biblical passage (chaps. 8 and 9) on giving and stewardship.

Galatians

AUTHOR

Both external and internal evidence of the Pauline genuineness of Galatians is abundant from the first century on; by the second century Galatians had become a rather popular Epistle. Irenaeus, Tertullian, and Clement of Rome quote it freely and ascribe it to Paul. It is validated by the Old Syriac, the Old Latin, and the Muratorian Canon.

Internal evidence is also strong. Every sentence of the Epistle clearly reflects the life and character of its author. Twice he calls himself Paul (1:1; 5:2). The historical background of Galatians readily harmonizes with the Acts, and its contents are so presented as to lie far beyond the reach of a forger, even if an adequate purpose could be found for such a forgery. Critical attempts to deny Pauline authorship to Galatians have been dismal failures.

BACKGROUND AND DATE

The Galatians were residents of the Roman province of Galatia. This included not only the territory of Galatia proper, inhabited mainly by Celts from Gaul, but also portions of Lycaonia, Pisidia, and Phrygia, all located toward the south. Paul and Barnabas established churches among these people in the cities of Antioch (of Pisidia), Iconium, Lystra, and Derbe on their first missionary tour (Acts 13, 14). Most scholars hold that these churches were the ones which Paul addressed in Galatians 1:2. Some believe, however, that the Galatian churches were peopled by residents of northern Galatia, the old territorial designation of the Celts' original settlement in the third century

B.C. This included the region in and near the cities of Pessinus, Ancyra, and Tavium (Acts 16:6).

However, Paul's reference to Barnabas (Gal. 2:1, 9, 13) would be unexplainable in a letter sent to northern Galatia. In addition, the Galatians were personal acquaintances among whom Paul had worked (4:13-15). In the south Galatian cities there were Jews who might well have introduced the legalistic error mentioned in the Galatian Epistle (Acts 13:14-51; 14:1; 16:1-3). Moreover, Acts 16:6 gives no hint of a protracted mission in Northern Galatia, as would be required by the Northern Galatian theory. Nor does the view of the Church Fathers lend support to this view. In the second century the Roman province was again restricted to ethnic Galatia, and the double meaning of the term which had been current in the apostolic era disappeared. The Church Fathers simply adopted the designation of their day.

The question of the date and place of writing of this Epistle cannot be answered decisively, and views vary among exponents of the Northern and Southern Galatian theories. The most plausible view is that the Epistle was written about the same time Paul wrote to the Corinthians and the Romans (approximately A.D. 55 or 56) and most likely from Macedonia or Greece on the third missionary tour.

IMPORTANCE AND PURPOSE

The Epistle to the Galatians is the Magna Charta of Christian liberty. Along with the Epistle to the Romans, Galatians became the battle cry of the Protestant Reformation. Martin Luther considered it in a special sense his own Epistle. Under inspiration Paul penned it as a powerful polemic against legalistic teachers who came in to undermine his proclamation of the gospel of the grace of God. These legalists professed to be Christians, acknowledging Jesus as the Messiah. However, they violated the simplicity of the gospel of free grace by insisting that circumcision and obedience to the Mosaic Law must be added to faith in Christ in order to assure salvation (2:16; 3:2, 3; 4:10, 21; 5:2-4; 6:12). Their teaching was a mixture of Judaism and Christianity, based on the false premise that Christianity could operate only within the sphere of the Mosaic Law. Faith in Christ was not sufficient, according to them. Had these legalists gone unchallenged, Christianity would have become a mere sect of Judaism. The challenge called forth a masterpiece of inspired logic and doctrinal truth. With flying colors the Apostle vindicates Christianity on the sole basis of the redemptive work of Christ. Men are both justified and sanctified by what God has done for them in Christ through grace. In no sense is their acceptance in either time or eternity based on works they perform or on rituals they observe. The Book of Galatians echoes the simplicity of justification and sanctification so masterfully expounded in the Epistle to the Romans.

OUTLINE

Introduction (1:1-5)
A. Vindication of Paul's Apostolic Authority (1:6 — 2:21)
    1. The occasion of his vindication (1:6, 7)
    2. The authenticity of his gospel (1:8-10)
    3. The divine origin of his apostleship (1:11-24)
    4. The official endorsement of his apostleship (2:1-10)
    5. The consistency of his conduct (2:11-21)
B. Defense of Paul's Doctrine of Justification (chapters 3, 4)
    1. The defection of the Galatians (3:1-5)
    2. The witness of Abraham (3:6-9)
    3. The redemptive work of Christ (3:10-14)
    4. The Law and the Abrahamic Covenant (3:15-18)
    5. The function of the Law (3:19-22)
    6. The superiority of faith over Law (3:23 — 4:11)
    7. The Apostle's appeal against a return to bondage (4:12-20)
    8. The relation between the Old and New Covenants (4:21-31)
C. Exposition of God's Blessing of Liberty (chapters 5, 6)
    1. Its imperilment by legalism (5:1-12)
    2. Its definition (5:13-15)
    3. Its proper use (5:16-26)
    4. Its practical manifestation (6:1-10)
    5. Its relation to the cross (6:11-16)
    6. Its price (6:17)
    7. Its benediction (6:18)

JUSTIFICATION
AND THE PURPOSE OF THE LAW

Since Paul in Galatians demonstrates that justification is by faith and faith alone (3:1 — 4:31), the question naturally arises, "What then is the purpose of the Mosaic Law?" (3:19a). The Apostle's answer (3:

19b-29) presents the following purposes. The Mosaic law was placed by the side of ("added to") grace (the grace of God shown to men in anticipation of the cross) that had operated from the fall and ever since the fall of man "for the sake of transgressions." It was given to reveal clearly to *all* men through the nation Israel that sin is the transgression of God's moral law as reflected in the Decalogue (Exod. 20:1-17) and that sin involves personal guilt (Rom. 5:13).

Moreover, the Mosaic Law was intended to demonstrate to fallen mankind the incurable sinfulness of the old Adamic nature. The Law not only failed to keep man from sinning but actually provoked him to sin more. This fact was advertised to the fallen race by the priesthood and sacrificial system of the Mosaic system, which pointed to God's forgiving grace to be realized in Christ. Thus the Mosaic Law was to be superimposed only temporarily over the grace which God had permanently covenanted with Abraham and his descendants. The Law was to remain in effect only until "the seed (Christ) should come" (3: 19). In Christ all of God's promises of grace would be fully realized.

The Law of Moses was also added in order to conclude all of mankind under sin (3:22; cf. Rom. 3:19-23). Through the example of the nation Israel it showed sinful men everywhere that salvation by grace through faith is God's only way of saving lost sinners (3:22, 23).

The Mosaic Law as a specific administration of God marked a period of child training for the Jew, and through him presented a lesson to the entire race. The law functioned as a pedagogue, training the Jew with "do's" and "don'ts" appropriate to childhood until he arrived at spiritual adulthood in Christ (3:24, 25). At this point mature and informed love was expected to respond spontaneously to the benefit conferred by grace. In this sense the Law was preparatory to the present age of spiritual adulthood (3:25-29), in which "faith" as the principle of salvation "has come," that is, has been demonstrated by the Law of Moses to be the only way of salvation for guilty sinners in all ages (3:23, 25).

During this present period of spiritual adulthood *all* believers have the mature status of "sons of God" rather than mere "children" (minors) under the Law (3:26). All of them have also been baptized by the Spirit into spiritual union with Christ (3:27) and have thus "put on Christ," thereby laying aside the boyish toga (Mosaic Law observances) for the adult toga (faith in Christ—3:27). Spiritual union with Christ means that all human distinctions are laid aside (3:28) and that the believer inherits through Christ the promises of faith given to Abraham (3:29).

SANCTIFICATION
AND THE PURPOSE OF THE LAW

Since the Apostle demonstrates that sanctification (as well as justification) is by faith and faith alone, the question may be asked, "What relation does sanctification have to the Law?" In dealing with this problem we must remember that the Decalogue given to Israel at Sinai (Exod. 20:1-17) is an expression of the eternal moral law of God, a timeless reflection of God's holy character and attributes. Its particular Mosaic mold and dress (Exod. 20:1-17) was adapted to the nation Israel so that they could be an example of God's dealings in grace with the fallen race as a whole.

The Mosaic Law was given by God to demonstrate to all the world that lost sinners could be neither justified nor sanctified in the sight of God by self-righteousness or law-keeping (5:1-26). Both justification and sanctification are granted to sinners when God imputes the righteousness of Christ to them at the moment of belief. This positional sanctification (in contrast with experiential sanctification) is as changeless and secure as justification, since both rest on God's eternal approval of the person and work of Christ.

In distinction to positional sanctification, which is changeless and secure because it depends entirely on God's faithfulness, *experiential* sanctification (the present-tense aspect of sanctification) is subject to constant change. It depends on the believer's constant exercise of faith in his positional privileges in Christ, as well as on continual reliance on the indwelling Holy Spirit for power to live a holy life. The purpose of the Mosaic Law was to drive men to Christ for both salvation and practical holiness of life.

Thus the Apostle also presents the human responsibility in experiential sanctification. "Walk *by the Spirit*" (5:16, RSV). What this involves is not observing certain ordinances, performing certain good deeds, or "trying harder"; instead, it involves a simple adjustment to the Holy Spirit. Experiential sanctification is produced by the Holy Spirit when we trust God for power to live holy lives (5:16-18). It is accomplished not by "works of the flesh" (5:19-21) but by "the fruit of the Spirit" (5:22-26).

THE BELIEVER
AND HIS RELATION TO THE LAW

But the question remains, "What is the relation of the justified and sanctified believer to the Law of Moses? Does the fact that he could never be saved by the Law mean that the Ten Commandments of the moral law of God no longer have any claim upon him?" By no means. But it does indicate that in their Mosaic mold, as an intrinsic part of the Mosaic Covenant, they do not apply even to saved Jews now, who are "not under the law, but under grace" (2:19; 4:4-7; cf. Rom. 6:14; 7:4). How much less do they apply to saved Gentiles, who were never under the Mosaic Law or Covenant in any sense!

But another problem calls for consideration. Was humanity without God's moral law before the giving of the Mosaic Law to Israel? Was the Gentile world during the legal era without such law? Has the human family since the close of the Mosaic age been without such a legal requirement? Certainly not. (Though the revelation of law was not made as clearly and publicly as it was to Israel.) The fact is that *all* humanity, saved as well as lost, has always been under God's eternal moral law. This will be the basis of God's judgment of the works of the unsaved (eventuating in degrees of punishment in hell—Rev. 20:11-15) as well as the basis of his judgment of the deeds of the saved (eventuating in reward or loss of reward in heaven—2 Cor. 5:10).

Meanwhile, under the New Covenant of grace the Holy Spirit works in the new nature of the believer, making him willing to obey God's will and to comply with his moral law (Heb. 10:16). So far is the life of the dedicated believer removed from the anarchy of self-will that he is described as "inlawed to Christ" (1 Cor. 9:21). The new "law of Christ" (6:2) is now his delight. Moreover, through the indwelling Spirit the righteousness of God's eternal law is fulfilled in him (5:16-18; cf. Rom. 8:2-4). The "commandments" in the distinctively Christian Scriptures refer to those instructions in righteousness which God requires all of his creatures to keep and which his redeemed people are empowered to keep by the Holy Spirit (2 Tim. 3:16, 17; Rom. 13:8-10; 1 Cor. 9:8, 9; Eph. 6:1-3).

FALLING FROM GRACE

Often misunderstood, the phrase "fallen from grace" (Gal. 5:4) means abandoning the true gospel of grace (faith and *faith alone* as the way of salvation) for some admixture of legalism, thereby becoming entangled in the legal yoke of bondage and denying the full efficacy of Christ's atoning work. It involves doing what the Galatians did, namely, being "removed from him that called (them) into the grace of Christ unto another gospel, which is not another; but there are some that trouble you, and would pervert the gospel of Christ" (Gal. 1:6, 7). It has nothing to do with an imagined "losing one's salvation."

CHRISTIAN LIBERTY AND LAW

Christian liberty is an outgrowth of salvation by grace and is realized by the believer in and through Jesus Christ (Gal. 4:3-5). Christian liberty is freedom from the Mosaic Law—not only the yoke of Old Testament ritual ordinances fulfilled in Christ (4:3; Col. 2:20), but the moral law in its Mosaic dress. For example, the fourth Commandment, requiring Sabbath observance, was never imposed upon either the Gentiles or the Church, but only upon the nation Israel. The Decalogue (Exod. 20:1-17) was inseparably bound up with the Mosaic Covenant, and was fulfilled by Christ just as completely as the priesthood and sacrifices of the Mosaic system.

This fact does not imply that Christian liberty means freedom from all moral law, since moral law is a reflection of the eternal character of the Creator. God's law is in the world by virtue of his own personal presence here. Christian liberty is deliverance from the *curse* of both the Mosaic Law and God's eternal moral law. Both condemn every sinner in Adam and confine him to salvation in Christ (3:13).

Christian liberty, far from granting freedom to commit sins, consists of freedom *from* sin and from committing sins (Rom. 6:7, 18). Since he is now "inlawed to Christ" (1 Cor. 9:21 and initiated into "the law of Christ" (Gal. 6:2), the believer as a Spirit-indwelt and Spirit-empowered son (4:1-7) has the inner desire and power to live out the moral law of God. He knows that his response to the eternal moral law of God determines what his works will be. He realizes, too, that he will be judged for his works as a prelude to heaven, even as the unsaved will be judged for theirs as a prelude to hell.

For this reason Christian liberty must never be misused as a cloak for sin. While the believer should guard against any threat to his true liberty under the gospel, he must also constantly keep in mind that his very freedom has brought him into total subjection to Christ, whose bondservant he is and whom he must always obey (Rom. 12:1). This is a paradox. But the Christian discovers that he enjoys his greatest liberty when he is most completely enslaved to the Lord Jesus Christ.

Ephesians

AUTHOR

None of the Pauline Epistles has a stronger chain of evidence authenticating its early and continued use than this Epistle. Clement of Rome, Ignatius, Polycarp, Hermas, Clement of Alexandria, Tertullian, Irenaeus, and others all attest their recognition of the Epistle.

Internal evidence is also strong. The author twice calls himself Paul (1:1; 3:1), and the subject matter and distinctive revelation of Church truths are clearly Pauline. The Epistle is written in Paul's usual epistolary style, including greeting and thanksgiving, doctrinal discussion, practical exhortations, and personal matters. The style and language are clearly Paul's. Nearly every sentence has overtones of what Paul has said elsewhere, especially in Colossians. Scholars have pointed out that of 155 verses in Ephesians, 78 are echoed in Colossians in varying degrees of similarity. The explanation of this similarity undoubtedly lies in the fact that Paul wrote the two Epistles within a short span of time.

BACKGROUND AND DATE

The Epistle was evidently addressed to the church at Ephesus, the most important city in the Roman province of Asia. It was located on the west coast of what is now Asiatic Turkey. The main part of the city, with its theater, baths, libraries, agora, and marble-paved streets, was situated between the mountain ranges of Koressos and the Cayster River, which connected the port with the sea. But the famous Temple of Artemis (Diana), then one of the seven wonders of the

Sheep graze near the tumbled remains of an Ephesian edifice. (*Russ Busby photo*)

world, lay one-and-one-half miles to the northeast, rendering the city a great cult center of the fertility goddess.

Paul founded the church at Ephesus upon returning from his second missionary tour (Acts 18:19-21). Later he spent three years there after returning from his third tour (Acts 19:1–20:1). As one of the Apostle's Prison Epistles, Ephesians was apparently written from Rome in A.D. 61 and sent to proconsular Asia with Tychicus (6:21, 22) along with two other Prison Epistles, Colossians and Philemon (Col. 4:7-9; Philem. 1:10).

Although addressed to "the saints at Ephesus" (1:1), the letter was evidently intended to circulate among the neighboring churches as well. The omission of the phrase "at Ephesus" in three of the oldest and most reliable manuscripts (Vaticanus, Sinaiticus, and Papyrus 46) suggests that early copyists were for some reason reluctant to localize the letter when it was intended for reading in other churches in the vicinity. Evidently the Apostle had in some way indicated this universal intent, possibly by a footnote. The early Church, however, construed from the textual evidence that the Epistle was addressed at least principally to the Ephesians. Hence the Muratorian Canon, Irenaeus, Tertullian, Clement of Alexandria, and Origen speak freely of the letter as the Epistle to the Ephesians.

IMPORTANCE AND PURPOSE

Among the Pauline letters none is more sublime and profound than the Epistle to the Ephesians. It expounds the glory of the Church as the "body of Christ" and unfolds the believer's heavenly blessings in Christ. The expression "the heavenlies," which designates the exalted realm of the believer's position in Christ, occurs five times in the letter (1:3, 20; 2:6; 3:10; 6:12).

The letter represents the high-water mark of Church truth as revealed to the Apostle Paul (see 3:1-10). Hence the term *mystery*, denoting truth unrevealed until the proper time for its revelation in the divine program, is found six times (1:9; 3:3, 4, 9; 5:32; 6:19). The fact of the believer's position in Christ permeates the entire thought of the Epistle, occurring about ninety times; the metaphor of the body, describing the believer's union with Christ, occurs eight times (1:23; 2: 16; 3:6, 15; 4:4, 12, 16; 5:23). The metaphor "walk," denoting conduct within the body, is the heart of the practical appeal of the Epistle and occurs frequently (2:2, 10; 4:1, 17; 5:15).

The union of the believer with the crucified, risen, ascended, and exalted Christ (1:19-23) is the basis of the believer's standing in grace in the body of Christ, the Church (1:3-14). By *standing* is meant the believer's unchanging position before God, the realm in which the Father sees the believer accepted and exalted in Christ. To these believers Ephesians expresses the sentiment of Matthew 3:17: "This is my beloved Son, in whom I am well pleased."

The believer's position (1:3-14) is related to the triune God. Chosen in Christ by the Father (1:3-6), redeemed by the Son (1:7-12), and sealed by the Holy Spirit (1:13, 14), the believer is placed "in the heavenlies" with Christ (1:13). So wonderful is this placement in Christ that the Apostle pauses in his doctrinal exposition to pray that the believers may experience the power of this incomparable position in their daily lives (1:15-23).

In chapter 2 Paul describes the power of God manifested in our salvation (2:1-10) and its miraculous union of Jew and Gentile into one body, the Church (2:11-22). In chapter 3 the Apostle reveals that he himself is the divinely commissioned messenger of this mystery (3:1-13); then he pauses to pray for the experiential realization of these blessings (3:14-21). This ends the doctrinal portion of the Epistle.

In the practical section (chapters 4 — 6) the Apostle exhorts his readers to "walk" (live day by day) worthily of their exalted vocation in union with the exalted Christ (4:1 — 6:9). He realizes that when we understand and depend on our position in Christ we will inevitably precipitate conflict with Satan and his demonic hosts (6:10-20). So he describes the believer's full armor of God. Depending on this armor assures sweeping victory for the believer.

OUTLINE

Salutation (1:1, 2)
A. Union with Christ Expounded (chapters 1 — 3)
    1. It is effected by the triune God (1:3-14).
        (a) Chosen by the Father (1:3-6)
        (b) Redeemed by the Son (1:7-12)
        (c) Sealed by the Spirit (1:13, 14)
    2. It is realized in human experience by prayer (1:15-23).
        (a) By knowing it (1:15-18)
        (b) By believing it (1:19-21)
        (c) By counting upon the exalted Christ (1:22-23)
    3. It is granted to us in salvation (2:1-10).
    4. It is manifested in the union of Jew and Gentile (2:11-18).
    5. It is illustrated by God's living temple (2:19-22).
    6. It is revealed as a mystery through Paul (3:1-12).
    7. It is apprehended by prayer (3:13-21).
B. Union with Christ Experienced (4:1 — 6:20)
    1. By a worthy walk (4:1 — 6:9)
        (a) By a consistent life (4:1-3)
        (b) By striving for unity (4:4-6)
        (c) By the use of the gifts of the risen Christ (4:7-16)
        (d) By a consistent life as a new man in Christ (4:17-29)
        (e) By a walk as a Spirit-indwelt believer (4:30-32)
        (f) By a walk as God's beloved child (5:1-17)

   (g) By being Spirit-filled (5:18-21)
   (h) By proper family relations (5:22 — 6:9)
  2. By a worthy warfare (6:10-20)
   (a) The believer's strength (6:10, 11)
   (b) The believer's foe (6:12)
   (c) The believer's resources (6:13-20)
C. Personal Note and Benediction (6:21-24)

THE PAULINE CONCEPT OF THE CHURCH

In Paul's letters the Church appears in two aspects — the local church (an organized assembly of professing Christians in a particular location) and the universal or true Church (the aggregate of all true believers of this age). The universal Church is that entity referred to in the New Testament Epistles as the *body of Christ*. All believers between Pentecost and Christ's second advent are part of this body.

In Ephesians the Apostle is evidently writing to this universal Church, for he addresses "the saints and faithful in Christ Jesus" everywhere. (The words "at Ephesus" in 1:1 are not found in the oldest manuscripts.) The doctrinal presentation of the mystical Church and the absence of anything about church order confirms the view that the Apostle has in mind the doctrine of the universal Church.

The true Church, as the Apostle presents it in Ephesians, is united with each member and with Christ by the baptism of the Holy Spirit (the "one baptism" — see Eph. 4:4, 5; 1 Cor. 12:12, 13). As the body of Christ, the Church is headed by Christ himself (1:22, 23) and constitutes a holy temple for the "habitation of God through the Spirit" (2:21, 22). It is "one flesh" with Christ (5:30, 31) and is espoused to him as a chaste virgin to one husband (2 Cor. 11:2-4). At Christ's return for the Church its living members will be translated to heaven and its deceased saints will be resurrected with glorified bodies (1 Thess. 4:13-17).

The local church may not be identical with the true Church, for it frequently has unsaved people in its membership. It meets for worship, praise, prayer, fellowship, testimony, the ministry of the Word, discipline, and the furtherance of the gospel to the ends of the earth (Acts 13:1-4; 20:7; 1 Cor. 5:4, 5; Phil. 4:14-18; 1 Thess. 1:8; Heb. 10:25). Every such local church is to be centered in Christ and its regenerated members led by the indwelling Spirit (1 Cor. 3:16, 17). In addition to "saints" (regenerated members), the local church is to include bishops (elders) and deacons (Phil. 1:1; 1 Tim. 3:1-13).

TRUE ECUMENICITY

In an Epistle that expounds the doctrine of the true Church and features the unity of God's people, we could well expect to find specific guidelines for solving the complex problems of unity that have always faced the Church. The Epistle to the Ephesians provides these guidelines, and sheds especially helpful light on the current trend toward religious ecumenicity. In particular, Ephesians presents *right conduct* and *sound doctrine* as the criteria for differentiating between legitimate and illegitimate ecumenicity.

Right conduct is described as behavior worthy of the believer's position in Christ (4:1-3). Basic to the maintenance of working unity within the body of Christ are the virtues of humility, meekness, long-suffering, and forbearing love (4:2). The Holy Spirit alone can produce this real-life unity. Hence it is referred to as the unity of the *Spirit* (4:3). It cannot be successfully imitated by humanly-devised schemes of church amalgamation.

Sound doctrine is basic to the right conduct discussed above (4:4-6). Doctrinal capitulation not only jeopardizes a worthy walk but destroys the foundation of true ecumenicity. Compromise of Christian truth precludes the unity of the Spirit. It substitutes a superficial veneer of man-made harmony in the place of the genuine "bond of peace" (4:3).

The doctrinal essentials that underlie true ecumenicity are clearly specified by the Apostle, and involve the recognition of the following truths: 1) "one body" composed of all who are truly regenerated. Christian unity does *not* embrace unregenerate religionists, no matter what their ecclesiastical or religious pretensions and credentials may be; 2) "one Spirit" — the Holy Spirit of God, who alone inspires and teaches Christian truth (John 16:13). The Holy Spirit must be distinguished from demonic spirits that instigate errors upon which false religions and cults are built (1 Tim. 4:1, 2; 1 John 4:1-6); 3) "one hope of your calling" — the divine calling in Christ "before the foundations of the world" (1:4-6), comprising the saved elect and these alone; 4) "one Lord" — the only Savior, the God-Man, Christ Jesus, the Head of the Body and the center of its unity. Religious teachings that deny or detract from Christ's absolute deity and full saviorhood and recognize other "saviors" and different ways of salvation produce a spurious unity that is artificial and unscriptural; 5) "one faith" in the body of Christian truth "once for all delivered to the saints" (Jude 1:3). This faith centers in the gospel of grace (2:8, 9) and springs out of the death and resurrection of Christ and the great salvation he purchased (2:1-10); 6) "one baptism" — that of the Spirit (1 Cor. 12:13), by which the "one body" is brought into union with Christ, the Head (chaps. 1 — 3; Rom. 6:3, 4); 7) "one God and Father of all (believers), who is above all (created beings), and through all (his own purposes), and in you all (believers)." This is the sevenfold test of Scripture to be applied to all proposals of amalgamation.

THE CHURCH AND SPIRITUAL CONFLICT

The Ephesian letter reveals important information about the Satanic forces leveled against the Church as a whole and against each individual member (6:10-12). Ephesians shows that Satan now attacks Christians in much the same way that he attacked Christ when he was here on earth.

The attacking force is specified as both Satan and his organized army of demon helpers, gradated as "principalities," "powers," "age rulers of this darkness," and "wicked spirits in the heavenlies" (6:12, literal translation). The Christian warrior's resources spring from his position "in the Lord;" he is to "be strong" (literally, "strengthen himself") in the "power" of Christ's "might" (6:10).

The believer's position in Christ constitutes his great resource against the foe; it is described under the figure of a Roman soldier fully equipped for battle (6:13-18). As the believer depends on his secure position in Christ he is pictured as standing against the foe (6:13, 14). As the result of the believer's steadfastness and prevailing prayer the enemy is vanquished and driven from the field (6:18-20). Because the Church is composed of individual members, it enters the spiritual conflict in proportion to their power and victory. Both the individual and group aspects of spiritual conflict and conquest are described in the Ephesian Epistle.

Philippians

AUTHOR

External attestation of the genuineness of Philippians is ample among the Church Fathers. Internal evidence is also strong. Scholars therefore generally recognize its authenticity, though some express doubt as to its unity, alleging that the present letter is a blending of two original letters of Paul addressed to the Philippians. One letter (1: 1—3:1; 4:21-23) is supposed to be addressed to the Church in general and the other (3:2—4:20) to more prominent members of it. It is imagined that the Apostle would not have been able to turn abruptly from the grateful and commendatory tone in 1:1—3:1 to a sharply critical one at 3:2, where he inveighs boldly against the Judaizers (as in Galatians). But the Apostle's abruptly critical tone in the last four chapters of Second Corinthians shows that he was indeed capable of changing his tone suddenly when it was called for.

BACKGROUND AND DATE

The church at Philippi was established by Paul on his second missionary tour (Acts 16:6-40) as the result of a clear divine leading, including a supernatural directing vision (Acts 16:6-11). The church was conceived in joy and born in a prison (Acts 16:25-34). This radiant letter, addressed to this same assembly some years later, was also penned from a prison. At the time of the writing of the Epistle the church was well established, as may be inferred from the address. Included are not only "saints in Christ Jesus" but also "bishops" (elders) and "deacons" (1:1).

The immediate occasion of the Epistle was to acknowledge a donation of money from the church. The gift was brought to the Apostle by Epaphroditus, one of the members of the Philippian assembly (4: 10-18). The whole letter is permeated with a spirit of tenderness; it is addressed to a group of believers who were especially dear to the Apostle's heart, having shared his joyful faith and devotion to Christ (2 Cor. 8:1-6).

Paul wrote this gracious Epistle while in prison (1:12-16). Thus Philippians is grouped with Ephesians, Colossians, and Philemon as a "Prison Epistle." The most widely held view is that all four letters were composed during the imprisonment at Rome (Acts 28:30) during the years A.D. 61-62. The allusions to the praetorian guard (1:13) apparently refer to the Emperor's residence on the Palatine. In Rome detachments of the *praetoriani* had charge of prisoners in imperial custody. The reference to "Caesar's household" (4:22) also seems to support Rome as the place of imprisonment.

However, the Emperor's huge staff of domestic and civil servants was somewhat like present-day civil service, and was not confined to the capital. Detachments of *praetoriani* were also sent to the provinces. Therefore some scholars believe that Caesarea, where Paul was in prison for two years (Acts 24:27), was the place of writing. Others hold that it was Ephesus (1 Cor. 15:32). However, if the Prison Epistles were indeed all written at one location, Rome seems to be the most probable site.

IMPORTANCE AND PURPOSE

The Epistle to the Philippians is one of the most intimate and personal of Paul's letters. It is filled with tender affection and spontaneous joy. Its theme is the joy of knowing Christ, the concept of rejoicing occurring no less than sixteen times in the letter. The church at Philippi in ancient Macedonia was the first assembly established by Paul in Europe. It was in a sense his best-loved congregation, for it entered more sympathetically into his sufferings and needs than any other assembly (4:14-20). The church at Thessalonica was also close to Paul's heart, but the ties that bound him to the Philippians were even closer than those that held him to the Thessalonians. The Apostle highly commends the church and expresses no misgivings about its loyalty to him.

Although Philippians is more of a letter than a treatise, it contains a distinct theological emphasis. Christ's person, work, humiliation, incarnation, death, resurrection, and exaltation are expounded in an instructive context and in closest connection with human experience (2:1, 5; 3:10). The doctrines of salvation (2:8-10), the coming of the Lord (3:20), glorification (3:21), and prayer (4:6) are also found among the practical admonitions.

The overall purpose of the Apostle in writing to the Philippians was to present the joy which Christ gives as our life (chap. 1), our example (chap. 2), our goal (chap. 3) and our sufficiency (chap. 4). Other secondary purposes are made to contribute to this primary one. The Apostle's secondary purposes are as follows: 1) to express appreciation to the Philippians for their fellowship and progress in the faith (1:3-11); 2) to share with them his hopes and fears (1:12-26); 3) to exhort them to unity and consistency of testimony (1:27–2:18); 4) to explain his purpose in sending Timothy and Epaphroditus to them (2: 19-30); 5) to warn them against legalistic teachers (3:1-14); 6) to urge the reconciliation of two women (Euodias and Syntyche) who were at odds (4:2, 3); 7) to exhort them to joyfulness, prayerfulness, and the pursuit of all that is good (4:4-9); 8) to thank them for their recent gift (4:10-20); and 9) to convey greetings (4:21-23).

OUTLINE

A. Joy in Christ Our Life (chapter 1)
   1. Greetings (1:1, 2)
   2. Thanksgiving, fellowship, and confidence (1:3-7)
   3. Triumph over suffering (1:8-18)
   4. Expectation of deliverance (1:19-30)
B. Joy in Christ Our Example (chapter 2)
   1. Christian humility and its example in Christ (2:1-11)
   2. Christian service and its basis in Christ (2:12-16)
   3. Apostolic burdens and sufficiency in Christ (2:17-30)
C. Joy in Christ Our Goal (chapter 3)
   1. True goal versus false goals (3:1-6)
   2. One goal versus other goals (3:7-14)
   3. One goal and Christian maturity (3:15-19)
   4. One goal and the believer's hope (3:20-21)
D. Joy in Christ Our Sufficiency (chapter 4)
   1. Secret of our steadfastness (4:1-5)
   2. Secret of God's peace (4:6-9)
   3. Secret of Paul's testimony (4:10-20)
E. Closing Greeting (4:21-23)

VICTORIOUS CHRISTIAN LIVING

In Philippians 3:1-14 the Apostle expounds the life of victory in Christ. Such an experience not only *can be* but *ought to be* enjoyed by every believer. Paul shows that to be victorious the believer must first recognize Christ as his true goal in life. Christ then grants joyful victory based on what he accomplished at Calvary. The believer must be careful to avoid false, legalistic goals, for these violate God's grace and detract from the all-sufficiency of Christ's atoning work (3:2, 3). The Apostle employs his own example to warn against trusting legal righteousness in order to find acceptance with God (3:4-6). Christ must be the sole object of the believer's faith for righteousness (3:7-9).

The victorious believer must also understand his position of union with Christ (3:10). His clear-cut aim must be to *know* Christ—not just theologically but in day-to-day joyful living. This incomparable knowledge releases "the power of Christ's resurrection" in the believer, enabling him to walk in "newness of life" (Rom. 6:4; Eph. 1:19-23) and thereby to overcome sin, self, the world, the flesh, and the devil. But this experience of spiritual victory is inseparable from "the fellowship of Christ's sufferings" (the cross). For resurrection power in the Christian life springs out of Christ's death, to which the victorious saint must be "made conformable." A literal translation would be "constantly molded into the form of" Christ's death.

The victorious believer must rely on his position of union with Christ (3:10). By doing so he experiences the victory called "the resurrection *(exanastasis)* of the dead" (3:11; cf. Rom. 6:11). In this verse the Apostle is not referring to the resurrection of the believer's body *(anastasis)* but is describing victorious Christian living here and now. The Apostle calls this "an out-resurrection from among the dead" because not all Christians take full advantage of Christ's resurrection power.

The victorious believer must constantly press forward toward Christ, the true goal in life (3:12-14). Day-to-day victory in the Christian life cannot be achieved in one climactic experience of permanent triumph; it requires constant pursuit. To this end the believer has been "laid hold of" by Christ (3:12). The Apostle uses his own life as an example of this (3:13, 14). He pressed on toward Christ, the goal, with the utmost concentration of purpose in order to attain and maintain a life of dynamic victory.

CHRISTIAN PERFECTION

The Apostle connects Christian perfection (3:12, 15) with his teaching on victorious Christian living (3:1-14; see the exposition in the preceding section). "Let us, therefore, as many as be perfect, be thus minded" (3:15). To be "perfect" (Greek *teleios*, "mature") means to be "grown up" both doctrinally and experientially. Those who have this maturity understand the doctrines of holiness and sanctification and, as the consequence of faith in God's truth, live the victorious Christian life. As noted previously, the Apostle calls this a *spiritual* resurrection—the "*out*-resurrection" from among those who are dead to sin by virtue of their position in Christ (3:11).

The word "perfect" as Scripture uses it of unglorified men does not refer to sinless perfection. Old Testament characters described as "perfect" were obviously not sinless (Gen. 6:9; 1 Kings 15:14; 2 Kings 20:3; 1 Chron. 12:38; Job 1:1, 8; Psa. 37:37). The Hebrew and Greek words translated "perfect" usually contain the concept of "completeness in all details" (Hebrew *tamem;* Greek *katartizō*) or "reaching a goal" or "achieving a purpose" (Greek *teleios*).

As with sanctification, three stages of perfection are revealed in Scripture: 1) *positional perfection*. This phase is absolute and unchangeable. It is possessed by every believer by virtue of his eternal union with the infinitely perfect Christ (Matt. 3:17; Col. 2:10; Heb. 10:14); 2) *experiential perfection*. This phase is relative, progressive, and changeable. It depends on the believer's knowledge of his position in Christ and on moment-by-moment faith. This is the aspect of perfection which the Apostle deals with in Philippians 3:1-14 and refers to in 3:12, 15; 3) *ultimate perfection*. This is the final phase of perfection and is equivalent to glorification (Phil. 3:20, 21). Positional perfection guarantees ultimate perfection, since both are grounded on what Christ has done for the believer and not on what the believer may do for Christ. Perfection in all its phases is based on faith rather than works. Experiential perfection produces good works, but strictly as the result of the operation of the Spirit in response to faith (Gal. 5:16-26). Perfection is through the Spirit and not the law; Christian character is produced by the Spirit and not by self-effort (John 15:1-5).

PHILIPPIANS VERSUS
THE ERROR OF ANTINOMIANISM

It is significant that the Apostle, having set forth the sound scriptural view of experiential sanctification (3:1-14), should warn against two common erroneous views of it—unsound legalistic perfectionism (3:15; see above for correct view) and dangerous licentious antinomianism (3:17-21).

This latter perversion of sanctification holds that since Christ's obedience and death satisfied the demands of the Law, the believer is free from obligation to observe it. This error overlooks the fact that *only as a system of curse and penalty* and *only in its Covenant associations* has the Law been abolished by Christ's death. As a transcript of the holiness of God the moral law of God is as eternal as is God himself; its demands as a moral rule for *all* mankind are therefore changeless (Matt. 5:17-19, 48; Rom. 10:4; Gal. 3:13).

The antinomian error also ignores the fact that God has imparted to the believer a totally new nature which possesses Christ's spirit of obedience and holiness (Rom. 8:9, 10, 15; Gal. 5:22-25; 1 John 1:6; 3: 6). By giving us the spirit of obedience and sonship Christ liberates us from the Law as an outward compulsion. At the same time he guards against lawlessness by fulfilling the essence of the Law within us through the power of the Holy Spirit.

The Apostle summarizes the error of the antinomian libertines by branding them "enemies of the cross of Christ" (3:18). They are akin to those who say, "We have fellowship with him" while they actually "walk in darkness" (1 John 1:6), or to those who say, "Let us do evil, that good may come" (Rom. 3:8). These errorists are determined to "continue in sin that grace may abound" (Rom. 6:1). Although they claim to belong to Christ they deny being "dead indeed unto sin" or "alive unto God" in union with Christ (Rom. 6:11). In denying the efficacy of the death of Christ to deliver from the power of sin they become enemies of the cross (3:18).

The lawlessness of the lives of these libertines is evident. Their end is "destruction." They invite premature physical death as the ultimate in severe chastening (1 Cor. 5:5; 11:30-32; 1 John 5:16). The Apostle hints at the extreme carnality and licentiousness of their conduct. Their "god is their appetite." Their "glory is their shame." Their joy is in "earthly things." Their tragic error caused the Apostle bitter weeping (3:18).

Colossians

AUTHOR

The Epistle is satisfactorily attested externally by Justin Martyr, Irenaeus, Clement of Alexandria, Tertullian, Origen, the Old Latin and Syriac Versions, and the Muratorian Fragment. Internal evidence is also satisfactory. Paul alludes to himself as author three times (1:1, 23; 4:18), and the style and theological concepts are characteristically Pauline. The Epistle's close affiliations with the Letter to Philemon, which is generally accepted as genuine, also argue for the authenticity of Colossians (cf. Col. 4:10-14 with Philem. 1:23, 24; Col. 4:17 with Philem. 1:2).

BACKGROUND AND DATE

Colossians, like Romans, was written to a church which Paul had not personally founded and apparently had not visited (1:4, 7, 8; 2:1). Paul evidently bypassed the cities of the Lycus Valley of Asia Minor on both his second and third missionary tours. Yet the Apostle considered Colosse, Laodicea, and Hierapolis as his parish, probably because the churches in these towns were indirectly founded by him as the result of his three-year ministry at Ephesus, when he had a powerful evangelistic outlet to the entire province of proconsular Asia (Acts 19: 10, 26).

It is likely that both Epaphras and Philemon were converted under the Apostle's Ephesian ministry (Philem. 1:19, 23). At any rate Paul dispatched Epaphras to preach to the Colossians (Col. 1:7); he in all likelihood evangelized Laodicea and Hierapolis as well (Col. 4:12, 13).

The population of Colosse in Phrygia was composed of native Phrygians, Greek colonists, and Jews. The latter were descended from Jewish families transported from Mesopotamia and Babylon to the provinces of Phrygia and Lydia by Antiochus the Great (223-187 B.C.). It was this Jewish element that was doubtless responsible for the introduction into the Lycus Valley of the Judaic-Gnostic heresy that was causing confusion at Colosse.

During the more than two years of Paul's absence from the province of Asia some apparently Judaistic Christians had introduced erroneous teaching at Colosse. This heresy had a distinctly Jewish element, an ascetic element, and a Greek philosophic (Gnostic) element. The Jewish element appears in the Apostle's reference to circumcision, ordinances, foods and drinks, festal days, new moons, and sabbaths (Col. 2:11-16). The ascetic element shows itself in Paul's reference to ordinances—"touch not, taste not, handle not" (Col. 2:20-23). The speculative element is seen in the warning against "philosophy and vain deceit" (Col. 2:8). There was a denial of the full deity of Christ (2:9; cf. 1:19) and the error of angel-worship (2:18, 19). In Galatia the error consisted of mixing law and grace. At Colosse it consisted of a Judaic-Gnostic-Christian syncretism.

Apparently Epaphras and his fellow-workers at Colosse were unable to deal with the situation and went to Rome to consult Paul about it (1:7, 8). Perhaps the Colossians had hoped for a visit from Paul (2:1-3). Since the Apostle was a prisoner of Rome and a visit was impossible, he wrote a letter. He sent it by Tychicus and Onesimus (4:7-9), since Epaphras apparently could not return at this time (4:12; cf. Philem. 1:23).

Paul was a prisoner at the time but was free to preach (4:10, 18; Acts 28:30, 31). Demas was still with him (4:14; 2 Tim. 4:10). We may conclude, then, that the time of writing was near the close of Paul's first imprisonment at Rome, about A.D. 61.

IMPORTANCE AND PURPOSE

Colossians is a strong polemic against an error that later developed into the heresy called Gnosticism. This false system that threatened the Colossian church assigned to Christ a position subordinate to the true Godhead and undervalued the uniqueness and complete efficacy of his redemptive work. It taught that between the infinitely holy God and this earth there were a host of angelic intermediaries, of which Christ was one. The error included the worship of angels (2:18) and a legalistic asceticism (2:20-22).

In refuting this incursion of error the Apostle presents a masterly exposition of the person and work of Christ that makes the Epistle of tremendous importance. In setting forth the dignity of Christ as the Head of the Church, Colossians is related to Ephesians, which presents the exaltation of the Church as the body of Christ. The Apostle meets the challenge of false teaching at Colosse by positive presentation of the truth rather than by point-by-point refutation. After expressing his apostolic solicitude and concern for the Colossians (1:1-8), Paul breathes a prayer for their spiritual welfare (1:9-23) in which he presents the nature of redemption (1:13, 14), the glory of Christ's person (1:15-19), the all-sufficiency of Christ's work (1:20-23), and the overall glory of Christ as proclaimed by the Apostle in his ministry (1:24-29). The Apostle proceeds to show that Christ is the answer to doctrinal error (2:1-7), including the peril of philosophy (2:8-13), the peril of legalism (2:14-17), the peril of false mysticism (2:18, 19), and the peril of asceticism (2:20-23).

The Apostle demonstrates that Christ is also the answer to dynamic Christian living (3:1—4:18). Union with him is the basis of a heavenly walk (3:1-4). It enables the believer to pronounce death on a sinful life (3:5-7), to put on the new man (3:8-17), and to conduct a heavenly walk in all relationships of life (3:18—4:6). It is also the basis of Christian fellowship (4:7-18).

OUTLINE

Introduction: Apostolic Solicitude (1:1-12)
A. The Person and Work of Christ (chapter 1)
    1. All-sufficiency of Christ's redemption (1:13, 14)
    2. Supreme glory of Christ's person (1:15-19)
    3. Completeness of Christ's work (1:20-23)
    4. Glory of Christ proclaimed in Paul's ministry (1:24-29)
B. Refutation of Doctrinal Errors (chapter 2)
    1. Conflict of error (2:1-7)
    2. False philosophy (2:8-13)
    3. Legalism (2:14-17)
    4. False mysticism (2:18, 19)
    5. Asceticism (2:20-23)
C. Exposition of Christian Living (chapters 3, 4)
    1. Heavenly walk with Christ (3:1-4)
    2. Conquest of sin through Christ (3:5-7)

3. New life in Christ (3:8-17)
4. Godly behavior from Christ (3:18 — 4:6)
5. Fellowship with believers in Christ (4:7-18).

THE PROBLEM OF RELIGIOUS RELATIVISM

Though Colosse was a comparatively small and insignificant town when Paul wrote to it in the first century A.D., the issues in the church there were vitally important. Moreover, it is becoming increasingly evident that the problem in the Colossian community is peculiarly pertinent to our own day of religious pluralism. The world is rapidly opening up to embrace the so-called Gnostic notion of Christ, namely, that he fits in with all religions and systems. As Ephesians presents the Church as the body of Christ and furnishes the divine criterion for distinguishing true ecumenicity from false, so Colossians furnishes the gauge to test true religion from false.

The Colossian errors are also today's errors. In the face of a Babel of cults on one hand and an infidel "liberalism" within the fold of professing Christianity on the other hand, the crucial question again needs to be answered, "What think ye of Christ? Whose son is he?" (Matt. 22:42).

Paul answers this question by proving the uniqueness of the Christian faith and its inevitable clash with all other systems of religion and human philosophy. This uniqueness is bound up in the *person* of Christ and his redemptive *work*. With Paul, arguments over such questions as Christ's virgin birth, sinless life, vicarious death, bodily resurrection, ascension, glorification in heaven, and second coming have no place. The Christ whom Paul presents is very God of very God (1:15a), the eternal Creator and Sustainer of the universe (1: 15b-17), the God-Man who is Head of the Church (1:18a), the crucified and risen Redeemer, the Firstborn from among the dead (1:18, 19), and the Reconciler of lost and estranged humanity (1:20-23).

The Apostle eliminates all pretenders to Christ and his position of supreme exaltation. He refutes those who would impose upon salvation any requirement except faith in the finished, redemptive work of Christ. He sounds the death knell to all human formulations of doctrine (2:8). He repudiates all those who would in any way depreciate Jesus Christ. He does so by declaring that "the fullness of the Godhead" dwells in him (2:9, 10). He is "the mystery" revealed (1:27; 2:2). In him are "all the treasures of wisdom and knowledge" (2:3). Christian maturity and practical sanctification rest solely on union with Christ (3:1–4:6).

The Epistle to the Colossians furnishes the answer to the religious relativism of today, which would make Christ *a* Savior instead of the *only* Savior and *a* way to God instead of the *only* way to God. The Apostle gives the lie to the popular pluralism of the hour that sends missionaries not to win the heathen to Christ but merely to share mutually the common residuum of truth claimed to underlie all religions, and that does not view the gospel as centering in Christ at all, but in the notion that each man may find God in his own particular religion.

1 Thessalonians

AUTHOR

External evidence for Pauline authorship is adequate from before the time of Clement of Alexandria. Marcion included the Epistle in his Canon, and it is found in the old Syriac and Old Latin Versions. The Muratorian Canon includes First Thessalonians. Irenaeus quotes it by name, and Clement of Alexandria ascribes it to Paul. After this period frequent references to the Epistle occur.

Internal evidence points clearly to Pauline authorship. Twice the writer calls himself Paul (1:1; 2:18). The historical allusions dovetail with Paul's life as set forth in the Book of Acts (cf. 2:2 with Acts 16: 22, 23; 2:17 with Acts 18:5; 3:4 with Acts 17:5). The Epistle itself is a mirror reflecting the life and character of the Apostle. It shows Paul's deep concern for his converts (3:1, 2), his consuming desire for their spiritual welfare (3:8-11), his great tenderness (2:7), his joy at their steadfastness (3:6, 7), and his deep sympathy in their distress (4:13-18).

Ruins of Caesarea, Mediterranean port used by the Apostle Paul *(Russ Busby photo)*

BACKGROUND AND DATE

The general events accompanying the founding of the church at Thessalonica on Paul's second missionary tour are outlined by Luke in Acts 17:1-9. Thessalonica was the capital of the Roman province of Macedonia. It was a free city, governed by its own officials, called "politarchs" (Acts 17:6, 8). The three-week synagogue ministry there (Acts 17:2) was apparently only an initial phase of Paul's work in this important town, for he refers to the believers there as Gentiles (1:9; 2:14; cf. 2:9 and 2 Thess. 3:8 with Acts 17:4). How long Paul stayed on his first visit is conjectural—possibly several months. Implacable hatred and venomous persecution by the local Jews drove the Apostle to Berea (Acts 17:5, 10).

Because he had to leave in such haste, the Apostle was deeply concerned about the welfare of the Thessalonian converts; thus he sent Timothy back to see how they were faring. Timothy brought back good news when he returned to the Apostle at Corinth (cf. Acts 18:5). The Thessalonians were standing true (1:3-10; 2:14; 3:6-9), though they had certain problems. Some of these were ethical, with special reference to sexual matters (4:3-8), but the main difficulty was prophetic. They were concerned about the coming of the Lord for his own (4:13-

18). They were under the misapprehension that those believers of their number who had died would be at a disadvantage as compared with those who were alive when the Lord returned. They also had difficulties regarding the day of the Lord (5:1-11).

To allay their misgivings Paul wrote to the Thessalonians immediately, expressing his joy at Timothy's good news and explaining that his abrupt departure from them was through no choice of his own (as his enemies had alleged). He described the coming of the Lord and explained why the deceased saints would suffer no disadvantage. He also distinguished this prophetic event from the day of the Lord.

It would appear from the Book of Acts that First Thessalonians was written during the latter part of Paul's second visit to Corinth. The year A.D. 50 (or perhaps 51) is the most probable date. Second Thessalonians was written shortly thereafter.

IMPORTANCE AND PURPOSE

First Thessalonians is important because it is not only the earliest of Paul's thirteen letters but, with the possible exception of the Epistle of James, it is probably the earliest writing of the entire New Testament. The Epistle is also significant because of its theme of Christ's return. In fact the second advent is such a prominent theme in both First and Second Thessalonians that together they have been called "the eschatological Epistles of Paul." First Thessalonians is also important because of the clear picture it presents of the Apostle Paul's ministry and of the life of an early Christian church.

OUTLINE

A. The Exemplary Church (chapter 1)
    1. Its faith, hope, and love (1:2-4)
    2. Its faithful discipleship (1:5-7)
    3. Its clean break with idolatry (1:8-10)
B. The Exemplary Pastor (chapter 2)
    1. The apostolic example (2:1-12)
    2. The response of the Thessalonians (2:13-16)
    3. The apostolic concern (2:17-20)
C. The Exemplary Individual (chapter 3)
    1. The apostolic solicitude (3:1-8)
    2. The apostolic intercession (3:9-13)
D. The Exemplary Walk (chapter 4)

1. Demands moral purity (4:1-8)
2. Demonstrates brotherly love (4:9, 10)
3. Displays integrity and honest industry (4:11, 12)
4. Derives dynamic from the Lord's coming (4:13-18)
E. Exemplary Watchfulness (chapter 5)
   1. The day of the Lord and the need for vigilance (5:1-11)
   2. Practical exhortations (5:12-22)
   3. Prayer for experiential sanctification (5:23-24)
   4. Conclusion (5:25-28)

THE LORD'S COMING (4:13-18)

In this passage the Apostle presents the central paragraph in all of Scripture dealing with Christ's coming for his own. Some have termed this important event the "rapture" or "catching away" of the Church. The Apostle discloses with incisive clarity certain revealed truths about this important phase of Christ's second advent.

The rapture is the blessed hope of the believer (4:13; Tit. 2:13).

The believer is exhorted in the light of the rapture not to grieve over the death of loved ones in the same way as do unbelievers, who have no hope beyond the grave. For a believer, death is only "falling asleep" as far as the body is concerned. At the coming of the Lord the body will be resurrected in the sense of being awakened from the sleep of death. This vital truth had been so subject to ignorance and misunderstanding that the Apostle had to declare concerning it, "I would not have you ignorant" (4:13).

The coming of the Lord is only for those who have believed the gospel (4:14).

At the heart of the gospel is the vicarious death and physical resurrection of Jesus Christ (1 Cor. 15:2-4). On this basis (1 Cor. 15:20, 52) God will bring with him through Jesus those who have "fallen asleep in death" (4:14, *Amplified Bible*). When Christ returns, God will bring the soul and spirit of all believers with him to be united with their risen and glorified bodies (4:14). The Christian dead will be united to the living and glorified Christ in glory. They will not miss the coming of the Lord, for God has promised to bring them with Christ when he returns (3:13).

These truths of the Lord's coming constitute a divine revelation from Christ to the Apostle Paul (4:15). It is by the Lord's own authoritative word (John 14:1-4) that Paul declares that those who are alive at Christ's coming will have no advantage over the Christian dead except that they will never have passed through physical death. The Apostle refers to this in First Corinthians: "Take notice! I tell you a mystery — a secret truth, an event decreed by the hidden purpose or counsel of God. We shall not all fall asleep (in death), but we shall all be changed (transformed)" (1 Cor. 15:51, *Amplified Bible*). The saints who are living at the time of the Lord's coming "shall in no way precede (into His presence) or have any advantage at all over those who have previously fallen asleep (in Him in death)" (4:15, *Amplified Bible*).

The coming of the Lord will involve the descent into the upper air of the glorified Lord himself (4:16).

This has been called "a secret coming," but it will be secret only to the unsaved. To those who are "in Christ" it will be exceedingly grand and glorious. The "shout" (the cry of triumph over death — 1 Cor. 15:54-57), the voice of the Archangel (Michael, who apparently figures prominently in the stages of the first resurrection — Dan. 12:1, 2; Jude 1:9), and the trumpet of God (1 Cor. 15:52) are all connected with the first resurrection to life. The unsaved, living or dead, have no part in this. This is emphasized by the Apostle when he declares that the dead *in Christ* will rise at this time. Because believers are united to the risen Lord by the baptism of the Spirit (Rom. 6:4; Col. 3:1-4) they fall asleep "in Jesus" when they die and thus constitute "the dead in Christ."

The coming of the Lord will occasion the resurrection of deceased believers and the simultaneous translation of living saints (4:17).

"Then we, the still living who remain (on the earth), shall simultaneously be caught up along with (the resurrected dead) in the clouds to meet the Lord in the air; and so always — through the eternity of the eternities — we shall be with the Lord!" (4:17, *Amplified Bible*). The expression "caught up" comes from a Greek word (*harpazō*) which literally means "to seize upon, to claim for oneself eagerly, to snatch out or away, to carry off speedily." To accomplish this grand event the living saints will immediately receive a sinless, deathless body like the resurrected one which our Lord now possesses (Rom. 8:23; 1 Cor. 15:50-53; Phil. 3:20, 21). The deceased saints will receive this same kind of glorified body by the act of resurrection — the raising of their mortal bodies from the grave.

The coming of the Lord for his own as revealed here must not be confused with his coming with his own (4:17b).

The rapture described here is the first stage of the Lord's coming. He does not at this time actually come down to the surface of the earth. "Clouds" and "air" imply simply the lower atmosphere *above* the earth. His resurrected and translated saints are snatched up from the earth to meet him *in the air,* after which they receive their rewards. His coming *with* his saints is *after* their rewards have been dispensed; it is then that they come to reign with him as he sets his feet upon the earth and conquers his enemies (Zech. 14:1-4; Rev. 19:11-16).

The coming of the Lord is the basis of solid comfort for the Christian (4:18).

The curtain of the future has been lifted enough to make our hearts leap with joy and hope. The Apostle's exhortation is practical, loving, and nonspeculative. "Therefore comfort and encourage one another with these words" (4:18, *Amplified Bible*).

FIRST THESSALONIANS AND THE DAY OF THE LORD (5:1-11)

Having just described the coming of the Lord for his own, the Apostle distinguishes it from the day of the Lord, which *follows* this event. While the coming of the Lord for his own inaugurates "the day of Christ" in heaven, with rewards for the glorified Church saints (1 Cor. 1:8; 5:5; 2 Cor. 1:14; Phil. 1:6, 10; 2:16), it ushers in "the day of the Lord" on the earth. By contrast, the day of the Lord concerns the earth judgments which take place prior to the establishment of the kingdom over Israel (Acts 1:6, 7; 3:19-21). Church saints will not participate in it because they will previously have been removed from the earth (4:13-18).

The earth judgments of the day of the Lord will eventuate in "the times and seasons" of Israel's restoration. The nation's repentance and conversion will bring "the times of refreshing" from the presence of the Lord and "the . . . times of restitution of all things, which God hath spoken by the mouth of all his holy prophets since the world began" (Acts 3:19-21). Because this was a well-known revelation of the Old Testament (Isa. 2:6-22; 11:1 — 12:6; Jer. 30:5-9; Zech. 14:1-21), the Apostle declares that he had no need to write about it to the Thessalonians (5:1). They knew perfectly well from the Old Testament that that day would come upon the wicked "as a thief in the night" (5:2).

Expecting world peace, the godless of earth will at that time be swiftly engulfed in the cataclysmic judgments described in Revelation chapters 6—19. They are "in darkness," in contrast to believers, who are of the light (5:4-8). Believers will be taken out of the world at the coming of the Lord for his saints (4:13-18); this event marks the beginning of the day of the Lord.

The Apostle emphasizes this truth by declaring that "God hath not appointed us" (believers) "to wrath but to obtain salvation by our Lord Jesus Christ" (5:9). That the "wrath" is God's manifestation of judgment against sinners *on the earth* during the day of the Lord (cf. Rev. 6:17; 14:10; 16:1) rather than eternal condemnation in hell is plain from the context. That the "salvation" is the climax of the coming of the Lord for his own (4:13-18) is demonstrated by 5:10: "Who died for us, so that whether we are still alive or are dead (at Christ's appearing) we might live together with Him and share His life" (*Amplified Bible*). This we believers will do at the Lord's coming for us, either by resurrection (if we have died in Christ) or by translation (if we are still living when he returns).

THE LORD'S COMING AND SANCTIFICATION

The Apostle wrote to the Thessalonians not only to correct erroneous views concerning the Lord's coming but to exhort them to moral purity (4:3-8) and holiness of life (4:9-12) in the light of the sanctifying effect of this "blessed hope" (1:9, 10; 2:12, 19; 3:13; 4:1-12, 5:4-11, 23, 24). Paul is in full accord with the Apostle John in emphasizing the fact that "everyone who has this hope in him *purifies himself, even as he is pure*" (1 John 3:3). The Apostle Paul, however, points out that "purifying oneself" is the result not of self-effort or legalistic fleshly striving but of adjustment to the Holy Spirit, so that God actually does the sanctifying rather than the believer.

Sanctification is the work of God and not an attainment of man; it is by faith and not by works (5:23a). "The very God of peace" (literally "the God of peace *himself*") "sanctify you wholly." Paul is viewing sanctification as a whole in all three tenses — past, present, and future. Not only is the sanctifying operation emphatically *all* of God in *all* its aspects ("God himself" is intensive), but it is also the gateway to a deeper peace: "The God *of peace himself* sanctify you wholly."

Sanctification comprehends the entire man (5:23b). It involves man's spirit, that higher part of man by which the regenerated man knows God (1 Cor. 2:11). It also comprehends man's soul (the seat of his intellect, affections, and will), which becomes consecrated to God in salvation and used by him in dedication. Sanctification also extends to the body, which as God's holy temple is indwelt by the Spirit. The body is to be presented to God (Rom. 12:1) in order to glorify him (1 Cor. 6:19, 20).

Sanctification is God's provision to keep us blameless in our life in this world (5:23c). The entire man may be preserved blameless until death or translation at the Lord's coming for his own (3:13; 4:16, 17; 5:10). "Blameless" means "free of specific moral or spiritual fault."

Sanctification has its incentive in God's faithfulness (5:24). God's character guarantees sanctification: "Faithful is he." God's call assures sanctification: "Faithful is he who calls you" (cf. Rom. 8:30). God's power effects sanctification: "who also will do it." Those who seek the power for holy living in themselves and their own faithfulness are doomed to failure and disappointment. For victorious living, occupation with self must give way to occupation with Christ; self-effort must yield to faith in God's provision in Christ and human strength must be displaced by divine power. Then a holy life will be the spontaneous result.

2 Thessalonians

AUTHOR

The external evidence for the early use and Pauline authenticity of Second Thessalonians is even earlier and more extensive than for that of First Thessalonians. Justin Martyr, Irenaeus, Tertullian, Clement of Alexandria, the Muratorian Canon, the Old Syriac, the Old Latin, and Marcion's Canon evidence its authenticity. The internal evidence reinforces the external evidence. Twice the writer names himself as Paul (1:1; 3:17). The vocabulary, style, and theological and eschatological concepts are all Pauline. Attempts by critics to establish Second Thessalonians as a forgery have been dismal failures.

BACKGROUND AND DATE

Apparently neither Paul nor any of his associates had returned to Thessalonica since the sending of the First Epistle. But the new teaching concerning the day of the Lord had caused great confusion. Whether it arose from a forged letter purporting to come from Paul, an alleged revelation from the Spirit, or a miscomprehension of Paul's First Epistle is not certain. In any case news of increased persecution against the Church, misunderstanding of Paul's teaching regarding the return of the Lord, and the idleness and dreamy expectation of some of the Thessalonians (3:6-12) prompted this letter to them.

The interval between the writing of the two Epistles was scarcely more than six months—a year at the very most. The condition of the Thessalonian church as described in both Epistles is practically identical. The same excitement prevailed concerning the coming of the Lord; Silas and Timothy were still with the Apostle (2 Thess. 1:1); the same group in the church continued in fanatical neglect of their everyday work (cf. 2 Thess. 3:6-14 with 1 Thess. 2:9; 4:10-12). It is very likely, therefore, that Paul wrote Second Thessalonians while still in Corinth, not more than a year later than First Thessalonians. This would place the date at late A.D. 50 or early A.D. 51.

IMPORTANCE AND PURPOSE

Second Thessalonians has much in common with First Thessalonians. Both are prophetic and deal with the coming of the Lord for his own and the day of the Lord following it. However, the Second Epistle was written to correct apparent misunderstanding of certain prophetic themes in the First Epistle. The Thessalonian believers had somehow gotten the erroneous notion that the trials they were going through were those of "the day of the Lord" (2 Thess. 2:1, 2). The Apostle had told them in First Thessalonians that they were to wait for the coming of the Lord for his own, and that as believers they were to be "delivered from the wrath" to be manifested in the day of the Lord (1 Thess. 1:10). He had also instructed them that as "sons of light" believers were not to experience "the wrath" of the day of the Lord; this was reserved for the unsaved, who were in darkness (5:1-8). Instead, God's people were to be taken out of the world by rapture (5:9, 10) before the events of that time of judgment would take place on the earth.

To clarify the wrong ideas which the Thessalonians had gotten about the coming of the Lord, whether from misunderstanding his first letter, from false teaching, from a forged letter (2:2), or from forgetting what he had taught them while he had been with them (2:5), the Apostle in his second letter to them clearly presents the removal of the Church *before* the day of the Lord. In addition he describes the events of the day of the Lord, the Man of Lawlessness, the latter-day demonic delusion (2:1-12), and the coming of the Lord in glory (1:5-10).

The Apostle also continues the theme of sanctification and holy living which he began in the first Epistle (2:13-15). Particularly singled out are the idle and disorderly (cf. 1 Thess. 4:11, 12); these are exhorted to work while awaiting the Lord's return (3:6-15).

OUTLINE

Salutation (1:1-4)
A. The Lord's Coming and Comfort (1:5-12)
    1. The reasons for their sufferings (1:5, 6)
    2. The basis for their comfort (1:7-10)
    3. The prayer for their blessing (1:11, 12)
B. The Lord's Coming and the Day of the Lord (2:1-12)
    1. The rapture and the day of the Lord (2:1-5)
    2. The rapture and the Holy Spirit (2:6, 7)
    3. The rapture and the man of sin (2:8, 9)
    4. The rapture and demonic deception (2:10-12)
C. The Lord's Coming and Christian Living (2:13 – 3:15)
    1. Believers are chosen to salvation and sanctification (2:13-17)
    2. Believers are chosen for a prayer ministry (3:1-5)
    3. Believers are to practice disciplinary separation (3:6)
    4. Believers are to be exemplary in life (3:7-9)
    5. Believers are to seek to cure disorders (3:10-15)
D. Conclusion (3:16-18)

THE TIME OF THE RAPTURE

Three present-day schools of interpretation exist. *Pretribulationism* holds that the removal of the Church will occur *before* the great tribulation. *Midtribulationism* maintains that this removal will take place *in the middle of* the great tribulation. *Posttribulationism* equates the rapture with Christ's second advent in glory and holds that it occurs *at the end of* the great tribulation.

Posttribulationism cannot be squared with the Apostle's teaching in Second Thessalonians, for the whole point of Paul's correction of the Thessalonian misconception is that the coming of the Lord for his own occurs *before* the day of the Lord (2 Thess. 2:1-5). Paul buttresses this teaching by revealing that the day of the Lord is *followed* by Christ's coming with his own in power and glory (2 Thess. 2:8).

Midtribulationism, while differentiating the rapture from the coming of Christ in glory, cannot be reconciled with Paul's clear revelation that the rapture occurs *before* the day of the Lord. The events of the first half of Daniel's seventieth week are part of the day of the Lord and are open and public, so that the truth of the imminency of the rapture as taught in the New Testament would be nullified by midtribulationism.

Paul is evidently arguing for a pretribulation rapture in Second Thessalonians 2:1-5. The Apostle describes the first phase of Christ's coming as the personal appearance of Christ in the clouds coupled with our gathering together to him (2:1; 1 Thess. 4:13-18). The apostasy occurs *before* the apocalyptic judgments of the day of the Lord burst upon a Christ-rejecting world (2:3). Then the Man of Lawlessness, the Antichrist of the end-time, is to be revealed (Dan. 11:36; Zech. 11:15-17; Rev. 13:1-10; 19:20; 20:10). He will arrogate to himself divine honors and deceive the nation Israel (2:4; Dan. 9:27).

THE RAPTURE OF THE CHURCH AND THE DEPARTURE OF THE SPIRIT

At Pentecost the Holy Spirit came and took up residence in the newly formed Church (John 16:7, 8, 13; Acts 2:4; 1 Cor. 6:19; Eph. 2:22). In the same sense in which he came when the Church began, he will leave when the Church is completed and raptured to heaven. This means that the Spirit will resume his pre-Pentecostal presence, as in Old Testament times. This important truth is revealed by the Apostle. He who has been indwelling the Church (John 14:16; 1 Cor. 6:19; Eph. 2:22) and has been restraining evil will continue to do so until "he is taken out of the way" (literally "comes out of the midst"). This takes place when the Church, indwelt by the Spirit, is glorified and caught up to meet Christ in the air (1 Thess. 4:13-17). Only when the divine Restrainer departs with the glorified Church can and will "the apostasy" take place (2:3) and "the lawless one" and "the mystery of iniquity" be revealed. Paul reveals clearly that the Church will be caught up before the day of the Lord and the unbridled demonism and deception of that time (2:8-12).

THE TWO PHASES OF CHRIST'S SECOND ADVENT

Not only does the Apostle in the Thessalonian letters differentiate between the two aspects of Christ's advent, but the rest of the New Testament likewise does so (John 14:1-3; Tit. 2:13; 1 John 3:1-3). The first or "rapture" phase is most fully expounded in First Thessalonians (see especially 4:13-18). This is Christ's coming *for* his saints. The second phase of Christ's advent is *with* his saints to judge the ungodly and destroy the Man of Lawlessness. This aspect is touched upon in First Thessalonians 3:13 and 5:1-6 and in Second Thessalonians 1:7-10 and 2:1-12. The latter aspect, with its accompanying judgments, climaxes the Old Testament day of the Lord (cf. Isa. 2:6-22).

Apparently because of the severity of their persecutions (1:4-7), the Thessalonians had begun to wonder whether they had failed to qualify for the rapture and whether the day of the Lord had already come (2:2). It is because of this uncertainty that Paul urged the Thessalonians to remain steadfast in their belief in the pre-tribulation rapture. The following chart will illustrate the New Testament teaching on the second advent.

THE TWO PHASES OF CHRIST'S SECOND ADVENT	
Phase 1 — the Rapture	*Phase 2 — the Revelation*
Christ's coming *for* his Church (1 Thess. 4:13-18). He comes to resurrect and translate his saints (4:16, 17).	Christ's advent *with* his Church (Rev. 19:11-16). He comes to slay his foes and set up his earthly kingdom (Acts 1:6).
Christ does not actually come to the earth but instead meets his glorified saints in the air (1 Thess. 4:17). This coming is hidden from the unsaved.	Christ's feet stand on Olivet (Zech. 14:4). He comes as a glorious Conqueror and King (Rev. 19:16). This coming is public to every eye (Rev. 1:7).
This coming is imminent, expected and awaited by the Church (1 Thess. 1:10; Tit. 2:13). No prophetic event will intervene. Occurs *before* the day of the Lord (2 Thess. 2:1-5).	This advent is not imminent but is preceded by definite signs (Matt. 24:29-31), although it will come upon sinners like a thief. Occurs following the day of the Lord (2 Thess. 2:8).
Not revealed in the Old Testament because the Church was not made known there except in types, which were unrevealed until the antitype appeared (Eph. 3:1-10).	Emblazoned on the pages of the Old Testament as a part of the day of the Lord and the prediction of the Davidic millennial kingdom (Dan. 7:9-12; Zech. 14:3-7; Mal. 3:1-6).
Precedes the revelation of the Antichrist (2 Thess. 2:3) and the final great apostasy (2:2). Precedes the consummation of "the mystery of iniquity" and worldwide rebellion (2:7).	Follows the career of Antichrist and is the means of his destruction (2 Thess. 2:8-10; Rev. 19:20; 20:10). Crushes the final apostasy and rebellion.

The Pastoral Epistles

First and Second Timothy and Titus are commonly called "Pastoral Epistles." This eighteenth-century designation, though practical, is not entirely accurate. The letters furnish invaluable instructions for pastors and important directions for the conduct and administration of local churches, but Timothy and Titus were not pastors in the usual present-day sense of that term. They were rather the Apostle's special envoys dispatched to act in a pastoral capacity in order to meet a specific need or to carry out a special assignment.

Modern criticism has shown a marked tendency to deny Pauline authorship to the Pastoral Epistles, despite clear statements of Pauline authorship in the three letters (1 Tim. 1:1; 2 Tim. 1:1; Tit. 1:1) and other objective internal evidence. Arguments against Paul's authorship are largely inferential, with objective proof lacking. The arguments, involving alleged variations in style and vocabulary between the Pastorals and the other Pauline letters, are tenuous and inconclusive. The claim that the theology is different and that grace is no longer central is unsupportable (cf. 1 Tim. 1:14; 2 Tim. 1:9; Tit. 3:4-6). It is true that good works as the *fruit* of faith are featured in the Pastorals, since the *nature* of faith and its *precedence* over works of Law had been thoroughly expounded in preceding letters.

The contention that the errors exposed in the Pastorals belong to the second century and that these letters could therefore not have been authored by Paul is far-fetched. It is claimed that the Pastorals controvert second-century Marcionism (e.g., 1 Tim. 6:20), a heresy with erroneous views of Christ's person. But this and other supposed allusions to second-century "isms" have no objective foundation, since the errors are essentially the same as in certain other Pauline Epistles. The allegation that the church organization in the Pastorals is too advanced for the first century is purely imaginary. The chronological argument—that no place for the Pastorals occurs in the Acts or in the life of Paul, and that they are therefore not genuine—is an argument drawn largely from silence and is thus inconclusive.

The Book of Acts points toward Paul's release rather than his execution (Acts 23:12-35; 28:21, 30, 31), as do Paul's Prison Epistles (Phil. 1:25-27; 2:24; Philem. 1:22). Clement of Rome and Eusebius bear witness to two Roman imprisonments, with ample room for the writing of the Pastoral Epistles in the interval between the two.

As to internal evidence, the epistolary form of the Pastorals and the Apostle's descriptions of himself are similar to the other Pauline letters. All of the objective evidence favors Pauline authorship.

1 Timothy

AUTHOR

See the preceding comments under "The Pastoral Epistles."

BACKGROUND AND DATE

Released from his first Roman imprisonment and apparently on his way to Asia Minor, Paul left Titus on the island of Crete to complete the organization of its churches (Tit. 1:5). At Ephesus the Apostle was joined by Timothy, who had evidently returned from Philippi (Phil. 2:19-23). Paul left for Macedonia, instructing Timothy to stay on at Ephesus in order to meet a great need there (1 Tim. 1:3, 4). From Macedonia Paul wrote his First Letter to Timothy in Ephesus and a letter to Titus in Crete. The most likely date for these would be A.D. 64-66.

IMPORTANCE AND PURPOSE

The central theme of the Epistle is stated in 3:15: "That thou mayest know how thou oughtest to conduct thyself in the house of God, which is the Church of the living God, the pillar and ground of the truth." Hence the letter concerns itself with church organization, the qualification and duties of various church officers, and the general conduct and responsibility of church members. Local churches were rapidly increasing in number during the close of the apostolic era, and these assemblies needed clear teaching about such matters as order, creed, and discipline. The Pastorals supply this important need.

Paul had four main goals in addressing this Epistle to Timothy: 1) to encourage him to expose false teaching (1:3-7, 18-20; 6:3-5, 20, 21); 2) to furnish the young pastor with written credentials authorized by Paul himself (1:3, 4); 3) to instruct Timothy in the organization and management of the local church (3:14, 15); and 4) to exhort him to pastoral diligence and fidelity (4:6—6:2).

OUTLINE

Salutation (1:1, 2)
A. Importance of Sound Doctrine (chapter 1)
  1. The pastor and unsound teachers (1:1-7)
  2. The Law and the gospel of Christ (1:8-11)
  3. The gospel and evangelism of sinners (1:12-17)
  4. The admonition to faithful pastoral work (1:18-20)
B. The Importance of Prayer and Public Worship (chapter 2)
  1. The Church and public prayer (2:1-8)
  2. The order of women in Christian society (2:9-15)
C. The Importance of Church Government (chapter 3)
  1. The qualifications of elders (3:1-7)
  2. The qualifications of deacons (3:8-13)
  3. The Church and revealed truth (3:14-16)
D. The Importance of a Faithful Pastor (chapters 4—6)
  1. The faithful pastor and error (4:1-6)
  2. The faithful pastor and self-discipline (4:7-16)
  3. The faithful pastor and various Christians (5:1-22)
  4. The faithful pastor and apostolic advice (5:23-25)
  5. The faithful pastor and social classes (6:1-5)
  6. The faithful pastor and materialistic gain (6:6-10)
  7. The faithful pastor as a man of God (6:11-16)
  8. The faithful pastor and wealthy believers (6:17-19)
  9. The faithful pastor and an appeal to watchfulness (6:20, 21)

THE RELATION OF THE LAW
TO THE GOSPEL

The Apostle deals briefly but incisively with this momentous question as he faced the errors of the legalists at Ephesus (1:8-11). In

Galatians Paul had dealt with the justification and sanctification of the believer in relation to the Law. Now in First Timothy he relates the Law to the gospel of grace. He first declares that *the Law itself is good* (1:8a; cf. Rom. 7:12): "We know the law is good." It is good because it reflects the holiness of God. However, *the Law must be used lawfully*, that is, for the purpose for which it was designed (1:8b). The Apostle declares that it was never intended to make bad people good, but rather to convict bad people of their sinfulness and to drive them to Christ to be saved (Rom. 3:21-28; Eph. 2:8-10). Therefore, the Law is not to be misused in the case of the "righteous (justified) man" as a means of either justifying or sanctifying him. The Law was *intended for the sinner, to reveal to him his sin and its penalty apart from Christ* (1:9, 10).

The Law must be used properly, *in accord with the gospel of grace* (1:11). Although the Law can neither justify, sanctify, nor glorify the believer, the gospel of Christ accomplishes and guarantees all of these things. It is therefore fitly called "the gospel of the glory of the blessed God." Because every believer has been given a new nature at the moment of conversion and is securely indwelt by the Holy Spirit, he manifests the ethics of God's eternal moral law in his upright way of life (2 Cor. 3:11; Rom. 8:1-15). This holy life is not the result of the works of the flesh or of legalistic strivings, but is "the fruit of the Spirit" (Gal. 5:22, 23).

THE ORDER OF WOMEN
IN CHRISTIAN SOCIETY

The Apostle treats this important aspect of Christian living and public worship in First Timothy 2:9-15. The Christian woman's demeanor and dress are to be consonant with her position in Christ and are never to violate Christian propriety (2:9, 10). In her relation to her husband she is to be characterized by a spirit of teachableness and quiet submission (2:11). In the first Corinthian letter Paul had dealt with the order of the sexes (1 Cor. 11:1-16). There he pointed out that the woman is subordinate to the man (denoted by her headdress), even as the man is subordinate to Christ. As a token of this a woman should not pray or prophesy with her head unveiled or uncovered.

In prescribing proper conduct in the Church and in Christian circles, the Apostle resumes the subject of the order of the sexes in his instructions to Timothy. He indicates that any lack of teachableness or quiet submission on the part of a Christian wife toward her husband is highly improper, particularly in a woman professing godliness. The

Apostle hints at the confusion which results when women forget their proper place in public worship and teach men or usurp authority over them (2:12). Women have a wide sphere of teaching, but not where men are directly involved. New cults have been started or abetted by women who refused to abide by God's Word on this point.

The Apostle establishes the doctrinal basis for the Christian ideal of subjection in First Timothy 2:13-15 (compare Genesis 3:16); it is a strikingly relevant issue in our own day, when the "liberation" of women is a militant cause and when the need for Christian balance is especially needed. Paul points out that Adam was created as the federal head of the race before Eve was formed (Gen. 2:7, 18; Rom. 5:12). Eve was formed from Adam and not Adam from Eve (Gen. 2:18-22). The woman rather than the man was deceived (Gen. 3:1-6) and is still particularly vulnerable to doctrinal deception. The woman will be "saved," that is, rescued or preserved from insubordination, deception, doctrinal error, and other evils or improprieties that threaten her, by the queenly grace of motherhood.

A Christian mother who possesses the essential qualities of "faith and love and holiness with sobriety" (3:15) can make a priceless contribution to the work of Christ and the upbuilding of the Church. The marriage that is strengthened by these hallowed virtues results in God-fearing youth who further the health and growth of the Church and the well-being of society.

THE DIVINE CRITERION TO DIFFERENTIATE FALSE RELIGIONS FROM TRUE

After relating the local church to revealed truth (1 Tim. 3:14-16) and tracing the origin of error, cultism, and false religion to demonism (4:1-6), the Apostle pauses to set forth the doctrinal norm or standard by which the countless varieties of religious teaching can be tested. This doctrinal touchstone is found in First Timothy 3:16: ". . . Great is the mystery of godliness: God was manifest in the flesh, justified in the Spirit, seen of angels, preached unto the Gentiles, believed on in the world, received up into glory." By this doctrinal formula all the cults of Christianity, as well as Judaism and all the non-Christian faiths of the world, can be evaluated and their truth or falsity determined.

This criterion of truth summarizes the essential verities of the Christian faith. It shows how lost and ungodly sinners can be restored to "godliness" (God-likeness) by being accepted before an infinitely holy God on the basis of the finished work of Christ. It contains the following elements: 1) the incarnation. "He who (God, the eternal Word) was manifest in the flesh" (cf. John 1:1, 14); 2) Christ's death and resurrection. He was "justified in the Spirit," that is, he was personally vindicated by the Holy Spirit by the act of physical resurrection; 3) Christ's divine person and complete redemptive work as attested by the unfallen angels. He was "seen by angels"; 4) the evidence of Christ's saving power. He was "believed on in the world"; 5) the divine validation of Christ's redemptive work. He was "received up into glory."

How good of God not to abandon us to our own fallible judgment in a realm so baffling as the religious! In a day of apostasy and false ecumenism how grateful we ought to be for the divinely revealed standard by which all doctrinal error can be exposed!

THE SOURCE OF DOCTRINAL ERROR AND FALSE RELIGIONS

Having presented the criterion of truth (3:16), the Apostle proceeds to reveal the origin of error. He shows that heresies spring from *doctrines of demons* (4:1, 2). This disclosure is of the utmost importance to the Church in her function as the "pillar and ground" of the truth (3:14, 15). The Holy Spirit declares that error is instigated not primarily by false teachers but by evil spirits or demons who inspire susceptible human beings. The result is called "doctrines of demons" (4:1).

As an illustration that false doctrine is demon-originated the Apostle chooses a type of legalistic asceticism current at the time (4:3, 4). It forbade marriage and thereby incriminated God by implying that this God-ordained institution was evil. It likewise disallowed certain foods created by God to be received with thanksgiving and prayer. The demonic impress in this error, illustrative of many that Satan tries to introduce, is apparent. It displays Satan's pride (Isa. 14:12-14), his slander of God's goodness (Gen. 3:5), and his treacherous falsehood (Gen. 3:4).

2 Timothy

AUTHOR

Refer to the comments under "The Pastoral Epistles."

BACKGROUND AND DATE

Paul was a prisoner in Rome (1:8, 16, 17; 2:9), with martyrdom facing him (4:6-8). Severely tested by loneliness (4:10, 11), he wrote to Timothy, who was presumably at Ephesus (since Priscilla and Aquila—4:19; cf. 1 Tim. 1:3—as well as Onesiphorus—1:16-18; 4:19—were apparently residing there).

After Paul had written First Timothy and Titus (evidently from Macedonia), he proceeded to Nicopolis, where he intended to spend the winter (Tit. 3:12). Nicopolis was the capital of Epirus; it lay north of Achaia on the west coast of Greece. Nicopolis was a Roman colony, like Philippi, and Paul may have planned to use it as a base for evangelizing Epirus. Although there were other towns named Nicopolis ("city of victory"), this was the only one of sufficient standing to warrant Paul's residence through an entire winter. In addition, its geographical location northwest of Crete would favor a meeting with Titus.

At Nicopolis Paul was apparently arrested and taken to Rome (1:16, 17). There in prison he wrote Second Timothy. Soon afterward, according to tradition, the noble Apostle died a martyr's death on the Ostian way, west of the capital. Paul seems to have been executed shortly before Nero's death on June 8, A.D. 68. Second Timothy was clearly written shortly before Paul's martyrdom. The Epistle may therefore be dated in the autumn of 67 or the spring of 68.

IMPORTANCE AND PURPOSE

Paul's Second Letter to Timothy is undoubtedly the Apostle's last in a total of thirteen that have come down to us. In this noble Epistle he displays the fortitude and resiliency of character that mark a great warrior and missionary of Christ. Although the Apostle was now a prisoner without human hope, he was courageously resigned to an inevitable death sentence. Paul's faith, subject to the utmost test, proved to be completely adequate. His message is a farewell from a man of indomitable spirit. In the Epistle he urges others to "endure hardship, as a good soldier of Jesus Christ" (2:3). Meanwhile he himself became the great exponent of what he challenged others to be. His triumphant spirit in the face of martyrdom has moved countless souls to take up their cross and follow Christ bravely and dauntlessly to the end.

But despite his approaching death, Paul did not ignore the specific needs of his younger co-worker. In writing this Epistle Paul charted the course of the faithful pastor in a day of doctrinal declension (chap. 1) and warned about the spiritual conflict which a good soldier of Jesus Christ must engage in if he would remain true to his call (chap. 2). He described the apostasy (3:1-5) and outlined its dire results (3:6-9) in persecution and suffering (3:10-13), together with the all-important role which the inspired and fully authoritative Word plays in the battle (3:14-17). The remedy for apostasy is the preaching of the inspired Word (4:1-4); this will be accompanied by rewards for the faithful preacher (4:5-8). Advice and instructions are given concerning fellow workers (4:9-13), as well as a warning concerning evil workers (4:14, 15). The faithful pastor must not lose heart at man's failure (4:16). He must rely instead on God's faithfulness (4:17, 18).

OUTLINE

Introduction (1:1, 2)
A. Pastoral Fidelity in Apostasy (chapter 1)
  1. Commendation of Timothy's faith (1:3-5)
  2. Encouragement to continued faithfulness (1:6-14)
  3. Warning against disloyalty (1:15)
  4. Reassurance in fidelity (1:16-18)
B. Spiritual Conflict in Apostasy (chapter 2)
  1. Standing true to grace (2:1, 2)
  2. Striving for mastery (2:3-10)
  3. Relying on God's faithfulness (2:11-19)

4. Separating from sin (2:20-22)
5. Avoiding foolish strife (2:23, 24)
6. Cultivating positive virtues (2:25, 26)
C. Defense of the Word in Apostasy (chapter 3)
    1. Prediction of apostasy (3:1-9)
    2. Apostolic warning (3:10-13)
    3. Believer's resource (3:14-17)
D. Faithfulness of God in a Day of Apostasy (chapter 4)
    1. He is Judge—therefore preach the Word (4:1-5)
    2. He will reward fidelity—therefore trust him (4:6-8)
    3. He never fails—therefore put confidence in him (4:9-18)
Conclusion (4:19-22)

THE CHRISTIAN'S RESOURCES IN TIMES OF APOSTASY

The Apostle indicates these resources as 1) faith (1:5); 2) the Holy Spirit (1:14); 3) the Word of God (3:14-17); 4) the grace of Christ (2:1); 5) the Lord's faithfulness and power (2:13, 19; 4:17, 18); 6) separation from heretics and apostates (2:20, 21); and 7) the Lord's sure reward (4:7, 8).

APOSTASY AND CHRISTIAN PROFESSION

The term "apostasy" comes from the Greek word *apostasia*, "a falling away," which in turn comes from *aphistasthai*, "to stand away from." It denotes a professed Christian who deliberately rejects the central facts of Christianity and turns away from Jesus Christ and his atoning sacrifice (1 John 4:1-3; 2 Pet. 2:1). Apostasy, unlike error or heresy, is never associated with regeneration and true saving faith. Error may be caused by simple ignorance (Acts 19:1, 2), and heresy may be traced to demonic delusion and Satanic deception (1 Tim. 4:1, 2; 2 Tim. 2:25, 26). Either of these may at times be true of regenerated believers. Apostates, however, deliberately depart from the faith (Jude 1:3) which they once professed intellectually but never enjoyed experientially. They forsake the *faith* of a Christian but not the *outward veneer and profession* of Christianity. They have "a form of godliness" but have denied (renounced) "the power of it" (2 Tim. 3:5).

Paul graphically describes apostates as rejecting "sound doctrine" and instead "after their own lusts heaping to themselves teachers, having itching ears." They "turn away their ears from the truth" and have "turned unto fables" (2 Tim. 4:3, 4). The Apostle Peter fully exposes apostates (2 Pet. 2:1-22), demonstrating that they are unsaved, having never experienced regeneration and the new nature. He graphically portrays their old nature under the figure of a dog and a sow: "But it is happened unto them according to the true proverb: the dog is turned to his own vomit again; and the sow that was washed to her wallowing in the mire" (2 Pet. 2:22; cf. Prov. 26:11).

Apostasy is irremediable; it awaits divine judgment (2 Thess. 2:10-12; 2 Pet. 2:17-21; Jude 1:11-15; Rev. 3:14-16). God's judgment is seen in the case of the angels that fell (Matt. 25:41; Jude 1:6), in the case of Israel (Deut.28:15-68; Isa. 1:5, 6; 5:5-7), and in the case of Christendom (2 Thess. 2:10-12). Of course, no sinner is beyond the reach of the grace of God in Christ. But an apostate must come as a lost sinner in order to accept the Savior for salvation. This means that he must renounce his apostasy and thus cease to be an apostate.

INSPIRED SCRIPTURE AND APOSTASY

The great bulwark against error and apostasy is the Word of God. The recognition of the Bible as the fully inspired and completely authoritative guide in matters of doctrine and morals is the believer's protection against error and apostasy. In times of doctrinal declension this or that doctrine of the faith may come under attack and be denied. But in a day of apostasy, as in both Paul's day and today, the Bible is rejected as the inspired and authoritative voice of God; as a result the very foundations of the faith are rejected. Once the full inspiration and authority of Scripture are renounced, the whole structure of doctrine is threatened with collapse.

The Apostle realized these important facts. Hence in Second Timothy, his Epistle that combats and exposes apostasy, he gives us the classic passage on the inspiration of Scripture (3:14-17). He sets forth the pivotal role which the Scriptures played in Timothy's life from childhood (3:14, 15; cf. 1 Tim. 1:1, 2; 2 Tim. 2:1, 2). God's Word, he points out, has the power to make one "wise to salvation" through faith centered in the person and work of Christ (3:15). Then he sets forth the inspiration and usefulness of Scripture (3:16, 17).

The correct rendering of this pivotal passage is: "All Scripture is God-breathed and profitable. . . . " This teaches that 1) *the entire Bible is fully inspired by God.* The inspiration of the Old Testament is indicated by direct assertion and the rest of canonical Scripture by clear implication. 2) *All Scripture is a product of God*—it is "God-breathed" (*theopneustos*). Not only was it breathed *into* the human agents, but through them it was breathed *out* by God. Without depriving the human authors of intelligence, individuality, literary style, or personal feelings, God supernaturally directed the writing of the Sacred Oracles. As a result the Scriptures recorded his comprehensive and infallible revelation to man with perfect accuracy. 3) *Since it is God-breathed, all Scripture in the original autographs is inerrant and fully authoritative.*

Having expounded the full inspiration of the Word, the Apostle outlines the usefulness of Scripture, particularly as the antidote against error and apostasy. He shows that all of Scripture is useful 1) "for *doctrine*" (teaching and systematizing Christian truth); 2) "for *reproof*" (censure of wrongdoing); 3) "for *correction*" (setting right what is wrong); 4) "for *instruction in righteousness*" (both God's own intrinsic righteousness and the righteous conduct which he requires of his saints); and 5) that "the man of God may be perfect," completely furnished "for all good works."

THE PREACHING OF THE WORD AND APOSTASY

As the antidote against apostasy, the Apostle solemnly enjoins the heralding of the Word (4:1, 2). Realizing how essential this activity is, the Apostle stresses the accounting which Christ's servants will be required to give regarding their treatment of God's truth. "Preaching the Word" means proclaiming it both authoritatively and systematically. A task of such unparalleled importance must be performed both "in season" (conveniently, opportunely) and "out of season" (inconveniently, inopportunely).

The Apostle leaves no doubt about the reason for his solemn charge to preach the Word constantly (4:3, 4). It is that the Word of God exposes and counteracts apostasy. Apostates cannot tolerate sound doctrine. They multiply teachers who will cater to their illegitimate desires. They have "itching ears," eager to be entertained by some novel error or unsound theory. They knowingly turn their ears from the truth of the Word. The result is that they adopt myths and fables (2 Thess. 2:10-12).

THE LORD'S COMING AND APOSTASY

In times of apostasy the faithful minister is to encourage himself with the prospect of the Lord's coming for his own (John 14:1-3).

"Henceforth there is laid up for me a crown of righteousness, which the Lord, the righteous Judge, will award to me on that day, and not only to me but also to all who have loved his appearing" (4:8). The Scriptures inculcate in believers an eager expectation of the Lord's coming for his own (1 Thess. 4:13-18).

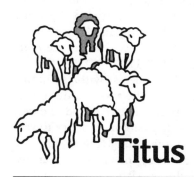

Titus

AUTHOR AND DATE

Paul apparently wrote the Epistle to Titus from Macedonia between his Roman imprisonments during A.D. 64-66. See comments under "The Pastoral Epistles."

BACKGROUND

Though he is not mentioned in the Acts of the Apostles, Titus is referred to quite frequently in Paul's Epistles, particularly in Second Corinthians and Galatians. He was born of Gentile parents (Gal. 2:3) and was a member of the delegation from Antioch who accompanied Paul and Barnabas to the first Church Council (Acts 15:2; Gal. 2:1-3). During the third missionary tour Titus was twice dispatched on urgent missions to Corinth, in which he was quite successful. It is not strange that he should be entrusted with an important assignment in the island of Crete. After the completion of this assignment he is said to have gone to Dalmatia, a region on the eastern coast of the Adriatic Sea (2 Tim. 4:10).

IMPORTANCE AND PURPOSE

Paul's letter to the young pastor Titus is much like his first letter to Timothy in that it features church order and sound doctrine. Titus had proved his ability in previous assignments and was charged with considerable responsibility on the island of Crete. He was given authority to appoint elders in the various churches there (1:5), to rebuke insubordinates (1:13; 3:10), to teach sound doctrine (2:1), and to exercise general oversight over the churches.

The Apostle's purpose in this letter is much the same as in his first letter to Timothy. After his first imprisonment in Rome Paul evidently stopped at Crete, for he left Titus there to carry on the work. Crete is a mountainous island about 156 miles long and 7 to 35 miles wide; it lies at the southern end of the Aegean Sea. Cretans are mentioned among those present at Pentecost (Acts 2:11).

After a lengthy salutation (1:1-4), Paul deals with scriptural church organization, urging Titus to complete the task facing him in Crete (1:5). The Apostle lists the qualifications to be required of elders (1:6-16). He then proceeds to outline proper pastoral ministry toward various groups, including the aged (2:1-3), the young (2:4-8), and servants (2:9-15). He then relates pastoral ministry toward Christian living that adorns the gospel (3:1-11). He closes with greetings and instructions concerning good works (3:12-15).

OUTLINE

Salutation (1:1-4)
A. The Church Adorning the Gospel (1:5-16)
   1. By proper organization (1:5)
   2. By qualified elders (1:6-9)
   3. By a firm stand against false elders (1:10-16)
B. The Pastor Adorning the Gospel (2:1-15)
   1. By his teaching ministry to the aged (2:1-4)
   2. By his teaching and example to the young (2:5-8)
   3. By his teaching and example to servants (2:9, 10)
   4. By his teaching and experience of the gospel of grace (2:11-15)
C. The Church Members Adorning the Gospel (3:1-11)
   1. By exemplary behavior before the world (3:1, 2)
   2. By comprehending the grace of God (3:3-7)
   3. By a life of good works (3:8-11)
D. Closing Greetings and Instructions (3:12-15)

SCRIPTURAL CHURCH ORGANIZATION

Both First Timothy and Titus give invaluable instruction about the need for scriptural organization of the local church. In Crete the problem was not the absence in the local church of persons having the qualifications of elders, for the Holy Spirit raises up and equips such (Acts 20:28). The problem was instead *the recognition and appointment* of qualified and Spirit-prepared elders. Whether Titus was to appoint such men or the church to elect them under his supervision is not stated. The important thing is not *how it is done* but that it *actually be done,* and that the qualified and Spirit-prepared men be duly installed in their important office.

The terms "elder" (Greek *presbuteros,* "an elderly man") and "bishop" (Greek *episkopos,* "overseer") apparently denote the same person, for they are used interchangeably (cf. Acts 20:17, 18; Tit. 1:5, 7). The term "elder" seems to refer to the office and the term "bishop" to the elder's general duty of overseeing the flock of God.

Eldership in the New Testament always occurs in the plural. The idea of *one* elder ruling or officiating over the church in the sense of an ecclesiastical dictatorship is foreign to Scripture. This practice is nevertheless sometimes found in churches that otherwise regard themselves as Bible-centered.

The functions of elders are clearly outlined in Scripture. These include 1) teaching and preaching (1 Tim. 5:17); 2) guarding the faith from error and distortion (Tit. 1:9); and 3) overseeing the spiritual interests of the local church (1 Tim. 3:4, 5; 5:17; John 21:15, 16, 17; Acts 20:28; Heb. 13:17; 1 Pet. 5:2). Not every elder will necessarily perform all these functions. Often these duties are distributed among the several elders.

THE GOSPEL OF GRACE AND GODLY LIVING

In combating the tendency to loose living and general immorality among the Cretans (1:12, 13), the Apostle penned one of the most comprehensive and concise New Testament summations of the relation of the gospel of grace to a godly life (2:10-14). In doing so he achieves a perfect balance of doctrine and practical living. The believer who accepts "the grace of God that bringeth salvation" (2:11) will in his life "adorn the doctrine of God, our Savior, in all things" (2:10). The Greek word translated "adorn" means "to decorate, to embellish." A consistent, godly life is an adornment to the grace of God which appeared to us in salvation.

Beginning with the incarnation ("the grace of God . . . hath appeared" — 2:11), this doctrine is related to a life that denies evil and does good here and now (2:12). The doctrine of the return of Christ is made the incentive for godly conduct ("looking for that blessed hope" — 2:13). The great truth of redemption is presented as God saving us, not *in* our sins (cf. Matt. 1:21) but *from* our sins and "all iniquity" in order to purify for himself a people for his own possession, "zealous of good works."

The doctrinal significance of this great passage as a refutation of both lawless abuse of grace and legalistic self-righteousness can scarcely be overstated. The Apostle in his great doctrinal Epistles (especially Romans and Galatians) had expounded the far-reaching truth of justification and sanctification by God's grace *alone,* apart from the works of the Law. Now he shows that such salvation, far from leading to license, is inseparably wedded to a pure, holy life produced by the Holy Spirit in the believer.

JUSTIFICATION AND GOOD WORKS

The second great doctrinal passage in the Epistle to Titus (3:4-8) complements the first one (2:10-14; see above) and likewise relates God's grace to a holy and useful life. However, there is this difference: the first passage features God's grace as manifested in salvation in general. The second passage relates divine grace specifically to justification and good works. In previous writings the Apostle had repeatedly propounded the far-reaching truth of justification by God's grace through faith, *totally* apart from works of law or self-effort. Did this mean that the justified believer was free to live a loose or lawless life, devoid of good works? Of course not. The Apostle's reply is, "This is a faithful saying, and these things I will that thou affirm constantly, that they who have believed in God might be *careful to maintain good works.* These things are good and profitable" (3:8; cf. Eph. 2:8, 9 with Eph. 2:10).

But it is significant that the Apostle in exhorting to good works does not in one iota minimize God's grace in salvation or justification ("being justified by *his grace*" — 3:7). Instead, he extols the all-sufficiency of divine grace, totally apart from works, to save and sanctify the lost. This he does in a passage which meets or exceeds in grandeur anything he had ever penned in Romans or Galatians about God's unmerited favor manifested in justification.

However, in relating justification apart from works to a justified life *that produces good works,* the Apostle stresses the fact that God saved us by the *"washing* of regeneration" in order to deliver us from the penalty and power of sin and by the *"renewing* of the Holy Spirit" in order to provide the inner dynamic for a holy life of good works (3: 5). That this inner dynamic is completely adequate for the production of such good works is also emphasized: ". . . which he *shed on us abundantly* through Jesus Christ our Savior" (3:6).

Philemon

AUTHENTICITY

This priceless letter demonstrates the power of the gospel of grace and the blessing of Christian fellowship in action. Marcion's Canon and the Muratorian Fragment (the earliest existing lists of Pauline writings) contain Philemon even though they omit the Pastoral Epistles. In the fourth century Philemon was questioned not so much for its authenticity as for its supposed triviality. Most scholars, however, have placed a high value on the tact, grace, delicacy of feeling, and Christian affection which adorn this letter, and have regarded it worthy of canonicity in the highest sense.

The letter is much more than a mere chance correspondence between two people. If we look beyond its personal and informal nature we see careful composition and observance of literary forms. It is important to note that both individuals and a church were recipients of this letter by the Apostle (1:2). Although Philemon is specifically named, his family and church are presumably linked with him, as in Romans 16:5 and Colossians 4:15.

BACKGROUND AND DATE

Paul is imprisoned (vv. 9, 10). The occasion is the same as that in the Epistle to the Colossians. Onesimus is to accompany Tychicus, the bearer of the Colossian letter (Col. 4:9). Paul's party in Philemon 1:23, 24 is almost identical with that in Colossians 4:10-14. The place is evidently Rome, during Paul's first imprisonment, in A.D. 61 or 62. Some scholars, however, single out Ephesus as the place of writing and date the Epistle at about A.D. 55. Rome was a haven for displaced persons of every description, and Ephesus too was large enough to get lost in. It is very unlikely that Onesimus would have stayed in proconsular Asia, knowing the stiff penalty which his defection as a slave involved.

This stone found at Caesarea bears the name of Pontius Pilate. *(Russ Busby photo)*

IMPORTANCE AND PURPOSE

The core of the Epistle is an appeal by Paul on behalf of a runaway slave from Colosse named Onesimus (Col. 4:9). Onesimus' conduct was in sharp contrast to his name, which means "useful" (v. 11).

By some means, possibly through his fellow-townsman Epaphras (Col. 4:12), the renegade slave had been brought into contact with Paul in prison. The result was a radical conversion. Not only so, but a deep love was engendered in Paul for his new "son" in the faith, in whom the veteran saw great potential.

Onesimus was in grave danger of severe punishment from his offended owner, Philemon. Under contemporary law frightful penalties could be imposed not only on derelict slaves but also on those who harbored them. It was at this point that the Apostle interposed with Philemon, a brother in the Lord (vv. 7, 20). He does not command but earnestly entreats (vv. 8, 9) that the master will receive his returning slave as he would Paul himself (v. 17). Paul solemnly offers to underwrite all the slave's debts (vv. 18, 19).

It is possible that Paul is asking for more than clemency. Some scholars think the Apostle is asking for Onesimus himself (v. 10), rather than merely pleading in his behalf. The request would then mean that Paul is asking that Onesimus be released to him for Christian service (vv. 11-14). The slave would from then on stand in an unspeakably closer and more permanent relationship than the old domestic one (vv. 15, 16). In any case Philemon owed his own introduction to Christ to Paul (v. 19).

OUTLINE

Introduction: Greeting to Philemon (1-3)
A. Commendation of Philemon (4-7)
    1. His love and faith (4, 5)
    2. Paul's prayer for him (6, 7)
B. Intercession for Onesimus (8-19)
    1. Plea for a runaway slave (8-10)
    2. Defense of a servant of Christ (11-16)
    3. Illustration of the principle of imputation (17-19)
C. Expression of Confidence (20, 21)
    1. Request of confidence (20)
    2. Assurance of confidence (21)
Conclusion (22-25)

AN EXQUISITE ILLUSTRATION
OF DIVINE IMPUTATION

Paul's eloquent intercession for Onesimus breathes the spirit of Christ's intercession for his own before the Father. Moreover, his plea for the runaway slave, now a servant of Christ (vv. 17, 18), perfectly illustrates imputation: "Receive him as myself; if he has wronged thee or owes thee anything, put that on my account."

In imputation (Gen. 15:6; James 2:23) the sinner's sins are reckoned or imputed to Christ's account, and Christ's righteousness is credited or imputed to the sinner's account, all on the basis of faith. As a result the sinner is not only forgiven and discharged of any sin or debt but is credited with the infinite righteousness of Christ and the riches of his salvation.

How exquisite that the Apostle should use this lofty and powerful appeal to Philemon, who had himself had his sins imputed to Christ and Christ's righteousness reckoned to him! Let Philemon deal with his runaway slave as God had dealt in grace with him!

CHRISTIANITY AND THE ISSUE OF SOCIAL INJUSTICE AND INEQUALITY

The Epistle of Philemon not only beautifully illustrates the liberating gospel of Christ and its central feature of imputation, but it also illustrates how this liberating message works to set enslaved humanity free from its social ills and injustices.

Philemon, the slave owner, became converted to Christ. Then his unsaved slave, Onesimus, robbed him and ran away. Converted to Christ, the recreant slave now sustained to his master the new relationship of "brother beloved" (v. 16). This new relationship was bound to affect the old relationship drastically, if not eventually dissolve it altogether. This was especially true under the influence of so strong a protagonist of Christ as Paul, who next to his divine Lord was the greatest emancipator of the human race that has ever been produced.

In the Epistle to the Galatians, the "Magna Charta of Christian Liberty," Paul the Emancipator penned these soul-stirring words that sound the death knell to prejudice, tyranny, and injustice, and show that in Christ's redemptive work lies the answer to the social problems that agitate present-day society. "For ye are all the sons of God by faith in Christ Jesus. For as many of you as have been baptized into Christ have put on Christ. There is neither Jew nor Greek, there is neither bond nor free, there is neither male nor female; for ye are all one in Christ Jesus" (Gal. 3:26-28).

"In Christ Jesus . . . there is *neither bond nor free.*" Slavery was one of the curses of the ancient world, especially in the Greco-Roman world of the first century A.D. Pagan people saw no more wrong in possessing slaves than we see in having domestic servants. Estimates of the slave population of the Roman Empire have been as high as sixty million! Under the provisions of Roman law, a slave was usually considered as property owned by another, possessing no rights at all, and, like any other form of personal property, disposable at the owner's whim. For the smallest offense a slave might be scourged, mutilated, thrown to the wild beasts, or otherwise inhumanly treated.

It is quite natural that some of the early Christians had slaves (see Eph. 6:9; Col. 4:1). The fact that the New Testament does not directly inveigh against slavery as a social evil does not mean that it condones the practice. Like the Epistle to Philemon, the New Testament as a whole exemplifies the Christian way of dealing with a grievous social evil. It does not advocate force or violence as the method of rooting out an injustice or inequality like slavery. It viewed the practice of slavery as a part of the order of the world that was passing away and which could not be eradicated instantly. It announced principles of righteousness and provisions of the gospel of redemption that would set men free in Christ and gradually and spontaneously cause the institution of slavery to vanish of itself. In the last resort the fraternity of the sons of God would see all its members free of their bonds. Even men outside this fraternity would come to see the essential injustice of an institution that treats human personality as so much chattel property and robs man of his dignity and right as a self-determining individual.

The Jewish-Christian and General Epistles

NATURE OF THE EPISTLES

The Jewish-Christian Epistles, which in most English versions follow the Pauline Epistles, consist of Hebrews, James and First Peter. These inspired books are addressed directly to Jewish believers. In the case of Hebrews the purpose is to expound the all-sufficiency and absolute finality of Messiah's redemptive work on the cross. It constitutes a warning to Jewish Christians of the peril of abandoning complete trust in Christ and going back to the fulfilled ritualism and legalism of Judaism as a means of either justification or sanctification before God.

The Epistle of James is a very early letter, having been written to Jewish believers before the gospel went out to the Gentiles and before the distinctive truths of the Church were revealed through the Apostle Paul. It instructs believers in the death, resurrection, and ascension of Christ in practical terms familiar to Old Testament saints.

First Peter is also addressed largely to Jewish believers of the Dispersion. Although it resembles James, it shows more advanced Christian truth than this very early Epistle. First Peter displays knowledge of most, if not all, of the Pauline Epistles, though these truths are molded to meet the needs of Jewish converts throughout the Roman Empire. Second Peter and Jude are more general, like the so-called General Epistles of First, Second, and Third John.

DIFFERENCE FROM PAUL'S EPISTLES

The Jewish-Christian and General Epistles differ significantly from the Pauline Epistles. The difference, however, is not that of conflict or disagreement but rather that of development and extension. Both present the same Savior, the same salvation, and the same hope. But as the Apostle to the Gentiles, Paul received the great spiritual revelations of the Church — an entity composed predominantly of saved Gentiles. The distinctive elements of this revelation, such as the nature, position, and destiny of the Church, are presupposed in the non-Pauline Epistles but are not expounded in any detail. The Epistle to the Hebrews, for example, expounds "so great salvation" from the viewpoint of its fulfillment of the Mosaic Covenant and its superiority to Judaism.

By way of further contrast, the inculcation of Christian living in the non-Pauline Epistles is grounded in the basic doctrines of Christianity, while in the Pauline Letters this same conduct is based on the more complex information of the believer's positional association with Christ in his death, burial, resurrection, and present session in glory (Rom. 6:1-11; Eph. 1:1-14; Col. 3:1-4).

Hebrews

AUTHOR

The Epistle is plainly anonymous and divinely intended to be so. All attempts to identify the author have been little more than futile guesses. Ancient traditions regarding the matter consisted of two divergent opinions, one (Tertullian's) attributing it to Barnabas and the other, the more dominating tradition (that of Clement of Alexandria and Origen), attributing it to Paul. The question of authorship was of greater importance in the early Church than it is today, for upon this issue depended the canonicity of the Epistle. The prevalence in Alexandria of the idea of Pauline authorship was responsible for early recognition of canonicity in the East; in the West canonicity was recognized by the time of Jerome and Augustine (about A.D. 400).

By the time of the Reformation, however, Erasmus, Luther, and Calvin were again disputing the Pauline authorship of the Epistle. Luther suggested that Apollos was the author. Other suggestions by later scholars include Philip the evangelist and Aquila and Priscilla. Scholars would do well to abide by Origen's caution and to leave the author incognito, as he was intended to be.

BACKGROUND AND DATE

The Epistle was evidently sent to Jewish Christians in Jerusalem and the surrounding regions. It seems clear that the Temple was still continuing (8:4, 13; 10:1, 8, 11; 13:10, 11). The readers had evidently been Christians for a long time and had suffered severely. A date of about A.D. 67-69 would thus seem to fit the internal evidence. Scholars who date the Epistle at A.D. 80-90 do so on insufficient evidence.

IMPORTANCE AND PURPOSE

From the standpoint of doctrinal contribution and literary excellence Hebrews stands among the greatest of the New Testament books. The work is unique in its explanation of the transition from Mosaic Law to Christian privilege and in its interpretation of the Old Testament symbols of Christ.

The writer especially undertakes to show the relationship of Christianity to Judaism. This problem had been a lively issue among Christians since the death, resurrection, and ascension of Christ and the giving of the Spirit, which marked the beginning of the Church age. To accomplish this goal the author expounds the superiority of the Son of God to everyone and everything else — to prophets and angels (1:4—2:18), to Moses and Joshua (3:1—4:13), and to Aaron and the Aaronic priesthood (typified by the Melchizedek priesthood — 5:1 — 8:5). He continues by demonstrating the superiority of the New Covenant to the Old Covenant (8:6—10:39) and the overall superiority of faith in God and his redemptive grace in Christ (11:1—13:17).

The author realizes the severe pressure upon Hebrew believers to turn back because of either fierce persecution from fellow Hebrews or the allurement of legalistic ordinances practiced by the nation for fifteen centuries. He therefore intersperses his masterly argument with periodic warnings against defection to legalism, each time prompting the Hebrew believer to press on in the grace of Christ (2:1-4; 5:11—6: 12; 10:19-39; 12:12—13:17). Often the correct meaning of these passages has been missed by failing to keep this important consideration in mind.

OUTLINE

Introduction: The Son, God's Final Revelation (1:1-3)
A. Christ's Superiority to the Angels (1:4—2:18)
    1. In his person and work (1:4-14)
    2. Parenthesis — warning against drifting (2:1-4)
    3. In his authority and perfect humanity (2:5-13)
    4. In his conquest of sin and death (2:14-18)
B. Christ's Superiority to Moses (3:1-19)
    1. As Son in contrast to a servant (3:1-6)
    2. Parenthesis — warning against unbelief (3:7-19)
C. Christ's Superiority to Joshua (4:1-13)
    1. In the rest he gives (4:1-8)
    2. In the redemption he provides (4:9-13)

D. The Superiority of Christ's Priesthood to Aaron's (4:14 – 10:39)
  1. Because of its redemptive accomplishment (4:14-16)
  2. Because of its higher qualifications (5:1-10)
  3. Parenthesis – warning against defection (5:11 – 6:12)
  4. Because of its superior order (6:13 – 7:22)
  5. Because of its efficacy and perpetuity (7:23-28)
  6. Because it is ministered in the heavenly sanctuary (8:1-5)
  7. Because it is ministered under the New Covenant (8:6 – 10:18)
    (a) It is superior to the Old Covenant (8:6 – 9:10)
    (b) It brings reality (9:11-14)
    (c) It is sealed by Christ's blood (9:15-22)
    (d) It assures a better sanctuary (9:23, 24)
    (e) It is based on a better sacrifice (9:25 – 10:10)
    (f) It involves a finished redemption (10:11-18)
  8. Parenthesis – appeal to faith in Christ (10:19-39)
E. The Superiority of Faith in Christ (11:1 – 13:17)
  1. Faith that envisioned Christ defined (11:1-3)
  2. Faith that envisioned Christ illustrated (11:4-38)
  3. Faith of Old Testament saints and ours compared (11:39-40)
  4. The race and goal of faith described (12:1-4)
  5. The disciplines of faith explained (12:5-11)
  6. Parenthesis – warning from Esau's example (12:12-17)
  7. Results of faith indicated (12:18-24)
  8. Parenthesis – warning against refusal to hear God's voice (12:25-29)
  9. Faith expressed in conduct (13:1-9)
  10. Faith attested in separation from Judaism (13:10-14)
  11. Faith exercised in spiritual worship and obedience (13:15-17)
Concluding Request and Benediction (13:18-25)

THE UNIQUENESS AND FINALITY OF CHRISTIANITY

The uniqueness of Christ and Christianity is the great theological contribution of the Epistle to the Hebrews. The author presents not *a* revelation of God, but *the* final and perfect revelation of God. This means not only that *Christianity supersedes all other faiths* (including Judaism) but that *Christianity itself can never be superseded.* Its salvation is eternal (5:9). So also is its redemption, its inheritance, and its covenant (9:12, 15; 13:20). Christ's offering is described as being "through the eternal Spirit" (9:14). The perfection and finality of the

Christian faith imbues the whole Epistle and furnishes the key for the comprehension of all its major themes.

Like the Pauline Epistles (notably Colossians), Hebrews gives the lie to present-day religious relativism and ecumenical pluralism, which make Christianity just another religion among the various religions of the world and just another way of salvation among many. In masterly fashion the writer to the Hebrews presents the person and work of Christ, demonstrating his superiority to *all* other intermediaries — prophets, angels, Moses, Joshua, and Aaron.

THE PERSON OF CHRIST. The opening chapter of the Epistle strikes the positive and exalted note of Christ's divine sonship. He is eternal, uncreated deity (1:2) — the Word who was with God and was himself God, but who became man (John 1:1, 14). The Son's role as eternal heir, exact replica of God's nature, and creator and sustainer of the universe is declared, as well as his role as redeemer of fallen man (1:2, 3). The Son is superior to the angels in his person and accomplishment (1:4-14), in his authority (2:5-9), in his perfect humanity (2:10-13), and in his conquest of sin and death (2:14-18).

The incarnation of the divine Son is emphasized. He was made a little lower than the angels (2:9), taking upon himself human nature (2:16, 17), and was made subject to all of the temptations which sinless humanity could be exposed to (4:15). His earthly life comes into focus in his temptations (2:18; 4:15), his agony of prayer (5:7), his perfect obedience (5:8), his teaching ministry (2:3), and his endurance of opposition (12:3). Christ's humanity is emphasized in his fulfillment of the Aaronic pattern; his deity is stressed in the fulfillment of the Melchizedek order (5:1 — 10:39).

THE WORK OF CHRIST. Christ's work in creating and sustaining the universe (1:2, 3) is presented as a prelude to his work in human redemption (1:3; 5:1 — 10:39). He is presented as the Redeemer-Priest who surpasses the two greatest Old Testament priests — Melchizedek and Aaron. He thoroughly fulfills both the eternal order of Melchizedek and the temporal and typical order of Aaron. It is against the background of the inadequacies of the Aaronic order that the writer to the Hebrews expounds the superiority of Christ's atoning work. The major superiorities are 1) the *personal nature* of the offering: he offered himself (9:14); 2) the *spiritual character* of the offering: he offered himself "through the eternal Spirit" (9:14); 3) the *permanent results* of his priestly work: he "obtained eternal redemption for us" (9:12); and

4) the *finality* of Christ's offering: he offered himself and entered the holy place once and for all (7:27; 9:12, 28; 10:10).

THE ISSUE OF THE BELIEVER'S SECURITY

In view of the eloquent presentation in Hebrews of the complete and eternal salvation which the all-sufficient Redeemer grants to the believing sinner, it is ironic that passages from this Epistle are frequently misinterpreted to teach that salvation is forefeitable and may be lost. The passage which is most widely abused in this way is the parenthetical exhortation to maturity and warning against defection recorded in 5:11−6:12. This passage concerns *truly regenerated converts from Judaism* who lapsed back into Mosaic legalism. They are therefore designated as immature (5:11-14), having failed to go on to "perfection" or mature status in "the grace and truth" that "came by Jesus Christ" (John 1:17). Instead, they were going back to the Mosaic Law and trusting in its ritual and precepts. They were occupied with what they were *doing* in order to be acceptable to God instead of relying upon what God *had done* for them in Christ to make them acceptable.

The spiritual declension of these Hebrew believers was due to a threefold cause. They were lingering in elementary truths instead of advancing to the deeper truths of grace. They were re-laying basic foundations instead of erecting the superstructure of grace on the existing foundation (6:1, 2). They were failing to appropriate God's power for gracious living and were instead lapsing back into legalistic self-effort.

The Apostle follows the cause of the sin by a clear analysis of its character (6:4-8). That it concerns genuinely regenerated believers is clearly evidenced (6:4, 5). However, they were Hebrew believers who failed to heed what they had heard from Christ through his Apostles and had neglected "such a great salvation" by reverting back to Mosaic legalism (2:1-4). They had remained in the wilderness of unbelief and self-occupation (although redeemed out of Egypt) instead of crossing over Jordan and entering the Canaan of God's rest by reposing in faith in Christ *alone* for their perfection (chaps. 3, 4). So they remained spiritual babies (5:11-14).

The essence of the sin of these believers was *doctrinal defection from the all-sufficiency of Christ's death* (6:6). It was falling from faith and grace to unbelief and works. It was "falling *along the way*" of grace (Greek *parapiptō*), similar to the "falling from" (*ekpiptō*, falling *out of*) grace in Galatians (5:4), with the difference that the former concerned Gentile believers and the latter Jewish believers. In neither case, however, is the issue forfeiture of salvation. The issue in both cases is leaving the gospel of pure grace for some legalistic admixture of works.

The sin was a contradiction of the Hebrew believers' initial repentance from the "dead works" of Judaistic observances (6:1). Consequently it involved the impossibility of restoration to repentance from "dead" religionism as long as it was persisted in. It was in reality a denial of the complete efficacy of Christ's death to save sinners (John 19:30). In reverting to ritual that had meaning only as it pointed ahead to Christ's sacrifice, this sin was tantamount to putting Christ back on the cross as an impostor and declaring that his death was not a fully sufficient atonement for sin. (In fact, this is the basic implication of all legalistic admixtures with grace.)

Such defection merits severe chastening of the believer (6:7, 8). The issue here is not salvation but rewards for Christian life and testimony (cf. 2 Cor. 5:10). Divine dealing with the believer is necessary because of lack of fruit (6:7), the presence of the curse of sin and the Law (6:8; cf. Gal. 3:13), and divine disapproval (*adokimos*, "not approved" – 1 Cor. 9:27). The cure of the sin (6:9-12) involves faith in God's grace in Christ (in order to show forth "the better things" inseparably connected with salvation – 6:9), keeping in mind God's justice and impartiality (6:10), and pressing on to maturity in grace (6:11, 12).

THE DOCTRINE OF ANGELS

In demonstrating the superiority of the Son over the angels the Epistle gives remarkable prominence to this order of created spirit beings.

ANGELS ARE RELATED TO BELIEVERS. They are "ministering spirits, sent forth to minister for them who shall be heirs of salvation" (1:14). This service evidently refers primarily to the physical safety and well-being of God's children (1 Kings 19:5; Psa. 34:7; 91:11; Dan. 6:22; Matt. 2:13, 19; Luke 22:43; Acts 5:19; 12:7-10). It would seem that this care begins in infancy and continues throughout life (cf. Heb. 1:14 with Psa. 91:11 and Matt. 18:10). Angels are said to observe us (Eccl. 5:6; 1 Cor. 4:9; Eph. 3:10), a fact which should influence our conduct for good. Man is made "a little lower than the angels" (Psa. 8:4, 5; Heb. 2:7). In the incarnation Christ assumed "for a little (time)" this lower place so that he might elevate the believer into his own sphere above the angels (Heb. 2:9, 10).

ANGELS ARE INCORPOREAL CREATURES. Though spirits (Psa. 104:4; Heb. 1:7) are normally invisible to human beings, angels are enabled upon occasion to become visible in the semblance of human form (Gen. 19:1, 5; Num. 22:22-31; Judg. 2:1; 6:11, 22; 13:3, 6; 1 Chron. 21:16, 20; Matt. 1:20; Luke 1:26; John 20:12; Acts 7:30; 12:7, 8; etc.). They are exceedingly numerous (Psa. 68:17; Matt. 26: 53; Heb. 12:22; Rev. 5:11). Their strength is far above natural or human power (2 Kings 19:35; Psa. 103:20). Their position is around God's throne as his servants (Psa. 103:20; Rev. 5:11; 7:11). Although referred to in Scripture by masculine pronouns, angels are apparently sexless. They are all direct creations of God and do not marry and propagate like human beings (Matt. 22:30; Mark 12:25).

THE ANGELS WILL ACCOMPANY CHRIST AND HIS SAINTS AT THE SECOND ADVENT (MATT. 25:31; REV. 19: 14). To them will be committed the preparation of the judgment of in-dividual Gentiles among the nations (Matt. 13:30, 39, 41, 42). How-ever, the coming age as a whole will not be subject to them. It will in-stead be in charge of Christ and his redeemed saints, for whom he was temporarily made a little lower than the angels (Heb. 2:7). Gabriel and Michael are archangels named in Scripture. The former is mentioned in connection with distinguished services (Dan. 8:16; 9:21; Luke 1:19, 26), while the latter is related to the nation of Israel and the resurrec-tions (Dan. 10:13, 21; 12:1, 2; Jude 1:9).

THE REALM OF THE FALLEN ANGELS INCLUDES SATAN AND HIS DEMONS (ISA. 14:12-14; EZEK. 28:11-17). Some of these angels are bound (Jude 1:6; 2 Pet. 2:4), whereas others are free with Satan to do his bidding. The doom of Satan and fallen angels is eter-nal hell — Gehenna (Matt. 25:41).

THE EXPERIENCE OF REDEMPTIVE REST

The demonstration of Christ's superiority over Joshua furnishes the writer of the Epistle to the Hebrews the occasion to expound the rest into which Christ's salvation brings the believer (4:1-13). The gospel of grace is presented as the source of salvation rest; it is pre-figured in the Canaan rest of the Old Testament (Num. 14:1-45; Psa. 95:8-11). Redemptive rest is *full trust* in the finished work of Christ, both for salvation of the soul and sanctification of the life. The gospel, which looked forward to Christ's atonement, was preached to Israel in the Old Testament. But because it was not received by faith (except for

Caleb and Joshua) the Israelites died in the wilderness and thus failed to enter the Canaan rest (Psa. 95:11; Heb. 3:11-19).

God's seventh-day creation rest (Heb. 4:3-8; Gen. 1:31—2:3) serves as a picture of the rest which the believer may enter spiritually now, as he fully relies on what Christ has done for him on the cross. Only Jesus, the greater "Joshua," can provide true rest (Heb. 4:8; Matt. 11:28-30). Christ's superiority to Joshua is seen in the redemption rest he provides. It is available for all believers as a "sabbath-keeping" (*sabbatismos,* "a state of cessation from all labor and self-effort"). It calls the believer to rest completely in Christ's perfect work of redemption, even as God rested from his own work of creation (4:10). It ceases from all self-effort, human merit, or legalistic claim as a means of attaining either salvation or sanctification (cf. Eph. 2:8-10). Through faith this God-given rest enjoys a daily experience of victory over Satan, self, and the world.

The rest, the writer shows, is to be diligently realized through faith (4:11). Unbelief robs us of it. The living Word of God is the object of faith which God uses to bring men into this rest (4:12, 13). Our ascended High Priest in the heavens is the guarantee of the rest (4:14-16). Such an approach to a life of victory was peculiarly appropriate to converts from Judaism, for they had been wedded to forms and ceremonies and legalistic observances for over fifteen centuries.

THE NEW COVENANT

One of the major reasons for the superiority of Christ's redemptive priesthood over Aaron's symbolic priesthood is the fact that it was ministered under a new and better covenant. The New Covenant (8:8-12; cf. Jer. 31:31-34; Matt. 26:28; Mark 14:24; Luke 22:20) is a covenant of unconditional blessing based upon the finished redemption of Christ. It secures blessing for the Church (Matt. 26:28; Mark 14:24) from the Abrahamic Covenant (Gen. 12:1-3; Gal. 3:13-20). In addition it guarantees covenant blessings to converted Israel (Jer. 31:31-34), including the promises of the Abrahamic, Palestinian, and Davidic Covenants. The New Covenant is unconditional, final, and irreversible. Its superiority over the Old or Mosaic Covenant appears from the following chart.

THE CONCEPT OF FAITH

One of the featured words of the Epistle is "faith." But it carries a different emphasis than the Pauline concept. Paul, writing mainly to

---

COMPARISON OF THE COVENANTS

The Old (Mosaic) Covenant	*The New Covenant*
Based on law and works.	Based on grace and faith.
Given by Moses (John 1:17).	Mediated by Christ (John 1:17).
Set forth in types and shadows (9:1-10).	Revealed in antitype and reality (9:11-14).
Limited, unsatisfactory, not gracious, conditional, enacted on inferior promises. Lacking finality and efficacy (8:6-13).	Unlimited in blessing, gracious, unconditional, possessing finality and efficacy (8:10-13).
Sealed by animal blood (9:15-22).	Sealed by Christ's blood (9:15-22).
Pertains to an earthly tabernacle.	Enacted in heaven (9:23, 24).
Its sacrifices are imperfect, repeatable, not expiatory (10:1-4).	Christ's sacrifice is perfect, final, fulfilling the old order (10:5-10, 15-18).
Inferior because of the inferior position of the Levitical priests (10:11-14).	Superior because of Christ's superior position, work, and present session (10:11-14).
A conditional covenant of works, making it a ministry of "condemnation" and "death" (2 Cor. 3:7-9) designed to lead the transgressor to Christ. Hence it was *ad interim* and temporary. Given solely to the nation Israel.	The covenant of unconditional blessing. Through Christ's redemption it secures blessing *for all mankind*, including the Church, from the Abrahamic Covenant (Gal. 3:13-20). It also secures Covenant blessings to converted Israel, including those of the Abrahamic, Palestinian, and Davidic Covenants.

Gentiles, stressed the dynamic concept of faith that accepts and rests in God's provision of salvation. The writer to the Hebrews, on the other hand, features faith as persevering against the temptation to lapse back into Mosaic legalism or to succumb to virulent persecution.

Faith in Hebrews is therefore defined not in its widest sense but simply as trust in God that holds out and endures to the end (11:1). Such faith enables men to receive divine approval and to understand spiritual truth (11:2, 3). It is illustrated by Old Testament worthies whose trust envisioned "the promise" (Christ) and persevered (11:4-40). They won divine approval as a result of their faith, but did not receive "the promise" in the sense of Christ's complete salvation or the fulfillment of the New Covenant. The perfection of the New Covenant will be realized for both Old Testament and New Testament saints when Christ returns to consummate salvation and to reign as absolute King and Lord (11:39, 40). Persevering faith is compared to a race with a goal (12:1-4). It is related to testings and chastenings (12:5-17). The results of persevering faith are specified. It delivers from the terror of the Law and introduces the believer to the blessings and relationship of grace (12:18-29). Such faith expresses itself in gracious, godly living (13:1-6), in a stable testimony (13:7-9), in a clear-cut separation from legalism (13:10-14), and in spiritual worship and obedience (13:15-17).

THE CONCEPT OF THE CHURCH

In the Epistle to the Hebrews the Church is related to the completed salvation which Christ has accomplished and the fruition of the persevering faith which the writer has expounded (12:18-24). The Church is seen glorified in the sinless eternal state, co-inhabiting the New Jerusalem with the glorified elect of every age (cf. Rev. 21:10–22:5; John 14:1-3). The writer declares that Abraham looked for this heavenly city (11:10), which God has prepared for his people (11:16) and which will be permanent (13:14). It is called "Mount Zion . . . the city of the living God, the heavenly Jerusalem" (12:22).

Inhabiting this celestial city as a part of its eternal splendor will be the glorified saints of this age, called "the church of the firstborn enrolled in heaven" (12:22, 23, literal translation). "The firstborn" is a reference to Christ (Rom. 8:29; Col. 1:15, 16; Heb. 1:6). The Church is the entity described by Paul as the Body of Christ, whose members are citizens of the heavenly city (Eph. 2:19; Phil. 3:20). The writer to the Hebrews relates the Church to the rest of glorified humanity (Heb. 11:39, 40). These others are designated "just men made perfect" (Heb. 12:23), and include perfected saints of the Old Testament, tribulation, and kingdom eras. Also inhabiting the City will be God in his unveiled glory (Rev. 21:3), as well as "Jesus, the Mediator of the New Covenant" (Heb. 12:24) and an uncounted host of unfallen angels (Heb. 12:22).

James

AUTHOR

Not until the Third Council of Carthage (A.D. 397) did the Epistle of James come to be generally recognized as canonical. Hesitation concerning its acceptance was due to uncertainty about the identification of the author, who styles himself simply as "a servant of God and of the Lord Jesus Christ" (1:1). When it became generally understood that James the brother of the Lord was the most likely author, and that he was called an "apostle" by Paul (Gal. 1:19), opposition against canonicity vanished.

James is referred to in the Gospels (Matt. 13:55; Mark 6:3). Like his brothers, he did not believe in Jesus during our Lord's ministry (cf. Mark 3:21, 31-35; John 7:3-9). After the Ascension, however, Jesus' brothers are found with those who were awaiting the promised Spirit (Acts 1:14). Paul mentions Christ's resurrection appearance to James (1 Cor. 15:7). James must already have shown gifts of leadership, for he soon became head of the Jerusalem Church (Acts 12:17; 15:13; 21: 18; Gal. 1:19; 2:9, 12).

BACKGROUND AND DATE

James wrote his Epistle for Christian Jews in the Dispersion (1:1). Representatives of this far-flung Jewish population in the Greco-Roman world were present at Pentecost, when the Spirit came and the Christian Church began (Acts 2:9-11). Some of these doubtlessly carried the gospel back to their native lands. It must be remembered that Jewish believers were the first Christian missionaries. The Christian movement was well on its way toward a wide outreach among the Jews of the Roman Empire *before* any Gentiles were admitted to gospel privilege (cf. Acts 4:36, 37; 9:2, 10, 14; 11:19, 20; 1 Pet. 5:13).

If the writer was indeed James, the Lord's brother, his Epistle was written before A.D. 62, the date of James' martyrdom, according to Josephus (*Antiquities XX*, 9, 1). That it was actually written much earlier, between A.D. 45 and 48 and before the first Church Council, is suggested by the following facts: 1) the Church order and discipline of the Epistle are very simple. The leaders are called "teachers" and "elders"; no reference is made to "bishops" (overseers) or "deacons." Believers still congregated in the synagogue (2:2). 2) The doctrine of the Epistle is also very elementary. There is a total absence of information about the character and destiny of the Church or the deeper theological meaning and implications of Christ's death. Even more significant is the absence of any information covering the relation of Gentiles to gospel privilege. All of the foregoing provides evidence that the Epistle must have been written about A.D. 48 or 49, before the Jerusalem Council.

IMPORTANCE AND PURPOSE

James is without doubt the most Jewish book in the New Testament—more so than even Matthew, Hebrews, or the Revelation. The letter is concerned mainly with the practical aspects of the Christian faith. It consists of maxims and advice for everyday conduct and is reminiscent of the wisdom literature of the Old Testament, especially Proverbs. There are practically no references to any of the central doctrines of the Christian faith. If the two passages referring to Christ were omitted (1:1 and 2:1), the whole Epistle might just as properly have appeared in the Old Testament.

The Epistle is addressed to Jewish believers, called "the twelve tribes scattered abroad" (1:1). It apparently circulated among the first converts to Christianity before the Gentiles came into gospel privilege and the great truths of the Church were revealed to Paul.

James in all likelihood intended his Epistle for all Christian Jews, wherever they were. Peter also wrote in part to the Jewish Dispersion (1 Pet. 1:1), but he evidently had the Western Dispersion especially in mind, since he wrote to Jewish believers in Asia Minor. The believers there would perhaps be less likely to know the Epistle of James.

These Jewish believers were undergoing intense persecution from their fellow countrymen and were being discriminated against. Their spiritual state was low. Strife, faction, and bitter speaking were common. Many acted as if knowing the truth were sufficient, as if faith without works met all requirements. Temptation to materialism was great and oppression of the poor was a common evil. These conditions among his fellow Jewish believers prompted the strict and righteous James to write this Epistle.

James presents a living faith in Christ as the panacea for the trials and ills that faced his Jewish brothers in the Dispersion. Such a vital trust would enable his brothers in the Christian faith to meet persecutions and testings courageously and victoriously. It would also rid them of their erroneous notion that a mere intellectual assent to Christian truth was sufficient. Living faith, in contrast to such "dead" (ineffective and nonexistent) faith, would change their lives and make them productive of good works. This would turn out to be the cure for their spiritual ills.

OUTLINE

Salutation (1:1)

A. Living Faith Tested by Trials (chapter 1)
1. The purpose of trials (1:1-4)
2. Wisdom for trials (1:5-12)
3. God's role in trials (1:13-18)
4. God's Word and trials (1:19-25)
5. Genuine religion and trials (1:26, 27)

B. Living Faith Attested by Works (chapter 2)
1. Dead faith is manifested in partiality (2:1-9)
2. Dead faith results in judgment (2:10-13)
3. Dead faith is useless (2:14-20)
4. Living faith attests a man's righteousness (2:21-26)

C. Living Faith Evidenced by Conduct (chapters 3—5)
1. Living faith controls the tongue (3:1-12)
2. Living faith manifests heavenly wisdom (3:13-18)
3. Living faith resists worldliness (4:1-5)
4. Living faith demonstrates humility (4:6-10)
5. Living faith avoids slander (4:11, 12)
6. Living faith counteracts secularism (4:13-17)
7. Living faith courageously meets persecution (5:1-11)
8. Living faith shuns swearing (5:12)
9. Living faith is exercised in prayer (5:13-18)
10. Living faith maintains a diligent witness (5:19, 20)

JAMES AND TRUE RELIGION

The subject of true religion is especially timely today because so many people have (in Paul's terminology) "a form of godliness" but have denied (renounced) "the power of it" (2 Tim. 3:5). In James' terminology such religionists do not practice "true religion" (1:26, 27). James points out what false religion is. It is, according to him, the expression of "dead works" produced by the flesh and the result of "dead" (nonexistent) faith.

Because man has been created religious he remains so even in his fallen state. As a result the world is full of empty religion, not only in the non-Christian faiths of the world but also within the fold of professing Christianity. James cites an example of such false religion by describing an unruly tongue that yields itself to slander and backbiting while claiming to be religious.

When religion (*outward* religious service) is genuine, it is the expression of a true *inward* faith. James cites an illustration of this. Such true religion is manifested 1) *in social consciousness* (looking after such helpless people as orphans and widows) and 2) *in separation from sin*. A truly religious person keeps himself clean of the world's smut and taint.

Many Christians today practice scriptural separation from apostasy and sin but are woefully deficient in a sense of social obligation and involvement. On the other hand, many professing Christians are extremely lax in scriptural separation from evil but are nevertheless vocal and active in social activity, some even to the extent of renouncing the gospel of redemption for a so-called "social gospel."

THE RELATION OF JUSTIFICATION TO WORKS

James shows that faith unverified by works is a "dead" faith—not really faith at all, but simply intellectual assent. Such a faith cannot save a man. It is just as useless as telling a destitute person to be fed and clothed but doing nothing to help him (2:14-16). James is here demonstrating that works and saving faith are inseparable. He does not question that faith is the way of salvation and *the only way*. But he does question that such living faith can ever be divorced from the works which prove its very existence. To offer God a faith separated from good works is to rise little higher than the demons, who believe and shudder but nevertheless remain incorrigibly wicked (2:17-19).

"Living" faith, that is, faith wedded to works, proves a man righteous. It attests that a man has been justified (declared righteous before God). Two examples of living or saving faith (faith with works) are given—Abraham, the classic man of faith in Scripture (2:21-24), and Rahab, the harlot (2:25). James teaches that Abraham was justified (vindicated) by works when he offered up Isaac (Gen. 22:9-12). Since

Abraham had already been justified by faith in the sight of *God* (Gen. 15:6), his supreme act of faith in offering his only son provided incontrovertible vindication of his faith in the sight of *men* as well.

In similar manner Rahab's saving faith was demonstrated before *men* when she hid the spies, sent them back by another route, and hung out the scarlet cord (Josh. 2:1-21; Heb. 11:31). James further illustrates this important principle with the analogy of the death of the body. When the body dies the spirit departs. Likewise, when faith is separated from works it is a dead, lifeless thing which can neither secure our righteous standing before God nor demonstrate our justification before men.

JAMES'S AND PAUL'S DOCTRINE OF JUSTIFICATION COMPARED

Martin Luther contended that James contradicts Paul on the matter of justification. He called James's letter "a right strawy Epistle" and held that it was not on a par with other canonical books. However, this personal judgment of the great reformer is not supported by any patristic evidence or sound exegesis. That James does not contradict Paul, who declares that Abraham was justified by faith apart from works (Rom. 4:2-5), appears from the following chart.

JUSTIFICATION COMPARED	
Justification in the Pauline Epistles	*Justification in the Epistle by James*
Paul employs the term "justified" in the sense of being *judicially declared righteous before God*. Paul is speaking *Godward*.	James uses the term in the sense of being *proved righteous before men*. James is speaking *manward*.
Abraham enjoyed justification by faith apart from works (Gen. 15:6) long before he offered up Isaac.	Abraham was justified (vindicated) by works when he offered up Isaac (Gen. 22:1-12) because he was already justified by faith.
Paul sets forth the truth itself.	James offers the corrective for the abused truth.
Paul's Epistles are beamed toward Gentiles, lost in sin, with no legal righteousness to offer to God.	James's Epistle is aimed at Jewish believers tempted to substitute a head knowledge of the Law for a heart experience of grace manifested in a holy life.

JAMES'S TEACHING ON DIVINE HEALING

Instructions for the physically ill (5:14, 15) direct that the sick Hebrew believer was to call for the elders of the assembly and ask them to anoint him with oil and pray for him. The Talmud shows that using oil for anointing the sick was generally practiced among the Jews. Our Lord and his disciples adopted the practice (Mark 6:13). Oil was also commonly used for medicinal purposes in the ancient Near East (Isa. 1:6; Luke 10:34). Its use here in James may symbolize either the employment of medicinal means for healing or, more likely, the healing power of the Holy Spirit.

James's stress, however, is not on the oil but on the "prayer of faith"; it is this which "saves the sick." This special type of prayer is *breathed by the Holy Spirit* through the human agent and is *always in God's will.* Since it is *not* always God's will to heal, this special "prayer of faith" is not always given; healing by God's power is thus *not* always effected. Chastening, testing, refining, and other factors influence the Lord's healing of a believer's illnesses (cf. 1 Cor. 11:30-32; 2 Cor. 12:7-9; 1 Tim. 5:23; 2 Tim. 4:20). Consequently, those who pray for the sick need the gift of "discerning of spirits" to ascertain the state of the ailing saint *in relation to the will of God* (1 Cor. 12:10). They also need "faith by the same Spirit" and "gifts of healing" (1 Cor. 12:9) in order to pray the prayer of faith after the will of God has been determined in each case.

For so-called "faith healers" to insist that it is *always* God's will to heal a believer who is in right relation with God is extremely perilous. Healings that are forced under the halo of the will of God may turn out not to be in the will of God at all, but instead may prove to be the "faith healer" forcing his own will under the disguise of God's will. Demonic spirits are waiting to take over when God's will is flouted, either consciously or unconsciously, deliberately or ignorantly. When demonic healings occur, there is *always* a price tag. The malady may be transferred from the physical to the mental, emotional, or spiritual realm, or there may be ensnarement in error or cultism or bondage to fanaticism of some sort.

DIVINE HEALING TODAY

God can and *does* heal today, but *not always.* James' passage on healing has often been misused by "faith healers." The fact that James 5:14-16 was never addressed to a Gentile church (James 1:1) and dates *very early* (A.D. 45-48 — before Gentiles were admitted to gospel privilege) is often overlooked. The nation Israel had not yet been set aside (cf. Acts 28:17-29), and the passage is based on a healing covenant made with Israel (Exod. 15:26). Under this covenant James 5:14-16 guaranteed Hebrew believers instantaneous and complete healing in response to faith in Christ (cf. Acts 3:6, 16; 4:30; 5:12-16; 6:8; 8:7, 8). This efficacious faith for healing was divinely imparted to the *apostolic* Jewish Christian elders in response to their claim upon the promises of Israel's healing covenant.

But the all-important point for the correctly instructed Christian minister to see is that now that the nation Israel and her healing covenant have been set aside while the great Gentile Church is being called out, the "prayer of faith" is divinely given and operative in the established Gentile Church *only when it is God's will to heal.* This is the reason why *nowhere* in any of the Church Epistles is anything said about anointing the sick with oil (cf. 2 Cor. 5:7). When "the prayer of faith" is prayed, however, and God heals the sick today, it is *always* on the basis of the divine will. God's will must be determined in each case and the petition offered in accordance with his divine purpose. Healings that flout this principle run the risk of being effected by demonic power, with perilous results to the one who is "healed." This is true no matter how sincere, well-meaning, or even godly the "faith healer" may be.

1 Peter

AUTHOR

The author is "Peter, an apostle of Jesus Christ" (1:1). Everywhere in the Epistle there are reminiscences of Peter's personal acquaintance with our Lord; he claims to have been "a witness of the sufferings of Christ" (5:1; cf. 3:18 and 4:1). He writes with deep per-

A street scene in the old part of Jerusalem *(Russ Busby photo)*

sonal feeling about the person of Christ and his sufferings (2:19-24). He pleads with his readers to remember that they are sharing in the sufferings of Christ (4:13). His admonition to "feed the flock of God"

(5:2) recalls Christ's own words to Peter, "Feed my lambs" and "Feed my sheep" (John 21:15-17). His injunction "Gird yourselves with humility" (5:5) apparently has in mind Christ's girding of himself with a towel when he washed the disciples' feet (John 13:3-5).

Scholars have also noted a correspondence between Peter's speeches in Acts and his words in the Epistle. Acts 10:34 recalls First Peter 1:17. Acts 2:32-36 and 10:40, 41 recall First Peter 1:21. Acts 4:10, 11 brings to mind First Peter 2:7, 8. Internal evidence strongly indicates that Peter wrote the Epistle toward the end of his career. The same recognition of the equality of Gentile and Jewish Christians that appears in the latter part of the Acts is found in the Epistle.

Attestation of the genuineness of the Epistle appears in its recognition in the early Church as a true work of the Apostle Peter. Its acknowledgement in the Second Epistle (2 Pet. 3:1) is amply corroborated by the early Church Fathers, especially Polycarp and Irenaeus.

Peter simply and unpretentiously introduces himself to his readers as "an apostle of Jesus Christ" (1:1). There is nothing in his two Epistles or in his early or later career that would substantiate the notion that he was the founder of the church at Rome or its first bishop. In the book of Acts Peter appears as the chosen instrument (Matt. 16:16-18) to present "such a great salvation" of the new age (Heb. 2:3) to Jews (Acts 2). Somewhat later he and John healed the crippled man (Acts 3:1-11) in the Temple and preached the sermon on the future fulfillment of Israel's covenants (Acts 3:12-26). He and certain other Apostles were arrested and tried before the Sanhedrin (Acts 4:1-22). As a leader of the Jerusalem Church, Peter was faced with disciplining Ananias and Sapphira (Acts 5:1-11).

Following a period of spectacular power in the early Church, Peter and other apostles were again subject to persecution and imprisonment by Jewish officials (Acts 5:12-40). After Stephen's martyrdom Peter introduced gospel opportunity to the half-Jew Samaritans (Acts 8:1-15) and later to pure Gentiles (Acts 10:1-48). He was imprisoned under Herod Agrippa I (A.D. 41-44) and miraculously released (Acts 12:7-11). Following Paul's first missionary tour, Peter took a leading role in the first Church Council in Jerusalem (Acts 15:7-11).

At Antioch Peter was reprimanded by Paul for hypocritically withdrawing from fellowship with Gentile believers (Gal. 2:11-14). Peter traveled extensively in the later years of his life, often with his wife (1 Cor. 9:5). He apparently had an extensive ministry in Asia Minor, especially in Pontus, Cappadocia, and Bithynia, areas Paul did not visit. His martyrdom was predicted by our Lord (John 21:18, 19).

BACKGROUND AND DATE

Peter addressed his Epistle to Christians who resided in the Roman provinces of Pontus, Galatia, Cappadocia, Asia, and Bithynia in Asia Minor (1:1). These provinces are probably listed in the order which the messenger, Silvanus (5:12), was to follow in delivering the letters to the churches concerned. "The exiles of the dispersion" (1:1, RSV) are evidently "elect" believers in general. James wrote to "the twelve tribes in the dispersion" (James 1:1, RSV), who were Jewish Christians outside Palestine, apparently of the Eastern dispersion (see under James).

However, Peter does not address his readers as "the twelve tribes." He evidently had Gentile as well as Jewish believers in mind (cf. 1:14; 2:9, 10; 4:3-5). His readers were "aliens and exiles" (2:11) in the sense of pilgrims and sojourners on earth (cf. Heb. 11:13-16; 13:14). He regarded Christians as dispersed among the heathen. Some scholars think that this statement may refer literally to members of the Roman church dispersed to the provinces as a result of Nero's fanatical persecutions.

The Epistle was written from "Babylon" (5:13), which some think is a pseudonym for the city of Rome (cf. Rev. 14:8; 18:2, 10, 21). However, numerous scholars believe that the literal city on the Euphrates is intended. Since Peter died in perhaps A.D. 66 or 67, this Epistle was in all likelihood written as late as A.D. 65, for it shows acquaintance with Colossians, Ephesians, and Philippians. Recent attempts to date First Peter in the reign of Emperor Trajan during the persecutions under Pliny's governorship of Bithynia-Pontus (A.D. 110-111) have not been very successful.

IMPORTANCE AND PURPOSE

First Peter is the Epistle of triumphant suffering and radiant hope. Seven different words are used for suffering in the letter. Hope in the midst of suffering is produced by the prospect of a glorious future inheritance (1:4, 5) to be realized in the advent of the Chief Shepherd (5:4). The sufferings of Christ provide the foundation of the Epistle (1:11; 2:21, 23; 5:1), and our suffering Lord is held up as an example to all of God's suffering children (2:21; 4:1, 2).

The Apostle warns God's people to expect suffering (4:12), for it is often consonant with the will of God (4:19). Saints are not to be upset by adversity (3:14), but are to bear it patiently (2:23; 3:9), even joyfully (4:13), knowing that fellow-believers also suffer (5:9). Peter is careful to show the value of suffering righteously (1:6, 7; 2:19, 20; 3: 14; 4:14). But he warns against suffering as an evildoer (2:20; 4:15). The Epistle is thus more practical than doctrinal.

OUTLINE

A. Present Suffering in View of Future Glory (1:1-25)
　　1. Suffering in the light of assured salvation (1:1-12)
　　2. Suffering in the light of the Lord's coming (1:13-22)
　　3. Suffering in the light of the Word of God (1:23-25)
B. Present Suffering in View of Christ's Passion (2:1 — 4:6)
　　1. Suffering in view of Christian growth (2:1-3)
　　2. Suffering in view of identity with Christ and his own (2:4-10)
　　3. Suffering in view of Christian character and conduct (2:11-20)
　　4. Suffering in view of Christ's example (2:21-25)
　　5. Suffering in view of God's order for the home (3:1-7)
　　6. Suffering in view of harmonious living (3:8-12)
　　7. Suffering in view of a good conscience (3:13-17)
　　8. Suffering in view of Christ's triumph (3:18-22)
　　9. Suffering in view of Christ's example for victory (4:1-6)
C. Present Suffering in View of Christ's Advent (4:7 — 5:11)
　　1. Suffering and impending judgment (4:7-19)
　　2. Suffering and reward for service (5:1-4)
　　3. Suffering and vigilant conduct (5:5-9)
　　4. Suffering and Christian maturity (5:10, 11)
Concluding Greeting (5:12-14)

FOREKNOWLEDGE, ELECTION, AND FOREORDINATION

The Apostle Peter describes believers as "elect according to the foreknowledge of God" (1:2). Foreknowledge is that attribute of God by which all things are known to him from the beginning. Consequently, God knew from eternity who would be saved from the fallen human race. Election is that gracious and sovereign act of God by which from eternity certain are chosen from the human race for himself (John 15:16, 19; 1 Thess. 1:4; Eph. 1:4; 1 Pet. 1:2; 2 Pet. 1:10). Election is based on God's sovereign purpose or decree (Rom. 9:11; Eph. 1:11) and is in accordance with his foreknowledge (1 Pet. 1:2). However, nowhere does Scripture reveal exactly how God's foreknowledge determines his elective choice. This is the realm of the infinite; it is un-fathomable to the finite human mind. In any case the Scriptures teach both that men bear moral responsibility for their choices and that the sovereign God works out all things according to his infinite wisdom and good pleasure.

Peter speaks also of foreordination. He declares that Christ the Savior "verily was foreordained before the foundation of the world," but was manifested in his Saviorhood "in these last times" for the elect (1:20). Foreordination is that operation of God's will in which everything he has decreed from eternity past is brought to realization in time. It is the believer's assurance that what God has predetermined for his own saints (the elect) will not be nullified. In this latter sense it is tantamount to predestination (Rom. 8:29, 30; Eph. 1:5, 11).

REDEMPTION

Peter declares that believers "were not redeemed with corruptible (perishable) things, like silver and gold . . . but with the precious blood of Christ" (1:18, 19). The word translated "redeemed" (*lutroō*) means "ransomed," that is, "bought back from bondage." The neces-sity for redemption springs out of the fact that the sinner is enslaved to Satan and sin (John 8:34; Rom. 6:17, 20). Redemption itself is God's undertaking on the basis of free and unmerited favor and choice. It is made possible by Jesus Christ, the Redeemer (1 Cor. 1:30; Gal. 3:13; 4:45; Eph. 1:7; Tit. 2:14). The basis is the shed blood of Christ. Re-demption is both past and future. The price has been paid once, and believers are thereby redeemed for all time. However, they wait in ex-pectation for the final fulfillment of that which is already theirs by faith (Rom. 8:23). Those who are redeemed (ransomed, delivered from bondage) once belonged to Satan as slaves. Now they belong to God as free men (1 Cor. 6:20). Their chief purpose in life is now to glorify their Redeemer (2:9).

THE PRIESTHOOD OF THE BELIEVER

Peter teaches that believers are "a holy priesthood, (offering up) spiritual sacrifices, acceptable to God by Jesus Christ" (2:5). He calls *all* Christians "a royal priesthood" (2:9; cf. Rev. 1:6). He emphasizes that every believer, being made one with Christ himself by faith, is constituted a priest before God in the tabernacle in heaven. In the Old Testament economy a priest had to mediate between God and the people by serving at the altar. A high priest also mediated for them in the Holiest Place before the Shekinah glory of the divine presence.

But Christ himself has now become the believer's high priest (Heb. 4:14; 5:10; 7:27; 9:11). Through Christ alone the humblest believer may now obtain access into the immediate presence of God. How ironic that the Apostle Peter, who declares so plainly that the only valid New Testament priesthood is that which includes every believer, should be connected by men with a hierarchical system of ecclesiastical priestism that would shut the believer out of his God-given privilege of access to God through Christ alone!

Never in the New Testament is the term "priest" (*hierus*) applied to an apostle or an ordained elder in the Church except as he shared in the universal priesthood of all believers. Recovery of this great New Testament truth furnished one of the great emancipating impulses of the Protestant Reformation and brought multitudes back to fellowship with God.

VICARIOUS ATONEMENT

The Apostle Peter presents the vicarious, atoning work of our Lord in one of the clearest and most incisive passages on the subject in the Bible. He declares that Christ "his own self bore our sins in his own body on the tree, that we, being dead to sins, should live unto righteousness; by whose stripes ye were healed" (2:24). Vicarious atonement means substitutionary reconciliation. The term "vicarious" derives from the Latin *vicarius*, meaning "substituted," "delegated." The expression "atonement" is from the Greek *katallagē*, denoting "an exchange," " a reconciliation," and "restoration to divine favor" (Rom. 5:11; 11:15; 2 Cor. 5:18, 19). It comprehends the thought of appeasing God's infinitely holy wrath against sin by a sufficient and satisfying sacrifice substituted for the guilty sinner. Christ, the "lamb without blemish and spot" (1:19), who died as a vicarious (substitutionary) sacrifice for sin, took the place of and died in the stead of the sinner. Thus he made atonement by reconciling the guilty sinner to God.

Three great facts underlie the doctrine of substitutionary atonement: 1) the sinner lies under the wrath of God and is therefore utterly undone and lost (Rom. 1:18; 3:19; 6:23); 2) by God's grace Christ willingly offered himself as a sin-bearer and substitute (Isa. 53:6; 2 Cor. 5: 21); and 3) God willingly accepted the atoning death of Christ, so that the sinner thereby secures the benefits of reconciliation and fellowship with God (Rom. 5:1-11).

In the old economy the blood sacrifices had to be repeated because they were typical and educatory and could not really remove sin forever. When offered by faith, however, these sacrifices were acceptable because they envisioned the future death of Christ and drew in advance upon the merit of his atonement (Rom. 3:25). Since the time of his death there has been absolutely no need for further sacrifice (Heb. 9:11-15; 10:1-14).

THE BROTHERHOOD OF MAN

The Apostle Peter speaks of honoring "all men" and loving "the brotherhood" (2:17). In a day when the humanistic notion of "the brotherhood of man and the fatherhood of God" has become a popular slogan in ecumenical Christianity, the concept involved must be clearly understood within the limits imposed by Scripture. There is a sense, of course, in which all men are brothers; it is the sense in which they are descended from Adam as the father of the race. But the fall of man and the entrance of sin into the human family destroyed that brotherhood and alienated men not only from God as their Father but also from their fellow men as their brothers.

For this reason Scripture is silent concerning a supposed brotherhood that includes the unsaved (Malachi 2:10 was spoken only to Jews within the covenant relationship). Exponents of the "brotherhood" of fallen man ignore not only the fall and its consequences but also the necessity of Christ's redemptive work in restoring alienated humanity to God. Scripture does speak, however, of a brotherhood which is the result of regeneration and adoption into the family of God. This new spiritual relationship is emphasized by Peter (1:2, 23; 2:2, 10; etc.) and by all the New Testament writers (e.g. John 3:3-5; Gal. 3:27; etc.). Through Christ believers are brought back into right relationship not only with God but also with one another as God's children and heirs (1 John 3:2; Gal. 3:26). Only those who have believed on the Lord Jesus Christ are accounted as God's children in the scriptural sense. Because of this they are brothers to all who confess the same Father and Lord.

THE NOTION OF A "SECOND CHANCE"

The idea that the Lord Jesus between his death and resurrection descended into Hades and there preached to the unsaved dead, giving them a second chance, has sometimes been erroneously attributed to the Apostle Peter. "Being put to death in the flesh but made alive by the Spirit, by whom also he went and preached unto the spirits in prison, who at one time were disobedient, when once the longsuffering of God waited in the days of Noah, while the ark was preparing, in which few, that is, eight souls, were saved by water" (3:18-20, *New Scofield Bible*).

"Quickened" or "made alive by the Spirit" refers to Christ's physical resurrection and not to a supposed quickening of his human spirit, since his spirit did not and could not die and therefore needed no quickening. Only his human *body* could die, and this was what was made alive by the Holy Spirit (Rom. 8:11). Through the Holy Spirit Peter declares that Christ "went and preached unto the spirits in prison." The preaching was not done by Christ personally, but by "the Spirit of Christ," who was in Old Testament prophets (1:11). Just as the Spirit of Christ testified through these prophets about Christ's future sufferings and glory, so the Spirit of Christ preached through Noah (Gen. 6:3) to the antediluvian sinners for 120 years while the ark was being built. Hence "the spirits in prison" were not in prison when Christ preached through Noah by his Spirit, but were living men in Noah's day.

BAPTISM

Peter declares that "corresponding" to the ark in which eight persons "were brought safely through the water . . . baptism now saves you—not the removal of dirt from the flesh, but the appeal to God for a good conscience—through the resurrection of Jesus Christ" (3:21, *New American Standard Bible*). That Peter is referring *primarily* to Spirit baptism and only secondarily and figuratively to water baptism is shown by the following facts.

Only Spirit baptism can save. The unanimous testimony of Scripture is that no mere external rite can place one "in Christ." Therefore, Peter *must* be referring to the spiritual reality when he declares, "baptism now saves you." Peter was well acquainted with Paul's Epistles and the truth of Spirit baptism as revealed to the Apostle to the Gentiles (cf. 2 Pet. 3:15, 16).

Water baptism saves figuratively rather than actually. Peter uses the flood as an illustration. How were "the few, that is, eight" souls of the preflood generation "saved"? It was *by* or *through* water. The flood water was that which cut them off from the sinners of that day, who were doomed under divine judgment. In the same way we are saved by spiritual baptism through removal from the sphere of sin and condemnation.

But this aspect of spiritual baptism is only negative. If this were the total picture, the eight antediluvians would have perished *in* the water rather than being saved *by* or *through* the water. They were saved by *entering the ark.* The believer is saved by Spirit baptism not because he is merely cut off from a state of sin and judgment, but because he is positively placed in the antitypical ark, Christ, by the Spirit's baptism. Likewise, the Israelites were saved from Egypt (the world) and Pharaoh (Satan) by the waters of the Red Sea, having been "baptized into Moses (picturing Christ) in the cloud and in the sea" (1 Cor. 10:2). Paul expounds the same truth in Romans. Spirit baptism *disconnects* the believer from his lost position "in Adam" (Rom. 5:12-21) before joining him to Christ (Rom. 6:3, 4).

No mere external rite can save. Peter is extremely careful to point this out by the qualifying definition, "Baptism now saves you— *not the removal of the dirt of the flesh.*" Then he adds the positive statement, ". . . but the appeal to God for a good conscience."

Spirit baptism directly connects with Christ's resurrection. "Baptism now saves you . . . through the resurrection of Jesus Christ." The intervening words are a parenthesis. Spiritual baptism (but not ritual baptism) has the most *direct* connection with Christ's resurrection. There was not, nor could there be, any spiritual baptism until after Christ's resurrection, ascension, and giving of the Spirit (Acts 1: 5; 11:14-16). Water baptism is intended to portray outwardly what spiritual baptism has *already* accomplished inwardly. It pictures the believer's separation from sin and union with Christ.

2 Peter

AUTHOR

Considering external evidence, Second Peter has less historical support for its genuineness than any other New Testament book. This is because it is a brief Epistle, addressed to no specific person or church, and contains little new doctrinal information. Internal evidence, however, is substantial. The writer calls himself Simon Peter (1:1). The autobiographical allusions are true to the facts, as in the case of the transfiguration (1:16-18) and Christ's prediction of Peter's martyrdom (1:12-14; cf. John 21:18, 19). Noah is spoken of as a preacher of righteousness (2:5), which is also the correct meaning in First Peter 3:18-20.

The allusion to Paul's Epistles (3:15, 16) does not necessarily imply that all thirteen had already been written. Peter simply includes the letters he had come to know. There is no evidence that the error which Peter exposes and denounces belongs to a later period than Paul's. The earnestness, the apostolic tone, and the lofty, chaste character of the teaching render it impossible to believe that the Epistle is a second-century forgery, as some critics contend.

BACKGROUND AND DATE

It seems clear that Second Peter was written to the same people as First Peter (cf. 3:1 and see 1 Peter). When the Apostle alludes to the recipients of his letter as those who "have obtained a like precious faith with us" (1:1), he most assuredly included at least some Gentile Christians. In 3:15 Peter probably had Paul's Epistles to the Galatians, Colossians, and Ephesians in mind (cf. 1 Pet. 1:1). He distinguishes between the things Paul wrote specifically to them (3:15) and the rest of Paul's Epistles (3:16). Believers, mainly Jewish converts scattered throughout "Pontus, Galatia, Cappadocia, Asia, and Bithynia" (1 Pet. 1:1), are apparently the addressees.

A philosophical Gnosticism with intellectual and antinomian characteristics (chap. 2) had gained entrance. Its unsound teachings were producing lawless and immoral living (2:10, 13, 14, 18, 19-22). The danger was spreading and posed a real threat (2:1-3, 18, 19). The Apostle Paul had been confronted with this heresy at Colosse and had dealt with it in the Colossian letter. But the error still persisted. Precisely what relationship Peter sustains to his readers is not clear. Perhaps he had visited them. Along with others, he had made known to them "the power and coming of our Lord Jesus" (1:16). His concern for them led him to pen this Epistle, especially since false teachers were flouting the truth of Christ's second advent (chap. 3).

Second Peter was written before the Epistle of Jude, since Jude apparently alludes to Second Peter (2:1—3:3; cf. Jude 1:4-16). This is more probable than that Peter cites Jude, since the latter quotes from tradition or possibly the apocryphal books of the Assumption of Moses and of Enoch, while Peter scarcely quotes at all. Jude (1:17, 18) almost certainly alludes to Second Peter 3:1-3, the unusual word "mockers" (*empaiktēs*) being found in each passage. Moreover, the false teachers in Second Peter are in a sense still future (2:1, 2, 12). In Jude they are already present (1:4, 8, 10-13, 16).

Apparently, then, Second Peter was written not long after First Peter and before the Epistle of Jude. The years A.D. 66 or 67 would seem to meet requirements.

IMPORTANCE AND PURPOSE

The subject of First Peter is *suffering* and its purpose is *consolation*. The theme of Second Peter is *false teachers and false teachings* and its purpose is *warning*. The Apostle's antidote for false teaching is true spiritual knowledge (cf. John 16:12, 13). The words "know," "knowledge," etc. are found no less than sixteen times in the Greek text (1:2, 3, 5, 6, 8, 12, 14, 16, 20; 2:9, 20, 21 (twice); 3:3, 17, 18). In six of these instances is found an intensified form of the word denoting full or complete knowledge (1:2, 3, 8; 2:20, 21). The knowledge (*epignōsis*) which Peter describes springs out of faith that rests on facts; it is imparted to the believer in fullness and precision by the Holy Spirit.

The golden text of Second Peter may be taken as 3:18: "But grow in grace and in the knowledge of our Lord and Savior, Jesus Christ." The Apostle shows that true knowledge is understanding God's grace in Christ. As a result of faith which brings such knowledge, believers are empowered to overcome sin and to confirm their call and election. The Christian faith is not founded on myths or man-made legends. It rests on the personal witness of those who saw the glory and majesty of Christ (chap. 1).

True knowledge of Christ's grace is perennially threatened by false teachers. By their lawless lives and unsound doctrine they deny the Redeemer. They promise freedom, but all the while they themselves are enslaved by lust. Their punishment is inescapable (chap. 2).

True knowledge of the future is perverted by false teachers; they reject the truth of Christ's second coming and misconstrue God's patient delay of judgment. But Christ's return to judge is inevitable. The destruction of the ungodly and the renovation of the earth by fire are likewise certain. Knowledge of this inspires God's own to live righteously.

OUTLINE

Salutation (1:1, 2)
A. True Knowledge from God (chapter 1)
   1. Centers in Christ (1:3-5)
   2. Promotes spiritual growth (1:6-9)
   3. Confirms Christ's call and our election (1:10, 11)
   4. Is based on eyewitness testimony of Christ's glory (1:12-18)
   5. Is founded on the authoritative Word (1:19)
   6. Is communicated by the Holy Spirit (1:20, 21)
B. False Knowledge from False Teachers (chapter 2)
   1. Inroads of their error (2:1-3)
   2. Punishment of their error (2:4-10)
   3. Their character and conduct (2:11-16)
   4. Dire consequences of their deception (2:17-22)
C. True Knowledge of the Future (chapter 3)
   1. Denied by rejectors of Christ's second advent (3:1-4)
   2. Centers in God's set plan for the future (3:5-7)
   3. Finds explanation in God's forbearance toward sinners (3:8, 9)
   4. Will be realized in cataclysmic judgment (3:10)

5. Fosters a holy life (3:11, 12)
6. Will eventuate in a sin-cleansed eternity (3:13)
7. Furnishes the basis for godly exhortation (3:14-18)

DIVINE ELECTION
AND CHRISTIAN CONDUCT

The Apostle insists on the validation of the believer's "calling and election" by the cultivation of Christian virtues (1:4-14). "Therefore (because of the peril of falling into spiritual ignorance and sin), brothers, be all the more diligent to make certain about his calling and choosing you" (literal translation). From God's point of view the Christian's election is certain. It is subject to no contingency, since it is the result of God's sovereign and immutable choice and is based on the total efficacy of Christ's finished work of redemption (cf. Eph. 1:4-6).

However, believers have the responsibility in life and testimony *to make their calling and election certain and assured before men.* This can be done only by employing the spiritual resources they are endowed with in grace (1:2-4), thus manifesting maturity (1:5-10). If they validate and confirm God's call and election before men by a virtuous life, Peter declares that they will *"in no wise"* (emphatic negative) "fall" (stumble so as to fail the grace of God bestowed on them).

ENTRANCE INTO GOD'S KINGDOM

If believers validate their divine calling and election before men by a virtuous life (1:5-10), the Apostle declares that "an entrance shall be ministered (to them) abundantly into the everlasting kingdom of our Lord and Savior, Jesus Christ" (1:11). Believers spiritually enter the kingdom of God when they are born again (John 3:3-5).

The entrance which Peter speaks of is the literal entrance into the eternal kingdom at the resurrection and glorification of the redeemed body (1 Thess. 4:13-18; Phil. 3:20, 21). Spiritual regeneration on the basis of faith in God's grace *assures* entrance to *every* born-again believer. Validating our calling and election before men by faithful service and a virtuous life will assure an abundant, full, and victorious entrance, with honors and awards for the faithful (1 Cor. 3:9-15; 9:27; 2 Cor. 5:10).

The prospect of this glorious future easily becomes dimmed. Thus Peter did not wish to be "negligent" in reminding God's people of "these things," though they knew them and were "established in the present truth" (1:12). Peter had in mind those gospel truths which were formerly promised to Old Testament saints but are now present with believers as an arrived reality.

INSPIRATION AND AUTHORITY
OF THE WRITTEN WORD

It is highly significant that, in dealing with the general theme of true knowledge from God as opposed to false knowledge from apostate teachers, the Apostle Peter should touch upon the pivotal subject of the source of authority in matters of spiritual knowledge. This is always a crucial issue in times of apostasy — today as in the days of the Apostles.

In expounding this subject Peter first lays the foundation by demonstrating *the authority of the apostolic testimony* (1:16-18). The inspired witness of the apostles precludes deception or imposture. They did not follow "cunningly devised fables," that is, man-concocted myths. Their witness is supported by divine revelation and the firsthand evidence of eyewitnesses (1:16; Matt. 17:1, 5). They saw the transfigured, glorified Christ on the mountain. Peter saw with his own eyes "that great One's majesty" (this is the emphasis of the Greek). Significantly, too, they had a personal revelation of "the power and coming of our Lord Jesus Christ," since the transfiguration was a portrayal in miniature of the second advent (Matt. 17:1-8; Mark 9:2-8; Luke 9:28-36). Peter also heard the voice of "the majestic glory" (God) with James and John in the "holy mountain" (1:17, 18).

Having established the authority of the apostolic testimony, Peter then declares *the inspiration and authority of the written Word* (1:19-21). The written Scriptures not only contain and preserve the authority of the apostolic testimony, but are themselves attested through fulfilled prophecy. "And we have the prophetic word (the Old Testament Scriptures) made more sure" (literal translation). In other words, Old Testament prophecies concerning Christ's first advent were fulfilled by the events of the New Testament era. Prophecies about the second advent received a foretaste of their fulfillment in Christ's transfiguration, which Peter, James, and John witnessed.

Through the Holy Spirit Peter declares that the Scriptures are of divine origin — that they are directly inspired by God (1:20, 21). An expanded translation of the Greek text has this emphasis: "For *not by the will of man* (emphatic) was any prophecy ever borne to us, but, on the contrary, men being borne along by the agency of the Holy Spirit spoke *from God* (emphatic)" (1:21).

Since Scripture is composed of the words of God spoken through human authors as directed by the Holy Spirit, no part of it is "of any private interpretation" or "its own interpretation." It is not to be isolated from what the Scripture declares elsewhere. Scripture is to be interpreted by both its own context and other relevant passages of Scripture, that is, by both the *immediate* connection in chapter and book as well as the broadest connection of all sixty-six books that make up the Bible. God's voice must not be stifled by the interjection of man's voice. God must be allowed to speak by the Spirit in interpretation, even as he has spoken by the Spirit in inspiration. The *authority* of God's voice must be recognized. Before this authority men's ideas and philosophies must bow in utter subjection.

FULFILLED PROPHECY AND INSPIRATION

Peter declares, "We have a more sure word of prophecy" (literally, "the prophetic word made more sure" — 1:19). Prophecy is made "more sure" by fulfillment. As Peter points out, fulfilled prophecy is a remarkable attestation of inspiration. Predictions of future events in the Bible were spoken so long before the events transpired that in no possible way could mere human precognition have foreseen them. Moreover, these predictions are so minute in detail and specific in character as to exclude the possibility of an unusual coincidence or a chance guess.

The Word of God has a large prophetic or predictive element woven into the warp and woof of its fabric. Hundreds of predictions concerning Israel, the nations, and historical personages have come to pass exactly as foretold. Through the power of God these amazing forecasts have been fulfilled by men who were ignorant of them, who disbelieved them, or who struggled in desperation to avoid their fulfillment. These predictions have been so ancient, so unique, so improbable, and so detailed and definite that no human mind could have anticipated them. They prove conclusively that the Scriptures which contain them are beyond any question inspired by God alone.

APOSTATE TEACHERS AND THEIR DOOM

Second Peter and Second Timothy have a great deal in common. Among other similarities, both envision the widespread departure from the faith that will culminate in the great apostasy of "the last days" (2:1 – 3:7, 2 Tim. 3:1-9, 13). The main thrust of Second Peter is the eloquent and comprehensive denunciation of apostasy and apostate teachers (2:1 – 3:5). These men had departed from the Christian faith (Jude 1:3), which they once professed intellectually but never enjoyed experientially. They had abandoned the faith of a Christian but retained the outward veneer and profession of Christianity.

The Apostle outlines the activity and influence of these apostate teachers (2:1-3) and declares their sure judgment. "Their judgment from long ago (in God's purpose and plan) is not idle, and their destruction is not asleep" (literal translation). Their ruin is illustrated by the case of the fallen angels (2:4), the sinners who perished in the flood (2:5), and the wicked inhabitants of Sodom and Gomorrah, who were consumed by fire (2:6-10). The presumption and greed of these false teachers are condemned (2:10-16), their empty intellectualism is denounced (2:17, 18), and their bondage to sin is exposed (2:19-22). Their spiritual ignorance and opposition to the prophetic Word (3:1-7; cf. 1:16-21) lead them to scoff at the truth of Christ's second coming.

THE SECOND ADVENT OF CHRIST AND HOLY LIVING

The Apostle shows that denying Christ's advent, as the apostate teachers were doing, was in line with their immoral and lawless conduct and was a deterrent to holy living (3:1-7). These "scoffers" walked "after their own lusts" (3:3). They made light of the second advent by espousing a uniformitarian view of history, flouting the idea of supernatural catastrophism suggested by the second advent. They say, "Where is the promise of his coming?" After all these centuries Christ's coming has not occurred, and their sneer is, "It never will!" They assume that all things in the natural world will continue as they have, with no major upset. Their ungodly assumption and their denial of the Word of God are refuted by both *Bible history* – the restoration of the chaotic earth (Gen. 1:1-31) and the flood (3:5, 6; cf. Gen. 6:1 – 8:22) – and *Bible prophecy* – the coming renovation of the earth by fire (3:7, 10-12).

Peter appeals to holy living in view of this fiery catastrophe and the coming dissolution of the old earth in preparation for a "new heavens and a new earth, in which righteousness dwells" (3:13). He is in perfect accord with the Apostle Paul (Tit. 2:11-13) and John (1 John 3: 1-3), who also present the Lord's coming as an incentive to a holy life.

THE DAY OF THE LORD
AND THE DAY OF GOD

Peter unfolds a new revelation about the day of the Lord. He relates this extended period to the cataclysm of fire (3:7, 10-12). Old Testament prophecy had clearly related that day to the earth judgments culminating in the advent of Messiah in glory and his subsequent reign over the millennial earth (Isa. 2:6-22; 4:1-6; cf. Rev. 4—19).

Peter's new revelation stresses the *consummation* of that day. He calls this climactic and final aspect of it "the day of God" (3:12). This day involves the ultimate and final catastrophe of time, when the earth is consumed in a fire-bath and the "new heavens and new earth" of the sinless state are created. The "day of God" envisions the time when sin, death, and hell are isolated in Gehenna (Rev. 20:11-14) and Christ surrenders the mediatorial kingdom to the Father (1 Cor. 15:24-28; Rev. 20:7—22:21).

GOD'S TIMETABLE
AND THE DIVINE PURPOSE

Peter rebuffs those who scoff at the second advent of Christ by showing that human concepts of time are not the limited context in which God accomplishes his purposes for time and eternity. Peter quotes Psalm 90:4 to demonstrate that God operates in eternity, and is not restricted by the time limitations which bind a finite creature like man (3:8).

Peter also shows that, even though God is not bound by time, he is always punctual (3:9). One day with him is "as a thousand years, and a thousand years as one day." He is not "slack" (remiss). He does not delay in the sense of being indecisive or remiss in keeping his promises, as some men erroneously interpret his patience. Instead, God has a purpose in his patience. "He is longsuffering, not wishing that any should perish, but that all should come to repentance" (cf. Gen. 6:3; 1 Tim. 2:4; 1 Pet. 3:20). He gives sinners time to consider their evil ways and to turn from their iniquity.

1 John

AUTHOR

The external evidence for the genuineness of First John is early and strong. Polycarp quotes First John 4:2, 3 in his Epistle to the Philippians. The Muratorian Fragment, the Old Syriac, Irenaeus, and Clement of Alexandria add their evidence, as do Cyprian, Origen, and Dionysius of Alexandria. Eusebius places First John among the books accepted canonically.

The author himself claims to be an eyewitness of Christ (1:1-4; 4:14). He is clearly the same person as the author of the fourth Gospel. Although the author does not state his name in either the Epistle or the Gospel, the early Church on solid grounds of internal evidence attributed both works to the Apostle John. There are striking resemblances between these two works in style, language, and thought patterns. Among the resemblances are the following distinctive words and expressions: *word, light, eternal life, love, new commandment, lay down one's life, take away sins, works of the devil, murderer, overcome the world, pass from death unto life, Savior of the world, Paraclete, begotten of God, joy-fulfilled, bear witness,* etc.

A few technical words, such as *propitiation, anointing,* and *parousia,* occur in only one of the works. But this is no evidence against Johannine authorship. Not even the blindest critic would insist that an author has to use his entire vocabulary every time he writes. The same simple, straightforward Hebraic style with use of parallelism characterizes both the fourth Gospel and the Epistle. Authorship of both by the Apostle John is the only logical conclusion.

BACKGROUND AND DATE

There is scarcely a clue from the testimony of the Epistle itself as to whom the Letter was addressed. The warning against idols (5:21), the sparse reference to the Old Testament, the absence of any reference to Hebraic legalism, and the general address to the family of God would at least indicate that its original readers were not primarily Hebrew believers.

The only significant indication of the original destination of John's First Epistle comes from early Church tradition. Irenaeus writes, "Then, again, the Church of Ephesus founded by Paul and having John remaining among them permanently until the time of Trajan, is a true witness of the tradition of the apostles" (*Against Heresies III:* 3, 4). (Emperor Trajan ruled during A.D. 98 to 117.)

It seems that John was active not only in the church at Ephesus but also in the assemblies of proconsular Asia (Rev. 2, 3). No doubt John visited neighboring districts and organized new churches. What would be more likely than to suppose that he directed First John to these Gentile converts?

John's immediate purpose in writing the Epistle was apparently to refute the twin error of Cerinthian Gnosticism and antinomian Nicolaitanism. The first of these errors was a philosophic perversion of the person and work of Christ. Cerinthus lived during the period A.D. 80-100 and was educated in Egypt, according to Irenaeus. He taught that the world was created not by God himself but rather by a certain power far separated from him. He declared that Jesus was merely the natural son of Mary and Joseph (though more righteous and prudent than other men). At Jesus' baptism "the Christ" as a spirit and in the likeness of a dove descended upon him, endowing him with miraculous gifts. At Jesus' death "the Christ" departed from him, so that Christ did not die, since he was a spirit being incapable of death. Thus only the *human* Jesus died and rose again, according to the Cerinthian heresy.

Although Irenaeus declares that the Nicolaitans were heretical followers of Nicolas ("a proselyte of Antioch" —*Against Heresies I:* 26, 3; *III:* 11, 1), there is no real historical basis for this identification. It is apparently an inference rather than a fact. The same is apparently true of Irenaeus' identification of the Nicolaitans as antinomian libertines. So far, all that we know definitely about the Nicolaitans of John's day is contained in Revelation 2:6. In all likelihood the name there is symbolic (like Jezebel in Rev. 2:20) and refers to the rise of a priestism that placed clergy over laity (*nikao,* "conquer" and *laos,* "people").

To combat the Cerinthian error John outlines the reality of the incarnation (1:1-4). He also delineates the practical aspects of the sin question (1:5 – 2:6) and describes the responsibility of "little children" in the Father's family to love one another (2:7-11) and to avoid being enamored of the evil world (2:12-17). He warns against heretical teaching (2:18-29) and admonishes the little children to live consistently in the light of the Lord's return (2:18 – 3:12) and to prove the reality of their salvation by their testimony before men (3:13-24).

Israel's modern parliament building, the Knesset, in Jerusalem *(IGTO photo)*

John gives the criterion for detecting false teachers (4:1-4) and describes their wordly outlook (4:5, 6). The Apostle presents another urgent entreaty to practice brotherly love (4:7-21). He presents faith as the principle which overcomes the world (5:1-8), gives assurance of salvation (5:9-15), and enables the believer to avoid sinning (5:16, 17). He closes with those things of which the believer has sure knowledge (5:18-21).

The date at which the Apostle John wrote his First Epistle can be determined approximately by the events of early Church history. The destruction of Jerusalem had scattered early believers, some of whom had migrated to Asia Minor. Tradition places John, Philip, and Andrew among these. As noted previously, Irenaeus claimed that John lived to the Trajan era (A.D. 98-117). From these and other considerations conservative scholars conclude that the Apostle wrote his Gospel at approximately A.D. 85-90 and his First Epistle a little later (since the Epistle assumes the reader's acquaintance with the Gospel).

IMPORTANCE AND PURPOSE

First John is best described as a family letter from the Father to his "little children" in the world. An intimate and tender word is employed for "children." It is a diminutive meaning "born-ones" who are beloved and cherished in the family circle. This is only one of many tender touches that make this Epistle one of the most intimate of the inspired writings. In First John the sin of the believer is treated as a child's offense against the Father; it is dealt with as a family matter (1:9; 2:1). The Epistle is addressed exclusively to believers; hence other ethical and moral problems are hardly mentioned.

OUTLINE

A. Family Fellowship and the Father (chapters 1 – 3)
   1. The basis of fellowship (the incarnation) (1:1-4)
   2. The conditions of fellowship (1:5-10)
      (a) Walking in the light (1:5-8)
      (b) Confessing our sins (1:9, 10)
   3. Christ's advocacy and fellowship (2:1, 2)
   4. Obedience and fellowship (2:3-6)
   5. Brotherly love and fellowship (2:7-11)
   6. Spiritual maturity and fellowship (2:12-14)
   7. Worldliness as a threat to fellowship (2:15-17)
   8. Doctrinal defection as a foe to fellowship (2:18-23)
   9. Abiding in Christ as a prerequisite to fellowship (2:24-29)
   10. Holy living as a prerequisite to fellowship (3:1-10)
   11. Brotherly love as an expression of fellowship (3:11-18)
   12. Christian assurance and fellowship (3:19-24)
B. Family Fellowship and the World (chapters 4, 5)
   1. False teachers of the world destroy fellowship (4:1-6)
   2. Love is the supreme manifestation of fellowship (4:7-18)
   3. Divine love is an incentive to fellowship (4:19-21)
   4. Faith is the ground of fellowship (5:1-5)
   5. The testimony of God's Son and the Spirit produce fellowship (5:6-12)

6. Prayer furthers fellowship (5:13-15)
7. Sin in the saint breaks fellowship (5:16, 17)
8. Assured knowledge fortifies fellowship (5:18-21)

FIRST JOHN AND THE GOSPEL OF JOHN

The Gospel of John describes *the Son of God*. The Epistle discusses mainly *the sons of God*. The Gospel stresses regeneration, while the Epistle stresses fellowship. The Gospel opens with the living Word existing in face-to-face fellowship with the Father "in the beginning"; the Epistle opens with the Word of life moving toward salvation of the Father's chosen ones "from the beginning." The following chart shows further comparisons.

COMPARISON OF JOHN'S GOSPEL AND FIRST EPISTLE	
Gospel of John	*First Epistle of John*
Presents the Son of God	Features the sons of God
Attests the Savior of the world	Instructs those saved out of the world
Stresses regeneration of lost sinners	Emphasizes fellowship in God's family
Written that men might believe and be saved from sin (20:30, 31)	Written that those saved might not go on sinning (2:1)
Presents the believer's Advocate (Chap. 17)	Urges the believer to use his Advocate (2:1)
Christ the Light of the world (8:12)	"Walking in the light" in fellowship (1:7)
Faith to receive life from God (3:16)	A righteous life the proof before men (2:29)
The coming of the Lord as a comfort (14:1-3)	The coming of the Lord as a warning (2:28)
How redemption was provided	How redemption is to be appropriated

JOHN'S WRITINGS
AND THE EPISTLES OF PAUL

In Paul's letters the doctrine of justification is prominent. In John's writings the doctrine of regeneration dominates. Paul presents unsaved men as outside God's favor and under divine wrath. John views them as outside the family of God, separated from the fellowship and joy of the family circle. Paul expounds the full theological perspective of the redemptive work of Christ. He especially stresses the nature, position, and destiny of the Church, the body of Christ. In contrast, John defines the person and work of the Redeemer as a historical event to be applied to the life of the believer in an intimate Father-son-family relationship.

Although John and Paul have different tasks to perform and different emphases to make, there is no disagreement, only perfect accord as inspired recorders of divine revelation. One supplements the other. For each the cross is the foundation of all his teaching. Its provisions constitute the only way a sinner can be saved and begin the Christian life. Its dynamic is the only way that those who are saved can continue on in Christian victory, fellowship, and blessing.

THE INCARNATION AND FELLOWSHIP

True Christian fellowship *must* be based on truth. The foundational truth of Christianity is the incarnation of the eternal Word, who was "with God" and "was God" (John 1:1; Prov. 8:23). In the Gospel John declares that it was God the Word who became incarnate (John 1:1, 14) and that this incarnate Word was the Creator of all things (John 1:3). The Gnostic, Cerinthus, had denied this basic truth. He declared that the world was created not by God himself but by some power far separated from him.

In introducing the incarnate Word the Apostle John refers to him in his eternal, preincarnate deity: "that which was from the beginning" (1:1; 2:13; John 1:1). He then documents his own personal witness to the incarnation of the eternal Word. He especially emphasizes the evidence which the human senses provide in attesting the genuine humanity of Christ: ". . . which we have heard, which we have seen with our eyes, and our hands have handled, of the Word of life." The "Word of life" describes Christ as the eternal Word of God who became incarnate to bring life to people dead in sin (John 3:16). The same Word who was eternally co-existent with the Father became revealed to men in the incarnation (1:2).

The Apostle thus at the outset refutes the error of Cerinthus, who denied the incarnation and substituted a kind of "apotheosis," by which a sinful, fallen man became indwelt by deity in the person of the eternal Word, "the Christ." Cerinthus taught that the eternal Word did not assume humanity by the operation of the Holy Spirit in the womb of the Virgin Mary (cf. Matt. 1:18-25; Luke 1:35; John 1:14) but was rather the natural offspring of Mary and Joseph and consequently a sinner like all of Adam's fallen race. At his baptism "the Christ," a spiritual, noncorporeal being, descended upon and indwelt him. He departed from him at death, since as a Spirit "the Christ" could not die. Only the human Jesus died and rose again.

Cerinthus thereby denied the incarnation — the union of God and man in the person of Jesus Christ. This was accompanied by a denial of Christ's sinless conception by the Holy Spirit (the virgin birth), a denial of the real and sinless humanity of Jesus Christ, and a denial of Christ's redemptive death. The heresy denied every basic teaching of the Christian faith. It offered no real Savior. It destroyed the very basis of the family of God and the fellowship of the Father's children in the family circle. This evil heresy did have one good result, however — it called forth the Apostle John's clear definition of the person and work of our Lord Jesus and the reality of his incarnation.

THE QUESTION OF "SINLESS PERFECTION"

This Epistle has sometimes been misconstrued to teach that a believer can in this life reach a spiritual plateau in which he is immune from the possibility of sinning. First John 3:9 has frequently been used as the basis of this misinterpretation. "Whosoever is born of God *doth not commit sin,* for his (God's) seed (nature) remains in him, and he cannot sin because he is born of God." Does this verse teach "sinless perfection" — that a believer can reach the place where he cannot sin? That it appears on the surface to teach this is due to the fact that the real meaning of the Greek tenses has been obscured in translation.

First John 3:9 may be paraphrased as follows to give the precise meaning of the original: "Whosoever is born of God," that is, who is regenerated and possesses a new nature, "does not go on *practicing* sin." The present tense denotes continuous action. The reason given is "for his (God's) seed," that is, the new divine nature implanted in the believer at regeneration, "remains in him" (present tense, "continues to abide in him") "and he cannot sin" (present tense again, "he is not able to go on practicing sin").

The Apostle shows that the practice of sin as the common custom of life is not possible with the regenerate, as it is with the unregenerate. Nor are they confirmed in the direction of sin, for they have a new divine nature given by God that *cannot* sin. But the question is, Why then do believers sin and require cleansing? The answer is that as long as the believer is still in this world he has the old nature alongside the new divine nature. Although the new nature cannot sin, the old nature can and does sin. However, the new nature cannot allow the *practice* of sin in the believer; through the indwelling Spirit it resists the habitual manifestation of sin.

That sinless perfection is not attainable in our unglorified bodies of this present life is due to the fact that the old nature is not removed until glorification. The Apostle John is careful to point this out. "If we say that we have no sin" (the sin nature as the principle or root of sin) "we deceive ourselves, and the truth is not in us" (1:18). Believers who imagine that they stand above the possibility of sinning are self-deceived. They lose sight of God's unsullied holiness (1:5), the presence of the old nature, their proneness to sin as a result, and their continual need of confession and cleansing (1:7, 9).

If believers say they "have not sinned" (a perfect tense in the Greek, denoting past action *continuing into the present*), they "make God a liar" by denying what his Word teaches and what their own experience should prove to them (1:10). The Apostle warns that the holiest and most mature saint still possesses an old nature. Not only *can* he sin but he must continually "walk in the light" as God is in the light (1:7) in order *not* to sin.

CONFESSION AND FELLOWSHIP

The Apostle teaches that if a believer sins he is to confess it immediately. Otherwise fellowship with the Father is broken. "If we confess our sins he is faithful and just (righteous) to forgive us our sins and to cleanse us from all unrighteousness" (1:9). The problem faced here by the believer who has sinned is not restoration to *salvation* but restoration to *fellowship*. The believer's *salvation* rests securely on the changeless person and merit of Christ. This unchanging basis enables the infinitely holy God, who "is light" and in whom "is no darkness at all" (1:5), to forgive the sins of his saints and yet remain "just" (righteous), totally uncompromising in his infinite holiness. It also enables God to remain "faithful" (cf. 1 Thess. 5:24) to his Word even though the sinning saint may be unfaithful.

While eternal salvation constitutes the unchanging basis upon which the Father-Son-child relationship of God's family rests, *fellowship* in the family is variable and changeable, depending on the believer's confession of sin and his walk "in the light" (1:6, 7).

To "confess one's sins" is to acknowledge them in a spirit of full avowal and admission. The word "confess" is from the Latin *con*, "together," and *fateri*, "to acknowledge," "to avow freely." Confession should be made to God as Father in the name of the Son, since the believer has been constituted a beloved child in the Father's family. God has promised to fully forgive and thoroughly cleanse the believer who confesses his sins (1:9). This promise is to be taken exactly as given. By faith the believer knows that God has forgiven him of his sin as soon as confession has been made. God's promise remains true even if the believer's emotions of guilt linger on. Fellowship with God and with fellow believers is restored, for "if we walk in the light, as he is in the light, we have fellowship with one another, and the blood of Jesus Christ his Son cleanseth us" ("keeps on cleansing us," present tense) "from all sin" (1:7).

CHRIST'S ADVOCACY
AND CHRISTIAN FELLOWSHIP

The Apostle presents Christ as the believer's advocate or defense lawyer in the court of heaven. "My little children, these things write I unto you, that ye sin not. And if any man sin, we have" (continually and unfailingly, a present tense) "an advocate with the Father, Jesus Christ the righteous" (2:1). As our legal representative our Lord never assumes the role of a prosecutor — despite the fact that charges are preferred against the believer before the Father's throne by Satan, the accuser of the brethren (cf. Rev. 12:10).

The heavenly Advocate's ministry is twofold. He advocates in behalf of the believer when he sins and intercedes for him in his weakness and immaturity. In the first chapter the Apostle expounds the effect of the believer's sin upon himself. In the second chapter, however, he contemplates the far more serious problem of the effect of the believer's sin upon God.

Recognizing this sin problem, some Christians assume that there is no specific cure for the believer's sin against God and that the saved one who has sinned must be prosecuted by the court of heaven and dismissed from his saved estate. Such a procedure would indeed be absolutely necessary were it not for the present advocacy of Christ. In this ministry our Lord pleads the complete efficacy of his atoning death for the specific sin or sins in question.

As the believer's advocate in heaven Christ pleads the fact that he bore the believer's sins. His resurrected and glorified human body bears witness to God's acceptance of his substitutionary work. Christ's redemptive work and God's acceptance of it therefore guarantee the sinning believer's acquittal and release. Condemnation is a legal and theological impossibility. Christ's complete effectiveness as the heavenly Advocate gains him the distinctive title of "Jesus Christ *the righteous*."

Christ's present advocacy in heaven is an inseparable part of his saviorhood. It is effective for *every* believer at all times. It remains in operation whether or not the believer understands it. Christ's advocacy is therefore not a subject of petition but rather an integral part of our "great salvation" (Heb. 2:3). It should evoke praiseful thanksgiving and confident rejoicing.

PROPITIATION AND FELLOWSHIP

In dealing with the problem of sin within the family circle of God's children, the Apostle sets forth the believer's advocate as his *propitiation*. "And he is the propitiation for our sins; and not for ours only, but also for the sins of the whole world" (2:2). Propitiation is the Godward side of Christ's redemptive work; it is the provision by which the infinitely holy God (1:5) can graciously extend mercy and forgiveness toward sinners. God's character has always been gracious and merciful, but his infinite holiness prevented him from extending this mercy toward fallen men.

But Christ made propitiation by dying on the cross and thus answering the just demands of God's holiness against sin. His own blood was, as it were, sprinkled over his sinless human body, the true mercy seat (Rom. 3:25; Heb. 9:5). God was now morally free to demonstrate limitless mercy and grace to the vilest of sinners.

God's propitious grace extends toward the unsaved as well as toward the sinning saint. "He is the propitiation for our sins: and not for ours only, but also for the sins of the whole world" (2:2). The death of Christ for the sins of the world altered the position of the entire human race in the sight of God. God recognizes what Christ did in behalf of the world whether men appropriate it or not.

The true gospel message is that God is propitious by virtue of what *Christ has done* and not as the result of anything the sinner might do or try to do. Thus all the burden is removed from both the sinner and the Christian, leaving him only to personally accept God's propitiousness through Christ. "Herein is love, not that we loved God, but that he loved us and sent his Son to be the propitiation for our sins" (4:10).

The blood-sprinkled body of Christ on the cross became the mercy seat for the sinner once and for all. There the God of righteousness can meet the sinner with salvation and the sinning saint with restoration to fellowship and joy. What otherwise would be a throne of awful judgment becomes the throne of infinite grace (cf. Heb. 4:16).

THE WORLD AND CHRISTIAN FELLOWSHIP

The Apostle John singles out "the world" (Greek *kosmos*) as the special enemy of God's children and a perennial peril to the destruction of Christian fellowship in the family circle. "Love not the world, neither the things that are in the world. If any man love the world, the love of the Father is not in him" (2:15; cf. Matt. 6:24; James 4:4). John is referring not to the material earth or to humanity in general but to those institutions of men set up in independence of God and headed by Satan. It is this Satanic system organized on principles of greed, selfishness, war, and godless commercialism that God does not love. The believer is likewise warned not to love it. If he does, his love for God will grow cold. This is the peril which the world presents.

Satan uses both this world system and the sin nature of the human body to generate prideful, godless living. This is the kind of life which Christ will destroy when he returns in glory. By contrast, "he who does the will of God remains forever" (2:17). He builds on the solid foundation of God's Word and will and rests securely in the knowledge that his life will stand in the day of judgment.

ABIDING IN CHRIST AND FELLOWSHIP

In John's writings abiding in Christ is presented not as a matter of maintaining *union* with Christ but of maintaining *communion* with him. Our union with Christ is eternally assured by his finished work of redemption. It is this secure relationship which makes fellowship or communion possible (Rom. 5:1-11). The Apostle John does not dwell at length on the believer's eternal union with Christ, because Paul had already expounded this in great detail, especially in the Book of Romans. Instead John challenges the believer to see if he is really "abiding in Christ" in his daily experience. "He that saith he abideth in him ought himself also to walk, even as he walked" (2:6). "He that loveth his brother abideth in the light, and there is no occasion of stumbling in him" (2:10; cf. 3:14). "Whosoever abideth in him sinneth not" (does not sin habitually, does not practice sin—a present tense in the Greek). "Whosoever sinneth" (constantly sins, a present participle) "hath not seen him, neither known him" (3:6). "And he that keepeth his commandments" (the eternal moral law of God) "dwelleth in him, and he in him" (3:24). Good works and holy living are the fruits of abiding.

John, like Paul, teaches that union with Christ is permanent and unchangeable (3:24b). Communion, however, is changeable and variable; it depends on keeping God's commandments and walking in God's light (1:7). In Paul's language it is "reckoning" (depending by faith) upon our union and experiencing it in our daily lives (Rom. 6:11).

TEST OF DOCTRINAL ORTHODOXY

The Apostle John in warning against doctrinal error as a foe to Christian fellowship gives a divine yardstick by which *all* religious untruth can be detected (4:1-6). This passage is comparable to the divine criterion for measuring truth described by the Apostle Paul in First Timothy 3:16, as well as to the pivotal Pauline passage that traces the source of all religious error to demonism (1 Tim. 4:1-6).

The particular demon-instigated and demon-propagated heresy which John refutes is Cerinthian Gnosticism. As discussed earlier, this error denies the true person and work of Christ. John shows that the demons propagate their false doctrines with great aggressiveness (4:1). The children in the Father's family need to remember that demonism is both the source and the dynamic of all false doctrine (4:1-3; 1 Tim. 4:1).

Because of the peril of demonic spirits the Apostle warns God's beloved not to believe every spirit, but to test the spirits, "whether they are of God." Many "spirits not of God" (i.e., demons or evil spirits) speak through false prophets. John warns that "many false prophets" have gone out into the world, parading as teachers of Christian truth but actually energized by demons. Such false teachers abounded not only in John's day but in our own day as well. Thus Paul's warning in First Timothy 3:16 and John's warning in First John 4:1-6 are especially timely for spiritually concerned believers today.

In First John 4:2, 3 John gives the acid test of error. The test centers in Christ's *deity* and *incarnation*. Confession of the truth involved in this basic issue is the touchstone that differentiates between true and false teachers. Every Christian heresy involves some erroneous teaching about the person and work of Christ.

The confession that "Jesus Christ is come in the flesh" embraces our Lord's true humanity. It acknowledges the reality of both his sinless human body before his death and his present resurrected and glorified human body installed at the right hand of the Father. It is the pledge and guarantee that the body of every believer will be glorified in the same way as Christ's body (cf. 3:1-3). This truth is brought out in the tense of the verb: "Jesus Christ *is come*" (*elēluthota*, a perfect tense—not a mere past historical fact but *present* and continuing in its blessed effects). Our Lord's glorified humanity in heaven assures a glorified body for *all* those united to him.

In this clear manner the Apostle John provides the authoritative test for distinguishing truth from error and the Holy Spirit from demon spirits. Together with the Apostle Paul (2 Tim. 3:13-17), he furnishes the criterion which God gives man to judge between the true and the false in the exceedingly complex realm of the religious. Those who heed man's voice instead of God's and ignore this divinely given chart expose themselves to the subtle snare of the Satanic and demonic. This peril often parades as "an angel of light" (2 Cor. 11:14) under the halo of the popular religious fads and cults of the day.

SIN THAT RESULTS IN PHYSICAL DEATH

In discussing prayer fellowship John shows that it is possible for a true believer to fall into serious and scandalous sin (5:16, 17). When a Christian sins a fellow Christian is to pray for him. God will in answer to prayer preserve the sinning Christian's physical life. (The Apostle is not speaking of eternal life, for this cannot be forfeited.) However, such prayer is effective only in instances where the sin is not "unto (physical) death."

"There is a sin unto death," that is, sin of such seriousness that it eventuates in *physical* (not spiritual) death. What the Apostle is warning against is persistent, wilful, deliberate sin that brings such dishonor upon God's salvation and the Savior that "the flesh is destroyed" (physical death occurs) so that "the spirit might be saved" (1 Cor. 5:1-5; Acts 5:1-11; 1 Cor. 11:30). This sin calls forth the ultimate in God's chastening of his own, the last recourse he uses with a disobedient and wilful child. Both Samson and Saul are Old Testament illustrations of this. David illustrates a sinning saint who came perilously close to committing this sin (2 Sam. 12:13; cf. 12:7-12).

The sin that entails physical death is *not to be prayed for*. It involves the operation of a fixed law of God that cannot be altered by prayer. All of the foregoing shows that *sin has different degrees of seriousness*. "All unrighteousness is sin," but there is "sin which is not unto (physical) death," involving less severe disciplinary action (5:17; cf. 1 Cor. 11:30; 2 Sam. 12:7-12).

SIN AND ITS REMEDY (1 JOHN 5:18-20)

John presents a threefold remedy for habitual sin. 1) *The new birth*

(5:18). "We know that everyone who has been born of God does not go on practicing sin" (present tense). This divine life keeps the believer from habitually practicing sin, as the unregenerate do. As a result Satan is unable to touch him. 2) *The believer's new position* (5:19). The believer is born into the family of God. "We know we are of God." By contrast, "the whole world" (the Satanic system of unregenerate humanity) "lieth in the wicked one." The world (the unsaved as a group) is under the power of Satan. 3) *The believer's comprehension of the truth* (5:20). This is an effective deterrent to the practice of sin. The spiritually healthy child of God moves in an atmosphere of truth, love, and light.

2 John

AUTHOR

Both the Second and Third Epistles of John are so similar in style, ideas, and character to the First Epistle that they must have been written by the same author. In the first verse of both the Second and Third Epistles the writer designates himself simply as "the elder" rather than as an apostle. But this is not evidence against authorship by John. Peter calls himself both "an apostle" (1 Pet. 1:1) and "a fellow elder" (1 Pet. 5:1). John could also certainly speak of himself as an elder. He may possibly have used the term in the sense of "advanced in years" or "aged." It is inconceivable that the letter could be a forgery, since a forger would certainly write under the guise of apostleship. There is no sound reason for rejecting authorship by the Apostle John.

BACKGROUND AND DATE

The letter is addressed to "the elect lady." Some scholars have interpreted this designation as a personification of one of the first-century churches. The reference to "some of your children" (v. 4) and "the children of your elect sister" (v. 13), as well as the tone of the letter, seem to indicate that a church is addressed rather than a family. However, many scholars conclude that John addressed the letter to a highly honored Christian matron with whom he was acquainted.

The time and place of writing of all three of John's Epistles are probably about the same, between A.D. 85 and 90 in the city of Ephesus.

IMPORTANCE AND PURPOSE

This extremely brief letter is concerned with God's own children "walking (living) in the truth" (v. 4) according to the "commandments" (the principles of righteousness reflected in God's character and required of all his creatures—v. 6). This is essential to resisting the encroachments of deceivers and false teachers (vv. 7-11). False doctrine is a peril that leads to disaster for any church or Christian. For this reason the author was intensely zealous that the truth of God's Word be wholeheartedly embraced and faithfully practiced in daily living.

OUTLINE

A. A Walk in Truth and Love (1-6)
    1. Greeting in truth and love (1-3)
    2. Commendation in truth and love (4)
    3. Exhortation to truth and love (5, 6)
B. A Threat to Such a Walk (7-11)
    1. Is presented by false teachers (7)
    2. Necessitates the utmost vigilance (8)
    3. Demands the keenest perception (9)
    4. Requires the most clean-cut separation (10, 11)
Conclusion: A Promised Visit and Personal Greetings (12, 13)

SOUND DOCTRINE AND CHRISTIAN LIVING

The urgent message of this significant Epistle centers around the vital dual issue of truth and right conduct. By the term "the truth" the

Apostle refers to both the Bible as God's written revelation of truth and the Lord Jesus Christ as the living embodiment of truth (cf. John 1:17; 14:6).

Orthodox Christian theology is not merely a matter of theory; it determines the way a Christian lives and forms the very foundation of the Christian message and mission. Only sound doctrine can produce sound experience. Rejection of the full inspiration and unquestioned authority of Scripture is the spawning ground for every type of false doctrine and consequent erratic conduct. This short letter provides insights into this problem not only as it threatened early Church life but also as it menaces the Church today.

The Apostle John clearly saw this peril of false doctrine in his day. He understood thoroughly how error dilutes the Christian witness and exerts its baneful effects in the lives of believers. His own love of the truth led him to pen an eloquent plea for a "walk (daily conduct) in truth" (v. 4) on the part of those who "have known the truth" (v. 1). He speaks about "love in the truth" (v. 1) "for truth's sake" (v. 2). His greeting from the triune God is "in truth and love" (v. 3). In the Gospel the Apostle declares, "And ye shall know the truth, and the truth shall make you free" (John 8:32). "New morality" and other errors in the Church today are not setting people free to happiness in right living but are enslaving them in lust and misery.

GOD'S COMMANDMENTS AND CHRISTIAN LIVING

The Apostle John connects truth inseparably with love and obedience to God's commandments. He speaks of loving *in the truth* (v. 1), of grace, mercy, and peace from God *in truth and love* (v. 3), and of *"walking in truth,* as we have received a commandment from the Father" (v. 4). He also speaks of the "commandment" from the beginning, that we "love one another" (v. 5). He declares "this is love, that we walk after his commandment" (v. 6).

Truth represents doctrine—the Word of God. "Thy word is truth" (John 17:17). The truth of the Word produces genuine love—the queen of all Christian virtues. A believer who loves God loves his fellow man and is, in John's terminology, "walking in truth" (v. 4) and walking "after God's commandments" (v. 6).

These "commandments" represent God's eternal moral law. They are as eternal as God is eternal; they are a reflection of his holy being and character. As given to the nation Israel in the Decalogue of the

Mosaic Covenant (Exod. 20:1-17) they were intended not as a way of salvation but as a means of showing to fallen man God's way of salvation through grace by faith. Yet even in their Mosaic wording the Commandments were summarized by love — love for both God (the first Table) and man (the second Table). See Deuteronomy 6:5; Leviticus 19:18; Matthew 22:35-40.

Now that the Mosaic Law has been fulfilled by Christ's loving sacrifice for fallen man, the new law of love is fulfilled in regenerated hearts by the indwelling Spirit (Rom. 5:5; Heb. 10:16). Our Lord in prospect of his redemptive work and the gift of the indwelling Spirit envisioned this new law of love (John 13:34). It was to be the fulfillment of the moral law of God not only in its Mosaic form in the Decalogue but also in its eternal form as the expression of God's relationship to all of his creatures of all time.

Christ therefore called the new law of love "a new commandment . . . that you love one another; as I have loved you, that you also love one another" (John 13:34). It is a *new commandment* (singular) in contrast to the *old commandments* (plural) of the Mosaic Decalogue; this single commandment of love embodied the essence of all ten of the Mosaic requirements.

The new law of Christ is a command to love with divine love. This love is produced in a believer's heart solely by the operation of the Holy Spirit. Through the Spirit this divine love is manifested spontaneously and without constraint in every believer who is "walking in truth" (v. 4). It is the "law of liberty" of James 1:25 and 2:12.

The Law of Moses, by contrast, was external and "dead" — trying to keep it was both a constraint and a bondage. It was simply beyond the ability of fallen human nature to completely obey it. The Law therefore exposed the depravity of all humanity.

Moses' Law demanded love (Lev. 19:18; Deut. 6:5; Luke 10:27), but Christ's new law of love (1 John 3:18, 23; 4:7-12, 19-21) takes the place of the external law by fulfilling it and supplying the internal reality and dynamic to keep it (Rom. 13:10; Gal. 5:14). Christ's law of love is "written in the heart" under the New Covenant (Heb. 10:16) and displayed in the believer's conduct by the power of the Holy Spirit.

REWARDS AND CHRISTIAN LIVING

In expounding the believer's "walk in truth" the Apostle John is careful to point out the peril of succumbing to error and falling prey to false teachers and deceivers (v. 7). This carries the risk of losing a "full reward" (v. 8). In broaching this subject of rewards the Apostle touches on a very important doctrine of Scripture.

A believer by steadfast faithfulness in service and good works will gain rewards or suffer loss of reward (1 Cor. 3:15). While no true believer can lose his salvation, some believers will receive less than a full reward (v. 8). In Pauline metaphor they will have failed to run the Christian race with full concentration on Christ (1 Cor. 9:27; Phil. 3: 10-14). The Apostle John warns that it is necessary to be constantly vigilant in order to receive a "full reward" at the judgment seat of Christ (2 Cor. 5:10). "Look to yourself" (be cautious and self-critical) in view of "the many deceivers" in the world, who deny the true person and full saving efficacy of Christ's finished redemption (v. 7). These "antichrists" use every possible trick of deception to lure God's people away from a walk of truth and the full reward that follows.

SEPARATION FROM SIN AND APOSTASY

This short Epistle also sheds light on the issue of separation from ecclesiastical apostasy. In our day this issue has been almost as vexing as the question of ecumenicalism (see discussion under Ephesians). Although separatist movements among Christians have often been tarnished by a spirit of censorious criticism and a conspicuous lack of love, it must still be said that Scripture does *not* condone compromise with apostasy and sin. There simply cannot be harmonious fellowship with religionists who deny the true person and work of Christ (vv. 9-11).

John states clearly that anyone who rejects "the doctrine of Christ," that is, the teaching of his full deity and perfect humanity as John has presented it (v. 9; cf. John 1:1, 14; 1 John 1:1-4; 4:1, 2), does not have God (cf. 1 John 2:19, 24). On the other hand, everyone who holds to this basic Christian tenet has both the Father and the Son (1 John 2:23). This admonition identifies apostates and apostasy (see discussion of apostasy in Second Timothy) and enjoins clear-cut separation from them on the part of every believer.

3 John

AUTHOR

The third letter of John is the shortest book of the New Testament. In style, vocabulary, and ideas it closely resembles the other Johannine writings. It was written by "the elder" (1:1; cf. 2 John 1:1), who is certainly John the Apostle, writer of the Gospel of John and First John (see remarks on Second John).

BACKGROUND AND DATE

The letter is addressed to "Gaius the beloved" (v. 1), of whom nothing is known, since the name was very common (cf. Acts 19:29; 20:4; Rom. 16:23; 1 Cor. 1:14). Whoever Gaius was, he was evidently a prominent member of a church in Asia Minor under John's supervision. Trouble had arisen in this assembly because of another influential member named Diotrephes. This domineering individual had refused to recognize messengers of the gospel sent by John to minister to the church. The only reason given for Diotrephes's opposition to these itinerant preachers was that he himself desired the place of preeminence. Perhaps he was ambitious to do all the teaching and was jealous of anyone else who came in this capacity.

The date of Third John is approximately the same as that of the other letters of John, that is, between A.D. 85 and 90.

IMPORTANCE AND PURPOSE

The Apostle penned the letter to voice his esteem of Gaius (v. 1), to assure him of his prayers for his health (v. 2), and to let him know of his joy at his stand for the truth (vv. 3, 4). John also commends him for having received the visiting preachers, urging him to continue this Christian hospitality (vv. 5-8). The Apostle promises to deal with Diotrephes, if he comes for a visit (vv. 9, 10), and commends Demetrius, who was likely the bearer of this Epistle (vv. 11, 12). The Apostle expresses the hope that he may be able to pay the church a visit and see Gaius face to face (vv. 13, 14).

OUTLINE

A. A Godly Life Commended (1-4)
  1. Greeting and well wishes (1, 2)
  2. Praise of a godly walk (3, 4)
B. Hospitality to Itinerant Ministers Lauded (5-8)
  1. Gaius' faithfulness mentioned (5)
  2. Gaius' hospitality exemplified (6)
  3. Gaius' hospitality encouraged (7, 8)
C. A Domineering Church Worker Denounced (9-11)
  1. He resisted the Apostle's authority (9)
  2. He insisted on his own way (10)
  3. A scriptural guideline set down (11)
D. A Godly Church Worker Praised (12)
  1. He is approved by his conduct (12a)
  2. He is approved by his doctrine (12b)
  3. He is approved by the Apostle (12c)
Conclusion: Intentions and Benediction (13, 14)

THE CHURCH AND THE PROBLEM OF ECCLESIASTICAL DOMINATION

The Third Letter of John anticipates a difficulty that has in varying degrees plagued the Church since Apostolic days. It is the problem of domineering individuals, groups of individuals, or ecclesiastical organizations. Third John presents the problem as crystallized in an individual. Diotrephes was perhaps a layman, but he illustrates the evil of domineering ambition on the part of anyone in the church—pastor, elder, deacon, or lay member. It was this spirit of pride and self-importance that led Diotrephes to slander "with malicious words" everyone who questioned his oppressive domination (cf. Prov. 9:8; 10:8; 12:1). Diotrephes's objects of slander included the Apostle John himself (v. 10).

Diotrephes intensified his dictatorial tactics by refusing hospitality to itinerant ministers of the gospel recommended by the Apostle John himself and by forbidding other church members to do so. Believers who exercised such hospitality he excommunicated from the church! (See verse 10.)

The Apostle Peter warned elders against being "lords over God's heritage," exhorting them rather to be "examples to the flock" (1 Pet. 5:3). The spirit of self-assertion which Diotrephes showed has crystallized in the Church in the invention of a priestly order that dominates over the so-called laity. It ignores the great truth of the priesthood of all believers, substituting instead the wholly unscriptural notion of a priesthood which is superior to ordinary believers.

The spirit of Diotrephes sometimes finds expression even in a church where the priesthood of all believers is taught and practiced. Occasionally a sound gospel preacher gets the notion that he must "run the church" as a God-ordained dictator. He listens to little advice from elders or deacons (if he has any) and tolerates no opposition. Those who dare to oppose him are put out of the church in true Diotrephene style. He spurns advice from older, more experienced men, as Diotrephes ignored the Apostle John.

The cure for the evil of ecclesiastical domination is rigid adherence to the Word of God and submissive reliance on the Holy Spirit's leading. The Holy Spirit never leads anyone to become an ecclesiastical dictator.

"The well-beloved Gaius" (vv. 1-4) and Demetrius, a believer of fine reputation for living out the truth (v. 12), are the Apostle's answer to unworthy intruders like Diotrephes.

Jude

AUTHOR

Similarities and allusions to Jude occur in the writings of Hermas, Polycarp, Theophilus of Antioch, and Tertullian. Although its canonicity was questioned by some because of alleged citations from the noncanonical books of Enoch and *The Assumption of Moses,* Jude's right to inclusion in the Canon was universally recognized by A.D. 350.

The author (1:1) was apparently the brother of James (bishop of Jerusalem and writer of the Epistle of James) and a half-brother of Christ (cf. Matt. 13:55; Mark 6:3). At first Jude or Judas was an unbeliever (John 7:3-5). Later, however, he became convinced of Christ's deity (Acts 1:14). Some scholars identify the author of the Epistle as the Apostle Judas (Luke 6:16; Acts 1:13), called elsewhere Lebbaeus or Thaddaeus (Matt. 10:3).

BACKGROUND AND DATE

The occasion of the Epistle was the appearance of a philosophic heresy which encouraged moral laxity and lawlessness. It was apparently the Gnosticism exposed elsewhere in the New Testament (notably in Colossians and Second Peter). Gnostic philosophy clashed sharply with Christianity in its assessment of all matter as evil. It denied the biblical doctrine of creation and the true incarnation of Christ, teaching that Christ's body could not have been real without at the same time being evil.

In the realm of Christian ethics the Gnostic philosophy taught a dual error. On one hand it prompted antinomianism (the belief that one is not obligated to keep the moral law) and on the other hand it fostered ascetic abuse of the body in order to promote spirituality. Both of these errors are clearly opposed by the Word of God.

Precisely where or when Jude wrote his Epistle is not known. The Epistle was apparently written not later than A.D. 81, when Domitian became Emperor. Hegesippus in the second century declares that Jude's two grandsons were arraigned before Domitian as descendants of David, but were dismissed as harmless peasants. Had Jude been alive, he too would probably have been brought before the Emperor. Jude apparently knew of Peter's writings. If so, his Letter cannot be earlier than A.D. 66 or 67. A date of about A.D. 75 would probably not be far afield.

IMPORTANCE AND PURPOSE

The Epistle of Jude contends for the faith against unbelief and apostasy. Jude's message is one of the most severe in the New Testament. But its severity is justified by the grave peril which Jude faced and combated. Like Second Peter, Jude concerns itself primarily with false teachers that had infiltrated the Church (cf. vv. 4-16 with 2 Pet. 2: 1 – 3:7). Jude denounces these false teachers in even stronger language than does Peter.

Both Second Peter and Jude deal with conditions that were already developing in their day. But both also envisioned the intensified apostasy that would prevail at the end of the age. In this respect Jude forms a fitting introduction to the Book of the Revelation.

OUTLINE

Salutation (1, 2)
A. Contending for the Faith (3, 4)
    1. Desire to expound salvation (3a)
    2. Necessity to contend for the faith (3b, 4)
B. Examples of Apostates (5-7)
    1. Israel in the wilderness (5)
    2. The fallen angels at the flood (6)
    3. The sinners of Sodom and Gomorrah (7)
C. Condemnation of False Teachers (8-16)
    1. Their presumption outlined and illustrated (8-10)
    2. Their woe predicted (11)

3. Their spiritual sterility indicated (12, 13).

4. Their judgment foretold (14, 15)

5. Their character reviewed (16)

D. Exhortation of God's People (17-23)

1. To remember apostolic warnings (17-19)

2. To build up themselves on their holy faith (20a)

3. To pray in the Holy Spirit (20b)

4. To keep themselves in the love of God and faith (21)

5. To show mercy toward the sinner (22)

6. To abhor the sinner's sin (23)

Concluding Doxology (24, 25)

JUDE AND THE COMMON SALVATION

Jude's original purpose was to write to believers concerning "the common salvation" (v. 3). This is deliverance from the world, the flesh, and the devil through the redemptive work of Jesus Christ. It is "common" in that it is offered to all, being based upon the glorious invitation "*Whosoever* will, let him take the water of life freely" (Rev. 22:17; cf. John 3:16). It is not confined to any particular nation, people, or race. Christ's redemptive work made the entire race salvable. God can justly redeem lost sinners who believe on Jesus.

Jude's exercise of "all diligence" in writing discloses his earnest zeal for the growth of God's people in the truth of the Word. That he felt compelled to write about "contending for the faith" instead of "the common salvation" (his original topic) is clearly providential. Salvation has been fully expounded by several other New Testament writers, notably the Apostle Paul. Jude's special topic has been important to the Church throughout its entire history, and never more so than today.

CONTENDING FOR THE FAITH

When Jude exhorted his readers to "contend for the faith" (v. 3) he employed a strong Greek word meaning "to zealously and earnestly contend" (*epagonizesthai*). An expanded definition would read, "to fight while standing on a fortress which is being attacked by a determined enemy; to hold the fortress at all costs."

Unfortunately, this concept of "contending strenuously in defense of the faith" has often been abused by sincere and well-meaning Christians. Too often the contending has been conducted in a spirit of pugnacious battling and censorious criticism devoid of meekness and love. Thus intellectual warfare has been waged at the expense of practical Christian living.

The contender for the faith is like a man walking a tightrope. Walking the rope requires two feats. The man must both stay on the rope (keep true to the faith) and move ahead with balance (keep true to the moral life of faith). If either of these endeavors is ignored the believer's testimony is lost. True scriptural zeal in contending for the faith *must* conform to the noble walk to which every believer is called. The militant must demonstrate "all lowliness and meekness, with longsuffering, forbearing one another in love." He must make every effort to "keep the unity of the Spirit in the bond of peace" (Eph. 4:1-3). He is responsible before God to keep the seven unities which the Spirit of God uses to maintain peace and purity in the Church.

These seven unities of Scripture consist of the following: "one body" (the true Church); "one Spirit" (the Holy Spirit); "one hope of our calling" (the hope of glorification); "one Lord" (Jesus Christ our Savior); "one faith" (the faith once-for-all delivered to the saints — Jude 1:3); "one baptism" (Spirit-baptism into Christ, of which water baptism is a symbol); and "one God and Father of all, who is above all, and through all, and in all" (Eph. 4:4-6).

THE CHRISTIAN FAITH

This is described as "the faith which was once-for-all delivered to the saints" (v. 3, ASV, RSV). This "faith" is the entire body of revealed truth which God expects Christians to believe, and is intimately tied to faith in everyday Christian living (Tit. 2:11-15; James 2:12-26). Believers are expected to defend "the faith" by both their sound words and their godly actions.

Jude's definition of "the faith" leaves room for no novel doctrines of any kind — such as the "ungodly men" of verse 4 were trying to introduce. The key word "once-for-all" (*hapax*) is employed of actions that are both final and permanently valid. It is this changeless quality of the Christian faith that Jude emphasizes. The Apostle Paul also stresses the same truth (cf. Gal. 1:8-12; 2 Tim. 3:16).

Today religious pluralism is attempting to "streamline" Christianity into a relativistic, ecumenical mold and to elevate the "good" of every religion and cult in the world to the level of Christian acceptability. Jude's definition of the Christian faith has thus never been more urgently needed. Like Jude, the Christian teacher is responsible to declare the changelessness of Christian principles of faith and practice. Although certain secondary applications of Christian truth vary from generation to generation in order to meet changing needs, *every principle of biblical truth remains forever the same.* This is "the faith delivered once-for-all to the saints" (v. 3).

ASSURED PUNISHMENT OF SIN

In treating the subject of rebellion and sin on the part of false teachers, Jude clearly points out the certainty of divine judgment upon deliberate and wilful sin. He presents three illustrations from history—the Israelites in the desert, the fallen angels at the time of the flood, and the sinners of Sodom and Gomorrah (vv. 5-7).

The first historical illustration involves the Lord's redeemed people (v. 5). Although they had faith to sprinkle the Passover blood (Exod. 12:1-40) and to be delivered out of Egypt, they were afterward destroyed at Kadesh-Barnea (Num. 14:1-45; 1 Cor. 10:1-5; Heb. 3:17-19) because of unbelief. The judgment of the redeemed involved physical death (cf. 1 Cor. 5:1-5; 11:30-32; 1 John 5:16).

The second historical warning relates to the fallen angels who cohabited with mortal women at the time of the flood (v. 6). Their immediate punishment for intrusion into the realm of another order of created beings (Gen. 6:1-4; 2 Pet. 2:4) was imprisonment in Tartarus. Their final doom will be consignment to the lake of fire after the great day of judgment (Rev. 20:11-15).

The third warning from history concerns the sinners of Sodom and Gomorrah (v. 7). Their destruction is intended to warn all transgressors of God's moral laws that punishment for sin is real (Rev. 19:20; 20:10, 14, 15; cf. Matt. 25:41). Jude's warning is especially striking in this day of apostasy, "new morality," and "God-is-dead" theology.

CONTENTION BETWEEN MICHAEL AND SATAN OVER THE BODY OF MOSES (v. 9)

Jude dramatizes the sinfulness of slander by contrasting the attitudes of apostate teachers and the archangel Michael. The apostates did not hesitate to slander exalted personages, possibly even angels ("dignities" literally means "glories"), while Michael refused to slander even a fallen angel (Satan). Jude's pointed contrast shows not only the pride of the apostates but also the seriousness of the sin of slander.

Contention about the body of Moses apparently arose because it was raised before its allotted time to appear in glorified form with Elijah (Matt. 17:3, 4). At the fall of man Satan had obtained "the power of death" over the whole human family (Heb. 2:14; cf. Gen. 2:17). He therefore challenged Moses' right to receive a glorified body *before* Christ's redemptive work had destroyed that power over believers. Michael in response simply claimed the redemptive power of Christ's sacrifice for Moses, as Zechariah had done for Israel in prospect of her future regeneration (Zech. 3:2). Further details about this incident are lacking because Scripture nowhere else mentions it.

RELIGIOUS NATURALISM

The religious naturalism so rampant today has been popularly designated "modernism." Though this name might seem to imply new concepts in religious thinking, the Book of Jude shows that the spiritually barren concepts of this error existed since the days of Cain. "The way of Cain" (v. 11) represents the religious but unsaved man who rejects the blood of Christ and instead attempts to offer his own good works to God (Gen. 4:3-8).

Jude exposes these same religious naturalists as mercenaries who "abandon themselves for the sake of gain to Balaam's error" (v. 11b, RSV; cf. 2 Pet. 2:15; Rev. 2:14). This error is the mistake of assuming that a righteous God could curse his chosen people because they had sinned (cf. Num. 22-24). It rejects the efficacy of Christ's death and ignores the higher morality of the cross, by which God can be righteous and at the same time eternally justify the believing sinner. Thus these false teachers reject the very essence of the Christian gospel.

Jude also denounces these men as partakers of Korah's sin of rebellion against the divine order in morality and religion (Num. 16:1-50; 26:9-11). Korah rejected the divine authority given to Moses as God's mouthpiece and to the Levites as God's priesthood. He demonstrated his rebellious attitude by intruding into the official activities of the priests. It is the mark of *all* false teachers to reject the authority of the Word of God and to pursue religious matters in their own way.

ENOCH'S PROPHECY
OF THE SECOND ADVENT

This prophecy, preserved as tradition in the noncanonical book of Enoch, is apparently cited by the Holy Spirit through Jude as divine truth (vv. 14, 15). Jude reveals that Enoch, "the seventh from Adam"

(Gen. 5:18-24; Heb. 11:5), envisioned the rise of these false teachers even in his day. He foretold that judgment would overtake them at Christ's second advent, when the latter-day apostates would be judged (v. 15).

The question arises, Does Jude ascribe this prophecy found in the apocryphal Book to the Enoch of Genesis 5? He apparently does. The difficulty may be resolved as follows. 1) There are reasons for thinking that the book of Enoch in the form now existing copied from Jude rather than Jude from the book of Enoch. Some later writer may have inserted the quotation in the original Book of Enoch. 2) The original prophecy of the patriarch Enoch may well have been appropriated by the author of the Book of Enoch without giving proper credit. 3) The Holy Spirit guided Jude in using this brief, true quotation from a non-canonical book, even as Paul was guided in referring to certain facts unrecorded in the Old Testament (2 Tim. 3:8; Gal. 3:19; Heb. 11:24) and in quoting certain true statements by pagan poets (cf. Acts 17:28; Tit. 1:12). In any case the earliest biblical prophecies of the Redeemer dwell on his second advent in glory rather than on his first coming in lowliness (cf. Gen. 3:15 with Rom. 16:20).

The Revelation

TITLE

The correct title of this great prophetic book is "The Revelation of Jesus Christ." The term "revelation" is from the Latin *revelatio*, "a revealing or uncovering," and the Greek *apokalupsis*, "an uncovering, a revelation." The phrase "of Jesus Christ" is objective genitive, indicating that the revelation or disclosure was not only *given to* Jesus Christ by God the Father but also *concerns* him (1:1). The great climactic events of history converge in Christ.

The sealed Golden Gate in Jerusalem's Eastern Wall, which some expect the returned Messiah to open *(Russ Busby photo)*

Soon after it was written the book came to be called "The Apocalypse of John" in order to differentiate it from many other "apocalypses" in circulation. In the fourth century the title was expanded to include the words "the Divine." This designation points to John the Apostle as the human instrument through whom the revelation came. The inspired title, however, is "The Revelation of (Concerning) Jesus Christ."

AUTHOR

External evidence to the Revelation as an authentic work of the Apostle John is substantial and completely adequate. Justin Martyr, Irenaeus, Tertullian, and Hippolytus in the West and Clement of Alexandria and Origen in the East give clear evidence of its genuineness. Victorinus, who wrote the earliest commentary of the Apocalypse that is still in existence, ascribes the book to John the Apostle. The Muratorian Fragment also received the work as apostolic and genuine.

Internal evidence is also ample. Four times the writer calls himself John (1:1, 4, 9; 22:8). As in the case of the fourth Gospel, the humility of the writer of the Apocalypse serves to identify him with the Apostle John. The author does not call himself an apostle but merely a "servant" of Christ (1:1) and a "brother and partaker with you in the tribulation and kingdom and patience which are in Jesus" (1:9).

The author of the Revelation was an exile on the small island of Patmos in the Aegean Sea (1:9). The Fathers declared that it was John the Apostle who was banished there, returning to the mainland after the death of Emperor Domitian. Irenaeus says that the Apostle John thereafter remained at Ephesus until the reign of Trajan.

Objections against apostolic authorship on linguistic grounds have not been successful. Differences in vocabulary, grammar, and general style between the Revelation and other Johannine writings are explainable on the basis of the apocalyptic nature of the subject matter. These differences are more than counterbalanced by a number of significant similarities in vocabulary, such as "the Word," "water of life," "little lamb," etc. The Hebraic style of the Revelation is to be expected in a book steeped in Old Testament imagery.

BACKGROUND AND DATE

John apparently came to Ephesus in the year A.D. 69 or 70 and worked among a number of churches in the province of Asia. The seven churches of Revelation (chaps. 2, 3) appear to have been in his circuit. He received the revelation while an exile on the island of Patmos, later returning to Asia (after the death of Domitian). The Apocalypse was no doubt intended for both the seven churches of Asia and the Christian Church at large.

On the basis of testimony by Irenaeus, Clement of Alexandria, Eusebius, and others that John was banished to Patmos and received his visions in the later part of Domitian's reign A.D. 81-96), the book is to be dated about A.D. 95 or 96.

DESCRIPTION AND INTERPRETATION

The Revelation belongs to the type of literature known as "apocalyptic." In this kind of writing the predictive element looms large and is couched in figures and symbols. These symbols are frequently unexplained and are to be interpreted *strictly on the basis of other biblical information.* The Revelation dovetails particularly well with such Old Testament apocalyptic and prophetic books as Daniel, Ezekiel, and Zechariah. Without a knowledge of these books in particular and Old and New Testament prophecy in general, the Revelation remains a sealed book. Attempts to interpret it on any basis other than the revealed prophetic Word itself have been complete failures.

The apocalyptic nature of the book is indicated in the opening verse. God sent and "signified" the revelation "by his angel to his servant John" (1:1). The word "signified" means "to put in the form of signs or symbols."

Since the time of its writing the Book of the Revelation has been interpreted in a number of different ways. Four of the major methods of interpretation are contrasted in the following table:

METHODS OF INTERPRETING THE BOOK OF REVELATION	
Allegorical ("Spiritualizing") Method	Mystical, allegorical approach. Denies any earthly millennial kingdom following the second advent. Fails to do justice to the prophetic nature of the book (1:3; 10:11; 22:7) and ignores the interpretive key (1:19) as well as the events preceding and succeeding the second advent. Fails to ground the book in Old Testament prophecy. Especially weak on prophecies of Daniel.
Preterist Method	Holds that the Book has already been essentially fulfilled in the Church's conflict with Judaism (Chaps. 4–11) and paganism (Chaps. 12–19). Chapters 20–22 describe the Church's present conflict. Ignores the interpretive key (1:19), attributes arbitrary meanings to the symbols of the book, and rejects indications of the short time-span of Chapters 4–19.
Continuous-Historical Method	Covers entire span of Church history (John's time to the end of time). Fails to correlate with Bible prophecy as a whole and has all the weaknesses of the Allegorical and Preterist Methods.
Futurist Method	This, we believe, is the *correct view* because 1) it uses the key (1:19) as guide, placing the bulk of the book (Chaps. 4–22) still in the future; 2) it grounds interpretation in Old Testament and New Testament prophecy; 3) it interprets the symbols biblically; and 4) it honors the truth of the imminent return of Christ for his own and his glorious advent to set up his kingdom (Acts 1:6).

OUTLINE

Introduction (1:1-11)

A. The Self-Revelation of Christ—the Things Seen (1:12-20)

        1. His relation to the churches (1:12-16)

        2. His message to the churches (1:17-20)

   B. Christ and His Church — the Things Which Are (chapters 2, 3)

        1. Ephesus, Smyrna, Pergamum, Thyatira (chapter 2)

        2. Sardis, Philadelphia, Laodicea (chapter 3)

   C. Christ and History's Consummation — the Things Which Shall Be Hereafter (chapters 4 — 22)

        1. The preparation in heaven (chapters 4, 5)

        2. The Great Tribulation on earth (chapters 6-18)

           a. The seal judgments (6:1 — 8:1)

           b. The trumpet judgments (8:2 — 11:19)

           c. The seven personages (chapters 12, 13)

           d. Preview of the end of the Tribulation (chapter 14)

           e. The bowl judgments (chapters 15, 16)

           f. The Judgment of Babylon (chapters 17, 18)

        3. The second advent and Armageddon (chapter 19)

           a. Rejoicing in heaven (19:1-6)

           b. Marriage of the Lamb (19:7-10)

           c. Advent in glory (19:11-16)

           d. Armageddon (19:17-21)

        4. The establishment of the kingdom (20:1-10)

           a. The binding of Satan (20:1-3)

           b. The millennial reign (20:4-6)

           c. The loosing of Satan and his final doom (20:7-10)

        5. The final judgment (20:11-15)

        6. The eternal state (chapters 21, 22)

           a. The sinless eternity (21:1-7)

           b. The isolation of the wicked (21:8)

           c. The New Jerusalem (21:9 — 22:5)

   Conclusion (22:6-21)

PROPHETIC FOREVIEW OF THE EARTHLY CAREER OF THE CHURCH

"The things seen" (1:19) included the vision of Christ (1:12-20). *"The things which are"* embraces the Church age (chaps. 2, 3). The fact that only seven of the churches of Asia are selected indicates that the Holy Spirit is symbolically comprehending the entire Church, since seven is the number of completion and perfection. It is incredible that in a prophecy covering the Church period ("the things that

are") there should be no such foreview. These messages must contain that foreview, for the Church does not appear after chapter 3. It is also evident that the messages to the seven churches reach beyond the immediate churches addressed and comprehend the entire Church of God.

PROPHETIC FOREVIEW OF THE CHURCH ON EARTH

A.D. *33-100   100-316   316-606   606-1520   1520-1750   1750-1900   1900-?*

Ephesus (Rev. 2:1-7). ⎯⎯⎯⎯⎯⎯⎯⎯⎯⎯⎯⎯⎯⎯⎯⎯⎯→
The Church characterized by good works, endurance, and separation from evil, but guilty of losing its initial love for Christ.

Smyrna (Rev. 2:8-11) ⎯⎯⎯⎯⎯⎯⎯⎯⎯⎯⎯⎯⎯⎯→
The Church under persecution by the Roman Emperors Hadrian (117), Septimius Severus (193), Maximin (235), Decius (249), Valerian (254), Aurelian (270), and Diocletian (284). Also harassed by Christ-hating Jews (2:9)

Pergamos (Rev. 2:12-17) ⎯⎯⎯⎯⎯⎯⎯⎯⎯⎯⎯⎯→
The Church compromising because of worldly favor. Held doctrine of Balaam—teaching that corrupts God's people with worldliness (Num. 31:15, 16). Also held doctrine of Nicolaitans (possibly antinomian license but more likely incipient laity-dominating clericalism).

Thyatira (Rev. 2:18-29) ⎯⎯⎯⎯⎯⎯⎯⎯⎯⎯→
The paganized Church of the Dark Ages and Middle Ages preceding the Protestant Reformation. Jezebel prefigures teachers who taught the errors and perversions that produced the Papal hierarchy and its perversions of biblical truth and Christian living. Plumbed "the depths of Satan" in occultism and heresy (2:24)

Sardis (Rev. 3:1-6) ⎯⎯⎯⎯⎯⎯⎯⎯→
The Church of the Reformation. Swept away rubbish of Romanism but failed to regain vibrant life of faith.

Philadelphia ⎯⎯⎯⎯⎯→
(Rev. 3:7-13)
The Church of worldwide evangelistic movements that has kept God's Word and has not denied Christ's name.

Laodicea →
(Rev.
3:14-22)
The apostate Church with unregenerate members who have embraced "liberal theology."

The primary importance of these messages is prophetic, since they delineate seven well-defined, successive periods of Church history. Each of these periods begins at a fairly specific time and continues to the end of Church history. Thus near the end of the Church age characteristics of all seven of the periods can be seen concurrently.

THE REVELATION
AND THE RAPTURE QUESTION

Does the Book of Revelation shed light on the controversial question of the time of the rapture? That the book supports a pretribulation rapture is indicated by the following considerations. A prophetic survey of the history of the Church is given in chapters 2 and 3. This constitutes "the things which are" (1:19), already existing in John's day and continuing throughout the entire Church age.

Chapters 4 to 22 constitute "the things which shall be hereafter" (4:1), that is, "after these (Church) things." In these chapters the Church no longer appears on earth but is instead seen glorified and rewarded in heaven (represented by the twenty-four elders in 4:4, 10, 11). This necessitates a pretribulation outtaking, since chapters 4 to 19 concern the tribulation (both the first and the second half). This agrees perfectly with Paul's description of the rapture in First Thessalonians and with his argument for the pretribulation outtaking in Second Thessalonians 2:1-10.

The invitation to John to "come up hither" (4:1), while not an explicit reference to the rapture of the Church, is certainly an implicit and symbolic representation of this event. This is suggested by the symbolic nature of the book and the pivotal change of time and place indicated by this verse, in accordance with the inspired interpretive key (1:19). (At this point in Revelation the Church age is consummated by the rapture and is followed by the Church in heaven).

Although the rapture is referred to in letters to two of the churches (2:25; 3:11) as a *doctrine*, it is not a featured part of the prophetic foreview of the Apocalypse. This is in accord with the primary objective of the book: to portray the events climaxing in the second advent, the prophetic kingdom, and the eternal state.

Whether or not Revelation 4:1 specifically symbolizes the rapture, this event must have occurred before the events of chapter 4, as evidenced by the subsequent chapters of the Revelation. The word "church," so common in chapters 2 and 3, does not occur again until 22:16 (cf. 19:7). The Church is completely absent from the scenes of the tribulation, which constitute the major portion of the book. People who are saved after the rapture of the Church are described as saved Israelites or saved Gentiles — never as members of the Church.

THE TWENTY-FOUR ELDERS AND THEIR IDENTITY (4:4, 10; 5:8, 14; 11:16; 19:4)

These elders clearly include the redeemed saints of the Church. Whether they also include Old Testament saints is not certain. They cannot represent angels, for the term "elder" is never applied to angels, nor do angels receive crowns or occupy thrones. These are promised only to redeemed men (Matt. 19:28; 2 Tim. 4:8; 1 Pet. 5:4; Rev. 2:10; 20:4). The 24 elders wear victor's crowns (*stephanoi*) won in the Christian career. The thrones they occupy indicate that they have already been judged for their works (1 Cor. 3:11-15; 2 Cor. 5:10). Their "white garments" distinguish them as a redeemed priesthood (1 Pet. 2: 9), active in priestly services (Rev. 5:8). They await the awarding of royal and judicial functions at Christ's advent in glory (20:4-6).

The number 24 is apparently representative of the full number of saints comprising the completed, glorified Church. When King David organized the priests into "courses" he established 24 heads of priestly families to represent the entire priesthood (1 Chron. 24:1-19). Thus the 24 elders of Revelation represent the priestly capacity of the entire Church in heaven. In Old Testament typology the Aaronic priests represent New Testament believers while Aaron, the high priest, typifies Christ.

THE SEVEN-SEALED BOOK (5:1-10)

This is the official document which guarantees dispossession of Satan and evil men from the earth prior to Christ's advent and kingdom. "Sealed with seven seals" denotes complete sealing; the document cannot be opened until a qualified personage appears to execute its contents. The distinguished personage who appears turns out to be none less than "the lion of the tribe of Judah . . . the root of David." By virtue of his divine-human nature and his fully efficacious death, Christ is uniquely qualified both to open the book and to administer its contents.

The transmittal of the scroll from God the Father to Christ as Executor (5:7-10) signals the inauguration of the tribulation judgments. Each sealed portion of the scroll specifies a particular judgment to be poured out on the world's wicked inhabitants (6:1 − 8:5).

After the full fury of six of the seven judgments has been poured out on the earth, God temporarily suspends further judgment while he enumerates the Jews and Gentiles who have been saved during the tribulation period (7:1-17). Then Christ breaks the seventh seal. Heaven's hosts react with stunned silence for about a half hour. Then God's wrath bursts forth on earth again with unprecedented fury. Seven trumpet judgments (8:7—11:19) and seven bowl judgments (16:2-21) combine to produce the greatest tribulation in the history of the world. A total of 13 chapters (6—18) is required to describe the horrors of this period.

THOSE SAVED IN THE TRIBULATION

After the rapture of the Church all who have rejected the clear preaching of the gospel will be delivered into demonic delusion and ultimate destruction (2 Thess. 2:7-12). Nevertheless, God will see fit to save multitudes of both Jews and Gentiles during the tribulation period. The 144,000 Jews of Revelation 7:1-8 represent those who are preserved from destruction and "sealed" for salvation (cf. Eph. 1:13, 14). Though all tribal genealogies have long since been obliterated from human records, God knows who and where the members of the various tribes are (Isa. 11:11-16; Ezek. 48:1-7).

The corresponding elect body of Gentiles saved during the tribulation is described in 7:9-17. They will also be preserved as an unglorified people on the earth to enter the earthly kingdom. They will have undergone unparalleled suffering and will have been brought to salvation by the preaching of the gospel of the kingdom (Matt. 24:13, 14). This is the good news of Christ's death and resurrection as it pertains to salvation in the light of the kingdom soon to be inaugurated. It is called "the everlasting gospel" (14:6), since Christ's death and resurrection pertain to God's eternal plan and purposes.

DEMONIC POWER AND DECEPTION
OF THE END-TIME

The Revelation discloses the awful outburst of demon power which the Apostle Paul predicted in Second Thessalonians 2:7-12. The locust symbolism (9:1-11) portrays the loosing of myriads of demons from the abyss, the prison of the demons (9:1-3; cf. Luke 8:30). These particular demons are imprisoned at present, but will be released during the tribulation period in order to delude and torment wicked earth-dwellers. Gross idolatry energized by demon worship will result in violence, occultism, sexual lawlessness, and immorality on a colossal scale (9:20, 21).

As the result of spiritual warfare in the heavenlies Satan and his demonic hosts will be cast down to the earth to augment the wickedness and diabolic fury of those days (12:7-12). With the rise of the Beast and the False Prophet (13:1-18), Satanic cunning and demonic delusion will reach their zenith (13:4, 14-18). The Battle of Armageddon will be energized and consummated by demon powers, who will delude the rulers of the earth and their armies in an attempt to take over the earth for Satan and to banish the name of God and his Christ (16:13, 14). But at the height of the battle Christ will return in majestic power to smash the Satanic world system. Satan and his demon hordes will be banished to the abyss (20:1-3) and Christ's millennial kingdom will be inaugurated.

After the millennium Satan and his demons will be released temporarily and will again inspire certain men to rebel against God (20:7-9a). This rebellion will consummate in the final downfall of evil, for God will not only destroy all wicked men but will remand Satan (and doubtless his hosts) to Gehenna forever (20:9b, 10). Death, hades, sin, Satan, demons, and wicked men will be isolated in this quarantine ward for all eternity. This will make possible a sinless eternity (chaps. 21, 22). With sin and sinners rigidly confined, never again to mar God's universe, the divine purpose will at last have been achieved.

THE MYSTERY OF GOD AND "THE LITTLE BOOK" (CHAP. 10)

The "mighty angel" who sets his foot on land and sea (10:2) symbolizes Christ in his right to claim the earth as his own (Psa. 2:7, 8). The angel's shout and the rumble of the seven thunders dramatize Christ's authority over the earth, now to be exercised "without delay" (10:6b, 7a). The theme of the little book is "the mystery of God" (10:7). This truth, previously hidden but now revealed, is the grand subject of the rest of the Revelation. It concerns Christ as the incarnate Redeemer and the imminent King of the earth.

The little book is apparently to be identified with the book which the prophet Daniel was told to seal up "until the time of the end" (Dan. 12:4, 9). The scroll was "sweet as honey" when first "eaten" (read and understood—see Ezek. 2:8, 9; 3:1-3), but "bitter" when the glowing promises of deliverance for Daniel's people, the Jews, were seen to be preceded by awful judgments.

THE SEVEN PERSONAGES OF REVELATION 12 AND 13	
The Person	*The Identification*
The Woman (12:1, 2)	Symbolizes Israel clothed in regal and governmental splendor, the 12 stars denoting her 12 tribes (Gen. 37:9). Her travail represents Israel's tribulation agony, during which she gives birth to the godly Jewish remnant (12:17; Mic. 5:2, 3).
The Dragon (12:3, 4)	Symbolizes Satan as the serpent (Gen. 3:1-5, 13-15). "Red" shows his murderous character (John 8:44). His diadem and horns identify him with the final form of Gentile power. He appears in historical perspective (cf. Isa. 14:12-14; Ezek. 28:12-15).
The Male Child (12:5, 6)	Christ prefigured in his *birth,* his *destiny of conquest* (Psa. 2:9), his *ascension,* and his *position on God's throne.*
Michael (12:7-12)	The archangel, special protector of the Jews (Dan. 12:1; cf. Dan. 10:13-21). He and his angels expel Satan and his angels from the heavenlies (Job 1:6; Eph. 2:2; 6:12).
The Remnant (12:17)	Satan turns against these godly Jews. They "keep the commandments of God" and bear witness to Jesus.
The Beast out of the Sea (13:1-10)	Head of revived Roman Empire, who arises out of the unsettled political condition ("the sea" — Isa. 57:20; Dan. 7:24-28). Has demon-inspired career of persecution of the saints (Dan. 7:21, 22).
The Beast out of the Earth (13:11-18)	The Prophet of the Beast (the Antichrist). Directs worship of the first beast through miraculous powers, giving life to the Beast's image. He is the culmination of fallen man's wickedness.

THE TWO WITNESSES (11:3-12)

These two miracle-workers of God are evidently members of the latter-day saved remnant of Israel. They are *Christ's* witnesses, the term "my witnesses" referring to Christ as symbolized by the mighty angel of chapter 10. They are "clothed in sackcloth" to symbolize their mourning over the grievous sin of Israel (cf. Joel 1:13; Jer. 4:8). Their message centers in Christ's imminent kingship over the earth.

The reference to "the two olive trees and the two lampstands" (Zech. 4:2, 3) point to Messiah as King-Priest, since Zechariah's olive trees indicate these two offices. He will soon rule as the light of the world over restored Israel, prefigured by the gold lampstand of Zechariah 4. Like Moses and Elijah, the two witnesses are endowed with the power of God. They effect drought like Elijah (1 Kings 17:1; James 5:17), turn water into blood (Exod. 7:19), and perform other signs like Moses (Exod. 7 — 10). They are murdered by the Beast, the leader of the revived Roman Empire, but not until after they have finished their testimony (11:7).

God then resurrects and translates the two witnesses in the cloud of the Shekinah glory (Ezek. 10:19; Matt. 17:5) and punishes their persecutors with an earthquake (11:11-13). Although the two witnesses have sometimes been associated with Moses and Elijah or Moses and Enoch, these identifications are hardly possible, since both of the witnesses are killed and resurrected. This could not be true of the actual Old Testament men, since they have already received glorified bodies (see Matt. 17:3).

THE SEVEN BOWL JUDGMENTS	
Bowl 1 (16:2)	Poured out upon those having the mark of the Beast. They are afflicted with a grievous ulcer.
Bowl 2 (16:3)	Poured out upon the sea, which becomes blood. Doubtless symbolic of the complete moral and spiritual death of godless society.
Bowl 3 (16:4-7)	Poured out upon fresh waters, which become blood. Doubtless symbolic of the moral pollution of all the sources of inspiration and refreshment.
Bowl 4 (16:8, 9)	Poured out upon the sun, which scorches men with heat. Men's blasphemy reveals their inveterately wicked character.
Bowl 5 (16:10, 11)	Poured out upon the throne of the Beast. His kingdom is plunged into gross darkness—physical, moral, and spiritual.
Bowl 6 (16:12-16)	Poured out upon the Euphrates River (1780 miles in length), symbolizing the removal of every barrier for the advance of "the kings from the east" to Armageddon.
Bowl 7 (16:17-21)	Poured out "upon the air," Satan's realm (Eph. 2:2). Worldwide earthquake signifies the consummation of God's wrath in judgment upon the Satanic world-system. Only one kingdom escapes. It is the kingdom of Christ, for it cannot be shaken (Dan. 2:44). Huge hailstones, about 100 pounds in weight, bring God's wrath to a close and prelude Messiah's glorious advent.

THE SEVEN BOWLS

The loosing of the seventh seal (8:1-6) completes the opening of the sealed scroll (5:1), so that its full contents (the trumpets and the bowls) may be released on the earth to free it from the grasp of Satan and wicked men. The seven trumpets announce three "woes." The fifth trumpet announces the first woe—the loosing of myriads of demons from the abyss (9:1-11). The sixth trumpet announces the second woe—evidently an infernal spirit army (9:13-21). The seventh trumpet announces the third woe—all the remaining judgments prior to the setting up of the kingdom (11:15—20:3), especially the terrible "bowl judgments" (16:2-21).

Chapter 16 introduces the seven bowls, which symbolize the consummation of God's wrath poured out on wicked men of the earth. This effusion of God's wrath eventuates in the Battle of Armageddon and the advent of Christ in glory as supreme King and absolute Lord (19:11-21).

THE VISION OF ECCLESIASTICAL BABYLON

Babylon symbolizes the world system headed by Satan. It consists of unsaved men led by Satan and his principles. In Revelation 17 the emphasis is on the religious or ecclesiastical aspects of this system, while in chapter 18 the stress is on the commercial aspects of Babylon. Actually the fall of Babylon had been briefly predicted as early as chapter 14: "Fallen, fallen" (14:8) is a Hebraism meaning "completely fallen" in the sense of totally doomed. Babylon's destruction is also foreseen in 16:19.

The doom of ecclesiastical Babylon is presented in detail in chapter 17 under the symbol of a harlot. This evil woman personifies the final form of religious apostasy and revolt against God. Representing corrupt religionism, especially as it will appear in the last days, she denotes a vast religious system that sacrifices truth in order to gain power in the Satanic world system. In Scripture symbolism a woman often portrays something out of place religiously (cf. Matt. 13:33; Rev. 2:20).

This system rises to power by exploiting the peoples ("waters") of the earth (17:1) and by prostituting truth and purity. It uses the state wherever possible, riding into power on political Babylon, the beast's kingdom, and the final form of Gentile world government (17:2, 3; cf. 13:1-10). The "golden cup" filled with "abominations" (idolatries) and "the filthiness of her fornication" portray her gross infidelity to God and his Word (17:4). The harlot represents all false religious movements from their inception in the ancient Babylon of Nimrod (Gen. 10:8-10) to their awful fruition in the apostate religionism of the tribulation period.

Ecclesiastical Babylon is guilty of murdering both Old Testament "saints" and New Testament "martyrs of Jesus" (17:6). In the terrible persecutions of the tribulation period this wicked system will collaborate with the Beast (the political power) in the wholesale murder of the true followers of Jesus (17:6).

THE DESTRUCTION
OF ECCLESIASTICAL BABYLON

The Beast, the end-time ruler of the *revived* Roman Empire, will turn against the harlotrous religious system and will destroy both it and its headquarters in the Beast's capital, the city of Rome (17:16-18). The end-time revival of the Roman power is foretold (17:8). It "was" (existed) in John's day, but today it "is not," exactly as foretold. ". . . Yet is" refers to the end-time, when it will return with Satanic powers from the abyss (cf. 2 Thess. 2:8-10; Rev. 9:1-11; 11:7; 13:2). However, its last-day form will be brief. It will go into perdition at Christ's second advent (19:20).

The form of government of the revived Roman Empire is specified (17:10). The seven heads represent the seven hills of Rome on which the harlot sits (17:9), as well as seven kings (17:10). These apparently allude to seven distinct forms of government which characterized the Roman Empire from 32 B.C. to A.D. 476. The "five . . . which had fallen" are kings, consuls, dictators, decemvirs, and tribunes. The "one" that "is" represents the imperial government of John's day. "The other" (the seventh) is still future; it will remain in full power for only three and one-half years (13:5).

The last king (17:11) rules the ten-kingdom federation and wars with the Lamb (16:14; 19:19) in the gigantic struggle for sovereignty over the earth (19:16). The evil system which has dominated and exploited the peoples of the earth (17:15) by riding into power on the Beast will find this deceptive ruler turning against it (17:16). God will fulfill his Word by allowing the Beast to utterly destroy ecclesiastical Babylon (17:17). The doom of this system is the just fate of the wicked harlot. Her lust for power in the Satanic world system invites her destruction (17:18).

THE DESTRUCTION
OF COMMERCIAL BABYLON

Her utter ruin is announced: "Babylon the great is fallen, is fallen" (18:2). Her godless commercialism is her undoing (18:2, 3). Elsewhere God's people are warned to separate from her (2 Cor. 6:14-18) because her cup of iniquity is full (cf. Gen. 15:16) and her punishment is overdue (18:6-8). She is bewailed by those who grew wealthy on her evil traffic (18:9-11) and her rich commerce (18:12-19).

Commercial Babylon's downfall is effected by God, who through Christ's redemptive work is the real destroyer of the Satanic world system in both its ecclesiastical and commercial aspects. The "millstone" thrown into the sea graphically represents Babylon's swift and terrible dissolution, for she is guilty of murdering God's people (18:21-24).

The Satanic world system is mentioned in more than 30 New Testament passages. Satan is its leader (John 12:31; 14:30; 16:11; Rev. 2:13). God regards it as thoroughly evil (Gal. 1:4; Col. 1:13; 2 Pet. 2:20; James 4:4). The Apostle John declared it to be limited and temporary (1 John 2:17), as Revelation 17 and 18 amply attest. Christ by virtue of his redemptive work sentenced it for destruction. At Christ's second advent (19:11-16) the wicked are slain and Satan is imprisoned in the abyss (19:11 − 20:3). As a result the greed, pride, and war that characterize this evil system (James 4:1-4) are brought to an end. No longer will Babylon be a snare to God's people in the kingdom age (cf. 1 John 2:16; Rev. 18:4, 5). Heaven thus rejoices at Babylon's fall (19:1-5).

THE MARRIAGE OF THE LAMB

This grand event honors Christ in his redemptive ministry, for it is featured as the marriage not of the Bride but of "the Lamb." The Bride, the wife-to-be, represents the Church (Eph. 5:25-33). The figure of the wife symbolizes the Church's future consummating union with Christ in public glory and dignity. It is the outward expression of the inner spiritual union between Christ and his Church (1 Cor. 12: 12, 13; Rom. 6:3, 4; Gal. 3:27; Eph. 5:25-33; Rev. 21:9).

The Bride is seen preparing herself for the wedding. This presupposes her fitness for this glorious event by virtue of Christ's finished redemptive work (Col. 1:12). It also includes the evaluation of her works at the judgment seat of Christ (1 Cor. 3:11-15; 2 Cor. 5:10). The Bride's robes represent Christ's righteousness imputed to her (Rom. 3: 21, 22) and manifested through her (Phil. 2:13).

The guests at the wedding are Old Testament saints (John 3:29). They are clearly distinguished from the Bride and are specified as "blessed" or "happy." The marriage supper is in sharp contrast to the supper of judgment of the wicked (19:17, 18). The judgment seat of Christ and the marriage of the Lamb are a necessary prelude to Christ's advent and kingdom rule.

CHRIST'S SECOND ADVENT IN GLORY

Christ's coming, described in symbolic vision (19:11-16), portrays the departure of the Redeemer-Conqueror from heaven with his saints and angels to claim his rightful kingship over the earth. His position "on a white horse" signifies his conquest in battle (Rev. 6:2; Psa. 45:4). He appears as both a judge and a warrior. His assured triumph is on the basis of his fidelity to the will of God (Phil. 2:5-11). His omniscient judgment is indicated by his "eyes as a flame of fire" (Rev. 1:14; 2:18). His inscrutable name and his many diadems attest his absolute power and lordship (Rev. 19:12). His garments "dipped in (his enemies') blood" (cf. Isa. 63:1-4) denote his vengeance upon his foes.

He comes as God and Creator (John 1:1, 3), since he is the "Word of God" as well as the Redeemer (John 1:1, 14). He has the right to reign in the dual role of Creator and Redeemer (Rev. 5:1-7). Associated with him in his triumph are "the armies of heaven" (saints and angels). The sharing of his conquest is indicated by the horse riders accompanying Christ on his own steed (19:14).

THE DESTRUCTION OF THE SATANIC WORLD SYSTEM

Christ's glorious return destroys this evil world system. Satan's hosts are put in the abyss (20:1-3) and Christ's enemies are slain (19: 15-21). Christ's conquest is supernatural. The "sharp sword" is not a material weapon but the omnipotent Word of God that spoke the universe into existence. This is the weapon that slays Christ's enemies (Isa. 11:4; Heb. 11:3). With Satan, his hosts, and wicked men put down, the world system collapses and is replaced by Christ's millennial kingdom.

Christ will rule as a peaceful Shepherd, but rebels will find his shepherd's staff a rod of iron (19:15; cf. 12:5; Psa. 2:9)—a symbol of relentless severity against evildoers. The figure of treading the vintage (19:15) shows that Christ will render unsparing judgment on evil (cf. Isa. 63:3, 6). He alone will have absolute authority as King par excellence and Lord par excellence. (19:16).

THE BATTLE OF ARMAGEDDON

This gigantic contest for the possession of the earth will be engineered and energized by demonic spirits (16:13, 14; cf. 1 Kings 22:20-

28). These demons, symbolized by frogs, will delude the nations into the supreme folly of attempting to oust God and Christ from the earth. Armageddon ("Hill of Megiddo"), in the plain of Esdraelon, is an ancient battlefield (cf. Judg. 6:19; 2 Kings 9:27; 2 Chron. 35:22). It represents the place of the gathering of the nations, even as the Valley of Jehoshaphat (Joel 3:2, 12) symbolizes the place of slaughter. This battle decides the question of who shall govern the earth—Christ or Satan.

Christ will settle the issue of Armageddon with the omnipotent word of his mouth. The colossal destruction of wicked men fighting against God under Satan's control will furnish the flesh for the great supper of God (19:17, 18). This awful supper on earth contrasts vividly with the blissful marriage supper of the Lamb in heaven. Armageddon ends in the total destruction of Christ's foes (19:19-21). The Beast and the False Prophet are both cast alive into Gehenna to be punished (19:20). Satan and his hosts are remanded to the abyss for the duration of Christ's earthly kingdom (20:1-3), to be cast into Gehenna after the final revolt (20:10).

THE MILLENNIUM

Christ's return, the binding of Satan, and the destruction of the Satanic world system open the way for the establishment of Christ's kingdom on the earth. It will supplant the Satanic world system that has operated since man's fall in Eden. The kingdom is both indicated in the Revelation and necessitated by Old Testament prophecy (cf. Isa. 9:1-7; 11:1—12:6; Ezek. 40:1—48:35; Zech. 12:1—14:21; etc.). The reason it is not more fully developed in Revelation is that it has already been thoroughly expounded in Old Testament prophecy.

John the Revelator fills in additional details (20:4-6). He outlines the classes of saints who will reign with Christ in the kingdom. *The first group* consists of all believers from Abel to the rapture of the Church (cf. Dan. 7:9, 10, ASV). *The second group* consists of the souls of the martyrs of the first part of the tribulation period (6:9-11). *The third group* consists of the martyrs of the last period of the tribulation, those who did not worship the Beast (13:15-17).

All of these groups belong to "the first resurrection" and are "blessed and holy"; they share in kingdom glory. They are separate from the unsaved ("the rest of the dead"), who are resurrected to perdition at the second resurrection (20:11-15). "The second death" (Gehenna) has no power over the saved. They will be king-priests of God associated with Christ, the great King-Priest (Zech. 6:9-15). They will reign over Israel with Christ during the thousand years of the earthly kingdom (Acts 1:6).

SATAN'S FINAL DOOM

Satan's earthly history does not end with his imprisonment in the abyss during the kingdom age. After his thousand-year imprisonment he will be temporarily released from the abyss. He will test man's loyalty to God under the ideal conditions of the Millennium, the last of God's ordered ages before the dawn of eternity (20:7). Satan will successfully deceive "the nations." This postmillennial rebellion will be reminiscent of the premillennial revolt (Ezek. 38, 39). Hence it is metaphorically called "Gog and Magog" (see "Ezekiel's Prophecies of Israel's Restoration," Ezekiel 37 – 39).

This consummating Satanic rebellion will be worldwide. It will constitute the final confederation against God, God's people, and the Holy City (20:7-9a). The rebels will be individuals among the kingdom nations who were never truly regenerated, who yielded only outward allegiance to Messiah's rigid rule (Psa. 2:9). Israel will remain loyal to her Messiah (Jer. 31:31-34; Rom. 11:26) and will doubtless be preserved as a glorified people in the new earth. The revolt will be completely crushed and will mark the end of God's toleration of evil on the earth (20:9b, 10).

Satan's final doom will then be executed. He will be consigned to his eternal fate in Gehenna, prepared for both him and all created human and angelic beings who have followed him (Matt. 25:41). He will join the Beast and False Prophet, who have been in Gehenna for a thousand years (20:10).

THE FINAL JUDGMENT

This judgment involves all the unsaved dead from Adam to the end of world history. It will include those who have been raised to condemnation in the second resurrection (John 5:29) as well as believers of the kingdom age who have died (since the first resurrection occurred before their death). This is why "the book of life" is opened (20:12, 15).

The unsaved face "a great white throne" (20:11). It is the greatest judgment ever held in that it comprises the largest number of persons ever judged at one time. The throne is white because it represents God's infinite holiness. Christ himself is the Judge (John 5:22), and each unsaved person faces him alone. Each is confronted with eternal hell in the lake of fire because he failed to appropriate Christ's salvation. Each is judged on the basis of his works (20:12, 13) and suffers degrees of punishment in Gehenna on the basis of his response to the moral law of God.

This judgment preludes eternity in that it represents God's final dealing with all sin and sinners prior to a sinless universe in the eternal state. Gehenna serves as the quarantine ward for all evil and evildoers. Its existence will make possible an eventual sinless universe (20:14, 15; cf. 21:8).

THE ETERNAL HOME
AND DESTINY OF THE REDEEMED

The eternal abode and the glory of the redeemed of all ages are symbolized by a magnificent city called "the new Jerusalem" (21:9—22:5). God's people have through the ages envisioned such a city (Heb. 11:10, 16; 13:14). It will be inhabited by God the Father (21:11), glorified Old Testament saints (Heb. 11:16), New Testament Church saints, hosts of unfallen angels, and our Lord Jesus Christ himself (Heb. 12:22-24). Both Israel and the Church share the glories of the city (21:12, 14), as well as tribulation and millennial saints.

The great wall of the city signifies the security of its inhabitants as they bask in God's unveiled glory. The city is apparently a solid golden cube 12,000 furlongs (1500 miles) long, wide, and high. This is equal to the colossal volume of 3,375,000,000 cubic miles.

The startling splendor of the city is an index to the glorious destiny and home of the redeemed in eternity. The apocalyptic imagery employs the figure of precious stones in order to convey to unglorified minds something of the indescribable beauty of their blissful future (21:18-21). No visible temple will be seen in the New Jerusalem, for the whole city will be suffused with the divine glory. Worship will be continuous and universal on the part of its inhabitants.

No external source of light will be needed to illuminate the city, for God himself will be manifested in unveiled glory (21:23, 24). Her gates will never be closed, for her enemies will all have been banished to Gehenna; all her citizenry will be sinless and undefiled (21:25-27).

PARADISE RESTORED

The marvelous revelation of an eventual sinless eternity is climaxed by the restoration of the paradise forfeited by man's fall. The complete removal of sin and its curse more than restores the blessings of the Edenic paradise. In paradise regained there will be a new heaven, a new earth, a new city, and a sinless universe.

The new paradise is symbolized and portrayed in terms of the old paradise in Eden. The "pure river of water of life, clear as crystal, proceeding out of the throne of God and the Lamb" (22:1) speaks of fullness of divine life and blessing (cf. Gen. 2:10; Zech. 14:8). The tree of life (22:2; cf. Gen. 2:9; 3:22) prefigures the complete fruition of eternal life. The leaves of the tree are for the health of the nations (22:2). There will be no more sickness, pain, or death in the eternal state (21:4), for there will be "no more curse" (cf. Gen. 3:16-19). All the toil, futility, and sin which have marred man's history will at last be past.

The glorified redeemed will joyfully submit to their sovereign Lord. They will see his face in ecstatic fellowship. They will be identified with their Lord by his name on their foreheads. They will reign with him in blissful fellowship forever.

Part Two

BIBLE
DICTIONARY

AARON (ăr'ŭn). The brother of Moses and Miriam and the first high priest of Israel. Although he had a sinful weakness common to fallen humanity (Exod. 32), in his high and holy calling he was a symbol of Christ, the Great High Priest. Both were divinely chosen. Aaron served as mediator between God and Israel. Christ is the only mediator between God and man (1 Tim. 2:5). Both had to be clean. As a sinner Aaron was purified through cleansing. As God incarnate Christ was intrinsically sinless. Both were perfectly clothed—Aaron with his coat, robe, and ephod and Christ in robes of glory and beauty. Both were crowned—Aaron with his miter and Christ with his many diadems (cf. Exod. 28:1-43). Both were consecrated and anointed—Aaron with oil and Christ with the Holy Spirit (cf. Lev. 8:22-30 with Matt. 3:16, 17 and John 17:16, 17). Both were blameless—Aaron outwardly and Christ totally. Christ is described as "holy, harmless, and undefiled" (Heb. 7: 26). Like Moses, Aaron was excluded from the Promised Land (Num. 20:12) and died on Mount Hor in Edom (Num. 20:23-29).

ABANA, ABANAH (à-bà'nà). Named Chrysorrhoas ("Golden River") by the Greeks, Abana is one of the rivers of Syria mentioned by Naaman the leper (2 Kings 5:12). It is probably to be identified with the modern Barada, which has its source in the Antilebanon mountains 18 miles northwest of Damascus. After flowing through the city, the river loses itself in the marshy lake, Bahret el-Kibliyen, about 18 miles to the east. It waters fertile gardens and orchards.

ABARIM (ăb'à-rîm). The eastern highlands of Moab (Num. 27:12; 33:47). The word indicates the passageways that opened up the plains or grazing lands facing Jericho.

ABDON (ăb'dŏn). One of the judges of Israel (Judg. 12:13).

ABEDNEGO (à-bĕd'nĕ-gō). The Babylonian name given to Azariah, Daniel's companion in exile (Dan. 1:7). He and his companions were delivered from the fiery furnace (Dan. 3:8-30). The name is a dissimilation of *Abed-Nebo (Nabu)*, "servant of the god Nabu," to avoid giving a heathen name to a Jew.

ABEL (ā'bĕl). The second son of Adam and Eve. He was murdered by his brother Cain (Gen. 4:1-8; Matt. 23:35). Abel was the first human being to die, the first person on earth to be murdered, and the first man to be associated with Christ and to present an offering acceptable to God. Christ's blood is said to be better than Abel's because it cries out for mercy while Abel's cries out for vengeance (Heb. 12:24). Abel prefigures the spiritual man justified by faith in atoning blood and a divinely approved substitute (Heb. 9:22; 11:4).

ABI (ä'bî) (abbreviated from Abijah, "the Lord is a father"). The mother of Hezekiah, king of Judah. Although she was the wife of the faithless Ahaz, this queen mother must have been a godly woman. Following her name and that of her son occurs the following significant biblical phrase: "And he (Hezekiah) did that which was right in the sight of the Lord" (2 Kings 18:3). Though handicapped by the godless weakness of her husband, Abi faithfully and tenderly instructed her young son and future king of Judah in the ways of the Lord. When Hezekiah assumed office he rooted out idolatry and was able to stand against the power of Assyria, evidently because of the faith he received at his mother's knee (2 Kings 18:1–20:21).

ABIATHAR (a-bī'a-thär) ("father of excellence"). The son of Ahimelech the priest. He was a co-priest with his father at Nob. He alone escaped the massacre of Saul, later joining David at Keilah (1 Sam. 22:20-23; 23:6). He assisted David spiritually and helped take the ark to Jerusalem (1 Chron. 15:11; 27:34). He became one of David's counselors (2 Sam. 15:35-37; 17:15). He was deposed from office by Solomon for conspiracy (1 Kings 1, 2).

ABIGAIL (äb'ï-gāl) (apparently "the father is rejoicing"). (1) The wife of Nabal. She was a woman of beauty, sagacity, and common sense, but was married to a sullen, foolish husband who took pains to insult David's kindness. On the death of Nabal (Hebrew, "fool"), she became one of David's wives (1 Sam. 25:3-44; 27:3; 2 Sam. 2:2). She was taken captive by the Amalekites when Ziklag was raided, but was rescued by David (1 Sam. 30:5, 18). She bore David a son named Chileab (2 Sam. 3:3) or Daniel (1 Chron. 3:1). (2) A half sister of David (1 Chron. 2:16). She was a daughter not of Jesse but of Nahash (cf. 2 Sam. 17:25). She was the mother of Amasa, at one time a commander in David's army (2 Sam. 19:13).

ABIHAIL (äb'ï-hāl) ("the father is strength"). (1) The wife of Abishur in the line of Judah's descendants to David (1 Chron. 2:29). (2) A wife of King Rehoboam and a descendant of Eliab, David's brother (2 Chron. 11:18). However, some interpret the text to mean that Abihail was the mother of Rehoboam's wife, Mahalath.

ABIHU (a-bī'hū) ("my father is he," i.e.

Jehovah). One of Aaron's sons. He saw God in his glory (Exod. 24:1, 9-11), yet dared to flout the ritual Law and was killed by holy fire (Lev. 10:1-7).

ABIJAH (a-bī'ja) ("my father is Jehovah"). (1) A son of Samuel (1 Sam. 8:2). (2) A priestly descendant of Eleazar (1 Chron. 24:4, 10; Luke 1:5). (3) A son of Jeroboam I (1 Kings 14:1-18). (4) A king of Judah, also called Abijam (2 Chron. 11: 20; 13:1; 1 Kings 14:31; 15:1). He was the son and successor of Rehoboam, censured for adherence to the corrupt religious policy of his father (1 Kings 15: 1-3). He won a great victory over the army of Jeroboam I (2 Chron. 13:1-19). His name also appears as Abijam, "father of sea (west)" in 1 Kings 14:31; 15:1. (5) Hezekiah's mother. See "Abi."

ABIMELECH (a-bĭm'ĕ-lĕk) ("the [divine] king is my father"). (1) A common surname of Philistine kings (Gen. 20:1-18; 21:22-32; 26:1-33). The titles "Pharaoh" among the Egyptians and "Agag" among the Amalekites offer parallels. (2) One of Gideon's sons. He massacred all his seventy brothers except Jotham. He reigned as king and died a violent death (Judg. 9: 1-57). (3) A priestly son of Abiathar (1 Chron. 18:16) according to the Massoretic Text, but perhaps a scribal error for Ahimelech (cf. 2 Sam. 8:17).

ABIRAM (a-bī'rám) ("the exalted one is [my] father"). (1) One of the rebels who fomented an uprising against Moses (Num. 16:1-3). (2) The eldest son of Hiel of Bethel. He rebuilt Jericho about 870 B.C., thus incurring the curse of God pronounced by Joshua (Josh. 6:26). The foundations of the city were laid at the cost of Abiram's life (1 Kings 16:34).

ABISHAG (äb'ï-shăg) (possibly "my father is a wanderer"). A very beautiful young woman called a "Shunamite," that is, a native of Shunem (1 Kings 1:3), a town near Jezreel and about five miles north of Mount Gilboa. She was brought to the aged David probably as a medical measure to restore the king's natural vigor (1 Kings 1:1-4, 15). Solomon regarded Abishag as David's wife and put Adonijah to death for treason when he requested her as his wife (1 Kings 2:13-25).

ABISHAI (a-bĭsh'ä-ī) ("father of gift" or "my father is Jesse"). A high officer in

David's army and the brother of Joab and Asahel (2 Sam. 2:18; 23:18; 1 Chron. 11: 20, 21).

ABITAL (ăb′ĭ-tăl) ("the father is dew"). One of David's wives and the mother of Shephatiah, who was born at Hebron (2 Sam. 3:3-5; 1 Chron. 3:3).

ABNER (ăb′nēr) ("father is light"). A cousin of King Saul and captain of his army. At Saul's death he obtained for Ishbosheth (Saul's son) the allegiance of all the tribes except Judah (2 Sam. 2:8-10). Alienated by Ishbosheth, he defected to David's side (2 Sam. 3:7-10) but was treacherously murdered by Joab.

ABOMINATION. The rendering of the Hebrew word which refers to gross affront to God through idolatry—the violation of the first and second commandments of the Decalogue (Exod. 20:1-7). Thus Molech (Milcom), the national god of the Ammonites, is called "the abomination of the Ammonites" (1 Kings 11:5) and "Chemosh, the abomination of Moab" (1 Kings 11:7).

ABOMINATION OF DESOLATION. Daniel refers to this future event (Matt. 24:15) as the forcible interruption of the Jewish ritual of worship by the Roman prince (cf. Dan. 9:27). This wicked ruler will break his covenant with the Jews in the middle of Daniel's seventieth week and will introduce idolatrous "abominations" that will render the restored sanctuary in Jerusalem "desolate." This sacrilege is foreshadowed by the profanation of the Jewish Temple in the time of the Maccabees (Dan. 11:21-29) by Antiochus IV Epiphanes (175-164 B.C.).

ABRAHAM (ā′brȧ-hăm). The great representative of justification by faith (Gen. 15:6; Rom. 4:1-25). His original name, Abram ("high or exalted father," Gen. 11:27−17:5), was changed to Abraham ("father of a multitude") at the time of ratification of the Abrahamic Covenant and the promise of future progeny (Gen. 17:5). He was called out of Ur in southern Babylonia at about 2000 B.C. and lived in Haran in the Balikh-Habur region of Northern Mesopotamia until his father, Terah, died. Then he entered Canaan, which his ancestors through Isaac and Jacob were to inherit and through whom the promised Redeemer

was to come (Matt. 1:1). His faith and obedience as a "sojourner and pilgrim" and his offering of Isaac are portrayed as outstanding illustrations of justifying faith in action (Heb. 11:8-19; James 2:20-23).

ABSALOM (ăb′sȧ-lŏm) ("father of peace"). The third son of David by Maacah, daughter of the King of Geshur (2 Sam. 3:30). He murdered his older half brother, Amnon, and fled to Geshur (2 Sam. 13:1-39). After three years of exile and two years of banishment from the court, he was received back into favor. David was repaid by Absalom's plot against his throne (2 Sam. 15:1-15). The result was tragic civil war and the death of the usurper (2 Sam. 18:9-17).

ACACIA. A tree found in several species in Sinai. The most common is an evergreen, ten to eighteen feet tall and adorned with yellow flowers. The wood is hard and durable and was used in the Tabernacle for the ark, the altars and their staves, the table boards, and the bars and pillars (Exod. 25:10, 13, 23, 28; 26: 15, 26; 27:1, 6). Acacias flourished in the Jordan Valley at Beth-Shittah (House of Acacia) and Shittim (Acacias).

ACCAD (ăk′ăd). A city of the lower alluvial plain of Shinar in ancient Sumer. It is identified with Akkadian *Akkadu* and Sumerian *Agâde* of the cuneiform inscriptions. It formed the original kingdom of Nimrod (Gen. 10:10) and is listed with such other archeologically known cities as Erech (Uruk) and Babel (Bâb-il). It was the capital of Sargon's empire during the twenty-second and twenty-third centuries B.C. The city was destroyed with the fall of the Akkadian dynasty; its site still awaits discovery.

ACCO, ACRE (ăc′kō; ā′kêr). A harbor and city-state on the bay of Acre, north of Mount Carmel. The city is first named in Egyptian sources in the Execration Texts of the nineteenth century B.C. It is also referred to in the Amarna Letters (1370 B.C.) and other later sources. At the time of Israel's conquest of Canaan, the tribe of Asher pressed toward the coast but did not drive out the inhabitants of Acco (Judg. 1:31, 32). In 733 B.C. Acco came under Assyrian domination. It was renamed Ptolemais in Hellenistic times and came under Roman domination in 65 B.C. Paul landed there on his third voyage (Acts 21:7). The modern name is Acre.

ACHAEANS (à-kē'ăns). Also called Mycenaeans, this people inhabited Mycenae and environs (in northeastern Peloponnesos in Greece) from 1400 to 1100 B.C. The splendor of Mycenaean civilization was brought to light by Heinrich Schliemann in his excavations at Mycenae in 1874-1876 and by later excavators. At the height of their power the Mycenaeans were able to contend successfully with the Minoans of Crete for control of the Aegean Sea. Driven from their native home in Greece by the barbaric Dorians around 1200 B.C., they sought new homes on the mainland of Asia Minor. Failing this, they swept down the Eastern Mediterranean. Rameses III (1195-1175 B.C.) defeated them and turned them back to Palestine and the Phoenician Coast, where they established themselves and mingled with the Semitic Phoenicians. See also under "Philistines" and "Phoenicians."

ACHAIA (à-kā'ya). The Roman province which comprised most of ancient Greece south of Macedonia (Acts 18:12, 27; 19: 21; Rom. 15:26; 1 Cor. 16:15; 2 Cor. 1:1; 9:2; 11:10; 1 Thess. 1:7, 8). The Achaian land appears in the Homeric poems as the home of the Achaians. At the time of Paul the proconsul of Achaia was Gallio (Acts 18:12) and the seat of administration was Corinth.

ACHAN (ā'kăn). A man of Judah who violated the sacrificial ban in the assault of Jericho. He and his family were put to death in the valley of Achor ("trouble, distress"), south of Gilgal (Josh. 7:1-26).

ACHISH (ā'kĭsh). A king of Gath in the time of David and Solomon. David resided incognito with him while fleeing Saul's anger (1 Sam. 21:10-15). Later Achish gave Ziklag to David (1 Sam. 21: 1-12).

ACHSAH (äk'săh) ("an anklet"). A daughter of Caleb, who promised to give her in marriage to anyone who would capture Kiriath-Sepher (a city near Hebron). Othniel, Caleb's younger brother or half brother, captured the town and received the maiden as his wife. At Achsah's request her father gave her the upper and lower springs (Josh. 15:16-19), thus evidently sharing with her as he had with his three sons (named in 1 Chron. 4:15).

ACRE (ā'kêr). See "Acco."

ADAD. A Syrian deity whose death was associated with summer drought. His name is combined with Rammam, the storm god, as Hadad-Rimmon (Zech. 12: 11).

ADAH (ā'dà) ("ornament" or perhaps "light"). (1) One of the two wives of Lamech and the first woman after Eve mentioned by name in the Bible. She was the mother of Jabal (whose descendants developed nomadic life) and of Jubal (who invented music – Gen. 4:19-22). As the two wives of Lamech, Adah and her sister Zillah are the first women in the Bible cited as being part of a polygamous household. They were in the godless line of Cain (Gen. 4:17-24). (2) One of the Canaanite wives of Esau and the daughter of Elon the Hittite (Gen. 36:2). She appears to be the same person as Bashemath (cf. Gen. 26:34). She and Esau's other wives were mothers of the Edomites, who subsequently migrated to Mount Seir (Gen. 36:8).

ADAM (ăd'əm). (1) The first human being created by God in his own image (Gen. 1: 27; 2:7). Through the creation of woman from man and procreation through the two sexes, mankind was created in Adam. In addition to being a proper name, the term denotes mankind as a whole. Adam was created innocent but fell into sin by disobedience, bringing physical, spiritual, and eternal death upon mankind (Gen. 2:17 – 3:24). God's plan of redemption centers in Christ, the last "Adam," who delivers fallen humanity from threefold death and bestows upon believers threefold life – physical, spiritual, and eternal (John 3:16; 1 Cor. 15:45; Rom. 5: 17). (2) A town east of the Jordan where the waters of the Jordan were dammed so that the Israelites could pass over (Josh. 3:9-17). The site is Tell ed-Damiyeh, located in the delta of the Jabbok shortly before it empties into the Jordan.

ADDER. In the King James Version this word is used to translate four Hebrew words that apparently refer to various species of venomous snakes. The *pethen* is the so-called "deaf adder" (because it is impervious to the voice of the snake-charmer—Psa. 58:4, 5). It is extremely venomous (Psa. 91:13) and seems identifiable with the *naja haje* of Egypt (Deut. 32:33; Job 20:14, 16; Isa. 11:8). The *akshūb* (Psa. 140:3; Rom. 3:13) is either a viper or an asp. The *siphŏni* (Isa. 11:8; 14:29; 59:5) is perhaps the Great Viper, translated in the King James Version as "cockatrice." The *shephĭphŏn* is the horned cerastes, a poisonous viper of Arabia and Egypt which reaches a length of three to six feet. It was worshiped at Thebes. It is mentioned in Genesis 49:17.

ADON, ADONAI (ä'dō-nī). Two closely related Hebrew words meaning "lord," "my lord," or "lordship." The primary designation of this name of Deity is *master;* it defines the relation of the Lord to the believer as a servant. The divine Lord and Master has a right to implicit obedience (Luke 6:46; John 13:13, 14). The servant has the right to divine direction in service (Isa. 6:8-12; cf. Exod. 4:10-12; Josh. 7:8-11).

ADONAI JEHOVAH (ä'dō-nī ji-hō'və). This compound name of Deity, translated "Lord God" in the King James Version, combines the Adonai character (see above) with the Jehovah meaning (see "Jehovah, Yahweh"). The prime emphasis is on the "Adonai" meaning (cf. Gen. 15:8; Deut. 3:24; 9:26; Josh. 7:7; 1 Kings 2:26; Isa. 7:7).

ADONIJAH (ă-dō-nī'jäh) ("my lord is Jehovah"). David's fourth son, who lost the succession of the throne to Solomon (1 Kings 1:5-53). Solomon executed him when his request for David's concubine, Abishag, was construed as a renewed attempt to claim the throne (1 Kings 2:13-25).

ADONIRAM (ă-dō-nī'răm) ("my lord is exalted"). An official in charge of forced labor under Solomon (1 Kings 4:6). He was stoned to death by the rebellious people, precipitating the division of the kingdom under Rehoboam. (cf. 1 Kings 12:18). He is evidently the same person as Adoram.

ADONIS (ə-dō'nĭs). The Greek representation of Tammuz. The death of this deity was associated with summer drought and the parching of vegetation.

ADONI-ZEDEK (ă-dō'nĭ-zĕ'dĕk) ("my lord is righteous"). An Amorite king of Jerusalem who joined a coalition of four other Canaanite kings against the Israelites and their allies at Gibeon. Joshua put these kings to death and buried them in a cave at Makkedah, where they had fled (Josh. 10:1-27).

ADOPTION. In regeneration a believer receives the nature of a child of God. By adoption (Greek *huiothesia,* "placing as a son") he receives the position of an adult son (Eph. 1:5; Gal. 3:23—4:7; 1 John 3:1, 2). The indwelling Spirit imparts the realization of sonship in the believer's present experience (Gal. 4:6). However, the full manifestation of sonship will not be witnessed till the resurrection, called "the redemption of the body" (Rom. 8:23; Eph. 1:14).

ADRAMMELECH (ă-drăm'mĕl-ĕk). (1) One of the sons of Sennacherib. He and his brother Sharezer murdered their father in 681 B.C. (2 Kings 19:37; Isa. 37:38). This event is also cataloged in the Babylonian Chronicle. (2) A pagan divinity imported from Sepharvaim to Samaria (2 Kings 17:31).

ADRAMYTTIUM (ă-dră-mĭt'tĭ-ŭm). A seaport in Mysia in the northwest part of the Roman province of Asia where Paul boarded "an Adramyttian ship" (Acts 27:2).

ADRIA, ADRIATIC (ā'drĭ-à). Originally the gulf into which the Po River of Northern Italy emptied. It was apparently named from the town of Adria located on this river. The name was later extended to include the entire body of water between the eastern shore of Italy and Illyricum, Dalmatia, Macedonia, and Achaia (Greece). In New Testament times it included the central Mediterranean Sea between Crete and Melita (Malta), where Paul was storm-tossed and shipwrecked.

ADULLAM (à-dŭl'lăm). A cave in which David hid from the murderous hate of Saul (1 Sam. 22:1). Nearby had existed a Canaanite city (Gen. 38:1, 2). Adullam was located in the territory of Judah (Josh. 12:15). It is mentioned by Micah (Mic. 1:15) and was inhabited after the exile (Neh. 11:30). It is identified with present-day Tell esh-Sheikh Madkhur, halfway between Jerusalem and Lachish.

ADUMMIM (a-dŭm′ĭm). A steep pass on the boundary between Judah and Benjamin (Josh. 15:7; 18:17) in the road from Jericho to Jerusalem. It is the traditional scene of the parable of the good Samaritan (Luke 10:25-37).

ADVENTS OF CHRIST. The two advents of the Messiah were foreseen in two aspects in the Old Testament—that of rejection and suffering (Isa. 53:1-9; Psa. 22:1-21) and that of earthly power and glory (Isa. 11:1-10; Jer. 23:5-8; Ezek. 37: 20-28). These two aspects frequently blended together into one picture. The prophets themselves were puzzled by this apparent contradiction (1 Pet. 1:10-12). It was solved by partial fulfillment. Christ was born at Bethlehem (Mic. 5:2) of a virgin (Isa. 7:14), and at the beginning of his public ministry announced that the predicted kingdom was "at hand" (Matt. 4:17). The rejection, crucifixion, death, burial, and resurrection of the King followed in due course. Both before his death and after his resurrection the King repeatedly announced his second advent in power and glory.

The second advent bears a threefold relationship—to the church, to the nation Israel, and to the Gentile nations. To the church it will mean the descent of the Lord into the air to raise believers who have died and to translate believers who are still living (1 Thess. 4:13-18; 1 Cor. 15:51, 52; Phil. 3:20, 21). This is a constant expectation and happy hope (John 14:1-3; Tit. 2:13). To Israel the Lord's return will mean national regathering, conversion, and establishment in kingdom blessing (2 Sam. 7:16; Zech. 14:1-9). To the Gentile nations Christ's advent will bring judgment and destruction of the present political world-system (Matt. 25:31-46). This will be followed by worldwide Gentile conversion and participation in kingdom blessing (Isa. 2:2-4; 11:10).

ADVOCACY OF CHRIST. This activity of the glorified Savior in heaven is carried on in behalf of sinning saints (1 John 2:1) in the presence of the Father. By virtue of the eternal efficacy of his sacrifice, the divine Advocate restores his erring ones to fellowship (John 9:10; Psa. 23:3).

AEGEAN SEA (ė-jē′ăn). This body of water is not specifically named in Scripture but is included in the reference to "islands of the sea" in Isaiah 11:11. It is directly connected with many places which Paul visited (e.g. Acts 20:13-16; 21:1, 2). This beautiful, island-dotted body of water was bounded by Macedonia on the north, the island of Crete on the south, Greece on the west, and Asia Minor on the east. Its name probably came from Aegeus, the father of Theseus, who drowned himself there.

AGABUS (ăg′a-bŭs). A prophet of Jerusalem who predicted a great famine, which took place in the reign of Emperor Claudius (A.D. 41-54). At Caesarea he dramatized a prediction of Paul's fate at Jerusalem (Acts 21:10, 11).

AGAG (ā′găg). Apparently the common title of the kings of the Amalekites (Num. 24:7). The name is specifically used of the king of the Amalekites spared by Saul in disobedience to God's command (1 Sam. 15:1-35).

AGAR (ā′gàr). The Greek form of Hagar.

AGE. An age is a period of time (Greek *aion*) in which God accomplishes certain purposes. Through Christ God programmed or arranged the successive ages of time (Heb. 1:2). Prominent in these time periods is the Mosaic age, extending from the giving of the Law at Sinai to the death of Christ. Concurrent with part of the Mosaic age is the era covered by "the times of the Gentiles," extending from the captivity of the Jews in 605 B.C. to the second advent of Christ. Following the Mosaic age is the church age, extending from Pentecost to the rapture. After this period the Tribulation and the second advent will witness the renewed divine dealing with Israel preparatory to the kingdom age. The latter will be inaugurated by the second advent of Christ and will end "the times of the Gentiles."

AGRICULTURALIST. The farmer was one of the oldest types of workers in Palestine. Good farming can be traced back to 7500 B.C. in the vicinity of Jericho, where irrigation was prominent. On the tributaries of the Jordan River irrigation cultures were common in the prehistoric period. But from the earliest times most of Palestine's farmers depended on rain. The long drought from June till October

A sower spreads seed in the stony Kidron Valley east of Jerusalem. (© *MPS*)

was broken by the "early rains." By November or early December the moistened earth was ready for plowing and sowing. The copious winter showers gave the crops their major moisture, but they were brought to maturity by the "latter rains" of March and April.

Wheat and barley constituted the chief grains. Various legumes, such as lentils, peas, and beans formed a second crop. Vegetables were also grown with onions and garlic. Various herbs and seeds furnished condiments. Farmers were busy harvesting the barley crop in April and May, and it preceded the wheat harvest by several weeks or sometimes a month. By that time a summer crop of millet had been sown on land left fallow through the winter. Sickles were used by the reapers.

AGRIPPA (á-grĭp'á). (1) "Herod the King" (Acts 12:1), the grandson of Herod the Great. He is known as Herod Agrippa I. He received from Emperor Caligula both his title and his territory (the regions northeast of Palestine). Galilee and Peraea were added to his territory in A.D. 39 and Judea and Samaria in A.D. 41. His sudden death at the age of 54 (A.D. 44) is narrated in Acts 12:20-23 and is corroborated by Josephus (*Antiquities* XIX: 8,2). (2) The son of Herod Agrippa I, known as Herod Agrippa II. He is best known to Bible readers for his encounter with Paul at Caesarea (Acts 25:13 – 26: 32), whom he banteringly charged with

trying to make a Christian of him (Acts 26:28).

AHASUERUS (á-hăz-ú-ē'rŭs). (1) Xerxes I, King of Persia during 485-465 B.C. and the husband of Esther (Esth. 1:2; 2:16, 17). (2) The father of Darius the Mede (Dan. 9:1).

AHAZ (ā'hăz). A wicked, idolatrous king of Judah (732-716 B.C.). His name means "he has grasped" and is an abbreviation of Jehoahaz. He refused to join an anti-Assyrian coalition with Pekah of Israel and Rezin of Damascus. The result was an invasion of Judah by these two powers (2 Kings 16:5; Isa. 7:1-9). Ahaz' trust in Assyria cost Judah a century-and-a-half of vassalage and financial drain.

AHAZIAH (ā-há-zī'á) ("the Lord has laid hold of"). (1) A king of Israel and the son and successor of Ahab. He ruled during 853-852 B.C. (1 Kings 22:51 – 2 Kings 1: 18). He was a weak ruler dominated by an idolatrous mother. During his brief reign Moab revolted (2 Kings 1:1) and Ahaziah's maritime venture with Jehoshaphat of Judah ended in disaster (2 Chron. 20:35-37). (2) A king of Judah and the youngest son of Jehoram (2 Chron. 22:1). He reigned barely a year, being slain by Jehu (2 Kings 9:16-28; 2 Chron. 22:6-9).

AHIJAH (á-hī'jáh). A prophet from Shiloh. He protested Solomon's idolatry and symbolically predicted the breakup of the kingdom (1 Kings 11:28-40). He also denounced Jeroboam's idolatry and foretold the extinction of his house and the eventual downfall of Israel (1 Kings 14: 1-16).

AHIKAM (á-hī'kăm) ("my brother has arisen"). A member of Josiah's deputation to the prophetess Huldah (2 Kings 22:12-14; 2 Chron. 34:20, 21). He became Jeremiah's benefactor (Jer. 26:24) and was the father of Gedaliah, the governor appointed by Nebuchadnezzar (2 Kings 25:22; Jer. 39:14).

AHIMAAZ (á-hĭm'á-ăz) ("my brother is wrath"). A son of Zadok and a helper of David during Absalom's revolt (2 Sam. 15:27, 36; 17:17-22). He was one of the messengers who brought news of Absalom's defeat (2 Sam. 18:19-32).

AHIMELECH (á-hĭm'é-lĕk) ("brother of a king"). The priest at Nob who was slain by Saul for giving David showbread and

Goliath's sword (1 Sam. 21:1 – 22:23).

AHINOAM (á-hǐn'ō-ăm) ("the brother is delight"). (1) Saul's wife, a daughter of Ahimaaz, and the first queen of Israel (1 Sam. 14:50). She presided over Saul's rustic palace-fort at Gibeah and suffered under her royal spouse when he became mentally unbalanced and spiritually oppressed by demon power. She had great consolation in her noble son, Jonathan (cf. 2 Sam. 1:26), who may have inherited her qualities. Ahinoam was also the mother of two other sons, Ishui and Melchisua, and two daughters, Merab and Michal (the latter becoming David's first wife). (2) One of David's eight wives. She was a native of Jezreel, a town at the head of the Valley of Jezreel (present-day Zerein), although Jezreel in Judah (Josh. 15:56; 1 Sam. 25:43) may be meant. Ahinoam and Abigail were taken captive by the Amalekites at Ziklag, but David and his 600 followers rescued them. After Saul's death David took Ahinoam and Abigail to reside at Hebron. Both undoubtedly witnessed David's anointing as king. Ahinoam bore Amnon, who was murdered by Absalom for dishonoring Tamar.

AHITHOPHEL (á-hǐth'ō-fĕl). One of David's advisors who defected to Absalom (2 Sam. 16:23; 15:12, 31).

AHITUB (á-hī'tŭb) ("brother of good"). A son of Phinehas, grandson of Eli (1 Sam. 14:3), and father of Ahimelech the priest (1 Sam. 22:9).

AHOLAH, OHOLAH (á-hō'läh) ("her tent"). A feminine name employed by Ezekiel to personify Samaria and the kingdom of Israel as a woman of loose character, unfaithful to the Lord (Ezek. 23:1-49). She is designated as the elder sister of Aholibah (representing Jerusalem and the Southern Kingdom), because the Northern Kingdom was the larger.

AHOLIBAH, OHOLIBAH (á-hōl'ǐ-bäh) ("my tent is in her"). See "Aholah."

AHOLIBAMAH, OHOLIBAMAH (á-hōl-ǐ-bā'mäh) ("my tent is a high place"). A wife of Esau and daughter of Anah the Hivite (Gen. 36:2). She is also called Judith ("praiseworthy") in Genesis 26:34.

AI (ā'ī). A Canaanite city near Bethel (Gen. 12:8) which was destroyed by Joshua (Josh. 7, 8). The site presently held to be Ai is et-Tell, located two miles eastsoutheast of Bethel and identified as modern Beitin. However, excavations at et-Tell yield confusing evidence that proves it is not the Ai of Scripture. Further archeological research will one day probably locate the true Ai.

AIJALON, PLAIN OF (ā'já-lŏn). See under "Plains of Scripture."

AKKADIANS (ə-kā'dē-əns). The Semitic Akkadians settled in Northern Babylonia about 3000 B.C. and gradually began to supersede the earlier non-Semitic Sumerians until they became dominant in both northern Babylonia (Akkad) and southern Babylonia (Sumer). This took place in the first Akkadian state under Sargon I and his successors (2371-2191 B.C.). The founding of Akkad (Agade) is attributed to Nimrod (Gen. 10:10). For a period the revival of Sumerian power threatened to put a stop to Akkadian expansion. About 2000 B.C., however, new Semitic invasions helped to drive the Sumerian culture out of existence. Akkadian became the official language of all Mesopotamia and, in succeeding centuries, the lingua franca of the ancient world. Early literary remains of the Sumerians, such as the Epic of Gilgamesh, were inscribed in Akkadian and preserved for posterity in cuneiform on clay tablets.

ALEXANDER (ăl-ĕx-ăn'dēr). (1) A common Hellenistic name (cf. Acts 4:6; 19:33). (2) A pernicious false teacher mentioned in 1 Timothy 1:20. (3) A coppersmith or metalworker who was a bitter enemy of Paul (2 Tim. 4:14).

Young Alexander the Great founded the Macedonian (Grecian) Empire. (© RTHPL)

ALEXANDER THE GREAT (ăl-ĕx-ăn'

dĕr). Destroyer of the Persian Empire. From 336 B.C. till his death in 323 B.C. he conquered the civilized world of the time. His generals founded a number of Hellenistic kingdoms out of his conquests. The Herods of the New Testament era constitute the epilogue to this era. Their Hellenizing influence produced the agonies of the Jews in the Maccabean age and resulted in the tensions that surrounded the Cross.

ALEXANDRIA (ăl-ĕg-zăn'drĭ-à). The cosmopolitan city founded by Alexander the Great in 331 B.C. about 14 miles from the westernmost mouth of the Nile. It was the capital of Egypt during the Hellenistic and Roman periods. It ranked with Rome as one of the most important cities of the Greco-Roman world. Its lighthouse (Pharos) was one of the seven wonders of the ancient world. Its great library was world-famous.

ALGUM (perhaps a variant form of Almug). A timber imported by Solomon from Ophir and Lebanon (1 Kings 10:11, 12). Its identity is uncertain. It is thought to be red sandalwood, native to India and Ceylon.

ALMOND. An early-blossoming nut tree of Palestine. It is called in Hebrew *shāqēd*, "the awakening one." Two varieties are common—the bitter, with gorgeous white blossoms, and the sweet, with roseate blossoms. Almonds were sent by Jacob to the Egyptian dignitary (Gen. 43:11). Aaron's rod budded with almond blossoms (Num. 17:8). The cups of the branches of the golden candlestick were in the form of almond blossoms (Exod. 25:33, 34). Jeremiah envisioned the rod of an almond tree, symbolizing the Lord's wakefulness (Jer. 1:11, 12).

ALMS. The Mosaic Law encouraged benevolence to the needy (Deut. 15:7-11; 24:19-22; Lev. 19:9, 10). Our Lord also commended true almsgiving (Matt. 19: 21; Luke 11:41; 12:33). He directed that it be done discreetly and sacrificially (Matt. 6:2-4; Luke 12:33, 34). He and his disciples practiced it (John 13:29). Paul encouraged cheerful giving (2 Cor. 9:6, 7; cf. Heb. 13:16). Paul was diligent in collecting for the poor of Jerusalem and Judea (Rom. 15:25-28; 1 Cor. 16:1; Gal. 2:10).

ALOES. The species *Aquilaria agallocha* or eaglewood, a tropical tree native to Southern Asia. It has fragrant wood and clustered flowers. It is used as an incense and spice ingredient, as well as in medicine and perfumery (Psa. 45:8; Prov. 7: 17; Song 4:14; John 19:39). Lign-aloes is probably referred to in Numbers 24:6.

ALPHA AND OMEGA (Grk. *'alpha; ōmega*). The first and last letters of the Greek alphabet. The expression "alpha and omega" frequently refers to Christ as "the first and the last," the eternal God. See Revelation 1:8; 21:6; 22:13.

ALPHAEUS (ăl-fē'ŭs). (1) The father of Levi the tax collector (Mark 2:14). He is generally identified with Matthew the Apostle. (2) The father of the apostle James (Matt. 10:3; Mark 3:18; Luke 6: 15; Acts 1:13).

ALTAR. A raised mound of earth or stone or other type of platform on which sacrifices were made (Exod. 20:24; 1 Sam. 14: 33-35; cf. Judg. 6:19-21; 13:19, 20). Indoor altars were fashioned of wood or metal, and horns were often added. Anyone who grasped these horns obtained divine protection (1 Kings 1:50; 2:28).

ALTAR OF BURNT OFFERING. The brass or bronze altar was situated at the threshold of the Tabernacle. It symbolized the fact that the shedding of blood is basic to man's access to God. It prefigures Christ as our burnt sacrifice, offering himself without spot to God (Exod. 27:1-8; Heb. 9:14). The bronze signifies divine judgment in action (Num. 21:9; John 3:14).

ALTAR OF INCENSE. Situated in the holy place in front of the veil, the altar of incense portrays Christ as the believer's intercessor (John 17:1-26; Heb. 7:25), through whom the believer's praise and prayer rise up to God (Heb. 13:15). The incense, offered twice daily, symbolizes prayer, which rises fragrantly and acceptably to heaven (Rev. 5:8; 8:3). The acacia wood overlaid with gold speaks of Christ's humanity united to deity (Exod. 30:1-5).

AMALEK, AMALEKITES (ăm'à-lĕk; ăm'à-lĕk-īts). Nomadic desert people who were descendants of Esau (Gen. 36: 12). At the time of the Exodus they were concentrated about Kadesh-barnea, southwest of the Dead Sea and west of Edom (Num. 13:29; 14:25). They clashed with Israel at Rephidim and were defeated (Exod. 17:8-13). Israel's foolhardy attempt to enter Palestine in self-will after their failure at Kadesh-barnea resulted in defeat by the Amalekites at Hormah (Num. 14:40-45). During the period of the Judges the Amalekites assisted the Moabites and the Midianites in their attempt to occupy and raid Israelite territory (Judg. 3:12-14; 6:1-6). Saul and David fought them (1 Sam. 15:1-33; 30:1-20). They were not completely defeated until Hezekiah's day (1 Chron. 4:43).

AMASA (ăm'á-sá). Commander of Absalom's rebel army (2 Sam. 17:25). He was defeated by Joab (2 Sam. 18:6-8) and pardoned by David. He replaced Joab as David's army commander (2 Sam. 19:13) but was treacherously murdered by Joab (2 Sam. 20:9-12).

AMAZIAH (ăm-á-zī'á) ("the Lord is mighty"). (1) A king of Judah (2 Kings 14:1-20) and a son of Joash (2 Chron. 24:27). He defeated the Edomites but was defeated by Israel. He fled to Lachish when a conspiracy was formed against him, and was murdered there (2 Chron. 25:1-28).

AMMINADAB (ăm-mĭn'á-dăb). Father-in-law of Aaron (Exod. 6:23) and an ancestor of David (Ruth 4:19; Matt. 1:4; Luke 3:33).

AMMONITES (ăm'mŏn-īts). Descendants of Lot (Gen. 19:38). They occupied Transjordan from the River Arnon on the south to the River Jabbok on the north. Their capital was at Rabbath-Ammon (present-day Amman, capital of Jordan). They were related to Israel but were in frequent conflict with the twelve tribes. They joined the Moabites in hiring Balaam to curse Israel (Deut. 23:3-6). Periodically they oppressed Israel (Judg. 3:13; 10:6-9) and were subdued by David (2 Sam. 11, 12). The Ammonites invaded Judah in Jehoshaphat's reign, but were defeated (2 Chron. 20:1-30). They paid tribute to Uzziah and Jotham (2 Chron. 26:8; 27:5). After the fall of Jerusalem they frustrated the attempt of the Jews to form a new community (2 Kings 25:25; Neh. 4:3, 7, 8). They were denounced as enemies of Israel by the prophets (Jer. 49:

1-6; Ezek. 25:1-7; Amos 1:13-15; Zeph. 2:8-11).

AMNON (ăm'nŏn) ("faithful"). David's firstborn son. He was murdered by Absalom for defiling the latter's sister Tamar (2 Sam. 13:1-29).

AMON, AMUN (ā'mŏn). (1) A king of Judah and son of Manasseh (2 Kings 21:19-26). His two-year reign was terminated by his assassination, probably as a victim of court intrigue. He followed the gross idolatry of his father. (2) A local god of Thebes (No). Through union with the sun-god, Amun became the chief Egyptian deity under the eighteenth dynasty (cf. Jer. 46:25; Nah. 3:8, RSV margin).

AMORITES (ăm'ŏ-rīts). A people of Canaan (Gen. 10:16) often listed with the Hittites, Perizzites, etc. as enemies of Israel (Exod. 33:2). They were dispersed throughout the central highland ridge and in the hill country east of Jordan. The name became a general designation for the inhabitants of Canaan (Gen. 48:22; Josh. 24:15). At the time of Israel's conquest of the land Amorite kings ruled most of East Jordan and had to be conquered (Josh. 12:1-6; Judg. 1:36).

From about 2500 B.C. Sumerian and Akkadian inscriptions refer to the Amorites as desert people unacquainted with civilized life. Their center of population was in the mountains of Basar (probably Jebel Bishri, north of Palmyra). About 2000 B.C. the Amorites moved into Babylonia in force. They were in part responsible for the fall of the powerful third dynasty of Ur, and took over the rule of several towns, including Larsa. They established a dynasty at Babylon. Under the great king Hammurabi they conquered the two other important Amorite states of Ashur and Mari (1750 B.C.).

Another Amorite group had settled in the Lebanon district and were engaged in horse trading. This Amorite kingdom flourished into the Amarna Period and the nineteenth dynasty in Egypt, when tribute was recorded from the state of Amor. The port of Amur apparently was Sumur (present-day Tell Simiriyan, south of Arvad; cf. Josh. 13:4). Other Amorite infiltrations into Syrian Palestine resulted in the numerous Amorite kingdoms that withstood Israel's conquest of Palestine (1400-1375 B.C.).

AMOS (ā'mŏs) ("burden"). A prophet who was a native of Tekoa in Judah, about six miles south of Bethlehem (Amos 1:1). He was a humble shepherd and dresser of sycamore trees (7:14, 15). He prophesied to the Northern Kingdom and clashed with the worldly, compromising high priest, Amaziah, at Bethel (765-750 B.C. – Amos 7:10-17).

AMPHIPOLIS (ăm-fĭp'ō-lĭs). The capital city of the first district of Macedonia. It was located about 30 miles southwest of Philippi on the Via Egnatia. Paul passed through this important city on his way to Thessalonica (Acts 17:1).

AMULET. An ornament or charm worn partly for adornment and partly as protection against evil spirits. While the wood amulet actually appears only once in the Bible (Isa. 3:20) in a list of feminine adornments, the earrings which Jacob buried at Shechem (Gen. 35:4) and the crescents which were hung from the necks of Midianite camels (Judg. 8:21) were also apparently amulets. Various kinds of amulets have been found in Palestinian excavations.

ANAH (ā'nắh) (perhaps "listening to"). The mother of Esau's wife, Oholibamah, and grandmother of Esau's children (Gen. 36:2, 14, 18, 25). She was apparently contemporary with Isaac's wife, Rebekah, who opposed her son's marriage with the Hittite line because it was descended from Hagar (Gen. 26:34, 35).

ANANIAS (ăn-à-nī'ăs) (The Greek form of Hananiah). (1) An early Christian who, with his wife Sapphira, sinned the sin that resulted in physical death (1 John 5:16) by lying to the Holy Spirit (Acts 5: 1-11). (2) A Christian at Damascus who was sent to restore sight to Saul of Tarsus after his conversion and to admit him to fellowship by baptism (Acts 9:10-18). (3) A high priest prominent in the political intrigues in Jerusalem from A.D. 48 to his assassination in A.D. 67.

ANATHEMA (à-năth'ě-mà). When a person, animal, or inanimate object was put under a ban or curse (Hebrew *ḥerem*) because of connection with idolatry (Exod. 22:20), it was said to be devoted to destruction or accursed (Lev. 27:28, 29).

In the case of a person or animal it was unredeemable and was to be put to death. In the case of an inanimate object indestructible by fire (such as silver or gold) it was to be put in the Lord's treasury. In the New Testament the ban or curse acquired a more generalized sense. It became expressive of very strong feeling (Rom. 9:3) or of reprehension or severe condemnation (1 Cor. 12:3; 16:22; Gal. 1:9).

ANATHOTH (ăn'à-thŏth). A priestly city in Benjamin, the birthplace of Jeremiah (Jer. 1:1). The name has been preserved in Anata, three miles north of Jerusalem. The original town, however, was situated at the ruin of Ras el-Karrubeh, about a half-mile to the southwest.

ANDREW (Greek *Andreas*, "manly"). The fisherman brother of Simon Peter (John 1:44; Matt. 4:18; Mark 1:16-18; Luke 6:14).

ANGEL OF THE LORD. This expression in the Old Testament usually indicates the presence of God in angelic form (Gen. 16:7-14; 22:10-18; Exod. 3:1-6; Judg. 2:1-5; 6:11-24; 13:1-23).

ANGELS. Angels are a special order of created beings. Unlike humans, they are purely spirit beings (Psa. 104:4; Heb. 1: 14). However, they have power to become visible in the semblance of human form (Gen. 19:1-22; 1 Kings 19:5-8; 2 Kings 1:3, 15; Acts 12:7-9). Wisdom and strength are chief attributes of the angelic order (2 Sam. 14:20; Psa. 103:20). They belong to the realm of the spiritual and supernatural and are very numerous (Psa. 68:17; Matt. 26:53; Heb. 12:22; Rev. 5:11). They are sometimes called "sons of God" (Gen. 6:2; Job 1:6; 2:1).

Angels are either fallen or unfallen. The host of fallen angels are apparently the demons. They followed Satan in the primeval revolt (Isa. 14:12-14; Ezek. 28: 11-19). Some of them are unbound and are free to do Satan's bidding. Others are chained in darkness, awaiting judgment (2 Pet. 2:4). Certain imprisoned demons will be let loose during the Great Tribulation (Rev. 16:12-14).

Unfallen angels function as "ministering spirits" to believers (Heb. 1:14). This ministry apparently begins in infancy and continues throughout our earthly life (Matt. 18:10; cf. Psa. 91:11). It particularly concerns physical safety and the well-being of God's children (1 Kings 19:5; Psa. 34:7; 91:11; Dan. 6:22; Matt. 2:13, 19; 4:11; Acts 5:19; 12:7-10). See also "Archangels" and "Cherubim and Seraphim."

ANIMALS. Ever since the fall of man, domestic animals have held an important place in the history of God's people. The shedding of sacrificial blood (typifying fallen man's need of a Redeemer) has always been the only way of access to God (Gen. 3:21; 4:1-7). Israelite religion streamed with the blood of sacrifices, for without the shedding of blood there is "no remission" (Heb. 9:7, 22; cf. Exod. 12:13; 29:16; 30:10; Lev. 1:5; Eph. 1:7; Col. 1:20; 1 Pet. 1:2; Rev. 1:5).

Domesticated animals also played a very important role in the daily lives of people in Bible lands. Oxen, sheep, and goats constituted the ordinary man's wealth, and a common word for cattle was *miqneh,* denoting "property." The patient ox served as a beast of burden and pulled the plowshare that tilled the earth. Sheep furnished wool for clothing. Goats furnished milk from which various dairy products were made. All of these animals furnished meat. But only those animals that chewed the cud and had split hoofs (such as the above) were clean and fit for food under the Mosaic Law (Lev. 11:1-8; Deut. 14:4-8). The ass was also a common beast of burden, but could not be yoked with an ox (Deut. 22:10). Crossbreeding was not allowed; hence mules had to be imported into Israel. Lambs and kids served as pets. Dogs in Israel were considered unclean and were rarely domesticated as household pets. In the Roman Empire, however, both dogs and cats were used as pets. The cat is not mentioned in the Bible.

ANISE (ăn′ĭs). A flavoring and condiment, the correct rendering in Matthew 23:23 being "dill." Dill *(Anethum gaveolens)* is of the same order as anise, resembling it in appearance and properties but being much more commonly grown. Anise *(Pimpinella anisum),* resembling caraway, was only occasionally cultivated in the East for use as a seasoning and a medicine. Dill is used in flavoring pickles

and yields an oil used in medicine.

ANKLET. "Bangles" or "anklets" are rendered "tinkling ornaments about their feet" (Isa. 3:18), from the Hebrew root meaning "rattle" or "tinkle." They appear in Isaiah's description of the luxurious articles of the daughters of Zion. Numerous ankle bracelets have been recovered by archeological excavations all over Palestine. Most of them are of bronze. At Lachish they are found in position in graves.

ANNA (ăn′à) (Greek form of Hebrew *Hannah,* "grace"). The first woman to acclaim Christ as the Messiah (Luke 2: 36-38). She was a widow, the daughter of Phanuel of the tribe of Asher. At the age of 84 she visited the Temple daily; she was there when the infant Jesus was brought in to be dedicated. As a prophetess she recognized him and proclaimed him as the long-promised Messiah.

ANNAS (ăn′ăs) (Greek for *Hanan,* contraction of *Hananiah,* "Jehovah is gracious"). A high priest at Jerusalem when John the Baptist began his ministry (Luke 3:2). He was deposed as high priest by the Roman procurator Valerius Gratus about A.D. 15. Although no longer officiating when Jesus was arrested, he still bore the honorary title (Luke 3:2; Acts 4:6; cf. John 18:13, 24).

ANNIHILATION. The erroneous belief that the wicked will be wholly destroyed and blotted out of conscious existence in eternity. Scripture shows the falsity of this notion (Jude v. 13; Rev. 14:9-11).

ANOINT, ANOINTING. Anointing with oil was a common custom in Bible lands (Deut. 28:40; Ruth 3:3; Mic. 6:15). Such anointing was a mark of respect which a host often paid his guests (Psa. 23:5; Luke 7:46). Anointing with oil was also a rite by which prophets (1 Kings 19:16; Psa. 105:15), priests (Exod. 40:15; Num. 3:3; Exod. 29:29; Lev. 16:32), and kings (1 Sam. 9:16; 10:1; 1 Kings 1:34) were officially inaugurated into their office. Under the Jewish economy the sick were also anointed with oil (Mark 6:13; James 5:14).

The Messiah was the "Anointed One" par excellence (Psa. 2:2; Isa. 61:1; Luke 4:18). Christians are also anointed with the Holy Spirit by God (2 Cor. 1:21).

ANT. Any of a group of black or red insects, generally wingless, that live in colonies. The ant furnishes an example of industry and forethought. That the ant of Palestine stores food on which to live in winter is intimated in the Bible (Prov. 6: 6-8; 30:24, 25) and clearly asserted in similar Arabic maxims.

ANTELOPE. A ceremonially clean animal fit for food and captured in nets. It is clear that the gazelle, a species of antelope, was found in biblical Palestine. But it is not certain that other antelopes had their habitat there. Some take the animal to be one of the hollow-horned mammals (*Bovidae*) generally classified as antelopes.

ANTICHRIST. The Antichrist of the last days is "the man of sin," "the son of perdition" (2 Thess. 2:3), the devil-indwelt opposer of Christ (Rev. 13:1-10). "Many antichrists" (1 John 2:18) and those who have the "spirit of antichrist" (1 John 4: 3) precede and prepare the way for the final Antichrist, the "vile person" of Daniel 11:21. The denial of the incarnation of the eternal Word (John 1:14) is the supreme mark of all antichrists.

ANTIOCH (ăn′tĭ-ŏk). (1) A great Hellenistic city in northwest Syria (modern Antakya, Turkey). It ranked with Rome and Alexandria as one of the three greatest cities of the Greco-Roman world. Through its seaport, Seleucia Pieria, it was a great commercial emporium connecting land and sea routes east and west. It was also a great cultural center and the metropolis from which early Christianity spread to Asia Minor and Europe. The church there (Acts 13:1) fostered Paul's great missionary tours (Acts 13:2 − 20: 38). (2) A Hellenistic city founded by Seleucus I (300 B.C.) in the lake district of southwest Asia Minor. In 188 B.C. the city was declared free after the defeat of Antiochus III by the Romans. Antony made it a part of the domain of the Galatian king Amyntas in 36 B.C. After Amyntas' death the city was incorporated in the Roman province of Galatia (25 B.C.). Paul preached in the synagogue to a congregation of Jews who had settled there in Seleucid days and to Greek-speaking Gentiles (Acts 13:14-43). The ancient site has been found two miles to the east of

modern Yalvac; some of its ancient splendor has been unearthed.

ANTIOCHUS THE GREAT (ăn-tī′ŏ-kŭs) (Greek, "withstander"). Antiochus III (223-187 B.C.), king of Syria, sixth ruler of the dynasty of the Seleucidae. He won a great victory at Paneas in 198 B.C., thereby gaining a dominant position in the East. He was defeated by Rome at Magnesia in 190 B.C.

ANTIOCHUS EPIPHANES (ăn-tī′ŏ-kŭs e-pĭf′ȧ-nēz). The eighth ruler of the house of Seleucidae during 175-163 B.C. (1 Macc. 1:10; 6:16). A fanatical Hellenizer, he clashed with the Jews and persecuted them insanely. He robbed and desecrated the Temple, commanded the sacrifice of swine, destroyed the sacred Hebrew books, and forbade circumcision. His outrages precipitated the Maccabean revolt (1 Macc. 1:41-53). He died shortly after receiving news of the Jewish uprising (1 Macc. 6:1-16).

ANTIPAS (ăn′tĭ-pȧs) (a shortened form of Antipater). A son of Herod the Great, he inherited the Galilean and Perean portions of his father's kingdom. He imprisoned and executed John the Baptist (Mark 6:14-28) and had a brief encounter with Jesus when the latter was sent to him by Pilate for judgment (Luke 23:7, 15). Our Lord called him "that fox" (Luke 13:31, 32). In A.D. 39 he was deposed by the Emperor Caligula, and ended his days in exile.

ANTONIA, TOWER OF (ăn-tō′nĭ-ȧ). A palatial guard tower rebuilt by Herod the Great at the northwest corner of the Temple court at Jerusalem. It served as a royal residence as well as soldiers' quarters. The fortress is not explicitly named in Scripture. It is, however, alluded to as "barracks" (AV "castle") in Acts 21:34-37; 22:24; 23:10, 16, 32.

APE (Hebrew *qōph*, a loan word from Egyptian *gwf*, "monkey"). It is impossible to identify with exactness the "apes" which Solomon's Red Sea Tarshish fleet (1 Kings 10:22) brought back from Ophir (apparently located in Somaliland, Africa). It is likely that these animals were not apes at all (tailless) but were instead monkeys (having tails) or baboons. These were well-known in Egypt, where the god Thoth was frequently represented by a baboon. The commonest baboon in this area is the Arabian species (*papio hamadyas*) found in Arabia, Abyssinia, and the Sudan.

APHRODITE (ăf-rə-dī'tē). A goddess identified with the Semitic Ashtoreth (Astarte), who mourned the dead Adonis. Sacred prostitution of the Fertility Cult was associated with this polluted deity. See "Ashtoreth."

APOLLONIA (ăp-ŏ-lō'nĭ-à). A Greek city in Macedonia through which Paul and Silas passed on the way to Thessalonica (Acts 17:1). The city was situated on the Via Egnatia, 30 miles from Amphipolis and 38 miles from Thessalonica.

APOLLONIUS (ăp'ŏ-lō'nĭ-ŭs). An official under Antiochus Epiphanes who persecuted the Jews (1 Macc. 1:29-32; 2 Macc. 5:24-26). He was defeated and slain by Judas Maccabeus (1 Macc. 3:10).

APOLLOS (à-pŏl'lŏs). An Alexandrian Jew and disciple of John the Baptist (Acts 18:24-28). He knew only John's preparatory baptism, but was taught the truth of the Spirit's baptism and the Christian message by Priscilla and Aquila. Under Paul's ministry Apollos' disciples received the Holy Spirit (Acts 19:1-7), for which John's baptism prepared the way.

APOSTASY. A doctrinal departure by professed believers who have never been regenerated and who deliberately reject the cardinal Christian truths of Christ's deity and redemptive sacrifice (1 John 4:1-3; 2 Pet. 2:1). Apostasy differs from error and heresy, which are consonant with saving faith. Apostasy is irremediable, and awaits divine judgment (2 Pet. 2:1-3).

APOSTLE. The word denotes a "messenger," a "delegate," one "dispatched with orders." Apostles were chosen by the Lord himself and were endued with sign-gifts and miraculous powers attesting their office (Matt. 10:1; Acts 5:15, 16; 16:16-18). An apostle was also an eyewitness of the resurrected Christ (Acts 1:22; 1 Cor. 9:1). Except in the general sense of a "messenger for Christ," apostles have not existed since the early days of the Church.

APOTHECARY. The King James Version's rendering for a perfumer (one who prepared cosmetics and mixed fragrant unguents). A typical king is pictured in 1 Samuel 8:13 as requiring the services of "perfumers" (RV margin, RSV) as well as "cooks and bakers." Archeology illustrates the reference. The great palace at Mari on the middle Euphrates had its own perfumery in the eighteenth century B.C. It supplied large quantities of various ointments for the royal officials, for personal use, and for ritual festivals and banquets.

APPHIA (ăf'ĭ-à). A Christian woman at Colosse or Laodicea mentioned by Paul in his letter to Philemon (verse 2). She may have been Philemon's wife.

APPLE (Hebrew *tappuaḥ*, Arabic *tuffakh*). A tree and its fruit probably to be identified with our apple tree (*Pyrus malus*). Some scholars try to identify it as the apricot, the citron, or the quince, but serious objections exist against these identifications. The apple tree was well known and extensively cultivated in ancient times. Parts of Palestine are suitable for the cultivation of this tree.

APRICOT. It is questionable that the apricot was established in Palestine in biblical times. See under "Apple." "Apples of gold" (Prov. 25:11) are evidently not apricots.

AQABA, GULF OF. (ä'kà-bä). Although not named in Scripture, this body of water is suggested in the biblical allusion to Solomon's copper fleet which sailed from Elath and Ezion-Geber (1 Kings 9:26, 27). It constitutes the eastern arm of the Red Sea, which today gives Israel access to the sea on the south. The Sinai Peninsula separates it from the western arm of the Red Sea (the Gulf of Suez).

ARABAH (ăr'à-bäh). See under "Valleys of Scripture" and "Wilderness."

ARABIANS. A general term for the inhabitants of the huge peninsula of Arabia. It is bordered by the Fertile Crescent on the north, the Red Sea and the Gulf of Aqabah on the west, the Indian Ocean on the south, and the Persian Gulf and Gulf of Oman on the east. Its area is about one-third that of the United States. The interior is largely desert, but important kingdoms flourished on the southwestern coasts. The main reason for the prosperity of these kingdoms was their location on the incense trade routes from the countries of the south coast and Ethiopia.

The "table of the nations" in Genesis 10 lists a number of South Arabian peoples as the descendants of Joktan, a son of Eber of the family of Shem. He is listed as the progenitor of Almodad, Sheleph, Hazarmaveth, Jerah, Hadoram, Uzal, Diklah, Obal, Abimael, Sheba, Ophir, Havelah, and Jobab (Gen. 10:25-29). Modern tribes in south and southwest Arabia claim that pure Arabs are descended from Joktan.

A number of north Arabian tribes are listed as springing from Abraham through Keturah and Hagar (Gen. 25:1-4, 12-16). Among Esau's descendants a number of Arabian peoples are mentioned (Gen. 36:1-18). At the time of Jacob two groups of Abraham's descendants appear as caravan traders — the Ishmaelites and the Midianites (Gen. 37: 25-36). In Solomon's reign contacts with Arabia became prominent after the famous visit of the Queen of Sheba (1 Kings 10:1-13) and the tribute received from "the kings of Arabia" (2 Chron. 9: 14) and the "steppe dwellers" ("children of the East"). (These were the people occupying the semi-desert regions to the east and south of Palestine.) In the ninth century Jehoshaphat received tribute from the Arabians (2 Chron. 17:11). In Hezekiah's time the Arabs were very familiar to the Jews; some were even hired to defend Jerusalem against Sennacherib. Arabians were coming into prominence as traders in the closing years of the kingdoms of Judah (Jer. 25:23, 24; Ezek. 27: 21, 22).

ARAD (ā′răd). A Canaanite city of the Negeb in the Mosaic era (Num. 21:1-3). The city was destroyed later by the Israelites, and its site was occupied by the nomadic Kenites (Judg. 1:16). The modern site is about 16 miles south of Hebron.

ARAMEANS (ăr′à-mē′äns). A Semitic people named with Elam and Assyria in Genesis 10:22, 23 and 1 Chronicles 1:17. The Arameans infiltrated Mesopotamia and Syria from the Arabian desert fringes from the third millennium onward. By Abraham's time (2000 B.C.) numbers of them were settled in the Balikh-Habur region (near Haran), called Aram-Naharaim or Paddan-aram (Gen. 28:5). Contact between the Hebrews and Arameans goes back to patriarchal times (Deut. 26:5). The maternal ancestry of Jacob's children is Aramaic.

By the middle of the eleventh century B.C. Aramaic states began to appear north and east of Canaan. Aram-Zobah rose to power on the eve of the Hebrew monarchy (1 Sam. 14:47; 2 Sam. 8:3; 10:6). It lay north of Damascus and its power extended to Hamath on the northwest. It had to be subdued by David, who laid the foundation of Solomon's empire (2 Sam. 8:3-11). Aram-Damascus rose to power toward the end of Solomon's reign and waged intermittent war with the Northern Kingdom during most of its national existence. The Aramean power which was centered in Damascus was crushed only a decade before the fall of Israel in 722 B.C.

Aram-maacah was another Aramaic principality. It was situated east of the Jordan near Mount Hermon (Josh. 12:5; 13:11). Geshur was still another Aramaic kingdom near Maacah and Dan (Judg. 18:29). The Arameans exerted a powerful influence in the ancient Near East. Their language became the lingua franca of the Bible world by the time of Jesus.

Mount Ararat, viewed from the village of Kinakin, as engraved by T. Fielding in early 1800s (© *RTHPL*)

ARARAT (ăr′à-răt). A country in Armenia in the vicinity of Lake Van (Assyrian *Urartu*). The mountains of this region were the resting place of the ark after the deluge (Gen. 8:4). The murderers of Sennacherib fled to "the land of Ararat" (2 Kings 19:37; Isa. 37:38). This event is substantiated by the *Babylonian Chronicle* (III:34-38) for the year 681 B.C.

ARAUNAH (à-rä′nà). A Jebusite from whom David purchased a threshing floor on Mount Moriah in order to construct an altar to the Lord (2 Sam. 24:18-25). The place afterward became the site of Solomon's Temple (2 Chron. 3:1). Araunah is called Ornan in Chronicles and Ornah in the Hebrew text of 2 Sam. 24:16.

ARCHANGELS. Michael and Gabriel are mentioned by name in Scripture (Dan. 8:16; 10:13; Luke 1:19; Jude 1:9; Rev. 12:7). The noncanonical book of Enoch also mentions Uriel, Raphael, Raquel, Saraqael, and Remiel. The archangel Michael sustains a particular relation to Israel and to the resurrections (Dan. 10:13, 21; 12:1, 2; 1 Thess. 4:16; Jude 1:9). Gabriel is employed in the most distinguished services (Dan. 8:16; 9:21; Luke 1:19, 26).

ARCHELAUS (är-kė-lā'ŭs) ("leader of people, chief"). A son of Herod the Great and brother of Herod Antipas. He ruled Judea as an ethnarch when Joseph and Mary returned from Egypt (Matt. 2:22). He was deposed and banished to Gaul for his cruelty about A.D. 6.

ARCHEOLOGY. Palestinian archeology is the handmaid of Bible history. This rapidly developing science illustrates and expands biblical backgrounds. It selects those material remains of Palestine and its adjacent countries which relate to the biblical period and narrative. The basic method of this science is to dig into the successive occupational layers of so-called "tells" or mounds which have accumulated over ancient towns. The

CLASSIFICATION OF ARCHEOLOGICAL PERIODS (ISRAEL)

Stone Age

Palaeolithic (Use of flint and stone tools only)	Before 10,000 B.C.
Mesolithic	10,000
Neolithic	7000-5000
Pre-pottery	7000
Pottery	5000

Chalcolithic Age — 4000-3200

Early (Transition from stone to bronze artifacts)	4000-3800
Middle	3800-3600
Late	3600-3200

Bronze Age

Early Bronze (EB) = Early Canaanite (EC) I	3200-2900
Early Bronze (EB) = Early Canaanite (EC) II	2900-2600
Early Bronze (EB) = Early Canaanite (EC) III, IV	2600-2200
Intermediate Bronze = Middle Canaanite (MC)	2200-1950
Middle Bronze (MB) = Middle Canaanite (MC) I	1950-1750
Middle Bronze (MB) = Middle Canaanite (MC) II	1750-1550
Late Bronze (LB) = Late Canaanite (LC) I	1550-1400
Late Bronze (LB) = Late Canaanite (LC) IIa	1400-1300
Late Bronze (LB) = Late Canaanite (LC) IIb	1300-1200

Iron Age

Iron Age (IA) I = Early Israelite I	1200-1050
Early Israelite II	1050-970
Iron Age (IA) II = Middle Israelite II	970-840
Middle Israelite III	840-580
Iron Age (IA) III = Late Israelite III	
Late Israelite IV	580-330

Hellenistic Period

Hellenistic Age I	330-165
Hellenistic Age II = Maccabean	165-63
Hellenistic Roman Period	63 B.C. — A.D. 70
Roman Period	A.D. 70-330

farther down the archeologist digs, the older are the remains uncovered. Each layer or stratum has come to be dated by the artifacts and pottery it yields. As a result, definite archeological periods can be outlined and described.

ARCHER. Whether on foot or on horseback, archers constituted an important part of ancient armies. The bow and arrow as weapons figure prominently in the wars of Israel. The bow was normally made of seasoned wood. The bowstring was commonly ox-gut. Arrows were made of reeds or light wood and were tipped with metal. The bow varied in length. The battle bow (Zech. 9:10) was sometimes as much as five feet in length. To string a battle bow the lower end had to be held down by the foot to fasten the string in a notch. For this reason archers were called "bow treaders" in Hebrew. Certain tribes of Israel became famous for their bowmen (cf. 1 Chron. 5:18; 12: 2; 2 Chron. 14:8).

ARCHITECT. Before the period of the monarchy in Israel the architect did not figure prominently. But with the advent of the monarchy his skills became necessary in order to build the walled town and the higher area which formed a "fort within a fort." During the prosperous united monarchy the architect came into prominence as public buildings and private homes became more pretentious and demanded more skill in planning.

The Phoenicians were famous as architects and craftsmen. Hiram of Tyre (979-944 B.C.) supplied both David and Solomon with the architectural skill and artisans necessary to build royal residences and the famed Temple in Jerusalem (cf. 2 Sam. 5:11; 2 Chron. 2:13, 14; 4:11-16). See also "Builder."

AREOPAGITE (ăr-ė-ŏp′á-gīt). A member of the venerated council of the Areopagus, so called because it convened on the Hill of the Areopagus at Athens (Acts 17: 19, 22). In New Testament times it still retained great prestige despite curtailment of many of its ancient powers. For example, it still retained special jurisdiction in matters of morals and religion. It was therefore quite natural that Paul, considered a "setter forth of strange gods," should be subjected to its adjudi-

cation (Acts 17:18).

ARISTARCHUS (ă-rĭs-tär′kŭs) (Greek, "best ruling"). A Macedonian of Thessalonica who accompanied Paul at Ephesus (Acts 19:29), traveled with him to Troas (Acts 20:4, 6), and sailed with him to Rome (Acts 27:2). He was also at one time a fellow-prisoner of Paul (Col. 4:10).

ARK OF THE COVENANT (Exod. 25: 10-22). A sacred container made of acacia wood (symbolizing Christ's humanity) and overlaid with pure gold (denoting Christ's deity). The ark represents Christ as possessing God's law in his heart, since it held the Decalogue (Exod. 25:21, 22). It also held a pot of manna, illustrating Christ as Life-sustainer. Later it also held Aaron's rod that budded (Num. 17: 10), portraying Christ in resurrection.

The mercy-seat was the gold top or lid of the ark. It illustrates how the divine throne was transformed from a throne of judgment into a throne of grace by the atoning blood sprinkled upon it. The two cherubim above the mercy-seat guarded the holiness of God's throne, symbolized by the Shekinah glory enthroned above it.

ARK OF NOAH. The ship which Noah was told to build (Gen. 6:14-16) is typical of Christ as the preserver of his people from judgment (Heb. 11:7). This preservation specifically embraces the remnant of Israel who will turn to the Lord during the Great Tribulation (Isa. 2:10, 11; 26: 20, 21). The "pitch" (Gen. 6:14) speaks of Christ's atoning work which keeps out the waters of judgment. The word rendered "pitch" (kopher) is the same root which is elsewhere rendered "atonement" (Lev. 17:11, etc.).

ARMAGEDDON (är-má-gĕd′ŏn). The Mount of Megiddo is the ancient hill which the fortress of Megiddo overlooked (Rev. 16:16). It will be the focal point of the great advance of the armies of the Beast and False Prophet as they attempt to annihilate the Jews and banish the name of Christ from the earth. Here the demon-driven armies of the nations (Rev. 16:13, 14) will be destroyed by the return of Christ in glory in fulfillment of the "smiting stone" prophecy of Daniel 2:35.

ARMLET. A band or bracelet clasping the upper arm. King Saul wore one (2 Sam.

1:10). Israelite men wore such armlets in the desert (Num. 31:50). Closely allied to the male armlet was the feminine bracelet, to which Isaiah makes reference as an item of luxurious adornment (Isa. 3:20). Excavations of Palestinian tombs indicate that both armlets and bracelets bound on the wrist were common (Gen. 24:22, 30, 47; Num. 31:50; Ezek. 16:11; 23:42).

Bronze armor of Roman officers in first centuries of Christian era, as seen in Naples museum (*HPS photo*)

ARMOR. Both defensive and offensive armor and weapons of war are summarized in the Hebrew term *kēlim* (Gen. 27:3; 1 Sam. 17:54) and the Greek term *hopla* (2 Cor. 10:4). The Hebrew term *nesheq*, "weapons," is also sometimes employed (2 Kings 10:2).

ARMY, ISRAELITE. No regular army existed in Israel previous to the reign of Saul. In premonarchical times the nation depended on divinely prepared military leaders in a time of crisis. Such a leader would often perform a heroic deed (Judg. 6:11–8:3). As a consequence, all able-bodied men would rally to his call. Sometimes, however, the response would not be complete (Judg. 5:16, 17).

After the establishment of the kingdom, a strong army became imperative not only for defense against hostile neighbors but also for offensive action to increase the borders of the realm. The nu-cleus of Saul's army was formed from permanent warriors selected by the king. David followed Saul's general military policy but greatly augmented the nation's military force (2 Sam. 15:18). Because of his efficient army David was able not only to defend the realm he had, but also to subdue neighboring peoples who proved hostile to his growing power. As a result he was able to carve out the empire which his son Solomon inherited.

From Solomon's time onward the army became an important institution in Israel. After the division of the kingdom both Israel and Judah had to support large armies. They frequently faced each other as foes, as well as hostile neighboring states. This situation made military strength imperative.

The Composition of the Israelite Army. The general levy of nonprofessional soldiers was divided into thousands, hundreds, fifties, and tens, each section with its own commander. This system seems to have come down from the Mosaic period (Exod. 18:24-26). The national army was supported by roving bands of marauders (Judg. 11:3). The backbone of the military, however, was the infantry. Cavalry did not play a prominent role until the reign of Solomon. This monarch introduced horses and chariots on a large scale (1 Kings 10:26; cf. 1 Kings 9:22), despite the prohibitions of the Law (Deut. 17:16; 20:1). The stables uncovered at Megiddo reveal that there was space for 450 horses (1 Kings 4:26; cf. 1 Kings 9:15, 19).

The archer was a very necessary part of the army. The bow and arrow figure prominently on Assyrian and Egyptian reliefs (Gen. 21:20; 48:22; 2 Sam. 1:18; 2 Chron. 35:23). In early Israel soldiers were maintained by booty (unless the booty was under the "ban"–1 Sam. 30:24) or by the produce of the land around their encampment. Later, under the monarchy, soldiers received regular pay (1 Kings 4:27).

The Israelite Military Camp. Guarding the central military base (*mahaneh*) was of the utmost importance (Judg. 7:19). Soldiers slept in tents or brush arbors (2 Sam. 11:11). The whole camp was deployed in a circle or square (Num. 2) and was surrounded by a "barricade." A force always remained behind in battle to guard the camp (1 Sam. 25:13).

ARMY, ROMAN. In the New Testament era Rome ruled Palestine and the then-known world. The basic unit was the "century" — one hundred men commanded by a "centurion." The legion, 6000 men, was divided into ten cohorts. Sometimes a small cavalry division was attached. The auxiliary cohorts were customarily named with particular titles, such as "the Italian band" (Acts 10:1) or "the Augustan band" (Acts 27:1), and were frequently divided into ten centuries.

ARNON (är'nŏn). The river flowing into the Dead Sea opposite En-gedi. It marked the boundary between Moab to the south and Ammon to the north (Judg. 11:18). It formed the southern border of Reubenite territory at the time of the conquest (Deut. 3:12, 16). Arnon is sometimes known as the "Wadi Mojib."

ARTAXERXES (är-tà-zērk'sēz). The third son of Xerxes and his successor to the throne of Persia (465-424 B.C.). In the seventh year of his reign (458 B.C.) he permitted Ezra to conduct a group of exiles back to Jerusalem (Ezra 7:1-10). Later he permitted Nehemiah to return and build the walls of Jerusalem (Neh. 13:6).

ARTEMIS (är'tĕ-mĭs). See "Diana."

ARTISAN. Skilled workers in metal, wood, or stone were present among the Hebrews (Exod. 38:23; 2 Sam. 5:11). Although not themselves distinguished by unusual inventiveness or artistry, the Hebrews nevertheless appreciated and even imported extraordinary talent for special projects like Solomon's Temple. Bezaleel of Judah was divinely gifted for artistic work on the Tabernacle (Exod. 31:1-11; 35:30-35). Ironworking was learned from the Philistines (1 Sam. 13: 19-21). The secrets of dyeing were acquired from the Phoenicians (2 Chron. 2: 7). The Hebrew word for artisan (*ḥārāsh*) signifies "one who cuts in" to "carve" or "devise" something artistic and useful (Exod. 38:23; 2 Sam. 5:11; 2 Chron. 24: 12).

ARVAD (är'văd). The northernmost of the Phoenician cities (Ezek. 27:8, 11). It is an island (1 Macc. 15:23) about two miles from the mainland and 125 miles north of Tyre (cf. Gen. 10:18). Arvad is present-day Ruwad.

ASA (ā'sà) ("physician" or perhaps a shortened name for "the Lord has healed"). A king of Judah from 911 to 870 B.C. He was a reformer (1 Kings 15:9-15; 2 Chron. 14:1-5; 15:16). He defeated an invasion of Ethiopians (2 Chron. 14:9-15) and thwarted Baasha's attempt to fortify Ramah. The king became diseased in his feet (1 Kings 15:23; 2 Chron. 16:12).

ASAHEL (ās'à-hĕl) ("God has made"). A nephew of David who served in David's army. He was famous for his valor and fleetness (2 Sam. 2:18). He was slain by Abner (2 Sam. 2:18-23).

ASAPH (ā'săf) ("collector"). A Levite (1 Chron. 6:39, 43) charged with the sacred music and song of the Tabernacle and whose descendants carried on the art (1 Chron. 25:1-7). Twelve Psalms (50 and 73 — 83) are attributed to the family of Asaph.

ASENATH (ās'ĕ-nǎth) (Egyptian, "belonging to the goddess Neith"). The daughter of Potiphera, priest of the great national temple of the sun at On (Heliopolis), seven miles northeast of modern Cairo. She became Joseph's wife and bore him two sons, Manasseh and Ephraim, who were adopted by her father-in-law, Jacob (Gen. 41:45, 50-52; 46:20).

ASH. A Palestinian tree formerly of uncertain identification but now established as the laurel. It flourishes on the central highland ridge as far south as Hebron.

ASHDOD (ăsh'dŏd). A city of the Philistine Pentapolis, seat of the worship of Dagon (Josh. 13:3; 1 Sam. 5:1-8; 6:17). It is called Azotus in the New Testament (Acts 8:40).

ASHER (ăsh'ēr) ("happy"). The eighth son of Jacob (Gen. 30:12, 13), the progenitor of the tribe that bore his name.

ASHERAH (à-shē'rà). The Hebrew form of the name of a Canaanite goddess. She appears in the Amarna Letters as Ashirtu (Ashratu). In the Ras Shamra literature from Ugarit in north Syria she is known as "Asherat, Lady of the Sea" and as the Mistress of the Gods. In the Old Testament she is associated with Baal (Judg. 3:7).

In addition to referring to the goddess

personally, the name "Asherah" also refers to the image of the goddess. The Israelites were ordered to cut down and burn the Asherim of the Canaanites (Exod. 34:13; Deut. 12:3) and were forbidden to harbor the idol beside God's altar (Deut. 16:21). See also "Grove."

ASHKELON, ASKELON (ăsh'kĕ-lŏn). A seacoast city of the Philistine Pentapolis. It is situated 12 miles north of Gaza in a valley on the Mediterranean coast (2 Sam. 1:20; Jer. 47:5-7; Amos 1:8; Zeph. 2:4; cf. Zech. 9:5).

ASHTORETH (ăsh'tō-rĕth). The "mother goddess," occupying a central place in the Fertility Cult and the groves or tree plantations dedicated to her (Isa. 1:29; Hos. 4:13). She corresponds to Ishtar of the Babylonians, Isis of the Egyptians, and Astarte of the Greeks. She was called "Queen of Heaven" (Jer. 44:19).

ASIARCHS. The administrators of the league of cities of the Roman province of Asia. The asiarchs were elected annually and were drawn from the wealthiest and most aristocratic citizens. From their ranks came the honorary high priests of the provincial cult of "Rome and the Emperor," established by the league in 29 B.C. Its headquarters were in the city of Pergamum. These chiefs of Asia (Acts 19:31) were patrons of the festivals and games at Ephesus. They were friendly to Paul.

ASP. See *pethen* under "Adder." The asp is of the same genus as the deadly cobra. It has a hood which it dilates when it is about to strike its victim.

ASS. (1) The wild ass (Hebrew ᶜarōd and pere'). It belongs to the genus *Asinus,* which contains several species of asses, both wild and domesticated. The ass genus belongs to the family of horses *(Equidae).* The wild ass is poetically described in Job 39:5-8. This species is known today as the onager *(Equus onager),* which is still extant in parts of Western and Central Asia. The wild ass of Syria *(Asinus hemippus)* is somewhat smaller than the onager (Job 24:5; 39:5; Psa. 104:11). The domestic ass is descended from the onager. It was domesticated probably as early as Neolithic times. (2) The domestic ass (Hebrew ḥamōr). It is a subspecies descended from

the onager. Tamed onagers appear in Mesopotamia in the third millennium B.C.. As a work animal the ass was used for carrying loads (Gen. 42:26; 1 Sam. 16:20; 25:18) and for agricultural work (Isa. 30:24). As a riding animal it was used before the horse became common (Num. 22:21; 2 Sam. 17:23; 2 Kings 4:24), even by people of position (Judg. 10:4; cf. Zech. 9:9; Matt. 21:1-7; John 12:14, 15). The meat of the animal was commonly eaten among the nations, as Xenophen and Pliny attest. But it was prohibited to Israelites by the Mosaic dietary laws (Lev. 11:1-8; Deut. 14:3-8; cf. 2 Kings 6:25). As an economic asset in an agricultural economy, the possession of an ass was a bare minimum for existence (Job 24:3).

ASSARION. See "Coins and Money."

ASSHUR (ăsh'ŭr). A city of Assyria situated on the Tigris River in Northern Iraq. The modern site has been excavated and has yielded many important texts and monuments. Asshur was the core of Assyria and its early capital. Asshur was also the chief god of the Assyrian pantheon, and was worshiped there from about 3000 B.C. Other capital cities at different periods were Calah, Nineveh, and Dur-Sharrukin.

ASSOS (ăs'ŏs). A seaport of Mysia in the Roman province of Asia (Acts 20:13, 14). At Troas Paul sent his associates around Cape Lectum by ship while he made the twenty-mile journey to Assos by land.

ASSURANCE-SECURITY. The believer's *security* rests in his position of union with Christ as a result of his faith in the complete efficacy of Christ's redemptive death and resurrection. The believer's *assurance* is realized when he rests confidently in his position in Christ as described by the written Word of God (John 3:14-18, 36; 5:24; 10:27-29; Rom. 3:21-23; 4:5; 5:1, 2; 6:23; 1 John 5:10-13). Assurance is the believer's full conviction that he possesses a salvation in which he will be kept eternally by God through Christ's fully efficacious redemption (2 Tim. 1:12).

ASSYRIANS (ă-sīr'ĭ-ăns). A semitic people whose center of power was located at Asshur on the upper Tigris River (cf. Gen. 10:10, 11) and whose capital in the heyday of imperial power was Nineveh. Called "the giant of the Semites," Assyria under ruthless conquerors from Ashurnasirpal II (884-859 B.C.) to Ashurbanipal (668-630 B.C.) became a scourge to the Near East and particularly to the Kingdom of Israel. Israel fell to Shalmaneser V in 722 B.C., and Judah almost succumbed to Sennacherib in 701 B.C. Assyria was finally defeated by the combined forces of the Babylonians, Medes, and Scythians. Nineveh was destroyed in 612 B.C. (Nah. 3:1-3) and the last vestiges of Assyrian power were wiped out at Haran shortly afterward.

ASTROLOGY. An ancient pseudo-science that claims to predict human destiny by studying the supposed influence of the relative positions of the sun, moon, and stars. Horoscopes are formulated for individuals on the basis of the relative positions of the heavenly bodies at the moment of the person's birth. These charts of the signs of the Zodiac and the positions of the planets claim to point out important guidelines for a person's future. As a form of fortune-telling and occultism, astrology is strictly forbidden by Scripture (Deut. 17:2-5; Isa. 47:13, 14; Dan. 2:27, 28; 4:7) Through its origin in ancient star worship it violates the first commandment of the moral law (Exod. 20:1-6). Astrology is experiencing a modern-day revival, along with spiritism, magic, card laying, palmistry, psychometry, and other occult phenomena.

ASYLUM. In ancient Israel any homicide, even an accidental one, initiated the action of the "avenger of blood" (*goel*). The nearest relative of the victim was responsible for putting the killer to death. However, the law acted to protect the unintentional killer. It provided safety at any shrine or altar whose horns he was quick to grasp (1 Kings 1:50; 2:28). Six cities, easily accessible, were appointed as places of refuge from the avenger of blood (Deut. 19:1-10). Intentional killers could be dragged from the altar and the city of refuge and executed by the *goel* (Exod. 21:12-14; Deut. 19:11-13). If a killing was proved unintentional, the acquitted had to settle in the city of refuge to avoid the avenger of blood. After the Exile an amnesty was declared for

unintentional killers so that they could return home without fear. See also "Cities of Refuge."

ATHALIAH (ă-thà-li'àh) ("the Lord is exalted"). The daughter of Ahab and Jezebel (2 Kings 8:18, 26; 2 Chron. 21:6; 22:2). She was married to Jehoram, king of Judah. As his queen (2 Kings 8:18; 2 Chron. 21:6) and as queen of the land for six years (841-835 B.C.), Athaliah was a proponent of Baal-Melkart. She was the only ruling queen of Judah, and represents a northern intrusion into the otherwise uninterrupted Davidic dynasty in Judah. She possessed all the cunning craftiness and idolatrous wickedness of her infamous mother, Jezebel. Also like Jezebel, Athaliah met a violent death.

ATHENS (ăth'ĕnz). The chief city of Attica and the capital of modern Greece. It was the intellectual and artistic center of the Greco-Roman world. It was visited by Paul (Acts 17:15 – 18:1). The name of the city was apparently derived from the goddess Athena.

ATONEMENT. The doctrine of forgiveness of sins by means of Christ's expiatory sacrifice. According to Scripture the sacrifice of the Old Testament only "covered" the offerer's sin (cf. Heb. 10:1-4). But since the Israelite's offering implied the obedience of faith in recognition of the future redemptive provision, God suspended judgment of the sin in anticipation of Christ's sacrifice (Rom. 3:25). Christ's death finally "put away" the sins committed previously "in the forbearance of God." The New Testament form of the doctrine thus regards the crucifixion of Jesus Christ as an act of atonement for the sins of the world (John 1:29). By Christ's death sinners are rendered salvable. However, only those who actually trust in God's provision are actually saved. The New Testament word translated "atonement" really means "reconciliation." "Not only so, but we also joy in God through our Lord Jesus Christ, by whom we have now received the reconciliation" (Rom. 5:11, *New Scofield Bible*).

ATONEMENT, DAY OF. *Yom Kippur* (the tenth day of the seventh month in the Hebrew calendar) marked the climax of access to God within the limits of the Old

Testament doctrine of atonement. On that most solemn occasion the high priest (a figure of Christ) entered the Most Holy Place to make annual atonement for the nation (Lev. 16:1-34). The expiation was only for a year but envisioned the once-for-all removal of sin by Christ's death (Exod. 30:10; Heb. 9:7, 8; 10:19).

In contrast to the sinless Christ, the high priest had to offer for himself as well as for the people (cf. Heb. 7:26, 27 with Lev. 16:6).

The high priest selected two goats and cast lots concerning their role in the sacrifice. The one on which "the Lord's lot" fell was slain, portraying Christ's vindication through death of the divine holiness expressed in the Law (Lev. 16:8-10, 15-17; Rom. 3:24-26). The other goat was sent forth into the wilderness as a "scapegoat," portraying Christ's expiation of our sin from the presence of God (Lev. 16:20-22; Rom. 8:33, 34; Heb. 9:26). The high priest's entrance into the Most Holy Place prefigures Christ's entrance into heaven itself (Heb. 9:24) to present the infinite merits of his shed blood before God's throne. See "Azazel."

ATTALIA (ăt-á-lī'á). A harbor city on the southwest coast of Asia Minor from which Paul and Barnabas sailed back to Syrian Antioch (Acts 14:25). It was founded by Attalus II of Pergamum (159-138 B.C.). The town still exists as present-day Antalya.

ATTALUS (ăt'ə-ləs). The King of Pergamos, either Attalus II Philadelphus or his nephew, Attalus III Philometor (138-133 B.C.) (1 Macc. 15:22).

AUGUSTUS (á-gŭs'tŭs). An honorific title of the Roman Emperors meaning "revered" or "reverend." When rendered in Greek (sebastos), it bore implications of divinity. In 27 B.C. the title was bestowed upon the founder of the Empire, who was its ruler at the time of Jesus' birth (Luke 2:1). His full name was Gaius Julius Caesar Octavianus. Used as a name by itself, Augustus refers to "Caesar Augustus" or Octavian (27 B.C.—A.D. 14), its most illustrious bearer. The title was borne by later Roman emperors and in its feminine form (Augusta) by empresses. See also "Caesar."

AUREUS. Called also "golden denarius" (denarius aureus), this gold coin was introduced by Julius Caesar in his financial reforms of 49 B.C. It is referred to by Josephus (Antiquities XIV: 8, 5) but is not mentioned in the Bible.

AUROCHS. The wild ox (Bos primigenius). Tiglathpileser I (1115-1102 B.C.) is pictured on Assyrian reliefs hunting this animal in the Lebanon region. In later centuries the aurochs became extinct; however, it is survived by its descendant, the domesticated ox. The wild species was distinguished from the domesticated animal in that it had a flatter forehead and large horns with double curvature.

AXE. See "Battle-Axe."

AZARIAH (ăz-á-rī'á) ("the Lord has aided"). A king of Judah from 767 to 740 B.C. He was more commonly known as Uzziah (cf. 2 Kings 15:1-7; 2 Chron. 26: 1-23). "Azariah" was also the name of at least a score of other less prominent people in the Old Testament.

AZAZEL (á-zā'zĕl). The word occurs only in the ritual of the Day of Atonement (Lev. 16:8, 10, 26). It apparently indicates "dismissal" or complete removal of sin from the camp of God's people. The word is used as an infinitive, "in order to remove." Some scholars interpret it as denoting the "scapegoat," the "goat that goes away." Others take it to denote a desolate region (cf. Lev. 16:22).

AZEKAH (á-zē'kä). A fortress city south of the Valley of Aijalon (Tell ez-Zakariyeh) and nine miles north of Beit Jibrin (Josh. 10:10, 11; 15:35; 1 Sam. 17:1). Rehoboam strengthened its fortifications about 918 B.C. (2 Chron. 11:5, 9). Mentioned in the fourth Lachish Letter, it was one of the last of Judah's fortified cities to fall to the Chaldeans in 588 B.C. (Jer. 34:7).

AZOTUS (á-zō'tŭs). The New Testament form of Ashdod.

AZUBAH (á-zū'báh) ("forsaken"). (1) The wife of Caleb, one of Judah's descendants. By him she had three sons (1 Chron. 2:18, 19). (2) The daughter of Shilhi, wife of King Asa of Judah. She was the mother of King Jehoshaphat of Judah, who reigned during 870-848 B.C. She was evidently a very godly woman, belonging to that group of queen mothers in Kings and Chronicles whose biographies begin, "And his mother's name was" and "he did that which was right in the sight of the Lord" (2 Chron. 20:31, 32). Her husband was a godly man and her son Jehoshaphat became a godly king.

B

BAAL (bā'ál). The great fertility god of the Canaanites. The Hebrew name means "master," "husband," or "lord." Baal was the son of El in the Ugaritic literature. Female deities associated with these male gods were Anath and Asherah. This fertility cult was extremely debased and presented a continual peril to Israelite worship of the one true God. Besides being grossly immoral, the Baal cults practiced child sacrifice (cf. Jer. 19:5).

Ruins of the Temple of Jupiter in Baalbek, Lebanon (© MPS)

BAALBEK (bā'ăl-bĕk). A town in modern Lebanon famous for its ancient pagan ruins and temples.

BAASHA (bā'à-shà). The exterminator of the house of Jeroboam I and founder of the second brief dynasty of the Northern Kingdom (909-886 B.C.), fulfilling the prophecy of Ahijah (1 Kings 15:25-33). He continued the apostate religious policy of Jeroboam and thereby earned stern prophetic rebuke (1 Kings 15:34 – 16:6).

BABYLON (băb'ĭ-lŏn). A great city of antiquity whose ruins are located on a branch of the Euphrates River near the modern town of Hilla, southwest of Bagdad. Its history goes back to dim antiquity (cf. Gen. 11:1-9). The city boasted a great temple tower or "ziggurat." The city reached its pinnacle of glory under Nebuchadnezzar II (605-562 B.C.). Its walls, gates, temple tower, and other buildings made it famous (cf. Dan. 4:30).

BABYLONIANS. The people who occupied the eastern end of the Fertile Crescent from Hit on the Euphrates to the Persian Gulf. The heart of Babylonia was the fertile alluvial plain of Shinar (Gen. 11:2) between the Euphrates and the Tigris in the last two hundred miles of the course of these two great rivers as they flowed to the sea. The Babylonians in the course of centuries became a blend of original non-Semitic Sumerians, Semitic Akkadians, Amorites, and later Hurrian and Kassite stock. The Semitic strain predominated.

The Early Dynastic Period (2800-2500 B.C.) saw the advent of kingship and the powerful city-states of Eridu, Batibirra, Larak, Sippar, Shuruppak, Kish, and Uruk (Erech). The Sargonid Semitic dynasty followed (2371-2191 B.C.). See "Akkadians." This Semitic state conquered the various city-states and extended its power to the Mediterranean region. Gudea of Lagash (2150 B.C.), however, staged a Sumerian revival and dominated Ur and the southern cities toward the end of this period.

The powerful Third Dynasty of Ur (2113-2006 B.C.) evidently witnessed Terah and Abraham's migration (Gen. 11:31). With the fall of Ur the Amorites took control (1894-1595 B.C.) under a vigorous dynasty in which Hammurabi (1792-1750 B.C.) ruled over an empire, as the Mari Letters show. This period was followed by the rule of the Kassites (1595-1174 B.C.), who invaded Babylonia from the eastern hills and gradually took over the country.

After this period Assyria began to dominate this region and held it in complete control from 745 to 626 B.C. The Neo-Babylonian or Chaldean Empire (626-539 B.C.) witnessed the exile of Judah under Nebuchadnezzar II (605-562 B.C.), Amel-Marduk or Evil Merodach (562-560 B.C.), Neriglissar (560-556 B.C.), Labashi-Marduk (556 B.C.), and Nabonidus, assisted by his son Belshazzar (556-539 B.C.).

Cyrus the Great took possession of Babylon on October 16, 539 B.C., and encouraged the return of the Jews to Palestine (Ezra 1:1-11). From 539 to 332 B.C. the Achaemenid line of Persian kings ruled Babylonia as part of their far-flung empire. Alexander the Great captured Babylon in 331 B.C. and ruled the region as part of his extensive realm until his death in 323 B.C. A Hellenistic line ruled until 312 B.C. From then until 64 B.C. the country passed into the hands of the Seleucids. From 64 B.C. it passed to the Parthians, until it was conquered by the Arabs in A.D. 641.

BADGER. A burrowing animal with thick, short legs and long-clawed forefeet. It existed in Bible lands. However, the Hebrew *tahash* (Exod. 26:14; 35:7;

Num. 4:25; Ezek. 16:10), whose skin was used for the outer covering of the Tabernacle and for sandals, was not the badger but the seal, especially the dugong (*Halicore hemprichii*). It has a round head and fish-like tail and exists in large numbers in the Red Sea.

BAKER. Bread made principally of barley or wheat was the basic food of the ancient world and was considered the staff of life (cf. Lev. 26:26). From earliest times the word "bread" was used for food in general (Gen. 3:19; Prov. 6:8, Hebrew). Those who prepared it, whether humble peasant housewife or chief baker in a palace (cf. Gen. 40:1), had an honorable task.

Flour mixed with water and seasoned with salt was kneaded in a special trough. To this was added leaven in the form of a small bit of fermented dough until the whole batch was leavened and ready for baking. Unleavened bread was baked for special occasions. The baking was done over a fire, on heated stones, on a griddle, or in an oven. The oven baking usually produced the best results.

BALAAM (bā'làm) ("swallower or conqueror of the nation"). A diviner-prophet (Josh. 13:22; cf. Num. 22:1 – 24:25) who was hired by the King of Moab to curse Israel, but was instead compelled by God to bless his people. As a typical mercenary prophet (2 Pet. 2:15), he erred in reasoning from natural morality that God must curse Israel because of her evil. He forgot the higher morality of the Cross, by which God can redeem the believing sinner without sacrificing his own justice (Rom. 3:26). Balaam's doctrine (Rev. 2:14) was his advice to corrupt the people who could not be cursed (Num. 31:15, 16; 23:8).

BALM, BALM OF GILEAD (gĭl'e-ăd). A resin apparently obtained in Gilead (Gen. 37:25; Jer. 8:22; 46:11) and exported from Palestine (Gen. 37:25; Ezek. 27:17). It was used as a healing ointment (Jer. 51:8). The balm cannot now be identified with any plant in Gilead. It has been claimed to be mastich, a product of the mastich tree (*Pistacia lentiscus*), common in Palestine. It is a bushy evergreen whose pale yellow gum was used for incense and as an ointment. Its leaves and berries and the oil from its bark were used as medicine. Classical authors have associated biblical "balm" with Mecca balsam (still imported into Egypt from Arabia).

BAPTISM. Ritual washing for purification from uncleanness of various sorts was common in the Old Testament (cf. Heb. 6:2; 9:10). Uncleanness was associated with childbirth, menstruation, contact with a corpse, certain diseases, idolatry, etc. Converts from heathenism were baptized. The Essenes baptized. John the Baptist employed the rite to signify repentance from sin. John's baptism was preparatory and introductory to Christ's spiritual baptism (Matt. 3:11; Mark 1:8; Luke 3:16; John 1:33; Acts 1:5; 11:15, 16).

Christ "baptized with the Holy Spirit" in the primary sense of providing "so great salvation" (Heb. 2:3). After his ascension the Holy Spirit came and "baptized" believers into union with the glorified Christ (1 Cor. 12:12, 13; Rom. 6:3, 4; Gal. 3:27).

BARABBAS (bär-ăb'ás) ("son of Abba"). A bandit (John 18:40) arrested for political violence (Mark 15:7). Pilate offered to release either him or Jesus. The crowd chose Barabbas.

BAR-JESUS (bär-jē'sŭs) ("son of Joshua"). A magician and false prophet. Under demonic power he tried to dissuade Sergius Paulus, the proconsul of Cyprus, from accepting the gospel (Acts 13:6-12).

BAR-KOCHBA (bär-kôkh'bä). The leader of the second Jewish revolt against the Romans (A.D. 132-135). He was hailed as "Messiah, the Son of a Star," the *bar kochba* of Numbers 24:17.

BARLEY. One of the most ancient of cereals. In Palestine it is commonly cultivated in winter and harvested in May (Ruth 1:22). Several varieties belong to the genus *Hordeum*. It formed one of the essential staple foods of ancient Bible lands.

BARNABAS (bär'ná-bás) ("son of prophetic consolation"). A companion of Paul on his first missionary tour (Acts 13:1 – 15:39).

BARTHOLOMEW (bär-thŏl'ŏ-mū). One of the Twelve Apostles. His first name was apparently Nathanael (John 1:45; cf.

Matt. 10:3; Mark 3:18; Luke 6:14; Acts 1:13).

BARUCH (bä'rŭk) ("blessed"). Jeremiah's friend and scribe (Jer. 36:1-32). The prophet placed the deed for some property in Baruch's hands (Jer. 32:6-16). He was taken to Egypt with Jeremiah (Jer. 43:1-7).

BARZILLAI (bär-zĭl'á-i) ("made of iron"). A wealthy Gileadite who befriended David during Absalom's rebellion (2 Sam. 17:27-29). David later rewarded him (2 Sam..19:31-40).

BASEMATH (băs'ĕ-măth). (1) One of Esau's wives, the daughter of Elon the Hittite (Gen. 26:34). (2) Another of Esau's wives, a daughter of Ishmael (Gen. 36:3, 13, 17). She was also called Makalath (Gen. 28:9). (3) A daughter of Solomon who was married to one of his twelve tax collectors (1 Kings 4:15).

BASHAN (bä'shăn). A mountainous region (cf. Psa. 68:15) east of Lake Huleh and the Lake of Galilee with elevated peaks reaching 2320 feet. Bashan was noted for its superior livestock (Deut. 32: 14; Ezek. 39:18).

BAT (Hebrew *ᶜaṭallēph*). Under Mosaic Law the bat was classed with fowls and was ceremonially unclean (Lev. 11:13, 19; Deut. 14:11, 12, 18). Strictly speaking, the bat is a quadruped rather than a bird, and as such has teeth rather than a bill and is covered with hair instead of feathers. Its "wing" is really a featherless membrane connecting its front and rear legs.

BATHSHEBA (băth-shē'bà) ("daughter of the oath or seventh day"). The wife of Uriah the Hittite. King David committed adultery with her and plotted her husband's death in battle. Then David married her. After the death of the illicit child, Bathsheba gave birth to Solomon. The sordid tale is told in 2 Samuel 11.

BATTERING-RAM. A military machine used by Assyrians, Babylonians, and other ancient peoples to beat down the walls of besieged cities. It was generally a large beam with a head of iron somewhat resembling the head of a ram.

BATTLE-AXE. A military weapon with a wood handle and a metallic axe-head. It was commonly used in battle by the Hittites, Assyrians, Babylonians, and Elamites. The "battle-axe" of Jeremiah 51:20 (Hebrew *mēphiṣ*, "scatterer") is really a club, doubtlessly imbedded with iron nails. Herodotus mentions such a weapon carried by Assyrian troops in Xerxes' army.

BEANS. The common broad bean (*Vicia faba*) is well known in Palestine. With wheat, emmer, barley, and millet it furnished the basic diet of the population as a whole in Bible times.

BEAR. In Bible times bears roamed in forests over Palestine. The Syrian form of the brown bear is still found in parts of the Middle East, including Lebanon (though not in Palestine proper). David killed a bear near Bethlehem (1 Sam. 17: 34-37). Near Bethel two female bears mauled a group of children who had mocked Elisha (2 Kings 2:23, 24). The bear figures prominently in Daniel's vision of the end of Gentile world power (Dan. 7:5).

BEAST, THE. A prophetic term denoting the great tyrant of the last days of world history. He will be Satan's agent of wrath against God and his Tribulation saints. The beast is described by several other biblical titles. In Daniel 7:8 he is called the "little horn"; in Daniel 9:27 and Matthew 24:15 he is seen as a desolator; in 2 Thessalonians 2:3 he is termed the "man of sin"; and in Revelation 13:1 he is described as a "beast out of the sea."

BEE. The name is correctly applied to several families of the order *Hymenoptera*, including solitary bees and bumblebees as well as honey bees (Hebrew *deborāh*). The honey bee is clearly referred to in Judges 14:8, Deuteronomy 1:44, and Psalm 118:12. In Isaiah 7:18 the prophet illustrates the Palestinian custom of calling honey bees by whistling for them: "The Lord shall hiss (whistle) for the bee that is in the land of Assyria."

"Abraham's Well" at Beersheba, today covered by a pumping station (© MPS)

BEERSHEBA (bē'ĕr-shē'bà). The chief city of the Negeb, famous from patriarchal times (Gen. 21:25-31; 26:32, 33). It was a religious sanctuary (Gen. 46:1-5). It marked the southernmost boundary of Israelite population (Judg. 20:1; 1 Chron. 21:2). See also under "Springs, Wells, and Pools."

BEETLE. The King James Version's rendering (Lev. 11:22) of a particular kind of leaping insect (Hebrew *hargōl*). It is not a beetle as defined in today's English, but is instead some type of grasshopper, locust, or cricket.

BEHEMOTH (bě-hē'mŏth) (plural of Hebrew *behēmāh*, "beast," an intensive plural denoting a large beast). A quadruped commonly taken as the hippopotamus of the Nile (*Hippopotamus amphibious*). Job pictures it eating grass like an ox and frequenting streams and rivers (Job 40:15-24). The hippopotamus is a large, amphibious animal with a huge tusk and short, stout legs. Its strength is incredible. Today these great beasts are only found far in the interior of Africa on the Upper Nile.

BELIAL (bē'lĭ-àl) ("worthless, destructive, wicked"). A Hebrew word used in expressions of contempt, as in Judges 19: 22 and 1 Samuel 25:17, 25. In later times Belial became a designation of Satan, the Evil One (2 Cor. 6:15).

BELIEF. To "believe" in the biblical sense involves more than mere intellectual assent to a fact. The New Testament concept of believing (*pisteuo*) means *to trust in, to have faith in, to repose upon, to commit oneself to* (a person or an object). To truly believe therefore includes not only the passive assent of the mind but also the action of the will. "Whosoever believeth in him" (John 3:16) means *whoever trusts in God's Son so as to become united to him in life and destiny.* See also "Faith."

BELIEVER. A person who has exercised saving faith in Christ (1 Tim. 4:12). Compare Acts 2:44; 11:17; 13:48; Ephesians 1:13. All such are permanently sanctified in their position "in Christ" and are thus saints by calling (Rom. 1:7; 8:27; 1 Cor. 1:2). See also "Saint."

BELSHAZZAR (běl-shäz'ĕr) ("Bel has protected his kingship"). A regent of

Babylon during the reign of his father, Nabonidus (553-539 B.C.). He was warned of the approaching doom of the Neo-Babylonian Empire by the aged Daniel (Dan. 5:1-31) and was slain when the Persian troops gained access to the city through the dry riverbed of the diverted Euphrates.

BENAIAH (bĕ-nā'yà). A valiant man under David (2 Sam. 23:20-22) who supervised David's bodyguard (2 Sam. 8:18). He remained faithful to David during Absalom's rebellion (2 Sam. 20:23) and escorted Solomon to Gihon to be anointed as king (1 Kings 1:38).

BENEDICTIONS. In ancient Israel priests were charged with blessing people in God's name (Num. 6:23-27). In postexilic Judaism it became a custom to invoke blessings as additions to prayers in doxologies. The practice was followed in Christian doxologies (cf. Heb. 13:20, 21; Jude 1:24, 25).

BENHADAD (bĕn-hā'dăd) ("son of the god Hadad"). The name of several Aramaean kings at Damascus (890-770 B.C.). At least two of these are mentioned in Scripture: Benhadad I (1 Kings 15:18), possibly the same person as Benhadad II, foe of Ahab (874-853 B.C.); Benhadad III or II (796-770 B.C.), the son of Hazael (2 Kings 13:22-25), mentioned also in the stele of Zakir, king of Hamath.

BENJAMIN (bĕn'jà-mĭn) ("son of the right hand"). Jacob's youngest son by Rachel (Gen. 35:16-20). He was the progenitor of one of the twelve tribes of Israel.

BERNICE (bĕr-nī'sē) ("victorious"). The eldest daughter of Herod Agrippa I, king of Judea (A.D. 41-44). She was married to Herod, King of Chalcis, who died in A.D. 48. She accompanied her brother, Herod Agrippa II, so constantly that scandal arose. She was with him when Paul made his defense before him (Acts 25:23; 26:30). Her loose character appears in the fact that she afterward became the mistress first of Vespasian and then of Titus.

BESOR (bē'sōr). A brook (Wadi Ghazzeh) which flows into the Mediterranean Sea about five miles south of Gaza. Two hundred of David's men remained here while 400 others pursued the Amalekites (1 Sam. 30:9, 10).

BETHANY (bĕth'à-nĭ). A small village about a mile-and-a-half east of Jerusalem on the eastern slope of the Mount of Olives. It was the home of Mary, Martha, and Lazarus (John 11:1) and the site of Christ's Ascension (Luke 24:50, 51).

BETH-AVEN (bĕth-ā'vĕn). A wilderness region located east of Bethel and near Ai (Josh. 7:2; 18:12). The site served as a boundary mark for Benjamin's apportionment (Josh. 18:12).

BETHEL (bĕth'ĕl). (1) A city about twelve miles north of Jerusalem on the main north-south ridge road. Although it is identified with present-day Beitin, there are difficulties in relating it to its environment, and some nearby location may yet prove to be the ancient site. The original city, Luz, was built before the time of Abraham (Gen. 12:8). It was Jacob who named it Bethel (Gen. 28:16-19). Jeroboam I lifted Bethel to new prominence when he made it the Northern Kingdom's chief sanctuary and the rival of Jerusalem (1 Kings 12:25-33). (2) An eminence or "mountain" (Josh. 16:1; 1 Sam. 13:2; etc.) on the watershed near the city of Bethel.

BETHESDA (bĕ-thĕz'dà). See under "Springs, Wells, and Pools."

BETH-HORON (bĕth-hō'rŏn). A town near the border of Benjamin (Josh. 18:14), a Levitical city (Josh. 21:20, 22). It consisted of a lower city (Josh. 16:3; 18:13) fortified by Solomon (1 Kings 9:17), as well as an upper town (Josh. 16:5; 2 Chron. 8:5).

Bethlehem today, looking from the west (© *MPS*)

BETHLEHEM (bĕth'lĕ-hĕm). A town in Judah which was the birthplace of Christ (Matt. 2:1, 5, 6), the home of David (1 Sam. 17:15; 20:6), and the adopted home of Ruth (Ruth 1:19-22). There was also a Bethlehem in Galilee (Josh. 19:15).

BETH-PEOR, BAAL-PEOR (bĕth-pē'ôr;

bā'ăl-pē'ŏr). A place about five miles northeast of the upper extremity of the Dead Sea in Transjordan. Moses was buried near this location (Deut. 34:6).

BETH-REHOB (bĕth-rē'hŏb). A town and region in the vicinity of Dan. It comprised the territory between Mount Lebanon and Mount Hermon (Judg. 18:28). It was occupied by the Arameans (2 Sam. 10:6).

BETHSAIDA-JULIAS (bĕth-sā'ĭ-dá). A fishing village on the Sea of Galilee during the Roman period (Matt. 11:21; Mark 6:45; John 1:44). A new city was constructed by Philip the tetrarch and named Julias in honor of the Roman imperial family.

BETHSHAN, BETHSHEAN (bĕth-shē'-ăn). A Bronze Age fortress city which guarded the entrance of the Valley of Jezreel from the east. In later years it was renamed Scythopolis. Its present-day remains are identified with Tell el-Husn near Beisan. Excavation of the city has yielded important archeological remains. During biblical times the city changed hands several times (cf. Josh. 17:11-18; Judg. 1:27, 28; 1 Sam. 31:7-12; 1 Kings 4:7, 12).

BETH-SHEMESH (bĕth-shē'mĕsh). A town on the border of Judah (Josh. 15:10) and a Levitical city (Josh. 21:13, 16). It was placed in Solomon's second district (1 Kings 4:7-9). It is identified with Tell er-Rumeileh, about fifteen miles west-southwest of Jerusalem. There was also a Beth-shemesh in Issachar (Josh. 19:22) and one in Naphtali (Josh. 19:38).

BEZALEL (bĕz'á-lĕl) ("in the shadow of God's protection"). A craftsman who fashioned much of the ornamental work of the Tabernacle in the desert (Exod. 31: 1-11; 35:30-35).

BILDAD (bĭl'dăd) ("Bel has loved"). One of Job's friends and would-be comforters (Job 2:11; cf. Chaps. 8, 18, 25).

BILHAH (bĭl'há) ("foolish, stupid"). Rachel's handmaid, given to her by her father, Laban, at the time of her marriage with Jacob. At her mistress' request she became one of Jacob's secondary wives and thereby the mother of Dan and Naphtali (Gen. 30:1-8). Later she committed adultery with Reuben (Gen. 35:22).

BINDING AND LOOSING. Power claimed by Jewish religious authorities to forbid or permit practices covered directly or indirectly by the Law of Moses. The Pharisees of Jesus' day claimed such power. On the basis of his full confession of the deity of Christ, Peter was given this power (Matt. 16:13-19). It was also shared by the other apostles (Matt. 18:18). Peter's use of this authority in declaring the gospel of forgiveness (John 20:23) is illustrated in Acts 10:44-48. Paul also used it (Acts 13:38, 39). The power is resident not in the preacher personally but in the gospel which he proclaims and the Savior which he presents under the authority of the Holy Spirit. See "Keys of the Kingdom of Heaven."

BISHOP. See "Elder."

BITHIAH (bĭ-thī'á) ("daughter of the Lord"). A daughter of Pharaoh and wife of a Judahite named Mered (1 Chron. 4: 17). Her name apparently indicates that she became a convert to the worship of Israel's God.

BITTER HERBS. Herbs eaten with the Paschal lamb during the Passover (Exod. 12:8; Num. 9:11). They were symbolic of the bitter experiences of the enslaved Hebrews in Egypt prior to the Exodus. The herbs may refer to endives, chicory, lettuce, watercress, or "star thistles." Horseradish is now commonly used in Europe and America as "bitter herbs" with the Paschal lamb, but it was not known in Bible times.

BITTERN (Hebrew *qippōd*). Possibly a marsh bird. Such a bird by the name of bittern is common today around Lake Huleh, north of the Sea of Galilee. But many scholars categorize the biblical bittern not as a bird at all but rather a porcupine or lizard.

BLACKSMITH. See "Smith."

BLASPHEMY. Blasphemy refers principally to reviling God by word or action (Num. 15:30; Isa. 37:6) or directly cursing him (Lev. 24:11; Rev. 16:9). Notorious enemies of God are full of blasphemies (Rev. 13:1, 5, 6; 17:3). The Jews accused Jesus of this crime because he claimed to forgive sins (Matt. 9:3; Mark 2:7; Luke 5:21) and to be Christ the Son of God (Matt. 26:63-65; Mark 14:61-64; John 10:30-33). Those who oppose the gospel commit blasphemy (1 Tim. 1:13) and bring discredit on Christ by their actions (Rom. 2:24; James 2:7).

The reviling of human authority is dangerously similar to blaspheming God himself, since all authority is granted by God (Acts 13:45; 18:6; Jude 1:8-10). In its weaker sense blasphemy may denote slander of any person (1 Cor. 4:13; 1 Pet. 4:4). Blasphemy against the Holy Spirit is apparently attributing Christ's works to Satan (Matt. 12:31, 32; Mark 3:28-30; Luke 12:10).

BLESSINGS AND CURSINGS. Power-laden words for good or ill, spoken on the occasion of religious celebrations or other special occasions and often accompanied by gestures and symbolic actions. In the patriarchal period the blessing of a dying father was transmitted to his heir (Gen. 27:1-29). Such blessings were irrevocable (Gen. 27:30-40). In early premonarchic Israel blessings and cursings were apparently a customary part of the festival of covenant renewal (Deut. 11:26-32).

Blessing formulas are found in the New Testament also, such as the Beatitudes (Matt. 5:3-12) and the benedictions found in the introductions and concluding portions of the Pauline letters. Curses appear seldom (cf. Mark 11:12-14), although the Book of Revelation contains both benedictions and woes (1:3; 8:13; 11:18; 14:13; 19:9; 22:7, 14, 18, 19). The ultimate blessing has been bestowed upon mankind through Christ Jesus.

BLOOD. Blood was regarded as the vehicle of life. Eating of flesh with the blood in it was accordingly forbidden among the Hebrews and early Christians (Acts 15:20).

BLOOD OF CHRIST. The blood of Christ was of infinite value (Rom. 5:9; Eph. 1:7; 2:13; Col. 1:14) because it represented his sinless life and vicarious death. "For the life of the flesh is in the blood" (Lev. 17:11). It was not the blood in the veins of the sacrifice but the blood of the slain victim upon the altar which was efficacious. "And I have given it (the blood) to you upon the altar to make an atonement for your souls; for it is the blood that maketh an atonement for the soul" (Lev. 17:11). Salvation by the mere imitation or influence of Christ's life is unknown in Scripture. It is the *death* of Christ that saves. His life is to be imitated only after the benefits of his death have been appropriated.

BLUE. The cord of blue upon the borders of the priests' garments (Num. 15:38) denotes the fact that the servants of God were to be heavenly in obedience and character. As the heavenly color, blue signified separation from earthly ambitions and desires.

BOAR. The wild swine, especially the male of the species (Psa. 80:13). The wild boar is three or more feet long. It has teeth projecting beyond the upper lip, constituting formidable tusks with which the boar rips open its enemies. The animal is still extant in the ravines east of the Jordan, in the swamps of the waters of Merom, in Lebanon, and in the Plain of Sharon.

BOAZ (bō'ăz) (probably "in him is strength"). Kinsman and husband of Ruth and ancestor of David and Christ (Ruth 2:1 – 4:22; Matt. 1:5).

BOGAZKÖY. The ancient capital of the Hittite Empire. Its present name is Hattusa. Here thousands of cuneiform tablets were unearthed in the archeological resurrection of the long-lost Hittites. The ruin is located in the great bend of the Halys River in Asia Minor (Anatolia).

BOHAN, STONE OF (bō'hăn). A landmark on the border between Judah and Benjamin (Josh. 15:6). It was in the wilderness region southwest of Jericho and not far from the Jordan River. It was known as "the Reubenite's thumb" (from *bohen*, "thumb").

BOOK. Books in Bible times were actually scrolls. These were documents written on strips of leather or papyrus. The scrolls were rolled up (Isa. 34:4) and often sealed (Rev. 5:1). Certain scrolls are mentioned by name in the Old Testament, such as the Book of the Covenant (Exod. 24:7), the Book of the Law (2 Kings 22:8), the Book of the Wars of the Lord (Num. 21:14), and the Book of Jasher (Josh. 10:13).

BOOK OF LIFE. In the Old Testament the term refers to physical life. "Let them be blotted out of the book of the living" (Psa. 69:28) means "let them die physically." Such is also the case in Exodus

32:32, 33, where Moses prays to be blotted out of God's book, and in Daniel 12:1, where all who "shall be found written in the book" will survive the Great Tribulation. Isaiah's reference to "everyone that is written among the living in Jerusalem" (Isa. 4:3) also embraces the *physically* living.

In the New Testament the book of life has reference to *eternal* life and the roster of believers (Phil. 4:3; Rev. 3:5; 22:19). At the Great White Throne judgment everyone not enrolled in the book of life is consigned to Gehenna (Rev. 20:12-15). This is the book of life of the slain Lamb, in which the names of the elect are recorded (Rev. 13:8; 21:27). The same idea occurs in Luke 10:20 and Acts 13:48.

BOOTHS, FEAST OF. Sometimes called the "Feast of Tabernacles," this Jewish event was one of three great annual festivals celebrated in the autumn at the end of the agricultural year (Lev. 23:34; Deut. 16:13). The pilgrims were to live in arbor shelters, reminiscent of Israel's wanderings.

BOTTLE-MAKER. Biblical "bottles" were usually tanned and sewn skins of animals. They were serviceable, but were subject to wear and tear (Josh. 9:4; Matt. 9:17).

BOW AND ARROW. See under "Archer."

BOX TREE. The *Boxus longifolia*, a small tree up to twenty feet high with small evergreen leaves and hard, fine-grained wood. The box, fir, and pine were the glory of Lebanon.

BOZEZ (bōz′ĕs). One of two crags near Gibeah, in the mountain pass through which Jonathan attempted to surprise the Philistine garrison (1 Sam. 14:4-6).

BOZRAH (bŏz′rà). A town in Edom mentioned in Genesis 36:33, Isaiah 34:6, Jeremiah 49:13, and Amos 1:12. It was on the King's Highway, which ran through Transjordan to Ezion-geber on the Gulf of Aqabah. It was situated about 50 miles south-southeast of the southern extremity of the Dead Sea.

BRACELET. See "Armlet."

BRAMBLE, BRIER. Apparently a variety of *Rhamnus,* quite common in the Dead Sea area, the Jordan Valley, and at Jerusalem. Thorn bushes and brambles were often used as fences to protect vineyards

and other cultivated areas (cf. Isa. 5:5; Song 2:15). The term "brier" is the rendering of no less than six Hebrew words referring to various types of burrs, thistles, and other prickly plants and shrubs (Judg. 8:7, 16; Isa. 9:18; 10:17; 55:13; Ezek. 2:6; 28:24; Mic. 7:4). The Greek word *tribolos* (caltrop, burr, thistle) occurs in Matthew 7:16 and Hebrew 6:8.

BRASS. See "Bronze."

BREASTPLATE. The breastpiece was fastened by gold chains to the shoulderpieces of the priest's ephod. It consisted of a square pouch that was a repository for the Urim and Thummim and an oblong gold setting containing twelve precious stones engraved with the names of the Israelite tribes, one on each stone (Exod. 28:15-21, 29, 30). This foreshadows Christ as our Great High Priest (Heb. 3:1; 7:26; 9:11). He now represents us before God (Rom. 8:33, 34; Heb. 7:25; 9:24), bearing our names before him much as the High Priest of Israel carried the names of the tribes of Israel on his shoulders and on his breast (cf. Isa. 49:16).

BRICKMAKER. Brickmaking was the labor of peasants and the enslaved Israelites in Egypt. The craft as practiced in Egypt is graphically and accurately described in Exodus 5:6-19. Archeology reveals that straw and stubble were regularly used during this period. The chemical decay of the straw in the bricks increased the plasticity and strength of the clay.

In Egypt and Mesopotamia sun-dried bricks were common. Kiln-baked bricks were used for facings and pavement construction. In Palestine sun-dried bricks were the norm. House walls were frequently of brick construction on a stone foundation. Bricks in Mesopotamia and Egypt were often impressed with the ruler's name. Nebuchadnezzar II (605-562 B.C.) used at least five different stamps.

BRIDE. See under "Engagement" and "Marriage, Jewish."

BRIDE OF CHRIST. The Church is now viewed as a "chaste virgin" espoused or betrothed to Christ (cf. 2 Cor. 11:2) and still unmarried. The betrothal is legally binding and represents the individual members of the body of Christ. The Rapture represents the coming of the Bridegroom for his bride (1 Thess. 4:13-18). This event heralds the approaching marriage, when the bride becomes "the Lamb's wife," a figure of glorification and association with Christ in rule and destiny. The Marriage Supper of the Lamb in heaven (Rev. 19:7-9) is celebrated just prior to the Second Coming of Christ to the earth to set up his kingdom rule in association with the glorified Church and resurrected Old Testament saints.

The marriage of the Lamb is the consummation of the union of Christ and the Church as his bride. The figure is in keeping with the oriental custom of marriage, which consisted of the betrothal, the marriage, and the marriage supper. The subsequent marriage feast (Matt. 25:1-13) with the ten virgins represents Israel at the end of the Tribulation. The five wise virgins prefigure the saved remnant, while the five foolish ones prefigure the professing but unbelieving part of the nation. Only those who possess the "oil" of the Holy Spirit (i.e., only true believers — cf. Rom. 8:9) can enter the kingdom. All others are excluded.

BRIER. See "Bramble, Brier."

BRONZE. In Scripture symbolism bronze represents divine judgment, as in the bronze altar and the bronze serpent (portraying God's judgment of sin) and in the bronze laver (symbolizing self-judgment of sin).

BRONZE SEA. A large vessel of cast bronze made by Hiram of Tyre for Solomon's Temple (1 Kings 7:23-26; 2 Chron. 4:2-5). It doubtless corresponded in use to the bronze laver of the Tabernacle. The molten sea was a copper bowl 15 feet in diameter and 7½ feet high. It rested on twelve oxen. When the Temple was plundered by the Babylonians the bronze sea was broken up and carried to Babylonia (2 Kings 25:13).

BROOM. A twiggy, nearly leafless bush which bears clusters of pink-white flowers. It grows in the Jordan Valley, Arabia, and the Peninsula of Sinai. The large stalk of the broom was used as fuel (Job 30:4) and made into charcoal (Psa. 120:4).

BUCKLER. A type of small shield (2 Chron. 14:8). It was a piece of defensive armor worn on the left arm. In early times bucklers were either of wood or wicker or else of wood covered with leather and sometimes ornamented with metal plates. The leather was oiled before battle to preserve it and make it glisten (Isa. 21:5). Smaller than the shield proper, the buckler was convenient for intercepting quick thrusts of the sword (Judg. 5:8; 2 Kings 19:32; Isa. 37:33). See also "Shield."

BUILDER. A builder was either a skilled or an unskilled workman (2 Chron. 34:11). The humble peasant was a builder in the sense that he constantly had to repair his thatched roof and mend his house with sundried clay or bricks. Large projects required skilled stonemasons and carpenters as well as porters and untrained workers. Important edifices were planned and constructed under the close supervision of a "masterbuilder" or architect (Greek *architectōn* — 1 Cor. 3:10). The chief builder checked the progress of the building with a "plumb line," a cord weighted with a heavy object (cf. Amos 7:7, 8; Zech. 4:10; 2 Kings 21:13).

BULRUSH. See "Papyrus."

BURIAL. Under Mosaic Law (Deut. 21:23) a corpse was to be buried on the day of death. The relatives of the deceased prepared the body for interment. Christ brought the hope of the resurrection of the body into clear focus (John 11:1-45). The rite of water baptism symbolizes the believer's identification with Christ in his death, burial, and resurrection (Rom. 6:3-6; Col. 2:12). See also under "Funerals, Jewish."

BURNING BUSH. A thorny bush (Hebrew *seneh*, Greek *batos*) which Moses saw aflame and from which the Lord spoke (Exod. 3:2-4; Mark 12:26). It was probably a form of the acacia (*Acacia vera* or *nilotica*), the Egyptian thorn, common in the Sinai Peninsula.

BUTCHER. The country farmer or shepherd served as his own butcher. In the walled cities, however, the occupation of butcher and meat salesman became a trade. Cattle had to be slaughtered, cleaned, and prepared for market. In the absence of refrigeration this was a daily occupation. At kings' courts or in the case of important people, servants were charged with this duty, which was included in the functions of a cook (cf. 1 Sam. 9:23). The Talmud speaks of a "street of the butchers" in Jerusalem.

BUTLER (Hebrew *mashqeh*, "one giving drink"). A court servant who tasted the king's wine. Butlers or cupbearers were often foreigners who became confidants of the king. A cupbearer at a Palestinian court is pictured on an ivory from Megiddo. Nehemiah was the cupbearer to Ar-taxerxes I of Persia (464-423 B.C.). The "butler" of the Pharaoh at the time of Joseph (Gen. 40:1-23) was the royal cupbearer. Cupbearers were part of Solomon's glittering court (1 Kings 10:5; 2 Chron. 9:4).

BYBLOS, BYBLUS. See "Gebal."

BYZANTIUM (bĭ-zăn'shĭ-ŭm). Constantinople or Istanbul, a Greek city. In the fourth century A.D. it was made the capital of the Roman Empire.

CABUL (kā'bŭl). A town in Asher (Josh. 19:27) ceded by Solomon to Hiram, King of Tyre (1 Kings 9:10-13).

CAESAR (sē'zẽr). The designation of the Roman Emperors after Julius Caesar. The name was used by Julius' adopted son, Augustus, the first Roman Emperor (27 B.C.-A.D. 14; see Luke 2:1). Afterward it was assumed in turn by each of his successors, so that it became a title. References to various Caesars occur in 28 places in the New Testament. Tiberius Caesar (A.D. 14-37) is mentioned in Luke 3:1 and 23:2, Mark 12:14-17, and John 19:12-15. Claudius Caesar (A.D. 41-54) is referred to in Acts 11:28, 17:7, and 18:2. Nero (A.D. 54-68) is apparently intended in Acts 25:8, 26:32, 27:24, and 28:19 and Philippians 4:22.

Other Caesars living during the New Testament period but not mentioned in the Bible include Caligula (A.D. 37-41), Galba (A.D. 68-69), Otho (A.D. 69), Vitellius (A.D. 69), Vespasian (A.D. 69-79), Titus (A.D. 79-81), Domitian (A.D. 81-96), Nerva (A.D. 96-98), and Trojan (A.D. 98-117).

CAESAREA (in Palestine) (sĕs-à-rē'à). A city established by Herod the Great on the site of a former coastal station called Strato's Tower (Acts 8:40; 10:1; 18:22; 23:33; 25:6). It was a brilliant Hellenistic city with both a harbor and an amphitheater. It was the administrative center of the Roman government in Palestine.

Lofty source of the Jordan River, near Mount Hermon and Caesarea Philippi (© *MPS*)

CAESAREA PHILIPPI (sĕs-à-rē'à fĭ-lĭp'ĭ). A capital city founded by Philip the tetrarch, son of Herod the Great (Matt. 16:13; Mark 8:27). It was located at the pagan cult center of Panias (Banias) near the headwaters of the Jordan River.

CAIAPHAS (kā'yȧ-fäs). Joseph Caiaphas officiated as the Jewish high priest from about A.D. 18 to 36, when he was deposed by Vitellius, the governor of Syria. Caiaphas is mentioned in the biblical account of the raising of Lazarus (John 11:47-53), the trial of Jesus (Matt. 26:57; John 18:24), and the trial of Peter and John (Acts 4:6-22).

CAIN (kān) ("acquisition"). The firstborn son of Adam and Eve. He became the world's first murderer (Gen. 4:1-8). Cain pictures man in his natural condition—lost and in desperate need of divine grace and atonement by shed blood (Eph. 1:7; Col. 1:14).

CALAMUS (Greek *kalamos*, "a reed"; Hebrew *keneh bosēm*, "reed of fragrance," and *kāneh*, "cane, reed"). An ingredient of the holy anointing oil (Exod. 30:23) and apparently also of certain sacrifices (Isa. 43:24; Jer. 6:20). It was imported (Jer. 6:20; Ezek. 27:19) from Europe and India. The calamus from Europe was evidently the *Acorus calamus*, common sweet sedge.

CALEB (kā'lĕb) ("dog"). One of the twelve scouts who explored Canaan (Num. 13). Through faith in God he was ready to enter the land immediately (Num. 13:30). Later he exercised the faith necessary to claim his inheritance (Josh. 14:6-14).

CALENDAR, HEBREW. Although the Old Testament gives clear evidence that the ancient Hebrews possessed a roughly calculated calendar, they have nowhere given a complete account of their system. The precise determination of this system still remains a problem of biblical research. The Hebrews probably always had a lunar-solar calendar. Such calendars were widely used throughout the ancient Near East from very early times.

1. *The Year.* The Hebrew word for "year" (*shanāh*, from the root "to change") is so named from the succession of the seasons. In Jewish civil time-reckoning the year began with the autumn equinox in the seventh month of Tishri (Exod. 23:16; 34:22). The Jewish religious year, however, began in the spring (Exod. 12:2; Deut. 16:1, 6). This was the "beginning of months" to the Jews in commemoration of their joyous departure from the bondage of Egypt.

2. *The Months.* The Hebrew calendar year consisted of lunar months. The primitive Hebrew word for "month" (*yerah*), like cognates in other Semitic languages, was related to the word for "moon" (*yareah*). Each month was calculated to consist of 29 or 30 days. Since the lunar year was about 11 days less than the solar year, some method of correction was necessary. However, precisely how the Hebrews adjusted the lunar year to the solar year is not known. Possibly they inserted a second Adar (twelfth month) or second Elul (sixth month) within the lunar cycle of 3, 6, 11, 14, 17, or 19 years.

Important for controlling the calendar was the observation of the autumnal equinox, "the going out of the year" (Exod. 23:16), and the spring equinox, "the return of the year" (1 Kings 20:26; 2 Chron. 36:10). The lunar year began when the thin crescent of the new moon was first visible nearest the spring equinox while the sun was in Aries (Josephus, *Antiquities* III: 8, 4). Then the Passover on the fourteenth day of Nisan coincided with the first full moon (Exod. 12:2-6).

The months were usually designated numerically in all periods, although other names were sometimes used. Each month had connections with the seasons of the year and the annual festivals.

The early (pre-exilic) names of the months, now identifiable only for the first, second, seventh, and eighth months, are probably local descriptive names of the Palestinian seasons. This is known to be true of Abib; it means "the ripening of grain" (Exod. 13:4). The names of Ziw (1 Kings 6:1, 37), Ethanim (1 Kings 8:2), and Bul (1 Kings 6:38) are now uncertain in meaning. In the post-exilic period the names of the Babylonian calendar were adopted.

3. *The Seasons.* Despite the fact that the Hebrews employed a calendar based on lunar months, as farmers they frequently indicated the time of the year by reference to the seasons. The agricultural calendar followed well-defined periods—the

dry season (April—September) and the rainy season (October—March). The latter was again subdivided into "seed-time" (November—December) and "harvest" (April—June; cf. Gen. 8:22).

4. *The Gezer Calendar.* This calendar was discovered in the city of Gezer in 1908. It is an agricultural calendar roughly inscribed in stone, apparently by a schoolboy of the tenth century B.C. It

THE HEBREW CALENDAR YEAR

Month	Pre-exilic Name	Post-exilic Name	Bible Reference	Present-day Equivalent	Season	Festival
1	Abib	Nisan	Exod. 12:2 Neh. 2:1	March-April	Spring Latter Rains Barley Harvest Flax Harvest	14, Passover 15-21, Un-leavened Bread 16, First-fruits
2	Ziw	Iyyar	1 Kings 6:1, 37	April-May	Dry Season Begins	
3		Siwan	Esth. 8:9	May-June	Early Figs	6, Pentecost, Feast of Weeks
4		Tammuz	Ezek. 8:14	June-July	Grape Harvest	
5		Ab		July-August	Olive Harvest	
6		Elul	Neh. 6:15	August-September	Dates, Summer Figs	
7	Ethanim	Tishri	1 Kings 8:2	September-October	Early Rains	1, Trumpets 10, Atonement 15-21, Taber-nacles 22, Solemn Assembly
8	Bul	Marheshwan	1 Kings 6:38	October-November	Plowing	
9		Kislev	Neh. 1:1	November-December	Sowing	25, Dedica-tion
10		Tebet	Esth. 2:16	November-December	Rains	
11		Shebat	Zech. 1:7	January-February	Almond Blossoms	
12		Adar	Ezra 6:15	February-March	Citrus Fruit Harvest	13, Purim (Lots)

lists the farming operations for the year: two months of storage, two months of planting grain, two months of spring growth, one month of hoeing up flax, one month of barley harvest, one month of harvesting everything else, two months of vine pruning, and one month of summer fruit.

5. *Other Methods of Calculating Time.* Historical events in the monarchical pe-

riod are commonly dated by the reigning years of rulers (2 Kings 3:1, 8:16; 12:1). Sometimes a memorable event is used in dating, such as the Exodus (1 Kings 6:1), the sojourn in Egypt (Exod. 12:40), the seventy-year exile in Babylon (Ezek. 33: 21), or the earthquake during Uzziah's reign (Amos 1:1; Zech. 14:5). In the post-exilic books of Haggai and Zechariah the datings are by the reign of the Persian kings (Hag. 1:1; Zech. 1:1, 6; etc.).

6. *Time Reckoning in the New Testament.* The New Testament writers usually referred to time in terms of the current Jewish calendar. Among the days of the week the Sabbath is frequently cited. Also mentioned is "the preparation," that is, the day before the Sabbath (Mark 15: 42; cf. John 19:31). Friday of the Passover week is referred to as "the preparation of the Passover" (John 19:14). The "first day of the week" (literally "one day after the Sabbath") received a new meaning after Christ's resurrection from the dead on that day (Acts 20:7; 1 Cor. 16:2).

Numerous references to the various Jewish festivals are found in the New Testament, especially in the Gospel of John (cf. John 2:13, 23; 5:1; 6:4; 7:2, 37; 10:22; 11:55, 56). References are also found in Matthew 26:2; Mark 14:1; Luke 22:1; Acts 2:1; 12:3, 4; 18:21; 20:6; 20: 16; 27:9; 1 Corinthians 16:8.

As in the post-exilic books of Haggai and Zechariah, dates in the New Testament are sometimes reckoned by reference to Gentile rulers. An elaborate reference is given in Luke 3:1, 2, where secular as well as religious authorities are named. Elsewhere in the New Testament Herod the Great is referred to (Matt. 2:1; Luke 1:5), as well as provincial governors Quirinius (Luke 2:2) and Gallio (Acts 18:12) and Roman Emperors Augustus (Luke 2:1), Tiberius (Luke 3:1), and Claudius (Acts 11:28).

7. *The Sectarian Calendar.* Minor calendar differences existed between the Sadducees and the Pharisees. Far more significant, however, is the cleavage between those in Judaism who subscribed to the sectarian calendar (known from the Book of Jubilees and now also from the Qumran Literature) and those who followed the traditional Jewish calendar.

Jesus and his disciples may have followed the sectarian calendar, thus possibly clarifying why they kept the Passover before his arrest while the chief priests and their aides did not keep it until after his crucifixion (cf. John 18:28).

CALF, GOLDEN. At Mount Sinai the Israelites turned to the worship of a golden bull (Exod. 32). Similar idolatrous representations were erected by Jeroboam I at the cult centers of Bethel and Dan (1 Kings 12:28, 29). They were doubtless similar to representations of the Egyptian deity Apis, even though the invisible God of Israel was regarded as enthroned above the bulls. In any case the statues were a dangerous innovation and a temptation to idolatry because of the pronounced bull affiliations of Baal, the great Canaanite deity.

CAMEL (Hebrew *gāmāl*, Greek *kamelos*). Most of the Bible references are to the one-humped *Camelus dromedarius* or Arabian camel. The species has two main types, the slow, burden-bearing camel (Gen. 37:25) and the swift dromedary (1 Sam. 30:17). A camel is an excellent beast of burden (Gen. 37:25; 1 Kings 10:2; Isa. 60:6); it can carry 450 to 550 pounds. A riding camel can cover between 65 and 75 miles in a day and is admirably adapted to desert or semi-desert areas. It eats desert plants and can go for several days without water. Its flat feet enable it to walk on the sand without sinking. Camel's hair was woven into cloth (Matt. 3:4).

Ageless vehicle of the Middle East may outlast the pyramids. *(Russ Busby photo)*

CAMEL DRIVER. Domesticated camels were employed to a limited degree beginning with the patriarchal period (from 2000 B.C.; cf. Gen. 12:16; 24:35; 30:43; 32:7; Job 1:3, 17; 42:12). In the thirteenth century the camel became widely used in caravan trade, superseding the earlier horse and the still earlier ass as a beast of burden. Men often conducted trade caravans as a permanent occupation, much as truckers today.

CAMPHIRE. See "Henna."

CANA (kā'nà). A town in Galilee (present-day Khirbet Qana) about eight miles north of Nazareth. It was here that Jesus changed water into wine (John 2:1-11; 4:46). Nathanael was a native of this town (John 21:2).

CANAANITES (kā'nà-nīts). The inhabitants of Canaan (the more ancient name of Palestine). As a geographical place name Canaan is apparently derived from "Hurrian," meaning "belonging to the land of red purple." This colorful designation derives from the commercial dye obtained from murex shells found on the Mediterranean coast and constituting an important item of trade of the seafaring Phoenicians. By the time of the Conquest the term "Canaan" designated Palestine in general. The term "Palestine" is of later Greek derivation and refers to Philistia, where the Philistines (Peleste) settled in large numbers in the twelfth century B.C.

The Canaanites inhabited the Syro-Palestinian coastland, particularly Phoenicia proper (Gen. 10:15-19; 12:5; 13:12; Num. 13:17-25). They were merchants and traders, specializing in the commerce of purple dye.

The Canaanites were mixed in race though predominantly Semitic. Fertility rites were prominent in their religion. Their pantheon and ritual are now well-known from the Ugaritic literature of the fourteenth century B.C. See also "Phoenicians."

CANDACE (kăn'dà-sē). A term applied to the reigning queens of the Ethiopian kingdom of Meroe in what is today the Sudan. Candace was a title roughly equivalent to "queen." The Candace whose treasurer Philip baptized was apparently the reigning queen mother not long after A.D. 30. The title was well known to ancient historians.

CANKERWORM (Hebrew *yelek*, "licker"). Undoubtedly the locust in the larva stage of its development. Joel 1:4 is probably intended to describe the various destructive stages of the locust as it grows to maturity rather than four separate animals, as in the King James Version.

CAPERNAUM (ká-pēr'na-ŭm). A town on the northwestern shore of the Lake of Galilee at the borders of Zebulun and Naphtali. There Jesus began his public ministry (Matt. 4:12-16; cf. Mark 1:21; Luke 4:31; John 2:12). The site is present-day Tell Hum (Hebrew Kefar Nahum); it is mentioned in Jewish sources. Its most prominent ruin is a synagogue built about A.D. 200.

CAPHTOR (kăf'tŏr). An ancient name of Crete. It was the home of the Caphtorim (Deut. 2:23), one of the Hamitic peoples listed in the Table of the Nations as descended from Mizraim or Egypt (Gen. 10:14; 1 Chron. 1:12). Caphtor is the land from which the Philistines came (Jer. 47:4; Amos 9:7); they are thus presumably the same people as the Caphtorim (Deut. 2:23).

CAPPADOCIA (kăp-à-dō'shĭ-à). A region of Asia Minor north of Cilicia and south of Pontus. The Old Persian name was *Katpatuka* (Greek *Kappadokia*, Latin *Cappadocia*). After being a part of the Persian Empire, it became an independent kingdom about 255 B.C. In A.D. 17 it became a Roman province (Acts 2:9; 1 Pet. 1:1).

CAPTAIN. This term is used in English versions to render several Hebrew words, mainly because little is known of army ranks in Bible times. Three of the more common Hebrew words so rendered are *rab, sar,* and *pehah. Rab* means literally "one who is great" or "chief." It is employed principally by Assyrian and Babylonian officers, for example *rab tabbaḥim*, "captain of the guard" (2 Kings 25:8-21; Jer. 39:9 – 52:30), Rabshakeh, and Rabsaris (2 Kings 18:17). *Sar* literally means "prince" and *pehah* means "governor, commander" (1 Kings 20:24; 2 Kings 18:24; Isa. 36:9).

CARCHEMISH (kär'kè-mĭsh). The Syro-Hittite capital located on the great bend of the upper Euphrates River. It was captured by the Assyrians (Isa. 10:9). It was the place where the battle between Necho of Egypt and Nebuchadnezzar of Babylon was fought in 605 B.C. (2 Chron. 35:20; Jer. 46:2).

CARMEL, MOUNT (kär'mĕl). The promontory overlooking the bay of Haifa. There Elijah contended with the priests of Baal (1 Kings 18:19). Carmel (Hebrew *karmel*, "garden land") is actually a range of hills some 30 miles long, extending from the northwest to the southeast, from the south shore of the bay of Acre to the plain of Dothan. Mount Carmel proper is the main ridge at the northwest end.

CARPENTER. Both Joseph (Matt. 13:55) and Jesus (Mark 6:3) pursued the ancient trade of carpentry (Greek *tektōn*). In Old Testament times the "worker in wood" (Hebrew *harāsh cesim*) performed the various tasks required in the construction of wood buildings and furniture. He even made such agricultural implements as yokes, plows, and threshing instruments (2 Sam. 24:22; Isa. 28:27, 28). Carpenters also made carts, chariots (Song 3:9), and idols (Isa. 44:13-17). Phoenician craftsmen built ships (Ezek. 27:5, 6) and supplied the skill for erecting public buildings in the Davidic-Solomonic era (2 Sam. 5:11; 1 Kings 5:18).

CARTHAGE (kär'thĭj). The chief Punic city of North Africa, originally a Tyrian colony. It was the historic rival of Rome until destroyed in 146 B.C.

CASSIA (kăsh'ĭ-à) (Hebrew *ḳiddāh*). An aromatic wood and an ingredient of the holy anointing oil (Exod. 30:24). Cassia is derived from the bark of a species of the cinnamon tree (cf. Psa. 45:8).

CAT. There is no reference to the cat in the Bible. This seems to indicate that the animal was not commonly known or kept as a pet in Western Asia during the biblical period. Greek zoologists knew the cat, which was probably first domesticated in Egypt. Bastet, a cat goddess, was the guardian deity of Bubastis. The cat was also closely connected with the sun-god, Re.

CATAPULT. A military machine employed by the Greeks and Romans for hurling stones against the parapets of walled towns. King Uzziah's "slings to cast stones" were giant catapults (2 Chron. 26:14).

CATERPILLAR. See "Locust."

CAUDA (kow'dà). A small island about 23 miles off the southeastern coast of Crete. Paul's ship ran under its lee when caught in the violent storm off Crete (Acts 27:16). Some ancient authorities call it Clauda (as in the King James Version). It is modern Gavdho.

CAVE. Caves are numerous in a limestone country like Palestine. In biblical times they were sometimes used as temporary homes (cf. Gen. 19:30; 1 Kings 19:9). They were natural tombs (Gen. 49:29-32; John 11:38). In periods of war and oppression they were ideal as places of refuge (Judg. 6:2; 1 Sam. 13:6; 24:3); the most notable cases were the caves at Makkedah (Josh. 10:16-27) and Adullam (1 Sam. 22:1; 2 Sam. 23:13). Sometimes caves were converted into storehouses or cisterns. See also under specific cave.

CEDAR, CEDAR OF LEBANON (Latin *Cedrus libani*, Hebrew *'erez*). One of the most famous trees of antiquity (1 Kings 5:6), reaching a height of 100 feet or more and a trunk diameter of 6 to 10 feet (Isa. 2:13; Ezek. 17:22; 31:3). Its fine timber was sought for the construction of palaces and temples (2 Sam. 5:11; 1 Kings 5:5, 6; 7:1-12; Ezra 3:7) and ships' masts (Ezek. 27:5). It was fragrant (Song 4:11) and was employed in ceremonial purification (Lev. 14:4; Num. 19:6). This noble tree still survives in the mountains of Syria and flourishes in the Taurus mountains of Asia Minor.

CELIBACY. The practice of remaining unmarried. Celibacy is nowhere commanded in Scripture, although the Apostle Paul describes circumstances under which it could be wise for an individual to abstain from marrying (1 Cor. 7:7-9, 25-40).

CENCHREA (sĕn'krė-à). The seaport of Corinth. It connected Corinth by sea to the East, as Lechaeum connected it with the West.

CENSER. A shallow, open-topped pan of bronze or gold (Exod. 27:3; 1 Kings 7:50) used for carrying live embers from the altar. When incense was placed on the sacred fire in these pans, they functioned as censers (Lev. 10:1; Num. 16:6; Rev. 8: 3-5). The right to use the censer in the Temple worship was a God-ordained prerogative of the Aaronic priesthood (Num. 16:1-35; 2 Chron. 26:16-21).

CENTIPEDE. A general name for any

small, crawling animal with many feet. All such were declared unclean and were not to be eaten (Lev. 11:41, 42).

CENTURION. A Roman army officer who commanded a century (100 men). There were ten centurions in a cohort and sixty in a legion. The centurions were subordinate to the six tribunes of each legion and often deferred to them (Acts 22:26). However, the centurions were the backbone of the Roman army and controlled the discipline and efficiency of the legion as a military unit.

The importance of centurions in the Roman army and in the life of the empire is reflected in their prominence in the New Testament. The first Gentile to confront Jesus was a centurion (cf. Matt. 8:5-13; Luke 7:2-10). The first Gentile to confess that Jesus was the Son of God was also a centurion (Matt. 27:54; Mark 15:39). The first Gentile to be introduced to the gospel of grace was Cornelius the centurion (Acts 10:1-48). Paul was delivered to a Roman centurion for safe conduct to Rome (Acts 27:1).

CEPHAS (sē′făs) (Greek *kēphas*, from Aramaic *kepha*, "stone or rock"). The Aramaic equivalent of "Peter" (Greek *petros*, "a stone"). The name given to Simon by Christ (John 1:42). See "Peter."

CHALDEANS (kăl-dē′ăns). Originally a semi-nomadic tribe which occupied the desert between North Arabia and the Persian Gulf (cf. Job 1:17). They settled in southern Babylonia around Ur (cf. Gen. 11:28; Acts 7:4). They were distinct from the Aramaeans. In the eighth century B.C. Chaldean power increased and Marduk-apla-iddina II, chief of the Chaldean district of Bit-Yakin, seized the throne of Babylon in 721-710 B.C. and again in 703-702 B.C., when he sought help from the West. He is the Merodach-Baladan of the Bible (2 Kings 20:12-19; Isa. 39:1).

In 626 B.C. a native Chaldean governor by the name of Nabopolasser came to the Babylonian throne. He founded a dynasty which ruled over a great empire. Among his successors were Nebuchadnezzar II (605-562 B.C.), Amel-Marduk or Evil-Merodach (562-560 B.C.), Nabonidus, and Belshazzar (556-539 B.C.). In Daniel's time the name Chaldea designated Babylonia as a whole (Dan. 1:1-4). The Chaldeans were prominent as a priestly class and were schooled in traditional astrology and philosophy (Dan. 1:17-20).

CHAMBERLAIN. The Hebrew word *saris* denotes a eunuch, an official in charge of the private quarters of a king or noble. As in the case of the cupbearer, the chamberlain had opportunity to gain the personal favor and confidence of his sovereign. Such an example was Nathanmeleck in the reign of Josiah (2 Kings 23:11). These officials were originally and customarily eunuchs, since they had access to the bedrooms of the palace women.

Chameleon—the animal that can "change its spots" (© *MPS*)

CHAMELEON. One of the numerous reptiles of the lizard family (Lev. 11:30). This particular lizard has the faculty of changing its color to blend with the objects surrounding it when in danger. This ability is due to the presence of both clear and pigment-bearing cells in its skin. See also "Lizard."

CHAMOIS (Hebrew *zemer*). A cloven-hoofed ruminant (Deut. 14:5) formerly thought to be the chamois, an alpine species never found near Palestine. More correct is "mountain sheep," commonly called "Barbary sheep," *Ammotragus lervia*. The mouflon (*Ovis musimon*) may also have been included.

CHANCELLOR. A Persian commanding official in the court of Artaxerxes (464-423 B.C.). The title probably denoted the office of Intelligence. See Ezra 4:8, 9, 17.

CHARIOT. Heavy, two-wheeled vehicles

drawn by asses and employed for war and peace in the third millennium B.C. in southern Babylonia (as demonstrated by discoveries at Ur and Kish). The true chariot, of lighter construction and drawn by the fleeter horse, did not come into use in Bible lands until the middle of the second millennium B.C. The Hittites and Egyptians adopted the horse-drawn chariot, as did many of the small city-states of Syria-Palestine (Gen. 41:43; 46: 29; 50:9). The Egyptian chariotry pursued Israel (Exod. 14:5-9, 23-28). The chariot became common in Israel during and after the time of David and Solomon (2 Sam. 8:4; 1 Kings 9:17-19; 10:28, 29). Ahab had a large chariotry, bringing 2000 chariots to the battle of Qarqar in 853 B.C. During the divided kingdom of Israel the chariot-driver was an important person in times of both war and peace in both Judah and Israel.

CHARM. See "Amulet."

CHEBAR RIVER (kē'bär). The Kabari Canal at Nippur in Babylonia (running east of the city). There Ezekiel saw his visions (Ezek. 3:15-22; 10:15).

CHEDORLAOMER (kĕd-ōr-lā-ō'mēr). An Elamite king (unidentified) who led a coalition that invaded the Jordan Valley in the time of Abraham (about 2000 B.C.).

CHEESE. In a pastoral country like Syria-Palestine milk and its by-products of butter and cheese were important staple items of diet. Cheese was frequently presented as a gift (1 Sam. 17:18; 2 Sam. 17: 29). In time, cheesemaking became an important trade. The Tyropean Valley west of the city of David was the "Valley of the Cheese-Makers."

CHEMOSH (kē'mŏsh). The chief deity of the Moabites (Num. 21:29; Jer. 48:46). Solomon built a sanctuary to this deity at Jerusalem (1 Kings 11:7). It was later destroyed by Josiah (2 Kings 23:13). Chemosh is prominent in the Mesha Stone and is compounded with Athtar, the Venus Star. This indicates that Chemosh may have been the manifestation of this astral deity.

CHERITH (kē'rĭth). A brook or wadi in Transjordan where Elijah took refuge from Jezebel at God's direction (1 Kings 17:3-5). It was apparently in Gilead, but the precise location is uncertain.

CHERUBIM AND SERAPHIM (chĕr'ŭb-ĭm; sĕr'ä-phĭm). The cherubim are celestial beings of the angelic order, evidently guardians of God's holiness (Gen. 3:24; Exod. 25:18-22). In Ezekiel 10 the chariot-throne of God, still upborne by cherubim, becomes mobile. Representations of cherubim from Samaria and Gebal (Byblos) depict a composite figure with a human face, an animal body with four legs, and two large wings.

The seraphim are mentioned only in Isaiah's vision (Isa. 6:1-13). They were human in form but had six wings. Like the cherubim, they seem to be an order of angelic beings responsible for certain functions of guardianship and worship. See also "Angels."

CHIEF PRIEST. See "High Priest."

CHILIARCH. A Roman commander of one thousand men. The word is usually translated "chief captain" in the King James Version. See also "Centurion."

CHINNERETH, CHINNEROTH (kĭn'ē-rĕth; kĭn'ē-rōth). The Old Testament name of the Sea of Galilee (Josh. 12:3). Some scholars think the name is derived from *kinnor*, the Hebrew word for "harp," since the lake is somewhat harp-shaped.

CHIOS (kī'os). One of the larger islands in the Greek Archipelago off the coast of Asia Minor in the Aegean Sea. It lies south of Lesbos at the entrance of the Gulf of Smyrna. Paul's ship passed by it on his last voyage to Palestine (Acts 20: 15).

CHITTIM, KITTIM (kĭt'ĭm). The island of Cyprus. Kittim denotes the Kitians, the people of Kit or Kiti (the ancient town of Kition located on the southern coast of Cyprus). Chittim is present-day Larnaka. The name Kition was extended not only to the entire island (Isa. 23:1, 12) but to the coastlands of the Eastern Mediterranean as well (Jer. 2:10; Ezek. 27:6; Dan. 11:30). The broader use is seen in the Apocrypha (1 Macc. 1:1; 8: 5) and in the Dead Sea Scrolls (the *Habbakuk Commentary*).

CHLOE (klō'ē) ("the verdant"). A woman whose household informed Paul at Ephesus that there were divisions among the Corinthian Christians (1 Cor. 1:11). She must have been well known to Paul and the Corinthian church in order to be able to vouch for the reliability of Paul's informants.

CHORAZIN (kô-rā′zĭn). A town of Galilee which lay north-northwest of Capernaum (Matt. 14:21; Luke 10:13).

CHOSEN PEOPLE. The Jewish people, selected by God to be separate from the other nations and to enjoy his special blessings (Deut. 7:6). This selection had a fourfold purpose: 1) to furnish mankind with a witness of the unity of God amid universal idolatry (Deut. 6:1-5; Isa. 43: 10-12); 2) to demonstrate to the Gentiles the blessedness of serving the true and only God (Deut. 33:26-29); 3) to receive, preserve, and transmit the written Word of God (Deut. 4:5-8; Rom. 3:1, 2); and 4) to be the human vehicle for the Messiah, the world's Savior (Gen. 3:15; 12:3; 22: 18; 28:10-14; 49:10; Isa. 7:14; Mat. 1:1; Rom. 1:3). Israel is now temporarily set aside in her national election (Rom. 11:1-25). She will be regathered and restored to national favor at the second advent of Messiah (Zech. 12:1 – 14:21; Luke 1:31-33). See also "Jews" and "Israelites."

CHRIST. See "Jesus Christ."

CHURCH, TRUE. The aggregate of all regenerated believers who have lived at any time during the period between Pentecost and the Rapture. All such are united to Christ and to one another by the baptism of the Spirit (1 Cor. 12:12, 13; Rom. 6:3, 4; Col. 2:12; Gal. 3:27). The Church is also pictured as Christ's "body," with Christ personally as the "head" (Eph. 1:22, 23). It is also described as a holy "temple" for God to live in by the Spirit (Eph. 2:21, 22). The Church is also seen espoused to Christ as a pure virgin to one husband (2 Cor. 11:2); she will be glorified at Christ's return in the air.

The Church is being formed by the crucified, risen, and ascended Lord Jesus Christ. He is exalted at God's right hand and is made "head over all things to the church" (Eph. 1:20-23). The new age of the Church was foretold by our Lord himself (Matt. 16:18) and was ushered in at Pentecost, when the Holy Spirit was given, received, and deposited in the new people of God (Acts 2:1-47; cf. John 14: 16, 26; 16:12-15). The age will end when

the Church is completed at the Rapture (1 Thess. 4:13-18; 1 Cor. 15:53, 54). See also "Bride of Christ."

CILICIA (sĭ-lĭsh′ĭ-à). A region in southeastern Asia Minor known as "Kizzuwatna" to the Hittites, "Khillaku" to the Assyrians, and "Kilikia" to the Greeks. It is called Kue in the Old Testament (1 Kings 10:28 RSV; 2 Chron. 1:16 RSV). It was the fourth satrapy of the Persian Empire. Cilicia Pedias ("lowland"), in which Tarsus was located, was distinguished from Cilicia Trachea ("rugged"), the mountainous western part.

CILICIAN GATES (sĭ-lĭsh′ĭ-án). A narrow pass from Syria-Cilicia which gives access to the interior of Asia Minor through the Taurus Mountains.

CINNAMON. A fragrant wood (Song 4:14; Rev. 18:13) used as an ingredient in the holy anointing oil (Exod. 30:23) and to perfume beds (Prov. 7:17) and other articles of furnishing or dress. The cinnamon tree is native to Ceylon and belongs to the laurel family. The bark yields a fragrant, yellow oil employed in perfumery.

CIRCUMCISION. God initiated this rite as the sign of the Abrahamic Covenant and a token of justifying faith in divine grace on the part of the circumcised (Gen. 17:10-14; Rom. 4:11, 12). Abraham was justified before God by faith *before* he was circumcised (Gen. 15:6). But his willing submission to the rite was a token of his faith in God's Word and his assent to the gospel of salvation by grace through faith, totally apart from works.

The Jewish generation newly departed from Egypt was circumcised at Gilgal (Josh. 5:2-9). The "reproach of Egypt" (bondage to Pharaoh) was "rolled away" at that time. Circumcision became a reminder that the Israelites were saved by God's grace and delivered from slavery to sin and Satan. Old Testament circumcision is analogous to New Testament water baptism, in which the believer identifies himself with Christ in death and resurrection (Rom. 6:1-11; Col. 2:11, 12). *Spiritual* circumcision is appropriating what Christ has provided for us and enjoying the new life of victory (Rom. 2: 28, 29; Phil. 3:3).

CITIES OF REFUGE. The six cities of

refuge, three on each side of the Jordan (Num. 35:6-34; Deut. 4:41-43; 19:1-13), illustrate Christ as the sinner's shelter from judgment (Rom. 8:1, 33, 34; Heb. 6: 17-20; cf. Psa. 46:1; 142:5). The refugee had to remain in the city of refuge until the death of the contemporary high priest. Then he was free to leave with impunity. Likewise the death of Christ, the Great High Priest, sets the sinner free. See "Asylum."

CLAUDA (klô'dà). See "Cauda."

CLAUDIA (klô'dĭ-à) (probably from Latin *claudos*, "lame"). A Christian woman, probably a Roman, who sent greetings to Timothy (2 Tim. 4:21). She is mentioned as the mother (or wife) of Linus, the first bishop of Rome, in the *Apostolic Constitutions* VII:46.

CLAUDIUS (klô'dĭ-ŭs). The fourth Roman Emperor (A.D. 41-54), a nephew of Tiberius. He banished all Jews from Rome (Acts 18:2).

CLEANSING. Scripture describes the fallen race in Adam as unclean and unfit for God's presence or fellowship. The once-for-all bath of regeneration cleanses not only from "dead works," which are powerless to save, but from the sins that are powerful to condemn (Rev. 1:5; 1 Cor. 6:11; 1 John 1:7). Although the believer is cleansed permanently from all guilt of the Law (Heb. 10:1-14), he incurs daily defilement in his earthly pilgrimage. His daily sins must be confessed so that unbroken fellowship with the Father and the Son may be maintained (1 John 1:8-10). This cleansing is illustrated by Jesus' washing of his disciples' feet (John 13:1-17) and by the cleansing of the laver in the Old Testament. The ceremonial approach to God involved first the bronze altar of sacrifice (symbolizing the Cross) and then the laver of cleansing (symbolizing cleansing from daily defilement). See Exodus 40:6, 7.

CLEMENT (klĕm'ĕnt) ("kind, merciful"). A Christian at Philippi who assisted Paul (Phil. 4:3).

CLEOPAS (klē'ò-pàs). One of two disciples who conversed with the risen Christ on the Emmaus Road (Luke 24:18).

CLEOPATRA (klē-ò-pǎt'rà). The Queen of Egypt from 52 to 30 B.C. Through her relations with Mark Antony she ob-

tained part of the coast of Palestine and the revenue of Jericho. She ruled as coregent with her son by Julius Caesar. Octavian's victory at Actium precipitated her downfall. She thereupon committed suicide, and Egypt became a Roman Province.

CLOTHING AND DRESS. The Bible does not present a detailed description of the various kinds of clothing which were worn in Palestine, except in the case of the Mosaic priesthood. However, a fair idea of the general dress may be formed by piecing together scattered biblical references. This is adequately supplemented by references in extra-biblical written records from Egypt, Asia Minor, Mesopotamia, and Syria-Palestine and from tomb paintings, seal impressions, and other archeological sources. For example, the tomb of Khnumhotep at Benihasan in Egypt displays a group of Asiatics arriving in Egypt with eyepaint. Their clothing is vividly colored and furnishes information about the clothing of the Hebrew patriarchs and other nomadic peoples during the twelfth Egyptian Dynasty (about 1870 B.C.).

Materials for Clothing. Skins of animals, wool, linen, and goat's hair were the common materials available in Palestine. The most widely used material was wool spun from the fleece of sheep. When spun from goat's hair it supplied a cheap material for the poor as well as the coarse sackcloth worn by mourners (1 Kings 21: 27; Job 16:15; Jonah 3:6). Cotton was woven from the fibers of a plant (*Gossypium herbaceum*) evidently introduced from India by Persian times (Esth. 1:6; 8:15). It was not generally available in Palestine during the Old Testament period.

Mosaic law prohibited the wearing of mixed materials, such as wool and linen (Lev. 19:19; Deut. 22:11). The regulation reminded Israelites of their separation to God and their responsibility to observe God's ordained order. For the same reason one sex was not to wear the clothes of the opposite sex (Deut. 22:5).

Dyes and Colors. White was the commonly preferred color of the Hebrews, the art of bleaching being known in early times (2 Kings 18:17; Isa. 7:3; Mal. 3:2; Mark

9:3). Scarlet was obtained from the juices of crushed cochineal insects found in oak trees. Black-purple or red-violet ("Tyrian" or "imperial" dye) was made from the mollusks *pupura* and *murex*, native to the Eastern Mediterranean coast. These dyes were used mainly for coloring expensive garments for royalty and nobility (Judg. 8:26; Prov. 31:22; Luke 16:19; Rev. 18:12, 16). They were also used in the Tabernacle fabric (Exod. 26:31). The "blue, purple, and crimson" were variations of these dyes (2 Chron. 3: 14; cf. John 19:2, 5).

In Palestine yellow dyes were made from ground pomegranate rind. The Phoenicians used safflower and turmeric. Blue was secured from the indigo plant imported from Syria or Egypt, where it had previously been transplanted from India.

Distinction between Male and Female Clothing. There was a general resemblance between the dress of men and women in biblical antiquity, the distinctions being far less marked than in western lands. But the differences were sufficiently obvious, for men and women were strictly prohibited from wearing one another's clothing (Deut. 22:5). Women wore finer materials with greater color and ornamentation, as well as veils and headcloths.

The most common items of dress were the shirt-tunic and the robe, comprising the basic inner and outer garments of both sexes. Women wore fine underwear (*sadin*) in addition (Prov. 31:24; Isa. 3: 23). See also specific item of clothing.

COAT OF MAIL (Hebrew *shiryon*). Armor which protected the torso and was made of scale-like plates of bronze (1 Sam. 17:5, 38). In Israelite times the coat of mail or cuirass was made of leather for the soldier and of bronze for the commander or general. Goliath had metal armor composed of bronze scales because he was the champion of the Philistines (1 Sam. 17:5). Ahab wore a cuirass when he was struck with an arrow "between the scale armor and the breastplate" (1 Kings 22:34 RSV), that is, between the leather flaps of the cuirass at the waistline. Jeremiah 46:4 and 51:3 refer to the cuirass as an exceptionally light-armored coat consisting of tiny iron plates fastened to a leather coat.

Such coats of metal date at least as early as the fifteenth century B.C., as is attested by discoveries at Ras Shamra, Boghazkeui, Nuzi, and Alalah. The later Greek equivalent of the metal cuirass was the *thorax*—armor used to protect war elephants (1 Macc. 6:43). Compare Paul's reference to "the breastplate of righteousness" in Ephesians 6:14.

COCKATRICE. See "Adder."

Pieces of silver—the price of infamous betrayal (© MPS)

COINS AND MONEY.

1. *The Pre-Coinage Period.* Prior to the introduction of coinage in the eighth century B.C., farm produce that could be bartered was the common medium of exchange. This consisted of such perishable commodities as wool, wheat, barley, and dates, and such non-perishable items as metals, timber, wine, honey, and livestock.

Metals as an exchange commodity were also used in commercial transactions. The most common of these in the ancient Near East was silver (cf. Gen. 13:2). Silver became so popular as a commodity that the Hebrew word for it became practically synonymous with the idea of money (cf. Gen. 17:13). Solomon bought chariots at 600 shekel-weight of silver and horses at 150 (1 Kings 10:29; cf. Lev. 5:15). Until the post-exilic era the *shekel* retained its literal meaning of a weight rather than a coin. The less-common gold was often listed following the silver (Gen. 13:2; 2 Kings 18:14).

Metal used for currency was circulated in the form of jewelry, objects in everyday use, or in various shapes (Gen. 24:22; Josh. 7:21; Isa. 13:12). Gold and silver were also circulated in the form of ingots, vessels, or dust. Bags or pouches were used to carry currency (Gen. 42:35; 2

Kings 5:23; Prov. 7:20; Hag. 1:6). Copper was often transported in the form of flat, circular disks.

Metals employed as currency had to be weighed out (Hebrew *shaqal*, "to weigh," hence *shekel*). The weighing was performed by the purchaser and verified by the seller in the presence of witnesses (Gen. 23:16; Jer. 32:9, 10). Standards varied from locality to locality; hence the expression "the silver current with the merchant" (Gen. 23:16, literal translation). Metals were also stamped with the place of origin (such as Ophir, 1 Kings 10:11, or Parvaim, 2 Chron. 3:6) or classified with respect to their refinement.

2. *The Period of Coined Money.* A coin is a piece of metal impressed with a seal attesting its title and weight so that it is acceptable on sight. Coinage first appeared in Asia Minor in the late eighth century B.C., when early silver specimens were recovered at Aegina. The first *staters* appeared when the proverbially rich Croesus (561-546 B.C.) minted *staters* in electrum (an alloy of gold and silver); his coins became dubbed "Croesides."

Coins were apparently introduced into the Persian Empire by Darius I (521-486 B.C.) after the conquest of Lydia. He gave his name to the thick gold *daric*, a 130-gram coin. It was familiar to the Jews in exile (Ezra 2:69 RSV; Neh. 7:70, 71 RSV).

The spread of coinage into Judah was apparently slow, possibly because of the images impressed into the coins. For example, the silver *shekels* of Nehemiah 5:15 and 10:32 may have been weights rather than coins. But the popularization of coins by Phoenician traders in the fifth and fourth centuries eventually began to have its effect on Judah. By the second century B.C., Syria and Palestine were under strong Hellenizing influence and the Greek *talent* and *drachma* began to be used widely. Their use continued well into New Testament times.

Although there is archeological evidence that the Jews attempted to mint their own coins in the fourth century B.C., it was not until the era of the Maccabees that they were successful in doing so. In 141 or 140 B.C. Antiochus VII granted permission to Simon Maccabeus to issue native coinage (1 Macc. 15:6), which appeared in circulation from that time on.

Money from a total of three different sources circulated in Palestine during this era. First was the official imperial coinage of Rome. Second was the provincial coinage minted at Antioch and Tyre; it was essentially Greek. Third was the local Jewish money, probably coined at Caesarea. Certain cities and client kings were also accorded the right to mint their own bronze coins.

Along with such a variety of coinage in circulation came an obvious need for money-changers. This was especially true at the Jewish feasts, when Jews from various parts of the Empire came to pay their poll tax to the Temple treasury (cf. Matt. 21:12; Mark 11:15; Luke 19:45, 46; John 2:13-17).

Coins commonly used during the New Testament era are described below.

Assarion (Greek *assarion*). A Roman copper coin translated "farthing" in the King James Version of Matthew 10:29 and Luke 12:6. It was worth a quarter of the bronze *sestertius* and one-sixteenth of the silver *denarius*. It was equal to roughly one cent in American money.

Denarius (Greek *denarion*). This standard Roman silver coin was equal to the Greek *drachma* and was equivalent to about 16 cents in today's money. Twenty-five *denarii* constituted the gold *aureus*. It is translated "penny" in the King James Version of Matthew 22:19. It was the average day's pay for a farm laborer in Palestine (Matt. 20:1-16).

Drachma (Greek *drachmē*). The silver *drachma* was the basic Greek coin while the silver *denarius* was the basic Roman coin. The two coins were roughly equal in value, each being worth about 16 cents. There were 100 *drachmai* to the *mina* and 6000 to the *talent*. It is the piece of silver referred to in Luke 15:8-10. The *didrachmon* or *double drachmon* was substituted for the *half-shekel* required for the annual Temple tax. The *tetradrachma* (*quadruple drachma* or *stater*) equaled one shekel, the tax for two people.

Lepton (Greek *leptos*). This is the famous "widow's mite" (Mark 12:42; Luke 21:2); the term denoted the smallest piece of money imaginable. It is the only Jewish coin alluded to in the New Testament. The *leptos* was bronze and was equal in value to one-half the Roman *quadrans* or one-eighth the *assarion*.

Mina (Greek *mna*). The "pound" of Luke 19:12-26. It is equivalent to one hundred denarii (about 16 dollars in present American currency).

Quadrans (Greek *kodrantēs*). The smallest Roman coin, equivalent in value to one-quarter of the copper *assarion*. It could be paraphrased "the last penny" in Matthew 5:26. (The coin is equivalent in value to about one-quarter of an American penny).

Sestertius. A Roman coin equivalent to one-quarter of a *denarius*. It is not referred to in the Bible.

Shekel. During the first revolt (A.D. 66-70) the Jews proudly coined their own silver for the first time, issuing shekels, half-shekels, and quarter-shekels.

Stater. The *tetradrachma*. See under "Drachma."

Talent. A unit of monetary reckoning rather than an actual coin. The Roman-Attic talent was equivalent to 240 *aurei*, roughly 960 American dollars. In Matthew 18:24, ten thousand talents signifies a very large sum of money. In Matthew 25:15-28 the silver talent is probably intended.

COLORS. Blue, purple, scarlet, fine-twined linen, and gold were prominent in the Tabernacle and priesthood, picturing various aspects of the person and work of Christ (cf. Exod. 26:31, 32, 36, 37, etc.). Blue, the color of the heaven, speaks of separation from evil and a heavenly walk. Purple, the color of royalty, portrays Christ's kingly role. Scarlet, the color of blood, speaks of Christ's atoning work. White, the color of purity, suggests Christ's sinlessness. Gold bespeaks Christ's deity.

COLOSSE (kŏ-lŏs′ĕ). A city in the Roman province of Asia in the western part of what is now Turkey. It was situated 10 miles up the Lycus Valley from Laodicea on the main road from Ephesus to the

east. Paul wrote his "Epistle to the Colossians" to the church in this city. The modern site (near Khonai) is not inhabited.

COMMANDMENTS. Commandments are principles of action which the Creator requires of all his creatures. They derive from the moral law of God, which is as eternal as God himself because it is a reflection of his eternally holy character and being. The commandments are summarized in the law of love — love of the creature for the Creator and love of the creature for his fellow-creatures (cf. Deut. 6:5; 10:12; Matt. 22:37-40). Sin entered the universe when Lucifer and a host of other angels broke the moral law of God. Human beings sinned for the same reason. Yet both fallen angels and fallen men will continue to be judged for their response to the eternal moral law, since God did not change when his creatures sinned.

Since fallen angels and unsaved men will be judged according to their works (their reaction to the moral law of God — Rev. 20:11-15), there will be degrees of punishment in Gehenna. Unfallen angels and redeemed men will also be judged according to their reaction to the moral law of God. This necessitates degrees of reward in heaven and the sin-cleansed universe (Rom. 14:10; Gal. 6:7; 1 Cor. 3:11-15; 2 Cor. 5:10; Eph. 6:8; Col. 3:24, 25).

The Ten Commandments from Sinai (Exod. 20:1-17) are an adaptation of the eternal moral law of God to the exigencies of the Mosaic Covenant made with the elect nation Israel. God imposed his moral law directly and dramatically upon Israel in order to display his covenant grace through them and to demonstrate to all the world the benefits of serving the one true God. This does not mean that non-Jews are free to ignore God's eternal moral law. All men are obligated to keep the law in its eternal features by virtue of their creaturehood.

The Mosaic Decalogue contains one commandment — that of Sabbath observance — which is unique to the Jewish people and which was never imposed on any other nation (Exod. 20:8-11). Observance of the Sabbath was a strict moral obligation of the covenant people. Breaking it was punishable by death (Exod. 31: 14; Num. 15:32-36).

All the other commandments of the Decalogue are universally binding upon all mankind in every age and are set forth in the New Testament under grace. No fallen man can keep these commandments to merit salvation before God. However, all men are to keep them outwardly as the basis of human law and are required to do so. For this they will give account both to God in the final judgment and to their fellow men in this life. See under "Decalogue."

CONCUBINE. A woman in biblical times who sustained a semi-married relationship with a man. She was less privileged than a wife but more privileged than a mistress in the modern sense. In biblical times the wife was on an equal social basis with her husband while the concubine was a bondmaid, quite frequently the servant of the wife (Gen. 29:24, 29) and often a captive taken in war (Deut. 21:10-14). A Hebrew woman might become a concubine by first falling into the condition of servitude. However, her position and treatment came under special restrictive legislation (Exod. 21:7-11).

The concubine's children were not accounted illegitimate, but constituted a kind of supplementary family. Their names frequently occur in the patriarchal narratives (Gen. 22:24). Their position and inheritance depended on the desire of the father (Gen. 25:6). Unlike a wife, a concubine could be rejected without a bill of divorce.

The whole system of concubinage, like polygamy, was clearly a perversion of the divine order of the sexes (Gen. 2:24). God permitted it to exist temporarily, but under limitations unheard of among neighboring pagan peoples. Scripture does not attempt to minimize the sad consequences resulting from the practice of polygamy and concubinage, even when it occurred among Bible heroes (Gen. 16:1-16).

CONEY (Hebrew *shāphān*). Not the English coney (the rabbit) but the rock badger, the *Hyrax syriacus*. It looks like a rabbit, even moving its jaws as if it were chewing the cud like the rabbit, but it does not actually ruminate. The rock badger lives among the rocks (Psa. 104: 18; Prov. 30:26). It is found in sections of Palestine and the Sinai Peninsula.

CONFESSION. Confession of Christ as Savior is that heart-response to God by which faith in Christ as one's Sin-Bearer is sealed (cf. Rom. 10:9, 10; 1 John 4:2, 3, 15). Confession as an act of a sinning saint involves not salvation but fellowship. The sinning Christian turns to the Father in full acknowledgement of his sin and accepts God's estimate of it. On the divine side, cleansing and forgiveness are provided in the faithfulness of God, since Christ has borne the sin in question (1 John 1:9).

CONSCIENCE. An inborn moral monitor found in every man. Conscience lifts man above the animal level. Rejection of God's revelation of himself in nature and in Scripture results in demonic delusion, idolatry, and a desensitized conscience (1 Tim. 4:1, 2).

CONSUL. The title of the two chief military and political magistrates in the Roman Republic. Although they are not mentioned in the Bible, a certain consul named Lucius is mentioned in 1 Maccabees 15:16.

CORBAN. An offering or oblation (Mark 7:11). The term in post-exilic Judaism refers to a gift consecrated to God for religious purposes. The Mishna declares that anything set apart by the use of the term, even rashly, could not thereafter be used for any other purpose. Christ refers to this special use of the word in Mark 7: 11.

CORIANDER (Hebrew *gad*). A plant bearing pink and white blossoms and yielding white seeds and small globular fruit used as a condiment. Manna resembled coriander seed (Exod. 16:31; Num. 11:7).

CORINTH (kōr'ĭnth). A commercial metropolis at the western end of the isthmus between central Greece and the Peloponnesus. It controlled trade routes across the isthmus through its western port, Lechaeum, and its eastern outlet at Cenchrea. Augustus made it the capital of the province of Achaia; it was ruled by a proconsul. Paul stayed eighteen months in Corinth on his second tour

(Acts 18:1-18). To the church there he penned 1 and 2 Corinthians.

CORMORANT (Hebrew *shālāk*). A ceremonially unclean bird (Lev. 11:13, 17; Deut. 14:12, 17). It is apparently the common cormorant *(Phalacrocorax carbo)*, a large water bird of the pelican family. The bird is found in Palestine along the Maritime Coast and on the Sea of Galilee. Another species, the pygmy cormorant, is sometimes found along the streams of Palestine which empty into the Mediterranean.

CORN. The term "corn" is an archaic generic designation for the staple cereals cultivated in Palestine. So truly are these grains the staff of life that the term "corn and wine" figuratively comprehends the entire vegetable produce of the field (Gen. 27:28; Deut. 7:13). The chief cereals were wheat, emmer, barley, and millet. Certain legumes, such as beans and lentils, were also basic staples.

CORNELIUS (kôr-nē'lĭ-ŭs). A Roman centurion who became the first Gentile to receive the gospel of Christ and the great salvation ministered by the outpoured Spirit (Acts 10:1-48).

COS, COOS (kŏs; kō'ŏs). An island of the Aegean Sea off the coast of Caria in Asia Minor. It lay about a day's sail between Miletus and Rhodes (Acts 21:1). The island is famous as the birthplace of Hippocrates and the site of the medical school which he founded there in the fifth century B.C.

COUNSELOR. In Old Testament times counselors were members of the king's court (2 Chron. 25:16; Isa. 1:26; 3:3). In some instances the counselor was apparently next in power to the king himself (Mic. 4:9; cf. Job 3:14; 12:17). In New Testament times counselors were members of advisory or legislative bodies.

The Greek word *bouleutēs* denotes a "decider" or "deliberator." Joseph of Arimathea, a member of the Sanhedrin or Jewish supreme court, was such an official (Mark 15:43; Luke 23:50). See also "Chancellor."

COW (Hebrew *ʿeglah*). Cows were domesticated early in human history. Abraham and other patriarchs herded cows (Gen. 13:2; 32:15). Egypt and Palestine afforded excellent pasturage (Gen. 41:2; Deut.

7:13; 1 Sam. 6:7). Cows' milk served as food (2 Sam. 17:29), together with the milk of camels and goats (Gen. 32:15; Prov. 27:27).

COZBI (kŏz'bĭ) (Akkadian *kuzbu*, "voluptuousness"). A Midianite woman slain at Shittim by Phinehas, grandson of Aaron (Num. 25:6-8, 14, 15; cf. Psa. 106:30, 31). The woman was a seducer and was guilty of immorality and complicity with Baal worship. As a princess (daughter of Zur, head of a chief tribe in Midian), her influence for evil was great. She beguiled Zimri, prince of a chief house of Simeon. Phinehas slew both Zimri and Cozbi with a javelin to cleanse Israel and stay a plague caused by complicity with idolatry (Num. 25:6-8, 14, 15).

CRAFTSMAN. See "Artisan."

CRANE (Hebrew *āgūr*). A large, elegant migrating bird that emits a chattering sound (Isa. 38:14). It is a long-legged wading bird, migrating south from Europe and Asia at the approach of winter.

CREATION. The account of the origin of the earth and the universe as contained in the Word of God. It is the authoritative answer to the fiction of evolution. The choice in the matter is to believe either God's revelation or man's theorizing. Direct creation by God answers the basic problem. The theory of evolution merely drives the idea of origin back into oblivion, leaving the central problem of a first cause no nearer solution. Moreover, it ignores the marvelous design and purpose manifested everywhere in the natural world.

The Bible account of creation is simple and elevated in tone, in contrast to the crass polytheistic concepts of the ancient world. But the creation of the world out of nothing makes sense only to those who have faith in the God of revelation, infinite in power and wisdom (Heb. 11:3). The visible universe is then understood to proceed from the invisible God. On earth man is made in God's image as the mysterious projection of the unseen into the seen. Christ is both the perfect projection and the Author of creation (John 1:1-3; Col. 1:15-17).

CRETE (krēt). A mountainous island about 156 miles long and 7 to 35 miles broad which is situated at the southern extremity of the Aegean Sea. It is evidently referred to as "Caphtor" in the Old Testament (Jer. 47:4; Amos 9:7). In the New Testament, Cretans are mentioned among those present at Pentecost (Acts 2:11). The island figures prominently in the account of Paul's journey to Rome (Acts 27:7-22). His vessel sailed past Salmone at the eastern end and put in at a port called Fair Havens (near Lasea in the center of the south coast). The ship missed the better wintering berth at Phenice in the southwest and was plunged into the terrible storm recounted in Acts 27. After his imprisonment Paul apparently revisited Crete, where he left Titus to carry on the work. The heyday of Cretan civilization was reached about 1750-1400 B.C.

CRETANS (krē'tāns). The inhabitants of the island of Crete (Caphtor). Their culture flourished under Minoan civilization of the second millennium B.C. and was centered at their capital of Knossos on the north-central coast of the island, facing the Aegean Sea. Crete became part of the Hellenic world when their domination of the Aegean Sea was brought to an end by the Achaeans. The Philistines came from Caphtor or Crete (Jer. 47:4; Amos 9:7) and were the "Cherethites and Pelethites" of David's bodyguard (2 Sam. 8:18). Jews came from Crete to celebrate Pentecost at Jerusalem (Acts 2:11). Paul sailed along the coast of Crete on his voyage to Rome (Acts 27:7-22). Christianity was planted in the island and Titus was appointed as overseer of the churches (Tit. 1:5).

CROCODILE. The word "crocodile" does not occur in the King James Version but is thought to be the reptile described as "leviathan" in Job 41. Egypt was the habitat of the crocodile.

CROSS. The framework of wood on which Christ was nailed. Theologically the word denotes the central meaning of Christ's sufferings and redemptive death on that instrument of torture (Gal. 6:14). The Cross reveals what the world is and judges it in the light of divine holiness and grace (John 12:31-33). See also "Crucifixion."

CROWN. A reward to be bestowed on believers at the judgment seat of Christ for faithful service to the Savior (1 Cor. 3:12-14; 2 Cor. 5:10). Several crowns are described in Scripture: *the incorruptible crown*, a reward for those who discipline bodily appetites (1 Cor. 9:24, 25); *a crown of life* for those who successfully endure testings (James 1:12); *the victor's crown* (2 Tim. 4:8) for those who finish their course and love Christ's appearing; *the faithful pastor's crown* (1 Pet. 5:4) for those who diligently shepherd God's flock; and *the martyr's crown* for those who are "faithful to death" (Rev. 2:10).

CRUCIFIXION. Oriental in origin, the inhuman practice of nailing a criminal to a wooden cross was adopted by the Romans as a punishment for especially loathsome criminals. Crucifixion was considered a dishonorable death, and was not inflicted on Roman citizens except for treason against the state. Usually the victim was scourged first and then compelled to carry the transverse beam of the cross to the place of execution. His crime was written on a placard and hung around his neck or carried ahead of him. The placard was then fastened to the cross as a warning to others. This is why the crosses, although erected outside city walls (cf. Heb. 13:12), were placed near busy highways and heavily frequented sites (cf. Matt. 27:36, 39, 55; Mark 15:29, 35, 40; Luke 23:35, 48, 49).

CUBIT. See under "Weights and Measures."

CUCUMBER. The *Cucumis chate*, very common in Egypt, was somewhat sweeter than the common cucumber, *Cucumis sativus*. The Israelites longed for it in the desert, together with the leeks and onions of Egypt (Num. 11:5). The cucumber was cultivated in Palestine with other similar vegetables and melons (Isa. 1:8).

CUMMIN. A fennel-like plant yielding white flowers and seeds which were eaten with food as a spice or relish (Isa. 28:25, 27). The Pharisees were meticulous about tithing it (Matt. 23:23). Caraway seeds have largely supplanted cummin as a condiment, being more tasty and nutritious.

CURSE. The entrance of sin into the human family brought with it the curse (Gen. 3:7-19). This involved the shame caused by sin (Gen. 3:7), estrangement from God (3:8, 9), fear (3:10), degradation of the serpent (3:14), a struggle between Satan's people and God's people (3:15), female childbirth problems and female subordination to man (3:16), a hostile, thorn-producing earth which required laborious cultivation (3:17-19), and threefold death—spiritual, physical, and eternal. The Old Testament ends with the curse still in effect (Mal. 4:6). The New Testament begins (Matt. 1:1) with Christ, who came to remove the curse by becoming a curse for us on the Cross (Gal. 3:13; Rev. 21:3, 4; 22:3).

The curse as an uttered imprecation was forbidden against 1) a leader of the people, as a representative of God (Exod. 22:28); 2) a deaf person (Lev. 19:14); 3) one's parents, as representatives of the Lord (Exod. 21:17; Lev. 20:9; Matt. 15:4; Mark 7:10); and 4) most important of all, God himself (Lev. 24:10-16). See also "Blessings and Cursings."

CUSH (kŭsh). (1) A son of Ham and the progenitor of the Arabian tribes of Seba, Havilah, Sabtah, Raamah, and Sabteca (Gen. 10:6-8). (2) The territory south of Egypt. It was the "Ethiopia" of classical writers and is present-day Northern Sudan. Syene or Seveneh (modern Aswan) was the frontier between Egypt and Ethiopia in the first millennium B.C. (Ezek. 29:10, RSV; cf. Psa. 68:31; 87:4; Zeph. 2:12; 3:10; Esth. 1:1). The Ethiopians (Nubians) were dark-skinned (Jer. 13:23). The runner who bore news of Absalom's death to David was a Cushite (2 Sam. 18:21, 23), as was Ebed-Melek of Jeremiah's day (Jer. 38:7) and Queen Candace's minister (Acts 8:27).

CUTHAH (kū'thȧ). A Mesopotamian city north of Babylon. From Cuthah the Assyrians deported people to Samaria (2 Kings 17:24). It is modern Tell Ibrahim.

CYPRESS (Hebrew *te ʿashur*). The cypress tree is native to Palestine and has recently been found growing wild in Gilead and Edom. It is cultivated widely in Palestine. The tree grows to forty or more feet in height and has globular, seed-bearing cones.

CYPRIOTS (sĭp'rĭ-ŏts). Inhabitants of the island of Cyprus in the Eastern Mediterranean. Its people were anciently called Kittim and were descendants of Javan (Gen. 10:4). A seafaring people, they gave the name "Kittim" or "Chittim" not only to the entire island of Cyprus but also to the coastlands of the eastern Mediterranean (Isa. 23:1, 12; Jer. 2:10; Ezek. 27:6).

CYPRUS (sī'prŭs) (Latin *cyprium*, "copper"). An Eastern Mediterranean island about 60 miles west of the coast of Syria and about the same distance south of the coast of Asia Minor. It is about 140 miles long and 60 miles wide at its broadest point. Its ancient name was Kittim or Chittim. The island was famous for its copper mines. Cyprus came under the government of Rome in 58 B.C. It was first an imperial province (27-22 B.C.) but later became a senatorial province under a pro-consul. This was its government when it was visited by Barnabas and Paul (Acts 13:4) and later by Barnabas and Mark (Acts 15:9). Paul sailed by it at least twice without landing (Acts 21:3; 27:4).

CYRENE, CIRENE (sī-rē'nė). A Greek colony founded in the seventh century B.C. In Roman times it formed a province with Crete, and the general area of Libya west of Egypt was called Cyrenaica (Matt. 27:32; Mark 15:21; Luke 23:26; Acts 2:10; 11:20; 13:1).

CYRUS (sī'rŭs). Cyrus II the Great, founder of the Persian Empire (559-530 B.C.). He is mentioned in the Book of Isaiah (44:28; 45:1-14). He conquered Babylon and repatriated the Jews (cf. Ezra 1:1-4).

D

DAGGER (Hebrew *hereb*). An easily handled, short sword used for stabbing. In the King James Version the word is translated "dagger" only in the Ehud story (Judg. 3:15-23). Weapons less than 16 inches in length are normally called daggers by archeologists. The Hebrews, however, apparently made no such distinction. Since Ehud's weapon was a cubit in length (about 17.5 inches), it could properly be translated "sword." Numerous daggers have been found in Bronze and Iron Age archeological sites throughout Egypt, Palestine, and Mesopotamia. The dagger was normally worn in a small sheath.

DALMANUTHA (dăl-mà-nū′thà). A district and town on the western shore of the Lake of Galilee (Mark 8:10). It is apparently the same place as Meijdel, Taricheae, Magadan, and Magdala (Matt. 15:39).

DALMATIA (dăl-mā′shĭ-à). A Roman province roughly equivalent in territory to Illyricum. It was bound on the north by Pannonia, on the east by Moesia, on the south by Macedonia, and on the west by the Adriatic Sea (cf. 2 Tim. 4:10).

DAMARIS (dăm′à-rĭs). An Athenian woman who believed the message of Paul when he preached before the Areopagus (Acts 17:34). The name, mentioned only here in Scripture, may be a variant of "Damalis" ("heifer"), a fairly common name in biblical times.

DAMASCUS (dà-măs′kŭs). An important trade city located east of the Anti-Lebanon Mountains in a well-watered plain of gardens and orchards. It was associated with Abraham (Gen. 14:15; 15:2). From about 931 to 732 B.C. it was the center of Aramean power in Syria, and its inhabitants frequently warred with Israel (1 Kings 11:24; 22:1-40). It was conquered by Assyria in 732 B.C. (2 Kings 16:9). Christianity made early converts there (Acts 9:10, 19). Although Damascus was actually located in the Roman province of Syria, it was regarded as part of Decapolis. An officer of the Nabataean king Aretas had authority there (2 Cor. 11:32).

DAN. (1) A town and cult center at the headwaters of the Jordan River southwest of Mount Hermon. It was the northernmost town of Israel (Deut. 34:1; 1 Kings 4:25). Formerly called Laish, it was renamed by the tribe of Dan (Judg. 18:29). Jeroboam I made it one of his centers of worship (1 Kings 12:28, 29). It was denounced by the prophets (Amos 8:14). The modern site is Tell el-Qadi. Caesarea Philippi was located in this general region. (2) Jacob's son by Bilhah (Gen. 30:5, 6). His future was predicted in Genesis 49:16, 17.

DANCING. Both secular and religious dancing were common among the Israelites, as among other peoples of antiquity. The dance stressed the happy events of life (Jer. 31:4, 13), such as victories (1 Sam. 18:6; 21:11; 29:5; 30:16), weddings and festal occasions (Matt. 14:6; Mark 6:22), and the wine harvest (Judg. 9:27). Music and dancing provided part of the prodigal son's homecoming festivities (Luke 15:25).

Dancing was also a religious practice among Israel's neighbors. The priests of Baal danced around altars (1 Kings 18:26) and the Phoenicians danced to Baal Melcarth. Israelites also sometimes danced as an act of worshipful joy to the Lord (2 Sam. 6:14; cf. Psa. 68:25).

DANIEL (dăn'yĕl) ("God has judged"). The great Old Testament prophet of the "times of the Gentiles" (605 B.C. to the second advent of Christ). His prophecies form the foundation of the prophetic disclosures of the entire Book of Revelation, especially as these predictions relate to the Great Tribulation and the reinstatement of the nation Israel at the second advent (Dan. 2:31-45; 9:24-27; 12:1-13; cf. Rev. 6:1 – 19:16; 20:1-9).

DARIUS (dà-rī'ŭs). Darius I the Great (522-486 B.C.), the Persian monarch of the Behistun Inscription and the benefactor of the Jews during the building of the Temple and the ministry of Haggai and Zechariah (520-515 B.C.).

King Darius and his crown prince, Xerxes, greet subjects in this bas-relief in Persepolis, Iran. (*OI-UC photo*)

DARIUS THE MEDE (dà-rī'ŭs; mēd). The son of Ahasuerus or Xerxes, who ruled Babylon on the death of Belshazzar (Dan. 9:1; cf. 5:30, 31; 6:1). Some scholars identify him with Gubaru, governor of Babylon and the region beyond the Euphrates River. Others identify him with Cyrus the Great.

DATHAN (dā'thăn). One of the men who rebelled against Moses' leadership (Num. 16:1-35; Psa. 106:17).

DAUGHTER. The word "daughter" occurs in the Scriptures more than 200 times. Daughters are mentioned by name less frequently than sons, since the family lineage and name ran in the line of the son. Hence fathers frequently regarded their daughters less highly than their sons. A father might even sell his daughter as a bondwoman (Exod. 21:7), though

not to a foreigner (Exod. 21:8).

In addition to the many daughters mentioned by name in Scripture, dozens are cited by reference to their fathers or other people. A few of the more significant unnamed daughters of Scripture are described below.

1. *Adam's Daughters.* Adam lived for a total of 930 years (Gen. 5:5). He had sons and daughters for 800 years after he begot Seth, who was born when Adam was 130 years old (Gen. 5:3, 4). Doubtless Adam also had sons and daughters before Seth was born. The reason these are not mentioned in the genealogy of Genesis 5:3-5 is that among all of Adam's children only Seth was in the messianic line (Gen. 4:25). (In the table from Adam to Noah only the messianic links are given.) There is every reason to believe that Adam had many sons and daughters both before and after Seth's birth. It is inconceivable that he would postpone obeying God's command to "be fruitful and multiply and fill the earth" (Gen. 1:28) for well over a century!

It is also inconceivable that Eve (whose conception of children was greatly increased as a result of the fall – Gen. 3:16) would have had no progeny in the 120 or so years intervening between Abel and Seth, especially since she and Adam were fully mature and capable of bearing children from the day of their creation.

Adam's sons and daughters therefore undoubtedly constituted a multitude of people – perhaps hundreds – by the time Seth was born into the messianic line. By the time of his death Adam may well have had thousands of children.

2. *Daughters of Men.* Some scholars interpret the "daughters of men" of Genesis 6:2, 4 as women from the unrighteous line of Cain, and the "sons of God" mentioned in these verses as the more upright line of Seth. However, this interpretation scarcely comes to grip with the scope of the passage.

The "daughters of men" are simply mortal women (Gen. 6:1-6). The "sons of God" are angels (Job 1:6; 2:1) or evil spirit beings that had illicit experiences with the human race. The occasion was a terrifying outburst of occultism that threatened the breakdown of God's ordained human and angelic orders in creation (Jude 1:6, 7). The impending catastrophe necessitated the destruction of the race by a flood. The "Nephilim" or "giants" of Genesis 6:4 were the monstrous offspring of this wicked intercourse between fallen angels and the human race.

3. *Daughters of the Philistines.* Philistine women whom Israelite men were not to marry (2 Sam. 1:20). They are also called "the daughters of the uncircumcised," since they had no part with God's covenant people (cf. Gen. 17:9-14).

4. *Daughters of Zion.* A figurative expression for the worldly-minded women of Jerusalem (Isa. 3:16). The prophet Isaiah denounced their vanity (Isa. 3:16-26).

5. *Jephthah's Daughter.* The only child of Jephthah, the ninth judge of Israel. When war broke out between Israel and the Ammonites, Jephthah (who had been cast out of his father's house by his brothers as illegitimate) was recalled out of the land of Tob to raise an army to fight the Ammonites (Judg. 11:1-29). It was then that Jephthah made a tragic vow to devote to the Lord as a burnt offering whatever came forth from the doors of his house to meet him (Judg. 11:30, 31).

Jephthah won a great victory. But upon his return to his home in Mizpeh he was greeted first by his only daughter. As a result Jephthah felt bound by his vow to devote his daughter to the Lord as a burnt offering. It is not certain whether she was actually offered as a human sacrifice or whether she was devoted to celibacy in the service of the Lord's Tabernacle. Whatever the vow entailed, it at least meant that she could not marry or bear children (Judg. 11:37-40).

6. *King's Daughter.* "The king's daughter" (Psa. 45:13) is a foreign princess about to be wed to a king of Israel. The whole Psalm is messianic. Portrayed are the supreme beauty of the King (Psa. 45: 1, 2), his coming in glory (Psa. 45:3-5; Rev. 19:11-16), and his deity and reign (Psa. 45:6, 7; Isa. 11:1-5; Heb. 1:8, 9). The King's daughter is associated with him in earthly rule as queen (the glorified Church—Psa. 45:9-13). The virgin companions of the queen (Psa. 45:14, 15) would seem to be the Jewish remnant (Rom. 11:5; Rev. 14:1-5). The Psalm closes with a description of the earthly fame of the King (Psa. 45:16, 17).

7. *Lot's Daughters.* Lot's two daughters became guilty of shameful incest with their father. Through this act the elder daughter became the ancestress of the Moabites and the younger one became the ancestress of the Ammonites (Gen. 19:30-38). Lot had been warned by angels to leave the wicked city with his wife and two daughters (Gen. 19:12-16). Lot's worldly wife met judgment when she turned back. She left her carnal stamp on her two daughters and husband, whose careers ended in shame.

8. *Pharaoh's Daughter.* An Egyptian princess who saved the life of the baby Moses (Exod. 2:5-10). She was thus unwittingly preparing Israel's great deliverer and lawgiver (Acts 7:20-22). Under the cruel decree of her father, one of the Pharaohs of Egypt (probably Thutmose III, about 1490-1450 B.C.), the child would otherwise have been doomed to die, since all male children had been ordered slain in order to curb the rapid increase of the Hebrews.

Moses' mother tried to hide her baby. When she could no longer do this, she placed him in a little basket-boat she had made and set him afloat among the reeds of the Nile where the princess came to bathe. The bold plan of faith worked. Pharaoh's daughter saw the child, took him to her heart, and adopted him as her own. Moses was educated in the highest Egyptian circles and was prepared by God for his great life's work. God used the gentleness of a great princess to work out his divine plan.

9. *Philip's Daughters.* Four unmarried women of New Testament times who had the gift of prophecy (Acts 21:9). Their father, Philip, was an evangelist (Acts 21:8). He evangelized Samaria (Acts 8:5-8), preached to and baptized the Ethiopian eunuch (Acts 8:26-40), and was a church deacon (Acts 6:5).

10. *Priest's Daughter.* The daughter of a Jewish priest was strictly forbidden to have illicit sexual relations (Lev. 21:9). Such a sin would profane the holy calling of her father, from whose family a high degree of purity was expected. The penal-

ty for harlotry in such a case was burning with fire, so serious was such a crime considered.

11. *Seth's Daughters.* Like his father, Adam, Seth had many sons and daughters both before and after the birth of the messianic heir. Enosh was born when Seth was 105 years old. Enosh alone is mentioned by name because, like his father, Seth, he was in the messianic line. Seth's daughters were granddaughters of Adam. However, Adam also had a multitude of great-grandchildren, great-great-grandchildren, etc. by the time Seth was born. In fact, by the time of Seth's birth the population of the earth was substantial. By Enosh's time men were extremely numerous on the earth.

12. *Shem's Daughters.* The genealogy of Genesis 11:10-32 lists the Semitic line from the Flood to Abraham. Those in the line of Messiah who begot sons and daughters were Shem, Arpachshad, Salah, Eber, Peleg, Reu, Serug, Nahor, Terah, and Abraham. These constitute ten messianic links in the line from Adam to Noah and ten from Noah to Abraham.

Shem's generations (Gen. 11:10-32) mark an important turning point in God's dealings with men. Until this point God had dealt with the whole Adamic race. Now he concentrated in the Semitic line, from which the Redeemer was to come.

DAVID (perhaps "beloved" or possibly from Babylonian *dawidum,* "chief"). Israel's second and most beloved king, founder of the Davidic dynasty, which lasted till the Babylonian exile. He is famous as the ancestor, forerunner, and foreshadower of the Lord Jesus Christ, David's "son" and Lord (Psa. 110:1; Rev. 22:16). His brilliant career is outlined from 1 Samuel 16:1 to 1 Kings 2:11.

DAVID, CITY OF. The original Jebusite stronghold on the southeastern side of the city of Jerusalem. It was taken by David and made the capital of the kingdom of the twelve tribes (2 Sam. 5:6-9).

DAY. (1) That part of the solar day which is light (Gen. 1:5, 14; John 11:9). (2) A period of 24 hours (Matt. 17:1; Luke 24: 21). (3) A period set aside for some special purpose, as "the day of atonement"

(Lev. 23:27). (4) An extended period of time during which certain revealed purposes of God are to be worked out (Gen. 2:4; 2 Pet. 3:10).

DAY OF CHRIST. In all New Testament references, the day of Christ is related to the Rapture of the church and the judgment seat of Christ (1 Cor. 1:8; 5:5; 2 Cor. 1:14; Phil. 1:6, 10; 2:16; 2 Thess. 2:2).

DAY OF THE LORD. In contrast to the day of Christ, which involves blessing and reward for saints in heaven, the day of the Lord involves judgment on unbelieving Jews and Gentiles during the Tribulation (Isa. 2:12; Joel 1:15; Mal. 4: 5, 6). The day of the Lord encompasses a prolonged period when God openly intervenes in human affairs. The period extends from the Rapture of the church until the dawn of the eternal state, with the end of the period merging into the "day of God" (2 Pet. 3:10-12).

DAYSMAN. A mediator (Job 9:33; 1 Tim. 2:5). Job longed for someone who understood both God and man and was able to draw both of them together (Job 9:32, 33; 16:21; 23:3, 4). Job's longing has been thoroughly fulfilled in our Lord Jesus Christ. In him God became man in order to bring man to God (1 Tim. 2:5). See also "Mediation."

DEACON. The basic meaning of deacon (Greek *diakonos*) is "servant" (Matt. 20: 26; 23:11; Mark 10:43; etc.) or "helper" (1 Thess. 3:2). The term is employed of a church official dedicated to the service of God and man (Phil. 1:1; 1 Tim. 3:8).

DEACONESS. A Christian woman who served the church (Rom. 16:1).

Mineral riches—potassium and magnesium—are dug at the south end of the Dead Sea. (© *MPS*)

DEAD SEA. The highly saline body of water which forms the terminus of the Jordan River. It is about 48 miles long, 6 to 9 miles wide, 1300 feet deep in spots, and 1280 feet below sea level. Masada, the famous fortress of the Maccabees and Herod the Great, once guarded a Roman road that passed through the shallow waters of the southern end. The earthquake-ridden cities of Sodom and Gomorrah also lie beneath these shallow southern waters. The Dead Sea is called the "Salt Sea" in Genesis 14:3, the "Eastern Sea" in Ezekiel 47:18, and the "Sea of Arabah" in Deuteronomy 4:49 RSV.

DEATH. Threefold death—spiritual, physical, and eternal—is the result of the fall of man and the curse of sin that followed (Gen. 2:17). Spiritual death (separation from the life of God and fellowship with God) came upon all who are "in Adam," that is, the entire human race. Both eternal death (everlasting separation from God in Gehenna) and physical death also eventually overtake all who are "in Adam." But all who have been regenerated are "in Christ" and are blessed with threefold life—spiritual life, eventual triumph over physical death in glorification of the body, and eternal life that delivers from eternal death.

DEBIR (dē'bĭr). (1) A Canaanite city taken by Israel (Josh. 10:38, 39; 15:15; Judg. 1:11). It became a Levitical city in Judah (Josh. 21:15; 1 Chron. 6:58). It is identified with present-day Tell Beit Mirsim and has been excavated. (2) A town on the border of Gad (Josh. 13:26). It is also called Lo-debar (2 Sam. 9:4; 17:27). The town is modern Umm ed-Dabar.

DEBORAH (dĕb'ô-rà) ("a bee"). (1) Rebekah's nurse, who came with her from Mesopotamia to Canaan. She was highly esteemed by Jacob's family. When she died she was buried with much sorrow under an oak below Bethel, the place being named "Allon-bacuth" (RSV) or "oak of weeping" (Gen. 35:8). Rachel's death in childbirth shortly afterward has been tied to the death of Deborah and the absence of her professional skill to aid her mistress (Gen. 35:19). (2) A prophetess and judge. She summoned Barak to fight against Sisera and went with him to battle (Judg. 4:4-24). After a great victory with the Lord's help, she composed a song of triumph (Judg. 5:1-31). She was a gifted administrator and judge as well as an intrepid leader. She judged Israel between Ramah and Bethel under a palm tree named in her honor (Judg. 4:4, 5). Deborah ranks among the great heroines of the Bible.

DECALOGUE. See "Commandments."

DECAPOLIS (dė-kăp'ô-lĭs). The Greek name for a league of approximately ten Hellenistic or Hellenized cities and accompanying territories in the Roman period. The cities included Scythopolis (west of the Jordan), certain cities east of Perea, and Dion, Abila, and Damascus. In the New Testament, Decapolis appears as the Gentile territory bordering on Galilee and Perea (Matt. 4:25; Mark 5:20; 7:31).

DEDICATION, FEAST OF. Held on 25 Kislew (our November or December), this Jewish celebration lasted eight days. It commemorated the cleansing of the Temple and altar by Judas Maccabeus in 165 B.C. (John 10:22; 1 Macc. 4:47-59). The prominence of lamps and lighting in the Feast gave rise to its popular name of "Feast of Lights."

DEITY. See "God."

DELILAH (de-lī'là). A seductive woman of Sorek (apparently a Philistine) with whom Samson was infatuated (Judg. 16:4). When Samson, the hero of the tribe of Dan, had humiliated the Philistines on repeated occasions, they bribed Delilah to find out the secret of his great strength (Judg. 16:5). After resisting her wiles three times, Samson finally succumbed and told her the secret of his power—his uncut hair, the symbol of his dedication to the Lord (Judg. 16:7-20; cf. 13:2-5). She then turned him over to the Philistines, who imprisoned him (Judg. 16:21). Delilah represents the worldly seductress who lures a man of God to ruin by compromise with sin.

DEMAS (dē'màs). Paul's fellow-laborer (Col. 4:14; Philem. 1:24). He later deserted the Apostle for worldly reasons (2 Tim. 4:10).

DEMETRIUS I SOTER (dė-mē'trĭ-ŭs, so'tǝr) ("belonging to Demeter," the goddess of agriculture). The King of Syria from 162 to 150 B.C. (1 Macc. 7:1-4). It was in battle with him that Judas Maccabeus lost his life (1 Macc. 9:1-19).

DEMONS. Evil spirits (Matt. 12:43-45) who are probably fallen angels. They are Satan's agents (Matt. 12:26, 27) and, like him, oppose the Word and will of God. As invisible spirits they can enter and control the body of both human beings and animals (Mark 5:2-13). All demons are evil in that they oppose God. Many are openly unclean and vicious (Matt. 8: 28; 9:33; 10:1; Mark 1:23; 5:2-13; 9:17-27; Luke 6:18). Others, however, are deceptively "good," educated, refined, and religious (1 Tim. 4:1, 2; 1 John 4:1-3). These are the most dangerous because they impose themselves on undiscerning people as spirits from God, thereby deluding the unwary into error, false religions, and erratic conduct. Like their leader, Satan, they often masquerade as "angels of light" (2 Cor. 11:14).

Evil spirits may exercise a varying degree of control over both saved and unsaved people. They may simply harass their victim from without or, if the victim permits entry by seriously violating God's moral law, they may enter in and inhabit the person's body. A person becomes especially vulnerable to demon influence or possession if he dabbles in occultism, in which he violates the first two commandments of the Decalogue and insults God's deity. Such inhabiting demons may inflict certain physical maladies (Matt. 12:22; 17:14-18; Luke 13:16) as well as certain mental and spiritual disorders. (However, it is essential that demon-inflicted maladies be distinguished from other disorders to which men are subject. For example, some mental problems are the legitimate domain of psychologists and psychiatrists, whereas other disorders can be corrected only by expulsion of the demon or demons through the ministry of a Spirit-filled servant of God.)

DEPRAVITY. A theological term which describes what the infinitely holy God sees as he looks on unsaved men. This depravity contrasts sharply with what *man* sees when he looks at himself or his fellow men. The phrase "total depravity" does not imply that there is no good of any kind in unsaved people but rather that the unsaved are totally unqualified to enter heaven on the basis of their own

merit (Rom. 3:10-18; 5:12; Eph. 2:1-3). They are all "in Adam" and "under sin" and are therefore confined to faith in Christ, God's gracious gift, as their only means of salvation (John 3:18; Eph. 2:8, 9).

DERBE (dĕr′bē). A town of the Lycaonian district of Roman Galatia. It was the most easterly place visited by Paul and Barnabas (Acts 14:6, 7). Beyond lay the client kingdom of Antiochus. The site has been identified as modern Kerti Huyuk, 13 miles north-northeast of Karaman and 60 miles southeast of Lystra.

DESERT. See "Wilderness."

DEVIL (Greek *diabolos*, "slanderer"). Satan, the great fallen angel and the accuser of God's people (Rev. 12:9, 10). He seeks to "devour them as a lion" (1 Pet. 5: 8) and to delude them as an "angel of light" (2 Cor. 11:14). He is called "Belial" ("worthless and no good" — 2 Cor. 6: 15), "Satan" ("adversary" — Job 2:1), and "that old Serpent" (Rev. 12:9).

DEVILS. See "Demons." ("Devils" in the King James Version always refers to demons. There is only one "devil" — Satan himself.)

DIANA (dī-ă′nà). The Latin name for Artemis, the Greek goddess of the moon and the hunt. Her temple at Ephesus was one of the seven wonders of the ancient world (Acts 19:27). The local silversmiths, who made small votary shrines for Artemis, instigated a riot when Paul's powerful ministry cut into their lucrative trade (Acts 19:23-41). Inscriptions from Ephesus label this deity "Artemis the Great" (cf. Acts 19:27, 28, 34).

DIBON (dī′bŏn). An important Moabite city where the Mesha Stone was found (Num. 21:30; 32:3). It was claimed by the Israelites (Num. 32:34; Josh. 13:9) as a Moabite city (cf. Isa. 15:2; Jer. 48:18).

DIETARY LAWS. Israel was called to be a holy nation. The Mosaic Code distinguished between clean and unclean animals (Lev. 11:1-47). Only clean animals were to be eaten by a holy people. This regulation served a hygienic purpose and was also intended as a guard against idolatrous practices. In keeping with this concept, the Jews washed their hands before touching food and practiced meticulous ceremonial cleanliness (Mark 7:4).

DINAH (dī'nȧ) (perhaps "judgment"). A daughter of Jacob by his concubine Leah (Gen. 30:21). She was either seduced or raped by the young Hivite prince Shechem, the son of Hamor (Gen. 34:1, 2). Shechem afterward wished to take her in honorable marriage (Gen. 34:3, 4). Her brothers outwardly agreed, on condition that the Hivites be circumcised (Gen. 34: 7-17). But while the males were recovering, Simeon and Levi, two of Dinah's full brothers, killed all the males of the place, including Hamor and Shechem (Gen. 34:24-29). Jacob was horrified at the slaughter and denounced it on his deathbed (Gen. 49:5-7). By this outrageous crime the district of Shechem fell to Jacob as tribal chief. However, he bequeathed it not to those responsible for the crime but to Joseph (Gen. 48:22).

DIOTREPHES (dī-ŏt'rė-fēz). ("nurtured by Zeus"). The professed disciple who refused to recognize the authority of the Apostle John. He domineeringly sought the preeminence (3 John 1:9) to the dethronement of Christ (cf. Col. 1:18). He illustrates church dictators who substitute self for Christ.

DISCIPLE. Christ enunciated stringent requirements for being his disciple. A true disciple must "hate" his life (Luke 14:26), "bear his cross" (Luke 14:27), and forsake everything (Luke 14:33). If taken at face value Christ's terms of discipleship are met by very few believers today.

DISPERSIONS OF ISRAEL. On the basis of her unchangeable covenants Israel is guaranteed ultimate possession of the land of promise (Deut. 30:1-8). Clearly predicted were three dispersions and three regatherings. The three dispersions have already occurred: that into Egypt (Gen. 15:13-16), that of the captivities (Israel in 722 B.C. and Judah in 586 B.C.—cf. Jer. 25:11, 12; Dan. 9:1, 2), and the present dispersion (having begun with the destruction of Jerusalem in A.D. 70 and continuing until Christ's second advent). It is at the second advent that Israel will be regathered for the last time (Deut. 30:1-3; Ezek. 37:21-28).

DIVINATION. The pagan and occult counterpart of biblical prophecy. It involves consultation of heathen gods for guidance with respect to the future. Divinatory methods embrace astrology, necromancy, spiritism, interpretation of dreams, and occult visions. Less familiar methods entail the use of arrows and the examination of animal livers (Ezek. 21: 21). Divination by rods (Hos. 4:12) and by psychic clairvoyance (Acts 16:16-18) was also practiced in the ancient world. Divination was forbidden in Israel because of its demonic implications (Deut. 18:9-12).

DIVINITY OF KINGS. In ancient times kings, like priests, were frequently anointed as sacred persons. Among the pagans the king was regarded as the visible representative of the national deity and was accorded divine honors.

DIVORCE. The original creatorial relationship which God established between the sexes was strict monogamy. A man was to leave his parents and be joined to his wife, thereby entering a permanent and unbreakable union in which the two parties became "one flesh" (Gen. 2:24; Matt. 19:4-6; Mark 10:6-9). The earliest fragments of sacred history and the earliest laws evidence the radical perversion of the original divine order (Gen. 4:23; 16:1, 2; Exod. 20:17). The Mosaic Law attempted only to curb these perversions by imposing restraints on what by that time had become established custom. Our Lord reminded the Pharisees of this fact by showing them that divorce under the Law was a concession to the hardness of the human heart (cf. Deut. 24:1-4) and that "from the beginning it was not so" (Matt. 19:7, 8; Mark 10:2-12).

The Mosaic statute, although a concession to human weakness, was evidently aimed at encouraging reconciliation and thus preserving the original covenant of Genesis 2:24. Such a divorce proceeding would take time, invite reflection, and enlist the unbiased counsel of magistrate and priest. It would thus tend to effect a reconciliation. The Mosaic statute was certainly not slanted to ignore God's hatred of marital infidelity and the breaking of the marriage tie (Mal. 2:14-16).

Christ's teaching on divorce and remarriage is based strictly on the original relationship which the Creator established between the sexes (Gen. 2:24). He does not concede to custom or accommodate human weakness, as does the Law of Moses. He forbids divorce and remarriage completely, with only one exception – the crime of adultery (Matt. 5:32; 19:9). He even declares that the union of a divorced woman with another man is adulterous, both for herself and for her husband. (In stating this, Christ evidently puts the woman on the same plane as the man. This is in contrast to the Mosaic Code, which did not permit a woman to separate from her husband for any reason.)

The Apostle Paul supplements but does not alter the teaching of our Lord. If a rift develops between a Christian couple they must be reconciled if possible. If this is not possible they may separate but must not remarry (1 Cor. 7:10, 11). If one party of an unsaved couple becomes converted he or she is to attempt to win his or her mate to the Lord (1 Cor. 7:13, 14, 16). If the unsaved partner finds the new faith intolerable, the believer is not to prevent him (or her) from leaving (1 Cor. 7:15). Believers must never marry unbelievers (2 Cor. 6:14).

DOEG (dō'ĕg) ("fearful, timid"). An Edomite and the chief of King Saul's herdsmen. It was he who informed Saul of Ahimelech's aid to David. As a result of Doeg's deceit Ahimelech and the priests at Nob were massacred by Saul (1 Sam. 22:6-19).

DOG. Dogs were domesticated long before Israel's history began. But in the Bible dogs appear mainly as scavengers, haunting the streets and refuse dumps of the city. They were considered unclean and vicious (Psa. 59:6, 14; Exod. 22:31; 1 Kings 14:11; 16:4; cf. Psa. 22:16, 20). However, shepherd dogs are mentioned (Job 30:1). In the New Testament the dog apparently appears as a pet (Matt. 15: 26, 27; Mark 7:27, 28).

DOLMEN. A sepulchral monument consisting of a large slab of stone placed on other unhewn stones. Some think these stone arrangements found throughout Palestine were erected as primitive altars and offering tables for the dead.

DOMITIAN (dȯ-mǐsh'ȧn). The Roman emperor from A.D 81 to 96. It was he who banished the Apostle John to the Island of Patmos.

DONKEY. See "Ass."

DOR (dōr). A town on the Mediterranean Coast south of Mount Carmel and north of Tantura. A Canaanite town, it was allotted to Manasseh even though it was in Asher (Josh. 17:11; cf. Judg. 1:27). It was later reckoned to Ephraim. It was a harbor town in the Hellenistic and Roman era.

DORCAS (dôr'kăs) ("gazelle"). A Christian woman of good works who was also called Tabitha. She was a friend and helper of the poor who lived in Joppa. When she died, Peter was summoned; he called her back to life. The incident caused many to believe on the Lord Jesus Christ (Acts 9:36-43). Dorcas is famous as a woman who unselfishly gave herself to help the needy and poor.

DOTHAN (dō'thȧn). A town in the fertile plains of the hill country about a dozen miles north of Shechem (Gen. 37:17; 2 Kings 6:13). Excavations reveal that the site, Tell Dotha, was occupied from the Early Bronze Age to the Assyrian invasions of the eighth century.

DOVE. A name for various species of pigeons. They constitute a family called *Columbidae*. Four species abound in Palestine – the ringdove or wood pigeon, the stock dove, the rock dove, and the ash-rumped rock dove. The dove is described as having a plaintive voice (Isa. 38:14) and as being gentle and affectionate (Song 2:14; 5:2) but not particularly sagacious (Hos. 7:11). It was used in Temple sacrifices (Matt. 21:12; Luke 2: 24). Its gentle, harmless nature (Matt. 10: 16) makes it a fit symbol of the Holy Spirit (Luke 3:22). See also "Pigeon."

DRAGON. A mythological monster conceived as a huge serpent with wings and claws. This may be the implication of some of the Old Testament allusions. In the New Testament the dragon (Greek *drakōn*) is an apocalyptic figure of Satan, that "old serpent the devil" (Rev. 12:3, 14; 13:2; 16:13; 20:1-3). In some of the Old Testament passages the dragon seems to refer to the crocodile ("leviathan" – Isa. 27:1; 51:9). The association with Egypt, the habitat of the crocodile, suggests the same possibility in Ezekiel 29:3 (compare Jeremiah 51:34).

DRAWER OF WATER. In Bible lands water had to be carried from cisterns and springs, which were sometimes quite a distance away. Those who carried the water often had an assigned daily responsibility. An illustration of this is furnished by the Gibeonites, who were assigned to draw water and cut wood for the Tabernacle and the priests and Levites (Josh. 9:21, 23, 27).

DRESSER OF SYCAMORE FRUIT. The original text of Amos 7:14 indicates that Amos was a dresser or tender of sycamore fruit. This involved slitting the top of each fig to guarantee its ripening. The sycamore-fig (*Ficus sycmorus*) has evergreen leaves and yields an edible fruit. King David appointed an overseer to superintend the olive and sycamore trees (1 Chron. 27:28; cf. Psa. 78:47). Zacchaeus climbed such a tree to see Jesus (Luke 19:4).

DROMEDARY. See "Camel."

DRUSILLA. (drū-sĭl'á). The third and youngest daughter of Agrippa I, King of Judea. Her brother, Agrippa II, had her married to Azizus, king of Emesa. When Felix was procurator of Judea (A.D. 52-60), he fell in love with Drusilla. Goaded on by the petty tyranny of her sister, Bernice, Drusilla defied the Jewish law, left her husband, and married Felix, a Gentile and an idolater. It is understandable why Felix trembled when Paul, then a prisoner, reasoned before him and Drusilla of righteousness, temperance, and judgment to come (Acts 24:24, 25).

DUGONG. See under "Badger."

DUMAH (dū'má). A town of Arabia (Gen. 25:14; 1 Chron. 1:30; Isa. 21:11) located about halfway across the Peninsula between Palestine and Southern Babylonia.

DYES AND COLORS. See under "Clothing and Dress."

EAGLE. The Hebrew word *nesher* is undoubtedly as much a generic term as the English word "eagle," including besides the true eagle (of the family *Accipitridae* of the genus *Aquila*) other large birds of prey, particularly the griffon vulture (Mic. 1:16; Matt. 24:28). The eagle was classified as unclean (Lev. 11:13). It was the monarch of the birds and the largest flying creature to be found in Bible lands. It had a majestic sweep in flight (Prov. 23:5; Isa. 40:31; Obad. 1:4). It swooped down on its prey (Job 9:26) and nested in inaccessible places (Job 39:27; Jer. 49:16). However, the eagle showed great solicitude for its young (Deut. 32:11). The allusion to the renewal of its youth (Psa. 103:5) doubtless refers poetically to its very long life. Ancient naturalists knew the difference between the eagle and the vulture. The vulture is generally a car-

rion-eating bird (cf. Matt. 24:28) with an unfeathered neck and head, and is a somewhat more social creature than the eagle.

EARRING. An ornament of both men and women, the earring was a ring (*nezem*) worn in the earlobes (Gen. 35:4; Exod. 32:2, 3; 35:22; Prov. 25:12; Job 42:11). The earring was the characteristic ornament of the Ishmaelites (Judg. 8:24-26). Their kings were also adorned with crescent-shaped amulets and eardrops (Judg. 8:26).

EBAL (ē'bál). A 3085-foot-high mountain peak in the central highland ridge northeast of Mount Gerizim. Both Mount Ebal and Mount Gerizim overshadow Shechem (modern Nablus). The natural amphitheater between these two peaks has wonderful acoustical properties. It was from these two mountains that the Mosaic blessings and curses were intoned upon the Jewish people (Deut. 11:26-30; 27:11 – 29:1).

EBED-MELECH (ē'bĕd-mē'lĕk) ("king's servant"). An Ethiopian palace eunuch in Zedekiah's time (597-586 B.C.). He was a credit to his race, assisting Jeremiah in his release from prison (Jer. 38:7-13).

EBER (ē'bēr) ("other side, region beyond"). A descendant of Shem and progenitor of the Hebrews (Gen. 10:22, 24; 11:16-26), of various Arabian tribes (Gen. 10:25-30), and of certain Aramaean tribes descended from Nahor (Gen. 11:29; 22:20-24). Eber originally belonged to the region beyond the Euphrates; it was from this locale that his name was probably derived.

EBONY. A hard, black wood used for inlaying. It was apparently obtained from India or Ceylon (Ezek. 27:15). Merchants of Dedan traded with it in the markets of Tyre. The Greeks were familiar with a black ebony from Ethiopia and a variegated species from India.

ECBATANA (ĕk-băt'ȧ-nȧ). The capital of ancient Media. It lay southwest of the Caspian Sea and was a royal city of Persia (Ezra 6:2; 2 Macc. 9:3). The city is modern Hamadan.

EDEN (ē'dĕn). (1) The original habitation of man. It was located somewhere in lower Babylonia in the Tigris-Euphrates country (Gen. 2:10-14). The Pishon and Gihon were probably canals that connected the Tigris and Euphrates as ancient riverbeds. (2) The land conquered by the Assyrians. It is the same as Bit-Adini or Beth-eden in the Balikh-Habur region of northwest Mesopotamia (Ezek. 27:23; Amos 1:5; Isa. 37:12).

EDOM (ē'dŏm) ("red"). A name of Esau, the older son of Isaac (Gen. 25:30; 36:1, 8, 19).

EDOMITES (ē'dŏ-mīts). A people descended from the Hebrews through Esau, the brother of Jacob and the grandson of Abraham (Gen. 36:9). They occupied the area south of the Dead Sea from the Wadi Zered to the Gulf of Aqabah, a 100-mile-long depression (Deut. 2:12; Judg. 11:18). The rugged terrain has peaks rising to 3500 feet. While not a fertile land, good arable areas are found (Num. 20:17, 19). The capital was Sela, situated on a small plateau behind Petra. Other important towns were Bozrah and Teman. In Bible times the King's Highway passed along the eastern plateau (Num. 20:17). Israel was refused passage over this road during the Exodus (Num. 20:14-21). Despite this discourtesy the Israelites were forbidden to hate their Edomite relatives (Deut. 23:7, 8). However, the contacts of Israel with Edom were fraught with bitter wars and lingering animosities.

Saul fought with the Edomites (1 Sam. 14:47). David conquered them (2 Sam. 8: 13, 14), enabling Solomon to build a port at Ezion-Geber (1 Kings 9:26-28) and to exploit the copper mines of the region, as attested by archeology. Later kings of Judah also warred with Edom. Uzziah dominated the country and restored the port at Elath (2 Kings 14:22). Ahaz lost control of Edom and it became a vassal state of Assyria after about 736 B.C. See also "Idumeans."

EGLAH (ĕg'lȧ) ("heifer"). One of David's eight wives, probably the least known. She was the mother of Ithream (2 Sam. 3: 5; 1 Chron. 3:3).

EGYPT, RIVER OF (ē'jĭpt). Modern Rhinococura (Wadi el Arish), 45 miles southwest of Gaza on the borders of Egypt (Gen. 15:18; Num. 34:5).

The Sphinx and Pyramids of Gizeh, Egypt, near Cairo, mark the tombs of royalty. (© *MPS*)

EGYPTIANS (ė-jĭp'shȧns). According to the Table of the Nations, Mizraim (Egypt) was the son of Ham and the brother of Canaan, Put, and Cush (Gen. 10:6). Ancient Egyptians were Hamites and belonged to the white race, which in prehistoric times migrated in successive waves into the country of Egypt. In later times other migrations from Babylonia (largely Semitic) left their influence upon the people and their language. In the course of history a Nubian element was also injected into the Egyptian mixture. This remarkable people occupied the fertile ribbon of the Nile Valley from the second cataract in Semneh (present-day Aswan) to the Mediterranean Sea, a distance of some 800 miles.

The Egyptians had from prehistoric times organized their country under two divisions, Upper and Lower Egypt (giving rise to the dual form of the Hebrew name "Mizraim"). At about 2900 B.C. the country was united under Menes. Manetho, a priest of the third century B.C., wrote a history of Egypt which divided the period 2900-332 B.C. into 30 royal dynasties. During this period the marvelous civilization of the Nile Valley was developed. This information has been brought to light by archeological research from about A.D. 1800 to the present. Because Egypt figures so prominently in the pages of the Bible, these archeological findings have shed great light on much of the Old Testament.

EHUD (ē'hŭd) (probably shortened from "Abihud"). The second judge of Israel. He slew Eglon of Moab and delivered and judged Israel (Judg. 3:15–4:1).

EKRON (ĕk'rŏn). One of the five principal Philistine cities (Josh. 15:45, 46). It has recently been identified with Khirbet al-Muqannac, about 25 miles west of Jerusalem. The ark was taken there after it had been removed from Gath (1 Sam. 5:10-12). The city is prominent in the records of the Assyrian Kings Sennacherib and Esarhaddon.

EL (ĕl). See "Elohim."

ELAM (ē'lăm) (probably from Akkadian *elamtu*, "highland"). A son of Shem and progenitor of the Elamites.

ELAMITES (ē'lȧ-mīts). The inhabitants of the highland region beyond the Tigris River and east of Babylonia. Their capital was at Susa. They are listed among the sons of Shem (Gen. 10:22), probably because of their periodic invasions into Babylonia and their amalgamation with the Semites who had been exiled there. Sargon of Akkac conquered Elam around 2150 B.C. Ur was destroyed by the Elam-

ites at about 2000 B.C., not long after Abraham and Terah had left the cities. In the eighteenth century B.C. Elam's expansionist aspirations were thwarted by Hammurabi. During the Kassite period Elam seems to have held the position of a province, having been conquered by Kurigalzu II about the middle of the fourteenth century. Elamite power revived intermittently thereafter. Shutruk-Nahunte (1200 B.C.) was able to raid Babylon and carry off the famous Law Code of Hammurabi, rediscovered in A.D. 1902 at Susa. By 1130 B.C. Nebuchadnezzar I had conquered Elam so thoroughly that it remained in comparative eclipse for three centuries.

In the eighth century B.C. Elam allied itself with Babylonia against Assyrian aggression. The struggle ended with the complete destruction of Elam's power by Ashurbanipal in about 645 B.C. In the Chaldean and Persian periods Elam held a subordinate position.

ELATH, ELOTH (ē'lăth; ē'lŏth). Sometimes called Ezion-Geber, Elath was a settlement at the north end of the Gulf of Aqabah. It is first mentioned as a stopping place for Israel during her exodus from Egypt (Num. 23:35, 36; Deut. 2:8). In about 955 B.C. Solomon developed copper and iron mining and smelting in the Arabah north of Ezion-geber (at the site of modern Tell el-Kheleifeh, two-and-a-half miles west of Aqabah). Old Elath (Ezion-geber-Elath) served as the terminal point for Solomon's trading fleet to Ophir and Arabia. The Edomites intermittently controlled this region (2 Kings 14:22).

ELDAD (ĕl'dăd) ("God has loved"). An elder who (with Medad) assisted Moses in governing Israel (Num. 11:24-30).

ELDER. A person of age and experience who was considered well qualified to rule. The Jews (Exod. 3:16; Num. 11:25) as well as the Egyptians (Gen. 50:7), the Moabites, and the Midianites (Num. 22:7), had elders. They acted as judges and filled various civil capacities (Deut. 21:1-9; Josh. 20:1-6) throughout the entire period of Old Testament history (2 Sam. 5:3; 1 Kings 8:1-3; 20:7; 2 Kings 19:1, 2; Ezek. 8:1). In the Hellenistic period Jewish synagogues were normally governed by a council of elders under the chairmanship of a "ruler of the synagogue." In religious matters all Jews were subject to the 71-member Sanhedrin. During the New Testament period the high priest was chairman *ex officio* of this august body.

The Christian church also followed the practice of employing men of age and experience in matters of ruling. The elder *(zaqen)* of the Old Testament became the presbyter *(presbuteros)* of the New Testament. Paul and Barnabas ordained elders in all the Gentile churches (Acts 14:23). The Apostle directed Titus to do the same in Crete (Tit. 1:5).

The elders at Ephesus (Acts 20:17-35) are also called "overseers" or "bishops" (Greek *episcopoi* — Acts 20:28), suggesting that the terms "presbyter" and "bishop" are interchangeable in New Testament usage. All elders were of equal rank; the eldership acted in a corporate capacity. The term "presbytery" *(presbuterion)* is employed to describe the body of elders that ordained Timothy (1 Tim. 4:14).

Duties of elders or presbyters included visitation of the sick (James 5:14), preaching and teaching (1 Tim. 5:17), general oversight of the local congregation (1 Pet. 5:1-4), receiving and dispensing gifts (Acts 11:29, 30), and rendering decisions on problems (Acts 15:1-6; 16:1-4).

ELEAZAR (ĕ-lē-ā′zăr) ("God has helped"). A priest, the third son of Aaron and the father of Phinehas (Exod. 6:23, 25; 28:1). He became chief of the Levites when his brothers Nadab and Abihu were killed for failing to offer sacrifices in the manner God had prescribed (Lev. 10:1-7; Num. 3: 4, 32). He succeeded Aaron upon the latter's death (Num. 20:22-29; Deut. 10:6).

ELECTION. The sovereign right of God to choose who from among his created beings shall be granted a position of special favor. Scripture reveals two major elections: 1) the nation Israel (Matt. 24: 1 — 25:46; Rom. 9:1-18; 11:1-36) and 2) the church of Christ (John 17:1-26; Rom. 8:28-39; Eph. 1:4-6). These two entities of God's people must be differentiated if Bible truth is to be understood.

Election is based on five divine decrees:

1) the decree to create; 2) the decree to permit the fall of man; 3) the decree to elect some to salvation; 4) the decree to provide a Savior; and 5) the decree to save the elect. The theological questions involved have divided believers into two main categories — Calvinists and Arminians.

The five points of Calvinism are 1) total depravity (utter inability of fallen man to redeem himself); 2) unconditional election; 3) a limited redemption; 4) efficacious grace; and 5) perserverance of the saints.

The opposing five points of Arminianism are 1) conditional election according to divine foreknowledge; 2) a universal redemption (although only those who believe are actually saved); 3) salvation by grace bestowed at birth; 4) resistible grace; and 5) possible falling from grace.

Israel's election guarantees 1) an everlasting nation; 2) an everlasting possession of their land; 3) an everlasting throne; 4) an everlasting king; and 5) an everlasting kingdom (2 Sam. 7:4-17; 1 Chron. 17:3-15).

ELEPHANT. A genus of large animals with ivory tusks native to Asia and Africa. This huge animal was used in wars (1 Macc. 1:17; 3:34; 6:37; 2 Macc. 14:12) during the time of the Seleucid kings. Maccabean coins depict the elephant.

ELEPHANTINE (ĕl′-ĕ-făn-tī-nĕ). The site of a Jewish military colony adjacent to Syene (modern Aswan) in the sixth and fifth centuries B.C. From this place came the important Aramaic documents known as the Elephantine Papyri.

ELI (ē′lī) ("high," possibly a contraction for "God is high"). A high priest and judge of Israel for forty years (1 Sam. 1: 1 — 4:18). Eli was a godly man but failed to exercise parental authority. As a result his two sons disgraced the priesthood and brought judgment upon both the house of Eli and the nation of Israel.

ELIAKIM (ĕ-lī′á-kīm). A high official of Hezekiah's court who conferred with the Assyrians (2 Kings 18:18-37; Isa. 36:3-22; cf. 2 Kings 19:2; Isa. 37:2). Isaiah commended Eliakim and promised him such exalted blessings from God that he must be regarded as a messianic type (Isa. 22:20-25).

ELIEZER (ĕl-ĭ-ē'zēr) ("God is a helper"). A citizen of Damascus and Abraham's steward (Gen. 15:2; cf. 24:2).

ELIHU (e-lī'hū) ("God is He" or "He is God"). One of Job's friends who gave counsel during Job's sufferings (Job Chaps. 32–37).

ELIHU (é-lī'hū) ("God is he" or "He is "the Lord is God"). A great prophet of the ninth century B.C. who fought Baal worship (1 Kings 18:17–19:18). He rebuked kings (1 Kings 21:20-22; 2 Kings 1:16). He was a mighty intercessor (1 Kings 17:20-22; 18:36-40; James 5:17) and performer of miracles (1 Kings 17:10-24) but was prone to discouragement (1 Kings 19:4) and was fallible in judgment (1 Kings 19:14, 18). He was divinely and signally honored (2 Kings 2:11; Matt. 17:3).

ELIPHAZ (ĕl'ĭ-făz) (possibly "God is fine gold"). One of Job's friends from Teman in Arabia (Job 2:11; 4:1; 15:1; 22:1; 42:7, 9). He was a religious dogmatist who gloried in his wisdom and tried to press Job into the mold of his own experience.

ELISABETH (é-lĭz'à-bĕth) ("God is an oath," i.e., the absolutely faithful One). The wife of the priest Zacharias and the mother of John the Baptist. She was of the house of Aaron and bore the Greek equivalent of the name of Aaron's wife, Elisheba. She was a relative of Mary of Nazareth. Inspired by the Holy Spirit, Elisabeth welcomed Mary as the mother of the promised Messiah (Luke 1:41-45).

ELISHA (é-lī'shà) ("God is salvation"). (1) Elijah's successor in prophetic ministry in the Northern Kingdom (1 Kings 19:16-21). He witnessed Elijah's translation and received a double portion of his spirit in order to conduct a miracle-filled ministry to offset the apostasy and inroads of Baalism (2 Kings Chaps. 2–13). He became a model spiritual leader, characterized by mercy (2 Kings 2:19-22), unselfishness (2 Kings 5:8-10, 15, 16, 25, 26), and patient endurance (2 Kings 5:17-19). (2) Apparently Kittim or Cyprus, the "Alashia" of the Amarna Letters and the Egyptian and cuneiform sources. These texts indicate that Alashia exported copper from the east coast of Cyprus. Elishah was the eldest son of Javan (Gen. 10:4).

ELISHEBA (é-līsh'é-bà). The wife of

Aaron and the ancestress of the entire Levitical line. She bore Aaron four sons: Nadab, Abihu, Eleazar, and Ithamar (Exod. 6:23). From these last two sons descended the long line of priests who ministered in the sanctuary and taught God's Law.

ELKANAH (ĕl-kā'nà) ("God has created"). The father of Samuel (1 Sam. 1:19, 20). He was a Levitical descendant (1 Sam. 1: 1).

ELM. See "Terebinth."

ELOHIM (ĕ-lō'hĭm). The primary word for God in the Old Testament, occurring in hundreds of passages. The noun is plural in form but singular in meaning when referring to God. The triunity of God is intimated in the Old Testament and clearly revealed in the New Testament. The singular form of the word, "El," denotes either "God" or "a god." (In the Ugaritic literature El refers to the chief god of the Canaanite pantheon, the father of Baal). In Scripture the singular form usually occurs in compound names such as 1) *El Olam,* "the everlasting God," expressing the eternity of the divine Being (Gen. 21:33); 2) *El Elyon,* "God the Highest" and "the Possessor of heaven and earth" (Gen. 14:18, 22); 3) *El Gibbor,* "Mighty God" (Isa. 9:6); and 4) *El Shaddai,* "Almighty or all-sufficient God" (Gen. 17:1), the name by which he revealed himself to the patriarchs prior to Israel's redemption out of Egypt (Gen. 28:3; 35:11; 48:3). See also "Adonai," "Adonai Jehovah" and "Jehovah."

ELYMAS (ĕl'ĭ-mäs). A magician and false prophet who through demonic power opposed Paul and Barnabas at Paphos in Cyprus (Acts 13:8-11).

EMBALMING. Out of religious motives the Egyptians attempted to preserve the bodies of their dead for the longest possible time. They thus developed the complicated art of embalming and mummification. The burial of Jacob and Joseph followed this custom (Gen. 50:1-3, 26), though the Israelites did not practice embalming themselves.

EMBROIDERING. The Israelites knew the art of embroidery (cf. Exod. Chaps. 27, 28, 35, 36, 38, 39). They probably learned it from the Egyptians, who also practiced it (Ezek. 27:7). The Jews employed embroidery freely in making the priestly vestments and materials of the Tabernacle. The robes of Assyrian and Babylonian kings were also richly embroidered, as the monuments attest.

EMMAUS (ĕ-mā'ŭs). A village near Jerusalem where Jesus appeared to two disciples after his resurrection (Luke 24:13). The town is possibly to be identified with present-day Colonia Amasa, about seven miles from Jerusalem.

EMMER. A kind of inferior wheat with more modest growth characteristics than durum wheat (Exod. 9:32; Isa. 28:25; Ezek. 4:9). This plant, called "rye" or "fitches" in the King James Version, is *Triticum dioccum*. No evidence exists that rye, fitches, or spelt were grown in biblical times in Palestine. Emmer, however, has been found in old Egyptian tombs, indicating that it was almost certainly grown in the Near East.

EMPEROR. A title of the ruler of the Roman Empire. It is derived from the Latin *imperator*, which was originally bestowed temporarily on a general who had been victorious in battle. Julius Caesar, however, retained the title permanently. Through his example it came to signify supreme military authority. It was employed by Augustus and his successors in this sense. Peter uses the term "king" *(basileus)* to refer to the Emperor (1 Pet. 2:13, 17). The title "Augustus" (the rendering of the Greek word *sebastos*, "revered, reverend") as well as the title "Caesar" occur in Acts 25:21, 25. Ideally the emperor ruled as *princeps* or "head of state." But corruption and abuse of power led to military autocracy, with the Emperor ruling his people as an imperator ruled his troops. Worse still, the title "Augustus" led to emperor worship. See "Emperor Cult" below.

EMPEROR CULT. From the time of Augustus (31 B.C. – A.D. 14) Roman emperors accepted the eastern belief in the divinity of kings. As a result they bore divine titles and were worshiped as Jupiter incarnate. Temples to the god Augustus and the goddess Roma were established throughout the Empire. Belief in imperial divinity was used as a means of keeping subject peoples loyal to Rome. Although the Jews were exempted from emperor worship, the Christians were not. They were looked upon as subversives and frequently suffered martyrdom for refusing to offer sacrifice and burn incense before the Emperor's image.

ENCHANTMENT. This term denotes the practice of the occult arts, notably magic and sorcery (Exod. 7:11, 22; 8:7). Magicians used various bizarre rituals and mutterings to enlist demonic powers (Isa. 8:19). Any resort to these methods of imposture was strictly prohibited by the Mosaic Law (Lev. 19:26). But occultism flourished in idolatrous pagan religions (2 Kings 17:17), even in the Christian era (Acts 13:6-8). See also "Demons," "Divination," and "Magic."

EN-DOR (ĕn'dôr). A village about four miles south of Mount Tabor (Josh. 17:11, 12). It was the home of the spirit medium whom King Saul consulted (1 Sam. 28:7).

ENGAGEMENT (Betrothal). In ancient Israel marriage was preceded by a period of betrothal. In earliest times the betrothal was largely a matter of business, and concerned chiefly the parents and near family friends (Gen. 21:21; 24:3). Distinction was clearly made between the betrothed and the married (Deut. 20:7). Later, under the second Jewish commonwealth, a legal ceremony for the betrothal was established by the rabbinical law. But at all periods of Israelite history betrothal was regarded as more than merely a promise to marry. It was considered the initial act of marriage and, like marriage itself, was dissoluble only by death or divorce.

Faithlessness to the betrothal vow was regarded as adultery and was punished as such (Lev. 19:20; Deut. 22:23-27). This is why Joseph was contemplating divorcing his betrothed wife, Mary, until he was apprised by the angel that her child was supernaturally conceived by the Holy Spirit (Matt. 1:18-25). After the betrothal a period of time (longer or shorter according to circumstances) was allowed to elapse before the nuptials (Gen. 24:55, 67; Deut. 20:7; Judg. 14:1-3, 7, 8). Later this period of time became established by talmudic law as a month for widows and a full year for virgins.

Between betrothal and marriage no sexual intercourse was allowed between the betrothed (Matt. 1:18). The ceremony of betrothal consisted of the simple act of the bridegroom handing to the bride or her representative a written engagement or a token of money. This was done in the presence of witnesses and was accompanied with the words "Be thou consecrated (wedded) to me." Since medieval times a ring has taken the place of the coin as the customary sign of betrothal.

Before the betrothal actually took place it was customary to agree upon a dowry. Customarily this was presented to the bride's parents (Exod. 22:16, 17; 1 Sam. 18:25), though sometimes it was given to an older brother (Gen. 24:53; 34:12). The dowry was considered a present to the bride or her parents for the purpose of sealing the engagement or enabling the bride to assume a worthy place in her future home (cf. Gen. 31:15). In rabbinical law, established at least by 100 B.C., the dowry was defined as a settlement upon the wife and was made as indispensable as is the marriage license today.

The dowry varied according to the circumstances of those concerned. Ordinarily it ranged from 30 to 50 shekels (approximately 20 to 30 dollars in terms of today's money). Other types of dowries were sometimes agreed upon (Gen. 29: 18; Josh. 15:16). Sometimes parents themselves bestowed presents on their daughters at the time of their betrothal (Gen. 29:24, 29; Tobit 10:11).

ENGRAVING. Engraving on ivory, bone, and precious stones was a skilled art in ancient Bible lands. Examples of Canaanite ivories come from Lachish (fourteenth century B.C.), Hagor (thirteenth century B.C.), and Tell Beit Mirsim. Ivories from Megiddo (twelfth century B.C.) and Samaria in Ahab's time (ninth century B.C.) are very similar to contemporary ivories from Arslan Tash (Syria) and Nimrud (Iraq). Some of the ivories are inlaid with gold, lapis-lazuli, colored stones, and glass.

Precious and semi-precious stones were also cut and carved. Inscribed seals have been recovered in jasper, agate, onyx, jade. opal, amethyst, and chalcedony. The modern method of facet cutting was not used. Instead, the stones were rounded and polished. Frequently they were also engraved and sculptured.

ENOCH (ē'nŭk) ("dedicated"). A pre-flood patriarch who lived a godly life and was translated to heaven at the age of 365 years (Gen. 5:18-24; Heb. 11:5). Jude refers to a prophecy of Enoch (Jude 1:14, 15), which is also recorded in the Book of Enoch.

EPAPHRAS (ĕp'á-frăs). A fellow-laborer of Paul who excelled in intercessory prayers (Col. 4:12).

EPAPHRODITUS (ĕ-păf-rò-dī'tŭs) ("lovely, charming"). A trusted messenger between Paul and the churches (Phil. 2:25; 4:18).

EPHAH (ē'fá). See under "Weights and Measures."

EPHESUS (ĕf'ē-sŭs). The principal city of the Roman province of Asia on the west coast of what is now Asiatic Turkey. The city was located at the mouth of the Cayster River between the mountain ranges of Koressos and the sea. It has been extensively excavated. The Temple of Diana was uncovered about a mile to the northeast. Christianity may well have been introduced to Ephesus by Paul's friends Aquila and Priscilla. Paul made a short visit there himself on his second missionary tour (Acts 18:18, 19). On his third tour he ministered there for over two years (Acts 19:8-10).

EPHOD (ē'fŏd). The linen ephod was apparently a simple, kimono-type article of priestly dress worn by the priests of Nob (1 Sam. 22:18), by Samuel (1 Sam. 2:18), and by David (2 Sam. 6:14). This ordinary ephod is to be distinguished from the high priest's ephod of costly material inwrought with gold, purple, and scarlet (Exod. Chaps. 28, 39). This latter garment reached from the chest to the hips. A special ephod was also used for oracular purposes (1 Sam. 21:9).

EPHRAIM (ē'frá-ĭm) ("doubly fruitful"). (1) The second son of Joseph by Asenath and the progenitor of a tribal family (Gen. 41:52; Num. 1:10). (2) The hill country of Central Palestine, extending from Bethel (12 miles north of Jerusalem) to the plain of Shechem (Josh. 17:15).

EPHRATHAH, EPHRATH (ĕf'rá-tá; ĕf'răth) ("fruitfulness"). One of the wives of Caleb and the mother of Hur (1 Chron. 2:19).

EPHRON (ē'frŏn). A hill or mountainous area between Nephtoah and Kiriath-Jearim (northwest of Jerusalem). The region defined part of the border of Judah (Josh. 15:9).

EPICUREANS (ĕp-ĭ-kŭ-rē'ănz). The founder of this philosophic school, Epicurus (341-270 B.C.), taught that happiness is to be attained by serene detachment which banishes all fear of divine intervention in life or of punishment after death. He conceived the gods as following to perfection the life of serene detachment (including detachment from human beings). Death, according to Epicurus, brings a dispersion to our constituent atoms. Paul encountered devotees of this school at Athens (Acts 17:18-20). It is not surprising that they found Paul's doctrine of the resurrection both strange and unpalatable. A later perversion of the original Epicurean philosophy has given the term "epicure" its modern connotation. (The original Epicureans did not advocate the pursuit of extravagant or illicit pleasure.)

ERASTUS (ê-răs'tŭs) ("beloved"). An assistant whom Paul sent to Macedonia (Acts 19:22; 2 Tim. 4:20). The official at Corinth, a convert of Paul, may be the same person (Rom. 16:23).

ERECH, URUK (ē'rĕk; ōō'rŏok). Modern Warka. It was founded around 4000 B.C. and was the leading city of Sumer and Babylonia. Its archeological finds include ziggurats and early pictograph tablets.

ERIDU (ā'ri-dōō). A city of Sumer and Babylonia. In the Sumerian king list it appears as the oldest city of Sumer. Found in this city (present-day Abu Shahrein) were the earliest writings on clay tablets.

ESARHADDON (ê-sär-hăd'ŏn) ("Asshur has given a brother"). Sennacherib's son and successor on the throne of Assyria, reigning from 680 to 668 B.C. He subdued Egypt and lifted Assyria to the zenith of power.

ESAU (ē'sô) ("hairy"). The elder son of Isaac and the twin brother of Jacob by Rebekah (Gen. 25:21-26). He was a skillful hunter but a secular-minded man, trading his birthright for a fleshly craving (Gen. 25:29-34; Heb. 12:16).

ESDRAELON, PLAIN OF (ĕs-drā-ē'lŏn). See under "Plains."

ESHCOL, BROOK OF (ĕsh'kŏl). A stream and wadi near Hebron where the Hebrew scouts cut down a cluster of grapes (Num. 13:23).

ESSENES (ĕs-sēnz'). A monastic religious order from about the time of Christ. The Essenes were a small sect rather than an influential party like the Pharisees or Sadducees. Philo, Josephus, and Pliny furnished the only sources of information on this reformation group in Judaism until the discovery of the Dead Sea Scrolls in 1947. This group or a similar one is now well-known as the result of the excavations of their headquarters at Qumran (on the northwest shore of the Dead Sea). The recovery of their Book of Discipline has substantiated ancient sources. They retired from society to pursue prayer and the practice of God's laws in order to offset the darkness and evil work in the world.

ESTHER (ĕs'tēr) (Akkadian *ishtar* or Persian *stara*, "star"). A beautiful Jewish maiden who became queen of Persia and thereby saved the Jews in the Empire from destruction. Esther's cousin and former guardian, Mordecai, had aroused the enmity of Haman, the prime minister. Haman goaded the king to authorize the massacre of all Jews in the Empire (Esth. 3:8-15). Mordecai informed Esther of the diabolical plot and urged her to appeal to the king. At the risk of her life Esther interceded (Esth. 4:15 – 5:4), telling the king that the edict would mean the destruction of her and her people. She persuaded her royal husband to issue a new decree which permitted the Jews to take vengeance on their enemies. Meanwhile Haman's wickedness was exposed and he was executed on the gallows which he had prepared for Mordecai. The Jews annihilated their foes and Mordecai became the new prime minister. Then Mordecai and Esther instituted the annual fest of Purim to commemorate Jewish deliverance from destruction (Esth. 9: 20-32).

ETAM (ē'tăm). A rock where Samson hid after slaughtering a number of the Philistines (Judg. 15:8). It is somewhere in the vicinity of Zorah.

ETERNAL LIFE. When Adam sinned, the human race incurred threefold death—spiritual, physical, and eternal (Gen. 2:17). In Adam "all die" (1 Cor. 15:22) in this threefold sense. Unregenerate man is dead spiritually (Eph. 2:1), without contact or fellowship with God. He must also die physically and be eternally separated from God (Rev. 20:11-15). Eternal life "in Christ" abrogates this three-fold death. Spiritual death gives way to spiritual life as a present possession (Rom. 6:23; 1 John 3:14). Physical death is conquered in the resurrection and glorification of the body (1 Cor. 15:50-54) or in the translation of the living at the Lord's coming (1 Thess. 4:13-18). Eternal death is cancelled by eternal life. No one possessing eternal life will ever be cast into eternal hell (Gehenna). Eternal life is as eternal as Christ himself and is imparted to the believer at the new birth (John 3:3-17).

ETHBAAL (ĕth'bá-ăl) ("with him is Baal"). A Phoenician king and father of the infamous Queen Jezebel (1 Kings 16:31).

ETHIOPIA (ê-thĭ-ō'pĭ-à). See "Cush."

ETHNARCH. A Greek term meaning "ruler of the people." It was a title of royalty bestowed upon a client king. It was higher than "tetrarch" but lower than "king" (1 Macc. 14:47). Archelaus, son of Herod the Great, "king" of Judea, was not deemed worthy of the title that his father bore but was appointed merely as an "ethnarch" (Josephus, *Antiquities* XVII: 11,4). Josephus and Matthew used popular terminology in referring to Archelaus as "king" (*Antiquities* XVIII:4,3).

The only actual use of the term "ethnarch" occurs in 2 Corinthians 11:32. This ruler was probably the appointed representative of the Nabatean king Aretas (9 B.C.-A.D. 39), who controlled Damascus. However, if the city was Roman-controlled, the ethnarch was a Nabatean with functions similar to the Jewish ethnarch in Jerusalem.

EUNICE (û-nī'sĕ) ("blessed with victory"). A pious Jewess and the mother of Timothy (2 Tim. 1:5). Godly training by Timothy's mother (and grandmother, Lois) contributed to the stalwart Christian character of the young pastor, whom Paul commended as "my dearly beloved son" (2 Tim. 1:2).

EUODIA (û-ō'dĭ-à) ("good journey, success"). A Christian woman in the church at Philippi. She and Syntyche were advised by Paul to resolve their difficulties and to get along with each other amicably (Phil. 4:2).

EUPHRATES (û-frā'tēz) (Hebrew *Perath*). The largest river in West Asia. It is called "the river" (Deut. 11:24) and flows for 1200 miles to the Persian Gulf from its two main effluents in East Turkey. Along with the Tigris, it has formed the rich alluvial plain of lower Babylonia. Many important cities of antiquity, including Babylon, were situated on its banks in the southern plain, which was the cradle of civilization (cf. Gen. 2:14).

EUTYCHUS (û'tĭ-kŭs) ("happy, fortunate"). A young man of Troas who fell asleep during Paul's long sermon and fell to his death from a window. He was miraculously revived by Paul (Acts 20:7-12).

EVE (ēv) (Hebrew *Hawwah*, "life"). The first woman, named "life" because she was to become the mother of the entire subsequent human race (Gen. 3:20). She was created from man (Gen. 2:21, 22) in order to be "a helper fit for him" (Gen. 2:18, RSV).

EVERLASTING FATHER. An honorific messianic title or appellative. It is literally "Father of Eternity," meaning "the Eternally Existing One" (Isa. 9:6). Eastern kings were also honorifically described as living forever (Dan. 2:4).

EVIL-MERODACH (ē'vĭl-mĕ-rō'dăk) (Akkadian *Amel-Marduk*, "man of Marduk"). Nebuchadnezzar's son and successor (562-560 B.C.). He released Jehoiachin of Judah from a 37-year imprisonment (2 Kings 25:27-30; Jer. 52:31-34). This event is corroborated by cuneiform records of the era. Evil-Merodach was slain in a palace coup and was succeeded in the throne by Neriglissar, the chief conspirator.

EXORCISM. Expulsion of demons by the power of God through the name of Christ can be Satanically imitated by its occult counterpart, called exorcism. The exorcist (Matt. 12:27; Acts 19:13) casts out demons by magical conjurations, incantations, and occult rigmaroles. The dispossessions are not genuine; Satan does not actually cast out his own demons (cf. Matt. 12:22-30) but simply relocates and regroups them for further attacks. But Christ practiced genuine demon expulsion (Mark 5:1-13), as did the Apostles and other early Christians.

EZEKIEL (ė-zēk'yĕl) ("God strengthens"). One of the major prophets of the Old Testament. Ezekiel prophesied in Babylonian exile, about 593 to 571 B.C. (Ezek. 1:1-3). Before the fall of Jerusalem he predicted the same fate for the wicked city as had Jeremiah (Ezek. Chaps. 1-24). He stressed the Lord's justification in sending his people into exile (cf. Ezek.

18:25-30; 33:17-20). His great prophecies center in hopeful predictions, and include a full vision of the final restoration of Israel (Ezek. Chaps. 33-48).

EZION-GEBER (ē'zĭ-ŏn-gē'bĕr). See "Elath."

EZRA (ĕz'ra) ("help"). A learned scribe of priestly descent who led one of the contingents of Jews returning from exile in about 458 B.C. (before Nehemiah rebuilt the walls in 445 B.C.). He labored to eliminate all paganistic influences from Jewish life (see books of Ezra and Nehemiah). Ezra is credited with important influence in determining the canonicity of certain Old Testament books.

FADUS, CUSPIUS. The Roman procurator of Judea after the death of Agrippa I in A.D. 44. He ruthlessly suppressed patriotic outbreaks.

FAIR HAVENS. A small bay situated on the south coast of Crete a few miles east of Cape Matala (Acts 27:8). It was the last place Paul's ship could stay in order to avoid the northwest wind.

FAITH. In its simplest concept faith is personal confidence in God. It brings with it the blessing of honoring God. Faith can be exercised in several important ways. 1) *Saving faith* is the Spirit-induced confidence which causes a person to trust Christ as his sin-bearer (Acts 16:31; Eph. 2:8, 9). 2) *Serving faith* is the confidence in God which prompts a believer to yield his redeemed life to God's will (Rom. 12:1, 2). 3) *Sanctifying faith* denotes the believer's confidence in

Christ as his source of sustaining grace and divine power (Rom. 6:11). 4) *Responsive faith* is a working belief which produces the fruit of the Spirit (Gal. 5:22, 23). 5) *Creedal or doctrinal faith* is trust in the body of revealed truth (1 Cor. 16: 13; Col. 1:23; 2:7; Jude 1:3). Faith pleases God and frees him to act on behalf of those who honor him by believing his Word (Heb. 11:6). See also "Belief."

FALL OF MAN. By disobeying God mankind fell from a state of innocence and incurred threefold death—immediate spiritual death, gradual physical death, and eventual eternal death (Gen. 2:17; 3: 1-15; 5:5; Rev. 19:20; 20:10, 14, 15). By Adam's sin all mankind came under the power of sin and death (Rom. 5:12; 1 Cor. 15:21, 22). Men can be released from this state of alienation and condemnation only by faith in Christ's atoning death on

"Adam and Eve Seal" found near Nineveh—dated by A.E. Speiser at about 3500 B.C. (*UMP photo*)

the cross (Rom. 5:13-21). See also "A-tonement" and "Redemption."

FALLOW DEER (Hebrew *yahmūr*, "brown goat"). In North Galilee the name *yahmūr* is still given to the roebuck (*Capreolus capraea* or *Cervus capreolus*). It is a dark reddish-brown in summer and a yellowish-gray in winter, with a large patch of white on the rump. It has antlers with three points and casts its horns every year. It is common in Europe and Asia. It was a ceremonially clean animal and was used for food (Deut. 14:5; 1 Kings 4:23). Some scholars identify the *yahmūr* with the bubale, a bovine antelope whose flesh is a delicacy.

FAMILY, JEWISH. As a result of common descent from Abraham and close tribal and inter-tribal unity, the family unit was viewed by the ancient Hebrews as the compact and basic institution of their society. The Hebrew concept of a house always included the thought of a family. A single word was used to designate both the dwelling and its inhabitants (see Genesis 46:31). In its original connotation the word embraced the concept of something built up or built together, each member being considered a vital and inseparable part of the structure (Gen. 16:2; 30:3; Deut. 25:9). The structure was in turn considered an inseparable part of the larger family unit, the clan and the tribe.

In harmony with their high view of the family, the Hebrews regarded children as one of life's greatest blessings (Psa. 113: 9; 127:3-5). They were earnestly prayed for when not given, and their birth occasioned a time of great rejoicing (Gen. 15: 2-5; 1 Sam. 1; Ruth 4:11). The hope of Israel lay in the birth of a future child who would be the Savior, the promised "Seed of the woman" (Gen. 3:15; Isa. 9: 6, 7).

The consideration which the Bible gives to children and childhood is both significant and delightful. It shows up conspicuously against the dark background of compassionless paganism, where children were often exposed or killed, frequently in the name of religion. Parental love toward offspring gilds the pages of Scripture (Gen. 37:34, 35; 2 Sam. 19:4; cf. Psa. 103:13). But this affection was not a weak indulgence. Rigorous discipline and training were part and parcel of it (Prov. 10:1; 13:24; 23:14; 29:15) on the part of both the parents and the state (Exod. 13:8; Deut. 4:9; 6:7; 11:19; 31:13). The fundamental philosophy of education was that "the fear of the Lord is the beginning of wisdom" (Prov. 1:7; 9:10). The mother and grandmother were featured in this godly training (cf. 2 Tim. 1:5; 3:15).

The Jewish firstborn son had a privileged position, even during the father's lifetime (Gen. 43:33). At his father's death he received twice as much of the father's estate as any other child (Deut. 21:17). He also assumed the position of father and head of family. Along with these rights went the duty of providing for the mother, if living, as well as other dependent members of the household. When the father acted as family priest the firstborn also inherited this function (Gen. 27:29; Deut. 21:17; cf. Num. 3:41).

The firstborn son might sell his birthright if he desired (Gen. 25:29-34; Heb. 12:16, 17). In such a case the father would direct how his property was to be distributed after his decease. The idea of a will in a technical sense is not mentioned until the Epistle to the Galatians (Gal. 3:15).

Ordinarily daughters did not inherit property. It was expected that they would be provided for by the eldest brother or by a husband (Gen. 31:14, 15). When there were no male children, daughters became joint-heirs of their father's estate if they did not marry outside the family line.

Even then they could sometimes claim their portion if the husband assumed the family name of his wife. When a family consisted only of unmarried daughters their names were entered in the registers of families as representatives of the father's house (Num. 27:1-11).

FARMER. See "Agriculturalist."

FATHERHOOD OF GOD. God is the Father of our Lord Jesus Christ (2 Cor. 1:3) in the sense that Christ is the eternal Son of the Father with respect to his deity. He is said to be "the God . . . of our Lord Jesus Christ" (John 20:17; 2 Cor. 11:31; Eph. 1:3; 1 Pet. 1:3). God is also the Father of all men in the restricted sense of being their Creator (Luke 3:38; Acts 17:28). Spiritually the unsaved are "children of the devil" (John 8:44). God's covenant relation to the elect nation Israel is prefigured in a Father-son relationship (Exod. 4:22; Deut. 32:6; Isa. 63:16; 64:8).

FATHOM. See under "Weights and Measures."

FEAST OF TABERNACLES. See "Booths, Feast of."

FELIX, ANTONIUS (fē'lĭx). The Roman procurator of Judea from A.D. 52 to 59. He married Drusilla, Herod Agrippa I's daughter. Nero recalled him because of his greed and cruelty. He kept Paul in prison at Caesarea because no bribe was offered (Acts 23, 24).

FESTUS, PORCIUS (fĕs'tŭs, pôr'shĭ-ŭs). The Roman procurator of Judea from A.D. 60 to 62. Paul refused his proposal to be tried at Jerusalem and instead appealed to Caesar (Acts 25). Festus was one of the better governors.

FIG TREE. One of the most popular trees because of its delicious fruit and heavy shade. The common species (*Ficus carica*, Num. 13:23; 20:5; Matt. 7:16) was extensively cultivated in Palestine in biblical times. To "sit under one's vine and fig tree" symbolized prosperity and security (1 Kings 4:25; Mic. 4:4; Zech. 3:10). The tree bears successively three kinds of fruit: 1) the late (autumn) figs (Jer. 8:13; 29:17), the main crop from August until winter; 2) the green or winter figs (Song 2:13; Rev. 6:13), which, in the absence of ripening weather, spend the winter on the branches and ripen in the spring; and

Fig tree with its first fruit (© *MPS*)

3) the first-ripe figs (Isa. 28:4; Jer. 24:2; Hos. 9:10; Mic. 7:1; Nah. 3:12), the most delicious figs, those that cling to the tree and ripen in the summer from June onward. Apparently a healthy tree had fruit on it for about ten months. Jesus evidently expected green figs on the tree he cursed (Matt. 21:18, 19).

FINGER RING. This was properly the signet-ring of a king, taken from the hand and given as a token of authority (Gen. 41:42; Esth. 3:10; 8:2). It was frequently employed in the sealing of official documents and messages (Esth. 3:12; 8:8, 10). Closely related to it was the seal ring, *hotham*, which bore the name of the wearer and was usually carried on a cord around the neck (Gen. 38:18). It was sometimes also worn on the hand (Jer. 22:24). This was the *sphragis* of the New Testament (Rom. 4:11; 1 Cor. 9:2; 2 Tim. 2:19; Rev. 5:1, 2; 6:1-12; 7:2; 8:1; 9:4).

FIR TREE (Hebrew *berosh*, botanically in the genus *Pinus*). Two varieties of these evergreen, cone-bearing trees are native to the hills of Palestine and Lebanon— *Pinus brutia* and *Pinus halepensis*. The latter is called the Syrian or Aleppo pine (Isa. 41:19; 55:13). In Gilead there are extensive forests of *Pinus carica* on the higher elevations. The stone pine (*Pinus maratima*) grows on the coast and in sandy plains and has edible seeds. This is probably the tree referred to in Hosea 14:8. The true fir of the region is *Abies cili-*

cica, growing in the higher heights of Lebanon (2 Sam. 6:5; Song 1:17; 1 Kings 5:8; Isa. 14:8; Zech. 11:2). It was used (along with cedar) in Solomon's Temple (1 Kings 5:8), for ship planks (Ezek. 27:5), and for musical instruments (2 Sam. 6:5).

FISH. Fish constituted an important part of the diet of the people of Bible lands. While in Egypt Israel ate fish freely (Num. 11:5). The Nile and its several branches in the Delta yielded a variety of fish (Isa. 19:8). Fishing also constituted an important industry in the Mediterranean, though it was largely in the hands of the Phoenicians in the north (Neh. 13:16) and the Philistines in the south. The fishing industry of Palestine centered in the Sea of Galilee, which swarmed with many varieties of fish. Fish were sold at Jerusalem (Neh. 13:16) and elsewhere. Fishing figures prominently in the life of our Lord and his disciples (Mark 1:16-20; Luke 5:4-7; John 21:1-14).

FISHERMAN. Fish abounded in Egypt (Num. 11:5). A tomb painting from Thebes from the fifteenth century B.C. shows an Egyptian dignitary spearing fish in the marshes with a two-pronged lance from a papyrus skiff. The Sea of Galilee swarmed with fish (Luke 5:6). Even today 24 species abound.

At least seven of Jesus' disciples were fishermen (Matt. 4:18, 21; John 1:44; 21:2). On the Sea of Galilee they used small boats propelled by oars (John 6:19) and probably sails as well. Night fishing was common (Luke 5:5; John 21:3). Nets were frequently used (Matt. 4:18; Luke 5:4). Sometimes nets were dragged to the shore (Matt. 13:48; John 21:8). The fish were then sorted and the unwanted ones thrown away (Matt. 13:48).

FISH MERCHANT. The fisherman sold his catch to a trader. At Jerusalem there was a Fish Gate, through which traders brought their fish to sell to the people (Zeph. 1:10). Fish also abounded at Tyre, and Tyrian fish merchants lived in Jerusalem in post-exilic times (Neh. 13:16). Often the fish were sold roasted rather than fresh. The salting and drying of fish in preparation for shipment to distant places became a flourishing industry, employing many workers. The fish

which the Tyrians sold in Jerusalem and the fish from the Lake of Galilee were in all probability prepared in this way. The fish used to feed the five thousand and the four thousand (Matt. 14:15-21; 15:32-38) were probably the dried and salted variety.

FLAGS. Reeds growing by the brink of the Nile River (Hebrew *suph,* Exod. 2:3, 5; Isa. 19:6). The word denotes aquatic vegetation, whether seaweeds (Jonah 2:5) or freshwater reeds. Moses' mother made the tiny boat for her son out of "bulrushes" or papyrus. The Red Sea in Hebrew is *yam suph,* "Sea of Reeds." Another Hebrew word is used in Job 8:11 to denote flags or reeds, and probably also aquatic vegetation in a general sense. See also "Papyrus."

FLAX. A small plant cultivated for its bark (which furnishes the fiber out of which linen is woven) and for its seeds (out of which linseed oil is extracted—Isa. 42:3; Matt. 12:20). The flax plant was grown in Egypt and elsewhere (Exod. 9:31). Its fine fibers were woven like wool (Isa. 19:9; Prov. 31:13; Hos. 2:5). Its stalks were spread on rooftops to dry in the sun (Josh. 2:6).

FLEA. A small flying insect mentioned in 1 Samuel 24:14 and 26:20. The flea is parasitic on man and beast and is an aggravating pest in Palestine.

FLESH. The word "flesh" has two general meanings in Scripture. It sometimes refers simply to the human body (John 3:6; 6:51; 1 Cor. 15:39; Eph. 5:31). Frequently, however, it refers to the sin nature acting within the human body. At conversion the believer receives a new nature, but the old nature is never eradicated. However, as the Christian yields to the indwelling Holy Spirit the fruit of the Spirit is produced in his life, thereby displacing the strong sinful desires of the old Adamic nature (Gal. 5:16-26).

FLORUS, GESSIUS. The Roman procurator from A.D. 64 to 66. His unprincipled conduct precipitated open revolt against Roman rule.

FLY. A two-winged insect of the order *Diptera,* especially the domestic fly, *Musca domestica.* The fly was so annoying that the people of Ekron worshiped a deity which they called Baal-zebub or "lord of flies" because he was considered able to ward them off (2 Kings 1:2). The dog-fly, a voracious biting insect of Egypt, is mentioned in Exodus 8:21 and Psalm 105:31.

FOREKNOWLEDGE. God's prior, determinative knowledge of all future events. The biblical concept of foreknowledge emphasizes God's own plan for man's future rather than God's prior knowledge of man's free choices (cf. Job 23:13, 14; Psa. 139:1-24; Jer. 1:5; Acts 2:23; 15:18; Rom. 8:28, 29; 1 Pet. 1:2).

FOREST. During the Middle Bronze Age (2000-1500 B.C.) the hill country of Palestine was covered with forests. In later centuries of Israelite occupation some of this forest land was cleared for settlements and farming. Still, considerable areas of woodland remained intact. One wooded area stretched from the Mediterranean Sea to the hill country of Ephraim (Josh. 17:15, 18). Another was located in Judah (1 Sam. 22:5). "The Forest of Ephraim" is specifically named (2 Sam. 18:6) and is generally supposed to have been in Transjordan near Mahanaim. The most famous forests were in Lebanon, whose renowned firs and cedars supplied woods for temples and kings' palaces (1 Kings 7:2). Part of the Jordan Valley was a luxuriant jungle with abundant wildlife. Some of the more significant forests of Scripture are described below.

Arabia, Forest in (Isa. 21:13). In this huge peninsula rainfall was scarce; even in the southwest, with its higher rainfall, forests were rare, being replaced by thickets of scrub and small trees. Arabia consists of the huge area bounded by the Fertile Crescent on the north, the Indian Ocean on the south, the Red Sea on the west, and the Persian Gulf and the Gulf of Oman on the east.

Beth-aven, Wood near (1 Sam. 14:25). A place where the Israelites collected honey. Beth-aven ("house of nothingness or idolatry") was located in the territory of Benjamin, near Ali, east of Bethel (Josh. 7:2), and west of Michmash (1 Sam. 13:5; cf. 14:23). It lay on the border of the wilderness (Josh. 18:12), which consisted of a heavily wooded area. This was possibly near the forest between Jericho and Beth-

el, where bears attacked the children who taunted the prophet Elisha (2 Kings 2:24).

Carmel, Forest of (2 Kings 19:23). Mount Carmel is the 1740-foot-high main ridge at the northwest end of a range of hills which extends southeast from the Bay of Acre to the plain of Dothan. Anciently it was densely vegetated, with its luxuriant growth reflected in Amos 1:2 and 9:3, Micah 7:14, and Nahum 1:4. In Song of Solomon 7:5 "the forest of Carmel" is an apt figure for thick, bushy hair. Parts of the forest were apparently cultivated to the summit with fruit trees and orchards (Isa. 33:9; 35:2; Jer. 50:19). The forest probably consisted chiefly of fruit trees (Mic. 7:14), although thickets of prickly oak and juniper covered the hills of the Carmel range.

Ephraim, Wood of (2 Sam. 18:6). The site of the battle between King David's men and Absalom's rebels. It was evidently located in Transjordan in the general vicinity of Mahanaim of Gilead (2 Sam. 17:24).

Forest of the South (Ezek. 20:45-49). The forest land of Judah, in which the Lord promised to kindle a fire to devour "every green tree and every dry tree" (the trees representing people). These forests in the mountains of Judah are referred to in 2 Chronicles 27:4 as the place where King Jotham built forts.

Lebanon, Forest of (2 Kings 19:23). The Lebanon mountains consist of two ranges running north and south, and are most famous for their forests of gigantic cedars. Fir trees and cypresses also abounded here (1 Kings 5:6-10; 2 Kings 19:23; Isa. 60:13; Zech. 11:1). Lebanon supplied timber for kings' palaces, temples, and masts for Phoenician ships. Lebanon formed the northwest boundary of the Promised Land (Deut. 1:7).

FORGIVENESS. During the Old Testament period sins were "covered" in anticipation of Christ's coming sacrifice (Acts 17:30; Rom. 3:25). Christ's great work of atonement was prefigured by the animal sacrifices (Heb. 9:13, 14). In this New Testament era the believer enjoys full forgiveness the moment he places his faith in Christ (Acts 13:38, 39). The believer never faces condemnation, for all his trespasses—past, present, and future—have been forgiven (John 3:18; 5: 24; Col. 2:13). However, when a believer sins he forfeits *fellowship* with the Father and the Son. He must accordingly confess his sin and claim the forgiveness which the Father extends (1 John 1:9 – 2: 2).

If a believer persists in unconfessed sin he will be chastised by the Father, though not condemned with the world (1 Cor. 11:31, 32). The ultimate in God's chastening is "the sin unto (physical) death" (1 John 5:16; cf. John 15:2; 1 Cor. 11:30). In this case God removes the severely sinning saint from this life so that he will not be "condemned with the world" (1 Cor. 11:31, 32).

The unpardonable sin was attributing to Satan the power of the Holy Spirit in the earthly ministry of Christ (Matt. 12: 22-32). This sin is not possible now and is inconsonant with the gospel of "whosoever will." Rejecting Christ as Savior is the nearest present-day equivalent.

FOX. Several species of foxes and the closely-related jackal are found in Palestine. They are members of the *Canidae* or dog family. Foxes usually remain solitary, while jackals run in packs. The Hebrew term *shucal* and the Greek term *alōpēx* apparently include both of these species. These animals eat fruit and vegetables, notably grapes (Song 2:15). It is probable that the 300 animals caught by Samson were jackals (Judg. 15:4), since foxes are extremely difficult to catch. The jackal devours carrion (Psa. 63:10), which the fox is loathe to do. See also "Jackal."

FRANKINCENSE. A white, aromatic gum resin with an odor similar to that of balsam, especially when burnt. The frankincense tree consists of a number of species, several native to India and others coming from the Somali coast of Africa and South Arabia. It was an ingredient in the holy anointing oil (Exod. 30:34) and the meal offerings (Lev. 2:1, 2). Pure frankincense was poured on the showbread (Lev. 24:7; 1 Chron. 9:29). Frankincense was imported to Palestine from Arabia (Isa. 60:6; Jer. 6:20).

FRINGED GARMENT. The common robe of the ancient East had a fringed edge, in which the Israelites were required to insert a blue thread to remind them that they were God's people. The Pharisees ceremoniously enlarged these fringes (Matt. 23:5).

FROG. An amphibious animal (Exod. 8:3). The frog of the Old Testament is probably *Rana punctata*, the spotted frog of Egypt. In Revelation 16:13, 14 the noisy, croaking frogs represent demonic agencies that stir up wicked men to fight against God at Armageddon.

FRUITBEARING. Fruitfulness is the result of union with Christ (John 15:1-5). This union is symbolized by the vine and the branches. The believer is "in Christ" much as a branch is in the vine. Three conditions of fruitbearing are indicated: 1) cleansing or pruning (John 15:2, 3); 2) abiding (John 15:4), that is, relying on Christ. In this condition the life of Christ flows through the believer much as the life of the vine enters the branches; and 3) obedience to Christ's commandments (John 15:10, 12, 14).

FULLER. Before fabrics were dyed it was necessary to cleanse their fibers of natural oils or gums. This cleansing and bleaching process was the duty of the fuller. He worked near a supply of water so that fabrics could be cleansed by treading them on stones submerged in water. For this reason the fuller was called a "trampler" (Hebrew *kabas*). Several references to the "fuller's field" at Jerusalem occur in the Bible (2 Kings 18:17; Isa. 7:3; 36:2).

For cleansing, natron or niter was sometimes imported from Egypt. It was mixed with white clay and used as soap (Prov. 25:20; Jer. 2:22). Alkali was supplied by burning the soda plant (*Salsola kali*). Malachi refers to "fuller's soap" (Mal. 3:2; cf. Mark 9:3).

FUNERALS, JEWISH. It was customary for Hebrews to take formal and affectionate leave of those about to die (Gen. 49). The lifeless body was then washed and wrapped in a linen cloth (Matt. 27:59; John 11:44). Sweet-smelling spices were laid in the folds of the enveloping shroud. This was intended to offset any odor produced by rapid decay of the unembalmed body. It also served as a medium for the expression of love and respect, much as flowers do today.

Embalming was not ordinarily practiced among the Hebrews (Gen. 50:2, 26). Burial in the ground or, if possible, in a rock tomb usually took place on the same day as death. This was necessitated by the rapid deterioration of the unembalmed corpse and the fact that the dead body was ceremonially defiling (Num. 19:11-16). The corpse was usually carried to its place of interment on a bier attended by a procession in which hired mourners took part.

The Israelites, in contrast to the Greeks and Romans, did not practice cremation. They interred but did not burn their dead, in harmony with the Egyptians and with other Semites. The bones of Saul and his sons were burned only to preserve their bodies from insult. After being reduced to ashes they were respectfully buried (1 Sam. 31:8-13). Exposing corpses to birds of prey was regarded as the acme of indignity (1 Kings 14:11; Jer. 16:4). Rizpah, Saul's concubine, watched the bodies of his seven sons in order to prevent this disgrace from befalling them (2 Sam. 21:10).

The Hebrews often buried entire families in the same tomb (Gen. 47:29, 30; Judg. 8:32; 16:31; Ruth 1:17). Thus Joseph of Arimathaea underwent a significant sacrifice in offering his family sepulchre as a place of interment for the body of Jesus (Matt. 27:57-60). The Hebrews distinguished clearly between the tomb of the body and the spirit world where the soul went (Gen. 25:8). Rock tombs were sealed with huge stones (Mark 16:1-4; John 20:1).

Lamentation for the dead began at the moment of death and continued unabated until after the burial or entombment. Hired professional mourners, generally women, joined their lamentations with the family and friends (Mark 5:38, 39). They wept, uttered cries of grief, beat their bodies, pulled out their hair, threw dust on their heads, tore their garments, put on sackcloth, and fasted (Gen. 37:34; 2 Sam. 13:31; 19:4).

Expressly forbidden to both priests (Lev. 21:5) and the people at large (Lev. 19:27, 28; Deut. 14:1) were bodily lacerations, ritualistically trimmed beards, baldness between the eyes, and "rounded" (mutilated) corners of the head.

The usual period of mourning lasted seven days (Gen. 50:10), although in unusual cases it might be as long as thirty days, as in the death of Aaron (Num. 20:28, 29) and Moses (Deut. 34:5-8). The custom of making an offering for the dead appears first in an apocryphal book in the second century B.C. (2 Macc. 12: 43).

FURLONG. See under "Weights and Measures."

GAASH, BROOKS OF (gā'ăsh). Seasonal streams apparently issuing from Mount Gaash near Timnath-Serah in the mountains of Ephraim. One of David's heroes came from this region (2 Sam. 23:30).

GABBATHA (găb'à-thà). A place in Jerusalem called "the Pavement" (Greek *lithostrotos* — John 19:13). It was located at or near the Tower of Antonia, north-west of the Temple area. It is buried beneath the present-day Church of the Daughters of Zion.

GAD (găd). Jacob's seventh son and a progenitor of one of the tribes of Israel (Gen. 30:10, 11; 46:16; 49:19).

GADARA (găd'ȧ-rȧ). A locality near the southeast shore of the Lake of Galilee in the district of Gadara. It lay six miles southeast of the Lake near the gorge of the Yarmuk. It was in this town that Jesus healed two demon-possessed men (Matt. 8:28-34; Mark 5:1-17; Luke 8:26-37).

GAIUS CALIGULA (gā'yŭs kȧ-lĭg'ū-lȧ). The Roman Emperor from A.D. 37 to 41. He was an eccentric, impious ruler who claimed to be divine and foolishly attempted to have his statue erected in the Jewish Temple at Jerusalem. His career came to an early end by assassination.

GALATIANS (gȧ-lā'shĭ-ȧns). A Celtic tribe that invaded Asia Minor in the third century B.C. Called Gauls, these Indo-European people gradually settled in the territory in which were located the old Phrygian cities of Pessinus and Tavium. Ancyra (modern Ankara) became their capital. Under Roman rule the Galatians were given autonomy. During the reign of their last king, Amyntas (25 B.C.), their territory was greatly enlarged on the south to include part of Phrygia, Pisidea, Lycaonia and Isauria. After the death of Amyntas this enlarged region was made a Roman province. In 7 B.C. still other additions were made. In Paul's day the term "Galatia" referred to both the original Galatic region and the larger territory of the Roman Province.

GALBANUM (găl'bȧ-nŭm). A fragrant spice which constituted one of the four ingredients of the holy incense (Exod. 30:34). It was made from the gum of two umbelliferous plants native to Persia.

GALILEE, SEA OF (găl'ĭ-lė). Palestine's largest lake, located near the northeast corner of the country along the Jordan River. It is also called "the lake of Gennesaret" (Luke 5:1) and "the sea of Tiberias" (John 21:1). This latter name was derived from the city of Tiberias, which had been founded by Herod Antipas on

Calm moments on the Sea of Galilee (© *MPS*)

the western shore of the lake about A.D. 20. In Old Testament times the lake was named "the sea of Chinneroth." The lake is about 13 miles long, 7 miles across at its widest point, and 695 feet below sea level. It is mentioned a number of times in the Gospels in connection with the activities of Christ and his disciples. See also "Chinneroth."

GALL (Hebrew *rōsh*, Greek *cholē*). A bitter, poisonous herb (Deut. 29:18; 32:32) that grew commonly in the fields (Hos. 10:4). A drink of gall water is compared to a severe punishment (Jer. 8:14; 9:15; 23:15). While hanging on the Cross, Christ was offered sour wine mixed with gall (Matt. 27:34; Mark 15:36; Luke 23:36; John 19:29, 30; cf. Psa. 69:21).

GALLIO (găl'ĭ-ō). The Roman proconsul of Achaia at the time of Paul's first visit to Corinth (A.D. 51-52). Paul was accused before him but was acquitted. Gallio exhibited indifference regarding the Jews' hatred of the Apostle (Acts 18:12-17).

GAMALIEL (gȧ-mā'lĭ-ĕl) ("God has rewarded"). A renowned doctor of Jewish law (Acts 5:34) who had instructed Saul of Tarsus (Acts 22:3). He showed great wisdom and moderation in opposing persecution of the apostles. If their work were simply man's, he counseled, it would fail. If it were from God, opposition to it would be vain and wicked (Acts 5:34-40). It is possible that he was a secret believer in Christ (cf. John 12:42, 43).

GAMES, JEWISH. There is little indication that the Hebrews indulged to any great extent in diversion for its own sake. As a God-fearing and largely pastoral and agricultural people, they had little time or money during most of their history to engage in those pastimes that have corrupted more affluent pagan societies. What leisure the Israelites enjoyed was to a large extent expended on their religious activities and sacred festivals. Their social life was distinctly home- and God-centered, in line with their divine calling and mission.

Simple home pleasures included riddle-telling and witty repartee. Ballplaying and other games known to have been played in Egypt must at least occasionally have been enjoyed in Israel (cf. Isa. 22: 18). Jewish children played various youthful games (Zech. 8:5; Matt. 11:16, 17; Luke 7:31, 32). In David's time archery was a pastime for royal youths and others (1 Sam. 20:20; Job 16:12, 13).

Public games, on the other hand, were not welcomed by the Jews. The introduction of Greek sports and the gymnasium during the Maccabean era was resisted as an insult to the faith of their fathers (1 Macc. 1:14; 2 Macc. 4:12-14). The Apostle Paul refers to the Greek games for purposes of illustration, especially boxing and the foot race (1 Cor. 9:24-27; Phil. 3:14; 2 Tim. 2:5; 4:7, 8). He also makes reference to the gladiatorial contests, which were a common diversion of the debauched pagan society of the first century A.D.

GARDENER. Kings, courtiers, and people of nobility had palaces and estates that called for large numbers of workers skilled in all phases of horticulture. Spices and choice plants graced the gardens of the wealthy (Song 5:1; 6:2, 11), which were customarily walled (Song 4: 12) and often graced by a summerhouse (2 Kings 9:27). The palace at Jerusalem had the well-known "king's garden" (2 Kings 25:4; Jer. 39:4; 52:7; Neh. 3:15). Sumptuous pleasure gardens surrounded the Persian royal palaces (Esth. 1:5; 7:7, 8).

Fruit orchards, vegetable gardens, vineyards, and olive yards were often included in a pleasure garden (1 Kings 21:2; Amos 4:9; 9:14; Song 4:16; Eccl. 2:5). Even private citizens often had well-landscaped estates. Egyptian and Mesopotamian kings had splendid yards. The Canaanite kings of Ugarit had a fine garden gracing an inner court of the palace in the fourteenth and thirteenth centuries B.C.

GARLIC. A bulbous, onion-like plant which was popular in Egypt (Num. 11:5). It belongs to the onion family but has a stronger scent and flavor than the onion. It was eaten by the poor as a relish.

GATH (găth). One of the five Philistine cities (Josh. 13:3; 1 Sam. 17:4; 21:10; 2 Sam. 1:20; 2 Kings 12:17; Mic. 1:10). It was probably northwest of Lachish.

GAZA (gā'zä). One of the five Philistine cities (Gen. 10:19; Josh. 11:22; 13:3). Although it had been reckoned to Judah (Josh. 15:47), it was in Philistine hands again by the time of the Judges (Judg. 16: 21; 1 Sam. 6:17). In New Testament times it was an independent city (Acts 8: 26). It is present-day el-Gazzeh.

GAZELLE. A small antelope, the *Gazella dorcas*. It was ceremonially clean (Deut. 12:22; 14:5), was hunted (Prov. 6:5; Isa. 13:14), and was extremely fleet-footed (2 Sam. 2:18). It possessed great beauty and grace (Song 2:9; 8:14) and was very timid. It is found in Syria, Egypt, and Arabia.

GEBAL (gē'băl). A Phoenician seaport on a bluff overlooking the Mediterranean Sea north of Sidon. It adjoins the Lebanese village of Jebeil. The Greeks named the city Byblus ("papyrus"), for here they saw scrolls made from imported Egyptian papyrus reeds. The territory of the Gebalites is mentioned in Joshua 13: 5. Its stonemasons were employed by Solomon (1 Kings 5:18, RSV). Their shipbuilders were skillful in caulking (Ezek. 27:9).

GEDALIAH (gĕd-à-lī'à) ("the Lord is great"). The appointed governor of Judah after the fall of Jerusalem. He resided at Mizpah, where he was treacherously assassinated (2 Kings 25:22-26).

GEHAZI (gė-hā'zī) ("valley of vision"). Elisha's servant, who proved to be unholy and avaricious (2 Kings 5:20-27), in contrast to his master, who was dedicated and holy.

GEHENNA (gė-hĕn'à). The Aramaic form of the Hebrew word *Gehinnom*, "the Valley of Hinnom" (also called *Tophet*). This valley lay southwest of Jerusalem and was notorious as a place where children had been burned as sacrifices to

Moloch. Later the place was made a dumping ground for offal and a burning ground for garbage (cf. Mark 9:44, 46, 48). The valley came to symbolize the place of eternal punishment for the wicked. Theologically, "Gehenna" is identical in meaning with "the lake of fire," the eternal prison of the wicked (Rev. 19:20; 20:10, 14, 15).

GENTILES. A biblical term which refers to non-Jewish nations and individuals. God's purpose in this age is to "visit the Gentiles to take out of them a people for his name" (Acts 15:14). These, together with converted Jews, form the Church, the "body of Christ." The "fullness of the Gentiles" is the completion of this purpose—the time when the last member of the true church will have been called out (Rom. 11:25; 1 Cor. 12:12, 13; Eph. 4:11-13). The "times of the Gentiles" (Luke 21:24) covers the extended period from Judah's captivity (to Nebuchadnezzar in 605 B.C.) until the second advent of Christ and the inauguration of the kingdom age. The judgment of individual Gentiles will take place at Christ's return to establish his kingdom over Israel (Matt. 25:31-46).

GERAR (gē'rär). An ancient town south of Gaza (Gen. 10:19) where Abraham and Isaac lived (Gen. Chaps. 20, 21, 26). The site is identified with present-day Tell Jemmeh, eight miles south of Gaza.

Mount Gerizim towers over ruins of Shechem. (© MPS)

GERIZIM (gĕr'ĭ-zĭm). The mountain which forms the south boundary of the valley in which Nablus (ancient Shechem) lies. Mount Gerizim and the more elevated Mount Ebal face each other. When the Israelites conquered Central Palestine, Joshua carried out the directions of Moses, placing half of the tribes in front of Mount Gerizim in order to pronounce blessings and the other half in front of Mount Ebal in order to pronounce curses (Deut. 11:29, 30; 27:11-26). The erection of a Temple there in the fourth century B.C. made Gerizim a holy mountain of the Samaritans.

GEZER (gē'zēr). A Canaanite city (Josh. 10:33) in Ephraim (Josh. 16:10). It was captured by the Egyptians and presented to Solomon (1 Kings 9:15-17). It is present-day Tell Jezer, which has been excavated. It lies 23 miles west-northwest of Jerusalem in the low country just east of Gibbethon. Excavations have uncovered levels from Chalcolithic to Maccabean times. The Greek form of the name is Gazara (1 Macc. 4:15).

GIBBETHON (gĭb'ĕ-thŏn). A town in the original territory of Dan (Josh. 19:44). It was a Levitical city (Josh. 21:23). It later fell into Philistine hands (1 Kings 15:27; 16:15, 17).

GIBEAH (gĭb'ĕ-à). The capital of Saul's kingdom (1 Sam. 10:26; 15:34). Excavations reveal that the town which existed during the period of the Judges was destroyed about 1100 B.C. (compare Judges 19 and 20). Saul's fortress was destroyed about 1100 B.C. The present-day site is Tell el-Ful, about four miles north of Jerusalem.

GIBEON (gĭb'ĕ-ŏn). A Canaanite town (Josh. 9:3; 10:2) and the scene of Joshua's great victory (Josh. 10:1-14). It had a notable pool (2 Sam. 2:13). Illegitimate sacrifices were offered at its altar (1 Kings 3:4). The site exists today as El-Jib, about 11 miles northwest of Jerusalem.

GIDEON (gĭd'ĕ-ŏn) ("hewer, feller"). A reformer, Baal exterminator, deliverer, and judge of Israel (Judg. 6:11—8:35). Relying upon the Lord, he routed the invading Amalekites and won a great victory with only 300 soldiers (Josh. 7:1-25).

GIER-EAGLE (Hebrew rāhām). Apparently the Egyptian vulture (Neophron percnopterus). It was common in Palestine, where it breeds during its northern migration. It was ceremonially unclean (Lev. 11:18; Deut. 14:17).

GIFTS OF THE SPIRIT. Sovereign bestowments of the Holy Spirit upon individual believers in the church. They are given in order to produce various spiritual ministries. Nine of these gifts operated in the early church before the New Testament was written. These are specified in 1 Corinthians 12:7-11. Three of these—direct inspirational prophecies, supernatural languages, and direct inspirational knowledge (1 Cor. 13:8)—were required only temporarily. Their need disappeared after the New Testament was completed. Thus the Apostle Paul explained that these temporary gifts would be superseded by "the completed (final) thing" (the completed New Testament) and would then pass out of use (1 Cor. 13:10-13). First Corinthians 14 regulated the use of these gifts in the early church.

GIHON (gī'hŏn). (1) A river associated with the Garden of Eden. It was presumably an ancient waterway that connected the Tigris and the Euphrates Rivers (Gen. 2:13). (2) A spring east of Jerusalem. See under "Springs, Wells, and Pools."

GILBOA (gĭl-bō'à). A range of hills southwest of Bethshan which overlooked the eastern end of the Plain of Jezreel (Esdraelon). It was the scene of Saul's death in his first clash with the Philistines (1 Sam. 28:4 – 31:6).

GILEAD (gĭl'ê-ăd). The mountainous country east of the Jordan Valley. It extends from the northern end of the Dead Sea to the River Yarmuk south of the Sea of Galilee. North of this territory, held by the tribes Reuben, Gad, and half-Manasseh, was the territory of Bashan (Deut. 3: 12, 13; Josh. 13:24-31). The last interview between Jacob and Laban took place in this region (Gen. 31:20-25). It was famous for its cattle (1 Chron. 5:9) and balm (Jer. 8:22; cf. Gen. 37:25).

GILGAL (gĭl'gál). The place where the Israelites were circumcised and the reproach of Egypt was "rolled away" from them (Josh. 5:9). It lay between Jericho and the Jordan River (Josh. 4:19). It is mentioned in the time of the Judges

(Judg. 2:1; 3:19) and in Samuel's era (1 Sam. 7:16; 1 Sam. 11:14, 15; 15:12-33). David's subjects met him at Gilgal with a homecoming welcome after Absalom's revolt (2 Sam. 19:15, 40).

GIRDLE. A sash or belt worn around the waist. It was an important accessory for ancients who wore long, flowing robes. Men frequently wore utilitarian belts (as the soldier's belt in 2 Samuel 20:8), while women wore more decorative girdles (Prov. 31:24; Isa. 3:24). Men's belts frequently held knives or weapons. The linen "sash" of a priest was a distinctive item of priestly attire (Exod. 28:4; 29:9; 39:29; Lev. 8:7; 16:4).

The leather belt or girdle (Greek *zōnē*) was originally the lower section of a double girdle worn by women. In the New Testament it also appears as an article of clothing worn by men (Matt. 3:4; Mark 1: 6). "Girding the loins" involved tightening flowing garments securely about the body so that the wearer would not stumble as he walked. The expression also denotes a figure of speech for preparing for spiritual activity (1 Pet. 1:13).

GLASSMAKER. Before the Roman period glass items were a rare luxury. But by the eighteenth dynasty in Egypt (1546-1316 B.C.) a glass factory at El-Amarna in Egypt was producing imitations of stone and pottery wares. Samples of these have been found at Gezer, Lachish, Megiddo, and Hazor. Local products also appeared around this time. Glazes are mentioned in contemporary Assyrian and Hittite texts. Cobalt and manganese were employed as coloring agents. However, ancient glass products lacked transparency. Techniques to eliminate the impurities in glass were not perfected until the Roman period (cf. Rev. 4:26; 15:2; 21:18, 21).

GNAT. In biblical times, as now, gnats abounded in swamps and marshes. The Egyptians slept under nets to protect themselves from gnat bites (Herodotus 11:95). The Pharisees strained drinking water through a cloth to avoid swallowing an insect regarded as unclean (Matt. 23:24).

GOAT, DOMESTIC. Denoted by a number of different Hebrew and Greek words, the goat was one of the most common domestic animals in Bible times. The domestic goat (*Capra hircus*) belonged to the large family of hollow-horned ruminants. Every flock of goats had its own stately leader (cf. Jer. 50:8). The goat was admirably suited for a hilly and somewhat dry country. The flesh and milk of goats furnished food (Deut. 14:4; Prov. 27:27) and their hair was woven into cloth (Exod. 25:4; 35:26). They formed a very important part of a cattleman's wealth (Gen. 30:25-36). The goat served as an animal of sacrifice (Gen. 15:9; Exod. 12:5; Lev. 1:10).

GOAT, WILD. A species of ibex (*Capra beden*), which the Arabs call *badan* or *beden*. It is lighter in color than the European ibex, with slender, recurved horns. It was found in Egypt, Arabia, Persia, Moab, the Judean Wilderness, and the wilderness about Engedi.

GOD. God is a Spirit, infinite in being, glory, blessedness, and perfection. He is eternal, unchangeable, incomprehensible, and all-sufficient. He is omnipresent, omnipotent, and omniscient. He is gracious, absolutely loving, and slow to anger, but he "will not at all acquit the wicked" (Nah. 1:3). He is revealed in nature, the written Word, and the incarnate Word—Christ himself (John 1:1, 14). Through him God becomes visible to men (John 1:18). God can be "just and the justifier of him who believes in Jesus" (Rom. 3:26) because his holy Law—the Mosaic Decalogue—has been vindicated by Christ's death. See also "Adonai," "Adonai Jehovah," "Elohim," and "Jehovah."

GODS. The worship of pagan gods or their idol representations was strictly forbidden by the first commandment of the Law (Exod. 20:1-6). One reason for this stringent prohibition is that people who bow down to idol images are actually worshiping demons. These fallen spirit beings masquerade as "gods" and frequently indwell various idol images (Lev. 17:7; Deut. 32:17; Rev. 9:20). The Apostle Paul strongly cautions New Testament believers against falling into this severe sin (1 Cor. 10:19-21).

GOG (gŏg). The "chief prince" of Meshech and Tubal (Ezek. 38:2). He will lead the great Northern Confederacy in an invasion of Palestine in the end time (Ezek. 38, 39), before Christ's second advent and Israel's restoration (Ezek. 40–48).

Possible Golgotha, the "place of the skull," where Jesus Christ was crucified (*Russ Busby photo*)

GOLGOTHA (gŏl'gŏ-thä). Probably "Gordon's Calvary" near the Garden Tomb (Matt. 27:33; Mark 15:22; John 19:17). The word is the Aramaic equivalent of Latin *calvaria* (Calvary).

GOLIATH (gŏ-lī'ăth) ("an exile"). The Philistine giant of Gath who taunted God and his people but was slain by David (1 Sam. 17).

GOMER (gō'měr). (1) The daughter of Diblaim and the wife of Hosea the prophet (Hos. 1:3). Her unfaithfulness in marriage was used by the prophet as a dramatic parable of Israel's unfaithfulness to God. Apparently the Lord commanded Hosea to marry a practicing harlot, though it is possible that she became a harlot only after his marriage. At any rate the prophet felt the sting and insult of his wife's infidelity, even as the Lord felt the pain of Israel's apostasy (Hos. 1:2-9).

The names of Gomer's children (Hos. 1:6-9) depict Israel's deserved sufferings. "*Lo-ruhamah*" means "unpitied" and "*Lo-ammi*" means "not my people." The name of Gomer's previous child, *Jezreel* (Hos. 1:3-5), means "the Lord sows." It pointed back to the blood shed by Jehu in Jezreel (2 Kings 10:1-11) and forward to the approaching punishment of the Jehu dynasty. It also intimated the future restoration of the nation (Hos. 2:21-23; cf. Rom. 9:25, 26). (2) The Japhetic progenitor of the Cimmerians (the *Gimirrai* of the Assyrian records), who inhabited "the uttermost parts of the north" (Ezek. 38:6; cf. 10:2, 3).

GOMORRAH (gṏ-mŏr′rȧ). A town now under the shallow waters of the southern end of the Dead Sea in the valley of Siddim, near Sodom (Gen. 14:2-11). It was destroyed by God because of its overwhelming wickedness (Gen. 18:20 – 19: 25).

GOOSE. Geese were common in Egypt at an early period and were mentioned by Homer (ninth century B.C.).

GOPHER WOOD. The timber out of which Noah's ark was constructed (Gen. 6:14). Its precise identification is obscure, but the writer evidently refers to a conifer. The cypress tree, commonly used in shipbuilding, may have been intended.

GORGIAS (gôr′jĭ-ăs). A Syrian general whom Antiochus Epiphanes commanded to destroy the forces of the Maccabees (1 Macc. 3 – 5).

GOSHEN (gō′shĕn). A district in Egypt (in the Wadi Tumilat in the northeast part of the Nile Delta) where the cities of Raamses, Baal-zephon, Pibeseth, Pithom, and Succoth were located (Gen. 45:10; 46:28, 29; 47:1-6; Exod. 8:22).

GOSPEL. The word "gospel" means "good news." The good news is addressed to lost humanity and centers in God's grace, which rescues man from sin and restores him to God's image and fellowship. The gospel was first announced when God promised Adam and Eve that the "seed of the woman" would crush the serpent's head (Gen. 3:15). It was prefigured in the shed blood of the animal which God killed in order to clothe the naked sinners (Gen. 3:21). It was symbolized year after year in the blood of the animals that were offered in the Mosaic sacrificial system (Heb. 9:11-14, 19, 21).

When Christ, the true Sacrifice, was offered, the gospel in symbol became the gospel in reality (Heb. 9:11-15; 10:10-14). Sins which had previously been passed over were now instantly remitted for all those who had believed, whether before or after the Cross (Rom. 3:25, 26). The one human requirement for salvation is *faith in God's grace revealed in Christ's death and resurrection* (Rom. 10:8, 9; Eph. 2:8, 9). Absolutely no other requirement for salvation must be added or substituted. Any addition, change, or substitution corrupts the simple gospel of pure grace into "another gospel" – a heretical one which God's people are instructed to denounce (Gal. 1:6-9). This spurious gospel may parade under various seductive forms. The test, however, is simple. Does the alleged gospel question the total sufficiency of God's grace to save, keep, and perfect? If it does, perhaps by recommending some kind of human striving, it is to be branded "another gospel" and is to be rejected outright.

GOSPELS, THE FOUR. Precisely speaking, these are neither biographies of our Lord nor histories of his earthly life among men. They are rather feature portraits of the most unique personage ever to walk the paths of earth. Matthew presents Christ as the King of the Jews. Mark features him as the Perfect Servant. Luke portrays him as the Perfect Man. John shows that he is above all the Son of God. While each Gospel emphasizes a particular role of Christ, all four roles (and other characteristics as well) can be seen in every Gospel.

The four Gospels describe the Person who is the heart of the gospel (1 Cor. 15: 1-4; 2 Pet. 1:16). They are not a doctrinal exposition of the gospel, although occasional expository notes are found.

GOURD. A plant which the Lord prepared for Jonah (Jonah 4:6). The castor-oil plant is suggested by some scholars. Others suggest the bottle gourd, a rapid-climbing vine, as in Isaiah 1:8. The "wild gourds" of 2 Kings 4:39 are commonly identified with the colocynth. It resembles the cucumber in appearance but is poisonous. It is useful as a cathartic when carefully administered.

GOVERNMENT. Human government was established by God after the Flood. Man was expected to govern his fellow man for God. The institution of capital punishment showed that man was to govern under divine moral law and to preserve order and safety (Gen. 9:5, 6). A contributing cause of the lawlessness and violence that necessitated the Flood may have been the complete absence of governmental authority. But after the Flood human governmental authority was to be exercised even to the point of capital punishment. This God-given authority was never rescinded in succeeding dispensations and is thus applicable even today. The ultimate breakdown of human authority will be seen in the rampant violence and unbridled lawlessness of the Tribulation Period.

GOVERNOR (Greek *hēgemōn*). A ruler set up by a king to administer a specific territory or province. In the New Testament the word is used for Roman legates, procurators, and proconsuls (who ruled for the Roman Emperor—1 Pet. 2:14). The Roman governor of the province of Syria was a legate. The governor of Judea, on the other hand, was only a procurator (Matt. 27:2). The Roman governor of Egypt was a prefect. Quirinius was a proconsul (Luke 2:2). Felix (Acts 23:24) and Festus (Acts 24:27) were procurators.

GOZAN (gō'zăn). (1) A town and district southeast of Haran in northern Mesopotamia. It was a site to which certain Israelites were deported (2 Kings 17:6; 19:12; 1 Chron. 5:26). The modern site, Tell Halaf, has been extensively excavated and is famous for its pottery. (2) The Habor River, a tributary of the Euphrates now known as the Habur. The town of Gozan mentioned above was situated on the upper Habur River. See "Habor."

GRACE. Grace is the manifestation of God's love and mercy toward sinful men (2 Cor. 8:9; Tit. 2:11). God's essential nature includes both love (1 John 4:16), manifested in mercy and grace, and holiness (1 John 1:5), manifested in righteous judgment of sin. God cannot display his love until sin has been judged. In the miracle of Calvary, Christ simultaneously paid the full penalty for sin and exhibited the ultimate manifestation of grace. Now God is able to freely save lost men (Rom. 3:24). Grace functions totally apart from human merit or works; it rests completely in Christ (Eph. 2:8, 9).

Divine grace provides not only salvation but security. This is accomplished by the continuation of the divine work of grace despite the believer's imperfections. Ephesian 2:8 reads literally "By grace you are saved and continue to be." Grace also leads the believer into the divine will and the good works which the Author of grace has previously planned

that he should accomplish (Eph. 2:10).

Grace versus Law. In Scripture grace as a principle is contrasted with law as a principle (John 1:17; Rom. 6:14, 15). Under law God demands righteousness; under grace he bestows it (Rom. 3:21-24; 8:3, 4; Gal. 2:16; Phil. 3:9). Law connects with Moses and works; grace ties in with Christ and faith (John 1:17; Rom. 10:4-10). Under law obedience brings blessing (Deut. 28:1-14). Under grace blessing is bestowed as a free gift. When obedience does not respond to love, grace teaches and disciplines (Tit. 2:11, 12; 1 Cor. 11:31, 32).

An Arab woman works in a vineyard near Taiyibeh, ancient Ephraim, northeast of Jerusalem. (© *MPS*)

GRAPE. The common grapevine (*Vitis vinifera*), indigenous to western Asia south of the Caspian Sea (cf. Gen. 9:20, 21). It was cultivated in Egypt (Gen. 40: 9-11; Psa. 78:47), as is abundantly attested by Old Empire sculptures and reliefs. The grape flourished in Palestine (Gen. 14:18), especially in the central highlands near Hebron, Shiloh, and Shechem (Num. 13:23; Judg. 9:27; 21:20; Jer. 31: 5), but also in Transjordan (Isa. 16:8-10; Jer. 48:32) and Lebanon (Hos. 14:7). See also "Vine."

GRASS. A term used in the Bible to include all herbage on which cattle could graze. Grass, herbs, and trees are basic divisions of the vegetable kingdom (Gen.

1:11). Man's brief life on earth is compared to grass (Psa. 37:2; 103:15, 16; Matt. 6:30).

GRASSHOPPER. A leaping orthopterous insect with a four-jointed tarsus and long tapering antennae. Some think that the Hebrew *hāgāb* (Lev. 11:22; Num. 13:33; Eccl. 12:5; Isa. 40:22) is a true grasshopper while others regard it as a locust.

GREEKS. A Japhetic or Indo-Germanic people who in the course of history occupied the Greek mainland and archipelago. They are listed as the descendants of Javan in Genesis 10:4. They consisted of various migrating tribes, notably the Ionians of Homer, who lived in the coasts of Lydia and Caria and whose cities became commercial centers several centuries before those on the mainland. "Javan" was the name under which the Hebrews first became acquainted with the Greeks. In Assyrian records the Greeks were first mentioned by Sargon II (721-705 B.C.), who encountered them in a naval battle.

In the New Testament the term "Greek" may refer either to a native of Greece (Acts 16:1; 17:4) or to any well-cultured Gentile (Rom. 1:14-16; 10:12).

The Greeks were eminent in art, science, philosophy, and human culture (cf. 1 Cor. 1:22).

GROVE. A sacred pole in the form of a branchless tree trunk is often found in remains of Canaanite shrines. The cult object is in some way connected with the Canaanite goddess Asherah and represents an intrusion of polluted Canaanite religion into Israelite worship (1 Kings 14:15; 2 Kings 23:6). The Book of Deuteronomy and the Hebrew prophets inveigh against the asherahs.

GUILT. Guilt is liability for sin committed or wrong enacted. Divine grace has triumphed over sin by removing the guilt of all who trust in Jesus Christ's atoning death (Rom. 8:1). Adam's sin and guilt passed upon the whole race (Rom. 5:12-21), but this guilt has been borne by Christ on the cross and is forgiven all who believe (Col. 2:13, 14). The guilt and condemnation of sins committed—past, present, and future—is removed entirely as soon as an individual receives Christ's free gift of salvation (Rom. 3:24). Sin in the life of the believer is judged on a Father-child basis by divine chastening (Heb. 12:5-13).

HABAKKUK (ha-băk'ŭk) (perhaps "embrace"). One of the "Minor Prophets" who lived during the rise of the Chaldean Empire (625-615 B.C.). He stressed the truth that "the righteous shall live by his faith" (Hab. 2:4, RSV).

HABOR (hā'bôr). A river of Mesopotamia sometimes known as the River of Gozan. It flows southward through Gozan and

after a course of 190 miles meets the Euphrates. The River Balikh empties into the Euphrates, some 90 miles west of the Habor. The city of Haran, associated with Terah and Abraham (Gen. 11:31), is situated on the Habor River. The territory between these rivers was known as Padan-Aram ("field" or "plain" of Aram—Gen. 25:20; 31:18) and is identical with Aram Naharaim, "Aram of the Rivers."

HACHILAH (hȧ-kī'lȧ). A hill between Engedi and Ziph in the Wilderness of Judah west of the Dead Sea. There David was hidden when the Ziphites plotted to betray him to Saul (1 Sam. 23:19; 26: 1, 3).

HADADEZER (hȧ-dăd-ē'zẽr) ("Hadad is a help"). The king of the Aramaean state of Zobah in northern Syria. He was defeated by David (2 Sam. 8:3).

HADASSAH (hȧ-dăs'sȧ) (Hebrew "myrtle"). The Hebrew name of Esther, the wife of King Ahasuerus (Xerxes I, 486-465 B.C.). She saved her people from destruction. Her story is related in the Book of Esther.

HADES (hā'dēs). The unseen realm of the spirit world. In Old Testament times the soul and spirit of every person went there after death. The righteous, however, were separated from the wicked by a "great gulf" (Luke 16:25, 26). Since the time of Christ's resurrection, paradise or "Abraham's bosom" has apparently been transferred to "the third heaven" (2 Cor. 12:1-4). This is the immediate presence of God (1 Thess. 4:13-18; 2 Cor. 5:1-8).

All the unsaved, however, (both before and after Christ's resurrection) still go to Hades and are in conscious torment (Luke 16:22-24). At the Great White Throne Judgment, which preludes the eternal state (Rev. 20:11-15), the wicked will be raised. Then Hades becomes part of Gehenna or eternal hell. This eternal destiny of Satan, fallen angels, and unsaved humanity (Matt. 25:41) is called "the second death." It will consummate the first death and will involve eternal separation from God and his sin-cleansed universe (Rev. 20:14).

HAGAR (hā'gär) ("flight"). Sarah's Egyptian slave woman, evidently obtained during Abraham's visit to Egypt (Gen. 16:1; cf. 12:10). Despairing of a son of her own (at 76 years of age), Sarah gave Hagar to Abraham as a wife. Ishmael was born as a result. When Sarah finally gave birth to Isaac tension arose between the boys and their mothers. Eventually Sarah cast out both Hagar and Ishmael (Gen. 16:1-16; 21:1-21; Gal. 4:21-31). Muslim Arabs claim descent from Hagar.

HAGGAI (hăg'gȧ-ī) ("festal"). A post-captivity prophet who predicted the future millennial Temple (Hag. 2:1-19) and the final destruction of Gentile world power (Hag. 2:20-23).

HAGGITH (hăg'gĭth) ("festal"). One of David's eight wives and the mother of Adonijah (2 Sam. 3:4; 1 Kings 1:5). Adonijah's selfish attempts to exalt himself seem to be a reflection of his mother's character (cf. 1 Kings 1:5, 11; 2:13-25).

HALAH (hā'lȧ). A place in Assyria to which Israelites were deported from Samaria in 722 B.C. (2 Kings 17:6; 18: 11). It is possibly the same as Halakku (near Kirkuk) or Halhu (near Gozan).

HALAK (hā'lăk). A mountain in southern Palestine on the way to Mount Seir (Josh. 11:17; 12:7). It is probably modern Jebel Halaq, west of the ascent of Akrabbim and southwest of the Dead Sea.

HAM (hăm) ("hot"). One of Noah's sons (Gen. 5:32; 6:10; 9:18). His display of uncleanness on the occasion of his father's drunkenness (Gen. 9:20-27) furnished prophetic insight into the moral character of his descendants, notably the Canaanites. Their moral debauchery reached its height at the time of the conquest by Israel.

HAMAN (hā'măn). One of King Ahasuerus' favorite court officers (Esth. 3:1). Because Mordecai the Jew refused to bow to him Haman plotted the destruction of all Jews in the kingdom (Esth. 3:2-15). However, Queen Esther (herself a Jew) frustrated his plan and Haman was hanged on the court gallows (4:1 — 7:10).

HAMATHITES (hăm'ȧ-thīts). Citizens of the city-state of Hamath on the Orontes River (cf. Gen. 10:18). Hamath, the capital city, was located on one of the main trade routes to the south. King Toi was its ruler in David's day (2 Sam. 8:9, 10). Solomon controlled it as a vassal state (2 Chron. 8:4). Jeroboam II conquered it in about 778 B.C. (2 Kings 14:28), as did Sargon II in about 721 B.C. (2 Kings 18: 33, 34). Some of its inhabitants were settled in Samaria by the Assyrians (2 Kings 17:24). In classical times the city was known as Epiphaneia. Today it is known as Hamah. Extensive archeological diggings have been made at the site. "The entering in of Hamath" (modern Leb-weh, 14 miles northeast of Baalbeck) was the ideal northern boundary of Israel (Num. 34:8; Josh. 13:5; Amos 6:14).

HAMMOLEKETH (hă-mŏl'ē-kĕth ("the queen"). The mother of Abiezer, from whose line sprang the great hero and judge, Gideon (1 Chron. 7:18).

HAMMURABI (hàm-ōō-rä'bĕ). The sixth Amorite king of the first dynasty of Baby-lon (1790-1750 B.C.). He carved out the first Babylonian Empire, which included nearly all of Mesopotamia. He is famous for his Code of Laws, discovered at Susa in 1902.

HAMUTAL (hă-mū'tàl) (probably "fa-ther-in-law is dew"). The wife of King Josiah (641-609 B.C.) and the mother of Kings Jehoahaz and Jeremiah of Libnah.

HANNAH (hăn'à) ("grace, compassion"). The favorite of Elkanah's two wives. She devoted her son Samuel to the Lord be-fore he was born (1 Sam. 1:1-28). He be-came the last of the Judges and the first of the prophets—one of the truly great and godly men of Israel. Hannah's devo-tion to the Lord found fruition in her eminent son. Her trust has been an in-spiration to godly mothers through the centuries. Her triumphal ode (1 Sam. 2:1-10) glimpses the coming Messiah and the day of the Lord which precedes the establishment of his kingdom (1 Sam. 2:9, 10). Hannah's song was apparently in the mind of Mary when she voiced her gratitude upon learning that she was to give birth to Israel's promised Messiah (Luke 1:46-55).

HANUN (hā'nŭn) ("favored"). An Am-monite king who responded to David's overtures of kindness with gross insult, thus precipitating a disastrous war (2 Sam. 10:1-19).

HARAN, HARRAN (hā'răn) (from Ak-kadian *harranu,* "main road"). A town located about 20 miles southeast of Urfa (Edessa) on the river Balikh in northern Mesopotamia. It was on the main east-west trade routes (Ezek. 27:23). Terah settled there after leaving Ur (Gen. 11:31, 32). It was from Haran that Abraham journeyed to Canaan (Gen. 12:1-5). Like Ur, it was the center of worship for the moon-god, Sin. After the fall of Nineveh in 612 B.C. Haran became the capital of

Assyria until it fell to the Chaldeans in 609 B.C. The Greek form of the name is "Charran" (Acts 7:4).

HARP. See under "Music and Musical Instruments."

The hawk at rest (© *MPS*)

HAWK (Hebrew *nes*). Any of several small-to-medium-sized diurnal birds of prey of the suborder *Falcones.* Twenty species of the sparrow hawk alone exist. They were ceremonially unclean (Lev. 11:16).

HAZAEL (hăz'å-ĕl) ("God has seen"). An Aramaean courtier who murdered his master (Benhadad I or II) and seized the throne (1 Kings 19:15, 17). He became a terrible scourge to sinning Israel and re-sisted Assyrian advance westward.

HAZOR (hā'zŏr). An important Canaanite city (Josh. 11:1, 10-13; Judg. 4:2). It was fortified by Solomon (1 Kings 9:15) but was later taken by the Assyrians (2 Kings 15:29) and still later by the Babylonians (Jer. 49:28-30). The present-day site is Tell el-Qedah, about five miles south-west of Lake Huleh in Galilee.

HEALING. God heals today through both natural and supernatural means in re-sponse to the "prayer of faith" (James 5: 14-16). In order to be a "prayer of faith" a petition must be offered in harmony with God's Word and God's will. Sometimes it is not God's will to heal (cf. 2 Kings 13:14; 2 Cor. 12:7-9). Thus it is not al-ways possible to offer a "prayer of faith" with regard to healing. God has not made a healing covenant with the church, as he did with the nation Israel (Exod. 15:26).

Although "gifts of healings" (1 Cor. 12:9) are to be operative in the church today, God heals only on the basis of his highest glory and the greatest *ultimate* benefit for the believer. He often uses illness to chastise sinning saints (1 Cor. 11:30-32) and to test and refine victorious saints (2 Cor. 12:7-9; 2 Tim. 4:20). Multitudes of believers can testify to miraculous healing by God's power. But we must not ignore doctors and medical help. God does not perform miracles wastefully when he has provided effective natural methods of healing.

HEAVEN. The usual term for the eternal abode of the saved (Matt. 5:12; Col. 1:5; 1 Pet. 1:4). Heaven will apparently be only part of the future sin-cleansed universe. There will also be Gehenna (the Lake of Fire—Rev. 20:14, 15), "a new heaven and a new earth" (2 Pet. 3:13; Rev. 21:1), and a new Jerusalem (Rev. 21:2). See also "New Jerusalem."

HEBREWS. The term "Hebrew" is used in Scripture as a name for Abraham and his posterity (Gen. 14:13). The designation is derived from the name "Eber" (Gen. 10:21-31; 11:14-16). Some scholars think the term means "one from the other side, a crosser or nomad," referring to the Hebrews as men from the "other side" of the Euphrates (cf. Gen. 12:5; Josh. 24:2, 3). Others connect the term with the "Habiru" of antiquity. These were aliens, soldiers of fortune, mercenaries.

The Habiru are prominent in the Tell el Amarna Letters as a people who invaded Palestine. These Letters relate how Abdi-Heba of Jerusalem made frantic appeals to the Egyptian Pharaoh Akhnaton (1375 B.C.) in a situation which seems to correspond to the invasion under Joshua. The Israelites doubtless fitted the category of nomads or soldiers of fortune, but not all Habiru were Israelites. Israelites are clearly called Hebrews in Scripture (Gen. 40:15; 1 Sam. 4:6; 13:3; 2 Cor. 11:22). In the New Testament a Hebrew was a Jew who spoke the Hebrew or Aramaic language (in distinction to Jews who spoke Greek and were called Grecians—Acts 6:1). A "Hebrew of the Hebrews" (Phil. 3:5) was a thorough-going Hebrew in language, parentage, and religious custom.

Hebron shelters tombs of the patriarchs in Machpelah's Cave, covered by a mosque. (© *MPS*)

HEBRON (hĕb'rŭn). The highest town in Palestine, 3,040 feet above sea level. It lies 19 miles south-southwest of Jerusalem. Its older name was Kiriath-arba ("tetrapolis"). It was founded about 1720 B.C. in the era of Tanis (cf. Num. 13:22). The patriarchs had important associations with Hebron (Gen. 23). The *Haram el-Halil* (the "Enclosure of the Friend," i.e. Abraham) is the traditional site of the graves of Abraham, Sarah, Isaac, Rebekah, Jacob, and Leah (Gen. 49:29-32; 50:13). Hebron was visited by the Israelite spies (Num. 13:22) and was captured by Joshua (Josh. 10:36, 37). It was a city of refuge (Josh. 20:7) and David's first capital (2 Sam. 2:1-4, 11).

HEIFER, RED. The ordinance of the red heifer was instituted during the wilderness wanderings of the nation of Israel because of their wholesale contact with human death (cf. 1 Cor. 10:5-10). The use of the ashes of an animal for purification beautifully illustrates Christ's atonement as the basis for the believer's cleansing from defilement in his pilgrim walk (1 John 1:7–2:2; cf. John 13:5-10). The ashes were a memorial of an already accepted sacrifice. Death suggests the polluting effects of sin, which defile the believer's conscience and render him unworthy to "serve the living God" (Heb. 9:14).

HELAH (hē'là) ("ornament, necklace"). One of the two wives of Ashur, the ancestor of the inhabitants of Tekoa in Judah (1 Chron. 4:5, 7).

HELIOPOLIS (hē-lĭ-ŏp'ō-lĭs). (1) The famous Syrian cult city of Baalbeck. It lies on the lower slope of Antilebanus about 40 miles from Damascus. It is best known for its ruins of cultic temples. (2) The Greek name (meaning "City of the

Sun") for the temple city of "On" in Lower Egypt. The Hebrew name is Bethshemesh (Jer. 43:13). See "On."

HELL. See "Gehenna" and "Hades."

HELMET. In early Israel helmets were apparently worn only by kings or prominent military leaders. King Saul gave David his own helmet of bronze (1 Sam. 17:38). Hittite helmets were similar to skull caps, as depicted on wall reliefs at Karnak, Egypt. In Uzziah's prosperous reign Hebrew soldiers were supplied with helmets which were probably made of leather (2 Chron. 26:14). When bronze became common, the ordinary soldier wore a bronze helmet (1 Macc. 6:35).

Roman armor in New Testament times consisted of helmet, cuirass, and greaves. The earliest Roman helmet was a leather cap *(galea)*. Later the metal helmet *(cassis)* became prominent. It consisted of several parts: the cap itself, the elaborately decorated crest, two cheek pieces, and a hinged visor. Both metal and leather helmets were common in New Testament times. The helmet as a figure for salvation is part of the Christian warrior's equipment in Christ (Eph. 6:17).

HEMLOCK. Any of a group of poisonous weeds of the carrot family. It has small white flowers and finely divided leaves. True hemlock is apparently not mentioned in Scripture. See instead "Gall" and "Wormwood."

HENNA. A shrub that grows wild in Palestine. It has spiny branches with clusters of white, fragrant flowers. It originated in North India. Its leaves were pulverized into a paste and used as a cosmetic from earliest times. It was also used as a hair and fingernail dye. It is translated "camphire" in Song of Solomon 1:14 and 4:13.

HEPHZIBAH (hĕf'zĭ-bà) ("my delight is in her"). The wife of King Hezekiah (716-687 B.C.) and the mother of Manasseh (2 Kings 21:1). She knew the love and fellowship of a godly husband as well as the extreme waywardness and apostasy of an ungodly son (whose evil reign extended from about 686 to 642 B.C. and brought Judah to the brink of disaster).

HERDSMAN. In Bible times human wealth and the sacrificial worship of God revolved in large degree around cattle.

This was true under both nomadic and settled agricultural conditions. Tending sheep and goats was therefore a very common occupation. See also "Shepherd."

HERMES (hûr'mēz). The divine messenger of the gods in Greek mythology (Acts 14:12). He corresponded to Mercury in Roman mythology.

HERMON (hûr'mŭn). A 9100-foot-high mountain in the Antilebanon range. It is the highest mountain in the neighborhood of Palestine and is perpetually snowclad. Its melting ice provides a major source of water for the Jordan River. The summit has three peaks, with the southeast one being the highest. Mount Hermon was also called Mount Sion (Deut. 4:48), Sirion, and Senir or Shenir (Deut. 3:9). Its proximity to Caesarea Philippi has led some to suggest that Hermon was the "high mountain" of Christ's transfiguration (Mark 9:2).

HEROD THE GREAT (hĕr'ŭd). The king of Judea from 40 to 4 B.C. He was the son of Antipater, a Jew of Idumean descent. Through friendship with Antony and Octavian he was appointed "King of the Jews" by the Roman Senate in 40 B.C. By exercising shrewdness and duplicity as well as some native ability he secured his position as a loyal client king under Rome. He was detested by the Jews for his Idumean origin, his loyalty to Rome, and his devotion to pagan Greek culture. He was a lavish builder, the Temple in Jerusalem being but one of his many enterprises. It was during Herod's administration that Christ was born (Matt. 2:1).

HERODIAS (hĕ-rō'dĭ-às). The daughter of Herod the Great's son Aristobulus. Her first marriage was to her uncle Herod Philip (a son of Herod the Great), by whom she had a daughter, Salome. She then married Herod the tetrarch while her first husband was still living. Herod in turn divorced his wife, a daughter of the Nabataean king Aretas, in order to indulge his guilty passion for Herodias. After John the Baptist reproved the guilty pair (Mark 6:18) Herodias began to plot the death of John and had him imprisoned. Then, after her daughter Salome had delighted Herod at a state banquet, Herodias extorted from Herod the head of John the Baptist. The king feared and respected John, but because of his foolish oath he sent a soldier to behead the Baptist and bring his head on a platter (Matt. 14:3-12; Mark 6:17-29). When the tetrarch was subsequently banished, Herodias went with him into exile.

HERODIUM (hĕ-rō'dĭ-ŭm). The fortress and burial site of Herod the Great. It is present-day Jebel Fureidis, located about three miles southeast of Bethlehem.

HERON. Any of a family (*Ardeidae*) of wading birds with a long thin neck and long legs. Its food is fish and other aquatic animals found in the lake regions of Palestine, on the Kishon River, and on the Palestinian seacoast.

HESHBON (hĕsh'bŏn). Originally a city of Moab but later taken by the Amorites and made a royal city of Sihon (Num. 21: 26). Israel captured it and allotted it to Reuben (Num. 21:21-25; 32:1-37). Later it passed over to Gad (Josh. 31:39). Eventually Moab retook the city (Isa. 15:4; Jer. 48:2). The present site is Hisban, about fourteen miles east-northeast of the mouth of the Jordan River as it enters the Dead Sea.

HETH (hāth). The second son of Canaan and an ancestor of the Hittites (Gen. 10: 15), an ancient imperial people whose civilization has been resurrected by modern archeological research.

HEZEKIAH (hĕz-ė-kī'à) ("the Lord has strengthened"). A godly king of Judah from about 716 to 687 B.C. Because of his hatred of idolatry and faith in the Lord he was able to keep Jerusalem and Judah from collapsing under Assyrian advance in 701 B.C., as the Northern Kingdom had done in 722 B.C. (2 Kings 18—20; Isa. 36—39).

HIDDEKEL (hĭd'ė-kĕl). The ancient name of the Tigris River (Gen. 2:14; Dan. 10:4). The name derives from the Akkadian word *Idiglat*.

HIEL (hī'ĕl) (probably "God lives"). A native of Bethel who rebuilt Jericho and suffered the curse predicted by Joshua (Josh. 6:26; 1 Kings 16:34).

HIERAPOLIS (hė-ēr-ăp'ō-lĭs). A city of the Lycus Valley in the Roman province of Asia Minor. Hierapolis, Colosse, and Laodicea were the subjects of Epaphras' ministry (Col. 4:12, 13).

HIGH PLACES. Elevated sanctuaries of idolatrous cult worship. They were erected either on natural hills or on elevated structures. Mosaic law forbade these sanctuaries as an offense to the God of Israel (Deut. 12:2-4).

HIGH PRIEST. Aaron prefigures Christ as the Great High Priest who now represents us before God (Exod. 29:1-9; Heb. 3:1; 7:23-28; 9:11-24). Like Aaron, Christ bears our names on his shoulders and on his breast (Exod. 28:1-29).

In New Testament times the high priest was the president of the Sanhedrin. He presided at Jesus' trial (Matt. 26:57-65; Mark 14:53-63; John 18:19-24). The plural is used in the New Testament and by Josephus to denote 1) members of the Sanhedrin who belonged to high priestly families, 2) ruling or deposed high priests, and 3) adult male members of the most prominent priestly families (cf. Matt. 16:21; 26:47; 27:12, 41; Mark 14:1; Luke 23:13; John 7:32; 19:15; Acts 9:14; 22:30; 26:10).

HILKIAH (hĭl-kī'à) ("the Lord is the portion"). A high priest during King Josiah's reign. He discovered the Book of the Law in the Temple and conveyed it to King Josiah through Shaphan the scribe. After hearing the words of the book Josiah instituted the greatest religious revival of any king of Judah (2 Kings 22:8—23:25).

HILLEL (hĭl'lĕl). A famous Jewish spiritual leader who lived from about 30 B.C. TO A.D. 10. He was a leader of the Pharisees, a member of the Sanhedrin, and a leader of a specific school of thought.

HIPPOPOTAMUS. See "Behemoth."

HIRAM (hī'răm) (probably abbreviated from *Ahiram*, "the brother is exalted"). (1) A king of Tyre and an ally and friend of David and Solomon. He helped supply materials and workmen for the construction of the Temple (1 Kings 5). (2) An architect and skilled craftsman sent by King Hiram to Solomon (1 Kings 7:13-46). He was also called "Huram."

HISTORY. See under "Archeology."

HITTITES (hĭt'īts). An Indo-European people who settled in Asia Minor about the beginning of the second millennium B.C. Their name derived from "Hatti," the earlier inhabitants of the area, whom they absorbed. The Hittites founded an empire (about 1800 B.C.) whose capital was at Boghaz-keui (ancient Hattushash) at the great bend of the Halys River. There are two chief periods of Hittite power: the earlier Old Kingdom (1800-1600 B.C.) and the New Kingdom (about 1400-1200 B.C.). The Hittites were practically unknown before the advent of modern archeology, which rediscovered this long-lost imperial people.

In the Old Testament the Hittites appear as a great nation which gave its name to the whole region of Syria (Josh. 1:4) and as an ethnic group which inhabited Canaan from patriarchal times until after the Israelite settlement (Gen. 15:20; Deut. 7:1; Judg. 3:5). They were known as "the children of Heth" because of their progenitor, Heth (Gen. 10:15).

After the collapse of the new Hittite kingdom, 24 city-states of the Tabali (the "Tubal" of Genesis 10:2) became heirs to the Hittite home territory in Asia Minor. In Syria, seven city-states which had once belonged to the Hittite Empire preserved the name "Hittite" for several centuries. Their rulers were called "kings of the Hittites" (cf. 1 Kings 10:28, 29; 2 Kings 7:6). Hamath on the Orontes and Carchemish on the Euphrates were among the most important of the Syrian Hittite states until they were conquered by Assyria in the late eighth century B.C.

HIVITES (hī'vīts). An ancient people listed as one of the sons of Canaan (Gen. 10: 17) and as a separate group inhabiting Syria-Palestine. They are distinguished from the Canaanites, Jebusites, Perizzites, Gergashites, and Amorites (Exod. 3:8; Num. 13:29; Deut. 7:1). They were located principally in the Lebanon region and the Hermon range as far as the valley leading to Hamath (Judg. 3:3; Josh. 11:3; cf. 2 Sam. 24:7). They were conscripted for Solomon's building operations (1 Kings 9:20, 21). Hivites also settled in Shechem (Gen. 34:2) and near Gibeon (Josh. 9:7; 11:19).

HOGLAH (hŏg'là) (perhaps from Arabic *hajal*, "partridge"). One of the five daughters of Zelophehad (Num. 26:33). Because Zelophehad had no sons a law was enacted which gave the right of inheritance to a man's daughters in such cases (Num. 27:1-11). The daughters, however, were required to marry within their native tribe (Num. 36:1-12; cf. Josh. 17:1-6).

HOLINESS. The holiness of believers exists in three aspects. (1) *Positional.* God sees all believers as "in Christ" and thus regards them as possessing the holiness of Christ himself (Eph. 1:3-14; Rom. 4:22-25; Phil. 3:8, 9). (2) *Experiential.* Believers can translate their positional holiness into practical, everyday holy living as they rely on the power of Christ (Rom. 6:11-18). Faith translates positional holiness into experiential holiness. (3) *Ultimate.* Believers will experience complete perfection only after the rapture and first resurrection (1 Cor. 15: 42-49; 1 John 3:2).

HOLY SPIRIT. The third Person of the triune God. He indwells and seals every believer (John 14:16, 17; Rom. 8:9-16; 1 Cor. 3:16; Eph. 1:13, 14) and glorifies Christ (16:13, 14).

HOMER. See under "Weights and Measures."

HOPE. Hope is faith that looks forward to the future fulfillment of God's promises contained in his Word. Israel's hope is centered in Messiah's advent and kingdom (Luke 1:67-75; 2:38; Acts 26:6, 7; 28:20; Eph. 2:12). The Christian's hope is centered in Christ's return for his own (Tit. 2:12, 13; 1 John 3:2, 3).

HOPHNI (hŏf'nī) (perhaps "hollow of hand"). The brother of Phinehas. Both brothers were slain when the ark was taken by the Philistines (1 Sam. 2:22–4:11). The tragedy was a judgment from God for their greed and immorality.

HOR (hōr). A mountain in the Wilderness of Kadesh northeast of Kadesh-barnea. It was here that Aaron died (Num. 20:22-29). Some scholars identify the site as present-day Jebel Madeira, northeast of Kadesh on the northwest border of Edom (since the detour around Edom began at Mount Hor–Num. 21:4).

HOREB (hōr'ĕb). Probably Mount Sinai, "the mount of God" (Jebel Musa). It is in the Sinai Peninsula, west of the Gulf of Aqaba and about 55 miles from the tip of the Peninsula (where the Gulf of Suez and the Gulf of Aqaba meet the Red Sea). There Moses received the Decalogue from God (Exod. 19:1–31:18). Elijah fled there from the wrath of Jezebel (1 Kings 19:1-8).

HORMAH (hôr′mȧ). An important town southeast of Beersheba (Josh. 15:30; 1 Sam. 30:30). Its king was defeated by Joshua (Josh. 12:14; cf. Num. 21:1-3). It is identified with present-day Tell el-Mishash.

HORN. A symbol of power and authority. Compare "the horn of David" (Psa. 132:17; 92:10) and "the horn of the house of Israel" (Ezek. 29:21). "The little horn" — the man of sin, the Antichrist — will appear at a future time (Dan. 7:8).

HORNET. Any of several types of large, stinging wasps. Hornets were well known in Bible lands. God helped Israel by driving out the Canaanites with hornets (Exod. 23:28; Deut. 7:20; Josh. 24:12).

HORSE. The most important beast of burden, though not the first one to be domesticated. (The earlier domesticated ass came from the wild species in desert regions.) The horse was native to the grasslands of Europe and Asia. The first mention of a horse is found on a Babylonian tablet from the time of Hammurabi (about 1750 B.C.). Horses were employed in Egypt at the time of the Exodus (about 1440 B.C.), and the nations inhabiting Canaan used horses in battle (Josh. 11:1-4). David fought against these peoples (2 Sam. 10:18) but apparently observed the prohibition against multiplying horses (Deut. 17:16). Solomon disregarded the divine command and kept large numbers of horses at Hazor, Megiddo, and Gezer. They were specially imported from Egypt (1 Kings 10:28, 29). Horses drew war chariots (Josh. 11:4-9) and are mentioned prominently in the Book of Revelation (Rev. 6:2-8; 9:16, 17; 19:14-21).

HORSELEECH. A blood-sucking creature that clings to the body (Prov. 30:15). The leech is well known in Palestine and is used for medical treatment. The horseleech is a large variety (*Haemopsis sanguisuga*). The writer of Proverbs apparently refers to its insatiable thirst for blood (Prov. 30:15).

HOSEA (hŏ-zē′à) ("salvation"). A prophet of Israel in the latter part of the materially prosperous but morally declining era

of Jeroboam II (782-753 B.C.). His ministry was on the Lord's love for his sinning people.

HULDAH (possibly "weasel"). A prophetess during the reign of Josiah (640-609 B.C.). She was the wife of Shallum and the "keeper of the wardrobe" (2 Kings 22:14; 2 Chron. 34:22). The "wardrobe" doubtless included the priestly vestments and royal robes. She resided in the second or western quarter of Jerusalem. She was consulted on behalf of the king by Hilkiah, the chief priest, and others concerning the discovery of the Book of the Law in the Temple (2 Kings 22:14; 2 Chron. 34:22).

Huldah accepted the newly found Scriptures (doubtless lost during the idolatrous orgy of Manasseh's reign) as the Word of the Lord. With its authority she predicted approaching judgment upon Judah.

HULEH, LAKE (hoo′lĕ). The body of water which forms the headwaters of the Jordan River. It lies about 12 miles south of the ancient cult center of Dan.

HUMAN SACRIFICE. To propitiate the gods, especially in times of danger, the pagans of antiquity often sacrificed their children, especially the firstborn. This cruel custom was denounced and prohibited in the Mosaic Law (Lev. 18:21; 20:2). The obscene deities Molech and Baal were thought to be honored by this horrible practice (Jer. 19:5).

HUNTER. Hunting was not a common occupation or recreation in Palestine. It was usually practiced only to provide food or to defend against attacking wild animals (Exod. 23:29; Judg. 14:5, 6; 1 Sam. 17:34, 35). However, men like Ishmael (Gen. 21:20) and Esau (Gen. 25:27) were noted for their hunting prowess. By contrast, the Mesopotamians from the days of Nimrod (the mighty hunter of antiquity — Gen. 10:8) had a long record of hunting activity. Lions and other ferocious beasts were hunted avidly, as depicted on monuments and bas-reliefs.

Egyptians liked to hunt game and predatory birds, using dogs and cats to aid them. The mention of such delicacies as the partridge (1 Sam. 26:20), the gazelle, the hart (Deut. 12:15), and the roebuck (1 Kings 4:23) indicates hunting activity among these people. The hunter used bow and arrow (Gen. 27:3), nets (Isa. 51:20) and snares (Psa. 91:3). For dangerous animals such as bears he used pits (Ezek. 19:1-8). Hunting techniques were sufficiently familiar to biblical writers to be used in figurative speech (Job 18:10; Jer. 5:26; Rom. 11:9; Matt. 22:15).

HUR (hûr) ("splendor"). The man who held up Moses' arms during the battle with the Amalekites (Exod. 17:10-12). He assisted Aaron while Moses was absent on Mount Sinai (Exod. 24:14).

HURRIANS, HORITES (hŏŏr′ē-əns; hō′ rīts). A Caucasian people who spread southward and westward from Lake Van into Mesopotamia at about the beginning of the second millennium B.C. They gradually infiltrated into Palestine Syria and occupied Edom in Abraham's time (Gen. 14:6) but were in turn driven out of Edom by the descendants of Esau (Deut. 2:12, 22). They also occupied places in central Palestine, including Shechem, according to the Septuagint.

Before archeology resurrected the Hurrians, the Horites were thought to be cave dwellers (derived from Hebrew *hor,* a hole or cave). But the Horites are now known to have been the same people as the Hurrians. They are well known from numerous tablets uncovered from A.D. 1925 to 1941 at Nazu, southeast of Nineveh and near modern Kirkuk. As part of the kingdom of Mitanni, they rose to dominant leadership in Syria at Alalah, Ras Shamra, Asia Minor (Boghaz-keui), and East Assyria (Nazu) from about 1550 to 1150 B.C., at which time they were subdued by Assyria.

HYKSOS (hĭk′sŏs). An ethnically composite group of people which dominated Upper Egypt and most of Syria Palestine from about 1792 to 1550 B.C., the interval between the strong twelfth and eighteenth dynasties. The Hyksos were "rulers of foreign countries" who took control of Egypt. Their capital was the Delta city of Avaris, though there is no evidence that the foreign invaders controlled Upper Egypt at Thebes and beyond.

The foreigners introduced the horse and chariot into Egypt and extended the use of bronze for weapons. Their domination of the Delta is concurrent with Israel's sojourn in Egypt. Their expulsion by Ahmose (1570-1545 B.C.), the first ruler of the eighteenth dynasty, is doubtless connected in some way with Israel's enslavement under and subsequent deliverance from Amenhotep II, one of the other pharaohs of the dynasty.

HYSSOP. A common plant of Egypt. The Israelites used it before the Passover to apply blood from a slain lamb to the lintels and doorposts of their houses (Exod. 12:1-13, 21-28). The ritual symbolized faith in the shed blood of Christ, the true Lamb of God (John 1:29, 36; 1 Pet. 1:18, 19; Rev. 5).

I

IBZAN (ĭb′zăn) ("swift"). One of the minor judges who succeeded Jephthah (Judg. 12:8-10).

ICHABOD (ĭk′ā-bŏd) ("the glory is not").

The posthumous son of Phinehas and the grandson of Eli. His name perpetuates the spiritual significance underlying the capture of the ark by the Philistines and the death of Eli and his sons (1 Sam. 4:19-22).

ICONIUM (ĭ-cō'nĭ-ŭm). A town on the borders of Phrygia and Lycaonia. It became part of the Roman province of Galatia in 25 B.C. It was visited by Paul and Barnabas on their first missionary tour (Acts 14:1-7; 16:2). Paul refers to it in 2 Timothy 3:11.

IDUMEANS (ĭd'ŭ-mē'ăns). The post-exilic name of those Edomites who were forced out of their ancient homeland southeast of the Dead Sea by the growing pressure of the Nabataeans (an Arab tribe who conquered Edom proper). The new region south of Judea became known as "Idumea" and its Edomite refugees as "Idumeans." Idumean power grew and eventually extended as far north as Bethzur, only 15 miles south of Jerusalem. Throughout the Seleucid, Hasmonean, and Herodian periods Idumea changed hands frequently. In 164 B.C. Judas Maccabeus fortified Beth-zur to oppose an independent Idumea (1 Macc. 4:61) and ravaged its territory (1 Macc. 5:3, 65). Idumea was annexed to the Hasmonean state by John Hyrcanus in 125 B.C. Pompey separated it from Judea in 63 B.C.

In the Herodian line Idumea supplied the native ruling dynasty in Palestine for nearly a century and a half. Herod the Great, an Idumean, reannexed Idumea to Judea, but after his death it again exchanged hands. Not until after the First Revolt did the territory come under the rule of the procurator of Judea as a permanent part of the province of Syria. See also "Edomites."

ILLYRICUM (ĭ-lĭr'ĭ-kŭm). A Roman province (Rom. 15:19) also called Dalmatia. The latter designation eventually became the official one.

IMAGE. As representations of pagan gods, images were strictly prohibited to Israelites under the Mosaic Law (Exod. 20:1-6). Because of their connection with demonized pagan religion, these objects were an affront to the Lord. God's people were to love him supremely and remain completely separated from idolatry.

IMMANUEL (ĭ-măn'ū-ĕl). The prophetic name of the virgin-born Messiah (Isa. 7:14). The name portrayed both his humanity and his deity: "Immanu" means

"with us" and "El" means "God."

IMMORTALITY. The perpetual life of the believer's resurrection body. Believers will receive an immortal body at the rapture (the coming of Christ to the air—1 Thess. 4:13-18; 1 Cor. 15:51-54). Christ's resurrected and glorified body in heaven is immortal. Believers will receive a body like his. He alone now has "immortality dwelling in the light" (1 Tim. 6:16). He brought "life and immortality to light through the gospel" (2 Tim. 1:10).

IMPUTATION. The word means "to reckon over to one's account." Scripture sets forth three major aspects of imputation. First, *Adam's sin is imputed to all mankind* (Rom. 5:12-21). In a sense all men sinned with Adam, the federal head of the race. In so doing mankind incurred the penalty of death (Rom. 5:12-21). This is a case of literal imputation, that is, reckoning to each person something that was his prior to his birth.

Second, *mankind's sin is imputed to Christ*. Christ "bore our sins" (1 Pet. 2:24), was "made . . . to be sin" (2 Cor. 5:21), and had "laid on him" our iniquity (Isa. 53:5, 6). This is *judicial* imputation: although Christ never sinned in any way, our guilt was transferred to him.

Third, *God's righteousness is imputed to the believer*. This is the righteousness of God reckoned to the believer by virtue of faith in Christ (Rom. 4:5-8). This aspect of imputation constitutes the believer's acceptance and standing before God. It is constituted legal before God since Christ offered himself without spot to God (Heb. 9:14). It is applied directly on the basis of the fact that the believer is "in Christ" (1 Cor. 1:30; 2 Cor. 5:21; Heb. 10:14).

INCARNATION. The process whereby Christ the Word, who was with God and was God (John 1:1), became man (John 1:14). The second Person of the triune Godhead became a theanthropic Person, lived a sinless life in a real human body on earth, and died a vicarious death to provide salvation for fallen men. As a result, every person who trusts Christ is guaranteed a sinless, deathless, glorified body like Christ's present glorified body.

INCENSE. Fragrant substances, such as

gums, spices, and resins, which release a fragrant smoke when burned. The burning of incense was a common practice in worship. Sweet incense was prominent in Israelite ritual (Exod. 25:6; 35:8; 37:29). It was offered on an "altar of incense" (Exod. 30:1-10; Luke 1:8-10). The divinely approved incense was compacted of opobalsamum, onycha, galbanum, and pure frankincense (Exod. 30:34-38). See also "Galbanum" and "Frankincense."

INNOCENCE. Man was created innocent of sin. He was placed in a perfect environment with only a single test, and was warned of the consequences of disobedience (Gen. 2:16, 17). Tempted by Satan, man chose to disobey God, thereby falling from his position of innocence. The woman was deceived, while the man transgressed deliberately (1 Tim. 2:14). The economy of innocence ended when God judged man by expelling him from Eden (Gen. 3:22-24). Being a sinner, man now needed redemption (Rom. 5:12-21).

INSECTS. Insects belong to a large group of invertebrate animals characterized in the adult state by division of the body into head, thorax, and abdomen and possessing three pairs of legs and membranous wings. Bees, beetles, flies, wasps, etc. are insects. The term is sometimes also popularly applied to other small animals (usually wingless), including spiders, snails, scorpions, etc. The mild and dry climate of Palestine encourages the growth of multitudes of insects and other small creatures. These normally help to maintain a proper balance in natural wildlife. In Old Testament times God sometimes used insects to upset this balance and thereby discipline his wayward people.

INSPIRATION. Holy Scripture is "God-breathed" in its very words as well as in its thoughts (Matt. 5:17-19; 2 Tim. 3:16, 17). The term "inspired" means "in-breathed," that is, by God. This applies to "all Scriptures" — that of the Old Testament as well as the New. The sound position has always been that of verbal and plenary inspiration, which teaches that in the original manuscripts every word of every portion of Scripture is fully inspired and bears full divine authority. Abandonment of this doctrine leads to a host of errors and false doctrines. This truth is the mother and guardian of all other theological truths. It is true that God used men to write his Word, but these human writers were borne along by the Holy Spirit and were infallibly guided to record everything God intended (2 Pet. 1:21).

INTERCESSION. A form of prayer in which the petitioner stands between God and some great need (Rom. 8:26, 27). Prayer in all its forms is to be offered to the Father (Matt. 6:9) in the name of the Son (John 16:23, 24), and in dependence on the Holy Spirit (Eph. 6:18; Jude 1:20).

ISAAC (ī'zak) ("he laughs"). The child of faith and promise born to Abraham and Sarah in their advanced years (Gen. 21:1-3). He was in the line of the promised Redeemer and is a beautiful picture of Christ as the Son "obedient to death" (Gen. 22:1-10) and as the Bridegroom of a called-out bride (Gen. 24:1-67).

ISAIAH (ī-sā'a) ("the Lord saves"). A great Old Testament prophet, writer, statesman, teacher, reformer, and theologian. His ministry extended from about 740 to 687 B.C. His prophecies, which are literary masterpieces, abound in detailed messianic predictions; of all the prophetic books of the Old Testament, Isaiah is the most messianic.

ISHBOSHETH (ish-bō'shĕth) ("man of shame"; originally Ishbaal, "man of Baal"). Saul's son, who contested the throne of Israel with David. He was ultimately deserted by Abner and murdered by two of his captains (2 Sam. 2:8—4:12).

ISHMAEL (ish'mā-ĕl) ("God hears"). Abraham's son by Hagar (Gen. 16) and the progenitor of the Ishmaelites, who roamed the deserts like the "wild ass" (Gen. 16:12). Like Ishmael, their ancestor, the Ishmaelites were celebrated for their skill with the bow. Moslem Arabs claim descent from Ishmael.

ISHTAR (ish'tăr). The Babylonian goddess corresponding to Ashtoreth of the Canaanites (Judg. 2:13; 10:6; 1 Sam. 7:3-4; 12:10; 1 Kings 11:5). See "Ashtoreth."

ISLAND. The islands of the biblical world are located in the Mediterranean Sea, also called "the great sea" (Josh. 1:4), "the uttermost sea" (Deut. 11:24), and "the sea of the Philistines" (Exod. 23:31).

These islands are called "the isles of the Gentiles" (Gen. 10:5) or "the isles of the sea." They consist principally of the land masses of the eastern half of the Mediterranean, notably Caphtor (Crete) and Chittim (Cyprus), but also include insular Tyre and Arvad. In the New Testament a number of islands receive special interest as the result of Paul's missionary travels. The island of Patmos in the Aegean is specified in the Book of the Revelation as the place where John received his apocalyptic visions.

ISRAEL (ĭz′rā-ĕl) ("God strives"). The new name given to Jacob, the supplanter, after his night of wrestling at Penuel (Gen. 32:28). The name also stands for the whole body of Jacob's descendants in their calling and destiny before God (Psa. 73:1; Rom. 11:26). See also "Israelites" below.

ISRAELITES. Those Hebrews who descended from Abraham through Isaac and Jacob (Israel). They became the divinely chosen line through which the Messiah-Redeemer would eventually come. Through their deliverance out of Egyptian bondage they became a symbol of redemption for the whole fallen race. The twelve tribes became a nation at Sinai. The Mosaic Law with its priesthood and sacrificial system was given to them so they could show to all nations both the necessity of redemption and the need to obey the eternal moral law of God.

The Israelite nation conquered Palestine and settled in it under covenant to serve and honor the Lord. Repeated violation of the covenant resulted in divine chastisement during the era of the judges and under the kingdoms of Saul, David, and Solomon. The most serious blow

was the division of the kingdom under Rehoboam (931 B.C.) After this date the Northern Kingdom of ten tribes went its separate way until its fall to Assyria in 722 B.C. Judah continued until the fall of Jerusalem in 586 B.C. and the ensuing exile in Babylon.

Elements of the twelve tribes had become integrated with the Judeans or "Jews." The mixed Judeans or "Jews" in turn adopted the broader term of "Israelites." Their prophets foresaw a regathering of representatives from every tribe and the establishment of the converted and blessed nation under Messiah-Savior in the end time. This was viewed as a fulfillment of God's faithful covenants and promises made to the nation (Isa. 11, 12, 55; Ezek. 37). See also "Chosen People" and "Jews."

ISSACHAR (ĭs′à-kär) ("man of wages, a hired worker"). A son of Jacob by Leah and the progenitor of the tribe that bears his name (Gen. 30:17, 18; 35:23).

ITHAMAR (ĭth′à-mär) (possibly "land of palms"). The youngest son of Aaron (Exod. 6:23) and an ordained priest (Exod. 28:1). He was placed over the Gershonites and Merarites (Num. 4:28, 33).

ITALY (ĭt′à-lĭ) The name of the peninsula bordered on the east by the Adriatic Sea and on the south by the Ionian Sea (Acts 27:1, 6; Heb. 13:24).

ITTAI (ĭt′à-ī) ("with me"). A loyal follower of David; he was faithful through thick and thin (2 Sam. 15:18-22; 18:2-5).

ITUREA (ĭt′ū-rē′à). The territory of the Itureans (the "Jetur" of Gen. 25:15; 1 Chron. 1:31). It was located in the valley between Lebanon and Antilebanon. After the death of Herod the Great it became part of the tetrarchy of Philip (Luke 3:1).

JABBOK (jăb′ŏk). An eastern tributary of the Jordan River. It separated the Transjordan tribes of Gad and Manasseh. There Jacob wrestled with the celestial visitant (Gen. 32:22-24).

JABAL (jā′băl). A pre-flood patriarch and a progenitor of migrating cattle owners (Gen. 4:20).

JABESH-GILEAD (jā′bĕsh-gĭl′ė-ăd). An Israelite town east of the Jordan River. Saul routed the Ammonites who were besieging it (1 Sam. 11:1-11). It is probably to be identified with present-day Tell Abu-Kharaz, nine miles from Bethshan and two miles from the Jordan.

JABEZ (jā′bĕz) ("he makes sorrow"). A man of Judah whose mother named him Jabez because she bore him in sorrow and pain. But after praying for and receiving a special blessing he became more honorable than his brothers (1 Chron. 4:9, 10).

JABIN (jā′bĭn) ("he perceives"). (1) A Canaanite king of Hazor who was defeated by Joshua (Josh. 11:1-14). (2) Another Canaanite king at Hazor who was defeated by Deborah and Barak (Judg. 4:1-24; cf. Psa. 83:9).

JACKAL. A carrion-eating mammal that inhabits wilderness areas (Isa. 34:13, 14; 35:7; 43:20; Jer. 49:33; 51:37). The jackal has been dubbed "the lion's provider" because its cry apprises the lion that food is at hand. See also "Fox."

JACOB (jā′kŭb) (popular etymology, "one who takes by the heel or supplants"). The son of Isaac and Rebekah and the twin brother of Esau (Gen. 25:21-26). He illustrates the conflict of the two natures in a believer. As Jacob he was crafty, deceitful, and selfish. As Israel he displayed faith and obedience as a chosen instrument of God. As such he was also affectionate (Gen. 29:18), industrious (Gen. 31:40, 41), prayerful (Gen. 32:9-12), and divinely disciplined (Gen. 37:31-35; 42: 36-38). He became the founder of the Hebrew nation (Gen. 49:1-28) and a link in the messianic line.

JACOB'S WELL. See under "Springs, Wells, and Pools."

JAEL (jā′ĕl) ("wild goat"). The wife of the Kenite Heber. She slew Sisera by driving a tent pin through his head while he slept (Judg. 4:18-21). When the victorious Barak passed by, Jael called him to see her part in the battle (Judg. 4:22). Deborah praised Jael's deed (Judg. 5:1-6, 24-27), thereby revealing the cruelty of the human heart in times of war.

JAIR (jā′ēr) ("he enlightens"). A judge of Israel for 22 years, succeeding Tola (Judg. 10:1-3).

JAIRUS (jā′ĭ-rŭs) ("he enlightens"). A ruler of the synagogue. It was his daughter whom Jesus raised from death (Mark 5:22-42; Luke 8:41-56).

JAMBRES (jăm′brēz). One of the demon-energized magicians of Egypt (Exod. 7, 8). He opposed Moses, the true miracle-worker of God (Exod. 7:1-6). The names Jannes and Jambres do not occur in the Old Testament but are found in extra-biblical literature in other forms, as in the Zadokite Work. See also "Jannes."

JAMES (a form of the name "Jacob"). (1) James the son of Zebedee and the brother of John (Matt. 4:21; 17:1). He was one of the inner circle of Christ's disciples. (2) James the son of Alphaeus. He was also an apostle (Matt. 10:3; Mark 15:40; 16:1). (3) James the half brother of Jesus (Matt. 13:55; Mark 6:3; Gal. 1:19). He was a leader in the early church at Jerusalem (Acts 12:17; 15:13; 21:18; Gal. 2:9, 12) and the writer of the Epistle of James (1:1).

JANNES (jăn'ēz). One of the two Egyptian magicians who attempted to counterwork Moses. See also "Jambres." Compare 2 Timothy 3:8 with Exodus 7 and 8.

JAPHETH (jā'fĕth) ("let him enlarge"). Noah's second son and the progenitor of the peoples that spread to the northern and western regions of the earth after the Flood—Medians, Greeks, Romans, Gauls, Germans, Russians, etc. (Gen. 9:18, 19; 10:1-5).

JASON (jā'sŭn) ("healing"). (1) A Hebrew Christian (Rom. 16:21). (2) A believer at Thessalonica who befriended Paul and Silas (Acts 17:5-9).

JAVAN (jā'văn). The fourth son of Japheth (Gen. 10:2) and the progenitor of the Ionian Greeks (Ezek. 27:13; Joel 3:6).

JAVELIN. A type of light spear having a shaft of wood pointed with metal. It could be hurled at a target (1 Sam. 18:10, 11; 19:9, 10). An even lighter and shorter spear was also employed as a javelin (Josh. 8:18; Jer. 6:23; Job 39:23).

JAZER (jā'zẽr). A town which was occupied by the tribe of Gad (Num. 32:1-5; Josh. 13:24, 25). It was a Levitical city (Josh. 21:39). It is identified with present-day Khirbet Jazzir, 10 miles east of the Jordan and about 12 miles south of the River Jabbok.

JEARIM (jē'á-rĭm). A mountain near Beth-shemesh whose northern shoulder formed a boundary of the tribe of Judah (Josh. 15:10). It is situated northwest of Jerusalem in the central highland ridge.

JEDIDAH (jē-dī'dá) ("beloved"). The wife of king Amon (642-640 B.C.) and the mother of Josiah. Her evil husband was struck down by palace servants for his wickedness. He was succeeded by his eight-year-old son, who became one of the godly kings of Judah (640-609 B.C.).

Since his father was wicked, it was apparently his mother who influenced the youthful king in the ways of the Lord.

JEHO-ADDAN (jē'hō-ăd'ăn) (perhaps "the Lord is delight"). The wife of King Joash of Judah (835-796 B.C.) and the mother of King Amaziah (796-767 B.C.). Joash did well in his youth under the guidance of the priest Jehoiada. Later on he apostatized from the Lord and was murdered, even as he had murdered Zechariah the son of Jehoiada for pronouncing judgment upon evildoers (2 Chron. 24:15-22; 2 Kings 12:20; 2 Chron. 24:25). Amaziah also began well but ended his reign in idolatry. Like his father, he was murdered (2 Kings 14:17-20).

JEHOAHAZ (jĕ-hō'á-hăz) ("the Lord has laid hold of"). (1) A son and successor of Jehu. He reigned over the Northern Kingdom from about 813 to 798 B.C. Syrian aggression reduced his kingdom to its lowest ebb (2 Kings 13:1-9). (2) The son and successor of King Jehoram of Judah (2 Chron. 21:17). He was also called Ahaziah. (2) A son of King Josiah who was deposed by Pharaoh-necho (2 Kings 23:30-34). He was also called Shallum (1 Chron. 3:15).

JEHOASH, JOASH (jĕ-hō'ăsh, jō'ăsh) ("the Lord has bestowed"). (1) A king of Judah, a son of Ahaziah, and the father of Amaziah (2 Kings 11:21; 12:1-18). He escaped family massacre by being concealed until he was seven years old. His preservation provided continuance of the royal line. (2) The king of Israel from about 798 to 782 B.C. and a son and successor of King Jehoahaz (2 Kings 13:10, 25; 14:8-16). He raised the fortunes of Israel from their lowest ebb under Jehoahaz to greatness for his son, Jeroboam II.

JEHOIACHIN (jĕ-hoî'á-kĭn) ("the Lord establishes"). The king of Judah during 598 and 597 B.C. and a son of Jehoiakim. He was carried off to Babylon (2 Kings 24:8-16; 2 Chron. 36:9, 10). This event is also described in the Babylonian Chronicle. He was succeeded by his uncle Mattaniah, renamed Zedekiah (2 Kings 24:17; Jer. 37:1).

JEHOIADA (jĕ-hoî'á-dá) ("the Lord knows"). The high priest who made Joash king and saved the infant Jehoash from massacre (2 Kings 11:4-17).

JEHOIAKIM (jė-hoi'á-kĭm) ("the Lord has established"). A son of Josiah. Pharaoh-necho made him king instead of Jehoahaz. His reign (609-598 B.C.) was evil and he displayed himself as a frivolous and profane egotist (2 Kings 23:34-36; 24:1-4).

JEHORAM (jė-hō'răm; abbrev. **JORAM**) ("the Lord is exalted"). (1) The king of Israel during 852 and 851 B.C. He succeeded the brief reign of his brother Ahaziah (2 Kings 1:17). Elisha was active during his reign (2 Kings 1:17 – 9:28). (2) A son of Jehoshaphat and brother-in-law of Jehoram of Israel through marriage with Athaliah, Ahab's daughter (848-841 B.C.). His reign over Judah (2 Kings 8:16-24) stood in sad contrast to that of his godly father. His apostasy was rebuked by Elijah (2 Chron. 21:12-15).

JEHOSHAPHAT (jė-hŏsh'á-făt) ("the Lord judges"). A king of Judah (870-848 B.C.) and son of Asa (1 Kings 22:41-50; 2 Chron. 17:1 – 21:1). He was a godly king, one of the best of Judah (1 Kings 22:43). However, he manifested weakness in allying himself with wicked kings (1 Kings 22:1-36).

JEHOSHEBA (jė-hŏsh'ē-bá) ("the Lord is an oath"). The daughter of King Jehoram of Judah and the wife of Jehoiada the high priest. When Ahaziah and the royal seed were slain by Athaliah, Jehosheba hid Ahaziah's infant son, Joash, in the Temple until he could safely be declared the rightful king in the Davidic line (2 Kings 11:2; 2 Chron. 22:11).

JEHOVAH (jė-hō'vá), **YAHWEH.** The personal name of Israel's God. The Hebrews connected the word with *hayah*, "to be." In Exodus 3:14 the name is explained as "I am that I am," indicating either the eternal, self-existent One or "I will be what I will be," that is, "I will be all that is necessary for every occasion." See also "Adonai Jehovah."

JEHU (jė'hū) ("the Lord is he"). The king of Israel from 841 to 814 B.C. With a massive bloodbath he exterminated the house of Ahab and stamped out the worship of Baal (2 Kings 9:1 – 10:28). But his true inner character appears in his toleration of the corrupt worship of the Lord linked with the bull images at Dan and Bethel (2 Kings 10:29-31). Israel did not prosper under Jehu, and Hazael of Syria overran all her territory in Transjordan (2 Kings 10:32, 33). Jehu's submission to Assyria is depicted on the Black Obelisk of Shalmaneser III, but the picture was doubtless rendered for the purpose of pitting Assyria against Hazael.

JEPHTHAH (jĕf'thá) ("God opens"). One of the later Hebrew judges (Judg. 11:1 – 12:7), who delivered Israel from Ammonite oppression. He made a rash vow and kept it (Judg. 11:29-40).

JEREMIAH (jĕr'ė-mī'á) ("the Lord lifts up"). The great prophet of the last forty years of the Kingdom of Judah (626-586 B.C.) He is called "the weeping prophet." The sin and apostasy of Judah caused him to grieve inconsolably. His sufferings and persecutions were intense (Jer. 20:1-18; 38:6). His predictions of the fall of Jerusalem to the Chaldeans were fully realized, to the consternation of his foes.

Mound of ancient Jericho in foreground connects by road with modern Jericho to the south. (© *MPS*)

JERICHO (jĕr'ĭ-kō). An important city located in the Valley of the Jordan (Deut. 34:1, 3) on the west side of the river. It is situated about 10 miles from the north end of the Dead Sea and about 17 miles from Jerusalem. It guarded the gateway to Palestine from Transjordan. Jericho fell to Joshua and the Israelites but was placed under a curse (Josh. 6). It is mentioned in both the Old and New Testaments (Luke 10:30; 18:35; 19:1, 2; Matt. 20:29). Old Testament Jericho is identified with present-day Tell es-Sultan, about one mile northwest of er-Riha village. Herodian and New Testament Jericho are identified with the mounds of Tulul Abu el-ᶜAlayiq, one mile west of modern er-Riha. It was Herod's winter capital.

JERICHO, PLAINS OF. The city of Jericho was situated about five miles west of the Jordan River and about 10 miles from the northern tip of the Dead Sea. The low-lying terrain between the city, the river, and the Sea constituted "the plains of Jericho" (Josh. 4:13). These plains were part of the deep valley of the Jordan River (Deut. 34:3). The valley was called the Arabah and designated the Rift Valley, which extends from the Sea of Galilee to the Gulf of Aqabah. Today the Valley of the Jordan downstream to the Dead Sea is called the Ghor, meaning the "depression." The plural of the word "Arabah" describes certain wastelands around Jericho (Josh. 5:10; 2 Kings 25:5).

JEROBOAM I (jĕr-ō-bō'am) ("the people become numerous"). The first king of the Northern Kingdom (931-910 B.C.). He was the man who gave occasion for Israel

782 to 735 B.C. He was the son of Joash. During his reign Israel attained material prosperity and power but declined spiritually (2 Kings 14:23-28). Amos prophesied during this reign (Amos 1:1), calling the wayward people to come back to God and warning of impending judgment. Hosea also ministered during Jeroboam's lifetime (Hosea 1:1).

JERUBBAAL (jĕr'ŭb-bā'ăl) ("let Baal contend"). The name given to Gideon by his father (Judg. 6:32). Jerubbesheth ("Let *shame* contend") is the same name with the word "shame" (*bosheth*) substituted for the pagan deity (2 Sam. 11:21).

JERUSALEM. The sacred city and well-known capital of Judah, of Judea, and of world Jewry. It was called Urusalim in the Amarna Letters and was probably the "Salem" of Genesis 14:18. It was originally a Canaanite (Jebusite) city (Josh. 10:1-5). It was captured from the Jebu-

Airview of Jerusalem, looking southwest over Temple site near Muslim Dome of the Rock and toward distant Mediterranean (© *MPS*)

to sin by setting up the polluted worship of the Lord at Bethel and Dan (1 Kings 12:25 – 13:5; 13:33, 34). Jeroboam attempted to retain his kingdom through idolatry even though Solomon had lost his kingdom by committing this sin.

JEROBOAM II. The king of Israel from

sites by David (2 Sam. 5:6-9) and later became the capital of the United Kingdom (2 Sam. 20:3; 1 Kings 2:36). It was threatened by the Assyrians (2 Kings 18:35) and plundered by the Babylonians (2 Kings 24:10-16; 25:1-21). It was restored after the exile (Ezra 1:1-4) and harassed by Antiochus Epiphanes (1 Macc. 4:36-60) and later became the Hasmonean capital. It was Herod the Great's capital (Matt. 2:1-3) and the religious center of Judea in Roman times (Luke 2:42-45; John 2:13, 23; Acts 2:5; 8:1; Gal. 1:18; 2:1).

JERUSALEM, NEW. The city is the glorious symbol of the eternal abode and destiny of the redeemed of all ages (Rev. 21:10 – 22:5). Such a city has always been foreseen by God's saints (Heb. 11:10; 13:14; cf. John 14:1-3). The inhabitants of the eternal city will include God the Father, glorified Old Testament saints (Heb. 11:10), New Testament church saints, myriads of unfallen angels, and our blessed Lord himself (Heb. 12:22, 23). Both Israel and the church appear prominently in the city (Rev. 21:12, 14). The great wall of the city symbolizes the security of its inhabitants, who are bathed in God's radiant, unveiled majesty (Rev. 21:23-25; 22:5). The city is distinct from the new heaven and earth of the eternal state, for it comes down from God out of heaven (Rev. 21:10). See also "Zion."

JERUSHAH (je-rū'shà) ("possessed"). The wife of Azariah king of Judah and the mother of his successor, Jotham (2 Kings 15:33; 2 Chron. 27:1), who reigned from about 739 to 731 B.C. It is recorded that this mother's son "became mighty, because he prepared his ways before the Lord" (2 Chron. 27:6).

JESSE (jĕs'ė) (perhaps "man"). The father of David and a descendant of Ruth the Moabitess (Ruth 4:18-22).

JESUS CHRIST. In addition to being the central character of the Bible, our Lord Jesus Christ is the greatest of all men everywhere. He fulfills this role because he is the eternal Word, God become man (John 1:1-18; Phil. 2:5-11). He is the Creator of all things; nothing was made apart from him (John 1:3; Col. 1:16, 17; Heb. 1:2). He was "before all things," and "in him all things consist (hold together)" (Col. 1:17). He is the appointed "heir of all things," the "brightness of (God's) glory," and the "express image of his person" (Heb. 1:2, 3).

As the eternal Word, Christ the preincarnate Son became a man by the power of the Holy Spirit in the womb of the virgin Mary (Isa. 7:14; Matt. 1:18-25; Luke 1:35). He thus possessed a human body, soul, and spirit that were united to deity to form a unique, divine-human personality. As the God-man, Christ lived a sinless life, died a vicarious and sin-atoning death, and was raised with a glorified body that forever unites redeemed mankind with God. For when Christ had "by himself purged our sins," he "sat down at the right hand of the majesty on high" (Heb. 1:3).

Thus this greatest of all men is now in heaven as the glorified Son of Man, Jesus Christ "come in the flesh" (1 John 4:2). The Greek perfect participle denotes that he possessed not merely a temporary humanity by virtue of his incarnation, but instead, a genuine, permanent, glorified human body for all eternity. This provides an eternal link between God and redeemed mankind.

Christ is greater than Adam because he is Adam's Creator. He is greater than Abraham because he existed in past eternity and was the object of Abraham's faith (John 8:56-58). He is greater than Solomon because he is "the wisdom of God" (Matt. 12:42; 1 Cor. 1:30) as well as the Creator and Owner of the universe and the "heir of all things" (Col. 1:15-17; Heb. 1:3). He is greater than Jacob in the liberality of his gift. Jacob gave his people a well (John 4:12), but Christ gave his people rivers of living waters (John 4:13, 14; 7:37-39).

Christ's Genealogies. Matthew and Luke present genealogies of Christ. Matthew, addressing Jews, presents Christ as the son of David, tracing his lineage back 2000 years to Abraham (Matt. 1:1-17). Matthew thus introduces the rightful Heir to the Kingdom and proclaims Christ as the King of Israel. Luke, addressing non-Jews, traces Christ's lineage to the first man, Adam, the father of the human race (Luke 3:23-38). Luke thus presents Christ as the Son of Man. Both genealogies link Christ to the Old Testament with its promises and prophecies of redemption.

Our Lord Jesus Christ bears many exalted names and titles. A few of these are herewith described.

Lord is the name that expresses Christ's sovereignty and majesty, both as Sovereign of life and Ruler of the earth (1 Cor. 12:3; Rev. 19:16). By the dual right of creation and redemption he is the absolute King and Ruler of the earth and its people. At his second advent he will fully assume this rightful dignity (Rev. 19:16).

Jesus is the human name of Christ, the Son of God. The name comes from the Greek form of the Hebrew word for "Joshua," meaning "Jehovah is salvation" (cf. Acts 7:45; Heb. 4:8). He was to be called Jesus because he was to "save his people from their sins" (Matt. 1:21). However, his full title is "Lord Jesus Christ." "Lord" relates him to his eternal deity, "Christ" to his threefold office (Prophet, Priest, and King), and "Jesus" to his incarnation and saviorhood as the God-man.

Christ (Greek *Christos*, Hebrew *Mashiah*) means "the anointed one" and is our Savior's official name. The title presents our Lord in the light of the Old Testament foreview of him as Prophet (Deut. 18:15-19), Priest (Psa. 110:4), and King (2 Sam. 7:12, 13; Psa. 2:1-12; Isa. 9:6, 7). Prophets, priests, and kings were anointed with oil (1 Kings 19:16; 1 Sam. 16:13), but Jesus was anointed with the Holy Spirit (Isa. 61:1-3; Matt. 3:16, 17; Mark 1:10, 11; Luke 3:21, 22; John 1:32, 33).

Shiloh, meaning "peace" (Gen. 49:10), presents Christ as our Peacemaker. He *preached* peace (Eph. 2:17), he *makes* peace (Eph. 2:15), and he *is* our peace (Eph. 2:14).

Immanuel (Isa. 7:14) is a name which describes Christ in his incarnation. The name is composed of two parts and means "with *us*" (*Immanu*) is "God" (*El*). Along with this highly significant name, Isaiah presented a sign which involved the miracle of the virgin birth. The sign was divinely given — "the Lord himself" gave it (Isa. 7:14). It was presented to David's house and not simply to Ahaz ("you" is plural in Isaiah 7:14). The sign included the element of the miraculous (Isa. 7:11). It foresaw the perpetuation of the house of David until the ultimate sign of the ages should be realized. It involved a virgin (Matt. 1:22, 23). Although divine, the child would also be human (Isa. 7:15).

Wonderful Counselor (Isa. 9:6) describes Christ in his infinite wisdom (cf. Prov. 8).

The Mighty God (Isa. 9:6) emphasizes Christ's deity. The title connotes "God-Champion," Christ as a champion in battle.

Everlasting Father (Isa. 9:6) is literally "father of eternity" or "the eternal one." The title connotes both Christ's eternal personal existence and his authorship of all eternal life.

Prince of Peace (Isa. 9:6) describes the sovereign Lord who will effect a warless world in the coming kingdom.

The Branch describes the coming Messiah in his Temple-building role (Zech. 6:12-15; Ezek. 40–42; Mic. 4:1, 2). He will be highly glorified (Psa. 8:1; Isa. 52:13; Rev. 19:16). Messiah will be the "second man" who regains that dominion over the earth which had been lost by the "first man," Adam (Psa. 8; Heb. 1:6-10; 1 Cor. 15:45-49). In the coming kingdom, Messiah will combine in one Person the two offices of King-Priest.

The Word of God is the rich title which John applies to Christ in Revelation 19:13. The name means "the full expression of God" and aptly epitomizes the infinite glory of the Person of Christ.

JETHRO (jĕth'rō) ("preeminence, excellence"). A priest of Midian and the father-in-law of Moses (Exod. 3:1; 4:18; 18:1-12). He was also called Reuel, which means "friend of God" (Exod. 2:18).

JEWELRY. See specific item of jewelry.

JEWS. As used in the Bible, the term "Jew" in the pre-exilic era referred to citizens of the southern state of Judah (Neh. 1:2; Jer. 32:12; 40:11). In post-exilic times the name denoted the people of Israel in contrast to the Gentiles (Esth. 9:15-19; Dan. 3:8; Zech. 8:23; John 4:9; Acts 14:1). In the New Testament the term applied to anyone who was Jewish by both nationality and religion. In a few cases Jewish Christians were also called Jews (John 8:31; Acts 21:39; Gal. 2:13). See also "Chosen People" and "Israelites."

JEZEBEL (jĕz'ĕ-bĕl). A pagan queen of

Israel and the wife of Ahab (873-853 B.C.). She was the daughter of Ethbaal, priest-king of Tyre and Sidon. She was an ardent devotee of Baal Melqart, and provision was made for her to continue her pagan cult in her new home in Samaria. Her staff numbered 450 Baal prophets and 400 prophets of the goddess Asherah (1 Kings 16:31-33; 18:19). Her zeal for Canaanite religion brought her into conflict with Elijah, who thoroughly discredited the cult worshipers on Mount Carmel (1 Kings 18:1-40).

Jezebel's idea of an absolute monarchy also collided with the Hebrew covenant relationship between the Lord, the king, and the people. Her ruthless treatment of Naboth was a highhanded violation of Hebrew law and morality and sealed her doom and that of the house of Ahab (1 Kings 21). Her name became proverbial for wickedness and symbolic of idolatrous lawlessness (Rev. 2:20-23).

JEZREEL (jĕz'rĕ-ĕl). A town at the head of the Valley of Jezreel. It was part of Solomon's fifth district (1 Kings 4:12). Ahab had a palace there (1 Kings 21:1-16).

JOAB (jō'ăb) ("the Lord is father"). A nephew of King David and a general in his army (1 Sam. 26:6; 2 Sam. 2:1— 1 Kings 2:34). He was an overambitious man, whose apparent devotion to David was actually a cover-up for his own preeminence as commander of the army. Although a skilled general (attested by the many victories he won—2 Sam. 2:12-32; 11:1; 12:26-29; 20:4-22; 1 Chron. 11:6-9), Joab was vindictive and ruthlessly cruel (2 Sam. 3:22-27; 18:14; 20:9, 10; 1 Kings 11:16).

JOANNA (jō-ăn'à) ("the Lord has been gracious"). A woman of position who supported Christ in his public ministry by giving of her material means (Luke 8:3). She was the wife of Chuza, an important official of Herod Antipas (Luke 8:3). She was one of the women who attempted to show final respects to Christ's body and shared in announcing the resurrection to the Twelve (Luke 24:1-11).

JOB (jōb) (meaning uncertain, but possibly "one who came back to God"). The great biblical example of the suffering saint. His experiences probe the question of why the righteous suffer. A prime answer to the question is that the godly suffer in order to be refined and purified to the ultimate glory of God (Job 42:1-6).

JOCHEBED (jŏk'ĕ-bĕd) ("the Lord is glory"). A daughter of Levi and the mother of Moses, Aaron, and Miriam (Exod. 6:20; Num. 26:59). Her name is not recorded in the actual narrative of Moses' birth and miraculous preservation (Exod. 2:1-10).

JOEL (jō'ĕl) ("the Lord is God"). A prophet in the days of King Uzziah (767-739 B.C.). He foresaw the future day of the Lord under the figure of a locust plague and the promised pre-kingdom outpouring of the Spirit (Joel 1, 2). This latter event bears resemblance to the pentecostal effusion upon believing Jews when the church was born (Acts 2:14-21). Joel also envisioned the judgment of the nations which precedes Israel's establishment in full kingdom blessing (Joel 3).

JOHN ("the Lord is gracious"). The "beloved Apostle," a son of Zebedee and brother of James (who was martyred under Herod Agrippa I). John belonged to a family of Galilean fishermen until he and his brother were called to follow Jesus (Matt. 4:21, 22; Mark 1:19, 20). Later they were appointed apostles (Matt. 10:2). Their vehemence won them the nickname "sons of thunder" (Mark 3:17). With his brother James, John belonged to the inner circle at the raising of Jairus' daughter (Mark 5:37; Luke 8:51), at the transfiguration (Matt. 17:1; Mark 9:2), and at the agony in Gethsemane (Matt. 26:37; Mark 14:33). John occupied the place next to Jesus at the Last Supper (John 13:23). He was a prominent witness of the resurrection and the ascension (John 20:1-10; Acts 1:1-13). John wrote the fourth Gospel, the three Johannine Epistles, and the Revelation (cf. Rev. 1:9).

JOHN THE BAPTIST. The rugged, fearless preacher who was the forerunner of the Messiah (Matt. 3:1). He preached the baptism of repentance (Matt. 3:11; Mark 1:8) which was preparatory to Messiah's baptism with the Holy Spirit (John 1:32, 33; Acts 1:5; 2:1-21).

JOKTAN (jŏk'tăn). The progenitor (through Eber of the family of Shem) of 13 Arab tribes (Gen. 10:26; 1 Chron. 1:19-23).

JONADAB, JEHONADAB (jŏn'ȧ-dăb, jė̇-hŏn'ȧ-dăb) ("the Lord is bounteous"). A son of Rechab (Jer. 35:6). He followed a strict ascetic life (Jer. 35:6, 7) and aided Jehu in exterminating Baal worship from Israel (2 Kings 10:15, 23).

JONAH (jō'nȧ) ("a dove"). The first Hebrew prophet to be sent as a missionary to a pagan nation (Jonah 1:1, 2; 2 Kings 14:25). He attempted to flee from the instructions and presence of God but was chastised in the stomach of a large marine animal (Jonah 1). Thereupon he repented, obeyed the call of God, and preached in Nineveh with astonishing response (Jonah 2, 3). He reluctantly learned about the mercy of God (Jonah 4). Jonah symbolizes Christ in death, resurrection, and witness (Matt. 12:38-41). His experiences also parallel the history of the Jewish nation.

JONATHAN (jŏn'ȧ-thăn) ("the Lord has given"). The eldest son of Saul and a close friend of David. He was humble, loving, loyal, and unselfish. He was unswervingly devoted to David even though he knew that David would occupy the throne of Israel which would normally have been Jonathan's as the firstborn son (1 Sam. 18:1 – 20:42).

JOPPA (jŏp'pȧ). A town on the Mediterranean coast about 35 miles northwest of Jerusalem. It was the seaport for Jerusalem in Old Testament times (2 Chron. 2:16; Ezra 3:7). It was at Joppa that Jonah attempted to sail from the presence of God (Jonah 1:3). Peter had an extensive ministry in Joppa (Acts 9:36-43; 10:5-23). Joppa is now called Jaffa and still maintains a harbor.

JORAM, JEHORAM (jō'răm, jē-hō'răm). (1) The king of Judah from 848 to 841 B.C. He was the son of Jehoshaphat (2 Kings 8:16-19). (2) The king of Israel from 852 to 841 B.C. He was the son of Ahab (2 Kings 3:1-3).

JORDAN RIVER. The largest and most important river of the Holy Land. The name "Jordan" (Hebrew *yardēn*) has the appropriate meaning of "the Descender." Its spring-fed headwaters first collect in Lake Huleh, 230 feet above sea level. At Lake Tiberias, 10 miles south, the river descends to 700 feet below sea level. At the north end of the Dead Sea it plunges

Serpentine Jordan River twists between barren hills toward lowest spot on earth, the Dead Sea. (© *MPS*)

to 1,290 feet below sea level. The Jordan River is a snakelike stream, requiring more than 150 miles of riverbed to cover the 75 straight-line miles from Lake Huleh to the Dead Sea. No river is referred to more frequently in the Bible.

JOSEPH (jō'sěf) ("may he add"). (1) The eleventh of Jacob's 12 sons (Gen. 30:22-24). He is a remarkable prefiguration of Christ. Both were special objects of a father's love (Gen. 37:3; Matt. 3:17; John 3:35). Both were hated by their brothers (Gen. 37:4; John 15:25). The superior claims of both were rejected by their brothers (Gen. 37:8; Matt. 21:37-39; John 15:24, 25). The brothers of both conspired to kill them (Gen. 37:18; Matt. 26:3, 4). Each became a blessing among the Gentiles and gained a Gentile bride (Gen. 41:1-45; Acts 15:14). Joseph reconciled his brothers to himself and afterward exalted them (Gen. 45:1-15). Christ will do the same with his Jewish brethren at the second advent (Deut. 30:1-10; Hos. 2:14-18; Rom. 11:1, 15, 25, 26).

(2) The husband of Mary and foster-father of our Lord Jesus Christ (Matt. 1:16-25). A humble carpenter (Matt. 13:55), Joseph was present at the manger where Jesus was born. Although the unborn infant which Mary carried was not Joseph's, he believed the angelic message about his wife's chastity (Matt. 1:18-24). He was blessed with the knowledge that the promised Messiah was to be a member of his own modest family and that

Mary was to bear the sinless Son of Man and Son of God.

JOSEPH OF ARIMATHEA (ăr'ĭ-mȧ-thē'ȧ). The man who gave his tomb to Jesus (Matt. 27:57-60; Mark 15:43-46; Luke 23:50-53; John 19:38-42). By this gift the virgin-born Savior was buried in a virgin tomb.

JOSEPHUS, FLAVIUS (jō-sē'fȧs, flā'vē-ȧs). A famous Jewish historian who lived from about A.D. 30 to 100. He was appointed commander of the army in Galilee at the outbreak of the Jewish revolt. He accompanied Vespasian's son Titus to Rome and received Roman citizenship and honors. His historical works include *The Jewish War* and *The Antiquities of the Jews.*

JOSHUA (jŏsh'ū-ȧ) ("the Lord is salvation"). As a slave in Egypt Joshua knew the lash of the oppressor's whip. As a scout in the wilderness he believed God and prepared to possess the land of Canaan (Num. 13:1 – 14:10). As a servant he was unswervingly loyal to God and Moses. As a savior he led the people into the land and vanquished their foes. As a statesman he allotted the land, set up the Tabernacle, and established the cities of refuge. As a saint he was filled with the Spirit (Deut. 34:9), enjoyed the presence of God (Josh. 1:5; 6:27), and obeyed the will of God (Num. 32:11, 12; Josh. 5:13-15). He is a symbol of Christ as the captain of our salvation, the leader who gives us rest (Heb. 3:7 – 4:11).

JOSIAH (jō-zī'ȧ) ("the Lord heals"). The king of Judah from 641 to 608 B.C. He was a good king, initiating revival and obeying the Word of God (2 Kings 22:1 – 23:30). He repaired the Temple, stamped out heathen worship, observed the Passover, and called the nation back to God. He met death at the hands of Pharaoh-Necho at the age of 39.

JUBILEE (jōō'bĭ-lē). Under the Mosaic Law every seventh year was a sabbatical year for the land. Sowing and pruning were forbidden. After seven sabbatical years or 49 years, the fiftieth year was a "jubilee year," when all slaves were released and all alienated property was returned to its ancestral owners (Lev. 25). This humane law showed that God owned the land, and that it was not to be alienated from the Lord's people permanently. Earth will one day celebrate its eternal jubilee in the new heaven and new earth (Rev. 21:1 – 22:5; cf. Rom. 8: 19-23).

JUDAH (jōō'dȧ) ("let him be praised"). The fourth son of Jacob and the founder of the kingly tribe of Israel (Gen. 29:35; Num. 26:19-22), from whom Messiah-King came. On account of their sins Reuben, Simeon, and Levi were passed over by Jacob and the blessing of the birthright was bestowed on Judah instead (Gen. 49:1-12).

JUDAISM (jōō'dȧ-ĭz'm). God's special relation with the Jews. The Apostle Paul refers to it as the religion of the Jews (Acts 26:5; Gal. 1:13; cf. James 1:26, 27). Although some similarities exist, Judaism is to be clearly distinguished from Christianity or what the New Testament writers designate as "the faith" (Jude 1:3) and "this way" (Acts 9:2; 22:4; cf. 18:26). Old Testament Judaism was conditioned by God's covenants with and promises to Israel, and looked forward to Christ. When Israel rejected Christ, God turned to the Gentiles to take out of them a heavenly people for his name (Acts 15:14). These are in contrast to God's earthly people, Israel. The latter will turn to Christ at his glorious second advent.

JUDAS (jōō'dȧs, jōō'dȧ) (1) A half-brother of Jesus, a brother of James, and the writer of the Epistle of Jude (Matt. 13: 55; Mark 6:3; Luke 6:16; Acts 1:13; Jude 1:1). (Jude is the English form of Judas.) See "Jude." (2) A Galilean who fomented an anti-Roman rebellion shortly after the birth of Christ (Acts 5:37). (3) A man with whom Paul lodged at Damascus (Acts 9:11). (4) A prophet (surnamed Barsabas) who was dispatched with Silas to Antioch (Acts 15:22).

JUDAS ISCARIOT. The false disciple who betrayed Christ and then committed suicide. Iscariot means " a man of Kerioth" (a city in Moab). Judas Iscariot was the treasurer of the apostolic band (John 13:29) and pilfered the money entrusted to him (John 12:6). He was so controlled by Satan as to be called "a devil" (John 6: 70, 71). His acts, however, were included in God's foreknown plan, despite Judas' inclusion as one of the twelve apostles.

He was chosen "that the Scriptures might be fulfilled" (Matt. 26:47-56; Zech. 11:12, 13; Psa. 109:5-8; Acts 1:16). He is called "a son of perdition," the designation of the Antichrist, the Man of Sin (2 Thess. 2:3). Some scholars therefore believe that Judas was the Devil incarnate and feel that the Antichrist will be Judas brought back from "his own place" (Acts 1:25).

JUDAS MACCABEUS. The warrior son of Mattathias. He was the valiant leader of the revolt against enforced Greek paganism (166-160 B.C.). He was slain in the battle of Elasa (1 Macc. 9:1-18). "Judas" is the Greek form of "Judah."

JUDGE. The first judges in Jewish history were appointed at Jethro's advice to assist Moses in settling cases of dispute (Exod. 18:13-27). They were God's earthly representatives for justice (Exod. 21:6; 22: 8; Psa. 82). The Mosaic Law made provision for the appointment of judges and officers to assist in dispensing justice (Deut. 16:18). Strict justice and absolute fairness were required (Deut. 1:16-18; 16:19, 20; 24:17, 18). In more important cases judges were assisted by priests who functioned as assessors (Deut. 17:8-13). During the period of the Conquest, the judges participated in the national assemblies (Josh. 8:33; 24:1).

During the period of the judges, the judge was more than simply a judicial arbiter representing God. He was first and foremost a "savior" and "deliverer" (Judg. 3:9), divinely raised up and charismatically empowered by God's Spirit to deliver Israel from her enemies (Judg. 6: 34). The same word in kindred Semitic dialects was used for the chief magistrates of Carthage and as a synonym for "king" at Ugarit.

Under the monarchy, judges performed both judiciary and executive functions (1 Chr. 26:29). Jehoshaphat displayed zeal for righteousness and appointed judges and officers city by city (2 Chron. 19:4-7). Ezra set judges over the people after the exile (Ezra 7:25). See also "Officer."

In the New Testament, Christ is declared to be the Judge of all mankind (John 5:22, 23, 27, 30). This fact is emphasized in apostolic preaching (Acts 10: 42; 17:31; Rom. 2:16). Christ will specif-

ically be the judge of believers' works (Rom. 14:10; 2 Cor. 5:10). The basis of judgment for the unsaved in Gehenna will also be their works (Rev. 20:12, 13). Thus *all men* will be judged for their works—their response to the eternal moral law of God.

JUDGMENT. The once-popular concept of a single general judgment cannot be sustained from a careful inductive study of God's Word. Eight well-defined and separate judgments appear in Scripture. These are briefly described below.

God's Judgment of Sin. When Christ died he bore all the sin and guilt of every believer (1 Cor. 15:3; Heb. 9:26-28; 1 Pet. 2:24; 3:18). When he was lifted up on the Cross, the world was judged and Satan was defeated (John 12:31). The result was the justification and security of every believer (John 5:24; Rom. 5:9; 8:1; 2 Cor. 5:21; Gal. 3:13).

The Believer's Judgment of Self. Believers must confess and forsake the sins they commit if they are to avoid chastisement by their heavenly Father (Heb. 12:7; 1 Cor. 11:31, 32). If confession is neglected, the Father's chastening follows, though never condemnation with the unsaved (1 Cor. 11:32; 5:5).

Christ's Judgment of the Believer's Works. This event is often termed "the judgment seat of Christ" (Rom. 14:10; 2 Cor. 5:10). At issue in this judgment is not the salvation of the believer but the rewards for his Christian service (1 Cor. 3:11-15). The event occurs immediately after the rapture (Christ's coming for his own). See 1 Corinthians 4:1-5 and 2 Timothy 4:8. This judgment is in no sense a condemnatory trial for sins, since even the least devoted believer will be saved "so as by fire" (1 Cor. 3:15).

The Judgment of All Unsaved. This event is often called the "Great White Throne judgment" (Rev. 20:11). It involves every unsaved person that has ever lived, and possibly angels and millennial saints as well. The unsaved are judged on the basis of their works (Rev. 20:12, 13). Everyone whose name is not written in the book of life is cast into the lake of fire (Rev. 20:15).

The Judgment of the Nations. This judgment takes place when Christ returns in glory to establish his kingdom over Israel (Matt. 25:31-33). The basis of judgment is the treatment of Christ's "brothers" (the Jewish remnant at the end time). The result will be admittance to or exclusion from the kingdom as individuals in the nations (Matt. 25:34-46).

The Judgment of Israel. The subjects of this judgment are Israelites regathered from worldwide dispersion at the end of the Tribulation period (Ezek. 20:33-38). At issue is the opportunity to enter the millennial kingdom (Mal. 3:2-5; 4:1-3).

The Judgment of Fallen Angels. Revelation 20:10 indicates that Satan (and presumably his angels) will be condemned with finality immediately following the millennial age. This judgment may include angels who cohabited with humanity prior to the Flood (Gen. 6:1-4; 2 Pet. 2:4; Jude 1:6). Evil angels will be cast into Gehenna, the Lake of Fire (Rev. 20:10).

JUDGMENT IN THE GATE. In Old Testament times, civil law cases were often heard at the gateway to a city. Either the elders of the city or the king himself would dispense justice at this location (Deut. 22:15; Ruth 4:1, 2; 2 Sam. 15:2; Prov. 31:23).

JUDITH (Hebrew feminine form of *Yehu-di,* "a Judean, a Jew"). (1) A wife of Esau and a daughter of Beeri the Hittite (Gen. 26:34). She is probably identical with the "Aholibamah" of Genesis 36:5. Esau's carnality and marriage to a pagan woman reveal his character and help explain why he was willing to forfeit his birthright (Gen. 25:29-34; 26:34, 35). (2) The heroine of the apocryphal book of Judith. By her valor this beautiful and devout Jewish widow of Bethulia (a pseudonym for Shechem) saved her city from Nebuchadnezzar's invading army under Holophernes.

JUNIPER. See "Broom."

JUSTICE. A virtue which God possesses in absolute perfection because of his infinite holiness. The gospel of grace, involving the death of Christ, is the solution to the problem of how God can remain just and nevertheless pardon guilty sinners (Rom. 3:25, 26).

JUSTIFICATION. A judicial act by which God declares a sinner righteous in his sight on the basis of Christ's substitutionary death on the Cross (Rom. 3:25, 26; 4:24, 25). Justification originates in the grace of God (Rom. 3:24; Tit. 3:4-7). It is received by faith alone, exclusive of works (Rom. 4:1-5; Gal. 2:16).

KADESH (kā'dĕsh). (1) A Canaanite city (Josh. 12:22) identified with present-day Tell Qades. It was a city of refuge and a Levitical city (Josh. 20:7). Barak lived there (Judg. 4:6). It was captured by Tiglath-Pileser III (2 Kings 15:29). (2) A city on the Orontes River (2 Sam. 24:6, RSV). It is identified with present-day Tell Nebi Mend.

KADESH-BARNEA. ᶜAin Qedeis or possibly Khirbet el-Qudeirat, a town in the desert of Paran south of Judah. From it the Israelite spies were sent out to explore Canaan (Num. 13:26).

KANAH (kā'nà). A river which runs west from the watershed at the heel of the Michmethath Valley, four miles south of Shechem. It constitutes the natural boundary between Ephraim and Manasseh (Josh. 16:8). The river is now known as Wadi Qana.

KASSITES (kăs'īts). An Indo-European people from the region of the Zagros mountains. They invaded and dominated Babylon from about 1500 to 1100 B.C., establishing a dynasty that ruled for half a millennium. The Kassite period is obscure historically, but it is known that the horse, which was a divine symbol of the Kassites, became common in Babylonia only after their entry.

KEILAH (kē-ī'là). Khirbet Qila in the Shephelah of Judah (Josh. 15:44). It is associated with David (1 Sam. 23:1-13). The town was located about eight miles northwest of Hebron.

KENITES (kē'nīts). A Midianite tribe (Judg. 1:16; 4:11) who inhabited the copper-yielding region southeast of the Gulf of Aqabah. Since their name means "smith," they are thought to have been itinerant artisans in metal. Balaam's parable implies that the Kenites were at home in Edom and the Wadi Arabah (Num. 24:20-22). They in all likelihood exploited the rich mineral deposits of this region. Hobab the Midianite (of the family of the Kenites) accompanied the Israelites as a scout on their march from Mount Sinai to Canaan (Num. 10:29-32).

After the conquest of Canaan the Kenites cast their lot with Judah and settled southeast of Hebron (Judg. 1:16). In Abraham's time a branch of the Kenites had settled in Canaan or its vicinity (Gen. 15:18, 19; Num. 24:20-22). It was perhaps this group which maintained friendly relations with Israel in the Saul-David era (1 Sam. 15:6; 27:10; 30:29), perhaps as itinerant smiths (cf. 1 Chron. 2:55). See also "Midianites."

KETURAH (kē-tū'rà) ("incense"). Abraham's wife after Sarah's death (Gen. 25:1). From her came the tribes of Zimram, Jokshan, Medan, Midian, and other Arabian peoples (1 Chron. 1:32). Her progeny were not placed on the same level with Isaac and were not in the line of the coming Redeemer. Abraham therefore endowed them with gifts and sent them eastward while he still lived (Gen. 25:6).

KEYS OF THE KINGDOM OF HEAVEN. A key is a symbol of power and authority (Isa. 22:22; Rev. 3:7). The keys given to Peter (Matt. 16:19) represent the divine authority granted him to open the gospel of grace to Jews at Pentecost (Acts 2:37-40), to racially mongrel Samaritans (Acts 8:14-17), and to pure Gentiles in the house of Cornelius (Acts 10:34-48). There was no other assumption of authority by Peter (Acts 15:7-11).

KHIRBET KERAZEH. See "Chorazin."

KIDRON, KEDRON (kĭd'rŏn, kē'drŏn). A seasonal stream which starts north of Jerusalem, flows past the Temple Mount and the Mount of Olives, and empties into the Dead Sea by way of the Wilderness of Judea. David passed over Kidron when he fled from Absalom (2 Sam. 15:23). There Hezekiah and Josiah destroyed pagan idols (1 Kings 15:13). Our Lord passed over Kidron to Gethsemane (John 18:1). The brook is present-day Wadi en-Nar.

KING (Hebrew *melek*). A monarch who rules by birth or acclaim. In Old Testament times the king normally administered a large territory surrounding a central walled city. He was also head of the army, supreme arbiter, and absolute master of the lives of his subjects. He had power to impose taxes and exact personal labor. Pagans either equated the king with their chief god or made him his representative.

In Egypt the pharaoh was usually looked upon as identical with the god. In Assyria he was regarded as representing the god. But in Israel the king, as well as prophets, priests, and judges, was regarded simply as God's representative (1 Sam. 10:1). He was divinely chosen and was expected to follow God's laws and to administer justice in God's place (Isa. 11:1-5; Jer. 33:15). He also had responsibilities as a judge (1 Kings 3:28) and as a proclaimer of the Law (2 Kings 23:2; cf. Judg. 17:6).

The term "king" is also frequently applied to the ultimate Ruler of all creation, God himself (1 Sam. 12:12; Psa. 47:7; Isa. 6:5; 1 Tim. 1:17). Special emphasis is given by Scripture to Christ's kingly role (Psa. 2:6; Zech. 9:9; Matt. 2:2; 21:5; Rev. 17:14; 19:16). Every Old Testament prophecy of the coming millennial kingdom bears witness to this glorious role which Christ will assume. He will occupy the Davidic throne as David's Lord and Heir (2 Sam. 7:16; Psa. 89:20-37; Isa. 11:11-16; Jer. 33:19-21). Christ came as a king (Luke 1:32, 33), was rejected as the king of Israel (Mark 15:12, 13; Luke 19:14), and died as a king (Matt. 27:37). At his second advent he will come as King par excellence (Rev. 19:16). His earthly reign as King will be mediatorial until he has vanquished all his enemies (1 Cor. 15:25-28). Then his mediatorial kingdom will merge into the eternal kingdom (2 Sam. 7:16; Psa. 89:36, 37; Isa. 9:6, 7; Luke 1:33; 1 Cor. 15:28).

KINGDOM. A sphere of rule and authority. Before man's fall the dominion of the earth belonged to Adam and Eve (Gen. 1: 26-28). When they sinned they lost this dominion and Satan became "prince of this world" (Matt. 4:8-10; John 14:30). After the Flood human government was instituted under the Noahic Covenant, which is still God's intended charter for all human government (Gen. 9:1-17).

KINGDOM OF GOD. The rule of God over all intelligences in heaven and on earth who willingly submit to the Creator. Among human beings, only those who are born again fall into this category.

KINGDOM OF HEAVEN. The rule of God over the earth at any given time. The kingdom of heaven has been manifested in various aspects throughout the centuries. In its theocratic aspect it was established by Moses (Exod. 19:3-6) and later continued under the judges (Josh. 1:1-5; Judg. 2:16-18) and the kings (1 Sam. 10: 1; 16:1-13; 1 Kings 9:1-5). It ended at the captivities (Ezek. 21:25-27; cf. Jer. 27:6-8; Dan. 2:36-38).

The theocratic kingdom will one day be restored (2 Sam. 7:8-16; Psa. 89:3, 4, 20, 21, 28-37). The prophets expound features of the kingdom as follows. (1) It will be Davidic, established under David's virgin-born Heir (Isa. 7:13, 14; 9:6, 7; 11:1), who will also be Immanuel, the God-Man (Jer. 23:5, 6; Ezek. 34:23; 37: 24; Hos. 3:4, 5). (2) It will be heavenly in origin and authority but will be estab-

lished on the earth (Isa. 2:2-4; 4:3-5; Joel 3:1-17). (3) It will be established first over regathered and converted Israel. Then it will become universal (Psa. 2:6-8; 22:22-31; 24:1-10). (4) The second advent of Christ will usher in the earthly kingdom (Deut. 30:3-5; Psa. 2:1-9; Matt. 24, 25). (5) The Davidic Covenant has not been set aside (Psa. 89:33-37); it is yet to be fulfilled (Acts 15:14-17).

The kingdom of heaven as announced by John, the Apostles, and Christ himself (Matt. 3:2; 4:17) was rejected (Matt. 12:1-50). This demonstrated that fallen man must have salvation provided for him before he could be ready for kingdom participation (Matt. 16:21). The kingdom was thus postponed until the risen, ascended, and glorified Redeemer would return (Rev. 19:11-16). Not until the millennial reign of Christ will the kingdom of heaven become a realization. Meanwhile the *mystery* form of the kingdom is already in existence (Matt. 13:11); Christ is already ruling in the hearts of his believers.

KING'S HIGHWAY. An important trade route from Ezion-geber (on the Red Sea) to Damascus. It passed through Edom and Transjordan. In later Roman times the route was called Trajan's Road. Under Turkish rule it was known as the Sultan's Road. It is the present-day Tariq es-Sultani. Note the ancient Israelites' attempted use of the route in Numbers 20: 14-21; 21:21-23.

KINSMAN-REDEEMER. The *go'el* or kinsman redeemer beautifully typifies Christ. The redeemer had to be a relative (Lev. 25:48, 49; Ruth 3:12, 13; Gal. 4:4, 5; Heb. 2:14, 15). He had to be capable of redeeming (Ruth 4:1-12; Gal. 3:13; 4:4, 5; Rev. 5:9, 10). He effected redemption by paying the just demand in full (Lev. 25:25-27; Gal. 3:13; 1 Pet. 1:18, 19).

KISH (kĭsh). (1) A Benjamite and the father of King Saul (1 Sam. 9:1, 2). (2) An important ancient Sumerian city of lower Babylonia. It was the center of kingship in the Early Dynastic period of Sumerian history.

KISHON (kī'shŏn). A river known today as Nahr el-Muqatta. It originates in the hills of Galilee, drains the plain of Esdraelon, and empties into the Bay of

Acre, east of Mount Carmel. Barak won his famous victory over Sisera at the Kishon River (Judg. 4:1-17; 5:21). It was at Kishon that Elijah slaughtered the prophets of Baal (1 Kings 18:40). The river was also known as "the waters of Megiddo" (Judg. 5:19).

KITTIM. See "Cypriots."

KOHATH (kō'hăth). The second son of Levi (Gen. 46:11). His descendants held special offices in sanctuary service (Num. 3:27-32).

KORAH (kō'rà) ("held"). A Levitical leader who with Dathan and Abiram rebelled against the authority of Moses and Aaron. They died under God's judgment in an earthquake (Num. 16:1-35).

KUE. See "Cilicia."

LABAN (lā'băn) ("white"). The grandson of Nahor (Abraham's brother). Laban lived at Haran in Padan-aram in the region of the Balikh and Habur Rivers of Mesopotamia (Gen. 28:5; 29:4, 5). His sister Rebekah married Abraham's son Isaac (Gen. 24). When Jacob fled Esau's wrath he went to his Uncle Laban, serving him twenty years for Laban's daughters Rachel and Leah and for a herd of cattle (Gen. 28:1 – 31:55). Laban mixed the true worship of Jehovah with the worship of household gods (Gen. 31:19, 30-35).

LACHISH (lā'kĭsh). A fortified city in the lowland of Judah (Josh. 15:33, 39). It is located at Tell ed-Duweir, five miles south-southwest of Beit Jibrin. It was captured by Sennacherib of Assyria in 701 B.C. and made the base of his operations against Jerusalem (2 Kings 18:14, 17; 19:8 cf. Isa. 36:2; 37:8). It was one of the last places to fall to the Babylonians before Jerusalem's destruction (Jer. 34:7). It was reoccupied after the Exile (Neh. 11:30). The mound of the city has been excavated, yielding the famous Lachish Letters of about 589 B.C.

LAMECH THE CAINITE (lā'mĕk). Born of a godless line of ancestors, Lamech practiced polygamy, boasted of self-defensive murder, and exulted in the use of the sword for that purpose (Gen. 4:18-24).

LAMECH THE SETHITE. The son of Methuselah and the father of Noah. A God-fearing man, Lamech rested his faith in the divine promise of the removal of the curse of sin (Gen. 5:25-31). He was in the line of the coming Messiah-Redeemer (Luke 3:36).

Bronze lamps used by Romans and Christians (© MPS)

LAMP. Ancient lamps were usually simple bowls made of wood, clay, or metal and containing oil and a wick. As time progressed lamps became more sophisticated. By the New Testament era a lamp would often have a long spout for the wick and a hole in which to pour the oil. Mass production of lamps was facilitated by the use of molds, one for the bowl and another for the lid.

LANCE (Hebrew *romaḥ*). A type of heavy spear (Num. 25:7; Judg. 5:8; 1 Kings 18:28; 2 Chron. 11:12). Troops with heavy armor carried this weapon, which was a feature of Egyptian soldiery (Jer. 46:4). It was a spear with a long shaft, and was employed for thrusting rather than hurling (Num. 25:7, 8). It is frequently mentioned in connection with the shield, since both were used in battle array. As the Assyrian monuments illustrate, the opposing front lines would face each other shield-to-shield with lances protruding.

LAODICEA (lȧ-ŏd'ĭ'sē-ȧ) (in Anatolia). A city of Phrygia which was probably introduced to Christianity at the same time as Colosse (cf. Col. 4:13-17). It was the site of one of the seven churches of Asia mentioned in Revelation 2 and 3. See especially Revelation 3:14-22. The present-day site is Eski-Hissar, near Denizli.

LAUREL. The *Laurus nobilis,* an evergreen tree with elliptical leaves and cream-white flower clusters. Its fruit is a black berry somewhat smaller than an olive. Laurel oil is extracted from the plant for medicinal purposes. The leaves are used as a condiment in flavoring pickles. The laurel is native to Palestine and the Mediterranean regions. It is mentioned only once in the Bible (Isa. 44:14).

LAW. Israelites as well as other ancient peoples of Bible times had codes of laws. The Mosaic Code was roughly paralleled by the Accadian Laws of Eshnunna (about 1850 B.C.), the Sumerian Code of Lipit-Ishtar (about 1900 B.C.), the Code of Hammurabi (about 1700 B.C.), the Hittite Laws (about 1500 B.C.), and the Middle Assyrian Laws (twelfth century B.C.). The Law given by God through Moses was distinct from other laws of the ancient world in its divine origin and authority and its high moral and spiritual tone.

LAW, BIBLE DOCTRINE OF. The word "law" is used in several different ways in the Bible. Five of the more important uses are described below.

(1) *The Eternal Moral Law of God.* This is the eternal, unchangeable law of God which applies at all times to all of his created intelligences. It was first introduced in written form in the Ten Commandments of the Mosaic Law (Exod. 20:1-17). Nine of the commandments underly all governmental laws. The fourth commandment, the requirement to observe the Sabbath, was given to Israel alone.

(2) *Governmental Law.* This is human law, determined by society but based on God's eternal moral law. All human beings are subject to some kind of governmental law (Rom. 13:1-7).

(3) *The Law of Moses.* The Law of Moses consists of the entire set of ordinances given to the Israelites by God through Moses. The Law is commonly divided into three parts: the moral law, the civil law, and the ceremonial law.

The moral law comprises the Ten Commandments (Exod. 20:1-17) and embraces the moral government of Israel (and, in principle, all other societies as well). The Ten Commandments may be succinctly summarized in the law of love to God and man (Matt. 22:34-40; Rom. 13:10; Gal. 5:14; James 2:8). It is this underlying principle of love which makes the essence of the Decalogue applicable to all mankind.

The second part of the Mosaic Law, the civil law, outlines the requirements for correct social relationships for the nation Israel (Exod. 21:1 – 23:33).

The third part of the Mosaic Law, the ceremonial law (sometimes called "the ordinances"), provided detailed regulations for Israel's worship (Exod. 25:1 – 31:18).

When Christ died on the Cross, the entire Mosaic system of law was abrogated as a test of human obedience (John 1:17; Rom. 10:4; 2 Cor. 3:6-11). However, the eternal moral principles which underly the Law of Moses have never been abolished. It is these very principles which are amply re-expressed throughout the New Testament, especially in the Epistles. Thus the *righteousness* of the Law (its underlying ethic) is fulfilled in every believer (Rom. 8:4).

(4) *The Law of Christ.* The law of Christ

includes all the principles of the eternal moral law of God as adapted to the teachings of grace (1 Cor. 9:20, 21; Gal. 6:2). Far from being an outlaw, the believer has been "inlawed to Christ" (1 Cor. 9: 20, 21, literal translation). The Spirit-filled believer exhibits the righteousness of Christ himself (Rom. 6:13; 1 Cor. 1: 30; Phil. 3:9).

(5) *The Law as the Will of God.* This includes all of God's revealed will for all people at all times. Paul's discussion in Romans 7:1 – 8:4 goes beyond the Law of Moses to include this facet of law.

LAWYER (Greek *nomikos,* from *nomos,* "law"). In biblical usage, an Israelite who was trained in the Law of Moses. In the New Testament the title is used synonymously with "scribe" and "teacher of the law" (cf. Matt. 22:35; Mark 12:28). By Christ's time many Jewish lawyers had departed from the Word of God. They concerned themselves mostly with traditions of men that actually set aside the commandments of God. Hence they merited severe censure from Christ (Luke 11:45-52).

LAZARUS OF BETHANY (lăz′ȧ-rŭs). The brother of Mary and Martha. It was he whom Jesus resurrected from death (John 11:1-44). This stupendous miracle of Christ so antagonized the Sanhedrin that they plotted to kill both Jesus and Lazarus (John 11:45-54; 12:10, 11).

LAZARUS THE BEGGAR. The destitute man who went to "Abraham's bosom" upon his death (Luke 16:19-31). The lesson of the story is that the accumulation of riches without regard to eternal destiny represents the ultimate folly in life.

LEAH (lē′à) ("wild cow" or "gazelle"). The elder daughter of Laban. She became Jacob's first wife and bore him six sons and a daughter. Laban tricked Jacob into marrying his less attractive elder daughter in addition to the younger and more beautiful Rachel (Gen. 29:15-30). To the less favored Leah were born Reuben, Simeon, Levi, and Judah (Gen. 29: 31-35), and later Issachar, Zebulun, and Dinah (Gen. 30:14-24). Her handmaid, Zilpah, bore Gad and Asher (Gen. 30:9-13). Leah and her children accompanied Jacob to Palestine (Gen. 31). She was buried with Abraham, Sarah, Isaac, and Rebekah in the Cave of Machpelah at Hebron (Gen. 49:31).

The majestic cedars of Lebanon (© *MPS*)

LEBANON (lĕb′à-nŏn). A mountain range in Syria. The name is sometimes also applied to the surrounding regions (Josh. 13:5). The name is derived from a Hebrew root meaning "to be white," an appropriate description of the white limestone of the high ridge of Lebanon and of the glittering snow that caps its peak for six months of the year. The southernmost peaks (which are a continuation of the hills of North Galilee) rise to a height of nearly 6200 feet behind Sidon. The east-west gorge of the Litany River marks the beginning of the 100-mile-long Lebanon range, whose highest peak reaches a height of almost 10,000 feet at a point east-southeast of Tripoli.

LEBANON, TREES OF. See under "Forest."

LEBBAEUS (lĕ-bē′ŭs). One of the twelve apostles. He was also called Thaddeus (Matt. 10:3; Mark 3:18). He was apparently also the "Judas" of Luke 6:16 and Acts 1:13.

LEEK. A tall herb resembling garlic. Its leaves and bulb are widely eaten as both a vegetable and a flavoring. The leek, *Allium porrum,* has always been a favorite dish in both Palestine and Egypt. It was one of the delicacies which the discontented Israelites longed for in the desert (Num. 11:5). The leek is still commonly sold in the markets of the Near East.

LENTIL. An annual plant with pinnate leaves and white flowers with violet stripes. Lentil seeds have been a favorite food in Near Eastern countries since biblical times (Gen. 25:34; 2 Sam. 17:27-29). The parched seeds could be carried easily on a long journey and were suitable for emergency needs (Ezek. 4:9). The "red pottage" of Esau was made of lentils (Gen. 25:29-34), and lentils were among the staples offered to David at Mahanaim (2 Sam. 17:28). A field of lentils is referred to in 2 Samuel 23:11, 12.

LEOPARD (Hebrew *nārmēr*). Any of several kinds of spotted cats, including the true leopard of Africa and Southern Asia (*Felis pardus*), the cheetah or hunting leopard, and several other wild cats of Palestine. The leopard was very swift (Hab. 1:8) and fed on smaller animals (Isa. 11:6). It sometimes attacked humans (Hos. 13:7, 8), lurking for its victims near villages (Jer. 5:6). Its ordinary habitat was the mountains (Song 4:8).

LEVI (lē'vī) ("joined, attached"). (1) Jacob's third son and an ancestor of Moses and Aaron. It was from Levi's lineage that the Old Testament priestly service was staffed (Exod. 28:1; Num. 1:47-54). (2) An alternative name for the Apostle Matthew (cf. Matt. 9:9-13 with Luke 5:27-32). See "Matthew."

LEVIATHAN. A large aquatic animal described at length in Job 41 and mentioned in several other poetic passages of Scripture. It is usually assumed to be the crocodile.

LEVIRATE MARRIAGE (lĕv'ĭ-rāt). The Mosaic Code provided that if a man died childless, his brother or male next of kin should marry his widow. The firstborn of this second marriage would then continue the name of the deceased (Deut. 25:5-10). This "kinsman-redeemer" practice is beautifully illustrated in the Book of Ruth. The removal of the shoe (Deut. 25:7-10; Ruth 4:7) arose from the custom of walking on the soil as a declaration of one's right of acquired possession. If a man refused this obligation, the widow took off his shoe and spat in his face.

LEVITES (lē'vīts). Sometimes this name denotes the entire tribe of Levi, including the priests, the descendants of Aaron (Exod. 6:25; Lev. 25:32; Num. 35:2;

Josh. 21:3). Frequently, however, the designation applies only to those descendants of Levi who were not priests. The priests offered the sacrifices and performed the ritual worship of the Tabernacle while the Levites handled the more routine duties.

LIBNAH (lĭb'nȧ) (in Judah). A Canaanite city captured by Joshua (Josh. 10:29, 30). It was located in the lowlands (Josh. 15:42) and was a Levitical town (Josh. 21:13). Its inhabitants revolted from Jehoram, king of Judah (2 Kings 8:22). Sennacherib attacked it (2 Kings 19:8). It is identified as present-day Tell es-Safi, about eight miles south of Ekron.

LIBYANS. The inhabitants of Libya, west of Lower Egypt. These hostile people first appear as "Lubim" in Egyptian texts of the twelfth and thirteenth centuries B.C. and in the Hebrew Bible (Nah. 3:9; cf. "Libyans" in Dan. 11:43). From the twelfth to the eighth century B.C. they entered Egypt as settlers, raiders, or soldiers in the armies of the Pharaohs. Lubim are prominent among the troops of Shishak (2 Chron. 12:3) and Zerah (2 Chron. 14:9; 16:8) and among the forces of the Ethiopian pharaohs that failed to protect No-Amon (Thebes) from Assyrian devastation (Nah. 3:9). Some scholars equate Phut or Put with Cyrenaica, the region around Cyrene (Gen. 10:6).

LICE (Hebrew *kinnām, kinnīm*). A small insect of somewhat uncertain identification. It has been variously identified as lice, gnats, sandflies, fleas, and mosquitoes.

LILY. A bulbous plant which produces a beautiful flower. A number of varieties flourish in Palestine, including the "lily of the valleys" (Song 2:1), the hyacinth, the anemone, and the madonna lily, as well as varieties of iris and gladioli (cf. Song 2:16; 4:5; 6:3; Matt. 6:28). The "lilies of the field" (Matt. 6:28; Luke 12:27) apparently refer to families of flowers which include the narcissus, the cyclamen, and the Palestinian chamomile (a common, daisy-like bloom).

LINEN EPHOD. A simple, white linen priestly robe (as distinguished from the more elegant high priestly garment). Samuel wore one (1 Sam. 2:18), as did the priests (1 Sam. 22:18; Hos. 3:4). David also wore such a garment when the ark of the Tabernacle was transferred to Jerusalem (2 Sam. 6:14).

LION. Lions are mentioned dozens of times in the Bible. They were once common in Europe and Asia and were also found in Palestine. The lion was proverbial for strength (2 Sam. 1:23; Prov. 30:30) and courage (2 Sam. 17:10). It had the habit of crouching before springing on its victim (Gen. 49:9). It preyed on small animals (1 Sam. 17:34, Isa. 11:6, 7) as well as man (1 Kings 13: 24). The lion lurked in thickets and forests (Jer. 4:7; 5:6; 25:38). It was especially common in the Jordan jungle (Jer. 49: 19). Satan is compared to a lion (1 Pet. 5: 8). Our Lord is called "the Lion of the tribe of Judah" (Rev. 5:5; cf. Gen. 49:9).

LIZARD. In the warm, dry climate of Palestine lizards of many varieties exist. Some forty species are found. They were regarded as unclean and were thus not used as food by the Hebrews (Lev. 11:30, 31). The green lizard, the wall lizard, the sand lizard, the monitor lizard, and the gecko are especially numerous.

LO-AMMI (lō-ăm′ī) ("not my people"). A name given by Hosea to his son (Hos. 1: 8-10; 2:23). It symbolized Israel's temporary rejection by the Lord because of her sin and apostasy.

Locust—food and foe of the Middle East (© *MPS*)

LOCUST (Hebrew *'arbeh;* Greek *'akris*). The locust is distinguished from the grasshopper by the shortness of its antennae. Locusts were clean insects (Lev. 11: 21, 22) and are still used as food by the poor (cf. Matt. 3:4). They are prepared by roasting or drying in the sun and removing the head, wings, legs, and intestines. The locust was, and still is, the scourge of the Middle East. Locusts blown by the wind into the Nile Valley constituted the eighth plague in the days of the Exodus (Exod. 10:3-20). The female deposits her eggs in the earth in April or May. They hatch in June, producing wingless larvae.

These then enter the pupa state, where they develop rudimentary wings. At this stage (Joel 1:4) the insects are more voracious than in any other stage of their development. In a month or so they cast their pupas or nymph skins and become full-grown insects, ready to participate in another wave of destruction.

LOGOS. A Greek word which means "a thought" or "the expression or utterance of a thought." It is an appropriate designation of Christ, since all the treasures of the divine wisdom are embodied in him (Col. 2:2, 3). From past eternity and especially in the incarnation, Christ has perfectly expressed the inmost nature of God (John 1:1-18; 14:9-11; Col. 1:12-20; Heb. 1:1-4).

LOIS (lō′ĭs). The mother of Eunice and the grandmother of Timothy (2 Tim. 1:5). Both women were devout Christians. Their godly example in teaching Timothy has been a source of inspiration for countless mothers to "train up a child in the way he should go" and to believe that "when he is old he will not depart from it" (Prov. 22:6).

LORD. The English word "Lord" is a translation of the Hebrew words *Yahweh, Adonai,* and *Adon* as well as the Aramaic word *mar* and the Greek word *kurios. Kurios* is used in a number of ways in the New Testament. It can refer to God (Acts 2:34; cf. Psa. 110:1), to Christ (Luke 10: 1), or to human masters (Matt. 18:23-35). It can mean simply "Rabbi" or "sir" (Matt. 8:6). Those who addressed Christ as "Lord" in the Gospels sometimes acknowledged his full deity by the title (as in John 20:28) while at other times they meant nothing more than the usual polite form of address (as in John 9:35, 36).

Because they were well versed in the vocabulary of the Old Testament, the early Christians associated the word "Lord" with God himself. They thus expressed the deity of Christ when they referred to him as "Lord." The Apostle Paul frequently alluded to Christ by his full and official title—the Lord Jesus Christ (1 Thess. 1:1; 2 Cor. 13:14; etc.).

LORD'S DAY. The weekly remembrance of our Lord's resurrection. It is identified with "the first day of the week" (Sunday).

Scripture says very little about this day (cf. Rev. 1:10). We do know, however, that the day represents the initiation of a new order rather than a change of the Sabbath. It celebrates the New Creation with the resurrected Christ as its Head. The Sabbath, by contrast, was connected with the Old Creation (Exod. 20:8-11; 31:12-17; Heb. 4:4). The Lord's day is in no sense a "Christian Sabbath." It has no connection with Mosaic legalism. It is a day to be honored solely by New Testament believers.

LORD'S SUPPER. One of two ordinances of the Christian church. It is intended to be a commemoration of Christ's atoning death and victorious resurrection (Matt. 26:26-28; Mark 14:22-24; Luke 22: 19, 20; 1 Cor. 11:23-28). The bread and the cup are beautiful, easily understood symbols of Christ's body and blood broken and shed for our sins (1 Cor. 11:24, 25).

LO-RUHAMAH (lō-rōō-hȧ′mȧ) ("not pitied"). The name given by the prophet Hosea to his second child. It symbolized God's anger against sinning Israel and warned that God would not pity his covenant people when he chastened them for their idolatry (Hos. 1:2, 6). The cruel lash of Assyria would be pitiless upon the back of God's wayward people.

LOT (probably "covering"). Abraham's nephew, who accompanied the patriarch from Mesopotamia to Canaan (Gen. 11: 27 – 12:5). He began his life experiences in faith as a justified believer (2 Pet. 2:8), but through unbelief and worldly greed he made a costly error of choice (Gen. 13: 5-13). As a result he lost everything except his own life and the lives of his two daughters (Gen. 19:1-30). Because of their pagan environment in childhood, even Lot's daughters ended up disgracing him (Gen. 19:31-38).

LOVE OF GOD. One of God's essential attributes is love (1 John 4:8, 16). His divine love embraces the whole world (John 3:16; Heb. 2:9; 1 John 2:2) but is directed especially toward the redeemed (Rom. 5:5). God's love is sacrificial (2 Cor. 8:9; 1 John 3:16, 17) and can be communicated toward his children (Rom. 5:5; 1 John 4:7, 11). If we love God we will reject the present evil world system (1 John 2:15-17). God also shows special love toward his eternally elect nation, Israel (Jer. 31:3). Though now temporarily set aside, Israel will be restored at Christ's second advent (Rom. 11).

LUCIFER (lū′sĭ-fēr) ("the light-bearer"). A name applied to the king of Babylon as a description of his glory and pomp (Isa. 14:12-14). The passage is a veiled reference to Satan, the real power behind the government of Babylon (Dan. 10:13; cf. Eph. 6:12).

LUD (lŭd) A region in Western Anatolia sometimes known as Ludu or Lydia. Its capital was Sardis. Gyges founded the Lydian kingdom in the seventh century B.C. Its last king, Croesus, was defeated by Cyrus the Persian. Lydian mercenaries were employed in Egyptian armies.

LUKE (meaning uncertain). A Christian physician and companion of Paul (Col. 4: 14; 2 Tim. 4:11). He was the inspired penman of the Gospel of Luke and the Book of the Acts. He was thus the first church historian. The Gospel of Luke presents Christ as the perfect man. It stresses themes of pardon and redemption and emphasizes joy and praise (Luke 1:14; 2:10, 13: 15:7). See especially the Magnificat of Mary (Luke 1:46-55), the Benedictus of Zechariah (Luke 1:67-79), the Gloria in Excelsis of the angels (Luke 2:14), and the Nunc Dimittis of Simeon (Luke 2:29-32).

LUMBERMAN. The modern lumberjack finds a parallel in the lumberman of antiquity, who hewed timber in the cedar forests of the Lebanon region. Together with firs and cypress trees, this area furnished the finest building materials in the ancient east. Hiram I of Tyre had timber cut in the Lebanon region for Solomon's Temple (1 Kings 5:6-9). The finest of Lebanon and Antilebanon (Sirion) were also felled to provide ships for Tyrian traders (Ezek. 27:5) and sacred barges for Egypt. Fine furniture was made from Lebanese cedar (Song 3:9). Wood for the second Temple at Jerusalem was also hewn in Lebanon (Ezra 3:7).

LUZ (lŭz). The ancient name for Bethel. The name was changed in Jacob's day (Gen. 28:19; 35:6; Josh. 18:13). It is now identified with Beitin, about a dozen miles north of Jerusalem. See "Bethel."

LYCAONIA (lĭk'à-ō'nĭ-à) The district of Asia Minor in which Lystra was located. Its natives were non-Greeks (Acts 14:6, 11).

LYDIA (lĭd'ĭ-à) (perhaps "a Lydian, woman of Lydia"). A businesswoman from Thyatira whom Paul met at Philippi. She became the first Christian convert in Europe (Acts 16:11-40). She and her household were baptized, and she acted as host to the apostle and his party. Lydia sold purple-dyed goods which she had brought to Philippi from Thyatira. She was a woman of means. Her generosity was characteristic of the Philippian church, from whom Paul accepted gifts because of his special love for them and their love for him (Phil. 1:3, 8; 4:1, 15-19).

LYSIAS (lĭs'ĭ-ăs). The chief captain of the Roman garrison at Jerusalem. He rescued Paul from the mob of hostile Jews (Acts 23:12 – 24:9).

LYSTRA (lĭs'trà). A city in Asia Minor in which Paul was stoned (Acts 14:8-20). It was also the home of Timothy (Acts 16:1, 2). It is present-day Zoldera, about 24 miles southwest of Iconium.

MAACHAH (mā'à-kà). (1) The wife of Machir son of Manasseh (1 Chron. 7:15, 16). (2) A concubine of Caleb son of Hezron (1 Chron. 2:48). (3) The wife of Jehiel and an ancestress of King Saul (1 Chron. 8:29; 9:35). (4) A daughter of Talmai king of Geshur. She became one of David's wives and bore him Absalom (2 Sam. 3:3). (5) The wife of King Rehoboam (930-913 B.C.). She was either the daughter or granddaughter of Absalom (1 Kings 15:2; 2 Chron. 11:20-22) and the mother of King Abijam (913-910 B.C.). After Abijam's death she remained queen mother. However, Asa, her grandson, removed her from this position because she made an idolatrous image of an Asherah, a Canaanite fertility goddess (2 Chron. 15:16).

MACEDONIANS (măs'ė-dō'nĭ-àns). The inhabitants of the country north of Greece. Macedonia came into prominence under Philip of Macedon (359-336 B.C.) and his world-conquering son, Alexander the Great (336-323 B.C.). Under Alexander's successors the country declined until it was conquered by the Romans in 168 B.C. It was made a province in 142 B.C. The Macedonian Empire is referred to in Daniel 8:5-8. Macedonia is prominent in the missionary call of Paul (Acts 16:6-10) and the introduction of the Christian gospel into Europe (Acts 16:11-40).

MACHPELAH (măk-pē'là). A cave and field near Hebron which Abraham purchased as a burial place (Gen. 23:9). Later Abraham, Isaac, Rebekah, and Jacob were buried here. The modern site of the burial cave is incorporated in the southern end of the sacred Haram al-Halil at Hebron.

MAGI (mā'jī). Originally an Iranian priestly order of wise men, astrologers, and soothsayers (similar to the Hindu Brahmin). Later the name was applied to any sage, especially eastern, such as the Magi who came to Jerusalem at Christ's birth (Matt. 2:1-10).

MAGIC. The operation of Satanic and demonic power in opposition to God's Word and will. Magic is the Satanic counterfeit of miracle. It attempts to use supernatural power independent of and in opposition to God (Exod. 7:10 – 8:7; 2 Thess. 2:7-10; Rev. 13). It is a phenomenon of demon-energized occultism.

MAGISTRATE. In the Old Testament the word occurs in Ezra 7:25 as the translation of the Hebrew word *shôphet* or "judge." In Judges 18:7 the word "magistrate" means a civil authority who exercised restraint against evil. Luke used the term to refer to civil authorities in general (Luke 12:11, 58). Paul was beaten by magistrates at Philippi (Acts 16:19-24, 35-38).

MAGOG (mā'gŏg). A son of Japheth and his descendants (Gen. 10:2). They are the Scythians. When Ezekiel employed the terms Gog and Magog (Ezek. 38:2; 39:6) he used them primarily in a historical sense but also applied them to the future rise of the Prince of the Northern Confederacy (Gog) and his scope of rule (Magog).

MAHALATH (mā'hă-lăth) ("sickness"). (1) One of Esau's wives. She was the daughter of Ishmael, Abraham's son (Gen. 28:9) and may have been the same person as Basemath. (2) A granddaughter of David and one of the eighteen wives of Solomon's son, King Rehoboam (2 Chron. 11:18).

MAHANAIM (mā'hà-nā'ĭm). A locality in Transjordan associated with Jacob (Gen. 32:2). David once took refuge there (2 Sam. 17:23-29). It was the center of Solomon's seventh district. It is perhaps located east of Penuel near the River Jabbok.

MAKKEDAH (mă-kē'dà). A cave where the defeated Amorite kings fled for refuge and were slain by Joshua. The town of Makkedah was located in the lowlands a few miles southwest of Bethshemesh and a few miles north of Azekah near the Vale of Elah (Josh. 10:10, 16).

MALACHI (măl'à-kī) ("my messenger"). The last of the Old Testament prophets and the author of the Book of Malachi (written about 400 B.C.). Malachi was the prophet who stressed God's electing love. He declares that Jacob's election was a demonstration of divine grace, and that Israel as a son had dishonored his Father by his sin (Mal. 1, 2). Judgment of the sinners and blessing for the penitent are shown to be certain. The coming day of the Lord is given as an example of judgment and the second advent of Christ is presented as the hope of blessing for the righteous (Mal. 3, 4).

MAMRE (măm'rĕ). A place in Hebron where Abraham and Isaac sojourned (Gen. 13:18; 18:1). The field of Machpelah was nearby (Gen. 25:9; 49:30).

MAN. God's special, direct creation, placed on earth in order to demonstrate God's plan of redemption (Gen. 1:1 – 3: 15). Through the redemption of man God will show to all creation how he will deal with sin and ultimately achieve a sinless universe (Rev. 21:1 – 22:5).

MAN OF SIN. The last-day Antichrist, the embodiment of Satan's power (Luke 4:5, 6). His rule on earth will be terminated by the glorious coming of Christ (2 Thess. 2:8-12; Rev. 20:10). He is the "little horn" of Daniel 7:8, the "willful king" of Daniel 11:36, the "abomination of desolation" of Matthew 24:15, and the first "beast" of Revelation 13:1-10.

MANASSEH (mà-năs'ĕ) ("causing to forget"). (1) Joseph's older son, born of Asenath. Like his brother, Ephraim, Manasseh was half Egyptian (Gen. 41: 50-52). In his dying prophecy Jacob conferred the primary blessing upon Ephraim instead of Manasseh (Gen. 48:8-20). (2) A wicked king of Judah from 687 to 643 B.C. He was the son of good King Hezekiah. He filled Jerusalem with idolatry and violence (2 Kings 21:1-16). He became subject to Assyria and paid tribute to Esarhaddon (680-669 B.C.). and Shalmaneser III (669-633 B.C.). Later he repented of his wickedness (2 Chron. 33:12-19).

MANDRAKE. The *Mandragora officinarum*, a stemless perennial herb with thick, branched roots which often resemble the lower parts of the human body. It was called the "love apple" and was sometimes used as an aphrodisiac (Gen. 30:14-16). In Palestine it is common in

UNGER'S GUIDE

fields of the Mediterranean zone.

MANNA. A divinely provided food which constituted the main diet of the Israelites during their sojourn in the desert (Exod. 16). Attempts to explain the phenomenon on a natural basis have failed. Some authorities attempt to identify the manna with certain lichens, or with a substance exuded from tamarisk trees, or with the excrement of certain scale insects living on tamarisk trees. Although the identifications are based on substantial findings, the substances involved are quantitatively far insufficient to have supported the large number of people involved. The manna must therefore have been supernaturally provided, as stated in Scripture.

MANTLE OF DISTINCTION (*'addereth*). Such a garment was worn by kings and prophets (Jonah 3:6). Achan stole this kind of apparel (Josh. 7:20, 21). Elijah had such a mantle (1 Kings 19:13, 19; 2 Kings 2:8, 13, 14). It was a sign of the prophet's office (Zech. 13:4). John the Baptist wore a mantle of camel's hair (Matt. 3:4; Mark 1:6). The robe of mockery placed on Christ was the Roman soldier's mantle, simulating that of royalty (Matt. 27:28, 31; Mark 15:17; John 19:2, 5).

In the New Testament the robe or stole was worn as a mark of honor, as by the scribes (Mark 12:38; Luke 20:46), the restored prodigal (Luke 15:22), the martyrs (Rev. 6:11), and the redeemed (Rev. 7:9, 13). See also "Robe."

MARA (mä′rà) ("bitter, sad in spirit"). The name chosen by Naomi when she returned to Bethlehem. It expressed the sorrow that came to her while she sojourned in Moab (Ruth 1:20).

MARAH (mä′rà). See under "Springs, Wells, and Pools."

MARDUK (mär′dŏŏk). The Mesopotamian hero-god. He was thought to be the head of the Babylonian pantheon, the creator of mankind, and the ruler of human destiny.

MARESHAH (mà-rē′shà). A town in the lowlands of Judah (Josh. 15:44). It had been fortified by Rehoboam (2 Chron. 11: 8) and was the scene of King Asa's victory over the Ethiopian invaders (2 Chron. 14:9-15). It was located at Tell Sandahanna, a few miles northeast of Lachish.

In the Hellenistic period the town was called Marisa.

MARI (mä′rē). A city-state on the Middle Euphrates. It was conquered by Hammurabi about 1765 B.C. Previously it was the capital of the kingdom of Mari. The administration and personal records of Mari, dating from the eighteenth century B.C., have been recovered. The modern site is Tell el-Hariri, near Abou Kemal.

MARK (Latin *marcus*, "a large hammer"). John Mark was a Jew and a son of Mary, a Christian matron at Jerusalem (Acts 12: 12). Mark accompanied Paul and Barnabas on their first missionary tour (Acts 13:5) but later dropped out in failure (Acts 13:13; 15:38). However, Mark recovered himself and won back his place in apostolic esteem, becoming a valued colleague of Paul (Col. 4:10, 11; Philem. 1:24; 2 Tim. 4:11; 1 Pet. 5:13). Mark wrote the Gospel of Mark, presenting the Son of God as the Perfect Servant, an especially appealing theme for Roman readers.

MARRIAGE. An institution established by God from the beginning of human existence (Gen. 2:21-25) and designed for the welfare and happiness of mankind. Monogamy is God's ideal for man's highest happiness (Gen. 2:24). However, plural marriages are recorded in the Old Testament, sometimes even of the most prominent saints. With the advance in relationship between God and his saints in the New Testament, the more exalted ideal of one wife and one husband is clearly enjoined (Eph. 5:22, 33).

MARRIAGE, JEWISH. The betrothal was consummated by the wedding festivities. These were mostly social in character and ordinarily lasted from one to two weeks (Judg. 14:12, 17). Guests were invited and summoned by special messenger (Luke 14:17). When the wedding day arrived, the bridegroom went in procession to the bride's house to bring her to his own house or that of his father. Special groomsmen, called "friends of the bridegroom," attended him in New Testament times and later. The "children of the bridechamber" (Matt. 9:15) refer to another class, the guests invited to the wedding. At the actual wedding no services of a priest were thought necessary.

Deeply veiled, the bride was led away from her home amid the well wishes of parents and friends (Ruth 4:11, 12). Sometimes, if circumstances required, the wedding festivities were celebrated at the bride's house (Gen. 29:22). A wealthy bridegroom sometimes distributed garments suitable for the occasion among his guests (Matt. 22:11). The bridal procession sometimes took place at night amid the blaze of torches and accompanied by singing, dancing, and merrymaking (Matt. 25:1-10). Under the Law of Moses the bridegroom was exempt from all public duties for one year following his marriage (Deut. 24:5).

In view of the sanctity of marriage God provided special laws to protect the marital union from violation. The sin of adultery was originally punished by stoning both participants to death (Lev. 20:10; Deut. 22:22). Nor did the Mosaic Law condemn only the outward act. Like our Lord (Matt. 5:27, 28), it also condemned the inner sin of lust (Exod. 20:17).

Under Mosaic Law a husband who suspected his wife of infidelity could subject her to a grueling ordeal which no guilty person could well pass through without betraying her guilt (Num. 5:11-31). Conversely, the Law protected the wife from unfounded suspicions of premarital infidelity (Deut. 22:13-21). See also "Engagement."

MARRIAGE OF THE LAMB. The marriage of Christ and his bride, the church (Rev. 19:7-9). The figure of marriage symbolizes the glory which redeemed church saints will share with Christ through all eternity (Rev. 21:9 – 22:5).

On Mars Hill in Athens the Greeks' wisest men concluded that Jesus' resurrection was only a fairy tale (Acts 17). (*Russ Busby photo*)

MARS HILL ("Hill of Ares," the god of war). The place at Athens where the Apostle Paul addressed the Court of the Areopagus (Acts 17:19). It was one of the lower hills west of the Acropolis. The seats of the judges and others connected with the court can still be seen in the rocks.

MARTHA (mär'thȧ). (Aramaic, "lady, mistress"). The woman to whom Christ first proclaimed, "I am the resurrection and the life" (John 11:24, 25). With her brother Lazarus and her sister Mary she resided at Bethany, a small town on the Mount of Olives (about two miles from Jerusalem). The trio loved Jesus sincerely, but of the two sisters Mary had the greater appreciation of spiritual things while Martha concerned herself more about the routine duties of hospitality. For this she was gently rebuked by Christ (Luke 10:38-42). Both sisters were true believers (John 11:21-32) and were honored by one of Christ's most celebrated miracles, the raising of their brother Lazarus from death (John 11:1-44). The supper where Mary anointed Christ's head (John 12:1-3) was at the house of Simon the leper (Matt. 26:6, 7; Mark 14:3). It is possible that Martha may have been the wife or widow of Simon.

MARY (mâr'ĭ) (from Hebrew *Miryam;* same as "Miriam"). (1) Mary the mother of Jesus. With respect to the birth of Jesus Christ, Mary was a virgin. She was "found with child of the Holy Spirit" (Matt. 1:18) before she had sexual union with Joseph (Matt. 1:24, 25). This was the fulfillment of the "virgin birth" prophecy made 700 years earlier by the Prophet Isaiah (Isa. 7:14; Matt. 1:22, 23). Christ's miraculous conception and virgin birth are also proclaimed by Luke (Luke 1:34-38) and are required by John's account, for God could become man (John 1:1-5, 14) only by such supernatural conception.

After Jesus' birth Mary had other children who were Christ's half brothers and sisters and the natural offspring of her husband, Joseph (Matt. 12:46-50; Mark 3:31-35; Luke 8:19-21). Mary appeared at the marriage in Cana of Galilee (John 2:1-11) and with other women at the Cross (John 19:25-27). After the ascension she was with the apostles in the upper room in Jerusalem (Acts 1:12-14). This is the last notice of her in Scripture. (2) Mary of Bethany. She with her sister Martha and brother Lazarus were close friends of Jesus and frequently entertained him in their home at Bethany (Luke 10:38-42). Mary also anointed the Lord with ointment (John 11:2; 12:1-8) in anticipation of his approaching death. (3) Mary Magdalene. Magdala was a town near Tiberias at the southern end of the fertile Plain of Gennesaret on the shore of the Sea of Galilee. It was a prosperous town, predominantly Gentile, and had a reputation for licentiousness. When Mary met Christ she was saved from both her sins and her severe demonic oppression (Luke 8:2; Mark 16:9). She became a devoted disciple of Christ (Luke 8:1-3; Mark 15:40, 41). Mary Magdalene appeared at the crucifixion (Mark 15:40; John 19:25), came to the tomb to anoint Jesus' body (Mark 16:1; Luke 23:55 — 24: 1), reported the fact of the empty tomb to the Eleven (Luke 24:1-11), and saw the risen Christ (John 20:11-18). (4) Mary the wife of Clopas. She was one of the women standing near the Cross (John 19:25). Clopas or Cleophas is apparently to be identified with Alphaeus (Matt. 10:3; Mark 3:18; Luke 6:15), the two names being variant forms of the same Aramaic original. Thus Mary and her husband Clopas were the parents of the Apostle James (Mark 3:18), Joses (Mark 15:40), and Levi (Mark 2:14). (5) Mary the mother of Mark. It was her son who authored the second Gospel and accompanied Paul and Barnabas in their missionary work (Acts 12:25; 15:36-41; cf. 2 Tim. 4: 11). The sole reference to this Mary occurs in Acts 12:12. Her house in Jerusalem was a meeting place for Christians, and Peter went there after his escape from prison (Acts 12:6-19). (6) Mary of Rome. A resident of Rome, she greatly assisted the missionary cause (Rom. 16:6).

MASADA (mȧ-sā'dȧ). An ancient Hasmonean stronghold on the west side of the Dead Sea. It lies about 11 miles south of En-gedi and opposite El Lisan. It was formidably fortified by Herod the Great. Like the Herodium and Machaerus, it held out tenaciously but unsuccessfully against the Romans. It is present-day es-Sebbeh, which has been carefully excavated.

MASON. Stonemasons worked on fine public buildings and sumptuous private dwellings (Amos 5:11). Palestinian limestone being soft and destructible, blocks of harder stones for the Temple and other public buildings were cut and worked in the Lebanon region (1 Kings 6:7). The stones were cut with saws (1 Kings 7:9) and trimmed with picks or axes.

The stonemason also quarried out hillside tombs at various locations, as well as rock cisterns for water storage at Jericho, Lachish, Megiddo, and Gibeon. Under Herod the Great's regime, massive blocks of stone were used for building purposes and were so carefully dressed that they could be aligned without mortar. Masons also cut inscriptions in rocks, as in the case of the Siloam Tunnel at Jerusalem.

MATTATHIAS OF MODIN (măt-ȧ-thī'ȧs, mō'dĭn). An aged Jewish priest who refused to compromise with the paganization program of Antiochus Epiphanes. He killed Antiochus' officer and the Jew who was willing to offer a profane sacrifice. Escaping with his five sons, he initiated the Maccabean revolt. The uprising was led by his sons — Judas (166-160 B.C.), Jonathan (160-142 B.C.), and Simon (142-134 B.C.). The latter inaugurated a period of Jewish independence (143-63 B.C.).

MATTHEW ("gift of the Lord"). A Jewish tax-collector who was also named Levi (cf. Matt. 9:9 with Luke 5:27). When Christ called him he immediately left all to follow the Lord (Luke 5:28). To celebrate the occasion, Matthew entertained Christ and others at a feast in his own house (Luke 5:29). Matthew wrote the Gospel which bears his name. He presents Christ as the Son of David and the King of the Jews.

MATTHIAS (mă-thī'ăs) (probably shortened from Mattathias, "gift of the Lord"). A disciple chosen by lot to succeed Judas Iscariot (Acts 1:23, 26). Tradition identifies him with the Seventy (Luke 10:1).

MEDES (mēdz). An Indo-European people who conquered and settled the country of Media east of the Zagros Mountains, south of the Caspian Sea, and north of Elam. They are the "Madaï" of the "table of the nations" (Gen. 10:2). The Medes became prominent in Assyrian records beginning with Shalmaneser III in the ninth century. Under Cyaxares (650-612 B.C.) Media allied itself with Babylonia, and with Scythian aid they were able to overthrow Assyria between 616 and 612 B.C. Meanwhile Persia, which lay south and east of Media, rebelled against Median power and Cyrus the Great became king of Media and Persia. The conquerors and the conquered were both of the fine Aryan race. The result was a dual nation, Media-Persia, which became a world empire until destroyed by Alexander the Great (cf. Dan. 2:39; 7:5). The two-horned ram of Daniel (Dan. 8:3-7, 20) symbolizes Media and Persia. One horn (Persia) was higher than the other (Media) and came up last. Though the Median power arose first, the Persian power later attained the ascendancy. See also "Persians."

MEDIATION. A ministry of reconciling persons at odds with each other. Christ is the great Mediator between God and man (1 Tim. 2:5). As a Prophet he represents God to man. As a Priest he represents man to God (Heb. 9:15). As a King he will reign as God over the earth (Psa. 2).

MEGIDDO (mė-gĭd′ō). A strategic fortified town which once guarded the mountain pass leading to the Plain of Esdraelon. It was taken by Thutmose III in the fifteenth century B.C. Its people opposed Joshua but remained in Canaanite control (Josh. 12:21; 17:11; Judg. 1:27). The city fell into Solomon's fifth district (1 Kings 4:12) and was fortified by him (1 Kings 9:15; cf. 2 Kings 9:27; 23:29). The modern site, Tell el-Mutesselim, has been extensively excavated and reveals occupational levels from the early fourth millennium until about 350 B.C.

MELCHIZEDEK (mĕl-kĭz′ĕ-dĕk) ("king of righteousness"). The priest and king of Salem or "peace" (Heb. 7:2). Melchizedek met Abraham and blessed him (Gen. 14:18-20; Heb. 7:1-3). He thus prefigures Christ's priesthood (Heb. 7). Christ alone can bring us peace, since he is our righteousness (1 Cor. 1:30). Melchizedek's genealogy is purposely omit-

ted to make him typify more strikingly the mystery of Christ's birth and the eternity of his priesthood. Christ had no human father and no divine mother. As the only-begotten of the Father, Christ was without priestly pedigree. Melchizedek's greatness is seen in the tithes which Abraham paid him. Christ himself is infinitely greater than Melchizedek and thus deserves our all.

MELITA (mĕl′ĭ-tà). Modern Malta, a central Mediterranean island about 60 miles south of Sicily. It is about 95 square miles in area. Paul's ship was driven there from Crete and wrecked (Acts 27: 9—28:1). The Apostle spent three months on the island before resuming his journey to Rome via Syracuse, Rhegium, and Puteoli (Acts 28:11-13). In the tenth century B.C. Melita was occupied by the Phoenicians. The island's name in that language means "refuge," a reminder that the island has often proved a haven to storm-battered sailors. The site of Paul's shipwreck is probably "Saint Paul's Bay," eight miles northwest of the modern town of Valetta.

MELON. The plant commonly named watermelon (*Citrullus vulgaris*), which the Hebrews ate in Egypt (Num. 11:5). Melons of all sorts were grown in Egypt, and these are included in the reference to the watermelon.

MEMPHIS. An ancient Egyptian city on the west side of the Nile River and about 19 miles above the apex of the delta. It was the capital of the earlier dynasties until power was transferred to Thebes. To the Hebrews it was known as Noph (Isa. 19:13) and Moph (Hebrew text of Hosea 9:6). Some Jews settled there after the fall of Jerusalem and Gedaliah's murder (Jer. 44:1). Most of the ruins of Memphis have been carried to Cairo for construction purposes, so that the ancient city is now almost non-existent. However, 20 pyramids and the celebrated sphinx still remain.

MENAHEM (mĕn′à-hĕm) ("comforter"). A murderer and usurper of the throne of Israel. He reigned for about 10 years, from 752 to 742 B.C. (2 Kings 15:14-22). He rose to power in the period of civil war that marked the end of the Jehu dynasty.

MEPHIBOSHETH (mė-fĭb′ō-shĕth). A

son of Jonathan and grandson of King Saul. He is also called "Meribbaal," "striver against Baal." (The "Baal" element was changed to *bosheth*, Hebrew for "shame.") Mephibosheth became crippled as a child when his nurse dropped him while fleeing from the news of the death of Saul and Jonathan (2 Sam. 4:4). He at first lived in exile under David, the new king, but was later reinstated because of a previous covenant between David and Jonathan (1 Sam. 20:11-17; 2 Sam. 9). The story of Mephibosheth illustrates God's grace to the redeemed sinner.

MEROM (mē'rŏm), **WATERS OF.** Copious springs situated between Lake Huleh (Semechonitis) and the Lake of Galilee. The springs lie about 10 miles west of the Jordan River in Upper Galilee at the village of Merom. The Waters of Merom flow southeastward into the Lake of Galilee. Joshua routed the Hazor confederacy there (Josh. 11:5-8).

MESHECH (mē'shĕk). A son of Japheth and progenitor of the "Mushki" of the Assyrian records of the ninth century B.C. They inhabited the regions northeast of Cilicia (Gen. 10:2; cf. Ezek. 27:13; 32:26; 38:2; 39:1) and will participate in the great Northern Confederacy that will attack Palestine in the future.

MESHULLEMETH (mē-shŭl'ē-mĕth) ("recompensed, repaid"). The wife of King Manasseh of Judah (686-642 B.C.). She became the mother of King Amon (642-640 B.C.). The Bible states that her son "did that which was evil in the sight of the Lord, as Manasseh his father had done" (2 Kings 21:19-22). The implication is that Meshullemeth, too, was an ungodly person.

MESSIAH (mē-sī'ȧ). The ancient custom of consecrating priests, prophets, and kings by anointing them with oil led to the description of such persons as "anointed ones" (messiahs). The promised "Seed of the woman," the virgin-born Christ (Gen. 3:15; Isa. 7:14), held the three offices of Prophet, Priest, and King and was thus the Messiah par excellence.

As the suffering Messiah our Lord experienced rejection and death at his first advent (Isa. 53; Psa. 22:1-21). At his second advent he will appear as the ruling Messiah-King and Lord supreme (Rev. 19:11-16).

METHUSELAH (mē-thū'zĕ-lȧ) (probably "man of a javelin"). The oldest of the pre-flood patriarchs (Gen. 5:21-27).

MICAH THE EPHRAIMITE (mī'kȧ, ē'frȧ-ĭm-īt). An Israelite idolater during the time of the judges. He hired a Levite to act as priest for an image, thus linking idolatry to the ancient Levitical order in open violation of the Word of God (Judges 17, 18).

MICAH THE PROPHET. A native of Moresheth near Gath, about 20 miles southwest of Jerusalem in North Philistia (Mic. 1:1). He ministered from about 750 to 700 B.C. He espoused the cause of the poor and called for social righteousness (Mic. 6:8). He foresaw Christ's birth in Bethlehem as the coming Prince of Peace (Mic. 5:2; 4:3).

MICAIAH (mī-kā'yȧ) ("who is like the Lord?"). A prophet who foretold the death of Ahab at Ramoth-gilead (1 Kings 22). He ranks with all true and faithful spokesmen for God.

MICHAL (mī'kăl) ("who is like God?"). The younger daughter of Saul (1 Sam. 14:49). Saul had offered Michal to David on the condition that he kill 100 Philistines. David performed the feat and received Michal as his wife (1 Sam. 18:22-27). When Michal helped David escape from Saul's plot to kill him, the unscrupulous king gave her to another man despite her marriage to David (1 Sam. 25:44). Eventually David retrieved his wife (2 Sam. 3:12-16). Later Michal despised David as he danced before the Lord when the ark was brought up to Jerusalem. As a result she died childless (2 Sam. 6:12-23).

MICHMASH (mĭk'măsh). The location of a Philistine encampment about seven miles northeast of Jerusalem (1 Sam. 13:1-5). Exiles from Michmash returned from the Captivity (Ezra 2:27; Neh. 7:31; Neh. 11:31). Jonathan Maccabaeus exercised judgeship there (1 Macc. 9:73). The pass still retains the name "Mukhmas."

MIDIANITES (mĭd'ĭ-ăn-īts). A nomadic desert people who had descended from Abraham through Keturah (Gen. 25:1-6). It was Midianite traders (with a caravan of Ishmaelites) who bought Joseph and carried him to Egypt (Gen. 37:25-28, 36).

The Midianites joined with the Moabites in hiring Balaam to curse Israel (Num. 22–24). See also "Kenites."

MIDWIFE. Midwives are first mentioned in the Bible in the story of Jacob. They assisted Rachel (Gen. 35:16, 17) and Tamar (Gen. 38:28). The Hebrew word denotes "one who helps to bear" by cutting the umbilical cord, washing the infant, and salting and wrapping it (Ezek. 16:4). Women in childbirth customarily crouched down on a pair of stones or on a birthstool of similar design (Exod. 1:16). The process is well illustrated from ancient Egyptian sources.

MILCAH (mĭl′kà) ("counsel"). (1) A daughter of Haran and a sister of Lot. She became the wife of Nahor (Gen. 11:29) and the grandmother of Rebekah (Gen. 22:20-23). (2) One of the five daughters of Zelophehad (Num. 26:33; 27:1; Josh. 17:3).

MILE. See under "Weights and Measures."

MILETUS (mĭ-lē′tŭs). A principal seaport city of Ionia. It was founded by Ionian Greeks in the tenth century B.C. In New Testament times it was a city of the Roman province of Asia (Acts 20:15, 17; 2 Tim. 4:20). Miletus was about 36 miles south of Ephesus on the south shore of the bay of Latmus.

MILLENNIUM. The thousand-year period of Christ's royal reign on earth. It is the time during which God will fulfill all the covenants and promises which he has made to Israel. The millennium occurs after the church age and the Tribulation and prior to eternity itself.

MILLER. After threshing and winnowing, grain was either crushed in a mortar with a pestle or ground in a stone mill. This process of reducing grain to flour was usually done in the home. In large households or in a royal court like Solomon's the services of a miller were required. The miller was usually a member of the baking staff.

MILLO (mĭl′ō) (Hebrew "a fill"). Apparently a citadel or fortress at Shechem (Judg. 9:6, 20) and at Jerusalem. It existed at the time of David (2 Sam. 5:9) and was rebuilt by Solomon (1 Kings 9:15, 24; 11:27). Hezekiah strengthened it against attack by the Assyrians (2 Chron. 32:5).

Sluice gate regulates flow of mineral-laden Dead Sea for mining of potash. (© *MPS*)

MINING. Copper and iron were mined within the confines of Solomon's empire (Deut. 8:9). His extensive mining operations at Ezion-geber required large numbers of laborers for both the mining and the refining of these ores. Silver was usually mined in the form of the sulphide ore of lead (galena) but was also occasionally mined in its native state (Jer. 6:29, 30). Sources of silver and lead were Asia Minor, Southern Greece, Armenia, Persia, and the islands of the Aegean Sea. Tin alloyed with copper produced bronze. Gold was mined and used for jewelry and currency from early times. Turquoise was mined before 3000 B.C. at Magharah and Serabit el-Khadim in West Sinai. See Job 28:1-11 for a vivid description of ancient mining practices.

MINOANS (mĭ-nō′əns). A people on the island of Crete who attained a high degree of culture in the second millennium B.C. Their capital was at Knossos. See also "Cretans."

MINT. An herb of the genus *Mentha*, of which there are several species (Matt. 23:23). Horsemint grows wild and is the commonest species in Syria.

MIRACLE. A supernatural act in which God temporarily transcends the laws of nature in order to accomplish some special purpose.

MIRIAM ("rebellion, stubbornness"). The sister of Aaron and Moses (Exod. 15:20; Num. 26:59). Though she was gifted as a prophetess, her career was tarnished by insubordination to Moses as God's spokesman. When Moses married a Cushite woman, Miriam and Aaron used the occasion to criticize their brother's superior influence and position as God's mouthpiece. They claimed that God had spoken by them as well (Num. 12). For this serious breach of God's order Miriam was struck with leprosy. Later she was healed through Moses' intercession.

Although not actually mentioned by name, it was certainly Miriam who watched over the ark that held the infant Moses (Exod. 2:1-11). It was also Miriam who led the women of Israel in triumphal song after crossing the Red Sea (Exod. 15:20, 21). She did not enter Canaan, but died at Kadesh and was buried there (Num. 20:1).

MITHRAISM (mĭth'rə-ĭz'ĕm). A religion which blended worship of the Iranian sun-god, Mithras, with the Fertility Cult. It produced a mystery faith that observed a Lord's Day on Sunday and a sacrament of bread and wine. It resembled Christianity in so many ways that it was regarded by the early church as a demonic counterfeit invented to delude mankind. Mithraism was formally suppressed in the fourth century A.D. It left many monuments which were destroyed in lands which Mohammedans overran, but which remain in parts of Germany.

MIZPAH, MIZPEH (mĭz'pà). (1) Tell en-Nasbeh, eight miles north of Jerusalem (Josh. 18:26). It was an early sanctuary site (Judg. 20:1). It was later associated with Samuel (1 Sam. 7:5, 15, 16; 10:17) and was fortified by King Asa (1 Kings 15:22). It was the seat of Gedaliah's government after the fall of Jerusalem in 586 B.C. (2 Kings 25:23; Jer. 40:6-12). It was reoccupied in the post-exilic period (Neh. 3:19). Excavations reveal Asa's fortifications. (2) The place in Gilead where the pillar called Mizpeh was set up by Laban (Gen. 31:48, 49). The place also figures in the career of Jephthah (Judg. 10:17; 11:29). (3) Mizpeh in Moab (1 Sam. 22:3). It has not been located in modern times.

MIZRAIM (mĭz'rà-ĭm). The second son of Ham and the progenitor of the Egyptians and other Hamitic peoples (Gen. 10:6, 13).

MOABITES. The descendants of Lot through an incestuous union with his older daughter (Gen. 19:30-37). They occupied the territory east of the Dead Sea from the Brook Zered to the Arnon. At the time of Israel's entrance into Palestine Moab refused Israel permission to travel along the "King's Highway" which crossed the plateau (Judg. 11:17). Balak king of Moab hired Balaam to curse Israel (Num. 22–24; Josh. 24:9). In the period of the judges Eglon, king of Moab, overran part of Israel (Judg. 3:12-30). Elimelech of Bethlehem migrated to Moab and his sons married Moabite women, Orpah and Ruth. Ruth married Boaz and became the ancestress of David (Ruth 4:13-22) and of Christ (Matt. 1:5-16). Saul fought the Moabites (1 Sam. 14:47), David subdued them, and Solomon ruled them. After Solomon's death Moab broke free and remained so until subdued by Omri, as the Moabite Stone recounts.

During the reign of Jehoshaphat, Judah was invaded by a confederacy of Moabites, Ammonites, and Edomites (2 Chron. 20:1-30). Moab was tributary to Assyria and was later subdued by the Chaldeans, Persians, and various Arab groups.

MOLE. The reference in Isaiah 2:20 is not to the common mole (which does not exist in Palestine) but to the mole rat (*Spalax typhlus*), a common animal in the Holy Land. It is mole-like in appearance but is not of the same order, being a rodent. Unlike the mole, it feeds on vegetables rather than insects. It is also larger than the mole.

MOLECH, MOLOCH (mō'lĕk, mō'lŏk). A degraded deity worshiped by the Ammonites and associated with the sacrifice of children in fire. The Mosaic Law prescribed death for any Israelite who offered his child to Molech (Lev. 18:21; 20:2-5).

MONEY. See "Coins and Money."

MONEY-CHANGERS. The trade arose because money for the Temple, including the required half-shekel (Exod. 30:13), had to be in Tyrian standard coin and not in the current Roman standard (the Roman coins had pagan embellishments). An exchange surcharge was made, leading to various bad practices. The "exchangers" (Matt. 25:27) were regular bankers (*trapezitai*). A specialized class of currency exchangers had a concession in the Temple precincts, most likely in the Court of the Gentiles (Matt. 21:12; Mark 11:15; John 2:14, 15). Our Lord overthrew the counters of these dealers at the lucrative Passover season, thus cleansing the holy precincts of commercialism tainted with covetousness and materialism.

MONOTHEISM. Belief in a single Supreme Being. This was the original faith of the human race and has been held by a faithful minority throughout world history. Monotheism formed the basis of the Mosaic Covenant (Exod. 20:1-7). It repudiated all idolatry and all physical representations of Deity.

MONTH. See under "Calendar, Hebrew."

MORDECAI (from Akkadian "Marduk," the chief Babylonian deity). A Jew of the Exile who reared his uncle's daughter, Hadassah (Esther). She in turn became queen of Persia under Xerxes (486-464 B.C.). Through the queen, Mordecai saved Xerxes' life by informing him of a plot (Esth. 2:21-23). Later, when Mordecai's enemy, Haman (a court favorite), determined to murder Mordecai and exterminate all Jews in the kingdom, God used Esther and Mordecai to save them and to have Haman executed (Esth. 2—10).

MOREH (mō'rĕ). A hill south of Mount Tabor (Judg. 7:1) at the entrance of the northern side of the Valley of Jezreel. It is about one mile south of Nain and about eight miles northwest of Gilboa. It is present-day Jebel Dahi. In the Gideon story the Midianites encamped in the valley by the Hill of Moreh to the north of Gideon's camp (Judg. 7:1).

MORESHETH-GATH (mō'rĕsh-ĕth-găth). The home town of Micah (1:1, 14; Jer. 26:18). ("Morasthite" means "of Moresheth."). Moresheth is identified with present-day Tell el Gudeideh, not far from Gath in Philistia.

MORIAH (mō-rī'à). One of the hills of Jerusalem on which Solomon built the Temple. It was traditionally believed to be the spot where Abraham offered his son Isaac (Gen. 22:2; cf. 2 Chron. 3:1).

MOSES. One of the greatest of all Bible heroes. He was educated in Egypt and could have attained great power and prestige there. But he chose to identify himself with God's persecuted people rather than to enjoy the pleasures of sin for a season (Exod. 2—5; Heb. 11:23-28). As Israel's leader he rose to his great destiny as deliverer, administrator, commander-in-chief, lawgiver, judge, author, and intermediary between God and his people. As a member of the tribe of Levi he consecrated his brother Aaron to the high priesthood and, under God's direction, constituted him the forefather of the priestly line.

Moses is a prefiguration of Christ. Both were preserved from perils in infancy (Exod. 2:2-10; Matt. 2:12-15). Both were great deliverers (Heb. 11:24-30; Matt. 1:21). Both fasted forty days (Exod. 34:28; Matt. 4:2). Both had power to control the sea (Exod. 14:21; Matt. 8:26). Both fed a multitude (Exod. 16:4-8; Matt. 14:14-21). Both were powerful intercessors (Exod. 32:11-14; John 17). Both spoke as the oracles of God (Deut. 18:15-22; John 7:46). Both left memorials (Exod. 12:14; Luke 22:19, 20). Both reappeared after death (Matt. 17:1-4; John 20: 11—21:25; Acts 1:3).

MOTH (Hebrew *ᶜash*, Greek *sēs*). The common clothes moth, as shown by the context of the Scripture references (Job 4:19; 13:28; 27:18; Psa. 39:11; Isa. 50:9; 51:8; Hos. 5:12; Matt. 6:19, 20; Luke 12: 33; James 5:2). The larva feeds on wool (Isa. 51:8). The moth flourishes in the mild climate of Palestine.

MOTHER. The Bible emphasizes the importance of the home and of godly family life. The influence of a mother in the rearing of children is repeatedly emphasized in Scripture. Ezekiel declares the proverb "Like mother, like daughter" (Ezek. 16:44, RSV). The Decalogue obligates children to honor the mother as well as the father (Exod. 20:12). Honoring parents demonstrates obedience to the will of God and results in divine blessing, since parents stand in the place of God until their children grow to maturity (Col. 3:20; Eph. 6:1-3; Exod. 20: 12b).

Both godly and ungodly mothers figure prominently in many of the Scripture accounts. While they are often mentioned by name, mothers also frequently remain unnamed. Some of the more significant unnamed mothers of Scripture are briefly described below.

David's Mother. She was a woman who shared the dangers as well as the triumphs of her illustrious son. While David was being hunted like a wild animal by King Saul, the safety of David's parents was also seriously threatened. He and his men therefore visited the king of Moab and requested asylum for his parents. This was granted and David's parents were protected as the king's guests while they were in danger of reprisals from King Saul (1 Sam. 22:3, 4).

Ichabod's Mother. She was the wife of the undisciplined and immoral priest, Phinehas (son of Eli). She represents a mother without hope. She received word of her husband's death in battle shortly before her son was to be born. She thereupon named him "Ichabod," meaning "inglorious, no glory," in commemoration of the tragic departure of Israel's glory (the ark of the Tabernacle had been captured by the Philistines). She then died in childbirth. The incident is related in 1 Samuel 4:19-22.

Micah's Mother. She represents a religiously confused and spiritually disoriented mother, unable to guide her son in the ways of the Lord (Judg. 17:1-6). Both she and her son lived in the lawless era of the Judges, when everyone "did what was right in his own eyes" (Judg. 17:6). Her son had stolen 1100 pieces of silver from her, but had returned them out of fear for the curse which she had pronounced on the thief. She thereupon pronounced the Lord's blessing on her son and commissioned a metal-worker to convert 200 pieces of the silver into two images!

Micah then prepared a shrine for the images, complete with priest, ephod, and teraphim (household deities). Though Micah's mother is not mentioned again after this incident, her idolatry corrupted a whole tribe of Danites, who stole the images and carried them to Laish-Dan (Judg. 18:7-31).

Peter's Wife's Mother. After Jesus had cleansed a leper (Matt. 8:1-4) and healed the servant of a centurion (Matt. 8:5-13), he healed Peter's wife's mother of a fever. The Savior simply touched her hand and

"the fever left her" (Matt. 8:14, 15). Luke the physician calls it a "great" or "high" fever, probably indicating acute malaria, then common in the region of Capernaum and Bethsaida.

After being healed, Simon Peter's mother-in-law "ministered unto them." The writers of all three synoptic Gospels report this remarkable detail. It is not surprising that she who owed her life and strength to Christ should be eager to serve him. She represents a great host of mothers who have become outstanding servants of the Savior after being healed by his touch.

The Mother from Shunem. Called the Shunnamite because of her residence in Shunem (near Jezreel), she is called "great" in the King James Version (2 Kings 4:8). This indicates that she was wealthy and influential. But her story shows that she was also great in faith, wisdom, and generosity. She offered hospitality to the prophet Elisha and prepared a "prophet's chamber" for him. Her generosity was rewarded by the Lord when the prophet informed her that she was to have a son.

Later, when the boy was about 12 years old, he died of apparent sunstroke after helping his father in the fields. With the poise of faith his mother hurried 16 miles to Carmel to get Elisha. He returned with her and restored the child to life.

During a very severe famine Elisha urged the woman to go to Philistia. She did so, remaining away seven years. Upon returning home she found that her house had been appropriated by others. Through Elisha's mediation it was restored to her by the king. The mother from Shunem represents the generous and faithful mother who allows God's blessings to flood her life. Her story is told in 2 Kings 4:1-37 and 8:1-6.

The Mother from Tekoa. A wise and clever woman who was engaged by David's general, Joab, to effect the recall of Absalom from his banishment. Because Absalom had murdered his half-brother, Amnon, for defiling his sister Tamar, the king had banished him to the Aramean principality of Geshur (his mother's native land). The mother from Tekoa presented herself before the king as a suppliant for mercy for one of her two sons. When the woman obtained a decision in favor of her own son, she quickly showed the king the parallel to his son Absalom. By this means she secured Absalom's recall (2 Sam. 14).

The Harlot Mothers. During Solomon's reign (971-931 B.C.) two prostitutes appeared before the king in a dispute over the possession of a child. A baby had been born to each of these women, both of whom lived in the same house. One child was smothered to death at night when the mother accidentally overlaid it. Boldly this woman took her own dead child and laid it beside the other woman, taking the living child as her own.

When the two appeared before Solomon, the king devised a clever test to reveal the true mother. He called for a sword and ordered that the living child be cut in two, with half to be given to each mother. The real mother showed her love by relinquishing her child to the other woman. The false mother, on the other hand, agreed to have the baby cut in two. In addition to illustrating the wisdom of Solomon, the story shows the triumph of motherly love over even the most severe test (1 Kings 3:16-28).

The Model Mother. Her price is "far above rubies" and her excellencies are eloquently portrayed in Proverbs 31:10-31. The preceding chapters in Proverbs sound a solemn warning against the woman who is not virtuous. But this portrait paints the ideal woman in her most glorious role of housewife and mother. She is fully trustworthy (v. 11). She does only good to her husband (v. 12). She is industrious and provident (vv. 13-19). She is considerate, kind, and generous (v. 20). She is thrifty, prosperous, strong, and happy of disposition (vv. 21-25). She is wise and kind of speech (v. 26). She is busy in doing good and is never idle (v. 27). She wins the love and respect of her husband and children (v. 28) and excels in virtue (v. 29). Her crowning grace is her fear of the Lord, which is reflected in her words and deeds (vv. 30, 31).

MOUNTAIN. A large part of the charm of Palestine and Transjordan lies in its mountains and rolling hills. The central highlands of Palestine consist of a moun-

tain range beginning at the Lebanons where peaks of over 6000 feet above sea level are found. The highest peak in Palestine is Jebel Jermaq in Upper Galilee (3962 ft.). Lower Galilee consists of a number of ridges not exceeding 2000 feet in height. The "hill country of Ephraim" is a broad limestone ridge interspersed with fertile valleys and plains. Mount Ebal (3083 ft.) and Mount Gerizim (2889 ft.), with the city of Shechem nestled between them, was the place where the coastal road and the north-south trunkline met.

The mountains of Ephraim present no marked difference from the hill country of Judah except that they are not quite as high. As they approach Jerusalem the hills decrease to an altitude of about 2600 feet; they rise again as they go south until the highest point, 3346 feet, is reached just north of Hebron. East of this central ridge between Jerusalem and Hebron is the desolate Wilderness of Judah, a wild, arid wasteland. On the west the terrain declines gently to the lowlands or "shephelah." This area was important for both agriculture and defense. Such fort towns as Lachish, Debir, Libnah, Azekah, and Beth-shemesh guarded the interior territories. To the south the hills descend gently to the semi-arid *negeb* or southland between Beer-sheba and Kadesh Barnea.

The eastern hills of Transjordan form a plateau or tableland cut by four rivers: the Yarmuk, the Jabbok, the Arnon, and the Zered. Because of its elevation this region receives considerable rainfall and is thus fertile and agriculturally productive. But the rainfall decreases eastward as the terrain changes rapidly from steppe to desert. Mountains reach to 3900 feet in Gilead and rise nearly as high in Ammon and Moab.

Other important mountains in Bible lands are those of the Sinai Peninsula. Mount Sinai is located here, as well as other peaks up to 8600 feet in elevation. Other lofty mountain ranges include the Taurus range of Asia Minor (with peaks of over 12,000 feet), the Mountains of Armenia (where Noah's Ark rested), and the Zagros Mountains east of Mesopotamia. The Pindus Mountains of central

Looking from the ruins of Jericho to traditional Mount of Temptation (*Russ Busby photo*)

Greece and the Apennines of Central Italy are also significant.

MOURNING RITES. Acts of lamentation included weeping, wailing, tearing of garments, gashing the body, wearing sackcloth, heaping dust or ashes on the head, sitting in an ash heap, and playing dirges on musical instruments (cf. Jer. 16:6-8; 2 Sam. 1:11, 12; 13:31; 14:2; Ezek. 7:18; Amos 8:10). See also under "Funerals, Jewish."

MULE (Hebrew *pered*). The mule is a crossbreed between the horse and the ass (1 Kings 18:5). It is frequently mentioned with horses (Psa. 32:9). It became popular for riding and transportation (2 Sam. 13:29; 2 Kings 5:17). It was well known from David's time onward. Mules were obtained from Armenia by the Tyrians (Ezek. 27:14).

MUSIC AND MUSICAL INSTRUMENTS. Though music did not attain the level of development in Israel which it attained elsewhere, especially among the Greeks, its importance was nevertheless great in both the social and religious life of the Israelites. To Jubal is ascribed the invention of music (Gen. 4:21), while his brother Jabal is said to be the ancestor of shepherds. Shepherds have always been fond of music. David was famous as a skilled lyrist. In Greek mythology Pan, the patron of shepherds, was credited with inventing the flute.

Music was popular and indispensable at public feasts and family festivities. Singing and dancing brightened every festive occasion (Gen. 31:27; Judg. 11:34). Singing men and women and skilled instrumentalists graced every royal court and every home of the great (2 Sam. 19:35; Amos 8:3), as shown by tomb paintings and archeological remains. Singing to the accompaniment of lyre and tambourine was an intrinsic part of feasting (Job 21:12). Such festivities sometimes led to drunkenness and immorality (Isa. 5:12; Amos 6:5, 6).

Music also played a prominent role in times of mourning. It may have originally been intended to drive away evil spirits. David's lyre-playing relieved Saul of demonic pressure (1 Sam. 16:23).

Music played a dominant role in the worship of the Lord. Israelites knew how to sing to God and praise him in song and dance. As newly freed slaves from Egypt they worshiped God with a full array of musical instruments (Exod. 15:20). The subsequent history is repeatedly highlighted by joyful music in the worship of the Lord (2 Sam. 6:5; Psa. 150:1-6).

The musical instruments of the Bible are somewhat better known today than when the King James Version was translated, though precise knowledge of the various instruments is still somewhat scant despite the contributions of modern archeological research.

The instruments mentioned in the Bible can be divided into three main groups: strings, wind, and percussion.
Strings: *harp, psaltery, sackbut.*
Wind: *clarinet, flute, horn, trumpet.*
Percussion: *bells, cymbals, gong, sistrum, timbrel.*

These instruments are listed and described in alphabetical order below.
Bells. Two types are mentioned. One type is literally "strikers," from the Hebrew root "to strike." It was fastened to the hem of the high priest's robe (Exod. 28:33; 39:25, 26). These bells apparently had no clappers, but produced a pleasant sound simply by striking against each

other at every movement of the high priest. The other type, literally "jingle bells" (from a Hebrew root meaning "to rattle, to jingle"), were used as ornaments or amulets on horses (Zech. 14:20). These produced both melody and rhythm.

Clarinet (from Hebrew *ḥālal*, "to pierce"). This was an actual reed woodwind (not merely a pipe or flute). It was the most popular of the woodwinds in the ancient Near East (1 Sam. 10:5; Isa. 5: 12; 30:29; Jer. 48:36). Its Greek counterpart is mentioned in Matthew 9:23 and 11:17, Luke 7:32, 1 Corinthians 14:7, and Revelation 18:22. It was practically identical with the Greek *aulos* (1 Cor. 14: 7). Long before Israel's existence the double clarinet is mentioned in Akkadian tablets; many ancient representations of this instrument have been found.

Cymbals. In certain ritual and priestly functions two round metal plates were clashed together (1 Chron. 13:8; 15:19; 16:5, 42; 2 Chron. 5:12, 13; 29:25; Ezra 3:10; Neh. 12:27). Another type of cymbal consisted of two cups, one held stationery in the hand and the other brought down upon it (2 Sam. 6:5; Psa. 150:5).

Flute. This is the King James translation of the Aramaic word *mashrōqitha* (Dan. 3:5). It is derived from the root *shāraq*, meaning "to hiss" or "to whistle." The word describes the hissing sound characteristic of pipe or flute music. The instrument mentioned in Daniel 3:5 is probably of this general type.

Gong. A bronze gong was commonly used at weddings and other joyous occasions. It was the "sounding brass" of 1 Corinthians 13:1. In its smaller form it appeared as a kind of handbell.

Harp. The *kinnor* (usually translated "harp" in the King James Version) is the first musical instrument mentioned in the Bible (Gen. 4:21). It is used in this passage as a general description for all stringed instruments. When used in other passages it is uncertain whether the word denotes the simple lyre (which has a sounding box under the upper part of the strings) or an actual harp. (A harp is triangular, is held upright, and usually has at least nine strings. The lyre usually had only five to eight strings).

Ancient Egyptian tomb paintings represent foreigners playing lyres with plectrum in their hands. Elaborate tenstringed harps were also depicted on the tomb paintings.

Horn (Hebrew *shōphār*, from Akkadian *shapparu*, "wild ibex"). The ram's horn (Josh. 6:4, 8, 13) was the Jewish signaling instrument par excellence. It sounded all signals in both war and peace. It announced the new moon, the beginning of the sabbath, the death of a notable, and many other events. In its strictly ritual usage it carried the cry of the people to God. At special occasions God or his angels also sound the *shōphār* (Isa. 27: 13; Zech. 9:14; Rev. 8:2, 6, 12; 9:1, 13). It was not so much a true musical instrument as a signaling device.

The *yobēl* (Exod. 19:13) was also a ram's horn used for signaling. Its special function was to announce the beginning of the Year of Jubilee (Lev. 25:9-17).

Psaltery (Hebrew *nēbel*). A stringed instrument, either a portable harp, lute, or guitar with a bulging resonance body at the lower end (1 Sam. 10:5; Psa. 71:22; Isa. 14:11; Amos 5:23; 2 Chron. 5:12; Neh. 12:27). The cithara, harp, lyre, and psaltery were all very similar stringed instruments. It is no longer possible to differentiate between them clearly in every Scripture reference.

Sackbut (Aramaic *sabbekâ*). A stringed instrument of uncertain appearance. It may have been a large, many-stringed harp. (The word incorrectly translated "sackbut" in the King James Version was a trombone-like wind instrument.)

Sistrum. A small, hand-held noisemaker which was fitted with metal pieces that rattled when it was shaken. The oldest sistrums were found at Ur, Kish, and other early sites. It came to Palestine and Egypt from Mesopotamia. The only biblical mention of this is in 2 Samuel 6:5, where it is incorrectly translated "cornet" in the King James Version.

Timbrel (Hebrew *toph*). A percussion instrument known from remote antiquity. It was a type of tambourine and was generally played by women as an accompaniment to songs and dances at festivals. It is mentioned frequently in the Old Testament, both alone and with other instruments (Gen. 31:27; Exod. 15:

20; Judg. 11:34; 1 Sam. 10:5; 18:6; Job 21:12; Isa. 5:12; Jer. 31:4). It was sometimes used in religious services (Psa. 68: 25; 81:2; 149:3; 150:4).

Trumpet (Hebrew *ḥaṣoṣerâ*, from a root meaning "to shatter"). A priestly instrument par excellence. Its function was almost the same as that of the horn (*shophar*). Trumpets were employed in pairs (Num. 10:1-10) and were made of silver and other metals. The question of whether the pitch of the trumpet could be standardized so that groups of trumpeters could play simultaneously (as in 2 Chronicles 5:12) has been settled by the Dead Sea Scrolls. The Scroll of the War of the Sons of Light and the Sons of Darkness assigns numerous complicated signals in unison. Trumpets were used to terrorize an enemy (Judg. 7:19, 20) and to introduce rituals and sacrifices.

MUSTARD. The plant whose seed was used by Christ as an illustration of something which develops rapidly from small beginnings, such as the kingdom of heaven (Matt. 13:31, 32; Mark 4:31, 32; Luke 13:19) or the faith of a person (Matt. 17: 20; Luke 17:6). Some equate the plant with the black mustard (*Sinapis nigra*), since in New Testament times its seeds were cultivated for their oil and for culinary purposes. Others identify it with white mustard (*Sinapis alba*). Though both varieties have reportedly attained a height of 15 feet, they normally do not exceed four feet at maturity.

MUTILATION. Religious frenzy in demon-oriented pagan religions often caused the priests and devotees to gash themselves with knives (1 Kings 18:28) and to otherwise mutilate themselves.

MYCENAE. A prominent city of Bronze Age Greece. It is known for its tombs of Achaean kings. The site gives its name to "Mycenaean" civilization, which spread over the Aegean region after the fall of the empire of the Minoans and reached as far as Rhodes and Asia Minor.

MYRA (mī'rà). A seaport of Lycia (Acts 27: 5), Myra was a province of southwestern Asia Minor bordered on the north by Caria and Pisidia and on the east by Pamphylia. On his voyage to Rome, Paul landed at Myra and subsequently took an Alexandrian freighter bound for Italy.

MYRRH (Hebrew *mōr*, Akkadian *murru*). The resin exuded from the stems and branches of a low, shrubby tree, either the *Commiphora myrrha* or the closely related *Commiphora kataf*. The gum hardens to form an oily, yellowish-brown resin as it exudes from the shrub. Myrrh was an ingredient of the sacred anointing oil (Exod. 30:23-33). It was used in cosmetics and perfumery, being highly valued for its aromatic qualities (Psa. 45:8; Prov. 7:17; Song 3:6; 4:14; 5:5, 13). It was presented by the Magi as a present to the infant Jesus (Matt. 2:11) and was mixed with the wine which was offered to Christ on the Cross (Mark 15:23). It was also one of the spices employed at his burial (John 19:39). The myrrh carried by the Ishmaelites to Egypt was apparently the resin of the *Cistus villosus*, commercial ladanum (Gen. 37:25; 43:11).

MYRTLE TREE (Hebrew *hadas*). A beautiful Palestinian evergreen with fragrant leaves and scented white flowers. It attains a height of about 30 feet. The tree flourished in mountain glens (Zech. 1:8-11). Booths were made of its branches at the Feast of Tabernacles (Neh. 8:15). It symbolizes the Israelite nation preserved through humiliation and suffering for future kingdom glory (Zech. 1:8-11; cf. Isa. 41:19; 55:13). The tree still adorns the hills of Palestine.

MYSTERIES. (1) Secrets of the ancient cults of Babylon and Rome. (2) Any work or purpose of God which was revealed for the first time in the New Testament Canon. Instead of consisting of secrets to be withheld, New Testament mysteries are wonderful truths to be revealed to believers (1 Cor. 4:1). Before the New Testament was established in permanent written form, the temporary spiritual gifts of direct inspirational prophecies, knowledge, and languages (1 Cor. 13:8-13) operated in the apostolic church in order to enable believers to receive these truths in public services (1 Cor. 13:2). As the written New Testament began to be circulated among the churches these mysteries became available through biblical study and exposition. The temporary gifts were then superseded by the completed New Testament canon, the "completed thing" of 1 Corinthians 13:10.

N

NAAMAH (nā'à-mà) ("sweet, pleasant"). (1) A daughter of Lamech and a sister of Tubal-cain (Gen. 4:22). She is the first daughter cited by name in the Bible. Her brother was the originator of the ancient craft of metalworking. (2) One of Solomon's 700 wives. She was an Ammonite woman and became the mother of Rehoboam, Solomon's successor on the throne of Israel (1 Kings 14:21, 31; 2 Chron. 12:13). As an Ammonite princess born of Israel's inveterate enemies, Naamah was a corrupting force. Solomon built for her a high place for the worship of her national god, Molech. Her son Rehoboam's life and death was a monument to his father's sin and folly and a reflection of his mother's hatred for the true God of Israel.

NAAMAN (nā'à-măn) ("pleasant"). A captain in the army of Benhadad, king of Damascus. He was cured of leprosy by Elisha the prophet (2 Kings 5).

NABAL (nā'bàl) ("foolish"). A wealthy but churlish sheepmaster. He was as foolish as his name implied (1 Sam. 25:1-43). He was temporarily saved from death (for refusing to help David in a time of distress) by his beautiful wife. But God subsequently struck Nabal dead, and his widow became a wife of David (25:39-42).

NABATEANS (năb'à-tē'ănz). An Arab people apparently descended from Ishmael and Edom (Gen. 25:13; 29:9). Their capital was at Petra. From the time of their first known king, Aretus I (170 B.C.), they became influential through the control of trade routes from India and China across Arabia. They brought silks, spices, and other luxuries to the Greco-Roman world. The Nabateans developed not only commerce but agriculture and the arts as well. They were a remarkably gifted people and had good relations with the Jews in the period of the Hasmoneans and Herodians. Several of their kings with the dynastic name of Haretath (Aretas) came in contact with biblical history. Aretas IV was the father-in-law of Herod Antipas. He attempted to seize Paul at Damascus (2 Cor. 11:32).

NABONIDUS (năb'ō-nī'dŭs) (Akkadian *Nabuna^cid*, "the god Nabu is exalted"). The last king of the Neo-Babylonian Empire (556-539 B.C.), whose son Belshazzar (Dan. 5) was co-regent from the third year of his reign to the fall of the city in 539 B.C.

NABOPOLASSAR (năb'ō-pō-lăs'âr) (Akkadian, "Nabu protect the son"). The king of Babylon from 625 to 605 B.C. He created the Neo-Babylonian Empire upon the ruins of the Assyrian Empire. He was the father of Nebuchadnezzar.

NABOTH (nā'bŏth) (from the Arabic *nabata*, "grow, sprout"). The man whom Jezebel arranged to have murdered in order to obtain his vineyard (1 Kings 21: 1-14).

NADAB (nā'dăb) ("liberal"). A son of Aaron who, with his brother Abihu, was slain by the Lord for offering priestly sacrifices in an unauthorized manner (Lev. 10:1, 2).

UNGER'S GUIDE

NAHUM (nā′hŭm) ("consolation, comfort"). A Hebrew prophet (c. 620 B.C.) who predicted the fall of Nineveh and the Assyrian Empire.

NAIN (nā′ĭn). A town where Jesus raised a widow's son to life (Luke 7:11-15). It is still called Nein and is located in the northwest corner of the eminence called Little Hermon. Nein is about two miles west-southwest of Endor and five miles south-southeast of Nazareth.

NAMES. Bible names frequently have a significant meaning and often carry a character designation, as in the case of Jacob (Gen. 27:36). The various names of deity describe God's character. To believe on Christ's name means to trust him as Redeemer-Savior. Works done "in his name" are accomplished directly by his power (Acts 16:18; cf. Luke 24:47). Prayer "in Christ's name" identifies the petitioner with him, so that the petition is as effective as though Christ himself had made the request (John 14:14; 16:23; cf. Rom. 10:13).

NAOMI (nā′ō-mī; nȧ-ō′mĭ) ("my pleasantness"). An Israelite woman who emigrated to Moab with her husband, Elimelech, because of famine. There their two sons, Mahlon and Chilion, took wives. But Elimelech and the two sons died in Moab, leaving three widows. Ruth, one of the daughters-in-law, elected to go back to Bethlehem with Naomi, but Orpah, the other daughter-in-law, chose to remain in Moab.

Back in Bethlehem, Naomi introduced Ruth to Boaz, her kinsman, and a levirate marriage between the two was consummated. Ruth beautifully portrays the believing remnant of the nation Israel, which will ultimately come in touch with the mighty Kinsman-Redeemer. Through him they will inherit the kingdom blessings. Naomi pictures the nation Israel in her sorrows outside the land and her ultimate restoration to the land through the believing remnant of the last days (cf. Isa. 10:21, 22; Mic. 4:7). Little wonder that Ruth became, through Boaz's child Obed, the ancestress of both David and David's Lord, the divine Kinsman-Redeemer (Ruth 4:17-22).

NAPHTALI (năf′tȧ-lī) ("my wrestling"). A son of Jacob and the progenitor of an Israelite tribe (Gen. 30:8; Gen. 46:24).

NATHAN (nā′thăn) ("he has given"). A prophet in the time of David and Solomon. He confronted David with his scandalous sin (2 Sam. 12:1-14). Nathan wrote a history of the period (1 Chron. 29:29).

NAZARETH (năz′ȧ-rĕth). A Galilean town situated in a high valley among the most southerly limestone hills of the Lebanon range. To the south is a magnificent view and a sharp descent to the Plain of Esdraelon. The village of Nazareth was Christ's home for about 30 years (Luke 2:39; 4:16).

NAZARITE, NAZIRITE (năz′ȧ-rīt; năz′ĭ-rīt) ("dedicated, separated"). A designation given to an Israelite who vowed special consecration to the Lord. Abstinence from wine (a symbol of natural joy—Psa. 104:15) symbolized the Nazarite's joy in the Lord alone (cf. Psa. 97:12; Hab. 3:18; Phil. 3:1; 4:4, 10). Long hair, naturally a reproach to man (1 Cor. 11:14), symbolized the Nazarite's willingness to bear reproach for the Lord.

The Nazarite symbolism was perfectly fulfilled in Christ, who was "holy, harmless, undefiled, and separate from sinners" (Heb. 7:26). He was completely separated to the Father (John 1:18; 6:38). He allowed no mere natural claim to direct him from God's will (Matt. 12:46-50; John 2:2-4).

NEAPOLIS (nē-ăp′ō-lĭs) (in Italy). Naples, near Pompeii on the bay of Naples (on the west-central coast of Italy).

NEAPOLIS (in Macedonia). The port of Philippi, which lay on Paul's route during his second missionary tour (Acts 16:11).

NEAPOLIS (in Palestine). The site of ancient Nablus (near Shechem). In the Roman period the city was called Colonia Julia Neapolis.

NEBO (nē′bō). (1) The mountain in the range of Abarim from which Moses viewed the promised land (Num. 27:12; Deut. 32:49; 34:1). Christian tradition identifies it with Jebel en-Neba (2,630 ft.) 17 miles east of the northern end of the Dead Sea. However, some scholars prefer Jebel Osha, a considerably higher mountain (3,303 ft.) which is farther to the north, overlooking Jericho. This site would better fit the description in Deuteronomy 34:1, 2. The mountain was named from the Babylonian god Nabu. (2) The Babylonian deity Nabu, son of Bel (Marduk). He symbolized the national power of Babylon (Isa. 46:1). He was considered the god of learning — writing, astronomy, and all science. A temple, Ezida ("the House of Knowledge"), was dedicated to him in each of the larger cities of Babylonia and Assyria.

NEBUCHADNEZZAR (nĕb'ŭ-kăd-nĕz'ẽr) (Akkadian *Nebuchadrezzar*, "Nabu defend the boundary"). The king of Babylon from 605 to 562 B.C. He was used by God as an instrument to chastise his disobedient people. He inaugurated "the times of the Gentiles" (Luke 21:24; cf. Dan. 4:34-37; Rev. 11:15-17). Nebuchadnezzar was one of the greatest builders and rulers of ancient times (cf. Dan. 4:29, 30).

NECHO II (nē'kō). The second ruler of Egypt's twenty-sixth dynasty. He reigned from 609 to 593 B.C. He slew Josiah of Judah at Megiddo in 608 B.C. He set Jehoiakim on the throne of Judah (2 Kings 23:29-34). He was completely routed from Asia by Nebuchadnezzar.

NECKLACE. Neck-pendants (Song 4:9; cf. Judg. 8:26; Prov. 1:9) were common in the ancient Near-Eastern world of antiquity. The tombs of Egypt and the excavated sites of Babylonia and Assyria have yielded necklaces of fine workmanship and beauty.

NEHEMIAH (nē'hĕ-mī'à) ("the Lord has comforted"). The cup-bearer of the king of Persia at Shushan (Susa). He obtained royal permission and help to rebuild the walls of Jerusalem. He was both a soldier and a statesman. As the governor of Jerusalem he overcame all types of difficulties in the completion of his patriotic task (see the Book of Nehemiah).

NEHUSHTA (nĕ-hŭsh'tà) ("of bronze"). The wife of King Jehoiakim (609-598 B.C.) and the mother of King Jehoiachin (598-597 B.C. — 2 Kings 24:8). She was taken prisoner with her son when the Babylonians took possession of Jerusalem in 597 B.C. and was carried away with other leading citizens to Babylon (2 Kings 24:12-15). Nehushta suffered severely in these terrible times. She saw her

wicked husband revolt against the Babylonians and perish in disgrace (Dec. 6, 598 B.C.). Her son Jehoiachin ruled only three months and ten days. His evil reign is described in 2 Kings 24:8, 9 and 2 Chronicles 36:9, 10. Jeremiah predicted the end of his rule and dynasty (Jer. 22: 24-30).

Evidently Nehushta and her son were treated as royal hostages in Babylon, for he is named in Babylonian tablets as receiving rations with his five sons. Nebuchadnezzar's successor in 561 B.C. transferred Jehoiachin from prison to the royal palace (2 Kings 25:27-30; Jer. 52:31-34). Whether Nehushta was still living and shared this good fortune is not known.

NERO (nē'rō). The Roman Emperor from A.D. 54 to 68. He was a monster of iniquity. He accused Christians of setting the great fire in Rome in A.D. 54 and had them tortured and killed. Doubtless Paul and perhaps Peter met death under him. When the Jewish Revolt broke out in Judea, Nero dispatched Vespasian to quell it. While the war raged, he was forced from the throne and committed suicide.

NETHINIM (nĕth'ĭ-nĭm). The name means "those who are given." David and the princes had given these people for the service of the Levites (Ezra 8:20). They are called "temple slaves" in 1 Esdras 5: 29 and Josephus (*Antiquities* XI:5, 1).

NETTLE. A number of related weeds with stinging hairs (Job 30:7). This weed overspreads the sluggard's unworked garden (Prov. 24:31) and an untilled countryside (Zeph. 2:9). The plant is not further identified. The Roman pill nettle (*Urtica pilulifera*) is common in Palestine. It is referred to in Isaiah 34:13 and Hosea 9:6. See also Proverbs 24:31, where a modification of the word in the plural is rendered "thorns."

NEW COVENANT. Secured in Christ's blood, this covenant guarantees the personal revelation of the Lord to every believer (Heb. 8:11) and the complete removal of sins (Heb. 8:12; 10:17). It rests on an accomplished redemption (Matt. 26:27, 28; 1 Cor. 11:25). It assures the perpetuity, future conversion, and kingdom blessing of a repentant Israel, with whom the new covenant will also someday be ratified (Jer. 31:31-34; Heb. 10:9).

NEW JERUSALEM. The eternal residence and destiny of the redeemed of all ages (Rev. 21:9–22:5). The city will be part of the new heaven and new earth (Rev. 21:1, 2) in the sin-cleansed universe.

NICODEMUS (nĭk'ȯ-dē'mŭs) ("victor over the people"). A Pharisee and Jewish teacher who came to Jesus by night and was instructed in the necessity of experiencing the new birth (John 3:1-21). Nicodemus must have experienced this new birth, for he later spoke for Christ (John 7:45-52) and honored him (John 19:39, 40).

NICOLAITANS (nĭk'ȯ-lā'ĭ-tănz). A religious sect that lived licentiously while professing to be Christians (Rev. 2:6, 15). They apparently advocated pagan sexual laxity. References in Irenaeus, Clement, and Tertullian trace this heretical group as far back as A.D. 200.

NICOPOLIS (nĭ-kŏp'ȯ-lĭs). A city on the southwestern tip of Epirus (northwest of Achaia). It was founded by Augustus in 31 B.C. to commemorate his victory at nearby Actium. Paul hoped to winter there when he penned the Epistle to Titus (Tit. 3:12).

NIGHT HAWK (Hebrew *tahmās*). An unidentified bird listed as unclean (Lev. 11:16; Deut. 14:15). Though most English versions render it "night hawk," the bird is better known as the night jar or goatsucker (*Caprimulgus europaeus*). The Septuagint and Vulgate identify the Hebrew word with the owl.

The Nile River in Old Cairo, an area familiar to Joseph (© MPS)

NILE (nīl). The longest and most naviga-ble river in Bible lands, a 4000-mile waterway to the heart of Africa. It was called "the Nile" by the Greek and Romans. This life-giving stream with its annual inundation was the life of Egypt and made possible a mighty nation in the heart of a scorching desert. In it Moses was hid in a papyrus boat (Exod. 2:3). The Hebrews referred to the river as *Yeor*, which in the plural refers to the Nile River system (Isa. 7:18).

NIMROD (nĭm'rŏd) (from the Hebrew root *marad*, "to rebel"). An ancient Hamitic ruler and the founder of imperial power in Babylonia (Gen. 10:8, 9). This power is intimated to be evil in the sense of rebellion against God.

NINEVEH (nĭn'ē-vĕ). The ancient capital of the Assyrian Empire (Gen. 10:11; 2 Kings 19:36; Jonah 1:2; Nah. 1:1). It was situated on the Upper Tigris River above the Great Zab tributary. It is represented by the tells (mounds) of Quyunjik and Nabi Yunus. In its heyday it embraced a great metropolitan area including Calah (Nimrud) and Dur-Sharrukin (Khorsabad). The "three days' journey" of Jonah 3:3 probably refers to the whole administrative district, which was about 30 to 60 miles across (Hatra-Khorsabad-Nimrud). The city was destroyed by the Babylonians and Medes in 612 B.C. (cf. Nah. 2:8; 3:7; Zeph. 2:13) and was lost in oblivion until resurrected by modern archeology.

NIPPUR. A religious and cultural center of Sumer from about 4000 B.C. It has yielded much information to the excavator. It is present-day Nuffar, southeast of Babylon, between Kish and Isin.

NO. The capital of Upper and Lower Egypt in the Middle Kingdom and under the Eighteenth Dynasty. It is 330 miles upstream from Cairo. Its site on the two banks of the Nile is marked on the eastern side by two vast temple-precincts of the god Amun, now known by the Arabic names Karnak and Luxor. The western side is marked by a row of royal funerary temples from modern Qurneh to Medinet Habu. Behind this extends a vest necropolis of rock-cut tombs. Ashurbanipal of Assyria sacked Thebes in 663 B.C. (Nah. 3:8). But the city still remained important (Jer. 46:25; Ezek. 30:14-16). It was finally destroyed completely by the Roman prefect Gallus, in 30 and 29 B.C.

NOAH (nō'a) ("rest"). (1) The man who, with his wife and his sons and his sons' wives, was saved out of the deluge to begin life anew on a cleansed earth (Gen. 6–9). The biblical account of the Flood finds remarkable parallels in Sumerian and Babylonian cuneiform accounts of the same event. (2) One of the five daughters of Zelophehad who asked for and received an inheritance even though their father was deceased and they had no brothers (Num. 26:33; 27:1-11; 36:10-12; Josh. 17:3-6).

NOB (nŏb). A priestly city in Benjamin (1 Sam. 21:1; 22:9; Isa. 10:32). It is identified with et-Tor, a few miles east-northeast of Jerusalem.

NOPH (nŏf). See "Memphis."

NOSE RING. A woman's ornament commonly worn on the nose (Gen. 24:22, 30, 47, RSV). Proverbs 11:22 speaks of a "ring in a swine's snout" (cf. Hos. 2:13, RSV; Ezek. 16:12).

NUMBERS. The numbers of Scripture undoubtedly possess spiritual significance.

One denotes unity – one Lord, one faith, etc. (Deut. 6:4; Eph. 4:3-6). It is the unity between Christ and the Father (John 10:30), the union between believers and the Godhead (John 17:20, 21), the oneness existing among Christians (Gal. 3:28), and the union of man and woman in marriage (Matt. 19:6).

Two prefigures both unity and diversity. Man and woman comprise the basic family unit (Gen. 1:27; 2:20-24). Animals entered the ark two-by-two (Gen. 7:9). Two people can work together in companionship (e.g. Joshua's two spies and the two witnesses of Revelation 11:3-12). The Twelve and the Seventy were sent out two-by-two (Mark 6:7; Luke 10:1). The Law was given on two tablets. Sometimes the number two designates opposing forces (1 Kings 18:21; Matt. 7: 13, 14).

Three relates to the perfection of God in the Trinity (Matt. 28:19), the three heavens (2 Cor. 12:2), and God's mighty acts (Exod. 19:11; Hos. 6:2; Jonah 1:17; Matt. 12:40; 1 Cor. 15:4).

Four speaks of the earth and creative works. The name "Jehovah," which has only four letters in its original form (YHWH), connects God redemptively with man and the earth. There are four quarters or "corners" of the earth (Rev. 7:1; 20:8), as well as four winds (Jer. 49:36; Ezek. 37:9; Dan. 7:2). The number four is prominent in prophetic symbolism about the earth and its judgments (Zech. 1:18-21; 6:1-8; Rev. 9:13). Four major kingdoms constitute world history from Nebuchadnezzar (605 B.C.) till the second advent of Christ (cf. Dan. 2 and 7).

Five as a divisor of ten denotes a portion of a complete unit. The ten virgins represent the nation Israel before Christ's advent in glory (Matt. 25:1). The five wise virgins symbolize the believing remnant while the five foolish ones represent the unbelieving segment.

Six is the number of man. He was created on the sixth and final day of creation (Gen. 1:27); six days constitute his work week (Exod. 20:9; 23:12; 31:15); 666 denotes man's complete rebellion against God (Rev. 13:18).

Seven denotes fullness or completion (not perfection per se). The seventh or sabbath day marked God's rest upon completion of creation (Gen. 2:2, 3; Exod. 20:10). Compare the seventh year (Lev. 25:2-6) and the Jubilee year, which follows seven times seven years (Lev. 25: 8). The Feast of Unleavened Bread and the Feast of Tabernacles each lasted seven days (Exod. 12:15, 19; Num. 29:12). The latter foreshadowed Israel's kingdom rest and the completion of the divine economies in time, before the advent of eternity. The Day of Atonement, prefiguring completed redemption, fell in the seventh month (Lev. 16:29). Seven is prominent in Old Testament ritual (Lev. 4:6; 14:7; Num. 28:11; cf. 2 Kings 5:10). The Tabernacle candlestick had seven flames (a stem and six branches), symbolizing Christ as the full light of God (Exod. 25:32).

Eight appears to denote resurrection (Matt. 28:1) and the spiritual power released in the putting off of the flesh by circumcision (Gen. 17:1, 12; Phil. 3:5; Col. 2:10-13). It looks forward to the eternal state, as typified by the eighth day which ends the Feast of Tabernacles

(Lev. 23:39).

Nine (three times three) suggests perfection and completeness that looks forward to God as all in all in the eternal state. The basis of this is the death of Christ that occurred at the ninth hour (Mark 15:34).

Ten, the sum of seven and three, indicates completeness. Ten pre-flood patriarchs represent the complete messianic line. The 10 Egyptian plagues embrace the full divine judgment against the gods of Egypt. The Ten Commandments reflect the complete moral law of God required of Israel. The 10 virgins represent the entire nation Israel at Christ's coming (Matt. 25:1-10). Ten powers which cannot separate the believer from God's love (Rom. 8:38, 39) stand for *all* powers.

Eleven (twelve minus one) signifies a missing of God's elective purpose (Acts 1:26).

Twelve, like three, seven, and ten, is a number of completeness and is connected with the elective purposes of God—for example, the 12 tribes of Israel and the 12 Apostles (Gen. 49:28; Matt. 10:1). The Hebrew year was divided into 12 months and the day into 12 hours (John 11:9).

NUTS. Pistachio nuts (Hebrew *botnim*) are referred to in Genesis 43:11. They were not grown in Egypt and thus constituted an acceptable gift to Joseph (they were considered a delicacy in the land of the Nile). The pistachio is native to western Asia but was introduced into southern Europe and Palestine. It is no longer common in Bible lands. The nut referred to in Song of Solomon 6:11 is apparently the walnut (*Juglans regia*), referred to in the United States as the English walnut. It is cultivated in Galilee and along the slopes of Mount Lebanon and Mount Hermon.

OAK (Hebrew *'alla, 'allōn, 'ēla*). These three common Hebrew words designate only a few of the many species of the genus *Quercus* found in Palestine. The oak is a sturdy hardwood tree which lives to a great age. Its fruit is the acorn. Some Palestinian species are evergreen while others are deciduous. Bashan, the fertile region north of Gilead in Transjordan, was famous for its oaks (Isa. 2:13; Ezek. 27:6; Zech. 11:2). Absalom was caught in an oak (2 Sam. 18:9, 10). Dead people were frequently buried under an oak (Gen. 35:8).

OATH. A solemn adjuration employed to ratify an assertion and usually sealed by appeal to divine authority (cf. Heb. 6:16). Swearing in biblical times took the following common forms: (1) placing the hand under the thigh of the person to whom the promise was made (Gen. 24:2; 47:29); (2) dividing a slain animal and distributing the pieces (Gen. 15:10, 17; Jer. 34:18); (3) lifting up the hand or placing the hand on the head of the accused (Gen. 14:22; Lev. 24:14; Deut. 17:7); and (4) standing before the altar or (if distant from Jerusalem) positioning oneself toward the Temple (1 Kings 8:31; 2 Chron. 6:22). The sanctity of the oath was protected by the Law. The crime of perjury was very severe (Exod. 20:7; Lev. 19:12).

OBADIAH (ō'bȧ-dī'ȧ) ("servant of the Lord"). One of the Hebrew prophets who foretold Edom's destruction.

OFFICER. (1) *Old Testament usage.* The Hebrew word *shoter* signifies "one who writes or records." Officers apparently acted as overseers over the people (Prov. 6:7). At the same time they functioned as assistants or recorders, helping those under whom they served. It was such foremen who supervised the enslaved Israelites in Egypt and monitored the number of bricks they made. This type of supervisory function is abundantly illustrated in Egyptian records from the Mosaic era and earlier. It is therefore not surprising that officers were appointed alongside judges in the Mosaic Law (Deut. 16:18) and held prominent positions in subsequent Israelite history (Josh. 1:10; 8:33; 1 Chron. 26:29, 30; 2 Chron. 19:11; 26:11; 34:13). (2) *New Testament usage.* Luke refers to a police "officer" or bailiff (Greek *praktor*—Luke 12:58) whose duty it was, after sentence was passed, to collect debts under orders from the judge. The term in classical Greek denoted tax collectors and other officials of finance.

Other minor officers or servants (Greek *huperetēs*) are frequently referred to in the New Testament. John Mark was such an assistant or helper of Paul and Barnabas (Acts 13:5). Such assistants (RSV, "guards") performed duties for a board or court, such as the Sanhedrin (Matt. 5:25; 26:58; Mark 14:54; John 7:32; 19:6; Acts 5:22). Synagogue attendants belonged to this category (Luke 4:20). The apostles were such servants of Christ (Acts 26:16; 1 Cor. 4:1).

OG (ŏg). A king of the Amorites of Bashan (Deut. 3:1, 8). His rule extended from the River Jabbok to Mount Hermon (Deut. 3: 8; Num. 21:23, 24). He was conquered by the invading   raelites (Num. 21:32-35; Deut. 3:14) an his territory was allotted to the half-tribe. of Manasseh (Deut. 3: 13).

OIL TREE. Some identify this tree with the oleaster (*Elaeagnus angustifolia*), a shrub common in Palestine. It yields an inferior oil and a small fruit. But it is difficult to see how a mere shrub like the oleaster could furnish wood of large enough dimensions to construct the cherubim (1 Kings 6:23, 26), the doors of the oracle, and the door posts for the Temple entrance (1 Kings 6:31-33). The oil tree may well be the Aleppo pine (*Pinus halepensis*). It is called "oil tree" because of the tar and turpentine obtained from it.

OLEANDER (*Apocynaceae*). A beautiful evergreen tree with pink or white blossoms. It was enjoyed by Palestinians in both biblical and modern times. It is a stream-loving tree that keeps a ribbon of refreshing green alive along sun-baked stream beds in the summer. The oleander is thought by some to be the "rose of Sharon" of Song of Solomon 2:1.

OLIVE DRESSER. The olive was one of the most valuable trees in Palestine. With the vine, its cultivation constituted an important and lucrative industry (1 Sam. 8:14; 2 Kings 5:26) which employed many workers. But the task of cultivating the trees and harvesting the fruit was only part of the work connected with the olive crop. The harvest had to be transported to the presses in baskets on the backs of donkeys. The berries were then crushed in a shallow rock cistern by an upper millstone or simply by the feet of the harvesters (Deut. 33:24; Mic. 6:15). The oil was then cleansed of impurities by a settlement process and stored in jars or rock cisterns.

OLIVE TREE. The olive tree of Palestine is the common *Olea europaea*. It has leathery, dusty, green leaves and small, whitish flowers. It is a distinct feature of the Palestinian landscape. It is a long-lived, gnarled tree, often surviving for centuries. The fruit furnished food to eat and oil to illuminate ancient homes. In order to remain fruitful an olive tree has to be cultivated. If its care is neglected it degenerates into a wild olive tree. The process of grafting a cutting from a wild olive tree into a cultivated tree is alluded to in Romans 11:17, 24. In horticulture the reverse procedure was normally followed. A cutting from the cultivated tree was grafted into the wild (uncultivated) olive tree in order to alter its nature. The olive tree is a symbol of peace, prosperity, beauty, and divine blessing (Psa. 52:8; Jer. 11:16; Hos. 14:6).

The Mount of Olives and Garden of Gethsemane, across the Kidron Valley from the Temple site (© MPS)

OLIVET. A small range of four summits which overlooks Jerusalem and the Temple area from the east across the Kidron Valley (Zech. 14:4; Matt. 21:1). In Christ's day the Mount of Olives (as Olivet was frequently known) was thickly wooded with olive trees. But it was stripped bare when Jerusalem was destroyed by Titus.

OMRI (ŏm′rī). The king of Israel from 880 to 873 B.C. and the founder of a dynasty which was continued in his son Ahab (873-853 B.C.) and Ahab's sons, Ahaziah (853-852 B.C.) and Joram (852-841 B.C.). Omri transferred his capital from Tirzah to Samaria. He followed the idolatries of Jeroboam (1 Kings 16:26). As the founder of the Omride dynasty he was well known by the Moabites (as the Moabite Stone attests), but his reputation among the Assyrians is proved by their reference to Jehu (a king of a different dynasty) as *mār Hûmri* or "successor of Omri."

ON (ŏn). Present-day Tell Husn, northeast of Memphis in Lower Egypt. It was a center for sun-worship. The Greek form of the name, Heliopolis, means "City of the Sun" (cf. Isa. 19:18, RSV; 43:13, RSV). The city was the home of Joseph's Egyptian wife (Gen. 41:45, 50).

ONESIMUS (ŏ-nĕs′ĭ-mŭs) ("useful, profitable"). A slave of Philemon whom Paul led to Christ at Rome and whom the Apostle returned to his Christian master as a brother beloved (Philem. 1:10-19). A native of Colosse, Onesimus accompanied Tychicus from Rome to that city with the letters of Colossians and Philemon (Col. 4:7-9).

ONESIPHORUS (ŏn′ĕ-sĭf′o-rŭs) ("profit-bringer"). A believer at Ephesus who befriended Paul (2 Tim. 1:16; 4:19).

ONIAS III (ŏ-nī′ăs). A Jewish high priest who suffered exile and death because of his loyalty to Judaism and opposition to Hellenism on the eve of the Maccabean Revolt (second century B.C.). He became a legendary figure (2 Macc. 3, 4).

ONION. A bulbous-root plant popular in Egypt as an article of food (Num. 11:5). It is the *Allium cepa*, cultivated from earliest times in Egypt and other parts of the East.

ONO (ō′nō). A town in the Plain of Ono (Neh. 6:2) near Lydda. The town is first mentioned in the lists of Thutmose III (1490-1436 B.C.). The Benjamites rebuilt it after the conquest of Canaan (1 Chron. 8:12) and reoccupied it after the Exile (Neh. 11:31-35).

OPHEL (ō′fĕl). The southeast hill of Jerusalem and the original Jebusite settlement and citadel at that city. It was captured by David. Its fortifications were improved by Jotham (2 Chron. 27:3). In a city of Moab, according to the Moabite Stone, Mesha built the wall of "the ophel," that is, "the bulge or hill" of the citadel.

OPHIR (ō′fẽr). A source of gold in the Arabian Peninsula or possibly on the East African Coast (Gen. 10:29; 1 Kings 9:28; 10:11; 22:48; cf. Job 22:24; Isa. 13:12).

ORACLE. According to pagan belief, either the utterances which the gods delivered or the temple chambers in which these messages were given. The oracular shrine of Apollo at Delphi was the most famous of these pagan temples. In contrast to the pagan usage, the Bible employs the word "oracle" in a much more exalted sense. In Old Testament usage the oracle was the inner shrine or Holiest Place. In New Testament usage oracles *(logia)* refer to the inspired Old Testament Scriptures in whole or in part (Acts 7:38; Rom. 3:2; Heb. 5:12; cf. 1 Pet. 4:11).

ORPAH (ôr′pă) ("neck"). The wife of Chilion and the sister-in-law of Ruth. She chose to remain in her native Moab while Ruth determined to follow her mother-in-law to Palestine (Ruth 1:14-22). In the beautiful typology that underlies this romance of redemption, Orpah symbolizes the unbelieving majority of the Jewish people that will choose to remain scattered among the nations in the day of Israel's return to her homeland. Ruth portrays the believing remnant of Israel that will trust in God's redemptive provision and will come in contact with the great Kinsman-Redeemer, Christ.

ORDINATION. In an ecclesiastical sense this term refers to setting men apart to a particular spiritual service (Mark 3:14; John 15:16; Acts 6:1-6; 13:2; Gal. 1:1; 1 Tim. 4:14; Tit. 1:5). Those who carry on the Christian ministry are apparently vested with the authority to ordain men to carry on the work of the gospel.

OSPRAY, OSPREY. An unclean bird (Lev. 11:13; Deut. 14:12). It is probably to be identified with a dark brown eagle, *Pandion haliaetus,* found along the Maritime Coast and the marshy lagoons of the Kishon.

OSSIFRAGE (Latin for "bone-breaker"; Hebrew *peres,* "breaker"). An unclean bird (Lev. 11:13; Deut. 14:12) commonly identified with the bearded eagle, whose chief haunts are the ravines of the Arnon. The ossifrage stands over three feet high and has about a nine-foot wingspread. It crushes its victim, often by dropping it on a rock from a great height.

OTHNIEL (ŏth'nĭ-ĕl). The first of the judges of Israel (Josh. 15:17; Judg. 1:13; 3:9).

OWL (Hebrew *kōs*). A ceremonially unclean bird (Lev. 11:17; Deut. 14:16) which frequents desolate places (Psa. 102:6). The reference is likely to the little owl *(Athene glaux),* which is very common in Palestine in ruins, tombs, rocks, thickets, and olive orchards. Another

species (Hebrew *yanshūph*), also ceremonially unclean (Lev. 11:17; Deut. 14:16) and frequenting waste places, was the great owl (Isa. 34:11). This bird is apparently to be identified with the Egyptian eagle owl *(Bubo ascalapus),* common in caves and ruins in the Petra area and around Beer-sheba. Some scholars think the night owl is referred to in Isaiah 34:14.

Strong oxen pull together under a yoke, as they have for centuries. *(Russ Busby photo)*

OX. The male of the species *Bos taurus.* It was domesticated early in human history. So common was the ox that the plural (oxen) was frequently used to denote cattle in general. The ox was in common use in Palestine in the time of Abraham, about 2000 B.C. (Gen. 12:16; 21:27; 20:14), and in Egypt at the time of the Exodus (1440 B.C.). This patient beast was used for plowing (1 Kings 19:19), for transport (Num. 7:3; 2 Sam. 6:6), and for trampling out grain at the threshing floor (Deut. 25:4). The ox was sometimes used for food (1 Kings 1:25; cf. Matt. 22:4) and was one of the sacrificial animals (Num. 7:87, 88; 2 Sam. 24:22).

PADAN-ARAM (pā'dăn-ā'răm) ("field or plain of Aram"). The Balikh-Habur region of northern Mesopotamia (Gen. 25: 20; 28:5-7; 31:18; 33:18). It is the same as Aram-Naharaim, "Aram of the two rivers."

PAINTER. Skilled artists were employed in antiquity to paint scenes on walls. A notable example is the Investiture fresco from Mari on the Middle Euphrates. Doubtless the Hebrew followed the same custom, although no examples have survived. However, excavations have uncovered pigments. Red ocher was used for painting on walls and wood (Jer. 22: 14; Ezek. 23:14).

PALM TREE (Hebrew *tāmār,* Greek *phoinix*). The date palm (*Phoenix dactylifera*) has a single upright stem and towers to a height of 60 to 80 feet, terminating at the top in a circle of feathery, perennially green leaves. The fruit of the palm was an important article of food (Joel 1:12). It was a tree of beauty and furnished the motif for carvings in various parts of Solomon's Temple and other sanctuaries (1 Kings 6:29, 32, 35; Herodotus II:169). Its expansive leaves were used as tokens of victory and peace (John 12:13; Rev. 7:9). In biblical times the palm tree flourished in Egypt and Palestine. Phoenicia took its Greek name from the date palm. The psalmist compared the righteous to the palm tree (Psa. 92: 12).

PALMERWORM. The migratory locust at a certain stage of its growth. See "Locust."

PALMYRA (păl-mī'rə). An oasis in the desert between Syria and Iraq. It was Old Testament Tadmor (2 Chron. 8:4), apparently also called "Tadmor in the wilderness" (1 Kings 9:18). It is located about 140 miles east-northeast of Damascus and about 120 miles from the Euphrates. Its surviving ruins are impressive.

PAMPHYLIA (păm-fĭl'ĭ-à). A Roman province west of Lycia and east of the Kingdom of Antiochus and Cilicia Trachea on the southern coast of Asia Minor. Paul landed at its seaport, Attalia, after his voyage from Paphos in Cyprus during his first missionary tour (Acts 13: 13). He departed from Attalia to return to Syrian Antioch (Acts 14:24). The city of Perga was located just northeast of Attalia. Paul preached there (Acts 14:25).

PANEAS. Modern Baniyas, located at one of the sources of the Jordan. It was renamed by Herod Philip, who took it as his capital. See "Dan" and "Caesarea Philippi."

PAPHOS (pā'fŏs). A Hellenistic Roman town (modern Kuklia) in the southwest extremity of Cyprus. It was called Old Paphos to distinguish it from the newer seaport town about 10 miles to the northwest. New Paphos was the capital of the Roman province of Cyprus and the residence of the proconsul. It was the center of Aphrodite worship and contained a celebrated temple dedicated to the goddess. Paul visited the town on his first tour (Acts 13:6-13). New Paphos is modern Baffo.

PAPYRUS (pà-pī'rŭs) (Hebrew *gōmē*). A giant sedge with a triangular stock which rises eight to ten feet and is terminated by a tuft of flowers. It grows in the Sharon plain (near the Sea of Galilee) and in the Huleh swamps. In antiquity it flourished on the Nile. The Egyptians used it to make baskets, boats, shoes, and paper as early as the third millennium B.C. Papyrus grows in mire (Job 8:11). The tiny ark of the baby Moses was made of papyrus, as were many larger boats (Isa. 18:2). See also "Flags."

PARACLETE (păr'à-klēt). The Greek word which designates one of the roles of the Holy Spirit (John 14:16, 17, 26; 15:26; 16:7). It means "someone called alongside to help" and is frequently translated "comforter." The word sometimes also describes the personal intercessory work of Christ in heaven (1 John 2:1).

PARADISE. A Greek word derived from ancient Iranian and meaning "a garden with a wall." The Jews identified paradise with that part of hades to which the soul and spirit of the righteous went between death and the resurrection. Christ mentioned paradise in the account of the rich man and Lazarus (Luke 16:19-31). Since the resurrection of Christ, however, paradise has apparently been transferred to the third heaven, where Christ sits enthroned (Eph. 4:8-10; 2 Cor. 12:4; Rev. 2:7). Paul was evidently caught up to paradise when he was stoned at Lystra (2 Cor. 12:1-6).

Now the spirits of departed believers are "with the Lord" in heaven (2 Cor. 5:8; Phil. 1:23). Their bodies await resurrection or translation (Rom. 8:23; 1 Cor. 15:35-57; Phil. 3:20, 21).

PARAN (pā'răn). A mountain mentioned in the Song of Moses (Deut. 33:2). It was apparently a prominent peak in the mountain range on the west shore of the Gulf of Aqabah in the Wilderness of Paran.

PARTHIANS (pàr'thĭ-ănz). An Iranian people who originally inhabited the territory southeast of the Caspian Sea. They were a subject people under the Persians, but revolted under the Seleucids and became an independent state in the third century B.C. under Arsaces I. Mithridates I (174-138 B.C.) founded the Parthian Empire, which extended westward to the Euphrates and adjoined the eastern provinces of the Roman Empire. From 64 B.C. to A.D. 226 the Parthians set limits to the Roman rule in the east. From 40 to 37 B.C. Parthian forces overran Asia Minor and Syria. They plundered Jerusalem and placed Antigonus, the last ruler of the Hasomeans, on the throne. Jews from Parthia were present at Jerusalem at Pentecost (Acts 2:9). Parthian power was not broken till the Persian family of Sassan instituted the second Persian or Sassanian Empire in A.D. 226.

PARTRIDGE (Hebrew *qōrē*, "crier" or "caller"). The rock partridge (*Alectoris graeca*). It is commonly hunted in the mountains of Palestine (1 Sam. 26:20). The partridge, of which several species exist in Palestine, was a large, fine bird. Jeremiah compares those who amass ill-gotten gain to a partridge (Jer. 17:11).

PATARA (păt'à-rà). A seaport city of southwest Lycia. Paul took ship there for Phoenicia on his last trip to Palestine (Acts 21:1). It possessed a famous shrine to Apollo.

PATHROS (păth'rŏs). The region of Upper Egypt (Isa. 11:11; Jer. 44:1, 15; Ezek. 29:14; 30:14). Pathros is Egyptian for "Southland."

PATMOS (păt'mŏs) One of the Sporades islands in the Greek Archipelago. It lies off the southwest coast of Asia Minor and is about 30 miles south of Samos. It is about ten miles long and six miles wide and is barren and rocky. There John was banished and received the visions recorded in the Book of the Revelation (Rev. 1:9).

PAUL ("little"). The great Apostle to the Gentiles, whose original name was Saul. He was one of the great men of the Bible and of all history. He was a convert from Pharisaic Judaism to Christ (Phil. 3:5) and was a tentmaker by trade (Acts 18:3). He was highly educated under Gamaliel (Acts 22:3). He became transformed from a rabid persecutor of Christianity to the world's greatest expositor of Christ. He was both a missionary of the Cross and the writer of 13 of the New Testament Epistles. The spread of Christianity to Europe and the western world is due in large part to the indefatigable zeal and labors of this mighty herald of the Cross.

PEACOCK (Hebrew *tukkiyīm*). The peacock is a native of India. Solomon's ships of Tarshish brought them from Ophir (India or Arabia). However, some scholars identify Ophir with the northeastern African Coast or Somaliland (Egyptian Punt) and identify the *tukkiyīm* as a type of monkey or baboon.

PEKAH (pē'kä) ("he has opened"). A conspirator against King Pekahiah. After seizing the throne he reigned from 739 to 731 B.C. He allied himself with Rezin of Damascus against Judah under Ahaz (Isa. 7:1-9). Pekah was subsequently murdered by Hoshea, who then seized the throne (731 B.C.).

PEKAHIAH (pĕk'à-hī'à) ("the Lord has opened"). The son and successor of Menahem (741-739 B.C.). He was assassinated by Pekah, who usurped the throne (2 Kings 15:23-26).

PELEG (pē'lĕg) ("division"). A son of Eber. In his time the earth "was divided" (Gen. 10:25). Possibly the division referred to the scattering of the descendants of Noah. Some associate the division with the incident at the tower of Babel, when the Lord scattered the builders over the face of the earth (Gen. 11:7-9).

PELICAN. A ceremonially unclean bird (Lev. 11:18; Deut. 14:17). It lived "in the wilderness" (Psa. 102:6), a description for swampland as well as arid desert. The drained swamps of the northern Jordan valley are still visited by migratory flocks of white pelicans.

PELLA (pĕl'à). Canaanite Pehel. It is mentioned in early Egyptian records and in the Amarna Letters. It was rebuilt by the Greeks under the name Pella. It was a city of the Decapolis, located in Transjordan about seven miles southeast of Scythopolis. After the fall of Jerusalem it became the center of a Christian community as a result of refugees from Judea.

PELOPONNESUS (pĕl'ə-pə-nē'sùs). The peninsula south of the Isthmus of Corinth. It was part of the Roman province of Achaia.

PELUSIUM (pē-lū'shĭ-ŭm). A fortress town east of the Nile Delta. It guarded the approach to Egypt. It is called "Sin" in the King James Version (Ezek. 30:15).

PENNINAH (pē-nĭn'à) ("coral"). One of Elkanah's two wives, the other being Hannah (1 Sam. 1:1, 2). Penninah taunted Hannah because the latter was childless. She displayed an ungracious spirit and had an unpleasant disposition. But Hannah was a woman of faith, and her trust in God resulted in the birth of Samuel, one of the greatest leaders and men of God that graced Israel's history (1 Sam. 1:1-20).

PENNY. See "Denarius" under "Coins and Money."

PENUEL, PENIEL (pē-nū'ĕl). The place where Jacob wrestled with the angel (Gen. 32:30). It was plundered by Gideon (Judg. 8:8-17) and fortified by Jeroboam I (1 Kings 12:25). It is identified with Tulul edh-Dhanab, north of the River Jabbok and about four miles east of Succoth in Transjordan.

PEOR (pē'ôr). A mountain east of the Jordan River that overlooked the desert. It was the place from which Balaam blessed Israel (Num. 23:28). The site is somewhere to the north of the Dead Sea and opposite Jericho, but its exact location is uncertain.

PERATH. See "Euphrates."

PERFECTION. In the sense of sinlessness in experience, perfection is not attainable in this life, for the sin nature is not removed until the glorification of the body at the Lord's coming and the resurrection (Phil. 3:20, 21). However, perfection in position (God's assessment of the believer) is assured by the Christian's position "in Christ" (Heb. 10:14). In this respect every believer is regarded as absolutely and infinitely perfect – as perfect as Christ himself.

Although sinless perfection is not possible in an unglorified body, progressive maturity and spiritual adulthood are to be experienced by every Spirit-filled believer (1 Cor. 2:6; 13:11; 14:20; Phil. 3:15; 2 Tim. 3:17). Ultimate perfection will be realized by the believer when his body is glorified and conformed to the image of Christ (Col. 1:28; Eph. 4:12, 13; 1 Thess. 3:13; 1 John 3:1-3; 1 Pet. 5:10; Jude 1:24, 25).

PERFUMER. Cosmetics and perfumery constituted an important industry in antiquity. Painting of the face and the body was common, particularly of the eyes and lashes (cf. 2 Kings 9:30; Jer. 4:30; Ezek. 23:40). Such eye paint consisted of lead sulphide rather than antimony, as is commonly supposed. Red ocher (oxide of iron) may have served as rouge and lipstick. Nails were dyed from a product made from the henna plant. Even face powder was used by the Sumerians. Perfumes figure prominently in the Song of Solomon (cf. 1:3, 12; 3:6; 4:6; 5:1; 8:14). See also "Apothecary."

PERGA (pûr′ga̍). A city of Pamphylia visited by Paul on his first tour (Acts 13: 13, 14; 14:25). It is northeast of the seaport Attalia. The present-day site is Murtana.

PERGAMUM (pûr′ga̍-mŭm). The splendid ancient capital of the Attalid kingdom. In Roman times it was in the province of Asia and was the center of the emperor-worship cult (Rev. 2:12, 13). Its church was one of the seven churches of Asia (Rev. 1:11; 2:12-17). Pergamum is modern Bergama.

PERSEPOLIS (pûr-sĕp′ō-lĭs). The Persian capital from the reign of Darius I the Great (521-486 B.C.). It displaced Pasargadae. It was destroyed by Alexander the Great and resurrected by modern archeological excavations. Persepolis is located about 175 miles east of the northern extremity of the Persian Gulf in the heart of Persia (modern Iran).

Mound of Susa—biblical Shushan—in Iran, the site of the winter residence of Darius the Great; spire among buildings at left marks traditional tomb site of Daniel. *(OI-UC photo)*

PERSIANS. An Indo-European people who established a great empire that dominated the ancient world from 550 B.C. to 330 B.C. The empire eventually stretched from the coast of Europe to the borders of India and from the Black Sea and the Caspian Sea to Ethiopia. Cyrus the Great was its founder. The Persians were noble-minded and generous and revered one supreme God. They had few temples and no altars or images. When Cyrus conquered Babylon he found an oppressed race who abhorred idols (like the Persians) and embraced a religion somewhat like his own. Cyrus thus determined to restore this people to their own country. This is recorded in the remarkable edict appearing in the first chapter of Ezra (1:2-4).

Darius I (the Great, 521-486 B.C.) granted the Jews the privilege of completing their Temple and even aided the work by grants from his own revenues (Ezra 6:1-5). Darius was succeeded by Xerxes (486-465 B.C.), who was apparently the Ahasuerus of Esther. Artaxerxes I (465-423 B.C.) is the monarch who showed favor toward Ezra (Ezra 7:11-28) and Nehemiah (Neh. 2:1-9). Other Persian kings reigned until the Empire collapsed under the attack of Alexander the Great in 330 B.C.

PERSIS (pûr′sĭs) (Greek for "Persian"). A Christian woman whom Paul commended for her labor for the Lord (Rom. 16:12). The name is frequently found in the papyrii and inscriptions, especially in connection with female slaves.

PETER (a "rock, a stone," the Greek form of the Aramaic surname "Cephas"). The great fisherman-apostle (Matt. 4:18; John 1:40). He was introduced to Christ by his brother, Andrew. Contact with the Lord transformed him from a reed to a rock. He became the leader and spokesman of the Twelve and, along with James and John, one of the inner circle of Jesus' friends. These three were privileged to witness the raising of Jairus' daughter (Mark 5:37), the transfiguration (Matt. 17:1-13), and the agony in Gethsemane (Matt. 26:37-46). He confessed Christ's deity (Matt. 16:16-19) and was given "the keys of the kingdom of heaven" to loose the gospel to Jews at Pentecost (Acts 2: 16), Samaritans in Samaria (Acts 8:14), and Gentiles at Caesarea (Acts 10:34-48). The outpoured gift of the Spirit transformed him into a fearless witness. He wrote First and Second Peter.

PETRA (pē'trả) (Greek equivalent of the Hebrew word *sela^c*, "rock"). A site in Edom (Isa. 16:1; cf. Obad. 1:3) situated in a rock basin on the eastern side of the Wadi Arabah. It is about 50 miles south of the southern end of the Dead Sea. About 300 B.C. the Nabataeans took over the site and converted the great valley to the north (some 4500 feet long and 740 to 1500 feet across) into the amazing rock-cut city of Petra. The massive rock plateau, Umm el-Biyara, which towers 1000 feet above the city, was the site of the great high place. Other altars stood on neighboring heights. The dynasty of Nabataean kings that ruled in Petra contained several kings with the name "Aretas." One of these is mentioned in 2 Corinthians 11:32.

PHARAOH (fâr'ō) A biblical title employed as a name of the king of Egypt. The word means "the great house" and derives from the Old Kingdom designation of the royal palace as "The Great House." This became a common exponent of authority in such titles as "Superintendent of the Domain of the Great House." By 1800 B.C. this name for the palace had attracted to itself some of the divine titles attributed to the name of the king. By 1500 B.C. the term came to be applied to the occupant of the palace, the king of Egypt himself.

PHARISEES (fâr'ĭ-sēz). A lay fellowship originating in the second century B.C. and dedicated to the strict observance of the Mosaic Law. The name comes from the Hebrew word *Perushim,* meaning "those separated" from sinners and lawbreakers. In Christ's day the Pharisees had degenerated into self-righteous, hypocritical religionists (cf. Matt. 23:13-36). But in their earlier days they had exerted great influence for good because of their purity, piety, and championship of national independence during the Maccabean period. They laid the foundations of orthodox Judaism.

PHAROS (fâr'ōs). An island which had a usable port prior to the founding of Alexandria. It later became the site of a lighthouse called "pharos" that marked the harbor of Alexandria.

PHARPAR (fär'pär). One of the two streams of Damascus mentioned by Naaman (2 Kings 5:12). It is present-day Awaj. Some 40 miles in length, it flows eastward from Hermon south of Damascus.

PHEBE, PHOEBE (fē'bḛ) ("radiant"). A Christian deaconess in the church at Cenchrea, the eastern seaport of Corinth (Rom. 16:1, 2). She evidently relocated to Rome and was a helper or patron to many.

PHILADELPHIA (fĭl'á-dĕl'fĭ-à). (1) A city in Asia Minor founded by Attalus Philadelphus. It lies about 28 miles southeast of Sardis. It was one of the seven churches of the Revelation (Rev. 1:11; 3:7-13). It is present-day Alasehir. (2) A city of the Decapolis, former Rabbah, or Rabbath Ammon. It was captured by Ptolemy II and renamed Philadelphia. See "Rabbah."

PHILEMON (fĭ-lē'mŏn) ("loving"). A believer at Colosse to whom Paul returned a runaway but converted slave. Paul addressed one of the New Testament Epistles to Philemon.

PHILETUS (fĭ-lē'tŭs) ("worthy of love"). A first-century heretic who taught that the resurrection had already occurred (2 Tim. 2:17, 18).

PHILIP (fĭl'ĭp). (1) One of the twelve apostles (Matt. 10:3; John 1:43-48; 6:5, 6; 12:20-23; 14:8-12; Acts 1:13). (2) A son of Herod the Great and the husband of Herodias. He was disinherited by his father and lived a private life (Matt. 14:3; Mark 6:17; Luke 3:19).

PHILIP OF MACEDON. The father of Alexander the Great. By conquest he raised Macedonia to a dominant position (359-336 B.C.) in Greek affairs.

PHILIP THE DEACON. One of the seven Greek-speaking believers chosen to manage the material needs of the church at Jerusalem (Acts 6:5). He became an evangelist (Acts 8:4-8; 21:8). He won and baptized the eunuch of Ethiopia (Acts 8:26-39). He resided in Caesarea and had four unmarried daughters (Acts 8:40; 21:8, 9).

PHILIP THE TETRARCH. The ruler of Iturea and Trachonitis (Luke 3:1). He enlarged Paneas and named it Caesarea. It became known as Caesarea Philippi

(Matt. 16:13) to distinguish it from Caesarea on the Mediterranean.

PHILIPPI (fĭ-lĭp′ĭ). A city of Macedonia rebuilt by Philip II of Macedon and named after himself (it had originally been called Krenides). It was evangelized by Paul on his second tour (Acts 16:11-40; 20:6; 1 Thess. 2:2; Phil. 4:15). The site is called Filibedjik today.

PHILISTIA (fĭ-lĭs′tĭ-à). The southern maritime plain of Palestine. It received its name from the Philistines (Exod. 15: 14; Psa. 60:8; Joel 3:4).

PHILISTINES (fĭ-lĭs′tēnz). A people descended from Casluhim, the son of Mizraim (Egypt), the son of Ham (Gen. 10:14). These people had settled in southeastern Palestine as early as the patriarchal age. But the great wave of them came from Caphtor (Crete) in the early twelfth century B.C. They settled in five main cities — Gaza, Ashkelon, Ekron, Ashdod, and Gath. They became a formidable power in the era of Saul and David, but were decisively defeated by David. They reasserted their aggressiveness in the time of Ahaz (Isa. 9:8-12). Their last scriptural mention is in Zechariah's prophecy, during the post-exilic period (Zech. 9:5-7). The Philistines were eventually assimilated by the Jews, for they are not mentioned in the New Testament.

PHILO (fī′lō). A famous Jewish and Hellenistic philosopher of Alexandria, Egypt (20 B.C. — A.D. 50). His ministry was to present biblical truth in categories that would appeal to the educated Greek. He employed allegory and personified divine wisdom as the "Logos." Philo's writings proved useful to the church and have been preserved through the centuries.

PHINEHAS (fĭn′ē-ăs) ("Egyptian, Nubian"). (1) A faithful priest and the grandson of Aaron (Exod. 6:25; Num. 25:1-18). (2) The younger of Eli's two degenerate sons, who was killed in battle when the ark was taken by the Philistines (1 Sam. 1:3; 2:34; 4:11-22).

PHOENICIANS (fė-nĭsh′ĭ-ȧnz). A seafaring people who occupied the coastal strip of the Mediterranean from the Ladder of Tyre (about 14 miles south of Tyre) to Ugarit on the north. Important Phoenician towns were Tyre, Sidon, Gebal (Byblos), Arvad, and Ugarit (Ras Shamra). The Phoenicians were apparently the product of the mingling of Canaanites and Achaeans. The Semitic element predominated. As artisans, traders, and skilled seamen, the Phoenicians were the merchant marine of antiquity. They established colonies in North Africa and Spain, even venturing as far as Britain.

The heyday of Phoenician history spanned from about 1150 to 880 B.C. Sidon was the most powerful city-state in the period of the Judges. But by the time of David and Solomon Tyre had gained the ascendancy. Hiram (979-945 B.C.) was the ally of Solomon. He furnished craftsmen and materials for constructing the Temple at Jerusalem (1 Kings 5:1-18). Western civilization owes its alphabet to the Phoenicians.

PHYLACTERIES. Small leather pouches which contained passages from the Pentateuch inscribed with Exodus 13:2-16 and Deuteronomy 6:4-9, 13-23. They were worn on the forehead and upper left arm during morning prayer, except on sabbaths and holy days. They were a literal representation of Deuteronomy 6:8: "The sign upon thy hand and frontlets between thine eyes." The term "phylactery" derives from a Greek word connoting an amulet. The practice of wearing them tended to substitute ritual for reality and even degenerated into a pagan superstition in some cases.

PHYSICIAN. The word for physician is rarely used in the Bible (Hebrew *rapha*ʾ, "healer"; e.g. Exod. 15:26; Jer. 8:22; Greek *iatros*; Mark 5:26; Luke 8:43). The biblical terms imply substantially the same meaning as "doctor" in present-day parlance. Israel's faith differed sharply from pagan religions in its clear-cut separation between the offices of priest and physician.

Remedies varied with the times. Poultices and local applications were frequently used (Isa. 1:6; 38:21; cf. Luke 10:34; Mark 5:26). Sometimes the remedy was linked with superstition (Gen. 30: 14-16). Wine is mentioned as a stimulant (Prov. 31:6) and a remedy (1 Tim. 5:23).

PIGEON. A number of doves are found in Palestine. The Hebrew word *yōnāh* is usually translated "dove." However, in the passages in Leviticus and Numbers it is rendered "pigeon." The dove was domesticated in antiquity and was widely used for both food and message-carrying. See also "Dove."

PILLARS. Stones, whether naturally occurring or artificially erected, attracted Semitic peoples as places of worship. Jacob set up a stone and poured oil over it (Gen. 28:18). Some of these stones were commemorative, marking covenants, boundaries, or battles (Gen. 31:45). Others were funeral monuments (Isa. 19: 19; Gen. 35:20). The twelve stones taken by Moses to build an altar (Exod. 24:4) and the twelve stones set up by Joshua after crossing the Jordan (Josh. 4:1-9) probably became relics, eventually to be linked with pagan deities. The prophets inveighed against these dangers (Jer. 2: 26-28). King Hezekiah was praised because he destroyed the pillars from the high places (2 Kings 18:4).

PILATE (pī′làt). The Roman procurator of Judea and Samaria from A.D. 26 to 36, a period that included the public ministry of Christ (Luke 3:1). He was intolerant of the religious scruples of his subjects and ruthless in asserting Rome's authority. His treatment of Jesus resulted from a shriveled conscience and a withdrawal from official responsibility. His insistence on crucifying Jesus as "King of the Jews" evidenced his scorn of the Jewish Sanhedrin (Matt. 27:36, 37; Mark 15:1-14; Luke 23:1-4, 38; John 18:28 – 19:22).

PINE TREE. The translation of the Hebrew word *tidhar* (Isa. 41:19; 60:13). The fir tree and the pine are botanically in the genus *Pinus,* and the reference is doubtless one of the species of evergreen coniferous trees native to the hills of Palestine and Lebanon.

PISGAH (pĭz′gà). A ridge crowning a hill or mountain. Such ridges or "pisgahs" are common in Transjordan (Num. 21: 20; cf. Num. 23:13, 14). The "pisgah" to which Moses was bidden to ascend in order to view the Promised Land from every point of the compass (Deut. 3:27) is carefully described in Deuteronomy 34:1 as "the mountain of Nebo to the top of (the) Pisgah, that is over against Jericho." If Nebo is Jebel Osha, Moses was able to see the entire Promised Land from this vantage point.

PISHON, PISON (pī′shŏn). The Pishon and the Gihon were associated with the Garden of Eden (Gen. 2:10-14). They were presumably canals which connected the ancient Tigris and Euphrates riverbeds.

PITHOM (pī′thŏm). A stone city built by the oppressed Israelites in Egypt (Exod. 1:11). It was located in Goshen, the extreme northeast portion of the Delta. It was about 30 miles east of Pibeseth (Bubastis). Probably Tell er-Retabeh.

PLAIN. The principal region of flat or gently rolling plains in Palestine is the coastal plain, along the Mediterranean Sea. From Sidon southward to the Ladder of Tyre is the Plain of Phoenicia, varying from four to ten miles in width. The plain of Acco extends from the Ladder of Tyre southward to Mount Carmel. It is bordered by the hills of Upper and Lower Galilee and is scarcely wider than the Phoenician Plain. Cradled in the Central Highland ridge to the southwest of the Plain of Acco is the Plain of Megiddo or Esdraelon, called also the Great Plain. South of Mount Carmel to the Wadi Zerqah is the narrow Plain of Dor. From the Wadi Zerqah to Joppa is the beautiful, fertile Plain of Sharon and south of it to the Brook Besor the large Plain of Philistia.

PLANE TREE. A deciduous tree (*Platanus orientalis*) which stands 30 to 50 feet high and has a broad, ovate crown and large, deep-lobed, hairy leaves (Gen. 30:37; Ezek. 31:8). It thrives on riverbanks in the northern part of Palestine.

POLITARCHS (pŏl′ĭ-tärks). The senior board of magistrates, five in number and later six, at Thessalonica. They were technically called politarchs. This title is attested for a number of Macedonian states. The King James Version calls them "rulers of the city" (Acts 17:6, 8). Since Thessalonica was a free city and the capital of the province of Macedonia, the politarchs of Thessalonica carried heavy responsibilities. As the Acts passage shows, the politarchs controlled the city under Roman supervision. This consisted of a proconsul of praetorian rank supported by a legate and a quaestor.

POLYGAMY. The custom of having more than one wife at the same time. The practice was a violation of the original monogamous standard set by the Creator at the beginning (Gen. 2:24). Fallen man very early disregarded this divine arrangement and entered into polygamous unions (Gen. 4:19). Polygamy soon became common, especially among men of rank and wealth. Even certain men in the godly messianic line practiced polygamy (cf. Gen. 16:3, 4; 25:1, 6; 28:9; 29:23, 28). However, the practice of the patriarchs was devoid of the shameful degradation associated with polygamy in pagan lands.

The Mosaic Law discouraged polygamy. Everywhere it recognized the original, divinely instituted principle of monogamy in distinguishing between the first or legitimate wife and those taken in addition to her. It prohibited second marriages in certain cases. If a man took more than one wife, his matrimonial obligations were clearly prescribed (Exod. 21:10, 11).

Polygamy persisted down to New Testament times, but with diminishing prevalence. It disappeared rapidly in the face of the clearer light and higher claims of Christianity.

POMEGRANATE (Hebrew *rimmon*). A small tree (*Punica granatum*) which grows wild in many eastern countries. It was much prized and cultivated in Bible lands from earliest times. It has bright green leaves, blossoms with scarlet petals, and a large, leathery calyx. The orange-like fruit has a hard red rind fitted with innumerable seeds in a bright red pulp. Several places in the Bible bear its name: Rimmon (Josh. 15:32), Gath-rimmon (Josh. 19:45), and En-rimmon (Neh. 11:29). A refreshing drink is made from pomegranate juice; a syrup called grenadine is squeezed from its seeds; and an astringent medicine is extracted from its blossoms. The pomegranate is as prominent in Palestinian art as the lotus is in Egyptian motifs. Ornamental pomegranates adorned the high priests' vestments (Exod. 28:33), the capitals of Solomon's Temple pillars (1 Kings 7:20), and the silver shekel of Jerusalem struck in Maccabean times (143-135 B.C.).

POMPEII. A Roman city southeast of Naples in Italy. It was destroyed by the eruption of Vesuvius in A.D. 79. It was covered with volcanic ash and resurrected by modern archaelogy.

PONTUS (pŏn'tŭs). The southern coastal region of the Black Sea (Pontus Euxinus) east of Bithynia. Part of it was incorporated into the province of Galatia and part united with Bithynia to form another province (Acts 2:9; 18:2; 1 Pet. 1:1).

POOL. See "Springs, Wells, and Pools."

POPLAR TREE (Hebrew *libneh*, "white"). Rods of this tree were peeled by Jacob in deceiving Laban (Gen. 30:37). It appears to be the white poplar (*Populus albus*), so named because the undersides of its leaves are white. It has thick foliage and provides dense shade.

PORTER. As used in the King James Version this word denotes a gatekeeper, from the Latin *portarius*, the attendant at the *porta* or gate (cf. Mark 13:34; John 10:3).

Levitical porters were a class of servants (together with the Nethinim) who assisted the priests and Levites in duties at the Temple (Ezra 7:7), including guarding the gates (2 Chron. 8:14; 35:15).

POTIPHAR (pŏt'ĭ-fêr) (Egyptian, "he whom Re has given"). The captain of Pharoah's guard (Gen. 39:1). His wife tried to seduce Joseph (Gen. 39:7-20).

Sensitive and strong fingers mold fine pottery. (© *MPS*)

POTTER. The potter was an important artisan in Bible lands after the invention of the potter's wheel in the late fourth millennium B.C. The professional potter's workshop is illustrated by discoveries at such cities as Lachish and Qumran. The potter sat on the edge of a small pit in which the wheels were located. These were customarily two stones, one pivoted over the other, which were turned with the potter's feet. Pottery assumed various styles during successive periods, thereby helping the archeologist to date the various strata of excavated sites.

PRAETOR (prē'tôr). Almost a synonym for the Greek word *strategoi*. It is used five times in Acts 16 to designate the highest officials of the Roman Colony of Philippi. In general it denotes the *duumviri* or chief magistrates of Roman Colonies.

PRAETORIUM (prē-tō'rĭ-ŭm). The palace occupied by Pontius Pilate at Jerusalem. In it the judgment seat was erected (Mark 15:16; Matt. 27:27; John 18:28; 19:9). Some take it to be the castle of Antonia. Herod's palace at Caesarea also had a praetorium (the "judgment hall" of Acts 23:35). The Praetorium Guard at Rome guarded the imperial palace and its occupant, the Emperor.

PREDESTINATION. God's total plan with respect to humanity is called predestination or foreordination. His purpose to act in such a manner that certain men will believe and be saved is called election. His purpose to act in such a manner that certain will disbelieve and therefore be lost is called reprobation.

PREFECT. The Praetorium prefect was a Roman military officer who commanded the Praetorian guards. The office came to have a civil aspect and the prefect, like a proconsul, ruled a province. Egypt was administered by a prefect.

PRESBYTER. See "Elder."

PRIEST. Although not technically a worker or artisan, both the high priest and the ordinary priests played a very significant role in the religious and social life of Israel under the Mosaic Covenant. Only when apostasy from God's Law developed did the people treat the priesthood and its sacrificial system with negligence or disrespect. In Israel the worship of God was intimately bound up with every phase of life, ennobling and purifying it. By contrast, in pagan Semitic cultures the veneration of heathen deities debased virtually every phase of life.

Engraving of Hebrew priest and Ark of the Covenant (*HPS photo*)

PRIESTHOOD. The priest is man's representative before God. In Old Testament times the patriarch functioned as the priest over his household (Gen. 8:20; Job 1:5). Melchizedek the priest symbolized Christ's priesthood in both person and order (Gen. 14:17-20; Psa. 110:1-4; Heb. 6:20 – 7:28). The Aaronic high priest likewise symbolizes Christ, while the regular priest symbolizes the believer. The New Testament believer is constituted a priest on the basis of the once-for-all, efficacious sacrifice of Christ. He offers worship, sacrifice, and intercession (Heb. 13:15, 16).

PRIESTHOOD OF CHRIST. Christ was set apart as Priest (as well as Prophet and King) at his baptism (Matt. 3:15-17; Heb. 5:1, 2; 7:23-25; 9:24). Christ's earthly service, bodily sacrifice, and heavenly intercession are all comprehended by his priesthood.

PRISON-KEEPER. In Egypt the "keeper of the prison" elevated Joseph to be in charge of all the prisoners there (Gen. 39: 20-23). In Jeremiah's time the palace guardrooms served as a temporary prison (Jer. 32:2, 8, 12; 33:1). Ahab had Micaiah imprisoned on rations of bread and water (1 Kings 22:27). Defeated kings were often imprisoned by their conquerors (cf. Jer. 24:1, 5; 52:11).

John the Baptist was incarcerated in Herod's fortress at Machaerus (east of the Dead Sea). The Apostles were imprisoned in "a public place of watching"

(Acts 5:18). Peter was imprisoned and guarded by four soldiers (Acts 12:3-6). At Philippi Paul was placed in custody in the town jail under the charge of a jail-keeper (Acts 16:24). At Caesarea Paul was imprisoned in Herod's castle (Acts 23:35). At Rome he was allowed to remain in his own house, but with a soldier chained to him (Acts 28:16, 30).

PRISCA (pris'kȧ) ("old woman"). Same person as Priscilla.

PRISCILLA (prĭ-sĭl'ȧ) ("little old woman"). The wife of Aquila, a tentmaker by trade. Paul met these Jewish Christians at Corinth (Acts 18:1-3). They were his fellow-passengers from Corinth to Ephesus, as Paul traveled to Syria (Acts 18:18, 19). They were instructed accurately in the gospel and were able to show the disciples of Apollos the difference between the baptism of John and the baptism of the Spirit (Acts 18:24 — 19:7). Paul regarded Priscilla very highly. In three out of five verses she is named before her husband (Acts 18:1-3, 18, 26; Rom. 16:3; 2 Tim. 4:19).

PROCONSUL (prō'kŏn-sŭl). In the Roman Empire as organized by Augustus, "proconsul" became the title of governors of provinces which required no standing army and were ruled by the Senate. Sergius Paulus was proconsul of Cyprus when Paul and Barnabas visited that island in about A.D. 47 (Acts 13:7). Gallio was proconsul of Achaia (A.D. 51-52) while Paul ministered in Corinth (Acts 18:12-17).

PROCURATOR (prŏ-cū-rā'têr). The designation of the financial officer of a province in Roman imperial administration. The title was also used of a Roman province of the third class, such as Judea. But in the New Testament the procurator of Judea is described as "governor" (Greek *hēgemōn*). The procurators were commonly of the equestrian order. They had auxiliary troops to assist them. They were free to exercise necessary authority but were subject to the superior authority of the imperial legate of Syria. Caesarea was their capital, though they took up residence in Jerusalem on important occasions.

During A.D. 6-41 and 44-66 Judea was administered by imperial procurators.

Three are listed in the New Testament. Of these, Pontius Pilate (A.D. 26-36) is the best known. Antonius Felix (A.D. 52-59) is mentioned in Acts 23:24-35 and Porcius Festus (A.D. 59-62) is referred to in Acts 24:27 and 25:12.

PROPHET. Like the priest, the prophet represented God to the people and constituted a characteristic feature of early Hebrew society. Because of the ever-present threat of the false prophet and the pagan counterpart, the diviner (cf. Deut. 18:20-22), constant vigilance had to be exercised against the incursion of false religion and demon-energized paganism with its threat of occult supernaturalism (Deut. 18:9-14). The coming Great Prophet (the Messiah) was constantly held out as the expectation of every godly Israelite (Deut. 18:15-19; cf. John 1:21, 45; 6:14; Acts 3:22, 23; 7:37).

PROPITIATION. Propitiation is in no sense the placating of a vengeful God. It is instead the satisfying of the righteousness of a holy God, so that it is possible for him to show mercy without compromising his infinite holiness. This satisfaction was procured by Christ's death on the Cross. In prospect of the Cross God righteously forgave sins in the Old Testament period (Rom. 3:25).

Propitiation (Greek *hilastērion*) means "that which expiates or makes propitious." The place of propitiation in the Old Testament was the mercy seat sprinkled with atoning blood on the Day of Atonement (Lev. 16:14; Heb. 9:11-15). Christ is our "propitiation" (1 John 2:2; 4:10), indicated by the Greek word *hilasmos*. Christ's New Testament fulfillment of the Old Testament sacrifices demonstrates that he completely satisfied the demands of a holy God for judgment on sin.

PROSTITUTION, SACRED. A concomitant of debased Canaanite paganism. Both male and female prostitutes were attached to the heathen temples as devotees of the polluted gods and goddesses. Canaanite religion features violence, war, and sexual immorality. Sacred prostitution in times of apostasy desecrated the holy Temple at Jerusalem (1 Kings 15:12; 2 Kings 23:7).

PSALTERY. See under "Music and Musical Instruments."

PTOLEMAIS (tŏl′ė-mā′ĭs). The Hellenistic city and port, formerly known as Acre or Acco. It was built during Ptolemaic rule over Palestine (1 Macc. 5:22; 11:22; 12:45; Acts 21:7).

PUAH (pū′à) (probably Ugaritic *pgt*, "girl"). One of the two Hebrew midwives ordered by the Pharaoh to kill all male children (Exod. 1:15). They were probably heads of a larger group of midwives. Puah had the courage to defy the tyrant's commands.

PUBLICAN. A tax collector for the Roman government. Jews who held this position were hated by their countrymen.

PUL (pŭl; pōōl). Another name for Tiglathpileser III (745-727 B.C.). He was the "Pulu" of the Babylonian dynastic tablets.

PUNT. The east coast of Africa in Egyptian records. It was the source of myrrh and other exotic products. It corresponds today to Somaliland and perhaps also the coast of Arabia.

PURIFICATION. Any legal or ritual uncleanness among the Jewish people had to be removed by various washings or sacrifices (Lev. 11:24; 15:1, 2; 17:15). This pointed to the defilement of sin and the necessity of its eventual remission by the sacrifice of Christ on the Cross. The Day of Atonement, which most graphically sets forth these truths, was therefore the supreme feast of purification for the Temple and the whole nation (Lev. 16).

PURIM (pū′rĭm), **FEAST OF.** This postexilic festival was observed on the fourteenth and fifteenth day of the month Adar. It celebrates the deliverance of the Jews from the plot of their enemy, Haman, a minister of Xerxes I (485-465 B.C.). The execution was fixed by lot or "Pur" for the thirteenth of Adar. After the Jews had permission to massacre their enemies, they rested and made the fourteenth of Adar a day of joyful feasting (Esther 9:20-32). The Second Book of Maccabees mentions the feast.

PURPLE. A color prominent in the tabernacle and its ritual. It typifies Christ in his kingship (Exod. 25:4; 26:1; 39:3; Num. 4:13). See also "Blue," "Scarlet," and "Gold."

PUTEOLI (pū-tē′ỏ-lī). The port where Paul landed in Italy (Acts 28:13). The present-day site is Pozzuoli, near modern Naples.

PYGARG (pī′gärg) (Hebrew *dīshōn*). A clean animal (Deut. 14:5) identified with the white-rumped antelope or addax. It has twisted and ringed horns. It is native to northeast Africa, but its range extended to the southeastern frontier of Palestine.

QANTIR. A town in Lower Egypt in the northeast part of the Nile Delta. It is considered by some to be the site of Raamses.

QARQAR. A town south of Hamath on the Orontes River. It is the place where the famous battle was fought in 853 B.C. between Shalmaneser III and a coalition of 12 kings of Syria-Palestine, including Ahab of Israel. The present-day site is Khirbet Qarqur.

QUAIL. The smallest species of the partridge subfamily. (The quail is about eight inches long.) It is migratory, arriving in Palestine and Sinai in immense numbers in March. Quail fly with the wind, and if the wind changes course and the birds become exhausted in flight, a whole flock of them may fall to the ground and lie stunned (Num. 11:31-34; Psa. 78:26-31; cf. Josephus, *Antiquities* III; 1, 5).

QUIRINIUS (kwĭ-rĭn'ĭ-ŭs). The Roman legate of Syria who instituted the census of the Jews decreed by Caesar Augustus (Luke 2:1-3). (This census apparently took place in 6 B.C., when Quirinius was first associated with the government of Syria.)

R

RA (rä). The national god of Egypt during the greater part of its history. His veneration was a form of sun-worship, and was carried out under the insignia of the solar disc encircled by the poisonous uraeus serpent.

RAAMSES (rā'ăm-sēz). A town in Egypt built by the Israelites (Exod. 1:11; Num. 33:3, 5). It was also called Zoan, Avaris, and Tanis at various times. It was located in the northeast section of the Nile Delta and is commonly identified with present-day San el-Hagar.

RAB (răb) (Hebrew *rab*, "great one, a chief, captain"). A title employed of certain Assyrian and Babylonian officers (2 Kings 25:8-20; Jer. 39:9–52:30). See also "Captain."

RABBAH (răb'à). The capital of Ammon (Deut. 3:11; Josh. 13:25). It was captured by David's army (2 Sam. 11:1; 12:26-31). It was sometimes called Rabbath-ammon.

RABBI. A Jewish title of honor used during the New Testament period. It comes from the Hebrew word *rab*, meaning "great," "master," or "teacher." *Rabbi* means "my teacher." The word eventually became a stereotyped form of reverential address for recognized Jewish teachers. *Rabboni* is a heightened form of *rabbi* and was used in addressing Christ (Mark 10:51; John 20:16). *Rabbi* was applied once to John the Baptist (John 3: 26) and some 12 times to our Lord (e.g. John 1:38, 50; 3:2, 26; 6:25).

RACHEL (rā'chĕl) ("ewe, a female sheep"). The younger daughter of Laban and Jacob's favorite wife. She became the mother of Joseph and Benjamin. Jacob worked seven years for Rachel (Gen. 29: 27-30) after being duped into marrying Jacob's older daughter, Leah (Gen. 29: 15-26). Rachel was barren for years and eventually gave Jacob her handmaid, Bilhah, to bear him children (Gen. 30:1-8). Bilhah gave birth to Dan and Naphtali. Then Rachel bore Joseph (Gen. 30:22-24). Later, in Canaan, she also bore Benjamin but died in childbirth and was buried near Ramah (Gen. 35:16-20).

RAHAB (rā'hăb) ("wide, broad"). The harlot who sheltered the men dispatched by Joshua to spy out Jericho (Josh. 2:1-21). She hid the two men on the roof of her house in stalks of flax. While she gave a false lead to the king's police, she let down the men from her house (which was built on the city wall) and enabled them to escape. She confessed to them that she knew the Lord to be the God of heaven and asked the spies to swear that when Israel took Jericho they would spare her house. The identification would be a scarlet cord tied to her window. In the subsequent conquest of the city only Rahab and her family were spared (Josh. 6:17, 22-25). Rahab is included among the heroes of faith in Hebrews 11 (v. 31). She is also cited as an example of saving faith in action (James 2:25). She is included in our Lord's genealogy (Matt. 1:5).

RAMAH (rā′mà). A town in Benjamin (Josh. 18:25) fortified by Baasha, king of Israel, but demolished by King Asa of Judah (1 Kings 15:17-22). It is associated with Rachel, the mother of Joseph and Benjamin (Jer. 31:15; Matt. 2:18). It is present-day er-Ram, about five miles north of Jerusalem.

RAMOTH-GILEAD (rā′mōth-gĭl′ē-ăd). A city of refuge in the tribe of Gad (Deut. 4: 43; Josh. 20:8; 21:38). It was in northern Transjordan, in Solomon's sixth district (1 Kings 4:13). It was in Ramoth-Gilead that the Syrians defeated Israel under Ahab (1 Kings 22:3-40) and Joram (2 Kings 8:28; 9:14-26). The site is present-day Tell Ramith, about 30 miles due east of Bethshan.

RAS-SHAMRA (räs-shäm′rá). The present-day site of the Canaanite-Phoenician city of Ugarit. Excavations here have uncovered a temple, library, and royal archives. The Ugaritic literature, rendered in alphabetic cuneiform, is of immense importance in evaluating the religion and morality of the Canaanites.

RAVEN. The bird referred to in Scripture is black in color (Song 5:11), feeds on carrion (Prov. 30:17), and is ceremonially unclean (Lev. 11:15). It is the common raven (*Corvus corax*). It is found all over Palestine. The name is also applied to the hooded crow, which is very similar in appearance. Noah sent a raven from the ark (Gen. 8:7). Elijah was fed by ravens (1 Kings 17:2-7).

REBEKAH, REBECCA (rĕ-bĕk′à) (probably from the root "to tie fast"). The daughter of Bethuel, Abraham's nephew in Padan-Aram (Gen. 22:23). Abraham sent his steward to Mesopotamia to find a bride for Isaac (Gen. 24). He found Rebekah as the result of divine leading. She proved barren, but in answer to prayer she finally bore twins, Esau and Jacob (25:20-26).

RECHABITES (rē′kăb-ītz). The descendants of Rechab (2 Kings 10:15-28). They formed an association to return to simple nomadic life, rejecting the comforts of sedentary life and advocating an austere and godly manner of living (Jer. 35). The Rechabites differed from the prophets. They protested the dangers which religious faith faces in an advanced civilization and sought to flee from them. The prophets, however, demonstrated that the essence of faith resides in the heart and cannot be quenched by external circumstances.

RECONCILIATION. The change which Christ's death produced in the relationship between God and fallen men. As a result of Calvary, God can justly show mercy where previously only judgment could be rendered. This reconciliation was totally God's undertaking. Man had no part in it (2 Cor. 5:19). This aspect of reconciliation constituted the lost race salvable.

There is another aspect of reconciliation, however, that actually saves men. This is accomplished by God in the believing sinner himself. As a result he becomes changed in his rebellion toward God and appropriates the reconciliation provided by Christ on the Cross (Rom. 5: 11). Christians can participate in the ministry of reconciliation by imploring sinners to be "reconciled to God" (2 Cor. 5:19, 20).

RECORDER (Hebrew *mazkir*, "one who causes to remember"). An aide to the king whose responsibilities included the chronicling of state events (cf. 2 Kings 21:25). Some scholars construe the office as that of an executive administrator or prime minister. Others take it to mean simply a herald or court announcer.

RED HEIFER. The sacrifice of the red heifer symbolized the death of Christ as the basis for the believer's cleansing from the daily defilement of sin (Num. 19). Death was required (Num. 19:2, 3), as well as sevenfold sprinkling of the blood before the tabernacle (Num. 19:4). (The sprinkled blood signifies the believer's public confession of faith in the finished work of Christ—Heb. 9:12-14; 10:10-12.) Then the slain heifer was burned. Its ashes were preserved and mixed with water as needed to sprinkle those defiled by sin (Num. 19:5-22). This pictures the Holy Spirit using the Word of God to convict the believer of the defilement of sin (water being a type of both the Spirit and the Word—John 7:37-39; Eph. 5:26). The convicted believer then acknowledges that the guilt of his sin has been met by Christ's death (1 John 1:7). He accordingly confesses the evil as unworthy of a saint, and is forgiven and cleansed (John 13:3-10; 1 John 1:7-10).

The Red Sea, near traditional area of Moses' crossing with Israelites (© *MPS*)

RED SEA. In modern geography, the large body of water that separates northeast Africa from Arabia. Its northern two arms, the Gulf of Suez and the Gulf of Aqabah, continue the sea northward on the western and eastern sides of the Sinai Peninsula. However, the term which is used in the Hebrew Old Testament is not the *Red* Sea but the *Reed* Sea—the *yam suph* or "sea of (papyrus) reeds." The term designates (a) the region of the Bitter Lakes in the Egyptian Delta north of Suez along the line of the Suez Canal

(Exod. 13:18; 14:1, 2); (b) the Gulf of Suez (Num. 33:10, 11 and possibly Exod. 23:31); and (c) the Gulf of Aqabah (Num. 14:25; Deut. 1:40; 2:1; Num. 21:4; Judg. 11:16; cf. 1 Kings 9:26).

REDEEMER. The first promise of the Redeemer given to the fallen race envisioned both the incarnation and the virgin birth of the eternal Word of God in his appearance as "the Seed of the Woman" (Gen. 3:15). The messianic line begins at this point and continues through Abel, Seth, Noah (Gen. 6:8-10), Shem (Gen. 9:26, 27), Abraham (Gen. 12:1-4), Isaac (Gen. 17:19-21), Jacob (Gen. 28:10-14), Judah (Gen. 49:10), and David (2 Sam. 7:5-17) and then culminates in Christ himself (Isa. 7:10-14; Matt. 1:20-23).

REDEMPTION, NEW TESTAMENT. The central idea of redemption is "deliverance by payment of a price." Christ's work in fulfilling Old Testament types and promises of redemption is summarized by three Greek words. (1) *Agorazo* means "to buy in the market" and pictures man as a slave "sold under sin" (Rom. 7:14) and condemned to death (Gen. 2:17; John 3:18, 19; Rom. 6:23). However, fallen man is subject to redemption by the purchase price of the blood of the Redeemer (1 Cor. 6:20; 7:23; 2 Pet. 2:1; Rev. 5:9). (2) *Exagorazo* means "to buy out of the market" by purchasing and removing from sale. This is what Christ did for us (Gal. 3:13; 4:5). His deliverance is final and complete. (3) *Lutroō* means "to set loose or free" and is used commonly to indicate the release of a slave (Luke 21:28; Rom. 3:24; 8:23; 1 Cor. 1:30; Eph. 1:7; 4:30; Col. 1:14; Heb. 9:15). After the redemption by Christ's blood the Holy Spirit empowers the believer to experience the deliverance in his daily life (Rom. 8:2).

REDEMPTION, OLD TESTAMENT. Israel's national redemption out of Egypt illustrates all human redemption. All redemption is based entirely on God's grace (Exod. 3:7, 8) and is implemented solely by the blood of Christ (Exod. 12:13, 23, 27; 1 Pet. 1:18, 19) and by divine power (Exod. 6:6; 13:14; Rom. 1:16; 1 Cor. 1:18, 24).

A lost estate could be redeemed by a

kinsman (Lev. 25:25). This custom furnishes a beautiful picture of Christ's redemption, as in the Book of Ruth. A redeemer must be a near relative (fulfilled in the incarnation). He must be capable of redeeming (fulfilled in the all-efficacious blood of Christ—Acts 20:28; 1 Pet. 1:18, 19). He must be willing to redeem (witnessed in Christ's delight in the Father's will and his voluntary obedience in death—Phil. 2:5-8; Heb. 10:4-10). He must be free from the calamity which made redemption necessary (fulfilled in Christ's sinlessness and Saviorhood). See also "Kinsman-Redeemer."

REGENERATION. A vital aspect of salvation in which the divine nature is imparted to the believer (John 3:1-6; Tit. 3: 5; 1 Pet. 1:23; 2:2) and he becomes a son in the Father's family (Gal. 3:26). In regeneration the believer is reborn by the Spirit through the Word (John 3:5) and receives a new, eternal life. He thereupon becomes an heir of God and a joint heir with Christ (Rom. 8:17). The sole condition of the new birth is unreserved faith in the crucified Christ (John 3:14-18).

REHOBOAM (rē′hō-bō′ăm) ("the people is enlarged"). The son and successor of Solomon. His folly split the kingdom. He followed the false philosophy that the subjects existed for the sovereign instead of the sovereign for the subjects. He heeded unsound advice and failed to give God first place (1 Kings 12:1—14:31; 2 Chron. 10:1—12:16).

REMNANT. A minority of humanity that has remained faithful to the Lord in every age since the fall of Adam. In Elijah's day it was seven thousand people who had not been corrupted by Baal worship (1 Kings 19:18; Rom. 11:1-5). In Isaiah's day it was "very small" (Isa. 1:9). Today it is composed of members of the true Church (cf. Rom. 11:4, 5). In the tribulation it will be the 144,000 Israelites (Rev. 7:3-8) and a great number of Gentiles (Rev. 7:9). A remnant will enter the kingdom age (Zech. 12:6—13:9).

REPENTANCE. Repentance is that change of attitude toward sin that enables a person to trust Christ as Savior. Repentance is inseparable from saving faith. Nor can saving faith ever be exercised apart from repentance. This vital newness of mind is a part of believing and is therefore sometimes used as a synonym for believing (cf. Acts 17:30; 20:21; 26: 20; Rom. 2:4; 2 Tim. 2:25; 2 Pet. 3:9). Repentance cannot be *added* to faith as a condition of salvation (John 3:16; Acts 16:31; Eph. 2:8, 9), for repentance and faith are two sides of the same coin. The one cannot occur without the other (Acts 20:21).

Believers who have sinned may repent as a separate act. But this is totally different from being saved over again (cf. 2 Cor. 7:8-11). Israel, God's covenant nation, was also called on to repent (Matt. 3:2). As in the case of the New Testament believer, this was not a gospel call but rather a challenge to return to a prior spiritual relationship (cf. Matt. 4:12-17).

RESURRECTION, THE FIRST. The raising of the new and heavenly body to reunion with the redeemed soul and spirit. This resurrection occurs in stages and will ultimately embrace all of God's elect saints from Adam to the end of the kingdom age (1 Cor. 15:22, 23; 1 Thess. 4:13-17; Rev. 20:4-6, 12, 13).

The final phase of the first resurrection occurs at the same time as the second resurrection—at the end of the kingdom age. It includes saints who have died during the millennium. Their names will appear in the "book of life" (Rev. 20:12, 13). Christ himself constituted the "firstfruits" of the first resurrection (1 Cor. 15:23).

RESURRECTION, THE SECOND. This is the "resurrection of condemnation" (John 5:28, 29). It constitutes the "great white throne" judgment (Rev. 20: 11-15) and includes every unsaved person from the fall of Adam to the creation of the new heavens and earth. These unsaved will be judged according to their works (deeds), that is, according to their response to the moral law of God, and will suffer degrees of punishment. This sentence involves eternal separation from God rather than simple annihilation (cf. Rev. 19:20 with 20:10).

RETURN OF CHRIST. Scripture declares the certainty of this event (John 14: 1-3; Acts 1:10, 11). Christ's return will be an actual occurrence and not simply a process. It is to be personal and corporeal or bodily (Matt. 23:39; 24:30; Phil. 3:20, 21; 1 Thess. 4:13-17). It occurs in two distinct stages: first, Christ's coming *for* his saints, when he raises the dead and transforms the living (1 Thess. 4:13-17; 1 Cor. 15:51-53; Phil. 3:20, 21; 1 John 3: 1-3); second, Christ's coming *with* his saints, when he conquers his enemies, destroys the Satanic world system, and establishes his earthly kingdom over Israel and the nations (Rev. 19:11−20:4; cf. Zech. 14:1-9; Luke 1:31-33; 1 Cor. 15: 24-28).

REUBEN (rōō'bĕn) ("behold a son"). Jacob's firstborn son. He forfeited his family status through gross misconduct (Gen. 29:31, 32; 35:22). This cost him his birthright (Gen. 49:3, 4). He fathered the Jewish tribe that bore his name (Num. 26:5-7).

REUEL (rōō'ĕl) ("God is a friend"). An alternate name for Jethro, Moses' father-in-law (Exod. 2:18).

REUMAH (rōō'mȧ) ("exalted"). A concubine of Nahor, Abraham's brother (Gen. 22:24). Her four sons were ancestors of Aramean tribes located in the regions north of Damascus.

RHEGIUM (rē'jĭ-ŭm). A city on the coast of Italy opposite Messina in Sicily. Paul's vessel touched at this port after leaving Syracuse (Acts 28:13). Rhegium is present-day Reggio.

RHODA (rō'dȧ) (Greek for "rose"). A maid in the house of John Mark's mother in Jerusalem. She announced Peter's arrival after the angel had released him from prison (Acts 12:13). Rhoda served both her mistress and the larger fellowship of the church.

RHODES (rōdz). The southernmost large island of the Aegean Sea. It lies off the southwestern extremity of Asia Minor and points toward Crete, about 95 miles to the southwest. The city of Rhodes, situated at the northeast tip of the island (about 65 miles from the mainland), was passed by Paul on his last journey to Palestine (Acts 21:1). The city was famed as a commercial mecca and for the huge statue of Apollo known as the "Colossus of Rhodes."

RIBLAH (rĭb'lȧ). A city south of Hamath in Syria (Ezek. 6:14, RSV). Here the Babylonians punished captive kings of Judah (2 Kings 23:33; 25:6, 20; Jer. 39:5; 52:9).

RIGHTEOUSNESS. God's righteousness is absolute, being the expression of his infinitely holy character. His divine righteousness is seen in his person (James 1:17; 1 John 1:5) as well as his purposes and plans (Rom. 3:25, 26). Imputed righteousness is the intrinsic righteousness of God imputed to the believer through Christ at conversion (1 Cor. 1:30; 2 Cor. 5:21; cf. Rom. 3:21, 22). God's righteousness was also imputed to Old Testament saints by virtue of their prospective faith in Christ (Gen. 15:6; Rom. 4:3; Gal. 3:6; James 2:23; cf. John 8:56; Heb. 11:13).

RIVERS AND STREAMS. The usual word for river in Hebrew is *nāhār*, signifying a constantly flowing stream, such as the rivers of Eden (Gen. 2:10, 13, 14), the Euphrates (Deut. 1:7), the rivers of Ethiopia (Isa. 18:1), and the rivers of Damascus (2 Kings 5:12). Sometimes the word is applied to canals, like the Chebar (Ezek. 1:1, 3; 3:15; 10:15). The great rivers of the Bible are the Nile, Tigris, the Euphrates, and the Jordan. In the New Testament the missionary journeys of Paul are associated with important cities located on rivers. (However, the rivers themselves, such as the Cydnus at Tarsus, the Orontes at Syrian Antioch, and the Tiber at Rome, are not named in Scripture.)

Another frequent Hebrew word, *nahal*, denotes a seasonal watercourse known as a *wadi*. In summer it is a dry riverbed or ravine. In the rainy season, however, it may become a raging torrent. The Jabbok was such a wadi (Deut. 2:37), as well as the brook Cherith (1 Kings 17:3).

Among the rivers of Palestine not named in the Bible are the Yarmuk, an eastern tributary of the Jordan River south of the Sea of Galilee, and the Auja (present-day Yarkon), which flows into the Mediterranean Sea at modern Tel-Aviv. The Nile is also unnamed in Scripture. "The river of Egypt" (Gen. 15:18) is probably not the Nile but rather the *Wadi el ͨArish*, south of Gaza.

RIZPAH (rĭz'pȧ) ("hot stone or coal"). A concubine of Saul. After Saul's death, Abner, the head of the army, took Rizpah as his wife (2 Sam. 3:7). This act was tantamount to a claim to the throne (cf. 1 Kings 2:22). Consequently Ishbosheth, Saul's son and nominal ruler, challenged Abner's loyalty. Abner in retaliation began negotiations to support David as king (2 Sam. 3:7-21).

Later, when famine came as a divine punishment for Saul's treacherous murder of the Gibeonites, David made recompense to the aggrieved Gibeonites by handing over seven of the sons of Saul (the two sons of Rizpah and five of Merab) to be hanged (2 Sam. 21:1-9). Then Rizpah showed intense love and fortitude by protecting the bodies from birds and beasts of prey until burial could be made (2 Sam. 21:10-14). This devotion led David to undertake proper burial of the bones of Jonathan and Saul along with those of the men who had been hanged.

ROBE (*simlah*). The ordinary outergarment of biblical times. It is still worn by modern *fellahin*. The robe was essentially a square piece of cloth thrown over one or both shoulders. There were openings for the arms at the sides. A cloak, which even the poorest person possessed, could not be given in loan, since it was used at night as a covering (Exod. 22:25-27; Deut. 24:13). It was removed during manual labor (Matt. 24:18; Mark 10:50). It was often used to hold a variety of objects (Exod. 12:34; Judg. 8:25; 2 Kings 4:39). A variety of the robe, a *sadin*, was a shawl-like wrap (Judg. 14:12, 13; Prov. 31:24).

ROBE (*me͑il*). This, too, was an outer, coat-like garment. Samuel's mother made one each year for her son (1 Sam. 2:19), and he wore one on significant occasions (1 Sam. 15:27; 28:14). Saul (1 Sam. 24:4, 11) and Jonathan (1 Sam. 18:4) wore one, as did David on the occasion of the transfer of the ark to Jerusalem (1 Chron. 15:27). This was the garment which was customarily ripped in times of grief or distress (Ezra 9:3, 5; Job 1:20; 2:12). The ephod of the priest was worn over the *me͑il* (Lev. 8:7; cf. Exod. 29:5). This garment may be similar to the *qumbaz* of modern Palestine—the long, loosely-fitting robe worn over all other clothing.

ROCK. Rocks abound in the hilly and mountainous sections of Palestine. Often the rocks are of such size and formation as to constitute well-known landmarks. They also afford shelter, shade, and defense. Little wonder that God is often described as a Rock!

Relief sculpture on Arch of Titus in Rome portrays Roman soldiers plundering treasures of Jerusalem Temple in A.D. 70. (*HPS photo*)

ROMANS. A Latin people strongly influenced by Etruscan culture. Rome, the center of their power and expansion, was founded about 753 B.C. Gradually this people extended their control over Italy and the entire Mediterranean world. The term "Roman" gradually acquired a broader meaning then simply an inhabitant of Rome (1 Macc. 8:1; Acts 2:10) or a representative of the Roman government (Acts 25:16; 28:17). It came to include anyone who had rights of citizenship in the Empire (Acts 16:21, 37, 38; 22:25-29). According to Valerian and Porcian laws no magistrate could arrest, scourge, or kill a Roman citizen. The life of one so privileged could not be taken except by the vote of a general assembly.

Rome became dominant in Jewish affairs from the time of Pompey in 63 B.C. Herod the Great was the vassal king of Rome, having been enthroned through Antony and Octavian. After the dethronement of Herod's son, Archelaus, Rome ruled Judea through procurators, except for the brief reign of Herod Agrippa I (A.D. 41-44).

Christianity was outlawed by the Romans, and early believers frequently suffered great persecution. The Emperor cult was diametrically opposed to the Christian faith. Although Rome resisted the gospel, Christianity nevertheless made great strides throughout the Empire, finally attaining imperial favor in the fourth century A.D. under Emperor Constantine.

ROME. The famous city on the Tiber River in Italy. It was the residence of the Emperor and the seat of the Roman government (Acts 28:14-16; Rom. 1:7, 15).

ROSE, ROSE OF SHARON (Hebrew *ḥabaṣṣeleth*). This is apparently not a true rose but instead the white narcissus, the crocus, the meadow saffron, or the anemone. (However, true roses apparently existed in Palestine in the biblical period. At least four wild species are still found in Palestine.) But the "rose" of the Old Testament was some common, bulbous plant that carpeted the Plain of Sharon.

RUE (Greek *peganon*). A plant which the Pharisees scrupulously tithed. It is native to Bible lands and was cultivated as a medicine and a condiment. It is identified as the *Ruta gaveolens,* a shrub with pinnate, bluish-green leaves and yellow flowers (Luke 11:42).

RULER OF THE SYNAGOGUE. During the Hellenistic period, Jewish synagogues were normally governed by a council of elders under the leadership of a "ruler of the synagogue." Several such rulers are mentioned: (1) Jairus, whose daughter Jesus raised from death (Mark 5:22-43); (2) an unnamed man who was angered because Jesus healed on the sabbath (Luke 13:10-17); (3) those who allowed Paul to speak in the synagogue at Antioch of Pisidia (Acts 13:14, 15); (4) Crispus, a convert at Corinth (Acts 18:8); and (5) Sosthenes, a ruler of the Corinthian synagogue at the time of Paul's first visit (Acts 18:17).

RUTH (rōōth) (apparently a contraction from *reᶜuth,* "a female companion"). The Moabite woman who by faith clung to Naomi and her God and accompanied Naomi back to Bethlehem (Ruth 1:1-22). In her act of faith Ruth illustrates how the believing remnant of the Israelite nation will someday return to the land in a saving relationship with Christ, the great Kinsman-Redeemer (portrayed by Ruth's marriage to Boaz). Naomi represents the sorrowing Israelite nation outside the land in dispersion, as well as her eventual return to Messiah through a believing remnant. The Book of Ruth illustrates God's redemptive ways with Israel and the nations through the Kinsman-Redeemer.

SACRIFICE. Fallen man's divinely appointed avenue of approach to God was always through animal-sacrifice until Christ himself died as the ultimate offering. Animal sacrifice was instituted immediately after the fall of Adam and was reiterated on several occasions thereafter (Gen. 3:21; 4:3-7; 8:20-22; 12:7; 33:18-20; Exod. 12:3-14). The slain animals in all cases prefigured Christ as the substitute sufferer for our sins. This is why they had to die through the shedding of blood (Heb. 9:22).

The death of Christ fulfilled all sacrificial types. The Father made the sacrifice (John 3:16; Rom. 8:32). It was substitutional (Lev. 1:4; Isa. 53:5, 6; 2 Cor. 5:21; 1 Tim. 2:6; 1 Pet. 2:24), voluntary (John

10:18), redemptive (1 Cor. 6:20; Gal. 3: 13; Eph. 1:7), propitiatory (Rom. 3:25; 1 John 2:2), reconciling (Rom. 5:10; 2 Cor. 5:18, 19; Col. 1:21, 22), efficacious (John 12:32, 33), and revelatory (1 John 4:9, 10).

The spiritual sacrifices which believers offer involve the priestly functions of self-dedication (Rom. 12:1, 2), praise (Eph. 5:20; Heb. 13:15), and giving of substance (Phil. 4:18).

The animal sacrifices in the future millennial kingdom (Ezek. 43:19-27) will be purely retrospective or commemorative—they will look back to the finished work of Christ.

SAFFRON (Hebrew *karkōm*). A fragrant plant with light violet flowers veined with red. The dried and pulverized stigmas yield a yellow dye. Olive oil was perfumed with saffron and food was spiced with it. It also served as a medicine (Song 4:14).

SAILOR. The Hebrews displayed little enthusiasm for the sea. Throughout their history they had few ports, the best harbors being held by alien maritime peoples (particularly the Phoenicians). However, Solomon did build a navy at Eziongeber which required many sailors (1 Kings 9:26-28). Jehoshaphat did the same, but his venture was frustrated (1 Kings 22:48). These ships were apparently manned mainly by Phoenician sailors in cooperation with the Phoenician fleet.

SAINT (Greek *hagios*, "a holy one"). A frequent New Testament designation of a believer in Christ. Every believer is a saint because of his holy standing in Christ. According to Scripture, sainthood depends not on personal merit but on the finished work of Christ. Sainthood is thus not a vague future possibility but a present privilege in Christ (1 Cor. 1:2).

SALAMIS (săl'à-mĭs). A Greek city on the east coast of Cyprus (the island which Paul and Barnabas began evangelizing on their first missionary tour—Acts 13:4-6). It is located north of present-day Famagusta.

SALEM (sā'lĕm). The name "Salem" as used in Genesis 14:18 apparently refers to the city of Jerusalem. This identification is supported by Psalm 76:2 and by ancient Jewish tradition.

SALOME (sà-lō'mē) (feminine form of Solomon, "peaceable"). (1) Zebedee's wife and the mother of James and John (Mark 15:40; 16:1). She was one of the women who witnessed the crucifixion (Matt. 27:56). She also took sweet spices to the sepulchre on the morning of the resurrection (Mark 16:1). (2) The daughter of Herodias by her first husband, Herod Philip. She is not actually named in the Gospel accounts but is certainly the girl who danced before Herod Antipas (Matt. 14:6; Mark 6:22). Josephus identifies her as Salome. Her evil mother used the occasion and the foolish oath of Herod to have John the Baptist beheaded. Salome later married her great-uncle, Philip the Tetrarch.

SALT SEA. See "Dead Sea."

SAMARIA (sà-mâr'ĭ-à) (1) The capital of the Hebrew Northern Kingdom. It was founded by Omri in the ninth century B.C. (1 Kings 16:24). The Assyrians took it in 722 B.C. (2 Kings 17:5, 6). The native population was displaced by foreigners (2 Kings 17:24), who practiced a mixed worship of the Lord (2 Kings 17:29). It later became the capital of an Assyrian and then of a Persian province (Ezra 4:17). Herod the Great rebuilt it and renamed it Sebaste. (2) The central highland ridge extending from Galilee in northern Palestine to Judea in southern Palestine (Jer. 31:5). "The hill of Samaria," on which Omri built the capital of the Northern Kingdom, was purchased for two talents of silver (about four thousand dollars) from a man named Shemer (1 Kings 16:23, 24).

SAMARITANS (sà-mâr'ĭ-tăns). The descendants of the colonists whom Shalmaneser V, king of Assyria, brought from Cutha, Babylon, Hamath, and other foreign places after he had conquered Samaria in 722 B.C. (2 Kings 17). Two later Assyrian kings, Esarhaddon and Ashurbanipal, added other pagan deportees. The first settlers were overrun by lions and appealed for a priest of the Lord to teach them the faith of Israel. The result was a mixed worship of Jehovah. The Jews despised the Samaritans for this (John 4:9). The Samaritans in turn obstructed the efforts of Ezra and Nehe-

Samaritan chief priest and ancient scroll in Nablus, ancient Shechem (© *MPS*)

miah to rebuild Jerusalem and reestablish the sanctuary (cf. Ezra 4:2-24). Jews contemptuously called Samaritans "Cuthites" because they came from Cutha and other pagan cities.

SAMOS (sā'mŏs). One of the larger islands in the Aegean Sea. It is situated off the coast of Asia Minor southwest of Ephesus. A narrow strait runs between Samos and the mainland at Trogillium. Paul sailed through this body of water on his way home from his third missionary journey (Acts 20:15). Emperor Augustus made Samos a free state in 17 B.C.

SAMOTHRACE (săm'ō-thrās). A small, mountainous island of the northeastern Aegean Sea off the coast of Thrace. A town by the same name was situated on the northern side. Paul sailed northwest from Troas to Neapolis, reaching Samothrace in one day and Neapolis the next (Acts 16:11).

SAMSON (săm'sŭn) ("little sun"). A judge of Israel who rescued God's people from the Philistines (Judg. 13:1 – 16:31). As long as Samson kept his Nazarite vow he was invincible. But his ultimate violation of his vow culminated in a tragic ending (Judg. 16:30). Samson was a man of contrasts. He was occasionally Spirit-possessed (Judg. 13:25; 15:14), but he frequently yielded to carnal appetites (Judg. 16:1-4). He was mighty in physical strength (Judg. 16:3-14) but weak in resisting temptation (Judg. 16:15-17). He was courageous in battle with the Philistines (Judg. 15:1-4) but cowardly in resisting the world, the flesh, and the Devil.

SAMUEL (săm'ū-ĕl) ("asked of God"). The last of the judges and the first of the prophets (Acts 3:24; 13:20). As a judge he exercised spiritual discernment and enforced the law and authority of the Lord (1 Sam. 7:15-17). As a prophet (1 Sam. 2:27-36; 3:19-21) his faithfulness rebuked the unfaithfulness of Eli. As a priest he interceded (1 Sam. 7:9), offered sacrifices (1 Sam. 7:9, 10), and anointed kings (1 Sam. 10:1; 16:13).

SANDALS. For the protection of the feet the Hebrews, like other eastern peoples, wore sandals. In their simplest form sandals consisted simply of pieces of leather bound to the soles of the feet by thongs (Gen. 14:23; Isa. 5:27; Mark 1:7; John 1: 27). Tomb paintings and other archeological remains reveal that sandals varied greatly in style, even resembling shoes or boots at times.

SAPPHIRA (să-fī'rà) (Aramaic "fair one"). A Christian in the first church in Jerusalem. She was the wife of Ananias (Acts 5: 1). Like Samson and Saul, Ananias and Sapphira committed the "sin unto (physical) death" (Acts 5:1-11; cf. 1 John 5:16). They yielded themselves to Satan by lying to the Holy Spirit regarding their financial commitment.

SAR (Assyrian *sharru*, "king"). A leader or chieftain of Israel (Num. 21:18), of Midian (Judg. 7:25; 8:3), or of the Philistines (1 Sam. 29:3). The word is also used of a noble or official under a king (Gen. 12: 15; Isa. 30:4) or of a military captain or general (1 Sam. 12:9; 1 Kings 1:25). It was sometimes employed as a term of rank and dignity (Isa. 23:8).

SARAH (sā'rà) ("a princess"). The wife of Abraham and the mother of Isaac, the child of promise in the line of Messiah (Gen. 11:29-31; 21:1-5). Sarai (the earlier form of her name) was childless for years. When she was about 76 years old, she doubted that God's promise of posterity would ever be fulfilled. She therefore prevailed upon her husband to take Hagar, her handmaid, as a secondary wife. Abraham yielded to her unbelief and became the father of Ishmael (Gen. 16). Several years later Sarai gave birth to Isaac through divine promise and power. Sarai's name was then changed to Sarah, meaning "princess" (Gen. 17:15).

Sarah died at Hebron at the age of 127 years. She is listed as a hero of faith despite her doubts (Heb. 11:11).

SARDIS (sär'dĭs). The brilliant capital city of Lydia. Its position of wealth and power under Croesus ended abruptly when the city fell to Cyrus the Persian (549 B.C.). Now only a small village (Sart) remains near the site of the ancient city. One of the seven letters of the Revelation is addressed to the church in Sardis (Rev. 3:1-6). Excavations have uncovered the ancient splendor of the city.

SARGON (sär'gŏn) (Assyrian *Sharru-ukin,* "he has established the kingship"). The Assyrian emperor from 722 to 705 B.C. He is described in some detail in the inscriptions at his palace at Khorsabad. He is named only once in Scripture, in Isaiah 20:1.

SATAN. See "Devil."

SATRAP. A designation of various grades of governor under the Persian Empire. The word is derived from the Old Persian and means "protector of the realm." The satraps had their own courts and were endowed with considerable authority (cf. Esth. 8:9; 9:3).

SAUL (sôl) ("asked for, demanded"). The first king of Israel (1030-1010 B.C.). He was a man who began well but finished in tragedy and untimely death. Although God-anointed (1 Sam. 10:1), humble (1 Sam. 9:21), and self-controlled (1 Sam. 10:27) in his early years, Saul later became disobedient and self-willed (1 Sam. 13:8-14). He rejected God's sovereignty over his kingship, and God in turn rejected him as king. He committed "the sin unto (physical) death" (1 John 5:16) and sealed his doom by resorting to occultism (1 Sam. 28:7-14).

SAUL OF TARSUS. The name of the Apostle Paul before his conversion and dedication to Christ (Acts 7:58).

SCAPEGOAT. The goat which symbolically carried away the sins of the Jewish people on the Day of Atonement (Lev. 16:10). The scapegoat typifies that aspect of Christ's work which puts away our sins from God's presence (Heb. 9:26). The goat slain (the Lord's lot — Lev. 16: 8, 9) portrays that facet of Christ's atonement which vindicates the divine holiness as expressed in the Law (Rom. 3:24-26).

SCARLET. A color which symbolizes safety through sacrifice (as in the scarlet line of Rahab — Josh. 2:21; Heb. 9:19-22). Scarlet was a prominent color in the Tabernacle ritual and symbolism (Exod. 25:4; 28:5, 6; 35:6, 23, 25; 38:18; Lev. 14:4; Num. 4:8). See also "Blue" and "Purple."

SCORPION. An anthropod commonly found in hot, dry countries. About a dozen kinds are found in Palestine. The scorpion's tail is armed with a poisonous sting which inflicts great pain (Rev. 9:5, 10). Rehoboam threatened to punish his subjects with scorpions (1 Kings 12:11), which were probably whips armed with sharp points to cause pain like a scorpion sting.

SCRIBE (Hebrew *sopher;* Greek *grammateus, nomikos*). Jewish experts in the Law of Moses. They originated after the Exile. The scribes instituted the synagogue service. Some were members of the Sanhedrin (Matt. 16:21; 26:3). They transmitted unwritten legal decisions (oral law) in their effort to apply the Mosaic Law to daily life. However, they eventually claimed that their oral law was more important than the written Law, thereby substituting human tradition for the Word of God (Mark 7:6-13).

SCULPTURE. The Canaanites possessed considerable artistic ability, and examples of their skill in sculpture have been recovered in Canaanite ruins in various Palestinian sites, such as Hazor and Tell Beit Mirsim. However, the works of their neighbors (such as the sculptured sarcophagus of Ahiram of Byblos) are much better known. Volute capitals found at Megiddo and Samaria were the forerunners of the Ionic type. Ossuary workers at Jerusalem have left us several chests engraved with six-pointed stars, rosettes, and flowers.

SCYTHIA (sĭth'ĭ-à). The region north of the Black Sea. It was the home of the uncivilized people known as Scythians. They were proverbially "barbarians" to Greeks and Romans (cf. Col. 3:11).

SCYTHOPOLIS (sĭth-ŏp′ə-lĭs). The Greek name of ancient Beth-shan (present-day Tell el-Husn). It is mentioned in the apocryphal books of Judith and Maccabees. In the time of Christ it was a city of the Decapolis. Scythopolis was thoroughly Hellenic and had a hippodrome, theater, and pagan temples.

SEA. The most prominent sea in the Bible is the Mediterranean. It lies west of Palestine, forming its entire western border. The Hebrew word for sea (*yām*) also means "west" or "westward," that is, "seaward." This large and beautiful body of water provided a most important means of travel and trade, linking the Holy Land with the civilized world of the time through such seaports as Joppa in Old Testament times and Caesarea in New Testament times. The Mediterranean Sea made accessible the long southern seaboard of Europe and the opposite coast of North Africa. Venturesome mariners passed through the straits of Gibraltar and out into the Atlantic, thereafter sailing to Africa or the British Isles. The Red Sea and the Persian Gulf opened up exploration of the east coast of Africa and the coastal regions of Arabia. Points in Asia were accessible across the Indian Ocean.

The Hebrews displayed little enthusiasm for the sea. Solomon depended heavily on Phoenician craftsmen both to build and operate his commercial fleet at Ezion-geber on the Red Sea (1 Kings 9: 26-28). Once every three years this fleet of vessels transported refined copper to Africa and South Arabia in exchange for gold, silver, ivory, apes, peacocks, and other exotic products (1 Kings 10:22). The Phoenicians, Israel's neighbors on the northwest, were thus the true sailors of antiquity. Egyptians, Greeks, Romans, and Carthaginians also plied the sea. Numerous accounts of voyages of these various peoples have come down to us. Paul's famous voyage to Rome in New Testament times shows how important sea traffic was.

SEAL. A symbol of the indwelling Holy Spirit as the security of the believer (Eph.

1:13, 14; 4:30; 2 Cor. 1:22). A seal signifies a finished transaction (Jer. 32:9, 10; John 17:4; 19:30), ownership (Jer. 32:11, 12; 2 Tim. 2:19), and security (Esth. 8:8; Dan. 6:17).

SEASONS. See under "Calendar, Hebrew."

SECOND DEATH. The "lake of fire," the eternal isolation ward for all sin and sinners (Rev. 21:8). It is called the *second death* because it follows physical death. The second death involves everlasting separation from God in sins (Matt. 25:41-46; 2 Thess. 1:7-9).

SEIR (sē′ir). (1) A mountain south of the Dead Sea in the land of Edom (Gen. 14: 6; Ezek. 35:15). (2) The mountainous land of Edom itself (Gen. 32:3; 36:21). This was Esau's home (Gen. 32:3). (3) Esau's descendants, who overcame the original inhabitants, the Horites (Gen. 14:6; 36:20; Deut. 2:12).

SELA (sē′là). The capital of Edom (2 Kings 14:7; Isa. 16:1). It was later called Petra by the Greeks. See "Petra."

SENNACHERIB (sĕ-năk′ĕr-ĭb). The king of Assyria from 705 to 681 B.C. He was the son and successor of Sargon II. Sennacherib overran Judah under Hezekiah in 701 B.C. He besieged Jerusalem but failed to take the city, as his own records confirm (2 Kings 18:13 – 19:34). God miraculously delivered Jerusalem and Judah (2 Kings 19:35, 36). The tyrant was murdered by two of his sons. Esarhaddon, a third son, succeeded him (2 Kings 19:37).

SEPARATION. God's people are to separate themselves from every sinful or defiling activity. Separation represents the human side of sanctification. Old Testament illustrations include Abraham's separation from Ur with its idolatry and Israel's separation from Egypt by the Exodus.

The New Testament teaches that the believer has been separated from his old position of slavery to sin in Adam by the redemptive work of Christ (Rom. 5:12 – 6:23). Believers are expected to shun unholy alliances of any kind (2 Tim. 2: 20, 21; 2 John 1:9-11). Separation from all sin must be followed by joining oneself actively to God in dedicated service (Rom. 12:1, 2).

SERAPHIM. See "Cherubim and Seraphim."

SERPENT. A reptile which creeps on its belly (Gen. 3:14). Palestine has some eighteen species of snakes. The "fiery serpents" of Numbers 21:6 were a poisonous species found in Arabia and the Sinai Peninsula. Their bite caused burning fever and thirst. The serpent symbolized sin and its outcome—death. The bronze replica of the serpent portrayed Christ's judgment and conquest of sin (Num. 21:9; John 3:14-16). See also "Adder," "Asp," and "Viper."

SETH (sĕth) ("appointed, substituted"). The third son of Adam and Eve. He was born after Cain had murdered Abel. Seth served as Abel's substitute in the perpetuation of the messianic line (Gen. 4:25, 26).

SHALMANESER (shăl-măn-ē'zĕr) (Assyrian, "the god Shulman is chief"). The name of several Assyrian emperors. Shalmaneser III (859-824 B.C.) clashed with a coalition of kings at Qarqar in 853 B.C. "Ahab the Israelite" was a member of this federation. Shalmaneser III received tribute from "Jehu, son of Omri," an event not mentioned in the Old Testament but portrayed on the Black Obelisk. Shalmaneser V (727-722 B.C.) vanquished Hoshea of Israel (2 Kings 17:3) and besieged Samaria for three years, until it fell in 722 B.C. (2 Kings 17:5, 6). This event is also recorded in the Babylonian Chronicle.

SHARON (shăr'ŭn). A large, fertile plain which spans 50 miles between Carmel and Joppa and extends ten miles back to the hills of Samaria. It is fertile (Isa. 35:2) and rich in vegetation (1 Chron. 27:29). Lydda was at its southern limits (Acts 9:35). The Plain of Sharon is the garden spot of Palestine.

SHEAR-JASHUB (shē'ăr-jä'shŭb) ("a remnant shall come back"). The infant son of Isaiah, whom he had with him (probably in his arms) when he announced the virgin-birth prophecy (Isa. 7:13-16). The child served to make the prophecy relevant to King Ahaz.

SHEBA (shē'bà). A region in South Arabia. Her queen visited Solomon (1 Kings 10:1-13). Sheba was a proverbial source of gold (Psa. 72:15) and incense (Jer. 6:

20; Isa. 60:6; Ezek. 27:22). At the capital city, Marib, archeology has unearthed examples of Sabaean art and architecture, notably the temple of the moon-god.

SHECHEM (shĕ'kĕm). (1) A city in central Palestine in the hill country of Ephraim (Josh. 20:7). It is in the vicinity of Mount Gerizim (Judg. 9:7) and lies about 31 miles north of Jerusalem and 6 miles southeast of Samaria. Shechem had patriarchal associations (Gen. 12:6; 33:18; 37:12). It was a city of refuge and a Levitical town (Josh. 20:7; 21:21). Joseph was buried there (Josh. 24:32). Shechem was the focal point for the assembly of Israel (Josh. 24:1; 1 Kings 12: 1). It was fortified by Jeroboam I (1 Kings 12:25) and was the first capital of the Northern Kingdom. (2) A Hivite prince who disgraced his princely dignity and suffered the consequences at the hands of Jacob's sons, Simeon and Levi (Gen. 34).

SHEEP. Sheep and goats were the most common of the small domestic animals in Bible times. Sheep were raised from earliest human history (Gen. 4:2). The sheep was a ceremonially clean animal under Mosaic Law and could therefore be used for food (Lev. 11:1-3). Its milk supplied many dairy products (Deut. 32: 14; Isa. 7:21, 22). Cloth was woven from its wool (Job 31:20; Prov. 27:26; Ezek. 34:3). As a clean animal the sheep was used in sacrifice (Exod. 20:24; Num. 22: 40). The sheep and the sheepcote furnish much of the redemptive imagery of the Bible (cf. Isa. 53:7; John 1:29; 1 Pet. 1: 18, 19).

SHEKEL. See under "Weights and Measures" and "Coins and Money."

SHEKINAH (shĕ-kī'nà). The radiant and glorious light which denoted the presence of the invisible God among his people (Exod. 40:34-38; Ezek. 43:2-4). The Shekinah resided beneath the overspread wings of the cherubim, above the mercy seat in the most holy place. God's glory also appears in the New Testament (Luke 2:9; 2 Cor. 3:18; Rev. 15:8; Rev. 21:23).

SHELOMITH (shĕl'ŏ-mĭth) (feminine form of *Shelomi*, "peaceful, complete"). A Danite woman whose son was stoned to death in the wilderness for blaspheming the name of the Lord (Lev. 24:10-23).

The incident shows the gravity of cursing God's name.

SHEM (shĕm) ("name, renown"). A son of Noah and a perpetuator of the messianic line. The Jewish people are "Shemites" or "Semites."

SHEMA (shē'mȧ). The initial Hebrew word of Deuteronomy 6:4. *Shema*ᶜ means "Hear!" The full verse forms a concise Jewish confession of faith. In Hebrew liturgy the *Shema*ᶜ refers to Deuteronomy 6:4-9 and 11:13-21 and Numbers 15:37-41. Deuteronomy 6:4 has become a slogan of Judaism, emphasizing its monotheistic faith.

SHEPHERD. Shepherding is probably the most sentimentally appealing occupation of Bible countries, since it pictures the guarding of human souls. Shepherds have existed since the time of Abel (Gen. 4:2). A shepherd's responsibility is clearcut and challenging. He must find pasturage and water in an arid, stony land (Psa. 23:2). He must protect his charges from the storm and the wild beast (Amos 3:12) and must retrieve any lost animal (Ezek. 34:8; Matt. 18:12). Christ is pictured as the Shepherd of Israel (Gen. 49:24; Psa. 23:1; Isa. 40:11), the Good Shepherd (John 10:1-18), and the Chief Shepherd (Heb. 13:20; 1 Pet. 2:25; 5:4). Christ's pastors are his under-shepherds (1 Pet. 5:2).

SHEOL (shē'ŏl). An Old Testament Hebrew word meaning "grave" (Gen. 42:38; Job 14:13; Psa. 88:3). It is a place of sorrow (2 Sam. 22:6; Psa. 18:5; 116:3) to which the wicked are consigned while fully conscious (Psa. 9:17; Ezek. 32:21). *Sheol* is equivalent to the New Testament word *hades* (Luke 16:19-31). See also "Gehenna."

SHIELD (Hebrew *ṣinnâ*). A large shield designed to cover the whole body. It was either oval or rectangular in shape and was as large as a door. Hence the Greek name was *thureos*, derived from *thyra*, "a door." (This large shield is inaccurately rendered "buckler" or "target" in the King James Version.)

All nations of antiquity employed shields in heavy-armed infantry (2 Chron. 14:8). Goliath, the Philistine champion, had a special shield-bearer (1 Sam. 17:7). Shields were usually made of wood or wickerwork overlaid with leather. Sometimes shields of gold or bronze were used (1 Kings 10:16, 17; cf. 14:26, 27).

SHILOH (shī'lō). (1) A city located about nine miles north of Bethel. It was an early assembly place of Israel (Josh. 18:1). The tabernacle was erected in Shiloh (Josh. 18:1; 1 Sam. 1:3). The site is present-day Seilun. (2) A symbolic name for Messiah. Rule in Judah will not depart until he comes; then his sovereignty will include the whole world (Gen. 49:10).

SHILOAH. See under "Springs, Wells, and Pools."

SHIMEI (shĭm'ĕ-ī) (shortened from *Shima*ᶜ*yahu*, "the Lord has heard"). The man who cursed David maliciously (2 Sam. 16:5-14). David bore the insult patiently, but Solomon later executed Shimei (1 Kings 2:36-46).

SHINAR (shī'när). The lower alluvial plain of the Tigris-Euphrates Rivers. In this region were located such ancient cities as Babylon, Erech, (Uruk), Akkad (Agade), and Calneh (Gen. 10:10). It was here that the Tower of Babel was attempted (Gen. 11:2-4).

SHIPHRAH (shĭf'rȧ) ("fair one"). One of the Hebrew midwives in Egypt who refused to obey the royal command to kill all Jewish male babies (Exod. 1:15-17). The name appears in a list of Egyptian slaves. The Aramaic form, Sapphira, occurs in the New Testament (Acts 5:1). God blessed Shiphrah and her companions for their integrity (Exod. 1:20, 21).

Egypt's pharaoh Shishak recorded here his battle victory over Judah's Rehoboam. (© *MPS*)

SHISHAK (shī'shăk). Pharaoh Sheshonq

I (945-924 B.C.), the founder of the twenty-second Egyptian dynasty. He invaded Palestine in the fifth year of Rehoboam (925 B.C.) and subdued Judah (1 Kings 14:25, 26; 2 Chron. 12:2-12). He also overran Israel, as is evident from his stele found at Megiddo and from his exploits recorded at the temple of Amun in Thebes.

SHIRT-TUNIC (Hebrew *kuttoneth,* Greek *chitōn*). A linen or woolen frock made short or long and with or without sleeves. It was worn next to the skin and frequently reached to the knees or ankles. It became prominent about 1400 B.C. and was the normal dress after 1200 B.C. The garment was similar for both sexes, though the woman's garment was fuller and of richer material than the man's.

The Bible also refers to a long, half-sleeved, shirtlike tunic which reached to the ankles (Gen. 37:3, 23, 31-35). The famous Benihasan painting illustrates such garments in white and various colors. It was worn by princes (2 Sam. 13: 18, 19), by Christ (John 19:23), and by the high priest at Christ's trial (Mark 14:63).

SHITTIM (shĭt'ŭm). See "Acacia."

SHOMER (shō'mēr) ("keeper, guard"). The mother of Jehozabad, one of the servants who murdered King Joash (Jehoash) of Judah (2 Kings 12:21; 2 Chron. 24:26). The name is also spelled Shamer (1 Chron. 7:34) and Shimrith (2 Chron. 24:26). Shomer was a Moabite woman.

SHUNEM (shoo͞'něm). A town in the territory of Issachar near Jezreel (Josh. 19: 18). It was the site of the Philistine camp before the battle of Gilboa (1 Sam. 28:4). It was here that Elisha miraculously raised the son of the Shunamite woman (2 Kings 4:8-37). Abishag was brought to David from this city (1 Kings 1:3, 15). The site is identified with present-day Solem.

SHUSHAN, SUSA (shoo͞'shăn, soo͞'sà). One of the three royal cities of the Persian Empire (Dan. 8:2; Neh. 1:1). The palace which Darius I built in Shushan constitutes one of the outstanding architectural features of the fifth century B.C. (cf. Esth. 1:2, 5; 2:3; 3:15).

SICILY. A large island at the toe of the foot of Italy. Paul sailed the narrow straits between this island and the Italian mainland on his trip to Puteoli and Rome. The famous city of Sicily was Syracuse, located at the southeastern extremity of the island.

SIDDIM (sĭd'ĭm), **VALLEY OF.** Originally a fertile, well-watered region south of the Lisan peninsula of the Dead Sea. It was later submerged by earthquake action (Gen. 14:3, 10).

SIDON (sī'dŏn). The chief Phoenician city before the rise of Tyre in the tenth century B.C. (Gen. 10:19; 1 Chron. 1:13). The city lay 25 miles northeast of Tyre. The present-day site is Saida in Lebanon. The city is prominent in both the Old Testament (Judg. 1:31; 1 Kings 17: 9; Isa. 23:2; Joel 3:4-8) and the New Testament (Matt. 11:21; Acts 27:3).

SILAS (sī'làs). Apparently the same person as Silvanus (2 Cor. 1:19; 1 Thess. 1: 1; 2 Thess. 1:1; 1 Pet. 5:12), the Latinized form of the name Silas. He was a member and prophet of the church at Jerusalem (Acts 15:32) and a delegate of the apostolic council (Acts 15:22). Silas was apparently a Roman citizen (Acts 16: 37) and spiritually qualified to take Barnabas' place as Paul's companion (Acts 15:40; cf. 16:19-29). He was also associated with Peter (1 Pet. 5:12).

SILOAM, POOL OF. See under "Springs, Wells, and Pools."

SILVER. In the Tabernacle symbolism, silver pictures redemption. When the Tabernacle was first constructed Moses was commanded to collect from every Israelite a half-shekel of silver (Exod. 30: 11-16), called "atonement money." Its purpose was "to make atonement for your souls" (Exod. 30:16). The silver collected in this manner was used for the sockets of the sanctuary and for the rods and hooks. As a result the Tabernacle rested on silver sockets. The curtains of the door (the way of access) were hung from silver rods and hooks (Exod. 27:17). But the atonement money was only a *token* payment. The actual redemption was not by silver or gold but by Christ's own blood (1 Pet. 1:18, 19).

SIMEON (sĭm'ē-ŭn) ("hearing"). One of Jacob's sons (Gen. 29:33). He took part in the massacre at Shechem (Gen. 34) and was rebuked for his bloody act by the dying Jacob (Gen. 49:5-7).

SIMEON OF JERUSALEM. A devout believer at Jerusalem who awaited the coming of the Messiah and saw his faith rewarded (Luke 2:25-34).

SIMON (sī'mŏn) **THE JUST.** A famous high priest of the third century B.C. He was lauded by Jesus Ben Sira in the apocryphal book of Ecclesiasticus.

SIMON THE MACCABEE. One of the five sons of the priest Mattathias, who fought for the Jewish faith against Hellenistic paganism. Simon became the successor of his brother Jonathan and established the Hasmonean dynasty (143-135 B.C.), which lasted till the rise of Herod the Great (37 B.C.).

SIMON MAGUS. A magician and sorcerer of Samaria who attempted to purchase the gifts of the Spirit with money (Acts 8: 9-24).

SIN. God is infinitely holy and is not the author of sin (Hab. 1:13; Tit. 1:2; James 1:13; 1 John 1:5). The "evil" God is said to create (Isa. 45:7) connotes "adversity" or "calamity." He has ordered that sorrow and misery shall be the inescapable results of sin. God did not create sinners, either angelic or human. The original universe was sinless (Job 38:4-7). Sin began among the angels in Lucifer's revolt (Isa. 14:12-14; Ezek. 28:11-19). Man was created in innocence and freedom of choice. But he fell and introduced sin into the human family (Gen. 3:1-19; Rom. 5:12-21; 1 Cor. 15:22). Because God is infinitely holy and separate from sin, fallen angels and Christ-rejecting men must face eternal separation from God. Unbelievers who regard hell as inconsonant with a God of love fail to comprehend God's full-orbed character (Nah. 1:3).

SIN. A city at the extreme northeast of the Nile Delta. The Greeks called it Pelusium. It is present-day Tell Farama and is located about 32 miles east of Raamses across Lake Menzaleh.

SINAI (sī'nī). The mountain in the Sinai Peninsula where the Law was given to Moses (Exod. 19:1-6; Gal. 4:24). It is the same as Mount Horeb. The precise identification of Mount Sinai is uncertain. Jebel Musa (7,370 feet) or Jebel Serbal (6,825 feet) are the most likely possibilities.

SINGER. Both men and women singers had a prominent part in the tabernacle and temple worship as developed by David and subsequent kings (cf. 1 Chron 9:33; 15:19; 2 Chron. 5:13). Singers and instrumentalists graced all the royal courts of antiquity.

SION, SIRION (sī'ŭn, sĭr'ĭ-ŏn). A synonym for Mount Hermon or one of its three peaks (Deut. 4:48). Sirion was the Canaanite name for Mount Hermon, as used in the Old Testament by the Sidonians (Deut. 3:9; cf. Psa. 29:6).

SISERA (sĭs'ēr-à). A Canaanite general who commanded the army of Jabin, king of Hazor (Judg. 4:2), in battle against Deborah and Barak. He was slain by Jael after his army suffered defeat (Judg. 4:1-31).

SLAVERY. The practice of slavery was regulated but not instituted by the Mosaic Law. The Law mitigated the hardship of slavery and guaranteed certain rights to everyone. A Hebrew could be reduced to servitude by selling himself in order to pay his debts and support his family (Lev. 25:25, 39). He could also fall into slavery as the result of theft (Exod. 22:1, 3). Sometimes a person became a servant through the exercise of paternal authority. This was limited to the sale of a daughter as a servant, frequently with the hope that she would become the concubine of the purchaser (Exod. 21:7-11).

The Mosaic Law humanely provided for the termination of all servitude at the end of six years of service (Exod. 21:2; Deut. 15:12). The Year of Jubilee (every fiftieth year) also ended all servitude (Lev. 25:39-41). Of course, the satisfaction or remission of all valid claims against the servant also resulted in his freedom. A servant who preferred to remain perpetually in the service of his master could signify his intention by having his ear pierced with an awl in the presence of judicial authorities (Exod. 21:6).

The Law prohibited cruel and inhumane treatment of servants (Lev. 25:39-43) and enjoined kindness and liberality (Deut. 15:12-15). However, some aspects of slavery in Israel might seem stringent when compared with modern, Christianized practices. For example, a father could sell his young daughter to a Hebrew with the hope that the purchaser or his son would marry her (Exod. 21:7-9). In this case the purchase money was considered a dowry given to the parents of the bride. Doubtless the consent of the maid had to be obtained, as the later Rabbis contend. In any case she was protected by law against exploitation (Exod. 21:7-11).

Enslavement of Hebrews by fellow Hebrews fell into gradual disuse, especially after the exile. Great numbers of Jews, however, were reduced to slavery as war prisoners by Phoenicians, Philistines, Romans, etc.

Non-Hebrew slaves were commonly war captives of the Canaanites and other foreign nations (cf. Num. 31:26-30). Some were purchased from foreign slave-dealers (Lev. 25:44, 45). The children of slaves remained slaves, being "born in the house" (Gen. 14:14; 17:12; Eccl. 2:7). The average price of a slave was 30 shekels (Exod. 21:32). He was the property of his master and could be sold freely as an article of personal possession (Lev. 25:45, 46).

Provision was made for the physical protection of the slave (Exod. 21:20; Lev. 24:17, 22). Loss of bodily members was to be recompensed by granting the servant liberty (Exod. 21:26, 27). Religious provision was also made for him in circumcision (Gen. 17:12) and participation in the Passover and other religious festivals (Exod. 12:44; Deut. 12:12, 18; 16:11, 14). The Mosaic legislation thus made slavery similar to hired service. As a result slavery almost disappeared among the Jews long before the Christian era. Christianity itself announced the full freedom in Christ which eventually abolished slavery completely as an institution in Christianized lands.

SLING. A simple weapon used chiefly by shepherds to ward off prowling beasts from their flock. David was armed with a sling and developed great skill in using it (1 Sam. 17:40, 49, 50). It was also used as a weapon of war among the Assyrians, Babylonians, and Egyptians. Stones for ammunition were abundant in Palestine, and Israelites employed companies of slingers as an important sector of their armed forces (Zech. 9:15). The Benjamites were famous as skilled slingers (1 Chron. 12:2).

The sling was made of a strip of leather which was broadened in the center to form a cavity for the stone. Both ends of the leather strip were held firmly in one hand while the loaded sling was whirled rapidly around the head. Then one end was released suddenly. With proper control the stone could strike its target with deadly force.

SMITH. Fine work in gold, silver, and copper was executed by Palestinians long before the advent of the iron age (about 1200 B.C.). When iron smelting methods were learned by Israelites in the Davidic-Solomonic era, a variety of metal instruments began to be produced by smiths. Plow blades, axes, forks, tips for ox-goads, knives, swords, daggers, lances, spears, and other weapons of war became common under David and Solomon.

Smiths' workshops began to dot the land. Metal was melted in a furnace heated by coals (Isa. 54:16). The molten metal was beaten on an anvil while still hot (Isa. 41:7). Joints were soldered or riveted together (Isa. 41:7). See also "Artisan."

SMYRNA (smûr′nȧ). A city of the Roman province of Asia. Smyrna was the site of one of the seven churches of the Revelation (Rev. 1:11; 2:8-11). It is present-day Izmir, located on a bay opening to the Aegean Sea.

SOCIAL LIFE, JEWISH. The ancient Hebrews, like most Orientals, were a highly social people. Their spiritual calling and organization contributed to this result. The entire family was expected to appear before the Lord at the sanctuary during pilgrimage festivals (Deut. 16:14). Other occasions for social gatherings were sheep-shearings, grain and fruit harvests, the weaning of children, the wedding seasons, and the normal entertaining of guests. The private home, the city gate, the marketplace, and the public well all served as places of social interchange.

Hospitality was normal for a people bound to each other and the Lord in a covenant relationship. Hospitality was exemplified by the earliest patriarchs

(Gen. 18:1-8) and was repeatedly enjoined by the Mosaic Law (e.g. Deut. 10:19). The greeting of guests was ordinarily warm and profuse (Gen. 23:7, 12). "Peace be to you" was a common greeting, equivalent to our "Hello" (1 Sam. 25:6; 1 Chron. 12:18).

SOCOH (sō'kồ). (1) A town in Solomon's third district (1 Kings 4:10). It is probably present-day Tell er-Ras, near the Plain of Sharon. (2) A town in the lowlands of Judah (Josh. 15:35; 1 Sam. 17:1). (3) A town in the hill country of Judah (Josh. 15:48). It is probably present-day Khirbet Shuweikeh, between Hebron and Beersheba.

SODOM. A city formerly located south of the Dead Sea (Gen. 10:19; 14:2-12). It was apparently submerged by the waters of the Dead Sea when it was destroyed by God (Gen. 19:24, 25).

SOLDIER. In early Israel there was no regular army. Recruits were enlisted on a voluntary basis when a crisis arose. Military leaders were raised up by God in the theocracy and were enabled to muster men quickly for battle, sometimes as the result of performing a heroic deed (Judg. 6:24-34). When the theocracy gave way to the monarchy, a standing army was formed. King Saul selected a contingent of private warriors. Under David the same policy prevailed, but the force was greatly increased (2 Sam. 15:18). The general levy of nonprofessional military men was divided into thousands, hundreds, fifties, and tens. Each category had its own commander. (This order apparently dated from Moses' time but had fallen into temporary disarray during the chaotic Period of the Judges.)

The archer was prominent in battle. Cavalry became important in the Solomonic era despite the prohibition of Deuteronomy 17:16. Solomon employed horses and chariots on a huge scale (1 Kings 10:26), as his stables at Megiddo attest (1 Kings 4:26). Soldiers were maintained by booty, by the produce of the land where they camped, and (under David and Solomon) by regular pay (1 Kings 4:27).

SOLOMON ("peaceable"). A son of David and his successor to the throne of Israel (971-931 B.C.). He was the wisest, wealthiest, and most famous king of Israel, but in the end his sensuality and apostasy became his undoing. Though he was the wisest of men, sin turned him into a fool. He became a disillusioned man of the world, as seen in the book of Ecclesiastes. His earlier brilliant reign under God's blessing witnessed great commercial expansion and building operations, notably the magnificent Temple (1 Kings 3:1 – 11:43).

SONSHIP. The relation into which a person enters when he is saved and admitted to God's family (John 1:12, 13; 3:5; Rom. 8:16, 17). This is effected by regeneration (the new or second birth, accomplished by the Holy Spirit through God's Word).

With regard to the elect nation Israel, sonship expresses the covenant relationship of this people with the Lord (Exod. 4:22, 23; Hos. 11:1). With regard to God's relation to the human race as a whole, sonship expresses the *creatorial* relationship of man to God (Luke 3:38; Acts 17:28). This does not mean that all men are *spiritually* related to God, for Scripture teaches that they are not (Eph. 4:17, 18).

SONSHIP OF CHRIST. Christ bears five distinct relationships of sonship: Son of God, Son of Adam, Son of Abraham, Son of David, and Son of Mary. As the Son of God Christ is the unique Son from all eternity, coeternal and coequal with the Father (Matt. 16:16). As the Son of Adam or Son of man Christ is revealed in his human aspect (Matt. 8:20). As the Son of Abraham Christ appears in the messianic line and is therefore related to the Abrahamic Covenant (Matt. 1:1). As the Son of David Christ is associated with the Davidic Covenant (Matt. 21:9). As the Son of Mary Christ is related to the incarnation (Matt. 1:25).

SOPATER (sō'pà-tẽr) ("of sound parentage"). A believer from Berea who accompanied Paul on his return from his third missionary tour (Acts 20:4; Rom. 16:21).

SORCERY. A general term for the practice of the occult arts (fortune-telling, divination, magic, spiritism, witchcraft, etc.). Sorcery was practiced at the Egyptian court (Exod. 7:11; 8:7, 18). The "magicians" resisted Moses by appealing to demonic powers masquerading as Egyptian deities. By this means they were able to counterfeit some of God's miracles displayed through Moses. Daniel also encountered occult workers in Babylonia in the sixth century B.C. (Dan. 2:2). They also tried to imitate the power of God through demonic means. Such demon-energized practitioners of false religions constantly threatened the pure faith of God's people (Isa. 2:6; Jer. 27:9; Mic. 5:12).

The clairvoyant medium with whom Paul clashed at Philippi (Acts 16:16-18), as well as Simon of Samaria (Acts 8:9-11) and Bar-Jesus of Paphos in Cyprus (Acts 13:6-11), practiced the occult arts in demonized religionism. All employment of sorcery was sternly forbidden by the Mosaic Law (Lev. 19:31; 20:6; Deut. 18:9-12).

SOUL AND SPIRIT. The immaterial part of man. The soul is related to life, action, and emotion. The spirit knows (1 Cor. 2:11) and is capable of communication with God when enlivened by the Holy Spirit (Job 32:8; Prov. 20:27; Psa. 18:28). The terms "soul" and "spirit" are sometimes used interchangeably, but they are nevertheless distinct (Heb. 4:12; 1 Cor. 15:44).

SOWER. Since sowing was done by hand in Bible days, the sower was a common figure in Palestine. Christ used this phase of the farmer's work to illustrate the Word of God planted in men's hearts (Matt. 13:1-9, 18-23).

SPARROW (Hebrew *ṣippōr*). Several species of sparrows are common in Palestine, such as the house sparrow, the Italian sparrow, the tree sparrow, and the rock sparrow. The Greek *strouthion* (Matt. 10:29; Luke 12:6, 7) implies not only the sparrow but a group of other small birds such as were, and still are, killed and offered for sale in Palestinian markets.

SPEAR. A weapon used from very ancient times. Metal-tipped spears became popular after the advent of metallurgy. Spears were often carried by kings and princes, military leaders, and individual warriors (1 Sam. 17:45; 19:9; 2 Sam. 2:23; cf. 2 Sam. 21:16).

The *logchē*, the spear which pierced Christ's side (John 19:34), was almost certainly the Roman *pilum*, a javelin with a three-foot iron shaft inserted into a wooden shaft of the same length. In New Testament times all legionnaires were equipped with such a weapon.

SPICES (Hebrew *bōsem*). A vegetable substance which has aromatic and pungent qualities (Song 4:16; cf. Exod. 25:6; 1 Kings 10:10; Song 4:10). The chief spices were myrrh, calamus, cassia, and cinnamon (Exod. 30:23, 24). Arabia was the principal producer of spices (1 Kings 10:2; Ezek. 27:22).

SPIDER (Hebrew *ᶜakkābīsh*). There are innumerable species of Spiders in Palestine. The "spider" in Proverbs 30:28, however, is probably actually the gecko. See "Lizard."

SPIKENARD (Hebrew *nērd;* Greek *nardos*). A fragrant oil obtained from the *Nardostachys jatamansi,* native to North India. In Bible times spikenard was very precious because of the long distance it had to be imported. It was sealed in alabaster containers, which were opened only on very special occasions (John 12:3).

SPIRITISM. Alleged communication with the dead through a spirit medium. The practice is a form of the occult arts and actually consists of the impersonation of dead persons by demonic spirits. This occult activity is severely condemned by God's Word (Lev. 19:31; 20:6, 27; Deut. 18:9-12; 1 Sam. 28:1-25).

SPIRITUAL GIFTS. Endowments given by the Holy Spirit to individual believers for the purpose of benefiting the church (1 Cor. 12:8-11; Rom. 12:3-8; Eph. 4:7-11). Certain gifts were meant to be temporary (1 Cor. 13:8) and were to be superseded by "the completed (final) thing" (1 Cor. 13:10), the completed New Testament Scriptures (1 Cor. 13:9-13).

SPRINGS, WELLS, AND POOLS. Water is a precious commodity in Palestine, since rainfall is not abundant. However, the geological structure of Palestine has provided it with many springs (Deut. 8:7). Since the presence of a permanent spring frequently made a particular site habitable for human beings, the Hebrew or Arabic words for "spring" often occur as a common element in place names.

For example, ᶜAin es Sultan is the fountain that determined the site of ancient Jericho.

Unlike a spring or fountain, which is provided by nature, a well is a manmade phenomenon. Successful wells are obtained by sinking a shaft or boring a hole into a natural underground spring (Gen. 24:11-14; John 4:11). Rainwater or well water was often stored in a cistern — a natural or manmade rock storage tank. The Pool of Siloam was supplied by both rainwater and springs. Sometimes water was conducted through channels from a cistern to nearby towns and gardens (Eccl. 2:6). In certain dry regions water was nearly as precious as gold. For this reason wells were sometimes the objects of fierce disputes (Gen. 21:25).

Some of the more significant springs, wells, and pools of Scripture are described below.

Beer-lahai-roi (bē'ēr-là-hī'roi) ("well of the Living One who sees me"). A well on the road through the wilderness between Kadesh and Bered (Gen. 16:7, 14; 24:62). Bedouins identify it with present-day Ain Muweileh, about 12 miles northwest of Kadesh and 50 miles south of Beersheba.

Beer-sheba (bē'ēr-shē'bà) ("well of the seven"). A place in south Judah where Abraham dug a well and where he and the king of Gerar made a treaty (Gen. 21: 22-32). The present city is 48 miles southwest of Jerusalem and two miles west of Tell es-Sebaᶜ, the original site of the ancient town.

Bethesda (bě-thēz'dà). A pool at Jerusalem where Jesus healed an infirm man (John 5:2). It had five porticoes. Excavators have discovered in the northeast sector of the city a five-porched pool which appears to be this site.

Elim (ē'lĭm) ("large trees"). The second stopping place of the Israelites after crossing the Red (Reed) Sea. It was an oasis with twelve springs (Exod. 15:27; 16:1; Num. 33:9, 10). Biblical references suggest that it is situated on the west side of the Sinai Peninsula, on the Gulf of Suez. It is probably presentday Wadi Gharandel, about 40 miles southeast of Suez.

En-dor (ĕn'dôr) ("spring of habitation"). Modern ᶜIndur, on the north shoulder of Little Hermon and six miles southeast of Nazareth in the tribe of Manasseh (Josh. 17:11). Fugitives from Sisera's defeated army perished there (Psa. 83:9, 10). The spirit medium consulted by Saul lived there (1 Sam. 28:7).

En-gedi (ĕn-gē'dī) ("spring of the goat"). A small oasis with a fresh-water spring located on the west mid-shore of the Dead Sea. The site was allotted to Judah (Josh. 15:62). En-gedi was a fertile spot in the midst of a desolate wilderness. It was a favorite hiding place for fugitives because food and caves were found nearby (Song 1:14; 1 Sam. 23:29; 24:1-7).

Gihon (gī'hŏn). A spring to the east of Jerusalem at which Solomon was anointed king (1 Kings 1:33, 38, 45). Hezekiah cut a tunnel through solid rock to conduct the water of Gihon to the pool of Siloam (2 Chron. 32:30). About 2000 B.C. the Jebusites cut a passage through the rock so that buckets could be let down a shaft to collect the water from the underground conduit.

Jacob's Well. This was located near Sychar. The site is identified with the village of Askar on the southeastern slope of Mount Ebal, about a half-mile to the north of Jacob's well. However, some scholars identify Sychar with ancient Shechem. Jesus met the woman of Samaria at Jacob's well and led her to a knowledge of salvation (John 4:5-29).

King's Pool. Probably the Lower or Old Pool of Jerusalem. See "Old Pools."

Marah (mä'rà). A spring of brackish water in the desert of Shur on the way to Sinai. Here Moses was divinely directed to cast a certain tree into the waters in order to make them potable (Exod. 15:23-25). Marah is probably to be located at Ain Hawarah, about 47 miles from Suez and a few miles inland from the Red Sea.

Old Pool. The Lower Pool or King's Pool, located near the Fountain Gate. The Old Pool is situated about 35 feet southeast of the Upper Pool and opens into the Kidron Valley. Modern buildings prevent archeologists from verifying that the Upper Pool was really Hezekiah's or that its waters overflowed directly to the Lower Pool. John 9:7-11 probably refers to the Old Pool.

Pool of Hebron (hē'brŭn). Hebron was

originally named Kiriath-arba, "tetrapolis." It is 19 miles south-southwest of Jerusalem and is the highest town in Palestine, rising 3,040 feet above sea level. There are 25 springs of water and 10 large wells in the area. The pool was doubtless a rock-hewn reservoir.

Pool of Samaria (sȧ-mā'rĭ-ȧ). A reservoir on the north side of the city. It was cut out of rock and cemented. It was beside this pool that Ahab's servants washed the bloodstained chariot in which Ahab's body was brought home from Ramoth-Gilead (1 Kings 22:38).

Siloam (sĭ-lō'ăm) ("conducted"). The Upper Pool of Jerusalem. It is located near a bend in the old wall beneath Ophel. It is a rectangular reservoir measuring 58 feet long by 18 feet wide by 19 feet deep. It was the termination of Hezekiah's tunnel, which had been cut through the rock from the spring of Gihon. In 1880 bathers in the Upper Pool found the entrance to Hezekiah's tunnel and the famous inscription commemorating the cutting of the 1,777-foot aqueduct.

Solomon's Pools. These were located in the valley of Etam (Urtas) near Bethlehem and supplied water to Jerusalem. Three in number, the pools are about 200 feet wide, as much as 600 feet long, and 50 feet deep. They supplied water for Jerusalem from at least as early as Roman times.

Waters of Shiloah (shĭ-lō'ȧ). The gently flowing stream from the Gihon spring. It originally flowed outside the city wall to the Old Pool, but was later diverted by Hezekiah's tunnel to the Upper Pool of Siloam, within the city limits. Shiloah or Siloah is apparently identical with the Old or Lower Pool, the Pool of Shelah, and the King's Pool. See also "Old Pool."

STACTE (stăk'tē) (Hebrew *nāṭāph;* Greek *stactē*). One of the ingredients of the sacred anointing oil (Exod. 30:34). It is probably the gum of the storax tree.

STAFF (Hebrew *shēbeṭ*). A support carried by travelers (Gen. 32:10; Mark 6:8), shepherds (Psa. 23:4), old men (Zech. 8:4), and men of rank (Gen. 38:18). This accessory was a walking stick and was frequently carved and ornamented. It was as welcome a companion and support to the ancient Hebrews on the hilly roads of Palestine as the Alpine stick is to climbers of the Alps. It was also a kind of protective weapon (1 Sam. 17:43; 2 Sam. 23:21). The disciples of our Lord, despite the meagerness of their outfit, were allowed to carry a staff (Mark 6:8).

STEPHANAS (stĕf'ȧ-năs) ("crowned"). A convert of Paul's at Corinth (1 Cor. 1:16). He also visited the apostle later and brought him aid (1 Cor. 16:15, 17).

STEPHEN (stē'vĕn) ("wreath or crown"). The first Christian martyr. He was one of the seven deacons appointed to supervise benevolent work (Acts 6:5-8). He was also a powerful preacher (Acts 7:1-53). Stephen was stoned to death by Jewish leaders (Acts 7:54 – 8:3). He was full of faith (Acts 6:5), grace (Acts 6:8, RV), power, the Scriptures (Acts 7:1-53), wisdom (Acts 6:3, 10), courage (Acts 7:51-56), and love (Acts 7:60).

STEWARD. An official who manages the affairs of a large household, overseeing the service of the master's table, directing the household servants, and controlling the household expenses on behalf of the master. Jesus employed the figure in parables (Luke 16:1-9). The master of a vineyard is also called a steward (Matt. 20:8; Luke 8:3).

STOICISM. A school of philosophy founded by Zeno (300 B.C.). Stoicism taught that men should cultivate moral virtue and be masters of themselves under every circumstance. The important thing was growth in character – not pleasure or the pursuit of happiness. Stoicism was possibly the most noble of the pagan philosophies, even paralleling Christian teachings in some points. However, Stoicism could not offer Christ's deliverance from sin or the Holy Spirit's dynamic for righteousness. Paul encountered disciples of Stoic and Epicurean thought at Athens (Acts 17:18).

STONE. A prominent scriptural symbol portraying Christ. Christ became a stumblingstone to Israel because he came to earth as a servant instead of a conquering king (Isa. 8:14, 15; Matt. 21:44; Rom. 9:32, 33; 1 Cor. 1:23; 1 Pet. 2:8). Christ is related to the church as her foundation (1 Cor. 3:11) and chief cornerstone (Eph. 2:

20-22; 1 Pet. 2:4, 5). He is related to the nations in judgment as "the stone cut without hands" (Dan. 2:34), who will destroy the Satanic world system at the second advent. Whoever falls on this stone in faith and contrition will be broken and will find salvation. But those on whom the stone falls in judgment will be ground to dust (Matt. 21:44). See also "Rock."

STONECUTTER. The art of carving and setting precious stones was an important occupation in Bible times. The jewels on the breastplate of the high priest (Exod. 28:15-21) were cut with the names of the twelve tribes of Israel. Jewels for the noble and wealthy (Exod. 11:2; Isa. 3:18-21) also called for the skilled gem cutter. Precious and semiprecious stones were not cut in facets, as in contemporary art, but were rounded and polished and sometimes engraved and sculptured.

Another kind of stonecutter worked not as a jeweler but as a mason, dressing large blocks of building stone. Hiram of Tyre and Solomon obtained large groups of workmen to cut cedar and other trees in Lebanon and to dress fine building stones, which had to be measured and cut to very exact dimensions (1 Kings 6:7; 7:9).

STORAX TREE (*Styrax officinalis*). A resinous shrub or tree which abounds in Galilee. It grows to a height of 15 or 20 feet and produces fragrant flowers. The extracted juice of the bark is called storax and is used in medicine and perfumery.

STORK (Hebrew *ḥāsīdāh*, "affectionate"). The *Ciconia alba*, a white, heron-like bird which migrates through Palestine in the Spring. There is also the black stork, *Ciconia nigra*, which is common in the Dead Sea area. It is a ceremonially unclean bird (Lev. 11:19; Deut. 14:18).

SUCCOTH (sŭk'ŏth). A town in Goshen on the northeast frontier of Egypt. It lay along the route of the Exodus (Exod. 12: 37; 13:20; Num. 33:5, 6). Succoth is identified with present-day Tell el Mashkuta, east of Pithom and not far from Lake Timsah. There was also a Succoth in the Arabah. It is mentioned in Genesis 33:17, Joshua 13:27, Judges 8:5, 1 Kings 7:46, and Psalm 60:6.

SUFFERING. The doctrine of suffering wrestles with the question of why the righteous suffer. Elihu's idea, that suffering is educational and disciplinary (Job 32 – 37), was apparently all that Job himself ever recognized (Job 42:5, 6).

The New Testament teaches that Christ's sufferings were infinite. What he suffered from the Father was humanly incomprehensible and cannot be shared by anyone else (Psa. 22:1; Matt. 27:46; 2 Cor. 5:21). What Christ suffered from men may be shared by others (John 15: 18-20).

The believer may suffer with Christ (Acts 9:15, 16; Rom. 8:16-18; 1 Pet. 4:12-16). He may also suffer because of chastening from the Father. This may be corrective (John 15:2; 1 Cor. 11:29-32; Heb. 12:3-13) or preventive (2 Cor. 12:1-10). In either case it refines and matures the saint, educates him in obedience, and enlarges his spiritual life and ministry.

SUMERIANS (sü-mĕr'ē-ənz). A remarkable non-Semitic people who came from the far east (Gen. 11:2) and settled in the rich alluvial plain of southern Babylonia before 3000 B.C. They called their new home Shumer or Sumer (biblical Shinar – Gen. 11:2). Prehistoric dynasties of Sumerian rulers were associated with such ancient cities as Erech, Ur, Nippur, Kish, and Lagash. Each city-state had its own local god, who was regarded as the actual ruler. Sumerian history flourished from 3000 to 2000 B.C., until it was interrupted by Akkadian (Semitic) domination under Sargan of Agade (2380-2160 B.C.).

After 2000 B.C. Sumer, like Akkad, fell to the Amorites. The conquerors eventually adopted Sumerian laws and culture. The Sumerians were intellectual and inventive and influenced all subsequent civilization on the Tigris-Euphrates Valley and the Fertile Crescent.

SURVEYOR. The builder or architect needed the services of a surveyor to lay out the site of a new edifice. This was done with a measuring line consisting of a rope or cord (2 Sam. 8:2; Zech. 2:1), single-filament string (1 Kings 7:15), or twisted linen thread (Ezek. 40:3). The space was marked in cubits (1 Kings 7: 15, 23). In New Testament times a reed rod was similarly employed (Rev. 11:1; 21:15).

SUSANNA (sū-zăn'à). A woman who gave Christ some of her material possessions (Luke 8:3). She is listed with Joanna, the wife of Herod's steward, and others who had been blessed both spiritually and physically by Christ's ministry.

SWEET CANE. See "Calamus."

SWINE. A ceremonially unclean animal (Lev. 11:7; Deut. 14:8). It was prohibited as food to Jews by the Mosaic Law. The pig was the emblem of filth and coarseness (Prov. 11:22; Matt. 7:6; 2 Pet. 2:22). To feed swine was the lowest state to which a Jew could sink (Luke 15:15). Partaking of pork at idolatrous feasts was the height of degeneration and apostasy among Jews (Isa. 65:4; 66:17).

SWORD (Hebrew *hereb*). The most frequently mentioned weapon in the Bible. The straight blade was made of iron (1 Sam. 13:19) and was at times two-edged (Psa. 149:6). It was usually kept in a sheath fastened to the left side of the waist-belt.

SYCAMINE TREE (Greek *sykaminos*). The black mulberry (*Morus nigra*), a small, stocky tree with edible fruit (Luke 17:6).

SYCAMORE. See "Sycomore tree."

SYCHAR (sī'kàr). Modern Askar, the place where Jacob's Well was located (John 4:5). It is on the eastern slope of Mount Ebal, about a half-mile north of Jacob's Well. Some scholars suggest a location at ancient Shechem.

SYCOMORE TREE (Hebrew *shiqma*; Greek *sykomōraia*). The sycomore-fig, a tree with a short trunk but a total height of 30 to 40 feet. It has evergreen leaves. The sycomore flourishes in Egypt and the lowlands of Palestine (1 Kings 10:27; 2 Chron. 1:15; 9:27). It produces edible fruit (1 Chron. 27:28; Psa. 78:47). Amos was a tender or dresser of the fruit (Amos 7:14). The dressing operation consisted in cutting off the top of each fig to aid its ripening. Zaccheus climbed a sycomore to see Jesus (Luke 19:4). The Bible sycomore is not to be confused with the North American plane tree (Platanus), also known as sycamore.

SYNAGOGUE (*sunagōgē*, "a bringing together, an assembly"). The traditional place at which Jews met to read the Scripture and pray. Archeologically, the oldest synagogue attested by an inscription is the one near Alexandria, Egypt, and dates from the reign of Ptolemy II (247-221 B.C.). For such an institution to have been formed abroad, it must already have existed in Israel itself. By New Testament times the synagogue was an established institution both in Palestine and throughout the Roman world—wherever Jews resided (Mark 1:21, 39; Luke 4:20, 28; 6:6; Acts 13:5; 14:1; 17:1; 18:4). The synagogue appears prominently in the ministry of both Christ and the apostles.

SYNTYCHE (sĭn'tĭ-chē) ("coincidence, success"). A woman believer at the church in Philippi who was exhorted by Paul to settle her differences with another woman believer, Euodia (Phil. 4:2).

SYRIA (sĭr'ĭ-à) See "Damascus."

SYRIANS. See "Arameans."

T

TABERNACLE AND TEMPLE. The Old Testament Tabernacle contains a vast array of biblical typology and appears prominently in New Testament interpretation (e.g., Heb. 9:1 – 10:39). The Tabernacle lasted almost 500 years, until it was replaced by Solomon's Temple. No typology of the Temple is expounded in the New Testament, but the figure of a temple is employed to symbolize the believer's body (1 Cor. 3:16, 17; 6:19). Both the local church (2 Cor. 6:16) and the entire mystical Church (Eph. 2:21) are also pictured as a temple.

A model of the Israelite tabernacle, prepared by Shick (© *MPS*)

Solomon's magnificent edifice endured for about 376 years, until it was destroyed by Nebuchadnezzar II in 486 B.C. Zerubbabel completed a temple in 515 B.C. It was replaced by Herod's magnificent edifice, which was destroyed by the Romans in A.D. 70, only a few years after its completion. In the end times the Jews will build a temple which will ultimately become occupied by the man of sin (2 Thess. 2:4). The millennial Temple (Ezek. 40 – 44) will be established by Christ himself and will be used for the duration of the kingdom age (Isa. 2:1-5). The unveiled presence of God will constitute the "temple of God" in the New Jerusalem of the eternal state (Rev. 21:3, 22).

TABERNACLE, FEAST OF. See "Booths, Feast of."

TABITHA (tăb′ĭ-thȧ). The Aramaic name for Dorcas. See "Dorcas."

TABOR (tā′bẽr). A rounded mountain rising from the Plain of Jezreel to 1,843 feet above sea level. Deborah summoned Barak and his army to assemble at Mount Tabor (Judg. 4:6). The view from its summit is breathtaking. A fourth-century tradition connects this mountain with the site of Christ's transfiguration. However, this identification is unlikely, since a town crowned the summit in New Testament times.

TAHPANHES (tä′păn-hēz). An important Egyptian settlement in the east Delta (Jer. 2:16; 44:1; 46:14; Ezek. 30:18). It is identified with present-day Tell Defneh, southeast of Tanis. Later the Greek trading settlement of Daphnae was established there. Jeremiah went to Tahpenhes with Jewish refugees (Jer. 43:7-13).

TAHPENES (tä′pē̇-nēz) (probably "the wife of the king"). An Egyptian queen, probably one of the rulers of the Twenty-first Dynasty at Tanis in the Delta

UNGER'S GUIDE

(during the Davidic-Solomonic era, 980-931 B.C.). During David's reign young Hadad of Edom had fled to Egypt. The reigning Pharaoh received him cordially and wedded him to the sister of the queen. After David's death Hadad returned to Edom and opposed Solomon (1 Kings 11:19, 20).

TALENT. See under "Weights and Measures."

TALMAI (tăl'mī) ("plowman" or possibly "big"). (1) A son of Anak who was ousted from Hebron by Caleb (Num. 13:22; Josh. 15:14; Judg. 1:10). (2) A king of the Aramean principality of Geshur. His daughter was one of David's wives and the mother of Absalom (2 Sam. 3:3; 13:37).

TAMAR (tā'mēr) ("date palm"). (1) Judah's daughter-in-law, the Canaanite wife of his eldest son, Er. After Er's death she remained a widow for a long time because Judah's second son, Onan, refused to marry her and his third son was withheld beyond the promised time (Gen. 38:1-23). In anger and impatience Tamar, disguised as a harlot, offered herself to Judah. As a result she bore him twins, Perez and Zerah (Gen. 38:24-30). She is recalled as the ancestress of the tribe of Judah in Ruth 4:12, 1 Chronicles 2:4, and Matthew 1:3. Tamar was a quick-witted widow who protected herself and her family rights under the Mosaic Law of Levirate marriage. She was not a promiscuous woman and was more righteous and honorable than Judah himself (Gen. 38:26). As the mother of Perez she became an ancestor of King David. (2) A daughter of King David by Maacah. She was Absalom's full sister. Tamar was raped and grossly insulted by Amnon, her half-brother (son of Ahinoam). Absalom took Tamar to his house, where she remained. When King David failed to punish his son for the despicable crime, Absalom took the matter into his own hands and had Amnon murdered (2 Sam. 13:1-39). This story is an awesome sequel to David's own sin (2 Sam. 11:1 – 12:23) and represents part of the divine chastisement upon the king himself. (3) A daughter of Absalom and a beautiful woman (2 Sam. 14:27). She was doubtless named after Absalom's sister,

who had been so shamefully treated by Amnon. Tamar apparently became the wife of Uriel and the mother of Maacah (King Rehoboam's wife – 2 Chron. 13:2).

TAMARISK. A small tree with minute, scale-like, evergreen leaves and striking pink flowers. It is considered a holy tree by Arabs. Three common species are found in desert areas of southern Palestine and Beersheba. Saul resided beneath a tamarisk in Ramah (1 Sam. 22:6, RSV) and the bones of Saul and his sons were interred beneath one in Jabesh-Gilead (1 Sam. 31:13).

TANIS. An Egyptian city on the Tanitic branch of the Nile (in the eastern part of the Delta). It was built seven years after Hebron and was thus in existence during Abraham's time (Num. 13:22). Certain kings of the Twelfth Egyptian Dynasty made Tanis their capital in order to repel invasions from the east. The Hyksos also used it as their capital, fortifying it and renaming it Avaris. Rameses II (1290-1224 B.C.) later named the city Raamses in his own honor. The modern site is San el-Hagar.

TANNING. Treating the skins of animals in order to obtain leather. Tanning was an important craft in Bible times. The common method was to remove the hairs by soaking in lime, then to treat the sundried skins with sumach pods, pine bark, oak bark, or leaves. The finest leathers were treated with mineral salts (usually alum) procured from the Dead Sea or imported from Egypt.

Leather used for many articles, including sandals and girdles (2 Kings 1:8; Matt. 3:4), containers for water or other liquids (Gen. 21:14; Matt. 9:17; Judg. 4:19), and numerous military items (2 Sam. 1:21; Isa. 21:5).

TAPHATH (tā'fäth) ("a drop"). A daughter of King Solomon. She became the wife of the son of Abinadab, one of the king's officials in charge of the region of Dor (1 Kings 4:11).

TARES (Greek *zizanion*). The bearded darnel (*Lolium temulentum*). It is a poisonous grass which is practically indistinguishable from wheat while both are in the blade. However, it is easily distinguished (though hard to separate) when they both come into ear (Matt. 13:25-30).

TARSUS. The capital of Cilicia and the home of the Apostle Paul (Acts 21:39; 22:3). The city lies on the Cydnus or Tarsus River and was prominent from Mycenean Times.

TAX COLLECTOR. The "publican" (Greek *telōnēs*) collected taxes or customs for the Roman Empire. As early as 212 B.C. such an order of publicans had existed and become active in a number of provinces. The system was vulnerable to abuse. Although the worst cases were apprehended and brought to justice, extortion and malpractice were characteristic of the *publicani* system from its inception.

The word *architelōnēs* in Luke 19:2 seems to suggest that Zacchaeus had contracted for the taxes of Jericho and supervised various collectors. If these were Jews, they were particularly despised (Matt. 5:46) and were classed with "sinners" because of their free association with Gentiles (Matt. 11:19; Luke 5:30; 15:1).

TEIL TREE. See "Terebinth."

TEKOA (tê-kō′à). A town six miles south of Bethlehem. Tekoa was near the Wilderness of Tekoa (2 Chron. 20:20) and was the home of the prophet Amos (Amos 1:1). The town was fortified by Rehoboam (2 Chron. 11:5, 6). Tekoa is present-day Tekua.

TEMA (tē′mà). A city in Arabia about 225 miles southeast of Petra (Job 6:19; Isa. 21:14).

TEMAN (tē′măn). A district inhabited by a tribe descended from Esau (Gen. 36:11). The territory was in Edom (Jer. 49:20), apparently in the northern part (Ezek. 25:13), where the inhabitants were noted for their wisdom (Jer. 49:7). Teman was on the King's Highway about five miles southeast of Petra (modern Tawilan).

TEMPLE. See "Tabernacle and Temple."

TEMPTATION OF CHRIST. Temptation is not sin, for Christ was tempted as we are but remained sinless (Heb. 4:15; Matt. 4:1-11). Because Christ was impeccable (incapable of sinning), his temptations can be likened to an attack on an impregnable fortress. Christ's victory over all temptations demonstrated his sinlessness (John 8:46; 14:30).

TEMPTATION OF GOD. Men tempt or test God when they challenge him to prove the truth of his words or the justice of his ways (Exod. 17:2-7; Num. 14:22; Psa. 78:18, 41, 56; 95:9; 106:14; Acts 15:10). The place name "Massah" was a memorial to such an instance of tempting God (Exod. 17:7; Deut. 6:16). The sin is sternly forbidden (Deut. 6:16; Matt. 4:7; 1 Cor. 10:9).

TEMPTATION OF MEN. Satan tests God's people within certain limits established by God himself (Job 1:12; 2:6; 1 Cor. 10:13). Satan is "the tempter" (Matt. 4:3; 1 Thess. 3:5) and a perpetual enemy of God's saints (1 Pet. 5:8). However, God overrules Satan's temptations for his own beneficent purposes (Matt. 4:1; 6:13). God also tests his people in order to reveal the condition of their hearts (Gen. 22:1; Exod. 16:4; 20:20; Deut. 8:2). Through trials he purifies them (Psa. 66:10; Isa. 48:10; Zech. 13:9; 1 Pet. 1:6, 7), matures them (James 1:2-12), and leads them into an enlarged assurance of his love (Gen. 22:15-18; Rom. 5:3-5). Men also test their fellow men in order to explore their capacities (1 Kings 10:1). Christ's opponents tempted him in order to test the validity of his Messiahship (Mark 8:11), examine his doctrines (Luke 10:25), and dissect his assertions (Mark 12:15).

Soldier touches stones considered part of the Temple in Jesus' day. *(Russ Busby photo)*

TEN LOST TRIBES. The idea of ten lost tribes which are "known only to God and later to be found by him" is a misconception of 2 Kings 17:7-23 (compare 2 Chronicles 6:6-11). The notion has given rise to serious errors which identify these alleged "lost tribes" with the Anglo-Saxon peoples, various gypsy groups, or certain people of Central Asia or Africa. Those "cast out" in the Northern Kingdom were excluded from the promise of restoration to the land (2 Kings 17:23). But this does not mean that only the tribes of Judah and Benjamin remained. From the division of the kingdom in 931 B.C. until the fall to Assyria in 722 B.C. multitudes of the ten tribes returned to the Davidic dynasty and the true worship of the Lord (1 Kings 12:16-20; 2 Chron. 11:16, 17; 2 Chron. 19:4; 20:1, 10, 11; 34: 5-7; etc.).

In God's view *all* the tribes were represented in the kingdom of Judah when it was taken to and repatriated from Babylon. Our Lord came to the entire nation (Matt. 10:5, 6) and was rejected by the entire nation. Tribes other than Judah are mentioned in the New Testament (Matt. 10:5, 6; Luke 2:36; Acts 4:36; 26: 7; Phil. 3:5; James 1:1).

Israel is still in age-long rejection, but she is being supernaturally preserved by God even though she does not acknowledge his divine care (Isa. 11:11-13; Hos. 3:4, 5; Rom. 11:1-12). Some of Israel has already returned to the land. A thorough spiritual restoration will eventually follow, and the ancient political rift will be healed (Ezek. 37:15-28). Then the kingdom will be established by the returning Messiah (Amos 9:13-15; Zech. 12:9-14; Rom. 11:25-27).

TERAH (tē'rå) (Akkadian *turahu,* "ibex"). The father of Abraham. He evidently worshiped Sin, the moon god (Josh. 24:2), who had temples at both Ur and Haran. Terah failed to renounce his idolatry and died in Haran (Gen. 11:25-32).

TERAPHIM (tĕr'å-phēm). Images of deities kept in homes for family protection (Gen. 31:19; 1 Sam. 19:13). The law against graven images (Exod. 20:1-6) forbade this pagan-influenced custom.

TEREBINTH (Hebrew *'ela,* A.V. "teil tree" Isa. 6:13 and "elm" Hos. 4:13). The tree referred to is now generally recognized as the Palestinian terebinth (*Pistacia terebinthus*) or turpentine tree.

TETRARCH. The Romans gave this title to the ruler of part of a province. It originally denoted the ruler of one-fourth (Greek *tetrarchos*) of a region, especially the four regions of Thessaly. When Herod the Great's will was contested by his sons after the death of the client king in 4 B.C., Caesar Augustus gave the title of tetrarch to two of them. Antipas was appointed tetrarch of Galilee and Perea, and Philip was appointed tetrarch of Gaulonitis, Batanea, and other areas northeast of the Sea of Galilee.

In the New Testament the term *tetrarch* is actually used only in reference to Herod Antipas (Matt. 14:1; Luke 3:19; 9:7; Acts 13:1). However, the cognate verb is applied to Antipas, Philip, and Lysanias (Luke 3:1).

THADDAEUS (thă-dē'ŭs). One of Christ's Twelve Apostles (Matt. 10:3; Mark 3:18). He was also called Lebbaeus and is sometimes identified with the Jude who wrote the Epistle of Jude.

THEBES (thēbz). See "No."

THEOCRATIC KINGDOM. When the times of the Gentiles have run their course, the mediatorial kingdom of God on earth will be restored to Israel (Acts 1: 6). This will take place when Messiah returns in power and glory to reign over the nations (Rev. 19:11 − 20:6; Mic. 4:1-8; Psa. 2:1-12). Christ's millennial rule will be a phase of the universal kingdom of God (1 Cor. 15:24). The theocratic kingdom was established at Sinai, with the Shekinah glory (the visible symbol of God's presence) as the divine Ruler (Exod. 40:34-38). The glory also entered and filled Solomon's Temple (2 Chron. 7:1, 2). The Shekinah departed from Jerusalem when the kingdom collapsed at the Babylonian captivity (Ezek. 11:23).

THEOPHANY. Any preincarnate appearance of God the Son. The form was angelic or human (Gen. 12:7; 18:1, 2), manifested glory (Isa. 6:1-4; Ezek. 1:4-28), or unspecified (Gen. 17:1).

THEOPHILUS (thē-ŏf'ĭ-lŭs) ("loved by God"). The Christian of position and prominence to whom Luke addressed both his Gospel (Luke 1:3) and the Acts (1:1).

THESSALONICA (thĕs'å-lō-nī'kà). The capital of one of the Macedonian districts during the Roman period. The city was originally called Thermae ("Hot

Springs") but was renamed Salonica or Thessalonica in honor of the wife of Cassander of Macedon. Thessalonica was a free city from 42 B.C. onward. Paul had an effective ministry there (Acts 17:1-13; Phil. 4:16; 1 Thess. 1:1; 2 Thess. 1:1).

THEUDAS (thū'dȧs). (1) A Jewish insurrectionist before A.D. 6 (cf. Acts 5:36). His precise identity is a historical puzzle. (2) A magician who led many followers to the Jordan River with the promise that the river would be divided at his command. The Roman procurator Fadus (A.D. 44-46) dispersed the crowd and beheaded Theudas.

THISTLE. Numerous thistles with flowerets of various colors are found in Bible lands. The milk thistle, the star thistle, the cocklebur, and the teasel are only a few. Thorny weeds and bushes of various kinds also abound. The thorny burnet, the thorny caper, the prickly pear, and the acanthus are common. The box thorn and the bramble are used for hedges. Various hawthorns flourish. In most passages where thistles and thorns are alluded to, the terms are generic rather than specific.

THOMAS ("twin"). One of the Twelve Apostles of Christ. He was also called Didymus (Greek "twin"). He earned the title of "Doubting Thomas" because of his hesitance in accepting the witness of Christ's resurrection (John 20:19-29). Yet he had previously been willing to go with Jesus to Lazarus' tomb at the risk of death at the hands of the Jews (John 11:16). Thomas' great confession of faith (John 20:28) is a highwater mark in the Gospel of John.

THORN. See "Thistle."

THRACE (thrās). The non-Greek "barbarian" country north of the Aegean Sea. It was overrun by the Persians and became part of the Persian Empire. It did not become a Roman Province until the time of Vespasian (A.D. 69-70).

THRONE. Various thrones are named in Scripture. The throne of God represents the seat of God's universal government (Isa. 2:2; Matt. 5:34; Acts 7:49; Heb. 8:1; Rev. 4:2; 3:21). The throne of David is the earthly seat of power which Christ will occupy as a "throne of glory" (Matt. 19:28; 25:31; Psa. 2:6; 2 Sam. 7:16; Psa.

89:36; Luke 1:32). The great white throne (Rev. 20:11, 12) is the site at which God will judge the wicked before the eternal state. The throne of Satan (Matt. 12:26; Col. 1:16; Rev. 2:13) represents the earthly power which Satan exercises. The throne of the Twelve Apostles represents their sphere of kingdom authority (Luke 22:30). The throne of grace is the immediate presence of God's power available to the petitioning saint in this age (Heb. 4:16). The throne of the church is represented by the session of the 24 elders in heaven (Rev. 4:4).

THUTMOSE III. The most powerful of the Egyptian pharaohs (1500-1450 B.C.). He was probably the oppressor of the enslaved Israelites. In fifteen campaigns he conquered Syria-Palestine and most of Western Asia. With his spoils he built great temples at Karnak.

THYATIRA (thī-à-tī'rà). A Greek city of proconsular Asia (Acts 16:14). It was one of the seven churches addressed in the Revelation (Rev. 2:18-29).

THYINE WOOD (Greek *thyinos*). This is thought to be wood from the sanderac-tree (*Tetraclinis articulata*), a small, coniferous tree native to North Africa. The wood is handsome, dark, and fragrant. It was used extensively in the Greco-Roman world for cabinetmaking. Some scholars have identified thyine with the wood of the almug-tree.

The city of Tiberias clings to the western shore of the Sea of Galilee. (© *MPS*)

TIBERIAS (tī-bēr'ĭ-ŭs). A town constructed by Herod Antipas, tetrarch of Galilee. It was named in honor of then-reigning

Emperor Tiberius (John 6:1, 23; 21:1). The present site is Tabariyeh, about 12 miles from the point at which the Jordan River enters the Lake of Galilee.

TIBERIUS CAESAR. The Roman Emperor from A.D. 14 to 37. This period spanned the ministry and crucifixion of Christ. One of the last actions of this elderly stepson of Augustus was to recall Pontius Pilate from Judea. In his later career Tiberius was under the influence of the villanous schemer Sejanus until the latter's execution.

TIGLATHPILESER (tǐg'lȧth-pǐ-lē'zẽr) ("my trust is in the son of Esharra," i.e. the god Ninib). The king of Assyria from 745 to 727 B.C. He was also called Pul or Pulu (2 Kings 15:19-29; 16:7, 10; 1 Chron. 5:6, 26; 2 Chron. 28:20). He was a great warrior and conqueror and acted as God's scourge to punish the sinning Northern Kingdom.

TIGRIS (tī'grǐs). One of the four streams associated with the Garden of Eden. It is also called the Hiddekel (Gen. 2:14). With the Euphrates, it formed the two great rivers of Mesopotamia in antiquity. From its source in the Mountains of Armenia the Tigris runs 1,146 miles to become a tributary of the Euphrates 40 miles from the Persian Gulf. However, in antiquity the Tigris emptied separately into the Persian Gulf, which extended much farther inland. Centuries of silting have extended the coastline of lower Babylonia out to sea. Nineveh, Assur, and Calah were among the ancient cities located on the Tigris River.

TIME. See under "Calendar, Hebrew."

TIMES OF THE GENTILES. The period during which non-Jews dominate God's chosen people. The period extends from the time of Nebuchadnezzar (605 B.C.) to the advent of Christ and his establishment of the kingdom (Luke 21:24; Dan. 2:34, 35, 44).

TIMNA (tǐm'nȧ). A woman listed as the concubine of Eliphaz the son of Esau in order to show the close relationship between Edomites and Horites (Hurrians). Timna was the sister of Lotan, one of the native Horite inhabitants of Edom (Gen. 36:22; 1 Chron. 1:39).

TIMNAH (tǐm'nȧ). A town near Philistia on the border of Judah (Josh. 15:10; 19: 43; Judg. 14:1, 5; 2 Chron. 28:18). It is identified with present-day Tell el-Batashi, about five miles south of Gezer. (2) A town in the hill country of Judah (Josh. 15:57; Gen. 38:12-14. It is present-day Tibnah, about fourteen miles southeast of Jerusalem.

TIMNATH-SERAH (tǐm'nȧth-sē'rȧ). Joshua's place of burial in the hill country of Ephraim (Josh. 24:29, 30). It is identified with present-day Khirbet Tibneh, about thirteen miles southwest of Shiloh.

TIMOTHY (tǐm'ō-thē) ("honored by God"). A young believer of Lystra who became Paul's companion and son in the faith (Acts 16:1). Paul addressed 1 and 2 Timothy to this young pastor. His name is joined with the Apostle's in a number of Paul's Epistles. Timothy was sent to various churches as a special pastor.

TIRZAH (tûr'zȧ) ("pleasantness"). (1) The youngest of Zelophehad's five daughters (Num. 26:33; 27:1; Josh. 17:3). (2) A Canaanite city whose king was defeated by Joshua (Josh. 12:24). It was the capital of the Northern Kingdom until Omri moved the seat of government to Samaria (1 Kings 15:21, 33; 16:6, 8, 15, 23; 2 Kings 15:14-16). It is identified with present-day Tell Far͏ᶜah, about seven miles northeast of Nablus.

TISHBE (tǐsh'bè). The home of Elijah "the Tishbite" (1 Kings 17:1). Tishbe was located just north of the Brook Cherith and about eight miles east of the Jordan River. It is identified with present-day Lisdib.

TITHING. The ancient custom (Gen. 14: 17-20) of giving a tenth of one's income to God. Under the Mosaic Law tithing was the primary means of supporting the Levitical priesthood (Lev. 27:30-33; Num. 18:21-26; Deut. 14:22-29). Under grace, giving is to be performed spontaneously — not out of necessity or legal pressure (2 Cor. 9:7). Giving is to be proportionate to God's blessing (1 Cor. 16:2). Grace giving ought to exceed the tithe rather than to justify dodging it or coming short of it.

TITUS (tī'tŭs). (1) The Roman Emperor from A.D. 79 to 81. He succeeded his father, Vespasian. When Vespasian was proclaimed Emperor he left Titus in Palestine to complete the task of crushing the Jewish revolt. Titus captured Jerusalem and destroyed the Temple, although it is said that he tried to restrain his troops from the Temple destruction. (2) A companion of Paul and a faithful pastor in Crete (Gal. 2:3; Tit. 1:4). The Epistle of Titus was written to him, probably after Paul's release from his first imprisonment.

TOB (tŏb). A city and district in South Hauran (Judg. 11:3-5). The town is apparently preserved in present-day et-Taiyibeh, between Bozrah and Edrei (near the sources of the Yarmuk River). Tob was an Aramean city (2 Sam. 10:6-13).

TOBIAH (tô-bī'à) ("the Lord is good"). An Ammonite who opposed the rebuilding of the walls of Jerusalem by Nehemiah (Neh. 2:10; 4:3, 7).

TONGUES. A supernatural sign to Jews in the Book of Acts. At Pentecost (Acts 2:1-8) it was a sign to the Jews (together with the wind and the fire) of a change from the Mosaic economy to the age of the church and grace. At Caesarea (Acts 10:46) supernatural languages were a sign to Peter and the Jews with him that the Gentiles had received identically the same gift of the Spirit as the Jews at Pentecost (Acts 11:17). At Ephesus (Acts 19:6) the sign of tongues demonstrated to the Jews that, no matter what their religious activity or fidelity to Old Testament religious ceremonies or beliefs might be, salvation was now possible only on the ground of faith in Christ's atoning sacrifice ministered to them by the outpoured Spirit.

In the early church (1 Cor. 12:7-11) tongues were a gift or sovereign bestowment of the Spirit. Along with the gift came extrabiblical prophecies and knowledge directly from God himself. These temporary provisions met the need for teaching in the primitive assembly (1 Cor. 13:8). After the New Testament Scriptures were written, they provided the *permanent* instruction in righteousness for the churches. Chapter 14 of 2 Corinthians regulates the gifts of tongues and direct inspirational prophecy and knowledge in the primitive assembly.

TOPHET (tō'fĕt). The name for the high place in the Valley of Hinnom (south of Jerusalem) where human sacrifices and other idolatrous abominations were practiced (2 Chron. 33:6; Jer. 7:31). King Josiah defiled the place (2 Kings 23:10). As a result of its idolatrous connections and its defilement (perhaps as the site of the city dump), the names for the valley (Hebrew *Ge-Hinnon*, Greek *Gehenna*) came to symbolize sin and its eternal punishment (Matt. 5:22; 10:28; Mark 9:43, 45, 47; Luke 12:5; James 3:6). Theologically, Gehenna is identical with the lake of fire (Rev. 19:20; 20:10-15) and the second death (John 8:24; Rev. 21:8).

TOWN CLERK. The *grammateus* (Acts 19:35) was customarily the secretary of a board of magistrates. His duty was to make an accurate record of official decisions. In the large and influential city of Ephesus he was evidently the president of the assembly. As such he was the principal municipal officer, the executive responsible for such situations as the riot over Paul (Acts 19:21-41). His important position is attested by coins and inscriptions from Ephesus and by the fact that his administration dated the year.

TRACHONITIS (trăk-ȯ-nī'tĭs). The Greek designation of the rugged country north of the Hauran. Herod the Great subdued its turbulent tribes and added the country to the Tetrarchy of Philip (Luke 3:1).

TRANSFIGURATION. A portrayal in miniature of Christ's second advent in glory (Matt. 17:1-9). All the elements of this great coming event were present: (1) Christ was seen as the glorified Son of man. (2) Moses appeared in glorified form, representing the redeemed who have entered the kingdom through death. (3) Elijah, likewise glorified, represented the redeemed who have entered the kingdom by translation (1 Thess. 4:14-17). (4) Peter, James, and John were seen unglorified, representing the Jewish remnant who will then enter the kingdom in unglorified bodies. (5) The multitude at the foot of the mountain (Matt. 17:14-21) represented the nations who will be ushered into the blessings of the kingdom after its restoration to Israel (Acts 1:6; Isa. 11:10-12).

TRIBULATION. The Greek word for tribulation, *thlipsis*, may denote (1) a trial of any kind or (2) the Great Tribulation. The latter usage refers to the seventieth week of Daniel (Dan. 9:24-27), the period of worldwide trouble and anguish following the rapture of the church (2 Thess. 2: 1-7). Then the mystery of iniquity will unfold and the Antichrist, the Man of Sin, will be manifested (2 Thess. 2:8-12; cf. John 5:43). This period represents the time of God's judgments on a Christ-rejecting world (Psa. 2:5). The period will witness the casting of Satan into the earth and his restriction to this sphere (Rev. 12:9-12). He will be joined by myriads of wicked demons now confined in the abyss (Rev. 9:1-20).

The awful suffering and bloodshed of the Tribulation will be climaxed by the battle of Armageddon (Rev. 16:13-16). Christ will return in glory to slay his enemies, destroy the Satanic world system (Rev. 19:11–20:3), and inaugurate his kingdom reign (Rev. 20:4-10). The Tribulation period is foretold in detail by both the major and minor prophets of the Old Testament (e.g., Jer. 30:5-7; Zech. 12:1–14:3).

TROAS (trō'ăz). A seaport of Mysia in northwest Asia Minor. Troas lies on the Aegean Sea about ten miles south of ancient Troy. It was an important city in New Testament times. It was here that the Apostle Paul experienced the missionary vision which called him to Europe (Acts 16:8-10; 2 Cor. 2:12). Paul stayed at Troas briefly on his third tour (Acts 20:6; cf. 2 Tim. 4:13).

TROPHIMUS (trŏf'ĭ-mŭs) ("nourishing"). A Gentile believer at Ephesus who accompanied Paul to Jerusalem. The Apostle was falsely accused of having brought Trophimus into the Temple in violation of the Mosaic Law (Acts 20:4; 21:29). Trophimus later became ill at Miletum (2 Tim. 4:20).

TRUMPETS, FEAST OF. A feast known as the "day of blowing the trumpets" (Num. 29:1) or the "memorial of blowing of trumpets" (Lev. 23:24). Held on the first day of the civil year, this feast prefigures the future regathering of Israel.

TRYPHENA (trī-fē'nà) ("dainty"). A Christian worker in the early church at Rome. Paul sent greetings to her and commended her for faithful service to God (Rom. 16:12).

TRYPHOSA (trī-fō'sà) ("delicate"). A woman linked with Tryphena as a worker in the Lord (Rom. 16:12). Possibly they were sisters or even twins, since their names are derived from the same Greek root. Both names also occur in extrabiblical literature.

TYRANNUS (tī-răn'ŭs) ("an absolute sovereign, a tyrant"). An Ephesian teacher of philosophy or rhetoric. Paul discussed Christianity in Tyrannus' school when he no longer had access to the synagogue (Acts 19:9).

TWO WITNESSES. Evidently two Jewish witnesses of the latter-day remnant who are endued with power to perform miracles like Moses and Elijah (Rev. 11: 3-13). They command drought (cf. 1 Kings 17:1), turn water to blood (cf. Exod. 7:19), and perform other signs (cf. Exod. 7–10). Their message stresses Christ's lordship over the earth and his imminent kingly reign.

After the two witnesses have completed their testimony, they are killed by the Beast (the head of the revived Roman Empire—Rev. 13:1-10; 17:8), who ascends out of the abyss. Their bodies, however, are resurrected and translated to heaven and their enemies are punished (Rev. 11:11-13).

TYCHICUS (tĭk'ĭ-kŭs) ("fortuitous"). A missionary companion of Paul (Acts 20: 4). He carried several Pauline Epistles to their recipients (Eph. 6:21; Col. 4:7). Paul proposed to send him as a messenger to Titus in Crete (Tit. 3:12). Later he was sent to Ephesus (2 Tim. 4:12).

TYPE. An illustration of truth woven into the fabric of Scripture. Most types occur in the Old Testament and prefigure various aspects of the life, death, and resurrection of Christ. Types form an important unifying bond between the Old and New Testaments and constitute an important evidence for the divine inspiration of Scripture. Some biblical personages who typify Christ include Adam (by contrast as well as parallelism), Melchizedek, Isaac, Moses, Aaron, Joshua, David, Solomon, and Jonah. All Old Testament sacrifices offered in obedience to God typify some aspect of the person or work of Christ. The tabernacle with all its rich symbolism also pointed dramatically to the promised Savior. Christ has totally fulfilled the Old Testament types in his life, death, resurrection, and ascension. Now the spiritual realities prevail.

TYRE (tĭr). An ancient Phoenician city and fortress situated on an island. Tyre was close to the Palestinian coast and about 25 miles south of Sidon (Josh. 19: 29). Alexander the Great captured the insular city in 333 B.C. by constructing a causeway from the mainland to the island. Hiram of Solomon's time built a breakwater that made the harbor one of the best on the entire coast. Tyre was still important in New Testament times (Matt. 15:21; Mark 7:31; Acts 12:20; 21: 3). The "Ladder of Tyre" was a pass through the mountains to the Plain of Phoenicia.

ULAI (ū'lī). A river east of Susa in southwest Persia (Dan. 8:2). It is Assyrian Ulai and classical Eulaeus. The river has changed its course in modern times. The present Upper Kherkhah and Lower Karun rivers were apparently once a single stream which flowed into the delta at the north of the Persian Gulf.

UNICORN. "See "Aurochs."

UR (ûr). The city in South Iraq (ancient Sumer) which Terah and Abraham left in order to go to Haran (Gen. 11:28, 31; 15: 7). Ur is identified with modern Tell el-Muqayyar, near Eridu. The site has yielded a rich store of objects from Sumerian royal tombs and a famous ziggurat or temple tower.

URARTU (ōō-rär'tōō). See "Ararat."

URIAH (ū-rī'à) ("the Lord is light"). The Hittite husband of Bathsheba and one of David's generals. He was sent to his death by David in order to conceal David's sin of adultery (2 Sam. 11:1-25).

URUK (ōō'rōōk). See "Erech."

UZAL (ū'zăl). An Arabian trading center located on the incense route through Sheba (in southeast Arabia). Uzal was connected with other similar trading centers, such as Muza, Eden, Timna, Marib, Shabwa, and Canneh in Sheba and Hazarmaveth in the southern extremity of the Arabian Peninsula.

UZZAH (ŭz'à) ("the Lord is strength"). A man of an unknown tribe who was struck dead for touching the Ark in violation of the Law (2 Sam. 6:2-7).

UZZIAH (ŭ-zī'à) ("the Lord is strength"). The king of Judah from 767 to 739 B.C. Uzziah (also called Azariah) brought Judah to the height of power and prosperity (2 Chron. 26:1-15). However, he intruded into the priests' office and was stricken with leprosy (2 Chron. 26:16-23).

VALLEYS OF SCRIPTURE. The primary valley of Palestine is the Rift Valley or the *Arabah*. The Jordan River descends rapidly through this valley. The narrow flood plain (the Zor) is covered with dense thickets of tamarisk and thorn scrub. The Zor is separated by the higher Rift Valley floor, called the Ghor, by badlands of grey saline marl. The northern (Syrian) part of the Rift Valley contains the Orontes and Leontes Rivers in the plain between the Lebanon and Anti-Lebanon Mountains. The southern part of the Rift Valley consists of the Dead Sea, 1,285 feet below sea level, and that portion of the Arabah that extends to the Gulf of Aqaba. Other significant valleys of Scripture are described briefly below.

Achor. A valley in northeast Judah where Achan was put to death (Josh. 7:24-26). It is the first place name on the copper scroll from Qumran. It is about four miles in length and is centered on the Wadi Qumran, northeast of the Dead Sea and ten miles south of Jericho.

Baca. A narrow valley mentioned in Psalm 84:6. Its name means "valley of the balsam tree." Baca poetically symbolizes a waterless place of testing and trial.

Decision, Valley of. A symbolic name given to a valley outside Jerusalem. It is apparently the same as the Valley of Jehoshaphat (Joel 3:2, 12, 14), where the judgment of the nations takes place.

Eshcol. The valley or wadi a few miles north of Hebron. There the scouts who had been sent out by Moses gathered a huge cluster (Hebrew *eshkol*) of grapes (Num. 13:23, 24).

Gibeon, Valley of. A narrow stretch of level terrain between the hills near the city of Gibeon. The valley is about six miles north of Jerusalem and is the site at which Joshua's army mustered for a great victory over the Amorite kings (Josh. 10: 1-15).

Hebron, Valley of. The region from which Jacob sent the lad Joseph to visit his brothers in Shechem (Gen. 37:14). The city of Hebron is situated partly in a valley and partly on a slope about 3000 feet above sea level. Hebron lies about 19 miles south-southwest of Jerusalem in a well-watered area of vineyards and olive groves.

Hinnom. A narrow valley to the south of Jerusalem. It is also called "the valley of the sons of Hinnom." Hinnom is identified with the Wadi er-Rababeh, which encircles the city on the west and meets the Kidron Valley on the southeast (Josh. 15:8; 18:16). It was defiled by gross idolatry (2 Chron. 33:6) and later became a burning ground for garbage and dead bodies (2 Kings 23:10). The name *Gehinnom* became shortened to *Gehenna*, which eventually came to symbolize the eternal fires of hell (Matt. 5:22; 18:9).

Jehoshaphat, Valley of. The designation which the prophet Joel gives to the place where Christ will judge the nations before his glorious return (Joel 3:2, 12). The name means "the Lord judges" and is apparently used symbolically rather than topographically. However, the great end-time earthquake will change the topography of the land to make the Kidron "a very great valley" (Zech. 14:4) and a suitable theater for judgment. See also "Decision, Valley of."

Jezreel, Valley of. The southeastern part of the plain of Esdraelon (the Greek form of Jezreel). The Vale of Jezreel proper is the valley that slopes down from the city of Jezreel to Bethshan, the fortress town commanding the Jordan Rift Valley. The Hill of Moreh lies to the north and Mount Gilead to the south. Esdraelon is the triangular, alluvial plain guarded on the east by Bethshan. At the northwest, on the slopes of the Carmel spur, the towns of Megiddo, Joknean, Taanach, and Ibleam controlled the main mountain passes and the north-south routes through West Palestine. These towns, together with Jezreel and Bethshan, also controlled the vital road running east and west from the Jordan Valley (the only route not blocked by ranges of hills).

Jordan. The "Vale of Siddim," the circular area of land at the southern end of the Dead Sea. Before the destruction of Sodom and Gomorrah the Jordan Valley was luxuriant in vegetation (Gen. 13:10). Since this cataclysm the region has been covered by the Dead Sea.

Kidron. A small valley through which the Brook Kidron flowed. Christ and his disciples crossed Kidron to get to the Garden of Gethsemane (John 18:1). On the west side of the Kidron is the Gihon or "Virgin's Fountain," a spring whose waters were diverted into a reservoir to supply the needs of Jerusalem.

Lebanon, Valley of. The plain between the two parallel ranges of mountains that extend northward parallel with the coast of Phoenicia. The coastal range is Lebanon and the inland range is Anti-Lebanon. The valley was called the *Biqaᶜ*, the Hebrew word for a wide valley between mountain ranges.

Rephaim. A valley which extends southwest from Jerusalem in the general direction of Bethlehem (Josh. 15:8; 18:16; 2 Sam. 23:13, 14). Rephaim was quite fertile and was presumably once inhabited by the Rephaim, a people of large stature.

Shittim, Valley of. The camping place of the Israelites before the invasion of Canaan (Num. 25:1; Josh. 2:1; 3:1). It is probably to be identified with Tell Kefren, an eight-by-fifteen-mile area east of the Jordan River on the plains of Moab opposite Jericho. Joel mentions "the valley of Shittim" ("the vale of acacia trees"). Some scholars identify the area with the Kidron ravine or the Wadi es-Sant (Joel 3:18).

VASHTI (vāsh'tĭ) (possibly Persian *vashti*, "one who is desired"). The wife of King Ahasuerus (Xerxes I, 486-465 B.C.), according to the Book of Esther (1:9-22). On the seventh day of a great banquet King Ahasuerus sent for Queen Vashti to parade her beauty before his guests. When Vashti refused to appear, the king banished her and proclaimed throughout his realm that every man should be lord in his own house (Esth. 1:22). Vashti's deposal occasioned a search for other beautiful maidens and the eventual selection of Esther as the new queen.

VEIL (*ṣaᶜiph*). Some kind of covering (probably a shawl or scarf) which Rebekah put on when she approached Isaac prior to their marriage (Gen. 24:65). It seems that the veil identified a marriageable maiden and that it was removed at the marriage ceremony. Such a veil was used by Tamar to trick Judah (Gen. 38:14-19).

The mantle (*redid*) worn by the women of Jerusalem (Isa. 3:23) and the young women in Canticles (Song 5:7) was apparently a summer dress (Septuagint *theristron*), like the stoles worn by women in modern times. The mask with which Moses covered his face (Exod. 34:33-35) is termed a "veil" or "hood" (*kalumma*) in 2 Corinthians 3:13-16.

The veils worn by Muslim women in the East today have little parallel in the Bible. They are largely the offshoot of Mohammed's teachings concerning the status of women.

VEIL OF THE TABERNACLE. The curtain of blue, purple, and scarlet that separated the Holy Place from the Most Holy Place (Exod. 26:31) in the Old Testament Tabernacle. The veil symbolized Christ's human body (Heb. 10:20), showing that only through Christ's vicarious death could fallen man be justified (Rom.

3:24; 5:1, 2, 9-11). When Christ died on the Cross the veil was torn down the middle supernaturally (Matt. 27:51), thereby providing unhampered access to the Holy of Holies in the Temple. Now faith in Christ gives instant approach to God, showing that "by the deeds of the law shall no flesh be justified in God's sight" (Rom. 3:20).

VESPASIAN (vĕ-spā'zhē-ən). The Roman emperor from A.D. 70 to 79. He was called by Nero to put down the Jewish Revolt in Palestine. In the midst of his task, which he carried out with grim relentlessness, he was called to Rome to become Emperor. His son, Titus, finished the war in Judea.

VINE. The word usually designates the common grapevine (*Vitis vinifera*). In Bible times Palestine was a land of vineyards and olive orchards. Prophets like Isaiah (5:1-7), poets like Asaph (Psa. 80:8-19), and Christ himself (John 15:1-8) often used the figure of the vine to teach spiritual truths. See also "Grapes."

Muscle power turned these stones into a productive winepress. (*Russ Busby photo*)

VINEDRESSER. Keeping vineyards and oliveyards was a major phase of agriculture in Palestine. Sitting under one's vine and fig tree was a figure of contentment and of security against enemy invasion (1 Kings 4:25). In preparing a vineyard a good site had to be chosen (Isa. 5:1) and the soil had to be prepared. The stones taken out of the soil were used as a wall to keep out larger animals. (Isa. 5:2, 5). A hedge of prickly thorn was also planted to keep out smaller animals (Isa. 5:5). A tower or house for the householder was erected, where a watch was maintained throughout the vintage period (Isa. 1:8; 5:2). The vines were chosen for fine quality and were arranged in rows about eight feet apart for easy cultivation. Pruning was done in the spring (Lev. 25:3; John 15:2). After the grapes were picked, they were carried to nearby winepresses, where the juice was trampled out by foot (Amos 9:13). The juice was stored in new, expandable goatskin bags (Matt. 9:17) or in large pottery or stone containers. Appropriate time was then provided for the juice to ferment adequately. Large quantities of grapes were also dried and molded into raisin cakes (1 Sam. 25:18).

VIPER (Hebrew '*eph*ᶜ*eh*). A poisonous snake which was common in the Negeb (Isa. 30:6; 59:5). Job refers to its deadly nature (Job 20:16). This or a closely related poisonous reptile (Greek *echidna*) attacked the Apostle Paul's hand while he was on the Island of Melita (Acts 28:3). The *echidna* was well known to the Jews (Matt. 3:7). It was probably the common viper (*Vipera communis* or *Pelias berus*), common on the Mediterranean coast.

VIRGIN BIRTH. The virgin birth of Christ is a necessary link in the whole golden chain of marvels that cluster around the person and work of our Lord Jesus Christ. To deny the fundamental fact of Christ's sinless conception is to invalidate all the other glorious realities of his unique career. His virgin birth is implicit in the first redemption prophecy, which specifies the Seed of the *woman* (Gen. 3:15). Isaiah clearly foretold Christ's virgin birth in the great messianic sign of Isaiah 7:14. This involved the miracle of the virgin birth because it was *divinely* given — "the Lord himself" gave it. It was given to the Davidic house — "to *you*" (plural) — not merely to Ahaz. It involved a stupendous miracle — "deep as Sheol" and "high as heaven."

The child's name, Immanuel, means "*with us*" (humanity) "*is God*" (deity), thereby declaring Christ's incarnation. *All* references to Christ in the New Testament presuppose him to be God incarnate, possessing a sinless human body generated in the womb of the virgin Mary by the Holy Spirit (Luke 1:35).

VOW. A specific dedication of oneself or one's possessions to the Lord. Vows were common in the Old Testament era (1 Sam. 1:11, 21; 2 Sam. 15:7, 8; Job 22:27; Psa. 65:1; etc.). Usually the vow was in the nature of a pious bargain, with the person making the vow expecting some specific deliverance or favor from God (Gen. 28:20-22; Judg. 11:30, 31). Vows were common under the Mosaic Law (Lev. 7:16; 22:18, 21, 23; 27:2-29; Num. 15:3). They were not to be made lightly (Prov. 20:25; Eccl. 5:4, 5). Vows were totally voluntary (Deut. 12:6), but once made they were to be conscientiously fulfilled (Deut. 23:21-23).

The Apostle Paul made at least one vow (Acts 18:18). He also assumed liability for a vow which four of his associates had taken (Acts 21:23-26). Paul's enemies also made a conspiracy under oath (similar to a vow) with the intent of killing the Apostle (Acts 23:12-14).

WADI. See "Rivers and Streams."

WAISTCLOTH. A garment which reached from the waist to the knee. It was a common item of dress in the Near Eastern world before the Israelite period. It disappeared as civilian attire during the latter part of the Bronze Age and survived only as a military garment (Isa. 5:27). Other primitve garments included animal skins and hairy cloaks or mantles. These were sometimes worn by poor people (Ecclesiasticus 40:4), as a badge of other-worldliness (2 Kings 1:8; Matt. 3:4), or as a symbol of grief (Gen. 37:24; Jonah 3:6).

Breeches or pants covering the hips and thighs were required for Hebrew priests (Exod. 28:42; 39:28), but were otherwise unknown in antiquity except among the Persians. The *paṭish* ("hosen") of Daniel 3:21 may have been breeches or pants, but the meaning of the word is uncertain.

WALK. A very common metaphor in both the Old Testament (Psa. 1:1) and the New Testament (Rom. 6:4; Eph. 4:1).

Since walking is performed a step at a time, it furnishes a very apt illustration of living moment by moment (Col. 1:10; 1 Thess. 4:12).

WASHINGS. Old Testament washings typify both regeneration and daily cleansing of the redeemed (from day-to-day defilements). The washing of Aaron and his sons (Exod. 29:4) symbolizes regeneration (Tit. 3:5). The washing at the laver, on the other hand, signifies daily cleansing (Exod. 30:18, 21; cf. 1 John 1:9). Both appear in John 13:10.

WATCHMAN. Watchmen in Bible lands were of two types—those who guarded vineyards against thieves or marauding animals and those who manned watchtowers on city walls to warn of human enemies. Such watchtowers have been unearthed at Tell Beit Mirsim and Tell en-Nasbeh. Herod the Great erected three massive defense towers in Jerusalem, called Hippicus, Phasael, and Mariamne. Watchmen were sometimes also stationed on city walls (2 Sam. 18:24-27).

Watchtowers were erected in pastures or vineyards from earliest times (Gen. 35:21). Sometimes the structures were used as living quarters during the harvest season.

WATER. See "Springs, Wells, and Pools."

WEAPON. Both offensive and defensive armor and weapons of war are summarized in the Hebrew term *kēlim* (Gen. 27:3; 1 Sam. 17:54) and the Greek term *hopla* (2 Cor. 10:4). The Hebrew term *nesheq*, "weapons," is also sometimes employed (2 Kings 10:2).

WEASEL (Hebrew *ḥōlēd*). An unclean quadruped (Lev. 11:29) found in Palestine. The weasel is a flesh-eating mammal with short legs and a long, bushy tail.

WEAVER. Weaving provided work for both men and women (Exod. 35: 35; 2 Kings 23:7). The hangings of the Tabernacle in linen and goats' hair were produced by a weaver (Exod. 26:1, 7), as were the priestly robes (Exod. 39:1) and our Lord's seamless garment (John 19:23). Guilds of weavers were formed (1 Chron 4:21). Egyptian and Babylonian weavers possessed great skill (Josh. 7:21; Isa. 19:9).

Spinning was known before weaving and consists of the production of yarn from short fibers by the use of a spindle. Weaving, on the other hand, involves two series of threads. The longitudinal thread is called the warp and the transverse one is labeled the woof. The weaving of the two sets of threads is accomplished on a loom. Weaving was such a common feature of everyday life that numerous figures of speech were derived from it (1 Sam. 17:7; 2 Sam. 21:19; Job 7:6). Yarn was produced in linen and wool (Lev. 13:47), in byssus or fine Egyptian linen (Prov. 31:22), and in goats' hair or camel's hair (Exod. 35:26; Matt. 3:4).

WEEKS, FEAST OF. The Jewish Feast of the Harvest, celebrated seven weeks after the sickle was put to the grain (Deut. 16:9, 10). The one-day event, also called Pentecost, is observed on the fiftieth day after the offering of the sheaf of grain during the Passover celebration.

WEIGHTS AND MEASURES.

Early Standards of Weight. Everyday transactions between people demanded some system of weighing things. In early times almost any object could be employed as a standard. Stones and pieces of metal soon became popular weights. These were frequently carved into shapes of various animals and other configurations. Many of these weights have been recovered from excavated sites. Weights were commonly carried in a bag (Deut. 25:13; Prov. 16:11; Mic. 6:11). This enabled a buyer to compare his own weights with those at the place of purchase. Tomb paintings show that balances equipped with plummets were used in Egypt and elsewhere before Israelite times.

Common Old Testament Weights. The Hebrew weights closely followed the Babylonian, consisting principally of the shekel, the mina, and the talent. In earlier times the proportion was 60 shekels to a mina and 60 minas to a talent. Later the proportion of 50 shekels to a mina was adopted. The shekel was also divided into the half-shekel, the quarter-shekel, and the twentieth-shekel.

However, under the Babylonian system there were two standards, the Royal and the Popular, with the former being somewhat heavier. Each of these was in turn divided into a heavy and a light form, the latter being half the weight of the former. The following tables of Babylonian and Israelite weights are derived from recovered artifacts and provide approximate conversions to modern measures.

For convenience the Israelite shekel may be considered about the same weight as an American half-dollar, the mina about one and one-fourth pounds in weight, and the talent about 75 pounds. The discovery of the pim (equal to two-thirds of a shekel) has clarified a once-obscure biblical passage (1 Sam. 13:19-21).

The beka (Gen. 24:22) is defined in Scripture as a half-shekel (Exod. 38:26). This is substantially confirmed by archeological findings. The gerah is one-twentieth of a shekel (Exod. 30:13; Lev. 27:25). A "third of a shekel" is referred to in 1 Samuel 13:21.

New Testament Weights. Only two weights are alluded to in the New Testament. The litra (John 12:3; 19:39) was a

TABLE OF BABYLONIAN WEIGHTS, ROYAL STANDARD

Unit	Metric Weight	U. S. Weight
Light Talent	30.6 kilograms	69.6 pounds
Light Mina	525 grams	1.2 pound
Light Shekel	8.4 grams	0.3 ounce
Heavy Talent	61.2 kilograms	138 pounds
Heavy Mina	1.05 kilograms	2.3 pounds
Heavy Shekel	16.7 grams	0.6 ounce

TABLE OF BABYLONIAN WEIGHTS, COMMON STANDARD

Unit	Metric Weight	U. S. Weight
Light Talent	30 kilograms	66 pounds
Light Mina	500 grams	1.1 pound
Light Shekel	8.3 grams	0.3 ounce
Heavy Talent	60 kilograms	132 pounds
Heavy Mina	1.0 kilogram	2.2 pounds
Heavy Shekel	16.7 grams	0.6 ounce

TABLE OF OLD TESTAMENT WEIGHTS

Unit	Metric Weight	U. S. Weight
Talent (3000 shekels)	34.3 kilograms	75.6 pounds
Mina (50 shekels)	571 grams	1.26 pound
Shekel	11.4 grams	0.4 ounce
Pim (2/3 shekel?)	7.6 grams	0.3 ounce
Beka (1/2 shekel)	5.7 grams	0.2 ounce
Third of a shekel	3.8 grams	0.1 ounce
Gerah (1/20 shekel)	0.6 gram	8.8 grains

Roman measure of weight equal to 327.45 grams (just under 12 ounces avoirdupois). (The King James Version renders litra as "libra," from which we have acquired the abbreviation "lb." for pound.)

The hailstones of Revelation 16:21 are said to weigh a talent. If this refers to the Old Testament talent of 3000 shekels, the hailstones would weigh about 75 pounds. Some scholars maintain that this talent equalled 125 librae, about 90 pounds. Others construe a light talent of 45 pounds.

A stone weight of one talent (© *MPS*)

Old Testament Dry Measures. The Old Testament terms were the same as those used throughout the ancient Near East. They were derived from various types of containers.

roughly seven liters or 1½ gallons (dry measure).

Omer. One-tenth of an ephah (Exod. 16:36), equivalent to about two liters or two quarts (dry measure).

Issaron. Apparently the equivalent of an omer or one-tenth of an ephah (Exod. 29:40; Lev. 14:10).

Cab (Hebrew *kab*). According to Rabbinical sources, one-eighteenth of an ephah, roughly the same as a liter or a quart (dry measure).

New Testament Dry Measures.

Koros. The Greek name for the Hebrew kor, equivalent to about 50 U.S. gallons (dry measure).

TABLE OF OLD TESTAMENT DRY MEASURES		
Unit	*Metric Volume*	*U.S. Volume* *(Dry Standard)*
Homer or Cor	220 liters	50 gallons
Half-Homer	110 liters	25 gallons
Ephah	22 liters	5.0 gallons
Seah	7.3 liters	6.6 quarts
Omer or Issaron	2.2 liters	2.0 quarts
Cab	1.2 liter	1.1 quart

Homer (Hebrew *ḥomer*, Akkadian *imēr*). "A donkey's load," a standard dry measure (Ezek. 45:11). The homer was equal to the cor and contained ten baths or ephahs (Ezek. 45:11-14). This was equivalent to about 220 liters or 50 U.S. gallons (dry measure).

Cor (Hebrew *kōr*, Akkadian *gur*). A large dry measure equal to the homer (cf. 1 Kings 4:22; 2 Chron. 2:10; 27:5).

Half-Homer (Hebrew *lethek*, Ugaritic *lth*). About 110 liters or 25 gallons (dry measure). The term occurs only in Hosea 3:2.

Ephah (Hebrew *ᵓephah*). A measure equal to the liquid *bath* or one-tenth of a homer (Ezek. 45:11). This is equivalent to about 22 liters or five gallons (dry measure).

Seah (Hebrew *seah*, Akkadian *sutu*). Probably one-thirtieth of a cor or one-third of an ephah (Isa. 40:12). This is

Modius. The "bushel" of Matthew 5:15, Mark 4:21, and Luke 11:33. It contained about 2.3 U.S. gallons (dry measure).

Choinix. A measure mentioned in Revelation 6:6 and equivalent to a little less than a quart (dry measure).

Saton. The Greek name (Matt. 13:33; Luke 13:21) for the Hebrew seah, equivalent to about 1.5 pecks.

Old Testament Liquid Measures. In addition to dry measures of capacity there were liquid measures. These varied as much as the dry measures. Even today the English gallon differs from the American gallon and the Connecticut bushel of 2,748 cubic inches differs from the Colorado bushel of 2500 cubic inches. In fact no worldwide, uniform standard of measures existed until the metric system was formulated. However, the numerical values of ancient measures have been

TABLE OF OLD TESTAMENT LIQUID MEASURES		
Unit	*Metric Volume*	*U.S. Volume*
Cor	220 liters	58 gallons
Bath	22 liters	5.8 gallons
Hin	3.7 liters	3.9 quarts
Log	1.8 liter	1.9 quart

determined closely enough to be of value to the Bible student.

Cor (Hebrew *kor*). A measure equal to the homer. It was used to measure oil, and, like the homer, it was said to contain ten baths (Ezek. 45:14). This is equivalent to about 220 liters or 58 liquid gallons.

Bath (Hebrew *bath*; Greek *batos*, Luke 16:6 only). The liquid equivalent of the ephah (Ezek. 45:11, 14). It was an exact and standard measure (Ezek. 45:10). Its modern equivalent is best calculated as 22 liters (about 6 gallons). The recovered examples from Lachish and Tell Beit Mirsim are fragmentary, however, and cannot be reconstructed with certainty. The estimated equivalents thus range between 20.9 and 46.6 liters.

Hin. The Hebrew hin ("a pot") was originally the designation of the vessels employed as a measure of oil (Exod. 29:40), of wine (Lev. 23:13), and of water (Ezek. 4:11). The hin was one-sixth of a bath, according to Josephus.

Log (Hebrew *log*). One-twelfth of a bath, according to Jewish tradition. It occurs only in Leviticus 14:10 as a measure of oil.

New Testament Liquid Measures.

Xestes. One-sixteenth of the Latin modius, or slightly less than a pint (Mark 7:4, 8).

Batos. The Greek counterpart of the Hebrew bath. It is referred to as a measure of oil in Luke 16:6. Josephus says the bath contained 72 sextarii or 4.5 modii. This would be equivalent to about 40 liters or 10 U.S. gallons.

Metretes. A Greek liquid measure referred to in John 2:6. It was approximately equal to the Hebrew bath (about 6 U.S. gallons).

Old Testament Units of Length. In ancient times units of length were derived from members of the human body (such as the finger, hand, palm, forearm, or foot) or from such loosely determined distances as a bowshot, a stone's throw, or the distance one could legally travel on a Sabbath day (Acts 1:12).

The following conversions were commonly used in Old Testament times:

4 fingerbreadths	= 1 handbreadth
3 handbreadths	= 1 span
2 spans	= 1 cubit
6 cubits	= 1 reed

When measurements became more precise, a standardized unit of length had to be agreed upon. The cubit was selected for this purpose.

Cubit (Hebrew *ʾamma*; Akkadian *ammatu*; Latin *cubitus*). The distance from the elbow to the fingertip. Four of these "natural" cubits constitute the height of a typical man.

However, a more precisely defined cubit was used as the standard of Hebrew measurements. The best calculations yield a value of 17.5 inches. This commonly accepted value agrees well with the ancient figure for the length of the Siloam tunnel, 1200 cubits. Based on the configuration of a half-sphere, Solomon's bronze laver of 1000 baths yields a cubit of 17.51 inches (see 1 Kings 7:23-26). The Egyptians used a cubit of 17.6 inches, a value only slightly larger than that of the standard Hebrew cubit.

The "long" or royal cubit was a handbreadth ("palm") longer than the standard cubit of six palms (Ezek. 40:5). It measured 20.4 inches. The Babylonian

TABLE OF OLD TESTAMENT LINEAR MEASURES		
Unit	*Metric Length*	*U.S. Length*
Reed	2.64 meters	8 feet, 8 inches
Reed (Ezekiel)	3.1 meters	10 feet, 2 inches
Cubit	44.5 centimeters	17.5 inches
Cubit (Ezekiel)	52 centimeters	20.5 inches
Span	22 centimeters	8.7 inches
Palm	7.4 centimeters	2.9 inches
Finger	18 millimeters	0.7 inch

cubit was 19.8 inches, attested by thirty fingers marked on a statue of Gudea. This was "three fingers" shorter than the Egyptian royal cubit, which, according to Herodotus, was 20.65 inches.

Reed (Hebrew *ganeh*). A unit equal to six cubits. It was exact enough to be mentioned in Scripture as a unit of length (Ezek. 40:5).

Span (Hebrew *zereth*). The distance from the thumb to the little finger in the outstretched hand. It was considered half a cubit (1 Sam. 17:4; Exod. 28:16; Ezek. 43:13).

Palm (Hebrew *tephah*). A "handbreadth," the width of the hand at the base of the four fingers (about 2.9 inches). See Exod. 25:25; 37:12; Ezek. 40:5; Psa. 39:5.

Finger (Hebrew *esba*). One-fourth of a handbreadth (Jer. 52:21). It was the smallest unit in everyday use in the ancient biblical world. It is commonly computed to be 0.73 inches.

Distance. Unlike the measurement of objects, which could be accomplished with a fair degree of precision, the ancient computation of distances was a much more approximate undertaking. Examples of distance standards include a bowshot (Gen. 21:16), a day's journey (Num. 11:31; 1 Kings 19:4), and the length of a plowed furrow (1 Sam. 14:14).

New Testament Units of Length.

Cubit. The custom of relating measurements to parts of the human body was continued in New Testament times. The basic unit remained the "forearm"

(Greek *pēchys*), that is, the cubit. However, the length of the Jewish cubit under the Roman Empire evidently measured 21.6 inches.

Fathom (Greek *orgyia*). The length of the outstretched arms (about 6 feet). The term was derived from the verb *orego*, "I stretch."

Furlong (Greek *stadion*). One hundred orgiai (about 607 feet), supposedly the exact length of the Olympian race course. Compare the English word stadium.

Mile (Greek *milion*). The Greek transliteration of the Roman *mille pasuum*, "a thousand paces." It consisted of 8 stadia (1,618 English yards). It was calculated on the basis of 5 Roman feet (each of 11.65 inches) to the pace (4 feet, 10.25 inches).

Sabbath Day's Journey. This was fixed at 2000 cubits in the Talmud. It is referred to in Acts 1:12.

Measures of Area. In Egypt the cubit of square measure was employed for area measurements. This was defined as an area one linear cubit wide and 100 linear cubits long. One hundred cubits of area constituted approximately two-thirds of an acre. Babylonian and Assyrian criteria for measuring area were frequently computed by units of agricultural capacity. An area was measured by the quantity of seed, such as barley, necessary to sow it properly.

In Israel areas were customarily measured by the *ṣemed*, translated "acre" in the King James Version (1 Sam. 14:14;

Isa. 5:10). It was defined as the amount of land which a pair of yoked animals could plow in one day. In Babylonia this amount was stipulated as 6,480 square cubits (about two-fifths of an acre). In later times this constituted essentially the Latin *jugerum* of 28,800 square Roman feet (about five-eighths of an acre).

WELL. See "Springs, Wells, and Pools."

WHALE. As used in the King James Version of the Old Testament, this term signifies any large marine animal (Gen. 1:21). The same is true of the Greek word *kētos* (Matt. 12:40). The rhinodon, the shark, the whale, the dolphin, the sea dog, and the seal are included in this general term. True whales are found in both the Mediterranean Sea and the Red Sea. The Hebrew term for "great fish," *dāg gādhōl* (Jonah 1:17), is rendered by the Septuagint as "great whale," *kētos mega*. Hence the word *kētos* passed into Matthew 12:40, giving rise to the idea that Jonah was necessarily swallowed by an actual whale.

Wheat mixed with tares gave Jesus a poignant spiritual illustration, told in Matthew 13. (© *MPS*)

WHEAT. Wheat was cultivated throughout the biblical world. Egypt was the granary of the Mediterranean region. Vast quantities of wheat were shipped annually to Rome from Alexandria (Acts 27:6, 38). Wheat cultivated in Palestine was of the common variety, *Triticum vulgare*. It was sown in November or December, after the rains began. Harvest came from April till June, depending on weather and locality.

WIDOW. In Old Testament times widows were the special object of the Lord's care. They were not to be wronged or neglected (Exod. 22:22; Isa. 1:17; Prov. 15:25; Mal. 3:5). The New Testament denounces those who "devour widows' houses" (Matt. 23:14; Mark 12:40; Luke 20:47). The neglect of widows became a temporary problem in the early church (Acts 6:1). Paul had much to say to Timothy, the young pastor, concerning the care of widows (1 Tim. 5:3-6). James declares that "pure religion and undefiled before God and the Father is to visit . . . widows in their affliction" (James 1:27). Some especially significant widows are briefly described below.

The Widow of Zarephath. This good woman of great faith gave the prophet Elijah a home, providing for him during the famine that raged in Israel at the time. As a reward of her trust in the Lord her oil and meal did not diminish and her boy was restored to life (1 Kings 17:8-24).

The Widow Whose Oil Multiplied. She was a recipient of the considerate ministry of Elisha (2 Kings 4:1-7). Her godly husband had died, and her two sons were in danger of being sold into slavery to satisfy creditors. All the woman had in her house was a pot of oil. The prophet directed her to borrow as many containers as she could, shut herself and her sons in their house, and empty the pot of oil into these vessels. In obedient faith she did so. The oil did not stop until all the containers were full. Her blessing was proportionate to her faith in gathering pots.

Elisha then directed her to sell the oil, pay her debts, and live on the remaining money. Her faith saved her family and brought the blessing of God into her life.

The Widow with Two Mites. She is enshrined among the spiritual heroes of the Bible because of the sacrifice and love for God that prompted her total giving. This widow's "mite" was a very small coin, worth scarcely one-eighth of a cent. But even though this impoverished widow seemed unnoticed in the swarming crowds that cast gifts into the Temple treasury during Passover Week, Jesus did not leave her devotion unnoticed, but preserved it for all future generations in the safekeeping of his praise. "This poor widow has cast more in than all they who have cast into the treasury. For all they did cast in of their abundance, but she of her want did cast in all she had, even all her living" (Mark 12:43-44; cf. Luke 21: 1-4).

The Importunate Widow. She appears as a figurative character in one of Jesus' parables (Luke 18:1-8). Her grievance was brought before a godless and callous judge who had no compassion for her or regard for the justice of her cause. Only by dint of dogged persistence did she finally get the judge to act in her behalf. Christ used the illustration to show that God, the righteous and compassionate Judge, will surely hear the cry of his persecuted people during the Great Tribulation preceding Christ's second advent (Luke 18:7, 8). He will answer them speedily, despite his seeming delay and the apparent triumph of evil.

The Hellenistic Jewish Widows. These women were widows of Hellenists, that is, Jews who spoke Greek and adopted many Greek customs. Even in the early church a tension existed between the Hellenists and the more conservative Hebrews. The Hellenists complained that their widows were being neglected in the philanthropic activities of the church (Acts 6:1).

The problem was resolved by appointing seven deacons (Acts 6:2-7). These officers were entrusted with the temporal responsibilities of the church. The apostles were thereby freed to devote themselves to prayer and Bible teaching.

WIFE. Wives play a very important role in the Bible; the word "wife" or "wives" is found almost 400 times. The monogamous standard was God's order from the beginning. "Therefore shall a man leave his father and his mother, and shall cleave unto his wife; and they shall be one flesh" (Gen. 2:24). But after Adam's fall polygamy with its attendant evils became common. Beginning with Lamech of the godless line of Cain (Gen. 4: 19), polygamy spread even to some of God's choicest saints. It invariably introduced trial and grief into the family circle. Monogamy has always been God's pattern for the greatest family happiness.

The Law of Moses forbade coveting a neighbor's wife (Exod. 20:17) and discouraged divorce (Deut. 24:1-4). The New Testament stipulated monogamy for believers (1 Cor. 7:2). Divorce is permitted only under certain circumstances (Matt. 5:32; Mark 10:2-12; 1 Cor. 7:10-17). Nowhere, however, does God's Word penalize an innocent marital partner for the sin of the mate.

Many wives mentioned in Scripture played important roles of various types, some good and some evil. In a number of cases the names of these wives are not given. Some of the more significant unnamed wives are briefly described below.

Cain's Wife. "And Cain knew his wife; and she conceived and bore Enoch" (Gen. 4:17). Bible skeptics often want to know who Cain's wife might have been. The question is based on the assumption that there were no women available to Cain, since his parents were the first human beings to appear on earth. This presupposition overlooks several important facts. It fails to take into account the phenomenal fertility of Adam and Eve after the fall. God greatly multiplied the conception and childbearing activity of the woman after she had sinned (Gen. 3: 16). Eve bore many children in addition to Cain, Abel, and Seth. In fact, Adam did not father Seth until he was 130 years old (Gen. 5:3). (Seth took the murdered Abel's place as the son in the messianic line — Gen. 4:25). In all probability Adam fathered many sons and daughters during this period of well over a century. In addition to numerous sons and daughters, he probably had many generations of descendants. By the time Adam was 130 years old there may well have been thousands of women from which Cain could have selected a wife!

Lot's Wife. Christ referred to Lot's wife in warning believers against the perils of worldliness and materialism. His stark words were, "Remember Lot's wife" (Luke 17:32). The Old Testament summarizes her tragic career with the words, "But (Lot's) wife looked back from behind him, and she became a pillar of salt" (Gen. 19:26). Lot's wife had lived in Sodom, enjoying all the luxuries and pleasures that her wealthy and compromising husband could provide. When destruction overtook the city, her heart remained with her possessions and pleasures. As a result she became engulfed in God's judgment on those wicked cities.

Moses' Ethiopian Wife. Apparently a second wife whom Moses married in the wilderness. She is distinct from Zipporah, his first wife (a daughter of the Midian priest, Jethro), whom Moses had married before he became the deliverer and leader of Israel. His sister, Miriam, and brother, Aaron, rebelled against Moses' leadership because of his marriage to this woman of a different race. But the Lord severely rebuked them and reaffirmed Moses' leadership and authority (Num. 12:1-16).

Peter's Wife. She remains strictly in the background, though she doubtlessly witnessed her mother's healing by Christ (Mark 1:30; Luke 4:38, 39). She must have entertained Christ often, since their home in Capernaum appears to have been Jesus' headquarters while there. Commonly referred to as Simon's (Cephas') wife, she frequently traveled with her husband, as did the wives of the other apostles (1 Cor. 9:5).

Pilate's Wife. After a dream on the night of Christ's arrest, the wife of the Roman procurator of Judea dispatched a message to her husband, imploring him not to condemn Jesus of Nazareth. She held strong convictions of right and wrong. Moreover, she had the courage to testify of Christ's innocence when the forces of evil were clamoring for his death. The few quoted words of Pilate's wife have immortalized her: "Have thou nothing to do with that just man" (Matt. 27:19).

Potiphar's Wife. A woman remembered solely for her wickedness (Gen. 39:1-20). She was an Egyptian of high social position, the wife of the chief of Pharaoh's bodyguard. Hence she moved in a circle of elegance and splendor (about 1870 B.C.). A spoiled, selfish woman, Potiphar's wife knew nothing of Joseph's God and the high standards of morality of those who worshiped him. Serving only the gods of sensual pleasures, she tried to seduce Joseph. When Joseph resisted her advances, she seized his outer garment and falsely accused him to her husband. Her husband, believing her, cast Joseph into prison.

Potiphar's wife represents the evil of humanity apart from the redemptive grace of God. Both she and Jezebel represent pagan women who manifest utter disregard of right and wrong—the basis of the eternal moral law of God. Both women dramatize the close relationship of idolatry and immorality.

Samson's Wife. This Philistine woman, whom Samson insisted on marrying because she "pleased him well" (Judg. 14:3), ended up giving him nothing but trouble (Judg. 14:15-20). However, the Lord overruled the hero's folly and ultimately used Samson to deliver Israel from the encroachments of the Philistines (Judg. 15:1-8).

Solomon's Many Wives. Solomon's enormous harem of 700 wives and 300 concubines testified to both his wealth and his growing apostasy from the Lord (1 Kings 11:1-8). Solomon's many marriages, first with the Pharaoh's daughter (1 Kings 3:1) and then with various foreign princesses, cemented his political ties with various countries. All of Solomon's wives lived in luxury and splendor. He built a special palace for Pharaoh's daughter (1 Kings 7:8-12).

However, the Bible does not indicate that a single one of Solomon's wives learned to trust the God of Israel. Instead, these pagan women turned the king's heart away from God. This "wisest of men" played the part of a fool by forsaking the Lord (1 Kings 11:1-13). The king violated God's law (Deut. 17:17) and paid a terrible price for his folly.

The Unbelieving Wife. The Apostle Paul declares that such a wife is sanctified by her believing husband (1 Cor. 7:14). Though he is a Christian and she is not, his faith stamps the marriage as holy and in a sense sanctifies the offspring of the union. The children are not, of course, saved by their parents' faith. However, in a certain sense they enjoy the blessings of the converted parent's Christian faith. (The Apostle presupposes that the believing parent will lead the child to accept the gospel of redemption and will rear him in Christian truth.)

The same principle applies to unsaved husbands. "The unbelieving husband is sanctified by the wife" (1 Cor. 7:14). This truth is meant to encourage a Christian husband or wife to claim his or her entire family for the Lord and to trust God to save all its unconverted members.

WILDERNESS. Since large areas of Palestine and the Near East are arid and mountainous, desert or wilderness conditions are common. The commonest Hebrew word for such a region, *midbar*, denotes barren areas of sand dunes or rock as well as steppes and pasture lands (Deut. 32:10; Job 38:26; Psa. 65:12; Joel 2:22). The same description applies to *erēmos*, the Greek word for wilderness regions (Matt. 14:15; Luke 9:10).

The term "Jeshimon" (Hebrew *yeshimon*, "a waste" or "desert") is identified principally with the Wilderness of Judah, a barren, rugged region extending from Masada to Khirhet Qumran (1 Sam. 23:24; 26:1). The designation is also sometimes applied to the rugged region north of the Dead Sea and east of the Jordan River (Num. 21:20; 23:28).

The term "Arabah," in addition to its use as a proper name for the long, barren Rift Valley from the Dead Sea to the Gulf of Aqabah, is also sometimes used in a general way of steppe and scrubland or of barren desert (Jer. 17:6; Job 39:6). Exceptionally arid regions are specifically designated as such by the words *ṣiyya* (Job 30:3; Psa. 78:17) or *tōhu* (Job 6:18; 12:24).

The more significant wildernesses of Bible lands are described briefly below.

Damascus. The semi-desert region beyond the fertile city of Damascus. It was the site at which Elijah anointed Hazael to be the king of Aram.

Edom. Edom proper is a rugged, mountainous region which extends about 100 miles southward from Moab on both sides of the Arabah (the great depression from the Dead Sea to the Gulf of Aqabah). The Wilderness of Edom was the Arabah at the southern extremity of the Dead Sea.

En-gedi. The rugged, mountainous country around En-gedi proper. Because it abounded in caves and deep ravines, the Wilderness of En-gedi was a frequent hiding place for hunted people.

Judah. A portion of the region between the Central Highland Ridge and the Dead Sea. It included the Valley of Berachah, the Ascent of Ziz, the Wadi Murab-

baᶜat, and part of the Brook Kidron. It was in the Wilderness of Judah that the Dead Sea Scrolls were found.

Kadesh-Barnea. The desert region in the vicinity of the city of Kadesh-Barnea. The locale is the same as Meribah (Exod. 17:7; Num. 20:13) and Meribath-Kadesh (Deut. 32:51). It was in Kadesh-Barnea that the people of Israel chose to disbelieve God and wander in the desert for a whole generation.

Paran. The desert plateau region in which Israel wandered for 38 years. It included practically the entire eastern half of the Sinai Peninsula. The region was bounded roughly by Mount Sinai, the Wilderness of Shur, the Wilderness of Zin, and the Gulf of Aqabah.

Shur. The barren country through which Israel marched for three days immediately after crossing the Red Sea. It was also called the Wilderness of Etham (Num. 33:8). The region extended from the frontier fortresses of Egypt to the River of Egypt.

Sin. The wilderness through which the Israelites passed on their journey from Elim (by the Red Sea) to Rephidim and Mount Sinai (Num. 33:11, 12). It was the general region northwest of Mount Sinai.

Life is precarious in wilderness regions, such as this in the Sinai Peninsula. (© *MPS*)

Sinai. The territory in the general vicinity of Mount Sinai. The Wilderness of Sinai included the south-central portion of the tip of the Sinai Peninsula, about midway between the Gulf of Suez and the Gulf of Aqabah. Some scholars locate Mount Sinai at Jebel Helal, south and east of the Brook of Egypt.

Tekoa. The region surrounding the city of Tekoa (about six miles south of Bethlehem). The Prophet Amos came from this area (Amos 1:1).

Zin. The rugged country ranging from Kadesh-Barnea in northeast Sinai to the Ascent of Akrabbim, between Edom and Judah (Josh. 15:1-4; cf. Num. 34:1-5).

Ziph. The rugged country near the town of Ziph in the hill country of Judah (Josh. 15:55). David fled from King Saul to the Wilderness of Ziph on at least two occasions (1 Sam. 23:12-18; 26:1-25).

WILFUL KING. Evidently the "little horn" of Daniel 7:24-26, the head of the revived Roman power preceding Christ's glorious advent. Some expositors, however, identify the wilful king as an apostate Palestinian Jew in league with the Roman beast. The wilful king will flout the God of Israel, ridicule the messianic hope, and honor the Roman beast (Rev. 13:11-18). The wilful king will be destroyed at Christ's second coming (Dan. 11:45).

WILL. The ability of conscious, rational creatures to choose and accomplish a course of action. The relationship of God's sovereignty and man's will has always challenged the ingenuity of theologians. Attempts to harmonize this relationship have resulted in two major schools of thought on the issue: Calvinism and Arminianism.

It is quite clear, however, that the will of man is a faculty designed and created by God to execute his purposes. Human will (as well as angelic will) thus *accomplishes* divine purposes rather than thwarting them. Satan's introduction of sin into the universe took the form of rebellion against God in five "I wills" thundered against the divine will (Isa. 14:13, 14).

Scripture teaches that Satan dominates the wills of unsaved men (Eph. 2:2). The saved are urged to yield their redeemed bodies to the Lord in order to be able to know and do God's perfect will (Rom. 12:1, 2). There is nothing higher for a believer than to find the will of God and to walk in it. This is God's gracious goal in saving him (Eph. 2:8-10).

God's will is either directive or permissive. His directive will includes the doctrines of decrees, election, predestination, and foreordination. God's permissive will allows man his own choice. This often results in second best or even outright sin.

God's will is the correct standard of comparison for every motive, thought, and action. Man's highest purpose in life is achieved when he finds and fulfills God's perfect will. Christ himself came to perform fully the will of the Father (John 6:38). Every yielded believer should say, as Christ did, "Not my will, but thine, be done" (Luke 22:42).

WILLOWS. The willow tree is commonly found alongside streams in Palestine (Job 40:22; Isa. 15:7; 44:4; Ezek. 17:5). The "willows of the brook" (Lev. 23:40) and the "willows" of Babylon (Psa. 137:2) are now usually regarded as species of the poplar. A few scholars, however, identify them with the aspen.

WINNOWER. In biblical days grain was harvested with a sickle, tied into sheaves, and carried to the threshing floor. Threshing floors were usually located on soil coated with marly clay or on rocky hilltops. The sheaves were laid about a foot deep and were trampled by animals until the grain was separated and the stocks chopped into bits. Sometimes a wooden sled with stones or nails was used to loosen the grain. The winnower then tossed the mass into the wind with a wooden pitchfork. The chaff was blown away and the remaining grain was put into bags.

WOLF. The Palestinian wolf is a variety of the European species (*Canis lupus*). It belongs to the same genus as the dog, but cannot bark (it howls instead). The wolf is fierce and carnivorous (Heb. 1:8). It seeks its prey, often sheep (John 10:12), in the evening (Zeph. 3:3). Violent rulers and false teachers are compared to wolves (Ezek. 22:27; Matt. 7:15; Acts 20:29).

WOMAN. In a certain biblical sense woman plays a secondary role to man. Because of both creation and the fall, man bears a certain responsibility of headship over woman. Man was created before woman. Moreover, woman was made from man and for man (Gen. 2:7, 18-24; 1 Cor. 11:8, 9). Woman was also the first to sin (Gen. 3:6; 1 Tim. 2:14), thereby becoming subject to the rule of her husband (Gen. 3:16; 1 Cor. 11:3). However, the headship of man over woman does not imply that woman is inferior to man. It simply means that God has given man a broader and more defined sphere of leadership in human affairs than woman. For this reason male characters are more numerous and more prominent in biblical history (and world history) than female characters.

However, the prominence of male characters over female characters does not detract from the importance of women in Scripture. In their own sphere women, like men, often become God's instrument to accomplish certain divine purposes. If unbelieving and disobedient, women can become agents of Satan to oppose God's will. God's Word describes its women as candidly as it does the men.

In general, Hebrew women were held in the highest respect by Israelite men. Two women were prophetesses (Exod. 15:20; 2 Kings 22:14), and one was both a prophetess and a judge (Judg. 4:4). Hebrew women enjoyed full legal rights in the execution of justice (Num. 27:1-11; 1 Kings 3:16-28). They are portrayed in every virtue and excellence of character as mothers and wives in the home. The highly beneficent influence of mothers on their offspring, especially their sons, is emphasized in Scripture (2 Tim. 1:5).

Women of the Old Testament era were active in both indoor and outdoor responsibilities. They spun yarn (Exod. 35:26; Prov. 31:19), made clothing (1 Sam. 2:19), served as water-carriers (Gen. 24:15; 1 Sam. 9:11) or shepherdesses (Gen. 29:6; Exod. 2:16), gleaned in the harvest fields (Ruth 2:17), and prepared bread (Matt. 24:41).

The sacrifice, zeal, and fidelity of Hebrew women are exemplified in the devoted group that supported Jesus' ministry and ministered to him of their material possessions (Luke 8:2, 3). The noblest features of Hebrew womanhood are seen in such biblical personalities as Mary, Elisabeth, Anna, Eunice, Lois, and many more.

The great New Testament revelation that all believers of both sexes enjoy identical spiritual privileges in Christ gave womanhood a dignity and glory that it had never enjoyed even in ancient Israel (Gal. 3:28). Every region of the world that has accepted the rudiments of Christianity has elevated womanhood under the principle of the headship of man. Modern "woman's liberation" movements usually ignore the teachings of Christ and reject the order of the sexes which God established in the beginning of human history.

As with certain men of Scripture, numerous women are referred to but not named in the pages of the Bible. These include mothers, wives, daughters, and various others. Some of these unnamed personalities actually fulfill more important roles than certain other women who are mentioned by name.

Some of the more significant unnamed women of Scripture are briefly described below.

An Adulterous Woman. Probably a young woman, likely a first offender. However, she was apprehended in the act of adultery (John 8:3-11) and could therefore have been stoned to death, according to the Law of Moses (Lev. 20:10). In dealing with the woman and her accusers Christ raised new standards for marriage. Both men and women were expected to honor their marriage vows. Christ in no sense condoned the guilty woman's sin, but he did provide opportunity for repentance and a renewed life.

The Elect Lady. John's Second Epistle is addressed to "the elect lady and her children" (1:1). She was evidently a Christian matron who resided somewhere in the circuit of churches over which the aged Apostle John exercised spiritual oversight. Some consider the designation a name—"Lady Elect." Other scholars feel the title refers to a church and its members.

The Great Harlot of Revelation 17. A

figure of the final form of religious rebellion against God's Word (Rev. 17:1-18). The woman's harlotry symbolizes corrupt religionism, which compromises the truth of God's Word for worldly power. The woman rides into power on the beast, the final form of Gentile world government. She represents in fullest scope all apostate religious movements and mergers from their inception in ancient Babylon (Gen. 11:1-9) to their endtime consummation in apostate Christendom (Rev. 17:5).

The woman's crimes are enumerated (Rev. 17:6) and her destruction at the hands of the beast (governmental authority) which she rode into power is described (17:7-18).

The Lamb's Wife. The bride of Christ, a symbol of the New Testament church (Rev. 21:9). The figure of a wife symbolizes the church in glorious union with Christ in the kingdom. The figure of marriage represents the outward, public consummation of the inner spiritual union between Christ and his church (Eph. 5:22-32).

The bride's preparation for marriage presupposes her sanctification through Christ's imputed righteousness and follows the evaluation of her works at the judgment seat of Christ (Rom. 14:10; 2 Cor. 5:10). The bride's robes portray the righteousness of Christ graciously imputed to her by God on the basis of Christ's death (Rev. 19:8).

The Queen of Heaven. An ancient Semitic fertility goddess (Jer. 7:18; 44:17-19). She was worshiped by the apostates of Judah in the last terrible forty years before the Babylonian captivity.

The Shulamite. The young woman in the Song of Solomon (Song 6:13). The name is best interpreted as the feminine form of Solomon and a descriptive title, "the Solomoness." Solomon wooed and apparently won her.

The Sun-Clothed Woman. A supernatural symbol which apparently portrays the nation Israel clothed in regal and governmental splendor (Rev. 12:1, 2). The twelve stars signify her twelve tribes, as Joseph's dream suggests (Gen. 37:9). Her travail reflects the nation's suffering during the Great Tribulation (Jer. 30:5-7;

Isa. 26:15-18; 66:7), when she will give birth to the godly remnant.

The Ten Virgins. The five wise virgins symbolize the believing remnant of the nation Israel during the nation's judgment just prior to the establishment of the kingdom (Matt. 25:1-13). The five foolish virgins prefigure the unbelieving part of the nation. They are not ready for the coming of the Messiah; their profession proves to be a false one. Their lack of the Holy Spirit (symbolized by the oil) will exclude them from participation in the coming kingdom.

The Woman of Endor. A spiritistic medium whom Saul brazenly consulted after he himself had outlawed spiritism from his realm (1 Sam. 28:3, 9), in accord with the warnings of the Mosaic Law (Lev. 19:31; 20:6, 27; Deut. 18:9-11). God unexpectedly intervened in the visit, bringing up the actual spirit of Samuel to pronounce doom upon Saul for this last step toward ruin (1 Sam. 28:12-20).

The Woman with Leaven. A symbol of false teaching. The leaven which she hides in the meal represents erroneous doctrine propagated by false Christianity during this present age (Matt. 16:11, 12; Mark 8:15; 1 Cor. 5:6-8; Gal. 5:9).

The Woman of Samaria. The woman who met Christ at the well at Sychar in the plain of Shechem. Jesus displayed toward her a compassionate concern which transcended all social and religious prejudices. He recalled her sinful life but did not censure her. She opened her heart to his message of life and carried it back to others in Samaria. The result was an ingathering of souls (John 4:7-42).

The Woman with Seven Husbands. The hypothetical woman who married each of seven brothers, every one of whom died without leaving a child (Matt. 22:23-30). Her marriages were in accord with the early Levirate law, which obligated a man to marry his deceased brother's widow (Deut. 25:5-10). The hypocritical Pharisees and Sadducees tried to embarrass Christ by contriving the situation of a woman with seven successive husbands. Whose wife would she be in the resurrection? Christ responded by revealing their ignorance of the spiritual realm, where God grants glorified bodies to all his saints (Matt. 22:29, 30).

WOOD CARVER. Bezaleel and Aholiab performed intricate wood carving for the Old Testament Tabernacle (Exod. 35:30-35). The walls and doors of Solomon's Temple were executed in bas-relief of lotus flowers, lilies, and cherubim (1 Kings 6:18, 29, 32-35). Ezekiel's Temple also reveals elaborate carving (Ezek. 41:16-26). In its heyday Egypt boasted exquisite and highly developed wood carving.

WORD OF GOD. The beauties and excellencies of the written Word of God are extolled in Psalm 119 in a manner found nowhere else in the Bible. Scripture bears its own witness that it is God-breathed and fully authoritative (2 Tim. 3:16, 17). This full inspiration and authority extends not merely to parts of Scripture, but to every word in the entire Book.

The process by which God communicated his thoughts to inspired writers is outlined in 1 Corinthians 2:9-14. Unsaved men cannot discover the unseen things of God (1 Cor. 2:9, 14). God has, however, revealed these truths to his saints (1 Cor. 2:10-12). They are communicated in Spirit-taught words (1 Cor. 2:13). The Holy Spirit sovereignly chose words from the writer's own vocabulary (1 Cor. 2:13). These words are properly understood by the believer only through the illumination of the Holy Spirit (1 Cor. 2:15, 16).

WORLD (Greek *kosmos*). The present world system, organized and controlled by Satan. It is erected upon Satan's principles of greed, force, selfishness, ambition, lust, and war (Matt. 4:8, 9; Eph. 2:2;

6:12). The believer is warned against loving this evil system (1 John 2:15-17). To love it is to be at enmity with God (James 4:1-4). Accommodation to this evil system is a constant threat to the spiritual life of the believer.

The Greek word *aiōn*, often translated "world" in the King James Version, actually refers to an age or a period of time (Mark 10:30; Matt. 12:32; 24:3; 28:20). The Greek word *oikoumenē* means the inhabited earth, as referred to in prophetic and kingdom teaching (Luke 2:1; Matt. 24:14).

WORLD EMPIRES. In his visions Daniel saw four great world Empires which spanned the centuries from Nebuchadnezzar to the second advent of Christ (Dan. 2:31-45; 7:1-28). The fourth Empire will be revived in the end time (Rev. 13:3), only to be shattered by Christ (the Stone supernaturally cut out of the mountain) at his second coming (Dan. 2:34). The stone will in turn become "a great mountain" (the millennial kingdom) and will fill the whole earth (Dan. 2:35).

WORMWOOD. Any of several species of strong-smelling plants that yield a bitter, dark-green oil used in making absinthe (an alcoholic liquor). The biblical references to wormwood are either to *Artemisia herba-alba* or to *Artemesia judaica*. Every species of wormwood has a strong, bitter taste (Prov. 5:4; Lam. 3:15, 19).

WORSHIP. Old Testament worship centered around the altar of incense, a symbol of Christ as our Intercessor (John 17:1-26; Heb. 7:25). It is through him that our prayers and praises ascend to God. The altar of incense also symbolizes the believer-priest's sacrifice of praise and worship to God (Heb. 13:15; Rev. 8:3, 4).

Z

ZACCHAEUS (ză-kē'ŭs) (Greek form of Hebrew *Zaccai*). A prosperous tax collector for the Roman government who lived in Jericho. He overcame obstacles to come to Christ and later became his devoted disciple (Luke 19:1-10).

ZACHARIAH (zăk'á-rī'á). The king of Israel during part of 753 and 752 B.C. He was the son of Jeroboam II. Zachariah was assassinated after only a six-month reign (2 Kings 14:29; 15:8-12).

ZACHARIAS (zăk'á-rī'ás) ("the Lord has remembered"). (1) A righteous man who was murdered at the insistence of King Joash (835-796 B.C.) in the court of the Temple (2 Chron. 24:20-22). Christ referred to the event in Luke 11:51. (2) The father of John the Baptist (Luke 1:5-79).

ZALMON (zăl'mŏn). A mountain in the vicinity of the town of Shechem (Judg. 9:48). It is probably to be identified with the southern part of Mount Gerizim or with Jabal al-Kabir. A different mountain is rendered "Salmon" in Psalm 68:14, KJV. This mountain is possibly one of the high peaks of Bashan.

ZAREPHATH (zăr'ē-făth). A town belonging to Sidon (1 Kings 17:9; Luke 4:26). Here lived the widow who fed Elijah and for whom the Lord performed miracles (1 Kings 17:8-24). The name of the town still lingers in the form of "Sarafend," a present-day village near the ruins of ancient Zarephath.

ZEBEDEE (zĕb'ē-dē) ("the Lord has given"). The father of James and John. Like his sons, Zebedee was a Galilean fisherman (Matt. 4:21, 22) and a man of enough wealth to retain hired servants (Mark 1:20).

ZEBOIM (zē-bō'ĭm). One of the five cities of the Plain of Genesis 10:19. Its king was defeated by Chedorlaomer (Gen. 14:2, 8, 10). Zeboim was destroyed with Sodom and Gomorrah and now lies buried beneath the shallow southern waters of the Dead Sea.

ZEBULUN (zĕb'ū-lŭn) ("habitation, dwelling"). Jacob's tenth son and the progenitor of one of the twelve tribes of Israel (Gen. 30:19, 20; Num. 26:26, 27).

ZECHARIAH (zĕk-á-rī'á) ("the Lord remembers"). A prophet of the restoration who (with Haggai) encouraged God's people to complete the Temple during 520 to 515 B.C. Zechariah foresaw the first and second comings of Messiah. He particularly envisioned Israel's final regathering and establishment in millennial blessing under Messiah-King-Priest (Zech. 3:1 – 6:15; 9:1 – 14:21).

ZEDEKIAH (zĕd'ē-kī'á) ("the Lord is righteous"). (1) A false prophet who encouraged King Ahab to go up to Ramoth-Gilead. He clashed with the true prophet of God, Micaiah (1 Kings 22:11-28). (2) The last king of Judah (597-586 B.C.) before the fall of Jerusalem to the Babylonians. He was an evil king and his career ended in tragedy. First his sons were slain before his eyes, and then his eyes were put out and he was carried to Babylon in chains (2 Kings 24:18 – 25:7).

ZEPHANIAH (zĕf'á-nī'á) ("the Lord has hidden"). One of the minor prophets. He was a contemporary of Jeremiah (640-608

B.C.). Zephaniah had access to the royal court and was therefore doubtless instrumental in Josiah's religious reformation (2 Kings 22:1–23:30). Zephaniah warned of approaching judgment upon both Israel (Zeph. 1) and the nations (Zeph. 2:1–3:8). He also foresaw Israel's kingdom blessing (Zeph. 3:9-20).

ZEPHATH (zē′făth). A Canaanite city which was destroyed and later renamed Hormah ("destruction"). Zephath was situated southeast of Beersheba, toward the borders of Edom. It is identified with present-day Tell el-Mishash. It was in Zephath that the presumptuous Israelites suffered defeat (Num. 14:39-45; Deut. 1: 44; cf. Num. 21:1-3). Zephath was originally allotted to the tribe of Judah but was later transferred to Simeon (Josh. 15: 30; 19:4). See also "Hormah."

ZERED (zē′rĕd). A brook which flows eastward into the south end of the Dead Sea. The Israelites crossed this wadi on their journey around the frontiers of Edom and Moab (Num. 21:12; Deut. 2: 13-14).

ZERUAH (zê-rōō′à) ("having a skin disease"). The mother of Jeroboam I, first king of the Northern Kingdom (931-910 B.C.). Zeruah was a widow at the time of Jeroboam's birth. Her husband, Nebat, had apparently been an official under King Solomon, and her son became an overseer of heavy work. As king of Israel Jeroboam introduced the idolatrous worship of the golden bulls at the cult centers of Dan and Bethel (1 Kings 12:25-33). No doubt Zeruah, being a widow at the time of Jeroboam's birth, was responsible for molding Jeroboam's life in a pattern of expediency and opportunism.

ZERUBBABEL (zĕ-rŭb′à-bĕl) (Akkadian, "seed of Babylon"). The governor of the Jewish remnant who returned from Babylon in 539 B.C. It was under his administration that Haggai and Zechariah prophesied and preached and that the Temple was rebuilt (515 B.C.). Zerubbabel was a son of Shealtiel and a relative of King David. He was also an ancestor of Christ (Matt. 1:12, 13; Luke 3:27).

ZERUIAH (zĕr′ōō-ī′à) (probably "one perfumed with mastix"). The mother of Joab, Abishai, and Asahel, three loyal supporters of David and commanders of his army (2 Sam. 2:18). The fact that her name appears some 25 times in connection with her sons seems to indicate that she exercised a beneficent influence on her sons' lives (1 Sam. 26:6; 2 Sam. 2:13, 18; 3:39; 8:16; etc.). Zeruiah was David's half-sister; like her sister Abigail, Zeruiah was a daughter not of Jesse but of Jesse's wife by an earlier marriage with Nahash (1 Chron. 2:16; cf. 2 Sam. 17:25).

ZIBIAH (zĭb′ĭ-à) ("gazelle"). The mother of Joash, king of Judah (835-796 B.C.), and the wife of King Ahaziah (841 B.C.). Zibiah's infant son was rescued from Athaliah's plot to kill all the royal seed. His aunt hid Joash in the Temple until he was seven years old. He was proclaimed king by the high priest, Jehoiada, after Athaliah was slain. His reign was good because of the influence of his mother and the high priest, Jehoiada (2 Kings 12:1-21).

ZIKLAG (zĭk′lăg). A town in south Judah (Josh. 15:31) which belonged to Simeon (Josh. 19:5). David took refuge there (1 Sam. 27:6; 30:1-6; 2 Sam. 1:1). It was settled after the exile (Neh. 11:28).

ZILPAH (zĭl′pà). The mother of Gad and Asher. Laban gave her to Leah as her maidservant (Gen. 29:24; 46:18). Leah, on the other hand, gave Zilpah to Jacob as his wife (Gen. 30:9; 37:2). She bore the patriarch two of his twelve sons (Gen. 30:10-13; 35:26).

ZION (zī′ŭn). The fortified hill southeast of Jerusalem which David captured from the Jebusites and made the capital of the United Kingdom (2 Sam. 5:7; 1 Kings 8: 1). In the Old Testament the name is used poetically for Jerusalem, and probably means "citadel" or "stronghold" (cf. 2 Kings 19:21; Psa. 48:1-14; 69:35; 133: 3; Isa. 1:8; 52:1).

The New Testament use of Zion refers not only to Jerusalem as a whole but to the entire nation of Israel (Rom. 11:26, 27). It also embraces the New Jerusalem, the symbolized abode and destiny of all the redeemed in eternity (Heb. 12:22, 23; Rev. 21:9–22:5).

Zion also has reference to the capital city of the millennial kingdom in the coming age (Isa. 1:27; 2:3; 4:1-6; Joel 3: 16; Zech. 1:16, 17; 8:3-8; Rom. 11:26).

ZIPPORAH (zĭ-pō′rà) ("swallow"). The

first wife of Moses and the mother of Gershom and Eliezer (Exod. 2:16-22). Moses met Zipporah in Midian. She was one of the seven daughters of Reuel (another name for Jethro). She and Moses apparently had little compatibility, she being a Midianite and he a Hebrew. She apparently opposed circumcising their son. This was a serious matter because circumcision was the symbol of the covenant between God and his people. Now called to deliver God's people out of Egypt, Moses recognized the seriousness of this reluctance. At an inn Moses evidently became violently ill. Zipporah in fright circumcised the child herself, and Moses' life was spared (Exod. 4:24-26). After this she became a nonentity until she, her sons, and her father, Jethro, joined Moses at Mount Sinai (Exod. 18:5). Zipporah seems to have been prejudiced and rebellious and of little help to her husband.

ZOAN (zō'ăn). A city of northeast Egypt known as Avaris in the Hyksos period, as Raamses under Rameses II, and as Tanis still later. See Num. 13:22; Psa. 78:12, 43; Isa. 19:11, 13; 30:4; Ezek. 30:14.

ZOAR (zō'ẽr). One of the cities of the Plain, probably the smallest of the five (Gen. 19:20, 22). Its original name was Bela (Gen. 14:2). Lot first interceded for Zoar, then fled from its impending destruction (Gen. 19:20 – 22:30). The site was in existence in the days of Isaiah and Jeremiah, apparently on the east (Moabite) side of the Dead Sea (Isa. 15:5; Jer. 48:34). Zoar is located a few miles from the present south-southeast shoreline of the Dead Sea.

ZOBAH (zō'bȧ). A powerful Aramean kingdom in the days of Saul and David. It lay west of the Euphrates (1 Sam. 14:47; 2 Sam. 8:3). It was also called Aram-Zobah (2 Sam. 10:6). David subdued the region and Solomon controlled it (cf. 1 Kings 11:23).

ZOPHAR (zō'fẽr) (perhaps "chirper," from Arabic *safara*, "to whistle"). One of Job's friends who boasted of his knowledge of God. Zophar was of little comfort or help to Job, for his dogmatism rested not upon God's Word but on what he thought he knew (Job 2:11; 11:1; 20:1; 42:9).

ZORAH (zō'rȧ). A town in the lowlands of Judah (Josh. 15:33). It was inhabited by the tribe of Dan (Josh. 19:41). Samson's father was a native of the place (Judg. 16:31). Some of the Danites who captured Laish were from Zorah (Judg. 18:2, 8, 11). Rehoboam fortified the town (2 Chron. 11:10). It was inhabited in the post-captivity period (Neh. 11:29). Zorah is located at Sarᶜa, on the north side of the Valley of Sorek and about 14 miles west of Jerusalem.

Part Three

BIBLE CONCORDANCE

CONCORDANCE
TO THE OLD AND NEW TESTAMENTS

PLAN OF THE WORK.—This Concordance is based on Cruden's and contains 40,000 references. Meanings of words and references of minor importance are stated first; the others follow in the order of the Books. The *inflexions* and *derivatives* of a word, and *phrases* in which it occurs, are *grouped* under it alphabetically; and are in the first instance set out in full in *italic*, but afterwards abbreviated, the *phrases* being represented by a dash ("—"), to avoid repetition and facilitate comparison.

ABASE, make low, &c.
Job 40. 11. every one proud *a.*
Is. 31. 4. lion will not *a.* himself
Ezek. 21. 26. *a.* him that is high
Dan. 4. 37. walk in pride is able to *a.*
Mat. 23. 12. exalt himself shall be *abased*
2 Cor. 11. 7. offence in *abasing* myself
ABATED, waters were, Gen. 8. 3, 11.
Lev. 27. 18. *a.* from thy estimation
Deut. 34. 7. nor his natural force *a.*
Judg. 8. 3. their anger was *a.* towards
ABHOR, greatly hate and loathe.
Lev. 26. 11. my soul shall not *a.* you
15. if your soul *a.* my judgments
30. my soul shall *a.* you
44. neither will I *a.* them
Deut. 23. 7. not *a.* an Edomite
1 Sam. 27. 12. made his people to *a.* him
Job 30. 10. they *a.* me, they flee
42. 6. I *a.* myself, and repent
Ps. 5. 6. Lord will *a.* the bloody
119. 163. I hate and *a.* lying
Jer. 14. 21. do not *a.* us for name's sake
Amos 5. 10. they *a.* him that speaketh
6. 8. I *a.* the excellency of Jacob
Mic. 3. 9. ye that *a.* judgment
Ex. 5. 21. made our savour *abhorred*
Lev. 26. 43. their soul *a.* my statutes
Deut. 32. 19. Lord saw it he *a.* them
1 Sam. 2. 17. men *a.* the offering
Job 19. 19. my inward friends *a.* me
Ps. 22. 24. nor *a.* affliction of afflicted
89. 38. hath cast off and *a.* anointed
106. 40. he *a.* his own inheritance
Prov. 22. 14. *a.* of the Lord shall fall
Lam. 2. 7. Lord hath *a.* his sanctuary
Zech. 11.8. their soul *a.* me
Rom. 2. 22. thou that *abhorrest* idols
Job 33. 20. his life *abhorreth* bread
Ps. 10. 3. covetous whom the Lord *a.*
36. 4 he *a.* not evil
107. 18. their soul *a.* all manner of meat
Is. 49. 7. him whom the nation *a.*
66. 24. be an *abhorring* unto all flesh
ABIDE, continue, bear.
Ex. 16. 29. *a.* ye every man in his place
Num. 35. 25. *a.* to death of high priest
2 Sam. 11. 11. ark and Israel *a.* in tents
Ps. 15. 1. who shall *a.* in thy tabernacle
61. 4. I will *a.* in tabernacle
61. 7. he shall *a.* before God for ever
91. 1. *a.* under shadow of Almighty
Prov. 7. 11. her feet *a.* not in her house
19. 23. that hath it shall *a.* satisfied
Hos. 3. 3. shall *a.* for me many days
3. 4. Israel shall *a.* without a king
Joel 2. 11. terrible; who can *a.* it
Mal. 3. 2. who may *a.* the day of his

Mat. 10. 11. there *abide* till ye go thence
Luke 19. 5. I must *a.* at thy house
24. 29. *a.* with us the day is far spent
John 14. 16. Comforter that he may *a.*
15. 4. *a.* in me and I in you, 7.
10. ye shall *a.* in my love, *a.* in his
Acts 20. 23. afflictions *a.* me
1 Cor. 3. 14. if any man's work *a.*
7. 8. good for them if they *a.* even as I
20. every man *a.* in the same
24. is called therein *a.* with God
Phil. 1. 24. to *a.* in the flesh is needful
25. know that I shall *a.* with you
1 John 2. 24. let that therefore *a.* in you
27. ye shall *a.* in him
28. little children *a.* in him
Ps. 49. 12. man in honour *abideth* not
55. 19. even he that *a.* of old
Eccl. 1. 4. the earth *a.* for ever
John 3. 36. wrath of God *a.* on him
8. 35. servant *a.* not, Son *a.* for ever
12. 24. except it die it *a.* alone
34. Christ *a.* for ever
15. 5. he that *a.* in me bringeth forth
2 Tim. 2. 13. yet he *a.* faithful
1 Pet. 1. 23. word of God *a.* for ever
1 John 3. 6. whoso *a.* in him sinneth not
24. hereby we know he *a.* in us
John 5. 38. not his word *abiding* in you
1 John 3. 15. no murderer hath eternal life *a.*
John 14. 23. make our *abode* with
ABILITY, in strength, wealth, &c., Lev. 27. 8.
Ezra 2. 69. Neh. 5. 8. Dan. 1. 4.
Mat. 25. 15. to every man according to his several *a.* Acts 11. 29.
1 Pet. 4. 11. as of the *a.* God giveth
ABLE men, such as fear God, Ex. 18. 21.
Lev. 14. 22. such as he is *a.* to get
Deut. 16. 17. every man give as he is *a.*
2 Chr. 20. 6. none is *a.* to withstand
Dan. 3. 17. God is *a.* to deliver
4. 37. walk in pride he is *a.* to abase
Mat. 3. 9. God is *a.* of these stones to raise up children, Luke 3. 8.
9. 28. believe ye I am *a.* to do this?
10. 28. are not *a.* to kill the soul
19. 12. he that is *a.* to receive it, let
Mark 4. 33. as they were *a.* to hear
John 10. 29. no man *a.* to pluck you
Rom. 4. 21. he was *a.* to perform
14. 4. God is *a.* to make him stand
1 Cor. 3. 2. neither yet now are ye *a.*
10. 13. tempted above that ye are *a.*
2 Cor. 9. 8. *a.* to make all grace abound
Phil. 3. 21. *a.* to subdue all to himself
2 Tim. 1. 12. *a.* to keep that which
3. 15. Scriptures *a.* to make wise
Heb. 2. 18 *a.* to succour the tempted

ABLE, Heb. 5. 7. *able* to save him from death
7. 25. *a.* to save to the uttermost
11. 19. *a.* to raise him from dead
Jas. 1. 21. *a.* to save your souls
4. 12. *a.* to save and to destroy
Jude 24. *a.* to keep you from falling
ABOLISH, make to cease.
Is. 2. 18. idols he shall utterly *a.*
51. 6. righteousness shall not be *abolished*
Ezek. 6. 6. your works may be *a.*
2 Cor. 3. 13. to the end of that *a.*
Eph. 2. 15. having *a.* in his flesh
2 Tim. 1. 10. Jesus Christ hath *a.* death
ABOMINABLE, very hateful, Lev. 7. 21; 11. 43;
18. 30. Is. 14. 19; 65. 4. Jer. 16. 18.
1 Chr. 21. 6. king's word was *a.* to Joab
Job 15. 16. how much more *a.* is man
Ps. 14. 1. have done *a.* works, 53. 1.
Jer. 44. 4. do not this *a.* thing I hate
Nah. 3. 6. I will cast *a.* filth on thee
Tit. 1. 16. in works deny him being *a.*
1 Pet. 4. 3. walked in *a.* idolatries
Rev. 21. 8. unbelieving and *a.* shall
ABOMINATION, what is very filthy, hateful,
and loathsome, as in, Is. 66. 3; idols, Ex.
8. 26.
Prov. 6. 16. seven things are an *a.* to Lord
11. 1. a false balance is *a.* to the Lord
20. they of froward heart are *a.*
12. 22. lying lips are *a.* to the Lord
15. 8. sacrifice of wicked is an *a.*
26. thoughts of wicked are an *a.*
16. 5. proud in heart is an *a.* to Lord, 3. 32.
20. 23. divers weights are an *a.* to the Lord
28. 9. his prayer shall be *a.*
Is. 1. 13. incense is an *a.* to me
Dan. 11. 31. *a.* that maketh desolate
12. 11. Mat. 24. 15. Mark 13. 14. *a.* of des.
Luke 16. 15. is *a.* in the sight of God
2 Ki. 21. 2. *abominations* of heathen
Ezra 9. 14. join people of these *a.*
Prov. 26. 25. seven *a.* in his heart
Jer. 7. 10. delivered to do all these *a.*
Ezek. 16. 2. cause Jerusalem to know her *a.*
20. 4; 23. 36.
18. 13. hath done all these *a.* shall die
Dan. 9. 27. for the overspreading of *a.*
Rev. 17. 5. mother of harlots and *a.* [Rom. 3. 7.
ABOUND, become very full, large, Prov. 8. 24.
Prov. 28. 20. faithful shall *a.* with blessings
Mat. 24. 12. because iniquity shall *a.*
Rom. 5. 20. offence might *a.* but where sin *a.*
grace did much more *a.*
6. 1. in sin that grace may *a.*
Phil. 1. 9. that your love may *a.* more
4. 12. both to *a.* and to suffer need
17. fruit that may *a.* to your account
18. I have all and *a.*
1 Thes. 3. 12. the Lord make you *a.* in love
2 Pet. 1. 8. these things be in you and *a.*
Eph. 1. 8. hath *abounded* toward us
1 Cor. 15. 58. always *abounding*
Col. 2. 7. *a.* therein with thanksgiving
ABOVE, higher, heaven, Ex. 20. 4.
John 3. 31. cometh from *a.* is *a.* all
8. 23. I am from *a.* ye are from beneath
John 19. 11. power given thee from *a.*
Gal. 4. 26. Jerusalem which is *a.* is free
Eph. 4. 6. one God who is *a.* all
Col. 3. 1. seek things which are *a.*
2. set your affection on things *a.*
Jas. 1. 17. every perfect gift is from *a.*
3. 15, 17. wisdom from *a.* is pure

ABSENT one from another, Gen. 31. 49. 2 Cor.
10. 1.
2 Cor. 5. 6. in body we are *a.* from the Lord
8. willing rather to be *a.* from the body
9. that whether present or *a.*
Col. 2. 5. though I be *a.* in the flesh
ABSTAIN from idols, Acts 15. 20.
1 Thes. 4. 3. ye should *a.* from fornication
5. 22. *a.* from all appearance of evil
1 Tim. 4. 3. commanding to *a.* from meats
1 Pet. 2. 11. *a.* from fleshly lusts
Abstinence from meats, Acts 27. 21.
ABUNDANCE, great fulness, and plenty,
Job 22. 11; 38. 34. Deut. 33. 19. 1 Chr.
22. 3, 4, 14, 15.
Deut. 28. 47. for the *a.* of all things
Eccl. 5. 10. he that loveth *a.* with
12. *a.* of rich not suffer him to sleep
Mat. 12. 34. out of the *a.* of the heart the mouth
speaketh, Luke 6. 45.
13. 12. shall have more *a.* 25. 29.
Mark 12. 44. cast in of their *a.*
Luke 12. 15. life consisteth not in *a.*
2 Cor. 8. 2. *a.* of their joy abounded
12. 7. through *a.* of revelations
ABUNDANT in goodness and truth, Ex. 34. 6.
2 Cor. 4. 15; 9. 12.
2 Cor. 11. 23. in labours more *a.*
1 Tim. 1. 14. grace of Lord exceeding *a.*
1 Pet. 1. 3. his *a.* mercy hath
Job 12. 6. God bringeth *abundantly*
Ps. 36. 8. shall be *a.* satisfied
Sol. 5. 1. yea drink *a.* O beloved
Is. 55. 7. he will *a.* pardon
John 10. 10. might have life more *a.*
1 Cor. 15. 10. laboured more *a.* than all
Tit. 3. 6. shed on us *a.* through Jesus
2 Pet. 1. 11. entrance ministered *a.*
ABUSE not my power, 1 Cor. 9. 18.
1 Cor. 7. 31. use world as not *abusing* it
ACCEPT, receive kindly in favour, Gen. 32. 20.
Acts 24. 3.
Lev. 26. 41. *a.* punishment of iniquity, 43.
Deut. 33. 11. *a.* work of his hands
2 Sam. 24. 23. Lord thy God *a.* thee
Job 13. 8. will ye *a.* his person, 10.
32. 21. not *a.* any man's person
42. 8. servant Job, him will I *a.*
Ps. 119. 108. *a.* freewill offerings
Prov. 18. 5. not good to *a.* person
Ezek. 43. 27. I will *a.* you, saith Lord
Mal. 1. 13. should I *a.* this of your
Gen. 4. 7. shalt thou not be *accepted*
19. 21. *a.* thee concerning this thing
Luke 4. 24. no prophet *a.* in his own
Acts 10. 35. worketh righteousness is *a.*
2 Cor. 5. 9. we may be *a.* of him
6. 2. heard thee in a time *a.* now is
Eph. 1. 6. made us *a.* in the beloved
Luke 20. 21. neither *acceptest* thou
Job 34. 19. *accepteth* not the person
Eccl. 9. 7. God now *a.* thy works
Hos. 8. 13. Lord *a.* them not
Gal. 2. 6. God *a.* no man's person
Heb. 11. 35. not *accepting* deliverance
Acceptable day of the Lord, Is. 58. 5.
Ps. 19.14. meditation of heart *a.*
Eccl. 12. 10. sought out *a.* words
Is. 49. 8. in an *a.* time I heard thee
61. 2. proclaim the *a.* year of the Lord, Luke
Dan. 4. 27. let my counsel be *a.* [4. 19.
Rom. 12. 1. sacrifice holy *a.* to God
Eph. 5. 10. proving what is *a.* to Lord

Phil. 4. 18. sacrifice *acceptable* well-pleasing
1 Pet. 2. 5. *a.* to God by Jesus Christ
Heb. 12. 28. serve God *acceptably*
1 Tim. 1. 15. worthy of *acceptation*
ACCESS, admission through Christ, Rom. 5. 2.
  Eph. 2. 18; 3. 12.
ACCOMPLISH, perform fully, finish, Lev.
  22. 21. Job 14. 6.
Ps. 64. 6. *a.* a diligent search
Is. 55. 11. it shall *a.* that I please
Ezek. 6. 12. thus will I *a.* my fury
Dan. 9. 2. would *a.* seventy years
Luke 9. 31. should *a.* at Jerusalem
Prov. 13. 19. desire *accomplished* is sweet to soul
Is. 40. 2. her warfare is *a.* her sin
John 19. 28. all things were now *a.*
1 Pet. 5. 9. same afflictions are *a.*
Heb. 9. 6. *accomplishing* service
ACCORD, hearty agreement, Acts 1. 14; 2. 1, 46;
  4. 24; 15. 25.
ACCOUNT, reckoning, esteem.
Job 33. 13. not *a.* of his matters
Ps. 144. 3. that thou makest *a.* of him
Eccl. 7. 27. one by one to find out *a.*
Mat. 12. 36. give *a.* in day of judgment
18. 23. would take *a.* of his servants
Luke 16. 2. give *a.* of stewardship
Rom. 14. 12. give *a.* of himself to God
Phil. 4. 17. fruit abound to your *a.*
Heb. 13. 17. as they that must give *a.*
1 Pet. 4. 5. shall give *a.* to him that
Ps. 22. 30. *accounted* to the Lord
Is. 2. 22. wherein is he to be *a.* of
Luke 20. 35. they which shall be *a.* worthy to
  obtain that world
21. 36. *a.* worthy to escape
22. 24. which should be *a.* greatest
Gal. 3. 6. *a.* to him for righteousness
ACCURSED, devoted to ruin.
Deut. 21. 23. hanged is *a.* of God.
Josh. 6. 18. keep from the *a.* thing
Is. 65. 20. one hundred years old shall be *a.*
Rom. 9. 3. wish myself *a.* from Christ
1 Cor. 12. 3. no man by Spirit calls Jesus *a.*
Gal. 1. 8, 9. preach other gospel be *a.*
ACCUSATION, Ezra 4. 6. Mat. 27. 37. Luke
  6. 7; 19. 8. John 18. 29. Acts 25. 18.
2 Pet. 2. 11. bring not a railing *a.* Jude 9.
ACCUSE, charge with crimes.
Prov. 30. 10. *a.* not servant to master
Luke 3. 14. neither *a.* any falsely
John 5. 45. that I will *a.* you to Father
1 Pet. 3. 16. falsely *a.* your good conversation
Tit. 1. 6. not *accused* of riot
Rev. 12. 10. *a.* them before our God, *accuser* of
  brethren is cast down
Acts 25. 16. have *accusers* face to face
2 Tim. 3. 3. false *a.* Tit. 2. 3.
John 5. 45. there is one that *accuseth*
Rom. 2. 15. thoughts *accusing* or
ACCUSTOMED to do evil, Jer. 13. 23.
ACKNOWLEDGE, own, confess.
Deut. 33. 9. neither did he *a.* his brethren
Ps. 32. 5. I *a.* my sin unto thee, and mine
51. 3. I *a.* my transgression
Prov. 3. 6. in all thy ways *a.* him
Is. 33. 13. ye that are near *a.* my might
63. 16. though Israel *a.* us not
Jer. 3. 13. only *a.* thine iniquity
14. 20. we *a.* our wickedness
Hos. 5. 15. till they *a.* their offence
1 Cor. 16. 18. *a.* them that are such
2 Tim. 2. 25. *acknowledging* the truth

ACKNOWLEDGE—Tit. 1. 1. *acknowledging* truth
Col. 2. 2. to the *acknowledgment* of the mystery
  of God and of the Father
ACQUAINT thyself with him, Job 22. 21.
Ps. 139. 3. *acquainted* with my ways
Is. 53. 3. man of sorrows, and *a.* with grief
Acquaintance, familiar friends or companions, Job
  19. 13; 42. 11. Ps. 31. 11; 88. 8, 18.
ACQUIT, hold innocent, Job 10. 14.
Nah. 1. 3. will not *a.* the wicked
ACTS of the Lord, Deut. 11. 3, 7.
Judg. 5. 11. rehearse righteous—
1 Sam. 12. 7. reason of all righteous—
Ps. 106. 2. utter mighty—
145. 4, 6. speak of thy mighty *a.*
Is. 28. 21. his *act* his strange *a.*
John 8. 4. taken in adultery in very *a.*
ACTIONS weighed, 1 Sam. 2. 3.
ADAMANT, Ezek. 3. 9. Zech. 7. 12.
ADD fifth part, Lev. 5. 16; 6. 5; 27. 13, 15, 19,
  27, 31.
Deut. 4. 2. shall not *a.* to word
29. 19. *a.* drunkenness to thirst
Ps. 69. 27. *a.* iniquity to their iniquity
Prov. 30. 6. *a.* not unto his words
Is. 30. 1. that they may *a.* sin to sin
Mat. 6. 27. *a.* one cubit, Luke 12. 25.
Phil. 1. 16. *a.* affliction to bonds
2 Pet. 1. 5. *a.* to your faith virtue
Rev. 22. 18. if any man *a.* unto these things, God
  shall *a.* unto him
Deut. 5. 22. he *added* no more
1 Sam. 12. 19. *a.* to all our sins this evil
Jer. 36. 32. were *a.* many like words
45. 3. Lord *a.* grief to my sorrow
Acts 2. 41. were *a.* 3,000 souls
47. Lord *a.* to the church . . . saved
5. 14. believers were the more *a.*
11. 24. much people was *a.* to the Lord
Prov. 10. 22. *addeth* no sorrow with
ADDER, poisonous serpent, Gen. 49. 17. Ps.
  58. 4; 91. 13; 140. 3. Prov. 23. 32. Is. 14. 29.
ADDICTED, devoted, 1 Cor. 16. 15.
ADJURE, to charge under pain of God's curse,
  1 Ki. 22. 16. 2 Chr. 18. 15. Mat. 26. 63.
  Mark 5. 7. Acts 19. 13. Josh. 6. 26. 1 Sam. 14. 24.
ADMINISTRATION, 1 Cor. 12. 5. 2 Cor. 9. 12;
  administered, 8. 19, 20.
ADMIRATION, undue regard, Jude 16. or
  wonder and amazement, Rev. 17. 6.
2 Thes. 1. 10. *admired* in them that believe
ADMONISH, warn, reprove.
Rom. 15. 14. able to *a.* one another
1 Thes. 5. 12. over you and *a.* you
2 Thes. 3. 15. *a.* him as a brother
Eccl. 4. 13. foolish king will no more be
12. 12. by these be *a.*   [*admonished*
Jer. 42. 19. know that I have *a.* you
Heb. 8. 5. as Moses was *a.* of God
Col. 3. 16. *admonishing* . . . in psalms
1 Cor. 10. 11. are written for our *admonition*
Eph. 6. 4. bring up in the nurture and *a.* of Lord
Tit. 3. 10. after first and second *a.* reject
ADOPTION, putting among God's children,
  Jer. 3. 19. 2 Cor. 6. 18.
Rom. 8. 15. received spirit of *a.*
23. *a.* redemption of our body
Gal. 4. 5. might receive *a.* of sons
Eph. 1. 5. unto *a.* of children
ADORN, deck out, Is. 61. 10. Jer. 31. 4.
1 Tim. 2. 9. women *a.* in modest
Tit. 2. 10. *a.* the doctrine of God our
Jer. 31. 4. *adorned* with thy tabrets

Luke 21. 5. *adorned* with goodly stones
1 Pet. 3. 5. holy women *a.* themselves
Rev. 21. 2. as bride *a.* for her husband
Is. 61. 10. as bride *adorneth* herself
ADULTERER, put to death, Lev. 20. 10.
Job 24. 15. eye of *a.* waits for twilight
Is. 57. 3. seed of the *a.* and the
Jer. 23. 10. land is full of *adulterers*
9. 2. Hos. 7. 4. they are all *a.*
Mal. 3. 5. I swift witness against *a.*
Heb. 13. 4. *a.* God will judge
Jas. 4. 4. ye *a.* and *adulteresses*
Prov. 6. 26. *adulteress* hunt for life
32. committeth *adultery* lacks
Mat. 5. 28. committed *a.* in his heart
2 Pet. 2. 14. having eyes full of *a.*   [Mark 7. 21.
Mat. 15. 19. out of the heart proceed *adulteries,*
Prov. 30. 20. way of *adulterous* woman
Mat. 12. 39. *a.* generation seeketh a sign, 16. 4.
   Mark 8. 38.
ADVANTAGE hath the Jew, Rom. 3. 1.
2 Cor. 2. 11. lest Satan get an *a.*
Luke 9. 25. what is a man *advantaged?*
ADVERSARY, opposer, enemy.
Ex. 23. 22. I will be an *a.* to thy *a.*
1 Ki. 5. 4. is neither *a.* nor evil
Job 31. 35. my *a.* had written a book
Mat. 5. 25. agree with thine *a.*
1 Tim. 5. 14. give no occasion to *a.*
1 Pet. 5. 8. your *a.* the devil as a
1 Sam. 2. 10. *adversaries* of Lord broken
Lam. 1. 5. her *a.* are the chief
Luke 21. 15. all your *a.* not be able
1 Cor. 16. 9. and there are many *a.*
Phil. 1. 28. and in nothing terrified by your *a.*
Heb. 10. 27. shall devour the *a.*
ADVERSITY, affliction, misery.
1 Sam. 10. 19. saved you out of *all a.*
2 Sam. 4. 9. redeemed my soul from—
2 Chr. 15. 6. God did vex with—
Ps. 10. 6. I shall never be in *a.*
31. 7. thou hast known my soul in *a.*
94. 13. give rest from days of *a.*
Prov. 17. 17. brother is born for *a.*
Eccl. 7. 14. in the day of *a.* consider
Is. 30. 20. give you the bread of *a.*
ADVICE, Judg. 19. 30. 1 Sam. 25. 33. 2 Sam.
   19. 43. Prov. 20. 18.
ADVOCATE with Father, 1 John 2. 1.
AFAR off, Gen. 22. 4; 37. 18. Ps. 65. 5; 138. 6.
   proud he knoweth *a.*
Ps. 139. 2. understandest thoughts *a.* off
Jer. 23. 23. not a God *a.*
Eph. 2. 17. preached peace to you *a.*
Heb. 11. 13. having seen promises *a.*
2 Pet. 1. 9. blind and cannot see *a.*
AFFAIRS, Ps. 112. 5. 2 Tim. 2. 4.
AFFECT, strive after, court.
Gal. 4. 17. they zealously *a.* you
18. good to be zealously *affected*
Lam. 3. 51. mine eye *affecteth* my heart.
Col. 3. 5. mortify inordinate *affection*
1 Thes. 2. 8. *affectionately* desirous
Rom. 12. 10. be kindly *affectioned*
1. 26. them to vile *affections*
Gal. 5. 24. crucify flesh with *a.*
AFFINITY, relation by marriage, 1 Ki. 3. 1.
   2 Chr. 18. 1. Ezra 9. 14.
AFFLICT, grieve, trouble, Gen. 15. 13. Ex. 1. 11;
   22. 22.
Ezra 8. 21. that we might *a.* ourselves
Lev. 16. 29, 31; 23. 27, 32. Num. 29. 7; 30. 13.
   shall *a.* your souls

Is. 58. 5. day for man to *afflict* his soul
Lam. 3. 33. doth not *a.* willingly   [Ps. 18. 27.
2 Sam. 22. 28. *afflicted* people thou wilt save,
Job 6. 14. to *a.* pity should be showed
34. 28. heareth the cry of the *a.*
Ps. 22. 24. not abhorred affliction of *a.*
119. 67. before I was *a.* I went astray
71. it is good that I have been *a.*
75. thou in faithfulness hast *a.* me
107. I am *a.* very
140. 12. wilt maintain cause of the a.
Prov. 15. 15. all days of *a.* are evil
Is. 49. 13. he will have mercy on *a.*
53. 4. smitten of God and *a.*
7. he was oppressed and *a.*
58. 10. satisfy the *a.* soul
Mic. 4. 6. gather her I have *a.*
Ex. 3. 7. seen the *affliction* of my people
2 Ki. 14. 26. Lord saw *a.* of Israel
Job 5. 6. *a.* cometh not forth of dust
36. 8. holden in cords of *a.*
15. delivereth poor in his *a.*
21. this chosen rather than *a.*
Ps. 25. 18. look upon my *a.* and pain
107. 10. bound in *a.* and iron
39. brought low through *a.*
119. 92. should have perished in *a.*
Is. 48. 10. chosen thee in furnace of *a.*
63. 9. in all their *a.* he was afflicted
Hos. 5. 15. in their *a.* they will seek
Amos 6. 6. not grieved for *a.* of Joseph
Obad. 13. not looked on their *a.*
Nah. 1. 9. *a.* not rise the second time
Zech. 1. 15. helped forward the *a.*
2 Cor. 4. 17. our light *a.* which is
Phil. 4. 14. communicate with my *a.*
1 Thes. 1. 6. received word in much *a.*
Heb. 11. 25. choosing to suffer *a.*
Jas. 1. 27. visit fatherless and widows in *a.*
Ps. 34. 19. *afflictions* of righteous
132. 1. remember David and all his *a.*
Acts 7. 10. delivered him out of all *a.*
20. 23. bonds and *a.* abide me
1 Thes. 3. 3. moved by these *a.*
2 Tim. 1. 8. partaker of *a.* of gospel
Heb. 10. 32. endured great fight of *a.*
1 Pet. 5. 9. the same *a.* accomplished
AFRAID, Lev. 26. 6. Num. 12. 8. Job 13. 21. Ps.
   56. 3; 119. 120.
Not be *afraid,* Ps. 56. 11; 112. 7. Is. 12. 2.
   Mat. 14. 27. Mark 5. 36. Luke 12. 4. 1 Pet.
   3. 6, 14. Heb. 11. 23.
AFRESH, crucify Son of God, Heb. 6. 6.
AGE is as nothing before thee, Ps. 39. 5.
Job 5. 26. to grave in full *a.*
John 9. 21. he is of *a.* ask him
Heb. 5. 14. meat to those of full *a.*
Tit. 2. 2, 3. *aged* men be sober
Ages, Eph. 2. 7; 3. 5, 21.
Col. 1. 26. mystery hid from *a.*
AGREE together, Acts 5. 9.
Mat. 5. 25. *a.* with thine adversary quickly
18. 19. if two shall *a.* on earth
1 John 5. 8. these three *a.* in one
Amos 3. 3. can two walk except *agreed*
Is. 28. 15. with hell at *agreement*
2 Cor. 6. 16. what *a.* hath temple . . . idols
ALIEN, stranger, Ex. 18. 3. Job 19. 15. Ps. 69. 8.
   heathens, Deut. 14. 21. Is. 61. 5. Lam. 5. 2.
   Heb. 11. 34.
Eph. 2. 12. *a.* from commonwealth
4. 18. *alienated* from life of God
Col. 1. 21. were sometime *a.*

ALIVE, Gen. 12. 12. Num. 22. 33.
1 Sam. 2. 6. killeth and maketh *a.*
15. 8. he took Agag *a.*
Luke 15. 24. my son was dead and is *a.*
Rom. 6. 11. *a.* unto God through Jesus
13. as those *a.* from the dead
7. 9. I was *a.* without the law once
1 Cor. 15. 22. in Christ all be made *a.*
1 Thes. 4. 15, 17. we *a.* and remain
Rev. 1. 18. I am *a.* for evermore
2. 8. was dead and is *a.*
ALLEGING, prove by quoting, Acts 17. 3.
ALLOW, deeds of fathers, Luke 11. 48.
Acts 24. 15. which themselves *a.*
Rom. 7. 15. that which I do I *a.* not
1 Thes. 2. 4. as we were *allowed* of God
Rom. 14. 22. in that which he *alloweth*
ALLURE, Hos. 2. 14. 2 Pet. 2. 18.
ALMIGHTY GOD, Gen. 17. 1; 28. 3; 35. 11;
43. 14; 48. 3. Ex. 6. 3. Num. 24. 4. Ruth 1. 20.
Ezek. 1. 24. 2 Cor. 6. 18. Rev. 1. 8; 4. 8;
15. 3; 16. 14; 19. 15; 21. 22.
Job 21. 15. what is the *Almighty*
22. 25. *A.* shall be thy defence
27. 10. delight himself in the *A.*
Ps. 91. 1. under shadow of *A.*
Rev. 1. 8. is to come, the *A.*
ALMOST all things, Heb. 9. 22.
Ex. 17. 4. *a.* ready to stone me
Ps. 73. 2. my feet were *a.* gone
94. 17. soul had *a.* dwelt in silence
Prov. 5. 14. I was *a.* in all evil in the congrega-
tion   [Christian
Acts 26. 28. *a.* thou persuadest me to be a
ALMS, Acts 3. 2, 3; 24. 17.
Mat. 6. 1. do not your *a.* before men
Luke 11. 41. give *a.* of such things
12. 33. sell that ye have, give *a.*
Acts 10. 2. gave much *a.* to people
4. thine *a.* are come up for memorial
ALONE, Jacob left, Gen. 32. 24.
Gen. 2. 18. not good for man to be *a.*
Num. 23. 9. dwell *a.* Deut. 33. 28
Deut. 32. 12. Lord *a.* did lead him
Ps. 136. 4. *a.* doeth great wonders
Eccl. 4. 10. woe to him that is *a.*
Is. 5. 8. that they may be placed *a.*
John 8. 16. I am not *a.*
17. 20. neither pray I for these *a.*
Gal. 6. 4. rejoicing in himself *a.*
Ex. 32. 10. *let me a.* that my wrath
Hos. 4. 17. Ephraim is joined to idols, let him *a.*
Mat. 15. 14. let them *a.*
ALTAR, Gen. 13. 4; 26. 25; 33. 20. Ex. 17. 15;
20. 24. Deut. 7. 5; 12. 3. Josh. 22. 10.
altar to Lord, Gen. 8. 20; 12. 7; 22. 9; 35. 1, 3.
Ex. 30. 27; 40. 10.
Judg. 6. 25. throw down *a.* of Baal
1 Ki. 13. 2. cried against *a.* O *a.*
Ps. 26. 6. so will I compass thine *a.*
43. 4. then will I go to the *a.* of God
Mat. 5. 23. if thou bring gift to *a.*
24. leave there thy gift before the *a.*
Acts 17. 23. found *a.* with inscription
1 Cor. 9. 13. they that wait at *a.* are partakers
with *a.* 10. 18. of the *a.*
Heb. 13. 10. we have an *a.* whereof
Rev. 8. 3; 9. 13. the golden *a.*
ALWAY(S), Deut. 5. 29. Job 7. 16.
Gen. 6. 3. Spirit not *a.* strive
Deut. 14. 23. learn to fear the Lord *a.*
1 Chr. 16. 15. mindful *a.* of covenant
Job 27. 10. will he *a.* call on God

Job 32. 9. great men are not *always* wise
Ps. 9. 18. needy not *a.* be forgotten
16. 8. I set the Lord *a.* before me
Prov. 5. 19. ravished *a.* with her love
28. 14. happy is man that feareth *a.*
Is. 57. 16. neither will I be *a.* wroth
Mat. 26. 11. have poor *a.* with you
28. 20. I am with you *a.* to the end
Luke 18. 1. men ought *a.* to pray
John 8. 29. I do *a.* things that please
Acts 10. 2. Cornelius prayed God *a.*
2 Cor. 6. 10. yet *a.* rejoicing
Eph. 6. 18. praying *a.* with all prayer
Phil. 4. 4. rejoice in the Lord *a.*
Col. 4. 6. your speech be *a.* with grace
AMBASSADOR, Prov. 13. 17. Is. 33. 7. 2 Cor.
5. 20. Eph. 6. 20.
AMEN, even so come, Rev. 22. 20.
2 Cor. 1. 20. promises of God in him *a.*
Rev. 3. 14. these things saith the *a.*
AMEND your ways, Jer. 7. 3, 5; 26. 13.
Jer. 35. 15. *a.* your doings
AMISS, 2 Chr. 6. 37. Dan. 3. 29. Luke 23. 41.
Jas. 4. 3.
ANCHOR, Acts 27. 30. Heb. 6. 19.
ANCIENT, wisdom is with, Job 12. 12.
Dan. 7. 9. the *a.* of days did sit
Ps. 119. 100. I understand more than *ancients*
ANGEL, who redeemed me, Gen. 48. 16.
Gen. 24. 7. send his *a.* before thee
Ex. 23. 23. my *a.* shall go before thee
Angel of the Lord, Ps. 34. 7. Zech. 12. 8. Acts
5. 19; 12. 7, 23.
Is. 63. 9. *a.* of his presence saved
Dan. 3. 28. sent his *a.* and delivered
6. 22. sent his *a.* and shut lions' mouths
John 5. 4. went down at a certain
Acts 6. 15. his face as face of an *a.*
23. 8. Sadducees say neither *a.* nor
Job 4. 18. *angels* he charged with folly
Ps. 8. 5. a little lower than *a.*
68. 17. chariots of God thousands *a.*
78. 25. man did eat *a.* food
104. 4. maketh his *a.* spirits
Mat. 4. 11. *a.* came and ministered
13. 39. reapers are the *a.*
18. 10. their *a.* behold face of my Father
24. 31. send his *a.* with trumpet
36. no, not *a.* of heaven, Mark 13. 32.
25. 31. all holy *a.* with him
Mark 12. 25. are as *a.* in heaven
Luke 20. 36. equal unto the *a.*
Acts 7. 53. law by disposition of *a.*
1 Cor. 6. 3. we shall judge *a.*
Col. 2. 18. beguile worshipping of *a.*
2 Thes. 1. 7. with his mighty *a.*
1 Tim. 3. 16. seen of *a.* preached unto
Heb. 2. 16. took not the nature of *a.*
12. 22. an innumerable company of *a.*
13. 2. entertained *a.* unawares
1 Pet. 1. 12. *a.* desire to look into
2 Pet. 2. 11. *a.* which are greater in power &
might, bring not railing
Jude 6. *a.* which kept not first estate
Rev. 1. 20. *a.* of seven churches
Angel of God, Gen. 28. 12; 32. 1. Mat. 22. 30.
Luke 12. 8; 15. 10. John 1. 51.
ANGER, let not the *a.* of my lord wax hot, Ex.
32. 22.
Deut. 29. 24. meaneth heat of this *a.*
Josh. 7. 26. from fierceness of his *a.*
Job 9. 13. if God will not withdraw *a.*
Ps. 27. 9. put not servant away in *a.*

Ps. 30. 5. his *anger* endureth but a moment
77. 9. hath he in *a.* shut up
78. 38. turned he his *a.* away
50. he made a way to his *a.*
85. 4. cause *a.* towards us to cease
90. 7. we are consumed by thine *a.*
11. who knoweth power of thine *a.*
103. 9. keep *a.* for ever, Jer. 3. 5, 12.
Prov. 15. 1. grievous words stir up *a.*
Eccl. 7. 9. *a.* resteth in the bosom of fools
Hos. 11. 9. not execute mine *a.*
14. 4. my *a.* is turned away from him
Mic. 7. 18. retaineth not *a.* for ever
Nah. 1. 6. who can abide his *a.*
Eph. 4. 31. let all *a.* be put away
Col. 3. 8. put off all these; *a.* wrath
Slow to anger, Neh. 9. 17. Ps. 103. 8. Joel 2. 13.
    Jonah 4. 2. Nah. 1. 3. Jas. 1. 19.
Ps. 106. 32. they *angered* him at waters
Gen. 18. 30. let not Lord be *angry*
Deut. 1. 37. Lord was *a.* with me
9. 20. Lord was *a.* with Aaron
1 Ki. 11. 9. Lord was *a.* with Solomon
Ps. 2. 12. kiss Son lest he be *a.*
7. 11. God is *a.* with wicked every day
76. 7. who stand when thou art *a.*
Prov. 14. 17. soon *a.* dealeth foolishly
22. 24. no friendship with an *a.* man
29. 22. *a.* man stirreth up strife
Eccl. 7. 9. be not hasty to be *a.*
Is. 12. 1. though thou wast *a.* with
Jonah 4. 9. I do well to be *a.* even
Mat. 5. 22. whoso is *a.* with brother
Eph. 4. 26. be *a.* and sin not
Tit. 1. 7. bishop must not be soon *a.*
ANGUISH, excessive pain.
Gen. 42. 21. saw the *a.* of his soul
Ex. 6. 9. hearkened not for *a.* of spirit
Ps. 119. 143. trouble and *a.* take hold
Jer. 6. 24. *a.* taken hold of us
John 16. 21. remember not *a.* for joy
Rom. 2. 9. tribulation and *a.* upon
ANOINT, with oil, to appoint, to qualify for office
    of king, priest, or prophet, Ex. 28. 41.
Dan. 9. 24. to *a.* the most holy
Amos 6. 6. *a.* with chief ointments
Mat. 6. 17. when fastest *a.* thy head
Rev. 3. 18. *a.* eyes with eyesalve
1 Sam. 2. 10. exalt the horn of his *anointed*
24. 6. seeing he is the *a.* of the Lord
1 Chr. 16. 22. touch not my *a.* Ps. 105. 15.
2 Chr. 6. 42. turn not away the face of thine *a.*
    Ps. 132. 10.
Ps. 2. 2. against the Lord and his *a.*
18. 50. mercy to his *a.* to David, 2 Sam 22. 51.
20. 6. the Lord saveth his *a.*
28. 8. Lord is saving strength of his *a.*
45. 7. *a.* thee with oil of gladness
84. 9. look upon face of thine *a.*
89. 38. wroth with thine *a.*
132. 17. ordained a lamp for mine *a.*
Zech. 4. 14. two *a.* that stand by the Lord
Hab. 3. 13. salvation with thine *a.*
Acts 4. 27. Jesus whom thou hast *a.*
10. 38. how God *a.* Jesus of Nazareth
2 Cor. 1. 21. who hath *a.* us is God
Ps. 23. 5. *anointest* my head with oil
1 John 2. 27. same *anointing* teacheth you of all
Jas. 5. 14. *a.* him with oil
ANSWER of peace, Gen. 41. 16. Deut. 20. 11.
Prov. 15. 1. soft *a.* turneth wrath
16. 1. *a.* of tongue is from the Lord
Job 19. 16. gave me no *a.* Sol. 5. 6.

Mic. 3. 7. there is no *answer* of God
Rom. 11. 4. what saith the *a.* of God
2 Tim. 4. 16. at my first *a.* no man
1 Pet. 3. 15. ready to give an *a.* to
21. the *a.* of a good conscience
Job 40. 4. what shall I *a.* thee
Ps. 102. 2. *a.* me speedily
143. 1. in thy faithfulness *a.* me
Prov. 26. 4, 5. *a.* fool according to his folly
Is. 14. 32. what *a.* messengers
58. 9. shalt thou call, and the Lord shall *a.*
66. 4. when I called none did *a.*
Mat. 25. 37. then shall righteous *a.*
Luke 12. 11. what thing ye shall *a.*
13. 25. he shall *a.* I know you not
21. 14. meditate not what to *a.*
2 Cor. 5. 12. somewhat to *a.* them
Col. 4. 6. know how to *a.* every man
Job 14. 15. thou shalt call and I will *a.* & 13. 22.
    Ps. 91. 15. Is. 65. 24. Jer. 33. 3. Ezek. 14. 4, 7.
9. 3. he cannot *a.* one
40. 5. once have I spoken, but I will not *a.*
Ps. 18. 41. to Lord but he *answered* not
81. 7. I *a.* thee in secret place
99. 6. called on the Lord and he *a.*
Prov. 18. 23. rich *answereth* roughly
13. he that *a.* matter before hear
27. 19. as in water face *a.* to face
Eccl. 10. 19. money *a.* all things
Tit. 2. 9. not *answering* again
ANT, Prov. 6. 6; 30. 25.
ANTICHRIST, I John 2. 18, 22. & 4. 3. 2 John 7.
APART, Ps. 4. 3. Zech. 12. 12. Jas. 1. 21.
APOSTLE, *one sent forth* by Christ to preach the
    gospel, found and uphold churches, Rom. 1. 1.
    1 Cor. 12. 28, especially the twelve eyewitnesses,
    Acts 1. 21, 22.
Rom. 11. 13. I am *a.* of Gentiles
1 Cor. 1. 1. am I not an *a.*
15. 9. not meet to be called an *a.*
2 Cor. 12. 12. signs of *a.* were wrought
Heb. 3. 1. consider *a.* and high priest
Mat. 10. 2. names of the twelve *apostles*
Luke 11. 49. send prophets and *a.*
1 Cor. 4. 9. God hath set forth us *a.*
15. 9. I am the least of the *a.*
2 Cor. 11. 13. false *a.*
Eph. 2. 20. built on foundation of *a.*
4. 11. gave some *a.* some prophets
Rev. 2. 2. say they are *a.* and are not
18. 20. holy *a.* and prophets, Eph. 3. 5.
21. 14. names of twelve *a.* of the Lamb
Acts 1. 25. part of this *apostleship*
Rom. 1. 5. received grace and *a.*
1 Cor. 9. 2. seal of my *a.* are ye
Gal. 2. 8. to *a.* of circumcision
APPAREL, Is. 63. 1. Zeph. 1. 8. 1 Tim. 2. 9.
    1 Pet. 3. 3. Jas. 2. 2.
APPEAR, Gen. 1. 9. Heb. 11. 3.
Ex. 23. 15. none shall *a.* before me empty, 34. 20.
    Deut. 16. 16.
1 Sam. 2. 27. did I *a.* to house of thy father
2 Chr. 1. 7. did God *a.* to Solomon
Ps. 42. 2. when shall I *a.* before God
Is. 1. 12. when ye *a.* before me who
66. 5. shall *a.* to your joy, but they
Mat. 6. 16. may *a.* to men to fast
23. 27. *a.* beautiful outward
Rom. 7. 13. sin that it might *a.* sin
2 Cor. 5. 10. we must all *a.* before the judgment
    seat of Christ.
Col. 3. 4. Christ *a.* ye also shall *a.*
1 Tim. 4. 15. thy profiting *a.* to all

Heb. 9. 24. to *appear* in the presence of **God** for us
28. *a.* second time without sin to
1 Pet. 5. 4. when chief shepherd *a.*
1 John 3. 2. not yet *a.* what we shall
1 Sam. 16. 7. man looketh on outward *appearance*, but the Lord on heart
John 7. 24. judge not according to *a.*
1 Thes. 5. 22. abstain from all *a.* of evil
Tit. 2. 11. grace *appeared* to all men
Heb. 9. 26. he *a.* to put away sin
2 Tim. 1. 10. manifest by *appearing* of Jesus
4. 1. judge quick and dead at his *a.*
8. all them that love his *a.*
Tit. 2. 13. look for glorious *a.* of great God
1 Pet. 1. 7. unto praise at *a.* of Jesus
APPETITE, Prov. 23. 2. Is. 29. 8.
APPLE of eye, Deut. 32. 10. Ps. 17. 8. Prov. 7. 2. Lam. 2. 18. Zech. 2. 8.
Apple tree, Sol. 2. 3. & 8. 5.
Apples, Prov. 25. 11. Sol. 2. 5; 7. 8.
APPLY heart to wisdom, &c., Ps. 90. 12. Prov. 2. 2.; 22. 17; 23. 12. Eccl. 7. 25.
APPOINT me thy wages, and I, Gen. 30. 28.
Is. 61. 3. *a.* to them that mourn in Zion
26. 1. salvation will God *a.* for walls
Mat. 24. 51. *a.* his portion with hypocrites
Luke 22. 29. I *a.* unto you a kingdom
Job 7. 1. an *appointed* time to man
14. 14. all the days of my *a.* time
30. 23. to house *a.* for all living
Ps. 79. 11. preserve those *a.* to die
Jer. 5. 24. reserve *a.* weeks of harvest
Hab. 2. 3. vision is for an *a.* time
1 Thes. 5. 9. God not *a.* us to wrath
Heb. 9. 27. *a.* to men once to die
APPREHENDED, lay hold of, grasp, Phil. 3. 12, 13. Acts 12. 4. 2 Cor. 11. 32.
APPROACH, come near to, marry.
Lev. 18. 6. *a.* to near of kin, 20. 16.
Ps. 65. 4. blessed is the man whom thou choosest and causest to *a.*
Jer. 30. 21. engaged heart to *a.* to me
1 Tim. 6. 16. light to which none can *a.*
Is. 58. 2. delight in *approaching* to God
Heb. 10. 25. as ye see day *a.*
APPROVE, prove, attest, test.
Ps. 49. 13. posterity *a.* their sayings
Phil. 1. 10. may *a.* things excellent
Acts 2. 22. man *approved* of God
Rom. 14. 18. acceptable to God, *a.*
16. 10. Apelles *a.* in Christ
1 Cor. 11. 19. *a.* be made manifest of men
Rom. 2. 18. *approvest* things excellent
Lam. 3. 36. to subvert the Lord *approveth* not
2 Cor. 6. 4. in all things *approving* ourselves
APT to teach, 1 Tim. 3. 2. 2 Tim. 2. 24.
ARE seven years, Gen. 41. 26, 27.
1 Cor. 1. 28. things which *a.* not
30. of him *a.* ye in Christ Jesus
8. 6. of whom *a.* all things
Heb. 2. 10. for and by whom *a.* all
Rev. 1. 19. write things that *a.*
20. *a.* angels; *a.* seven churches
ARGUE, Job 6. 25; 23. 4.
ARIGHT, set not their heart, Ps. 78. 8.
Ps. 50. 23. ordereth his conversation *a.*
Jer. 8. 6. but they spake not *a.*
ARISE for our help, Ps. 44. 26.
1 Chr. 22. 16. *a.* and be doing
Ps. 68. 1. let God *a.* and enemies be
Amos 7. 2. by whom shall Jacob *a.* 5.
Mic. 7. 8. when I fall I shall *a.*

Mal. 4. 2. Sun of righteousness *arise*
Ps. 112. 4. to upright *ariseth* light
Mat. 13. 21. persecution *a.* because
ARM of flesh with him, 2 Chron. 32. 8.
Ex. 15. 16. by greatness of thine *a.*
Job 40. 9. hast thou an *a.* like God
Ps. 44. 3. own *a.* did not save them, 77. 15.
89. 13. hast a mighty *a.*
Is. 33. 2. be thou their *a.* every
51. 5. mine *a.* shall judge; on my *a.*
9. put on strength, O *a.* of the Lord
53. 1. *a.* of Lord revealed, John 12. 38.
62. 8. Lord hath sworn by the *a.*
63. 12. led them by his glorious *a.*
Acts 13. 17. high *a.* brought he them
1 Pet. 4. 1. *a.* yourselves with same
Luke 11. 21. strong man *armed* keepeth
His arm, Ps. 98. 1. Is. 40. 10, 11; 59. 16. Jer. 17. 5. Ezek. 31. 17. Zech. 11. 17. Luke 1. 51.
Gen. 49. 24. *arms* of his hands made
Deut. 33. 27. underneath everlasting *a.*
ARMIES of living God, 1 Sam. 17. 26
Job 25. 3. any number of his *a.*
Ps. 44. 9. goest not with our *a.* 60. 10.
Sol. 6. 13. company of two *a.*
Rev. 19. 14. *a.* in heaven followed
ARMOUR of light, Rom. 13. 12.
2 Cor. 6. 7. by *a.* of righteousness
Eph. 6. 11, 13. put on whole *a.* of God
ARRAY, order of battle, 2 Sam. 10. 9. Job 6. 4. Jer. 50. 14.
ARRAY, to clothe, Esth. 6. 9. Job 40. 10. Jer. 43. 12. Mat. 6. 29. 1 Tim. 2. 9. Rev. 7. 13; 17. 4; 19. 8.
ARROGANCY, 1 Sam. 2. 3. Prov. 8. 13. Is. 13. 11.
ARROWS of the Almighty, Job 6. 4.
2 Ki. 13. 17. *arrow* of Lord's deliverance
Ps. 91. 5. nor for *a.* that flieth by day
Lam. 3. 12. set me as a mark for *a.*
Deut. 32. 23. I will spend mine *arrows* upon
Ps. 38. 2. thine *a.* stick fast in me
45. 5. thine *a.* are sharp in the heart
ASCEND into hill of Lord, Ps. 24. 3.
Ps. 139. 8. if I *a.* to heaven, Rom. 10. 6.
John 20. 17. I *a.* to my Father and
Prov. 30. 4. who hath *ascended* into heaven
John 3. 13. no man hath *a.* to heaven
Eph. 4. 8. when he *a.* up on high
Rev. 8. 4. smoke of incense *a.*
11. 12. *a.* up to heaven in a cloud
Gen. 28. 12. angels *ascending* and descending, John 1. 51. on Son of man
ASCRIBE greatness to God, Deut. 32. 3.
Job 36. 3. *a.* righteousness to my Maker
ASHAMED to lift face, Ezra 9. 6.
Gen. 2. 25. man and wife naked not *a.*
Ezek. 16. 61. remember ways and be *a.*
Mark 8. 38. be *a.* of me and my word
Rom. 1. 16. I am not *a.* of the gospel
6. 21. whereof ye are now *a.*
Not be ashamed, Ps. 25. 2; 119. 6, 80. Is. 49. 23. Rom. 9. 33. 2 Tim. 2. 15.
ASHES, Gen. 18. 27. Job. 2. 8; 13. 12; 30. 19; 42. 6. Ps. 102. 9. Is. 44. 20; 61. 3. Jer. 6. 26. Ezek. 28. 18. Mal. 4. 3.
ASK the way to Zion, Jer. 50. 5.
Jer. 6. 16. *a.* for the old paths
Mat. 7. 7. *a.* and it shall be given
11. give good things to them that *a.* him
20. 22. ye know not what ye *a.*
Luke 12. 48. of him they will *a.* more
John 14. 13, 14. whatsoever ye *a.* in my name, & 15. 16; 16. 23.

John 16. 24. *asked . . . . ask* and ye shall receive
Eph. 3. 20. above all that we *a.* or think
Jas. 1. 5. wisdom ask him *a.* of God
6. let him *a.* in faith, not wavering
4. 2, 3, because ye *a.* not; ye *a.* and receive not, because ye *a.* amiss
1 John 3. 22. whatsoever we *a.* we receive
5. 14, 15. *a.* according to his will
Mat. 7. 8. that *asketh* receiveth
ASLEEP, 1 Cor. 15. 6, 18. 1 Thes. 4. 13.
ASP, poisonous serpent, Deut. 32. 33. Job 20. 14, 16. Is. 11. 8. Rom. 3. 13.
ASS knows master's crib, Is. 1. 3.
Zech. 9. 9. riding on an *a.* Mat. 21. 5. John 12. 15.
ASSEMBLY of wicked, Ps. 22. 16.
Ps. 89. 7. God feared in the *a.* of saints
Heb. 12. 23. general *a.* of firstborn
Is. 4. 5. create on her *assemblies* a cloud
Heb. 10. 25. forsake not *assembling*
ASSUAGE, Gen. 8. 1. Job 16. 5, 6.
ASSURANCE, quiet confidence.
Is. 32. 17. effect of righteousness *a.*
Col. 2. 2. riches of full *a.* of understanding
1 Thes. 1. 5. gospel came in much *a.*
Heb. 6. 11. to full *a.* of hope unto the end
1 John 3. 19. of truth, and shall *assure* our hearts before him
ASTRAY, Ps. 119. 176. Is. 53. 6. Mat. 18. 12.
Luke 15. 4. 1 Pet. 2. 25.
ATHIRST, sore, called, Judg. 15. 18.
Rev. 21. 6. give to him *a.* of fountain
ATONEMENT (setting at one), pacifying, satisfaction for sin, Lev. 16. 11; 23. 27, 28; 25. 9. Ex. 30. 16. Num. 8. 19, 21; 16. 46; 28. 22.
ATTAIN to wise counsels, Prov. 1. 5.
Ps. 139. 6. high, I cannot *a.* unto it
Ezek. 46. 7. according as hand shall *a.*
Phil. 3. 11, 12. *a.* to resurrection of dead . . . not already *attained*
ATTEND to my cry, Ps. 55. 2; 61. 1; 66. 19; 86. 6; 142. 6.
Prov. 4. 1. *a.* to know understanding
20. *a.* to my words, 7. 24.
Acts 16. 14. she *attended* to things spoken
Attendance, 1 Ki. 10. 5. 1 Tim. 4. 13. Heb. 7. 13.
Rom. 13. 6.
Attent(ive), 2 Chr. 6. 40; 7. 15. Neh. 1. 6; 8. 3.
Ps. 130. 2. Luke 19. 48.
AUTHOR not of confusion, 1 Cor. 14. 33.
Heb. 5. 9. *a.* of eternal salvation
12. 2. Jesus *a.* and finisher of our faith
AUTHORITY, power to govern.
Mat. 7. 29. taught as one having *a.*
John 5. 27. *a.* to execute judgment
1 Cor. 15. 24. put down all *a.* and
Tit. 2. 15. rebuke with all *a.*
1 Pet. 3. 22. angels and *a.* subject
Rev. 13. 2. dragon gave him *a.*
AVAILETH, Esth. 5. 13. Gal. 5. 6; 6. 15. Jas. 5. 16.
AVENGE not, nor grudge, Lev. 19. 18.
Lev. 26. 25. *a.* quarrel of covenant
Deut. 32. 43. he will *a.* blood of his
Is. 1. 24. I will *a.* me of my enemies
Luke 18. 7. shall not God *a.* his elect
Rom. 12. 19. *a.* not yourselves
Rev. 6. 10. dost thou not *a.* our blood
Jer. 5. 9, 29. shall not my soul be *avenged* on such a nation, 9. 9.
Rev. 18. 20. God hath *a.* you on her
AVENGER, Num. 35. 12. Ps. 8. 2; 44. 16.
1 Thes. 4. 6. the Lord is the *a.* of all
2 Sam. 22. 48. God that *avengeth* me

Judg. 5. 2. praise for *avenging* Israel
AVOID it, pass not by it, Prov. 4. 15.
Rom. 16. 17. cause divisions, *a.* them
Avoided, i.e. escaped, 1 Sam. 18. 11.
AVOUCHED, Deut. 26. 17, 18.
AWAKE for thee, Job 8. 6.
Ps. 35. 23. *a.* to my judgment
139. 18. when I *a.* I am still with
1 Cor. 15. 34. *a.* to righteousness
Eph. 5. 14. *a.* thou that sleepest
Ps. 78. 65. Lord *awaked* out of sleep
73. 20. when *awakest* shalt despise
AWE, stand in *a.* sin not, Ps. 4. 4.
Ps. 33. 8. world stand in *a.* of him
AXE, Deut. 19. 5. 1 Ki. 6. 7. 2 Ki. 6. 5. Is. 10. 15. Jer. 51. 20.
Mat. 3. 10. *a.* laid to root of trees
Axes, 2 Sam. 12. 31. Ps. 74. 5, 6. Jer. 46. 22.

B

BABBLER, Eccl. 10. 11. Acts 17. 18.
1 Tim. 6. 20. avoiding profane and vain *babblings,* 2 Tim. 2. 16. Prov. 23. 29.
BABE leaped in her womb, Luke 1. 41.
Ps. 8. 2. out of mouth of *babes*
17. 14. rest of substance to *b.*
Is. 3. 4. *b.* shall rule over them
1 Cor. 3. 1. as unto *b.* in Christ
1 Pet. 2. 2. as newborn *b.* desire
BACK to go from Samuel, 1 Sam. 10. 9.
1 Ki. 14. 9. cast me behind thy *b.*
Ps. 129. 3. plowers plowed on my *b.*
Prov. 26. 3. rod for the fool's *b.*
Is. 38. 17. cast my sins behind thy *b.*
50. 6. gave my *b.* to smiters
Jer. 2. 27. turned their *b.* 32. 33.
18. 17. I will shew them *b.* not face
Ex. 33. 23. shall see my *b.* parts
Ps. 19. 13. keep *b.* thy servant from
53. 6. when God bringeth *b.* captivity
Acts 20. 20. kept *b.* nothing profitable
Neh. 9. 26. cast law behind *backs*
BACKBITERS, haters of God, Rom. 1. 30.
Ps. 15. 3. *backbiteth* not with his tongue
2 Cor. 12. 20. strifes, *backbitings*
BACKSLIDER in heart, Prov. 14. 14.
Jer. 3. 6. 12. return thou *backsliding* Israel, 14. 7; 31. 22; 49. 4.
8. 5. slidden back by perpetual *b.*
Hos. 11. 7. my people are bent to *b.*
14. 4. I will heal their *b.*
Jer. 2. 19. thy *backslidings* reprove
5. 6. and their *b.* are increased
Backward, Gen. 9. 23. went *b.* and covered
Is. 1. 4. they are gone away *b.*
59. 14. judgment is turned away *b.*
John 18. 6. went *b.* and fell to ground
BAG, sack, or pouch, Deut. 25. 13. Job 14. 17.
Prov. 16. 11. Is. 46. 6. Mic. 6. 11. Hag. 1. 6.
Luke 12. 33. John 13. 29.
BALANCE, Job 31. 6; 6. 2. Ps. 62. 9. Is. 40 12; 46. 6. Dan. 5. 27.
Prov. 11. 1. false *b.* abomination to Lord, 20. 23.
Hos. 12. 7. *b.* of deceit are in hand
Mic. 6. 11. count pure with wicked *b.*
BALD, 2 Ki. 2. 23. Jer. 16. 6; 48. 37.
Baldness, Lev. 21. 5. Deut. 14. 1. Is. 3. 24; 15. 2; 22. 12. Ezek. 7. 18.
BALM, Gen. 37. 25; 43. 11.
Jer. 8. 22. is there no *b.* in Gilead, 46. 11; 51. 8.
Ezek. 27. 17.

BANNER, Is. 13. 2. Ps. 20. 5.
  Ps. 60. 4. *b.* to them that fear thee
  Sol. 2. 4. his *b.* over me was love
  6. 4. terrible as army with *banners*
BANQUET, Esth. 5. 4. Dan. 5. 10.
BAPTISM of water, Mat. 3. 6, 7.
Baptism of John, Mat. 21. 25. Mark 11. 30. Luke
  7. 29; 12. 50; 20. 4. Acts 1. 22; 10. 37; 18. 25;
  19. 3, 4.
Baptism of repentance, Mark 1. 4. Acts 13. 24;
  19. 4.
Baptism of suffering, Mat. 20. 22, 23. Mark 10. 38, 39.
  Luke 12. 50.
  Rom. 6. 4. buried by *baptism,* Col. 2. 12.
  Eph. 4. 5. one faith, one *b.*
  1 Pet. 3. 21. *b.* doth now save us by
  Heb. 6. 2. doctrine of *baptisms*
BAPTIZE with water, with Holy Ghost, Mat.
  3. 11. Mark 1. 8. Luke 3. 16. Acts 1. 5. John
  1. 26, 28, 31, 33.
  Mark 1. 4. John did *b.* in wilderness
  5. were all *baptized* of him, 8.
  9. Jesus was *b.* of John, Mat. 3. 13, 14, 16.
  Luke 3. 21.
  Mark 16. 16. believeth and is *b.*
  Luke 3. 7. came to be *b.* 12.
  7. 29, 30. publicans *b.* lawyers not *b.*
  John 4. 1. Jesus *b.* more disciples
  Acts 2. 38. repent and be *b.* every one
  2. 41. received his word were *b.*
  8. 13. Simon believed and was *b.*
  48. Peter commanded them to be *b.*
  16. 15. she was *b.* and her household
  33. was *b.* he and all his
  18. 8. Corinthians believed and were *b.*
  22. 16. arise and be *b.* wash away
  Rom. 6. 3, 4. as . . . . *b.* into his death
  1 Cor. 1. 13. were ye *b.* in name of Paul
  10. 2. were all *b.* unto Moses
  12. 13. are all *b.* into one body
  15. 29. are *b.* for the dead
  Gal. 3. 27. as have been *b.* into Christ
  Mat. 28. 19. *baptizing* in name
BARE you on eagles' wings, Ex. 19. 4.
  Is. 53. 12. he *b.* the sin of many
  1 Pet. 2. 24. *b.* our sins in own body
BARN, Prov. 3. 10. Mat. 6. 26; 13. 30. Luke
  12, 18, 24.
BARREL of meal, 1 Ki. 17. 14.
BARREN, Gen. 11. 30; 25. 21; 29. 31. Judg.
  13. 2. Luke 1. 7.
  Ex. 23. 26. nothing shall be *b.*
  1 Sam. 2. 5. *b.* hath borne seven
  Ps. 113. 9. *b.* woman to keep house
  Sol. 4. 2. none is *b.* among, 6. 6.
  Is. 54. 1. sing, O *b.* Gal. 4. 27.
  2 Pet. 1. 8. neither *b.* nor unfruitful
BASE in my own sight, 2 Sam. 6. 22.
  1 Cor. 1. 28. *b.* things of this world
  2 Cor. 10. 1. who in presence am *b.*
  Ezek. 29. 14, 15. *basest* of kingdoms
  Dan. 4. 17. set up *b.* of men
BASTARD, not enter, Deut. 23. 2.
  Zech. 9. 6. *b.* shall dwell in Ashdod
  Heb. 12. 8. *bastards* and not sons
BATTLE, laws of war, Deut. 20. 1-20.
  Gen. 14. 8, 9. *b.* of four kings against five
  Josh. 8. 14. men of Ai against Israel to *b.*
  Judg. 8. 13. Gideon returned from *b.*
  20. 14. *b.* of children of Benjamin
  2 Sam. 2. 17. a very sore *b.* that day
  10. 8, 13. Ammon put *b.* in array
  21. 15. four *b.* against Philistines

  2 Chr. 13. 3. Abijah set *battle* in array
  14. 10. Asa set *b.* in array
  25. 8. be strong for the *b.*
  Ps. 140. 7. covered head in day of *b.*
  Eccl. 9. 11. *b.* not to the strong
  Jer. 8. 6. as horse rusheth into *b.*
  Rev. 16. 14. *b.* of great day of God
BATTLE-AXE, thou . . . , Jer. 51. 20.
BATTLEMENTS, parapet, Deut. 22. 8.
BEAM out of timber, Hab. 2. 11.
  Mat. 7. 3. considerest not *b.* in own eye
  Sol. 1. 17. *beams* of our house are cedar
BEAR, Gen. 49. 15. Deut. 1. 9, 31. Prov. 9. 12;
  30. 21. Lam. 3. 27.
  Gen. 4. 13. punishment greater than I can *b.*
  Num. 11. 14. not able to *b.* all this people
  Ps. 75. 3. I *b.* up the pillars of it
  91. 12. *b.* thee up in their hands
  Prov. 18. 14. wounded spirit who can *b.*
  Amos 7. 10. land not able to *b.* words
  Mic. 7. 9. I will *b.* indignation of Lord
  Luke 14. 27. whoso doth not *b.* cross
  John 16. 12. ye cannot *b.* them now
  Rom. 15. 1. strong *b.* infirmities of weak
  1 Cor. 3. 2. hitherto ye were not able to *b.* it
  10. 13. that ye may be able to *b.* it
  Gal. 6. 2. *b.* one another's burdens
  5. every man *b.* his own burden
  17. I *b.* in body marks of Lord Jesus
  Heb. 9. 28. offered to *b.* sins of many
  Bear fruit, Ezek. 17. 8. Hos. 9. 16. Joel 2. 22.
  Mat. 13. 23. Luke 13. 9. John 15. 2, 4, 8.
  Ps. 106. 4. favour thou *bearest* to
  Rom. 11. 18. *b.* not root but
  13. 4. *beareth* not sword in vain
  1 Cor. 13. 7. charity *b.* all things
  Ps. 126. 6. *bearing* precious seed
  Rom. 2. 15. conscience *b.* witness, 9. 1.
  Heb. 13. 13. *b.* his reproach
BEARD, 2 Sam. 10. 4; 19. 24; 20. 9. Ezra
  9. 3. Ps. 133. 2. Is. 15. 2. Jer. 41. 5; 48. 37.
BEARS, mentioned, 2 Sam. 17. 8. 2 Ki. 2. 24.
  Prov. 17. 12. Is. 59. 11. Lam. 3. 10. Dan. 7. 5.
  Hos. 13. 8. Amos 5. 19. Rev. 13. 2.
BEASTS, animals without reason, Gen. 1. 24, 25.
  3. 1.—*rather* 'living ones,' God's agencies,
  Ezek. 1. 5-25. Rev. 4. 6-9; 14. 3; 15. 7;
  19. 4.—heathen kingdoms, Dan. 7. 3-7;
  8. 3-8.—anti-christ, Dan. 7. 11. Rev. 11. 7;
  13. 1, 11; 15. 2; 16. 13; 17. 8; 19. 19; 20. 10.
  Ps. 73. 22. I was as a *beast* before thee
  49. 12. like *beasts* that perish, 20.
  Prov. 9. 2. wisdom killed her *b.*
  1 Cor. 15. 32. I fought with *b.* at Ephesus
BEAT, Prov. 23. 14. Is. 3. 15. Luke 12. 47, 48.
  1 Cor. 9. 26.
BEAUTY, garment for, Ex. 28. 2.
  1 Chr. 16. 29. in the *b.* of holiness, 2 Chr.
  20. 21. Ps. 29. 2; 96. 9; 110. 3.
  Ps. 27. 4. to behold *b.* of the Lord
  39. 11. makest his *b.* to consume
  Prov. 20. 29. *b.* of old men gray head
  31. 30. favour deceitful *b.* is vain
  Is. 3. 24. be burning instead of *b.*
  33. 17. see the king in his *b.*
  61. 3. give them *b.* for ashes
  Zech. 11. 7. two staves, *B.* and Bands
  Beautify, Ps. 149. 4. Is. 60. 13.
  Beautiful, Eccl. 3. 11. Sol. 6. 4; 7. 1. Is. 52. 1, 7;
  64. 11. Jer. 13. 20. Ezek. 16. 12, 13; Mat.
  23. 27. Acts 3. 2. Rom. 10. 15.
BED set for him, 2 Ki. 4. 10.
  Ps. 41. 3. make his *b.* in sickness

Sol 3. 1. on my *bed* I sought him
Is. 28. 20. *b.* is shorter than man
Heb. 13. 4. marriage *b.* undefiled
Rev. 2. 22. I will cast her into a *b.*
Amos 6. 4. lie on *beds* of ivory
BEFORE, in sight, Gen. 20. 15; 43. 15. Ex.
　22. 9. 1 Ki. 17. 1; 18. 15. 2 Ki. 3. 14.—
　(in time or place) Gen. 31. 2. Job. 3. 24. Josh.
　8. 10. Luke 22. 47. 2 Chr. 13. 14.—(in dignity)
　2 Sam. 6. 21. John 1. 15, 27.
Phil. 3. 13. those things which are *b.*
Col. 1. 17. he is *b.* all things
BEG, Ps. 37. 25; 109. 10. Prov. 20. 4. Luke 16. 3;
　23. 52. John 9. 8.
BEGGAR, 1 Sam. 2. 8. Luke 16. 20, 22.
Beggarly elements, Gal. 4. 9.
BEGIN at my sanctuary, Ezek. 9. 6.
　Gen. 49. 3. *beginning* of strength, Deut. 21. 17.
　Ex. 12. 2. the *b.* of months
　Ps. 111. 10. fear of the Lord is the *b.* of wisdom,
　　Prov. 1. 7; 9. 10.
　Eccl. 7. 8. better the end than the *b.*
　Mat. 24. 8. these are *b.* of sorrows
　Col. 1. 18. who is *b.* and firstborn
　2 Pet. 2. 20. end is worse than *b.*
　Rev. 1. 8. I am Alpha and Omega, *b.* and the end-
　　ing, 21. 6; 22. 13.
　3. 14. saith the *b.* of creation of God
BEGOTTEN dew drops, Job 38. 28.
　Ps. 2. 7. this day have I *b.* thee, Acts 13. 33.
　　Heb. 1. 5, 6.
　John 1. 14. only *b.* of the Father, 18.
　3. 16. gave his only *b.* Son, 18.
　1 Pet. 1. 3. *b.* us again to a lively hope
　1 John 4. 9. sent his only *b.* Son
　5. 1. loveth him that is *b.* of him
　Rev. 1. 5. Christ first *b.* of the dead
BEGUILE, Col. 2. 4, 18. Gen. 3. 13. 2 Cor. 11. 3.
BEGUN to fall, Esth. 6. 13.　　　[2 Pet. 2. 14.
　Gal. 3. 3. having *b.* in the spirit
　Phil. 1. 6. *b.* a good work in you
BEHAVE myself wisely, Ps. 101. 2.
　Ps. 131. 2. I *behaved* myself as a child
　Tit. 2. 3. in *behaviour* as becometh holiness
BEHELD not iniquity in Jacob, nor perverseness
　　in Israel, Num. 23. 21.
　Luke 10. 18. 1 *b.* Satan as lightning fall
　John 1. 14. we *b.* his glory
　Rev. 11. 12. their enemies *b.* them
BEHIND, Lev. 25. 51. Judg. 20. 40.
　Ex. 10. 26. not an hoof left *b.*
　Neh. 9. 26. cast law *b.* their backs
　Ps. 139. 5. beset me *b.* and before
　Is. 38. 17. cast my sins *b.* thy back
　Phil. 3. 13. forgetting things *b.*
　Col. 1. 24. fill up that is *b.* of affliction
BEHOLD with thine eyes, Deut. 3. 27.
　Job 19. 27. my eyes shall *b.* and not
　40. 4. *b.* I am vile
　Ps. 11. 4. his eyes *b.* his eyelids try
　7. his countenance doth *b.* upright
　17. 15. I will *b.* face in righteousness
　27. 4. desired to *b.* beauty of Lord
　37. 37. *b.* the upright man
　113. 6. humbleth himself to *b.*
　133. 1. *b.* how good and how
　Eccl. 11. 7. it is pleasant to *b.* sun
　Is. 24. 1. *b.* Lord maketh the earth empty
　32. 1. *b.* a king shall reign
　37. 7. *b.* I will send a blast
　40. 10. *b.* the Lord will come
　42. 1. *b.* my servant, mine elect
　48. 10. *b.* I have refined thee

Is. 49. 1. *behold* Lord's hand is not shortened
Hab. 1. 13. of purer eyes than to *b.*
Mat. 18. 10. their angels *b.* face of
John 17. 24. they may *b.* my glory
19. 5. *b.* the man, 14. *b.* your King
26. *b.* thy son, 27. *b.* thy mother
1 Pet. 3. 2. *b.* chaste conversation
Rev. 1. 7. *b.* he cometh with clouds
18. *b.* I am alive for evermore
3. 8. *b.* I set before thee an open door, 9.
11. *b.* I come quickly, 22. 7, 12.
20. *b.* I stand at the door
4. 2. *b.* a throne was set in heaven
9. 12. *b.* there come two woes more
11. 14. *b.* third woe cometh quickly
21. 5. *b.* I make all things new
Ps. 33. 13. Lord *beholdeth* all sons of men
Jas. 1. 24. he *b.* himself and goeth
Ps. 119. 37. turn eyes from *beholding* vanity
Prov. 15. 3. *b.* evil and good
2 Cor. 3. 18. open face *b.* as in glass
Col. 2. 5. joying and *b.* your order
Jas. 1. 23. like man *b.* natural face
BEING, Ps. 104. 33; 146. 2. Acts 17. 28.
BELIAL, *Heb.* worthlessness, Deut. 13. 13. Judg.
　19. 22; 20. 13. 1 Sam. 1. 16; 2. 12;
　10. 27; 25. 17, 25; 30. 22. 2 Sam. 16. 7;
　20. 1; 23. 6. 1 Ki. 21. 10, 13. 2 Chr.
　13. 7. 2 Cor. 6. 15.
BELIEVE, Ex. 4. 1. Num. 14. 11; 20. 12.
　Deut. 1. 32. ye did not *b.* the Lord
　2 Chr. 20. 20. *b.* Lord, *b.* prophets
　Is. 7. 9. not *b.* not established
　Mat. 9. 28. *b.* ye that I am able
　Mark 1. 15. repent and *b.* the gospel
　9. 24. Lord, I *b.* help my unbelief
　11. 24. *b.* that ye receive them
　Luke 8. 13. for a while *b.* and
　24. 25. slow of heart to *b.* all
　John 1. 12. even to them that *b.*
　6. 69. we *b.* and are sure thou art Christ
　John 7. 39. that *b.* him should receive
　8. 24. if ye *b.* not I am he, ye die
　11. 27. I *b.* that thou art the Christ
　40. if thou *b.* should see glory of God
　42. may *b.* thou hast sent me
　12. 36. *b.* in the light while ye have
　14. 1. ye *b.* in God, *b.* also in me
　17. 20. pray for them who shall *b.*
　20. 31. written that ye might *b.*
　Acts 8. 37. I *b.* Jesus Christ is the Son
　13. 39. all that *b.* are justified
　16. 31. *b.* on Lord Jesus and be saved
　Rom. 3. 22. on all them that *b.*
　10. 9. shalt *b.* in thine heart
　14. how shall they *b.* on him
　2 Cor. 4. 13. we *b.* and therefore speak
　Phil. 1. 29. not only to *b.* but suffer
　2 Thes. 2. 11. they should *b.* lie
　1 Tim. 4. 10. especially those that *b.*
　Heb. 10. 39. *b.* to saving of the soul
　11. 6. cometh to God must *b.* that he is
　Jas. 2. 19. devils also *b.* and tremble
　1 John 3. 23. his comm. . . . *b.* on Jesus Christ
Believe not, Is. 7. 9. John 4. 48; 8. 24; 10. 26;
　12. 39; 16. 9; 20. 25. Rom. 3. 3. 2 Cor. 4. 4.
　2 Tim. 2. 13. 1 John 4. 1.
Gen. 15. 6. *believed* in Lord, and he counted
　Rom. 4. 3. Gal. 3. 6. Jas. 2. 23.
Ps. 27. 13. fainted unless I had *b.*
116. 10. I *b.* therefore have I spoken
119. 66. I *b.* thy commandments　　[Rom. 10. **16.**
Is. 53. 1. who hath *b.* our report, John 12. **38.**

Jonah 3. 5. people of Nineveh *believed* God.
Mat. 8. 13. as thou hast *b*. so be it
21. 32. publicans and harlots *b*. him
John 4. 53. himself *b*. and his house
7. 48. have any of the Pharisees *b*. on
17. 8. have *b*. thou didst send me
Acts 4. 32. that *b*. were of one heart
8. 13. Simon *b*. and was baptized
11. 21. great number *b*. and turned
13. 48. were ordained to eternal life *b*.
Rom. 4. 18. against hope *b*. in hope
13. 11. salvation nearer than when we *b*.
Eph. 1. 13. after ye *b*. ye were sealed
1 Tim. 3. 16. God was *b*. on in world
2 Tim. 1. 12. know whom I have *b*.
Believed not, Ps. 78. 22, 32; 106. 24. Luke 24. 41.
Acts 9. 26. Rom. 10. 14. 2 Thes. 2. 12. Heb.
3. 18. Jude 5.
Believers, Acts 5. 14. 1 Tim. 4. 12.
Believest, Luke 1. 20. John 1. 50; 11. 26; 14. 10.
Jas. 2. 19.
Acts 8. 37. if thou *b*. with all thine heart
26. 27. *b*. thou prophets? I know thou *b*.
Believeth, Job 15. 22; 39. 24.
Prov. 14. 15. simple *b*. every word
Is. 28. 16. he that *b*. shall not make haste
Mark 9. 23. all things possible to him that *b*.
16. 16. he that *b*. shall be saved
John 3. 15, 16. *b*. in him not perish
18. that *b*. not is condemned already
36. *b*. on Son hath everlasting life
5. 24. *b*. on him that sent me
6. 35. *b*. on me shall never thirst
40. seeth Son, and *b*. have everlasting life, 47.
7. 38. that *b*. on me out of his belly shall flow
11. 25. *b*. in me though he were dead
26. he that *b*. in me shall never die
12. 44. *b*. in me, *b*. not on me, but
John 12. 46. *b*. on me should not abide in darkness
14. 12. *b*. on me the works that I do
Rom. 1. 16. power of God . . . to every that *b*.
3. 26. justifier of him that *b*. in Jesus
4. 5. worketh not, but *b*. on him
9. 33. *b*. on him shall not be ashamed, 10. 11.
10. 4. end of the law for righteousness to every one that *b*.
14. 2. one *b*. that he may eat all things
1 Cor. 7. 12. wife that *b*. not
13. husband that *b*. not
1 Cor. 13. 7. charity *b*. all
14. 24. come in one that *b*. not
2 Cor. 6. 15. he that *b*. with infidel
1 Tim. 5. 16. that *b*. have widows
1 Pet. 2. 6. *b*. on him not confounded
1 John 5. 1. whoso *b*. Jesus is Christ
5. overcometh world, but he that *b*.
10. he that *b*. on Son of God hath witness:
b. not God hath made him a liar
John 20. 27. be not faithless, but *believing*
31. that *b*. ye might have life
Acts 16. 34. *b*. in God with all his house
Rom. 15. 13. all joy and peace in *b*.
1 Tim. 6. 2. that have *b*. masters
1 Pet. 1. 8. yet *b*. ye rejoice with joy
2 Thes. 2. 13. *belief* of the truth
BELLOWS are burnt, Jer. 6. 29.
BELLY, on *b*. shalt go, Gen. 3. 14.
Num. 5. 21. *b*. to swell and thigh rot
25. 8. thrust them through the *b*.
Job 3. 11. when I came out of *b*.
15. 2. fill his *b*. with east wind
35. their *b*. prepareth deceit

Job 20. 15. God cast them out of his *belly*
Ps. 17. 14. whose *b*. thou fillest with
22. 10. art my God from mother's *b*.
44. 25. our *b*. cleaveth to the earth
Is. 46. 3. borne by me from the *b*.
Jonah 1. 17. *b*. of fish, Mat. 12. 40.
2. 1. prayed to God out of fish's *b*.
2. out of the *b*. of hell cried I
Hab. 3. 16. my *b*. trembled that I
Luke 15. 16. fill his *b*. with husks
John 7. 38. out of his *b*. shall flow
1 Cor. 6. 13. meats for *b*. and *b*. for
Phil. 3. 19. whose god is their *b*.
Rev. 10. 9. make thy *b*. bitter
Tit. 1. 12. Cretians slow *bellies*
BELONG, Lev. 27. 24. Luke 23. 7.
Gen. 40. 8. interpretations *b*. to God
Deut. 29. 29. secret things *b*. to Lord, **things**
revealed *b*. to us and children
Ps. 47. 9. shields of earth *b*. to God
68. 20. to God *b*. issues from death
Dan. 9. 9. to Lord *b*. mercies and **forgivenesses**
Mark 9. 41. because ye *b*. to Christ
Luke 19. 42. things that *b*. to thy peace
1 Cor. 7. 32. care for things *b*. to Lord
Ezra. 10. 4. this matter *belongeth* to
Ps. 3. 8. salvation *b*. to the Lord
62. 11. power *b*. to God, 12. *b*. mercy
Dan. 9. 7. righteousness *b*. to thee
8. to us *b*. confusion of face
Heb. 5. 14. strong meat *b*. to them
BELOVED—another hated, Deut. 21. 15.
Neh. 13. 26. Solomon *b*. of his God
Ps. 60. 5. thy *b*. may be delivered
127. 2. Lord giveth his *b*. sleep
Sol. 1. 14. *my beloved*, 2. 3, 9, 16, 17; 4. 16.
5. 2, 4-6, 8, 10, 16; 6. 2, 3; 7. 10, 13.
Is. 5. 1. *my beloved* hath a vineyard in a **fruitful**
Sol. 5. 9. thy *b*. more than another *b*.
Dan. 10. 11, 19. man, greatly *b*. 9. 23.
Mat. 3. 17. this is my *b*. Son, 17. 5.
Rom. 9. 25. *b*. which was not *b*.
11. 28. *b*. for the fathers' sake
16. 8. Amplias *b*. in the Lord
Eph. 1. 6. accepted in the *b*.
Col. 3. 12. elect of God and *b*.
4. 14. Luke the *b*. physician
2 Pet. 3. 15. *b*. brother Paul
Rev. 20. 9. they compassed *b*. city
BEMOAN, Jer. 15. 5; 16. 5; 22. 10; 31. 18; 48. 17.
BEND bow, Ps. 11. 2; 64. 3; 58. 7; 7. 12; 37. 14.
Lam. 2. 4; 3. 12. Is. 5. 28.
Jer. 9. 3. *b*. their tongues like a bow
Is. 60. 14. afflicted thee come *bending*
Zech. 9. 13. I have *bent* Judah for me
BENEATH, Prov. 15. 24. John 8. 23.
BENEFACTORS, Luke 22. 25.
BENEFITS, loadeth us with Ps. 68. 19.
Ps. 103. 2. forget not all his *b*.
116. 12. render to Lord for all his *b*.
BENEVOLENCE, due, 1 Cor. 7. 3.
BEREAVE soul of good, Eccl. 4. 8.
Jer. 15. 7. *b*. of children, 18. 21. Gen. 42. 36;
43. 14. Ezek. 5. 17; 36. 12, 13, 14. Lam. 1. 20.
Hos. 9. 12; 13. 8.
BESEECH God to be gracious, Mal. 1. 9.
2 Cor. 5. 20. as though God did *b*.
BESET me behind and before, Ps. 139. 5.
Hos. 7. 2. own doings have *b*. them
Heb. 12. 1. sin which doth so easily *b*. us
BESIDE waters, Ps. 23. 2. Is. 32. 20.
Sol. 1. 8. feed kids *b*. shepherds' tents
Is. 56. 8. *b*. those that are gathered

BESOM of destruction, Is. 14. 23.
BESOUGHT the Lord, Deut. 3. 23. 2 Sam. 12. 16.
  1 Ki. 13. 6. 2 Ki. 13. 4. 2 Chr. 33. 12. Ezra
  8. 23. 2 Cor. 12. 8.
BEST estate is vanity, Ps. 39. 5.
  Luke 15. 22. bring forth *b*. robe
  1 Cor. 12. 31. covet earnestly *b*. gifts
BESTEAD, placed, hardly, Is. 8. 21.
BESTOW a blessing, Ex. 32. 29.
  Luke 12. 17. room to *b*. my fruits
  1 Cor. 12. 23. *b*. more abundant honour
  13. 3. *b*. all my goods to feed the poor
  John 4. 38. *bestowed* no labour
  1 Cor. 15. 10. his grace *b*. on me
  2 Cor. 1. 11. gift *b*. on us by means
  8. 1. grace of God *b*. on churches
  Gal. 4. 11. lest *b*. labour in vain
  1 John 3. 1. love Father hath *b*. on us
BETIMES, 2 Chr. 36. 15. Job 8. 5; 24. 5.
  Prov. 13. 24. Gen. 26. 31.
BETRAY, Mat. 24. 10; 26. 21. Mark 13. 12;
  14. 18. Luke 22. 4, 21. John 13. 21.
BETROTH, Deut. 28. 30. Hos. 2. 19, 20.
BETTER than ten sons, 1 Sam. 1. 8.
  Judg. 8. 2. gleanings *b*. than vintage
  Prov. 15. 16. *b*. is little with fear of Lord
  17. *b*. is a dinner of herbs with love
  16. 8. *b*. is a little with righteousness
  16. much *b*. to get wisdom than gold
  17. 1. *b*. is dry morsel, and quietness
  27. 10. *b*. is a neighbour near than
  Eccl. 4. 9. two are *b*. than one
  13. *b*. is a poor and wise child than
  7. 1. *b*. is a good name than precious
  2. *b*. to go to the house of mourning than house
    of feasting
  3. *b*. is sorrow than laughter
  5. *b*. to hear rebuke of the wise than
  8. *b*. is the patient than proud in
  9. 16. wisdom is *b*. than strength
  18. wisdom is *b*. than weapons of
  Sol. 1. 2. love *b*. than wine, 4. 10.
  Rom. 3. 9. are we *b*. than they
  1 Cor. 9. 15. were *b*. for me to die
  11. 17. come not for the *b*. but worse
  Phil. 1. 23. with Christ is far *b*.
  2. 3. esteem others *b*. than themselves
  Heb. 1. 4. so much *b*. than angels
  6. 9. persuaded *b*. things of you
  7. 19. bringing in of a *b*. hope did
  22. Jesus made a surety of a *b*. testament
  8. 6. mediator of a *b*. covenant
  10. 34. a *b*. and an enduring substance
  11. 16. desire a *b*. country
  35. might obtain a *b*. resurrection
  40. God provided some *b*. thing
  12. 24. blood speaketh *b*. than Abel
  2 Pet. 2. 21. *b*. not to have known
BETWEEN thy seed and her, Gen. 3. 15.
  1 Ki. 3. 9. discern *b*. good and bad
  18. 21. how long halt *b*. two opinions
  1 Tim. 2. 5. one mediator *b*. God and men
BETWIXT Phil. 1. 23. In a strait *b*. two
BEWARE of men, Mat. 10. 17.
  Mat. 7. 15. *b*. of false prophets
  16. 6. *b*. of leaven of Pharisees, 11. Mark 8. 15.
  Luke 12. 15. *b*. of covetousness
  Phil. 3. 2. *b*. of dogs, *b*. of evil workers
  Col. 2. 8. *b*. lest any man spoil you
  2 Pet. 3. 17. *b*. lest being led away
BEYOND, go, over-reach, 1 Thes. 4. 6.
BID, Mat. 22. 9; 23. 3. Luke 14. 10.
BIDE, not in unbelief, Rom. 11. 23.

BILL, Deut. 24. 1, 3. Is. 50. 1. Jer. 3. 8. Mark
  10. 4. Luke 16. 6, 7.
BILLOWS, Ps. 42. 7. Jonah 2. 3.
BIND sweet influences, Job 38. 31.
  Job 31. 36. I would *b*. it as a crown
  Ps. 105. 22. *b*. his princes at pleasure
  149. 8. to *b*. their kings with chains
  Prov. 3. *b*. them about thy neck
  Is. 8. 16. *b*. up testimony, seal law
  Hos. 6. 1. smitten, and will *b*. us up
  Mat. 12. 29. first *b*. strong man and
  13. 30. *b*. them in bundles to burn
  16. 19. thou shalt *b*. on earth, 18. 18.
  22. 13. *b*. him hand and foot, and cast
Bindeth up, Job 5. 18. Ps. 147. 3.
BIRD hasteth to snare, Prov. 7. 23.
  Ps. 124. 7. soul is escaped as a *b*.
  Eccl. 10. 20. *b*. of air tell the matter
  Is. 46. 11. ravenous *b*. from the east
  Jer. 12. 9. heritage as a speckled *b*.
Birds, Gen. 15. 10; 40. 17. Lev. 14. 4. 2 Sam. 21. 10.
  Ps. 104. 17. Eccl. 9. 12. Sol. 2. 12. Is. 31. 5.
  Jer. 5. 27; 12. 4, 9. Mat. 8. 20.
BIRTH, 2 Ki. 19. 3. Eccl. 7. 1. Is. 66. 9. Ezek.
  16. 3. Gal. 4. 19.
BIRTHDAY, Gen. 40. 20. Mat. 14. 6.
BIRTHRIGHT, Gen. 25. 31, 32, 33; 27. 36;
  43. 33. 1 Chr. 5. 1. Heb. 12. 16.
BISHOP, 1 Tim. 3. 1, 2. Tit. 1. 7.
  1 Pet. 2. 25. return to *b*. of souls
  Phil. 1. 1. with *bishops* and deacons
BITE, Num. 21. 6, 8, 9. Eccl. 10. 8, 11. Jer. 8. 17.
  Amos 9. 3. Hab. 2. 7.
  Mic. 3. 5. prophets *b*. with their teeth
  Gal. 5. 15. if ye *b*. and devour one another
  Prov. 23. 32. at last it *biteth* like a serpent
BITTER, made their lives, Ex. 1. 14.
  Ex. 12. 8. with *b*. herbs, Num. 9. 11.
  Deut. 32. 24. devoured with *b*. destruction
  32. their grapes of gall, clusters are *b*.
  2 Ki. 14. 26. affliction was very *b*.
  Job 3. 20. life given to the *b*. in soul
  13. 26. write *b*. things against me
  Ps. 64. 3. their arrows even *b*. words
  Prov. 27. 7. every *b*. thing is sweet
  Is. 5. 20. woe them that put *b*. for sweet
  Jer. 2. 19. evil thing and *b*. that
  Col. 3. 19. be not *b*. against them
  Jas. 3. 14. if ye have *b*. envying
  Rev. 8. 11. because they were made *b*.
  10. 9. make thy belly *b*.
  Judg. 5. 23. curse *bitterly* inhabitants
  Is. 22. 4. I will weep *b*. 33. 7.
  Ezek. 27. 30. shall cry *b*. Zeph. 1. 14.
  Hos. 12. 14. provoked him most *b*.
  Mat. 26. 75. wept *b*. Luke 22. 62.
Bitterness of soul, 1 Sam. 1. 10.
  1 Sam. 15. 32. *b*. of death is past
  2 Sam. 2. 26. it will be *b*. in end
  Prov. 14. 10. heart knows its own *b*.
  Acts 8. 23. in gall of *b*. and bond of
  Rom. 3. 14. full of cursing and *b*.
  Eph. 4. 31. let all *b*. be put away
  Heb. 12. 15. root of *b*. springing up
BITTERN, Is. 14. 23; 34. 11.
BLACK, 1 Ki. 18. 45. Mat. 5. 36.
  Sol. 1. 5. I am *b*. 6.
Blackness of darkness, Heb. 12. 18. Jude 13.
BLAME, Gen. 43. 9; 44. 32. 2 Cor. 8. 20. Eph. 1. 4.
Blamed, 2 Cor. 6. 3. Gal. 2. 11.
Blameless, Gen. 44. 10. Josh. 2. 17. Judg. 15. 3.
  Mat. 12. 5. Phil. 3. 6. 1 Tim. 5. 7.
  Luke 1. 6. in ordinances of the Lord *b*.

1 Cor. 1. 8. be *blameless* in day of our Lord
1 Thes. 5. 23. be preserved *b*.
1 Tim. 3. 2. bishop must be *b*. Tit. 1. 6, 7.
10. office of deacon found *b*.
2 Pet. 3. 14. without spot and *b*.
BLASPHEME, revile God, &c.
Ps. 74. 10. enemy *b*. thy name
Mark 3. 29. *b*. against Holy Ghost not forgiven
Acts 26. 11. compelled them to *b*.
1 Tim. 1. 20. may learn not to *b*.
Jas. 2. 7. do they not *b*. that name
2 Ki. 19. 6. servants *blasphemed* me, Is. 37. 6.
Ps. 74. 18. foolish people have *b*.
Is. 52. 5. my name continually is *b*.
Rom. 2. 24. God is *b*. through you
1 Tim. 6. 1. name of God be not *b*.
Rev. 16. 9, 11, 21. *b*. God of heaven
Lev. 24. 16. *blasphemeth* put to death
Ps. 44. 16. voice of him that reproacheth and *b*.
Mat. 9. 3. scribes said this man *b*.
Luke 12. 10. to him that *b*. against the Holy
Ghost it shall not be forgiven
Blasphemer, 1 Tim. 1. 13. 2 Tim. 3. 2.
Blasphemy, 2 Ki. 19. 3. Is. 37. 3. Mat. 12. 31.
Mark 7. 22. Col. 3. 8. Rev. 2. 9.
BLAST, Ex. 15. 8. 2 Sam. 22. 16. 2 Ki. 19. 7.
Job 4. 9. Is. 25. 4.
Blasting, Deut. 28. 22. 1 Ki. 8. 37.
BLEMISH, your lamb shall be without, Ex. 12. 5;
29. 1. Lev. 1. 3, 10; 4. 23.
Dan. 1. 4. children in whom was no *b*.
Eph. 5. 27. church holy, without *b*.
1 Pet. 1. 19. as a lamb without *b*.
BLESS them that *b*. thee, Gen. 12. 3.
Gen. 22. 17. in blessing I will *b*. thee
Ex. 23. 25. *b*. thy bread and water
24. 1. pleased Lord to *b*. Israel
Num. 6. 24. Lord *b*. and keep thee
Ps. 5. 12. wilt *b*. the righteous
28. 9. *b*. thine inheritance and feed
29. 11. will *b*. his people with peace
67. 1. be merciful to us and *b*. us
115. 13. he will *b*. them that fear
132. 15. I will abundantly *b*. her
134. 3. the Lord *b*. thee out of Zion
Hag. 2. 19. from this day will I *b*.
Rom. 12. 14. *b*. them that persecute
Acts 3. 26. sent him to *b*. you
1 Cor. 4. 12. being reviled we *b*.
Bless the Lord, Deut. 8. 10. Judg. 5. 9. Ps. 16. 7;
26. 12; 34. 1; 103. 1, 21, 22; 104. 1, 35.
Bless thee, Ps. 63. 4; 145. 2, 10. Gen. 12. 2.
Gen. 1. 22. God *blessed* them and
2. 3. God *b*. the seventh day
Ex. 20. 11. the Lord *b*. the sabbath
Ps. 33. 12. *b*. whose God is the Lord
Prov. 10. 7. memory of the just is *b*.
Mat. 13. 16. *b*. are eyes, Luke 10. 23.
24. 46. *b*. is that servant whom his lord when he,
Luke 12. 37, 38.
Mark 10. 16. in his arms and *b*. them
Luke 1. 28, 42. *b*. art thou among women
45. *b*. is she that believed
48. all generations shall call me *b*.
Acts 20. 35. it is more *b*. to give
Rom. 1. 25. Creator *b*. for ever, 9. 5. 2 Cor.
11. 31. Eph. 1. 3. 1 Pet. 1. 3.
1 Tim. 1. 11. glorious gospel of the *b*. God
6. 15. *b*. and only potentate
John 12. 13. *b*. is he that cometh in
Rev. 14. 13. *b*. *are* dead which die in the Lord
Prov. 8. 32. *b*. *are they* that keep my ways
Is. 30. 18.—that wait for him

b. *are they* Mat. 5. 3-11.—poor in spirit—
mourn—meek—hunger and thirst—merciful
—pure in heart—peacemakers—persecuted
—when men revile you, Luke 6. 20-22.
Luke 11. 28.—that hear the word
John 20. 29.—that have not seen, and
Rom. 4. 7.—whose iniquities are forgiven
Rev. 19. 9.—called to marriage supper
22. 14.—that do his commandments
Num. 24. 9. *blessed is he* that blesseth
Ps. 32. 1.—whose transgression is
41. 1.—that considereth the poor
Dan. 12. 12.—that waiteth and cometh
Mat. 11. 6.—not offended in me
21. 9.—cometh in the name of the Lord, 23. 39.
Mark 11. 9. Luke 13. 35.
Rev. 1. 3.—readeth this prophecy
20. 6.—part in first resurrection
22. 7.—keepeth the sayings of this book
Ps. 1. 1. *b*. *is the man* that walketh not in the
counsel of the ungodly
32. 2.—to whom the Lord imputeth
34. 8.—that trusteth in him, 84. 12.
65. 4.—whom thou choosest
84. 5.—whose strength is in thee
94. 12.—whom thou chastenest
112. 1.—*that* feareth the Lord
Prov. 8. 34. *b*. *is the man that* heareth me,
Is. 56. 2.—doeth this, and son
Jer. 17. 7.—trusteth in the Lord
Jas. 1. 12.—endureth temptation
Blessedness, Rom. 4. 6, 9. Gal. 4. 15.
Gen. 12. 2. thou shalt be a *blessing*
27. 36. he hath taken away my *b*.
28. 4. give thee *b*. of Abraham
Deut. 11. 26. set before you a *b*. and a curse,
30. 19. Jas. 3. 9, 10.
23. 5. turned curse into *b*. Neh. 13. 2.
Neh. 9. 5. exalted above all *b*.
Job 29. 13. *b*. of him ready to perish
Ps. 3. 8. thy *b*. is upon thy people
109. 17. delighted not in *b*.
129. 8. the *b*. of Lord be upon you
Is. 65. 8. destroy it not, a *b*. is in it
Joel 2. 14. leave a *b*. behind him
1 Cor. 10. 16. cup of *b*. which we *bless*
Gal. 3. 14. *b*. of Abraham come on Gentiles
Blessings, Gen. 49. 25, 26. Josh. 8. 34. Ps. 21. 3.
Prov. 10. 6; 28. 20. Mal. 2. 2. Eph. 1. 3.
BLIND, Ex. 4. 11. Lev. 21. 18.
Job 29. 15. I was eyes to the *b*.
Ps. 146. 8. openeth the eyes of the *b*.
Is. 42. 7. to open the *b*. eyes, 18.
19. who is *b*. but my servant
43. 8. bring the *b*. people that have eyes
Mat. 11. 5. *b*. receive sight, Luke 7. 21, 22.
23. 16. woe to you *b*. guides, 24.
Luke 4. 18. recovery of sight to *b*.
2 Pet. 1. 9. lacketh these things is *b*.
Rev. 3. 17. thou art *b*. and naked
John 12. 40. *blinded* their eyes.
Rom. 11. 7. the rest were *b*.
2 Cor. 4. 4. god of this world *b*. the minds
1 John 2. 11. darkness *b*. his eyes
BLOOD of grapes, Gen. 49. 11; of Abel,
Gen. 4. 10, 11.
Job 16. 18. cover thou not my *b*. let
Ps. 9. 12. maketh inquisition for *b*.
72. 14. precious their *b*. in his sight
Is. 26. 21. earth shall disclose her *b*.
Ezek. 3. 18. his *b*. will I require
9. 9. land is full of *b*. and city full
16. 6. polluted in thine own *b*.

Mic. 3. 10. they build up Zion with *blood*
Mat. 26. 28. *b.* of new testament, Mark 14. 24.
     Luke 22. 20. 1 Cor. 11. 25.
27. 8. field of *b.* Acts 1. 19.
25. his *b.* be on us and on our children
Luke 13. 1. whose *b.* Pilate mingled
22. 44. as it were great drops of *b.*
John 1. 13. born not of *b.* nor of flesh
6. 54. drinketh my *b.* hath eternal life
55. my *b.* is drink indeed
56. drinketh my *b.* dwelleth in me
Acts 17. 26. made of one *b.* all nations
18. 6. your *b.* be on your own heads
20. 26. pure from the *b.* of all men
28. hath purchased with his own *b.*
Rom. 3. 25. through faith in his *b.*
1 Cor. 11. 27. guilty of body and *b.*
Col. 1. 20. peace through *b.* of cross
Eph. 1. 7. redemption through his *b.* even
     forgiveness of sins, Col. 1. 14.
Heb. 9. 20. the *b.* of the testament
10. 19. into holiest by *b.* of Jesus
12. 4. ye have not yet resisted unto *b.*
24. *b.* of sprinkling that speaketh
1 Pet. 1. 2. sprinkling of *b.* of Jesus
19. with precious *b.* of Christ
1 John 1. 7. *b.* . . . cleanseth from all sin
5. 6. came by water and *b.*
Rev. 1. 5. washed us in his own *b.*
6. 10. dost thou not avenge our *b.*
8. 7. hail and fire mingled with *b.*
16. 6. shed *b.* . . . given them *b.* to drink
17. 6. drunken with the *b.* of saints
Blood-guiltiness, Ps. 51. 14.
Bloody, Ex. 4. 25, 26. Ps. 5. 6; 55. 23.
BLOSSOM, man's rod, Num. 17. 5.
     Is. 5. 24. their *b.* shall go up as dust
27. 6. Israel shall *b.* and bud
35. 1. the desert shall *b.* as the rose
2. it shall *b.* abundantly and rejoice
Hab. 3. 17. the fig tree shall not *b.*
Ezek. 7. 10. rod hath *blossomed*
BLOT, Job 31. 7. Prov. 9. 7.
     Ex. 32. 32, 33. *b.* me out of thy book, Num. 5. 23.
     Ps. 69. 28. Rev. 3. 5.
Blot out their name or remembrance, Deut. 9. 14;
     25. 19; 29. 20. 2 Ki. 14. 27. Ps. 109. 13.
Blot out sin, transgression, iniquity, Neh. 4. 5. Ps.
     51. 1, 9; 109. 14. Is. 43. 25; 44. 22. Jer.
     18. 23. Acts 3. 19.
Col. 2. 14. *blotting* out handwriting
BLOW on my garden, Sol. 4. 16.
     Hag. 1. 9. I did *b.* upon it
John 3. 8. wind *bloweth* where it listeth
BLUSH to lift up my face, Ezra 9. 6.
     Jer. 6. 15. neither could they *b.* 8. 12.
BOAST, Ps. 10. 3; 34. 2; 49. 6; 52. 1. Prov. 20. 14;
     25. 14. Jas. 3. 5.
1 Ki. 20. 11. *b.* as he that putteth it off
Prov. 27. 1. *b.* not of tomorrow
Rom. 11. 18. *b.* not against the branches, but if
     thou *b.* thou bearest not the root
Eph. 2. 9. not of works lest any *b.*
Rom. 1. 30. proud *boasters*, 2 Tim. 3. 2.
Boasting, Acts 5. 36. Rom. 3. 27.
Jas. 4. 16. now ye rejoice in your *boastings*
BODY of heaven, Ex. 24. 10.
     Job 19. 26. worms destroy this *b.*
Mat. 6. 22. *b.* full of light, Luke 11. 34.
10. 28. that kill the *b.* Luke 12. 4.
26. 26. this is my *b.* 1 Cor. 11. 24.
John 2. 21. of the temple of his *b.*
Rom. 6. 6. *b.* of sin be destroyed

Rom. 7. 4. dead to law by the *body* of Christ
24. me from the *b.* of this death
8. 10. *b.* is dead because of sin
13. do mortify deeds of the *b.*
23. the redemption of our *b.*
1 Cor. 5. 3. absent in *b.* present in spirit
6. 18. every sin is without the *b.* but
19. *b.* temple of Holy Ghost
7. 4. wife not power of own *b.*
9. 27. I keep under my *b.* and bring
10. 16. communion of *b.* of Christ
11. 29. not discerning the Lord's *b.*
12. 14. the *b.* is not one member
27. ye are the *b.* of Christ
15. 44. sown natural *b.* raised spiritual *b.*
2 Cor. 5. 6. home in *b.* absent from Lord
8. to be absent from the *b.*
10. receive things done in *b.*
12. 2. whether in *b.* or out I cannot
Eph. 3. 6. fellow heirs of the same *b.*
4. 12. for edifying the *b.* of Christ
5. 23. he is the saviour of the *b.*
Phil. 1. 20. Christ magnified in my *b.*
3. 21. shall change our vile *b.*
Col. 1. 18. head of the *b.* the church
2. 11. putting off the *b.* of sins of flesh
2. 23. neglecting of the *b.*
Heb. 10. 5. a *b.* hast thou prepared
Jas. 3. 6. tongue defileth whole *b.*
Jude 9. disputed about *b.* of Moses
Heb. 13. 3. being also in the *b.*
1 Pet. 2. 24. in his own *b.*
Deut. 28. 11, 18, 53. fruit of the *b.* 30. 9. Ps.
     132. 11. Mic. 6. 7.
Rom. 8. 11. quicken your mortal *bodies*
12. 1. present your *b.* a living sacrifice
1 Cor. 6. 15. *b.* members of Christ
Eph. 5. 28. love wives as their own *b.*
Heb. 10. 22. *b.* washed with pure water
Luke 3. 22. Holy Ghost in a *bodily* shape
2 Cor. 10. 10. his *b.* presence is weak
Col. 2. 9. the fulness of Godhead *b.*
1 Tim. 4. 8. *b.* exercise profiteth little
BOLD as a lion, Prov. 28. 1.
     2 Cor. 10. 1. being absent am *b.*
11. 21. if any is *b.* I am *b.* also
Phil. 1. 14. are much more *b.* to speak
Mark 15. 43. went *boldly* unto Pilate
Heb. 4. 16. come *b.* to throne of grace
2 Cor. 7. 4. my *boldness* of speech
Eph. 3. 12. in whom we have *b.* and
Heb. 10. 19. *b.* to enter into the holiest
1 John 4. 17. *b.* in day of judgment
BOND of the covenant, Ezek. 20. 37.
     Job 12. 18. looseth *b.* of kings
Eph. 4. 3. unity of Spirit in *b.* of peace. charity *b.*
     of perfectness, Col. 3. 14.
1 Cor. 12. 13. *bond and free*, Gal. 3. 28. Eph. 6. 8.
     Col. 3. 11. Rev. 6. 15; 13. 16; 19. 18.
Ps. 116. 16. hast loosed my *bonds*
Acts 20. 23. *b.* and afflictions abide me
23. 29. worthy of death or of *b.*
Eph. 6. 20. I am an ambassador in *b.*
Phil. 1. 16. to add affliction to my *b.*
Col. 4. 18. remember my *b.*
2 Tim. 2. 9. suffer trouble even unto *b.*
Philem. 10. have begotten in my *b.*
Heb. 10. 34. compassion in my *b.*
11. 36. trial of *b.* and imprisonments
Ex. 13. 3. house of *bondage*, 20. 2.
1. 14. their lives bitter with hard *b.*
2. 23. sighed by reason of the *b.*
Rom. 8. 15. spirit of *b.* again to fear

1 Cor. 7. 15. sister is not under *bondage*
Gal. 4. 24. Sinai gendereth to *b.*
5. 1. entangled with the yoke of *b.*
Bondwoman, Gen. 21. 10. Gal. 4. 23, 30.
BONE of my bone, and flesh of my flesh, Gen.
    2. 23; 29. 14. Judg. 9. 2. 2 Sam. 5. 1;
    19. 13. 1 Chr. 11. 1.
Ex. 12. 46. not break a *b.* of it
John 19. 36. *b.* of him not be broken
Ps. 51. 8. *bones* thou hast broken may
Eccl. 11. 5. how the *b.* grow in the
Ezek. 37. 1. valley full of dry *b.*
3, 4, 5, 7. resurrection of *b.*
Mat. 23. 27. full of dead men's *b.*
His bones, Ps. 34. 20. Eph. 5. 30. Job 20. 11. Prov.
    12. 4.
Ps. 6. 2. heal me, *my bones* are vexed
22. 14. all—out of joint, 17. I may tell all—
32. 3.—waxed old through my roaring
35. 10.—shall say, Lord, who is like
38. 3. neither rest to—because of my sin
102. 3.—are burnt as an hearth
5.—cleave to my skin
BOOK, Gen. 5. 1. Esth. 6. 1.
Ex. 32. 32. blot me out of *b.*
Job 19. 23. O that they were printed in a *b.*
Ps. 40. 7. volume of *b.* Heb. 10. 7.
56. 8. tears, are they not in thy *b.*
139. 16. in *b.* members are written
Book of life, Phil. 4. 3. Rev. 3. 5; 13. 8; 17. 8;
    20. 12, 15; 21. 27; 22. 19.
Books, Eccl. 12. 12. Dan. 7. 10; 9. 2. John 21. 25.
    2 Tim. 4. 13. Rev. 20. 12.
BOOTHS, Lev. 23. 42, 43. Neh. 8. 14.
BORDER of his garment, Mark 6. 56.
BORN to trouble, man is, Job 5. 7.
Job 14. 1. *b.* of a woman, 15. 14; 25. 4. Mat.
    11. 11. Luke 7. 28.
Ps. 58. 3. go astray as soon as *b.*
87. 4. this man was *b.* there, 6.
Prov. 17. 17. brother *b.* for adversity
Eccl. 3. 2. a time to be *b.* and die
Is. 9. 6. unto us a child is *b.* a son
66. 8. shall a nation be *b.* at once
Mat. 11. 11. them *b.* of women
26. 24. better if he had not been *b.*
1. 13. *born of God,* 1 John 3. 9; 4. 7; 5. 1, 4, 18.
John 3. 3, 5, 7. *b.* again
4. can man be *b.* when old
5. *b.* of water and of the Spirit
6. *b.* of flesh is flesh; *b.* of Spirit is
Rom. 9. 11. children being not yet *b.*
1 Cor. 15. 8. one *b.* out of due time
Gal. 4. 23. he *b.* after the flesh, 29.
1 Pet. 2. 2. as new *b.* babes desire milk of
Jer. 15. 10. *borne* me a man of strife
BORROW, Deut. 15. 6; 28. 12.
Ex. 22. 14. *b.* of his neighbour, 3. 22; 11. 2;
    12. 35.
Mat. 5. 42. would *b.* of thee turn not away
Prov. 22. 7. *borrower* is servant to lender
Is. 24. 2. as with lender so with *b.*
BOSOM, Gen. 16. 5. Ex. 4. 6.
Num. 11. 12. carry them in *b.* as a
Deut. 13. 6. wife of thy *b.* 28. 54, 56.
Ps. 35. 13. prayer returned to own *b.*
74. 11. pluck thy hand out of thy *b.*
89. 50. how I do bear in my *b.*
Prov. 5. 20. why embrace the *b.* of a
17. 23. gift out of *b.* to pervert, 21. 14.
19. 24. hideth hands in *b.* 26. 15.
Eccl. 7. 9. anger resteth in *b.* of fools
Is. 40. 11. carry them in his *b.*

Is. 65. 6, 7. recompense into their *bosom.*
Ps. 79. 12. Jer. 32. 18.
Mic. 7. 5. her that lieth in thy *b.*
Luke 6. 38. men give into your *b.*
16. 22. carried into Abraham's *b.* 23.
John 13. 23. leaning on Jesus' *b.*
BOTH, Gen. 2. 25; 3. 7; 19. 36.
Zech. 6. 13. peace between *b.*
Eph. 2. 14. our peace made *b.* one
16. that he might reconcile *b.* to God
BOTTLE, Gen. 21. 14, 15, 19.
Ps. 56. 8. put my tears into thy *b.*
119. 83. I am like a *b.* in the smoke
Jer. 13. 12. every *b.* filled with wine
Job 38. 37. stay *bottles* of heaven
Mat. 9. 17. new wine into old *b.*
Mark 2. 22. new wine into new *b.*
BOUGHT, Gen. 17. 12, 13; 33. 19.
Deut. 32. 6. is not he thy father that *b.* thee?
Mat. 13. 46. sold all and *b.* it
1 Cor. 6. 20. *b.* with a price, 7. 23.
2 Pet. 2. 1. denying the Lord that *b.* them
BOUND Isaac, Gen. 22. 9.
Job 36. 8. if they be *b.* in fetters
Ps. 107. 10. being in affliction
Prov. 22. 15. foolishness *b.* in heart
Is. 61. 1. opening of prison to them that are *b.*
Mat. 16. 19. whatsoever ye bind on earth shall
    be *b.* in heaven, 18. 18.
Acts 20. 22. I go *b.* in the spirit
21. 13. ready not to be *b.* only, but
Rom. 7. 2. wife is *b.* to her husband, 1 Cor. 7. 39.
1 Cor. 7. 27. *b.* to a wife, seek not
2 Tim. 2. 9. the word of God is not *b.*
Heb. 13. 3. in bonds as *b.* with them
Is. 1. 6. not closed or *bound up*
Ezek. 30. 21. not—to be healed
34. 4. neither have ye—the broken
Hos. 13. 12. iniquity of Ephraim is—
BOUNTY, 1 Ki. 10. 13. 2 Cor. 9. 5.
Prov. 22. 9. *bountiful* eye be blessed
Ps. 13. 6. dealt *bountifully* with me, 116. 7; 119.
    17; 142. 7.
BOW in the clouds, Gen. 9. 13, 14, 16.
Gen. 49. 24. his *b.* abode in strength
Josh. 24. 12. not with sword nor *b.*
2 Sam. 1. 18. teach children use of *b.*
Ps. 7. 12. hath bent his *b.* and made
11. 2. lo, wicked bend their *b.*
44. 6. I will not trust in my *b.*
78. 57. turned aside like deceitful *b.*
Jer. 9. 3. bend tongue like *b.* for lies
Lam. 2. 4. bent his *b.* like an enemy
3. 12. bent his *b.* and set me as a mark
Hos. 1. 5. break the *b.* of Israel
7. I will not save them by *b.*
7. 16. turned like a deceitful *b.*
1 Sam. 2. 4. Ps. 37. 15. *bows,* 64. 3; 78. 9. Jer.
    51. 56.
Bow down thine ear, 2 Ki. 19. 16. Ps. 31. 2; 86. 1.
    Prov. 22. 17.
Job 31. 10. let others—upon her
Ps. 95. 6. let us worship and—
Gen. 23. 12. Abraham *bowed down* himself before
    the people, 27. 29.
Judg. 7. 5, 6.—on knees to drink
Ps. 38. 6. I am—greatly, I go mourning
145. 14. raiseth up all that be—146. 8.
Is. 2. 11. haughtiness of men—17.
BOWELS did yearn, Gen. 43. 30. 1 Ki. 3. 26.
    2 Chr. 21. 15, 18.
Ps. 71. 6. took out of mother's *b.*
Is. 63. 15. the sounding of thy *b.*

Jer. 4. 19. my *bowels* my *b*. I am pained
31. 20. my *b*. are troubled for him, Lam. 1. 20;
2. 11. Sol. 5. 4.
Acts 1. 18. all his *b*. gushed out
2 Cor. 6. 12. straitened in your own *b*.
Phil. 1. 8. I long after you in the *b*. of Christ
Col. 3. 12. put on *b*. of mercies
Philem. 7. *b*. of saints refreshed
20. refresh my *b*. in the Lord
1 John 3. 17. shutteth up *b*. of compassion
BOWL, Num. 7. 85. Eccl. 12. 6. Zech. 4. 2, 3;
9. 15; 14. 20.
BRAKE the tables, Ex. 32. 19; 34. 1.
1 Sam. 4. 18. Eli *b*. his neck and died
1 Ki. 19. 11. wind *b*. in pieces rocks
2 Ki. 11. 18. *b*. Baal's image, 10. 27.
23. 14. *b*. the images, 2 Chr. 31. 1.
Job 29. 17. *b*. the jaws of the wicked
Ps. 76. 3. *b*. the arrows of the bow
105. 16. *b*. the whole staff of bread
107. 14. *b*. their bands in sunder
Jer. 31. 32. my covenant they *b*. Ezek. 17. 16.
Dan. 2. 1. his sleep *b*. from him
6. 24. *b*. all their bones to pieces
Mat. 14. 19. blessed bread and *b*. and gave,
15. 36; 26. 26. Mark 6. 41; 8. 6; 14. 22.
Luke 9. 16; 22. 19; 24. 30. 1 Cor. 11. 24.
Mark 14. 3. she *b*. box and poured
Break down images—altars of Baal, 2 Ki. 10. 27;
11. 18. 2 Chr. 14. 3; 23. 17; 34. 4.—wall of
Jerusalem, 2 Ki. 14. 13; 25. 10. 2 Chr.
25. 23; 36. 19. Jer. 39. 8; 52. 14.—houses
of Sodomites—high places—altars—altar of
Bethel, 2 Ki. 23. 7; 8, 12, 15.
BRAMBLE, Judg. 9. 14. Luke 6. 44.
BRANCH, with clusters of grapes, Num. 13. 23.
Is. 17. 9; 18. 5.
Job 14. 7. tender *b*. thereof not cease
18. 16. shall his *b*. be cut off
Prov. 11. 28. righteous flourish as *b*.
Is. 4. 2. *b*. of the Lord be beautiful
9. 14. cut off *b*. and rush, 19. 15.
14. 19. cast out like an abominable *b*.
25. 5. *b*. of terrible be brought low
60. 21. *b*. of my planting, 61. 3.
Jer. 23. 5. to David righteous *b*.
Ezek. 8. 17. they put *b*. to their nose
Zech. 3. 8. bring forth my servant *b*.
6. 12. behold man whose name is *b*.
Mal. 4. 1. leave neither root nor *b*.
Mat. 24. 32. when *b*. is yet tender
John 15. 4. *b*. cannot bear fruit of itself
6. cast forth as a *b*. and is withered
Lev. 23. 40. take *branches* of palm-trees, Neh.
8. 15. John 12. 13.
Job 15. 30. flame shall dry up his *b*.
Ps. 80. 11. sent her *b*. unto the river
104. 12. fowls sing among the *b*.
Is. 16. 8. her *b*. are stretched out
17. 6. four or five in outmost fruitful *b*.
18. 5. take and cut down *b*. 27. 10.
Jer. 11. 16. the *b*. of it are broken, Ezek. 17. 6, 7;
19. 10, 11, 14.
Dan. 4. 14. hew down tree, cut off *b*.
Hos. 14. 6. his *b*. spread as olive
Zech. 4. 12. what be these two olive *b*.
John 15. 5. I am vine, ye are the *b*.
Rom. 11. 16. if root be holy, so are *b*.
17. if some of the *b*. be broken off
18. boast not against the *b*.
21. God spared not natural *b*. 24.
BRAND, Judg. 15. 5. Zech. 3. 2.
BRASEN, Num. 16. 39. 2 Ki. 18. 4; 25. 13.

2 Chr. 6. 13. Jer. 1. 18; 15. 20; 52. 20.
Mark 7. 4.
BRASS, Gen. 4. 22. Dan. 5. 4.
Num. 21. 9. made serpent of *b*.
Deut. 8. 9. out of hills mayest dig *b*.
28. 23. the heaven shall be *b*.
Job 6. 12. or is my flesh *b*.
41. 27. he esteemeth *b*. as rotten wood
Ps. 107. 16. broken the gates of *b*.
Is. 48. 4. thy neck iron, and brow *b*.
Dan. 2. 32. belly and thighs of *b*.
Zech. 6. 1. were mountains of *b*.
1 Cor. 13. 1. as sounding *b*. and
Rev. 1. 15. feet like fine *b*. 2. 18.
BRAWLER, 1 Tim. 3. 3. Tit. 3. 2.
Prov. 21. 9; 25. 24. *brawling* woman
BREACH be upon thee, Gen. 38. 29.
Num. 14. 34. know my *b*. of promise
Judg. 21. 15. Lord made *b*. in tribes
2 Sam. 6. 8. Lord made *b*. on Uzzah
Job 16. 14. breaketh *b*. upon *b*.
Ps. 106. 23. Moses stood in the *b*.
Is. 30. 13. this iniquity shall be as *b*.
58. 12. called the repairer of the *b*.
Lam. 2. 13. thy *b*. is great like the sea
Ps. 60. 2. heal *breaches* thereof
BREAD shall be fat, Gen. 49. 20.
Ex. 16. 4. I will rain *b*. from heaven
23. 25. he will bless thy *b*. and water
Lev. 21. 6. *b*. of their God they offer
Num. 14. 9. they are *b*. for us
21. 5. soul loatheth this light *b*.
Deut. 8. 3. not live by *b*. only, Mat. 4. 4.
Ruth 1. 6. visited his people giving *b*.
1 Sam. 2. 5. hired themselves for *b*.
25. 11. take my *b*. and my water
1 Ki. 18. 4. fed them with *b*. and water
Neh. 5. 14. not eaten *b*. of governor, 18.
9. 15. gavest them *b*. from heaven
Ps. 37. 25. nor his seed begging *b*.
78. 20. can he give *b*. also
80. 5. feedest them with *b*. of tears
102. 9. I have eaten ashes like *b*.
132. 15. satisfy her poor with *b*.
Prov. 9. 17. *b*. eaten in secret is pleasant
20. 17. *b*. of deceit is sweet
22. 9. giveth of his *b*. to the poor
31. 27. she eateth not *b*. of idleness
Eccl. 9. 11. neither yet *b*. to the wise
11. 1. cast thy *b*. upon the waters
Is. 3. 1. away whole stay of *b*. 7.
30. 20. Lord give you *b*. of adversity
55. 2. money for that which is not *b*.
10. give seed to sower, *b*. to eater
58. 7. deal thy *b*. to the hungry
Lam. 4. 4. the young children ask *b*.
Ezek. 18. 7. hath given *b*. to hungry
Hos. 2. 5. give me my *b*. and water
Amos 4. 6. want of *b*. in all your places
Mal. 1. 7. ye offer polluted *b*. on mine
Mat. 4. 3. these stones be made *b*.
4. not live by *b*. alone, Luke 4. 4.
6. 11. this day our daily *b*.
7. 9. son ask *b*. will he give a stone, Luke 11. 11.
15. 26. meet to take the children's *b*.
26. 26. took *b*. and blessed it
Mark 8. 4. satisfy these men with *b*.
Luke 7. 33. neither eating *b*. nor
15. 17. servants have *b*. enough
24. 35. known in breaking of *b*.
John 6. 32. Moses gave you not that *b*.
33. the *b*. of God is he that cometh
34. evermore give us this *b*.

John 6. 35. I am the *bread* of life, 48. true *b.* 32.
50. this is the *b.* that cometh down
13. 18. he that eateth *b.* with me
Acts 2. 42. breaking *b.* and in prayer
46. breaking *b.* from house to house
20. 7. came together to break *b.*
27. 35. he took *b.* and gave thanks
1 Cor. 10. 16. *b.* we break is it not
17. we many are one *b.* and one body
11. 26. as often as ye eat this *b.* 27.
2 Cor. 9. 10. minister *b.* for your food
Deut. 16. 3. *bread of affliction*, 1 Ki. 22. 27.
2 Chr. 18. 26. Is. 30. 20.
Gen. 3. 19. *shall eat bread*, 28. 20. Ps. 14. 4;
127. 2. Prov. 25. 21. Eccl. 9. 7. Mark 7. 5.
Luke 14. 15. 1 Cor. 11. 26. 2 Thes. 3. 12.
1 Sam. 2. 36. *piece of bread*, Prov. 6. 26; 28. 21.
Jer. 37. 21. Ezek. 13. 19.
Lev. 26. 26. *break staff of bread*, Ps. 105. 16.
Ezek. 4. 16; 5. 16; 14. 13.
Gen. 19. 3. *unleavened bread*, Ex. 12. 8, 15,17,18,
20; 13. 6, 7. Mark 14. 12. Luke 22. 7. Acts
12. 3; 20. 6. 1 Cor. 5. 8.
BREAK, Gen. 19. 9. Ex. 34. 13.
Ezra 9. 14. again *b.* commandments
Ps. 2. 3. let us *b.* their bands asunder
9. shalt *b.* them with a rod of iron
10. 15. *b.* thou arm of the wicked
58. 6. *b.* their teeth in their mouth
89. 31. if they *b.* my statutes
34. my covenant will I not *b.* nor
Sol. 2. 17. till the day *b.* 4. 6.
Is. 38. 13. as a lion so will he *b.* all
42. 3. bruised reed not *b.* Mat. 12. 20.
Jer. 14. 21. *b.* not covenant with us
15. 12. shall iron *b.* northern iron
33. 20. *b.* my covenant
Ezek. 4. 16. *b.* of bread, 5. 16; 14. 13. Ps. 105. 16.
17. 15. *b.* covenant and be delivered
Hos. 1. 5. *b.* the bow of Israel, 2. 18.
Zech. 11. 10. might *b.* my covenant
Mat. 5. 19. *b.* one of least commandments
Acts 21. 13. mean ye to *b.* my heart?
1 Cor. 10. 16. bread which we *b.*
Ex. 23. 24. *break down*, Deut. 7. 5. Ps. 74. 6.
Eccl. 3. 3. Jer. 31. 28; 45. 4. Hos. 10. 2.
Ex. 19. 22, 24. *break forth*, Is. 55. 12. Jer. 1. 14.
Gal. 4. 27.
Is. 14. 7. *break forth into singing*, 44. 23; 49. 13;
54. 1; 55. 12; 52. 9.
Ex. 22. 6. *break out*, Is. 35. 6. Hos. 4. 2. Amos 5. 6.
Job 19. 2. *break in pieces*, 34. 24. Ps. 72. 4;
94. 5. Is. 45. 2. Jer. 51. 20, 21, 22. Dan.
2. 40, 44; 7. 23.
Ex. 19. 21, 24. *break through*, and gaze
Mat. 6. 19, 20. thieves—and steal
Jer. 4. 3. *break up* fallow ground, Hos. 10. 12.
Gen. 32. 26. let me go, day *breaketh*
Job 9. 17. he *b.* me with a tempest
Ps. 29. 5. voice of Lord *b.* cedars
46. 9. *b.* the bow and cutteth spear
119. 20. my soul *b.* for the longing
Prov. 25. 15. a soft tongue *b.* the bone
Eccl. 10. 8. *b.* a hedge, a serpent
Jer. 19. 11. as one *b.* a potter's vessel
23. 29. like a hammer that *b.* rocks
Luke 24. 35. known of them in *breaking* of bread
Acts 2. 42. *b.* of bread, 46.
Rom. 2. 23. through *b.* law dishonourest thou
God?
BREAST, John 13. 25. lying on Jesus' *b.* 21. 20.
Is. 60. 16. suck the *b.* of kings, 49. 23.
Lam. 4. 3. sea monsters draw out the *breast*

Breasts, Gen. 49. 25.
Job 3. 12. why *b.* that I should suck
21. 24. his *b.* are full of milk
Ps. 22. 9. I was upon my mother's *b.*
Prov. 5. 19. let her *b.* satisfy thee at
Sol. 1. 13. all night between my *b.*
4. 5. thy *b.* are like two roes, 7. 3.
7. 7. thy *b.* to clusters of grapes, 8.
8. 1. sucked the *b.* of my mother
8. a little sister, and she hath no *b.*
10. I am a wall, and my *b.* like towers
Is. 28. 9. weaned and drawn from *b.*
66. 11. satisfied with *b.* of her consolation
Ezek. 16. 7. thy *b.* are fashioned
23. 3. there were their *b.* pressed
8. and they bruised the *b.* of her virginity, and
poured
Hos. 2. 2. adulteries from between her *b.*
9. 14. miscarrying womb and dry *b.*
Joel 2. 16. gather those that suck *b.*
Luke 23. 48. smote *b.* and returned
Rev. 15. 6. *b.* girded with golden
Ex. 28. 4. *breastplate*, Rev. 9. 9, 17.
Eph. 6. 14. *b.* of righteousness
1 Thes. 5. 8. *b.* of faith and love
BREATH of life, Gen. 2. 7; 6. 17; 7. 15, 22.
Is. 2. 22. Hab. 2. 19.
Job 12. 10. in whose hands is *b.* of all
15. 30. by *b.* of his mouth
17. 1. my *b.* is corrupt, my days are extinct
33. 4. *b.* of Almighty given me life
34. 14. if he gather his spirit and *b.*
37. 10. by the *b.* of God frost is given
41. 21. his *b.* kindleth coals
Ps. 33. 6. made by *b.* of his mouth
104. 29. takest away their *b.*
135. 17. neither any *b.* in mouths
146. 4. *b.* goeth forth, he returneth
Eccl. 3. 19. they have all one *b.*
Is. 2. 22. whose *b.* is in his nostrils
11. 4. with *b.* of his lips slay wicked
30. 28. his *b.* an overflowing stream
33. the *b.* of the Lord doth kindle it
33. 11. your *b.* as fire shall devour you
42. 5. giveth *b.* unto the people
Jer. 10. 14. no *b.* in them, 51. 17.
Lam. 4. 20. the *b.* of our nostrils
Dan. 5. 23. in whose hand thy *b.* is
Acts 17. 25. giveth to all life and *b.*
Ps. 27. 12. *breathe* out cruelty
Ezek. 37. 9. come *b.* upon these slain
John 20. 22. he *breathed* on them
Acts 9. 1. *breathing* out slaughter
BREECHES, linen, Ex. 28. 42; 39. 28.
Lev. 6. 10; 16. 4. Ezek. 44. 18.
BREED, abundantly, Gen. 8. 17.
Deut. 32. 14. rams of *b.* of Bashan
Ex. 16. 20. *bred* worm and stank
Zeph. 2. 9. *breeding* of nettles
BRETHREN, we be, Gen. 13. 8.
Gen. 19. 7. *b.* do not so wickedly
24. 27. led me to house of my master's *b.*
42. 3. Joseph's ten *b.* went to buy corn
6. *b.* bowed down themselves
45. 16. Joseph's *b.* are come
49. 5. Simeon and Levi are *b.*
26. separate from *b.* Deut. 33. 16.
50. 15. Joseph's *b.* saw their father was dead
Num. 27. 4. give possession among *b.* 7.
10. if no *b.* . . . to his father's *b.* 11.
Deut. 17. 20. be not lifted up above *b.*
25. 5. if *b.* dwell together
33. 9. neither did he acknowledge his *brethren*

Deut. 24. let him be acceptable to his *brethren*
Josh. 6. 23. Rahab and *b*.
Judg. 9. 1. Abimelech . . . mother's *b*. 3.
2 Ki. 10. 13. we are *b*. of Ahaziah
1 Chr. 4. 9. more honourable than his *b*.
5. 2. prevailed above his *b*.
12. 2. Saul's *b*. of Benjamin
26. 7. *b*. were strong men
1 Chr. 27. 18. Elihu of *b*. of David
2 Chr. 21. 2. Jehoram and his *b*.
22. 8. Jehu found *b*. of Ahaziah
Job 6. 15. my *b*. dealt deceitfully
19. 13. put my *b*. far from me
Ps. 22. 22. declare thy name unto my *b*.
69. 8. become a stranger to my *b*.
Ps. 122. 8. for *b*. and companions' sakes
133. 1. for *b*. to dwell in unity
Prov. 6. 19. soweth discord among *b*.
17. 2. part of inheritance of *b*.
Hos. 13. 15. fruitful among his *b*.
Mat. 4. 18. Jesus saw two *b*. 21.
12. 48. who are my *b*.
19. 29. forsaken houses, or *b*. or sisters
20. 24. moved against the two *b*.
22. 25. seven *b* . . . married a wife. Mark 12. 20.
23. 8. all ye are *b*. Acts 7. 26.
25. 40. the least of these my *b*.
28. 10. go tell my *b*. that they go
Mark 10. 29. left house or *b*. Luke 18. 29.
Luke 14. 26. hate not *b*. own life also
16. 28. for I have five *b*.
21. 16. betrayed by *b*.
John 7. 5. neither did his *b*. believe
20. 17. go to my *b*. and say, I ascend
Acts 6. 3. *b*. look ye out seven men
7. 26. sirs, ye are *b*. why do ye
9. 30. when the *b*. knew
10. 23. certain *b*. from Joppa
11. 12. these six *b*. accompanied me
29. send relief to the *b*.
12. 17. shew these things to James and *b*.
14. 2. evil affected against *b*.
15. 3. caused great joy to all the *b*.
22. chief among *b*. 23. greeting to *b*.
32. exhort *b*. with many words
40. by *b*. unto the grace of God
17. 6. drew Jason and certain *b*.
10. *b*. sent away Paul and Silas, 14.
18. 18. Paul took leave of *b*.
27. *b*. wrote exhorting the disciples
20. 32. now *b*. I commend you to God
23. 6. men and *b*. I am a Pharisee
Rom. 8. 29. the firstborn among many *b*.
9. 3. accursed from Christ for my *b*.
1 Cor. 6. 5. to judge between his *b*.
8. 12. sin against the *b*.
15. 6. seen of above five hundred *b*. at once
Gal. 2. 4. false *b*. unawares brought in
1 Tim. 4. 6. put *b*. in remembrance
5. 1. entreat the younger as *b*.
Heb. 2. 11. is not ashamed to call them *b*.
1 Pet. 1. 22. unfeigned love of the *b*.
3. 8. love as *b*. be pitiful, courteous
1 John 3. 14. because we love the *b*.
16. to lay down our lives for the *b*.
3 John 10. neither doth receive the *b*.
Gen. 27. 29. *thy brethren*, 48. 22; 49. 8. Deut.
15. 7; 18. 15. 1 Sam. 17. 18. Mat. 12. 47.
Mark 3. 32. Luke 8. 20; 14. 12; 22. 32.
Jer. 12. 6.—have dealt treacherously
Rev. 19. 10. I am of—22. 9.
1 Ki. 12. 24. *your brethren*, 2 Chr. 30. 7, 9; 35. 6.
Neh. 4. 14. fight for—your sons

Is. 66. 5. *your brethren* that hated you
Acts 3. 22. raise up of—prophet like unto me,
7. 37. Deut. 18. 15.
BRIBES, 1 Sam. 8. 3. Amos 5. 12.
1 Sam. 12. 3. have I received any *b*.
Ps. 26. 10. right hand full of *b*.
Is. 33. 15. hands from holding *b*.
Job 15. 34. tabernacles of *bribery*
BRICK, Gen. 11. 3. Ex. 1. 14; 5. 7, 8, 14, 16, 18,
19. Is. 9. 10; 65. 3.
2 Sam. 12. 31. *brick-kiln*, Jer. 43. 9. Nah. 3. 14.
BRIDE, doth clothe with an ornament, Is. 49. 18.
Is. 61. 10. as a *b*. adorneth herself
Jer. 2. 32. can a *b*. forget her attire
Joel 2. 16. *b*. go out of her closet
John 3. 29. hath *b*. is the bridegroom
Rev. 21. 2. as *b*. adorned for husband
9. I will shew thee *b*. Lamb's wife
Mat. 9. 15. *bride-chamber*, Mark 2. 19.
BRIDEGROOM, Joel 2. 16. John 2. 9.
Ps. 19. 5. as *b*. coming out of chamber
Is. 61. 10. as a *b*. decketh himself
62. 5. as a *b*. rejoiceth over the bride
Jer. 7. 34. cease voice of *b*. and bride, 16. 9;
25. 10; 33. 11. Rev. 18. 23.
Mat. 9. 15. as long as the *b*. is with them, Mark
2. 19, 20. Luke 5. 34.
Mat. 25. 1. went forth to meet *b*. 6.
John 3. 29. friend of *b*. rejoiceth
BRIDLE for the ass, Prov. 26. 3.
Job 30. 11. let loose the *b*.
Ps. 32. 9. mouth held with *b*.
39. 1. I will keep my mouth as with a *b*.
Is. 37. 29. put my *b*. in thy lips, 30. 28. 2 Ki.
19. 28. Rev. 14. 20.
Jas. 3. 2. able to *b*. the whole body
1. 26. *bridleth* not his tongue
BRIEFLY, Rom. 13. 9. 1 Pet. 5. 12.
BRIERS, Judg. 8. 7, 16. Is. 7. 23, 24, 25; 32. 13.
Heb. 6. 8. Mic. 7. 4.
Is. 5. 6. come up *b*. and thorns
9. 18. wickedness . . . shall devour *b*. 10. 17.
27. 4. set *b*. against me in battle
55. 13. instead of *b*. shall come up myrtle
Ezek. 2. 6. though *b*. and thorns be
28. 24. no more a pricking *b*. unto
BRIGANDINE, coat of mail, Jer. 46. 4. put on
b. 51. 3. lifteth self in *b*.   [38, 39.
BRIGHT, Lev. 13. 2. *b*. spot, 2, 4, 19, 23, 24–26,
Job 37. 11. *b*. cloud, 21.
Sol. 5. 14. *b*. ivory
Jer. 51. 11. make *b*. the arrows
Ezek. 1. 13. fire was *b*. and out of
21. 15. sword made *b*. it is
Nah. 3. 3. *b*. sword and glittering
Zech. 10. 1. the Lord shall make *b*. clouds
Mat. 17. 5. a *b*. cloud overshadowed
Luke 11. 36. *b*. shining of a candle
Acts 10. 30. a man stood in *b*. clothing
Rev. 22. 16. *b*. and morning star
Brightness, 2 Sam. 22. 13. Ezek. 1. 4, 27, 28; 8. 2;
28. 7, 17.
Job 31. 26. beheld moon walking in *b*.
Is. 59. 9. we wait for *b*. but walk
Ezek. 10. 4. full of the *b*. of Lord's glory
28. 7. they shall defile thy *b*.
Dan. 4. 36. honour and *b*. returned
12. 3. *b*. firmament
Amos 5. 20. even very dark and no *b*. in it?
Hab. 3. 4. and his *b*. was as the light
Acts 26. 13. a light above *b*. of sun
2 Thes. 2. 8. Lord with *b*. of his coming
Heb. 1. 3. being the *b*. of his glory

BRIM, Josh. 3.15. 1 Ki. 7.26. 2 Chr. 4.2,5. John 2.7.
BRIMSTONE, Gen. 19. 24. Lord rained on
  Sodom and Gomorrah *b.* Luke 17. 29.
Deut. 29. 23. the whole land thereof is *b.*
Ps. 11. 6. rain snares, fire, and *b.*
Is. 30. 33. breath of L. like a stream of *b.*
34. 9. dust thereof into *b.*, land burning
Ezek. 38. 22. great hailstones, fire, and *b.*
Rev. 9. 17, 18. issued fire and *b.*
19. 20. cast into a lake of fire and *b.* 20. 10.
BRING a flood, Gen. 6. 17.
Josh. 23. 15. *b.* upon you all the evil
1 Ki. 8. 32. to *b.* his way on his head
Job 14. 4. who can *b.* a clean thing
33. 30. to *b.* back his soul from pit
Ps. 60. 9. who *b.* me into strong city
Eccl. 11. 9. God will *b.* thee into judgment,
  12. 14. Job 30. 23.
Sol. 8. 2. *b.* thee to my mother's house
Is. 1. 13. *b.* no more vain oblations
43. 5. I will *b.* thy seed from east
6. *b.* my sons from afar, 60. 9.
46. 13. I *b.* near my righteousness
66. 9. *b.* to birth and not *b.* forth
Hos. 2. 14. allure and *b.* her into wilderness
Zeph. 3. 5. every morning *b.* his judgment
Luke 2. 10. I *b.* you good tidings
8. 14. *b.* no fruit to perfection
John 14. 26. *b.* all to remembrance
Acts 5. 28. *b.* this man's blood on us
1 Cor. 1. 28. *b.* to nought things that are
4. 5. *b.* to light the hidden things
1 Thes. 4. 14. God will *b.* with him
1 Pet. 3. 18. that he might *b.* us to God
Gen. 1. 11, 20, 24. *bring forth,* 3. 16. Mat. 1. 21.
  Job 39. 1. Ex. 3. 10.
2 Ki. 19. 3. there is not strength to—
Job. 15. 35. they conceive mischief and—vanity.
  —iniquity, Is. 59. 4.
Ps. 37. 6. he shall—thy righteousness
92. 14. they shall still—fruit in old age
Prov. 27. 1. knowest not what a day may—
Is. 41. 21.—your strong reasons
42. 1.—judgment to the Gentiles, 3.
66. 8. shall earth be made to—in one day?
Zeph. 2. 2. before the decree—
Mark 4. 20.—fruit some thirtyfold
Luke 3. 8.—fruits worthy of repentance
8. 15. heard word—fruit with patience
John 15. 2. that it may—more fruit
Ps. 1. 3. *bringeth forth* fruit in his season
Hos. 10. 1. Israel . . . —fruit to himself
Mat. 3. 10. bring not forth good fruit, 7. 19; 12. 35.
  Luke 6. 43.
John 12. 24. if it die it bring much fruit
Jas. 1. 15. bring sin bring death
BROAD, Num. 16. 38, 39. Nah. 2. 4. Mat. 23. 5.
Job 36. 16. out of strait into *b.* place
Ps. 119. 96. commandment is exceeding *b.*
Is. 33. 21. Lord . . . a place of *b.* rivers
Mat. 7. 13. *b.* is way to destruction
BROKEN my covenant, Gen. 17. 14. Ps. 55. 20.
  Is. 24. 5; 33. 8; 36. 6. Jer. 11. 10; 33. 21.
  Ezek. 44. 7.
Ps. 34. 18. nigh them of *b.* heart
44. 19. sore *b.* us in place of dragons
51. 8. bones thou hast *b.* rejoice
17. *b.* spirit, *b.* and contrite heart
147. 3. healeth the *b.* in heart
Prov. 17. 22. a *b.* spirit drieth bones
Eccl. 4. 12. a threefold cord not *b.*
Is. 61. 1. bind *b.* hearted, Luke 4. 18.
Jer. 2. 13. hewed out *b.* cisterns

Jer. 5. 5. these have altogether *broken* the yoke
Dan. 2. 42. partly strong and partly *b.*
Hos. 5. 11. Ephraim *b.* in judgment
Mat. 21. 44. fall on stone shall be *b.*
BROOK, Num. 13. 23. Deut. 2. 13.
Ps. 110. 7. drink of the *b.* in the way
Job 20. 17. *brooks* of honey and butter
Is. 19. 6. *b.* of defence be emptied
BROTHER, for adversity, Prov. 17. 17.
Prov. 18. 19. a *b.* offended is harder
24. a friend that sticketh closer than a *b.*
27. 10. neighbour near, than *b.* far
Jer. 9. 4. trust not in any *b.* for
Mat. 10. 21. *b.* shall deliver up *b.* to death,
  Mark 13. 12. Mic. 7. 2.
Acts 9. 17. *b.* Saul receive thy sight
1 Cor. 5. 11. *b.* be a fornicator or
7. 15. *b.* or sister is not in bondage
8. 11. shall the weak *b.* perish
1 Thes. 4. 6. no man defraud his *b.*
2 Thes. 3. 15. admonish him as a *b.*
Jas. 1. 9. let *b.* of low degree rejoice
Ps. 35. 14. *my brother,* Sol. 8. 1. Mat. 12. 50;
  18. 21. 1 Cor. 8. 13.
Ps. 50. 20. *thy brother,* Mat. 5. 23, 24; 18. 15.
  Rom. 14. 10, 15.
Gen. 45. 4. *your brother,* Rev. 1. 9.
Zech. 11. 14. *brotherhood,* 1 Pet. 2. 17.
Amos 1. 9. *brotherly* covenant
Rom. 12. 10. affectioned with *b.* love
1 Thes. 4. 9. as touching *b.* love, ye
Heb. 13. 1. let *b.* love continue
2 Pet. 1. 7. to godliness *b.* kindness
BROUGHT me hitherto, 2 Sam. 7. 18.
Neh. 4. 15. God *b.* counsel to nought
9. 33. thou art just in all that is *b.* on us
Ps. 45. 14. be *b.* unto the king in raiment
79. 8. mercies prevent us: we are *b.* very low
106. 43. *b.* low for their iniquities
107. 39. *b.* low through oppression
Is. 1. 2. nourished *b.* up children
Mat. 10. 18. *b.* before governors, Mark 13. 9.
Luke 12. 16. ground of a rich man *b.* forth
1 Cor. 6. 12. not be *b.* under power
Gal. 2. 4. false brethren unawares *b.* in
1 Tim. 6. 7. *b.* nothing into world
Ps. 107. 12. *brought down,* Mat. 11. 23.
Deut. 33. 14. *brought forth,* Ps. 18. 19. & 90. 2.
  Is. 66. 7. Jas. 5. 18.
BRUISE . . . thou his heel, Gen. 3. 15.
Is. 53. 10. it pleased the Lord to *b.* him.
Rom. 16. 20. God of peace *b.* Satan
2 Ki. 18. 21. trustest staff of *bruised* reed
Is. 42. 3. *b.* reed, Mat. 12. 20.
53. 5. He was *b.* for our iniquities
Ezek. 23. 3. *b.* teats, 21.
Luke 4. 18. set at liberty the *b.*
Is. 1. 6. wounds, *bruises* and putrifying
BRUIT, report, Jer. 10. 22. Nah. 3. 19.
BRUTISH man knoweth not, Ps. 92. 6.
Ps. 94. 8. understand ye *b.* among people
Prov. 12. 1. that hateth reproof is *b.*
Jer. 10. 14. *b.* in knowledge, 51. 17.
BUCKET, nations as drop of a, Is. 40. 15.
Num. 24. 7. water out of his *buckets*
BUCKLER, 1 Chr. 5. 18, &c.,
Job 15. 26. runneth upon . . . his *bucklers*
Sol. 4. 4. a thousand *b.*
BUD, horn to, Ps. 132. 17. Ezek. 29. 21.
BUFFET, 2 Cor. 12. 7.—ED, Mat. 26. 67. 1 Cor.
  4. 11. 1 Pet. 2. 20.
BUILD walls of Jerusalem, Ps. 51. 18.
Ps. 102. 16. Lord shall *b.* up Zion

Ps. 127. 1. except the Lord *build* the house
Eccl. 3. 3. break down and a time to *b.* up
Mic. 3. 10. they *b.* up Zion with blood
Acts 20. 32. grace, which is able to *b.* you up
Heb. 11. 10. *builder* and maker is God
Ps. 118. 22. stone which the *builders* refused is
become head, Mat. 21. 42. Mark 12. 10. Luke
20. 17. Acts 4. 11. 1 Pet. 2. 7.
1 Cor. 3. 10. as a wise *master builder,*
Josh. 6. 26. cursed *buildeth* this city
Prov. 14. 1. every wise woman *b.* her house
Jer. 22. 13. woe to him that *b.* house
Amos 9. 6. *b.* his stories in heaven
Hab. 2. 12. *b.* a town with blood
1 Cor. 3. 10. another *b.* thereon
9. God's husbandry, ye are God's *building*
2 Cor. 5. 1. we have a *b.* of God, an house
Eph. 2. 21. all the *b.* fitly framed
Job 22. 23. return shalt be *built* up
Ps. 89. 2. mercy be *b.* up for ever
Mat. 7. 24. *b.* his house on a rock
Eph. 2. 20. ye are *b.* on foundation of
Heb. 3. 4. he that *b.* all things is God
1 Pet. 2. 5. *b.* up a spiritual house
BULLS (foes) compassed me, Ps. 22. 12.
Ps. 50. 13. will I eat the flesh of *b.*
68. 30. rebuke the multitude of *b.*
Heb. 9. 13. if *blood of b.* and goats
10. 4. the—cannot take away sins
Ps. 69. 31. than *bullock* with horns
Jer. 31. 18. as a *b.* unaccustomed to yoke
Ps. 51. 19. offer *bullocks* on thy altar
Is. 1. 11. delight not in blood of *b.*
BULRUSHES, Ex. 2. 3. Is. 18. 2: 58. 5.
BULWARKS, Ps. 48. 13. Is. 26. 1.
BUNDLE, Gen. 42. 35. Acts 28. 3.
1 Sam. 25. 29. bound in the *b.* of life
Mat. 13. 30. tares in *bundles* to burn
BURDEN, 2 Ki. 5. 17; 8. 9.
Ex. 18. 22. shall bear the *b.* with thee, Num.
23. 5. ass lying under his *b.* [11. 17.
Deut. 1. 12. how can I bear your *b.*
2 Sam. 15. 33. thou shalt be a *b.* unto
19. 35. servant be yet *b.* to my lord
2 Ki. 5. 17. given two mules' *b.* of earth?
9. 25. the Lord laid this *b.* upon him
2 Chr. 35. 3. not be *b.* on shoulders
Neh. 13. 19. no *b.* brought in on sabbath day,
Jer. 17. 21, 22, 24, 27.
Job 7. 20. so that I am a *b.* to myself
Ps. 38. 4. a *b.* they are too heavy for me
55. 22. cast thy *b.* upon the Lord
81. 6. I removed his shoulder from *b.*
Eccl. 12. 5. grasshopper shall be a *b.*
Is. 9. 4. thou hast broken the yoke of his *b.*
30. 27. the *b.* thereof is heavy: his lips full
Zeph. 3. 18. reproach of it was a *b.*
Zech. 12. 3. that *b.* themselves with
Mat. 11. 30. my yoke easy, my *b.* is light
Acts 15. 28. no greater *b.* than necessary
2 Cor. 12. 16. But be it so, I did not *b.* you
Gal. 6. 5. every man bear his own *b.*
Rev. 2. 24. put on you no other *b.*
Is. 13. 1. *b.* threatening of heavy judgments,
14. 28; 15. 1; 17. 1; 19. 1; 21. 1, 11; 22. 1;
23. 1. Ezek. 12. 10. Nah. 1. 1. Hab. 1. 1.
Zech. 9. 1: 12. 1.
Mal. 1. 1. *b.* of the word of the Lord
2 Cor. 5. 4. we groan being *burdened*
8. 13. not others eased and ye *b.*
Gen. 49. 14. *burdens,* Ex. 1. 11; 2. 11; 5. 4.
Is. 58. 6. to undo the heavy *b.* and let the
Lam. 2. 14. seen for thee false *b.*

Mat. 23. 4. bind heavy *burdens.* Luke 11. 46.
Gal. 6. 2. bear one another's *b.* and fulfil
Zech. 12. 3. Jerusalem *burdensome,* 2 Cor.
11. 9; 12. 13, 14. 1 Thes. 2. 6.
BURN upon altar, Ex. 29. 13, 18, 25. Lev. 1. 9,15;
2. 2; 3. 5, 11, 16; 5. 12; 6. 15; 9. 17.
Gen. 44. 18. let not thine anger *b.*
Deut. 32. 22. shall *b.* to lowest hell
Is. 27. 4. go through them and *b.*
Mal. 4. 1. day cometh shall *b.* as an oven
Luke 3. 17. chaff he will *b.* with fire
24. 32. did not our heart *b.* within us?
1 Cor. 7. 9. better marry than *b.* Rom. 1. 27.
2 Cor. 11. 29. who is offended and I *b.* not?
Ex. 3. 2. the bush *burned* with fire
Deut. 9. 15. the mount *b.* with fire
1 Cor. 3. 15. if man's work *b.* . . . himself saved
13. 3. though I give my body to be *b.* and
Heb. 6. 8. whose end is to be *b.*
12. 18. not come to the mount that *b.*
Ps. 46. 9. *burneth* the chariot, 83. 14.— a wood
Is. 9. 18. wickedness *b.* Prov. 16. 27.
Rev. 21. 8. lake which *b.* with fire
Gen. 15. 17. *burning* lamp, Rev. 4. 5.
Jer. 20. 9. his word *b.* fire shut up in bones
Ezek. 1. 13. *b.* coals forth at feet, Hab. 3. 5.
Luke 12. 35. loins girded, your lights *b.*
John 5. 35. a *b.* and a shining light
Ex. 21. 25. *b.* for *b.,* wound for wound
Deut. 28. 22. smite thee with extreme *b.*
2 Chr. 16. 14. a *b.* (burial); no *b.* 21. 19. Jer. 34.5.
Is. 3. 24. *b.* instead of beauty
4. 4. spirit of judgment and *b.* Mat. 3. 11.
Amos 4. 11. firebrand out of *b.*
Is. 33. 14. shall dwell with everlasting *burnings*
b. incense, Aaron & sons, 1 Chr. 23. 13. Korah, &c.,
Num. 16. 35. Jeroboam, 1 Ki. 13. 1. Uzziah,
2 Chr. 26. 16. Zacharias, Luke 1. 9. people,
1 Ki. 22. 43. Is. 65. 7.—to idols, Hos. 2. 13;
4. 13. Hab. 1. 16. Jer. 7. 9; 44. 17. Amaziah,
2 Chr. 25. 14. Ahaz, 28. 3.
Gen. 8. 20. *burnt-offerings,* Deut. 12. 6.
Hos. 6. 6. mercy, obey, contrition, justice, more
than—, 1 Sam. 15. 22. Ps. 51. 17. Is. 1. 11.
Mic. 6. 8. Jer. 7. 21.
Mark 12. 33. love neighbour more than—
Heb. 10. 6. in —for sin . . . no pleasure
Ps. 74. 8. *burned up* all the synagogues
Is. 64. 11. our beautiful house is—
Mat. 22. 7. destroyed and—their city
2 Pet. 3. 10. earth and works . . . shall be—
BURST thy bands, Jer. 2. 20.
Jer. 5. 5. yoke and *b.* bonds, 30. 8.
Prov. 3. 10. presses shall *b.* out = run over
Mark 2. 22. new wine *b.* bottles, Job 32. 19.
Acts 1. 18. he *b.* asunder in midst
BURY dead out of my sight, Gen. 23. 4.
Gen. 49. 29. *b.* me with my fathers
Ps. 79. 3. there was none to *b.*
Mat. 8. 21. first to go and *b.* my father
22. let the dead *b.* their dead, Luke 9. 60.
Rom. 6. 4. *buried* with him by baptism, Col. 2. 12.
1 Cor. 15. 4. he was *b.* and rose again •
Gen. 23. 4. a possession of a *burying* place
47. 30. bury me in their *b.* place
2 Chr. 26. 23. *burial,* Acts 8. 2.
Eccl. 6. 3. that he have no *b.*
Is. 14. 20. not joined with them in *b.*
Jer. 22. 19. buried with the *b.* of an ass
BUSH, in the, Deut. 33. 16. Mark 12. 26. Luke
20. 37. angel—, Ex. 3. 2. Acts 7. 35.
BUSHEL, Mat. 5. 15. Luke 11. 33.
BUSHY & black locks, Sol. 5. 11.

BUSINESS, Gen. 39. 11. Deut. 24. 5.
  Ps. 107. 23. do *b.* in great waters
  Dan. 8. 27. the king's *b.* Esth. 3. 9.
  Luke 2. 49. must be about my Father's *b.*
  Rom. 12. 11. not slothful in *b.*; fervent
  1 Thes. 4. 11. study to do your own *b.*
BUTTER, 2 Sam. 17. 29. *b.* and milk, Gen. 18. 8.
  Deut. 32. 14. Judg. 5. 25. Prov. 30. 33.
  Job 20. 17. the brooks of honey and *b.*
  Ps. 55. 21. words were smoother than *b.*
  Is. 7. 15. *b.* and honey shall he eat, 22.
BUY the truth, sell it not, Prov. 23. 23.
  Is. 55. 1. *b.* and eat, yea, *b.* wine
  Jas. 4. 13. *b.* and sell, and get gain
  Rev. 3. 18. I counsel thee to *b.* gold
  13. 17. no man *b.* or sell, save . . . mark
  Prov. 20. 14. it is naught saith *buyer*
  Is. 24. 2. as with *b.* so with seller
  Ezek. 7. 12. let not the *b.* rejoice, nor
  Mat. 13. 44. selleth all and *buyeth* that field
  Rev. 18. 11. no man *b.* their merchandise
BY and **BY,** immediately, Mat. 13. 21. Mark 6. 25.
  Luke 17. 7; 21. 9.
BYWORD, song and, Job 17. 6; 30. 9.
  1 Ki. 9. 7. Israel shall be a *b.*
  Ps. 44. 14. makest us a *b.*, Deut. 28. 37.

C

CAGE, Jer. 5. 27; (Babylon) Rev. 18. 2.
CAKE . . . tumbled into host, Judg. 7. 13.
  1 Ki. 17. 12. I have not a *c.* but meal
  Hos. 7. 8. Ephraim a *c.* not turned
Cakes, Gen. 18. 6. Judg. 6. 19. 2 Sam. 6. 19.
  Lev. 24. 5. bake twelve *c.* (shewbread)
  Jer. 7. 18. make *c.* to queen of heaven
CALAMITY at hand, Deut. 32. 35.
  Job 6. 2. my *c.* laid in the balances
  Ps. 18. 18. prevented me in day of my *c.*
  Prov. 1. 26. I will laugh at your *c.*
  19. 13. a foolish son is the *c.* of his father
  27. 10. nor go to brother's house in *c.*
  Jer. 18. 17. back not face in the day of *c.*
  46. 21. day of their *c.* is come, 48. 16; 49. 8, 32.
  Ezek. 35. 5. Obad. 13.
  Ps. 57. 1. until *calamities* be overpast
  141. 5. my prayer shall be in their *c.*
  Prov. 17. 5. glad at *c.* not unpunished
CALDRONS, 1 Sam. 2. 14. Job 41. 20. Ezek.
  11. 3, 7, 11. Mic. 3. 3. Jer. 52. 18, 19.
CALF, Gen. 18. 7. Lev. 9. 2. Job 21. 10. Ps. 29. 6.
  Is. 27. 10. Rev. 4. 7.
  Ex. 32. 4. made a molten *c.*, 20. Deut. 9. 16.
  Neh. 9. 18. Ps. 106. 19.
  Is. 11. 6. *c.* and young lion together
  Jer. 34. 18. *c.* in twain and passed between
  Hos. 8. 5. thy *c.* O Samaria, hath cast thee
  Luke 15. 23. bring the fatted *c.*
  1 Ki. 12. 28. made two *calves* of gold
  Hos. 14. 2. we will render the *c.* of our lips
  Mic. 6. 6. come with *c.* of a year old
  Mal. 4. 2. grow up as *c.* of the stall
  Heb. 9. 12. blood of goats and *c.*, 19.
CALKERS, Gebal, wise men thy, Ezek. 27. 9.
CALL them what Adam would, Gen. 2. 19.
  Gen. 24. 57. we will *c.* the damsel
  30. 13. *c.* me blessed, Prov. 31. 28.
  Deut. 4. 7. nigh as God in all we *c.* . . for
  26. I *c.* heaven and earth to witness, 30. 19.
  1 Sam. 3. 6. for thou didst *c.* me
  1 Ki. 8. 52. in all they *c.* for to thee

Job 5. 1. *Call* now if there be any to answer
  13. 22. *c.* thou, I will answer, 14. 15.
  27. 10. will he always *c.* upon God
  Ps. 4. 1. hear me when I *c.* O God
  14. 4. they *c.* not upon the Lord, 53. 4.
  49. 11. *c.* lands after their names
  77. 6. I *c.* to remembrance my song
  80. 18. quicken us and we will *c.* on thy
  86. 5. plenteous in mercy to all that *c.*
  145. 18. nigh to all that *c.* upon him
  Prov. 1. 28. then shall *c.* I will not answer
  Is. 5. 20. woe that *c.* evil good and
  22. 12. day the Lord did *c.* to weeping
  58. 9. thou *c.* and Lord will answer
  65. 24. before they *c.* I will answer
  Jer. 25. 29. *c.* for a sword upon all
  29. 12. shall ye *c.* and I will hearken
  Joel 2. 32. whosoever shall *c.* on Lord
  Jonah 1. 6. arise, *c.* upon thy God
  Zech. 13. 9. shall *c.* upon thy name
  Mal. 3. 12. all nations shall *c.* you blessed
  15. and now we *c.* the proud happy
  Mat. 9. 13. I am not come to *c.* righteous
  22. 3. *c.* them that were bidden
  23. 9. *c.* no man your father on earth
  Luke 1. 48. all generations *c.* me blessed
  6. 46. why *c.* ye me Lord, Lord and
  14. 12, 13. *c.* not friends . . . *c.* poor
  John 4. 16. *c.* thy husband and come
  13. 13. ye *c.* me Master and Lord
  15. 15. I *c.* you not servants, but friends
  Acts 2. 39. as many as the Lord shall *c.*
  24. 14. after the way they *c.* heresy
  Rom. 9. 25. I will *c.* them my people
  10. 12. rich in mercy to all that *c.* on him
  2 Cor. 1. 23. I *c.* God for a record on my
  Heb. 2. 11. not ashamed to *c.* brethren
  Jas. 5. 14. *c.* for the elders of church
  1 Pet. 1. 17. if ye *c.* on the Father
Call on the name of the Lord, Gen. 4. 26; 12. 9;
  13. 4; 21. 33; 26. 25. 1 Ki. 18. 24. 2 Ki.
  5. 11. Ps. 116. 4, 13, 17. Joel 2. 32. Zeph.
  3. 9. Acts 2. 21. Rom. 10. 13. 1 Cor. 1. 2.
I will call unto, or, *on the Lord,* 1 Sam. 12. 17. 2 Sam.
  22. 4. Ps. 18. 3; 55. 16; 86. 7.   [29. 12.
Call upon me, Ps. 50. 15; 91. 15. Prov. 1. 28. Jer.
  Gen. 21. 17. angel of God *called* to Hagar
  22. 11. angel of Lord *c.* to Abraham, 15.
  Ex. 3. 4. God *c.* him out of the bush
  Judg. 15. 18. athirst, and *c.* on the Lord
  2 Ki. 8. 1. Lord hath *c.* for a famine
  1 Chr. 4. 10. Jabez *c.* on the God of Israel
  21. 26. David *c.* on Lord and he answered
  Ps. 17. 6. I have *c.* upon thee, 31. 17.
  18. 6. in my distress I *c.* upon the Lord
  79. 6. not *c.* on thy name, Jer. 10. 25.
  88. 9. I have *c.* daily upon thee
  118. 5. I *c.* on the Lord in my distress
  Prov. 1. 24. I have *c.* and ye refused
  Sol. 5. 6. I *c.* him, he gave no answer
  Is. 41. 2. who *c.* him to his foot
  42. 6. I the Lord *c.* thee in righteousness
  43. 1. I have *c.* thee, 22. thou not *c.*
  48. 1. *c.* by the name of Israel, 45. 4.
  49. 1. the Lord *c.* me from the womb
  50. 2. when I *c.* was none to answer
  51. 2. I *c.* him alone, and blessed him
  61. 3. might be *c.* trees of righteousness
  62. 4. thou shalt be *c.* Hephzibah
  65. 12. I *c.* ye not answer, Jer. 7. 13.
  Lam. 1. 19. I *c.* for my lovers, they
  3. 55. I *c.* upon thy name, O Lord
  Hos. 11. 1. I *c.* my son out of Egypt

Amos 7. 4. the Lord *called* to contend by fire
Hag. 1. 11. I *c*. drought on the land
Mark 14. 72. Peter *c*. to mind the word
Luke 15. 19. not worthy to be *c*. thy son
John 1. 48. before that Philip *c*. thee
10. 35. if he *c*. them gods to whom
John 15. 15. but I have *c*. you friends
Acts 9. 21. destroy them which *c*. on this name
41. when he had *c*. the saints
10. 23, 24. *c*. in . . . *c*. together his kinsmen
11. 26. disciples were *c*. Christians first
13. 2. for work whereto I *c*. them
15. on whom my name is *c*.
19. 40. *c*. in question, 23. 6. I am, 24. 21.
Rom. 1. 1. *c*. to be an apostle, 1 Cor. 1. 1.
6. *c*. of Jesus Christ, 7. *c*. to be saints
2. 17. art *c*. a Jew and restest in the law
8. 28. the *c*. according to his purpose
30. predestinate, them he also *c*.
9. 24. whom he *c*., not of Jews only
1 Cor. 1. 9. faithful . . . were *c*.
26. not many wise, not many noble are *c*.
5. 11. if any man *c*. a brother be
7. 17. as the Lord hath *c*. every one, so let
18. *c*. circumcised? 21. *c*. servant?
24. every man wherein . . . *c*. abide with God
15. 9. not meet to be *c*. an apostle
Gal. 1. 6. *c*. you into grace of Christ
15. God who *c*. me by his grace
5. 13. ye have been *c*. to liberty; only use not
Eph. 2. 11. who are *c*. uncircumcision
4. 4. are *c*. in one hope of your calling
Col. 3. 15. peace of God to which ye are *c*.
1 Thes. 2. 12. God . . . . *c*. you unto kingdom
4. 7. God hath not *c*. us to uncleanness
2 Thes. 2. above all that is *c*. God
14. he *c*. you by our gospel to the obtaining
1 Tim. 6. 12. life, whereunto thou art *c*.
2 Tim. 1. 9. *c*. us with holy calling
Heb. 3. 13. exhort while it is *c*. to day
5. 4. *c*. of God, as was Aaron
11. 16. not ashamed to be *c*. their God
24. be *c*. the son of Pharaoh's daughter
Jas. 2. 7. name by the which ye are *c*.
1 Pet. 1. 15. as he that *c*. you is holy
2. 9. who *c*. you out of darkness
21. suffer . . . for even hereunto were ye *c*.
5. 10. God *c*. us to his eternal glory
2 Pet. 1. 3. *c*. us to glory and virtue
1 John 3. 1. we should be *c*. sons of God
Jude 1. preserved in Christ Jesus and *c*.
Rev. 17. 14. with him *c*. and chosen
19. 9. are *c*. unto the marriage supper
2 Chr. 7. 14. *called by my name*, Is. 43. 7; 65. 1.
Jer. 7. 10, 11, 14, 30; 25. 29; 32. 34; 34. 15.
Amos 9. 12.
1 Ki. 8. 43. *called by thy name*, 2 Chr. 6. 33.
Is. 4. 1; 43. 1; 45. 4; 63. 19. Jer. 14. 9;
15. 16. Dan. 9. 18, 19.
1 Ki. 8. 43. do all stranger *calleth* for
Ps. 42. 7. deep *c*. unto deep at the noise
147. 4. *c*. them by name, Is. 40. 26.
Is. 59. 4. none *c*. for justice nor for truth
64. 7. none that *c*. upon thy name
Hos. 7. 7. none among them that *c*.
Amos 5. 8. that *c*. for waters of the sea
Luke 15. 6. *c*. together his friends, 9.
John 10. 3. he *c*. his own sheep by name
Rom. 4. 17. *c*. things which be not as though
9. 11. not of works but of him that *c*.
Gal. 5. 8. persuasion not of him that *c*.
1 Thes. 5. 24. faithful is he that *c*.
Rom. 11. 29. the gifts and *calling* of God

1 Cor. 1. 26. ye see your *calling* brethren
7. 20. let every man abide in the same *c*.
Eph. 1. 18. know what is the hope of his *c*.
4. 4. called in one hope of your *c*.
Phil. 3. 14. prize of the high *c*. of God
2 Thes. 1. 11. count worthy of this *c*.
2 Tim. 1. 9. and called us with an holy *c*.
Heb. 3. 1. partakers of the heavenly *c*.
2 Pet. 1. 10. make your *c*. and election
Is. 41. 4. *c*. the generations from
Mat. 11. 16. sitting and *c*. their fellows
Mark 11. 21. Peter *c*. to remembrance
Acts 7. 59. stoned Stephen *c*. on God
22. 16. *c*. on name of Lord
1 Pet. 3. 6. obeyed Abraham *c*. him lord
CALM, Ps. 107. 29. Jonah 1. 11. great *c*., Mat.
8. 26. Mark 4. 39. Luke 8. 24.
CALVE (cow), Job 21. 10. (hinds), 39. 1. Ps. 29. 9.
Jer. 14. 5. See *Calf*.
CAME (of Christ), Mat. 20. 28. John 1. 11;
8. 14, 42; 18. 37. Rom. 9. 5. 1 Tim. 1. 15.
1 John 5. 6.
John 1. 17. grace and truth *c*. by Jesus Christ
Came again, spirit, Judg. 15. 19. 1 Sam. 30. 12.
soul, 1 Ki. 17. 22. Luke 8. 55.
Came down, 2 Ki. 1. 10, 12, 14. 2 Chr. 7. 1, 3.
Lam. 1. 9. John 3. 13; 6. 38, 41, 51, 58.
Rev. 20. 9.
Came forth, Num. 11. 20. Judg. 14. 14. Eccl. 5. 15.
Zech. 10. 4.
John 16. 28. I—from the Father
Came upon, God's Spirit, Num. 24. 2. Judg. 3. 10;
fear, 2 Chr. 14. 14. wrath, Ps. 78. 31.
2 Ki. 24. 3. Dan. 4. 28.
CAMEL, Gen. 30. 43. Lev. 11. 4.
Mat. 3. 4. raiment of *c*.'s hair, Mark 1. 6.
19. 24. it is easier for a *c*. to go through
23. 24. strain at gnat, and swallow *c*.
CAMP, Ex. 32. 17; 36. 6.
Ex. 14. 19. angel went before the *c*.
16. 13. quails came up and covered the *c*.
Num. 11. 26. prophesied in the *c*.
31. let the quails fall by the *c*.
Deut. 23. 14. Lord walketh in midst of *c*. there-
fore shall thy *c*. be holy
Judg. 13. 25. began to move him in *c*.
Heb. 13. 13. go unto him without the *c*.
Rev. 20. 9. compassed the *c*. of saints
CAN we find such a one, Gen. 41. 38.
Deut. 1. 12. how *c*. I alone bear your
32. 39. neither is there any that *c*. deliver
2 Sam. 7. 20. what *c*. David say more
2 Chr. 1. 10. who *c*. judge this people
Esth. 8. 6. how *c*. I endure
Job 11. *c*. the rush grow without mire
25. 4. how *c*. man be justified with God?
34. 29. who then *c*. make trouble?
Eccl. 4. 11. one be warm alone
Is. 49. 15. *c*. woman forget sucking child
Jer. 2. 32. *c*. maid forget her ornaments
Ezek. 22. 14. *c*. thine heart endure
37. 3. *c*. these bones live?
Amos 3. 3. *c*. two walk together except
Mat. 12. 34. how *c*. ye speak good things?
19. 25. who then *c*. be saved?
Mark 2. 7. who *c*. forgive sins but God?
19. *c*. children of bridechamber fast
3. 27. no man *c*. enter a strong man's
10. 38. *c*. ye drink of the cup that I
John 3. 4. how *c*. man be born when old?
9. how *c*. these things be, Luke 1. 34.
5. 19. Son *c*. do nothing of himself, 30.
6. 44. no man *c*. come to me except

John 6. 60. an hard saying, who *can* hear it?
9. 4. night cometh, when no man *c.* work
14. 5. how *c.* we know the way?
15. 4. no more *c.* ye, exept ye abide
1 Cor. 12. 3. no man *c.* say that Jesus is
  Lord
2 Cor. 13. 8. *c.* do nothing against the truth
1 Tim. 6. 7. we *c.* carry nothing out
Heb. 10. 11. *c.* never take away sins
Jas. 2. 14. not works? *c.* faith save him?
Cannot, Gen. 32. 12. *c.* be numbered for multitude,
  1 Ki. 3. 8. Hos. 1. 10.
Num. 23. 20. blessed, I *c.* reverse it
Josh. 24. 19. ye *c.* serve the Lord; for he
1 Sam. 12. 21. things which *c.* profit
1 Ki. 8. 27. heaven of heavens *c.* contain thee,
  2 Chr. 6. 18.
Ezra 9. 15. we *c.* stand before thee
Job 9. 3. he *c.* answer him one of a
12. 14. he breaketh down and it *c.* be
14. 5. appointed his bounds that he *c.* pass
28. 15. it *c.* be gotten for gold, neither
36. 18. a great ransom *c.* deliver thee
Ps. 40. 5. *c.* be reckoned up in order
77. 4. I am so troubled that I *c.* speak
93. 1. world established, that it *c.* be
139. 6. too high, I *c.* attain unto it
Is. 38. 18. the grave *c.* praise thee
44. 18. they *c.* see; they *c.* understand
20. he *c.* deliver his soul, nor say, Is there
45. 20. pray unto a god that *c.* save
56. 11. shepherds that *c.* understand
59. 1. neither his ear heavy, that it *c.*
Jer. 4. 19. I *c.* hold my peace, because
6. 10. are uncircumcised, they *c.*
7. 8. ye trust in lying words that *c.*
14. 9. as a mighty man that *c.* save
18. 6. *c.* I do with you as this potter?
29. 17. I like the vile figs that *c.* be
33. 22. the host of heaven *c.* be
Lam. 3. 7. hath hedged me, that I *c.* get
Mat. 6. 24. ye *c.* serve God and mammon
7. 18. a good tree *c.* bring forth evil fruit
19. 11. all men *c.* receive this saying
26. 53. thinkest thou I *c.* now pray to
27. 42. himself he *c.* save, Mark 15. 31.
Luke 14. 26. *c.* be my disciple, 27, 33.
John 3. 3. *c.* see (5. enter) kingdom of God
7. 34. thither *c.* come, 8. 21; 13. 33.
8. 43. because ye *c.* hear my word
14. 17. whom the world *c.* receive
15. 4. branch *c.* bear fruit of itself
16. 12. things to say, ye *c.* bear now
Acts 4. 20. we *c.* but speak the things
5. 39. if it be of God ye *c.* overthrow it
Rom. 8. 8. that are in the flesh *c.* please God
26. with groanings which *c.* be uttered
1 Cor. 10. 21. ye *c.* drink cup of the Lord
15. 50. flesh and blood *c.* inherit kingdom
2 Cor. 12. 2. body or out of body I *c.* tell
Gal. 5. 17. ye *c.* do the things that ye
2 Tim. 2. 13. he *c.* deny himself
Tit. 1. 2. God who *c.* lie promised
2. 8. sound speech *c.* be condemned
Heb. 4. 15. high priest which *c.* be
9. 5. we *c.* now speak particularly
12. 27. things which *c.* be shaken
28. kingdom that *c.* be moved
Jas. 1. 13. God *c.* be tempted with evil
1 John 3. 9. he *c.* sin because born of God
Canst, Ex. 33. 20. thou *c.* not see my face
Deut. 28. 27. thou *c.* not be healed
Job 11. 7. *c.* thou . . . find God?

Job 11. 8. what *canst* thou do? what *c.* thou
Mat. 8. 2. if thou wilt, thou *c.* make
Mark 9. 22. if thou *c.* do any thing have
John 3. 8. *c.* not tell whence it cometh
13. 36. thou *c.* not follow me now
CANDLE shall be put out, Job 18. 6; 21. 17.
  Prov. 24. 20.   *See* Jer. 25. 10.
Job 29. 3. when his *c.* shined on my head
Ps. 18. 28. the Lord will light my *c.*
Prov. 20. 27. spirit of man is *c.* of Lord
31. 18. her *c.* goeth not out by night
Mat. 5. 15. do men light a *c.* and put it, Mark
  4. 21. Luke 8. 16; 11. 33.
Luke 15. 8. light *c.* and sweep the house
Rev. 18. 23. light of *c.* shine no more
22. 5. they need no *c.* neither light
Zeph. 1. 12. search Jerusalem with *candles*
Ex. 25. 31. *candlestick,* 37. 17, 20. Lev. 24. 4.
  Num. 8. 2. 2 Ki. 4. 10. Dan. 5. 5.
Zech. 4. 2. behold a *c.* all of gold
Rev. 2. 5. I will remove thy *c.* out of his
1. 20. seven *candlesticks* are the seven churches
CANKER, 2 Tim. 2. 17. Jas. 5. 3.
CAPTAIN, Num. 2. 3; 14. 4.
Josh. 5. 14, 15. *c.* of the Lord's host
2 Chr. 13. 12. God himself is our *c.*
Heb. 2. 10 *c.* of their salvation perfect
CAPTIVE, Gen. 14. 14; 34. 29.
Judg. 5. 12. lead thy captivity *c.*
Is. 49. 24. or lawful *c.* be delivered
51. 14. *c.* exile hasteneth to be loosed
Jer. 22. 12. die whither they led him *c.*
Amos 7. 11. Israel be led away *c.*
2 Tim. 2. 26. taken *c.* by him at will
3. 6. lead *c.* silly women laden with
Deut. 30. 3. Lord will turn thy *captivity*
Job 42. 10. the Lord turned *c.* of Job
Ps. 14. 7. Lord bringeth back the *c.*
68. 18. lead *c.* captive, Eph. 4. 8.
78. 61. delivered his strength into *c.*
126. 1. turned again the *c.* of Zion
4. turn again our *c.* as streams in south
Jer. 15. 2. such as are for *c.* to *c.*
29. 14. I will turn away your *c.*
30. 3. bring again *c.* of my people, 32. 44; 33. 26;
  34. 22; 42. 12.
Hos. 6. 11. returned *c.* of my people
Zeph. 2. 7. Lord turn away their *c.*
Rom. 7. 23. bringing me to *c.* of sin
2 Cor. 10. 5. bringing into *c.* every
Rev. 13. 10. leadeth into *c.* go into *c.*
CARCASE, Num. 14. 29. Mat. 24. 28.
CARE, Luke 10. 40. 1 Cor. 7. 21.
Mat. 13. 22. *c.* of this world choke
1 Cor. 9. 9. doth God take *c.* for oxen
2 Cor. 11. 28. *c.* of all the churches
1 Tim. 3. 5. how shall he take *c.* of
1 Pet. 5. 7. casting all your *c.* on him
Ps. 142. 4. no man *cared* for my soul
John 12. 6. not that he *c.* for the poor
2 Ki. 4. 13. *careful* (anxious) for us
Jer. 17. 8. not *c.* in year of drought
Dan. 3. 16. not *c.* to answer thee
Luke 10. 41. Martha art *c.* and troubled
Phil. 4. 6. be *c.* for nothing; but by
10. were *c.* but ye lacked opportunity
Tit. 3. 8. *c.* to maintain good works
Is. 32. 9. *careless* daughters, 10, 11.
Mat. 22. 16. *carest* not, Mark 4. 38.
Deut. 11. 12. land thy God *careth* for
John 10. 13. hireling *c.* not for the sheep
1 Cor. 7. 32. unmarried *c.* for things of Lord,
  married *c.* for things of the world

1 Pet. 5. 7. *care* on him; for he *careth*
CARNAL, sold under sin, Rom. 7. 14.
Rom. 8. 7. *c.* mind is enmity against God
15. 27. minister to them in *c.* things
1 Cor. 3. 1. not speak but as to *c.*
9. 11. is . . . if we reap your *c.* things?
2 Cor. 10. 4. our weapons are not *c.*
Heb. 7. 16. law of a *c.* commandment
9. 10. *c.* ordinances imposed on them
Rom. 8. 6. to be *carnally* minded is death
CARPENTER, 2 Sam. 5. 11. Is. 41. 7. Jer. 24. 1.
   four *c.* Zech. 1. 20.
Mat. 13. 55. *carpenter's son*, Mark 6. 3.
CARRY us not up hence, Ex. 33. 15.
Num. 11. 12. *c.* them in thy bosom
Eccl. 10. 20. bird of the air shall *c.* voice
Is. 40. 11. *c.* lambs in his bosom
46. 4. even to hoar hairs will I *c.* you
Luke 10. 4. neither purse nor scrip
John 21. 18. *c.* thee whither thou
1 Tim. 6. 7. we can *c.* nothing out
Luke 16. 22. *carried* by the angels into
Eph. 4. 14. *c. about* with every wind
Heb. 13. 9.—with divers doctrines
Rev. 17. 3. *c.* me away in the spirit, 21. 10.
CART is pressed full, Amos 2. 13.
CASE (state), Ex. 5. 19. Ps. 144. 15.
CAST law behind backs, Neh. 9. 26.
Ps. 22. 10. *c.* upon thee from womb
55. 22. *c.* thy burden on the Lord
Prov. 1. 14. *c.* in thy lot among us
16. 33. the lot is *c.* into the lap
Eccl. 11. 1. *c.* thy bread upon the waters
Is. 2. 20. man *c.* his idols of silver
38. 17. hast *c.* all my sins behind thy back
Ezek. 23. 35. *c.* me behind thy back
Dan. 3. 20. *c.* into fiery furnace
Jonah 2. 4. I am *c.* out of thy sight
Mic. 7. 19. *c.* all their sins into the sea
Nah. 3. 6. *c.* abominable filth on thee
Mal. 3. 11. vine shall not *c.* her fruit
Mat. 3. 10. *c.* into fire, 7. 19. Luke 3. 9.
5. 25. thou be *c.* into prison
29, 30. *c.* it from thee . . . *c.* into hell, 18. 9.
7. 6. neither *c.* pearls before swine
13. 42. *c.* them into a furnace, 50.
18. 30. went and *c.* him into prison
22. 13. *c.* him into outer darkness
25. 30. *c.* unprofitable servant into
Mark 11. 23. be thou *c.* into the sea
12. 44. she of her want *c.* in all, Luke 21. 4.
Luke 1. 29. she *c.* in her mind what
12. 5. fear him . . . power to *c.* into hell
58. lest the officer *c.* thee into prison
John 8. 7. let him first *c.* a stone at her
Acts 16. 23. they *c.* them into prison
Rev. 2. 10. devil *c.* some into prison
22. I will *c.* her into a bed, and them
20. 3. *c.* him into the . . . pit
Lev. 26. 44. I will not *cast away*
2 Sam. 1. 21. shield is vilely—
Job 8. 20. God will not—perfect man
Ps. 2. 3. let us—their cords from us
Is. 41. 9. I will not *c.* thee *a.*
Ezek. 18. 31.—all your transgressions
Rom. 11. 1. hath God—his people, 2.
Heb. 10. 35. *c.* not *a.* your confidence
1 Cor. 9. 27. myself *a*—(disqualified)
Job 22. 29. when men are *cast down* then
Ps. 37. 24. though he fall . . . not be utterly—
42. 5. why art thou—11; 43. 5.
2 Cor. 4. 9.—but not destroyed
7. 6. comforteth those that are—

Ps. 44. 9. hast *cast off*, 23. *c. us* not *off* for ever,
   77. 7. will the Lord—for ever
71. 9. *c.* me not off in the time of old age
89. 38. thou hast—and abhorred, thou
94. 14. the Lord will not—his people
Jer. 31. 37. I will—all the seed of Israel
Lam. 3. 31. the Lord will not—for ever
Rom. 13. 12. let us—works of darkness
1 Tim. 5. 12. they—their first faith
Gen. 21. 10. *cast out* this bondwoman and her
   son, Gal. 4. 30.
Ex. 34. 24. I will—the nations before thee
Lev. 18. 24. which I—before thee
Deut. 7. 1.—many nations before thee
Ps. 78. 55. he—heathen also before them
80. 8.—the heathen and planted it
Is. 14. 19. thou art—of thy grave
26. 19. the earth shall—the dead
58. 7. poor that are—to thy house
66. 5. *c.* you out for my name's sake
Jer. 7. 15. I will *c.* you out (Judah), 15. 1.
16. 13. I will *c.* you out of this land
Mat. 7. 5. *c.* beam out of thine own eye
8. 12. children of the kingdom shall be—
12. 24.—devils but by Beelzebub
21. 12.—them that sold and bought
Mark 9. 28. why could not we *c.* him out?
12. 8. *c.* him out of the vineyard
16. 9. had—(of M. Magdalene) seven devils
17. in my name shall they—devils
Luke 6. 22.—your name as evil
John 6. 37. that cometh in no wise—
12. 31. prince of this world be—
Rev. 12. 9. and the great dragon was—
Ps. 73. 18. thou *castedst* them down
Job 15. 4. thou *castest* off fear
Ps. 50. 17. *c.* my words behind thee
Job 21. 10. cow *casteth* not her calf
Ps. 147. 6. *c.* the wicked to the ground
Jer. 6. 7. so she *c.* out wickedness
Mat. 9. 34. he *c.* out devils through Beelzebub.
   Mark 3. 22. Luke 11. 15.
1 John 4. 18. perfect love *c.* out fear
3 John 10. *c.* them out of the church
Job 6. 21. ye see my *casting* down
Rom. 11. 15. if the *c.* away of them be
2 Cor. 10. 5. *c.* down imaginations
1 Pet. 5. 7. *c.* all your care upon him
CASTOR and Pollux, Acts 28. 11.
CATCH every man his wife, Judg. 21. 21.
Ps. 10. 9. he lieth in wait to *c.* the poor
35. 8. his net . . . hid *c.* himself
109. 11. let the extortioner *c.* all he hath
Jer. 5. 26. they set a trap, they *c.* men
Mark 12. 13. they *c.* him in his words
Luke 5. 10. henceforth thou shalt *c.* men
CATTLE on a thousand hills mine, Ps. 50. 10.
Ps. 104. 14. grass to grow for the *c.*
Ezek. 34. 17. I judge between *c.* and *c.*
John 4. 12. drank thereof and his *c.*
CAUGHT and kissed him, Prov. 7. 13.
John 21. 3. that night they *c.* nothing
Acts 8. 39. Spirit of Lord *c.* away Philip
2 Cor. 12. 4. *c.* up into paradise
1 Thes. 4. 17. *c.* up together with
Rev. 12. 5. her child was *c.* up unto God
CAUL, *i.e.* net, Is. 3. 18. Hos. 13. 8.
CAUSE of both before judges, Ex. 22. 9.
Ex. 23. 2. not speak in a *c.* to decline
3. not countenance a poor man in his *c.*
6. nor wrest judgment of thy poor in *c.*
Deut. 1. 17. *c.* too hard for you bring
Job 5. 8. to God would I commit my *c.*

Ps. 9. 4. maintained my right and *cause*
35. 23. awake unto my *c.* my God, 27.
Prov. 18. 17. that is first in his own *c.*
25. 9. debate thy *c.* with thy neighbour
Eccl. 7. 10. what is *c.* . . . former days
Is. 51. 22. pleadeth *c.* of his people
Jer. 5. 28. *c.* of the fatherless, 22. 16.
Lam. 3. 36. to subvert a man in his *c.*
Mat. 19. 3. put away wife for every *c.*
2 Cor. 4. 16. for which *c.* we faint not
5. 13. if we be sober it is for your *c.*
Ex. 9. 16. *for this cause*, Mat. 19. 5. Eph. 5. 31.
John 12. 27; 18. 37. Rom. 1. 26; 13. 6.
1 Cor. 11. 30.
1 Tim. 1. 16—I obtained mercy
Ps. 119. 161. *without cause*, Prov. 3. 30. Mat.
5. 22. John 15. 25.
Job 6. 24. *c.* me to understand
Ps. 10. 17. wilt *c.* thine ear to hear
85. 4. *c.* thine anger towards us to cease
143. 8. *c.* me to know the way . . . walk
Is. 3. 12. lead thee, *c.* to err, 9. 16.
58. 14. I will *c.* thee to ride on high
66. 9. birth and not *c.* to bring forth
Jer. 3. 12. not *c.* my anger to fall
7. 3. *c.* you to dwell in this place, 7.
15. 4. *c.* them to be removed into all
11. *c.* the enemy to treat thee well
18. 2. I will *c.* thee to hear my words
32. 37. I will *c.* them to dwell safely
Lam. 3. 32. though he *c.* grief, yet he
Ezek. 36. 27. *c.* to walk in statutes
37. 5. *c.* breath to enter into you
Dan. 9. 17. *c.* thy face to shine upon thy
Prov. 7. 21. fair speech *caused*
26. 2. the curse *causeless* shall not
10. 5. a son *causeth* shame, 17. 2; 19. 26.
18. 18. the lot *c.* contentions to cease
19. 27. cease instruction that *c.* to err
Mat. 5. 32. *c.* her to commit adultery
2 Cor. 2. 14. always *c.* us to triumph
CAVE, a stone lay on it, John 11. 38.
Gen. 19. 30. Lot dwelt in a *c.*, he and
23. 19. buried Sarah his wife in the *c.*
25. 9. buried Abraham in the *c.*
49. 29. bury me with my fathers in the *c.*
Josh. 10. 16. hid themselves in a *c.*
Is. 2. 19. go to *caves* for fear of the Lord
Ezek. 33. 27. they that be in the *c.* shall die of
pestilence
Heb. 11. 38. wandered in *c.* of the earth
CEASE, day and night not, Gen. 8. 22.
Neh. 6. 3. why should the work *c.*
Job 3. 17. there wicked *c.* from troubling
Ps. 37. 8. *c.* from anger and wrath
46. 9. he maketh wars to *c.* unto end
Prov. 19. 27. *c.* to hear instruction
23. 4. *c.* from thine own wisdom
Acts 13. 10. wilt thou not *c.* to pervert
1 Cor. 13. 8. tongues, they shall *c.*
Eph. 1. 16. *c.* not to give thanks for
Col. 1. 9. *c.* not to pray for you
2 Pet. 2. 14. that cannot *c.* from sin
Ps. 12. 1. the godly man *ceaseth*
Prov. 26. 20. where no talebearer, strife *c.*
1 Thes. 5. 17. pray without *ceasing*, 2. 13.
1 Sam 12. 23. Acts 12. 5. Rom 1. 9. 2 Tim. 1. 3.
CEDAR wood, Lev. 14. 4. Num. 19. 6.
2 Ki. 14. 9. thistle sent to *c.* in Lebanon
Ps. 29. 5. voice of the Lord breaketh *c.*
92. 12. grow like a *c.* in Lebanon
Sol. 1. 17. beams of our house are *c.*
Ezek. 17. 3. great eagle took highest branch of *c.*

Ezek. 31. 3. the Assyrian was a *cedar* in
Lebanon
Sol. 5. 15. countenance excellent as *cedars*
Is. 9. 10. we will change them into *c.*
CELEBRATE, death cannot, Is. 38. 18.
CELESTIAL, 1 Cor. 15. 40.
CHAFF, storm carries away, Job 21. 18. Ps. 1. 4;
35. 5. Is. 17. 13; 29. 5; 41. 16. of summer
threshing, Dan. 2. 35. flame consumeth,
Is. 5. 24. Hos. 13. 3. he will burn, Luke 3. 17.
Is. 33. 11. ye shall conceive *c.*
Jer. 23. 28. what is the *c.* to the wheat
Zeph. 2. 2. before the day pass as *c.*
Mat. 3. 12. burn up *c.* in unquenchable
CHAIN-S, gold, Gen. 41. 42. Dan. 5. 7. (partition
by) 1 Ki. 6. 21. camel's, Judg. 8. 26. silver,
Is. 40. 19.
Ps. 73. 6. pride . . . as *c.*
Prov. 1. 9. (parent's) ornament of grace and *c.*
Is. 3. 19. Lord will take away thy *c.*
Ezek. 16. 11. I put a *c.* on thy neck
(Captive's), make a *c.* Ezek. 7. 23. *c.* heavy,
Lam. 3. 7. *See* Is. 45. 14. Jer. 40. 4. Ezek.
19. 4. Mark 5. 3. Rev. 20. 1.
Ps. 149. 8. to bind their kings with *c.*
Acts 12. 7. Peter's *c.* fell from his hands
28. 20. Israel I am bound with this *c.*
2 Tim. 1. 16. was not ashamed of my *c.*
2 Pet. 2. 4. delivered into *c.* of darkness
Jude 6. reserved in everlasting *c.*
CHALDEANS (*wise men* or Magi), Dan. 2. 2, &c.
(people), Job 1. 17. Is. 48. 20. Jer. 38. 2, &c.
Dan. 9. 1.
Is. 43. 14. C. whose cry is in the ships
Ezek. 23. 14. images of the *C.* portrayed
CHAMBER, Ps. 19. 5. Joel 2. 16.
Gen. 43. 30. Joseph entered *c.* and wept
Dan. 6. 10. windows in *c.* toward Jerusalem
Job 9. 9. maketh *chambers*
Ps. 104. 3. beams of *c.* in the waters
Prov. 7. 27. going down to the *c.* of death
Sol. 1. 4. the king brought me to his *c.*
Is. 26. 20. enter into *c.* and shut door
Mat. 24. 26. he is in the secret *c.*
CHANCE, happens, 1 Sam. 6. 9. Eccl. 9. 11.
by *c.*, 2 Sam. 1. 6. Luke 10. 31.
CHANGE, of raiment, Judg. 14. 12, 13. Zech. 3. 4.
changeable, Is. 3. 22.
Job 14. 14. wait till my *c.* come
Prov. 24. 21. with them given to *c.*
Job 17. 12. *c.* night into day
Ps. 102. 26, as a vesture *c.* them, Heb. 1. 12.
Jer. 13. 23. can Ethiopian *c.* his skin
Dan. 7. 25. think to *c.* times, laws
Mal. 3. 6. I am the Lord, I *c.* not
Rom. 1. 26. women did *c.* the natural
Phil. 3. 21. Christ shall *c.* our vile bodies
Heb. 7. 12. of necessity a *c.* of law
Dan. 3. 27. were coats *changed*, Job 30. 18.
Rom. 1. 23. *c.* the glory of God into
25. *c.* the truth of God into a lie
2 Cor. 3. 18. *c.* into the same image
Job 10. 17. *changes* and war are against me
Ps. 55. 19. they have no *c.* therefore
15. 4. sweareth to his hurt and *changeth* not
Dan. 2. 21. he *c.* times and seasons
CHANT to sound of viol, Amos 6. 5.
CHAPEL, it is the king's, Amos 7. 13.
CHARGE, Gen. 26. 5; 28. 6. Ex. 6. 13.
Ps. 91. 11. give his angels *c.* over thee, Mat. 4. 6.
Luke 4. 10.
Ps. 35. 11. to my *c.* things I knew not
Acts 7. 60. lay not to their *c.*, 2 Tim. 4. 16.

Acts 16. 24. received such a *charge*, thrust into
23. 29. nothing laid to his *c.* worthy   [prison
Rom. 8. 33. lay to *c.* of God's elect
1 Cor. 9. 18. make gospel without *c.*
1 Tim. 1. 18. this *c.* I commit to thee
6. 13. I give thee *c.* in the sight of God
Sol. 2. 7. I *c.* you,· O daughters of Jerusalem,
3. 5; 5. 8; 8. 4.
1 Tim. 6. 17. *c.* them that are rich
Job 1. 22. nor *charged* God foolishly
4. 18. *c.* his angels with folly, 15. 15.
Luke 9. 21; Mat. 12. 16. *c.* not make known
1 Thes. 2. 11. *c.* every one as a father
Chargeable, 2 Sam. 13. 25. Neh. 5. 15. 2. Cor.
11. 9. 1 Thes. 2. 9. 2 Thes. 3. 8.
CHARIOT, (Joseph), Gen. 41. 43. (Pharaoh), Ex.
14. 6; 15. 4. Sol. 1. 9.
Ex. 14. 25. and took off their *c.* wheels
2 Ki. 2. 11, *c.* of fire. 13. 14, *c.* of Israel.
Ps. 104. 3. who maketh the clouds his *c.*
Acts 8. 28. sitting in *c.* read Esaias
Josh. 17. 16. *chariots* of iron, Judg. 1. 19.
1 Sam. 8. 11. king take sons for his *c.*
2 Sam. 8. 4. David reserved . . . for a hundred *c.*
1 Ki. 10. 26. Solomon's *c.*, Sol. 3. 9.
6. 17. mountain full of *c.* and horses
18. 24. trust on Egypt for *c.*, Is. 31. 1.
Ps. 20. 7. some trust in *c.*, Is. 22. 18.
68. 17. the *c.* of God are twenty thousand
Sol. 6. 12. like the *c.* of Amminadib
Is. 21. 7. saw *c.* of asses
Hab. 3. 8. didst ride upon thine horses, and thy
c. of salvation
Zech. 6. 1. four *c.* between two mountains
Rev. 9. 9. sound of wings as of *c.*
Chariot cities (Solomon's), 2 Chr. 1. 14; 8. 6; 9. 25.
CHARITY edifieth, 1 Cor. 8. 1.
1 Cor. 13. 2, have not *c.* I am nothing. 4, *c.*
suffereth long. 8, *c.* never faileth
13. faith, hope, *c.* . . . but the greatest is *c.*
Col. 3. 14. above all these things put on *c.*
1 Thes. 3. 6. tidings of your faith and *c.*
2 Thes. 1. 3. *c.* of every one aboundeth
1 Tim. 1. 5. end of commandment is *c.*
2. 15. if they continue in faith and *c.*
4. 12. be thou an example in *c.*
2 Tim. 2. 22. follow righteousness, faith, *c.*
3. 10. known my doctrine, faith, *c.*
Tit. 2. 2. aged men be sound in *c.*
3 John 6. borne witness of thy *c.*
1 Pet. 4. 8. fervent *c.* . . . . *c.* shall cover sins
5. 14. greet one another with a kiss of *c.*
2 Pet. 1. 7, to brotherly kindness, *c.*
Jude 12. these are spots in your feasts of *c.*
Rev. 2. 19. I know thy works and *c.*
Rom. 14. 15. walkest not *charitably*
CHARMED, not, Jer. 8. 17.
charmers, Deut. 18. 11. Ps. 58. 5. Is. 19. 3.
CHASTE virgin, 2 Cor. 11. 2.
Tit. 2. 5. young women discreet, *c.*
1 Pet. 3. 2. your *c.* conversation, with
CHASTEN . . . rod of men, 2 Sam. 7. 14.
Ps. 6. 1. neither *c.* me in thy, 38. 1.
Prov. 19. 18. *c.* son while there is hope
Dan. 10. 12. to *c.* thyself before God
Rev. 3. 19. as many as I love, I *c.*
Ps. 69. 10. *chastened* soul with fasting
118. 18. the Lord hath *c.* me sore
1 Cor. 11. 32. *chastened* that we be not condemned
2 Cor. 6. 9. as *c.* and not killed
Heb. 12. 10. fathers for few days *c.* us
Ps. 94. 12. blessed whom thou *chastenest*
Deut. 8. 5. as man *chasteneth* his son

Prov. 13. 24. loveth him *chasteneth* betimes
Heb. 12. 6. whom the Lord loveth he *c.*
Job 5. 17. despise not thou *chastening* of the
Lord, Prov. 3. 11. Heb. 12. 5.
Is. 26. 16. when *c.* was upon them
Heb. 12. 7. if *c.*, God dealeth as with sons
11. no *c.* for present seemeth joyous
CHASTISE you seven times, Lev. 26. 28.
Deut. 22. 18. the elders shall *c.* him
Hos. 7. 12. *c.* as congregation heard
10. 10. my desire that I should *c.* them
Luke 23. 16. *c.* and release him, 22.
Job 34. 31. I have borne *chastisement* I will not
Is. 53. 5. *c.* of our peace was upon him
Jer. 30. 14. with the *c.* of a cruel one
Heb. 12. 8. without *c.* then are ye bastards
CHATTER like a crane, Is. 38. 14.
CHEEK, smite on, 1 Ki. 22. 24. Job 16. 10.—
judge, Mic. 5. 1.—right *c.*, Mat. 5. 39.—one
c., Luke 6. 29.
Sol. 1. 10. *cheeks* comely rows of jewels
5. 13. his *c.* are as a bed of spices
CHEER, Deut. 24. 5. Eccl. 11. 9.
Judg. 9. 13. wine which *cheereth* Ps. 104. 15.
Be of good c., Paul, Acts 23. 11; 27. 22, 25. son—
thy sins be forgiven, Mat. 9. 2.—it is I, 14. 27.
—; I have overcome the world, John 16. 33.
Cheerful feasts, Zech. 8. 19. *c.* giver, 2 Cor. 9. 7.
merry heart . . . *c.* countenance, Prov. 15. 13.
—*ness*, Rom. 12. 8.
Acts 24. 10. *cheerfully* answer for
CHERISHETH, as Lord the church, Eph. 5. 29.
as a nurse *c.* children, 1 Thes. 2. 7.
CHERUBIMS, between, 1 Sam. 4. 4. 2 Sam. 6. 2.
2 Ki. 19. 15. 1. Chr. 13. 6. Ps. 80. 1;
99. 1. Is. 37. 16. Ezek. 10. 7.
CHICKENS, hen gathereth, Mat. 23. 37.
CHIDE, not always, Ps. 103. 9.
CHIEF fathers, Num. 31. 26, &c. *c.* house, Josh.
22. 14, &c. *c.* men, 1 Chr. 7. 3, &c. *c.* priest,
2 Ki. 25. 18, &c. *c.* priests, Mat. 16. 21, &c.
c. of ways of God, Job 40. 19. strength, Ps.
78. 51. —nations, Jer. 31. 7. Amos 6. 1.
—Asia (*Asiarchs*), Acts 19. 31.
Mat. 20. 27. whoso will be *c.* among you
Luke 22. 26. is *c.*, as he that serveth
Eph. 2. 20. *c.* corner stone, 1 Pet. 2. 6.
1 Tim. 1. 15. sinners, of whom I am *c.*
Sol. 5. 10. the *chiefest* among ten thousand
CHILD (Isaac), Gen. 18. 13. (Joseph), 37. 30.
goodly *c.* (Moses), Ex. 2. 2. Heb. 11. 23.
(Samson), Judg. 13. 5. (Obed), Ruth 4. 16. the
c. Samuel, 1 Sam. 2. 21. (Bathsheba's), 2 Sam.
12. 14. (Jeroboam's), 1 Ki. 14. 3. (widow's),
1 Ki. 17. 21. Luke 7. 12. (John Baptist),
Luke 1. 36. (Jesus) the young *c.*, Mat. 2. 8.
thy holy *c.*, Acts 4. 27. (possessed), Mark 9. 21.
(nobleman's), John 4. 49.
Ps. 131. 2. quieted as a *c.* weaned
Prov. 20. 11. a *c.* known by his doings
22. 6. train up a *c.* in the way he, 15.
Eccl. 4. 13. better . . . wise *c.* than king
10. 16. woe when thy king is a *c.* Is. 3. 4.
Is. 7. 16. before *c.* knows to, 8. 4.
9. 6. for unto us a *c.* is born
Jer. 31. 20. Ephraim is he a pleasant *c.*?
Hos. 11. 1. when Israel was a *c.* I loved
Luke 2. 34. this *c.* is set for the fall
Gal. 4. 1. heir, as . . . is a *c.*, differs nothing
Rev. 12. 5. to rule with a rod of iron. *See* Is.
11. 8. *c.* . . . . a hundred years old, 65. 20.
1 Tim. 2. 15. saved in *childbearing*, if
1 Sam. 12. 2. *childhood*, Eccl. 11. 10.

1 Cor. 13. 11. put away *childish* things
Gen. 15. 2. *childless*, Jer. 22. 30. Luke 20. 28.
Child of hell, Mat. 23. 15. Acts 13. 10.
Little c., I know not, 1 Ki. 3. 7. *See* Jer. 1. 6.—
  shall lead, Is. 11. 6. receive one—,Mat. 18. 5.
Luke 9. 48. receive kingdom of God as—,
  Luke 18. 17. suffer *l. children*, Mat. 19. 14,
  &c. *See* John 13. 33. 1 John 2. 1; 4. 4. Gal.
  4. 19.
2 Sam. 12. 16. David besought God for *c.*
1 Ki. 3. 25. divide living *c.* in two
2 Ki. 5. 14. flesh like a *c.* Job 33. 25.
No child, Deut. 25. 5. 2 Sam. 6. 23.
Only c., Judg. 11. 34. Luke 9. 38. *first c.*, Jer. 4. 31.
  c. of old age (Sarah's), Gen. 21. 2. Heb. 11. 11.
  (Jacob's), Gen. 44. 20. (Shunammite's),
  2 Ki. 4. 16. (Elisabeth's), Luke 1. 7.
CHILDREN, Gen. 3. 16. in sorrow bring *c.*
Gen. 18. 19. command *c.* and household after
  him, Deut. 6. 7. *See* Josh. 4. 6, 21. 2 Sam.
  1. 18. Ps. 78. 5.
Gen. 30. 1. give me *c.* or else I die
Ex. 20. 5. iniquity of fathers upon the *c.*
13. 15. all firstborn . . . *c.* I redeem. Num. 3. 45,
  Levites instead of all the firstborn . . . *c.*
Lev. 25. 45. *c.* of strangers, 1 Ki. 9. 20. Is. 2. 6.
Num. 14. 33. your *c.* shall wander 40 years
Deut. 32. 5. their spot is not . . . *c.*
24. 16. fathers not (die) for *c.* nor *c.* for fathers,
  2 Ki. 14. 6. Jer. 31. 30.
1 Ki. 2. 4. if *c.* heed, . . . shall not fail, Ps. 89. 30.
2 Ki. 2. 24. two she bears tare forty-two *c.*
17. 31. Sepharvites burnt *c.* (= pass through
  fire to Molech). *See* 2 Chr. 28. 3; 33. 6. Is.
  57. 5. Mic. 6. 7. Ezek. 16. 21; 23. 39.
Ezra 2. 55. *c.* of Solomon servants, 1 Ki. 9. 20.
Ps. 17. 14. are full of *c.* *See* Ps. 127. 5.
69. 8. an alien to my mother's *c.*
72. 4. he shall save the *c.* of needy
82. 6. gods; all of you are *c.* of Most High
Prov. 17. 6. glory of *c.* are their fathers
20. 7. just, his *c.* blessed after him
31. 28. her *c.* rise and call her blessed
Is. 1. 2. I brought up *c.* and they rebelled
8. 18. I and *c.* whom Lord hath, Heb. 2. 13.
54. 13. great shall be the peace of thy *c.*
Jer. 3. 14. backsliding *c.*, wise to evil
7. 18. *c.* gather wood, . . . queen of heaven
Dan. 5. 13. *c.* of captivity, Ezra 4. 1.
Mal. 4. 6. turn the hearts of fathers to *c.*
Mat. 2. 18. Rachel weeping for *c.*, Jer. 31. 15.
5. 45. *c. of* Father in heaven. 8. 12,—kingdom
9. 15, bridechamber. 11. 19,—wisdom
15. 26, *c.* bread; 21. 15, *c.* crying Hosanna
Luke 6. 35. *c.* of the Highest
7. 32, *c.* in marketplace. 11. 7, in bed
16. 8. *c.* of this world, 20. 34. 1 Cor. 1. 26.
Acts 3. 25. ye are the *c.* of the prophets
Rom. 8. 17. if *c.* then heirs, . . . of God
9. 8. *c.* of promise, Gal. 4. 28. Acts 2. 39.
9. 26. there shall be called *c.* of living God
1 Cor. 14. 20. in malice be ye *c.* in understanding
2 Cor. 12. 14. *c.* not lay up for parents
Gal. 4. 3. when *c.*, were in bondage, 31.
Eph. 1. 5, adoption of *c.* 2. 3, *c.* of wrath
2. 2. *c.* of disobedience, 5. 6. Col. 3. 6.
4. 14. no more *c.* tossed with every wind
5. 1, as dear *c.* 1 Pet. 1. 14, as obedient *c.*
6. 1. *c.* obey your parents, Col. 3. 20.
4. fathers provoke not *c.*, Col. 3. 21.
1 Thes. 5. 5. *c.* of light, day, not of night
1 Tim. 5. 4. *c.* shew piety at home
Heb. 2. 14. as *c.* partakers flesh, He also

Heb. 12. 5. exhortation as unto *children*. **My son·**
  See Ps. 128. 3; 147. 13. Is. 54. 13. Lam. 4. 4·
  Nah. 3. 10. Mat. 23. 31, 37.
Children of the East, Gen. 29. 1. Judg. 6. 3; 7. 12;
  8. 10. wisdom of—, 1 Ki. 4. 30.
Children of God, peacemakers, Mat. 5. 9. —*c.* of
  resurrection, Luke 20. 36. gather—, John 11. 52.
  witness we are—, Rom. 8. 16. liberty of—,
  8. 21. *c.* of flesh not—, Rom. 9. 8. all—by
  faith in Christ Jesus, Gal. 3. 26.—manifest,
  1 John 3. 10. we love—, 5. 2. *c. of light*, John
  12. 36. Eph. 5. 8.
Children of Israel, Gen. 50. 25, &c.—increased,
  Ex. 1. 7,—as sand, 1 Ki. 4. 20, *see* Gen.
  22. 17. Hos. 1. 10. Neh. 9. 23 I will dwell
  among—, Ex. 29. 45. 1 Ki. 6. 13.—my
  servants, Lev. 25. 55, atonement money of—.
  Ex. 30. 16. —(10 tribes) and Judah shall come
  together, Jer. 50. 4. Hos. 1. 11. —days without
  king, 3. 4. as *c.* of Ethiopians unto me, O—,
  Amos 9. 7.
Children of men, fairer than, Ps. 17. 14. hearts of—
  before Lord, Prov. 15. 11.
Children to Abraham, Mat. 3. 9. *See* John 8. 39.
  seed of Abraham not all—, Rom. 9. 7. *c.* of faith
  . . . are—, Gal. 3. 7.
Children's children (sin visited on), Ex. 34. 7.
  (mercy until), Jer. 2. 9. Ps. 103. 17. *see* thy
  —,128. 6.—crown of old men, Prov. 17. 6.
CHOKE, Mat. 13. 7. Mark 4. 19. Luke 8. 14.
Mark 5. 13. herd ran . . . and were *choked* Luke
  8. 33.
CHOOSE, Num. 17. 5. man's rod whom I *c.*
Deut. 12. 5. place Lord God shall *c.*, 17. 10.
17. 15. set king over thee . . . Lord God *c.*
30. 19. life and death, . . . therefore *c.*
Josh. 24. 15. *c.* whom ye will serve
2 Sam. 24. 12. *c.* thee one of them
Neh. 9. 7. Lord God didst *c.* Abraham
Ps. 65. 4. blessed is the man whom thou *c.*
Prov. 1. 29. did not *c.* fear of the Lord
Is. 7. 15. refuse evil and *c.* good, 16.
14. 1. the Lord will yet *c.* Israel, 49. 7.
56. 4. *c.* the things that please me
Zech. 1. 17. I shall yet *c.* Jerusalem
Phil. 1. 22. what I shall *c.* I wot not
Heb. 11. 25. *choosing* affliction with people
Luke 6. 13. *chose* twelve . . . named apostles
Gen. 13. 11. Lot *c.* plain of
Judg. 10. 14. the gods, . . . ye have *chosen*
1 Sam. 16. 8. neither hath the Lord *c.* this
1 Ki. 8. 48. city thou hast *c.*, Ps. 132. 13.
Job 36. 21. iniquity *c.* rather than affliction
Prov. 16. 16. rather . . . *c.* than silver, 22. 1.
Is. 58. 5. is it such a fast that I have *c.*? 6.
Jer. 8. 3. death shall be *c.* rather than
33. 24 two families *c.* cast off?
49. 19. who is a *c.* man that, 50. 44.
Mat. 20. 16. many called, few *c.*, 22. 14.
Mark 13. 20. elect's sake . . . he hath *c.*
Luke 10. 42. Mary hath *c.* that good part
23. 35 Christ the *c.* of God,
John 15. 16. have not *c.* me, . . . I you
Acts 9. 15. *c.* vessel to me, 22. 14.
1 Pet. 2. 4. *c.* of God; 9. a *c.* generation
Rev. 17. 14. called, and *c.* and faithful
1 Cor. 1. 27. God hath *c.* the foolish
Eph. 1. 4.—us in him before foundation
2 Chr. 6. 6. *I have chosen*, Is. 42. I. (Mat.
  12. 18). Zerub . . . signet—Hag. 2. 23.
Ps. 119. 30.—way of truth; 173.—precept
Is. 44. 1. Israel, whom—, 41. 9; 43. 10.
48. 10.—thee in furnace of affliction

John 13. 18. I know whom—, 15. 16, 19.
My chosen, Is. 43. 20; 65. 15. Jacob *his c.*, Ps.
   105. 6, 43; 135. 4. Is. 41. 8.
CHRIST should be born, Mat. 2. 4.
  Mat. 16. 16. thou art the *C.* the Son
  23. 8. one is your master, even *C.,* 10.
  Mark 9. 41. because ye belong to *C.*
  Luke 2. 26. not die before seeing *C.*
  4. 41. the devils knew he was *C.*
  24. 26. ought not *C.* to have suffered
  46. it behoved *C.* to suffer and rise
  John 4. 25. Messias . . . which is called *C.*
  7. 26. that this is the very *C.*
  27. when *C.* cometh, no man knoweth
  41. shall *C.* come out of Galilee?
  42. *C.* cometh of the seed of David
  12. 34. that *C.* abideth for ever: and how
  Acts 8. 5. Philip preached *C.* to (Samaria)
  Rom. 5. 6. *C.* died for the ungodly
  8. while yet sinners, *C.* died for us
  8. 9. have not the Spirit of *C.,* he is none of
  10. if *C.* be in you, the body is dead
  15. 3. for *C.* pleased not himself; but
  1 Cor. 1. 24. *C.* the power of God and
  3. 23. ye are *C.*'s, and *C.* is God's
  5. 7. *C.* our passover is sacrificed
  15. 14. if *C.* be not risen, . . . our preaching vain
  16. if dead rise not, *C.* not raised
  2 Cor. 6. 15. what concord *C.* with Belial
  Gal. 2. 20. crucified with *C.*: *C.* liveth
  3. 13. *C.* hath redeemed us from curse
  4. 19. travail till *C.* be formed in you
  Eph. 2. 12. ye were without *C.*, aliens
  3. 17. that *C.* dwell in your hearts
  4. 20. ye have not so learned *C.*, if so
  5. 14. dead, and *C.* shall give thee light
  23. wife, as *C.* is head of the church; *see also* 24,
  6. 5. in singleness of heart, as unto *C.*   [25, 32.
  Phil. 1. 21. to me to live is *C.* and to die
  3. 8. all . . . but dung, that I may win *C.*
  4. 13. I can do all things through *C.*
  Col. 1. 27. *C.* in you hope of glory
  Rom. 8. 1. no condemnation . . . in *C. Jesus*
  2. the law of the spirit of life in—
  1 Cor. 1. 30. but of him are ye in—
  2. 2. not . . . you, save—and him crucified
  2 Cor. 13. 5. know ye not—is in you?
  Gal. 3. 28. ye are all one in—, 26.
  5. 6. in—neither circumcision nor uncircumcision
  Eph. 2. 10. created in—unto good works
  Phil. 2. 11. confess that—is Lord
  3. 3. rejoice in—no confidence in flesh
  12. for which I am apprehended of—
  Col. 2. 6. received—the Lord, 3. 24.
  1 Tim. 1. 15.—came into world to save
  2 Tim. 2. 3. as a good soldier of—
  3. 12. will live godly in—shall suffer
  Heb. 13. 8.—the same yesterday and to day
  Rom. 12. 5. many, one body *in Christ*
  1 Cor. 15. 18. fallen asleep—are perished
  19. if in this life only we have hope—
  2 Cor. 5. 17. if man be—new creature
  19. God was—reconciling the world
  12. 2. I knew a man—above fourteen years
  Gal. 1. 22. churches which were—
  Phil. 1. 13. so that my bonds—are manifest in all
    the palace
  2. 1. if there be any consolation—if any
  Col. 1. 2. saints and faithful—, Eph. 1. 1.
  1 Thes. 4. 16. the dead—shall rise first
  John 1. 25. *that Christ*, 6. 69.
  Mat. 16. 20. *the Christ*, 26. 63. Mark 8. 29;
    14. 61. Luke 3. 15; 9. 20; 22. 67. John 1. 20, 41;

  3. 28; 4. 29, 42; 7. 41; 10. 24; 11. **27**; **20**. **31**.
  1 John 2. 22; 5. 1.
John 11. 27. I believe that thou art *the Christ*
Rom. 6. 8. if we be dead *with Christ*
  8. 17. heirs of God and joint heirs—
  Gal. 2. 20. I am crucified— . . . I live
  Eph. 2. 5. quickened us together—
  Phil. 1. 23. desire to depart and be—
  Col. 2. 20. if ye be dead—from rudiments
  3. 3. dead, and your life is hid—in God
  Rev. 20. 4. souls . . . reigned—a thousand years
  Acts 26. 28. almost . . . to be a *Christian*
  11. 26. *Christians* first at Antioch
CHURCH, Acts 14. 27; 15. 3. 1 Cor. 4. 17;
  14. 4, 23. 3 John 9.
  Mat. 16. 18. this rock I will build my *c.*
  18. 17. tell it to *c.*: neglect to hear *c.*
  Acts 2. 47. the Lord added to *c.* daily
  5. 11. great fear came on all the *c.*
  8. 1. great persecution against the *c.*
  11. 26. assembled themselves with the *c.*
  15. 22. pleased elders, with the whole *c.*
  1 Cor. 14. 4. that *c.* receive edifying
  16. 19. *c.* in their house, Col. 4. 15.
  Eph. 1. 22. head over all . . . to the *c.*
  3. 10. known by *c.* . . wisdom of God
  5. 24. as *c.* is subject unto Christ
  25. as Christ loved the *c.* and gave
  27. present to himself a glorious *c.*
  32. I speak concerning Christ and the *c.*
  Phil. 3. 6. . . . zeal, persecuting the *c.*
  4. 15. no *c.* communicated with me
  Col. 1. 18. head of the body, the *c.*
  24. for his body's sake, which is the *c.*
  1 Tim. 5. 16. let not *c.* be charged
  Heb. 12. 23. assembly and *c.* of firstborn
  3 John 6. witness of charity before *c.*
  Acts 7. 38. *in the church*, 13. 1. 1 Cor. 6. 4;
    11. 18; 12. 28; 14. 19, &c. Eph. 3. 21. Col. 4. 16.
    the church of God, Acts 20. 28. 1 Cor. 1. 2;
    10. 32; 15. 9. 2 Cor. 1. 1. Gal. 1. 13. 1 Tim. 3. 5.
  9. 31. *churches* rest, 15. 41. confirming the *c.*
  16. 5. so the *c.* established in faith
  Rom. 16. 16. *c.* of Christ salute you
  1 Cor. 7. 17. and so ordain I in all *c.*
  14. 33. as in all *c.* of the saints
  34. women keep silence in the *c.*
  1 Thes. 2. 14. followers of *c.* . . . in Judaea
  2 Thes. 1. 4. we . . . glory in you in the *c.*
  Rev. 1. 4. seven *c.* which are in Asia
  2. 7. &c. hear what the Spirit . . . to *c.*
  22. 16. testify these things in the *c.*
CHURL, Is. 32. 5, 7.—*ish*, 1 Sam. 25. 3.
CIRCUIT, 1 Sam. 7. 16. Job 22. 14. Ps. 19. 6.
CIRCUMCISE the flesh, Gen. 17. 11.
  Deut. 10. 16. Lord will *c.* thy heart, 10. 16.
  Josh. 5. 2. *c.* again Israel, 4. Josh. did *c.*
  Jer. 4. 4. *c.* yourselves to the Lord
  Gen. 17. 10. every male shall be *circumcised*,
    14, 23, 26. Phil. 3. 5.
  21. 4. Abraham *c.* Isaac eight days old
  Jer. 9. 25. punish all *c.* with uncircumcised
  Acts 15. 1. except *c.* cannot be saved
  24. ye must be *c.* and keep the law
  16. 3. *c.* him because of the Jews
  Gal. 2. 3. neither compelled to be *c.*
  Col. 2. 11. in whom also ye are *c.*
  John 7. 22. Moses gave *circumcision*
  Acts 7. 8. God gave covenant of *c.*
  Rom. 2. 25. *c.* profiteth if thou keep law
  29. *c.* is that of the heart, in the spirit
  3. 1. what profit is there of *c.*? Much
  30. which shall testify *c.* by faith

Rom. 4. 9. cometh this blessedness on *circumcision*
11. he received the sign of *c*. [only?
15. 8. Christ was minister of the *c*.
1 Cor. 7. 19. *c*. is nothing, but the keeping
Gal. 2. 7. gospel of *c*. unto Peter
5. 6. neither *c*. availeth nor uncirc., 6. 15.
Phil. 3. 3. we are *c*. which worship
Col. 2. 11. with *c*. . . . without hands
Tit. 1. 10. deceivers, specially of *c*.
CIRCUMSPECT, Ex. 23. 13. see that ye walk
circumspectly, Eph. 5. 15.
CISTERN, 2 Ki. 18. 31. Prov. 5. 15.
Jer. 2. 13. hewed *cisterns*, broken *c*.
CITY (of Cain), Gen. 4. 17. *see* 11. 4. a *little c*. Gen.
19. 20. *see* Eccl. 9. 14.
Ps. 48. 2. *c*. of great King, Mat. 5. 35.
107. 4. they found no *c*. to dwell in
127. 1. except the Lord keep the *c*.
Prov. 16. 32. ruleth his spirit . . . taketh *c*.
Lam. 1. 1. How doth *c*. sit solitary
Sol. 3. 2. I will go about the *c*. in
Is. 1. 21. faithful *c*. become a harlot
22. 2. a tumultuous *c*., a joyous *c*.
25. 2. *c*. an heap. 26. 1, a strong *c*.
33. 20. look on Zion, *c*. of our solemnities
62. 12. sought out, a *c*. not forsaken
Jer. 3. 14. take you one of a *c*., two of a
29. 7. seek peace of the *c*. (Babylon)
Amos 4. 7. I rain on one *c*. not on
Zeph. 2. 15. this is the rejoicing *c*.
Zech. 8. 3. shall be called *c*. of truth
Mat. 5. 14. *c*. on hill cannot be hid
9. 1. his own *c*. (Capernaum), *see* 4. 13.
Luke 10. 8. whatsoever *c*. ye enter
12. tolerable for Sodom than for that *c*.
19. 41. he beheld the *c*. and wept over it
Heb. 11. 10. he looked for a *c*. which
16. he hath prepared for them a *c*.
12. 22. to the *c*. of the living God
13. 14. have here no continuing *c*.
Rev. 3. 12. name of the *c*. of my God
21. 18. *c*. was pure gold, 23. no sun
Neh. 11. 1, 18. *holy city*, Is. 48. 2; 52. 1. Dan.
9. 24. Mat. 4. 5; 27. 53. Rev. 11. 2; 21. 2;
22. 19.
Num. 35. 15. *c*. of *refuge*, Josh. 21. 13.
Luke 19. 17. authority over ten *cities*
Rev. 16. 19. the *c*. of the nations fell
Luke 15. 15. *citizen*, 19. 14. Acts 21. 39.
Eph. 2. 19. fellow *citizens* with the saints
CLAMOUR, Eph. 4. 31. Prov. 9. 13.
CLAY, Job 10. 9; 13. 12; 33. 6. vessel of *c*., Jer.
18. 4, *see* 2 Cor. 4. 7.
Job 4. 19, houses of *c*. 38. 14, it is turned as *c*.
to the seal
Is. 41. 25. on . . . as the potter treadeth *c*.
64. 8. we are the *c*., thou our potter, 45. 9. Jer.
18. 6. Rom. 9. 21.
Jer. 43. 9. hide them in the *c*. in kiln
Dan. 2. 33. feet part of iron, part of *c*.
John 9. 6. *c*. of spittle and anointed
Clay ground, 1 Ki. 7. 46. 2 Chr. 4. 17.
CLEAN beasts, Gen. 7. 2; 8. 20.
Lev. 10. 10. between unclean and *c*. 11. 47.
Ezek. 22. 26; 44. 23.
Job 14. 4. who bring *c*. out of unclean, 15. 14.
25. 4. can he be *c*. . . . born of a woman
Ps. 19. 9. the fear of the Lord is *c*.
Prov. 16. 2. ways of man are *c*. in his own
Is. 1. 16. wash you, make you *c*.; put
52. 11. be ye *c*. that bear the vessels
Jer. 13. 27. wilt thou not be made *c*.
Ezek. 36. 25. sprinkle *c*. water, be *c*.

Mat. 8. 3. I will, be thou *clean*, Luke 5. 13.
23. 25. make *c*. outside of, Luke 11. 39.
Luke 11. 41. all things are *c*. to you
John 13. 11. said he, Ye are not all *c*.
Rev. 19. 8. fine linen, *c*. and white
Job 17. 9. *clean hands*, Ps. 24. 4.
Ps. 51. 10. *clean heart*, 73. 1.
18. 24. *cleanness* of my hands in his sight
Amos 4. 6. *c*. of teeth in all cities
Ps. 19. 12. *cleanse* me from secret faults
51. 2. *c*. me from my sin
119. 9. shall a young man *c*. his way
Jer. 33. 8. I will *c*. them from all sin
Ezek. 36. 25. from idols will I *c*. you
Mat. 10. 8. heal sick, *c*. the lepers
2 Cor. 7. 1. let us *c*. ourselves from
Eph. 5. 26. *c*. with washing of water
Jas. 4. 8. *c*. your hands, ye sinners
2 Chr. 30. 19. though not *cleansed* accor.
Ps. 73. 13. I have *c*. my heart in vain
Ezek. 36. 33. *c*. you from all iniquities
Mat. 11. 5. the lepers are *c*.
Luke 17. 17. were there not ten *c*.?
Acts 10. 15. what God hath *c*., 11. 9.
1 John 1. 7. blood of Jesus Christ *cleanseth* us from
CLEAR the guilty, Ex. 34. 7. [all sin
Ps. 51. 4. be *c*. when thou judgest
Sol. 6. 10. looketh *c*. as the sun
Zech. 14. 6. light shall not be *c*. nor dark
CLEAVE to his wife, Gen. 2. 24. Mat. 19. 5.
Mark 10. 7. Eph. 5. 31.
Deut. 4. 4. ye did *c*. to the Lord, 10. 20; 11. 22;
13. 4; 30. 20. Josh. 22. 5; 23. 8.
Ps. 137. 6. tongue *c*. to the roof of my mouth
Rom. 12. 9. *c*. to that which is good
Ps. 22. 15. tongue *cleaveth* to my jaws
44. 25. our belly *c*. unto the earth, 119. 25.
CLIMB, 1 Sam. 14. 13. Joel 2. 7. Luke 19. 4.
Amos 9. 2. though *c*. up to heaven
John 10. 1. *climbeth* up some other way
CLOAK, Mat. 5. 40, &c. 2 Tim. 4. 13.
Is. 59. 17. clad with zeal as a *c*.
John 15. 22. have no *c*. for their sin
1 Pet. 2. 16. liberty *c*. of maliciousness
CLOSET, Joel 2. 16. Mat. 6. 6.
CLOTHE, God *c*. grass, Mat. 6. 30
Gen. 3. 21. Lord God . . . skins and *clothed*
Job 10. 11. *c*. me with skin and flesh
Ps. 35. 26. be *c*. with shame, 132. 18.
104. 1. *c*. with honour and majesty
109. 18. he *c*. himself with cursing
132. 9. priests be *c*. with righteousness
Is. 61. 10. *c*. with garments of salvation
Ezek. 16. 10. I *c*. thee with broidered
Zeph. 1. 8. *c*. with strange apparel
Zech. 3. 3. Joshua *c*. with filthy
Mat. 11. 8. *c*. in soft raiment, Luke 7. 25.
25. 36. naked, and ye *c*. me, 38.
2 Cor. 5. 2. desiring to be *c*. upon with
4. not unclothed, but *c*. upon
1 Pet. 5. 5. be *c*. with humility: for
Rev. 3. 5. be *c*. with white raiment
12. 1. a woman *c*. with the sun
19. 13. *c*. in vesture dipped in blood
14. *c*. in fine linen, clean and white
Job 24. 7. *clothing*, 24. 7. long, Mark 12. 38.
bright, Acts 10. 30. gay, Jas. 2. 3.
Ps. 45. 13. her *c*. is of wrought gold
Prov. 31. 25. strength and honour her *c*.
Is. 59. 17. garment of vengeance for *c*.
Mat. 7. 15, in sheep's *c*. 11. 8, soft *c*.
CLOUD, Gen. 9. 13. Ex. 14. 20.
Ex. 19. 9. Lord said, I come in thick *c*.

Is. 44. 22. blotted out as a thick *cloud*
1 Cor. 10. 1. our fathers were under the *c.*
Heb. 12. 1. so great a *c.* of witnesses
Rev. 11. 12. ascended up to heaven in a *c.*
Judg. 5. 4. *clouds* dropped water
2 Sam. 23. 4. a morning without *c.*
Ps. 36. 5. faithfulness reacheth to *c.*
57. 10. thy truth unto the *c.*, 108. 4.
104. 3. who maketh *c.* his chariot
Eccl. 11. 4. regardeth the *c.* shall not reap
Mat. 24. 30. coming in the *c.* of heaven, 26. 64.
     Mark 13. 26; 14. 62.
1 Thes. 4. 17. caught up in *c.*, to meet
2 Pet. 2. 17. *c.* carried with a tempest
Jude 12. *c.* without water, carried about
Rev. 1. 7. he cometh with *c.*
CLOVEN, Deut. 14. 7. tongues, Acts 2. 3.
COAL, 2 Sam. 14. 7. Is. 6. 6; 47. 14. Lam. 4. 8.
     Ps. 18. 8, 12; 120. 4; 140. 10.
Job 41. 21. his breath kindleth *coals*
Prov. 6. 28. can one go upon hot *c.*
25. 22. heap *c.* of fire on his head, Rom. 12. 20.
26. 21. as *c.* are to burning *c.*
Sol. 8. 6. *c.* thereof are *c.* of fire. *See* 1 Ki.
     19. 6 Is. 44. 12, 19. Hab. 3. 5.
John 18. 18. a fire of *c.* 21. 9.
COAT, Gen. 3. 21; 37. 3. Ex. 28. 4.
Sol. 5. 3. put off *c.*; how put it on
John 19. 23. the *c.* was without seam
21. 7. Peter girt his fisher's *c.*
Mat. 10. 10. neither two *coats,* Mark 6. 9.
Luke 3. 11. he that hath two *c.* let him
Acts 9. 39. *c.* and garments Dorcas
COLD, Gen. 8. 22. Job 24. 7; 37. 9.
Mat. 24. 12. the love of many shall wax *c.*
Rev. 3. 15. neither *c.* nor hot, 16.
COLLECTION, 1 Cor. 16. 1. Rom. 15. 26.
COME not to their secret, Gen. 49. 6.
Ex. 20. 24. where my name, I will *c.*
1 Sam. 17. 45. I *c.* to thee in name of
1 Chr. 29. 14. all things *c.* of thee, 12.
Job 22. 21. (so) good shall *c.* unto thee
38. 11. hitherto shalt thou *c.*, but no
Ps. 40. 7. lo I *c.*: in the volume, Heb. 10. 9.
65. 2. to thee shall all flesh *c.*
Eccl. 9. 2. all things *c.* alike to all
Sol. 4. 16. wind, *c.* thou south
Is. 1. 18. *c.* let us reason together saith Lord
35. 4. your God will *c.* and save you
55. 1. *c.* ye to the waters, John 7. 37.
3. incline your ear, and *c.* unto me
Jer. 3. 22. we *c.* to thee for thou art Lord
Hos. 6. 1. *C.* let us return unto the Lord
Mic. 6. 6. wherewith shall I *c.* before
Hab. 2. 3. it will surely *c.* it will not tarry
Mal. 3. 1. Lord suddenly *c.* to his temple
4. 6. lest I *c.* and smite the earth
Mat. 8. 11. *c.* from east and west
11. 3. art thou he that should *c.* or look we,
     Luke 7. 19, 20. Gen. 49. 10.
28. *c.* unto me all ye that labour and
16. 24. if any man will *c.* after me
17. 10. say scribes Elias must first *c.*
22. 4. all things ready, *c.* to marriage
Luke 7. 8. I say *c.* and he cometh
14. 20. married a wife, I cannot *c.*
John 1. 39. *c.* and see, 46; 4. 29. Rev.
     6. 1, 3, 5, 7; 17. 1; 21. 9.
5. 40. ye will not *c.* to me, that ye
6. 44. no man can *c.* to me, except
7. 37. if any man thirst, let him *c.*
14. 18. not leave you, I will *c.* to
Acts 1. 11. this Jesus shall so *c.* as

Acts 16. 9. *come* over into . . . and help us
1 Cor. 11. 26. shew Lord's death till he *c.*
2 Cor. 6. 17. *c.* out from among them
1 Tim. 4. 8. promise of the life to *c.*
Heb. 4. 16. *c.* boldly unto the throne of
7. 25. save them that *c.* to God by him
10. 37. he that shall *c.* will *c.*
Rev. 18. 4. *c.* out of her, my people
22. 17. the Spirit and the bride say, *c.*
Ps. 118. 26. *cometh* in name of the Lord
Is. 63. 1. who is this that *c.* from Edom
Mat. 3. 11. he that *c.* after me is
Luke 6. 47. whoso *c.*, heareth, doeth, is
John 3. 31. he that *c.* from above
6. 35. *c.* to me shall never hunger
37. *c.* to me, I will in no wise cast out
45. hath learned of Father *c.* unto me
Heb. 11. 6. that *c.* to God must believe
Jas. 1. 17. gift *c.* down from the Father
Heb. 10. 1. make the *comers* perfect
Ps. 19. 5. as bridegroom *coming* out
121. 8. the Lord shall preserve thy *c.* in
Mal. 3. 2. who may abide day of his *c.*
Mat. 24. 3. what the sign of thy *c.*, 27.
John 1. 27. *c.* after me is preferred before
1 Cor. 1. 7. waiting for the *c.* of our
15. 23. that are Christ's at his *c.*   [3. 13; 5. 23.
1 Thes. 2. 19. presence of Jesus Christ at his *c.*,
1 Pet. 2. 4. to whom *c.* as to a living stone
2 Pet. 1. 16. power and *c.* of L.
3. 12. hasting unto *c.* of day of God
1 Thes. 4. 15. *coming of the Lord,* 2 Thes. 2. **1.**
Jas. 5. 7, 8.   [CAME.]
COMELY, 1 Sam. 16. 18. Job 41. 12.
Ps. 33. 1. praise is *c.* (becoming), 147. 1.
Prov. 30. 29. yea, four are *c.* in going
Sol. 1. 5, black but *c.* 10, cheeks *c.*
6. 4. art *c.* as Jerusalem, Jer. 6. 2.
1 Cor. 7. 35, which is *c.* 12. 24, *c.* parts
Is. 53. 2. no form nor *comeliness*
Ezek. 16. 14. perfect through my *c.*
COMFORT in affliction, Ps. 119. 50.
Mat. 9. 22. be of good *c.*, Mark 10. 49.
Acts 9. 31. walking in *c.* of Holy Ghost
1 Cor. 14. 3. to exhortation and *c.*
2 Cor. 7. 4, am filled with *c.* Phil. 2. 1, *c.* of love
Col. 4. 11. these only . . . a *c.* to me
Gen. 5. 29. this stall *c.* us
Job 7. 13. my bed shall *c.* me, . . . then
Ps. 23. 4. thy rod and staff *c.*
Sol. 2. 5, *c.* with apples. Judg. 19. 5, bread
Is. 40. 1 *c.* ye my people
51. 3. Lord shall *c.* Zion, Zech. 1. 17.
61. 2. to *c.* all that mourn, Mat. 5. 4.
Jer. 31. 13. I will *c.* and make them
Lam. 1. 2. she hath none to *c.* her, 21.
2 Cor. 1. 4. be able to *c.* them . . . by *c.*
1 Thes. 4. 18. *c.* one another with these
5. 11. *c.* selves together, and edify one
14. *c.* feeble minded, support weak
2 Thes. 2. 17. Lord Jesus *c.* your hearts and
Is. 40. 2. *comfortably,* Hos. 2. 14. 2 Sam. 19. 7.
     2 Chr. 30. 22; 32. 6.
Gen. 24. 67. Isaac was *comforted*
37. 35. *refused to be c.*, Ps. 77. 2.
     Jer. 31. 15. Ra(c)hel weeping—, Mat. 2. 18.
Is. 49. 13. Lord hath *c.* his people
54. 11. tossed with tempest, not *c.*
Luke 16. 25. he is *c.*, thou tormented
Rom. 1. 12. *c.* . . . by mutual faith both
1 Cor. 14. 31. one by one all be *c.*
2 Cor. 1. 4. wherewith we are *c.* of God
7. 13. we were *c.* in your comfort

1 Thes. 3. 7. *comforted* over you by your faith
Job 16. 2, *comforters.* Ps. 69. 20, no *c.*
Is. 51. 12. I am he that *comforteth*
John 14. 18. not leave *comfortless*
Ps. 94. 19. *comforts,* Is. 57. 18.
COMMAND, Gen. 49. 33. 2 Chr. 8. 14.
Gen. 18. 19. Abraham will *c.* his children
Deut. 28. 8. Lord *c.* blessing, Lev. 25. 21.
Ps. 42. 8. Lord will *c.* his lovingkindness
Is. 45. 11. work of my hands, *c.* me
Mat. 4. 3. *c.* these stones be made bread
John 15. 14. if ye do whatsoever I *c.*
1 Cor. 7. 10. unto the married I *c.*
1 Tim. 4. 11. these things *c.* and teach
Ps. 111. 9. *commanded* his covenant
119. 4. *c.* us to keep thy precepts
133. 3. *c.* blessing, even life for ever
148. 5. Lord *c.* and they were created
Mat. 28. 20. whatsoever I have *c.* you
2 Cor. 4. 6. God who *c.* the light to
Heb. 12. 20. not endure that which was *c.*
Lam. 3. 37. when the Lord *commandeth*
Mark 1. 27, *c.* spirits. Job 9. 7, *c.* sun
Acts 17. 30. now *c.* all men to repent
1 Tim. 4. 3. *commanding* to abstain from meats,
    which God
Num. 23. 20. *commandment* to bless and
Ps. 119. 96. thy *c.* is exceeding broad
Prov. 6. 23. the *c.* a lamp; and law light
8. 29. waters not pass his *c.,* Job 38. 11.
Hos. 5. 11. willingly walked after the *c.*
Mat. 22. 38. is the first and great *c.*
Mark 7. 9. reject *c.* of God, Mat. 15. 6.
John 10. 18. this *c.* I received of my Father
12. 50. his *c.* is life everlasting
13. 34. a new *c.* give I unto you
15. 12. this is my *c.* that ye love one
Rom. 7. 8. sin taking occasion by the *c.*
9. when the *c.* came, sin revived
1 Tim. 1. 5. end of the *c.* is charity
Heb. 7. 16. not after law of carnal *c.*
2 Pet. 2. 21. turn from the holy *c.*
1 John 2. 7. an old *c.* which ye had, 8.
3. 23. this is his *c.* that we believe
Ex. 34. 28. wrote ten *commandments*
Ps. 111. 7. all his *c.* are sure, 119. 86.
112. 1. delight greatly in his *c.,* 119. 47.
119. 6. I have respect unto all thy *c.*
19. hide not thy *c.* from me
21. which do err from thy *c.*
35. make me to go in the path of thy *c.*
48. thy *c.* which I have loved
66. I have believed thy *c.*
73. give understanding to learn thy *c.*
127, I love thy *c.* 131, I longed for thy *c.*
143, thy *c.* . . . . my delights. 151, thy *c.* truth
172. all thy *c.* are righteousness
Mat. 15. 9. for doctrines *c.* of men
22. 40. on these two *c.* hang all the law
Mark 10. 19. knowest the *c.,* Luke 18. 20.
Luke 1. 6. walking in all the *c.* of Lord
Col. 2. 22. subject . . . after *c.* of men
1 John 3. 24. keepeth his *c.* dwelleth
2 John 6. love . . . we walk after his *c.*
Num. 15. 40. *do all,—these,—my,—his, c.* Deut.
    6. 25; 15. 5; 28. 1, 15; 19. 9; 27. 10;
    30. 8. 1 Chr. 28. 7. Neh. 10. 29. Ps.
    103. 18, 20; 111. 10. Rev. 22. 14.
COMMEND, Gen. 12. 15. Rom. 16. 1. *c.* selves,
    2 Cor. 3. 1; 5. 12; 10. 12.
Luke 23. 46. to thy hands I *c.* my spirit
Rom. 3. 5. if our unrighteousness *c.*
Acts 14. 23. *commended* them to Lord on

Rom. 5. 8. God *commendeth* his love
1 Cor. 8. 8. meat *c.* us not to God
2 Cor. 10. 18. not he that *c.* self is approved
3. 1. epistles of *commendation*
COMMISSION, Ezra. 8. 36. Acts 26. 12.
COMMIT adultery, thou shalt not, Ex. 20. 14.
    Deut. 5. 18. Mat. 5. 27; 19. 18. Rom. 13. 9.
    Lev. 5. 17. Luke 18. 20.
Gen. 39. 8, 22. *c.* (give in charge)
Job 5. 8. to God would I *c.* my cause
Ps. 31. 5. to thy hand I *c.* my spirit
37. 5. *c.* way (Prov. 16. 3. *c.* works) to Lord
Luke 12. 48. *c.* things worthy of stripes
16. 11. who *c.* to . . . riches?
John 2. 24. not *c.* himself to them
Rom. 1. 32. *c.* such things are worthy
1 Tim. 1. 18. this charge I *c.* unto
1 Pet. 4. 19. *c.* keeping of their souls
1 John 3. 9. born of God not *c.* sin
Luke 12. 48. *committed* much . . . ask
John 5. 22. *c.* all judgment to the Son
1 Tim. 1. 11. gospel *c.* to my trust, 1 Cor. 9. 17.
    2 Cor. 5. 19. Tit. 1. 3. Gal. 2. 7.
2 Tim. 1. 12. which I have *c.* to him
1 Pet. 2. 23. *c.* himself to him that
Jude 15. which they have ungodly *c.*
Ps. 10. 14. poor *committeth* himself
John 8. 34. who *c.* sin is servant of sin
1 John 3. 8. who *c.* sin is of the devil
COMMON, Num. 16. 29. *c.* bread, 1 Sam.
    21. 4, 5. Jer. 31. 5. the *c.* people, Lev. 4. 27.
    Mark 12. 37. Ezek. 23. 42.
Acts 2. 44. had all things *c.,* 4. 32.
10. 15. God cleansed call not *c.* (unclean)
1 Cor. 10. 13. temptation *c.* to man
Tit. 1. 4, *c.* faith. Jude 3, *c.* salvation
Mat. 28. 15. *commonly,* 1 Cor. 5. 1.
Eph. 2. 12. *commonwealth* of Israel
COMMUNE with, heart, Ps. 4. 4. another, Luke
    6. 11. (of God), Ex. 25. 22.
COMMUNICATE to him that teacheth in all
    good things, Gal. 6. 6.
Phil. 4. 14. *c.* with (share) my affliction
1 Tim. 6. 18. distribute, willing to *c.*
Heb. 13. 16. and to *c.* forget not
Gal. 2. 2. *communicated* that gospel
Phil. 4. 15. no church *c.* with me in
Eph. 4. 29. let no corrupt *communication,* Col.
    3. 8.
Luke 24. 17. what manner of *communications* are
1 Cor. 15. 33. evil *c.* . . . . good manners
10. 16. is it not the *communion* of the blood of
    Christ? *c.* of body of Christ?
2 Cor. 6. 14. what *c.* light with darkness?
13. 14. *c.* of the Holy Ghost be with you
COMPACT(ED), Ps. 122. 3. Eph. 4. 16.
COMPANY (caravan), Gen. 32. 8, 21.
Ps. 55. 14. to the house of God in *c.*
Prov. 29. 3. keepeth *c.* with harlots
Sol. 6. 13. as it were the *c.* of two armies
Acts 4. 23. own *c.* 6. 7, *c.* of priests
Rom. 15. 24. first filled with your *c.*
1 Cor. 5. 11. not to keep *c.,* if any
2 Thes. 3. 14. have no *c.* with him
Heb. 12. 22. an innumerable *c.* of angels
Ps. 119. 63. I am a *companion* of all
Prov. 13. 20. *c.* of fools shall be destroyed
Mal. 2. 14. thy *c.* and wife of covenant
Phil. 2. 25. Epaphroditus my *c.* in labour
Rev. 1. 9. your *c.* in tribulation
Ps. 45. 14. virgins, *companions* that
122. 8. for my *c.* sakes . . . Peace be
Is. 1. 23. thy princes *c.* of thieves

COMPARE God, Is. 40. 18; 46. 5.
2 Cor. 10. 12. *c.* ourselves . . . *c.* themselves
Ps. 89. 6. who in heaven be *compared*
Prov. 3. 15. not *c.* to wisdom, 8. 11.
Sol. 1. 9. *c.* my love to company
Rom. 8. 18. not worthy to be *c.*
1 Cor. 2. 13. *comparing* spiritual things with
COMPASS, circle, Ex. 27. 5; 38. 4. *fetch a c.*
2 Sam. 5. 23. 2 Ki. 3. 9. Acts 28. 13.
Ps. 5. 12. with favour *c.* him as with
26. 6. innocency: so will I *c.* thy altar
32. 10. mercy shall *c.* him about
Is. 50. 11. *c.* yourselves with sparks
Jer. 31. 22. a woman shall *c.* a man
Hab. 1. 4. wicked doth *c.* the righteous
Mat. 23. 15. ye *c.* sea and land to
Ps. 18. 4. sorrow *compassed* me, 116. 3.
118. 10, 12. all nations *c.* me about
Jonah 2. 3. floods *c.* me about, 5.
Ps. 139. 3. thou *compassest* my path
73. 6. pride *compasseth* them
Hos. 11. 12. Ephraim *c.* me with lies
COMPASSION, give them, 1 Ki. 8. 50. *See*
2 Chr. 30. 9.   [112. 4; 145. 8.
Ps. 78. 38. (God) full of *c.* 86. 15; 111. 4;
bowels of c., 1 John 3. 17. *moved with c.* (Jesus),
Mat. 9. 36; 14. 14. Mark 1. 41. the lord—,
Mat. 18. 27.
Zech. 7. 9. and shew mercy and *c.*
Deut. 30. 3. Lord turn captivity and *have c.*
Jer. 12. 15. return and—, Mic. 7. 19.
Lam. 3. 32. cause grief, yet will he—
Mat. 15. 32. I—on multitude, Mark 8. 2.
Mark 9. 22. canst do any thing—on us
Rom. 9. 15. will—on whom I will—
Heb. 5. 2. who can—on ignorant
10. 34,—*of* me in bonds. 1 Pet. 3. 8,—one
of another. Jude 22,—of some
Ex. 2. 6. babe wept. And she *had c.*
Mat. 20. 34. two blind men . . . Jesus—
Mark 5. 19. friends, tell how Lord—on
Luke 7. 13. Lord—and said, Weep not
15. 20. off, father saw him, and —
Lam. 3. 22. his *compassions* fail not
COMPEL to, go a mile, Mat. 5. 41. —bear
cross, Mark 15. 21. —come in, Luke 14. 23.
2 Chr. 21. 11. fornication and *compelled* Judah
Acts 26. 11. I *c.* them to blaspheme
2 Cor. 12. 11. I am a fool ye *c.* me
Gal. 2. 3. not *c.* to be circumcised
14. *compellest* Gentiles to live as Jews
COMPLAIN, Job 7. 11; 9. 27; 23. 2.
Lam. 3. 39. why doth a living man *c.*
Num. 11. 1. *complainers*, Jude 16.
Ps. 144. 14. *complaining* in streets
COMPLETE in him, Col. 2. 10; 4. 12.
COMPREHEND, things we cannot, Job 37. 5;
c. with saints, Eph. 3. 18. darkness *compre-
hended* not, John 1. 5.
Is. 40. 12, *c.* dust. Rom. 13. 9, briefly *c.*
CONCEAL his blood, Gen. 37. 26.
Job 6. 10. not *c.* words of Holy One, 27. 11.
Prov. 11. 13. faithful *c.* 12. 23, prudent *c.*
Ps. 40. 10 not *concealed* thy lovingkindness
CONCEIT, in own, Prov. 18. 11; 26. 5; 28. 11.
Rom. 11. 25; 12. 16.
CONCEIVE, Gen. 30. 38. Luke 1. 31.
Job 15. 35. they *c.* mischief, Is. 59. 4.
Ps. 51. 5. in sin did my mother *c.* me
Is. 7. 14. a virgin shall *c.* and bear a son
33. 11, *c.* chaff. 59. 13, *c.* falsehood
Heb. 11. 11. through faith Sara *c.*
Num. 11. 12. *conceived* all this people?

Job 3. 3. there is a man child *conceived*
Ps. 7. 14. hath *c.* mischief, and brought forth
falsehood
Jer. 49. 30. *c.* a purpose against you
Mat. 1. 20. *c.* in her is of the Holy Ghost
Luke 1. 36. Elisabeth . . . *c.* a son in old age
2. 21. Jesus so named before *c.*
Acts 5. 4. why hast thou *c.* in thy heart
Jas. 1. 15. lust hath *c.* it bringeth
CONCISION (a term of contempt = circum-
cision), Phil. 3. 2.
CONCLUDED (shut up) in unbelief, Rom. 11. 32.
Gal. 3. 22. *c.* all under sin
Acts 21. 25. *c.* that they observe no
Eccl. 12. 13. *conclusion* of the matter
CONCORD, 2 Cor. 6. 15. what *c.* hath Christ
CONCUBINE, Judg. 19. 1. 2 Sam. 16. 21. 1 Chr.
1. 32. 1 Ki. 11. 3. Dan. 5. 2.
CONCUPISCENCE, sinful lust, Rom. 7. 8.
Col. 3. 5. 1 Thes. 4. 5.
CONDEMN the land in, 2 Chr. 36. 3.
Job 9. 20. my own mouth shall *c.* me
10. 2. I will say to God, do not *c.* me
Ps. 37. 33. nor *c.* him when judged
94. 21. *c.* innocent blood, Mat. 12. 7.
Is. 50. 9. Lord will help me, who shall *c.*?
Mat. 12. 41. this generation and shall *c.* it
Luke 6. 37. *c.* not and ye shall not be *c.*
John 3. 17. sent not Son to *c.* world
8. 11. neither do I *c.* thee, go and sin no
Luke 23. 40. in same *condemnation*
John 3. 19. this is the *c.,* that light is
5. 24. shall not come into *c.* but is
Rom. 8. 1. no *c.* to them . . . in Christ Jesus
5. 16. judgment by one to *c.,* but free
2 Cor. 3. 9. the ministration of *c.*
1 Tim. 3. 6. fall into *c.* of the devil
Jas. 3. 1. receive the greater *c.*
5. 12. swear not, lest ye fall into *c.*
Jude 4. of old ordained to this *c.*
Mat. 12. 37. by thy words thou shalt be *condemned*
Rom. 8. 3. for sin, *c.* sin in the flesh
1 Cor. 11. 32. not be *c.* with world
Tit. 2. 8. sound speech cannot be *c.*
Prov. 17. 15. *condemneth* just . . . abomination
Rom. 8. 34. who is he that *c.*? It is Christ
14. 22. Happy is he he that *c.* not himself in
CONDESCEND to men, Rom. 12. 16.
CONFESS, Lev. 5. 5. Neh. 1. 6.
Lev. 26. 40. if they *c.,* 1 Ki. 8. 33, 35.
Ps. 32. 5. I will *c.* . . . and thou forgavest
Mat. 10. 32. shall *c.* me before men
Luke 12. 8. him will I *c.,* Rev. 3. 5.
Rom. 10. 9. *c.* with thy mouth Lord Jesus;
Jas. 5. 16. *c.* your faults . . . and pray
1 John 1. 9. if we *c.* our sins, he is faithful
4. 15. *c.* Jesus is Son of God, 4. 2, 3. 2 John 7.
Heb. 11. 13. *confessed,* John 1. 20.
Prov. 28. 13. *confesseth* and forsaketh
Mat. 3. 6. in Jordan *confessing* sins
Josh. 7. 19. *confession,* 2. Chr. 30. 22. Ezra
10. 11. Dan. 9. 4, 20.
Rom. 10. 10. *c.* is made to salvation
1 Tim. 6. 13. witnessed a good *c.*
CONFIDENCE, gold, my, Job 31. 24.
Ps. 65. 5. *c.* of all ends of the earth
118. 8. *c.* in man, Jer. 2. 37.
Prov. 3. 26. Lord be thy *c.,* 14. 26.
Jer. 48. 13. Israel ashamed of *c.* (idols)
Ezek. 29. 16. no more the *c.* of Israel
Mic. 7. 5. put no *c.* in guide, Prov. 25. 19.
Eph. 3. 12. in whom we have access with *c.*
Phil. 3. 3. we have no *c.* in the flesh

Heb. 3. 6. if we hold fast the *confidence*, 14.
1 John 3. 21. *c.* toward God, 2. 28; 5. 14.
Confident, 2 Cor. 5. 6. Phil. 1. 6.
CONFIRM feeble knees, Is. 35. 3.
Dan. 9. 27. shall *c.* the covenant
Rom. 15. 8. *c.* the promises, Heb. 6. 17.
1 Cor. 1. 8. shall *c.* you to the end
2 Cor. 2. 8. *c.* your love toward him
Is. 44. 26. *confirmeth* word of servant, Mark 16. 20.
CONFLICT, Phil. 1. 30. Col. 2. 1.
CONFORMED to image, Rom. 8. 29.
Rom. 12. 2. be not *c.* to this world
CONFOUND language, Gen. 11. 7.
Jer. 1. 17. lest I *c.* thee before them
1 Cor. 1. 27. foolish things to *c.* wise
Ps. 97. 7. *confounded* that serve images
Jer. 17. 18. not be *c.*, Ps. 69. 6.
Ezek. 16. 52. *c.* and bear shame, 54.
Mic. 3. 7. diviners *c.* 7. 16. nations be *c.*
Acts 2. 6. multitude *c.* 9. 22. *c.* the Jews
1 Pet. 2. 6. believeth shall not be *c.*
Ezra 9. 7. *confusion* of face, Dan. 9. 7.
Ps. 44. 15. my *c.* is continually before
71. 1. let me never be put to *c.*, 70. 2.
Is. 24. 10. city of *c.* 41. 29. images are *c.*
1 Cor. 14. 33. God is not author of *c.*
CONGREGATION, assembly, people; taber-
nacle *of c.* Ex. 27. 21. &c.; tent—Ex. 40. 2;
mount—Is. 14. 13.
C. of Israel (especially under Moses and Joshua;
frequently in Chronicles); rulers of *c.* Ex.
16. 22; elders of *c.* Lev. 4. 15; Judg. 21. 16;
chief of *c.* Num. 4. 34; 250 princes famous in
c., men of renown, 16. 2; 1. 16. *see* Josh. 9. 15;
22. 30; chief fathers of *c.* Num. 31. 26; *whole c.*
Ex. 16. 2. Judg. 21. 13.
Num. 14. 27. this evil *c.* (generally of Exod.)
Lam. 1. 10. heathen not enter *c.*, Neh. 13. 1.
Ps. 22. 25. the great *c.*, 35. 18; 40. 9.
Mic. 2. 5. cast a cord by lot in *c.*
Ps. 26. 12. *congregations*, 68. 26; 74. 4.
CONIES, Ps. 104. 18. Prov. 30. 26.
CONQUER, conquering and to, Rev. 6. 2.
Rom. 8. 37. more than *conquerors*
CONSCIENCE, John 8. 9. 1 Cor. 8. 7.
Acts 24. 16. a *c.* void of offence
Rom. 2. 15. *c.* bearing witness, 9. 1.
13. 5. not . . . , for *c.* sake, 1 Cor. 10. 28.
2 Cor. 1. 12. testimony of our *c.*
1 Tim. 3. 9. in pure *c.*, 2 Tim. 1. 3.
4. 2. having their *c.* seared with hot
Tit. 1. 15. their mind and *c.* is defiled
Heb. 9. 14. purge *c.* from dead works
10. 2. *c.* of sins; 1 Cor. 8. 7. *c.* of idol
Acts 23. 1. *good conscience*, 1 Tim. 1. 5, 19. Heb.
13. 18. 1 Pet. 3. 21.
CONSENT, Gen. 34. 15. with one *c.* Ps. 83.
5.
Luke 14. 18. by *c.* Hos. 6. 9.
Prov. 1. 10. entice thee, *c.* thou not
Rom. 7. 16. I *c.* to law . . . good
1 Tim. 6. 3. if *c.* not to wholesome
Ps. 50. 18. *consentedst* with a thief
Acts 8. 1. *consenting*, 22. 20. Rom. 7. 16.
CONSIDER in thy heart, Deut. 4. 39.
Deut. 32. 29. O that . . . *c.* their latter end
1 Sam. 12. 24. *c.* how great things he
Ps. 8. 3. when I *c.* thy heavens
Eccl. 7. 13. *c.* work of God, Job 37. 14.
Is. 1. 3. my people doth not *c.*
5. 12. neither *c.* operation of his hands
Hag. 1. 5. saith the Lord, *c.* your ways, 2. 15.
Mat. 6. 28. *c.* the lilies, Luke 12. 27.

2 Tim. 2. 7. *consider* what I say, and Lord give
Heb. 3. 1. *c.* Apostle and High Priest
10. 24. *c.* one another to provoke to
12. 3. *c.* him that endured such
Job 1. 8. hast *considered* my servant, **2. 3.**
Ps. 31. 7. hast *c.* my trouble, 9. 13.
77. 5. have *c.* days of old, the years
Mark 6. 52. *c.* not the miracle of loaves . . .
Rom. 4. 19. *c.* not his own body dead
Mat. 7. 3. *considerest* not the beam
Ps. 41. 1. blessed . . . *considereth* the poor
CONSIST, Col. 1. 17. Luke 12. 15.
CONSOLATION, son of, Acts 4. 36; 15. 31.
Luke 2. 25. waiting for *c.* of Israel
6. 24. woe rich, have received your *c.*
Rom. 15. 5. God of *c.* grant you to
2 Cor. 1. 5. our *c.* aboundeth by Christ
Phil. 2. 1. if therefore any *c.* in Christ
Heb. 6. 18. might have a strong *c.*
Job 15. 11. *consolations*, Is. 66. 11.
CONSTRAIN, Gal. 6. 12. Acts 16. 15.
2. Cor. 5. 14. for the love of Christ *constraineth*
1 Pet. 5. 2. not by *constraint*, but willingly
CONSUME, Deut. 5. 25; 7. 16; 28. 38.
Ex. 33. 3. lest I *c.* thee in the way
Ps. 78. 33. their days did he *c.* in vanity
Ezek. 4. 17. *c.* for iniquity, Ps. 37. 20.
2 Thes. 2. 8. Lord shall *c.* with the spirit of
Jas. 4. 3. *c.* it upon your lusts
Ex. 3. 2. bush was not *consumed*
Ps. 90. 7. we are *c.* by thine anger
119. 139. my zeal hath *c.* me, because
Prov. 5. 11. thy flesh and body are *c.*
Lam. 3. 22. of the Lord's mercies not *c.*
Gal. 5. 15. not *c.* one of another
Deut. 4. 24. Lord *consuming* fire, Heb. 12. 29.
Lev. 26. 16. *consumption*, Deut. 28. 22. Is.
10. 22, 23; 28. 22.
CONTAIN, John 2. 6. Rom. 2. 14.
1 Ki. 8. 27. heaven of heavens cannot *c.*
John 21. 25. world not *c.* the books
1 Cor. 7. 9. if cannot *c.*, let them marry
CONTEMN God, wicked, Ps. 10. 13.
Ezek. 21. 13. if sword *c.* the rod, 10.
Ps. 15. 4. a vile person is *contemned*
123. 3. we are filled with *contempt*
Dan. 12. 2. awake to shame and everlasting *c.*
Mal. 1. 7. table of the Lord *contemptible*
2. 9. have I made you *c.* before all
2 Cor. 10. 10. weak, his speech *c.*
CONTEND, Deut. 2. 9. Job 9. 3; 13. 8.
Is. 49. 25. I will *c.* with them that *c.*
50. 8. *c.* with me. 57. 16. not *c.* for ever
Jer. 12. 5. wearied thee, then how canst thou *c.*
with horses?
Amos 7. 4. the Lord God called to *c.* by fire
Jude 3. earnestly *c.* for the faith
Job 40. 2. *contendeth* with the Almighty
Hab. 1. 3. *contention*, Acts 15. 39. sharp *c.* Phil.
1. 16. preach Christ of *c.* 1 Thes. 2. 2.
Prov. 13. 10. by pride cometh *c.*, 22. 10.
17. 14. water, leave off *c.* before it be
18. 6. A fool's lips enter into *c.*, and
Jer. 15. 10. borne me a man of *c.* to
Contentions, Prov. 18. 18. of wife, 19. 13. *See*
23. 29. 1 Cor. 1. 11. Tit. 3. 9.
Prov. 21. 19. *contentious* woman, 27. 15. man,
26. 21. Rom. 2. 8. 1 Cor. 11. 16.
CONTENT, Josh. 7. 7. Prov. 6. 35.
Phil. 4. 11. state . . . therewith to be *c.*
1 Tim. 6. 8. food and raiment let us be *c.*
Heb. 13. 5. be *c.* with. Luke 3. 14. wages
1 Tim. 6. 6. godliness with *contentment*

CONTINUAL burnt offering, Ex. 29. 42. bread, Num. 4. 7. stroke, Is. 14. 6.
Rom. 9. 2. *c.* sorrow in my heart
Gen. 6. 5. heart was only evil *continually*
Ex. 28. 30. upon his heart before the Lord *c.*
Ps. 34. 1. his praise *c.* in my mouth
52. 1. goodness of God endureth *c.*
71. 3. habitation whereto I may *c.* resort
14. I will hope *c.* 73. 23. *c.* with thee
Prov. 6. 21. bind *c.* upon thine heart
Is. 58. 11. the Lord shall guide thee *c.*
Hos. 12. 6. turn and wait on thy God *c.*
Acts 6. 4. give ourselves *c.* to prayer
Heb. 13. 15. sacrifice of praise to God *c.*
Ps. 139. 16. *continuance*, Rom. 2. 7.
CONTINUE, Mat. 15. 32. Acts 26. 22.
1 Sam. 12. 14. *c.* following the Lord
Ps. 36. 10. O *c.* thy lovingkindness
102. 28. children of servants shall *c.*
119. 91. *c.* according to thine ordinances
John 8. 31. *c.* in my word. 15. 9.—love
Acts 13. 43. to *c.* in the grace of God
14. 22. to *c.* in the faith, 1 Tim. 2. 15.
Rom. 6. 1. shall we *c.* in sin that grace
Col. 1. 23. if ye *c.* in faith grounded
4. 2. *c.* in prayer, and watch in same with
1 Tim. 4. 16. doctrine; *c.* in them: for
2 Tim. 3. 14. *c.* thou in things learned
Heb. 13. 1. let brotherly love *c.*
Rev. 13. 5. to *c.* forty-two months
Neh. 5. 16. *continued*, Dan. 1. 21.
Luke 6. 12. *c.* all night in prayer
22. 28. *c.* with me in my temptations
Acts 1. 14. *c.* with one accord in prayer
2. 42. *c.* stedfastly in apostles' doctrine
20. 7. *c.* speech till midnight
Heb. 8. 9. *c.* not in my covenant
1 John 2. 19. would have *c.* with us
Gal. 3. 10. that *continueth* not in all things
1 Tim. 5. 5. *c.* in supplication and prayer
Heb. 7. 24. this man, because he *c.* ever
Jas. 1. 25. law of liberty, and *c.*
Continuing, Jer. 30. 23. in prayer, Rom. 12. 12. Acts 2. 46. *c.* in praise Heb. 13. 14.
CONTRADICT-ING-ION, Acts 13. 45. Heb. 7. 7. *c.* of sinners, 12. 3.
CONTRARY, Ezek. 16. 34. walk *c.* Lev. 26. 21. *c.* wind, Mat. 14. 24. Acts 27. 4.
Acts 18. 13. *c.* to the law, 17. 7; 23. 3.
26. 9. things *c.* to the name of Jesus
Rom. 11. 24. grafted *c.* to nature
Gal. 5. 17. Spirit against flesh: and . . . are *c.*
Col. 2. 14. of ordinances *c.* to us
1 Thes. 2. 15. not God, and are *c.* to all men
1 Tim. 1. 10. is *c.* to sound doctrine
CONTRITE heart, or spirit, Ps. 34. 18; 51. 17. Is. 57. 15; 66. 2.
CONTROVERSY, Deut. 17. 8; 21. 5; 25. 1. 2 Chr. 19. 8. Ezek. 44. 24. Is. 34. 8. Lord hath a *c.* Jer. 25. 31. Hos. 4. 1; 12. 2. Mic. 6. 2. 1 Tim. 3. 16. without *c.* great is the
CONVENIENT, Acts 24. 25. Philem. 8.
Prov. 30. 8. feed with food *c.* for me
Rom. 1. 28. over to do things not *c.*
Eph. 5. 4. talking and jesting not *c.*
CONVERSATION (manner of life), Gal. 1. 13.
Eph. 2. 3; 4. 22. 2 Cor. 1. 12.
Ps. 37. 14. such as be of upright *c.*
50. 23. ordereth his *c.* aright will I
Phil. 1. 27. *c.* be as becometh the gospel
3. 20. our *c.* (citizenship) is in heaven
1 Tim. 4. 12. an example of believers in *c.*
Heb. 13. 5. *c.* without covetousness

Jas. 3. 13. shew out of good *conversation* works
1 Pet. 1. 15. holy in all manner of *c.*
2. 12. *c.* honest among the Gentiles
3. 1. won by *c.* of the wives. 2. chaste *c.*
16. accuse your good *c.* in Christ
2 Pet. 2. 7. filthy *c.* 3. 11. in all holy *c.*
CONVERSION of Gentiles, Acts 15. 3.
CONVERT, Is. 1. 27. and be healed, 6. 10.
Jas. 5. 19. err, and one *c.* him, 20.
Ps. 51. 13. sinners be *converted* to thee
Is. 60. 5. abundance of sea, *c.* to thee
Mat. 13. 15. be *c.* and I heal, Mark 4. 12.
18. 3. except *c.* and become as children
Luke 22. 32. when *c.* strengthen brethren
Acts 3. 19. be *c.* and your sins blotted out
CONVINCE, refute, Job 32. 12. Tit. 1. 9. convict, Jas. 2. 9. 1 Cor. 14. 24, &c.
John 8. 46 (who) *convinceth* me of sin?
CORD, Josh. 2. 15. Ps. 118. 27. Jer. 10. 20. Mic. 2. 5. small *c.* John 2. 15.
Job 30. 11. loosed my *c.* (tent-*c.* life)
Eccl. 4. 12. threefold *c.* not quickly broken
Job 36. 8. *cords* of affliction
Ps. 2. 3. away their *c.* 129. 4. cut *c.*
Prov. 5. 22. *c.* of sins. Is. 5. 18.—vanity
Is. 54. 2. lengthen thy *c.*, strengthen
Hos. 11. 4. *c.* of a man, bands of love
CORN, Gen. 41. 49. Deut. 7. 13. Neh. 13. 5.
Deut. 25. 4. not muzzle ox that treadeth out *c.*, 1 Cor. 9. 9. 1 Tim. 5. 18.
Josh. 5. 11. eat of old *c.* of land, 12.
Job 5. 26. as a shock of *c.* cometh in
Ps. 65. 9. thou preparest them *c.*, 13.
72. 16. handful of *c.* in the earth
78. 24. given them *c.* of heaven to eat
Is. 62. 8. no more give *c.* to enemies
Ezek. 36. 29. call for *c.* and increase
Hos. 2. 8. I gave her *c.* . . . 9. I take my *c.*
10. 11. heifer . . . loveth to tread out *c.*
Zech. 9. 17. how great. . . ! *c.* shall
Mat. 12. 1. to pluck the *c.* [EAR.]
John 12. 24. *c.* of wheat, Mark 4. 28.
CORNER, Lev. 19. 9. 2 Ki. 14. 13.
Lev. 19. 27. mar *c.* Jer. 9. 26. utmost *c.*
Prov. 21. 9. dwell in *c.*, Amos 3. 12.
Is. 30. 20. teachers removed into *c.*
Zech. 10. 4. out of him came forth the *c.*
Mat. 6. 5. pray in *c.* of streets, Prov. 7. 8.
21. 42. head of *c.*, Acts 4. 11.
Job 38. 6. *c.* stone, Ps. 118. 22; 144. 12. Is. 28. 16. 1 Pet. 2. 6. Eph. 2. 20.
CORRECT son, Prov. 29. 17; 23. 13.
Ps. 39. 11. with rebukes dost *c.* man
94. 10. chastiseth heathen . . . shall not he *c.*?
Jer. 2. 19. own wickedness *c.* thee
10. 24. *c.* me, 30. 11. in measure, 46. 28.
Heb. 12. 9. fathers of . . . *corrected* us, 11.
Job 5. 17. happy man . . . God *correcteth*
Prov. 3. 12. whom the Lord loveth he *c.*
Job 37. 13. whether for *correction*
Prov. 3. 11. but be not weary of his *c.*
22. 15. rod of *c.* shall drive foolishness
Hab. 1. 12. established them for *c.*
2 Tim. 3. 16. Scripture profitable for *c.*
CORRUPT, Job 17. 1. Ps. 38. 5.
Ps. 14. 1. they are *c.*, 53. 1; 73. 8.
Mat. 6. 19. moth and rust doth *c.*, 20.
7. 17. *c.* tree, 12. 33. tree *c.* and fruit *c.*
1 Cor. 15. 33. evil communications *c.*
2 Cor. 2. 17. not as many which *c.* word
Eph. 4. 22. the old man which is *c.*
1 Tim. 6. 5. of *c.* minds, 2 Tim. 3. 8.

Jude 10. in those they *corrupt* themselves
Ex. 32. 7. thy people *corrupted* selves, Judg. 2. 19.
Hos. 9. 9. have deeply *c.* themselves
Mal. 2. 8. ye have *c.* covenant of Levi
2 Cor. 7. 2. we have *c.* no man
1 Cor. 9. 25. *corruptible*, 15. 53. 1 Pet. 1. 18, 23.
Job 17. 14. *corruption*, Ps. 16. 10; 49. 9. Is.
  38. 17. Dan. 10. 8. Jonah 2. 6. Acts 2. 31;
  13. 34. Rom. 8. 21. 1 Cor. 15. 42. Gal. 6. 8.
  2 Pet. 1. 4; 2. 19. mount of *c.* 2 Ki. 23. 13.
COST, Luke 14. 28. king's, 2 Sam. 19. 42. *c.*
  nothing, 24. 24. 1 Chr. 21. 24.
COUNCIL, the Hebrew, Ps. 68. 27. 2 Chr.
  28. 14 (*Sanhedrin*) Mat. 5. 22; 10. 17;
  26. 59. Mark 15. 1. Acts 4. 5, 15, &c.
COUNSEL, ask of God, Num. 27. 21, references
Num. 31. 16. *c.* of Balaam, 2 Pet. 2. 15.
1 Ki. 12. 8. *c.* of old men
Job 5. 13. *c.* of froward carried headlong
12. 13. Lord hath *c.* and understanding
21. 16. *c.* of wicked far from me, 22. 18.
Job 38. 2. who is this that darkeneth *c.*? 42. 3.
Ps. 1. 1. *c.* of ungodly. 14. 6. *c.* of poor
33. 10. *c.* of Lord stands for ever, Prov. 19. 21.
  Is. 46. 10; in my *c.* Jer. 23. 22.
55. 14. sweet *c.* 83. 3. taken crafty *c.*
Prov. 1. 25. set at nought all my *c.*
8. 14. *c.* is mine and sound wisdom
11. 14. where no *c.* is the people fall
20. 18. purpose established by *c.*
21. 30. no wisdom . . . nor *c.* against the Lord
24. 6. by wise *c.* make war, in multitude
27. 9. sweetness . . . friend by hearty *c.*
Is. 11. 2. spirit of *c.* and might
28. 29. Lord . . . wonderful in *c.*, Jer. 32. 19.
40. 14. with whom took he *c.*, Rom. 11. 34.
Zech. 6. 13. *c.* of peace between them
Luke 7. 30. rejected *c.* of God against
Acts 2. 23. by the determinate *c.*, 4. 28.
5. 38. if this *c.* be of men it will come
20. 27. declare to you all the *c.* of God
Eph. 1. 11. after the *c.* of his own will
Ezra 4. 5. *counsellor(s)*, 2 Sam. 15. 12. 1 Chr.
  26. 14; 27. 33. Mark 15. 43. 2 Chr. 22. 3.
  Job 3. 14; 12. 17. Dan. 3. 24.
Ps. 119. 24. thy testimonies are my *c.*
Prov. 11. 14. in multitude of *c.* safety
Is. 1. 26. restore *c.* as at beginning
9. 6. called Wonderful, *C.*, the mighty God
COUNT, Ex. 12. 4. Lev. 23. 15.
Num. 23. 10. who *c.* dust of Jacob, Gen. 15. 5.
Job 31. 4. doth not he *c.* all my steps
Ps. 139. 18. if I *c.* them . . . more than
Acts 20. 24. neither *c.* I my life dear
Phil. 3. 7, 8. I *c.* all things loss for Christ
13. I *c.* not to have apprehended
Jas. 1. 2. *c.* it all joy when ye fall
Gen. 15. 6. *counted* to him for righteousness, Ps.
  106. 31. Rom. 4. 3.
Is. 40. 17. *c.* to him less than nothing
Hos. 8. 12. law *c.* as a strange thing
Luke 21. 36. (*ac*) *c.* worthy to escape. Acts 5. 41.
  —suffer. 2 Thes. 1. 5.—of kingdom. 1 Tim.
  5. 17.—double honour. Heb. 3. 3.—more glory.
  10. 29. *c.* blood of covenant unholy
COUNTENANCE, Gen. 4. 5; 31. 2.
Num. 6. 26. Lord lift up his *c.* on thee
1 Sam. 1. 18. her *c.* was no more sad
16. 7. look not on his *c.* or height
Neh. 2. 2. why is thy *c.* sad, Eccl. 7. 3.
Job 29. 24. light of my *c.*, Ps. 4. 6.
Ps. 90. 8. secret sins in the light of thy *c.*
Sol. 2. 14. let me see thy *c.*

Mat. 6. 16. as hypocrites of a sad *countenance*
Acts 2. 28. full of joy with thy *c.*
COUNTRY, far, Mat. 21. 33; 25. 14. Mark 12. 1.
  Luke 15. 13; 19. 12; 20. 9. Prov. 25. 25.
Heb. 11. 14. declare plainly they seek a *c.*
16. they desire a better *c.* . . . an heavenly
2 Cor. 11. 26. *countrymen*, 1 Thes. 2. 14.
COURAGE, Josh. 2. 11. Acts 28. 15.
Num. 13. 20. be of good *c.*, Deut. 31. 6. Josh.
  1. 6; 10. 25; 23. 6. 2 Sam. 10. 12; 13. 28.
  1 Chr. 22. 13; 28. 20. Ezra 10. 4. Ps. 27. 14;
  31. 24. Is. 41. 6.
COURSE(S), 1 Chr. 23. 6. 1 Cor. 14. 27.
Acts 20. 24. finish my *c.* with joy
Eph. 2. 2. according to the *c.* of this world
2 Thes. 3. 1. word may have free *c.* and
2 Tim. 4. 7. finished my *c.*, Acts 13. 25.
Jas. 3. 6. the *c.* of nature, Ps. 82. 5.
COURT, Ex. 27. 9. Is. 34. 13.
Amos 7. 13. Bethel . . . it is the king's *c.*
Rev. 11. 2. *c.* without the temple leave
Ps. 65. 4. dwell *in* thy *c.* 84. 10. day—is
100. 4. enter his *c.* with praise
Is. 1. 12. who required, to tread my *c.*
62. 9. drink it in *c.* of my holiness
1 Pet. 3. 8. be pitiful, be *courteous*
Acts 27. 3. *courteously*, 28. 7.
COVENANT, God's with Noah, Gen. 9. 9.
  Abram, 15. 18. Israel, Ex. 6. 4. David, 2 Sam.
  23. 5. Hag. 2. 23.
Gen. 9. 12 (bow) token of the *c.*
17. 11. (circumcision)—13. in your flesh
Ex. 2. 24. God remembered his *c.*
24. 7. book of *c.* 34. 28. words of *c.*
Num. 10. 33. ark of *c.* Deut. 9. 15. tables of *c.*
25. 13. *c.* of everlasting priesthood
Judg. 2. 1. never brake *c.* with you
1 Chr. 16. 15. mindful of his *c.*, Ps. 105. 8.
Job 31. 1. I made a *c.* with mine eyes
Ps. 25. 14. fear him . . . shew them *c.*
50. 5. made a *c.* with me by sacrifice
74. 20. Have respect to the *c.*: for the
89. 3. *c.* with my chosen . . . sworn to David
132. 12. if thy children keep my *c.*
Prov. 2. 17. forgetteth *c.* of her God
Is. 28. 15. your *c.* with death, 18.
42. 6. give thee for a *c.* of people
54. 10. nor *c.* of my peace be removed
55. 3. everlasting *c.*, sure mercies of David
Jer. 14. 21. break not *c.* with us
31. 31. I make a *c.* with Israel
50. 5. to the Lord in a perpetual *c.*
Ezek. 20. 37. bring into the bond of *c.*
Dan. 9. 27. confirm *c.* with many for one
Hos. 6. 7. have transgressed the *c.*
10. 4. swearing falsely in making *c.*
Mal. 2. 4. *c.* with Levi, 14. wife of *c.*
Luke 1. 72. to remember his holy *c.*
Acts 3. 25. ye the children of the *c.*
Rom. 9. 4. adoption, and glory and *c.*
Heb. 8. 6. the mediator of a better *c.*, 7, 9.
C. breakers, Ps. 55. 20. Rom. 1. 31.
Gen. 9. 16. *everlasting covenant*, 17. 7. Lev.
  24. 8. 2 Sam. 23. 5. 1 Chr. 16. 17. Ps. 105. 10.
  Is. 24. 5; 55. 3; 61. 8. Jer. 32. 40. Ezek.
  16. 60; 37. 26. Heb. 13. 20.
Gen. 17. 9, 10. *keep, keepest, keepeth covenant*,
  Ex. 19. 5. Deut. 7. 9, 12; 29. 9; 33. 9. 1 Ki.
  8. 23; 11. 11. 2 Chr. 6. 14. Neh. 1. 5; 9. 32.
  Ps. 25. 10; 103. 18; 132. 12. Dan. 9. 4.
Gen. 15. 18. the Lord *made* a *c.* Ex. 34. 27. Deut.
  5. 2. 2 Ki. 23. 3. Job 31. 1.
Jer. 31. 31. *new c.*, Heb. 8. 8, 13; 12. 24.

Gen. 9. 15. *remember covenant*, Ex. 6. 5. Lev.
  26. 42, 45. Ps. 105. 8; 106. 45. Ezek. 16. 60.
  Amos 1. 9. Luke 1. 72.
Lev. 2. 13. *c. of salt*, Num. 18. 19. 2 Chr. 13. 5.
Deut. 17. 2. *transgressed the c.* Josh. 7. 11, 15;
  23. 16. Judg. 2. 20. 2 Ki. 18. 12. Jer. 34. 18.
  Hos. 6. 7; 8. 1.
Eph. 2. 12. *covenants* of promise
COVER, locusts, Ex. 10. 5. vail, 40. 3.
Ex. 21. 33. dig a pit and not *c.* it
33. 22. I will *c.* thee with my hand
Deut. 33. 12. Lord shall *c.* him all day
1 Sam. 24. 3. *c.* his feet, Judg. 3. 24.
Job 16. 18. O earth *c.* not my blood
Ps. 91. 4. *c.* thee with his feathers
Is. 11. 9. as the waters *c.* sea, Hab. 2. 14.
58. 7. naked that thou *c.* him
Hos. 10. 8. *c.* us, Luke 23. 30. Rev. 6. 16.
1 Cor. 11. 7. man ought not to *c.* his head
1 Pet. 4. 8. charity shall *c.* multitude of sins
Job 31. 33. if I *covered* my transgressions
Ps. 32. 1. whose sin is *c.*, Rom. 4. 7.
Lam. 3. 44. *c.* thyself with a cloud
Ps. 104. 2. *coverest* thyself with light
73. 6. violence *covereth* them as a garment
Prov. 10. 12. Hatred . . . love *c.* all sins
Is. 28. 20. *covering*, 1 Cor. 11. 15.
4. 6. *covert*, 16. 4; 32. 2. Ps. 61. 4. Jer. 25. 38.
COVET, Ex. 20. 17. Mic. 2. 2.
1 Cor. 12. 31. *c.* earnestly the best gifts
14. 39. *c.* to prophesy and forbid not
Acts 20. 33. *coveted*, 1 Tim. 6. 10.
Prov. 21. 26. *coveteth*, Hab. 2. 9.
Ps. 10. 3. wicked blesseth the *covetous*
Luke 16. 14. Pharisees who were *c.*
1 Cor. 5. 10. not company . . . with *c.*, 11.
6. 10. nor *c.* inherit kingdom of God
1 Tim. 3. 3. bishop must not be *c.*
2 Tim. 3. 2. in last days *c.*, boasters
2 Pet. 2. 14. exercised with *c.* practices
Ex. 18. 21. hating *covetousness*
Ps. 119. 36. incline my heart to thy testimonies
  and not to *c.*
Ezek. 33. 31. heart goeth after their *c.*
Luke 12. 15. beware of *c.*: for man's
Col. 3. 5. *c.* which is idolatry, Eph. 5. 5.
Heb. 13. 5. conversation without *c.*
CRAFT, Dan. 8. 25. Mark 14. 1. Acts 18. 3;
  19. 25; *craftsman*, Rev. 18. 22.
Job 5. 12. disappoint devices of *crafty*
15. 5. choosest tongue of the *c.*
5. 13. *craftiness*, 1 Cor. 3. 19. Luke 20. 23. 2 Cor.
  4. 2. Eph. 4. 14.
CREATE, Gen. 1. 1, &c. Deut. 4. 32.
Ps. 51. 10. *c.* in me a clean heart
Is. 4. 5. *c.* on every dwellingplace
45. 7. I form light and *c.* darkness
57. 19. I *c.* the fruit of the lips, peace
65. 18. rejoice in what I *c.*: I *c.* Jerusalem
Ps. 102. 18. people which shall be *created*
104. 30. forth thy spirit, they are *c.*
Is. 43. 7. I have *c.* him for my glory
Jer. 31. 22. *c.* new thing in the earth
Mal. 2. 10. hath not one God *c.* us
Eph. 2. 10. *c.* in Christ Jesus to good works
3. 9. *c.* all things by Jesus Christ, Col. 1. 16.
Col. 3. 10. after the image of . . . *c.* him
1 Tim. 4. 3. which God *c.* to be received
Rev. 4. 11. hast *c.* all . . . are and were *c.*
10. 6. *c.* heaven and things therein
Creation, whole, Rom. 8. 22. beginning of *c.*
  Mark 10. 6; 13. 19. Rom. 1. 20.
Rev. 3. 14. Witness, beginning of *c.* of God

Eccl. 12. 1. remember thy *Creator* in days
Is. 40. 28. the Lord *C.* of ends of earth
43. 15. I am . . . *C.* of Israel, your king
Rom. 1. 25. served creature . . . *C.*
1 Pet. 4. 19. souls . . . as to a faithful *C.*
Gen. 1. 20. *creature*, Lev. 11. 46.
Mark 16. 15. preach gospel to every *c.*
Rom. 8. 20. *c.* was subject to vanity
19. *c.* waiteth. 21. *c.* be delivered
2 Cor. 5. 17. man in Christ is a new *c.*
Gal. 6. 15. availeth anything but a new *c.*
Col. 1. 15. Son . . . firstborn of every *c.*
1 Tim. 4. 4. *c.* of God is
Heb. 4. 13. neither any *c.* not manifest
Is. 13. 21. houses . . . full of doleful *creatures*
Jas 1. 18. firstfruits of his *c.*
Ezek. 1. 5. *living creatures*, Rev. 4. 6, &c.
CREEP, Lev. 11. 31. Ps. 104. 20.
2 Tim. 3. 6. which *c.* into houses
Jude 4. *crept* in unawares . . . ungodly
CRIB, Job 39. 9. Prov. 14. 4. Is. 1. 3.
CRIME, Job 31. 11. Ezek. 7. 23.
CRIMSON, Is. 1. 18. Jer. 4. 30.
CROOKED serpent, Job 26. 13. Is. 27. 1.
Ps. 125. 5. their *c.* ways, Prov. 2. 15.
Eccl. 1. 15. *c.* cannot be made straight
Is. 40. 4. the *c.* made straight, Luke 3. 5.
Phil. 2. 15. *c.* generation, Deut. 32. 5.
CROSS, John 19. 17, 19, 25, 31. Luke 23. 26.
Mat. 10. 38. taketh not up his *c.* and followeth
  16. 24. Luke 9. 23; 14. 27.
1 Cor. 1. 17. lest the *c.* of Christ be of none
Gal. 5. 11. is the offence of the *c.* ceased
6. 14. glory save in the *c.* of Lord Jesus
Phil. 2. 8. obedient to death . . . of *c.*
3. 18. enemies of the *c.* of Christ
Col. 1. 20. peace through blood of his *c.*
2. 14. took . . . nailing it to his *c.*
Heb. 12. 2. for joy . . . endured the *c.*
CROWN, holy, Lev. 8. 9; Esth. 1. 11.
Ps. 89. 39. thou hast profaned his *c.*
Prov. 12. 4. virtuous woman is a *c.*
14. 24. *c.* of wise is their riches: but
17. 6. children's children are *c.* of old men
Sol. 3. 11. behold king Solomon with *c.*
Is. 28. 5. Lord of hosts for *c.* of glory
62. 3. a *c.* of glory in hand of the Lord
1 Cor. 9. 25. to obtain a corruptible *c.*
Phil. 4. 1. my joy and *c.*, 1 Thes. 2. 19.
2 Tim. 4. 8. laid up . . . a *c.* of righteousness
Jas. 1. 12. receive the *c.* of life which Lord
Rev. 2. 10. I will give thee a *c.* of life
3. 11. hold . . . , that no man take thy *c.*
Ps. 8. 5. Heb. 2. 9. *crowned with* glory and
  honour. Prov. 14. 18.—knowledge
Ps. 65. 11. *crownest* year with thy goodness
103. 4. *crowneth* thee with lovingkindness
Zech. 6. 11. *crowns*, Rev. 4. 4; (locusts) 9. 7;
  seven, 12. 3; ten, 13. 1; many, 19. 12.
CRUCIFY, Mat. 20. 19; 23. 34; 27. 31; 28. 5
  Mark 15. 27. Luke 23. 21.
Heb. 6. 6. they *c.* Son of God afresh, and put
Rom. 6. 6. old man is *crucified* with him
1 Cor. 1. 13. was Paul *c.*? 23. preach Christ *c.*
2 Cor. 13. 4. though *c.* through weakness
Gal. 2. 20. I am *c.* with Christ, I live
5. 24. Christ's have *c.* the flesh with
6. 14. world is *c.* to me, I to world
Rev. 11. 8. where also our Lord was *c.*
CRUEL, Prov. 11. 17. venom, Deut. 32. 33.
Gen. 49. 7. their wrath *c.*, Prov. 27. 4.
Is. 19. 4. a *c.* lord; Ps. 71. 4 *c.* man
Prov. 12. 10. mercies of wicked are *c.*

Sol. 8. 6. jealousy is *cruel* as the grave
Is. 13. 9. day of the Lord cometh, *c.* with
Jer. 6. 23. *c.* and have no mercy, 50. 42.
Heb. 11. 36. had trial of *c.* mockings
CRUMBS, Mat. 15. 27. Luke 16. 21.
CRY of Sodom, Gen. 18. 20. Esau, 27. 34.
Ex. 2. 23. their *c.* came up to God
22. 23. I will surely hear their *c.*
Ps. 9. 12. forgetteth not *c.* of humble
Jer. 7. 16. neither lift up *c.* for, 11. 11.
Mat. 25. 6. at midnight a *c.* made
Is. 40. 6. voice said, C. . . . what shall
42. 2. not *c.* nor lift up voice, Mat. 12. 19.
58. 1. *c.* aloud, spare not, shew my
Ezek. 9. 4. men that sigh and *c.* for
Jonah 3. 8. let . . . *c.* mightily to God
Luke 18. 7. *c.* day and night to him
19. 40. if . . . peace, stones would *c.* out
Rom. 8. 15. Spirit . . . *c.* Abba, Father
Ps. 22. 5. *cried* to thee and were delivered
34. 6. this poor man *c.* and Lord heard
138. 3. I *c.,* thou answeredst me
Lam. 2. 18. heart *c.* to Lord, Ps. 119. 145.
Hos. 7. 14. not *c.* with their heart
Prov. 2. 3. if thou *criest* after knowledge
Gen. 4. 10. brother's blood *crieth*
Prov. 1. 20. wisdom *c.* without; she
Mic. 6. 9. Lord's voice *c.* to the city
Prov. 19. 18. *crying,* Mat. 3. 3. strong *c.* Heb.
5. 7. no more *c.* Rev. 21. 4.
CUBIT, Ezek. 40. 23. stature, Mat. 6. 27.
CUMBER (trouble), Luke 10. 40; 13. 7.
CUP, Gen. 40. 11; 44. 2.
Ps. 16. 5. portion of my *c. See* 11. 6.
23. 5. my *c.* runneth over. 73. 10. a full *c.*
Ps. 116. 13. *c. of* salvation, Is. 51. 17. Zech.
12. 2.—trembling, Jer. 16. 7.—consolation,
25. 15. wine *c.* of fury, Lam. 4. 21. Ezek.
23. 31. Is. 51. 17. Babylon *c.* in Lord's
hand, Jer. 51. 7. *See* Rev. 17. 4.
Prov. 23. 31. when it giveth colour in *c.*
Ezek. 23. 33. *c.* of thy sister Samaria
Hab. 2. 16. *c.* Lord's right hand, Ps. 75. 8.
Mat. 10. 42. a *c.* of cold water only
20. 22. able to drink of the *c.* that I
23. 25. make clean outside of *c.* and
26. 39. let this *c.* pass from me
John 18. 11. *c.* which my Father hath given
1 Cor. 10. 16. *c.* of blessing which we
21. drink *c.* of the Lord and *c.* of devils
11. 25. this *c.* is the new testament
Rev. 16. 19. *c.* of his wrath, 14. 10.
CUPBEARER, 1 Ki. 10. 5. Neh. 1. 11.
CURIOUS, with care (*cura*), Ex. 35. 32. Acts
19. 19. *curiously,* Ps. 139. 15.
CURSE, bring on me, Gen. 27. 12, 13.
Deut. 11. 26. blessing and *c.,* 30. 1.
23. 5. turned *c.* to blessing, Neh. 13. 2.
Prov. 3. 33. *c.* of Lord in house of wicked
26. 2. *c.* causeless shall not come
Mal. 3. 9. ye are cursed with a *c.*
Is. 65. 15. *for,* or, *to be a c.* Jer. 26. 6; 49. 13;
(remnant of Judah), 24. 9; 25. 18, &c.; (—in
Egypt), 42. 18; 44. 8.
Gen. 8. 21. not again *c.* the ground
Ex. 22. 28. nor *c.* ruler of thy people
Lev. 19. 14. shalt not *c.* the deaf
Num. 22. 6. *c.* me this people, 17.
Judg. 5. 23. *c.* ye Meroz, *c.* bitterly
2 Sam. 16. 10. let him *c.* because Lord, 11.
Job 1. 11. he will *c.* thee to thy face, 2. 5.
2. 9. retain integrity? *c.* God and die
Ps. 109. 28. let them *c.* but bless

Prov. 11. 26. people shall *curse* him, 24. 24.
Eccl. 10. 20. *c.* not king in chamber
Jer. 15. 10. every one doth *c.* me
Mal. 2. 2. I will *c.* your blessings
Mat. 5. 44. bless . . . *c.* you, Rom. 12. 14.
Gen. 49. 7. *cursed* be their anger
Job 3. 1. Job *c.* his day, Jer. 20. 14.
Ps. 119. 21. proud *c.* which do err from
Jer. 11. 3. *c. be man* that obeyeth not
17. 5. *c.*—that trusteth in man, 48. 10. *c.* be he
that doeth work of Lord deceitfully.
Deut. 30. 19. *cursing,* Rom. 3. 14. Heb. 6. 8.
Ps. 10. 7; 59. 12; 109. 17.
CURTAIN, Ex. 26. 1. 2 Sam. 7. 2. Ps. 104. 2.
CUSTOM, Gen. 31. 35. Rom. 13. 7. Luke 4. 16.
1 Cor. 11. 16. Jer. 10. 3.
CUT, Lev. 22. 24. *See* Mal. 1. 13.
Zech. 11. 10. cut asunder, Mat. 24. 51. Luke
12. 46. Jer. 50. 23. Ps. 129. 4.
Luke 13. 7. cut down, Job 22. 16, 20. Jer. 48. 2.
Job 4. 7. cut off, 8. 14. Ps. 37. 9, 28; 76. 12;
90. 10; 101. 5. Prov. 2. 22. Mat. 5. 30; 18. 8.
Rom. 11. 22. 2 Cor. 11. 12. Gal. 5. 12.
Acts 5. 33. cut to heart, 7. 54.
CYMBAL, 2 Sam. 6. 5. Ezra 3. 10. Ps. 150. 5.
1 Cor. 13. 1. I am become as sounding brass, or a
tinkling *c.*

D

DAINTY, Job 33. 20. Prov. 23. 6.
Gen. 49. 20. he shall yield royal *dainties*
Ps. 141. 4. not eat their *d.* Prov. 23. 3.
DAM, not take with the young, Deut. 22. 6.
DAMNED (judged, condemned), who believe not,
Mark 16. 16. 2 Thes. 2. 12.
Rom. 14. 23. doubteth, is *d.* if he eat
2 Pet. 2. 1. *damnable* heresies
Mat. 23. 14. receive greater *damnation*
33. *d.* of hell. Mark 3. 29. eternal *d.*
John 5. 29. forth to resurrection of *d.*
1 Cor. 11. 29. eateth and drinketh *d.*
1 Tim. 5. 12. *d.* because . . . first faith
2 Pet. 2. 3. their *d.* slumbereth not
DANCE, Miriam, Ex. 15. 20, *see* Judg. 11. 34,
&c. daughters of Shiloh, Judg. 21. 21. satyrs,
Is. 13. 21. daughter of Herodias, Mat. 14. 6.
See Ex. 32. 19. Luke 15. 25.
Ps. 149. 3. praise him in *d.,* 2 Sam. 6. 14.
DANDLED on knees, Is. 66. 12.
DANGER of council, hell fire, Mat. 5. 21.
Acts 19. 27. craft in *d.* 40. we in *d.*
DARE, 1 Cor. 6. 1. 2 Cor. 10. 12.
Rom. 5. 7. some would even *d.* to die
Durst, Mat. 22. 46. Acts 7. 32. Jude 9.
DARK, it was, John 6. 17; 20. 1. *d.* places, Ps.
74. 20. Is. 45. 19. Lam. 3. 6; *d.* speeches, Num.
12. 8. *d.* sayings, Ps. 49. 4; 78. 2. Prov.
1. 6. *d.* sentences, Dan. 8. 23.
2 Sam. 22. 12. *d.* waters, Ps. 18. 11.
Job 24. 16. in *d.* dig through houses
Ps. 88. 12. thy wonders known in *d.?*
Ex. 10. 15. land *darkened,* Is. 5. 30.
Ps. 69. 23. let eyes be *d.,* Rom. 11. 10.
Mat. 24. 29. sun be *d.,* Luke 23. 45.
Rom. 1. 21. their foolish heart was *d.*
Eph. 4. 18. having the understanding *d.*
1 Cor. 13. 12. through a glass *darkly*
Gen. 1. 2. *darkness,* 15. 12. horror of *d.*
2 Sam. 22. 29. Lord will lighten my *d.*
Job 34. 22. no *d.* . . . where workers of
Ps. 104. 20. makest *d.,* and it is night

Is. 5. 20. *darkness* for light, and light for *d.*
45. 7. I form light and create *d.*
Mat. 6. 23. whole body full of *d.*
8. 12. outer *d.*, 22. 13; 25. 30.
John 1. 5. *d.* comprehended it not
3. 19. men loved *d.* rather than light
12. 35. light lest *d.* come upon you
Acts 26. 18. turn from *d.* to light
Rom. 13. 12. cast off works of *d.*, Is. 29. 18.
Ezek. 8. 12. Eph. 5. 11.
1 Cor. 4. 5. the hidden things of *d.*
2 Cor. 4. 6. light to shine out of *d.*
Eph. 5. 8. were sometimes *d.*, but
6. 12. the rulers of the *d.* of this world
1 Pet. 2. 9. called you out of *d.*
2 Pet. 2. 4. delivered into chains of *d.*
1 John 1. 5. in him is no *d.* at all
2. 8. *d.* is past, and the true light shineth
11. because *d.* hath blinded his eyes
Jude 13. blackness of *d.* for ever
Deut. 28. 29. *in darkness*, 1 Sam. 2. 9. Ps.
107. 10; 112. 4. Is. 9. 2; 50. 10. Mat. 4. 16;
10. 27. John 1. 5. 1 Thes. 5. 4.
DARLING, Ps. 22. 20; 35. 17.
DARTS, fiery, of devil, Eph. 6. 16.
DASH, 2 Ki. 8. 12; Ex. 15. 6. Is. 13. 16, 18.
Hos. 10. 14; 13. 16. Ps. 137. 9. Jer. 13. 14.
Ps. 2. 9. *d.* in pieces like a potter's vessel
91. 12. lest *d.* thy foot against a stone
DAUB, Ex. 2. 3. Ezek. 13. 10; 22. 28.
DAVID, for Christ, Ps. 89. 3. Jer. 30. 9. Ezek.
34. 23, 24; 37. 24, 25. Hos. 3. 5. Is. 55. 3.
DAY, Gen. 1. 5. for the *d.* breaketh, 32. 26.
Ps. 19. 2. *d.* unto *d.* uttereth speech
84. 10. a *d.* in thy courts is better than
118. 24. this is the *d.* which the Lord
Prov. 27. 1. what a *d.* may bring forth
Amos 6. 3. put far away the evil *d.*
Zech. 4. 10. despised the *d.* of small things
Mat. 6. 34. sufficient to the *d.* is the evil
John 8. 56. Abraham rejoiced to see my *d.*
1 Cor. 3. 13. the *d.* shall declare it
Phil. 1. 6. the *d.* of Jesus Christ, 2. 16. 2 Thes.
2. 2. 1 Cor. 1. 8.
1 Thes. 5. 5. children of the *d.*
Mat. 10. 15. *day of judgment*, 11. 22, 24; 12. 36.
Mark 6. 11. 2 Pet. 2. 9; 3. 7. 1 John 4. 17.
Is. 2. 12. *day of the Lord*, 13. 6, 9; 34. 8. Jer.
46. 10. Lam. 2. 22. Ezek. 30. 3. Joel 1. 15;
2. 1, 31; 3. 14. Amos 5. 18. Obad. 15.
Zeph. 1. 8, 18; 2. 2, 3. Zech. 14. 1. Mal. 4. 5.
1 Cor. 5. 5. 2 Cor. 1. 14. 1 Thes. 5. 2. 2 Pet.
3. 10. Rev. 1. 10.
Ps. 20. 1. Lord hear in *day of trouble*
50. 15. call on me in—91. 15.
59. 16. my defence and refuge in—
77. 2. in the—I sought the Lord, *see* 86. 7.
Is. 37. 3. This *d.* is a—and of rebuke, and of
blasphemy
Ezek. 7. 7. time is come,—is near
Nah. 1. 7. Lord is good, a strong hold in—
Hab. 3. 16. I might rest in—
Zeph. 1. 15. a—distress, desolation
Job 8. 9. *days* on earth as a shadow
14. 1. of few *d.* and full of trouble
32. 7. *d.* should speak, and multitude
Ps. 90. 12. teach us to number our *d.*
Prov. 3. 16. length of *d.* is in right
Eccl. 7. 10. former *d.* better than
11. 8. remember *d.* of darkness; many
12. 1. while the evil *d.* come not
Jer. 2. 32. forgotten me *d.* without
Gal. 4. 10. observe *d.*, months, and years

Eph. 5. 16. because the *days* are evil
1 Pet. 3. 10. love life and see good *d.*
Gen. 49. 1. *last days*, Is. 2. 2. Mic. 4. 1. Acts
2. 17. 2 Tim. 3. 1. Heb. 1. 2. Jas. 5. 3. 2 Pet.
3. 3.
Num. 24. 14. *latter days*, Deut. 31. 29. Jer.
23. 20; 30. 24. Dan. 10. 14. Hos. 3. 5.
Job 10. 20, *my days*, 17. 1, 11.
7. 6.—are swifter than a shuttle
16. let me alone,—are vanity
Ps. 39. 4. to know end, and measure of—
102. 3.—are consumed like smoke
11.—like shadow, 23. shortened—
Is. 39. 8. peace and truth in—
Jer. 20. 18.—are consumed with shame
Job 9. 33. *daysman*, or umpire
38. 12. *dayspring*, Luke 1. 78.
2 Pet. 1. 19. *day star* arise in your hearts
Ps. 61. 8. *daily* perform my vows
Prov. 8. 34. watching *d.* at my gates
Is. 58. 2. seek me *d.* and delight in
Acts 2. 47. added to church *d.* . . . . saved
Heb. 3. 13. exhort one another *d.*
DEACON, Phil. 1. 1. 1 Tim. 3. 8, &c.
DEAD, Gen. 20. 3; 23. 3.
Num. 16. 48. stood between *d.* and living
1 Sam. 24. 14. after a *d.* dog, . . . flea
Ps. 88. 10. shall *d.* arise and praise
115. 17. the *d.* praise not the Lord
Eccl. 9. 5. the *d.* know not any thing
10. 1. *d.* flies cause the ointment to
Mat. 8. 22. let the *d.* bury their *d.*
22. 32. not God of *d.* but of living, 31.
Luke 8. 52. she is not *d.* but sleepeth
John 5. 25. *d.* hear voice of Son of God
11. 25. though *d.* yet shall he live
Rom. 6. 8. *d.* with Christ, 11. *d.* to sin
Gal. 2. 19. I through law *d.* to the law
Eph. 2. 1. who were *d.* in trespasses
Col. 2. 13. being *d.* in your sins
1 Thes. 4. 16. *d.* in Christ rise first
2 Tim. 2. 11. *d.* with him, we shall live
Heb. 11. 4. being *d.* yet speaketh
Rev. 14. 13. blessed are *d.* . . . . in the Lord
Ps. 17. 9. *deadly*, Jas. 3. 8. Rev. 13. 3.
DEAF, Ex. 4. 11. Ps. 38. 13. Is. 29. 18; 35. 5.
Mic. 7. 16. Mark 7. 32.
Lev. 19. 14. thou shalt not curse the *d.*
Is. 42. 18. hear, ye *d.* and look, ye blind
19. or *d.* as my messenger that I sent?
43. 8. and the *d.* people that have ears
Mat. 11. 5. *d.* hear, dead are raised, Mark 7. 37.
DEATH, Gen. 21. 16. Ex. 10. 17.
Num. 23. 10. let me die *d.* of the righteous
Deut. 30. 15. set before you life and *d.*
Ps. 6. 5. in *d.* no remembrance of thee
68. 20. to Lord belong issues from *d.*
73. 4. have no bands in their *d.*: but
89. 48. liveth and shall not see *d.*
116. 15. precious . . . Lord is *d.* of saints
118. 18. not given me over to *d.*
Prov. 2. 18. her house inclineth to *d.*
8. 36. all they that hate me love *d.*
18. 21. *d.* and life in power of tongue
Eccl. 7. 26. more bitter than *d.* woman
8. 8. no man . . . hath power in the day of *d.*
Is. 25. 8. swallow up *d.* in victory
28. 15. We . . . made covenant with *d.*
38. 18. *d.* cannot celebrate thee
Jer. 8. 3. *d.* chosen rather than life
21. 8. I set before you way of life, way of *d.*
Hos. 13. 14. O *d.* I will be thy plagues
Mat. 16. 28. not taste of *d.*, Luke 9. 27.

Mat. 26. 38. sorrowful even unto *death*
John 5. 24. from *d.* to life, 1 John 3. 14.
8. 51. he shall never see *d.*, 52.
12. 33. what *d.* he should die, 21. 19.
Acts 2. 24. loosed the pains of *d.*
Rom. 5. 12. sin entered, and *d.* by sin
6. 5. planted in the likeness of his *d.*
9. *d.* hath no more dominion over
21. for the end of those things is *d.*
7. 5. to bring forth fruit unto *d.*
8. 2. free from law of sin and *d.*
6. for to be carnally minded is *d.*
38. *d.* nor life shall separate us from
1 Cor. 3. 22. or life, or *d.*, or things
11. 26. ye shew Lord's *d.* till he come
15. 21. by man came *d.*, by man also
54. *d.* is swallowed up in victory
55. O *d.* where is thy sting, Hos. 13. 14.
56. sting of *d.* is sin, and strength
2 Cor. 1. 9. sentence of *d.* in ourselves
10. deliver from so great a *d.*, and doth
2. 16. to one . . . savour of *d.* unto *d.*
4. 11. delivered to *d.* for Jesus' sake
12. *d.* worketh in us, but life in you
Phil. 2. 8. obedient to *d.* . . . the *d.* of cross
Heb. 2. 9. taste *d.* for every man
15. through fear of *d.* are subject to
11. 5. should not see *d.*, Luke 2. 26.
Jas. 1. 15. sin finished bringeth *d.*
1 Pet. 3. 18. put to *d.* in the flesh
1 John 5. 16. a sin unto *d.*, 17. not—
Rev. 1. 18. I have the keys of hell and *d.*
2. 10. be faithful unto *d.* and I will
20. 6. on such second *d.* hath no power
21. 4. there shall be no more *d.* nor
DEBATE, (plead) Prov. 25. 9. Is. 27. 8. (contention) Is. 58. 4. Rom. 1. 29. 2 Cor. 12. 20.
DEBT, Rom. 4. 4. Mat. 6. 12; 18. 27. Ezek.
18. 7. *debtor*, Gal. 5. 3. Rom. 1. 14; 8. 12;
15. 27. Luke 7. 41. Mat. 6. 12.
DECEASE, Luke 9. 31. 2 Pet. 1. 15.
DECEIT, Jer. 5. 27; 9. 6, 8.
Ps. 72. 14. redeem soul from *d.*
101. 7. worketh *d.* shall not dwell
Prov. 20. 17. bread of *d.* is sweet to man
Is. 53. 9. any *d.* in his mouth
Jer. 8. 5. they hold fast *d.* and refuse
Col. 2. 8. spoil through vain *d.*
Ps. 35. 20. *deceitful*, 109. 2. Prov. 11. 18;
14. 25; 23. 3; 27. 6.
5. 6. abhor bloody and *d.* man
55. 23. *d.* men shall not live half their days
78. 57. turn like a *d.* bow, Hos. 7. 16.
52. 4. Mic. 6. 12. Zeph. 3. 13.
Jer. 17. 9. heart *d.* above all things
Eph. 4. 22. according to the *d.* lusts
Ps. 24. 4. *deceitfully*, Jer. 48. 10. Job 13. 7. 2 Cor.
Mat. 13. 22. *deceitfulness* of riches   [4. 2.
DECEIVE, 2 Ki. 4. 28; 18. 29.
Prov. 24. 28. *d.* not with thy lips
Mat. 24. 4. take heed no man *d.* you
24. 24. if possible *d.* the very elect
1 Cor. 3. 18. let no man *d.* himself
1 John 1. 8. if we say . . . no sin, we *d.* ourselves
Deut. 11. 16. heart be not *deceived*
Job 12. 16. *d.* and the deceiver are
Is. 44. 20. a *d.* heart hath turned
Jer. 20. 7. O Lord, thou hast *d.* me
Ezek. 14. 9. if prophet be *d.*, I Lord *d.*
Obad. 3. thy pride hath *d.* thee
Rom. 7. 11. sin *d.* me, and by it slew me
1 Tim. 2. 14. Adam was not *d.* but
2 Tim. 3. 13. *deceiving* and being *d.*

Gen. 27. 12. Mal. 1. 14. *deceiver*, Mat. 27. 63.
2 John 7. 2 Cor. 6. 8. Tit. 1. 10.
Prov. 26. 19. *deceiveth*, Rev. 12. 9.
Gal. 6. 3. when nothing, *d.* himself
Jas. 1. 26. *d.* his own heart, 22.
DECENTLY, 1 Cor. 14. 40.
DECLARE (make known), Gen. 41. 24. Is. 42. 9.
Ps. 22. 22. I will *d.* thy name unto brethren
38. 18. I will *d.* my iniquity and
50. 16. what hast . . . to do to *d.* my statutes
78. 6. may *d.* them to their children
145. 4. shall *d.* thy mighty acts
Is. 3. 9. they *d.* their sin as Sodom
53. 8. who shall *d.* his generation
Acts 17. 23. worship, him *d.* I unto
20. 27. not shunned to *d.* all counsel
Rom. 3. 25. to *d.* his righteousness
Heb. 11. 14. say such things *d.* plainly
1 John 1. 3. seen and heard *d.* we
Rom. 1. 4. *declared* to be the Son of God
Amos 4. 13. *declareth* to man his thought
DECLINE, swerve, Deut. 17. 11. Ps. 44. 18.
DECREE, 2 Chr. 30. 5. of Nebuchadnezzar,
Dan. 3. 29. Cyrus, Ezra 5. 13. Darius, 6. 1.
Artaxerxes, 7. 21. Ahasuerus (Xerxes), Esth.
3. 15. Esther, 9. 32. Augustus, Luke 2. 1.
Ps. 2. 7. I will declare the *d.*
Prov. 8. 15. by me . . . princes *d.* justice
Jer. 5. 22. bound of sea by a perpetual *d.* Prov.
8. 29. *See* Ps. 148. 6. Job 28. 26.
Dan. 4. 17. *d.* of the watchers. *See* 24.
Zeph. 2. 2. before the *d.* bring forth
Is. 10. 1. *decreed*, 1 Cor. 7. 37.
10. 1. *decrees*, Acts 16. 4; 17. 7.
DEDICATE, Deut. 20. 5. 2. Sam. 8. 11. 1 Chr.
26. 30, 26, 27. Ezek. 44. 29.
Num. 7. 84. *dedication*, 2 Chr. 7. 9. Ezra
6. 16, 17. Neh. 12. 27. John 10. 22.
DEED, Judg. 19. 30. 2 Sam. 12. 14.
Rom. 15. 18. obedient by word and *d.*
Col. 3. 17. whatsoever ye do in word or *d.*
1 John 3. 18. love in *d.* and in truth
Ps. 28. 4. give them according to their *deeds,*
Jer. 25. 14. Rom. 2. 6. *See* Luke 23. 41. 2 Cor.
5. 10.
Neh. 13. 14. wipe not out my good *d.*
John 3. 19. because their *d.* were evil
Rom. 3. 20. by *d.* of law no flesh justified
8. 13. mortify *d.* of body, Col. 3. 9.
2 John 11. partaker of his evil *d.*
DEEP, Gen. 1. 2; 7. 11. Job 38. 30.
Ps. 36. 6. thy judgments a great *d.*
42. 7. *d.* calleth unto *d.* at the noise
1 Cor. 2. 10. yea, the *d.* things of God
2 Cor. 11. 25. I have been in the *d.*
Is. 31. 6. *deeply* revolted, Hos. 9. 9.
Mark 8. 12. sighed *d.* in spirit
DEFAME, 1 Cor. 4. 13. Jer. 20. 10.
DEFENCE, 2 Chr. 11. 5. Is. 19. 6.
Num. 14. 9. their *d.* is departed
Job 22. 25. the Almighty shall be thy *d.*
Ps. 7. 10; 59. 9. God is my *d.*, 16, 17; 62. 2, 6;
89. 18; 94. 22.
Eccl. 7. 12. wisdom is a *d.*, money is a *d.*
Is. 4. 5. on all the glory shall be *d.*
33. 16. place of *d.* the munitions of
DEFER, Is. 48. 9. Prov. 13. 12; 19. 11.
D. not, Eccl. 5. 4. Dan. 9. 19.
DEFILE, land, Lev. 18. 25. Is. 24. 5.
Dan. 1. 8. would not *d.* himself
Mat. 15. 18. they *d.* the man, 20.
1 Cor. 3. 17. if any *d.* temple of God
Mark 7. 2. *defiled* hands, *see* Sol. 5. 3.

Tit. 1. 15. mind and conscience is *defiled*
Heb. 12. 15. (by) bitterness many *d.*
Rev. 3. 4. have not *d.* their garments
21. 27. not enter any thing that *defileth*
DEFRAUD, Lev. 19. 13. *See* Mark 10. 19.
1 Sam. 12. 3. whom have I *defrauded*? 2 Cor. 7. 2.
1 Cor. 6. 7. law . . . why not rather be *d.*
DELAY, Ex. 32. 1. not *d.* 22. 29. Acts 9. 38.
Ps. 119. 60. I *delayed* not to keep
Mat. 24. 48. my lord *delayeth* coming
DELICATE, (dainty), Jer. 51. 34. (luxurious),
Deut. 28. 56. Is. 47. 1. Jer. 6. 2. Mic. 1. 16.
delicately, 1 Sam. 15. 32. Prov. 29. 21. Lam.
4. 5. Luke 7. 25.
DELIGHT, Ps. 1. 2. his *d.* is in the law of God,
119. 92.
16. 3. saints in whom is all my *d.*
40. 8. I *d.* to do thy will, O my God
94. 19. thy comforts *d.* my soul
Prov. 11. 1. just weight *his d.* 20. upright—.
15. 8. prayer of upright—
Sol. 2. 3. under his shadow with *d.*
Is. 1. 11. I *d.* not in blood of bullocks
Jer. 9. 24. in these things I *d.* saith Lord
Gen. 34. 19. *delight in* Jacob's daughter
Num. 14. 8. If Lord—us, then he will bring
Deut. 10. 15. Lord had a—thy fathers
1 Sam. 15. 22. hath Lord as great—offerings
2 Sam. 24. 3. Why doth the king—this thing?
Job 22. 26. thy—the Almighty, 27. 10.
Is. 55. 2. eat . . . good let your soul—
58. 2. take—approaching to God
Rom. 7. 22. I—law of God . . . but see
2 Sam. 22. 20. *delighted in* me. 1 Ki. 10. 9.
Esth. 2. 14. except the king—her, that
Ps. 22. 8. deliver him, seeing he—him
109. 17. he *d. not in* blessing, so let
Esth. 6. 6. king *delighteth* to honour,
Ps. 147. 10. he *d.* not in strength of horse
Prov. 3. 12. as father son in whom he *d.*
Is. 42. 1. elect in whom my soul *d.*
62. 4. Hephzibah, Lord *d.* in thee
Mic. 7. 18. because he *d.* in mercy
Prov. 8. 31. my *delights* with sons of men
Sol 7. 6. how pleasant, O love, for *d.*
Mal. 3. 12. ye shall be a *delightsome* land
DELIVER, Ex. 3. 8; 5. 18.
Job 5. 19. *d.* thee in six troubles
10. 7. none can *d.* out of thy hand
Ps. 33. 19. to *d.* their soul from death
50. 15. I will *d.* thee, and thou, 91. 15.
56. 13. wilt thou not *d.* my feet
74. 19. *d.* not the soul of thy turtle
Eccl. 8. 8. shall wickedness *d.* those
Ezek. 14. 14. should *d.* but own souls
34. 10. I will *d.* my flock from their mouth
Dan. 3. 17. our God is able to *d.* us
Hos. 11. 8. how shall I *d.* thee, Israel
Rom. 7. 24. shall *d.* me from body
1 Cor. 5. 5. to *d.* such a one to Satan
2 Tim. 4. 18. Lord shall *d.* me from
Heb. 2. 15. *d.* them who through fear
2 Pet. 2. 9. Lord knows to *d.* godly
Prov. 28. 26. walketh wisely shall be *delivered*
Is. 38. 17. love to soul, *d.* it from pit
49. 24, 25. prey . . . lawful captive *d.*?
Jer. 7. 10. *d.* to do all abominations
Ezek. 3. 19. hast *d.* thy soul, 21; 33. 9.
Dan. 12. 1. thy people shall be *d.*
Joel 2. 32. call on name of Lord . . . be *d.*
Mic. 4. 10. Babylon, there shalt thou be *d.*
Mat. 11. 27. all *d.* to me of my Father
Acts 2. 23. *d.* by determinate counsel

Rom. 4. 25. who was *delivered* for our offences
7. 6. now we are *d.* from the law, that
8. 32. (God) *d.* him up for us all
2 Cor. 1. 10. who *d.* us from so great a death,
and doth *d.*, and will *d.* us
4. 11. *d.* to death for Jesus' sake
1 Thes. 1. 10. *d.* us from wrath to come
1 Tim. 1. 20. whom I have *d.* to Satan
Jude 3. faith once *d.* to the saints
2 Ki. 5. 1. given *deliverance.* 13. 17. 2 Chr.
12. 7. Esth. 4. 14. Ps. 32. 7; 44. 4. Joel 2. 32.
Obad. 17. Luke 4. 18.
Gen. 45. 7. *great deliverance,* Judg. 15. 18.
1 Chr. 11. 14. Ps. 18. 50.
Ezra 9. 13. given us such *d.* as this
Heb. 11. 35. tortured, not accepting *d.*
DELUSION, 2 Thes. 2. 11. Is. 66. 4.
DEMAND (requirement), Dan. 4. 17.
DEMONSTRATION, 1 Cor. 2. 4.
DEN, Job 37. 8. Ps. 104. 22. (refuge) Judg. 6. 2.
Heb. 11. 38. Rev. 6. 15.
Jer. 9. 11. *den of dragons,* 10. 22.
Ps. 10. 9. *den of lions,* Sol. 4. 8. Dan. 6. 7, 24.
Amos 3. 4. Nah. 2. 12.
Jer. 7. 11. *den of robbers*
Mat. 21. 13. Mark 11. 17. *den of thieves*
DENY, 1 Ki. 2. 16. Job 8. 18.
Prov. 30. 9. lest I be full, and *d.* thee
Mat. 10. 33. shall *d.* me before men
16. 24. let him *d.* himself and take up
26. 34. before the cock crow thou shalt *d.*
me, 75. Mark 14. 30, 72.
Mat. 26. 35. I nor *d.* thee, Mark 14. 31.
2 Tim. 2. 12. if we *d.* him, he will *d.* us
Tit. 1. 16. but in works they *d.* him
1 Tim. 5. 8. hath *denied* the faith
Rev. 2. 13. hast not *d.* my faith
Tit. 2. 12. *denying* ungodliness and worldly
2 Pet. 2. 1. *d.* Lord that bought them
DEPART from us, Job 21. 14; 22. 17.
Hos. 9. 12. woe when I *d.*, Judg. 16. 20.
Mat. 7. 23. *d.* from me, ye that work
25. 41. *d.* from me, ye cursed, into
Luke 2. 29. lettest thy servant *d.* in peace
5. 8. *d.* from me . . . a sinful man, O Lord
Phil. 1. 23. having a desire to *d.* and
1 Tim. 4. 1. some shall *d.* from faith
Ps. 18. 21. not wickedly *departed* from my God,
119. 102. 2 Sam. 22. 22.
D. from evil, Ps. 34. 14; 37. 27. Prov. 3. 7; 13. 19;
14. 16; 16. 6, 17. to—is understanding, Job 28. 28.
Is. 59. 15. that—makes himself prey
Acts 20. 29. after my *departing,* wolves
Heb. 3. 12. unbelief, in *d.* from living God
2 Tim. 4. 6. *departure,* Ezek. 26. 18.
DEPTH, Job 28. 14; 38. 16. Prov. 8. 27. Mat.
18. 6. Mark 4. 5.
Rom. 8. 39. height nor *d.* . . . . separate us
Eph. 3. 18. breadth, length, *d.,* height
Ex. 15. 5, 8. *depths,* Ps. 68. 22; 71. 20; 130. 1.
Prov. 3. 20; 9. 18.
Mic. 7. 19. cast sins into *d.* of sea
Rev. 2. 24. have not known *d.* of Satan
DERISION, Job 30. 1. Ps. 2. 4; 44. 13; 59. 8;
119. 51. Jer. 20. 7, 8.
DESCEND (God), Ex. 19. 18; 33. 9.
Ps. 49. 17. glory not *d.* after him
Is. 5. 14. rejoiceth shall *d.* into it
1 Thes. 4. 16. Lord *d.* from heaven
Gen. 28. 12. angels of God ascending and
descending, John 1. 51. [32, 33.
Mat. 3. 16. the Spirit of God *d.*, Mark 1. 10. John 1.
DESERT (described), Jer. 2. 6;—(arid, *see* Jer. 17. 6.).

desert blossom as the rose, Is. 35. 1. make
rivers in *d.* 35. 6; 43. 19. set in *d.* fir tree,
41. 19. *d.* like garden of Lord, 51. 3. (trackless)
in *d.* highway, Is. 40. 3. *see* Mat. 3. 3. towers
in *d.,* wells, 2 Chr. 26. 10.
Mark 1. 45. Jesus . . . was without in *d. place*
Luke 1. 80. in *deserts* till day of shewing
Heb. 11. 38. wandered in *d.* and mountains
D. of the sea (Babylonia), Is. 21. 1.
D. (Heb. pasture ground) *of Wanderings,* Ex.
3. 1; 5. 3. (described) Jer. 2. 6. *see* Ps.
78. 40, &c. John 6. 31.
Wild beasts of d. Is. 13. 21, &c. asses in *d.*
Job 24. 5. owl of *d.* Ps. 102. 6. foxes in *d.*
Ezek. 13. 4.
DESIRE, whole, 2 Chr. 15. 15. Deut. 18. 6.
Gen. 3. 16. *d.* shall be to thy husband
Ex. 34. 24. nor any man *d.* thy land
Neh. 1. 11. who *d.* to fear thy name
Job 14. 15. wilt have a *d.* to the work of
21. 14. we *d.* not knowledge of thy ways
Ps. 38. 9. all my *d.* is, 2 Sam. 23. 5.
145. 16. satisfieth *d.* of every living thing
Prov. 10. 24. *d.* of righteous granted
11. 23. *d.* of righteous is only good
13. 19. *d.* accomplished is sweet
Eccl. 12. 5. *d.* fail because man goeth
Is. 26. 8. *d.* of our soul is to thy name
Hag. 2. 7. the *d.* of all nations shall
Luke 22. 15. with *d.* I have desired
Jas. 4. 2. *d.* . . . and cannot obtain
Rev. 9. 6. *d.* to die, and death shall flee
Ps. 19. 10. more to be *desired* are
27. 4. one thing have I *d.* of the Lord
Is. 26. 9. with my soul have I *d.* thee
Jer. 17. 16. neither have I *d.* woeful day
Hos. 6. 6. I *d.* mercy, not sacrifice
Ps. 37. 4. give *desires* of thine heart
Eph. 2. 3. fulfilling *d.* of the flesh
Ps. 51. 6. thou *desirest* truth in the
16. thou *d.* not sacrifice, else would
Job 7. 2. servant earnestly *desireth*
Ps. 34. 12. what man *d.* life and loveth
68. 16. hill which God *d.* to dwell in
Prov. 12. 12. wicked *d.* net of evil men
13. 4. soul of sluggard *d.* and hath not
21. 10. soul of wicked *d.* evil.
DESOLATE, 2 Sam. 13. 20. Job 15. 28; 16. 7.
Ps. 25. 16. Is. 49. 21; 54. 1. Mat. 23. 38.
Rev. 17. 16.
Is. 49. 6. *desolations,* 61. 4. Jer. 25. 9, 12. Ezek.
35. 9. Dan. 9. 2, 18, 26.
DESPAIR, 2 Cor. 4. 8; 1. 8. Eccl. 2. 20.
Job 6. 26. *desperate,* Is. 17. 11.
Jer. 17. 9. *desperately* wicked
DESPISE my statutes, Lev. 26. 15.
1 Sam. 2. 30. that *d.* me be lightly
Job 5. 17. *d.* not the chastening of the Almighty,
Prov. 3. 11.
Ps. 102. 17. will not *d.* their prayer
Prov. 23. 22. *d.* not mother when old
Amos 5. 21. I *d.* your feast days
Mat. 6. 24. hold to one, and *d.* the other
Rom. 14. 3. *d.* him that eateth not
1 Tim. 4. 12. no man *d.* thy youth
Gen. 16. 4. mistress was *despised* in
2 Sam. 6. 16. she *d.* him in her heart
Prov. 12. 9. is *d.* and hath a servant
Is. 53. 3. he is *d.* and rejected, Ps. 22. 6.
Zech. 4. 10. who *d.* day of small things
Luke 18. 9. righteous and *d.* others
Heb. 10. 28. that *d.* Moses' law died
Acts 13. 41. *despisers,* 2 Tim. 3. 3.

Rom. 2. 4. *despisest* riches of goodness
Job 36. 5. God *despiseth* not any
Prov. 11. 12. void of wisdom *d.* his neighbour;
14. 21. that—sinneth
13. 13. whoso *d.* the word shall be destroyed:
but he
15. 32. refuseth instruction *d.* his soul
19. 16. he that *d.* his ways shall die
30. 17. eye . . . *d.* to obey his mother
Is. 33. 15. *d.* gain of oppression
Luke 10. 16. *d.* you, *d.* me, *d.* him
1 Thes. 4. 8. *d.* not man but God
Heb. 12. 2. *despising* the shame
10. 29. done *despite* to the Spirit of grace
DESTROY, Sodom, Gen. 19. 13.
Ps. 101. 8. I will *d.* the wicked of land
Prov. 1. 32. prosperity of fools *d.*
Eccl. 7. 16. why shouldest *d.* thyself
Mat. 5. 17. not come to *d.* but to
21. 41. miserably *d.* those wicked men
John 2. 19. *d.* this temple, and I
Rom. 14. 15. *d.* not him with thy meat
20. for meat *d.* not work of God
1 Cor. 3. 17. defile temple of God shall God *d.*
6. 13. God shall *d.* both it and them
Jas. 4. 12. able to save and to *d.*
1 John 3. 8. might *d.* works of the devil
Hos. 4. 6. *destroyed* for lack of knowledge
13. 9. Israel, thou hast *d.* thyself
2 Cor. 4. 9. cast down, but not *d.*
Job 15. 21. *destroyer,* Ps. 17. 4. Prov. 28. 24.
Jer. 4. 7. 1 Cor. 10. 10.
Shall be destroyed, Esth. 4. 14. wicked, Ps. 37. 38;
92. 7. Prov. 13. 20; 29. 1. Aven, Hos. 10. 8.
death, 1 Cor. 15. 26.
Dan. 2. 44. kingdom . . . never be *d.*
Deut. 7. 23. *destruction,* 32. 24.
Job 5. 22. at *d.* and famine shall laugh
26. 6. *d.* before him hath no covering
31. 23. *d.* from God was a terror to me
Ps. 90. 3. thou turnest man to *d.*
91. 6. *d.* that wasteth at noonday
Prov. 10. 29. *d.* shall be to workers of iniquity,
21. 15. Job 21. 30; 31. 3.
15. 11. Hell and *d.* are before the Lord
16. 18. pride goeth before *d.*
18. 12. before *d.* . . . . heart is haughty
27. 20. hell and *d.* are never full
Jer. 4. 20. *d.* upon *d.* is cried, for
Hos. 13. 14. O grave, I will be thy *d.*
Mat. 7. 13. the way, that leadeth to *d.*
Rom. 3. 16. *d.* and misery are in their ways
1 Cor. 5. 5. for the *d.* of the flesh
2 Cor. 10. 8. not for your *d.,* 13. 10.
1 Thes. 5. 3. sudden *d.* cometh on them
2 Pet. 2. 1. bring on selves swift *d.*
3. 16. wrest . . . scriptures to their own *d.*
DETERMINED, 2 Chr. 25. 16. Job 14. 5.
Is. 10. 23; 28. 22. Dan. 9. 24. Acts 2. 23;
4. 28; 17. 26. 1 Cor. 2. 2.
DETESTABLE, Deut. 7. 26. Jer. 16. 18. Ezek.
5. 11; 7. 20; 11. 18; 37. 23.
DEVICE, Eccl. 9. 10. Job 5. 12. Ps. 33. 10.
Prov. 1. 31; 12. 2; 14. 17; 19. 21. Jer. 18. 11,
12, 18. 2 Cor. 2. 11.
DEVIL, Mat. 4. 5; 8. 16; 9. 32.
Mat. 4. 1. to be tempted of the *d.*
13. 39. the enemy that sowed is the *d.*
John 6. 70. twelve, and one of you is a *d.*
7. 20. thou hast a *d.,* 8. 48.
8. 44. of your father the *d.,* Acts 13. 10.
13. 2. *d.* having now put into, *see* 27.
Eph. 4. 27. neither give place to *d.*

1 Tim. 3. 6. fall into condemnation of *devil*
2 Tim. 2. 26. recover out of snare of *d.*
Jas. 4. 7. resist *d.* and he will flee
1 Pet. 5. 8. your adversary the *d.*
1 John 3. 8. to destroy the works of *d.*
10. children of God and children of *d.*
Rev. 2. 10. the *d.* shall cast some of
Lev. 17. 7. sacrifice to *devils,* Deut. 32. 17.
2 Chr. 11. 15. priests for *d.* (satyrs)
Ps. 106. 37. sacrificed their sons to *d.*
Mat. 4. 24. which were possessed with *d.,* 8. 16, 28, 33. Luke 4. 41; 8. 36.
10. 8. raise the dead, cast out *d.*
Mark 16. 9. cast . . . seven *d.,* Luke 8. 2.
Luke 10. 17. even *d.* are subject to us
1 Tim. 4. 1. heed to . . . doctrines of *d.*
Jas. 2. 19. *d.* believe and tremble
DEVISE not evil against, Prov. 3. 29.
Prov. 14. 22. do they not err that *d.* evil
Jer. 18. 18. *d.* devices against Jeremiah
Mic. 2. 1. woe to them that *d.* iniquity
Prov. 16. 9. a man's heart *deviseth* his ways
DEVOTED, Lev. 27. 21, 28. Num. 18. 14.
Ps. 119. 38. servant is *d.* to thy fear
Acts 17. 23. I beheld your *devotions*
DEVOUR, Gen. 49. 27. Is. 1. 7; 9. 12.
Prov. 30. 14. to *d.* the poor off the earth
Mat. 23. 14. ye *d.* widows' houses
2 Cor. 11. 20. if a man *d.* you
Gal. 5. 15. if ye bite and *d.* one another
Heb. 10. 27. which *d.* the adversaries
1 Pet. 5. 8. seeking whom he may *d.*
Is. 24. 6. curse *devoured* the earth
Jer. 3. 24. shame hath *d.* the labour
50. 17. Israel the king of Assyria hath *d.*
Hos. 7. 7. *d.* judges, Mal. 3. 11. I will rebuke *devourer*
Ex. 24. 17. *devouring fire,* Is. 29. 6; 30. 27, 30; 33. 14. *d.* words, Ps. 52. 4.
DEVOUT, Luke 2. 25. Acts 2. 5; 8. 2; 10. 2, 7; 13. 50. women, 17. 4, 17; 22. 12.
DEW, Gen. 27. 28. distil as *d.* Deut. 32. 2. of youth, Ps. 110. 3. of herbs, Is. 26. 19.
Hos. 6. 4. goodness is as the early *d.*
14. 5. I will be as *d.* to Israel
Mic. 5. 7. Jacob . . . as *d.* from Lord
DIADEM, Job 29. 14. Is. 28. 5; 62. 3.
DIAL of Ahaz, 2 Ki. 20. 11. Is. 38. 8.
DIE, Gen. 6. 17. Ex. 20. 19. Num. 16. 29.
Gen. 2. 17. thou shalt surely *d.,* 3. 4. 7. 1 Sam. 14. 44; 22. 16. 1 Ki. 2. 37, 42. Jer. 26. 8. Ezek. 3. 18; 33. 8, 14.
Gen. 3. 4. ye shall not surely *d.*
Job 14. 14. if a man *d.* shall he live again?
Ps. 82. 7. but ye shall *d.* like men
Prov. 23. 13. if . . . rod, he shall not *d.*
Eccl. 3. 2. time to *d.* 7. 17. why *d.* before
Is. 22. 13. to-morrow we shall *d.*
Jer. 31. 30. *d.* for his own iniquity
Ezek. 3. 19. *d.* in his iniquity, 33. 8.
18. 31. why will ye *d.* O . . . Israel, 33. 11.
Jonah 4. 3. better to *d.* than live
Mat. 26. 35. though I should *d.* with thee
Luke 20. 36. neither can *d.* any more
John 8. 21. ye shall *d.* in your sins, 24.
11. 50. expedient that one *d.* for people
Rom. 14. 8. we *d.* we *d.* unto the Lord
1 Cor. 9. 15. better for me to *d.* than
Phil. 1. 21. to live is Christ, to *d.* gain
Heb. 9. 27. appointed for men once to *d.*
Rev. 3. 2. that are ready to *d.*
Rom. 5. 6. Christ *died* for the ungodly
8. while yet sinners, Christ *d.* for us

Rom. 6. 10. for in that he *died* he *d.* unto sin
7. 9. command. came, sin revived and I *d.*
14. 9. to this end Christ *d.* and rose
1 Cor. 15. 3. Christ *d.* for our sins
2 Cor. 5. 15. he *d.* for all, that they
1 Thes. 5. 10. who *d.* for us that whether
Heb. 11. 13. these all *d.* in faith, not
Rom. 6. 9. being raised . . . *dieth* no more
14. 7. no man *d.* to himself
2 Cor. 4. 10. *dying,* 6. 9. Heb. 11. 21.
DIFFER, who maketh to, 1 Cor. 4. 7.
1 Cor. 15. 41. star *d.* Rom. 12. 6. gifts *d.*
Lev. 10. 10. *difference,* Jude 22.
Acts 15. 9. no *d.* Rom. 3. 22; 10. 12.
DILIGENCE, do thy, 2 Tim. 4. 9, 21.
Prov. 4. 23. keep thy heart with all *d.*
2 Pet. 1. 5. *give d.* Luke 12. 58. Jude 3.
10.—to make . . . election sure
Rom. 12. 8. ruleth, with *d.* 2 Cor. 8. 7. abound in all *d.*
Deut. 19. 18. *diligent,* Josh. 22. 5.
Prov. 10. 4. hand of *d.* maketh rich
12. 24. hand of *d.* shall bear rule
13. 4. soul of *d.* shall be made fat
Prov. 21. 5. thoughts of *d.* tend to plenty
Ps. 64. 6. *d.* search, 77. 6. *d.* inquisition. Deut. 19. 18.
Prov. 22. 29. man *d.* in his business, 27. 23.
2 Cor. 8. 22. (Titus) proved *d.,* more *d.*
2 Pet. 3. 14. be *d.* to be found of him
Ex. 15. 26. if *diligently* hearken to, Deut. 28. 1. Jer. 17. 24. Zech. 6. 15.
Deut. 4. 9. keep thy soul *d.* . . . forget
6. 17. *d.* keep the commandments, Ps. 119. 4.
Ps. 37. 10. *d.* consider, Jer. 2. 10.
Luke 15. 8. *d.* seek. Heb. 11. 6.—him
Heb. 12. 15. looking *d.* lest . . . fail of
1 Pet. 1. 10. prophets searched *d.* what
DIM, Moses' eye not *d.* Deut. 34. 7.
Is. 8. 22. *dimness* of anguish, Job 17. 7.
DIMINISH, Deut. 4. 2. &c. Prov. 13. 11.
Rom. 11. 12.—*ing* of them riches of Gentiles
DINNER, Prov. 15. 17. Luke 14. 12.
DIP, Ruth 2. 14. John 13. 26. Ps. 68. 23.
DIRECT, Eccl. 10. 10. Is. 45. 13.
Ps. 5. 3. will I *d.* my prayer to thee
Prov. 3. 6. he shall *d.* thy paths
Is. 61. 8. I will *d.* their work in truth
Jer. 10. 23. man that walketh to *d.* his steps
Ps. 119. 5. my ways were *directed* to keep
Is. 40. 13. who hath *d.* the Spirit of Lord
Prov. 16. 9. a man's heart deviseth his way: the Lord *directeth* his steps
DISCERN, Eccl. 8. 5. 2 Sam. 14. 17. *see* 1 Ki. 3. 9, 11. spiritually, 1 Cor. 2. 14.
Mal. 3. 18. *d.* between righteous and
Heb. 5. 14. to *d.* both good and evil
1 Cor. 11. 29. not *discerning* Lord's body
12. 10. to another *d.* of spirits
DISCHARGE, in war, Eccl. 8. 8.
DISCIPLE, John 9. 28; 19. 38.
Mat. 10. 24. *d.* is not above his master
42. cup of water in the name of a *d.*
Luke 14. 26. if . . . he cannot be my *d.*
Acts 21. 16. an old *d.* with whom
John 8. 31. then are ye my *disciples* indeed
DISCORD, soweth, Prov. 6. 14, 19.
DISCRETION, Ps. 112. 5. Prov. 1. 4; 2. 11; 3. 21. without *d.* 11. 22; 19. 11. to *d.* Is. 28. 26. heavens by *d.* Jer. 10. 12.
DISEASE, Ps. 38. 7. Eccl. 6. 2. healing *d.* Mat. 4. 23, &c.; 10. 1.
2 Chr. 16. 12. in his *d.* (Asa) sought not Lord
Diseases of Egypt, Ex. 15. 26.

Ps. 103. 3. who healeth all thy *diseases*
John 6. 2. miracles . . . on . . . *diseased*
DISFIGURE faces, Mat. 6. 16.
DISGRACE not throne, Jer. 14. 21.
DISHONOUR, Ezra. 4. 14. Prov. 6. 33.
Ps. 35. 26. clothed with *d.* 71. 13.
Rom. 1. 24. to *d.* their own bodies
1 Cor. 15. 43. it is sown in *d.* it is raised
2 Cor. 6. 8. approving . . . by honour and *d.*
Mic. 7. 6. son *dishonoureth* his father, Mat. 10. 35.
DISINHERIT (Israel), Num. 14. 12.
DISOBEDIENCE, 2 Cor. 10. 6. children of *d.*
Eph. 2. 2; 5. 6. Col. 3. 6.
Rom. 5. 19. by one man's *d.* many
Heb. 2. 2. if every *d.* received just
DISOBEDIENT, 1 Ki. 13. 26. Neh. 9. 26.
Luke 1. 17. *d.* to wisdom of the just
Rom. 1. 30. *d.* to parents, 2 Tim. 3. 2.
1 Tim. 1. 9. law made for lawless and *d.,*
Tit. 1. 16. in works deny him being . . . *d.*
1 Pet. 3. 20. which sometime were *d.* Tit. 3. 3.
DISORDERLY, 2 Thes. 3. 6, 7, 11.
DISPENSATION, a, 1 Cor. 9. 17. Eph. 3. 2.
Col. 1. 25. *d.* of fulness, Eph. 1. 10.
DISPERSED the (Jews), Is. 11. 12. Esth. 3. 8.
Zeph. 3. 10. John 7. 35.
DISPLEASED, Gen. 38. 10. 2 Sam. 11. 27.
1 Chr. 21. 7. Zech. 1. 2, 15. Is. 59. 15.
Mark 10. 14. 1 Ki. 1. 6. Ps. 60. 1.
Deut. 9. 19. *displeasure,* Ps. 2. 5; 6. 1; 38. 1.
DISPOSING is of the Lord, Prov. 16. 33.
Acts 7. 53. *disposition* of angels
DISPUTE, Job 23. 7. Mark 9. 33. Acts 6. 9; 9. 29;
17. 17; 19. 8, 9.
Rom. 14. 1. doubtful *disputations*
DISQUIETED, Ps. 39. 6; 42. 5, 11.
DISSEMBLE, Josh. 7. 11. Jer. 42. 20. Gal. 2. 13.
Ps. 26. 4. Prov. 26. 24.
Rom. 12. 9. *dissimulation,* Gal. 2. 13.
DISSENSION, Acts 15. 2; 23. 7, 10.
DISSOLVED, Ps. 75. 3. Is. 24. 19. 2 Cor. 5. 1.
2 Pet. 3. 11. Job 30. 22.
DISTINCTLY, read law, Neh. 8. 8.
DISTRACT, Ps. 88. 15. 1 Cor. 7. 35.
DISTRESS, this, Gen. 42. 21. Neh. 9. 37. *d.* of
nations, Luke 21. 25.
Gen. 35. 3. answered in day of my *d.*
2 Sam. 22. 7. in my *d.* I called on the Lord, Ps.
18. 6; 118. 5; 120. 1.
1 Ki. 1. 29. redeemed soul out of *d.*
Ps. 4. 1. enlarged me when in *d.*
Prov. 1. 27. when *d.* and anguish cometh
Is. 25. 4. strength to needy in *d.*
Zeph. 1. 15. day of trouble and *d.* 17.
Rom. 8. 35. from love of Christ? shall . . . *d.*
Gen. 32. 7. *distressed.* 2 Chr. 28. 20. *d.* Ahaz.
2 Sam. 1. 26. I am *d.* for thee
Ezek. 30. 16. Noph have *distresses:* 2 Cor. 6. 4.
approve *in d.:* 12. 10. pleasure—: Ps. 25. 17;
107. 6 &c. out of *d.*
DISTRIBUTE, to poor, Luke 18. 22; ready to,
1 Tim. 6. 18. to saints, Rom. 12. 13.
Job 21. 17. God *distributeth* sorrows in anger
Acts 4. 35. *distribution,* 2 Cor. 9. 13.
DITCH, 2 Ki. 3. 16. Job 9. 31. Ps. 7. 15. Prov.
23. 27. Is. 22. 11. Mat. 15. 14.
DIVERSITIES, 1 Cor. 12. 4, 6, 28.
DIVIDE, Gen. 1. 6, 14. Ex. 14. 16, &c.
Ps. 55. 9. destroy . . . *d.* their tongues
Is. 53. 12. will I *d.* him a portion
Luke 12. 13. to *d.* inheritance, 14.
Gen. 10. 25. *divided* (Peleg), Deut. 32. 8.
Josh. 19. 51. *d.* land by lot, Ezek. 45. 1.

Dan. 2. 41. kingdom *divided,* 5. 28; 11. 4.
Mat. 12. 25. kingdom and house *d.* . . . not stand
1 Cor. 1. 13. is Christ *d.?*
12. 11. *dividing* to every man severally
2 Tim. 2. 15. rightly *d.* the word of
Heb. 4. 12. to the *d.* . . . of soul and spirit
Judg. 5. 15, 16. *divisions,* Luke 12. 51.
DIVINE, Gen. 44. 5. 1 Sam. 28. 8. Prov. 16. 10.
Mic. 3. 11. prophets *d.* for money
Num. 22. 7. *divination,* 23. 23. Deut. 18. 10.
Ezek. 21. 21. Acts 16. 16.
Deut. 18. 14. *diviners,* 1 Sam. 6. 2. Is. 44. 25.
Mic. 3. 6, 7. Zech. 10. 2. Jer. 29. 8.
Heb. 9. 1. ordinances of *d.* service
2 Pet. 1. 3. his *d.* power hath given
4. partakers of the *d.* nature
DIVORCE, Jer. 3. 8. Lev. 21. 14; 22. 13. Num.
30. 9.
Deut. 24. 1, 3. *divorcement,* Is. 50. 1. Mat. 5. 31.
DO, right, Gen. 18. 25.
Mat. 7. 12. men *d.* to you, *d.* ye so
John 15. 5. without me ye can *d.* nothing
Rom. 7. 15. what I would that *d.* I not
Phil. 4. 13. I can *d.* all through Christ
Heb. 4. 13. with whom we have to *d.*
Rev. 19. 10. see thou *d.* it not, 22. 9.
Rom. 2. 13. *doers* of it shall be justified
Jas. 1. 22. be ye *d.* of word and not
His doing, Ps. 64. 9; 66. 5. the Lord's *d.,* 118. 23.
d. good, Acts 10. 38. *d.* God's will, Eph. 6. 6.
doings, Lev. 18. 3. Prov. 20. 11. Is. 1. 16.
Jer. 7. 3. according to his *d.,* 32. 19. Zech. 1. 4.
Well doing, Rom. 2. 7. 1 Pet. 2. 15; 3. 17; 4. 19.
not be weary in—Gal. 6. 9. 2 Thes. 3. 13.
DOCTOR, Acts 5. 34. Luke 2. 46; 5. 17.
DOCTRINE (teaching), Deut. 32. 2.
Is. 28. 9, make to understand *d.?* 29. 24.
Jer. 10. 8. the stock is a *d.* of vanities
Mat. 7. 28, &c. astonished at his *d.*
Mark 1. 27. what new *d.* is this? for
John 7. 17. he shall know of the *d.*
Acts 2. 42. apostles' *d.* and fellowship
Rom. 6. 17. form of *d.* delivered
16. 17. contrary to *d.* ye have learned
Eph. 4. 14. with every wind of *d.*
1 Tim. 5. 17. labour in word and *d.*
6. 3. *d.* according to godliness
2 Tim. 3. 16. scripture profitable for *d.*
Tit. 2. 7. in *d.* showing uncorruptness
10. may adorn *d.* of God our Saviour
Heb. 6. 1. principles of the *d.* of Christ
2. *d.* of baptisms and laying on of hands
Rev. 2. 14. *d.* of Balaam. 15. *d.* of Nicolaitans
Mat. 15. 9. teaching for *doctrines* the command-
ments of men, Col. 2. 22.
1 Tim. 4. 1. giving heed to *d.* of devils
Heb. 13. 9. strange *d.*
DOG, Ex. 11. 7. price of, Deut. 23. 18.
1 Sam. 17. 43. am I a *d.* 2 Ki. 8. 13.
Prov. 26. 11. to his vomit, 2 Pet. 2. 22.
Eccl. 9. 4. living *d.,* better than a dead lion
Is. 56. 10. dumb *dogs.* 11. greedy *d.*
Mat. 7. 6. give not that which is holy to *d.* See
Ex. 22. 31. Mal. 1. 13.
15. 27. *d.* eat of crumbs, Mark 7. 28.
Phil. 3. 2. beware of *d.* Rev. 22. 15. *See* 1 Ki.
21. 19. Mat. 15. 26. Luke 16. 21.
DOMINION, Gen. 1. 26; 27. 40; 37. 8.
Num. 24. 19. he that shall have *d.*
Job 25. 2. *d.* and fear are with him
Ps. 8. 6. over works of thy hands
49. 14. upright shall have *d.* over them
72. 8. *d.* from sea to sea, Zech. 9. 10.

Ps. 145. 13. thy *dominion* endureth through all
Is. 26. 13. other lords had *d.* over us
Dan. 4. 3. his *d.* is from generation to generation,
34. an everlasting *d.* 7. 14.
Rom. 6. 9. death hath no more *d.* over
2 Cor. 1. 24. not have *d.* over your faith
Jude 8. despise *d.* and speak evil of
25. to God *d.* 1 Pet. 4. 11; 5. 11.
Dan. 7. 27. all *dominions* shall serve
Col. 1. 16. thrones or *d.* or principalities
DOOR, Deut. 15. 17. Sol. 5. 4. Judg. 16. 3.
Gen. 4. 7. sin lieth at the *d.*
Ex. 12. 23. Lord will pass over the *d.*
Ps. 84. 10. *d.* keeper in the house of God
141. 3. keep *d.* of my lips
Prov. 26. 14. as *d.* turneth upon hinges, so doth
slothful on his bed.
Hos. 2. 15. valley of Achor *d.* of hope
John 10. 1. entereth not by the *d.* . . . . thief
7. I am *d.* of sheep. 9. I am the *d.*
Acts 14. 27. opened *d.* of faith to Gentiles
Col. 4. 3. God open *d.* of utterance
Jas. 5. 9. judge standeth before *d.*
Rev. 3. 8. set before thee an open *d.* 4. 1.
Ps. 24. 7. lift up ye everlasting *doors*
d. posts, Ex. 12. 7. Deut. 11. 20. Is. 6. 4.
Mal. 1. 10. shut *d.* Mat. 6. 6; 25. 10.
Mat. 24. 33. near, even at the *d.*
DOTE, Jer. 50. 36. Ezek. 23. 5. 1 Tim. 6. 4.
DOUBLE, Gen. 43. 12. Ex. 22. 4. Deut. 21. 17.
2 Ki. 2. 9. *d.* portion of thy spirit
1 Chr. 12. 33. *d.* heart, Ps. 12. 2.
Job 11. 6. secrets of wisdom *d.* to
Is. 40. 2. *d.* for her sins, Jer. 16. 18.
Jer. 17. 18 destroy with *d.* destruction
1 Tim. 3. 8. deacons not *d.* tongued
5. 17. worthy of *d.* honour
Jas. 1. 8. *d.* minded man, 4. 8.
Rev. 18. 6. *d.* to her, fill to her *d.*
DOUBT, Deut. 28. 66. Gal. 4. 20.
Mat. 14. 31. wherefore didst thou *d.*
21. 21. have faith and *d.* not, Mark 11. 23.
John 10. 24. how long . . . make us to *d.*
Rom. 14. 23. he that *doubteth* is damned
Luke 12. 29. neither be ye of *doubtful* mind
Rom. 14. 1. not to *d.* disputations
DOVE, Ps. 55. 6; 68. 13; 74. 19. Sol. 1. 15;
2. 14; 5. 2; 6. 9. Mat. 3. 16. Luke 3. 22. John 1. 32.
Is. 38. 14. mourn as *d.* 59. 11. Ezek. 7. 16.
Hos. 7. 11. Ephraim is like a silly *d.*
Is. 60. 8. fly as *doves* to their windows
Mat. 10. 16. wise . . . and harmless as *d.*
DOWN, Job 1. 7. *d.* sitting, Ps. 139. 2.
Is. 37. 31. *downward,* Eccl. 3. 21.
DRAGON, Ps. 91. 13. Is. 27. 1; 51. 9. Jer.
51. 34. Ezek. 29. 3. Rev. 12. 3—17; 13. 2, 4, 11;
16. 13; 20. 2.
Deut. 32. 33. *dragons,* Job 30. 29. Ps. 44. 19;
74. 13; 148. 7. Is. 13. 22; 34. 13; 43. 20. Jer.
9. 11; 14. 6. Mic. 1. 8. Mal. 1. 3.
DRAW, Gen. 24. 44. city, 2 Sam. 17. 13.
Job 21. 33. every man *d.* after him
Ps. 28. 3. *d.* me not with wicked
Sol. 1. 4. *d.* me, we will run after thee
Is. 5. 18. woe that *d.* iniquity with cords
John 6. 44. except the Father . . . *d.* him
Heb. 10. 38. if any man *d.* back, 39.
Ps. 73. 28. good for me to *d.* near God
Eccl. 12. 1. years *d.* nigh when thou . . . say
Is. 29. 13. *d.* near me with their mouth
Heb. 7. 19. by which we *d.* nigh to God
Jas. 4. 8. *d.* nigh to God, he will *d.*
Jer. 31. 3. with lovingkindness have I *drawn* thee

Ps. 18. 16. *drew* me out of waters, Ex. **2. 10.**
Hos. 11. 4. *d.* them with cords of a man
DREAD, Gen. 9. 2. Ex. 15. 16. Job 13. 11.
Deut. 1. 29. *d.* not, 1 Chr. 22. 13.
2. 25. I put *d.* of thee on nations
Is. 8. 13. let him be your *d.* Job 13. 11.
Gen. 28. 17. how *dreadful* is this place
Dan. 9. 4. great and *d.* God
Mal. 1. 14. my name is *d.* among
4. 5. great and *d.* day of the Lord
DREAM (Joseph), Gen. 37. 5; 40. 5; 41. 7.
Gen. 20. 3. God came to Abimelech in a *d.*
28. 12. (Jacob) *d.* 31. 11. angel to Jacob in *d.*
Num. 12. 6. I speak to prophet in *d.*
Job 20. 8. fly away as a *d.* Ps. 73. 20.
33. 15. in a *d.* in a vision of the night
Ps. 126. 1. we were like them that *d.*
Eccl. 5. 3. *d.* cometh through . . . business
Is. 29. 7. fight against Ariel be as *d.*
Jer. 23. 28. who hath a *d.* . . . . tell a *d.*
Dan. 2. 28. thy *d.* 4. 8. told *d.* 7. 1. had *d.*
Mat. 1. 20. angel appeared in a *d.*
2. 12. warned of God in a *d.,* 13, 19, 22.
27. 19. suffered many things in a *d.*
Acts 2. 17. old men *d. dreams,* Joel 2. 28.
Eccl. 5. 7. in multitude of *d.* . . . vanities
Dreamer (law of), Deut. 13. 1. Jer. 27. 9.
DRINK, Ex. 15. 24; 32. 20. Judg. 7. 5.
Job 21. 20. *d.* of wrath of the Almighty
Ps. 36. 8. *d.* of river of . . . pleasures
60. 3. wine of astonishment, Jer. 25. 15.
69. 21. vinegar to *d.* See Ruth 2. 14.
80. 5. givest them tears to *d.*
110. 7. *d.* of the brook in the way
Prov. 4. 17. *d.* the wine of violence
5. 15. *d.* out of own cistern, 2 Kings 18. 31.
Sol. 5. 1. *d.,* yea, *d.* abundantly
Is. 22. 13. let us eat and *d.* 1 Cor. 15. 32.
65. 13. my servants shall *d.* but ye
Hos. 4. 18. their *d.* is sour: they have
Amos 4. 1. say to masters, Bring, and let us *d.*
Mat. 10. 42. *d.* to one of these little ones
20. 22. able to *d.* of cup, Mark 10. 38.
25. thirsty, and ye gave me *d.,* 37, 42.
26. 27. *d.* ye all of it
29. not *d.* henceforth, 42. except I *d.* it
27. 34. gave him vinegar to *d.*
John 6. 55. my blood is *d.* indeed
7. 37. come to me and *d.* Is. 55. 1.
Rom. 12. 20. enemy thirst give *d.* Prov. **25. 21.**
14. 17. kingdom of God is not *d.*
1 Cor. 10. 4. did all *d.* same spiritual *d.*
21. cannot *d.* the cup of Lord and devils
11. 25. as often as ye *d.* it in remembrance
Lev. 10. 9. not *d.* wine nor *strong drink,* Judg.
13. 4. 1 Sam. 1. 15. Luke 1. 15.
Prov. 20. 1; 31. 4. nor for princes—
31. 5. lest they *d.* and forget the law
Is. 5. 11. follow—22. mingle—
28. 7. priest and prophet erred through—
Mic. 2. 11. prophesy to them of—
Job 15. 16. *drinketh* iniquity like water
John 6. 54. *d.* my blood . . . eternal life
1 Cor. 11. 29. eateth and *d.* unworthily
Heb. 6. 7. earth which *d.* in rain
Rev. 17. 2. *drunk* with wine of fornication
Deut. 21. 20. glutton and *drunkard*
Prov. 23. 21. *d.* and glutton shall come to poverty
26. 9. as thorn to hand of *d.,* so parable
Is. 24. 20. earth shall reel like a *d.*
1 Cor. 5. 11. with railer or *d.* . . . . not eat
Ps. 69. 12. *drunkards,* Is. 28. 1, 3. Joel **1. 5.**
Nah. 1. 10. 1 Cor. 6. 10.

Job 12. 25. stagger like a *drunken* man, Ps.
107. 27. Jer. 23. 9. Is. 19. 14.
Is. 29. 9. *d.*, . . . not with wine, 51. 21.
1 Cor. 11. 21. one is hungry, another *d.*
1 Thes. 5. 7. be *d.* are *d.* in the night
Deut. 29. 19. *drunkenness*, Eccl. 10. 17. Jer.
13. 13. Ezek. 23. 33. Luke 21. 34. Rom.
13. 13. Gal. 5. 21.
DROP, Deut. 33. 28. Judg. 5. 4. Ps. 68. 8.
Ps. 65. 11. thy paths *d.* fatness, 12.
Prov. 5. 3. *d.* as honeycomb, Sol. 4. 11.
Is. 40. 15. nations as a *d.* of a bucket
Sol. 5. 5. my hands *dropped* myrrh
Prov. 19. 13. continual *dropping*, 27. 15.
Drops, he maketh small, Job 36. 27. *d. of* dew,
38. 28.—night, Sol. 5. 5.—blood, Luke 22. 44.
DROSS, Ps. 119. 119. Is. 1. 25. Ezek. 22. 18.
DROWN, Sol. 8. 7. 1 Tim. 6. 9.
DROWSINESS clothe, Prov. 23. 21.
DRY, Judg. 6. 37. Job 13. 25. Prov. 17. 1. Is. 44. 3.
Jer. 4. 11. *d.* tree, Is. 56. 3. Ezek. 17. 24; 37. 2.
Hos. 9. 14.
DUE, Lev. 10. 13. Deut. 18. 3.
1 Chr. 15. 13. sought him not after *d.* order
Prov. 3. 27. withhold not good . . . is *d.*
Mat. 18. 34. pay all that was *d.*
Luke 23. 41. we receive *d.* reward . . . but
Rom. 13. 7. tribute to whom tribute is *d.*
Ps. 104. 27. meat in *due season*, 145. 15. Mat.
24. 45. Luke 12. 42.
Prov. 15. 23. a word in—how good is
Eccl. 10. 17. eat in—for strength
Gal. 6. 9. in—we shall reap, if we
Deut. 32. 35. foot slide in *due time*
1 Cor. 15. 8. as one born out of—
1 Tim. 2. 6. to be testified in—
Tit. 1. 3. hath in—manifested . . . word
DULL of hearing, Mat. 13. 15. Heb. 5. 11.
DUMB, Ezek. 3. 26, &c. Luke 1. 20.
Ps. 38. 13. I was as a *d.* man, 39. 2, 9.
Prov. 31. 8. open thy mouth for *d.*
Is. 35. 6. tongue of *d.* to sing
53. 7. as sheep before shearers is *d.*
56. 10. watchmen are all *d.* dogs
D. idols, Hab. 2. 18. 1 Cor. 12. 2. *devil*, Mat. 9. 33;
12. 22. Mark 9. 25. *d.* ass, 2 Pet. 2. 16.
DUNG of solemn feasts, Mal. 2. 3.
Phil. 3. 8. I count them but *d.*
Dunghill, 1 Sam. 2. 8. Is. 25. 10. Luke 14. 35.
DURABLE riches, Prov. 8. 18.
Is. 23. 18. merchandise . . . for *d.* clothing
DUST, Ex. 8. 17. Job 28. 6; 39. 14. *d.* thou art
and to *d.* shalt return, Gen. 3. 19. Job 10. 9;
34. 15. Ps. 104. 29. Eccl. 3. 20; 12. 7. sleep in
d. Dan. 12. 2. Job 17. 16.
D. before wind, Ps. 18. 42. Is. 29. 5; 41. 2.
Cast d. 2 Sam. 16. 13. Acts 22. 23.—on head, Josh.
7. 6. Job 2. 12.
Exalt out of d. 1 Sam. 2. 8. 1 Ki. 16. 2. Ps. 113. 7.
Lay in d. Ps. 7. 5. *see* Job 16. 15. Ps. 72. 9. Is.
26. 29. Lam. 3. 29. Amos 2. 7. Rev. 18. 19.
Number as d. (Abraham's seed), Gen. 13. 16.
28. 14. *d.* of Jacob, Num. 23. 10. 2 Chr. 1. 9.
see Is. 29. 5. gold—, Job 22. 24. Zech. 9. 3.
flesh—Ps. 78. 27.
Serpent of d. Deut. 32. 24. Is. 65. 25.
Small as d. Ps. 18. 42. stamp—Deut. 9. 21.
2 Ki. 23. 12. (metaph.), 2 Sam. 22. 43. 2 Ki. 13. 7.
Gen. 18. 27. am but *d. and* ashes
Job 30. 19. become like—, 42. 6. repent in—
Deut. 28. 24. make rain *d.* *See* Is. 5. 24.
Ps. 22. 15. brought me into *d.* of death
30. 9. shall the *d.* praise thee

Ps. 102. 14. thy servants . . . favour *dust* thereof
103. 14. remembereth that we are *d.*
Mat. 10. 14. shake off *d.* Acts 13. 51.
DUTY (rights) of marriage, Ex. 21. 10.
2 Chr. 8. 14. as *d.* of every day required
Eccl. 12. 13. this is the whole *d.* of man
Luke 17. 10. which was our *d.* to do
DWELL in holy hill, Ps. 15. 1. Is. 33. 16.
Ps. 23. 6. *d.* in house of Lord for ever, 27. 4.
84. 10. than to *d.* in tents of wickedness
120. 5. that I *d.* in tents of Kedar
132. 14. here will I *d.* for I desired
Is. 33. 14. who *d.* with devouring fire
Rom. 8. 9. Spirit of God *d.* in you, 1 Cor. 3. 16.
2 Cor. 6. 16. I will *d.* in them, Ezek. 43. 7.
Eph. 3. 17. that Christ may *d.* in hearts
Col. 1. 19. that in him should all fulness *d.*
3. 16. let the word of Christ *d.* in you richly
1 John 4. 13. know that we *d.* in him
Rev. 21. 3. he will *d.* with them, and
John 6. 56. *dwelleth* in me, and I in him
14. 10. Father that *d.* in me, he doeth
17. Spirit of truth; . . . *d.* with you
Acts 7. 48. *d.* not in temples, 17. 24.
Rom. 7. 17. sin that *d.* in me, 20.
18. in my flesh *d.* no good thing
Col. 2. 9. in Christ *d.* all fulness of Godhead
2 Tim. 1. 14. Holy Ghost which *d.* in us
Jas. 4. 5. spirit which *d.* in us lusteth
2 Pet. 3. 13. wherein *d.* righteousness
1 John 3. 17. how *d.* the love of God in him
4. 12. God *d.* in us, and his love is
15. confesseth Jesus is Son of God, God *d.* in him,
16. *d.* in love, *d.* in God
2 John 2. truth's sake which *d.* in us
1 Tim. 6. 16. *dwelling* in light
Heb. 11. 9. *d.* in tabernacles with Isaac
2 Pet. 2. 8. that righteous (Lot) *d.* among them
Ps. 87. 2. more than all *dwellings* of Jacob
John 1. 14. Word made flesh and *dwelt*
Acts 13. 17. *d.* as strangers in Egypt
2 Tim. 1. 5. faith *d.* first in grandmother

E

EAGLE, Deut. 28. 49. as swift as the *e.* flieth
Ezek. 17. 3. *See* Hab. 1. 8. Hos. 8. 1.
32. 11. as *e.* stirreth nest, beareth
Job 9. 26. *e.* hasteth to prey, Mat. 24. 28.
39. 27. mount as *e.* Is. 40. 31.
Ps. 103. 5. renewed like *e.*
Prov. 30. 19. too wonderful . . . way of *e.* in air
Jer. 49. 16. nest high as *e.* Obad. 4.
Mic. 1. 16. enlarge thy baldness as *e.*
Rev. 4. 7. (beast), Ezek. 10. 14. Dan. 7. 4. *See*
Lev. 11. 13. Prov. 23. 5. Dan. 4. 33.
12. 14. woman wings of great *e.*
Ex. 19. 4. bare on *eagles'* wings
2 Sam. 1. 23. swifter than *eagles*, Jer. 4. 13.
Prov. 30. 17. young *e.* eat it, Job 39. 30.
Lam. 4. 19. persecutors swifter than *e.*
EAR, bore his, Ex. 21. 6. Deut. 15. 17.
Ex. 29. 20. blood on tip of *e.* Lev. 8. 23.
2 Ki. 19. 16. bow down *e.* Ps. 31. 2; 86. 1.
2 Chr. 6. 40. *e.* attent, Ps. 130. 2. Neh. 1. 6.
Job 4. 12. mine *e.* received a little thereof
12. 11. Doth not *e.* try words, 34. 3.
36. 10. God openeth man's *e.* 15; 33. 16.
42. 5. heard of thee by hearing of *e.*
Ps. 94. 9. He that planted the *e.* shall
Prov. 15. 31. *e.* that heareth reproof
20. 12. The hearing *e.* and seeing eye
25. 12. wise reprover on an obedient *e.*

Is. 48. 8. time thine *ear* was not opened
50. 5. Lord God hath opened mine *e.*, and
Jer. 6. 10. *e.* uncircumcised, Acts 7. 51.
Amos 3. 12. As shepherd . . . piece of an *e.*
Luke 12. 3. spoken in *e.* 22. 50. (Malchus)
1 Cor. 2. 9. nor *e.* heard; 12. 16. if *e.* say
Give ear (to prayer), Ps. 5. 1; 17. 1; 39. 12; 54. 2;
    55. 1; 80. 1; 86. 6; 141. 1. —O heavens, Deut.
    32. 1. Is. 1. 2. —O princes, Judg. 5. 3. —O
    my people, Ps. 78. 1. *See* Is. 1. 10; 51. 4;
    —careless daughter, 32. 9. —house of king,
    Hos. 5. 1.—all inhabitants of world, Ps.
    49. 1. Is. 8. 9.—of land, Joel 1. 2. *See* 2 Chr.
    24. 19. Neh. 9. 30.
Ps. 17. 6. *incline ear* (to prayer), 71. 2; 88. 2;
    102. 2; 116. 2. Is. 37. 17. Dan. 9. 18.
45. 10.—, forget. 49. 4. —to parable
78. 1. —to words of my mouth, 4. 20.
Is. 55. 3. —and come unto me: hear
Jer. 7. 24; 11. 8. *nor inclined their ear*, 17. 23;
    25. 4; 35. 15; 44. 5.
Stop e. adder, Ps. 58. 4.—at (poor's) cry, *see* Is.
    33. 15. Zech. 7. 11. *e.* of deaf shall be unstopped,
    Is. 35. 5.
Deut. 29. 4. eyes to see and *ears* to hear
2 Sam. 7. 22. heard with *e.* Job 28. 22. Ps. 44. 1.
22. 7. my cry into his *e.* Jas. 5. 4.
Job 15. 21. a dreadful sound in his *e.*
33. 16. God openeth (man's) *e.* 36. 10, 15.
Ps. 34. 15. his *e.* open to cry, 1 Pet. 3. 12.
40. 6. my *e.* hast thou opened
115. 16. (idols) *have e. and hear not.* (Judah)—,
    Jer. 5. 21.
Is. 6. 10. make *e.* heavy, Mat. 13. 15. *See*
    Acts 28. 27. Rom. 11. 8; Is. 59. 1. Lord's *e.*
    not heavy that it cannot hear
32. 3. *e.* of hearers shall hearken
43. 8. deaf . . . have *e.* Jer. 5. 21. Ezek. 12. 2.
Mat. 11. 15. *e.* to hear, let him hear, 13. 9, 43.
    Rev. 2. 7; 3. 6; 13. 9.
13. 16. blessed your *e.*, . . . they hear
Mark 7. 33. Jesus put his fingers into *e.*
8. 18. having *e.* hear ye not?
Luke 9. 44. let sayings sink into your *e. See*
    Prov. 26. 17. Eccl. 1. 8. Ezek. 23. 25.
2 Chr. 6. 40. *thine ear(s)* be attent to
Ps. 10. 17. cause—to hear
Prov. 23. 12. apply—to words of knowledge
Is. 30. 21.—shall hear a word behind
Ezek. 3. 10. hear with—40. 4; 44. 5.
EAR (of corn), in the, Ex. 9. 31. Mark 4. 28. green
    e. Lev. 2. 14; 23. 14. *See* 2 Ki. 4. 42. cut off
    tops of *e.* Job 24. 24. reap, gathereth *e.* Is.
    17. 5.
EAR, to plough (*aro*), Deut. 21. 4. 1 Sam. 8. 12. Is.
    30. 24.
Earing time, Ex. 34. 21. Gen. 45. 6.
EARLY, Gen. 19. 2, 27. John 18. 28; 20. 1.
Ps. 46. 5. God shall help her and that right *e.*
57. 8. will awake *e.* 108. 2.
90. 14. satisfy us *e.* with thy mercy
Prov. 1. 28. seek me *e.* and not find
8. 17. that seek me *e.* shall find me
Is. 26. 9. with spirit I seek thee *e.*
Jer. 7. 13, &c. *rising up e.* and speaking; 11. 7.
    —and protesting; 7. 25; 26. 5, &c. 2 Chr.
36. 15.—and sending; Jer. 32. 33.—& teaching
Hos. 5. 15. in affliction will seek me *e.*
Jas. 5. 7. receive *e.* and latter rain
EARNEST (pledge) of Spirit, 2 Cor. 1. 22; 5. 5.
Eph. 1. 14. *e.* of inheritance
Rom. 8. 19. *e.* expectation of, Phil. 1. 20.
2 Cor. 7. 7. told us of your *e.* desire

Heb. 2. 1. more *earnest* heed
Job 7. 2. servant *earnestly* desireth shadow
Jer. 11. 7. I *e.* protested to fathers
Mic. 7. 3. do evil with both hands *e.*
Luke 22. 44. in agony, prayed more *e.*
1 Cor. 12. 31. covet *e.* the best gifts
2 Cor. 5. 2. in this we groan, *e.* desiring
Jas. 5. 17. prayed *e.* it might not rain
Jude 3. ye should *e.* contend for the faith
EARNETH wages, Hag. 1. 6.
EARRING, Gen. 24. 47; 35. 4. Ex. 32. 2; 35. 22.
    Num. 31. 50. Judg. 8. 24. Job 42. 11. Hos.
    2. 13. Ezek. 16. 12.
EARTH corrupt, Gen. 6. 11, 12, 13.
Gen. 11. 1. whole *e.* of one language
41. 47. *e.* brought forth by handfuls
Ex. 9. 29. *e.* is the Lord's, Deut. 10. 14. Ps.
    24. 1. 1 Cor. 10. 26, 28.
Num. 16. 32. *e.* opened her mouth, 26. 10.
    Deut. 11. 6. Ps. 106. 17. Rev. 12. 16.
Deut. 28. 23. *e.* under thee be iron
32. 1. hear O *e.* words of my mouth
Judg. 5. 4. *e.* trembleth and heavens
1 Sam. 2. 8. pillars of *e.* are Lord's
1 Chr. 16. 31. let *e.* rejoice, Ps. 96. 11.
Job 9. 6. shaketh *e.* out of her place
11. 9. longer than *e.*, broader than sea
16. 18. O *e.* cover not blood, Gen. 4. 10.
26. 7. and hangeth *e.* upon nothing
30. 8. base men, viler than the *e.*
38. 4. I laid the foundations of the *e.*
Ps. 33. 5. *e.* is full of the goodness of Lord
65. 9. visitest the *e.* and waterest it
67. 6. shall yield increase, 85. 12.
78. 69. like *e.* established for ever
89. 11. heaven and *e.* are thine
97. 4. *e.* saw and trembled, 2 Sam. 22. 8.
104. 24. *e. is full of* thy riches; Is. 6. 3. whole
    e.—thy glory, Ps. 72. 19.
115. 16. given to children of men
139. 15. in lowest parts of the *e.*
Prov. 25. 3. heaven for height and *e.* for depth
Eccl. 1. 4. *e.* abideth for ever
Is. 11. 4. smite *e.* with rod of mouth
9. *e.* full of knowledge of Lord, Hab. 2. 14.
13. 13. *e.* shall remove out of her place
24. 1. Lord maketh the *e.* empty
4. *e.* mourneth and fadeth, 33. 9.
5. *e.* is defiled. 19. *e.* is utterly broken down
20. *e.* shall reel to and fro like a drunkard
26. 19. *e.* shall cast out the dead
66. 1. *e.* is my footstool, where is
Jer. 22. 29. O *e. e. e.* hear word of the Lord
Ezek. 34. 27. *e.* shall yield increase
43. 2. the *e.* shined with his glory
Hos. 2. 22. *e.* shall hear the corn, and
Hab. 3. 3. and *e.* was full of his praise
Mat. 13. 5. stony ground . . . not much *e.*
John 3. 31. he that is of *e.* is earthly
Heb. 6. 7. *e.* which drinketh in rain
Ps. 67. 2. way be known *upon earth*
73. 25. none—I desire beside thee
Eccl. 5. 2. God is in heaven and thou—
7. 20. not a just man—sinneth not
10. 7. princes walking as servants—
Luke 5. 24. Son of man power—to forgive
Col. 3. 5. mortify members—
Earthen, Lev. 6. 28. Jer. 19. 1; 32. 14. Lam.
    4. 2. 2 Cor. 4. 7. *earthly*, John 3. 12, 31.
    2 Cor. 5. 1. Phil. 3. 19. Jas. 3. 15. *earthy*,
    1 Cor. 15. 47.
Earthquake, 1 Ki. 19. 11, 12. Is. 29. 6. Amos
    1. 1. Zech. 14. 5. Mat. 24. 7; 27. 54.

Rev. 8. 5; 11. 19. *A great earthquake,* Mat. 28. 2.
Acts 16. 26. Rev. 6. 12; 16. 8.
EASE, Job 12. 5; 16. 12; 21. 23. Ps. 25. 13;
123. 4. Deut. 28. 65. Is. 32. 9, 11. Jer. 46. 27;
48. 11. Ezek. 23. 42. Amos 6. 1. Zech. 1. 15.
Is. 1. 24. I will *e.* me of adversaries
Luke 12. 19. take thine *e.* and be merry
Mat. 9. 5. *easier,* 19. 24. Luke 16. 17.
Heb. 12. 1. sin which doth so *easily* beset us
Prov. 14. 6. knowledge is *easy* to him
Mat. 11. 30. my yoke is *e.* . . . my burden light
1 Cor. 14. 9. words *e.* to be understood
Jas. 3. 17. gentle, *e.* to be entreated
EAST, Gen. 28. 14. Mat. 2. 1. Ps. 103. 12.
Is. 43. 5. bring thy seed from the *e.*
Mat. 8. 11. many shall come from the *e.*
Gen. 41. 6. *east wind,* Ex. 14. 21. Ps. 48. 7. Is.
27. 8. Hos. 13. 15. Hab. 1. 9.
Children of the e. Judg. 6. 3. Gen. 29. 1.
EAT, Gen. 2. 16. of every tree . . . freely *e.*
Gen. 2. 17. of tree of knowledge thou shalt not *e.*
3. 14. *e.* dust. 17. in sorrow *e.* 18. *e.* herb of field.
19. in sweat of thy face *e.* bread
18. 8. angels, . . . did *e. See* Luke 24. 43.
27. 4. savoury meat, . . . that I may *e.*
Ex. 10. 5. (locusts), Joel 1. 4. Amos 7. 2.
12. 48. no uncircumcised shall *e.* thereof
16. 35. Israel did *e.* manna 40 years, until
Lev. 6. 29, &c. All the males . . . priests *e.* . . . it
is *most holy;* (viz., meat offering, 2. 3; 6. 18.
shewbread, 24. 9. *e. the holy* thing, 22. 14.)
See Deut. 18. 1. 1 Sam. 2. 36.
21. 22. (priest) *e.* bread of his God, both of *most
holy & holy. See* Ezra 2. 63. Ezek. 42. 13.
7. 21. (offerer) *e.* of the flesh of peace offering,
22. 30. *e.* sin offering in the holy place,
10. 17. Ezek. 44. 29. Hos. 8. 13.
8. 31. *e.* . . . at door of the tabernacle; 10. 13. *e.
in* the holy place. 14. —a clean place. Num.
18. 31. —every place
11. 2. beasts which ye shall *e.* [CLEAN.]
22. *e.* locusts. *See* Mat. 3. 4.
19. 25. planted . . . in fifth year *e.* the fruit
26. 38. land *e.* you up, Num. 13. 32.
Num. 6. 3. Nazarite . . . neither *e.* grapes
11. 5. fish we *e.* in Egypt, melons, leeks
Deut. 4. 28. gods which neither *e.* nor
14. 21. shall not *e.* anything that dieth
23. *e.* before Lord God tithe, firstlings
28. 55. *e.* children, 2 Ki. 6. 29. Lam. 2. 20.
Ezek. 5. 10. *e.* sons, Lev. 26. 29.
32. 38. gods, . . . *e.* the fat of their sacrifices
2 Sam. 9. 13, *e.* at the king's table, 19. 42.
1 Ki. 2. 7. 2 Ki. 25. 29. Dan. 1. 8.
1 Ki. 13. 9. *e.* no bread, drink no water
19. 5. angel touched . . . said, Arise and *e.*
21. 23. dogs shall *e.* Jezebel, 14. 11.
2 Ki. 4. 43. an hundred men? . . . *e.* and leave
Neh. 8. 10. *e.* the fat, drink the sweet
Job 1. 4. feasted, and called for their three sisters
to *e.* and drink
Ps. 22. 26. meek shall *e.* and be satisfied
53. 4. *e.* up my people as bread, 14. 4.
78. 25. did *e.* angels' food, John 6. 31.
106. 28. They . . . *ate* sacrifices of dead
128. 2. the labour of thine hands. *See* Eccl.
2. 24; 3. 13; 5. 18, &c. Is. 62. 9.
Prov. 1. 31. *e.* the fruit of their own way
13. 2. *e.* good by fruit of mouth, 18. 21.
25. 16. honey? so much as sufficient
Eccl. 9. 7. *e.* with joy . . . God accepteth
Sol. 5. 1. *e.,* O friends; drink, yea
Is. 1. 19. if obedient ye shall *e.*

Is. 3. 10. righteous *eat* of doings, Ps. 128. 2.
4. 1. we will *e.* our own bread, only let
7. 15. butter and honey shall he *e.* 22.
9. 20. *e.* his own arm. Jer. 19. 9. *e.* friend's flesh
(for hunger) [CHILDREN.]
11. 7. and the lion shall *e.* straw, 65. 25.
30. 24. young asses *e.* clean provender
37. 30. *e.* this year such as groweth of itself
51. 8. worm shall *e.* them as wool
55. 1. buy and *e.;* yea, come buy
2. *e.* that is good, let your soul delight
61. 6. ye shall *e.* the riches of the Gentiles
65. 4. which *e.* swine's flesh, 66. 17.
13. my servants shall *e.* but ye, 22.
Jer. 15. 16. words . . . I did *e.* Ezek. 3. 1.
Ezek. 4. 9. bread . . . 390 days *e.* thereof
13. Israel *e.* defiled bread among Gentiles
16. *e.* by weight, with care, 12. 18.
22. 9. *e.* upon the mountains, 18. 11.
Dan. 1. 12. let them give us pulse to *e.*
4. 33. did *e.* grass as oxen, Ps. 106. 20.
Hos. 4. 10. *e.* and not have enough
Amos 7. 12. there *e.* bread, and prophesy
9. 14. gardens, and *e.* fruit, Jer. 29. 5.
Mic. 3. 3. *e.* the flesh of my people
Zech. 7. 6. did not ye *e.* for yourselves?
Mat. 6. 25. no thought what ye shall *e.*
26. 26. Jesus said, Take *e.* this is my body,
Mark 14. 22. 1 Cor. 11. 24, 26, 28.
Mark 1. 6. *e.* locusts and wild honey
7. 5. *e.* bread with unwashen hands
28. dogs *e.* of children's crumbs
Luke 10. 8. *e.* things set before you
15. 23. let us *e.,* and be merry
22. 30. ye may *e.* and drink at my table
John 4. 31. Master. *e.* 32. I have meat to *e.*
6. 26. because ye did *e.* of the loaves
53. except ye *e.* the flesh of Son of man
Acts 2. 46. did *e.* . . . with gladness
1 Cor. 5. 11. with such, no not to *e.*
8. 7. some . . . *e.* as a thing offered to an idol
8. neither if we *e.* are we the better
10. 31. whether ye *e.* . . . do all to glory of
God
2 Thes. 3. 10. if not work, neither *e.*
Jas. 5. 3. rust . . . *e.* your flesh as fire
Rev. 2. 7. overcometh . . . *e.* tree of life
10. 9–11. *e.* little book . . . prophesy again
17. 16. shall *e.* her flesh, and burn
E. blood, Gen. 9. 4. flesh with life . . . blood shall ye
not *e., see* Lev. 17. 14. a perpetual statute *e.*
neither fat nor blood, *see* Lev. 3. 17; 17. 12.
Acts 15. 29. *e. with the blood,* 1 Sam. 14. 32.
Ezek. 33. 25.
E. of sacrifice (idolatrous), 1 Cor. 8. 4. Rev. 2. 14.
call to—Ex. 34. 15. Num. 25. 2. *e.* upon
mountains, Ezek. 18. 6; 22. 9. —*e.* bread,
Gen. 31. 54. *e.* bread before God, Ex. 18. 12;
24. 11. Deut. 12. 7. Ezek. 44. 3. 1 Chr.
29. 22. *e.* flesh, Deut. 12. 27. Jer. 7. 21. to
the high place to *e.,* 1 Sam. 9. 13.
Deut. 26. 14. not *eaten* in mourning
Ps. 69. 9. zeal of [for] thine house hath *e.* me up,
John 2. 17. Ps. 119. 139.
Prov. 9. 17. bread *e.* in secret is pleasant
Hos. 10. 13. having *e.* fruit of lies
Mat. 14. 21. *e.* were 5,000; 15. 38. —4,000
Luke 13. 26. *e.* . . . in thy presence
Acts 12. 23. (Herod) was *e.* of worms
Judg. 14. 14. out of *eater* came forth meat
Is. 55. 10. seed to the sower, bread to *e.*
Nah. 3. 12. fall into the mouth of the *e.*
Eccl. 4. 5. fool . . . *eateth* his own flesh

Mat. 9. 11. why *eateth* your master with publicans
and sinners, Luke 15. 2.
John 6. 54. whoso *e.* my flesh and drinketh
58. he that *e.* this bread shall live
Rom. 14. 6. he that *e. e.* to Lord; he that *e.* not,
to the Lord he *e.* not
14. 20. for that man who *e.* with offence
1 Cor. 11. 29. *e.* unworthily, *e.* damnation
1 Sam. 30. 16. *eating* and drinking, and dancing,
Ex. 32. 6. 1 Cor. 10. 7.
Mat. 11. 18. John came neither *e.* nor drinking.
19. Son of man came *e.*
24. 38. were *e.* and drinking, Luke 17. 27.
26. 26. as they were *e.* Jesus took
EDIFY (build up), Rom. 14. 19. 1 Thes. 5. 11.
1 Cor. 8. 1; 10. 23; 14. 17. Acts 9. 31.
Rom. 15. 2. please neighbour . . . to *edification*
1 Cor. 14. 3. speak unto men to *e.*
2 Cor. 10. 8. authority, for *e.* 13. 10.
1 Cor. 14. 12. may excel to *edifying*
2 Cor. 12. 19. we do all for your *e.*
Eph. 4. 12. for the *e.* of the body of Christ
16. increase of body to the *e.* in love
29. but that which is good to the use of *e.*
1 Tim. 1. 4. questions rather than godly *e.*
EFFECT of every vision, Ezek. 12. 23.
Is. 32. 17. *e.* of righteousness quietness
Mat. 15. 6. commdt. of God *of none effect*
Mark 7. 13. making word of God—
Rom. 3. 3. unbelief make faith of God without *e.*
9. 6. word of God had taken none *e.*
1 Cor. 1. 17. lest cross of Christ be made—
Gal. 5. 4. Christ is become of no *e.* to you
1 Cor. 16. 9. great door and *effectual*
2 Cor. 1. 6. which is *e.* in enduring
Eph. 3. 7. *e.* working of his power
Philem. 6. faith may become *e.* by
Jas. 5. 16. *e.* fervent prayer of righteous
Gal. 2. 8. *effectually*, 1 Thes. 2. 13.
EFFEMINATE, 1 Cor. 6. 9.
EGG, Deut. 22. 6. Job 6. 6; 39. 14. Is. 10. 14;
59. 5. Jer. 17. 11. Luke 11. 12.
ELDER, Gen. 10. 21. 2 John 1. 3 John 1.
Gen. 25. 23. *e.* serve younger, Rom. 9. 12.
1 Tim. 5. 1. rebuke not an *e.* but entreat
2. entreat *e.* women as mothers
1 Pet. 5. 1. *elders*, who am also an *e.*
5. younger submit yourselves to *e.*
Deut. 32. 7. ask *e.* they will tell thee
Ezra 10. 8. according to counsel of *e.*
Joel 2. 16. assemble *e.* Ps. 107. 32.
Acts 14. 23. ordained *e.* in every church
15. 23. *e.* and brethren send greeting
20. 17. Ephesus, called *e.* of church
1 Tim. 5. 17. *e.* rule well be counted
Tit. 1. 5. ordain *e.* in every city
Heb. 11. 2. *e.* obtained good report
Jas. 5. 14. sick . . . call for *e.* of church
Rev. 4. 4. four and twenty *e.* sitting, 5. 6; 11. 16;
19. 4; 7. 11; 14. 3.
ELECT, *chosen, choice one.*
Is. 42. 1. *e.* in whom my soul delighteth
65. 9. mine *e.* shall inherit it . . . dwell there
Mat. 24. 22. for *e.*'s sake days shortened
24. if possible deceive the very *e.*
31. gather his *e.* from the four winds
Luke 18. 7. God avenge his own *e.*
Rom. 8. 33. to the charge of God's *e.*
Col. 3. 12. put on as the *e.* of God
1 Tim. 5. 21. before the *e.* angels
2 Tim. 2. 10. I endure all things for *e.*'s sake
Tit. 1. 1. according to faith of God's *e.*
1 Pet. 1. 2. *e.* according to foreknowledge of God

1 Pet. 2. 6. corner stone, *elect*, precious
2 John 1. *e.* lady. 13. *e.* sister
1 Pet. 5. 13. church *elected* with you
Rom. 9. 11. purpose . . . according to *election*
11. 5. remnant according to the *e.* of grace
7. the *e.* hath obtained, the rest blinded
1 Thes. 1. 4. knowing . . . your *e.* of God
2 Pet. 1. 10. make your calling and *e.* sure
ELEMENTS (rudiments), Gal. 4. 9.
ELOQUENT, Ex. 4. 10. Acts 18. 24.
EMPTY pit, Gen. 37. 24. ears, 41. 27. pitchers,
Judg. 7. 16. 2 Ki. 4. 3.
Ex. 23. 15. none appear before me *e.* 34. 20.
Deut. 16. 16.
Deut. 15. 13. go away *e.* Gen. 31. 42.
2 Sam. 1. 22. sword returned not *e.*
Hos. 10. 1. Israel is an *e.* vine
Luke 1. 53. sent *e.* away, Mark 12. 3.
Is. 34. 11. stones of *emptiness*   [5. 20.
EMULATION, (rivalry) Rom. 11. 14. (envy) Gal.
ENCHANTMENT, Lev. 19. 26. Num. 23. 23.
Eccl. 10. 11. Is. 47. 9.
END of all flesh is come, Gen. 6. 13.
Deut. 32. 20. see what their *e.* shall be
Ps. 37. 37. the *e.* of that man is peace
39. 4. make me to know mine *e.*
73. 17. then understood I their *e.*
102. 27. and thy years shall have no *e.*
119. 96. seen an *e.* of all perfection
Prov. 5. 4. her *e.* is bitter as wormwood
Eccl. 4. 8. there is no *e.* of his labour
7. 2. mourning, . . . for that is the *e.* of all
8. the *e.* is better than the beginning
Is. 9. 7. of his government shall be no *e.*
Jer. 5. 31. what will ye do in the *e.*
17. 11. days, and at his *e.* shall be a fool
31. 17. and there is hope in thine *e.*
Lam. 4. 18. our *e.* is come, our *e.* is near
Ezek. 7. 2, 6. Amos 8. 2.
Ezek. 21. 25. when iniquity have an *e.*
Dan. 8. 19. at time appointed the *e.*
Hab. 2. 3. at the *e.* it shall speak
Mat. 13. 39. harvest is *e.* of world
24. 3. what . . . sign of the *e.* of world
6. but the *e.* is not yet, Luke 21. 9.
Rom. 6. 21. the *e.* of those things is death
22. ye have . . . and the *e.* everlasting life
14. 9. to this *e.* Christ both died and rose
1 Tim. 1. 5. *e.* of commandment is charity
Heb. 6. 8. whose *e.* is to be burned
16. oath . . . to them an *e.* of all strife
7. 3. beginning of days, nor *e.* of life
Jas. 5. 11. seen the *e.* of the Lord
1 Pet. 1. 9. receiving the *e.* of your faith
4. 7. the *e.* of all things is at hand
17. *e.* of those that obey not the gospel
Rev. 21. 6. beginning and *e.* 22. 13; 1. 8. 1 Sam.
3. 12.
Jer. 4. 27. *make a full end*, 5. 10, 18; 30. 11. Ezek.
11. 13.
Num. 23. 10. *last end*, Jer. 12. 4. Lam. 1. 9;
Dan. 8. 19;
Deut. 8. 16. *latter end*, 32. 29. Job 42. 12. Prov.
19. 20. 2 Pet. 2. 20.
Ps. 119. 33. *unto the end*, Dan. 6. 26. Mat.
24. 13; 28. 20. John 13. 1. 1 Cor. 1. 8. Heb.
3. 6, 14; 6. 11. Rev. 2. 26.
1 Tim. 1. 4. *endless*, Heb. 7. 16.
Ps. 22. 27. *ends* of the world remember
67. 7. *all ends of earth* shall fear him, Zech. 9. 10.
98. 3.—have seen the salvation, Is. 52. 10.
Prov. 17. 24. eyes of fool in—
Is. 45. 22. be ye saved—, Acts 13. 47.

1 Cor. 10. 11. *ends of the world* are come
ENDUED, Gen. 30. 20. 2 Chr. 2. 12, 13. Luke
24. 49. Jas. 3. 13.
ENDURE, Job 8. 15; 31. 23.
Gen. 33. 14. as children are able to *e.*
Ps. 30. 5. weeping may *e.* for a night
102. 26. they shall perish, but thou shalt *e.*
Prov. 27. 24. crown *e.* to every generation
Ezek. 22. 14. can thine heart *e.* or
Mark 4. 17. no root, and *e.* but for a time
13. 13. that shall *e.* unto end shall
2 Tim. 2. 3. *e.* hardness as a soldier
10. all things for the elect's sake
4. 5. watch thou, *e.* afflictions, do the
Heb. 12. 7. if ye *e.* chastening, God
Jas. 5. 11. we count happy which *e.*
Ps. 81. 15. should have *endured* for ever
Rom. 9. 22. *e.* with much longsuffering
2 Tim. 3. 11. what persecutions I *e.*
Heb. 6. 15. patiently *e.* he obtained
11. 27 *e.* as seeing him who is invisible
12. 2. *e.* cross. 3. *e.* contradiction
Ps. 30. 5. his anger *endureth* but a
100. 5. his truth *e.* to all generations
145. 13. thy dominion *e.* throughout
Mat. 10. 22. that *e.* to end shall be saved, 24. 13.
Mark 13. 13.
John 6. 27. meat which *e.* unto life
1 Cor. 13. 7. charity *e.* all things
Jas. 1. 12. blessed man that *e.* temptation
Ps. 9. 7. *endure for ever*, the Lord, 102. 12;
104. 31; his name, Ps. 72. 17; his seed,
89. 29, 36.
1 Chr. 16. 34, 41. *endureth for ever*, his mercy,
2 Chr. 5. 13; 7. 3; 20. 21. Ezra 3. 11. Ps.
106. 1; 107. 1; 118. 1, &c.; 136. 1–26.
Ps. 138. 8. Jer. 33. 11. his righteousness—,
Ps. 111. 3; 112. 3. his praise—, Ps. 111. 10.
truth of Lord—, Ps. 117. 2. thy judgments—,
119. 160. thy name—, 135. 13. word of Lord—,
1 Pet. 1. 25.
Ps. 19. 9. fear of the Lord . . . *enduring* for ever
Heb. 10. 34. better and *e.* substance
ENEMY, Ex. 15. 6, 9. Ps. 7. 5.
Ex. 23. 22. I . . . an *e.* to thine enemies
Deut. 32. 27. not that I feared wrath of the *e.*
1 Sam. 24. 19. find his *e.* will he let
Job 33. 10. counteth me for his *e.*
Ps. 7. 5. let the *e.* persecute my soul
8. 2. mightest still the *e.* and avenger
Prov. 27. 6. kisses of *e.* are deceitful
1 Cor. 15. 26. the last *e.* destroyed is death
Gal. 4. 16. am I become your *e.*
2 Thes. 3. 15. count him not as *e.*
Jas. 4. 4. friend of world, *e.* of God
1 Ki. 21. 20. *mine enemy*, Ps. 7. 4. Mic. 7. 8, 10.
Job 16. 9. Lam. 2. 22.
Ex. 23. 4. *thine enemy*, Prov. 25. 21. Rom.
12. 20. Mat. 5. 43.
Mic. 7. 6. man's *enemies* . . . men of own house
Rom. 5. 10. if when *e.* we were reconciled
1 Cor. 15. 25. put all *e.* under his feet
Col. 1. 21. *e.* in your mind by wicked
Gen. 22. 17. *his enemies*, Ps. 68. 1, 21; 112. 8;
132. 18. Prov. 16. 7. Is. 59. 18; 66. 6. Heb.
10. 13.
Deut. 32. 41. *mine enemies*, Ps. 18. 37, 48; 23. 5;
119. 98; 139. 22; 143. 12. Is. 1. 24. Luke 19. 27.
Deut. 32. 31. *our enemies*, Luke 1. 71, 74.
Ex. 23. 22. *thine enemies*, Num. 10. 35. Deut.
28. 48. &c., 33. 29. Judg. 5. 31. Ps. 21. 8;
92. 9; 110. 1. Mat. 22. 44. Heb. 1. 13.
Gen. 3. 15. I will put *enmity* between

Rom. 8. 7. carnal mind is *enmity* against God
Eph. 2. 15. abolished *e.* 16. slain *e.*
ENGAGED his heart, Jer. 30. 21.
ENJOIN, Job 36. 23. Heb. 9. 20. Philem. 8.
ENJOY, Num. 36. 8. Deut. 28. 41.
Lev. 26. 34. land *e.* her sabbaths, 43.
Acts 24. 2. we *e.* great quietness
Heb. 11. 25. *e.* pleasures of sin for season
ENLARGE, Ex. 34. 24. Mic. 1. 16.
Gen. 9. 27. God shall *e.* Japheth
Is. 54. 2. *e.* the place of thy tent
2 Sam. 22. 37. *enlarged* steps, Ps. 18. 36.
Ps. 4. 1. thou hast *e.* me when in distress
25. 17. troubles of my heart are *e.*
Is. 5. 14. hell hath *e.* herself, and opened
2 Cor. 6. 11. our heart is *e.* 13.
Esth. 4. 14. *enlargement*
Deut. 33. 20. he that *enlargeth* Gad
Hab. 2. 5. *e.* his desire as hell
ENLIGHTEN darkness, Ps. 18. 28. [*enlightened*
Eph. 1. 18. eyes of your understanding being
Heb. 6. 4. impossible for those once *e.*
ENOUGH, I have, Gen. 33. 9, 11.
Gen. 45. 28. it is *e.* Joseph . . . is yet alive
Ex. 36. 5. people bring more than *e.*
2 Sam. 24. 16. Lord said to angel, It is *e.*
1 Ki. 19. 4. it is *e.* . . . take way my life
Prov. 30. 15, 16. say not, it is *e.*
Mat. 10. 25. it is *e.* for disciple that
Mark 14. 41. it is *e.* . . . hour is come
Luke 15. 17. bread *e.* and to spare
ENRICHED, 1 Cor. 1. 5. 2 Cor. 9. 11.
Ps. 65. 9. *enrichest* it with the river of God
ENSAMPLE, 1 Cor. 10. 11. Phil. 3. 17. 1 Thes.
1. 7. 2 Thes. 3. 9. 1 Pet. 5. 3. 2 Pet. 2. 6.
ENSIGN, Is. 5. 26; 30. 17. Zech. 9. 16.
Is. 11. 10. stand for *e.* to the people, 12.
Ps. 74. 4. set up their *ensigns* for signs
ENTANGLE, Mat. 22. 15. Gal. 5. 1. 2 Tim.
2. 4. 2 Pet. 2. 20.
ENTER, Gen. 7. 13; 19. 23. Ex. 33. 9. Num.
20. 24. Dan. 11. 17, 40, 41.
Ps. 100. 4. *e.* his gates with thanksgiving
118. 20. gate . . . the righteous shall *e.*
Is. 2. 10. *e.* into the rock and hide
26. 20. *e.* into thy chambers, and shut
57. 2. righteous . . . shall *e.* into peace
Mat. 5. 20. no case *e.* into kingdom
6. 6. when thou prayest, *e.* into thy closet
7. 21. shall *e.* into kingdom of heaven
18. 8. it is better to *e.* into life halt
19. 24. hard for rich men to *e.* into the kingdom of
heaven, Mark 10. 25. Luke 18. 25.
25. 21. servant . . . *e.* thou into joy of thy Lord
Mark 14. 38. watch and pray, lest ye *e.* into
temptation, Luke 22. 46
Luke 13. 24. seek to *e.* but not able
24. 26. suffered . . . and *e.* into his glory
John 3. 4. can he *e.* the second time
5. he cannot *e.* into the kingdom of God
10. 9. I am the door; by me if any man *e.*
Acts 14. 22. thro' tribulation *e.* kingdom of God
Heb. 4. 3. believed do *e.* into rest
10. 19. *e.* into holiest by blood of Jesus
Rev. 15. 8. no man able to *e.* temple
22. 14. thro' gates enter into the city
Job 22. 4. will he *enter into* judgment, 34. 23.
not—judgment, Ps. 143. 2.
Prov. 4. 14.—path of wicked, and go not
23. 10.—the fields of fatherless
Mat. 26. 41. that ye—temptation
Ps. 119. 130. *entrance*, 2 Pet. 1. 11.
Luke 11. 52. *entered* not yourselves

John 4. 38. ye *entered* into their labours
Rom. 5. 12. sin *e.* into the world
5. 20. law *e.* that offence might abound
Heb. 4. 6. *e.* not because of unbelief
John 10. 1. *entereth* not by door, but climbeth up
Mat. 23. 13. *entering*, Luke 11. 52. Mark 4. 19;
   7. 15. 1 Thes. 1. 9. Heb. 4. 1.
ENTERTAIN strangers, Heb. 13. 2.
ENTICE, Ex. 22. 16. Deut. 13. 6. (Ahab) 2 Chr.
   18. 19, 20, 21. Prov. 1. 10.
Job 31. 27. *enticed*, Jas. 1. 14.
1 Cor. 2. 4. *enticing* words, Col. 2. 4.
ENTREAT, Gen. 12. 16; 23. 8. Ex. 8. 8; 9. 28;
   10. 17. Jer. 15. 11.
1 Sam. 2. 25. man sin who shall *e.*
1 Cor. 4. 13. being defamed, we *e.*
1 Tim. 5. 1. but *e.* him as a father
Jas. 3. 17. easy to be *entreated*
Prov. 18. 23. poor useth *entreaties*
2 Cor. 8. 4. praying us with much *entreaty*
ENVY slayeth silly one, Job 5. 2.
Prov. 3. 31. *e.* not the oppressor
14. 30. *e.* is the rottenness of bones
23. 17. let not thy heart *e.* sinners
27. 4. who is able to stand before *e.*
Is. 11. 13. *e.* of Ephraim shall depart
Ezek. 35. 11. do according to Edom's *e.*
Mat. 27. 18. for *e.* they delivered him
Acts 7. 9. moved with *e.* 17. 5; 13. 45.
Phil. 1. 15. some preach Christ . . . of *e.*
1 Tim. 6. 4. whereof cometh *e.*, strife
Tit. 3. 3. living in *e.*, hateful and
Jas. 4. 5. spirit in us lusteth to *e.*
Gen. 26. 14. Philistines *envied* (Isaac;) 30. 1.
   Rachel *e.* Leah; 37. 11. brethren *e.* (Joseph);
   Ps. 106. 16. they *e.* Moses
Eccl. 4. 4. work, for this a man is *e.*
1 Pet. 2. 1. laying aside all *envies*
Num. 11. 29. *enviest* thou for my sake
Ps. 37. 1. *envious*, 73. 3. Prov. 24. 1, 19.
Rom. 13. 13. not in strife and *envying*
1 Cor. 3. 3. *e.* and strife, and divisions
Gal. 5. 26. not . . . *e.* one another
2 Cor. 12. 20. debates, *envyings* Gal. 5. 21.
EPHOD, Ex. 39. 2. Judg. 8. 27; 17. 5. 1 Sam.
   2. 18; 21. 9; 23. 9; 30. 7. 2 Sam. 6. 14. Hos. 3. 4.
EPISTLE, Acts 15. 30; 23. 33. Rom. 16. 22. 1 Cor.
   5. 9. 2 Cor. 7. 8. Col. 4. 16. 1 Thes. 5. 27.
   2. Thes. 2. 15; 3. 14, 17. 2 Pet. 3. 1.
2 Cor. 3. 2. *e.* written in our hearts
   1. *epistles*, 2 Pet. 3. 16. (Paul's)
EQUAL, Job 28. 17, 19. Ps. 17. 2; 55. 13. Prov.
   26. 7. Lam. 2. 13.
Is. 40. 25. to whom make me *e.* 46. 5.
Ezek. 18. 25. way of the Lord is not *e.*
Mat. 20. 12. made them *e.* to us
Luke 20. 36. (not) die . . . *e.* to the angels
John 5. 18. making himself *e. with God*
Phil. 2. 6. thought not robbery to be—
Col. 4. 1. masters, give . . . just and *e.*
Rev. 21. 16. breadth, and height *e.*
Gal. 1. 14. *equals*; 2 Cor. 8. 14. *equality*
EQUITY, dost establish, Ps. 99. 4.
Ps. 98. 9. judge people with *e.*
Prov. 1. 3. wisdom, justice, judgment, *e.*
17. 26. nor to strike princes for *e.*
Eccl. 2. 21. labour is in wisdom, knowledge, *e.*
Is. 11. 4. reprove with *e.* for meek
59. 14. truth fallen, *e.* cannot enter
Mic. 3. 9. princes that pervert all *e.*
Mal. 2. 6. Levi walked with me in *e.*
ERR, 2 Chr. 33. 9. Is. 19. 14.
Ps. 95. 10. do *e.* in heart, Heb. 3. 10.

119. 21. *err* from thy commandments
Prov. 14. 22. not *e.* that devise evil
Is. 9. 16. the leaders cause to *e.* 3. 12.
30. 28. bridle . . . causing them to *e.*
35. 8. wayfaring men . . . shall not *e.*
Is. 63. 17. why made us to *e.* from thy
Jer. 23. 13. prophet *caused to e.* 32.
Hos. 4. 12. spirit of whoredom—
Mic. 3. 5. prophets make people *e.*
Mat. 22. 29. *e.* not knowing scripture
Jas. 5. 19. if any of you *e.* from truth
Num. 15. 22. and if you have *erred* . . . offer.
1 Sam. 26. 21. I . . . have *e.* exceedingly
Job 6. 24. understand wherein I have *e.*
Ps. 119. 110. I *e.* not from thy precepts
Is. 28. 7. priest and prophet have *e.* through
   strong drink
1 Tim. 6. 10. have *e.* from the faith
21. *e.* concerning the faith, 2 Tim. 2. 18.
Prov. 10. 17. *erreth*, Ezek. 45. 20.   [Dan. 6. 4.
2 Sam. 6. 7. *error*, Job 19. 4. Eccl. 5. 6; 10. 5.
Is. 32. 6. utter *e.* against the Lord
Dan. 6. 4. neither was any *e.* found
Rom. 1. 27. recompence of their *e.*
Jas. 5. 20. sinner from the *e.* of his way
2 Pet. 2. 18. them who live in *e.*
1 John 4. 6. know we . . . the spirit of *e.*
Jude 11. after the *e.* of Balaam
Ps. 19. 12. who understand his *errors*
Jer. 10. 15. vanity and work of *e.* 51. 18.
Heb. 9. 7. for the *e.* of the people
ERRAND, Judg. 3. 19. 2 Ki. 9. 5.
ESCAPE, Gen. 19. 17, 22; 32. 8.
Ezra 9. 8. leave a remnant to *e.*
Esth. 4. 13. think not that thou shalt *e.*
Job 11. 20. but (wicked) shall not *e.*
Ps. 56. 7. shall they *e.* by iniquity
71. 2. deliver me and cause me to *e.*
141. 10. let the wicked fall . . . whilst I *e.*
Prov. 19. 5. that speaketh lies shall not *e.*
Eccl. 7. 26. pleaseth God shall *e.* her
Is. 20. 6. we flee for help . . . how shall we *e.*
Jer. 11. 11. evil . . . shall not be able to *e.*
Ezek. 17. 15. shall he *e.* that doeth
Mat. 23. 33. *e.* the damnation of hell
Luke 21. 36. accounted worthy to *e.*
Rom. 2. 3. *e.* the judgment of God
1 Cor. 10. 13. temptation . . . a way to *e.*
1 Thes. 5. 3. they shall not *e.*
Heb. 2. 3. how shall we *e.* if we neglect
Ezra 9. 15. we remain yet *escaped*
Job 1. 15, 16, 17, 19. I only am *e.* to tell
Ps. 124. 7. our soul is *e.* as a bird out of snare
Is. 45. 20. *e.* of the nations
John 10. 39. he *e.* out of their hand
Heb. 12. 25. *e.* not who refused him
2 Pet. 1. 4. *e.* corruption of world, 2. 20.
2. 18. allure those that were clean *e.*
ESCHEW evil, Job 1. 8. 1 Pet. 3. 11.
ESPOUSALS, Sol. 3. 11. Jer. 2. 2.
Mat. 1. 18. *espoused*, 2 Cor. 11. 2.
ESTABLISH, STABLISH, Num. 30. 13. 1 Ki.
   15. 4. Deut. 28. 9. Job 36. 7.
Gen. 9. 9. *e.* my covenant, 17. 7, 19, 21. Ex. 6. 4.
   Lev. 26. 9. Deut. 8. 18. Ezek. 16. 60. *e.* an
   everlasting covenant
1 Sam. 1. 23. the Lord *e.* his word
2 Sam. 7. 12. I will *e.* his kingdom, 13.
2 Chr. 9. 8. God loved Israel to *e.* them
7. 18. *S.* throne of kingdom, 1 Chr. 17. 12.
Ps. 7. 9. but *e.* the just, 48. 8.
89. 2. thy faithfulness shalt thou *e.* in heaven
4. David . . . thy seed will I *e.* for ever

Ps. 90. 17. *establish* the work of our hands, ... *e.* thou
99. 4. thou dost *e.* equity
119. 38. *s.* thy word to thy servant
Prov. 15. 25. *e.* the border of the widow
Is. 9. 7. order it, and to *e.* it with judgment
49. 8. give thee for a ... to *e.* the earth
62. 7. no rest till he *e.* Jerusalem
Rom. 3. 31. yea, we *e.* the law
10. 3. to *e.* their own righteousness
16. 25. that is of power to *s.* you
1 Thes. 3. 13. *e.* your hearts, Jas. 5. 8.
2 Thes. 2. 17. *s.* in every good word
1 Pet. 5. 10. God of all grace *s.* you
Gen. 41. 32. the thing is *established*
Ex. 15. 17. which thy hands have *e.*
Ps. 40. 2. upon a rock, he *e.* my goings
78. 5. he *e.* a testimony in Jacob
93. 1. the world is *s.* 2. thy throne is *e.*
119. 90. hast *e.* the earth, and it abideth
Prov. 3. 19. (Lord) ... *e.* heavens, Ps. 148. 6.
4. 26. ponder ... let all thy ways be *e.*
12. 3. man not be *e.* by wickedness
16. 12. throne is *e.* by righteousness
20. 18. every purpose is *e.* by counsel
Is. 7. 9. if ye will not believe ... not be *e.*
16. 5. in mercy shall the throne be *e.*
Jer. 10. 12. *e.* the world by wisdom, 51. 15.
Hab. 1. 12. *e.* them for correction
Mat. 18. 16. of two or three witnesses every
    word may be *e.* 2 Cor. 13. 1.
Acts 16. 5. so were the churches *e.*
Rom. 1. 11. to the end ye may be *e.*
Col. 2. 7. built up in him, and ... *s.* in faith
Heb. 8. 6. upon better promises
13. 9. that the heart be *e.* with grace
2 Pet. 1. 12. *e.* in the present truth
Lev. 25. 30. *shall be established*, Deut. 19. 15. Ps.
    89. 21. 2 Cor. 13. 1.
2 Chr. 20. 20. believe in God, so ye—
Job 22. 28. decree a thing and it—
Ps. 102. 28. their seed—before thee
Prov. 12. 19. lip of truth—for ever
25. 5. throne—in righteousness, 29. 14.
Is. 2. 2. the Lord's house—, Mic. 4. 1.
54. 14. in righteousness thou—
Jer. 30. 20. their congregation—before me
Prov. 29. 4. king by ... *establisheth* the land
Hab. 2. 12. woe to him that *s.* a city
2 Cor. 1. 21. *s.* us with you is God.
ESTATE, STATE, Gen. 43. 7. Esth. 1. 7, 19.
Ps. 39. 5. man at his best *s.* is vanity
136. 23. remembered us in low *e.*
Prov. 27. 23. know *e.* of thy flocks
Mat. 12. 45. last *s.* is worse, Luke 11. 26.
Luke 1. 48. low *e.* of his handmaiden
Phil. 4. 11. in whatsoever *e.* ... content
Jude 6. angels that kept not their first *e.*
ESTEEM, Job 36. 19. Is. 29. 16, 17.
Ps. 119. 128. I *e.* all thy precepts
Is. 53. 4. we did *e.* him stricken of God
Phil. 2. 3. *e.* each other better than
1 Thes. 5. 13. *e.* them highly in love
Deut. 32. 15. and lightly *esteemed* the rock of his
    salvation
1 Sam. 2. 30. they that despise me shall be
    lightly *e.*
Job 23. 12. *e.* the words of his mouth
Luke 16. 15. is highly *e.* among men
Rom. 14. 5. *esteemeth* one day above
14. to him that *e.* it, it is unclean
Heb. 11. 26. *esteeming* reproach of Christ
ESTRANGED, Job 19. 13. Jer. 19. 4.
Ps. 58. 3. wicked are *e.* from the womb

Ps. 78. 30. not *estranged* from their lusts
Ezek. 14. 5. they are all *e.* from me
ETERNAL God thy refuge, Deut. 33. 27.
Is. 60. 15. make thee an *e.* excellency
Mark 3. 29. danger of *e.* damnation
Rom. 1. 20. even his *e.* power
2 Cor. 4. 17. exceeding and *e.* weight of
18. the things which are not seen are *e.*
5. 1. a house ... hands, *e.* in the heavens
Eph. 3. 11. according to the *e.* purpose
1 Tim. 1. 17. to the King *e.* ... be honour
2 Tim. 2. 10. salvation ... with *e.* glory
Heb. 5. 9. author of *e.* salvation unto all
9. 12. obtained *e.* redemption for us
14. through *e.* Spirit; 15. *e.* inheritance
1 Pet. 5. 10. *e.* glory; Jude 7. of *e.* fire
Mat. 19. 16. that I may have *eternal life*, Mark
    10. 17. Luke 10. 25.
25. 46. the righteous (shall go) into—
Mark 10. 30. and in the world to come—
John 3. 15. should not perish but have—
4. 36. wages, gathereth fruit unto—
6. 54. blood hath—and I will raise him up
68. we go? thou hast the words of—
10. 28. and I give unto them—17. 2.
12. 25. hateth his life ... shall keep it unto—
17. 3. this is—to know the only true God
Acts 13. 48. ordained to—believed
Rom. 2. 7. glory, honour, immortality, and ...—
6. 23. the gift of God is—through Jesus
1 Tim. 6. 12. lay hold on—19.
Tit. 1. 2. in hope of—which God
3. 7. heirs according to the hope of—
1 John 1. 2.—which was with the Father
3. 15. ye know that no murderer hath—
5. 11. record, ... God hath given—in his Son
13. that ye may know that ye have—20.
Jude 21. looking for the mercy ... unto—
ETERNITY, that inhabiteth, Is. 57. 15.
EUNUCH, 2 Ki. 9. 32; 20. 18.
Is. 56. 3. neither *e.* say, I am a dry tree
Mat. 19. 12. some *e.* born ... made *e.* ... selves *e.*
Acts 8. 27. of great authority, 39.
EVEN balance, Job 31. 6.
Ps. 26. 12. my foot standeth in an *e.* place
Sol. 4. 2. flock of sheep that are *e.* shorn
Luke 19. 44. lay thee *e.* with the ground
EVEN or **EVENING,** Gen. 1. 5, &c.; 19. 1.
    (between the evenings) Ex. 12. 6, 18.
1 Ki. 18. 29. at *e.* sacrifice, Ezra 9. 4, 5. Ps.
    141. 2. Dan. 9. 21.
Hab. 1. 8. horses more fierce than *e.* **wolves,**
    Zeph. 3. 3.
Zech. 14. 7. at *e.* time it shall be light
EVENT, Eccl. 2. 14; 9. 2, 3.   [4. 7; 14. 9.
EVER, a long time, constantly, eternally, Josh.
Deut. 19. 9. to walk *e.* in his way
Ps. 5. 11. let them *e.* shout for joy
25. 15. my eyes *e.* towards the Lord
37. 26. he is *e.* merciful and lendeth
51. 3. and my sin is *e.* before me
Luke 15. 31. son, thou art *e.* with me
John 8. 35. in house son abideth *e.*
1 Thes. 4. 17. shall we *e.* be with the Lord
5. 15. *e.* follow that which is good
2 Tim. 3. 7. *e.* learning, and never able to
Heb. 7. 24. this man continueth *e.*
25. he *e.* liveth to make intercession
Jude 25. to God be glory now and *e.*
Gen. 3. 22. and eat and live *for ever*
Deut. 32. 40. and say, I live—
Josh. 4. 24. fear the Lord your God—
1 Ki. 10. 9. Lord loved Israel—

1 Ki. 11. 39. afflict seed of David, but not—
Ps. 9. 7. Lord shall endure—102. 12.
12. 7. thou will preserve them—
22. 26. your heart shall live *for ever*
23. 6. dwell in house of the Lord—61. 4.
30. 12. give thanks to thee—52. 9.
33. 11. counsel of the Lord standeth—
37. 18. their inheritance shall be—
49. 9. he should still live—
73. 26. God the strength . . . and my portion—
74. 19. forget not congregation of poor—
81. 15. their time should have endured—
92. 7. that they shall be destroyed—
103. 9. (the Lord) will not keep his anger—
105. 8. remember . . . covenant—111. 9.
119. 111. thy testimonies as heritage—
146. 6. which keepeth truth—
Prov. 27. 24. riches are not—
Eccl. 1. 4. the earth abideth—
Is. 26. 4. trust in the Lord—for in Lord
32. 17. quietness and assurance—
40. 8. the word of our God shall stand—
57. 16. I will not contend—Gen. 6. 3.
Jer. 3. 5. will he reserve anger—12.
32. 39. that they may fear me—
Lam. 3. 31. the Lord will not cast off—
Mic. 7. 18. retaineth not his anger—
Zech. 1. 5. prophets, do they live—
John 6. 51. if any eat . . . shall live—58.
Rom. 1. 25. the Creator who is blessed—
9. 5. (Christ) is over all, God blessed—
2 Cor. 9. 9. his righteousness remaineth—
Heb. 13. 8. Jesus Christ, same . . . and—
1 Pet. 1. 23. the word of God abideth—
25. word of the Lord endureth—Is. 40. 8.
1 John 2. 17. doeth will of God abideth—
Ex. 15. 18. Lord reigneth *for ever and ever*
1 Chr. 16. 36. blessed be God—29. 10. Neh.
9. 5. Dan. 2. 20.
Ps. 10. 16. the Lord is king—
45. 6. thy throne, O God, is—Heb. 1. 8.
48. 14. this God is our God—52. 8.
111. 8. commandments stand fast—
119. 44. I will keep thy law—
145. 1. I will bless thy name—2, 21.
Mic. 4. 5. walk in the name of . . . God—
Gal. 1. 5. to whom be glory—Rom. 11. 36.
Phil. 4. 20. 1 Tim. 1. 17. Heb. 13. 21. 1 Pet.
4. 11. Rev. 1. 6, &c.
Rev. 4. 9. who liveth—Dan. 4. 34; 12. 7.
EVERLASTING hills, Gen. 49. 26.
Gen. 17. 8. Canaan, an *e.* possession, 48. 4.
21. 33. called on the name of Lord, *e.* God
Ex. 40. 15. *e.* priesthood, Num. 25. 13.
Deut. 33. 27. underneath are *e.* arms
Ps. 24. 7. lifted up ye *e.* doors
41. 13. blessed be God from *e.* to *e.*
90. 2. from *e.* to *e.* thou art, 106. 48.
103. 17. mercy of Lord from *e.* to *e.* 100. 5.
112. 6. righteous in *e.* remembrance
139. 24. lead me in the way *e.*
145. 13. *e.* kingdom, Dan. 4. 3.
Prov. 10. 25. righteous is an *e.* foundation
Is. 9. 6. The mighty God, the *e.* Father
26. 4. in the Lord Jehovah is *e.* strength
33. 14. who dwell with *e.* burnings
35. 10. songs of *e.* joy, 51. 11; 61. 7.
40. 28. the *e.* God . . . fainteth not
45. 17. Israel saved with *e.* salvation
55. 13. to the Lord for a name, an *e.* sign
56. 5. an *e.* name, 63. 12; from *e.* 16.
60. 19. the Lord shall be an *e.* light, 20.
Jer. 10. 10. true . . . living God, *e.* King

Jer. 20. 11. *everlasting* confusion never forgotten
23. 40. *e.* reproach. 31. 3. with *e.* love
Dan. 4. 34. *e.* dominion, 7. 14.
Mic. 5. 2. goings forth of old, from *e.*
Hab. 1. 12. art thou not from *e.*,
3. 6. *e.* mountains scattered;
Mat. 18. 8. cast into *e.* fire, 25. 41.
25. 46. shall go into *e.* punishment
Luke 16. 9. receive into *e.* habitations
2 Thes. 1. 9. punished with *e.* destruction
1 Tim. 6. 16. to whom be . . . power *e.*
2 Pet. 1. 11. *e.* kingdom of Lord Jesus Christ
Jude 6. reserved in *e.* chains
Rev. 14. 6. having the *e.* gospel
Dan. 12. 2. awake to *everlasting life*
Mat. 19. 29. shall inherit—
Luke 18. 30. in world to come—
John 3. 16. not perish but have—36.
4. 14. well of water springing up into—
5. 24. that heareth my word hath—
6. 27. meat which endureth to—
40. whoso believeth may have—47.
12. 50. his commandment is—
Acts 13. 46. yourselves unworthy of—
Rom. 6. 22. ye have . . . and the end—
Gal. 6. 8. shall of the Spirit reap—
1 Tim. 1. 16. believe on him to—
EVERMORE, Ps. 16. 11, &c. John 6. 34. 2 Cor.
11. 31. 1 Thes. 5. 16. Rev. 1. 18.
EVERY imagination evil, Gen. 6. 5.
Ps. 32. 6. for this *e.* one . . . godly pray
119. 101. *e.* evil way. 104. *e.* false way, 128.
Prov. 2. 9. understand *e.* good path
14. 15. simple believeth *e.* word
15. 3. eyes of Lord are in *e.* place
Eccl. 3. 1. a time to *e.* purpose
Is. 45. 23. *e.* knee shall bow, *e.* tongue swear,
Rom. 14. 11. Phil. 2. 11.
2 Tim. 2. 21. *e.* good (4. 18. *e.* evil) work
Heb. 12. 1. let us lay aside *e.* weight
1 John 4. 1. believe not *e.* spirit
EVIDENCE, Jer. 32. 10. Heb. 11. 1.
Evidently (visibly), Acts 10. 3. Gal. 3. 1.
EVIL, Gen. 2. 9, 17; 3. 5, 22.
Deut. 29. 21. I will separate him to *e.*
30. 15. life and good, death and *e.*
Josh. 24. 15. if it seem *e.* to you
Job 2. 10. shall we not receive *e.*
5. 19. there shall no *e.* touch thee
30. 26. looked for good *e.* came
Ps. 23. 4. I will fear no *e.* for thou
34. 21. *e.* shall slay the wicked
51. 4. have done this *e.* in thy sight
52. 3. lovest *e.* more than good
91. 10. no *e.* shall befall thee
97. 10. ye that love the Lord, hate *e.*
Prov. 5. 14. I was almost in all *e.*
12. 21. no *e.* shall happen to just
15. 3. beholding the *e.* and the good
31. 12. will do him good and not *e.*
Eccl. 5. 13. sore *e.*, riches kept to hurt
9. 3. heart of . . . men is full of *e.*
Is. 5. 20. call *e.* good, and good *e.*
7. 15. know to refuse the *e.* 16.
45. 7. I make peace and create *e.*
57. 1. taken away from the *e.* to come
59. 7. feet run to *e.* and make haste
Jer. 17. 17. art my hope in day of *e.*
18. 11. I frame *e.* against you,
29. 11. thoughts of peace and not of *e.*
44. 27. I will watch over them for *e.*
Lam. 3. 38. proceedeth not *e.* and good
Ezek. 7. 5. an *e.* an only *e.* is come

Dan. 9. 12. on us a great *evil*, 13, 14.
Amos 3. 6. shall there be *e.* in a city
5. 14. seek good and not *e.*
9. 4. set eyes on them for *e.*
Hab. 1. 13. purer eyes than to behold *e.*
Mat. 5. 11. all manner of *e.* against you
6. 34. sufficient to the day is *e.* thereof
Rom. 2. 9. on every soul that doeth *e.*
7. 19. *e.* which I would not that I do
21. I would do good *e.* is present with me
12. 17. recompense to no man *e.* for *e.*
21. be not overcome of *e.* but overcome *e.*
1 Cor. 13. 5. charity thinketh no *e.*
1 Thes. 5. 15. none render *e.* for *e.* 1 Pet. 3. 9.
22. abstain from all appearance of *e.*
1 Tim. 6. 10. love of money is the root of all *e.*
Tit. 3. 2. to speak *e.* of no man
Heb. 5. 14. discern both good and *e.*
Gen. 6. 5. thoughts of his heart only *e.* 8. 21.
Prov. 14. 19. *e.* bow before the good
15. 15. all the days of the afflicted are *e.*
Is. 1. 4. a seed of *e.*doers, 14. 20.
Mat. 5. 45. his sun to rise on *e.* and good
7. 11. if ye, being *e.*, know, Luke 11. 13.
Luke 6. 35. kind to unthankful and *e.*
John 3. 19. because their deeds were *e.*
Eph. 5. 16. because the days are *e.*
3 John 11. follow not that which is *e.*
Jude 10. speak *e.* of those things.
EXACT, Deut. 15. 2. Ps. 89. 22. Neh. 5. 7.
Luke 3. 13. *exactors*, Is. 60. 17.
EXALT self, Dan. 11. 14, 36. Obad. 4.
Ex. 15. 2. my father's God, I will *e.*
1 Sam. 2. 10. *e.* horn of his anointed
Ps. 34. 3. let us *e.* his name together
99. 5. *e.* Lord for he is holy, 107. 32.
118. 28. my God, I will *e.* thee, Is. 25. 1.
Ezek. 21. 26. *e.* him that is low
1 Pet. 5. 6. may *e.* you in due time
Num. 24. 7. his kingdom be *exalted*
2 Sam. 22. 47. *e.* be the God of my salvation
Neh. 9. 5. *e.* above all blessing
Job 5. 11. *e.* to safety, 36. 7.
Ps. 89. 16. in righteousness shall be *e.* 17.
Prov. 11. 11. by . . . of upright, city is *e.*
Is. 2. 2. Lord's house . . . *e.* Mic. 4. 1.
11. Lord shall be *e.* 17; 5. 16; 30. 18; 33. 5, 10.
40. 4. every valley *shall be e.* 49. 11. my high-
    ways—. 52. 13. my servant—
Hos. 13. 1. Ephraim was *e.* in Israel, he
Mat. 11. 23. Capernaum . . . *e.* to heaven
23. 12. humbleth himself shall be *e.*
Luke 1. 52. *e.* them of low degree
Acts 2. 33. by right hand of God *e.* 5. 31.
2 Cor. 12. 7. I be *e.* above measure
Phil. 2. 9. God hath highly *e.* him
Prov. 14. 34. righteousness *exalteth* a nation
Luke 14. 11. *e.* himself be abased, 18. 14.
2 Thes. 2. 4. *e.* himself above all that
EXAMINE, Luke 23. 14. Acts 4. 9; by scourging,
    22. 24, 29; 28. 18.
Ps. 26. 2. *e.* me, O Lord, and prove me
1 Cor. 11. 28. man *e.* himself, 2 Cor. 13. 5.
EXAMPLE, 1 Thes. 1. 7. Jas. 5. 10.
Mat. 1. 19. not make her a public *e.*
John 13. 15. I have given you an *e.*
1 Cor. 10. 6. these things were our *e.*
1 Tim. 4. 12. an *e.* of believers
Heb. 4. 11. the same *e.* of unbelief
8. 5. serve unto the *e.* and shadow
Jas. 5. 10. for an *e.* of suffering affliction
1 Pet. 2. 21. Christ . . . leaving us an *e.*
Jude 7. for an *e.* suffering the vengeance

EXCEED, Deut. 25. 3. 1 Ki. 10. 7.
Mat. 5. 20. except your righteousness *e.*
2 Cor. 3. 9. ministration of righteousness *e.*
Gen. 17. 6. *exceeding* fruitful
27. 34. Esau cried with *e.* bitter cry
Num. 14. 7. (Canaan) . . . *e.* good land
1 Sam. 2. 3. talk no more so *e.* proudly
1 Ki. 4. 29. gave Solomon wisdom *e.* much
1 Chr. 22. 5. house *e.* magnifical
Ps. 43. 4. I will go to God my *e.* joy
Mat. 5. 12. rejoice and be *e.* glad
Rom. 7. 13. might become *e.* sinful
2 Cor. 4. 17. a far more *e.* . . . weight*
7. 4. I am *e.* joyful in all tribulation
Eph. 1. 19. *e.* greatness of his power
2. 7. might shew *e.* riches of his grace
3. 20. him that is able to do *e.* abundantly
1 Tim. 1. 14. grace was *e.* abundant
2 Pet. 1. 4. *e.* great and precious promises
Jude 24. present you with *e.* joy
Gen. 13. 13. sinners before the Lord *exceedingly*,
    1 Sam. 26. 21. 2 Sam. 13. 15.
Ps. 68. 3. let (the righteous) *e.* rejoice
119. 167. thy testimonies I love *e.*
1 Thes. 3. 10. praying *e.* that . . . face
2 Thes. 1. 3. your faith groweth *e.*
EXCEL, Gen. 49. 4. 1 Ki. 4. 30.
Ps. 103. 20. angels that *e.* in strength
1 Cor. 14. 12. seek that ye may *e.* to
Gen. 49. 3. the *excellency* of dignity and
Ex. 15. 7. in greatness of thine *e.*
Deut. 33. 26. rideth in his *e.* on sky
Job 13. 11. his *e.* make you afraid
37. 4. thunders with voice of his *e.*
40. 10. deck thyself now with *e.*
Ps. 47. 4. *e.* of Jacob, whom he loved
68. 34. his *e.* is over Israel, and his
Is. 35. 2. see glory and *e.* of our God
Amos 8. the *e.* of Jacob, 8. 7.
1 Cor. 2. 1. not with *e.* of speech
2 Cor. 4. 7. *e.* of power be of God
Phil. 3. 8. all loss for *e.* of knowledge of Christ
Esth. 1. 4. *excellent* majesty, Job 37. 23.
Ps. 8. 1. how *e.* is thy name, 9.
16. 3. saints, *e.* in whom my delight
36. 7. how *e.* is thy lovingkindness
148. 13. the Lord, for his name alone is *e.*
Prov. 12. 26. the righteous is more *e.*
17. 27. man of understanding is of *e.* spirit
Is. 12. 5. Lord hath done *e.* things
Ezek. 16. 7. art come to *e.* ornaments
Dan. 5. 12. an *e.* spirit in Daniel, 6. 3.
Rom. 2. 18. more *e.* 1 Cor. 12. 31.—way
Phil. 1. 10. approve things that are *e.*
Heb. 1. 4. obtained a more *e.* name
11. 4. offered a more *e.* sacrifice
2 Pet. 1. 17. a voice from *e.* glory
Prov. 31. 29. thou *excellest* them all
Eccl. 2. 13. wisdom *excelleth* folly
2 Cor. 3. 10. reason of glory that *e.*
EXCESS, Mat. 23. 25. (wine) Eph. 5. 18.
EXCLUDE, Rom. 3. 27. Gal. 4. 17.
EXCUSE, Luke 14. 18. Rom. 1. 20; 2. 15.
EXECRATION, Jer. 42. 18; 44. 12.
EXECUTE, Num. 5. 30; 8. 11.
Ps. 149. 7. *e.* vengeance, Mic. 5. 15.
Hos. 11. 9. not *e.* fierceness of mine anger
Rom. 13. 4. a revenger to *e.* wrath
Ex. 12. 12. *execute judgment*, Deut. 10. 18.
    Ps. 119. 84. Is. 16. 3. Jer. 7. 5; 21. 12; 22. 3;
    23. 5. Mic. 7. 9. Zec. 7. 9; 8. 16. John 5. 27.
    Jude 15.
EXERCISE, Mat. 20. 25; *e.* self, Ps. 131. 1.

Acts 24. 16. 1 Tim. 4. 7. *exercised*, Heb. 5. 14;
12. 11.
2 Pet. 2. 14. *e.* lovingkindness, Jer. 9. 24.
EXHORT, Acts 2. 40; 11. 23; 15. 32; 27. 22.
2 Cor. 9. 5. 1 Thes. 2. 11; 4. 1; 5. 14. 1 Tim.
2. 1. 2 Tim. 4. 2. Tim. 1. 9; 2. 6, 9, 15. 1 Pet.
5. 1, 12.
2 Thes. 3. 12. *e.* by Lord Jesus Christ
Heb. 3. 13. *e.* one another daily, 10. 25. Jude 3.
Luke 3. 18. *exhortation*, Acts 20. 2. Rom. 12. 8.
1 Cor. 14. 3. 2 Cor. 8. 17. 1 Thes. 2. 3. 1 Tim.
4. 13. Heb. 12. 5. word of *e.* Acts 13. 15. Heb.
13. 22.
EXPECTATION, Luke 3. 15. Acts 12. 11.
Ps. 9. 18. *e.* of poor shall not perish
62. 5. on God; for my *e.* is from him
Prov. 10. 28. *e. of wicked* shall perish, 11. 7,
11. 23.—is wrath
23. 18. *e.* shall not be cut off, 24. 14.
Is. 20. 5. be ashamed of their *e.* 6.
Rom. 8. 19. *e.* of creature waiteth
Phil. 1. 20. according to earnest *e.*
Jer. 29. 11. give you an *expected* end
EXPEDIENT that one man die for the people,
John 11. 50; 18. 14.
John 16. 7. *e.* for you that I go away
1 Cor. 6. 12. all things not *e.* 10. 23.
12. 1. it is not *e.* for me to glory
EXPERIENCE, Gen. 30. 27. Rom. 5. 4.
2 Cor. 9. 13. by the *experiment* of
EXPERT in war, 1 Chr. 12. 33. Sol. 3. 8. Jer.
50. 9. in customs, Acts 26. 3.
EXPOUNDED, riddle, Judg. 14. 19. he *e.* Mark
4. 34. Luke 24. 27. Peter *e.* Acts 11. 4. Aq. &
Pris. *e.* 18. 26. Paul *e.* 28. 23.
EXPRESSLY, Ezek. 1. 3. 1 Tim. 4. 1.
EXTEND mercy, Ezra 7. 28; 9. 9. Ps. 109. 12.
e. peace like a river, Is. 66. 12.
Ps. 16. 2. my goodness *extendeth* not to thee
EXTINCT, Job 17. 1. Is. 43. 17.
EXTOL (God), Ps. 30. 1; 66. 17; 68. 4; 145. 1. Is.
52. 13. Dan. 4. 37.
EXTORTION, Ezek. 22. 12. Mat. 23. 25.
Ps. 109. 11. *Extortioner*, Is. 16. 4. Luke 18. 11.
1 Cor. 5. 10, 11; 6. 10.
EXTREME, Deut. 28. 22. Job 35. 15.
EYE for *e.* Ex. 21. 24. Mat. 5. 38.
Deut. 32. 10. apple of *e.* Ps. 17. 8.
Job 24. 15. no *e.* shall see me
Ps. 33. 18. the *e.* of the Lord on them
Prov. 20. 12. the seeing *e.* Lord hath
Eccl. 1. 8. the *e.* not satisfied, 4. 8.
Is. 64. 4. neither *e.* seen, 1 Cor. 2. 9.
Jer. 13. 17. mine *e.* shall weep sore, because
Mat. 6. 22. light of body is the *e.* Luke 11. 34.
18. 9. if thine *e.* offend thee, 5. 29.
Rev. 1. 7. every *e.* shall see him
Prov. 23. 6. *evil eye*, 28. 22. Mat. 6. 23; 20. 15.
Mark 7. 22. Luke 11. 34.
Job 16. 16. *eyelids*, 41. 18. Ps. 11. 4; 132. 4. Prov.
4. 25; 6. 4, 25; 30. 13. Jer. 9. 18.
Rev. 3. 18. *eyesalve*; Eph. 6. 6. *eyeservice*, Col. 3.
2 Sam. 22. 25. *eyesight*, Ps. 18. 24.   [22.
Luke 1. 2. *eyewitnesses*, 2 Pet. 1. 16.
Gen. 3. 5. your *eyes* shall be opened
Job 10. 4. hast thou *e.* of flesh
Ps. 15. 4. in whose *e.* a vile person
145. 15. *e.* of all wait on thee
Eccl. 2. 14. wise man's *e.* in his head
11. 7. pleasant for *e.* to behold sun
Is. 3. 16. walk with . . . wanton *e.*
29. 18. *e.* of blind see out of obscurity
32. 3. *e.* of them that see shall not dim

Is. 35. 5. *eyes* of blind shall be opened, 42. 7.
43. 8. blind people that have *e.*
Jer. 5. 21. have *e.* and see not, Is. 42. 20.
Hab. 1. 13. purer *e.* than to behold
Zech. 3. 9. on one stone seven *e.*
Mat. 13. 16. blessed are your *e.* for
18. 9. having two *e.* to be cast into hell fire
Mark 8. 18. having *e.* see ye not
Luke 4. 20. *e.* of all were fastened on him
10. 23. blessed are the *e.* which see
John 9. 6. anointed *e.* of blind man
Rom. 11. 8. *e.* that they should not
Eph. 1. 18. *e.* of your understanding
Heb. 4. 13. all open unto *e.* of him
2 Pet. 2. 14. *e.* full of adultery
1 John 2. 16. lust of the *e.* and pride
Rev. 1. 14. his *e.* as fire, 2. 18; 19. 12.
3. 18. anoint *e.* 4. 6, full of *e.* 8.
Deut. 13. 18. right in the *eyes of the Lord*,
1 Ki. 15. 5, 11; 22. 43.
Gen. 6. 8. Noah found grace in the—
1 Sam. 26. 24. my life be set by in—
2 Sam. 15. 25. find favour in—
2 Chr. 16. 9.—run to and fro, Zech. 4. 10.
Ps. 34. 15.—on righteous, 1 Pet. 3. 12.
Prov. 5. 21. ways of man before—
15. 3.—are in every place beholding
22. 12.—preserve knowledge
Is. 49. 5. shall I be glorious in—
Amos 9. 8.—on the sinful kingdom
Ps. 25. 15. *mine eyes* ever towards Lord
101. 6.—shall be upon the faithful
119. 148.—prevent the night watches
141. 8.—are unto thee, O God
Is. 1. 15. I will hide—from you
65. 12. did evil before—66. 4.
Jer. 9. 1. Oh that—were a fountain of tears
14. 17.—run down with tears
24. 6. I will set—upon them for good
Amos 9. 4. I will set—on them for evil
Luke 2. 30.—have seen thy salvation
Ps. 123. 2. *our eyes* wait on the Lord
Mat. 20. 33. that—may be opened
1 John 1. 1. which we have seen with—
Deut. 12. 8. right *in his own eyes*, Judg. 17. 6;
Job 32. 1. he was righteous—   [21. 25.
Neh. 6. 16. cast down *in their own eyes*
Ps. 139. 16. *thine eyes* did see my substance
Prov. 23. 5. set—on that which is not
Is. 30. 20.—shall see thy teachers
Jer. 5. 3. are not—upon the truth
Ezek. 24. 16. take away the desire of—25.

F

FABLES, 1 Tim. 1. 4; 4. 7. 2 Tim. 4. 4. Tit. 1. 14.
FACE, Gen. 3. 19; 16. 8.   [2 Pet. 1. 16.
Lev. 19. 32. honour the *f.* of old man
Num. 6. 25. Lord make his *f.* shine, Ps. 31. 16;
67. 1; 80. 3; 119. 135. Dan. 9. 17.
2 Chr. 6. 42. turn not *f.* Ps. 132. 10.
Ps. 17. 15. behold thy *f.* in righteousness
84. 9. behold the *f.* of anointed, 132. 10.
Ezek. 1. 10. *f.* of a man, Rev. 4. 7.
Hos. 5. 5. testify to his *f.* 7. 10.
Mat. 11. 10. my messenger before thy *f.* Mark
1. 2. Luke 7. 27; 9. 52.
Acts 2. 25. Lord always before my *f.*
1 Cor. 13. 12. but then *f.* to *f.*
2 Cor. 3. 18. with open *f.* beholding
Jas. 1. 23. his natural *f.* in a glass
FADE, we all *f.* as a leaf, Is. 64. 6.
Jas. 1. 11. rich man *f.* away in his ways
1 Pet. 1. 4. inheritance that *fadeth* not away

1. Pet. 5. 4. crown of glory that *fadeth* not away
FAIL, Deut. 28. 32. Job 11. 20.
Deut. 31. 6. Lord will not *f.* nor forsake, 8. Josh.
    1. 5. 1 Chr. 28. 20.
Ps. 12. 1. faithful *f.* from among men
77. 8. doth his promise *f.* for evermore
Lam. 3. 22. his compassions *f.* not
Luke 16. 9. ye *f.* they may receive you
17. one tittle of law to *f.* Mat. 5. 18.
22. 32. prayed that thy faith *f.* not
Heb. 12. 15. lest any *f.* of the grace
Sol. 5. 6. soul *failed* when he spake
Ps. 31. 10. my strength *faileth,* 38. 10; 71. 9.
    heart *f.* 40. 12. spirit *f.* 143. 7.
Luke 12. 33. treasure in heaven that *f.* not
1 Cor. 13. 8. charity never *f.*
Deut. 28. 65. shall give *failing* of eyes
Luke 21. 26. men's hearts *f.* them
FAINT, Deut. 25. 18. Judg. 8. 4, 5.
Is. 1. 5. head is sick, whole heart *f.*
40. 29. he giveth power to the *f.*
30. youths shall *f.* and be weary
31. wait on Lord shall walk and not *f.*
2 Cor. 4. 1. received mercy we *f.* not, 16.
Gal. 6. 9. shall reap if we *f.* not
Heb. 12. 5. nor *f.* when rebuked of
Ps. 27. 13. *fainted* unless I believed
Rev. 2. 3. hast laboured and not *f.*
Ps. 84. 2. soul *fainteth* for courts of Lord
    119. 81—for thy salvation
Is. 40. 28. God the Creator *f.* not
FAIR, Gen. 6. 2; 12. 11; 24. 16.
Prov. 7. 21. *f.* speech, Rom. 16. 18.
Sol. 1. 15. behold thou art *f.* 4. 1, &c.
Jer. 12. 6. they speak *f.* words
Acts 7. 20. Moses was exceeding *f.*
Gal. 6. 12. desire to make *f.* shew in
Ps. 45. 2. *fairer* than children of men
Dan. 1. 15. their countenance *f.*
FAITH, Acts 3. 16; 13. 8.
Deut. 32. 20. children in whom is no *f.*
Mat. 6. 30. clothe you, O ye little *f.* 8. 26;
    16. 8; 14. 31. Luke 12. 28.
8. 10. not found so great *f.* Luke 7. 9.
17. 20. *f.* as a grain of mustard seed
21. 21. have *f.* and doubt not
23. omitted judgment, mercy, and *f.*
Mark 4. 40. how is it ye have no *f.*
Luke 17. 5. Lord, increase our *f.*
6. if ye had *f.* ye might say to this
18. 8. shall (Son) find *f.* on the earth
Acts 3. 16. the *f.* which is by him
6. 5. Stephen, a man full of *f.* & Holy Ghost
7. company of priests obedient to *f.*
11. 24. good man, full of Holy Ghost and of *f.*
14. 9. that he had *f.* to be healed
16. 5. churches established in the *f.*
20. 21. *f.* toward our Lord Jesus Christ
Rom. 1. 5. for obedience to the *f.*
17. righteousness of God revealed from *f.* to *f.* . . . .
    The just shall live by *f.*
3. 3. make *f.* of God without effect
27. of works? Nay, but by the law of *f.*
4. 5. his *f.* is counted for righteousness
11. circumcision, a seal of righteousness of the
    f. 12. *f.* of Abraham, 16.
13. through the righteousness of *f.*
14. if of law be heirs, *f.* is made void
10. 8. the word of *f.* which we preach
10. 17. *f.* cometh by hearing, and hearing
12. 3. God dealt every man measure of *f.*
6. according to the proportion of *f.*
14. 22. hast thou *f.*? have it to . . . God

Rom. 16. 26. nations for the obedience of *faith*
1 Cor. 12. 9. *f.* by the same spirit
13. 2. though I have all *f.* to remove
13. now abideth *f.*, hope, charity
2 Cor. 4. 13. having the same Spirit of *f.*
Gal. 1. 23. preacheth the *f.* which
3. 2. Spirit by the hearing of *f.* 5.
12. the law is not of *f.* but the man
23. before *f.* came, we were under the law
25. after that *f.* is come, we are no
5. 6. but *f.* which worketh by love
22. but the fruit of the Spirit is . . . . *f.*
Eph. 4. 5. one Lord, one *f.*, one baptism
6. 16. above all taking the shield of *f.*
23. love with *f.* from God the Father
Phil. 1. 25. abide for your joy of *f.*
27. striving together for *f.* of the gospel
1 Thes. 1. 3. remember your work of *f.*
5. 8. putting on the breastplate of *f.*
2 Thes. 1. 4. glory for your *f.* 11. fulfil work of
    f. 3. 2. for all men have not *f.*
1 Tim. 1. 5. charity out of *f.* unfeigned
14. exceeding abundant with *f.*
3. 9. holding the mystery of *f.*
4. 1. in last days some shall depart from the *f.*
6. nourished up in the words of *f.*
5. 8. denied *f.* 12. cast off first *f.*
6. 12. fight the good fight of *f.*
2 Tim. 1. 5. unfeigned *f.* that is in thee
2. 18. overthrow the *f.* of some
22. follow righteousness, *f.*, charity
3. 8. reprobate concerning the *f.*
10. fully known my doctrine, manner of life, *f.*
4. 7. fought a good fight, . . . kept the *f.*
Tit. 1. 1. according to the *f.* of God's elect
Heb. 4. 2. not being mixed with *f.*
6. 1. dead works and of *f.* toward God
10. 22. draw near in assurance of *f.*
23. hold fast the profession of our *f.*
11. 1. *f.* substance of things hoped for
6. without *f.* impossible to please God
12. 2. Jesus the finisher of our *f.*
13. 7. whose *f.* follow, considering
Jas. 2. 1. have not of *f.* of Lord Jesus
17. *f.* if it hath not works, is dead, 26.
18. hast *f.* and I works; shew me thy *f.*
22. *f.* wrought with his works; by works *f.* made
5. 15. prayer of *f.* shall save   [perfect
2 Pet. 1. 1. like precious *f.* with us
1 John 5. 4. overcometh world, even our *f.*
Jude 3. contend earnestly for the *f.*
20. building up yourselves on holy *f.*
Rev. 2. 13. hast not denied my *f.*
19. I know thy works and *f.*
13. 10. here is the *f.* of the saints
14. 12. which keep the *f.* of Jesus
Hab. 2. 4. just shall live *by faith,* Rom. 1. 17.
    Gal. 3. 11. Heb. 10. 38.
Acts 15. 9. purifying their hearts—
26. 18. are sanctified—that is in me
Rom. 1. 12. comforted *by* mutual *f.*
3. 22. righteousness—of Christ
28. conclude a man is justified—
30. God, which shall justify circumcision—and
    uncircumcision through *f.*
5. 1. being justified—we have peace
2. have access—Eph. 3. 12.
Rom. 9. 32. not—but by the works of the law
11. 20. Thou standest—Be not highminded
2 Cor. 1. 24. of your joy; for—ye stand
5. 7. we walk—and not by sight
Gal. 2. 16. not justified, but—3. 24.
20. I live—of the Son of God

Gal. 3. 22. the promise *by faith* of Jesus Christ be
26. children of God—in Jesus Christ   [given
5. 5. for hope of righteousness—
Eph. 3. 17. Christ dwell in your hearts—
Phil. 3. 9. righteousness through *f.*
Heb. 11. 4.—Abel, 5.—Enoch, &c.
7. heir of righteousness which is—
Jas. 2. 24. justified by works, not—
Rom. 4. 19. not weak *in faith*
20. strong—giving glory to God
1 Cor. 16. 13. stand fast—quit you
2 Cor. 8. 7. ye abound—and utterance
13. 5. examine whether ye be—
Col. 1. 23. if ye continue—grounded
1 Tim. 1. 2. Timothy, my own son—
4. godly edifying which is—
2. 7. teacher of the Gentiles—
15. if they continue—and charity
3. 13. purchase great boldness—
2 Tim. 1. 13. —and love . . . in Christ Jesus
Tit. 1. 13. that they may be sound—2. 2.
3. 15. greet them that love us—
Heb. 11. 13. these died—not having
Jas. 1. 6. ask—nothing wavering
2. 5. poor, rich—heirs of kingdom
1 Pet. 5. 9. whom resist, stedfast—
Mat. 9. 2. J., *their faith,* Mark 2. 5. Luke 5. 20.
Acts 3. 16. *through faith* in his name
Rom. 3. 25. propitiation—in his blood
Gal. 3. 8. God would justify the heathen—
14. receive promise of Spirit—
Eph. 2. 8. by grace ye are saved—
Col. 2. 12.—of the operation of God
2 Tim. 3. 15. salvation—in Jesus
Heb. 6. 12.—and patience inherit promises
11. 3.—we understand the worlds
28.—Moses kept the passover
33.—subdued kingdoms, &c.
39. obtained a good report—2.
1 Pet. 1. 5. kept by power of God—
Mat. 9. 22. *thy faith* hath made thee whole,
    Luke 8. 48; 17. 19.
15. 28. O woman, great is—be it unto
Luke 7. 50.—hath saved thee, 18. 42.
22. 32. I have prayed that—fail not
Philem. 6. communication of—
Jas. 2. 18. shew me—without thy works
Luke 8. 25. where is *your faith?*
Rom. 1. 8.—is spoken of through
1 Cor. 2. 5. that—not stand in wisdom
15. 14.—is also vain, 17.
2 Cor. 1. 24. not . . . have dominion over—
10. 15. when—is increased, we   [1. 4.
Eph. 1. 15. heard of—in the Lord Jesus, Col.
Phil. 2. 17. sacrifice and service of—
Col. 2. 5. beholding stedfastness of—
1 Thes. 1. 8.—to God-ward is spread
3. 2. comfort you concerning—
5. I sent to know—lest the tempter
6. brought us good tidings of—
7. comforted in affliction by—
10. perfect that which is lacking in—
2 Thes. 1. 3.—groweth exceedingly
Jas. 1. 3. trying of—worketh patience
1 Pet. 1. 7. trial of—being precious
1. 9. receiving the end of *your faith*
1. 21. that—and hope might be in God
2 Pet. 1. 5. add to—virtue, and to virtue
Mat. 17. 17. O *faithless* and perverse generation,
    Mark 9. 19. Luke 9. 41.
John 20. 27. be not *f.* but believing
FAITHFUL, 1 Sam. 2. 35; 22. 14. 2 Sam. 20. 19.
    Neh. 13. 13. Dan. 6. 4. 1 Tim. 6. 2. 1 Pet. 5. 12.

Num. 12. 7. *faithful* in all my house
Heb. 3. 2, 5. Moses *f.* in all his house
Deut. 7. 9. He is God, the *f.* God keepeth covenant
Neh. 7. 2. a *f.* man, and feared God
9. 8. foundest (Abraham's) heart *f.*
Ps. 12. 1. *f.* fail from among men
31. 23. Lord preserveth the *f.*
89. 37. as a *f.* witness in heaven
101. 6. mine eyes be upon *f.* of the land
119. 86. thy commandments are *f.*
Prov. 11. 13. He that is of a *f.* spirit
13. 17. a *f.* ambassador is health
14. 5. a *f.* witness will not lie
20. 6. a *f.* man who can find?
27. 6. *f.* are the wounds of a friend
28. 20. *f.* man abound with blessings
Is. 1. 21. the *f.* city become an harlot
26. city of righteousness, *f.* city
8. 2. I took *f.* witnesses to record
49. 7. Lord is *f.* Holy One of Israel
Jer. 42. 5. the Lord be a *f.* witness
Hos. 11. 12. Judah is *f.* with saints
Mat. 25. 21. well done . . . *f.* servant
23. *f.* in a few things, Luke 19. 17.
Luke 12. 42. who is that *f.* steward
16. 10. *f.* in least is *f.* also in much
12. not *f.* in what is another man's
Acts 16. 15. judged me *f.* to the Lord
1 Cor. 1. 9. God is *f.* by whom ye
4. 2. required in stewards, a man *f.*
17. Timothy who is *f.* in the Lord
10. 13. God is *f.* who will not suffer
Eph. 1. 1. *f.* in Christ Jesus, Col. 1. 2.
6. 21. *f.* minister, Col. 1. 7; 4. 7, 9.
1 Thes. 5. 24. *f.* is he that calleth
2 Thes. 3. 3. but the Lord is *f.*, who
1 Tim. 1. 12. for he counted me *f.*
15. a *f.* saying and worthy of all acceptation, 4. 9.
    2 Tim. 2. 11. Tit. 3. 8.
3. 11. wives grave, . . . sober, *f.* in all
2 Tim. 2. 2. same commit to *f.* men
13. abideth *f.*: he cannot deny himself
Tit. 1. 6. one wife, having *f.* children
9. holding fast the *f.* word as taught
Heb. 2. 17. might be a merciful and *f.* high priest
10. 23. *f.* is he that promised 11. 11.
1 Pet. 4. 19. as unto a *f.* Creator
1 John 1. 9. he is *f.* and just to forgive
Rev. 1. 5. *f.* and true witness, 3. 14.
17. 14. they are chosen and *f.*
21. 5. words are true and *f.* 22. 6.
1 Sam. 26. 23. render every man his . . . *faithfulness*
Ps. 5. 9. no *f.* in their mouth
36. 5. thy *f.* reacheth to the clouds
40. 10. I have declared thy *f. See* 89. 1.
88. 11. or thy *f.* in destruction?
89. 1. make known thy *f.* to all generations
5. praise thy *f.* in the congregation
8. who is like to thy *f.* round about thee
24. my *f.* shall be with him (David)
33. no suffer my *f.* to fail
92. 2. to shew forth thy *f.* every night
119. 75. thou in *f.* hast afflicted me
90. thy *faithfulness* is unto all generations
143. 1. in thy *f.* answer me, and in thy
Is. 11. 5. *f.* the girdle of his reins
Lam. 3. 23. great is thy *f.*
Hos. 2. 20. I will betroth thee to me in *f.*
FALL, Num. 11. 31; 14. 29, 32.
Gen. 45. 24. *f.* not out by the way
2 Sam. 24. 14. *f.* into the hand of Lord
Ps. 37. 24. though he *f.* he shall not
45. 5. whereby people *f.* under thee

Ps. 141. 10. let wicked *fall* into their own nets
145. 14. the Lord upholdeth all that *f.*
Prov. 11. 5. wicked *f.* by own wickedness
24. 16. wicked shall *f.* into mischief
26. 27. diggeth pit shall *f.* in, Eccl. 10. 8.
28. 14. hardeneth his heart shall *f.*
Eccl. 4. 10. if they *f.* one will lift up
Is. 8. 15. many shall stumble and *f.*
Dan. 11. 35. them of understanding shall *f.*
Hos. 10. 8. and to the hills *f.* on us, Luke 23. 30.
Rev. 6. 16.
Mic. 7. 8. rejoice not when I *f.*
Mat. 7. 27. great was the *f.* of it
10. 29. sparrow not *f.* on the ground
15. 14. blind lead blind, both *f.* into ditch
Luke 2. 34. set for *f.* and rising of many
Rom. 11. 11. stumbled that they should *f.* . . .
   through their *f.* salvation is come
14. 13. occasion to *f.* in his brother's
1 Cor. 10. 12. take heed lest he *f.*
1 Tim. 3. 6. *f.* into condemnation of devil
6. 9. will be rich *f.* into temptation
Heb. 4. 11. *f.* after the same example
10. 31. fearful to *f.* into hands of living God
Jas. 1. 2. when ye *f.* into divers
2 Pet. 1. 10. if ye do these . . . shall never *f.*
3. 17. lest ye *f.* from stedfastness
Heb. 6. 6. impossible if . . . *fall away* to renew
Ps. 16. 6. *fallen* in pleasant places
Hos. 14. 1. thou hast *f.* by thine iniquity
Gal. 5. 4. justified . . . ye are *f.* from grace
Rev. 2. 5. remember whence thou art *f.*
Prov. 24. 16. just man *falleth* seven times
Rom. 14. 4. to his own master he *f.*
Ps. 56. 13. wilt not deliver (116. 8. hast delivered)
   my feet from *falling*
2 Thes. 2. 3. there come a *f.* away first
Jude 24. able to keep you from *f.*
FALLOW, Jer. 4. 3. Hos. 10. 12.
FALSE, Jer. 14. 14; 37. 14.
Ex. 23. 1. not raise a *f.* report
7. keep thee far from a *f.* matter
Ps. 119. 104. hate every *f.* way, 128.
Prov. 11. 1. *f.* balance abomination, 20. 23.
Jer. 14. 14. prophesy to you a *f.* vision
23. 32. against them that prophesy *f.* dreams
Zech. 8. 17. love no *f.* oath
Mal. 3. 5. witness against *f.* swearers
Mat. 24. 24. *f.* Christs, *f.* prophets
2 Cor. 11. 13. *f.* apostles, *f.* brethren
Gal. 2. 4. *f.* teachers, 2 Pet. 2. 1.
2 Tim. 3. 3. *f.* accusers, Tit. 2. 3.
Ps. 119. 118. their deceit is *falsehood*
144. 8. whose right hand is a . . . of *f.*
Is. 57. 4. are ye not . . . a seed of *f.*
59. 13. from the heart words of *f.*
Jer. 10. 14. molten image is *f.* 51. 17.
Lev. 6. 3. sweareth *falsely,* Jer. 7. 9.
19. 12. swear by my name *f.* Jer. 5. 2.
Ps. 44. 17. not dealt *f.* in covenant
Jer. 6. 13. every one dealeth *f.* 8. 10.
Zech. 5. 4. house of him that sweareth *f.*
Mat. 5. 11. evil against you *f.* for
Luke 3. 14. neither accuse any *f.*
1 Pet. 3. 16. be ashamed that *f.* accuse
Mat. 7. 15. *false prophets,* 24. 11, 24. Luke 6. 26.
2 Pet. 2. 1. 1 John 4. 1.
Ex. 20. 16. *false witness,* Deut. 5. 20; 19. 16.
Prov. 6. 19; 12. 17; 14. 5; 19. 5, 9; 21. 28;
25. 18; Mat. 15. 19; 19. 18. Rom. 13. 9.
1 Cor. 15. 15.
FAMILIAR, Job 19. 14. Ps. 41. 9. Lev. 19. 31;
   20. 6, 27. Is. 8. 19.

FAMILY, Gen. 10. 5. Lev. 20. 5.
Zech. 12. 12. mourn, every *f.* apart
Eph. 3. 15. whole *f.* in heaven are named
Ps. 68. 6. setteth the solitary in *families*
Amos 3. 2. known of all the *f.* of the earth
FAMINE, Gen. 12. 10; 41. 27.
Job 5. 20. in *f.* he shall redeem thee
Ps. 33. 19. keep them alive in *f.*
37. 19. in the days of *f.* be satisfied
Ezek. 5. 16. evil arrows of *f.* 6. 11.
Amos 8. 11. not a *f.* of bread   [Zeph. 2. 11.
FAMISH, Gen. 41. 55. Prov. 10. 3. Is. 5. 13.
FAN, Is. 41. 16. Jer. 4. 11; 51. 2. Mat. 3. 12.
FAR, Ex. 8. 28. Neh. 4. 19.   [Luke 3. 17.
Ex. 23. 7. keep thee *f.* from a false matter
Ps. 73. 27. *f.* from thee shall perish
Mark 12. 34. not *f.* from the kingdom
Eph. 2. 13. were *f.* off made nigh by
Phil. 1. 23. to be with Christ . . . is *f.* better
FARTHING, Mat. 5. 26; 10. 29.
FASHION, 1 Cor. 7. 31. Phil. 2. 8.
Job 10. 8. thy hands . . . *fashioned* me, Ps. 119. 73.
Ps. 139. 16. in continuance were *f.*
Ezek. 16. 7. thy breasts are *f.*
Phil. 3. 21. be *f.* like his glorious body
Ps. 33. 15. he *fashioneth* their hearts
1 Pet. 1. 14. not *fashioning* yourselves
FAST, 2 Sam. 12. 21. Esth. 4. 16.
Is. 58. 4. ye *f.* for strife; shall not *f.* as
Jer. 14. 12. when they *f.* I will not hear
Zech. 7. 5. did ye at all *f.* unto me
Mat. 6. 16. ye *f.* be not as hypocrites, *see* 18.
9. 14. why do we *f.* but thy disciples *f.* not, 18.
Luke 5. 33.
15. can children of bride-chamber *f.* . . . shall
   they *f.* Mark 2. 19, 20. Luke 5. 34, 35.
Luke 18. 12. I *f.* twice in the week
1 Ki. 21. 9. saying, proclaim a *f.* 12. 2 Chr.
20. 3. Ezra 8. 21. Is. 58. 3, 5, 6. Jer. 36. 9.
Joel 1. 14; 2. 15. Jonah 3. 5. Zech. 8. 19.
Acts 27. 9.
Judg. 20. 26. *fasted* that day, 1 Sam. 7. 6.
2 Sam. 1. 12. wept and *f.* till even
12. 16. David *f.* and lay all night on
Ezra 8. 23. we *f.* and besought the Lord
Is. 58. 3. why have we *f.* and thou
Mat. 4. 2. when he had *f.* forty days
Acts 13. 2, 3. ministered to Lord, *f.* and prayed
Neh. 9. 1. assembled with *fasting*
Esth. 4. 3. Jews *f.* and weeping, 9. 31.
Ps. 109. 24. my knees weak through *f.*
Jer. 36. 6. read the roll on *f.* day
Dan. 6. 18. king passed the night *f.*
9. 3. to seek by prayer and supplication with *f.*
Joel 2. 12. turn ye to me with *f.*
Mat. 15. 32. not send them away *f.*
Acts 10. 30. was *f.* till this hour
14. 23. ordained elders, prayed with *f.*
1 Cor. 7. 5. give yourselves to *f.*
Luke 2. 37. with *fastings* and prayers night and
   day
2 Cor. 6. 5. in *f.* (often, 11. 27.)
FASTENED, Job 38. 6. Eccl. 12. 11. Is. 22. 25.
FAT is Lord's, Lev. 3. 16; 4. 8.   [Luke 4. 20.
Prov. 11. 25. liberal soul shall be made *f.*
13. 4. soul of the diligent shall be made *f.*
15. 30. good report maketh bones *f.*
28. 25. trust in the Lord shall be made *f.*
Is. 25. 6. *f.* things full of marrow
11. 6. *fatling,* Mat. 22. 4.
Job 36. 16. be set on table . . . be full of *fatness*
Ps. 36. 8. satisfied with *f.* of thy house
63. 5. satisfied with marrow and *f.*

Ps. 65. 11. and thy paths drop *fatness*
Is. 55. 2. let your soul delight in *f.*
Jer. 31. 14. satiate the soul of priests **with** *f.*
Rom. 11. 17. root and *f.* of the olive-**tree**
FATHER, Gen. 2. 24; 4. 20, 21.
Gen. 17. 4. be a *f.* of many nations
Num. 11. 12. as *f.* beareth sucking child
2 Sam. 7. 14. I will be his *f.* Heb. 1. 5.
Job 29. 16. I was a *f.* to the poor
31. 18. brought up with me as with a *f.*
38. 28. hath the rain a *f.* or who
Ps. 68. 5. a *f.* of fatherless . . . is God
103. 13. as a *f.* pitieth his children
Is. 9. 6. the everlasting *F.,* prince of
Jer. 31. 9. I am a *f.* to Israel and
Mal. 1. 6. if I be a *f.* where is my honour
2. 10. Have we not all one *f.*?
John 5. 19. what he seeth the *F.* do
20. the *F.* loveth the Son, 3. 35.
21. as *F.* raiseth dead and quickeneth
22. *F.* judgeth no man but hath . . . the Son
26. as *F.* hath life in himself; so . . . Son
8. 18. *F.* . . . beareth witness of me
29. *F.* hath not left me alone
16. 32. I am not alone, *F.* is with me
Acts 1. 4. wait for the promise of the *F.*
7. times . . . *F.* put in his own power
Rom. 4. 11. the *f.* of all that believe
12. *f.* of circumcision, 16. the *f.* of us all
17. made thee a *f.* of many nations
1 Cor. 8. 6. *F.* of whom are all things
2 Cor. 1. 3. God and *F.* of our Lord, *F.* of mercies,
Eph. 1. 3, 1 Pet. 1. 3. *F.* of glory, Eph. 1. 17.
6. 18. I will be a *F.* to you and ye
1 Tim. 5. 1. intreat him as a *f.*
Heb. 1. 5. I will be to him a *F.* and
12. 9. subjection to the *F.* of spirits
Jas. 1. 17. gift . . . from the *F.* of lights
John 5. 17. *my Father* worketh and I
10. 30. I and—are one; 14. 20. I am in—, 10;
28.—is greater
Ezek. 16. 45. *your father* an Amorite
Mat. 5. 16. glorify—in heaven
23. 9. call no man—on earth
John 8. 41. ye do the deeds of—. . . . said . . .
We have one *F.,* even God
20. 17. I ascend to my *F.* and—
Ex. 15. 2. my *f.*'s God, and I will exalt
Neh. 9. 16. *our fathers* dealt proudly
Ps. 22. 4. —trusted in thee
39. 12. sojourner, as all my *f.* were
Lam. 5. 7. —have sinned . . . and we
Acts 15. 10. —nor we able to bear
Ex. 22. 22. not afflict . . . the *fatherless*
Deut. 10. 18. execute judgment of *f.*
Ps. 10. 14. thou helper of the *f.*
68. 5. a father of the *f.* . . . is God
146. 9. (Lord) relieveth the *f.* and widow
Is. 1. 17. judge the *f.,* plead for widow
Hos. 14. 3. in thee the *f.* findeth mercy
Jas. 1. 27. visit the *f.* in affliction
FAULT, Gen. 41. 9. Ex. 5. 16.
Mat. 18. 15. if trespass, tell him his *f.*
Luke 23. 4. I find no *f.* in him, 14. John 18. 38;
19. 4, 6.
1 Cor. 6. 7. utterly a *f.* among you
Gal. 6. 1. if a man be overtaken in a *f.*
Ps. 19. 12. cleanse thou me from secret *faults*
1 Pet. 2. 20. if when . . . buffeted for your *f.*
Jude 24. to present you *faultless*
FAVOUR, Gen. 39. 21. Deut. 33. 23.
1 Sam. 2. 26. Samuel in *f.* with the Lord
Job 10. 12. granted me life and *f.*

Ps. 5. 12. with *favour* wilt thou compass
30. 5. in his *f.* is life; weeping may endure
Prov. 31. 30. *f.* is deceitful, beauty vain
Luke 2. 52. in *f.* with God and man
Ps. 41. 11. know thou *favourest* me
FEAR, Gen. 9. 2. Ex. 15. 16.
Ps. 53. 5. in *f.* where no *f.* was
90. 11. according to thy *f.* so is wrath
119. 38. servant devoted to thy *f.*
120. flesh trembleth for *f.* of thee
Prov. 1. 26. mock when *f.* cometh
29. 25. *f.* of man bringeth a snare
Is. 8. 12. *f.* not their *f.* nor be afraid
29. 13. their *f.* toward me is taught
63. 17. hardened our heart from thy *f.*
Jer. 32. 40. put my *f.* in their hearts
Mal. 1. 6. if master where is my *f.*
Rom. 13. 7. render *f.* to whom *f.*
2 Tim. 1. 7. spirit of *f.* but of power
Heb. 2. 15. who through *f.* of death
12. 28. with reverence and godly *f.*
1 Pet. 1. 17. time of sojourning here in *f.*
1 John 4. 18. no *f.* in love, love casteth out *f.*
Gen. 20. 11. *fear of God* not in this place
2 Sam. 23. 3. ruleth men just, ruling in—
Neh. 5. 15. so did not I because of—
Ps. 36. 1. no—before eyes, Rom. 3. 18.
2 Cor. 7. 1. perfecting holiness in—
Job 28. 28. *fear of the Lord,* that is
Ps. 19. 9.—is clean, enduring for ever
34. 11. children, I will teach you—
Prov. 1. 29. they did not choose—
8. 13.—is to hate evil
10. 27.—prolongeth days
14. 26. in—is strong confidence
15. 33.—is instruction of wisdom
16. 6. by—men depart from evil
19. 23.—tendeth to life; satisfied
22. 4. by—are riches, honour, life
23. 17. be thou in—all day long
Is. 33. 6.—is his treasure
Acts 9. 31. walking in—and comfort
Ps. 2. 11. *with fear,* Phil. 2. 12.
Deut. 4. 10. learn to *f.* me
5. 29. such a heart that would *f.* me
28. 58. mayest *f.* this glorious name
1 Chr. 16. 30. *f.* before him all earth
2 Chr. 6. 31. that they may *f.* thee, 33.
Neh. 1. 11. servants, desire to *f.* thy name
Ps. 23. 4. I will *f.* no evil, for thou
31. 19. goodness laid up for those that *f.*
61. 5. heritage of them that *f.* thy name
86. 11. unite my heart to *f.* thy name
Jer. 10. 7. who would not *f.* thee
32. 39. heart that may *f.* me for ever
Luke 12. 5. *f.,* him, which . . . cast into hell,
Mat. 10. 28.
Rom. 8. 15. not received spirit of bondage again
to *f.*
11. 20. be not highminded, but *f.*
Heb. 4. 1. *f.* lest promise being left
12. 21. Moses said, I exceedingly *f.*
Rev. 2. 10. *f.* none of those things
11. 18. saints and them that *f.* thy name
Gen. 42. 18. this do and live, for I *fear God*
Ex. 18. 21. such as—men of truth
Ps. 66. 16. come and hear, all that—
Eccl. 5. 7. vanities, *f.* thou God
8. 12. shall be well with them that—
12. 13.—keep his commandments
Job 37. 24. therefore men do *fear him*
Ps. 25. 14. secret of the Lord is with *them that*
33. 18. eye of the Lord upon—   [*fear him*

Ps. 85. 9. salvation nigh to *them that fear him*
103. 13. as father, so Lord pitieth—
17. mercy everlasting upon—
147. 11. The Lord taketh pleasure in—
Luke 1. 50. his mercy on—from generation
Deut. 6. 2. mightest *fear the Lord*
13. thou shalt—thy God, 10. 20.
24.—our God for our good always
10. 12.—thy God to walk in his ways
14. 23. learn to—thy God, 17. 19; 31. 12, 13.
Josh. 4. 24. ye might—your God
24. 14. therefore—serve in sincerity
1 Sam. 12. 14. if ye will—and serve
24. only—and serve him in truth
1 Ki. 18. 12. thy servant did—2 Ki. 4. 1.
2 Ki. 17. 28. how they should—
Ps. 15. 4. be honoureth them that—
22. 23. ye that—trust in him, 115. 11.
33. 8. let all the earth—
115. 13. he will bless them that—
118. 4. let them that—say, his mercy
135. 20. ye that—bless the Lord
Prov. 3. 7.—and depart from evil
24. 21. my son—and meddle not
Jer. 5. 24. let us—that giveth rain
26. 19. did not he—and besought Lord
Hos. 3. 5. and shall—and his goodness
Jonah 1. 9. I—the God of heaven
Gen. 15. 1. *fear not*, I am thy shield
Num. 14. 9. Lord is with us—them
Deut. 1. 21.—neither be discouraged, 31. 8.
Josh. 8. 1; 10. 25.
Ps. 56. 4. I will not *f.* what flesh can do, 118. 6.
Heb. 13. 6.
Is. 41. 10.—for I am with thee, I will help
thee, 13; 43. 5.
Jer. 5. 22. *f.* ye not me, saith the Lord
30. 10. —O my servant Jacob, 46. 27, 28.
Mat. 10. 28.—them that kill the body
Luke 12. 32.—little flock
Ex. 1. 17. midwives *feared* God, 21.
14. 31. people *f.* Lord and believed
1 Sam. 12. 18. all people greatly *f.* Lord
Neh. 7. 2. Hanani *f.* God above many
Job 1. 1. that *f.* God and eschewed evil
Ps. 76. 7. thou art to be *f.*
89. 7. God is greatly to be *f.* in the
96. 4. Lord is to be *f.* above all gods
Mal. 3. 16. they that *f.* the Lord spake often
Acts 10. 2. one that *f.* God
Heb. 5. 7. was heard in that he *f.*
Gen. 22. 12. that thou *fearest* God
Job 1. 8. that *feareth* God, 2. 3.
Prov. 28. 14. happy man that *f.* alway
Ps. 25. 12. what man is he that *feareth the Lord*
112. 1. blessed is the man that—
Is. 50. 10. who among you—
Acts 10. 22. one that *f.* God and of good report
35. that *f.* God and worketh righteousness
13. 26. whosoever among you *f.* God
Ex. 15. 11. *fearful* in praises
Mat. 8. 26. why are ye *f.* Mark 4. 40.
Heb. 10. 27. certain *f.* looking for of
31. *f.* thing to fall into hands of the living God
Rev. 21. 8. *f.* and unbelieving shall have their part
Ps. 139. 14. I am *fearfully* and wonderfully made
55. 5. *fearfulness* and trembling
Is. 33. 14. *f.* hath surprised hypocrites
FEAST, Gen. 19. 3; 21. 8.
Prov. 15. 15. merry heart continual *f.*
Eccl. 10. 19. *f.* is made for laughter
Is. 25. 6. Lord make to all a *f.* of
1 Cor. 5. 8. let us keep *f.*, not with

FEEBLE, Gen. 30. 42. Job 4. 4.
Ps. 105. 37. not one *f.* person among
Is. 35. 3. confirm *f.* knees
Zech. 12. 8. he that is *f.* shall be as David
1 Thes. 5. 14. comfort the *f.* minded
Heb. 12. 12. lift up the *f.* knees
FEED, *fed*, Gen. 25. 30; 30. 36.
Ps. 28. 9. *f.* them and lift them up
37. 3. verily thou shalt be *f.*
49. 14. death shall *f.* on them
Prov. 10. 21. lips of righteous *f.* many
Is. 58. 14. *f.* thee with heritage of Jacob
Jer. 3. 15. pastors *f.* you with knowledge
Acts 20. 28. to *f.* the church of God
1 Cor. 13. 3. give my goods to *f.* poor
3. 2. I have *f.* you with milk, and
Prov. 30. 8. *f.* me with food convenient
Sol. 1. 8. *f.* kids beside shepherds' tents
Mic. 7. 14. *f.* thy people with thy rod
John 21. 15. *f.* my lambs, *f.* my sheep, 16, 17.
Rom. 12. 20. enemy hunger, *f.* him
1 Pet. 5. 2. *f.* flock of God among
Is. 44. 20. he *feedeth* on ashes
Sol. 2. 16. he *f.* among lilies, 6. 3.
Hos. 12. 1. Ephraim *f.* on wind
1 Cor. 9. 7. who *f.* a flock and eateth not
FEEL, *feeling*, Gen. 27. 12. Acts 17. 27. Eph. 4. 19.
Heb. 4. 15.
FEET, Gen. 18. 4; 19. 2; 49. 10.
1 Sam. 2. 9. keep *f.* of his saints
Neh. 9. 21. their *f.* swelled not
Job 12. 5. is ready to slip with his *f.*
29. 15. eyes to blind, *f.* to lame
Ps. 73. 2. my *f.* were almost gone
116. 8. delivered my *f.* from falling
119. 101. refrained my *f.* from every evil
105. thy word is a lamp to my *f.*
Prov. 4. 26. ponder path of thy *f.*
Is. 59. 7. their *f.* run to evil, and
Luke 1. 79. guide our *f.* into way of
Eph. 6. 15. *f.* shod with preparation
Heb. 12. 13. straight paths for your *f.*
Rev. 11. 11. they stood upon their *f.*
FEIGNED, 1 Sam. 21. 13. Ps. 17. 1. 2 Pet. 2. 3.
feignedly, Jer. 3. 10.
FELLOW, Gen. 19. 9. Ex. 2. 13.
Eccl. 4. 10. if they fall, one will lift up his *f.*
Acts 24. 5. a pestilent *f.* 22. 22.
Rom. 16. 7. my kinsmen and *f.* prisoners
2 Cor. 8. 23. my *f.* helper, 3 John 8.
Eph. 2. 19. *f.* citizens, 3. 6. *f.* heirs
Col. 1. 7. *f.* servant, 4. 7. Rev. 6. 11.; 19. 10;
4. 10. Aristarchus my *f.* prisoner   [22. 9.
Phil. 2. 25. *f.* soldier, Philem. 2.
4. 3. Philem. 1, 24. *f.* labourers, 1 Thes. 3. 2.
Ps. 45. 7. oil of gladness above *fellows*, Heb. 1. 9.
94. 20. have *fellowship* with thee
Acts 2. 42. continued . . . apostles' doctrine and *f.*
1 Cor. 1. 9. called to *f.* of Jesus Christ
10. 20. should have *f.* with devils
2 Cor. 6. 14. what *f.* hath righteousness with
unrighteousness
8. 4. *f.* of ministering to saints
Gal. 2. 9. gave us right hands of *f.*
Eph. 5. 11. no *f.* with works of
Phil. 1. 5. for your *f.* in the gospel
2. 1. if there be any *f.* of the spirit
3. 10. may know him and *f.* of his sufferings
1 John 1. 3. *f.* with us . . . our *f.* with Father
6. if we say we have *f.* with him
FERVENT in spirit, Acts 18. 25.
Rom. 12. 11. *f.* in spirit, serving Lord
2 Cor. 7. 7. *f.* mind toward me

Jas. 5. 16. *fervent* prayer of righteous
1 Pet. 4. 8. have *f.* charity among
2 Pet. 3. 10. melt with *f.* heat, 12.
Col. 4. 12. Epaphras always labouring *fervently*
    for you in prayers
1 Pet. 1. 22. love one another *f.*
FEW, Gen. 29. 20. Ps. 105. 12.
Mat. 7. 14. way to life, *f.* that find it
20. 16. many called, *f.* chosen, 22. 14.
1 Pet. 3. 20. *f.* . . . eight souls saved
Rev. 2. 14. I have *f.* things against
3. 4. thou hast a *f.* names in Sardis
FIDELITY, all good, Tit. 2. 10.
FIERCENESS of anger, Deut. 13. 17. Josh.
    7. 26. 2 Ki. 23. 26. Job 4. 9; 10. 16; 39. 24;
    41. 10. Ps. 85. 3. Jer. 25. 38. Hos. 11. 9.
FIERY law, Deut. 33. 2.
Num. 21. 6. *f.* serpents, 8. Deut. 8. 15.
Ps. 21. 9. make them as a *f.* oven
Eph. 6. 16. quench *f.* darts of wicked
Heb. 10. 27. *f.* indignation . . . devour
1 Pet. 4. 12. not strange the *f.* trial
FIGHT, 1 Sam. 17. 20. Ex. 14. 14.
Acts 5. 39. found to *f.* against God
23. 9. let us not *f.* against God
1 Tim. 6. 12. *f.* the good *f.* of faith
2 Tim. 4. 7. I have fought a good *f.*
Heb. 10. 32. a great *f.* of afflictions
FIGS, Gen. 3. 7. Is. 34. 4; 38. 21.
Jer. 24. 2. good *f.,* vile *f.* 29. 17.
Mat. 7. 16. gather *f.* of thistles?
Jas. 3. 12. can *f.* tree bear olive . . . vine *f.*
Judg. 9. 10. *fig tree,* 1 Ki. 4. 25. Mic. 4. 4.
Is. 36. 16. Hos. 9. 10. Nah. 3. 12. Hab.
    3. 17. Zech. 3. 10. Mat. 21. 19; 24. 32. Luke
    13. 6, 7. John 1. 48, 50. Rev. 6. 13.
FIGURE, Rom. 5. 14. 1 Cor. 4. 6. Heb. 9. 9, 24;
    11. 19. 1 Pet. 3. 21.
FILL, Job 8. 21; 23. 4.
Ps. 81. 10. open mouth wide, I will *f.* it
Jer. 23. 24. I *f.* heaven and earth
Rom. 15. 13. God *f.* you with all joy
Eph. 4. 10. ascended . . . might *f.* all
Ps. 72. 19. earth *filled* with his glory
Luke 1. 53. *f.* hungry with good things
Acts 9. 17. *f.* with the Holy Ghost, 2. 4; 4. 8, 31;
    13. 9, 52. Luke 1. 15.
Rom. 15. 14. *f.* with all knowledge
2 Cor. 7. 4. I am *f.* with comfort
Eph. 3. 19. be *f.* with all fulness of God
Phil. 1. 11. *f.* with fruits of righteousness
Col. 1. 9. *f.* with knowledge of his will
2 Tim. 1. 4. that I may be *f.* with joy
Eph. 1. 23. fulness of him that *filleth*
FILTH, Is. 4. 4. 1 Cor. 4. 13.
Ezek. 36. 25. from all *filthiness* will I cleanse you
2 Cor. 7. 1. cleanse from all *f.* of flesh and
Jas. 1. 21. lay apart all *f.*
Job 15. 16. more *filthy* is man
Ps. 14. 3. altogether become *f.* 53. 3.
Is. 64. 6. our righteousness as *f.* rags
Col. 3. 8. put off *f.* communication
1 Tim. 3. 3. greedy of *f.* lucre, 8. Tit. 1. 7, 11.
    1 Pet. 5. 2.
2 Pet. 2. 7. vexed with *f.* conversation
Rev. 22. 11. that is *f.* let him be *f.*
FINALLY, 2 Cor. 13. 11. Eph. 6. 10. Phil. 3. 1;
    4. 8. 2 Thes. 3. 1. 1 Pet. 3. 8.
FIND, Gen. 19. 11; 38. 22.
Num. 32. 23. your sin will *f.* you out
Prov. 1. 28. shall seek me and not *f.*
Sol. 5. 6. I sought but could not *f.*
Jer. 6. 16. shall *f.* rest to your souls

Jer. 29. 13. shall seek me and *find* me
Mat. 7. 7. seek and ye shall *f.* Luke 11. 9, **25.**
7. 14. way to life, few that *f.* it
10. 39. findeth life shall lose it; loseth life shall *f.*
    it, 16. 25.
11. 29. ye shall *f.* rest to your souls
John 7. 34. seek me, and shall not *f.*
2 Tim. 1. 18. may *f.* mercy of the Lord
Heb. 4. 16. may *f.* grace to help
Rev. 9. 6. seek death and shall not *f.*
Prov. 8. 35. whoso *findeth* me *f.* life
18. 22. whoso *f.* a wife *f.* a good thing
Eccl. 9. 10. whatsoever thy hand *f.* to do
Mat. 7. 8. that seeketh *f.* Luke 11. 10.
Is. 58. 13. not *finding* own pleasure
Rom. 11. 33. his ways past *f.* out
FINE, Job 28. 1. Is. 3. 23. Lev. 2. 1. Ps. 81. 16.
    Prov. 25. 4.
FINGER of God, Ex. 8. 19; 31. 18. Deut. 9. 10.
1 Ki. 12. 10. little *f.*   [Luke 11. 20.
John 20. 27. reach hither thy *f.*
Ps. 8. 3. heaven the work of thy *fingers*
Prov. 6. 13. he teacheth with his *f.*
Luke 11. 46. touch not . . . with one of your *f.*
FINISH transgression, Dan. 9. 24.
Acts 20. 24. *f.* my course with joy
2 Cor. 8. 6. *f.* in you the same grace
2 Tim. 4. 7. I have *finished* my course
John 17. 4. I have *f.* work, 19. 30.
Jas. 1. 15. sin when it is *f.* bringeth death
Heb. 12. 2. author and *finisher* of faith
FIRE, Ex. 3. 2; 9. 23, 24; 40. 38.
Gen. 19. 24. Lord rained brimstone and *f.*
Ps. 11. 6. rain *f.* and brimstone on wicked
39. 3. while musing the *f.* burned
Prov. 6. 27. can man take *f.* in his bosom
25. 22. heap coals of *f.* on head, Rom. 12. 20.
Sol. 8. 6. coals thereof are coals of *f.*
Is. 9. 18. wickedness burneth as a *f.*
10. 17. light of Israel for a *f.*
31. 9. Lord whose *f.* is in Zion
43. 2. walkest through *f.* not burnt
Jer. 23. 29. is not my word like *f.* 20. 9.
Amos 5. 6. lest Lord break out like *f.*
7. 4. Lord God called to contend by *f.*
Hab. 2. 13. labour in very *f.* for
Zech. 2. 5. I will be a wall of *f.*
Mal. 3. 2. he is like a refiner's *f.*
Mat. 3. 10. cast into the *f.* 7. 19.
12. burn with unquenchable *f.* Mark 9. 43, 44,
    46, 48. Luke 3. 17.
Luke 9. 54. command *f.* to come down
12. 49. am come to send *f.* on earth
1 Cor. 3. 13. revealed by *f.* and *f.* shall try every, 15.
Heb. 12. 29. our God is a consuming *f.*
Jude 23. pulling them out of the *f.*
Mat. 5. 22. hell *fire,* 18. 9. Mark 9. 47.
Lev. 10. 1. *strange fire,* Num. 3. 4; 26. 61.
FIRST, Mat. 10. 2. Esth. 1. 14.
Is. 41. 4. the Lord the *f.* and the last, 44. 6;
    48. 12. Rev. 1. 11, 17; 2. 8; 22. 13.
Mat. 6. 33. seek *f.* kingdom of God
7. 5. *f.* cast out the beam, Luke 6. 42.
19. 30. *f.* shall be last, 20. 16. Mark 10. 31.
Acts 26. 23. Christ *f.* rise from dead
Rom. 11. 35. who hath *f.* given to him
1 Cor. 15. 45. *f.* Adam, 47. *f.* man of earth
2 Cor. 8. 5. *f.* gave their own selves to the Lord
12. accepted, *f.* willing mind
1 Pet. 4. 17. if judgment *f.* being at us
1 John 4. 19. because he *f.* loved us
Rev. 2. 4. left *f.* love, 5. do *f.* works
20. 5. this is the *f.* resurrection, 6.

Mat. 1. 25. *firstborn,* Luke 2. 7.
Rom. 8. 29. *f.* among many brethren
Col. 1. 15. *f.* of every creature
18. *f.* from the dead
Heb. 12. 23. assembly and church of *f.*
Rom. 11. 16. if *firstfruit* be holy
Prov. 3. 9. honour the Lord with *firstfruits*
Rom. 8. 23. *f.* of the Spirit
1 Cor. 15. 20. Christ *f.* of them that slept, 23.
Jas. 1. 18. we a kind of *f.* of his creatures
Rev. 14. 4. redeemed are *f.* to God
FISH, Ezek. 29. 4, 5; 47. 9, 10.
Jer. 16. 16. *fishers,* Ezek. 47. 10. Mat. 4. 18, 19.
John 21. 7. Is. 19. 8.
FLAME, Ex. 3. 2. Judg. 13. 20.
Ps. 104. 4. ministers a *f.* Heb. 1. 7.
Is. 10. 17. his Holy One for a *f.*
2 Thes. 1. 8. in *flaming* fire taking
FLATTER, Ps. 78. 36. Prov. 2. 16; 20. 19.
Job 32. 21, 22. 1 Thes. 2. 5.
FLEE, Is. 10. 3; 20. 6. Heb. 6. 18.
Prov. 28. 1. wicked *f.* when no man
Mat. 3. 7. who warned you to *f.* wrath
1 Cor. 6. 18. *f.* fornication, 10. 14. *f.* idolatry
2 Tim. 2. 22. *f.* youthful lusts
Jas. 4. 7. resist the devil, he will *f.*
FLESH, Gen. 2. 21. 1 Cor. 15. 39.
Gen. 2. 24. they shall be one *f.* Mat. 19. 5. 1 Cor.
6. 16. Eph. 5. 31.
Job 10. 11. clothed with skin and *f.*
Ps. 56. 4. what *f.* can do to me
78. 39. remember they but *f.*
Jer. 17. 5. cursed that maketh *f.* his arm
Mat. 26. 41. spirit willing, *f.* weak
John 1. 14. the Word was made *f.*
6. 53. eat *f.* of Son of man, 52, 55, 56.
63. *f.* profiteth nothing, words are
Rom. 7. 25. serve with *f.* law of sin
9. 5. of whom concerning *f.* Christ
13. 14. make not provision for *f.*
1 Cor. 1. 29. that no *f.* should glory
2 Cor. 1. 17. purpose according to *f.*
10. 2. walked according to the *f.*
Gal. 5. 24. crucified *f.* with affections
Eph. 5. 30. members . . . of his *f.* and
6. 5. masters according to *f.*
Heb. 12. 9. we had fathers of our *f.*
Jude 7. going after strange *f.*
23. hating garment spotted by *f.*
John 8. 15. ye judge *after the flesh*
Rom. 8. 1. walk not—but Spirit, 9.
8. 5. they that are—mind things of *f.*
13. if ye live—ye shall die, 12.
1 Cor. 1. 26. not many wise men—
10. 18. Israel—Rom. 9. 8. Gal. 6. 13.
2 Cor. 5. 16. know no man—known Christ—
2 Pet. 2. 10.—in lust of uncleanness
Ps. 65. 2. to thee shall *all flesh* come
Is. 40. 7.—is grass, 1 Pet. 1. 24.
49. 26.—know I am thy Redeemer
Jer. 32. 27. I am the Lord, God of—
Joel 2. 28. I will pour my Spirit on—
Luke 3. 6.—shall see salvation of God, Ps. 98. 3.
John 17. 2. given him power over—
Rom. 7. 5. when we were *in the flesh*
8. 8. that are—cannot please God
1 Pet. 3. 18. he was put to death—4. 1.
Gen. 2. 23. *my flesh,* 29. 14. Job 19. 26. Ps. 63. 1;
119. 120. John 6. 51. 55, 56. Rom. 7. 18.
John 1. 13. born not of will *of the flesh*
3. 6. that which is born—is *f.*
Rom. 8. 5. after *f.* do mind things—
Gal. 5. 19. works—are manifest

Gal. 6. 8. soweth to *flesh* shall *of the flesh* reap
corruption
Eph. 2. 3. lusts of our *f.* desires—
1 Pet. 3. 21. not putting away filth—
1 John 2. 16. lust—lust of the eyes, pride
Mat. 16. 17. *flesh and blood* hath not revealed
1 Cor. 15. 50.—cannot inherit kingdom of God
Gal. 1. 16. I conferred not with—
Eph. 6. 12. we wrestle not against—but
Heb. 2. 14. children partakers of—
2 Cor. 1. 12. not with *fleshly* wisdom
Col. 2. 18. puffed up by his *f.* mind
1 Pet. 2. 11. abstain from *f.* lusts
FLOCK, Gen. 32. 5. Ps. 77. 20. Is. 40. 11;
63. 11. Jer. 13. 17, 20.
Zech. 11. 4. feed *f.* of slaughter, 7.
Acts 20. 28. take heed to the *f.* 29.
1 Pet. 5. 2. feed *f.* of God among you
FLOURISH, Is. 17. 11; 66. 14.
Ps. 72. 7. shall the righteous *f.* 16; 92. 12, 13, 14.
Prov. 11. 28; 14. 11.
132. 18. on himself shall crown *f.*
FOLLOW, Gen. 32. 4. Ex. 14. 4.
Ex. 23. 2. shall not *f.* a multitude
Deut. 16. 20. is just shalt thou *f.*
Is. 51. 1. hearken . . . that *f.* after righteousness
Hos. 6. 3. know if we *f.* on to know the Lord
Rom. 14. 19. *f.* things that make for peace
1 Cor. 14. 1. *f.* after charity
Phil. 3. 12. but I *f.* that I may apprehend
1 Thes. 5. 15. *f.* that which is good
1 Tim. 6. 11. *f.* after righteousness
2 Tim. 2. 22. *f.* faith, charity, peace
Heb. 12. 14. *f.* peace with all men
13. 7. whose faith *f.* considering end
1 Pet. 2. 21. leaving us example that ye *f.* his steps
Rev. 14. 13. their works do *f.* them
Ps. 23. 6. goodness and mercy shall *follow me,*
Mat. 4. 19; 9. 9; 19. 21. Luke 5. 27; 9. 59.
John 1. 43; 21. 19.
Mat. 16. 24. take up cross and—
Luke 18. 22. all thou hast, and—
John 12. 26. if any serve me let him—
Num. 14. 24. hath *followed* me fully
32. 11. wholly *f.* the Lord, Deut. 1. 36. Josh.
14. 8, 9, 14.
Rom. 9. 30. *f.* not after, 31. *f.* law of righteous-
ness
Ps. 63. 8. soul *followeth* hard after
Mat. 10. 38. taketh not cross and *f.* me
Mark 9. 38. he *f.* not us, Luke 9. 49.
FOLLY wrought in Israel, Gen. 34. 7. Deut. 22. 21.
Josh. 7. 15. Judg. 20. 6.
Job 4. 18. angels he charged with *f.*
Ps. 49. 13. their way is their *f.*
Prov. 26. 4. answer not fool according to *f.*
2 Tim. 3. 9. their *f.* shall be manifest
FOOD, Gen. 3. 6. Deut. 10. 18.
Job 23. 12. words more than necessary *f.*
Ps. 78. 25. men did eat angels' *f.*
146. 7. which giveth *f.* to the hungry
Prov. 30. 8. *f.* convenient for me
Acts 14. 17. filling our hearts with *f.*
2 Cor. 9. 10. ministered bread for *f.*
1 Tim. 6. 8. having *f.* and raiment
FOOL said in heart, Ps. 14. 1; 53. 1.
Jer. 17. 11. at his end shall be a *f.*
Mat. 5. 22. say to brother, Thou *f.*
Luke 12. 20. thou *f.* this night thy soul
1 Cor. 3. 18. let him become a *f.*
2 Cor. 11. 16. think me a *f.* 23. as a *f.*
Ps. 75. 4. *fools* deal not foolishly
94. 8. *f.* when will ye be wise

Prov. 1. 7. *fools*... wisdom, 22. *f.* . . . . knowledge
13. 20. companion of *f.* shall be destroyed
14. 8. folly of *f.* is deceitful
9. *f.* make a mock at sin
Eccl. 5. 4. he hath no pleasure in *f.*
Mat. 23. 17. ye *f.* and blind, 19.
Rom. 1. 22. professing to be wise became *f.*
1 Cor. 4. 10. are *f.* for Christ's sake
Eph. 5. 15. circumspectly, not as *f.*
Deut. 32. 6. *foolish* people and unwise
Ps. 5. 5. *f.* shall not stand in thy sight
73. 22. so *f.* was I and ignorant
Mat. 7. 26. like *f.* man which built . . . on sand
25. 2. ten virgins, . . . five *f.* 3, 8.
Rom. 1. 21. *f.* heart darkened
Gal. 3. 1. O *f.* Galatians, who hath
Eph. 5. 4. filthiness, nor *f.* talking
Tit. 3. 3. sometimes *f.* disobedient
Gen. 31. 28. done *foolishly*, Num. 12. 11. 1 Sam.
13. 13. 2 Sam. 24. 10. 1 Chr. 21. 8. 2 Chr.
16. 9. Prov. 14. 17. 2 Cor. 11. 21.
Job 1. 22. Job . . . not nor charged God *f.*
2 Sam. 15. 31. turn counsel into *foolishness*
Prov. 12. 23. heart of fools proclaimeth *f.*
14. 24. *f.* of fools is folly, 15. 2, 14.
22. 15. *f.* is bound in heart of a child
24. 9. thought of *f.* is sin
27. 22. bray a fool . . . yet will not his *f.* depart
1 Cor. 1. 18. cross to them that perish *f.*
21. God by *f.* of preaching to save
2. 14. they are *f.* to him; neither can he
3. 19. wisdom of world *f.* with God
FOOT shall not stumble, Prov. 3. 23.
Eccl. 5. 1. keep thy *f.* when thou
Is. 58. 13. turn . . . *f.* from sabbath
Mat. 18. 8. if thy *f.* offend thee, cut
1 Cor. 12. 15. if *f.* say, because I am not
Heb. 10. 29. trodden under *f.* Son of God
FORBEAR, Ex. 23. 5. 1 Cor. 9. 6.
Rom. 2. 4. goodness and *forbearance*, 3. 25.
FORBID, Mark 10. 14. Luke 18. 16; 6. 29.
Acts 24. 23; 28. 31.
1 Thes. 2. 16. *forbidding* to speak to Gentiles
1 Tim. 4. 3. *f.* to marry
FORCE, Mat. 11. 12. Heb. 9. 17.
Is. 60. 5. *forces* of Gentiles shall come, 11.
Job 6. 25. how *forcible* right words
FOREFATHERS, 2 Tim. 1. 3. Jer. 11. 10.
FOREHEAD, Ex. 28. 38. Lev. 13. 41.
Jer. 3. 3. thou hast a whore's *f.*
Ezek. 3. 8. thy *f.* strong against their *foreheads*
Rev. 7. 3. sealed in their *f.* 9. 4.
14. 1. Father's name written in *f.* 22. 4.
FOREIGNERS, Ex. 12. 45. Deut. 15. 3. Obad. 11.
Eph. 2. 19.
FOREKNOW, Rom. 8. 29; 11. 2.
Acts 2. 23. *foreknowledge* of God, 1 Pet. 1. 2.
FOREORDAINED, 1 Pet. 1. 20.
FORESEETH, Prov. 22. 3; 27. 12.
FOREWARN, Luke 12. 5.
FORGAT Lord, Judg. 3. 7. 1 Sam. 12. 9.
Ps. 78. 11. *f.* his works and wonders, 106. 13.
Lam. 3. 17. I *f.* prosperity
Hos. 2. 13. *f.* me, saith the Lord
Deut. 9. 7. remember and *forget* not
Job 8. 13. paths of all that *f.* God
Ps. 45. 10. *f.* thine own people, and
50. 22. consider this, ye that *f.* God
103. 2. *f.* not all his benefits
119. 16. will not *f.* thy words, 83, 93, 109, 141, 153, 176.
Prov. 3. 1. my son *f.* not my law
Is. 49. 15. woman *f.* sucking child

Jer. 2. 32. can a maid *forget* ornaments
Heb. 6. 10. God not unrighteous to *f.* your labour of love
13. 16. to do good and to communicate *f.* not
2. be not *forgetful* to entertain
Ps. 44. 24. *forgettest* our affliction
9. 12. he *forgetteth* not the cry of humble
Prov. 2. 17. *f.* covenant of her God
Jas. 1. 24. *f.* what manner of man
Phil. 3. 13. *forgetting* those things
Ps. 10. 11. God hath *forgotten*
42. 9. why hast thou *f.* me
77. 9. hath God *f.* to be gracious
119. 61. I have not *f.* thy law
Is. 17. 10. *f.* God of thy salvation
49. 14. Zion said, my Lord hath *f.* me
Jer. 2. 32. my people have *f.* me
3 21. have *f.* their God, Deut. 32. 18.
50. 5. covenant that shall not be *f.*
Heb. 12. 5. *f.* the exhortation
FORGAVE their iniquity, Ps. 78. 38.
Mat. 18. 27. *f.* him the debt, 32.
Luke 7. 42. frankly *f.* them both
43. love most, to whom *f.* most
Col. 3. 13. as Christ *f.* you, also do
Ps. 32. 5. *forgavest* the iniquity of
99. 8. thou wast a God that *f.* them
Ex. 32. 32. *forgive* their sin
Ps. 86. 5. thou art . . . ready to *f.*
Is. 2. 9. therefore *f.* them not
Jer. 31. 34. I *f.* their iniquity, 36. 3.
Mat. 6. 12. *f.* us our debts, as we *f.*
14. if ye *f.* men, 15. if you *f.* not
9. 6. Son of man hath power on earth to *f.*
Luke 6. 37. *f.* and ye shall be forgiven
17. 3. if he repent, *f.* him, 4.
23. 34. Father, *f.* them, they know not
2 Cor. 2. 10. to whom ye *f.* any thing
1 John 1. 9. faithful to *f.* us our sins
Ps. 32. 1. transgression is *forgiven*
85. 2. *f.* the iniquity of thy people
Is. 33. 24. people *f.* their iniquity
Luke 7. 47. to whom little is *f.* loveth
Rom. 4. 7. blessed . . . whose iniquities *f.*
Eph. 4. 32. as God hath *f.* you , Col. 3. 13.
Jas. 5. 15. if he have . . . sins, they shall be *f.*
1 John 2. 12. your sins are *f.* you
Acts 5. 31. repentance to Israel and *forgiveness*
26. 18. may receive *f.* of sins by faith
Col. 1. 14. redemption, even *f.* sins
Dan. 9. 9. to Lord belong mercies and *forgivenesses*
Ps. 103. 3. *forgiveth* thine iniquities
Ex. 34. 7. *forgiving* iniquity, transgression, sin,
Num. 14. 18. Mic. 7. 18.
Eph. 4. 32. *f.* one another, Col. 3. 13.
FORM, Gen. 1. 2. 1 Sam. 28. 14.
Is. 53. 2. hath no *f.* nor comeliness
Rom. 2. 20. hast *f.* of knowledge
6. 17. obeyed that *f.* of doctrine
Phil. 2. 6. who being in *f.* of God
7. took upon him the *f.* of a servant
2 Tim. 1. 13. hold *f.* of sound words
3. 5. having the *f.* of godliness
Is. 45. 7. *f.* light and create darkness
Ps. 94. 9. that *formed* the eye shall he not see?
Prov. 26. 10. God that *f.* all things
Is. 27. 11. *f.* them shew no favour
43. 21. this people I *f.* for myself
44. 2. *f.* thee from womb
54. 17. no weapon *f.* against thee shall prosper
Rom. 9. 20. thing *f.* say to him that *f.*
Gal. 4. 19. till Christ be *f.* in you
Jer. 10. 16. the *former* of all things, 51. 19.

Zech. 12. 1. *formeth* spirit of man within
FORNICATION, 2 Chr. 21. 11. Is. 23. 17.
Ezek. 16. 15, 26, 29.
John 8. 41. we be not born of *f.*
Acts 15. 20. abstain from *f.* 21. 25.
Rom. 1. 29. filled with *f.*, wickedness
1 Cor. 5. 1. there is *f.* among you
6. 13. body not for *f.* 18. flee *f.*
7. 2. to avoid *f.* have own wife
10. 8. neither let us commit *f.*
2 Cor. 12. 21. not repented of their *f.*
Gal. 5. 19. works of flesh, adultery, *f.*
Eph. 5. 3. *f.* and all uncleanness
Col. 3. 5. mortify . . . *f.* uncleanness
1 Thes. 4. 3. should abstain from *f.*
Jude 7. giving themselves to *f.*
Rev. 2. 14. and to commit *f.* 20.
21. I gave her space to repent her *f.*
9. 21. neither repented of their *f.*
14. 8. of the wine of her *f.* 17. 2.
Rev. 17. 4. filthiness of her *f.*
18. 3. committed *f.* with her, 9.
19. 2. did corrupt earth with her *f.*
Ezek. 16. 15. *fornications,* Mat. 15. 19.
1 Cor. 5. 9–11. *fornicators,* 6. 9. Heb. 12. 16.
FORSAKE, Deut. 12. 19; 31. 16.
Deut. 4. 31. (Lord thy God) will not *f.* thee,
31. 6, 8. 1 Chr. 28. 20. Heb. 13. 5.
Josh. 1. 5. I will not fail thee nor *f.* thee,
Is. 41. 17; 42. 16.
1 Sam. 12. 22. Lord will not *f.* his people,
8. 57. let him not leave nor *f.* us   [1 Ki. 6. 13.
Ps. 27. 10. when father and mother *f.*
94. 14. neither will he *f.* inheritance
Is. 55. 7. let the wicked *f.* his way
Jer. 17. 13. that *f.* thee be ashamed
Jonah 2. 8. *f.* their own mercy
Ps. 71. 11. God hath *forsaken* him
22. 1. My God, my God, why hast thou *f.* me,
Mat. 27. 46.
Is. 49. 14. the Lord hath *f.* me
54. 7. for a small moment have I *f.* thee
Jer. 2. 13. *f.* me the fountain, 17. 13.
Mat. 19. 27. we have *f.* all, 29. *f.* houses or
brethren, or sisters, &c.
2 Cor. 4. 9. persecuted but not *f.*
Prov. 2. 17. *forsaketh* guide of youth
28. 12. confesseth and *f.* shall find
Deut. 32. 15. *forsook* God which made him
Ps. 119. 87. I *f.* not thy precepts
2 Tim. 4. 16. all men *f.* me
FORTRESS and rock, Lord is my, 2 Sam.
22. 2. Ps. 18. 2; 31. 3; 71. 3; 91. 2; 144. 2. Jer. 16. 19.
FOUND, Gen. 26. 19; 31. 37.
Eccl. 7. 27. this have I *f.* that, 29.
Sol. 3. 1. I *f.* him not, 4. I *f.* him
Is. 55. 6. seek Lord while he may be *f.*
65. 1. *f.* of them that sought me not
Ezek. 22. 30. I sought a man *f.* none
Dan. 5. 27. weighed and *f.* wanting
2 Pet. 3. 14. be *f.* of him in peace
Mat. 7. 25. *founded* on a rock, Ps. 24. 2. Prov.
3. 19. Is. 14. 32.
Job 4. 19. whose *foundation* is in dust
Prov. 10. 25. righteous is an everlasting *f.*
Is. 28. 16. I lay in Zion a sure *f.*
Rom. 15. 20. build on another man's *f.*
1 Cor. 3. 10. laid *f.* 12. build on this *f.*
Eph. 2. 20. built on *f.* of prophets
1 Tim. 6. 19. lay up good *f.* for time
2 Tim. 2. 19. *f.* of God standeth sure
Ps. 11. 3. if *foundations* be destroyed
Heb. 11. 10. a city which hath *f.*

Rev. 21. 14. the city hath twelve *foundations*
Mat. 13. 35. *foundation of the world,* 25. 34.
John 17. 24. Eph. 1. 4. 1 Pet. 1. 20. Rev. 13. 8;
17. 8. Ps. 104, 5. Prov. 8. 29. Is. 51. 13, 16.
FOUNTAIN, Gen. 7. 11. Deut. 8. 7.
Deut. 33. 28. *f.* of Jacob on a land
Ps. 36. 9. with thee is *f.* of life
68. 26. bless Lord from *f.* of Israel
Prov. 5. 18. let thy *f.* be blessed
13. 14. law of wise is a *f.* of life
14. 27. fear of the Lord is a *f.* of life
Eccl. 12. 6. a pitcher broken at the *f.*
Sol. 4. 12. *f.* sealed, 15. *f.* of gardens
Jer. 2. 13. forsaken me, the *f.* of living waters
9. 1. that my eyes were a *f.* of tears
Joel 3. 18. a *f.* out of house of Lord
Zech. 13. 1. a *f.* opened for house
Jas. 3. 12. can *f.* both yield salt
Rev. 21. 6. give *f.* of life freely, 22. 17.
FOXES, Judg. 15. 4. Ps. 63. 10. Sol. 2. 15. Lam.
5. 18. Ezek. 13. 4. Mat. 8. 20. Luke 13. 32.
FRAGMENTS, Mat. 14. 20. Mark 6. 43;
8. 19, 20. John 6. 12, 13.
FRAIL I am, Ps. 39. 4.
FRAME, Ps. 103. 14. Is. 29. 16. Jer. 18. 11. Eph.
2. 21. Heb. 11. 3.
FREE, Ex. 21. 2. Lev. 19. 20.
2 Chr. 29. 31. as many as were of a *f.* heart
Ps. 51. 12. uphold with thy *f.* spirit
88. 5. *f.* among the dead, like slain
John 8. 32. truth shall make you *f.*
36. if Son make *f.* shall be *f.* indeed
Rom. 5. 15. so also is *f.* gift, 16, 18.
1 Cor. 7. 22. the Lord's *f.* man
Gal. 3. 28. bond nor *f.* Col. 3. 11.
2 Thes. 3. 1. word of Lord may have *f.* course
1 Pet. 2. 16. *f.* and not using liberty
Hos. 14. 4. I will love them *freely*
Mat. 10. 8. *f.* ye have received, *f.* give
Rom. 3. 24. justified *f.* by his grace
8. 32. with him *f.* give us all things
1 Cor. 2. 12. things *f.* given us of God
Rev. 21. 6. fountain of water of life *f.* 22. 17.
FRET, Ps. 37. 1, 7, 8. Prov. 24. 19.
Ezek. 16. 43. hast *fretted* me in all
Prov. 19. 3. his heart *fretteth* against **Lord**
FRIEND, Jer. 6. 21. Hos. 3. 1.
Ex. 33. 11. as a man speaketh to his *f.*
Deut. 13. 6. *f.* which is as his own soul
2 Sam. 16. 17. is this kindness to thy *f.*
2 Chr. 20. 7. Abraham thy *f.* Is. 41. 8. Jas.
2. 23.
Prov. 17. 17. *f.* loveth at all times
18. 24. a *f.* closer than a brother
27. 10. own *f.* father's *f.* forsake not
Sol. 5. 16. this is my beloved, . . . *f.*
Mic. 7. 5. trust ye not in a *f.* . . .
Prov. 18. 24. hath *friends* shew himself friendly
John 15. 13. lay down life for his *f.*
14. ye are my *f.* if, 15. called you *f.*
Prov. 22. 24. make no *friendship* with angry man
Jas. 4. 4. *f.* of the world is enmity with God
FROWARD, Job 5. 13. 1 Pet. 2. 18.
Deut. 32. 20. a very *f.* generation
Ps. 18. 26. with *f.* wilt shew thyself *f.*
101. 4. *f.* heart shall depart from
Prov. 4. 24. *f.* mouth, 6. 12; 8. 13.
10. 31. *f.* tongue, 11. 20. *f.* heart, 17. 20.
Is. 57. 17. went on *frowardly*
Prov. 6. 14. *frowardness* is in his heart
FRUIT, Gen. 4. 3. Lev. 19. 24.
Gen. 30. 2. withheld *f.* of the womb
Ex. 21. 22. hurt so that *f.* depart

2 Ki. 19. 30. bear *fruit* upward, Is. 37. 31.
Ps. 92. 14. shall bring forth *f.* in old age
127. 3. *f.* of womb is his reward
Prov. 11. 30. *f.* of righteous tree of life
Sol. 2. 3. his *f.* was sweet to taste
Is. 3. 10. eat the *f.* of their doings
27. 9. all the *f.* to take away sin
57. 19. create *f.* of the lips
Hos. 10. 1. empty vine bringeth *f.* to himself
Mic. 6. 7. *f.* of body for sin of my soul
Mat. 7. 17. good tree good *f.* 21. 19.
12. 33. *f.* good; tree known by his *f.*
26. 29. not drink of *f.* of vine till
Luke 1. 42. blessed is *f.* of thy womb
John 4. 36. gathereth *f.* to life eternal
15. 2. branch beareth not *f.* he taketh away; beareth *f.* he purgeth it
Rom. 6. 21. what *f.* 22. *f.* to holiness
7. 4. should bring forth *f.* unto God
15. 28. have sealed to them this *f.*
Gal. 5. 22. *f.* of Spirit is love
Eph. 5. 9. *f.* of Spirit is in all goodness
Phil. 4. 17. desire *f.* that may abound
Heb. 12. 11. peaceable *f.* of righteousness
Jas. 3. 18. *f.* of righteousness sown
Rev. 22. 2. yielded *f.* every month
Sol. 4. 13. pleasant *fruits*, 6. 11. *f.* of valley
7. 13. all manner of pleasant *f.*
Mat. 3. 8. *f.* meet for repentance
2 Cor. 9. 10. increase *f.* of righteousness
Phil. 1. 11. filled with *f.* of righteousness
Jas. 3. 17. full of mercy and good *f.*
FRUSTRATE, Is. 44. 25. Gal. 2. 21.
FULL, Gen. 15. 16. Ex. 16. 3, 8.
Deut. 34. 9. (Joshua) *f.* of spirit of wisdom
Ruth 1. 21. went out *f.* . . . . home empty
1 Sam. 2. 5. that were *f.* have hired
Job 5. 26. come to grave in *f.* age
Ps. 17. 14. are *f.* of children
Prov. 27. 7. *f.* soul loatheth honeycomb
30. 9. lest I be *f.* and deny thee
Luke 4. 1. Jesus *f.* of the Holy Ghost
6. 25. woe to you that are *f.*
John 1. 14. the Word was made flesh, *f.* of grace and truth
Phil. 4. 12. know both to be *f.* and
Col. 2. 2. riches of *f.* assurance
2 Tim. 4. 5. *f.* proof of thy ministry
Heb. 6. 11. to *f.* assurance of hope
10. 22. near in *f.* assurance of faith
Gen. 29. 27. *fulfil*, Ex. 23. 26.
Ps. 145. 19. *f.* the desire of them
Mat. 3. 15. us to *f.* all righteousness
Acts 13. 22. which shall *f.* all my will
Gal. 5. 16. shall not *f.* lust of flesh
6. 2. bear burden and so *f.* law of Christ
Phil. 2. 2. *f.* ye my joy, that ye be
Col. 4. 17. ministry . . . that thou *f.* it
Jas. 2. 8. if ye *f.* the royal law
Rev. 17. 17. put in their hearts to *f.* his will
Luke 21. 24. till times of . . . be *fulfilled*
Gal. 5. 14. law is *f.* in one word
Eph. 2. 3. *fulfilling* desires of flesh, mind
Job 20. 22. in *fulness* of sufficiency
John 1. 16. of his *f.* have we received
Rom. 11. 25. till *f.* of Gentiles become
15. 29. *f.* of blessing of the Gospel
Gal. 4. 4. when *f.* of time was come
Eph. 1. 10. dispensation of *f.* of times
23. *f.* of him that filleth all in all
3. 19. filled with the *f.* of God
4. 13. to the stature of *f.* of Christ
Col. 1. 19. in him should all *f.* dwell

Col. 2. 9. all the *fulness* of the Godhead
FURNACE, Deut. 4. 20. Jer. 11. 4. Ps. 12. 6.
Is. 31. 9; 48. 10. Dan. 3. 6, 11. Mat. 13. 42, 50.
Rev. 1. 15.
FURNISHED, Deut. 15. 14. Prov. 9. 2.
2 Tim. 3. 17. throughly *f.* to all good works
FURY is not in me, Is. 27. 4.
Is. 59. 18. repay *f.* to his adversaries
Jer. 6. 11. am full of *f.* of the Lord
10. 25. pour out thy *f.* on heathen

G

GAIN, Prov. 3. 14. Job 22. 3.
Is. 33. 15. despiseth *g.* of oppressions
Phil. 1. 21. to live is Christ, to die is *g.*
1 Tim. 6. 5. supposing *g.* godliness, 6. godliness with contentment is great *g.*
Mat. 16. 26. if he *g.* world
1 Cor. 9. 19. servant to all, that I might *g.*
Job 27. 8. hope of hypocrite though he hath *gained*
Mat. 18. 15. thou hast *g.* thy brother
Luke 19. 16. thy pound hath *g.* ten
Tit. 1. 9. convince *gainsayers*
Acts 10. 29. *gainsaying*, Rom. 10. 21. *g.* people
Jude 11. perished in the *g.* of Core
GALL, Job 16. 13; 20. 14, 25.
Deut. 29. 18. root beareth *g.* and wormwood
Ps. 69. 21. gave me *g.* for meat, Mat. 27. 34. *g.* to drink
Jer. 8. 14. given us water of *g.* 9. 15.
Lam. 3. 19. remembering . . . wormwood and *g.*
Acts 8. 23. in the *g.* of bitterness
GAP, to stand in, Ezek. 22. 30.
GARDEN, Gen. 2. 15; 3. 23; 13. 10.
Sol. 4. 12. a *g.* enclosed is my sister
16. blow on my *g.* 5. 1; 6. 2, 11.
Jer. 31. 12. soul as a watered *g.* Is. 58. 11.
GARMENT, Josh. 7. 21. Ezra 9. 3.
Job 37. 17. thy *garments* are warm
Ps. 22. 18. part my *g.* among them
Is. 9. 5. and *g.* rolled in blood
59. 17. put on *g.* of vengeance
Joel 2. 13. rend your hearts not *g.*
Mat. 21. 8. spread their *g.* in way
Acts 9. 39. coats and *g.* Dorcas made
Rev. 3. 4. have not defiled their *g.*
16. 15. watcheth and keepeth his *g.*
GATE, Gen. 19. 1; 34. 20, 24.
Gen. 22. 17. possess *g.* of his enemies
28. 17. house of God, *g.* of heaven
Job 29. 7. I went to *g.* prepared
Ps. 118. 20. this *g.* of the Lord
Mat. 13. enter strait *g.* Luke 13. **24.**
Heb. 13. 12. suffered without the *g.*
Ps. 9. 13. up from *gates* of death
24. 7. lift up heads, O *g.* 9. Is. 26. 2.
100. 4. enter his *g.* with thanksgiving
118. 19. open to me *g.* of righteousness
Is. 38. 10. go to *g.* of the grave
Mat. 16. 18. *g.* of hell not prevail
GATHER thee from all nations, Deut. 30. **3.**
Neh. 1. 9. Jer. 29. 14.
Ps. 26. 9. *g.* not my soul with sinners
Zeph. 3. 18. *g.* them that are sorrowful
Mat. 3. 12. *g.* his wheat into garner
7. 16. do men *g.* grapes of thorns
Eph. 1. 10. *g.* in one all things in Christ
Mat. 23. 37. *gathered* thy children as hen *g.*
John 4. 36. *gathereth* fruit unto life eternal
GAVE, Gen. 14. 20. Ex. 11. 3.
Ps. 81. 12. *g.* them up unto their own hearts' lust

Is. 42. 24. *gave* Jacob for a spoil
John 1. 12. *g.* power to become sons
3. 16. God *g.* his only begotten Son
1 Cor. 3. 6. God *g.* the increase, 7.
2 Cor. 8. 5. first *g.* themselves to Lord
Gal. 1. 4. who *g.* himself for our sins
2. 20. *g.* himself for me, Tit. 2. 14.
Eph. 4. 8. *g.* gifts unto men, 11. *g.* some apostles
1 Tim. 2. 6. *g.* himself a ransom for all
Ps. 21. 4. asked life of thee, thou *gavest* it
John 17. 4. work thou *g.* 22. glory thou *g.* 6. (men)
   thou *g.* me, 12; 18. 9. *g.* me, lost none
GENEALOGIES, 1 Tim. 1. 4. Tit. 3. 9.
GENERATION, Gen. 2. 4; 6. 9.
Deut. 32. 5. perverse and crooked *g.*
20. a very froward *g.* in whom
Ps. 14. 5. God is in *g.* of righteous
22. 30. accounted to Lord for a *g.*
24. 6. this is *g.* of them that seek
102. 18. written for the *g.* to come
112. 2. *g.* of upright shall be blessed
145. 4. one *g.* shall praise thy works
Mat. 3. 7. ye *g.* of vipers, 12. 34; 23. 33.
Acts 13. 36. had served his own *g.*
1 Pet. 2. 9. chosen *g.* royal priesthood
Ps. 33. 11. thoughts . . . to all *generations*
45. 17. name remembered in all *g.*
72. 5. fear thee . . . throughout all *g.*
79. 13. shew forth thy praise to all *g.*
89. 4. build thy throne to all *g.*
90. 1. our dwelling place in all *g.*
100. 5. his truth endureth to all *g.*
102. 24. thy years are throughout all *g.*
119. 90. thy faithfulness is to all *g.*
145. 13. dominion endureth to all *g.*
Col. 1. 26. mystery hid from ages and *g.*
GENTILES, Gen. 10. 5. Jer. 4. 7.
Is. 11. 10. to it shall *g.* seek, 42. 6. a light of *g.*
   49. 6. Luke 2. 32. Acts 13. 47.
60. 3. *g.* shall come to thy light
62. 2. *g.* shall see thy righteousness
Mat. 6. 32. after these things do the *g.* seek
Luke 21. 24. trodden of *g.* till times of *g.*
John 7. 35. dispersed among *g.,* teach *g.*
Acts 13. 46. we turn to the *g.*
14. 27. opened door of faith unto *g.*
Rom. 2. 14. *g.* which have not law
3. 29. is he not also God of *g.?* yea
11. 25. till fulness of *g.* be come
15. 10. rejoice, ye *g.,* with his people
12. reign over *g.;* in him shall *g.* trust, Mat.
   12. 21.
Eph. 3. 6. *g.* be fellowheirs, 8. preach among *g.*
1 Tim. 2. 7. teacher of *g.* 2 Tim. 1. 11.
3. 16. God in flesh, preached to the *g.*
GENTLE among you, 1 Thes. 2. 7.
2 Tim. 2. 24. servant of Lord must be *g.*
Tit. 3. 2. be *g.* shewing all meekness
Jas. 3. 17. wisdom from above is *g.*
1 Pet. 2. 18. not only to the *g.* but to
Ps. 18. 35. thy *gentleness* made me great
2 Cor. 10. 1. by the meekness *g.* of Christ
Gal. 5. 22. fruit of Spirit is longsuffering, *g.*
Is. 40. 11. *gently* lead those with young
GIFT, 1 Cor. 1. 7; 7. 7.
Ex. 23. 8. take no *g.* for a *g.* blindeth the wise,
   Deut. 16. 19. 2 Chr. 19. 7.
Prov. 17. 8. *g.* is a precious stone, 23.
18. 16. a man's *g.* maketh room for
21. 14. a *g.* in secret pacifieth anger
Eccl. 7. 7. a *g.* destroyeth the heart
John 4. 10. if thou knewest *g.* of God
Rom. 6. 23. *g.* of God is eternal life

Eph. 2. 8. it is the *gift* of God
Phil. 4. 17. not because I desire a *g.*
1 Tim. 4. 14. neglect not the *g.* that
Heb. 6. 4. tasted of heavenly *g.*
Ps. 68. 18. received *gifts* for men
Mat. 7. 11. good *g.* to your children
Rom. 11. 29. for *g.* and calling of God
Eph. 4. 8. captivity captive gave *g.* to men
GIRD with strength, Ps. 18. 32.
1 Pet. 1. 13. *g.* up loins of mind
Ps. 30. 11. *girded* me with gladness
Luke 12. 35. let your loins be *g.*
Eph. 6. 14. loins *girt* with truth
Is. 11. 5. *girdle,* Mat. 3. 4. Rev. 1. 13; 15. 6.
GIVE, Gen. 12. 7; 30. 31.
1 Ki. 3. 5. ask what I shall *g.* thee
Ps. 2. 8. I shall *g.* thee the heathen
29. 11. Lord will *g.* strength to his
84. 11. Lord will *g.* grace and glory
104. 27. mayest *g.* them their meat
109. 4. I *g.* myself to prayer
Jer. 17. 10. to *g.* every man according to his
   works, 32. 19. Rev. 22. 12.
Hos. 11. 8. how shall I *g.* thee up
Luke 6. 38. *g.* and it shall be given
John 10. 28. I *g.* to them eternal life
Acts 3. 6. such as I have *g.* I thee
20. 35. more blessed to *g.* than to receive
Rom. 8. 32. freely *g.* us all
Eph. 4. 28. have to *g.* to him that needeth
1 Tim. 4. 15. *g.* thyself wholly to them
2 Sam. 22. 50. *give thanks,* 1 Chr. 16. 8, 34,
   35, 41. Neh. 12. 24. Ps. 35. 18; 79. 13; 92. 1;
   105. 1; 107. 1; 118. 1; 136. 1.
Ps. 6. 5. in grave who shall—to thee
30. 4.—at the remembrance of his holiness, 97. 12.
119. 62. at midnight I will rise to—
Eph. 1. 16, &c. cease not to—for you
1 Thes. 5. 18. in every thing—Phil. 4. 6.
Mat. 13. 12. to him shall be *given*
11. it is *g.* to you to know mysteries
Luke 12. 48. to whomsoever much is *g.*
Rom. 11. 35. hath first *g.* to him
1 Cor. 2. 12. know things freely *g.* of God
2 Cor. 9. 7. God loveth cheerful *giver*
Ps. 37. 21. righteous . . . mercy and *giveth*
Prov. 28. 27. he that *g.* to poor shall
Is. 40. 29. *g.* power to the faint
42. 5. *g.* breath to people on earth
1 Tim. 6. 17. *g.* us richly all things
Jas. 1. 5. *g.* to all men liberally
GLAD, my heart is, Ps. 16. 9.
Ps. 31. 7. I will be *g.* and rejoice in
64. 10. righteous shall be *g.* in Lord
104. 34. I will be *g.* in the Lord
122. 1. *g.* when they said, Luke 15. 32.
Mark 6. 20. heard him *gladly,* 12. 37.
Luke 8. 40. people *g.* received him
Acts 2. 41. that *g.* received his word
2 Cor. 12. 15. I will very *g.* spend
Ps. 4. 7. put *gladness* in my heart
30. 11. hast girded me with *g.*
45. 7. anointed with oil of *g.* Heb. 1. 9.
51. 8. make me to hear joy and *g.*
100. 2. serve the Lord with *g.*
106. 5. rejoice in *g.* of thy nation
Is. 35. 10. obtain joy and *g.* 51. 11.
Acts 2. 46. eat their meat with *g.*
14. 17. filling our hearts with food and *g.*
GLASS, we see through, 1 Cor. 13. 12.
2 Cor. 3. 18. beholding as in a *g.*
Jas. 1. 23. beholding natural face in *g.*
Rev. 4. 6. a sea of *g.* 15. 2.

Rev. 21. 18. the city pure gold like clear *glass*
GLOOMINESS, Joel 2. 2. Zeph. 1. 15.
GLORY, Gen. 31. 1. Ps. 49. 16.
1 Sam. 4. 21. *g.* departed from Israel
1 Chr. 29. 11. the power and *g.* Mat. 6. 13.
Ps. 8. 5. crowned him with *g.* and honour, Heb. 2. 7.
73. 24. afterward receive me to *g.*
89. 17. art the *g.* of their strength
145. 11. speak of *g.* of thy kingdom
Prov. 3. 35. the wise shall inherit *g.*
16. 31. hoary head is a crown of *g.*
25. 27. to search their own *g.* is not *g.*
Is. 4. 5. upon all the *g.* shall be a defence
23. 9. Lord purposed it, to stain pride of all *g.*
24. 16. heard songs, even *g.* to the righteous
28. 5. Lord shall be for a crown of *g.*
Jer. 2. 11. changed their *g.* Ps. 106. 20.
Ezek. 20. 6. the *g.* of all lands, 15.
Hos. 4. 7. change their *g.* into shame
Hag. 2. 7. I will fill this house with *g.*
9. *g.* of this latter house greater
Zech. 2. 5. I will be a wall of fire, *g.*
8. after the *g.* hath he sent me
6. 13. build temple and bear the *g.*
Mat. 6. 2. may have *g.* of men
Luke 2. 14. *g.* to God in the highest
32. light of Gentiles, *g.* of thy people
John 1. 14. his *g.*, *g.* as of only begotten **Son**
17. 22. *g.* which thou gavest me I have
Rom. 2. 7. seek *g.* honour, immortality
11. 36. to whom be *g.* for ever, Gal. 1. 5. 2 Tim.
   4. 18. Heb. 13. 21.
16. 27. God only wise be *g.* through Christ
1 Cor. 11. 7. (man) is image and *g.* of God.
15. 43. sown in dishonour, raised in *g.*
2 Cor. 3. 18. changed . . . from *g.* to *g.*
4. 17. eternal weight of *g.*
Eph. 1. 6. praise of *g.* of his grace
3. 21. to him be *g.* in the church
13. my tribulation for you is your *g.*
Phil. 3. 19. whose *g.* is in their shame
Col. 1. 27. Christ in you hope of *g.*
3. 4. appear with him in *g.*
1 Thes. 2. 12. called you to his kingdom and *g.*
20. ye are our *g.* and joy, 19.
1 Tim. 3. 16. received up into *g.*
1 Pet. 1. 8. joy unspeakable, full of *g.*
11. the sufferings of Christ, *g.* follow, 21.
4. 13. his *g.* be revealed, 14. spirit of *g.*
5. 1. partaker of *g.* to be revealed
4. ye shall receive a crown of *g.*
10. called us to eternal *g.* by Christ
2 Pet. 1. 3. called us to *g.* and virtue
17. came a voice from excellent *g.*
Rev. 4. 11. worthy to receive *g.* 5. 12. Rom.
   16. 27. 1 Tim. 1. 17. 1 Pet. 5. 11. Jude 25.
Ps. 19. 1. *glory of God*, Prov. 25. 2. Acts
   7. 55. Rom. 3. 23; 5. 2. 1 Cor. 10. 31; 11. 7.
   2 Cor. 4. 6. Rev. 21. 11.
Ex. 16. 7. *glory of the Lord*, Num. 14. 21.
   1 Ki. 8. 11. Ps. 104. 31; 138. 5. Is. 35. 2;
   40. 5; 60. 1. Ezek. 1. 28; 3. 12, 23; 43. 5;
   44. 4. Luke 2. 9. 2 Cor. 3. 18.
Ps. 29. 9. *his glory*, 49. 17; 72. 19; 113. 4;
   148. 13. Prov. 19. 11. Is. 6. 3. Hab. 3. 3. Mat.
   6. 29; 19. 28; 25. 31. John 2. 11. Rom. 9. 23.
   Eph. 1. 12; 3. 16. Heb. 1. 3.
Job 29. 20. *my glory*, Ps. 16. 9; 30. 12; 57. 8;
   108. 1. Is. 42. 8; 43. 7; 48. 11; 60. 7; 66. 18.
   John 8. 50; 17. 24.
Ex. 33. 18. *thy glory*, Ps. 8. 1; 63. 2. Is. 60. 19;
   63. 15. Jer. 14. 21.
1 Chr. 16. 10. *glory* ye in his holy name

Ps. 64. 10. upright in heart shall *glory*
Is. 41. 16. shalt *g.* in Holy One of
45. 25. seed of Israel be justified, and *g.*
Rom. 4. 2. hath whereof to *g.* but not
5. 3. we *g.* in tribulations also
2 Cor. 5. 12. to *g.* on our behalf . . . them which
   g. in appearance, not in heart
11. 18. many *g.* after the flesh, I *g.* also
12. 1. it is not expedient for me to *g.*
9. will I rather *g.* in my infirmities
Gal. 6. 14. God forbid I should *g.* save
1 Cor. 5. 6. *glorying*, 9. 15. 2 Cor. 7. 4; 12. 11.
Lev. 10. 3. before all I will be *glorified*
John 7. 39. Jesus was not yet *g.*
12. 23. the hour is come that the Son of man
   should be *g.*
15. 8. herein is my Father *g.*
17. 10. all mine are thine, I am *g.*
Acts 3. 13. God of our fathers hath *g.* his Son
4. 21. all men *g.* God for that which was done
Rom. 1. 21. they *g.* him not as God
Gal. 1. 24. they *g.* God in me
2 Thes. 1. 10. be *g.* in his saints
3. 1. word have free course and be *g.*
Heb. 5. 5. even Christ *g.* not himself
Rev. 18. 7. how she hath *g.* herself
Ps. 50. 23. whoso offereth praise *glorifieth*
Is. 25. 3. strong people *glorify* thee
60. 7. I will *g.* house of my glory
Mat. 5. 16. *g.* your Father in heaven
John 12. 28. Father, *g.* thy name
17. 1. *g.* thy Son that Son *g.* thee
5. *g.* thou me . . . with the glory
21. 19. by what death he should *g.* God
1 Cor. 6. 20. *g.* God in your body and
1 Pet. 2. 12. *g.* God in day of visitation
Rev. 15. 4. who shall not fear thee, and *g.*
Ex. 15. 6. *glorious* in power
11. who is like thee, *g.* in holiness
Deut. 28. 58. fear this *g.* and fearful name
1 Chr. 29. 13. praise thy *g.* name
Ps. 45. 13. king's daughter all *g.* within
66. 2. make his praise *g.*
72. 19. blessed be his *g.* name, Neh. 9. 5.
87. 3. *g.* things spoken of thee, O city of God
111. 3. his work is honourable and *g.*
145. 5. speak of *g.* honour of thy
12. the *g.* majesty of his kingdom
Is. 4. 2. branch of Lord shall be *g.*
11. 10. his rest shall be *g.*
22. 23. be for a *g.* throne to his father's house
30. cause his *g.* voice to be heard
49. 5. I be *g.* in eyes of the Lord
60. 13. make the place of my feet *g.*
63. 12. his *g.* arm, 14. a *g.* name
Jer. 17. 12. a *g.* high throne from
Rom. 8. 21. *g.* liberty of children of God
2 Cor. 3. 7. ministration *g.* 8, 10, 11.
4. 4. light of *g.* Gospel should shine
Eph. 5. 27. present to himself *g.* church
Phil. 3. 21. vile body . . . like his *g.* body
Col. 1. 11. according to his *g.* power
1 Tim. 1. 11. according to the *g.* gospel of
Tit. 2. 13. looking for *g.* appearing
Ex. 15. 1. *gloriously*, Is. 24. 23.
GLUTTON, Deut. 21. 20. Prov. 23. 21.
Mat. 11. 19. *gluttonous*, Luke 7. 34.
GNASH, Job 16. 9. Ps. 35. 16; 37. 12; 112. 10.
Lam. 2. 16. Mark 9. 18.
Mat. 8. 12. *gnashing of teeth*, 13. 42, 50; 22.
   13; 24. 51; 25. 30. Luke 13. 28.
GNAT, strain at *g.*, swallow camel, Mat. 23. 24.
GNAW, Zeph. 3. 3. Rev. 16. 10.

GO, Judg. 6. 14. 1 Sam. 12. 21. Mat. 8. 9. Luke 10. 37. John 6. 68.

Job 10. 21. *I go*, Ps. 39. 13; 139. 7.

Mat. 21. 30. John 7. 33; 8. 14, 21, 22; 13. 33; 16. 5.

Ex. 4. 23. *let my people go*, 5. 1.

Gen. 32. 26. *not let go*, Ex. 3. 19. Job 27. 6. Sol. 3. 4.

Ex. 23. 23. *shall go*, 32. 34; 33. 14. Acts 25. 12.

1 Sam. 12. 21. *should go*, Prov. 22. 6.

Judg. 11. 35. *go back*, Ps. 80. 18.

Num. 22. 18. *go beyond*, 1 Thes. 4. 6.

Gen. 45. 1. *go out*, Ps. 60. 10. Is. 52. 11; 55. 12. Jer. 51. 45. Ezek. 46. 9. Mat. 25. 6. John 10. 9. 1 Cor. 5. 10.

Deut. 4. 40. *go well* with thee, 5. 16; 19. 13. Prov. 11. 10; 30. 29.

Job 34. 21. seeth all his *goings*

Ps. 17. 5. hold up my *g.* in thy paths

40. 2. set my feet . . . established my *g.*

68. 24. seen thy *g.*, O God, in sanctuary

Prov. 5. 21. he pondereth all his *g.*

20. 24. man's *g.* are of the Lord

Mic. 5. 2. whose *g.* are of old, from

GOAT, Lev. 3. 12; 16. 8, 21, 22.

Is. 1. 11. delight not in blood of . . . *goats*

Ezek. 34. 17. judge between rams and *g.*

Zech. 10. 3. I punished the *g.*

Mat. 25. 32, 33. set *g.* on his left hand

Heb. 9. 12. blood of *g.* 13, 19; 10. 4.

GOD, and *gods* for *men* representing God, Ex. 4. 16; 7. 1; 22. 28. Ps. 82. 1, 6.

John 10. 34; for *idols* put in God's place, Deut. 32. 21. Judg. 6. 31, and 140 other places; for devil, god of this world, 2 Cor. 4. 4; and for the true God about 3,120 times

Gen. 17. 1. I am Almighty *G.* Job 36. 5. Is. 9. 6; 10. 21. Jer. 32. 18.

7. a *G.* to thee and thy seed, Ex. 6. 7.

21. everlasting *G.* Ps. 90. 2. Is. 40. 28. Rom. 16. 26.

Ex. 8. 10. none like Lord our *G.* 1 Ki. 8. 23. Ps. 35. 10; 86. 8; 89. 6.

18. 11. Lord is greater than all *gods*

Deut. 10. 17. *G.* of gods, Josh. 22. 22. Dan. 2. 47. Ps. 136. 2.

32. 39. there is no *g.* with me, 1 Ki. 8. 23. 2 Ki. 5. 15. 2 Chr. 6. 14; 32. 15. Is. 43. 10; 44. 6, 8; 45. 5, &c.

Job 33. 12. *G.* is greater than man

Ps. 18. 31. who is *G.* save the Lord, 86. 10.

Mic. 7. 18. who a *G.* like thee

Mat. 6. 24. cannot serve *G.* and mammon

19. 17. none good but one, that is *G.*

Mark 12. 32. there is one *G.* and none other

John 17. 3. only true *G.* 1 John 5. 20.

Acts 7. 2. *G.* of glory appeared to Abraham

Rom. 3. 4. *G.* forbid: yea, let *G.* be true

8. 31. if *G.* be for us, who against

9. 5. over all, *G.* blessed for ever

15. 5. *G.* of patience, 13. *G.* of hope

1 Cor. 15. 28. that *G.* may be all in all

2 Cor. 1. 3. *G.* of all comfort

2 Thes. 2. 4. above all called *G.* Dan. 11. 36.

1 Tim. 3. 16. *G.* manifest in flesh

1 Pet. 5. 10. *G.* of all grace

1 John 4. 12. no man seen *G.* John 1. 18.

Deut. 10. 17. *great G.* 2 Sam. 7. 22. 2 Chr. 2. 5. Job 36. 26. Neh. 1. 5. Prov. 26. 10. Jer. 32. 18, 19. Dan. 9. 4. Tit. 2. 13. Rev. 19. 17.

Deut. 5. 26. *living G.* Josh. 3. 10. 1 Sam. 17. 26, 36. 2 Ki. 19. 4, 16; and 22 other places

Ex. 34. 6. *G. merciful*, Deut. 4. 31. 2 Chr. 30. 9.

Neh. 9. 31. Ps. 116. 5. Jonah 4. 2.

Gen. 49. 24. *mighty G.* Deut. 7. 21; 10. 17. Neh. 9. 32. Job 36. 5. Ps. 50. 1; 132. 2, 5. Is. 9. 6; 10. 21. Jer. 32. 18. Hab. 1. 12.

2 Chr. 15. 3. *true G.* Jer. 10. 10. John 17. 3. 1 Thes. 1. 9. 1 John 5. 20.

Gen. 39. 9. wickedness and sin *against G.* Num. 21. 5. Ps. 78. 19. Hos. 13. 16. Acts 5. 39; 23. 9. Rom. 8. 7; 9. 20. Rev. 13. 6. Dan. 11. 36.

Ps. 42. 2. *before God*, 56. 13; 61. 7; 68. 3. Eccl. 2. 26. Luke 1. 6. Rom. 2. 13; 3. 19. 1 Tim. 5. 21. Jas. 1. 27. Rev. 3. 2.

John 9. 16. *of God*, Acts 5. 39. Rom. 9. 16. 1 Cor. 1. 30; 11. 12. 2 Cor. 3. 5; 5. 18. Phil. 1. 28. 1 John 3. 10; 4. 1, 3, 6; 5. 19. 3 John 11.

Ex. 2. 23. *(un)to God*, Ps. 43. 4. Eccl. 12. 7. Is. 58. 2. Lam. 3. 41. John 13. 3. Heb. 7. 25; 11. 6; 12. 23. 1 Pet. 3. 18; 4. 6. Rev. 5. 9; 12. 5.

Gen. 5. 22. *with God*, 24; 6. 9; 32. 28. Ex. 19. 17. 1 Sam. 14. 45. 2 Sam. 23. 5. Job 9. 2; 25. 4. Ps. 78. 8. Hos. 11. 12. John 5. 18. Phil. 2. 6.

Gen. 28. 21. *my God*, Ex. 15. 2. Ps. 22. 1; 31. 14; 91. 2; 118. 28. Hos. 2. 23. Zech. 13. 9. John 20. 17, 28, and about 120 other places

Ex. 5. 8. *our God*, Deut. 31. 17; 32. 3. Josh. 24. 18. 2 Sam. 22. 32. Ps. 67. 6, and 180 other places

Ex. 20. 2. *thy God*, 5, 7, 10, 12. Ps. 50. 7; 81. 10, and 340 other places

2 Chr. 36. 23. *God of heaven*, Ezra 5. 11; 6. 10; 7. 12, 23. Neh. 1. 4; 2. 4. Ps. 136. 26. Dan. 2. 18, 19, 44. Jonah 1. 9. Rev. 11. 13; 16. 11.

Ex. 24. 10. *God of Israel*, Num. 16. 9. Josh. 7. 19; 13. 33; 22. 16, 24; 24. 23. Judg. 11. 23. Ruth 2. 12. Is. 41. 17. Jer. 31. 1. Ezek. 8. 4. Mat. 15. 31.

Rom. 15. 33. *God of peace*, 16. 20. 2 Cor. 13. 11. 1 Thes. 5. 23. Heb. 13. 20.

Ps. 24. 5. *God of his salvation, of our salvation*, 65. 5; 68. 19, 20; 79. 9; 85. 4; 95. 1.

Acts 17. 29. *Godhead*, Rom. 1. 20. Col. 2. 9.

GODLY, Ps. 4. 3; 12. 1; 32. 6. Mal. 2. 15. 2 Pet. 2. 9. 3 John 6.

2 Cor. 1. 12. in simplicity and *g.* sincerity

7. 9. sorrow after a *g.* manner, 10, 11.

Tit. 2. 12. live soberly, righteously and *g.*

Heb. 12. 28. with reverence and *g.* fear

1 Tim. 2. 2. quiet life in all *godliness*, 10; 3. 16; 6. 3, 5, 11. 2 Tim. 3. 5.

4. 7. exercise thyself to *g.* 6. 11.

8. *g.* is profitable to all things

6. 3. doctrine according to *g.* Tit. 1. 1.

6. *g.* with contentment is great gain

2 Tim. 3. 5. having a form of *g.* but

2 Pet. 1. 3. all that pertain to life and *g.*

6. to patience *g.* 7. to *g.* brotherly kindness

3. 11. . . . in all holy conversation and *g.*

GOLD, Gen. 2. 11; 13. 2. Is. 2. 7.

Job 23. 10. I shall come forth as *g.*

31. 24. if I made *g.* my hope, fine *g.*

Ps. 19. 10. more desired than *g.*, yea

119. 127. love . . . above *g.*, yea, fine *g.* 72.

Prov. 8. 19. my fruit is better than *g.*

Is. 13. 12. man more precious than fine *g.*

Zech. 13. 9. try them as *g.*

1 Cor. 3. 12. build on this foundation, *g.*

1 Tim. 2. 9. modest apparel . . . not *g.* 1 Pet. 3. 3.

1 Pet. 1. 7. trial of faith more precious than *g.*

Rev. 3. 18. buy of me *g.* tried in the fire

GOOD, Deut. 6. 24; 10. 13.

Gen. 1. 31. every thing was very *good*
2. 18. not *g.* for man to be alone
32. 12. thou saidst, I will do thee *g.*
50. 20. God meant it unto *g.*
2 Ki. 20. 19. *g.* is word of Lord, Is. 39. 8.
Ps. 34. 8. taste and see that Lord is *g.*
73. 1. truly God is *g.* to Israel
86. 5. Lord, art *g.*, ready to forgive
106. 5. may see the *g.* of thy chosen
145. 9. Lord is *g.* to all, 136. 1.
Lam. 3. 25. Lord *g.* to them that wait
Mic. 6. 8. shewed thee what is *g.*
Mat. 19. 17. Why callest thou me *g.?* . . . none *g.*
Rom. 3. 8. do evil that *g.* may come
7. 18. how to perform . . . *g.* I find not
1 Thes. 5. 15. follow that which is *g.* 3 John 11.
Neh. 2. 18. hand for this *good work*
Mat. 26. 10. wrought a—on me
John 10. 33. a—we stone thee not
2 Cor. 9. 8. abound to every—
Phil. 1. 6. begun a—will finish it
Col. 1. 10. fruitful in every—
2 Thes. 2. 17. establish you in every—
1 Tim. 5. 10. followed every—
Tit. 1. 16. to every—reprobate
3. 1. ready to every—
Heb. 13. 21. perfect in every—
John 10. 32. many *good works* I shewed you
Acts 9. 36. Dorcas was full of—
Rom. 13. 3. not a terror to—
Eph. 2. 10. created in Christ Jesus to—
1 Tim. 2. 10. (women professing godliness) with—
5. 10. reported of for—
25. the—of some are manifest
Tit. 3. 8. careful to maintain—14.
Heb. 10. 24. provoke to love and—
1 Pet. 2. 12. may by your—which
Ex. 33. 19. make my *goodness* pass
34. 6. God abundant in *g.* and truth
2 Chr. 6. 41. let saints rejoice in *g.*
Neh. 9. 25. delight themselves in *g.*
35. not served thee in thy great *g.*
Ps. 16. 2. my *g.* extendeth not to
23. 6. *g.* and mercy shall follow me
27. 13. believed to see *g.* of Lord
31. 19. how great is thy *g.* Zech. 9. 17.
33. 5. earth full of *g.* of Lord, 145. 7.
52. 1. the *g.* of God endureth
65. 4. satisfied with *g.* of thy house
11. crownest the year with thy *g.*
Is. 63. 7. great *g.* bestowed on Israel
Hos. 3. 5. fear the Lord and his *g.*
Rom. 2. 4. *g.* of God leadeth to repentance
11. 22. behold the *g.* and severity of God
Eph. 5. 9. fruit of Spirit in all *g.* Gal. 5. 22.
GOSPEL, Mark 1. 1, 15; 8. 35.
Mat. 4. 23. preaching *g.* of kingdom
Mark 16. 15. preach *g.* to every creature
Acts 20. 24. *g.* of grace of God
Rom. 1. 1. *g.* of God, 15. 16. 1 Tim. 1. 11.
1 Cor. 1. 17. but to preach the *g.*
4. 15. begotten you through the *g.*
2 Cor. 4. 3. if our *g.* hid, 4. glorious *g.*
11. 4. another ye, Gal. 1. 6.
Eph. 1. 13. *g.* of salvation, 6. 15. *g.* of peace
Phil. 1. 5. fellowship in the *g.*
27. as becometh the *g.* . . . . striving for faith of *g.*
Col. 1. 5. truth of *g.* Gal. 2. 5.
1 Thes. 1. 5. our *g.* came in power
Heb. 4. 2. unto us was *g.* preached
1 Pet. 4. 6. *g.* was preached to dead
Rev. 14. 6. everlasting *g.* to preach

GOVERNMENT, Is. 9. 6, 7; 22. 21. 1 Cor. 12. 28
2 Pet. 2. 10.
GRACE, Ezra 9. 8. Esth. 2. 17.
Ps. 84. 11. Lord will give *g.* and glory
Prov. 3. 34. *g.* to lowly, Jas. 4. 6.
Zech. 4. 7. with shoutings, crying, *g. g.* to it
12. 10. spirit of *g.* and supplications
Acts 18. 27. which had believed through *g.*
Rom. 3. 24. justified freely by his *g.*
5. 20. *g.* did much more abound
6. 14. not under law, but *g.*
11. 5. according to the election of *g.*
6. if by *g.* then not of works, otherwise *g.* no more *g.*
2 Cor. 12. 9. my *g.* sufficient for thee
Eph. 2. 5. by *g.* ye are saved, 8.
7. shew exceeding riches of his *g.* 1. 7.
4. 29. minister *g.* to the hearers
Tit. 3. 7. justified by his *g.*
Heb. 4. 16. come boldly to the throne of *g.*
13. 9. heart be established with *g.*
1 Pet. 3. 7. heirs of the *g.* of life
5. 5. and giveth *g.* to the humble
2 Pet. 3. 18. grow in *g.* and knowledge
Rom. 1. 7. *grace and peace* to you
Luke 2. 40. *grace of God,* Acts 11. 23; 13. 43;
 14. 3, 26; 15. 40; 20. 24, 32. Rom. 5. 15.
 1 Cor. 1. 4; 3. 10; 15. 10. Eph. 3. 2, 7. Heb.
 2. 9; 12. 15.
2 Cor. 1. 12. by—our conversation
6. 1. receive not—in vain
8. 1. of—bestowed on churches
9. 14. for the exceeding—in you
Gal. 2. 21. I do not frustrate—
Col. 1. 6. knew—in truth
1 Pet. 4. 10. stewards of manifold—
5. 12. this the true—wherein ye stand
Jude 4. turning—into lasciviousness
Acts 15. 11. *grace of our Lord Jesus Christ,*
 Rom. 16. 20, 24. 1 Cor. 16. 23. 2 Cor. 8. 9;
 13. 14. Gal. 6. 18. Phil. 4. 23. 1 Thes. 5. 28.
 2 Thes. 3. 18. Philem. 25.
Rev. 22. 21.—be with you all
Gen. 43. 29. God be *gracious* to thee
Ex. 22. 27. I will hear, for I am *g.* 33.
19. I will be *g.* to whom I will be *g.*
34. 6. Lord God merciful and *g.* 2 Chr. 30. 9.
 Neh. 9. 17, 31. Ps. 103. 8; 116. 5; 145. 8.
 Joel 2. 13.
Num. 6. 25. Lord be *g.* 2 Sam. 12. 22.
Job 33. 24. then he is *g.* to him
Ps. 77. 9. hath God forgotten to be *g.*
86. 15. compassion and *g.* 78. 38; 111. 4; 112. 4.
Amos 5. 15. may be, Lord will be *g.*
Jonah 4. 2. knew thou art a *g.* God
Mal. 1. 9. beseech God . . . be *g.* Is. 33. 2.
1 Pet. 2. 3. if ye have tasted that Lord is *g.*
Gen. 33. 5. *graciously,* 11. Ps. 119. 29.
Hos. 14. 2. receive us *g.*
GRANT, Job 10. 12. Prov. 10. 24. Rom. 15. 5.
Eph. 3. 16. 2 Tim. 1. 18. Rev. 3. 21.
GRAPES, of gall, Deut. 32. 32.
Sol. 2. 13. the tender *g.* 7. 7. clusters of *g.*
Is. 5. 4. wild *g.* Ezek. 18. 2. sour *g.*
Mic. 7. 1. *g.* gleanings of vintage
GRASS, Ps. 37. 2; 90. 5; 92. 7; 102. 4, 11. Is.
44. 4; 51. 12.
Ps. 103. 15. as for man his days like *g.*
Is. 40. 6. all flesh is *g.* 7, 8. 1 Pet. 1. 24. Jas.
1. 10, 11.
Mat. 6. 30. if God so clothe the *g.*
Rev. 8. 7. green *g.* 9. 4. not hurt *g.*
GRAVE, 1 Ki. 2. 9; 14. 13.
1 Sam. 2. 6. Lord bringeth down to *g.*

Job 5. 26. come to thy *grave* in full age
14. 13. hide me in the *g.* 17. 1, 13.
Ps. 6. 5. in *g.* who shall give thanks
Prov. 1. 12. swallow alive, as the *g.*
Eccl. 9. 10. nor wisdom in the *g.*
Is. 38. 18. *g.* cannot praise
Hos. 13. 14. the power of the *g.* O *g.* I will be thy
1 Cor. 15. 55. O *g.* where is thy victory
GRAVEN with an iron pen, Job 19. 24.
Is. 49. 16. have *g.* thee on the palms
Jer. 17. 1. sin *g.* upon table of heart
GREAT, Gen. 12. 2; 30. 8.
Deut. 29. 24. *g.* anger, 2 Chr. 34. 21.
1 Sam. 6. 9. *great evil,* Neh. 13. 27. Eccl. 2. 21.
Jer. 44. 7. Dan. 9. 12.
Ps. 47. 2. *great king,* 48. 2; 95. 3. Mal. 1. 14.
Mat. 5. 35.
Job 32. 9. *great men,* Jer. 5. 5.
Ex. 32. 11. *great power,* Neh. 1. 10. Job 23. 6.
Ps. 147. 5. Nah. 1. 3. Acts 4. 33; 8. 10.
Rev. 11. 17.
Ex. 32. 21. *so great,* Deut. 4. 7, 8. 1 Ki. 3. 9.
Ps. 77. 13; 103. 11. Mat. 8. 10; 15. 33.
2 Cor. 1. 10. Heb. 2. 3; 12. 1. Rev. 16. 18;
18. 17.
Job 5. 9. *great things,* 9. 10; 37. 5. Jer. 45. 5.
Hos. 8. 12. Luke 1. 49.
Gen. 6. 5. *great wickedness,* 39. 9. Job 22. 5.
Joel 3. 13. 2 Chr. 28. 13.
Job 33. 12. God is *greater* than man
Mat. 12. 42. *g.* than Solomon is here
John 1. 50. see *g.* things than these
4. 12. art thou *g.* than, 8. 53.
10. 29. my Father . . . is *g.* than all, 14. 28. *g.* than I
1 Cor. 14. 5. *g.* is he that prophesieth
1 John 4. 4. *g.* he that is in you, 3. 20. God *g.*
5. 9. witness of God is *g.* [than our heart
1 Sam. 30. 6. David was *greatly* distressed
2 Sam. 24. 10. I have sinned *g.* in that I
1 Ki. 18. 3. Obadiah feared the Lord *g.*
1 Chr. 16. 25. great is Lord and *g.* to be praised,
Ps. 48. 1; 96. 4; 145. 3.
2 Chr. 33. 12. humbled himself *g.*
Job 3. 25. thing I *g.* feared is come
Ps. 28. 7. my heart *g.* rejoiceth
89. 7. God is *g.* to be feared in the assembly
116. 10. I was *g.* afflicted
Dan. 9. 23. O man, *g.* beloved, 10. 11, 19.
Mark 12. 27. ye do *g.* err
Ex. 15. 7. *greatness* of thy excellency
Num. 14. 19. pardon (spare me, Neh. 13. 22.)
according to the *g.* of thy mercy
Deut. 32. 3. ascribe ye *g.* to our God
Ps. 66. 3. *g.* of thy power, 79. 11. Eph. 1. 19.
145. 3. his *g.* unsearchable, 6.
Is. 63. 1. travelling in *g.* of strength
GREEDY, of gain, Prov. 1. 19; 15. 27.
Is. 56. 11. they are *g.* dogs, never
1 Tim. 3. 3. not *g.* of filthy lucre, 8.
Eph. 4. 19. work uncleanness with *greediness*
GRIEF, Is. 53. 3, 4, 10. Heb. 13. 17.
Lam. 3. 33. nor *grieve* children of men
Gen. 6. 6. *grieved* him at his heart
Judg. 10. 16. his soul was *g.* for misery
Ps. 95. 10. forty years long was I *g.*
119. 158. I beheld transgressors and was *g.*
139. 21. *g.* with those that rise up
Is. 54. 6. woman forsaken and *g.*
Jer. 5. 3. stricken, they have not *g.*
Amos 6. 6. not *g.* for (Joseph's) affliction
Mark 3. 5. *g.* for hardness of hearts
Rom. 14. 15. if brother be *g.* with thy meat
Ps. 10. 5. ways are always *grievous*

Mat. 23. 4. burdens *grievous* to be borne
Acts 20. 29. shall *g.* wolves enter
1 John 5. 3. his commandments are not *g.*
Mat. 8. 6. *grievously* tormented, 15. 22.
GRIND the faces of poor, Is. 3. 15.
Mat. 21. 44. it will *g.* him to powder
Eccl. 12. 3. *grinders* cease because few, 4.
GROAN earnestly, 2 Cor. 5. 2, 4.
John 11. 33. (Jesus) *groaned* in spirit
Rom. 8. 22. whole creation *groaneth*
Ps. 6. 6. weary with my *groaning*
38. 9. my *g.* is not hid from thee
102. 20. to hear the *g.* of prisoner
Rom. 8. 26. *groanings* which cannot be uttered
GROUNDED, staff (*i.e.* of doom), Is. 30. 32.
Eph. 3. 17. rooted and *g.* in love
Col. 1. 23. if continue in the faith *g.*
GROW, Gen. 48. 16. 2 Sam. 23. 5.
Ps. 92. 12. *g.* like cedar in Lebanon
Hos. 14. 5. as a lily, 7. *g.* as a vine
Eph. 4. 15. *g.* up into him in all things
1 Pet. 2. 2. milk of word that ye may *g.*
2 Pet. 3. 18. *g.* in grace
Eph. 2. 21. *groweth* unto a holy temple
GRUDGE, Lev. 19. 18. Jas. 5. 9.
1 Pet. 4. 9. *grudging,* 2 Cor. 9. 7.
GUIDE unto death, Ps. 48. 14.
Ps. 73. 24. *g.* me with thy counsel
Prov. 2. 17. forsaketh *g.* of youth
Is. 58. 11. Lord shall *g.* thee continually
Jer. 3. 4. my Father, thou art *g.* of my youth
Luke 1. 79. *g.* our feet into way of peace
John 16. 13. *g.* you into all truth
1 Tim. 5. 14. bear children, *g.* house
GUILE, Ex. 21. 14. Ps. 55. 11. 2 Cor. 12. 16. 1 Th. 2. 3.
Ps. 32. 2. in whose spirit is no *g.*
34. 13. keep thy lips from *g.* 1 Pet. 3. 10.
John 1. 47. Israelite in whom no *g.*
1 Pet. 2. 1. laying aside malice and *g.*
GUILTY, Lev. 4. 13; 22. 27.
Ex. 34. 7. clear *g.* Num. 14. 18. Gen. 42. 21.
Rom. 3. 19. all world may become *g.* before God
1 Cor. 11. 27. *g.* of body and blood of
Jas. 2. 10. offend in one point, *g.* of all
Ex. 20. 7. not hold him *guiltless*

H

HABITABLE part, Prov. 8. 31.
HABITATION, 2 Chr. 6. 2; 29. 6.
Deut. 26. 15. look down from thy holy *h.*
Ps. 68. 5. Jer. 25. 30. Zech. 2. 13.
Ps. 26. 8. loved the *h.* of thy house
71. 3. be thou my strong *h.* whereunto
89. 14. are *h.* of thy throne, 97. 2.
91. 9. hast made Most High thy *h.*
Prov. 3. 33. he blesseth *h.* of just
Is. 33. 20. see Jerusalem a quiet *h.*
63. 15. behold from *h.* of thy holiness
Jer. 31. 23. Lord bless thee, O *h.* of justice
Jude 6. angels which left their own *h.*
Rev. 18. 2. Babylon is become *h.* of
Ps. 74. 20. earth full of *habitations* of cruelty
Luke 16. 9. receive into everlasting *h.*
HAIR(S), Job 4. 15. Sol. 4. 1.
Ps. 40. 12. more than *h.* of head, 69. 4.
Hos. 7. 9. gray *h.* are here and there
Mat. 5. 36. not make one *h.* white or
10. 30. *h.* of head numbered, Luke 12. 7.
1 Cor. 11. 14. long *h.* 1 Tim. 2. 9. broided *h.*
1 Pet. 3. 3. plaiting the *h.*

HALT, between two opinions, 1 Ki. 18. 21.
  Mic. 4. 6. assemble her that *halteth*
  Jer. 20. 10 watched for my *halting*
HAND, Gen. 3. 22; 16. 12.
  Deut. 33. 3. all his saints are in thy *h.*
  Ezra 7. 9. good *h.* of his God on him
  8. 22. *h.* of our God is upon all
  Job 2. 10. good at *h.* of God and not evil
  12. 6. into whose *h.* God bringeth
  Prov. 10. 4. *h.* of diligent maketh rich
  11. 21. though *h.* join in *h.* 16. 5.
  Is. 1. 12. who required this at your *h.*
  Mat. 22. 13. bind him *h.* and foot
  Luke 1. 74. out of *h.* of our enemies
  1 Pet. 5. 6. humble yourselves under . . . *h.* of
  Num. 11. 23. is the *Lord's hand* waxed short
  2 Sam. 24. 14. fall into—not of man
  Job 12. 9. —hath wrought this, Is. 41. 20.
  Is. 40. 2. received of the—double
  59. 1.—is not shortened that it
  Ps. 16. 8. he is at my *right hand,* I
  11. at thy—are pleasures for evermore
  18. 35. thy—hath holden me up
  48. 10. thy—is full of righteousness
  73. 23. hast holden me by my—
  110. 5. Lord at thy—shall strike kings
  137. 5. let my—forget her cunning
  139. 10. thy *h.* lead and thy—hold
  Prov. 3. 16. length of days is in her—
  Eccl. 10. 2. wise man's heart at his—
  9. 1. wise and their works in *h.* of God
  Sol. 2. 6. his—doth embrace me, 8. 3.
  Mat. 5. 30. if thy—offend thee, cut it off
  6. 3. not thy left *h.* know what thy—doeth
  20. 21. one on the—other on left
  25. 33. sheep on—goats on left, 34, 41.
  Mark 14. 62. sitting on—of power
  16. 19. sat on—of God, Rom. 8. 34. Col. 3. 1.
    Heb. 1. 3; 8. 1; 10. 12. 1 Pet. 3. 22. Acts 2. 33;
    7. 55, 56.
  Ps. 31. 5. into *thy (thine) hand* I commend my
    spirit, Luke 23. 46. cp. Acts 7. 59.
  145. 16. thou openest—and satisfiest
  Prov. 30. 32. lay—upon thy mouth
  Eccl. 9. 10. whatsoever—findeth to do
  Is. 26. 11. when—is lifted up, they
  Mat. 18. 8. if—or thy foot offend
  Acts 4. 28. to do whatsoever—and
  Gen. 27. 22. *hands* are the *h.* of Esau
  Ex. 17. 12. Moses'—were heavy
  Job 17. 9. clean *h.* shall be stronger
  Ps. 24. 4. clean *h.* and a pure heart
  119. 73. thy *h.* made . . . fashioned me
  Prov. 31. 20. reacheth *h.* to the needy
  31. give her of the fruit of her *h.*
  Is. 1. 15. spread forth your *h.* I will hide, . . . your
    h. full of blood
  Mic. 7. 3. do evil with both *h.*
  Mat. 18. 8. having two *h.* or feet
  9. 44. delivered into *h.* of men
  John 13. 3. given all things into his *h.*
  9. but also my *h.* and head
  2 Cor. 5. 1. house not made with *h.*
  Eph. 4. 28. working with his *h.*
  1 Tim. 2. 8. lifting up holy *h.*
  Heb. 9. 11. tabernacle, not made with *h.*
  10. 31. fearful thing to fall into the *h.* of the
    living God, 12. 12. *h.* which hang down
  Jas. 4. 8. cleanse your *h.* ye sinners
  1 John 1. 1. our *h.* handled . . . word of life
  Col. 2. 14. *handwriting* of ordinances
HANDLE me and see, Luke 24. 39.
  Col. 2. 21. taste not, *h.* not

  2 Cor. 4. 2. not *handling* word . . . deceitfully
HANG, Ps. 137. 2. Josh. 8. 29.
  Deut. 28. 66. thy life shall *h.* in doubt
  Mat. 22. 40. on these *h.* law and prophets
  Heb. 12. 12. hands which *h.* down
  Deut. 21. 23. *hanged* accursed of God, Gal. 3. 13.
  Mat. 18. 6. millstone *h.* about neck
  Job 26. 7. he *hangeth* the earth on nothing
HAPPEN, Jer. 44. 23. Rom. 11. 25.
  Prov. 12. 21. no evil shall *h.* to just 1 Pet. 4. 12,
    as though some strange thing *happened*
  1 Cor. 10. 11. these *h.* for ensamples
  Eccl. 2. 14. one event *happeneth* to them all
  8. 14. *h.* according to work of righteous
  9. 11. time and chance *h.* to all
HAPPY am I, for the daughters, Gen. 30. 13.
  Deut. 33. 29. *h.* art thou, O Israel
  1 Ki. 10. 8. *h.* are thy men, *h.* these
  Job 5. 17. *h.* the man whom God correcteth
  Ps. 127. 5. *h.* the man who hath his quiver
  128. 2. *h.* shalt thou be, and be well
  144. 15. *h.* people whose God is Lord
  146. 5. *h.* is he that hath God of Jacob
  Prov. 3. 13. *h.* the man that findeth wisdom, 18.
  14. 21. that hath mercy on poor, *h.* is he
  16. 20. who trusteth in Lord, *h.* is he
  28. 14. *h.* is man that feareth alway
  29. 18. he that keepeth law, *h.* is he
  Mal. 3. 15. we call the proud *h.*
  John 13. 17. *h.* ye if ye do them
  Rom. 14. 22. *h.* he that condemneth not
  1 Pet. 3. 14. suffer for righteousness' sake, *h.* are ye
  4. 14. reproached for the name of Christ, *h.* are ye
  1 Cor. 7. 40. *happier* if she so abide
HARD, Gen. 35. 16, 17. Ex. 1. 14; 18. 26. 2 Sam.
    13. 2. Ps. 88. 7.
  Gen. 18. 14. any thing too *h.* for the Lord
  2 Ki. 2. 10. thou hast asked a *h.* thing
  Ps. 60. 3. shewed thy people *h.* things
  Prov. 13. 15. way of transgressors is *h.*
  Jer. 32. 17. nothing too *h.* for thee, 27.
  Mark 10. 24. how *h.* for them . . . riches
  Acts 9. 5. *h.* for thee to kick, 26. 14.
  2 Pet. 3. 16. things *h.* to be understood
  Jude 15. of all their *h.* speeches
HARDEN, Ex. 4. 21. Deut. 15. 7. Josh. 11. 20.
    Job 6. 10; 39. 16.
  Heb. 3. 8. *h.* not hearts as in the provocation,
    15; 4. 7. Ps. 95. 8.
  Job 9. 4. *hardened* himself against (God)
  Is. 63. 17. *h.* our heart from thy fear
  Mark 6. 52. their heart was *h.* 3. 5.
  Heb. 3. 13. *h.* through deceitfulness
  Prov. 21. 29. *hardeneth* face, 28. 14. *h.* heart
  29. 1. he . . . reproved *h.* his neck shall be destroyed
  Prov. 18. 19. brother offended *harder* . . . won
  Jer. 5. 3. made faces *h.* than a rock
  Ezek. 3. 9. forehead *h.* than flint
  Mat. 19. 8. *hardness* of your hearts
  Mark 3. 5. grieved for the *h.* of their
  Rom. 2. 5. after thy *h.* and impenitent
  2 Tim. 2. 3. endure *h.* as a good soldier
  Gen. 34. 31. Josh. 2. 1. Judg. 11. 1. Prov. 7. 10.
    Is. 1. 21; 23. 15.
  Jer. 2. 20. play the *h.* 3. 1, 6, 8. Ezek. 16. 15, 16, 41.
    Hos. 2. 5; 4. 15.
  1 Cor. 6. 16. joined to *h.* is one body
  Heb. 11. 31. by faith *h.* Rahab
  Jas. 2. 25. Rahab *h.* justified by works
  Mat. 21. 31. *harlots* into kingdom of God
    before, 32.
  Rev. 17. 5. mother of *h.*
HARM, Gen. 31. 52. Acts 28. 5.

1 Chr. 16. 22. do my prophets no *harm*. Ps.
105. 15. Prov. 3. 30. Jer. 39. 12.
1 Pet. 3. 13. who is he that will *h*. you
Mat. 10. 16. *harmless*, Phil. 2. 15.
HARVEST, Gen. 8. 22; 30. 14.
Ex. 34. 21. in *h*. thou shalt rest
Is. 9. 3. according to joy in *h*.
Jer. 5. 24. appointed weeks of *h*.
8. 20. *h*. is past, summer is ended
51. 33. time of *h*. come, Joel 3. 13.
Mat. 9. 37. *h*. plenteous, 38. pray ye the Lord
of the *h*.
13. 39. *h*. is the end of the world
Rev. 14. 15. *h*. of earth is ripe
HASTE, Ex. 12. 11, 33. Is. 52. 12.
Ps. 31. 22. I said in my *h*. 116. 11.
38. 22. make *h*. help me, 40. 13; 70. 1, 5;
71. 12; 141. 1.
119. 60. I made *h*. and delayed not
Sol. 8. 14. make *h*., my beloved
Is. 28. 16. believeth shall not make *h*.
49. 17. thy children shall make *h*.
Ps. 16. 4. *hasten* after another god
Is. 5. 19. let him make speed and *h*.
60. 22. I the Lord will *h*. it in his time
Jer. 1. 12. I will *h*. my word
Prov. 20. 21. inheritance may be gotten *hastily*
14. 29. *hasty* of spirit, Eccl. 7. 9.
29. 20. *h*. in words? more hope of fool
HATE, Gen. 24. 60. Deut. 21. 15.
Lev. 19. 17. shall not *h*. thy brother
Deut. 7. 10. repayeth them that *h*.
Ps. 68. 1. let them that *h*. him flee
97. 10. ye that love the Lord, *h*. evil
119. 104. I *h*. every false way, 128.
113. 1 *h*. vain thoughts, 163. *h*. lying
139. 21. do not I *h*. them that *h*.
Prov. 8. 13. fear of Lord is to *h*. evil
36. all they that *h*. me love death
Jer. 44. 4. abominable thing that I *h*.
Amos 5. 10. they *h*. him that
15. *h*. the evil, and love the good
Luke 14. 26. and *h*. not his father
Rom. 7. 15. what I *h*. that do I
1 John 3. 13. marvel not if world *h*.
Rev. 2. 6. *h*. deeds, which I *h*. 15.
17. 16. these shall *h*. the whore
Prov. 1. 29. they *hated* knowledge
5. 12. how have I *h*. instruction
Is. 66. 5. your brethren that *h*. you
Mal. 1. 3. I *h*. Esau, Rom. 9. 13.
Mat. 10. 22. &c. shall be *h*. of all men
Luke 19. 14. his citizens *h*. him
John 15. 24. *h*. me and my Father, 18.
Eph. 5. 29. no man *h*. his own flesh
Tit. 3. 3. *hateful* and *h*. one another
Jude 23. *h*. garment spotted by flesh
Rom. 1. 30. backbiters, *haters* of God
Ps. 5. 5. *hatest* workers of iniquity
50. 17. seeing thou *h*. instruction
Ex. 23. 5. ass of him that *hateth*
Prov. 13. 24. spareth rod, *h*. his son
John 12. 25. *h*. his life in this world
1 John 2. 9. *h*. his brother is in darkness, 11;
3. 15; 4. 20.
Ex. 18. 21. men of truth, *hating* covetousness
HAUGHTY, my heart not, Ps. 131. 1.
Prov. 16. 18. *h*. spirit before fall, 18. 12.
21. 24. proud and *h*. scorner dealeth
Zeph. 3. 11. no more be *h*. because
Is. 2. 11. *haughtiness*, 17; 13. 11; 16. 6.
HEAD, Gen. 2. 10; 40. 13.
Gen. 3. 15. it shall bruise thy *h*. and

Gen. 49. 26. blessings on Joseph's *head* Deut. 33.
Ezra 9. 6. iniquity increased over *h*. [16.
Ps. 38. 4. iniquities gone over my *h*.
Prov. 16. 31. hoary *h*. is a crown of
20. 29. beauty of old men is gray *h*.
Eccl. 2. 14. wise man's eyes are in *h*.
9. 8. let thy *h*. lack no ointment
Sol. 5. 2. my *h*. is filled with dew
11. his *h*. is as most fine gold
Is. 1. 5. whole *h*. is sick and heart
6. from sole of foot even unto *h*.
Jer. 9. 1. Oh that my *h*. were waters
48. 37. every *h*. shall be bald
Ezek. 9. 10. their way on *h*. 16. 43.
Dan. 2. 28. visions of thy *h*. on bed
38. thou art this *h*. of gold, 32.
Zech. 4. 7. bring forth *h*.stone
Mat. 8. 20. not where to lay his *h*.
14. 8. give me *h*. of John Baptist
Rom. 12. 20. coals of fire on *h*. Prov. 25. 22.
Eph. 1. 22. gave him to be *h*. over all
4. 15. which is the *h*. even Christ
5. 23. husb. *h*. of wife, Christ *h*. of the church
Col. 1. 18. he is *h*. of the body, 2. 19.
Rev. 19. 12. on his *h*. many crowns
Ps. 24. 7. lift up your *heads*, 9.
Is. 35. 10. everlasting joy on *h*. 51. 11.
Luke 21. 28. lift up your *h*.
Rev. 13. 1. seven *h*. and ten horns
Job 5. 13. *headlong*, Luke 4. 29. Acts 1. 18.
2 Tim. 3. 4. *heady*, highminded
HEAL her now, O God, Num. 12. 13.
Deut. 32. 39. I wound, and I *h*.
2 Chr. 7. 14. and will *h*. their land
Ps. 6. 2. *h*. me, for my bones are
41. 4. *h*. my soul, for I have sinned
Is. 57. 18. seen his ways and will *h*. him
Jer. 3. 22. *h*. your backslidings, Hos. 14. 4.
17. 14. *h*. me, and I shall be *h*.
Hos. 6. 1. hath torn and he will *h*. us
Luke 4. 18. *h*. the brokenhearted
23. will say, Physician, *h*. thyself
John 12. 40. converted and I should *h*.
2 Chr. 30. 20. (Lord) *healed* the people
Ps. 30. 2. I cried . . . and thou hast *h*.
Is. 6. 10. convert and be *h*. Acts 28. 27.
53. 5. with his stripes we are *h*. 1 Pet. 2. 24.
Jer. 6. 14. *h*. hurt of daughter, 8. 11.
15. 18. wound . . . which refuseth to be *h*.
Hos. 7. 1. I would have *h*. Israel
Mat. 4. 24. and he *h*. them, 12. 15; 14. 14.
Heb. 12. 13. let it rather be *h*.
Jas. 5. 16. pray that ye may be *h*.
Rev. 13. 3. his deadly wound was *h*.
Ex. 15. 26. I the Lord that *healeth* thee
Ps. 103. 3. who *h*. all thy diseases
147. 3. he *h*. the broken in heart
Is. 30. 26. *h*. stroke of their wound
Jer. 14. 19. looked for time of *healing*
30. 13. thou hast no *h*. medicine
Mal. 4. 2. with *h*. in his wings
Mat. 4. 23. *h*. all manner of sickness
1 Cor. 12. 9. to another the gifts of *h*.
Rev. 22. 2. leaves were for *h*. nations
Ps. 42. 11. *health* of countenance, 43. 5.
Prov. 3. 8. shall be *h*. to thy navel
12. 18. the tongue of the wise is *h*.
Jer. 8. 15. looked for a time of *h*.
30. 17. I will restore *h*. and heal
HEAP coals, Prov. 25. 22. Rom. 12. 20.
Deut. 32. 23. I will *h*. mischiefs upon
Job 36. 13. hypocrites . . . *h*. up wrath
2 Tim. 4. 3. *h*. to themselves teachers

Jas. 5. 3. ye have *heaped* treasure
Ps. 39. 6. he *heapeth* up riches, and
Judg. 15. 16. *heaps* upon *h*. with the
HEAR, Gen. 21. 6; 23. 6.
Deut. 30. 17. if thou wilt not *h*.
1 Ki. 8. 30. *h*. in heaven thy dwelling
2 Ki. 19. 16. bow thine ear, and *h*.
2 Chr. 6. 21. *h*. from thy dwelling
Job 5. 27. *h*. it and know it for good
Ps. 4. 1. *h*. my prayer, 39. 12; 54. 2; 51. 8;
    84. 8; 102. 1; 143. 1. Dan. 9. 17, 19.
4. 3. Lord will *h*. 17. 6; 145. 19. Zech. 10. 6.
10. 17. thou wilt cause thine ear to *h*.
59. 7. who, say they, doth *h*.
66. 16. come and *h*. all ye that
115. 6. they have ears, but *h*. not
Prov. 19. 27. cease to *h*. instruction
Eccl. 5. 1. be more ready to *h*. than
Sol. 2. 14. let me *h*. thy voice, 8. 13.
Is. 1. 2. *h*. O heavens, and give ear
6. 10. lest they *h*. with ears, Deut. 29. 4.
55. 3. *h*. and your soul shall live
Mat. 10. 27. what ye *h*. in the ear
13. 17. to *h*. those things which ye *h*.
17. 5. this is my beloved Son, . . . *h*. ye him
18. 17. if he neglect to *h*. them
Mark 4. 24. take heed what ye *h*.
33. spake word . . . as they were able to *h*.
Luke 8. 18. take heed how ye *h*.
John 5. 25. they that *h*. shall live
Acts 10. 33. to *h*. all things that are commanded
Jas. 1. 19. every man be swift to *h*.
Rev. 3. 20. if any *h*. my voice, and open
Ex. 2. 24. God *heard* their groaning
Ps. 6. 9. Lord hath *h*. supplication
10. 17. hast *h*. desire of humble, 34. 6.
34. 4. I sought the Lord, and he *h*.
61. 5. thou hast *h*. my vows, 116. 1.
66. 19. verily God hath *h*. me, 18. 6.
118. 21. I will praise thee, for thou hast *h*. me
120. 1. I cried to Lord, and he *h*.
Is. 40. 28. hast thou not *h*. that God
Jer. 8. 6. I hearkened and *h*.
Jonah 2. 2. I cried to Lord and he *h*.
Mal. 3. 16. Lord hearkened and *h*.
Mat. 6. 7. be *h*. for much speaking
Luke 1. 13. thy prayer is *h*. and thy
John 3. 32. what he hath seen and *h*.
8. 6. wrote as though he *h*. them not
Rom. 10. 14. of whom they have not *h*.
1 Cor. 2. 9. eye not seen nor ear *h*.
Phil. 4. 9. things learned and received and *h*.
Heb. 4. 2. with faith in them that *h*.
5. 7. was *h*. in that he feared
Jas. 5. 11. ye have *h*. of patience of Job
Rev. 3. 3. how thou hast received and *h*.
Ex. 3. 7. *I have heard* their cry
6. 5.—the groaning, Acts 7. 34.
16. 12.—the murmurings, Num. 14. 27.
Job 42. 5.—of thee by the hearing
Is. 49. 8. in an acceptable time—
Jer. 31. 18.—Ephraim bemoaning
Jas. 1. 25. not a forgetful *hearer* but a doer
Rom. 2. 13. not *hearers* of the law just
Eph. 4. 29. minister grace to the *h*.
Jas. 1. 22. doers of word, not *h*.
Ps. 65. 2. O thou that *hearest* prayer
John 11. 42. I knew thou *h*. me
1 Sam. 3. 9. speak, thy servant *heareth*
Prov. 8. 34. blessed the man that *h*. me
Mat. 7. 24. whoso *h*. these sayings
Luke 10. 16. he that *h*. you *h*. me
John 9. 31. God *h*. not sinners, but

1 John 5. 14. ask according to his will he *heareth*
Rev. 22. 17. let him that *h*. say, Come
Job 42. 5. of thee by *hearing* of ear
Prov. 20. 12. the *h*. ear, and seeing
28. 9. turneth away his ear from *h*.
Rom. 10. 17. faith cometh by *h*. and *h*. by
Heb. 5. 11. seeing ye are dull of *h*.
2 Pet. 2. 8. in seeing and *h*. vexed his
HEARKEN to the Lord, Deut. 28. 15.
Deut. 28. 1. if thou *h*. diligently, 30. 10.
1 Sam. 15. 22. to *h*. better than fat of rams
Ps. 103. 20 angels *h*. to voice of his word
Is. 46. 12. *h*. unto me, ye stouthearted
51. 1. *h*. unto me, ye that follow
55. 2. *h*. diligently unto me, eat
HEART, Ex. 28. 30; 35. 5.
1 Sam. 1. 13. she spake in her *h*. only
10. 9. God gave him another *h*.
16. 7. but the Lord looketh on the *h*.
24. 5. David's *h*. smote him because
1 Chr. 16. 10. let the *h*. of them rejoice that
    seek the Lord, Ps. 105. 3.
22. 19. set *h*. . . . Lord your God
2 Chr. 17. 6. *h*. lifted up in Lord's ways
30. 19. prepareth his *h*. to seek God
Ps. 22. 26. your *h*. live for ever, 69. 32.
37. 31. law of his God is in his *h*.
51. 17. broken and contrite *h*. Is. 66. 2.
64. 6. inward thought, . . . and *h*. deep
78. 37. their *h*. was not right with
Prov. 4. 23. keep thy *h*. with diligence
10. 20 *h*. of wicked is little worth
14. 10. *h*. knoweth own bitterness
16. 9. a man's *h*. deviseth his way
27. 19. (answereth) *h*. of man to man
Eccl. 7. 4. *h*. of wise is in house of mourning
10. 2. wise man's *h*. at his right hand, a fool's *h*.
Sol. 3. 11. day of gladness of his *h*.   [at his left
Is. 6. 10. make *h*. of this people fat
57. 15. to revive the *h*. of contrite
Jer. 11. 20. triest reins and *h*. 17. 10.
12. 11. no man layeth it to *h*. Is. 42. 25.
17. 9. *h*. is deceitful above all things
24. 7. I will give them an *h*. to know
32. 39. give them one *h*. Ezek. 11. 19.
Lam. 3. 41. lift up our *h*. with hands
Ezek. 11. 19. take stony *h*., give *h*. of flesh
18. 31. make you a new *h*.
36. 26. new *h*., take stony *h*., give *h*.
Joel 2. 13. rend your *h*. not garments
Mal. 4. 6. turn *h*. of fathers
Mat. 6. 21. there will your *h*. be also
12. 35. of good treasure of *h*. Luke 6. 45.
15. 19. out of *h*. proceed evil thoughts, Mark 7. 21.
Luke 2. 19. pondered them in *h*. 51.
24. 25. O fools, slow of *h*. to believe
32. did not our *h*. burn within us
John 14. 1. let not *h*. be troubled, 27.
Acts 5. 33. were cut to the *h*. 7. 54.
11. 23. with purpose of *h*. cleave to
13. 22. found man after mine own *h*.
Rom. 10. 10. with *h*. man believeth
1 Cor. 2. 9. nor entered into *h*. of man
2 Cor. 3. 3. in fleshy tables of the *h*.
1 Pet. 3. 4. in hidden man of *h*.
1 John 3. 20. if *h*. condemn us, God
Deut. 11. 13. serve him *with all your h*. and soul,
    Josh. 22. 5. 1 Sam. 12. 20,—
Jer. 29. 13. search for me—
Deut. 6. 5. love God *with all thy h*. and soul,
    30. 6. Mat. 22. 37. Mark 12. 30. Luke 10. 27.
26. 16. keep and do them—and soul.
Prov. 3. 5. trust in Lord—

Deut. 30. 2. (re)turn to Lord *with all thy h.* and
  soul, 10. 2 Ki. 23. 25. (*his h.*). Joel 2. 12. (*your h.*).
1 Ki. 2. 4. walk bef. me *with all their h.* and soul
8. 48. return to thee—and soul
2 Chr. 15. 12. seek God of their fathers—and soul
15. 15. sworn—
22. 9. sought Lord *with all his h.* 31. 21. did it—
Zeph. 3. 14. sing . . . rejoice *with all the h.*
Ps. 86. 12. praise thee *with all my heart*
45. 1. *my heart* is inditing a good
57. 7.—is fixed, O God, 108. 1.
61. 2. when—is overwhelmed
73. 26. my flesh and—faileth, but
84. 2.—and my flesh crieth for the
109. 22.—is wounded within me
131. 1. Lord—is not haughty, nor
Sol. 5. 2. I sleep, but—waketh
Jer. 3. 15. give pastors according to—
Hos. 11. 8.—is turned within me
2 Ki. 20. 3. and with *perfect heart*, 2 Chr. 19. 9.
1 Chr. 28. 9. serve him with—29.
2 Chr. 16. 9. toward him whose—
Ps. 101. 2. within my house with a—
24. 4. clean hands and *pure heart*
Mat. 5. 8. blessed are the pure in *h.*
1 Tim. 1. 5. charity out of a—
2 Tim. 2. 22. call on Lord out of—
1 Pet. 1. 22. love with—fervently
Ps. 9. 1. praise thee, O Lord, *with my whole
  heart*, 111. 1; 138. 1.
119. 2. seek him—10.—have I sought
34. observe it—58. thy favour—69. keep thy
  precepts—
Jer. 3. 10. not turned unto me with whole *h.*
Col. 3. 23. do it *heartily* as to Lord
HEATH, Jer. 17. 6; 48. 6.
HEATHEN, Lev. 25. 44; 26. 45.
Ps. 2. 1. why do the *h.* rage, Acts 4. 25.
2. 8. give them the *h.* for
Gal. 3. 8. justify *h.* through faith
HEAVEN of *h.* cannot contain thee, 1 Ki. 8. 27.
  2 Chr. 2. 6; 6. 18.
Ps. 103. 11. as *h.* is high above the
115. 16. *h.* even heavens are Lord's
Prov. 25. 3. *h.* for height, and earth
Is. 66. 1. *h.* is my throne, Acts 7. 49.
Jer. 31. 37. if *h.* can be measured
Hag. 1. 10. *h.* is stayed from dew
Luke 15. 18. sinned against *h.* 21.
John 1. 51. see *h.* open and angels
Acts 3. 21. the *h.* must receive him
Ps. 73. 25. whom have I *in heaven*
Eccl. 5. 2. God is—thou upon earth
Heb. 10. 34. have—better substance
1 Pet. 1. 4. inheritance reserved—
Ps. 8. 3. when I consider *thy heavens*
19. 1. *the heavens* declare the glory of God
89. 11.—are thine, and earth also
Is. 65. 17. I create new *heavens* and a new earth,
  66. 22. Rev. 21. 1.
2 Cor. 5. 1. a house eternal in the *h.*
Eph. 4. 10. ascended far above all *h.*
2 Pet. 3. 12. *h.* being on fire shall be dissolved
Mat. 6. 14. *heavenly* Father, 26, 32; 15. 13;
  18. 35. Luke 11. 13.
John 3. 12. if I tell you of *h.* things
1 Cor. 15. 48. as is *h.* such the *h.* 49.
Eph. 1. 3. in *h.* places, 20; 2. 6; 3. 10.
2 Tim. 4. 18. unto his *h.* kingdom
Heb. 3. 1. partakers of *h.* calling
HEAVY, Num. 11. 14. Job 33. 7.
Prov. 31. 6. wine to those of *h.* hearts
Is. 6. 10. make their ears *h.* lest

Is. 58. 6. to undo the *heavy* burden
Mat. 11. 28. that labour and are *h.* laden
23. 4. bind *h.* burdens and grievous
Ps. 69. 20. I am full of *heaviness*
119. 28. my soul melteth for *h.*
Prov. 12. 25. *h.* in heart maketh it stoop
14. 13. end of that mirth is *h.*
Rom. 9. 2. I have great *h.* and sorrow
1 Pet. 1. 6. in *h.* through . . . temptations
HEDGE, Job 1. 10. Prov. 15. 19. Is. 5. 5. Hos.
  2. 6. Job 3. 23. Lam. 3. 7.
HEED, 2 Sam. 20. 10. 2 Ki. 10. 31.
Deut. 2. 4. take good *h.* to yourselves, 4. 15.
Josh. 22. 5. take diligent *h.* to do the
Ps. 119. 9. by taking *h.* thereto
Jer. 18. 18. not give *h.* to any of his
HEEL, his, shalt bruise, Gen. 3. 15.
Ps. 41. 9. lifted *h.* against me, John 13. 18.
Hos. 12. 3. he took his brother by *h.*
Ps. 49. 5. iniquity of *heels* shall compass
HEIFER, Num. 19. 2. Jer. 46. 20; 48. 34. Hos.
  4. 16; 10. 11. Heb. 9. 13.
HEIR, Gen. 15. 4; 21. 10.
Jer. 49. 1. hath Israel no sons . . . no *h.*
Rom. 4. 13. (Abraham) should be *h.* of the world
  through faith
Gal. 4. 7. if a son, then an *h.* of God
Heb. 1. 2. whom God appointed *h.*
11. 7. became *h.* of righteousness
Rom. 8. 17. *heirs* of God, joint *h.* with Christ
Gal. 3. 29. if ye be Christ's then Abraham's seed
  and *h.* according to the promise
Eph. 3. 6. Gentiles should be fellow *h.*
Heb. 6. 17. willing to shew *h.* of promise
1 Pet. 3. 7. *h.* together of grace of
HELD, Ps. 94. 18. Sol. 3. 4.
HELL, Mat. 18. 9. Mark 9. 43, 45.
Deut. 32. 22. shall burn to lowest *h.*
2 Sam. 22. 6. the sorrows of *h.*
Job 11. 8. it is deeper than *h.*; what
26. 6. *h.* is naked before him and
Ps. 9. 17. wicked be turned into *h.*
16. 10. not leave soul in *h.* Acts 2. 27.
55. 15. let them go down quick into *h.*
86. 13. delivered soul from lowest *h.*
139. 8. make my bed in *h.* thou art
Prov. 5. 5. her steps take hold on *h.*
7. 27. her house is the way to *h.*
9. 18. her guests are in depths of *h.*
15. 11. *h.* and destruction before the Lord
24. that he may depart from *h.*
23. 14. shalt deliver his soul from *h.*
27. 20. *h.* and destruction are never
Is. 5. 14. *h.* hath enlarged herself
14. 9. *h.* from beneath is moved to
15. thou shalt be brought down to *h.*
57. 9. debase thyself even to *h.* Ezek. 31. 16, 17;
  32. 21, 27.
Amos 9. 2. though they dig into *h.*
Jonah 2. 2. out of belly of *h.* cried I
Hab. 2. 5. enlargeth his desire as *h.*
Mat. 5. 22. be in danger of *h.* fire
29. body, eye, &c., be cast into *h.* 30.
10. 28. destroy soul and body in *h.*
11. 23. brought down to *h.* Luke 10. 15.
16. 18. gates of *h.* shall not prevail
23. 15. twofold more the child of *h.*
Luke 12. 5. power to cast into *h.*
16. 23. in *h.* he lift up his eyes
Acts 2. 31. his soul not left in *h.* 27.
Jas. 3. 6. tongue set on fire of *h.*
2 Pet. 2. 4. cast them down to *h.*
Rev. 1. 18. have keys of *h.* and

Rev. 6. 8. Death, and *Hell* followed with
20. 13. death and *h.* delivered up dead
14. death and *h.* were cast into lake
HELMET, 1 Sam. 17. 5. 2 Chr. 26. 14.
Eph. 6. 17. take the *h.* of salvation
1 Thes. 5. 8. an *h.,* hope of salvation
HELP meet for him, Gen. 2. 18.
Deut. 33. 29. Lord, shield of thy *h.*
Judg. 5. 23. came not to *h.* of Lord
Ps. 27. 9. thou hast been my *h.*
33. 20. he is our *h.* and shield
40. 17. my *h.* and deliverer, 70. 5.
46. 1. God a very present *h.* in trouble
60. 11. vain is *h.* of man, 108. 12.
71. 12. my God, make haste for my *h.*
89. 19. laid *h.* on one that is mighty
115. 9. Lord is *h.* and shield, 10, 11.
124. 8. our *h.* is in name of Lord
Hos. 13. 9. but in me is thy *h.*
Acts 26. 22. having obtained *h.* of God
2 Chr. 14. 11. nothing with thee to *h.*
Ps. 40. 13. make haste to *h.* me, 70. 1.
Is. 41. 10. I will *h.* thee, 13, 14; 44. 2.
63. 5. I looked and there was none to *h.*
Acts 16. 9. come to Macedonia, and *h.* us
Heb. 4. 16. find grace to *h.* in time
1 Sam. 7. 12. hitherto the Lord *helped* us
Is. 49. 8. in day of salvation I *h.*
Zech. 1. 15. *h.* forward affliction
Acts 18. 27. *h.* them much which believed
Rev. 12. 16. the earth *h.* the woman
Ps. 10. 14. art the *helper* of the fatherless
Job 9. 13. proud *helpers* do stoop
2 Cor. 1. 24. (we) are *h.* of your joy
3 John 8. fellow*h.* to the truth
Rom. 8. 26. Spirit *helpeth* our infirmities
1 Cor. 12. 28. *helps,* governments
HEM, Mat. 9. 20; 14. 36.
HEN, Mat. 23. 37. Luke 13. 34.
HERESY, Acts 24. 14. 1 Cor. 11. 19. Gal. 5. 20.
2 Pet. 2. 1.
HERITAGE appointed by God, Job 20. 29.
Ps. 16. 6. I have a goodly *h.*
61. 5. *h.* of those that fear thy name
119. 111. testimonies as *h.* for
Is. 54. 17. *h.* of Lord's servants, 58. 14.
Jer. 3. 19. goodly *h.* of the hosts
Joel 2. 17. give not thine *h.* to reproach, 3. 2.
1 Pet. 5. 3. not as lords over God's *h.*
HEW tables of stone, Ex. 34. 1. Deut. 12. 3.
Jer. 2. 13. *hewed* out cisterns
Hos. 6. 5. I *h.* them by prophets
Mat. 3. 10. *hewn* down, 7. 19. Luke 3. 9.
HID themselves, Gen. 3. 8.
Ps. 119. 11. word have I *h.* in heart
Mat. 10. 26. and *h.* that shall not be
11. 25. *h.* from wise, Luke 10. 21.
2 Cor. 4. 3. if gospel be *h.* it is *h.* to
Col. 2. 3. in whom are *h.* all treasures
3. 3. your life is *h.* with Christ
1 Cor. 4. 5. bring to light *hidden* things
1 Pet. 3. 4. the *h.* man of heart
Rev. 2. 17. give the *h.* manna
Gen. 18. 17. shall I *hide* from Abraham
Job 33. 17. and *h.* pride from man
Ps. 17. 8. *h.* me under the shadow
27. 5. in time of trouble he shall *h.*
30. 7. didst *h.* thy face and I was troubled
31. 20. shalt *h.* them in the secret of thy presence
51. 9. *h.* thy face from my sins
Is. 26. 20. *h.* thyself for a little
Jas. 5. 20. *h.* a multitude of sins, 1 Pet. 4. 8.
Rev. 6. 16. *h.* us from face of him

Job 13. 24. why *hidest* thou thy face, Ps. 30. 7;
44. 24; 88. 14; 143. 7.
Is. 45. 15. thou art a God that *h.* thyself
Job 34. 29. when he *hideth* his face
42. 3. who is he that *h.* counsel
Ps. 139. 12. darkness *h.* not from
Is. 8. 17. I will wait on Lord that *h.*
Hab. 3. 4. *hiding* of his power
Ps. 32. 7. *h.* place, 119. 114. Is. 32. 2.
HIGH, Deut. 12. 2. &c. places . . . upon *h.* mountains
Deut. 26. 19. make thee *h.* above all
1 Ki. 9. 8. at this house which is *h.*
1 Chr. 17. 17. man of *h.* degree
Job 11. 8. *h.* as heaven, what canst
Ps. 49. 2. both low and *h.,* rich and
89. 13. strong hand, and *h.* is right hand
97. 9. Lord art *h.* above all, 113. 4.
103. 11. as heaven is *h.* above earth
131. 1. or in things too *h.* for me
138. 6. though Lord be *h.* yet hath
Eccl. 12. 5. afraid of that which is *h.*
Is. 57. 15. I dwell in *h.* and holy place
Ezek. 21. 26. abase him that is *h.*
Rom. 12. 16. mind not *h.* things
2 Cor. 10. 5. every *h.* thing that exalteth itself
against knowledge of God
Phil. 3. 14. for the prize of the *h.* calling of God
Num. 24. 16. *Most High,* Deut. 32. 8. 2 Sam.
22. 14. Ps. 7. 17; 9. 2; 21. 7; 46. 4; 50. 14;
56. 2.
Ps. 47. 2. the Lord—is terrible
83. 18. Jehovah art—over all earth
Is. 14. 14. I will be like the—
Hos. 11. 7. called them to the—
Acts 7. 48.—dwelleth not in temples
Job 5. 11. set *on high* those that be
16. 19. witness . . . and my record is—
Ps. 107. 41. setteth the poor—
113. 5. like our God who dwelleth—
Is. 26. 5. bringeth down that dwell—
Luke 24. 49. be endued with power from—
Eccl. 5. 8. there be *higher* than they
Is. 55. 9. as heavens *h.* . . . . my ways *h.*
Heb. 7. 26. made *h.* than heavens
Ps. 18. 13. *Highest* gave his voice
Eccl. 5. 8. he that is higher than *h.*
Luke 1. 35. *H.* shall overshadow thee
2. 14. glory to God in the *h.* 19. 38.
6. 35. shall be the children of the *H.*
1. 28. thou that art *highly* favoured
16. 15. is *h.* esteemed among men
Rom. 12. 3. not think of self more *h.*
1 Thes. 5. 13. esteem very *h.* in love
Rom. 11. 20. be not *highminded* but fear
1 Tim. 6. 17. rich, that they be not—
Job 22. 12. *height,* Rom. 8. 39. Eph. 3. 18.
HILL, Ex. 24. 4. Ps. 68. 15, 16.
Ps. 2. 6. set King on holy *h.* of Zion, 3. 4;
15. 1; 43. 3; 68. 15; 99. 9.
Gen. 7. 19. all the high *hills* covered
49. 26. utmost bound of everlasting *h.*
Num. 23. 9. from the *h.* I beheld him
Ps. 65. 12. little *h.* rejoice on every
98. 8. *h.* be joyful together
114. 4. little *h.* skipped like lambs
Hos. 10. 8. *h.* fall on us, Luke 23. 30.
Hab. 3. 6. the perpetual *h.* did bow
HIND, 2 Sam. 22. 34. Ps. 29. 9. Prov. 5. 19. Sol.
2. 7; 3. 5. Hab. 3. 19.
HIRE, Deut. 24. 15. Is. 23. 18. Mic. 1. 7; 3. 11.
Luke 10. 7. Jas. 5. 4.
Job 7. 1. a *hireling,* John 10. 12, 13.

HITHERTO Lord helped, 1 Sam. 7. 12.
Job 38. 11. *h.* shalt thou come, but
John 16. 24. *h.* ye asked nothing in
1 Cor. 3. 2. meat; *h.* ye were not able
HOLD, Gen. 21. 18. Ex. 9. 2; 20. 7.
Judg. 9. 46. *h.* of house of the god Berith
Job 17. 9. righteous shall *h.* on way
Is. 41. 13. God will *h.* thy right hand   [64. 12.
62. 1, 6. for Zion's sake will I not *h.* my peace,
Jer. 2. 13. cisterns that can *h.* no water
Mat. 6. 24. *h.* to one, despise other
Phil. 2. 29. *h.* such in reputation
Heb. 3. 14. if we *h.* beginning of our confidence
1 Thes. 5. 21. hold *fast* that which is good
2 Tim. 1. 13.—form of sound words
Heb. 3. 6. if—confidence . . . of hope
4. 14. let us—our profession, 10. 23.
Rev. 2. 25. what ye have—till I come
3. 3. hast received and heard—and repent
11.—that which thou hast, that no man
Ps. 77. 4. *holdest* mine eyes waking
Rev. 2. 13. *h.* fast my name and hast
Job 2. 3. still he *holdeth* fast integrity
Ps. 66. 9. which *h.* our soul in life   [wise
Prov. 17. 28. fool when he *h.* his peace counted
Jer. 6. 11. I am weary with *holding*
Phil. 2. 16. *h.* forth the word of life
Col. 2. 19. not *h.* the Head, from
1 Tim. 1. 19. *h.* faith and a good conscience
3. 9. *h.* mystery of faith in a pure conscience
Tit. 1. 9. *h.* fast the faithful word
HOLY ground, Ex. 3. 5. *h.* sabbath, Ex. 16. 23;
31. 14, 15. *h.* nation, 19. 6. 1 Pet. 2. 9. *h.*
things, gifts, Ex. 28. 38. *h.* crown, 29. 6. *h.*
ointment, 30. 25. *h.* sanctuary, Lev. 16. 33.
h. house, 27. 14. *h.* tithe, 30. *h.* water, Num.
5. 17. *h.* instruments, 31. 6.
Lev. 11. 45. be *h.* for I am *h.* 20. 7.
1 Sam. 2. 2. there is none *h.* as Lord
21. 5. vessels of young men are *h.*
Ps. 22. 3. thou art *h.* . . . that inhabitest praises
99. 5. worship at his footstool, for he is *h.*
145. 17. (Lord is) *h.* in all his works
Prov. 20. 25. snare to man who devoureth . . . *h.*
Ezek. 22. 26. no difference between *h.*
Mat. 7. 6. give not that is *h.* to dogs
Luke 1. 35. *h.* thing which shall be born
Acts 4. 27. thy *h.* child Jesus, 30.
Rom. 7. 12. law *h.*, commandment *h.*
11. 16. if firstfruit *h.*, lump is also *h.*
12. 1. sacrifice, *h.*, acceptable to God
1 Cor. 7. 14. children unclean, now *h.*
2 Tim. 1. 9. called us with *h.* calling
3. 15. hast known the *h.* scriptures
Tit. 1. 8. sober, just, *h.*, temperate
1 Pet. 1. 15. be *h.* in all manner, 16.
2. 5. a *h.* priesthood, 9. *h.* nation
2 Pet. 1. 21. *h.* men of God spake as
Rev. 3. 7. saith he that is *h.* . . . true
4. 8. *h. h. h.* Lord God Almighty
15. 4. fear thee for thou only art *h.*
22. 11. he that is *h.* let him be *h.* still
Ex. 26. 33. *most holy* place, 1 Ki. 6. 16, &c.
Ezek. 44. 13; 45. 3.—altar, Ex. 29. 37.—meat,
sin, trespass, Lev. 6. 17; 14. 13. Num. 18. 9, 10.
—of land, Ezek. 48. 12.   [and *h.*
Lev. 21. 22. bread of his God both of *most h.*
2 Chr. 3. 8. made the—house
Ezek. 43. 12. whole limit shall be—
Jude 20. building yourselves in—faith
Ps. 42. 4. multitude that kept *holyday*, Is.
58. 13. Col. 2. 16. Ex. 35. 2.
Mat. 1. 18. child of *the Holy Ghost*, 20.

Mat. 3. 11. &c. baptize you with *the Holy Ghost,*
Acts 1. 5; 11. 16.
12. 31, &c. blasphemy against—
Mark 12. 36. David said by—Acts 1. 16.
13. 11. not ye that speak, but—
Luke 1. 15, 35.—shall come upon **thee**
2. 25.—was upon
26. revealed unto him by—
3. 22.—descended in bodily shape
12. 12.—shall teach you what to say
John 7. 39. for—was not yet given
14. 26. Comforter, which is—, whom
20. 22. receive—   [ment
Acts 1. 2. (Jesus) through—had given command-
8. after that—is come upon you
2. 38. receive gift of—10. 45. (Gentiles)
5. 3. Satan filled heart to lie to—
32. we are his witnesses . . . and so is also—
7. 51. ye do always resist—
8. 15. receive—17, 19.—given, 18.
9. 31. walking in the comfort of—
10. 38. anointed Jesus . . . with—
44.—fell on all, 15. 8. giving them—
13. 2. the—said, Separate me Barnabas and
4. they being sent forth by—
15. 28. it seemed good to—and us
16. 6. forbidden of—to preach in
20. 23. save that—witnesseth . . . that bonds
28. flock over which—made you overseers
21. 11. thus saith—so shall the Jews
Rom. 5. 5. love of God shed abroad . . . by—
9. 1. conscience bearing witness in—
14. 17. righteousness, peace, joy in—
15. 16. offering of Gentiles . . . sanctified by—
1 Cor. 2. 13. in words—teacheth
6. 19. your body temple of—not own
2 Cor. 6. 6. by—by love unfeigned
13. 14. communion of—be with you
1 Thes. 1. 5. in power and in—, 6. joy of—
2 Tim. 1. 14. good thing . . . keep by—
Tit. 3. 5. saved . . . by the renewing of—
Heb. 2. 4. God witness . . . with gifts of—
3. 7. wherefore, as—saith, to-day if
9. 8.—this signifying, that the way
1 Pet. 1. 12. preached gospel with—
2 Pet. 1. 21. men of God . . . moved by—
1 John 5. 7. Father, Word, and—. . . one
Jude 20. building up . . . praying in—
Luke 1. 15, 41, 67; 4. 1, *filled with,* or *full of the*
Holy Ghost, Acts 2. 4; 4. 8; 6. 3, 5; 9. 17;
11. 24; 13. 9, 52.
Ps. 51. 11. take not thy *Holy Spirit*
Is. 63. 10. rebelled and vexed his—
11. where is he that put his—within
Luke 11. 13. give—to them that ask
Eph. 1. 13. sealed with—of promise
4. 30. grieve not—of God, 1 Thes. 5. 19.
1 Thes. 4. 8. God, who hath given his—
Ps. 87. 1. *holy mountain,* Is. 11. 9; 56. 7; 57. 13;
65. 11, 25; 66. 20. Dan. 9. 16; 11. 45. Joel
2. 1; 3. 17. Obad. 16. Zeph. 3. 11. Zech. 8. 3.
Lev. 20. 3. *holy name,* & 22. 2, 32. 1 Chr.
16. 10, 35. Ps. 33. 21; 103. 1; 111. 9; 145. 21.
Is. 57. 15. Ezek. 36. 20.
Deut. 33. 8. *Holy One,* Job 6. 10. Ps. 16. 10;
89. 19. Is. 10. 17; 29. 23; 40. 25; 43. 15;
49. 7. Dan. 4. 13. Hos. 11. 9. Hab. 1. 12;
3. 3. Mark 1. 24. Acts 3. 14. 1 John 2. 20.
2 Ki. 19. 22. *Holy One of Israel,* Ps. 71. 22;
78. 41; 89. 18. Is. 1. 4; 5. 19, 24; 10. 20;
12. 6; 17. 7; 29. 19; 30. 11. &c.; 31. 1; 41. 14;
45. 11; 47. 4; 49. 7; 55. 5; 60. 9, 14. Jer.
50. 29; 51. 5. Ezek. 39. 7.

Deut. 7. 6. *holy people*, 14. 2, 21; 26. 19; 28. 9.
Is. 62. 12. Dan. 8. 24; 12. 7.
Ex. 28. 29, &c. *holy place*, Lev. 6. 16; 10. 17.
1 Ki. 8. 8. Ezra 9. 8. Ps. 68. 17. Eccl.
8. 10. Acts 6. 13. Heb. 9. 12, and about 25
other places
Ps. 5. 7. *holy temple*, 11. 4; 65. 4; 79. 1; 138. 2.
Jonah 2. 4, 7. Mic. 1. 2. Hab. 2. 20. Eph. 2. 21.
Is. 65. 5. for I am *holier* than thou
Heb. 9. 3. the *Holiest* tabernacle, 8; 10. 19.
1 Thes. 2. 10. how *holily* . . . we behaved
Ex. 15. 11. glorious in *holiness*
28. 36. *h*. to Lord, 39. 30. Is. 23. 18.
1 Chr. 16. 29. in beauty of *h*. Ps. 29. 2; 96. 9;
110. 3. 2 Chr. 20. 21.
2 Chr. 31. 18. sanctified themselves in *h*.
Ps. 30. 4. remembrance of his *h*. 97. 12.
47. 8. God sitteth on throne of his *h*.
60. 6. God hath spoken in his *h*. 108. 7.
89. 35. I have sworn by my *h*.
93. 5. *h*. becometh thine house, O Lord
Is. 35. 8. shall be called the way of *h*.
62. 9. drink it in the courts of my *h*.
Jer. 2. 3. Israel *h*. to Lord, Is. 63. 18.
23. 9. because of Lord and words of his *h*.
Amos 4. 2. Lord hath sworn by his *h*.
Obad. 17. on mount Zion . . . there shall be *h*.
Zech. 14. 20. on horse bells, *h*. to Lord
Mal. 2. 11. Judah profaned *h*. of Lord
Luke 1. 75. in *h*. and righteousness
Acts 3. 12. as though by our own . . . *h*.
Rom. 1. 4. Son of God . . . Spirit of *h*.
6. 22. fruit unto *h*. . . . end everlasting life
2 Cor. 7. 1. perfecting *h*. in fear of God
Eph. 4. 24. new man . . . created . . . in true *h*.
1 Thes. 3. 13. unblameable in *h*. before God
1 Tim. 2. 15. if they continue in . . . *h*.
Tit. 2. 3. behaviour as becometh *h*.
Heb. 12. 10. partakers of his *h*.
14. *h*. without which shall . . . see the Lord
HOME, Gen. 43. 16. 1 Ki. 13. 7. Deut. 24. 5.
Ruth 1. 21. Lord hath brought me *h*.
Job 39. 12. he will bring *h*. thy seed
Ps. 68. 12. tarried at *h*. divided spoil
Eccl. 12. 5. man goeth to his long *h*.
2 Cor. 5. 6. whilst at *h*. in body, absent
Tit. 2. 5. young women . . . keepers at *h*.
Jer. 2. 14. Israel a *homeborn* slave?
HONEST and good heart, Luke 8. 15.
Acts 6. 3. seven men of *h*. report, full
Rom. 12. 17. provide things *h*. in the sight of all
men, 2 Cor. 8. 21.
2 Cor. 13. 7. should do that which is *h*.
Phil. 4. 8. whatsoever things are *h*.
1 Pet. 2. 12. having your conversation *h*.
Rom. 13. 13. walk *honestly* as in day
1 Thes. 4. 12. walk *h*. towards them
Heb. 13. 18. willing to live *h*.
HONEY, Gen. 43. 11. Ex. 16. 31. Lev. 2. 11.
Judg. 14. 18. 1 Ki. 14. 3. Ezek. 27. 17.
Ps. 19. 10. sweeter than *h*. 119. 103.
81. 16. *h*. out of rock, Jer. 41. 8.
Sol. 4. 11. *h*. and milk under thy tongue
Is. 7. 15. butter and *h*. shall he eat, 22.
Mat. 3. 4. his meat locusts and wild *h*.
Rev. 10. 9. in mouth sweet as *h*. 10. 1 Sam.
14. 27. dipt in *honeycomb*, Prov. 5. 3; 16. 24;
24. 13; 27. 7. Sol. 4. 11; 5. 1. Luke 24. 42.
HONOUR, get *h*. Ex. 14. 17. Num. 22. 17. not for
h. Judg. 4. 9. 2 Chr. 26. 18. vanity of *h*. Eccl.
6. 2.
Gen. 49. 6. to their assembly, mine *h*.
1 Chr. 29. 12. riches and *h*. come of

Ps. 7. 5. lay mine *honour* in the dust
8. 5. crowned him with glory and *h*.
26. 8. place where thine *h*. dwelleth
49. 20. man in *h*. understandeth not
149. 9. this *h*. have all his saints
Prov. 3. 16. in left hand riches and *h*.
14. 28. the people is the king's *h*.
15. 33. before *h*. is humility, 18. 12.
20. 3. it is an *h*. to cease from strife
21. 21. followeth mercy findeth . . . *h*.
25. 2. *h*. of kings to search a matter
26. 1. *h*. is not seemly for a fool
29. 23. *h*. shall uphold the humble
Mat. 13. 57. prophet is not without *h*. save in his
own country, Mark 6. 4. John 4. 44.
John 5. 41. I receive not *h*. from men
Rom. 2. 7. in well doing seek glory, *h*.
9. 21. one vessel to *h*., another, 2 Tim. 2. 20.
12. 10. in *h*. preferring one another
2 Cor. 6. 8. by *h*. and dishonour, by evil report
Heb. 5. 4. taketh this *h*. to himself
1 Pet. 1. 7. found unto praise and *h*.
3. 7. *h*. to wife as weaker vessel
1 Sam. 2. 30. that *h*. me I will *h*.
15. 30. *h*. me before elders . . . and Israel
Prov. 3. 9. *h*. Lord with substance
Is. 29. 13. with their lips do *h*. me
John 5. 23. with Son as they *h*. Father
12. 26. serve me, him will my Father *h*.
1 Pet. 2. 17. *h*. all men, 1 Tim. 5. 3. *h*. widows
Heb. 13. 4. marriage is *honourable*
Ps. 15. 4. *honoureth* them that fear
Mat. 15. 8. *h*. me with lips, Mark 7. 6.
HOOF, Ex. 10. 26. Lev. 11. 3-7. Judg. 5. 22. Is.
5. 28. Mic. 4. 13.
HOOK, Ex. 26. 32. Job 41. 1. Ezek. 29. 4. Mat.
17. 27. *pruninghooks*, Is. 2. 4; 18. 5.
HOPE in Israel concerning this, Ezra 10. 2.
Job 11. 20. *h*. shall be as giving up ghost
Ps. 78. 7. might set their *h*. in God
Prov. 10. 28. *h*. of righteous shall be gladness
11. 7. *h*. of unjust men perisheth
14. 32. righteous hath *h*. in his death
19. 18. chasten thy son while there is *h*.
26. 12. more *h*. of a fool, 29. 20.
Is. 57. 10. saidst thou not, There is no *h*. Jer.
2. 25; 18. 12. Ezek. 37. 11.
Jer. 14. 8. the *h*. of Israel, Acts 28. 20.
17. 7. blessed whose *h*. the Lord is
50. 7. the *h*. of their fathers
Lam. 3. 29. if there be *h*.
Hos. 2. 15. valley of Achor for door of *h*.
Joel 3. 16. Lord will be the *h*. of his people
Zech. 9. 12. turn to the strong hold, ye prisoners
of *h*.
Acts 24. 15. have *h*. towards God
Rom. 5. 4. experience (worketh) *h*.
5. *h*. not ashamed   [seen is not *h*.
8. 24. we are saved by *h*.: but *h*. that is
15. 4. comfort of scriptures, have *h*.
1 Cor. 9. 10. that ploweth . . . plow in *h*. and that
thresheth in *h*. . . . partaker of his *h*.
13. 13. now abideth faith, *h*., charity
15. 19. if in this life only . . . *h*. in Christ
Gal. 5. 5. wait for *h*. of righteousness
Eph. 2. 12. no *h*. and without God
Col. 1. 23. not moved away from *h*. of Gospel,
27. Christ . . . the *h*. of glory
1 Thes. 4. 13. sorrow not as others which have
no *h*.
5. 8. for helmet, the *h*. of salvation
1 Tim. 1. 1. Jesus Christ who is our *h*.
Tit. 2. 13. looking for that blessed *h*.

Heb. 6. 11. to full assurance of *hope*
19. which *h*. we have as an anchor
1 Pet. 1. 3. begotten again to lively *h*.
3. 15. asketh a reason of *h*. in you
1 John 3. 3. every man that hath this *h*.
Ps. 16. 9. my flesh shall rest *in hope*
Rom. 4. 18. against *h*. believed—
5. 2. rejoice—of glory of God, 12. 12.
Tit. 1. 2.—eternal life God promised
Job 17. 15. where is now *my hope*
31. 24. if I have made gold—
Ps. 39. 7.—is in thee, 71. 5; Jer. 17. 17.
22. 9. didst make me *hope* on mother's
33. 18. . . . *h*. in his mercy, 22; 147. 11.
42. 5. *h*. thou in God, for, 11; 43. 5.
119. 49. thou hast caused me to *h*.
81. I *h*. in thy word, 114; 130. 5.
Lam. 3. 26. good that a man should *h*.
Rom. 8. 25. if *h*. for that we see not
1 Pet. 1. 13. be sober and *h*. to end
Ps. 119. 43. *I have hoped* in thy judgments
74, 147,—in thy word. 166,—for thy salvation
Heb. 11. 1. faith is the substance of things *hoped*
1 Cor. 13. 7. charity . . . *hopeth* all things   [*for*
Luke 6. 35. lend, *hoping* for nothing
HORN of my salvation, Ps. 18. 2.
1 Sam. 2. 1, my *h*. is exalted in the Lord, 10.
Ps. 92. 10. my *h*. as *h*. of unicorn
148. 14. he exalteth the *h*. of his
Mic. 4. 13. I will make thy *h*. iron
Rev. 13. 1. beast having ten *horns*, 17. 3, 7.
5. 6. lamb having seven *h*.
HORRIBLE, Ps. 11. 6; 40. 2. Jer. 5. 30; 18. 13;
23. 14. Hos. 6. 10. Jer. 2. 12. Ezek. 32. 10.
HORROR, Gen. 15. 12. Job 18. 20. Ps. 55. 5;
119. 53. Ezek. 7. 18.
HORSE and rider thrown, Ex. 15. 21.
Ps. 32. 9. be ye not as *h*. or mule
33. 17. *h*. is a vain thing for safety
147. 10. delighteth not in the strength of the *h*.
Jer. 8. 6. as *h*. rusheth into battle
Eccl. 10. 7. have seen servants on *horses*
Jer. 12. 5. canst thou contend with *h*.
Hos. 14. 3. we will not ride upon *h*.
Zech. 1. 8; 6. 2, 3, 6. *h*. red, white, black &
Rev. 6. 2, 4, 5, 8; 9. 17.
HOSPITALITY, Rom. 12. 13. 1 Tim. 3. 2.
Tit. 1. 8. 1 Pet. 4. 9.
HOST, Luke 10. 35. Rom. 16. 23. Ps. 27. 3;
33. 16; 103. 21; 108. 11; 148. 2. Is. 40. 26.
Luke 2. 13. Jer. 3. 19.
HOT, Ps. 38. 1; 39. 3. Prov. 6. 28. Hos. 7. 7.
1 Tim. 4. 2. Rev. 3. 15.
HOUR, Dan. 3. 6, 15; 4. 33.
Mat. 10. 19. given you in that same *h*.
24. 36. day and *h*. knoweth no man
25. 13. know neither day nor *h*.
Luke 12. 12. Holy Ghost shall teach you that
same *h*.
22. 53. this is your *h*. and power of darkness
John 2. 4. mine *h*. is not yet come
4. 23. *h*. cometh, and now is, 5. 25.
7. 30. *h*. was not yet come, 8. 20.
Rev. 3. 3. not know what *h*. I come
10. keep from the *h*. of temptation
17. 12. power as kings one *h*. with
18. 10. in one *h*. is thy judgment
HOUSE, Ex. 20. 17. Lev. 14. 36.
Ex. 12. 30. not a *h*. where . . . not one dead
Job 21. 28. where is the *h*. of prince
30. 23. *h*. appointed for all living
Prov. 3. 33. curse of Lord is in *h*. of
7. 27. her *h*. is the way to hell

Prov. 12. 7. *house* of the righteous shall stand
Eccl. 7. 2. go to the *h*. of mourning than *h*. of
12. 3. when keepers of *h*. tremble   [feasting
Sol. 2. 4. brought me to the banqueting *h*.
Is. 5. 8. woe to them that join *h*. to *h*.
60. 7. I will glorify the *h*. of my
64. 11. our holy and beautiful *h*.
Mat. 10. 13. if the *h*. be worthy
12. 25. a *h*. divided, Luke 11. 17.
23. 38. *h*. left desolate, Luke 13. 35; Jer. 12. 7.
Luke 12. 3. proclaimed on *h*.tops
John 14. 2. in my Father's *h*. are
Rom. 16. 5. church in their *h*. 1 Cor. 16. 19.
Col. 4. 15. Philem. 2.
2 Tim. 1. 16. mercy to *h*. of Onesiphorus
Heb. 3. 3. who built *h*. more honour than *h*.
2 John 10. receive him not to your *h*.
Ps. 105. 21. him lord of all *his house*
112. 3. wealth and riches shall be in—
Acts 10. 2. feared God with all—
16. 34. believing in God with all—
Heb. 3. 2. faithful in all—5, 6.
John 4. 53. believed and his *whole house*
1 Tim. 5. 8. specially for those of his own *h*.
Josh. 24. 15. as for me and *my house*
2 Sam. 23. 5. although—not so with God
Ps. 101. 2. will walk within—with
Mat. 12. 44. will return to—Luke 11. 24.
Acts 16. 15. judged me faithful . . . come into—
Deut. 6. 7. when thou sittest in *thine house*
Ps. 26. 8. I loved habitation of—
36. 8. satisfied with fatness of—65. 4.
Is. 38. 1. set—in order, for thou
Acts 11. 14. thou and all—saved, 16. 31.
Gen. 28. 17. *house of God* or *Lord*, Ps. 23. 6;
27. 4; 42. 4; 55. 14. Eccl. 5. 1. Is. 2. 3. Mic.
4. 2. 1 Tim. 3. 15. 1 Pet. 4. 17. Ex. 23. 19.
Josh. 6. 24, and about 100 other places
Job 4. 19. dwell in *houses* of clay
Ps. 49. 11. *h*. shall continue for ever
Prov. 19. 14. *h*. and riches are inheritance of fathers
Mat. 11. 8. wear soft clothing are in king's *h*.
19. 29. forsaken *h*., brethren, Mark 10. 29.
23. 14. devour widows' *h*. Luke 20. 47.
Luke 16. 4. may receive me into their *h*.
1 Cor. 11. 22. have ye not *h*. to eat . . . in
1 Tim. 3. 12. ruling . . . own *h*. well
2 Tim. 3. 6. creep into *h*. and lead
Tit. 1. 11. subvert whole *h*. teaching things which
they ought not
Acts 16. 15. baptized and her whole *household*
Gal. 6. 10. *h*. of faith
Eph. 2. 19. *h*. of God
Mat. 13. 52. like *householder*, 20. 1.
HOW long, Ps. 6. 3; 13. 1; 74. 9; 79. 5; 80. 4;
89. 46. Is. 6. 11. Jer. 4. 14. Dan. 8. 13;
12. 6. Mat. 17. 17. Luke 9. 41. Rev. 6. 10.
Job 15. 16. *how much more*, Prov. 21. 27. Mat.
7. 11. Luke 12. 24, 28. Heb. 9. 14.
Mat. 18. 21; 23. 37. *how oft*, Luke 13. 34. Job
21. 17. Ps. 78. 40.
HUMBLE person, save, Job 22. 29.
Ps. 9. 12. forgetteth not the cry of the *h*.
10. 12. forget not the *h*.
17. desire of the *h*.
34. 2. shall hear thereof, and be
Prov. 16. 19. to be of an *h*. spirit
Is. 57. 15. of contrite and *h*. spirit, to revive the
spirit of *h*.
Ex. 10. 3. thou refuse to *h*. thyself
Deut. 8. 2. to *h*. thee, and prove, 3, 16.
2 Chr. 7. 14. shall *h*. themselves
34. 27. didst *h*. thyself before God

Prov. 6. 3. *humble* thyself, make sure thy friend
Jer. 13. 18. *h.* yourselves
Mat. 18. 4. whosoever *h.* himself shall be exalted,
   23. 12. Luke 14. 11; 18. 14.
2 Cor. 12. 21. my God will *h.* me
Jas. 4. 6. giveth grace to *h.* 1 Pet. 5. 5.
4. 10. *h.* yourselves in the sight of Lord
1 Pet. 5. 6. *h.* yourselves under the mighty hand
   of God
Lev. 26. 41. if uncircumcised hearts be *humbled*
2 Ki. 22. 19. hast *h.* thyself before the Lord
2 Chr. 12. 6. princes . . . and king *h.* themselves
12. he *h.* himself, 32. 26; 33. 12.
33. 23. *h.* not himself before Lord, 36. 12.
Ps. 35. 13. I *h.* my soul with fasting
Is. 2. 11. lofty looks of man shall be *h.*, 9, 17.
5. 15. mighty man shall be *h.* and eyes of the
   lofty shall be *h.*
10. 33. haughty shall be *h.*
Jer. 44. 10. they are not *h.* unto this day
Lam. 3. 20. my soul is *h.* in me
Dan. 5. 22. hast not *h.* thy heart
Phil. 2. 8. *h.* himself and became obedient
Deut. 21. 14. *humbled her*, 22. 24, 29. Ezek.
   22. 10, 11.
Col. 3. 12. put on *humbleness* of mind
Ps. 113. 6. Lord who *humbleth* himself to behold
Mic. 6. 8. walk *humbly* with thy God
Prov. 22. 4. by *humility* are riches and honour,
   15. 33; 18. 12.
Acts 20. 19. serving Lord with all *h.*
Col. 2. 18. in a voluntary *h.* 23.
1 Pet. 5. 5. be clothed with *h.*
HUNGER, Ex. 16. 3. Deut. 28. 48.
Ps. 34. 10. young lions . . . suffer *h.*
Prov. 19. 15. idle soul shall suffer *h.*
Lam. 4. 9. sword better than slain with *h.*
Deut. 8. 3. suffered thee to *h.*
Is. 49. 10. shall not *h.* nor thirst, Rev. 7. 16.
Mat. 5. 6. blessed are they which do *h.*
Luke 6. 21. blessed are ye that *h.* now
25. woe to you that are full, ye shall *h.*
John 6. 35. cometh to me shall never *h.*
Rom. 12. 20. if thine enemy *h.* feed
1 Cor. 4. 11. we both *h.* and thirst
11. 34. if any man *h.* let him eat at
Ps. 107. 9. filleth the *hungry* soul with goodness
146. 7. God giveth food to the *h.*
Prov. 25. 21. if enemy be *h.* give him
27. 7. to the *h.* soul every bitter thing is sweet
Is. 58. 7. to deal thy bread to the *h.*
10. if thou draw out thy soul to the *h.*
65. 13. shall eat; but ye shall be *h.*
Ezek. 18. 7. given bread to the *h.* 16.
Luke 1. 53. filled the *h.* with good things
Phil. 4. 12. how to be full and to be *h.*
HUNT, 1 Sam. 26. 20. Job 38. 39.
Ps. 140. 11. evil shall *h.* the violent
Job 10. 16. thou *huntest* me as a fierce lion
HURT, Gen. 4. 23; 26. 29.
Josh. 24. 20. will turn and do you *h.*
Ps. 15. 4. sweareth to his own *h.*
Eccl. 5. 13. riches . . . to their *h.*
Jer. 6. 14. healed *h.* of the daughter, 8. 11, 21.
Rev. 2. 11. shall not be *h.* of second death
6. 6. *h.* not the oil and wine, 7. 3; 9. 4.
Ezra. 4. 15. *hurtful*, Ps. 144. 10.
1 Tim. 6. 9. fall into foolish and *h.* lusts
HUSBAND, Gen. 3. 6, 16; 29. 32.
Ex. 4. 25. bloody *h.* art thou to me, 26.
Is. 54. 5. thy Maker is thine *h.*
Mark 10. 12. if a woman put away her *h.*
John 4. 17. I have no *h.*

1 Cor. 7. 14. unbelieving *husband* is sanctified by
34. careth how she may please *h.*
2 Cor. 11. 2. espoused you to one *h.*
Eph. 5. 23. the *h.* is the head of wife, 24.
33. the wife reverence her *h.*
John 4. 18. thou hast had five *husbands*
1 Cor. 14. 35. let them ask *h.* at home
Eph. 5. 22. wives, submit to your *h.*
25. *h.*, love wives, as Christ, Col. 3. 19.
Col. 3. 18. wives, submit to your *h.*
1 Pet. 3. 1. subject to their own *h.*
7. ye *h.*, dwell with them according to knowledge
HUSBANDMAN, my Father is the, John 15. 1.
Jas. 5. 7. *h.* waiteth for precious fruit
1 Cor. 3. 9. ye are God's *husbandry*
HYMN, Mat. 26. 30. Eph. 5. 19. Col. 3. 16.
HYPOCRISY, Is. 32. 6. Mat. 23. 28. Mark
   12. 15. Luke 12. 1. 1 Tim. 4. 2. Jas. 3. 17.
   1 Pet. 2. 1.
Mat. 7. 5. *hypocrite*, Luke 6. 42; 13. 15.
Job 8. 13. the *h's.* hope shall perish
20. 5. joy of *h.* for a moment
27. 8. what is the hope of the *h.*
Is. 9. 17. every one is a *h.* and evil
Mat. 6. 2. *hypocrites*, 5, 16; 15. 7; 16. 3; 23.
   13, 14, 15, 23.
Job 15. 34. congregation of *h.* shall be desolate
Is. 33. 14. fearfulness hath surprised *h.*
Mat. 24. 51. appoint him portion with *h.*

I

IDLE, they be, Ex. 5. 8, 17.
Prov. 19. 15. an *i.* soul shall suffer
Mat. 12. 36. every *i.* word that men shall speak
20. 6. why stand ye all day *i.*
Luke 24. 11. words seemed as *i.* tales
Prov. 31. 27. *idleness*, Eccl. 10. 18. Ezek. 16. 49.
IDOL, 2 Chr. 15. 16; 33. 7.
Is. 66. 3. as if he blessed an *i.*
Zech. 11. 17. woe to the *i.* shepherd
1 Cor. 8. 4. an *i.* is nothing in world
Ps. 96. 5. gods of nations are *idols*
Is. 2. 8. land is full of *i.*; they worship the work
   of their own hands
Jer. 50. 38. they are mad upon *i.*
Hos. 4. 17. Ephraim is joined to *i.*
Acts 15. 20. abstain from pollutions of *i.*
Rom. 2. 22. thou that abhorrest *i.*
1 Cor. 8. 1. touching things offered to *i.*
1 John 5. 21. keep yourselves from *i.*
Rev. 2. 14. eat things sacrificed to *i.*
9. 20. not worship devils and *i.* of gold
1 Cor. 5. 10, 11. *idolater*, 6. 9; 10. 7. Eph.
   5. 5. Rev. 21. 8; 22. 15.
1 Sam. 15. 23. stubbornness as iniquity and
   idolatry
1 Pet. 4. 3. walked in . . . abominable *idolatries*
Acts 17. 16. city wholly given to *i.*
1 Cor. 10. 14. dearly beloved, flee from *i.*
Gal. 5. 20. *i.*, witchcraft, hatred
Col. 3. 5. covetousness, which is *i.*
IGNORANCE, sin through, Lev. 4. 2, 13, 22,
   27. Num. 15. 24, 25. Acts 3. 17.
Acts 17. 30. this *i.* God winked at
Eph. 4. 18. alienated from God through *i.*
Is. 63. 16. though Abraham be *ignorant* of
Rom. 10. 3. *i.* of God's righteousness
1 Cor. 14. 38. if man be *i.* let him be *i.*
Heb. 5. 2. can have compassion on *i.*
Acts 17. 23. *ignorantly*, 1 Tim. 1. 13.
ILLUMINATED, Heb. 10. 32.

IMAGE, Lev. 26. 1. Dan. 2. 31.
Gen. 1. 26. let us make man in our *i*. 27; 5. 1; 9. 6. Col. 3. 10.
5. 3. Adam begat son . . . after his *i*.
Ps. 73. 20. thou shalt despise their *i*.
Mat. 22. 20. whose is this *i*. and superscription, Luke 20. 24.
Rom. 8. 29. conformed to *i*. of Son
1 Cor. 15. 49. have borne *i*. of earthy shall also bear *i*. of heavenly
2. Cor. 4. 4. Christ is *i*. of God, Col. 1. 15.
Heb. 1. 3. express *i*. of his person
Rev. 13. 14. make an *i*. to the beast
Ex. 23. 24. break down *images,* 34. 13.
IMAGINE, Ps. 2. 1. Nah. 1. 9. Zech. 7. 10; 8. 17. Acts 4. 25.
Gen. 6. 5. every *imagination* of the thoughts . . . was evil, 8. 21. Deut. 29. 19. Prov. 6. 18. Lam. 3. 60, 61. Rom. 1. 21. 2 Cor. 10. 5.
IMMEDIATELY, Mark 4. 15. Acts 12. 23.
IMMORTAL, invisible, 1 Tim. 1. 17.
Rom. 2. 7. seek for glory, honour, *immortality*
1 Cor. 15. 53. this mortal put on *i*.
2 Tim. 1. 10. brought life and *i*. to light
IMMUTABLE Heb. 6. 17, 18.
IMPENITENT heart, Rom. 2. 5.
IMPERIOUS whorish woman, Ezek. 16. 30.
IMPLACABLE, Rom. 1. 31.
IMPORTUNITY, Luke 11. 8.
IMPOSSIBLE, Mat. 17. 20; 19. 26.
Luke 1. 37. with God nothing shall be *i*.
17. 1. it is *i*. but offences will come
Heb. 6. 4. *i*. for those once enlightened
18. in two things it was *i*. for God to
11. 6. without faith it is *i*. to please
IMPUDENT, Prov. 7. 13. Ezek. 2. 4.
IMPUTE, 1 Sam. 22. 15. Lev. 7. 18; 17. 4.
Rom. 4. 11. righteousness might be *imputed*
22. to him for righteousness, 24.
5. 13. sin is not *i*. when there is no law
Jas. 2. 23. *i*. unto him for righteousness
Ps. 32. 2. Lord *imputeth* not iniquity
Rom. 4. 6. *i*. righteousness without
2 Cor. 5. 19. not *imputing* trespasses
IN Christ, Acts 24. 24. Rom. 12. 5. 1 Cor. 1. 2, 30; 3. 1; 15. 18, 22. 2 Cor. 1. 21; 2. 14; 3. 14; 5. 17, 19; 12. 2. Gal. 1. 22. Eph. 1. 1, 3, 10, 12, 20; 2. 6, 10, 13. Phil. 1. 1, 13; 2. 1, 5; 3. 14. Col. 1. 2, 4.
1 Thes. 1. 1. *in God,* John 3. 21. Col. 3. 3.
Gen. 15. 6. *in the Lord,* Ps. 4. 5; 31. 24; 34. 2; 35. 9; 37. 4, 7. Is. 45. 17, 24, 25. Jer. 3. 23. Zech. 12. 5. 1 Cor. 1. 31; 4. 17; 7. 22, 39. Eph. 2. 21; 6. 10. Phil. 4. 2, 4. Col. 3. 18; 4. 7, 17. 1 Thes. 5. 12. Philem. 16, 20. Rev. 14. 13.
INCLINE heart, Josh. 24. 23. Judg. 9. 3. 1 Ki. 8. 58. Ps. 119. 36, 112; 141. 4.
Ps. 78. 1. *incline,* 40. 1; 116. 2. Prov. 2. 2; 5. 13. Jer. 7. 24, 26; 11. 8; 17. 23; 25. 4; 34. 14; 35. 15; 44. 5. Is. 55. 3.
INCLOSED, Ps. 17. 10; 22. 16. Sol. 4. 12; 8. 9. Lam. 3. 9.
INCONTINENT, 1 Cor. 7. 5. 2 Tim. 3. 3.
INCORRUPTIBLE(UN-) God, Rom. 1. 23.
1 Cor. 9. 25. but we an *i*. (crown)
15. 52. dead shall be raised *i*.
1 Pet. 1. 4. to an inheritance *i*.
23. not of corruptible seed, but of *i*.
1 Cor. 15. 42, 50, 53, 54. *incorruption*
INCREASE, Lev. 19. 25; 25. 7.
Lev. 25. 36. take no usury of him nor *i*., 37.
Num. 32. 14. risen up . . . an *i*. of sinful men

Deut. 16. 15. bless thee in all thine *increase*
Ps. 67. 6. earth yield her *i*., 85. 12.
Is. 9. 7. of the *i*. of his government
Ezek. 18. 8. neither taken any *i*., 13, 17.
1 Cor. 3. 6. I planted . . . God gave *i*., 7.
Col. 2. 19. increaseth with *i*. of God
Ps. 62. 10. if riches *i*. set not heart
Prov. 1. 5. wise will *i*. learning, 9. 9.
Eccl. 5. 11. when goods *i*. they are
Is. 29. 19. meek shall *i*. their joy
Luke 17. 5. Lord, *i*. our faith
John 3. 30. he must *i*. but I decrease
1 Thes. 3. 12. Lord make you to *i*.
2 Tim. 2. 16. *i*. to more ungodliness
Ezra 9. 6. iniquities are *increased*
Is. 9. 3. multiplied nation, not *i*. joy
Luke 2. 52. Jesus *i*. in wisdom and
Acts 6. 7. the word of God *i*. and the
Rev. 3. 17. I am rich and *i*. with goods
Eccl. 1. 18. *increaseth* knowledge, *i*. sorrow
Col. 2. 19. whole body . . . *i*. with increase of God
1 Chr. 11. 9. David went on *increasing*
Col. 1. 10. *i*. in knowledge of God
INCURABLE wound, Job 34. 6. Jer. 15. 18. Mic. 1. 9.
Jer. 30. 12. *i*. bruise. 15, *i*. sorrow
INDEED, 1 Ki. 8. 27. 1 Chr. 4. 10. Mat. 3. 11. John 1. 47; 4. 42; 6. 55; 8. 31, 36. 1 Tim. 5. 3, 5. 1 Pet. 2. 4.
INDIGNATION, Neh. 4. 1. Esth. 5. 9. Ps. 69. 24; 78. 49; 102. 10.
Is. 10. 5. staff in their hand is mine *i*.
Mic. 7. 9. I will bear the *i*. of Lord
Nah. 1. 6. who can stand before his *i*.
Mat. 20. 24. moved with *i*.
26. 8. when disciples saw it, they had *i*.
Rom. 2. 8. *i*. and wrath, tribulation
2 Cor. 7. 11. yea, what *i*., yea, what
Heb. 10. 27. fiery *i*. which shall devour
Rev. 14. 10. poured into cup of his *i*.
INDITING a good matter, Ps. 45. 1.
INEXCUSABLE, O man, Rom. 2. 1.
INFALLIBLE proofs, Acts 1. 3.
INFANT, 1 Sam. 15. 3. Job 3. 16. Is. 65. 20. Hos. 13. 16. Luke 18. 15.
INFIDEL, 2 Cor. 6. 15. 1 Tim. 5. 8.
INFINITE iniquities, Job 22. 5.
Ps. 147. 5. his understanding is *i*.
Nah. 3. 9. her strength, and it was *i*.
INFIRMITY, this is my *i*., Ps. 77. 10.
Prov. 18. 14. spirit of man will sustain *i*.
Heb. 5. 2. himself is compassed with *i*., 7. 28.
Mat. 8. 17. himself took our *infirmities*
Rom. 8. 26. the Spirit helpeth our *i*.
2 Cor. 12. 9. glory in my *i*.
10. pleasure in *i*.
1 Tim. 5. 23. wine for . . . and thine often *i*.
Heb. 4. 15. with the feeling of our *i*.
INFLAME (EN-) them, Is. 5. 11; 57. 5.
INFLICTED punishment, 2 Cor. 2. 6.
INFLUENCES of Pleiades, Job 38. 31.
INHABIT, Prov. 10. 30. Is. 65. 21, 22.
Ps. 22. 3. *inhabitest* the praises of Israel
Is. 57. 15. lofty One that *inhabiteth*
INHERIT, Gen. 15. 8. Ps. 82. 8.
1 Sam. 2. 8. make them *i*. throne of glory
Ps. 25. 13. his seed shall *i*. earth
37. 11. the meek shall *i*. the earth, Mat. 5. 5.
29. the righteous shall *i*. land, Is. 60. 21.
82. 8. O God, thou shalt *i*. all nations
Prov. 3. 35. wise shall *i*. glory; but
8. 21. that love me to *i*. substance
Mat. 25. 34. *i*. kingdom prepared for you

Mark 10. 17. what shall I do that I may *inherit* eternal life, Luke 10. 25; 18. 18.
1 Cor. 6. 9. unrighteous shall not *inherit the kingdom of God*
15. 50. flesh and blood cannot—
Gal. 5. 21. do such things shall not—
Heb. 6. 12. through faith . . . *i.* promises
1 Pet. 3. 9. that ye should *i.* blessing
Rev. 21. 7. overcometh shall *i.* all things
Num. 18. 20. I am thy part and thine *inheritance,* Deut. 10. 9; 18. 2. Ezek. 44. 28.
Deut. 4. 20. a people of *inheritance,* 9. 26, 29; 32. 9. 1 Ki. 8. 36. Ps. 28. 9; 33. 12; 68. 9; 74. 2; 78. 62, 71; 79. 1; 94. 14; 106. 5, 40. Is. 19. 25. Jer. 10. 16; 51. 19.
Ps. 16. 5. Lord is portion of mine *i.*
Prov. 19. 14. riches are *i.* of fathers
Eccl. 7. 11. wisdom is good with an *i.*
Acts 20. 32. *i.* among . . . sanctified, 26. 18.
Eph. 1. 11. in whom we obtained an *i.*
14. earnest of our *i.*
5. 5. any *i.* in the kingdom of Christ
Col. 1. 12. partakers of *i.* of saints
3. 24. shall receive the reward of *i.*
Heb. 9. 15. the promise of eternal *i.*
1 Pet. 1. 4. to an *i.* incorruptible
INIQUITY, Gen. 15. 16; 19. 15.
Ex. 20. 5. visiting *i.* of the fathers on children, 34. 7. Num. 14. 18. Deut. 5. 9.
34. 7. forgiving *i.* and transgression   [43.
Lev. 26. 41. accept the punishment of their *i.,*
Num. 23. 21. hath not beheld *i.* in Jacob
Job 4. 8. they that plow *i.* . . . reap same
5. 16. *i.* stoppeth mouth, Ps. 107. 42.
15. 16. man which drinketh *i.* like water
22. 23. put away *i.* far from thy tabernacles
34. 32. if I have done *i.* I will do no
Ps. 32. 5. mine *i.* have I not hid . . . and thou forgavest the *i.* of my sin
39. 11. with rebukes dost correct man for *i.*
51. 5. behold, I was shapen in *i.*
66. 18. if I regard *i.* in my heart
69. 27. add *i.* unto their *i.*
119. 3. they also do no *i.:* they walk
133. let not any *i.* have dominion
Eccl. 3. 16. place of righteousness there *i.* was
Is. 1. 4. people laden with *i.,* a seed
5. 18. woe to them that draw *i.* with
27. 9. by this shall *i.* of Jacob be purged
33. 24. people shall be forgiven their *i.*
53. 6. Lord laid on him the *i.* of us all
57. 17. for *i.* of his covetousness
59. 3. defiled . . . your fingers with *i.*
Jer. 2. 5. what *i.* have fathers found
3. 13. only acknowledge thine *i.*
31. 30. every one shall die for his own *i.*
50. 20. *i.* of Israel be sought for
Ezek. 3. 18. he shall die in his *i.,* 19; 18. 18; 33. 8.
18. 30. so *i.* shall not be your ruin
Dan. 9. 24. make reconciliation for *i.*
Hos. 14. 2. take away all *i.* and
Mic. 7. 18. a God . . . that pardoneth *i.*
Hab. 1. 13. thou . . . canst not look on *i.*
Mat. 7. 23. depart from me, ye that work *i.*
24. 12. because *i.* shall abound
Acts 8. 23. in gall . . . and bond of *i.*
Rom. 6. 19. uncleanness and to *i.* to *i.*
1 Cor. 13. 6. (charity) rejoiceth not in *i.*
2 Thes. 2. 7. mystery of *i.* doth already work
2 Tim. 2. 19. nameth . . . Christ depart from *i.*
Tit. 2. 14. he might redeem us from all *i.*
Jas. 3. 6. tongue is a fire, a world of *i.*

Ps. 18. 23. *mine iniquity,* 25. 11; 32. 5; 38. 18; 51. 2.
Job 34. 22. *workers of iniquity,* Ps. 5. 5; 6. 8; 14. 4; 92. 7. Prov. 10. 29; 21. 15. Luke 13. 27.
Lev. 16. 21. confess over him all *iniquities*
26. 39. pine in their iniquity and *i.* of their fathers
Ezra 9. 6. our *i.* are increased,
13. punished less than our *i.* deserve
Neh. 9. 2. confessed *i.* of fathers
Job 13. 26. to possess *i.* of my youth
Ps. 38. 4. mine *i.* are gone over my head
40. 12. mine *i.* have taken hold upon
51. 9. hide thy face . . . sins, blot out my *i.*
65. 3. *i.* prevail against me: as for
79. 8. remember not . . . former *i.*
90. 8. thou hast set our *i.* before thee
107. 17. fools, because of . . . *i.,* are afflicted
130. 3. if thou, Lord, mark *i.*
8. he shall redeem Israel from all *i.*
Prov. 5. 22. his own *i.* shall take the wicked
Is. 43. 24. hast wearied me with thine *i.*
Jer. 14. 7. our *i.* testify against us
Dan. 4. 27. break off . . . thine *i.* by shewing
Mic. 7. 19. he will subdue our *i.* and
Acts 3. 26. bless you in turning . . . from *i.*
Rom. 4. 7. blessed are they whose *i.* forgiven
Rev. 18. 5. God remembered her *i.*
Is. 53. 11. he shall bear *their iniquity(ies)*
Jer. 33. 8. I will cleanse them from all—and I will pardon all—
Ezek. 43. 10. may be ashamed of—
Heb. 8. 12. their sins and—will I remember no more, 10. 17.
Num. 14. 34. ye bear *your iniquities*
Is. 50. 1. for—have ye sold yourselves
59. 2.—have separated you and God
Jer. 5. 25.—turned away these things
Ezek. 24. 23. ye shall pine away for—
36. 31. lothe yourselves . . . for—33. I shall have cleansed you from all—
Amos 3. 2. I will punish you for all—
INJURED me, have not, Gal. 4. 12.
1 Tim. 1. 13. a persecutor and *injurious*
INK, 2 John 12. 3 John 13.
INNER, 1 Ki. 6. 27. Eph. 3. 16.
INNOCENT, Ps. 19. 13. Prov. 28. 20.
Gen. 20. 5. On . . . *innocency* of my hands
Ps. 26. 6. wash my hands in *i.,* 73. 13.
Dan. 6. 22. before him *i.* found in me
Hos. 8. 5. how long ere they attain *i.*
INNUMERABLE, Job 21. 33. Ps. 40. 12. Luke 12. 1. Heb. 11. 12; 12. 22.
INORDINATE, Ezek. 23. 11. Col. 3. 5.
INQUIRE after iniquity, Job 10. 6.
Ps. 27. 4. to *i.* in his temple
Eccl. 7. 10. thou dost not *i.* wisely
Is. 21. 12. if ye will *i. i.* ye: return
Ps. 78. 34. returned and *inquired* early after God
Ezek. 36. 37. I will yet for this be *i.* of by the house of Israel
Zeph. 1. 6. have not sought Lord, nor *i.* for him
Mat. 2. 7. Herod . . . *i.* of them diligently
1 Pet. 1. 10. of which salvation prophets *i.*
Judg. 20. 27. *inquired of Lord,* 1 Sam. 23. 2, 4; 30. 8. 2 Sam. 2. 1; 5. 19, 23; 21. 1. Jer. 21. 2.
Prov. 20. 25. after vows to make *inquiry*
INQUISITION, Deut. 19. 18. Ps. 9. 12.
INSCRIPTION to unknown God, Acts 17. 23.
INSPIRATION, Job 32. 8. 2 Tim. 3. 16.
INSTANT, Is. 29. 5; 30. 13. Jer. 18. 7. Rom. 12. 12. 2. Tim. 4. 2. Acts 12. 5.
Luke 7. 4. besought him *instantly*
Acts 26. 7. *i.* serving God day and

INSTRUCT, Deut. 4. 36; 32. 10.
Neh. 9. 20. thy good spirit to *i*. them
Job 40. 2. contendeth with Almighty *i*. him
Ps. 16. 7. my reins *i*. me in the night
Sol. 8. 2. mother's house who would *i*. me
Is. 28. 26. his God doth *i*. him
1 Cor. 2. 16. Lord that he may *i*. him
Is. 8. 11. Lord . . . *instructed* me that I
Phil. 4. 12. in all things I am *i*. both
Job 33. 16. sealeth their *instruction*
Ps. 50. 17. hatest *i*. and castest my
Prov. 4. 13. take fast hold of *i*.
5. 12. how have I hated *i*. and
19. 27. cease to hear *i*. that causeth
23. 12. apply thine heart to *i*. and
2 Tim. 3. 16. profitable for . . . *i*. in
Rom. 2. 20. an *instructor* of foolish
1 Cor. 4. 15. ten thousand *instructors* in Christ
INSTRUMENTS of cruelty, Gen. 49. 5.
Ps. 7. 13. prepared for him *i*. of death
Rom. 6. 13. neither yield members *i*. of un-
righteousness . . . but . . . *i*. of righteousness
Is. 32. 7. the *i*. also of the churl are evil
INTEGRITY of my heart, Gen. 20. 5.
Job 2. 3. still he holdeth fast his *i*.
27. 5. I will not remove mine *i*.
Ps. 7. 8. according to my *i*. that is
25. 21. let *i*. and uprightness preserve me
26. 1. I have walked in mine *i*.
Prov. 11. 3. *i*. of upright shall guide
INTERCESSION, Jer. 7. 16; 27. 18.
Is. 53. 12. bare the sin of many, and made *i*. for
the transgressors
Rom. 8. 26. Spirit maketh *i*. for us, 27.
34. who also maketh *i*. for us
11. 2. (Elias) maketh *i*. to God against Israel
Heb. 7. 25. he ever liveth to make *i*.
Is. 59. 16. there was no *intercessor*
INTERMEDDLE, Prov. 14. 10; 18. 1.
INTERPRETATION, Gen. 40. 5; 41. 11. Judg.
7. 15. Dan. 2. 4, 7, 36. 1 Cor. 12. 10; 14. 26.
2 Pet. 1. 20.
Job 33. 23. *interpreter*, one among a thousand
INTRUDING into things, Col. 2. 18.
INVENT, Amos 6. 5. Rom. 1. 30.
Ps. 99. 8. tookest vengeance of their *inventions*
106. 29. provoked him with their *i*.
39. went a whoring with their *i*.
Prov. 8. 12. find out witty *i*.
Eccl. 7. 29. men sought many *i*.
INVISIBLE, Rom. 1. 20. Col. 1. 15, 16. 1 Tim.
1. 17. Heb. 11. 27.
INWARD friends abhorred me, Job 19. 19.
Ps. 5. 9. *inward part*, 51. 6. Prov. 20. 27. Jer.
31. 33. Luke 11. 39.
Rom. 7. 22. *inward man*, 2 Cor. 4. 16.
Ps. 62. 4. curse *inwardly*
Mat. 7. 15. *i*. . . . ravening wolves
Rom. 2. 29. he is a Jew which is one *i*.
IRON sharpeneth iron, Prov. 27. 17.
Eccl. 10. 10. if the *i*. be blunt, put to
Is. 48. 4. neck is an *i*. sinew, and
Jer. 15. 12. shall *i*. break northern *i*.
Dan. 2. 33. legs of *i*., his feet part *i*.
4. 23. even with a band of *i*. and
5. 23. thou hast praised the gods of silver, and
gold, of brass, *i*.
1 Tim. 4. 2. conscience seared with a hot *i*.
ISSUES from death, Ps. 68. 20.
Prov. 4. 23. out of (heart) are the *i*. of life
ITCHING ears, 2 Tim. 4. 3.
IVORY, 1 Ki. 10. 18; 22. 39. Ps. 45. 8. Sol. 5. 14;
7. 4. Ezek. 27. 6. Amos 3. 15; 6. 4. Rev. 18. 12.

J

JEALOUS God, I am a, Ex. 20. 5; 34. 14. Deut.
5. 9; 6. 15. Josh. 24. 19.
Ezek. 39. 25. be *j*. for my holy name
Joel 2. 18. will Lord be *j*. for his land
Nah. 1. 2. God is *j*. and the Lord
Zech. 1. 14. I am *j*. for Jerusalem, 8. 2.
2 Cor. 11. 2. *j*. over you with godly *jealousy*
Deut. 29. 20. (Lord's) *j*. shall smoke
Ps. 79. 5. shall thy *j*. burn like fire
Prov. 6. 34. *j*. is the rage of a man
Sol. 8. 6. *j*. is cruel as the grave
Rom. 10. 19. provoke them to *j*. 11. 11.
1 Cor. 10. 22. we provoke Lord to *j*.
JEHOVAH. This name is translated Lord (in
capitals) about 2,000 times. (See *Index*.)
JERUSALEM, for the church, Is. 24. 23; 62. 1;
66. 10, 13. Jer. 3. 17. Joel 2. 32; 3. 16, 17.
Zech. 12. 10; 8. 22. Gal. 4. 25, 26. Heb.
12. 22. Rev. 3. 12; 21. 2. (See *Index*.)   [2.
JESHURUN,*i.e.* Israel,Deut.32.15;33.5,26.Is.44.
JESUS, or Joshua, Acts 7. 45. Heb. 4. 8.
JESUS the Saviour of men, Mat. 1. 21; 2. 1;
8. 29; 14. 1; 27. 37. 1 Cor. 12. 3. 2 Cor. 4. 5.
Eph. 4. 21. Heb. 2. 9; 12. 2. Rev. 22. 16. and
about 650 other places. (See *Index*.)
JEWS first, and also Greeks, Rom. 1. 16; 2. 9, 10
Rom. 2. 28, 29. not a *J*. which is one outwardly,
but a *J*. which is one inwardly
10. 12. no difference between *J*. and Greek
1 Cor. 9. 20. to Jew I became as a *J*.
Gal. 3. 28. neither *J*. nor Greek, Col. 3. 11.
Rev. 2. 9. say they are *Jews* and are not, 3. 9.
JOIN, Ex. 1. 10. Ezra 9. 14.
Prov. 11. 21. hand *j*. in hand, 16. 5.
Is. 5. 8. woe to them that *j*. house to house
Jer. 50. 5. let us *j*. ourselves to Lord
Acts 5. 13. durst no man *j*. himself
Hos. 4. 17. Ephraim is *joined* to idols
Num. 25. 3. Israel *j*. himself to Baal-Peor,
Ps. 106. 28.
Eccl. 9. 4. for him that is *j*. to living there is hope
Zech. 2. 11. nations shall be *j*. to Lord
Mat. 19. 6. what God hath *j*. let not
1 Cor. 1. 10. be perfectly *j*. together
Eph. 5. 31. shall be *j*. to his wife
Col. 2. 19. all body by *joints* and bands
Heb. 4. 12. dividing asunder of . . . *j*.
JOURNEY, Num. 9. 13. Rom. 1. 10.
JOY, 1 Chr. 12. 40. 2 Chr. 20. 27.
Neh. 8. 10. *j*. of Lord your strength
Esth. 8. 17. Jews had *j*. and gladness
Job 20. 5. *j*. of the hypocrite but for
Ps. 16. 11. thy presence is fulness of *j*.
43. 4. God my exceeding *j*.
51. 8. make me hear *j*. and gladness
12. restore to me *j*. of thy salvation
126. 5. that sow in tears shall reap in *j*.
Eccl. 9. 7. eat thy bread with *j*.
Is. 9. 3. hast not increased the *j*.: they *j*. . . . .
according to *j*. in harvest
12. 3. with *j*. shall ye draw water out
35. 10. with songs and everlasting *j*. . . . . shall
obtain *j*. and gladness
61. 3. give them the oil of *j*. for mourning
7. everlasting *j*. shall be to them
66. 5. he shall appear to your *j*.
Zeph. 3. 17. (Lord) will *j*. over thee with singing
Mat. 2. 10. rejoiced with great *j*.
13. 20. hear the word, and with *j*.
Luke 1. 44. babe leaped in womb for *j*.
15. 7. *j*. shall be in heaven over one

John 15. 11. your *joy* might be full, 16. 24.
16. 20. your sorrow be turned into *j*.
22. your *j*. no man taketh from you
17. 13. my *j*. fulfilled in themselves
Acts 20. 24. finish my course with *j*.
Rom. 15. 13. fill you with all *j*. and peace
2 Cor. 1. 24. we . . . are helpers of your *j*.
2. 3. my *j*. is the *j*. of you all
Gal. 5. 22. fruit of the Spirit is love, *j*.
Phil. 4. 1. brethren . . . my *j*. and crown
1 Thes. 1. 6. receive word with *j*. of
Heb. 12. 2. who for the *j*. set before
Jas. 1. 2. count it all *j*. when ye
1 Pet. 1. 8. rejoice with *j*. unspeakable
4. 13. be glad with exceeding *j*.
1 John 1. 4. write we that your *j*. may be full
Ezra 6. 22. Lord made them *joyful*
Ps. 35. 9. my soul shall be *j*. in Lord
63. 5. I will praise thee with *j*. lips
89. 15. people that know the *j*. sound
Eccl. 7. 14. in day of prosperity be *j*.
Is. 56. 7. make them *j*. in my house
61. 10. my soul shall be *j*. in God
2 Cor. 7. 4. exceeding *j*. in all our
Eccl. 9. 9. live *joyfully* with the wife
Heb. 10. 34. took *j*. spoiling of goods
Deut. 28. 47. servedst not Lord . . . with *joyfulness*
Col. 1. 11. longsuffering with *j*.
2. 5. *joying* and beholding your
Heb. 12. 11. no chastening . . . seemeth to be *joyous*
JUDGE, Deut. 17. 9; 25. 2.
Gen. 18. 25. shall not the *J*. of earth
Ex. 2. 14. who made thee . . . *j*., Acts 7. 27.
1 Sam. 2. 25. the *j*. shall *j*. him; but
Is. 33. 22. Lord is our *j*. . . . lawgiver
Ps. 68. 5. father of fatherless and *j*. of widows
75. 7. God is the *j*.: he putteth down, 50. 6.
Luke 12. 14. who made me a *j*. over
Acts 10. 42. to be the *J*. of quick and dead
2 Tim. 4. 8. Lord the righteous *J*.
Heb. 12. 23. are come to God the *J*.
Jas. 5. 9. the *J*. standeth before the door
Gen. 16. 5. Lord *j*. between me and thee, 1 Sam. 24. 12.
Deut. 32. 36. the Lord shall *j*. his people, Ps. 135. 14. Heb. 10. 30.
Ps. 7. 8. Lord shall *j*. the people: *j*. me
9. 8. Lord shall *j*. world in righteousness, 96. 13; 98. 9. Acts 17. 31.
Mic. 3. 11. heads thereof *j*. for reward
Mat. 7. 1. *j*. not, that ye be not judged
John 5. 30. as I hear I *j*. and my
12. 47. I came not to *j*. the world
Acts 23. 3. sittest thou to *j*. me
Rom. 2. 16. when God shall *j*. secrets of men
3. 6. then how shall God *j*. the world
14. 10. why dost thou *j*. thy brother
1 Cor. 4. 3. I *j*. not mine own self
5. *j*. nothing before the time
6. 3. know ye not that we shall *j*. angels
11. 31. if we would *j*. ourselves, we
14. 29. let prophets speak, . . . other *j*.
Col. 2. 16. let no man *j*. you in meat
2 Tim. 4. 1. who shall *j*. the quick and the dead, 1 Pet. 4. 5.
Jas. 4. 11. if thou *j*. the law
Ps. 51. 4. *judgest*, Rom. 14. 4. Jas. 4. 12.
7. 11. God *judgeth* the righteous
58. 11. he is a God that *j*. in earth
1 Cor. 2. 15. but he that is spiritual *j*. all things
4. 4. he that *j*. me is the Lord
Mat. 19. 28. *judging* twelve tribes, Luke 22. 30.
Deut. 1. 17. not respect persons in *j*.

Deut. 1. 17. the *judgment* is God's
Ps. 1. 5. ungodly not stand in the *j*.
9. 16. Lord is known by the *j*. he executeth
101. 1. I will sing of mercy and *j*.
143. 2. enter not into *j*. with thy servant
149. 9. to execute upon them the *j*.
Prov. 21. 15. it is joy to just to do *j*.
29. 26. ever man's *j*. cometh from Lord
Eccl. 11. 9. but know thou . . . God will bring thee into *j*., 12. 14.
Is. 1. 27. Zion shall be redeemed with *j*.
28. 17. *j*. also will I lay to the line
30. 18. Lord is a God of *j*., Job 35. 14.
42. 1. he shall bring *j*. to Gentiles
53. 8. he was taken from prison and *j*.
61. 8. I the Lord love *j*.
Jer. 5. 1. if there be any that executeth *j*.
8. 7. people know not the *j*. of Lord
10. 24. correct me, but with *j*.; not in
Dan. 4. 37. all whose . . . ways *j*.
7. 22. and *j*. was given to the saints
Hos. 12. 6. keep mercy and *j*., wait on
Amos 5. 7. who turn *j*. to wormwood
24. let *j*. run down as waters, and
Mat. 5. 21. be in danger of *j*., 22.
12. 20. till he send *j*. unto victory
John 5. 27. given him authority to execute *j*.
9. 39. for *j*. I am come into the world
16. 8. reprove the world of sin . . . and *j*.
Acts 24. 25. reasoned of . . . *j*. to come
Rom. 5. 18. *j*. came on all men
14. 10. must all stand before *j*. seat
1 Pet. 4. 17. *j*. begin at house of God
Jude 15. execute *j*. on all
Rev. 17. 1. shew thee *j*. of great whore
Ps. 19. 9. *judgments* of Lord are true
36. 6. thy *j*. are a great deep
119. 75. I know, O Lord, that thy *j*. are right
108. O Lord, teach me thy *j*.
120. am afraid of thy *j*.
Is. 26. 8. in way of thy *j*. . . . we waited
26. 9. when thy *j*. are in the earth
Jer. 12. 1. let me talk with thee of thy *j*.
Rom. 11. 33. how unsearchable his *j*.
JUST man, Noah was, Gen. 6. 9.
Lev. 19. 36. *j*. balance, *j*. weights, &c., Deut. 25. 15. Ezek. 45. 10.
Deut. 16. 20. that which is *j*. shalt thou follow
32. 4. a God of truth . . . *j*. and right is he
2 Sam. 23. 3. he that ruleth men must be *j*.
Neh. 9. 33. art *j*. in all that is brought upon us
Prov. 4. 18. path of *j*. is as shining
10. 6. blessings are on head of *j*.
11. 1. but a *j*. weight is his delight
12. 21. no evil shall happen to *j*.
17. 26. to punish the *j*. is not good
18. 17. in his own cause seemeth *j*.
20. 7. the *j*. man walketh in his integrity
24. 16. *j*. man falleth seven times
Eccl. 7. 15. there is a *j*. man that perisheth in his righteousness
20. there is not a *j*. man on earth
8. 14. be *j*. men, to whom it happeneth
Is. 26. 7. way of *j*. is uprightness; thou dost weigh the path of the *j*.
45. 21. no God beside me; a *j*. God
Ezek. 18. 9. he is *j*., he shall live
Hab. 2. 4. *j*. shall live by his faith, Rom. 1. 17. Gal. 3. 11. Heb. 10. 38.
Zeph. 3. 5. the *j*. Lord is in the midst [persons
Luke 15. 7. more than over ninety-nine *j*.
20. 20 who should feign themselves *j*.
John 5. 30. my judgment is *j*.

Acts 7. 52. shewed before the coming of *Just*
One, 22. 14.
24. 15. resurrection . . . both of *j*. and
Rom. 2. 13. not hearers of law are *j*.
3. 26. he might be *j*. and justifier
7. 12. commandment holy, *j*., and
Phil. 4. 8. whatsoever things are *j*.
Col. 4. 1. give . . . that which is *j*. and
Heb. 2. 2. received a *j*. recompence
12. 23. spirits of *j*. men made perfect
1 Pet. 3. 18. once suffered for sins, *j*. for the
Rev. 15. 3. *j*. and true are thy ways
Mic. 6. 8. to do *justly*, and love
Luke 23. 41. we indeed *j*., for we
1 Thes. 2. 10. how holily and *j*. we behaved
Gen. 18. 19. to do *justice* and
Job 37. 23. excellent in power, and in judgment,
and in plenty of *j*.
Ps. 89. 14. *j*. and judgment are the habitation of
thy throne
Prov. 8. 15. by me . . . princes decree *j*.
Jer. 31. 23. O habitation of *j*., 50. 7.
JUSTIFY not the wicked, Ex. 23. 7.
Deut. 25. 1. they shall *j*. the righteous
Job 9. 20. if I *j*. myself, mine own mouth
27. 5. God forbid that I should *j*.
33. 32. speak, for I desire to *j*. thee
Is. 5. 23. them which *j*. the wicked
53. 11. shall my servant *j*. many
Luke 10. 29. he, willing to *j*. himself
16. 15. ye are they which *j*. yourselves before
men
Rom. 3. 30. God shall *j*. circumcision
Gal. 3. 8. God would *j*. heathen
Rom. 4. 25. raised for our *justification*
5. 16. gift is of many offences unto *j*.
Job 11. 2. should a man full of talk be *justified*
13. 18. I know that I shall be *j*.
25. 4. how can man be *j*. with God?
32. 2. he *j*. himself rather than God
Ps. 51. 4. mightest be *j*. when thou speakest
Is. 43. 9. that they may be *j*., 26.
45. 25. in Lord shall the seed of Israel be *j*.
Jer. 3. 11. hath *j*. herself more than Judah
Ezek. 16. 51. thou . . . hast *j*. thy sisters in all
thine abominations, 52.
Mat. 11. 19. wisdom is *j*. of children, Luke
7. 35.
12. 37. by thy words thou shalt be *j*.
Luke 7. 29. *j*. God, being baptized of
Rom. 2. 13. doers of law shall be *j*.
3. 4. thou mightest be *j*. in thy sayings
20. there shall no flesh be *j*. in his
24. being *j*. freely by his grace
28. man is *j*. by faith without deeds
4. 2. if Abraham were *j*. by works
5. 1. being *j*. by faith, we have
9. being now *j*. by his blood, we shall be saved
8. 30. whom he *j*. them he also
1 Cor. 4. 4. yet am I not hereby *j*.
6. 11. ye are *j*. in name of the Lord
Gal. 2. 16. not *j*. by works of law . . . we might
be *j*. by faith of Christ, 17.
3. 11. no man is *j*. by the law
24. that we might be *j*. by faith
5. 4. *j*. by law, ye are fallen from grace
1 Tim. 3. 16. God . . . in flesh, *j*. in spirit
Tit. 3. 7. that being *j*. by his grace
Jas. 2. 21. Abraham *j*. by works when
25. was not Rahab the harlot *j*. by works
Rom. 3. 28. the *justifier* of him that
Prov. 17. 15. he that *justifieth* wicked
Is. 50. 8. he is near that *j*. me

Rom. 4. 5. him that *justifieth* the ungodly
8. 33. it is God that *j*.
1 Ki. 8. 32. *justifying* the righteous, 2 Chr. 6. 23.

K

KEEP, Gen. 2. 15; 33. 9.
Gen. 18. 19. *k*. the way of the Lord
28. 15. I am with thee and will *k*. thee
20. if God will be with me, and *k*. me
Ex. 23. 7. *k*. thee far from a false matter
20. I send an angel to *k*. thee in
Num. 6. 24. Lord bless thee and *k*. thee
Deut. 23. 9. *k*. thee from every wicked
29. 9. *k*. words of this covenant
1 Sam. 2. 9. he will *k*. the feet of his
1 Chr. 4. 10. thou wouldest *k*. me
Ps. 25. 10. to such as *k*. his covenant, 103. 18.
20. *k*. my soul, 17. 8. *k*. me as apple of eye
39. 1. *k*. my mouth with a bridle
89. 28. my mercy will I *k*. for him
91. 11. angels to *k*. thee in all thy ways
106. 3. blessed are they that *k*. judgment
119. 2. *k*. his testimonies, 88, 129, 146. *k*. thy
precepts, 4, 63, 69, 100. *k*. his statutes, 33.
k. his word and law, 17, 34, 57, 101, 136.
127. 1. except the Lord *k*. the city
140. 4. *k*. me, O Lord, from hands of wicked
141. 3. *k*. the door of my lips
Eccl. 5. 1. *k*. thy foot when thou goest
Is. 26. 3. thou wilt *k*. him in perfect
Jer. 3. 12. I will not *k*. anger for ever
Hos. 12. 6. *k*. mercy and judgment
Mic. 7. 5. *k*. the doors of thy mouth
Mal. 2. 7. priest's lips should *k*. knowledge
Luke 11. 28. hear word of God and *k*. it
1 Cor. 5. 8. let us *k*. the feast, not
11. not to *k*. company with such
9. 27. I *k*. under my body, and
Eph. 4. 3. endeavouring to *k*. unity
Phil. 4. 7. peace of God shall *k*. your
2 Thes. 3. 3. Lord shall stablish you and *k*. you
1 Tim. 5. 22. *k*. thyself pure
6. 20. *k*. that which is committed
2 Tim. 1. 12. able to *k*. that which I have
14. that good thing which was committed to thee,
k. by Holy Ghost
Jas. 1. 27. *k*. himself unspotted
2. 10. *k*. whole law, yet offend in one
Jude 21. *k*. yourselves in love of God
24. that is able to *k*. you from
Rev. 1. 3. blessed . . . that hear . . . and *k*.
3. 10. I will *k*. thee from the hour of
22. 9. them which *k*. sayings
Lev. 26. 3. *keep my commandments*
Deut. 5. 10. diligently—, 11. 1, 22.
13. 4.—his—and obey his voice, 11. 8.
Ps. 119. 60. I delayed not to—thy—
Prov. 4. 4.—my—and live, 7. 2.
Eccl. 12. 13. fear God, and—his—
Mat. 19. 17. if thou wilt enter into life—the—
John 14. 15. if ye love me—my—
1 John 2. 3. we know that we know him, if we—
his—
5. 3. this is the love of God that we—his—
Rev. 14. 12. here are they that—the—
Judg. 3. 19. *keep silence*, Ps. 50. 21. Eccl. 3. 7.
Is. 41. 1. Lam. 2. 10. Amos 5. 13. Hab. 2. 20.
1 Cor. 14. 28, 34.
Ps. 35. 22. *k. not s.* 50. 3; 83. 1. Is. 62. 6; 65. 6.
1 Ki. 8. 23. who *keepest* covenant and mercy,
2 Chr. 6. 14. Neh. 9. 32.

Ps. 121. 3. he that *keepeth* thee will not slumber
146. 6. which *k.* truth for ever
Prov. 13. 3. he that *k.* his mouth *k.* his life
29. 18. he that *k.* the law, happy is he
1 John 5. 18. that is begotten of God *k.* himself
Rev. 16. 15. blessed is he that . . . *k.* his garments
22. 7. blessed is he that *k.* . . . this prophecy
Ex. 34. 7. *keeping* mercy for thousands
Ps. 19. 11. in *k.* of them is great reward
Dan. 9. 4. *k.* the covenant and mercy
1 Pet. 4. 19. commit *k.* of their souls
Ps. 121. 5. the Lord is thy *keeper*
Sol. 1. 6. made me *k.* of vineyards
Eccl. 12. 3. when *keepers* of house shall
5. 7. *k.* took away my veil from me
Tit. 2. 5. chaste, *k.* at home
Deut. 32. 10. *kept* them as the apple of eye
33. 9. and *k.* thy covenant
Josh. 14. 10. Lord hath *k.* me alive
2 Sam. 22. 22. *k.* ways of Lord, Ps. 18. 21.
Ps. 18. 23. *k.* myself from mine iniquity
Job 23. 11. his way have I *k.* and
Ps. 17. 4. *k.* me from paths of the
30. 3. *k.* me alive, that I should not go
Sol. 1. 6. mine own vineyard not *k.*   [youth
Mat. 19. 20. all these things have I *k.* from my
Luke 2. 19. Mary *k.* all these things, and pondered them, 51.
John 15. 20. if they have *k.* my sayings
17. 6. they have *k.* thy word
12. that thou gavest me I have *k.*
Rom. 16. 25. *k.* secret since the world
2 Tim. 4. 7. I have *k.* the faith
1 Pet. 1. 5. *k.* by the power of God
Rev. 3. 8. hast *k.* my word, and not
KEY of house of David, Is. 22. 22. Rev. 3. 7.
Rev. 9. 1. *k.* of the bottomless pit, 20. 1.
Mat. 16. 19. *keys* of the kingdom of heaven
Rev. 1. 18. I have *k.* of hell
KICK, Deut. 32. 15. 1 Sam. 2. 29. Acts 9. 5;
KID, Is. 11. 6. Luke 15. 29.   [26. 14.
Sol. 1. 8. feed *kids* beside shepherds'
KILL, thou shalt not, Ex. 20. 13.
Eccl. 3. 3. time to *k.* and a time to heal
Mat. 10. 28. fear not them which *k.* body, but are not able to *k.* soul
Mark 3. 4. lawful to save life, or *k.*
1 Ki. 21. 19. hast thou *killed* and
Ps. 44. 22. are we *k.* all day long, Rom. 8. 36.
Luke 12. 5. after he hath *k.* hath power
Acts 3. 15. *k.* the Prince of life
2 Cor. 6. 9. as chastened, not *k.*
1 Thes. 2. 15. *k.* Lord Jesus and . . . prophets
Rev. 13. 10. that *k.* with sword must be *k.*
1 Sam. 2. 6. the Lord *killeth* and maketh
John 16. 2. who *k.* you will think he doeth
2 Cor. 3. 6. letter *k.* . . . . spirit giveth life
KIND, Gen. 1. 11. 2 Chr. 10. 7.
Luke 6. 35. he is *k.* to unthankful
1 Cor. 13. 4. charity suffereth long and is *k.*
1 Sam. 20. 14. while yet I live shew me the *kindness* of the Lord
2 Sam. 9. 3. may shew the *k.* of God
16. 17. is this thy *k.* to thy friend
Neh. 9. 17. a God . . . slow to anger and of great *k.* Joel 2. 13. Jonah 4. 2.
Ps. 117. 2. his merciful *k.* is great
141. 5. let righteous smite me; it shall be a *k.*
Prov. 19. 22. the desire of a man is his *k.*
31. 26. in her tongue is law of *k.*
Is. 54. 8. with everlasting *k.* will I have mercy
10. my *k.* shall not depart from thee

Jer. 2. 2. I remember thee, the *kindness* of
Col. 3. 12. put on bowels of mercies, *k.*
2 Pet. 1. 7. to godliness brotherly *k.*, to brotherly *k.* charity
Ps. 36. 7. how excellent is thy *lovingkindness*
10. O continue thy—unto them
63. 3. thy—is better than life
103. 4. who crowneth thee with—
Is. 63. 7. I will mention the—of Lord
Jer. 9. 24. the Lord which exercise—
31. 3. with—have I drawn thee
32. 18. thou shewest—to thousands
Hos. 2. 19. I will betroth thee . . . in—
Ps. 25. 5. remember . . . thy *lovingkindnesses*
KINDLE, Prov. 26. 21. Is. 10. 16.
Is. 30. 33. breath of Lord . . . doth *k.* it
Hos. 11. 8. my repentings are *kindled*
2 Sam. 22. 9. coals *k.* by it, Ps. 18. 8.
Ps. 2. 12. when his wrath is *k.* but a
Is. 50. 11. walk in . . . sparks that ye have *k.*
Luke 12. 49. fire on earth, what . . . if it be already *k.*?
KING, Gen. 14. 18; 36. 31.
Job 18. 14. bring him to *k.* of terrors
Ps. 10. 16. Lord is *K.* for ever and
24. 7. *K.* of glory shall come in, 9, 10.
33. 16. no *k.* saved by multitude of
47. 7. God is *K.* of all the earth, 6.
74. 12. God is my *k.* 5. 2; 44. 4.
Prov. 30. 31. a *k.* against whom is no
Eccl. 5. 9. *k.* himself is served by the field
8. 4. where word of *k.* is there is power
Sol. 1. 4. *k.* brought me into his chambers
12. while the *k.* sitteth at his table
7. 5. the *k.* is held in the galleries
Is. 32. 1. a *k.* shall reign in righteousness
33. 22. Lord is our lawgiver . . . our *k.*
43. 15. Creator of Israel, your *K.*
Hos. 3. 5. seek Lord their God and David their *k.*
7. 5. in day of our *k.* the princes
13. 11. I gave thee a *k.* in mine anger
Zech. 9. 9. behold, thy *K.* cometh
Luke 23. 2. he himself is Christ, a *k.*
John 6. 15. by force to make him *k.*
1 Tim. 1. 17. now unto the *K.* eternal
6. 15. *K.* of kings, and Lord of lords, Rev. 17. 14; 19. 16.
1 Pet. 2. 17. fear God, honour *k.*
Rev. 15. 3. just and true . . . *K.* of saints
Ps. 76. 12. terrible to *kings* of earth, 72. 11.
102. 15. *k.* of earth thy glory, Is. 62. 2.
144. 10. that giveth salvation to *k.*
149. 8. to bind their *k.* with chains
Prov. 8. 15. by me *k.* reign, and
Hos. 8. 4. they set up *k.* but not by
Mat. 11. 8. soft clothing in *k.* s' houses
Luke 22. 25. *k.* of Gentiles exercise
1 Cor. 4. 8. reigned as *k.* without us
1 Tim. 2. 2. giving of thanks . . . for *k.* and all
Rev. 1. 6. made us *k.* and priests to God, 5. 10.
Ex. 19. 6. be a *kingdom* of priests, and an
1 Sam. 10. 25. Samuel told people manner of the *k.*
1 Chr. 29. 11. thine is the *k.*, O Lord, Mat. 6. 13.
Ps. 22. 28. for the *k.* is the Lord's
Dan. 2. 44. in days of these kings shall God of heaven set up a *k.*
4. 17. the most High ruleth in *k.* of men, 25, 32.
7. 27. whose *k.* is everlasting *k.*, 14.
Mat. 12. 25. every *k.* divided against itself
13. 19. heareth the word of the *k.*
38. good seed are the children of *k.*
25. 34. inherit *k.* prepared for you
Mark 11. 10. blessed be the *k.* of our father David

Luke 12. 32. Father's good pleasure to give you the *kingdom*
19. 12. to receive for himself a *k.*
22. 29. I appoint unto you a *k.*, as my Father appointed to me
John 18. 36. my *k.* is not of this world
1 Cor. 15. 24. delivered up *k.* to God
Col. 1. 13. translated us into the *k.* of
2 Tim. 4. 18. preserve me to his heavenly *k.*
Jas. 2. 5. rich in faith, heirs of *k.*
2 Pet. 1. 11. an entrance . . . into everlasting *k.* of our Lord and Saviour
Rev. 1. 9. in *k.* and patience of Jesus
17. 17. to give their *k.* to the beast
Mat. 6. 33. *kingdom of God*, 12. 28; 21. 43. Mark 1. 15; 10. 14, 15; 12. 34; 15. 43. Luke 4. 43; 6. 20; 9. 62; 10. 9, 11; 13. 29; 17. 20, 21; 18. 16, 17, 29; 21. 31.
John 3. 3. except a man be born again, he cannot see—, 5.
Rom. 14. 17.—is not meat and drink
1 Cor. 4. 20.—is not in word, but
6. 9. unrighteous shall not inherit—
Eph. 5. 5. hath any inheritance in—
2 Thes. 1. 5. be counted worthy of—
Rev. 12. 10. salvation and strength and—
Mat. 3. 2. *kingdom of heaven*, 4. 17; 10. 7; 5. 3, 10, 19, 20; 7. 21; 8. 11; 11. 11, 12; 13. 11, 24, 31, 52; 16. 19; 18. 1, 3, 23; 20. 1; 22. 2; 23. 13; 25. 1, 14.   [our Lord
Rev. 11. 15. the *kingdoms* of this world are *k.* of
KISS the Son, lest he be angry, Ps. 2. 12.
Sol. 1. 2. let him *k.* me with the kisses
Rom. 16. 16. salute one another with an holy *k.*
1 Pet. 5. 14. greet . . . with *k.* of charity
Ps. 85. 10. righteousness and peace have *kissed* each other
Luke 7. 38. *k.* his feet and anointed
Prov. 27. 6. *kisses* of an enemy are deceitful
KNEES, Gen. 30. 3; 41. 43.
Job 4. 4. feeble *k.* Is. 35. 3. Heb. 12. 12.
Is. 45. 23. to God every *k.* shall bow, Rom. 14. 11. Phil. 2. 10. Mat. 27. 29. Eph. 3. 14.
Nah. 2. 10. *k.* smite together, Dan. 5. 6.
KNIFE, Prov. 23. 2; 30. 14.
KNIT, 1 Sam. 18. 1. Col. 2. 2, 19.
KNOCK, Mat. 7. 7. Rev. 3. 20.
KNOW, Gen. 3. 7; 4. 1; 42. 7.
Gen. 28. 16. Lord in this place, I *knew* it not
Deut. 34. 10. whom Lord *k.* face to face
Jer. 1. 5. before I formed thee . . . I *k.*
Mat. 7. 23. I never *k.* you: depart ye
Rom. 1. 21. *k.* God they glorified him not
1 John 3. 1. because it *k.* him not
John 4. 10. if thou *knewest* the gift of God
Deut. 8. 2. to *know* what was in thy
Josh. 22. 22. Israel he shall *k.*
1 Sam. 3. 7. Samuel did not yet *k.* Lord
1 Ki. 8. 38. shall *k.* every man plague of . . . heart
1 Chr. 28. 9. *k.* thou the God of
Job 5. 27. *k.* thou it for thy good
8. 9. for we are but of yesterday, and *k.* nothing
13. 23. make me to *k.* my transgression
22. 13. how doth God *k.*, Ps. 73. 11.
Ps. 4. 3. *k.* that Lord doth set apart the **godly**
9. 10. that *k.* thy name will trust in
46. 10. be still, and *k.* that I am God
51. 6. thou shalt make me to *k.* wisdom
73. 16. when I thought to *k.* this
139. 23. *k.* my heart . . . *k.* my
Eccl. 11. 9. *k.* thou that for all these things God will bring thee into judgment
Is. 58. 2. they seek me daily and delight to *k.*

Jer. 17. 9. heart deceitful . . . , who can *know* it
22. 16. was not this to *k.* me, saith Lord
24. 7. I will give them a heart to *k.*
31. 34. *k.* the Lord, for they shall all *k.* me
44. 28. shall *k.* whose words shall   [33. 33.
Ezek. 2. 5. shall *k.* that there . . . prophet hath,
Hos. 2. 20. in faithfulness, and thou shalt *k.* Lord
Mic. 3. 1. is it not for you to *k.* judgment
Mat. 6. 3. let not left hand *k.* what
7. 11. *k.* how to give good gifts, Luke 11. 13.
John 4. 42. we *k.* this is the Christ
7. 17. he shall *k.* of the doctrine
10. 4. sheep follow him, for they *k.*
14. and *k.* my sheep and am known
13. 7. knowest not now, but thou shalt *k.* 17. if ye *k.* these things, happy are. 35. by this shall all men *k.* that ye are my disciples
Acts 1. 7. it is not for you to *k.* the times
1 Cor. 2. 14. neither can he *k.* them
4. 19. and will *k.* not speech of them, but power
8. 2. knoweth nothing as he ought to *k.*
Eph. 3. 19. to *k.* love of Christ
Tit. 1. 16. profess they *k.* God, but
Ex. 4. 14. *I know*, Job 9. 2, 28; 13. 18.
Gen. 18. 19.—him that he will command
22. 12. now—that thou fearest God
2 Ki. 19. 27.—thy abode and thy
Job 19. 25.—my Redeemer liveth
Ps. 41. 11. by this—thou favourest
Jer. 10. 23.—that way of man is not in himself
29. 11.—thoughts that I think, saith Lord
Mat. 25. 12.—you not, Luke 13. 25, 27.
John 13. 18. *I know* whom I have chosen
Acts 26. 27.—that thou believest
Rom. 7. 18.—that in me, that is in my
1 Cor. 4. 4. for—nothing by myself
13. 12. now—in part; but then shall—
Phil. 4. 12.—how to be abased
2 Tim. 1. 12.—whom I have believed
1 John 2. 4. he that saith—him, and keepeth
Rev. 2. 2.—thy works, 9, 13, 19; 3. 1, 8, 15.
Hos. 6. 3. *we know*, 8. 2. John 4. 22. 1 Cor. 2. 12. 1 John 2. 3, 5.
John 16. 30. *thou knowest* all things
21. 15, 16.—all things—I love thee
Ps. 1. 6. Lord *knoweth* the way of
94. 11. Lord *k.* thoughts of man are
103. 14. he *k.* our frame, that we
138. 6. the proud he *k.* afar off
139. 14. my soul *k.* right well
Eccl. 9. 1. no man *k.* either love or
Is. 1. 3. ox *k.* his owner, and ass his
Jer. 8. 7. stork *k.* her appointed times
Zeph. 3. 5. the unjust *k.* no shame
Mat. 6. 8. Father *k.* things ye have need of
24. 36. of that day and hour *k.* no man
2 Tim. 2. 19. Lord *k.* them that are his
2 Pet. 2. 9. Lord *k.* how to deliver
1 John 3. 1. the world *k.* us not
Rev. 2. 17. a name which no man *k.*
Ps. 9. 16. Lord *known* by judgment
31. 7. hast *k.* my soul in adversities
67. 2. that thy way may be *k.* on earth
Is. 45. 4. thou hast not *k.* me, 5.
Mat. 10. 26. there is nothing hid that shall not be *k.*, Luke 8. 17; 12. 2.
Luke 19. 42. if thou hadst *k.* . . . . in this
Acts 15. 18. *k.* to God are all his works
Rom. 1. 19. *k.* that which may be *k.* of God
7. 7. I had not *k.* sin but by the law
1 Cor. 8. 3. the same is *k.* of, 13. 12.
Gal. 4. 9. *k.* God, or rather are *k.* of God
2 Tim. 3. 15. from a child thou hast *k.*

Rev. 2. 24. have not *known* the depths of Satan
Gen. 2. 17. *knowledge* of good and evil
1 Sam. 2. 3. the Lord is a God of *k.*
Ps. 19. 2. night unto night sheweth *k.*
73. 11. is there *k.* in the Most High
139. 6. such *k.* is too wonderful
Prov. 8. 12. I find out *k.* of witty inventions
9. 10. *k.* of the holy is understanding
14. 6. *k.* is easy to him that understandeth
19. 2. that the soul be without *k.* is not good
30. 3. nor have the *k.* of holy
Eccl. 9. 10. there is no . . . device nor *k.*
Is. 28. 9. whom shall he teach *k.*
53. 11. by his *k.* shall my righteous
Jer. 3. 15. pastors . . . feed you with *k.*
Dan. 12. 4. and *k.* shall be increased
Hos. 4. 6. are destroyed for lack of *k.*
Hab. 2. 14. earth filled with *k.* of the glory of
God, Is. 11. 9.
Mal. 2. 7. priest's lips should keep *k.*
Rom. 2. 20. a teacher . . . hast form of *k.*
3. 20. for by the law is *k.* of sin
10. 2. a zeal of God, but not according to *k.*
1 Cor. 8. 1. all have *k. K.* puffeth up
Eph. 3. 19. love of Christ which passeth *k.*
Phil. 3. 8. loss for excellency of the *k.* of
Col. 2. 3. treasures of wisdom and *k.*
3. 10. renewed in *k.* after image of
1 Pet. 3. 7. dwell with them according to *k.*
2 Pet. 1. 5. and to virtue *k.* and to *k.*
3. 18. grow in grace and in *k.* of Lord and
Saviour Jesus Christ

L

LABOUR, Gen. 31. 42; 35. 16.
Ps. 90. 10. yet is their strength *l.*
104. 23. man goeth to his . . . *l.* till even
128. 2. thou shalt eat the *l.* of thine
Prov. 14. 23. in all *l.* there is profit
Eccl. 1. 8. all things are full of *l.*
4. 8. yet is there no end of all his *l.*
Is. 55. 2. ye spend your *l.* for that which
John 4. 38. no *l.* . . . their labours
1 Cor. 15. 58. your *l.* is not in vain in
1 Thes. 1. 3. work of faith, *l.* of love
Prov. 23. 4. *l.* not to be rich; cease
Mat. 11. 28. come unto me all ye that *l.* and are
heavy laden
John 6. 27. *l.* not for the meat that
1 Thes. 5. 12. know them which *l.*
Heb. 4. 11. let us *l.* to enter into
Is. 49. 4. I have *laboured* in vain
John 4. 38. other men *l.* and ye
1 Cor. 15. 10. I *l.* more abundantly
Phil. 2. 16. I have not run in vain, neither *l.* in
vain
Luke 10. 7. the *labourer* is worthy of his hire,
1 Tim. 5. 18.
Mat. 9. 37. but *labourers* are few, Luke 10. 2.
1 Cor. 3. 9. *l.* together with God
Prov. 26. 6. he that *laboureth, l.* for
Eccl. 5. 12. sleep of *labouring* man is sweet
Col. 4. 12. Epaphras . . . *l.* fervently . . . in prayers
Rev. 14. 13. dead . . . may rest from *labours*
LACK, Hos. 4. 6. Mat. 19. 20. 2 Cor. 11. 9.
1 Thes. 3. 10. Jas. 1. 5.
LADEN with iniquity, Is. 1. 4.
Mat. 11. 28. labour and heavy *l.*
LADY of kingdoms, Is. 47. 5.
Is. 47. 7. I shall be a *l.* for ever
2 John 1. unto the elect *l.*

Esth. 1. 18. *ladies* of Persia
Judg. 5. 29. her wise *l.* answered her
LAMB, Ex. 12. 3.
Gen. 22. 7. where is *l.* for a burnt offering
8. God will provide himself a *l.*
2 Sam. 12. 3. had nothing save one little ewe *l.*
Is. 11. 6. wolf shall dwell with *l.*
53. 7. brought as *l.* to slaughter
John 1. 29. behold the *L.* of God, 36.
1 Pet. 1. 19. as a *l.* without blemish
Rev. 5. 12. worthy is *L.* that was slain
7. 14. washed their robes, and made them white
in blood of the *L.*, 12. 11.
17. *L.* in the midst of the throne shall feed them
13. 8. *L.* slain from foundation
John 21. 15. Jesus said to Peter, Feed my *lambs*
LAME, Lev. 21. 18. Mal. 1. 8, 13.
Job 29. 15. eyes to blind, feet to *l.*
Prov. 26. 7. legs of *l.* are not equal
Is. 35. 6. shall the *l.* man leap as an hart
Heb. 12. 13. lest . . . *l.* be turned out of way
LAMP, Gen. 15. 17. Ex. 27. 20. 1 Ki. 15. 4.
Mat. 25. 1, 3, 4, 7, 8.
2 Sam. 22. 29. thou art my *l.* O Lord
Job 12. 5. is as a *l.* despised . . . of him
Ps. 119. 105. thy word a *l.* to my feet
132. 17. I have ordained a *l.* for mine
Prov. 6. 23. the commandment is a *l.*
13. 9. *l.* of wicked shall be put out
Is. 62. 1. salvation as *l.* that burneth
Ex. 25. 37. *seven lamps,* 37. 23. Num. 8. 2. Zech.
4. 2. Rev. 4. 5.
LAND, Eccl. 10. 16, 17. Is. 5. 30.
Deut. 19. 14. not remove *landmark,* 27. 17. Job
24. 2. Prov. 22. 28; 23. 10.
LANGUAGE, Gen. 11. 1. Neh. 13. 24. Ps. 81. 5.
Is. 19. 18. Zeph. 3. 9.
LANGUISH, Is. 24. 4. Ps. 41. 3.
LASCIVIOUSNESS, Mark 7. 22. 2 Cor. 12. 21.
Gal. 5. 19. Eph. 4. 19. 1 Pet. 4. 3.
Jude 4. turning grace of God into *l.*
LAST end be like his, Num. 23. 10.
Lam. 1. 9. she remembered not *l.* end
Luke 11. 26. *l.* state . . . is worse than first
1 Pet. 1. 5. *last time,* 20. 1 John 2. 18.
Jude 18. should be mockers in the —
LATTER day, Job 19. 25. *l.* end, Prov. 19. 20.
l. house, Hag. 2. 9. *l.* time, 1 Tim. 4. 1.
LAUGH, Gen. 17. 17; 18. 12, 15.   [2 Tim. 3. 1.
Job 5. 22. at destruction . . . thou shalt *l.*
Ps. 2. 4. he that sitteth in heavens shall *l.*
37. 13. Lord shall *l.* at him
52. 6. righteous shall see and fear and *l.*
Prov. 1. 26. I will *l.* at your calamity
Luke 6. 21. blessed . . . that weep . . . ye shall *l.*
25. woe to you that *l.* . . . ye shall mourn
Job 8. 21. till he fill thy mouth with *laughing*
Ps. 126. 2. mouth filled with *laughter*
Prov. 14. 13. in *l.* heart is sorrowful
Eccl. 2. 2. I said of *l.*, It is mad
7. 3. sorrow is better than *l.*
Jas. 4. 9. let *l.* be turned to mourning
LAW, Gen. 47. 26. Prov. 28. 4.
Deut. 33. 2. from right hand went a fiery *l.*
Neh. 8. 7. caused people to understand *l.*
10. 28. separated from people . . . to *l.* of God
Job 22. 22. receive . . . *l.* from his mouth
Ps. 19. 7. *l.* of the Lord is perfect
37. 31. *l.* of his God is in his heart
78. 5. he . . . appointed a *l.* in Israel, 10.
119. 72. *l.* of thy mouth is better
Prov. 6. 23. *l.* is light, 13. 14. *l.* of wise
7. 2. keep my *l.* as apple of thine eye

Prov. 28. 9. turneth away his ear from hearing *law*
29. 18. keepeth the *l.* happy is he
Is. 2. 3. shall go forth *l.*, Mic. 4. 2.
8. 16. seal the *l.* among my disciples
20. to the *l.* and the testimony
42. 21. magnify the *l.* and make it
51. 7. people in whose heart is my *l.*
Jer. 18. 18. *l.* not perish from priest
31. 33. I will put *l.* in inward parts
Hos. 8. 12. written to him great things of *l.*
Mal. 2. 7. they should seek *l.* at his mouth
Luke 16. 16. *l.* and prophets were until John
John 1. 17. *l.* was given by Moses
19. 7. we have a *l.* and by our *l.* he
Acts 13. 39. not justified by the *l.* of Moses
Rom. 2. 12. sinned without *l.* perish without *l.*
13. not hearers of *l.* . . . but doers of *l.*
14. having not *l.* a *l.* to themselves
3. 20. by deeds of *l.* shall no flesh be justified, for
        by the *l.* is the
31. do we make void *l.*? . . . we establish the *l.*
4. 15. *l.* worketh wrath; where no *l.*
5. 13. sin is not imputed where no *l.*
7. 7. had not known sin but by *l.*
8. for without the *l.* sin was dead
9. I was alive without the *l.* once
12. the *l.* is holy, just, and good
14. *l.* is spiritual, but I am carnal
22. I delight in the *l.* of God   [my mind
23. *l.* in my members warring against *l.* of
8. 2. *l.* of Spirit . . . made me free from *l.* of sin
Rom. 10. 5. righteousness of *l.*, 9. 31. Phil. 3. 9.
1 Cor. 6. 1. Dare any of you . . . go to *l.*
6. 7. brother goeth to *l.* with brother
Gal. 2. 16. man not justified by works of the *l.* . . .
        by works of *l.* no flesh justified
19. I through the *l.* am dead to *l.*
3. 10. of works of *l.* are under curse
12. the *l.* is not of faith, but the
13. Christ redeemed us from curse of *l.*
5. 23. love, faith, against such is no *l.*
1 Tim. 1. 8. the *l.* is good, if a man use
9. that *l.* is not made for righteous
Heb. 7. 19. *l.* made nothing perfect
Jas. 1. 25. looketh into perfect *l.*
1 John 3. 4. sin transgresseth the *l.* . . . sin is the
        transgression of *l.*
Neh. 9. 26. cast *thy law* behind their backs
Ps. 40. 8.—is within my heart
94. 12. teachest him out of—
119. 70. I delight in—77, 92, 174.
18. wondrous things out of—
97. how I love—113, 163, 165, 167.
Ezek. 18. 5. do that is *lawful* and right, 33. 14, 19.
1 Cor. 6. 12. all things *l.* to me, 10. 23.
Is. 33. 22. Lord is *lawgiver*, Jas. 4. 12.
LAY, Gen. 19. 33, 35. Job 29. 19.
Eccl. 7. 2. the living will *l.* it to heart
Is. 28. 16. I *l.* in Zion . . . a tried stone
Mal. 2. 2. ye do not *l.* it to heart
Mat. 8. 20. hath not where to *l.* his head
Acts 7. 60. *l.* not this sin to their charge
15. 28. *l.* on you no greater burden
Heb. 12. 1. *l.* aside every weight
Jas. 1. 21. *l.* apart all filthiness and superfluity
        of, 1 Pet. 2. 1.   [3. 16.
John 10. 15. *lay down life*, 13. 37; 15. 13. 1 John
1 Tim. 5. 22. *lay hands*, Heb. 6. 2.
6. 12. *lay hold* on eternal life
Heb. 6. 18.—on hope set before us
Mat. 6. 20. *lay up* for yourselves
Ps. 62. 9. to be *laid* in the balance
89. 19. I *l.* help on one that is

Is. 53. 6. Lord hath *laid* on him the **iniquity** of
        us all
1 Cor. 3. 10. I have *l.* foundation, 11.
1 Sam. 21. 12. David *laid up* words
Ps. 31. 19. thy goodness . . . —for them
Sol. 7. 13. pleasant fruits . . . —for thee
Luke 1. 66.—in their hearts
12. 19. much goods—for many years
Col. 1. 5. hope which is—for you
2 Tim. 4. 8.—for me a crown of
Job 21. 19. God *layeth* up his iniquity
Prov. 2. 7. *l.* up wisdom, 26. 24. *l.* up deceit
Is. 56. 2. blessed is the man . . . that *l.* hold on it
57. 1. no man *l.* it to heart, 42. 25.
Jer. 12. 11. land desolate; no man *l.* it to heart
Heb. 6. 1. not *laying* again foundation
1 Tim. 6. 19. *l.* up . . . a good foundation
LEAD, Ex. 15. 10. Job 19. 24. Zech. 5. 7, 8. Gen.
        33. 14. Ex. 13. 21.
Ps. 5. 8. *lead me* . . . in thy righteousness
25. 5.—in thy truth, 27. 11.—in a plain path
61. 2.—to rock higher than I
139. 24.—in the way everlasting
Sol. 8. 2. I would *l.* thee . . . to my mother's house
Is. 11. 6. a little child shall *l.* them
40. 11. gently *l.* those with young
Mat. 15. 14. blind *l.* blind, Luke 6. 39.
1 Tim. 2. 2. may *l.* a quiet . . . life
Rev. 7. 17. Lamb . . . shall *l.* them to
Is. 55. 4. *leader* to people, 9. 16.
Ps. 23. 2 *leadeth* me beside still waters
Mat. 7. 13. broad is way that *l.* to
7. 14. straight is the gate and narrow is the way
        that *l.* to life
John 10. 3. calleth sheep and *l.* them out
Gen. 24. 27. *Lord led, leddest, leadest, leadeth,*
        48. Ex. 13. 18; 15. 13. Deut. 8. 2; 29. 5;
        32. 10, 12. Neh. 9. 12. Ps. 77. 20; 80. 1; 78. 14,
        53; 106. 9; 136. 16; 107. 7. Is. 48. 21; 63. 13,
        14. Jer. 2. 6, 17.
Rom. 8. 14. *led by Spirit*, Gal. 5. 18.
LEAF, Job 13. 25. Ezek. 47. 12. Rev. 22. 2.
LEAGUE with stones, Job 5. 23.   [3. 5.
LEAN not unto thine own understanding, Prov.
Job 8. 15. he shall *l.* upon his house
Mic. 3. 11. yet will they *l.* on Lord
Sol. 8. 5. *leaning* on her beloved
John 13. 23. *l.* on Jesus' bosom, 21. 20.
LEANNESS, Job 16. 8. Ps. 106. 15. Is. 10. 16.
Is. 24. 16. my *l.*, my *l.*, woe
LEAP, Sol. 2. 8. Is. 35. 6. Zeph. 1. 9.
6. 23. rejoice and *l.* for joy
Luke 1. 41. the babe *leaped* in her womb   [12, 13.
LEARN to fear me, Deut. 4. 10; 5. 1; 14. 23; 31.
Ps. 119. 71. might *l.* thy statutes, 73.
Prov. 22. 25. lest thou *l.* his ways
Is. 1. 17. *l.* to do well, seek
26. 10. yet will he not *l.* righteousness
Jer. 10. 2. *l.* not way of the heathen
Mat. 9. 13. *l.* what that meaneth
11. 29. *l.* of me, for I am meek
Tit. 3. 14. also *l.* to maintain good
Rev. 14. 3. no man could *l.* that song
Ps. 106. 35. *learned* their works
Is. 50. 4. given me tongue of the *l.*
John 6. 45. hath *l.* of Father cometh unto **me**
Acts 7. 22. Moses was *l.* in all wisdom
Eph. 4. 20. ye have not so *l.* Christ
Heb. 5. 8. though a Son, yet *l.* he
Acts 26. 24. much *learning* doth make thee **mad**
Rom. 15. 4. were written for our *l.*
2 Tim. 3. 7. ever *l.*, never able to
LEAST of thy mercies, Gen. 32. 10.

Jer. 31. 34. shall know me from *least* of them
Luke 16. 10. faithful in . . . *l*. is faithful
1 Cor. 6. 4. judge who are *l*. esteemed
15. 9. I am *l*. of the apostles
Eph. 3. 8. less than the *l*. of all saints
LEAVE father and mother and cleave to wife,
    Gen. 2. 24. Mat. 19. 5. Mark 10. 7. Eph. 5. 31.
1 Ki. 8. 57. let him not *l*. us, nor
Ps. 16. 10. not *l*. soul in hell, Acts 2. 27.
27. 9. *l*. me not, neither forsake me
Mat. 5. 24. *l*. there thy gift before
23. 23. and not to *l*. other undone
John 14. 18. will not *l*. you comfortless
27. peace I *l*. with you, my peace
Heb. 13. 5. I will never *l*. thee, nor forsake
LEAVEN, Ex. 12. 15. Lev. 2. 11.
Mat. 13. 33. kingdom of heaven is like *l*. 16. 6.
    beware of *l*. of Pharisees, Luke 12. 1. 1 Cor.
    5. 7, 8. purge out the old *l*. of   [5. 9.
1. Cor. 5. 6. a little *l*. leaveneth whole lump, Gal.
LEES, Is. 25. 6. Jer. 48. 11. Zeph. 1. 12.
LEGS, Ps. 147. 10. Prov. 26. 7.
LEND, Ex. 22. 25. Deut. 23. 19, 20.
Ps. 37. 26. merciful and *lendeth*, 112. 5.
Prov. 19. 17. giveth to the poor *l*. to Lord
22. 7. borrower is servant to *lender*
1 Sam. 1. 28. I have *lent* him to Lord
Jer. 15. 10. neither *l*. on usury, nor
LEOPARD, Sol. 4. 8. Is. 11. 6. Jer. 5. 6; 13. 23.
    Hos. 13. 7. Hab. 1. 8.
LESS, Ezra 9. 13. Job 11. 6. Is. 40. 17. Heb. 7. 7.
    Eph. 3. 8. Gen. 32. 10.
LETTER, Rom. 7. 6. 2 Cor. 3. 6.
LETTEST, -TETH, Luke 2. 29. 2 Thes. 2. 7.
LEVIATHAN, Job 41. 1. Ps. 74. 14.
LIBERAL, Prov. 11. 25. Is. 32. 5, 8. 2 Cor. 9. 13.
    1 Cor. 16. 3. *liberality*, 2 Cor. 8. 2.
Jas. 1. 5. ask of God that giveth to all men
LIBERTY, Lev. 25. 10. Jer. 34. 8.   [*liberally*
Ps. 119. 45. I will walk at *l*. for I seek
Is. 61. 1. anointed me to . . . proclaim *l*.
Luke 4. 18. to set at *l*. the bruised
Rom. 8. 21. *l*. of the children of God
Gal. 5. 1. stand fast in *l*. wherewith
13. use not *l*. for an occasion to
Jas. 1. 25. but whoso looketh into perfect law of
2. 12. be judged by the law of *l*.   [*l*.
LIE, Lev. 6. 3; 19. 11. Job 11. 3.
Ps. 62. 9. men of high degree are a *l*.
2 Thes. 2. 11. they should believe a *l*.
Num. 23. 19. God is not a man, that he should *l*.,
    neither son of man
Is. 63. 8. children that will not *l*.
Hab. 2. 3. it shall speak and not *l*.
Col. 3. 9. *l*. not one to another, Eph. 4. 25.
Tit. 1. 2. God that cannot *l*. hath promised
Heb. 6. 18. impossible for God to *l*.
Ps. 58. 3. wicked go astray . . . speaking *lies*
101. 7. that telleth *l*. shall not tarry
Hos. 11. 12. compasseth me with *l*.
1 Tim. 4. 2. speaking *l*. in hypocrisy
John 8. 44. he is a *liar* and the father
Rom. 3. 4. let God be true, every man a *l*.
1 John 1. 10. we make him a *l*., 5. 10.
2. 4. keepeth not commandments is a *l*.
Ps. 116. 11. I said . . ., All men are *liars*
Is. 44. 25. frustrateth tokens of *l*.
Tit. 1. 12. the Cretians are always *l*.
Rev. 2. 2. tried . . . and found them *l*.
Ps. 119. 29. remove . . . way of *lying*
163. I hate and abhor *l*. but love thy law
Prov. 12. 19. *l*. tongue but for a moment
Jer. 7. 4. trust ye not in *l*. words, saying

Hos. 4. 2. by swearing and *lying* . . . they
Jonah 2. 8. observe *l*. vanities
LIFE, Gen. 2. 7, 9; 42. 15; 44. 30.
Deut. 30. 15. set before thee . . . *l*. and good
32. 47. not a vain thing . . . it is your *l*.
1 Sam. 25. 29. soul of my Lord shall be bound in
    the bundle of *l*.
Job 10. 12. granted me *l*. and favour
Ps. 16. 11. shew me the path of *l*.
21. 4. asked *l*. of thee and thou gavest
36. 9. with thee is the fountain of *l*.
63. 3. lovingkindness better than *l*.
66. 9. God holdeth our soul in *l*.
91. 16. with long *l*. will I satisfy
Prov. 8. 35. whoso findeth me findeth *l*.
15. 24. way of *l*. is above to the wise
18. 21. death and *l*. in power of tongue
Is. 57. 10. hast found *l*. of thy hand
Mat. 6. 25. take no thought for your *l*.
John 1. 4. in him was *l*. and *l*. was light of
3. 36. believeth on Son hath everlasting *l*.
5. 40. not come to me, that ye might have *l*.
6. 35. I am the bread of *l*. 48. everlasting *l*.,
51. my flesh I give for *l*. of world   [40, 47
63. words I speak unto you are spirit and *l*.
8. 12. he that followeth me . . . shall have light of *l*.
10. 10. I am come that they might have *l*.
11. 25. I am the resurrection and the *l*.
John 14. 6. I am the way, the truth, and the *l*.
Rom. 5. 17. reign in *l*. by Jesus Christ, 21.
8. 2. law of Spirit of *l*. in Christ Jesus hath
6. to be spiritually minded is *l*. and
2 Cor. 2. 16. the savour of *l*. unto *l*.
3. 6. letter killeth, spirit giveth *l*.
4. 11. *l*. of Jesus might be manifest
5. 4. mortality swallowed up of *l*.
Gal. 2. 20. the *l*. I now live in flesh
Eph. 4. 18. alienated from *l*. of God
Col. 3. 3. your *l*. is hid with Christ
4. when Christ our *l*. shall appear
1 Tim. 2. 2. a peaceable *l*. in all godliness
4. 8. having promise of the *l*. that
2 Tim. 1. 10. brought *l*. and immortality to light
2 Pet. 1. 3. that pertain to *l*. and
1 John 5. 12. that hath Son hath *l*. . . . that hath
    not Son hath not *l*.
Job 2. 4. all man hath will he give for *his life*
Mat. 10. 39. findeth—shall lose it, and loseth—
    for my sake shall find   [for many
20. 28. Son of man came . . . to give—a ransom
Rom. 5. 10. being reconciled shall be saved by—
1 Ki. 19. 3, (Elijah went for—
4. O Lord, take away *my life*, 14.
Ps. 26. 9. gather not . . . —with bloody men
27. 1. the Lord is the strength of—
Jonah 2. 6. brought up—from corruption
John 10. 15. I lay down—for sheep, 13. 37.
Acts 20. 24. neither count I—dear
Ps. 17. 14. *this life*, Luke 8. 14; 21. 34. Acts
    5. 20. 1 Cor. 6. 3; 15. 19.
Prov. 4. 10. hear . . . and the years of *thy life*
Jer. 39. 18.—shall be for a prey, 45. 5.
Prov. 10. 16. tendeth (*un*) *to life*, 11. 19; 19. 23.
    Mat. 7. 14. John 5. 24. Acts 11. 18. Rom.
    7. 10. Heb. 11. 35. 1 John 3. 14.
LIFT *up* his countenance upon thee, Num. 6. 26.
Ps. 4. 6. Lord—light of countenance
7. 6. Lord—thyself because of rage
24. 7.—ye gates, —ye doors, and
25. 1. to thee I—my soul, 86. 4.
75. 4.—not the horn, 5.
121. 1.—mine eyes, 123. 1.
Eccl. 4. 10. one will—his fellow

Is. 33. 10. I will be exalted . . . I *lift up* myself
42. 2. he shall not cry, nor—. . . voice
Jer. 7. 16. neither—cry nor prayer, 11. 14.
Lam. 3. 41. let us—our hearts with
Heb. 12. 12.—hands . . . and feeble knees
Jas. 4. 10. Lord . . . shall *l.* you up
2 Chr. 17. 6. heart *lifted up* in ways of the Lord
83. 2. they that hate thee—the head
102. 10. thou hast—and cast me down
Is. 26. 11. Lord, when thy hand is—
Hab. 2. 4. his soul which is—is not upright
John 3. 14. so must Son of man be—
8. 28. when ye have—Son of man
12. 32. if I be—will draw all men, 34.
Ps. 3. 3. my glory and *lifter up* of
Prov. 2. 3. *liftest up* voice for understanding
Ps. 141. 2. *lifting up* of hands, 1 Tim. 2. 8.
LIGHT, Num. 21. 5. Deut. 27. 16. Judg. 9. 4.
    1 Ki. 16. 31. Ezek. 8. 17; 22. 7.
Is. 49. 6. it is a *l.* thing thou shouldest be my
Zeph. 3. 4. her prophets *l.* and   [servant
Mat. 11. 30. my yoke easy, my burden *l.*   [ment
2 Cor. 4. 17. our *l.* affliction which is but for a mo-
Ps. 62. 9. they are altogether *lighter* than vanity
Jer. 3. 9. *lightness* of whoredom, 23. 32.
LIGHT, Gen. 1. 3, 4, 5, 16; 44. 3.
Job 18. 5. *l.* of the wicked put out
25. 3. on whom doth not his *l.* arise
33. 30. enlightened with *l.* of living
Ps. 4. 6. lift up *l.* of thy countenance
36. 9. in thy *l.* shall we see *l.*
43. 3. O send out thy *l.* and thy truth
90. 8. our secret sins in *l.* of thy countenance
97. 11. *l.* is sown for the righteous
104. 2. coverest thyself with *l.* as a
112. 4. to the upright ariseth *l.* in
119. 105. thy word is . . . *l.* to my path
Prov. 4. 18. path of the just is as shining *l.*
6. 23. law is *l.* and reproofs . . . are way
15. 30. *l.* of the eyes rejoiceth the
Eccl. 11. 7. *l.* is sweet and a pleasant
Is. 5. 20. darkness for *l.* and *l.* for
30. the *l.* is darkened, Job 10. 22.
8. 20. because there is no *l.* in them
9. 2. walked . . . have seen a great *l.*
Is. 30. 26. *l.* of moon as *l.* of sun, *l.* of
42. 6. keep thee, and give thee for a . . . *l.*
45. 7. I form *l.* and create darkness
50. 10. walketh in darkness and hath no *l.*
58. 8. thy *l.* break forth as morning
60. 1. shine; for thy *l.* is come, 19, 20.
Zech. 14. 6. *l.* shall not be clear nor
7. evening time it shall be *l.*
Mat. 5. 14. ye are the *l.* of the world
16. let your *l.* so shine before men
Luke 2. 32. *l.* to lighten Gentiles   [of *l.*
16. 8. children of world wiser than the children
John 1. 4. the life was the *l.* of men
7. (John) came to bear witness of *l.*, 8.
9. true *l.* that lighteth every man
3. 19. loved darkness rather than *l.*
20. cometh not to *l.* 21. cometh to *l.*
5. 35. (John) a burning and a shining *l.*
8. 12. I am the *l.* of the world; he that followed
    me . . . shall have *l.* of life
12. 35, 36. walk while ye have the *l.*
Acts 13. 47. I have set thee for a *l.*
26. 18. turn them from darkness to *l.*
Rom. 13. 12. put on the armour of *l.*
2 Cor. 4. 4. lest *l.* of . . . Gospel . . . should shine
6. 14. what communion hath *l.* with darkness
Eph. 5. 8. walk as children of *l.*
14. awake . . . Christ shall give thee *l.*

1 Thes. 5. 5. ye are the children of *light*
1 Pet. 2. 9. called . . . to his marvellous *l.*
1 John 1. 5. God is *l.* and in him is
Rev. 21. 23. Lamb is *l.* thereof, 11.
Ps. 136. 7. *lights*, Ezek. 32. 8. Luke 12. 35. Phil.
    2. 15. Jas. 1. 17.   [Rev. 21. 23.
2 Sam. 22. 29. *lighten*, Ezra 9. 8. Ps. 13. 3; 34. 5.
Ex. 19. 16. *lightning*, Ps. 18. 14. Mat. 28. 3;
    24. 27. Luke 10. 18.
LIKE men, quit you, 1 Cor. 16. 13.
Heb. 2. 17. be made *l.* his brethren
1 John 3. 2. we shall be *l.* him
Gen. 1. 26. after our *likeness*
5. 3. Adam . . . begat a son in his own *l.*
Ps. 17. 15. satisfied when I awake with thy *l.*
Rom. 6. 5. *l.* of his death . . . *l.* of resurrection
8. 3. in *l.* of sinful flesh, Phil. 2. 7.
LILY, Sol. 2. 1, 2, 16; 4. 5; 5. 13; 6. 2, 3; **7. 2.**
Hos. 14. 5. Mat. 6. 28.
LINE upon *l.*, *l.* upon *l.* Is. 28. 10, 13.
Is. 28. 17. judgment will I lay to *l.*
34. 11. stretch out on it *l.* of confusion
2 Cor. 10. 16. not to boast in another man's *l.* of
Ps. 16. 6. *lines* are fallen unto me   [things
LINGER, Gen. 19. 16. 2 Pet. 2. 3.
LION, Gen. 49. 9. Judg. 14. 5, 18. Job 4. 10, 11;
    10. 16; 28. 8. Ps. 7. 2; 17. 12; 10. 9; 22. 13.
    Is. 38. 13.
Prov. 22. 13. there is a *l.* without, 26. **13.**
28. 1. righteous are bold as a *l.*
Is. 11. 6. calf and young *l.*, 7; 65. 25.
35. 9. no *l.* shall be there, nor
Ezek. 1. 10. face of a *l.* 10. 14. Rev. 4. 7.
Hos. 5. 14. be as young *l.*, Lam. 3. 10.
2 Tim. 4. 17. out of mouth of the *l.*
1 Pet. 5. 8. the devil as a roaring *l.*
Rev. 5. 5. *L.* of the tribe of Juda
LIPS, Ex. 6. 12, 30. Prov. 16. 10.
Ps. 12. 3. cut off all flattering *l.*
4. our *l.* are our own
17. 1, not feigned *l.* 31. 18, lying *l.*, 120. 2. Prov.
    10. 18; 12. 22; 17. 4, 7. Is. 59. 3.
63. 5. praise thee with joyful *l.*
Prov. 10. 21. *l.* of the righteous feed
26. 23. burning *l.* and wicked heart
Sol. 7. 9. *l.* of those that are asleep to speak
Is. 6. 5. man of unclean *l.* . . . people of unclean *l.*
57. 19. I create the fruit of the *l.*
Mal. 2. 7. priest's *l.* should keep knowledge
Ps. 51. 15. open thou my *lips*
63. 3.—shall praise thee, 71. 23.
141. 3. keep the door of—
17. 4. thy *lips*, 34. 13; 45. 2.
LITTLE, Ezra 9. 8. Neh. 9. 32.
Ps. 2. 12. when his wrath is kindled but a *l.*
8. 5. a *l.* lower than the angels, Heb. **2. 7.**
37. 16. a *l.* that a righteous man hath
Prov. 6. 10. *l.* sleep, *l.* slumber, 24. 33.
15. 16. better is *l.* with fear, 16. 8.
Is. 28. 10. here a *l.* and there a *l.*, 13.
54. 8. in a *l.* wrath I hid my face
Ezek. 11. 16. will I be to them as a *l.* sanctuary
Mat. 6. 30. O ye of *l.* faith, 8. 26; 14. 31; 16. 8.
Luke 12. 32. fear not, *l.* flock, it is
19. 17. been faithful in a very *l.*
1 Tim. 4. 8. bodily exercise profiteth *l.*
Rev. 3. 8. hast *l.* strength, and kept
LIVE, Gen. 3. 22; 17. 18.
Lev. 18. 5. if a man do, he shall *l.*, Neh. 9. 29.
    Ezek. 3. 21; 18. 9; 33. 13, 15, 16, 19. Rom.
    10. 5. Gal. 3. 12.
Deut. 32. 40. *live(th)* for ever, 1 Ki. 1. 31. Neh.
    2. 3. Ps. 22. 26; 49. 9. Dan. 2. 4; 3. 9; 5. 10;

6. 21. Zech. 1. 5. John 6. 51, 58. Rev. 4. 9; 5. 14; 10. 6; 15. 7.
Job 14. 14. if a man die, shall he *live*
Ps. 55. 23. bloody . . . men shall not *l.* out half
63. 4. bless thee while I *l.*, 146. 2.
118. 17. I shall not die, but *l.* and
Is. 38. 16. men *l.* . . . make me to *l.*
55. 3. hear, and your soul shall *l.*
Ezek. 16. 6. I said, when thou wast in thy blood, *L.*; yea, I said unto thee . . ., *L.*
18. 32. turn yourselves and *l.*, 33. 11.
Hab. 2. 4. just *l.* by faith, Rom. 1. 17, &c.
Mat. 4. 4. man shall not *l.* by bread alone but by every word, Deut. 8. 3.
John 14. 19. because I *l.* ye shall *l.*
Acts 17. 28. in him we *l.* and move
Rom. 8. 13. if ye *l.* after the flesh, ye
14. 8. whether we *l.*, we *l.* unto Lord
1 Cor. 9. 14. they which preach the Gospel *l.* of
2 Cor. 5. 15. which *l.* should not *l.* to themselves
6. 9. as dying, and behold we *l.*
13. 11. be of one mind, *l.* in peace
Gal. 2. 20. life I *l.* I *l.* by faith of Son of God
5. 25. if we *l.* in Spirit, walk in
Phil. 1. 21. to *l.* is Christ, 22.
2 Tim. 3. 12. all that will *l.* godly in
Titus 2. 12. we should *l.* soberly, righteously
Heb. 13. 18. willing to *l.* honestly
1 Pet. 2. 24. should *l.* to righteousness
1 John 4. 9. that we might *l.* through
Acts 23. 1. *lived* in all good conscience
Jas. 5. 5. ye have *l.* in pleasure
Rev. 18. 9. *l.* deliciously, Luke 7. 25.
Job 19. 25. my Redeemer *liveth*
Rom. 6. 10. in that he *l.*, he *l.* unto God
1 Tim. 5. 6. *l.* in pleasure dead while she *l.*
Heb. 7. 25. he ever *l.* to make intercession
Rev. 1. 18. he that *l.* and was dead
Acts 7. 38. received *lively* oracles
1 Pet. 1. 3. begotten again to a *l.* hope
2. 5. ye, as *l.* stones, are built up a
1 John 3. 16. *lives*, Rev. 12. 11.
Eccl. 7. 2. *living* will lay it to heart
Is. 38. 19. the *l.*, the *l.* shall praise
Jer. 2. 13. (Lord) fountain of *l.* waters
Mat. 22. 32. not God of dead, but of *l.*
John 7. 38. flow rivers of *l.* water
Rom. 12. 1. your bodies a *l.* sacrifice
14. 9. Lord both of dead and *l.*
1 Cor. 15. 45. first man Adam made a *l.* soul
Heb. 10. 20. by a new and *l.* way
1 Pet. 2. 4. coming as to a *l.* stone
Rev. 7. 17. lead them to *l.* fountains
LOAD, Ps. 68. 19. Is. 46. 1.
LO(A)THE themselves for evil, Ezek. 6. 9; 16. 5; 20. 43; 36. 31.
Num. 21. 5. soul *loatheth*, Prov. 27. 7.
Ps. 38. 7. *loathsome* disease
LOFTY eyes, Ps. 131. 1. Prov. 30. 13.
Is. 2. 11. *l.* looks humbled, 5. 15.
57. 15. I. One that inhabiteth
LOINS girt, Prov. 31. 17. Is. 11. 5. Luke 12. 35.
Eph. 6. 14. 1 Pet. 1. 13.   [18. 7. Jas. 5. 7.
LONG, Ps. 91. 16. Eccl. 12. 5. Mat. 23. 14. Luke
Ex. 34. 6. Lord God, *longsuffering*, Num. 14. 18.
Ps. 86. 15. Jer. 15. 15. Rom. 2. 4; 9. 22. 1 Tim. 1. 16. 1 Pet. 3. 20. 2 Pet. 3. 9, 15.
Gal. 5. 22. fruit of Spirit is . . . *l.*, Eph. 4. 2. Col. 1. 11; 3. 12. 2 Tim. 3. 10; 4. 2.
LONG Job 3. 21; 6. 8. Rom. 1. 11.
Ps. 119. 40. *I have longed* after thy precepts
131.—for thy commandments
174.—for thy salvation

Ps. 63. 1. my flesh *longeth* for thee
84. 2. my soul *l.* . . . for courts of Lord
107. 9. he satisfieth the *longing* soul
119. 20. my soul breaketh for the *l.*
LOOK, Gen. 13. 14. Ex. 10. 10.
Is. 8. 17. wait upon Lord . . . and I will *l.*
45. 22. *l.* unto me and be saved
66. 2. to this man will I *l.*
Mic. 7. 7. I will *l.* unto the Lord
Luke 7. 19. do we *l.* for another, 20.
2 Cor. 4. 18. we *l.* not at things seen
Phil. 2. 4. *l.* not every man on his own
3. 20. heaven, from whence also we *l.* for
Heb. 9. 28. to them that *l.* for him
1 Pet. 1. 12. angels desire to *l.* into
Gen. 29. 32. the Lord *looked* on my affliction, Ex. 2. 25; 3. 7; 4. 31. Deut. 26. 7.
Ps. 34. 5. they *l.* to him and were lightened
Sol. 1. 6. *l.* not upon me, because I am black, because the sun hath *l.* upon me
Is. 5. 7. he *l.* for judgment
22. 11. ye have not *l.* to the maker of
64. 3. didst terrible things we *l.* not for
Jer. 8. 15. we *l.* for peace, but, 14. 19.
Hag. 1. 9. ye *l.* for much, and it
Luke 2. 38. *l.* for redemption in Israel
22. 61. the Lord *l.* on Peter
Heb. 11. 10. *l.* for a city . . . builder . . . is God
1 John 1. 1. that which we have *l.* on
1 Sam. 16. 7. man *looketh* on outward appearance, but Lord *l.* on the heart
Ps. 33. 13. the Lord *l.* from heaven, 14. 2.   [27.
Prov. 14. 15. prudent man *l.* well to his goings, 31.
Sol. 2. 9. *l.* forth at the windows, 6. 10.
Mat. 5. 28. *l.* on a woman to lust
24. 50. come in a day he *l.* not for
Jas. 1. 25. *l.* into perfect law of
Is. 38. 14. mine eyes fail with *looking* upward
Luke 9. 62. no man . . . *l.* back is fit for kingdom of God
Tit. 2. 13. *l.* for that blessed hope
Heb. 10. 27. a certain fearful *l.* for
12. 2. *l.* to Jesus, the author and
2 Pet. 3. 12. *l.* for . . . day of God
Jude 21. *l.* for the mercy of our Lord
Ps. 18. 27. wilt bring down high *looks*
LOOSE, Deut. 25. 9. Josh. 5. 15.
Ps. 102. 20. to *l.* those appointed to death
Eccl. 12. 6. or ever the silver cord be *loosed*
Acts 2. 24. *l.* pains of death
1 Cor. 7. 27. bound to a wife? seek not to be *l.* Art thou *l.* . . . ? seek not a wife
Ps. 146. 7. the Lord *looseth* the prisoners
LORD, ascribed to God, Gen. 28. 16. Ex. 5. 2. 1 Cor. 12. 5; in about 300 other texts; and to man, Gen. 18. 12; 23. 11. Is. 23. 13. 1 Cor. 8. 5. 1 Pet. 5. 3, and in about 14 other places.
Ex. 34. 6. *L.*, the *L.* God, merciful
Deut. 4. 35. *L.* is God, 39. 1 Ki. 18. 39.
6. 4. *L.* our God is one *L.*, 10.
10. 17. *L.* of *l.*, Dan. 2. 47. 1 Tim. 6. 15. Rev. 17. 14; 19. 16.
Neh. 9. 6. art *L.* alone, Is. 37. 20.
Ps. 118. 27. God is the *L.*, 100. 3.
Mark 2. 28. Son of man is *L.* of sabbath
Acts 2. 36. made . . . Jesus . . . *L.* and Christ
Rom. 10. 12. for the same *L.* over all is rich unto all, Acts 10. 36.
14. 9. *L.* of the dead and of the living
1 Cor. 2. 8. *L.* of glory
8. 6. one God, one *L.* Jesus Christ
15. 47. *L.* from heaven
Eph. 4. 5. one *L.*, one faith, one baptism

Gen. 15. 6. he believed *in the Lord*
1 Sam. 2. 1. heart rejoiced—Ps. 32. 11; 33. 1;
35. 9; 97. 12; 104. 34. Is. 41. 16; 61. 10.
Joel 2. 23. Hab. 3. 18. Zech. 10. 7. Phil.
3. 1; 4. 4.
2 Ki. 18. 5. trust—Ps. 4. 5; 11. 1; 31. 6;
32. 10; 37. 3; 115. 9, 10, 11; 118. 8; 125. 1.
Prov. 3. 5; 16. 20; 28. 25; 29. 25. Is. 26. 4.
Zeph. 3. 2. she trusted not—
Ps. 31. 24. hope—130. 7; 131. 3.
34. 2. soul make her boast—
37. 4. delight thyself—7. rest—
Is. 45. 17. Israel shall be saved—
24.—have I righteousness
45. 25.—all seed of Israel be justified
Rom. 16. 12. labour—1 Cor. 15. 58.
1 Thes. 5. 12. over you—Col. 4. 7, 17.
Rev. 14. 13. blessed are dead which die—
LOSE, Eccl. 3. 6. Prov. 23. 8. Mat. 10. 39, 42;
16. 26. John 6. 39. 2 John 8.
Luke 15. 4. having an hundred sheep, if he *l.* one
1 Cor. 3. 15. *loss*, Phil. 3. 7, 8.
Ps. 119. 176. astray like *lost* sheep
Ezek. 37. 11. our hope is *l.*, we are cut
Mat. 5. 13. if salt have *l.* his savour
10. 6. to the *l.* sheep of . . . Israel, 15. 24.
18. 11. save that which was *l.*, Luke 19. 10.
Luke 15. 32. thy brother was *l.* and is found
2 Cor. 4. 3. gospel be hid, hid to them that are *l.*
LOT, Lev. 16. 8, 9, 10. Josh. 15. 1.
1 Sam. 14. 41. perfect *l.*, 42.
Ps. 16. 5. thou maintainest my *l.*
125. 3. rod of wicked not rest on *l.* of righteous
Prov. 16. 33. the *l.* is cast into lap
18. 18. *l.* causeth contentions to cease
Acts 1. 26. the *l.* fell on Matthias
Ps. 22. 18. cast *lots* upon my vesture, Mat.
27. 35. Mark 15. 24.
LOVE, Gen. 27. 4. 2 Sam. 13. 15.
2 Sam. 1. 26. passing the *l.* of women
Eccl. 9. 1. no man knoweth either *l.*
Sol. 2. 5. I am sick of *l.*, 5. 8.
8. 6. *l.* is strong as death
Jer. 2. 2. remember the *l.* of thine espousals
31. 3. loved thee with everlasting *l.*
Ezek. 16. 8. thy time was time of *l.*
33. 31. their mouth they shew much *l.*
Mat. 24. 12. *l.* of many shall wax cold
John 15. 9. continue ye in my *l.*, 10.
13. greater *l.* hath no man than this
Rom. 8. 35. who shall separate us from the *l.* of
Christ, 39.
12. 9. let *l.* be without dissimulation
13. 10. *l.* is the fulfilling of the law
15. 30. Christ's sake, and *l.* of Spirit
2 Cor. 5. 14. *l.* of Christ constraineth
Gal. 5. 6. faith which worketh by *l.*
13. by *l.* serve one another
22. fruit of the Spirit is *l.*, joy, peace
1 Thes. 1. 3. your labour of *l.*, Heb. 6. 10.
5. 8. breastplate of faith and *l.*
2 Thes. 2. 10. received not *l.* of truth
Heb. 13. 1. let brotherly *l.* continue
1 John 3. 1. what manner of *l.* Father bestowed
on us
4. 7. *l.* is of God. 8, 16, God is *l.*
4. 9. manifested the *l.* of God
18. there is no fear in *l.* . . . perfect *l.*
21. who loveth God *l.* his brother
Rev. 2. 4. thou hast left thy first *l.*
Sol. 7. 12. there I will give thee my *loves*
Eph. 1. 4. without blame before him *in love*
3. 17. grounded—4. 2. forbearing one another—

Eph. 4. 15. speaking truth *in love* 16.
5. 2. walk—as Christ hath loved
Col. 2. 2. knit together—and
1 Thes. 3. 12. abound—
5. 13. esteem very highly—
Luke 11. 42. *love of God*, John 5. 42.
Rom. 5. 5.—is shed abroad in our
2 Cor. 13. 14.—. . . be with you all
2 Thes. 3. 5. direct your hearts into—
1 John 2. 5. in him is—perfected
3. 16. perceive we—
4. 9. in this was manifested—towards   [ments
5. 3. this is the—that we keep his command-
Deut. 7. 7. his *love*, Zeph. 3. 17. Ps. 91. 14. Is.
63. 9. John 15. 10. Rom. 5. 8.
Lev. 19. 18. thou shalt *l.* thy neighbour as thyself,
34. Mat. 19. 19; 22. 39. Rom. 13. 8. Gal.
5. 14. Jas. 2. 8.
Deut. 6. 5. shalt *l.* Lord thy God with all thy
heart, Mat. 22. 37. Mark 12. 30. Luke 10. 27.
Deut. 10. 12. to fear the Lord . . . and to *l.*
Ps. 31. 23. *l.* Lord, all ye his saints
145. 20. Lord preserveth them that *l.* him
Sol. 1. 4. the upright *l.* thee
Zech. 8. 19. *l.* the truth and peace
Mat. 5. 44. *l.* your enemies, bless
John 13. 34. *l.* one another, 15. 12, 17. Rom.
13. 8. 1 John 3. 11, 23; 4. 7, 11, 12. 1 Pet.
1. 22.
14. 23. if a man *l.* me . . . my Father will *l.* him
1 Cor. 16. 22. if any man *l.* not Lord
Eph. 5. 25. *l.* your wives, Col. 3. 19.
2 Tim. 4. 8. all . . . that *l.* his appearing
1 Pet. 1. 8. having not seen, ye *l.*
2. 17. *l.* brotherhood, 3. 8.
1 John 2. 15. *l.* not world . . . if any *l.* world,
l. of Father not in him   [7–12, 16.
4. 19. we *l.* him because he first loved us,
Ps. 116. 1. *I love* Lord because, 18. 1.
119. 97. how—thy law, 113, 119, 127, 159, 163,
167; 26. 8.
2 John 1. whom—in the truth, and
Rev. 3. 19. as many as—I rebuke
Deut. 7. 8. because the Lord *loved* you, 33. 3.
1 Sam. 18. 1. *l.* (David) as his own soul, 20. 17.
2 Sam. 12. 24. and he called his name Solomon:
and the Lord *l.* him.
1 Ki. 3. 3. Solomon *l.* the Lord
10. 9. the Lord *l.* Israel
Hos. 11. 1. Israel was a child, then I *l.* him
Mark 10. 21. Jesus beholding him, *l.* him
Luke 7. 47. sins forgiven, she *l.* much
2 Tim. 4. 10. *l.* this present world
Heb. 1. 9. hast *l.* righteousness and
John 3. 16. God so *l.* the world that
19. men *l.* darkness rather than
12. 43. *l.* the praise of men more
13. 1. having *l.* his own . . . he *l.* them
23. one of his disciples whom Jesus *l.*, 19. 26;
20. 2; 21. 7, 20.
14. 28. if ye *l.* me, ye would rejoice
15. 9. as my Father *l.* me, so have I *l.*
16. 27. Father loveth you because ye *l.* me
17. 23. hast *l.* them as thou hast *l.* me
26. wherewith thou hast *l.* me
Rom. 8. 37. conquerors through him that *l.* us
9. 13. Jacob I *l.*, Esau I hated, Mal. 1. 2.
Gal. 2. 20. Son of God, who *l.* me
Eph. 2. 4. great love wherewith he *l.* us
5. 2. walk in love, as Christ *l.* us
25. love wives as Christ *l.* church
2 Thes. 2. 16. God, even our Father . . . *l.* us
2 Pet. 2. 15. *l.* wages of unrighteousness

1 John 4. 10. not that we *loved* God, but he *l.* us
Rev. 1. 5. unto him that *l.* us and washed us from
our sins in his own blood
12. 11. *l.* not their lives unto death
Ps. 146. 8. the Lord *loveth* the righteous
Prov. 3. 12. whom the Lord *l.* he correcteth,
17. 17. a friend *l.* at all times   [Heb. 12. 6.
21. 17. he that *l.* pleasure shall be poor
Sol. 1. 7. whom my soul *l.*, 3. 1, 4.
Mat. 10. 37. *l.* father or mother more
John 3. 35. Father *l.* the Son, 5. 20.
2 Cor. 9. 7. God *l.* a cheerful giver
3 John 9. *l.* to have preeminence
Rev. 22. 15. whosoever *l.* and maketh a lie
2 Sam. 1. 23. *lovely*, Sol. 5. 16. Ezek. 33. 32.
Phil. 4. 8.
Ps. 88. 18. *lover*, Tit. 1. 8. Ps. 38. 11. Hos. 2. 5.
2. Tim. 3. 2, 4.
LOW, Deut. 28. 43. Ezek. 17. 24.
Job 40. 12. look on every one that is proud and
bring him *l.*
Ps. 49. 2. both *l.* and high, rich and
136. 23. remembered us in our *l.* estate
Prov. 29. 23. man's pride shall bring him *l.*
Is. 26. 5. the lofty city, he layeth it *l.*, 25. 12.
32. 19. city shall be *l.* in a *l.* place
Luke 1. 48. he hath regarded the *l.* estate
52. exalted them of *l.* degree, Job 5. 11. Ezek.
21. 26. Jas. 1. 9, 10.
3. 5. every mountain and hill shall be brought *l.*
Ps. 63. 9. *lower* parts of the earth, 139. 15. Is.
44. 23. Eph. 4. 9.
Eph. 4. 2. *lowliness*, Phil. 2. 3.
138. 6. yet hath he respect to *lowly*
Prov. 3. 34. he giveth grace unto *l.*
11. 2. with *l.* is wisdom
Mat. 11. 29. learn of me, I am meek and *l.*
LUCRE, filthy, 1 Tim. 3. 3, 8. Tit. 1. 7. 1 Pet. 5. 2.
LUKEWARM, thou art, Rev. 3. 16.
LUMP, Is. 38. 21. Rom. 9. 21; 11. 16. 1 Cor.
5. 6, 7. Gal. 5. 9.
LUST, Ex. 15. 9. Ps. 78. 18. Jas. 4. 2.
Ps. 81. 12. up to their own hearts' *l.*
Mat. 5. 28. looketh on woman to *l.*
Rom. 7. 7. I had not known *l.* except the law
1 Cor. 10. 6. not *l.* after evil things
Gal. 5. 16. shall not fulfil *l.* of flesh
1 Thes. 4. 5. not in the *l.* of concupiscence
1 John 2. 16. *l.* of the flesh, and *l.* of
Gal. 5. 17. flesh *lusteth* against Spirit
Mark 4. 19. *lusts* of other things
John 8. 44. *l.* of your father ye will do
Rom. 6. 12. should obey it in the *l.*
13. 14. for the flesh, to fulfil the *l.*
24. crucified flesh with affections and *l.*
1 Tim. 6. 9. foolish and hurtful *l.*
2 Tim. 2. 22. flee youthful *l.*: but follow
3. 6. laden with sins, led away with divers *l.*
Tit. 2. 12. denying ungodliness and worldly *l.*
3. 3. divers *l.* and pleasures
Jas. 4. 3. consume it on your *l.*
1 Pet. 2. 11. abstain from fleshly *l.*
4. 2. no longer live to the *l.* of men
2 Pet. 3. 3. walking after own *l.*, Jude 16, 18.

M

MAD, Deut. 28. 34. 1 Sam. 21. 13.
Jer. 50. 38. they are *m.* upon idols
Hos. 9. 7. prophet is a fool, spiritual man is *m.*
John 10. 20. he hath a devil and is *m.*

Acts 26. 11. exceedingly *mad* against
24. much learning doth make thee *m.*
Deut. 28. 28. *madness*, Eccl. 1. 17; 2. 12; 9. 3;
10. 13. Zech. 12. 4. Luke 6. 11. 2 Pet. 2. 16.
MADE, Ex. 2. 14. 2 Sam. 13. 6.
Ps. 104. 24. in wisdom hast thou *m.* them all
139. 14. I am . . . wonderfully *m.*
Prov. 16. 4. Lord *m.* all things for
John 1. 3. all things were *m.* by him
Rom. 1. 3. Christ, *m.* of the seed of David
20. being understood by things that are *m.*
1 Cor. 1. 30. Christ . . . who of God is *m.* unto us
9. 22. *m.* all things to all men
Gal. 4. 4. *m.* of a woman, *m.* under law
Phil. 2. 7. *m.* in the likeness of men
MAGNIFY, Josh. 3. 7. 1 Chr. 29. 25.
Job 7. 17. man, that thou shouldest *m.*
Ps. 34. 3. *m.* the Lord with me
69. 30. *m.* him with thanksgiving
Is. 42. 21. *m.* the law, and make it
Luke 1. 46. my soul doth *m.* Lord
Acts 10. 46. spake with tongues, *m.* God
Gen. 19. 19. *magnified* thy mercy
2 Sam. 7. 26. let thy name be *m.* for
Ps. 35. 27. let Lord be *m.*, 40. 16; 70. 4.
138. 2. hast *m.* thy word above
Acts 19. 17. name of Lord Jesus was *m.*
Phil. 1. 20. Christ be *m.* in my body
MAID, Gen. 16. 2. Deut. 22. 14. Job 31. 1. Jer.
2. 32. Amos 2. 7. Zech. 9. 17.
MAJESTY, Dan. 4. 30, 36; 5. 18, 19. Job 40. 10.
Ps. 21. 5; 45. 3, 4.
1 Chr. 29. 11. thine, O Lord, is . . . *m.*
Ps. 29. 4. voice of Lord is full of *m.*
93. 1. (Lord) is clothed with *m.*, 104. 1.
145. 5. honour of thy *m.*
145. 12. glorious *m.* of his kingdom
Is. 2. 10. for glory of his *m.*, 19, 21.
Heb. 1. 3. right hand of *M.* on high
8. 1. throne of *M.* in heavens
2 Pet. 1. 16. eyewitnesses of his *m.*
Jude 25. to only wise God . . . be glory and *m.*
MAINTAIN my cause, 1 Ki. 8. 45. Ps. 9. 4;
140. 12. Job 13. 15.
Tit. 3. 8. careful to *m.* good works, 14.
Ps. 16. 5. thou *maintainest* my lot
MAKE, Gen. 1. 26; 3. 6, 21. Deut. 32. 35. 1 Cor.
4. 5. 1 Sam. 20. 38.
Job 4. 17. more pure than *maker*?
32. 22. my *m.* would soon take me
35. 10. where is God my *m.*
36. 3. ascribe righteousness to my *m.*
Prov. 14. 31. reproacheth his *m.*, 17. 5.
22. 2. Lord is the *m.* of them all
Is. 17. 7. day shall man look to his *m.*
22. 11. ye have not looked to the *m.* thereof
45. 9. woe to him striveth with *m.*
51. 13. forgettest the Lord thy *m.*
54. 5. thy *m.* is thy husband; the
Heb. 11. 10. builder and *m.* is God
MALE and female, Gen. 1. 27. Num. 5. 3. Mal.
1. 14. Mat. 19. 4. Gal. 3. 28.
MALICE, leaven of, 1 Cor. 5. 8.
1 Cor. 14. 20. in *m.* be children, but in
Eph. 4. 31. put away . . . with all *m.* Col. 3. 8.
Tit. 3. 3. living in *m.* and envy   [1 Pet. 2. 1.
MAMMON, Mat. 6. 24. Luke 16. 9.
MAN, Gen. 1. 26, 27. 2 Ki. 9. 11.
Job 4. 17. shall . . . *m.* be more just than God?
7. 17. what is *m.* thou shouldest be mindful of
him
11. 12. vain *m.* would be wise
14. 1. *m.* born of woman is of few days

Job 15. 14. What is *man*, that he should be clean?
25. 4. How can *m*. be justified with God?
6. much less *m*. that is a worm
Ps. 8. 4. what is *m*. that thou art mindful
10. 18. *m*. of earth may no more oppress
25. 12. what *m*. is he that feareth Lord
49. 12. *m*. being in honour abideth not
90. 3. thou turnest *m*. to destruction
104. 23. *m*. goeth forth to his work
118. 6. not fear; what can *m*. do
144. 3. what is *m*. that thou takest knowledge of
him; or son of *m*.
Prov. 20. 24. *m*.'s goings are of Lord
Eccl 6. 10. it is known that it is *m*.
7. 29. God made *m*. upright, but
12. 5. *m*. goeth to his long home
Is. 2. 22. cease ye from *m*. whose
Zech. 13. 7. awake against the *m*. that
Mat. 4. 4. *m*. shall not live by bread
26. 72. I know not the *m*., 74.
John 7. 46. never *m*. spake like this *m*.
Rom. 6. 6. old *m*. crucified with him
7. 22. delight in law of God after inward *m*.
1 Cor. 2. 11. what *m*. knoweth the things of a *m*.
save the spirit of *m*.
14. natural *m*. receiveth not things
11. 8. *m*. not of woman, but woman of *m*.
15. 47. first *m*. is of the earth earthy; second *m*.
2 Cor. 4. 16. though outward *m*. perish, yet
inward *m*. is renewed
Eph. 4. 22. put off . . . the old *m*. which
24. put on new *m*., Col. 3. 9, 10.
1 Pet. 3. 4. be the hidden *m*. of heart
Ex. 15. 3. Lord is *a man* of war
Num. 23. 19. God is not—that he
Is. 47. 3. I will not meet thee as—
53. 3.—of sorrows and acquainted
Jer. 15. 10. borne me—of strife and
31. 22. a woman shall compass—
Mat. 8. 9. I am—under authority
16. 26. what shall—give in exchange
John 3. 3. except—be born again, 5.
Acts 10. 26. I myself also am—
2 Cor. 12. 2. I knew—in Christ, 3.
Phil. 2. 8. in fashion as—he humbled
Mat. 16. 24. *if any man*, John 6. 51; 7. 17, 37.
Rom. 8. 9. 2 Cor. 5. 17. Gal. 1. 9. Rev. 22. 19.
Ps. 39. 5. *every man*, Prov. 19. 6. Mic. 4. 4; 7. 2.
Gal. 6. 4. Col. 1. 28. Heb. 2. 9.
87. 4. *this man*, Is. 66. 2. Mic. 5. 5. Luke 19. 14.
John 7. 46. Jas. 1. 26.
Prov. 1. 5. *a wise man* will hear
9. 8. rebuke—and he will love thee
14. 16.—feareth and departeth
Eccl. 2. 14.—eyes are in his head
10. 2.—heart is at his right hand
Jer. 9. 23. let not—glory in wisdom
Jas. 3. 13. who is—and endued with
Deut. 33. 1. *man of God*, Judg. 13. 6, 8. 2 Ki.
1. 9, 13. 1 Tim. 6. 11. 2 Tim. 3. 17.
MANDRAKES, Gen. 30. 14. Sol. 7. 13.
MANIFEST, Eccl. 3. 18. 1 Cor. 15. 27.
John 14. 21. *m*. myself to him, 22.
1 Cor. 4. 5. make *m*. counsels of hearts
Gal. 5. 19. works of the flesh are *m*.
1 Tim. 3. 16. God was *m*. in the flesh
1 John 3. 10. in this children of God are *m*.
Mark 4. 22, nothing hid . . . not be *manifested*
John 2. 11. forth his glory, and his
17. 6. I have *m*. thy name unto men
1 John 3. 5. was *m*. to take away sin, 8.
4. 9. in this was *m*. the love of God
Luke 8. 17. *made manifest*, John 3. 21. 1. Cor.

3. 13. 2 Cor. 4. 10; 5. 11. Eph. 5. 13.
Rom. 8. 19. *manifestation* of sons of God
1 Cor. 12. 7. *m*. of the Spirit is given
MANIFOLD mercies, Neh. 9. 19, 27.
Ps. 104. 24. how *m*. are thy works
Amos 5. 12. I know your *m*. transgressions
Luke 18. 30. *m*. more in this present
Eph. 3. 10. known by the church *m*. wisdom of God
1 Pet. 1. 6. in heaviness through *m*. temptations
4. 10. as good stewards of *m*. grace of God
MANNA, Ex. 16. 15. Num. 11. 6. Deut. 8. 3, 16.
Josh. 5. 12. Neh. 9. 20. Ps. 78. 24. John 6. 31,
Rev. 2. 17. give to eat of hidden *m*.   [49, 58.
MANNER, 1 Sam. 8. 9, 11. Is. 5. 17. Jer. 22. 21.
1 Thes. 1. 5, 9. 1 John 3. 1. *manners*, 2 Ki.
17. 34. Acts 13. 18. 1 Cor. 15. 33. Lev.
20. 23. Heb. 1. 1.
MANSIONS in my Father's house, John 14. 2.
MARK, set me as a, Job 7. 20; 16. 12. Lam. 3. 12.
Ezek. 9. 4. set *m*. on the foreheads, Rev.
13. 16, 17; 14. 9; 19. 20.
Phil. 3. 14. I press toward the *m*.
Ps. 37. 37. *m*. perfect man   [14. Jer. 2. 22.
130. 3. if thou shouldest *m*. iniquity, Job 10.
Rom. 16. 17. *m*. them which cause divisions
Gal. 6. 17. bear in my body *marks*
MARRIAGE, MARRIED, MARRY, Gen. 38. 8.
Deut. 25. 5.
Mat. 22. 2. king made a *m*. for his son
25. 10. that were ready went into *m*.
John 2. 1. there was a *m*. in Cana, 2.
Heb. 13. 4. *m*. is honourable in all
Rev. 19. 7. *m*. of Lamb is come, 9.
Jer. 3. 14. I am *married* to you, saith Lord
Luke 14. 20. I have *m*. a wife, and
Is. 62. 5. as a young man *marrieth* a virgin
1 Cor. 7. 9. better to *marry* than to burn
1 Tim. 4. 3. forbidding to *m*. and
5. 14. that younger women *m*. and
MARROW, to bones, Prov. 3. 8.
Job 21. 24. bones moistened with *m*.
Ps. 63. 5. soul is satisfied as with *m*.
Is. 25. 6. feast of fat things full of *m*.
Heb. 4. 12. dividing . . . joints and *m*.
MARTYR, Acts 22. 20. Rev. 2. 13; 17. 6.
MARVEL not, Eccl. 5. 8. John 3. 7; 5. 28. **Acts**
3. 12. 1 John 3. 13.
Ps. 48. 5. and so they *marvelled*, Mat. 8. 27;
9. 8, 33; 21. 20; 22. 22. Luke 1. 63. Acts 2. 7;
4. 13.
Mat. 8. 10. Jesus *m*. Mark 6. 6.
Job 5. 9. doeth *marvellous* things
10. 16. shewed thyself *m*. upon me
Ps. 17. 7. shew thy *m*. kindness, 31. 21.
98. 1. done *m*. things, Mic. 7. 15.
1 Pet. 2. 9. out of darkness into his *m*. light
1 Chr. 16. 12. remember his *m*. works, Ps. 9. 1;
105. 5.
Ps. 139. 14. *m*. are thy works, Rev. 15. 3.
MASTER, Is. 24. 2. Mal. 1. 6; 2. 12.
John 3. 10. art thou a *m*. of Israel
13. 13. ye call me *M*. and Lord
14. if I . . . your Lord and *M*. have washed your
Rom. 14. 4. to his own *m*. he standeth
Eccl. 12. 11. *masters* of assemblies
Mat. 6. 24. no man can serve two *m*.
23. 10. neither be ye called *m*.
Col. 4. 1. *m*. give your servants, Eph. 6. 9.
Jas. 3. 1. be not many *m*.
1 Cor. 3. 10. as a wise *masterbuilder*
MATTER, Ex. 18. 22; 23. 7. 1 Sam. 10. 16.
Job 19. 28; 32. 18. Ps. 45. 1. Dan. 7. 28.
Acts 8. 21. part nor lot in this *m*.   [2 Cor. 9. 5.

Job 33. 13. account of *matters*
Ps. 131. 1. exercise myself in great *m.*
1 Pet. 4. 15. busybody in other men's *m.*
MEAN, what, Ex. 12. 26. Deut. 6. 20; 29. 24.
   Josh. 4. 6, 21. Ezek. 17. 12. Acts 17. 20;
   21. 13. Ezek. 37. 18. Jonah 1. 6.
Ps. 49. 7. by any *means,* Jer. 5. 31. 1 Cor. 9. 22.
   Phil. 3. 11. 1 Thes. 3. 5.
Gen. 50. 20. but God *meant* it unto good
MEASURE, Lev. 19. 35. Deut. 25. 15.
Job 11. 9. the *m.* is longer than earth
Ps. 39. 4. to know . . . the *m.* of my days
Is. 27. 8. in *m.* when it shooteth
Jer. 30. 11. correct thee in *m.,* 46. 28.
Mat. 7. 2. with what *m.* ye mete
23. 32. fill up the *m.* of your fathers
John 3. 34. giveth not Spirit by *m.*
2 Cor. 1. 8. were pressed out of *m.*
12. 7. lest I be exalted above *m.*
Eph. 4. 7. according to the *m.* of . . . Christ
13. to the *m.* of . . . fulness of Christ
Rev. 11. 1. *m.* the temple of God
MEAT, Job 6. 7. Ps. 42. 3; 69. 21.
Ps. 104. 27. give them their *m.,* 145. 15.
111. 5. given *m.* to them that fear him
Prov. 6. 8. provideth her *m.,* 30. 25.
Hos. 11. 4. I laid *m.* unto them
Hab. 1. 16. portion is fat . . . *m.* plenteous
3. 17. the fields shall yield no *m.*
Hag. 2. 12. his skirt touch . . . *m.* shall it
Mal. 1. 12. his *m.* is contemptible
Mat. 6. 25. is not life more than *m.*
John 4. 32. I have *m.* to eat ye know not of
34. my *m.* is to do the will of him
6. 27. labour not for *m.* which perisheth
55. my flesh is *m.* indeed, and my blood
Rom. 14. 15. destroy not him with thy *m.*
17. kingdom of God is not *m.* and drink
1 Cor. 8. 8. *m.* commendeth us not to God
10. 3. did all eat same spiritual *m.*
6. 13. *meats* for belly, belly for *m.*
MEDDLE, 2 Ki. 14. 10. Prov. 17. 14; 20. 3, 19;
   24. 21; 26. 17.
MEDIATOR, is not *m.* of one, Gal. 3. 20.
Gal. 3. 19. by angels in hand of a *m.*
1 Tim. 2. 5. one *m.* between God and men
Heb. 8. 6. *m.* of a better covenant
9. 15. *m.* of new testament
12. 24. *m.* of new covenant   [Ezek. 47. 12.
MEDICINE, Prov. 17. 22. Jer. 30. 13; 46. 11.
MEDITATE, Isaac went to, Gen. 24. 63.
Josh. 1. 8. *m.* (in the law) day and night, Ps. 1. 2;
   119. 15, 23, 48, 78, 148.
Ps. 63. 6. *m.* on thee in the night watches
77. 12. I will *m.* also of all thy work, 143. 5.
Is. 33. 18. thine heart shall *m.* terror
Luke 21. 14. not *m.* before what ye shall answer
1 Tim. 4. 15. *m.* upon these things
Ps. 5. 1. consider my *meditation*
49. 3. *m.* of my heart shall be of understanding
104. 34. my *m.* of him shall be sweet
119. 97. (thy law) is my *m.* all the day
99. thy testimonies are my *m.*
MEEK, Moses was very, Num. 12. 3.
Ps. 22. 26. *m.* shall eat and be satisfied
25. 9. *m.* will he guide in judgment
37. 11. *m.* shall inherit the earth
147. 6. the Lord lifteth up the *m.*
149. 4. beautify *m.* with salvation
Is. 11. 4. reprove with equity for *m.* of
29. 19. *m.* shall increase their joy
61. 1. preach good tidings to *m.*
Amos 2. 7. that turn aside way of *m.*

Mat. 5. 5. blessed are the *meek*
11. 29. I am *m.* and lowly in heart
1 Pet. 3. 4. ornament of *m.* and quiet spirit
Ps. 45. 4. because of truth and *meekness*
Zeph. 2. 3. seek righteousness, seek *m.*
1 Cor. 4. 21. come . . . in the spirit of *m.*
2 Cor. 10. 1. beseech you by *m.* . . . of Christ
Gal. 5. 23. fruit of Spirit is . . . *m.*
6. 1. restore such an one in the spirit of *m.*
Eph. 4. 2. walk with lowliness, *m.*
1 Tim. 6. 11. follow after love, patience, *m.*
2 Tim. 2. 25. in *m.* instructing those
Tit. 3. 2. shewing all *m.* to all men
Jas. 1. 21. receive with *m.* engrafted word
3. 13. shew . . . works with *m.* of wisdom
1 Pet. 3. 15. reason of hope . . . with *m.*
MEET, help, for him, Gen. 2. 18.
Job 34. 31. it is *m.* to be said to God
Mat. 3. 8. fruits *m.* for repentance, Acts 26. 20.
1 Cor. 15. 9. not *m.* to be called an apostle
Col. 1. 12. *m.* to be partakers of inheritance
2 Tim. 2. 21. vessel . . . *m.* for master's use
Heb. 6. 7. bringeth forth herbs *m.* for them by
   whom it is dressed
Is. 47. 3. I will not *m.* thee as a man
Hos. 13. 8. I will *m.* them as a bear
Amos 4. 12. prepare to *m.* thy God
1 Thes. 4. 17. caught up to *m.* Lord
Is. 64. 5. thou *meetest* him that rejoiceth
MELODY in heart to Lord, Eph. 5. 19.
MEMBER, body not one, 1 Cor. 12. 14.
Jas. 3. 5. tongue is a little *m.* and
Ps. 139. 16. and in thy book all my *members* were
   written
Mat. 5. 29. one of thy *m.* perish
Rom. 6. 13. neither yield your *m.* as
7. 23. I see another law in my *m.*
12. 5. every one *m.* one of another
1 Cor. 6. 15. your bodies *m.* of Christ
12. 12. body is one, and hath many *m.*
Eph. 4. 25. we are *m.* one of another
5. 30. *m.* of his body, his flesh and
Col. 3. 5. mortify your *m.* on earth
MEMORY cut off, Ps. 109. 15.
Ps. 145. 7. utter *m.* of thy great goodness
Prov. 10. 7. *m.* of the just is blessed
Eccl. 9. 5. *m.* of them is forgotten
Is. 26. 14. made all their *m.* to perish
1 Cor. 15. 2. if ye keep in *m.* what I
Ex. 3. 15. my *memorial* to all generations
13. 9. be for *m.* between thine eyes
17. 14. write this for a *m.* in book
Hos. 12. 5. God of hosts; Lord is his *m.*
Mat. 26. 13. be told for a *m.* of her
Acts 10. 4. alms are come up for a *m.* before God
MEN, Gen. 32. 28; 42. 11.
Ps. 9. 20. know themselves to be but *m.*
17. 14. *m.* which are thy hand
82. 7. ye shall die like *m.* and fall
Eccl. 12. 3. strong *m.* shall bow
Is. 31. 3. Egyptians are *m.,* not God, Ezek. 28. 2.
Hos. 6. 7. they like *m.* have transgressed
Mat. 7. 12. ye would that *m.* should do to you
Eph. 6. 6. *m.* pleasers, Col. 3. 22. 1 Thes. 2. 4.
MENSTRUOUS, Is. 30. 22. Lam. 1. 17. Ezek.
   18. 6. come near a *m.* woman
MENTION, Ex. 23. 13. Job 28. 18.
Ps. 71. 16. make *m.* of thy righteousness
Is. 26. 13. by thee only will we make *m.* of
62. 6. ye that make *m.* of the Lord
Rom. 1. 9. make *m.* of you in my prayers, Eph.
   1. 16. 1 Thes. 1. 2. Philem. 4.
MERCHANT, Hos. 12. 7. Mat. 13. 45.

Is. 23. 18. *merchandise* . . . be holiness, Mat.
  22. 5. John 2. 16. 2 Pet. 2. 3.
MERCY, Gen. 19. 19; 39. 21.
Ex. 34. 7. keep *m.* for thousands, Deut. 7. 9.
  1 Ki. 8. 23. Neh. 1. 5; 9. 32. Dan. 9. 4.
Num. 14. 18. Lord is . . . of great *m.*
Ps. 23. 6. goodness and *m.* shall follow
25. 10. all paths of Lord are *m.* and
33. 18. them that hope in his *m.,* 147. 11.
52. 8. I trust in the *m.* of God
57. 3. God shall send forth his *m.*
66. 20. not turned away . . . his *m.*
69. 13. in multitude of thy *m.,* 16.
86. 5. plenteous in *m.* to all, 103. 8.
101. 1. I will sing of *m.* and
103. 17. *m.* of the Lord is from everlasting
106. 1. *his m. endureth for ever,* 107. 1; 118. 1;
  136. 1-26. 1 Chr. 16. 34, 41. 2 Chr. 5. 13;
  7. 3, 6; 20. 21. Ezra 3. 11. Jer. 33. 11.
Prov. 16. 6. by *m.* and truth iniquity is purged
20. 28. *m.* and truth preserve king
Hos. 6. 6. I desired *m.* and not sacrifice
10. 12. reap in *m.* 12. 6. keep *m.*
14. 3. in thee fatherless findeth *m.*
Jonah 2. 8. they . . . forsake their own *m.*
Mic. 6. 8. to do justly, and love *m.*
7. 18. because he delighteth in *m.*
20. and the *m.* to Abraham
Luke 1. 50. *m.* is on them that fear
78. through tender *m.* of our God
Rom. 9. 23. on vessels of *m.* prepared
15. *m.* on whom I will have *m.*
11. 31. through your *m.* they obtain *m.*
15. 9. might glorify God for his *m.*
2 Cor. 4. 1. as we have received *m.*
1 Tim. 1. 13. I obtained *m.* because I did it
  ignorantly, 2. grace, *m.,* and peace, Tit. 1. 4.
  2 John 3. Jude 2.
2 Tim. 1. 18. that he may find *m.* in
Heb. 4. 16. we may obtain *m.* and
Jas. 2. 13. shall have judgment without *m.* that
  shewed no *m.*; and *m.* rejoiceth
3. 17. full of *m.* and good
5. 11. Lord is very pitiful and of tender *m.*
Gen. 32. 10. not worthy of least of all the *mercies*
1 Chr. 21. 13. great are his *m.*
Is. 55. 3. sure *m.* of David, Acts 13. 34.
Dan. 9. 9. to the Lord our God belong *m.* and
Rom. 12. 1. I beseech you by *m.* of God
2 Cor. 1. 3. Father of *m.* and God of
Col. 3. 12. put on bowels of *m.*
Ps. 25. 6. *tender mercies,* 40. 11; 51. 1; 77. 9;
  79. 8; 103. 4; 119. 77, 156; 145. 9.
Prov. 12. 10.—of wicked are cruel
Gen. 19. 19. *thy mercy(ies),* Num. 14. 19. Neh.
  13. 22. Ps. 5. 7; 6. 4; 13. 5; 25. 7; 31. 7, 16;
  33. 22; 36. 5; 44. 26; 85. 7; 86. 13; 90. 14;
  94. 18; 108. 4; 57. 10; 119. 64; 143. 12.
Ex. 34. 6. Lord God *merciful* and gracious,
  2 Chr. 30. 9. Neh. 9. 17, 31. Ps. 103. 8. Joel
  2. 13. Jonah 4. 2.
Ps. 18. 25. with *m.* thou wilt shew thyself *m.*
37. 26. he is ever *m.* and lendeth
117. 2. his *m.* kindness
Is. 57. 1. *m.* men are taken away
Jer. 3. 12. I am *m.,* saith the Lord
Mat. 5. 7. blessed are the *m.*
Luke 6. 36. be . . . *m.,* as your Father also is *m.*
Heb. 2. 17. a *m.* and faithful high priest
8. 12. I will be *m.* to their unrighteousness
MERRY, be, Luke 12. 19; 15. 23–32.
Jas. 5. 13. is any *m.?* let him sing
Is. 24. 7. *merryhearted,* Prov. 17.22. Eccl. 9. 7.

Prov. 15. 13.
MESSAGE from God, Judg. 3. 20. Hag. 1. 13.
  1 John 1. 5; 3. 11.
Job. 33. 23. if there be a *messenger*
Is. 42. 19. who is blind or deaf, as my *m.*
Mal. 2. 7. he is the *m.* of the Lord
Is. 14. 32. one answer *messengers* of nation
44. 26. that performeth counsel of his *m.*
MESSIAH(IAS), Dan. 9. 25, 26. John 1. 41; 4. 25.
MIDST, Ps. 22. 14; 46. 5; 110. 2. Prov. 4. 21.
  Is. 4. 4; 41. 18. Ezek. 43. 7, 9. Joel 2. 27.
  Zeph. 3. 5, 12, 15, 17. Phil. 2. 15. Rev. 1. 13;
  5. 6.   [them
Rev. 7. 17. Lamb in *m.* of the throne shall feed
MIGHT, Gen. 49. 3. Num. 14. 13.
Deut. 6. 5. love Lord with all thy . . . *m.*
2 Ki. 23. 25. turned to Lord with *m.*
2 Chr. 20. 12. no *m.* against this great company
Ps. 76. 5. none of men of *m.* found
145. 6. men speak of the *m.* of thy terrible acts
Eccl. 9. 10. findeth to do, do it with thy *m.*
Is. 40. 29. to them that have no *m.*
Zech. 4. 6. not by *m.* . . . but by Spirit
Eph. 3. 16. strengthened with *m.*
6. 10. be strong . . . in power of his *m.*
Col. 1. 11. strengthened with all *m.*
Deut. 7. 23. with *mighty* destruction
10. 17. a great God, a *m.* and a
Judg. 5. 23. help of Lord against the *m.*
Ps. 24. 8. Lord strong and *m.,* . . . *m.* in battle
Is. 5. 22. *m.* to drink wine, men of
Jer. 32. 19. great in counsel, *m.* in work
1 Cor. 1. 26. not many *m.* are called
2 Cor. 10. 4. weapons . . . but *m.* through God
Ps. 93. 4. Lord on high is *mightier*
Acts 18. 28. *mightily,* Col. 1. 29.
19. 20. so *m.* grew word of God
MILK, Gen. 18. 8; 49. 12.
Job 10. 10. hast poured me out as *m.*
Sol. 4. 11. and *m.* under thy tongue
5. 1. drunk my wine with my *m.*
Is. 55. 1. buy wine and *m.* without
Joel 3. 18. the hills shall flow with *m.*
Heb. 5. 12. such as have need of *m.*
1 Pet. 2. 2. desire sincere *m.* of word
MIND, Gen. 26. 35. Lev. 24. 12.
1 Chr. 28. 9. serve him with . . . willing *m.*
Neh. 4. 6. people had a *m.* to work
Is. 26. 3. whose *m.* is stayed on thee
Luke 12. 29. neither be ye of doubtful *m.*
Acts 17. 11. with readiness of *m.*
20. 19. serving Lord with all humility of *m.*
Rom. 7. 25. with *m.* I serve law of God
8. 7. carnal *m.* is enmity against [1 Cor. 2. 16.
11. 34. who hath known the *m.* of the Lord,
1 Cor. 1. 10. joined together in the same *m.*
2 Cor. 8. 12. be first a willing *m.* it is
13. 11. be of one *m.,* live in peace, Phil. 1. 27;
  2. 2; 4. 2. 1 Pet. 3. 8.
2 Tim. 1. 7. given (spirit) of . . . sound *m.*
Tit. 1. 15. their *m.* and conscience
1 Pet. 5. 2. not for filthy lucre, but ready *m.*
Rom. 8. 5. of flesh do *m.* things of
12. 16. *m.* not high things, but condescend
Phil. 3. 16. walk by same rule, *m.* same thing
19. glory in their shame, *m.* earthly things
2 Cor. 3. 14. *minds* were blinded
Phil. 4. 7. God . . . keep your hearts and *m.*
Heb. 10. 16. in their *m.* will I write
12. 3. wearied and faint in your *m.*
2 Pet. 3. 1. stir up your pure *m.* by
Rom. 8. 6. to be carnally *minded* is death;
  but to be spiritually *m.* is life and peace

Rom. 11. 20. be not high*minded* but fear
15. 5. God grant you to be like*m*.
Tit. 2. 6. men exhort to be sober *m*.
Ps. 8. 4. thou art *mindful* of him?
111. 5. ever *m*. of his covenant, 1 Chr. 16. 15.
    Ps. 105. 8.
MINISTER, Josh. 1. 1. Luke 4. 20.
Mat. 20. 26. let him be your *m*.
Acts 26. 16. to make thee a *m*. and
Rom. 13. 4. he is the *m*. of God to thee
15. 8. Christ was *m*. of circumcision
16. be *m*. of Jesus Christ to the Gentiles
Eph. 3. 7. was made a *m*. according
4. 29. may *m*. grace unto hearers
Rom. 15. 25. *m*. to saints, Heb. 6. 10.
15. 27. *m*. to them in carnal
2 Cor. 9. 10. *m*. bread for your food
1 Pet. 4. 11. if any man *m*., let him
1 Tim. 4. 6. shalt be a good *m*. of Jesus
Heb. 8. 2. *m*. of the sanctuary
Ps. 103. 21. *ministers* of his that do
104. 4. his *m*. a flaming fire, Heb. 1. 7.
Joel 1. 9. the priests, the Lord's *m*.
Luke 1. 2. eyewitnesses and *m*. of the
Rom. 13. 6. they are God's *m*.
1 Cor. 3. 5. *m*. by whom ye believed
4. 1. account of us as *m*. of Christ
2 Cor. 3. 6. made us able *m*. of new testament
6. 4. approved ourselves . . . to of God
11. 23. are they *m*. of Christ? so
Mat. 4. 11. *ministered*, Luke 8. 3. Gal. 3. 5.
    Heb. 6. 10. 2 Pet. 1. 11.
Heb. 1. 14. all *ministering* spirits   [9. 1, 13.
Luke 1. 23. *ministration*, Acts 6. 1. 2 Cor. 3. 7, 8;
Acts 6. 4. give ourselves . . . to *ministry*
20. 24. finish *m*. which I have received
2 Cor. 4. 1. seeing we have this *m*.
5. 18. given to us *m*. of reconciliation
6. 3. that the *m*. be not blamed
Col. 4. 17. take heed to *m*. that thou
1 Tim. 1. 12. putting me into the *m*.
2 Tim. 4. 5. make full proof of thy *m*.
Heb. 8. 6. obtained more excellent *m*.
MIRACLE, Mark 6. 52; 9. 39. Luke 23. 8. John
    2. 11; 6. 26; 10. 41; 11. 47. Acts 2. 22; 4. 16;
    6. 8; 19. 11. 1 Cor. 12. 10, 28, 29. Gal. 3. 5.
    Heb. 2. 4.
MIRTH, Prov. 14. 13. Eccl. 2. 2; 7. 4. Is. 24. 8,
    11. Jer 7. 34; 16. 9.; 25. 10. Hos. 2. 11.
    Ezek. 21. 10.
MISCHIEF, Gen. 42. 4; 44. 29.
Job 15. 35. they conceive *m*.
Ps. 10. 14. thou beholdest *m*. and
23. 3. *m*. is in their hearts, 10. 7.
36. 4. he deviseth *m*. upon his bed
94. 20. which frameth *m*. by a law
Prov. 10. 23. sport to a fool to do *m*.
11. 27. he that seeketh *m*. it shall
24. 16. wicked shall fall into *m*.
MISERY, Job 3. 20. Lam. 3. 19.
Judg. 10. 16. his soul grieved for *m*.
Prov. 31. 7. drink and remember his *m*. no more
Eccl. 8. 6. the *m*. of man is great   [ways
Rom. 3. 16. destruction and *m*. are in their
Job 16. 2. *miserable* comforters are ye all
1 Cor. 15. 19. are of all men most *m*.
Rev. 3. 17. knowest not thou art . . . *m*.
MOCK when fear cometh, Prov. 1. 26.
Prov. 14. 9. fools make a *m*. at sin
1 Ki. 18. 27. Elijah *mocked* them
2 Chr. 36. 16. *m*. messengers of God
Prov. 17. 5. whoso *mocketh* the poor
30. 17. eye that *m*. at his father

Prov. 20. 1. wine is a *mocker*, strong drink is raging
Is. 28. 22. be not *mockers*, lest your bands
Jude 18. there should be *m*. in last
MODERATION known to all, Phil. 4. 5.
MODEST apparel, 1 Tim. 2. 9.
MOMENT, Ex. 33. 5. Is. 27. 3.
Num. 16. 21. consume them in a *m*. 45.
Job 20. 5. joy of hypocrite but for a *m*.
Ps. 30. 5. his anger endureth but a *m*.
Is. 26. 20. hide thyself, as it were, for a little *m*.
54. 7. for a small *m*. have I forsaken
1 Cor. 15. 52. in a *m*., in the twinkling
MONEY, Gen. 23. 9; 31. 15.
Eccl. 7. 12. wisdom is defence, and *m*.
10. 19. *m*. answereth all things
Is. 55. 1. he that hath no *m*., come
2. wherefore do ye spend *m*. for that
Mic. 3. 11. the prophets divine for *m*.
Acts 8. 20. thy *m*. perish with thee
1 Tim. 6. 10. love of *m*. root of all evil
MORROW, Ex. 8. 23; 16. 23.
Prov. 27. 1. boast not thyself of to *m*.
Is. 22. 13. to *m*. we die, 1 Cor. 15. 32.
Mat. 6. 34. take no thought for *m*.
Jas. 4. 14. know ye not what shall be on *m*.
MORTAL man be just, Job 4. 17.
Rom. 6. 12. let not sin reign in your *m*. body
8. 11. raised Christ . . . quicken *m*. bodies
1 Cor. 15. 53. *m*. put on immortality
2 Cor. 5. 4. *mortality* swallowed up
Col. 3. 5. *mortify* your members on earth
MOTE, Mat. 7. 3, 4, 5. Luke 6. 41.
MOTH, Job 4. 19; 27. 18. Ps. 39. 11. Is. 50. 9;
    51. 8. Hos. 5. 12. Mat. 6. 19, 20. Luke 12. 33.
MOTHER, Gen. 3. 20; 21. 21. Judg. 5. 7. 2 Sam.
    20. 19. 1 Ki. 3. 27. Gal. 4. 26.
Ps. 27. 10. when father and *m*. forsake me
71. 6. out of my *m*.'s bowels, 139. 13.
Mat. 12. 49. behold my *m*. Mark 3. 34, Luke
John 19. 25-27, his [Jesus'] *m*.   [8. 21.
MOVE, Ex. 11. 7. Judg. 13. 25.
Acts 17. 28. in him we live and *m*.
20. 24. none of these things *m*. me
Ps. 15. 5. never be *moved*, 21. 7; 46. 5; 55. 22;
    62. 2, 6; 66. 9; 112. 6; 121. 3. Prov. 12. 3.
Col. 1. 23. be not *m*. away from hope
1 Thes. 3. 3. no man be *m*. by these
Heb. 12. 28. kingdom which cannot be *m*.
2 Pet. 1. 21. spake as . . . *m*. by the Holy Ghost
Rom. 7. 5. when in flesh, *motions* of sins
MOURN, Neh. 8. 9. Job 5. 11.
Is. 61. 2. to comfort all that *m*.
Mat. 5. 4. blessed are they that *m*.
Jas. 4. 9. be afflicted and *m*. and
Mat. 11. 17. we have *mourned* unto you
1 Cor. 5. 2. and have not rather *m*.
Eccl. 12. 5. *mourners* go about streets
Is. 57. 18. restore comforts to him and to his *m*.
Ps. 30. 11. turned . . . my *mourning* to dancing
Is. 61. 3. to give . . . the oil of joy for *m*.
Jer. 9. 17. call for the *m*. women
31. 13. I will turn their *m*. into joy
Joel 2. 12. with fasting and with weeping and
    with *m*.
Jas. 4. 9. laughter be turned to *m*.   [21. 16.
MOUTH of babes and sucklings, Ps. 8. 2. Mat.
Ps. 37. 30. *m*. of righteous speaketh wisdom
Prov. 10. 14. *m*. of foolish is near destruction
10. 31. *m*. of just bringeth forth wisdom
12. 6. *m*. of upright shall deliver
14. 3. in *m*. of fools is a rod of pride
15. 2. *m*. of fools poureth out foolishness
18. 7. a fool's *m*. is his destruction

Prov. 22. 14. *mouth* of strange women is a pit
Lam. 3. 38. out of *m.* of the Most High pro-
ceedeth not evil and good
Mat. 12. 34. out of abundance of heart *m.*
Luke 21. 15. will give you a *m.* and   [speaketh
Rom. 10. 10. with the *m.* confession is made
Lam. 3. 29. putteth *his mouth* in dust
Mal. 2. 7. they should seek law at—
Ps. 17. 3. *my mouth* not transgress
39. 1. I will keep—with a bridle
49. 3.—shall speak of wisdom
51. 15.—shall shew thy praise, 63. 5.
71. 15.—shall shew thy righteousness
Eph. 6. 19. that I may open—boldly
Ps. 81. 10. open *thy mouth* wide
103. 5. who satisfieth—with good
Prov. 31. 8. open—for the dumb in
Eccl. 5. 6. suffer not—to cause thy flesh
MULTITUDE, Gen. 16. 10; 28. 3. Ex. 12. 38;
23. 2. Num. 11. 4.
Job 32. 7. *m.* of years should teach wisdom
Ps. 5. 7. in *m.* of thy mercy
10. cast out in *m.* of their transgressions
33. 16. no king saved by the *m.* of
51. 1. according unto the *m.* of thy tender
mercies, 106. 7, 45.
94. 19. in the *m.* of my thoughts
Prov. 10. 19. in *m.* of words wanteth not sin
11. 14. in *m.* of counsellors safety, 15. 22; 24. 6.
Eccl. 5. 3. *m.* of business, . . . *m.* of words
Jas. 5. 20. hide *m.* of sins, 1 Pet. 4. 8.
MURDER, Rom. 1. 29. Mat. 15. 19. Gal. 5. 21.
Rev. 9. 21.
Job 24. 14. *murderer* rising with light
John 8. 44. (devil) was a *m.* from the
Hos. 9. 13. bring forth children to *m.*
1 Pet. 4. 15. none suffer as a *m.*
MURMUR, Deut. 1. 27. Ps. 106. 25. Jude 16.
MUSE, Ps. 39. 3; 143. 5.   [Ex. 16. 7. Phil. 2. 14.
MUSIC, Lam. 3. 63. Amos 6. 5.
MUSTARD seed, Mat. 13. 31; 17. 20.
MUZZLE, Deut. 25. 4. 1 Cor. 9. 9. 1 Tim. 5. 18.
MYSTERY of kingdom, Mark 4. 11.
Rom. 11. 25. not . . . be ignorant of *m.*
16. 25. according to revelation of *m.*
1 Cor. 2. 7. wisdom of God in a *m.*
Eph. 1. 9. made known *m.* of, 3. 3.
3. 4. my knowledge in *m.* of Christ
9. fellowship of the *m.*
6. 19. make known *m.* of gospel
Col. 1. 26. *m.* which hath been hid
27. glory of this *m.* among Gentiles
2. 2. acknowledgment of *m.* of God
4. 3. open a door to speak *m.* of Christ
2 Thes. 2. 7. *m.* of iniquity doth
1 Tim. 3. 9. holding *m.* of the faith
16. great is the *m.* of godliness
Rev. 1. 20. write the *m.* of seven stars
10. 7. *m.* of God should be finished
1 Cor. 4. 1. stewards of the *mysteries* of God
13. 2. prophecy and understand all *m.*
14. 2. in the spirit he speaketh *m.*

N

NAIL, Judg. 4. 21; 5. 26.
Is. 22. 23. fasten him as a *n.* in a
Zech. 10. 4. out of him came the *n.*
Eccl. 12. 11. *nails* fastened by the masters
NAKED, Gen. 2. 25; 3. 7, 11.
Ex. 32. 25. when Moses saw the people were *n.*

2 Chr. 28. 19. he made Judah *naked*
Job 1. 21. *n.* came I out of my mother's womb
Mat. 25. 36. *n.* and ye clothed me, 38.
1 Cor. 4. 11. we hunger and thirst and are *n.*
2 Cor. 5. 3. clothed we shall not be found *n.*
Heb. 4. 13. all things are *n.* and open
Rev. 16. 15. keepeth his garments, lest he walk *n.*
NAME, Ex. 34. 14. Lev. 18. 21.
Ps. 20. 1. the *n.* of God of Jacob
109. 13. let their *n.* be blotted
Prov. 10. 7. the *n.* of the wicked shall rot
22. 1. a good *n.* is rather to be chosen than great
riches
Eccl. 7. 1. good *n.* better than precious ointment
Is. 55. 13. shall be to the Lord for *n.*
56. 5. a *n.* better than of sons and
62. 2. thou shalt be called by new *n.*
Jer. 13. 11. for a people, and for a *n.*
32. 20. made thee *n.* as at this day
33. 9. shall be to me a *n.* of joy, a
Mic. 4. 5. walk in the *n.* of the Lord
Mat. 10. 41. receive prophet in *n.* of
Luke 6. 22. cast out your *n.* as evil
Rom. 2. 24. *n.* of God is blasphemed
Col. 3. 17. do all in the *n.* of Lord
2 Tim. 2. 19. that nameth *n.* of Christ
Heb. 1. 4. obtained more excellent *n.*
1 Pet. 4. 14. reproached for *n.* of Christ
1 John 3. 23. believe on *n.* of Son, 5. 13.
Rev. 2. 17. new *n.* written, which no man
3. 1. thou hast a *n.* that thou livest
12. write on him the *n.* of my God, and the *n.* of
the city of my God . . . and will write upon
him my new *n.*
14. 1. his Father's *n.* written in their foreheads,
22. 4.
Eph. 1. 21. every *n.* that is named
Phil. 2. 9. a *n.* above every *n.*
Ps. 76. 1. *his name* is great in Israel
72. 17.—shall endure for ever
106. 8. he saved them for—'s sake
Prov. 30. 3. what is—and what is his
Is. 9. 6.—shall be called Wonderful
Zech. 14. 9. shall be one Lord and—one
John 20. 31. ye might have life through—
Rev. 3. 5. confess—before my father
13. 17. or the number of—15. 2.
Ex. 23. 21. *my name* is in him
3. 15. and this is—for ever,
Is. 48. 9. for—'s sake I defer anger
Ezek. 20. 9. wrought for—sake, 14, 22.
Mal. 1. 14.—is dreadful among the
2. 2. lay it to heart, to give glory to—
Mat. 10. 22. hated of all for—'s sake
John 14. 13. ask in—15. 16; 16. 23, 26.
16. 24. asked nothing in—
Acts 9. 15. a chosen vessel to bear—
Rev. 2. 3. for—'s sake hast laboured, and
13. holdest fast—3. 8. not denied—
2 Chr. 14. 11. in *thy name* we go
Ps. 8. 1. how excellent is—in all, 9.
48. 10. according to—so is thy
75. 1.—is near, thy wondrous works declare
138. 2. praise— . . . thy word above all—
Sol. 1. 3.—is as ointment poured
Is. 26. 8. desire of our soul is to—
64. 7. none that calleth on—   [9. Dan. 9. 6.
Jer. 14. 7. do it for—'s sake, 21. Jos. 7. 9. Ps. 79.
Mic. 6. 9. man of wisdom shall see—
John 17. 12. I kept them in—26.
Ex. 23. 13. no mention of the *name(s)* of other
gods, Deut. 12. 3. Ps. 16. 4.
28. 12. Aaron bear their *n.* before Lord

Ps. 49. 11. call lands after their *names*
Luke 10. 20. *n.* written in heaven
Rev. 3. 4. hast a few *n.* in Sardis
NARROW, 1 Ki. 6. 4. Prov. 23. 27. Is. 28. 20;
    49. 19. Mat. 7. 14.
NATION, Gen. 15. 14; 21. 13.
Gen. 20. 4. wilt slay a righteous *n.*
Num. 14. 12. make of thee a greater *n.*
2 Sam. 7. 23. what one *n.* . . . . is like thy people
Ps. 33. 12. blessed is *n.* whose God is Lord
147. 20. not dealt so with any *n.*
Is. 1. 4. Ah sinful *n.*, a people laden
2. 4. *n.* shall not lift sword against *n.*
49. 7. him whom the *n.* abhorreth
66. 8. shall a *n.* be born at once
Mat. 24. 7. *n.* rise against *n.*, Mark 13. 8.
Luke 7. 5. he loveth our *n.* and he hath built
Acts 10. 35. in every *n.* he that feareth (God)
Rom. 10. 19. by a foolish *n.* I will
Phil. 2. 15. in midst of a crooked . . . *n.*
1 Pet. 2. 9. ye are an holy *n.*, Ex. 19. 6.
Rev. 5. 9. redeemed us . . . out of every *n.*
Gen. 10. 32. *nations*, 17. 4, 6, 16.
Ps. 9. 20. *n.* may know themselves
113. 4. Lord high above all *n.*
Is. 2. 2. all *n.* shall flow unto it
40. 17. *n.* before him are as nothing
55. 5. *n.* that knew thee not shall
Jer. 4. 2. *n.* shall bless themselves in
Zech. 2. 11. many *n.* be joined to Lord
Mat. 25. 32. before him be gathered all *n.*
Acts 14. 16. suffered all *n.* to walk in
Rev. 21. 24. *n.* of them that are saved
NATURE, Rom. 2. 27. Jas. 3. 6.
Rom. 1. 26. that which is against *n.*
2. 14. do by *n.* things contained in
1 Cor. 11. 14. doth not *n.* itself teach
Gal. 4. 8. them which by *n.* are no gods
Eph. 2. 3. by *n.* the children of wrath
Heb. 2. 16. took not on him *n.* of angels
2 Pet. 1. 4. partakers of divine *n.*
Deut. 34. 7. *natural(ly)*, Rom. 1. 26, 27, 31;
    11. 21, 24. 1 Cor. 2. 14; 15. 44, 46. 2 Tim. 3. 3.
    Jas. 1. 23. 2 Pet. 2. 12. Phil. 2. 20. Jude 10.
NAUGHT, it is, saith the buyer, Prov. 20. 14.
Jas. 1. 21. superfluity of *naughtiness*
1 Sam. 17. 28. the *n.* of thine heart
NEAR, Ps. 119. 151; 148. 14. Is. 55. 6; 57. 19.
    Jer. 12. 2.
NECESSARY, Job 23. 12. Acts 13. 46; 15. 28.
    Tit. 3. 14. Heb. 9. 23.
Rom. 12. 13. *necessity(ies)*, Acts 20. 34. 1 Cor.
    9. 16. 2 Cor. 6. 4; 9. 7; 12. 10. Philem. 14.
    Heb. 9. 16.
NECK, Sol. 1. 10. Is. 48. 4. Rom. 16. 4.
Acts 15. 10. yoke on *n.* of disciples
2 Ki. 17. 14. hardened their *necks*, Neh.
    9. 16, 17, 29. Jer. 7. 26; 19. 15.
NEED of all these things, Mat. 6. 32.
Mat. 9. 12. they that are whole *n.* not
Luke 15. 7. just persons which *n.* no repentance
Heb. 4. 16. grace to help in time of *n.*
1 Pet. 1. 6. if *n.* be, ye are in heaviness
1 John 2. 27. *n.* not that any man
Rev. 3. 17. rich . . . and have *n.* of nothing
21. 23. the city had no *n.* of sun
22. 5. and they *n.* no candle
Eph. 4. 28. give to him that *needeth*
Luke 10. 42. one thing is *needful*
Ps. 9. 18. *needy* not alway forgotten
72. 12. he shall deliver the *n.*
113. 7. lifteth *n.* out of dunghill
Is. 14. 30. *n.* shall lie down in safety

NEGLECT to hear, Mat. 18. 17.
1 Tim. 4. 14. *n.* not the gift that is in thee
Heb. 2. 3. if we *n.* so great salvation
NEIGH, Jer. 5. 8; 8. 16; 13. 27.
NEIGHBOUR, Ex. 3. 22; 11. 2.
Ex. 20. 16. not bear false witness against thy *n.*
    Deut. 5. 20.
Lev. 19. 13. thou shalt not defraud thy *n.*
17. thou shalt in any wise rebuke thy *n.*
18. shalt love thy *n.* as thyself, Mat. 19. 19;
    22. 39. Rom. 13. 9. Gal. 5. 14. Jas. 2. 8.
Ps. 15. 3. nor doeth evil to his *n.*
Prov. 27. 10. better is a *n.* that is near
Jer. 31. 34. teach no more every man his *n.*
Luke 10. 29. who is my *n.*, 36.
Rom. 13. 10. love worketh no ill to his *n.*
15. 2. let every one of us please his *n.*
NEST, Job 29. 18. Ps. 84. 3. Prov. 27. 8. Is.
    10. 14. Hab. 2. 9. Mat. 8. 20.
NET, Job 18. 8; 19. 6. Ps. 9. 15; 25. 15; 31. 4;
    35. 7, 8; 57. 6; 66. 11. Is. 51. 20. Hab.
    1. 15, 16. Mat. 13. 47. Ps. 141. 10. Eccl. 7. 26.
NEW, Lord make *n.* thing, Num. 16. 30.
Judg. 5. 8. chose *n.* gods, Deut. 32. 17.
Eccl. 1. 9. and there is no *n.* thing under the sun,
    10.   [2 Pet. 3. 13. Rev. 21. 1.
Is. 65. 17. *n.* heavens and a *n.* earth, 66. 22.
Jer. 31. 22. created a *n.* thing in earth
Ezek. 11. 19. a *n.* spirit within you, 36. 26.
Mat. 9. 16. putteth *n.* cloth unto an old garment
17. neither put *n.* wine in old bottles
13. 52. bringeth forth . . . things *n.* and old
Mark 1. 27. what *n.* doctrine is this, Acts 17. 19.
John 13. 34. a *n.* commandment I give unto you,
    1 John 2. 7, 8.
Acts 17. 21. to hear some *n.* thing
1 Cor. 5. 7. that ye may be a *n.* lump
2 Cor. 5. 17. if any man be in Christ, he is a *n.*
    creature; behold, all things are become *n.*
Gal. 6. 15. neither circumcision nor uncircum-
    cision, but a *n.* creature
Eph. 4. 24. put on *n.* man, Col. 3. 10.
1 Pet. 2. 2. as *n.* born babes desire
Rev. 2. 17. a *n.* name written, which no man
    knoweth, 3. 12. Is. 62. 2.
5. 9. sung a *n.* song, 14. 3. Ps. 33. 3. Is. 42. 10.
Rom. 6. 4. should walk in *newness* of life
7. 6. we should serve in *n.* of spirit
NIGH, Lev. 25. 49. Num. 24. 17.
Deut. 4. 7. who hath God so *n.* unto
30. 14. word is very *n.* to thee, Rom. 10. 8.
Ps. 34. 18. Lord is *n.* them of broken heart
145. 18. Lord is *n.* them that call on
Mat. 15. 8. draweth *n.* unto me with their mouth
Eph. 2. 13. made *n.* by blood of Christ
17. peace to . . . them that were *n.*
NIGHT, Gen. 1. 5, 14; 26. 24.
Ex. 12. 42. this is that *n.* of the Lord
Ps. 19. 2. *n.* unto *n.* sheweth knowledge
30. 5. weeping may endure for a *n.*
139. 11. *n.* shall be light about me
Is. 21. 11. Watchman, what of *n.*?
Jer. 14. 8. turneth aside to tarry for a *n.*
Luke 6. 12. continued all *n.* in prayer
12. 20. this *n.* thy soul be required
John 9. 4. *n.* cometh when no man
Rom. 13. 12. *n.* is far spent; day is at hand
Rev. 21. 25. shall be no *n.* there, 22. 5.
Ps. 134. 1. *by night*, Sol. 3. 1. John 3. 2; 7. 50;
    19. 39.
Job 35. 10. giveth songs *in the night*
Ps. 16. 7. instruct me—seasons
42. 8.—his song shall be with me

Ps. 77. 6. I call to remembrance my song *in the night*
119. 55. I have remembered thy name . . . —
Is. 30. 29. ye shall have a song as—
59. 10. stumble at noonday as—
John 11. 10. if a man walk—he stumbleth
1 Thes. 5. 7. sleep—and . . . are drunken—
NOBLE, Ezra 4. 10. Esth. 6. 9. Jer. 2. 21. Acts 17. 11.
1 Cor. 1. 26. not many *n.* are called
Ex. 24. 11. *nobles,* Num. 21. 18.
Neh. 13. 17. contended with *n.* of Judah
Ps. 149. 8. bind . . . their *n.* with fetters
Prov. 8. 16. by me princes rule, and *n.*
Eccl. 10. 17. when thy king is son of *n.*
Luke 19. 12. *nobleman,* John 4. 46, 49.
NOISOME, Ps. 91. 3. Rev. 16. 2.
NOSE, Prov. 30. 33. Is. 65. 5.
Is. 2. 22. breath in *nostrils,* Lam. 4. 20.
NOTHING, Gen. 11. 6. Ex. 9. 4; 12. 10. Num. 6. 4; 16. 26. Josh. 11. 15.
2 Sam. 24. 24. which doth cost me *n.*
1 Ki. 8. 9. *n.* in ark save the two tables
Neh. 8. 10. send to them for whom *n.* is prepared
Job 6. 21. for now ye are *n.*
8. 9. of yesterday, and know *n.*
26. 7. hangeth earth on *n.*
34. 9. it profiteth a man *n.*
Ps. 17. 3. tried me, and shalt find *n.*
49. 17. when he dieth, shall carry *n.* away
119. 165. *n.* shall offend them
Prov. 13. 4. sluggard desireth and hath *n.*
7. maketh himself rich, yet hath *n.*
Is. 40. 17. nations before him as *n.*
Jer. 10. 24. lest thou bring me to *n.*
Lam. 1. 12. is it *n.* to you, all ye that
Luke 1. 37. with God *n.* shall be impossible
John 14. 30. prince of this world . . . hath *n.* in me
15. 5. without me ye can do *n.*
1 Cor. 1. 19. bring to *n.* understanding
13. 2. I am *n.,* 2 Cor. 12. 11.
2 Cor. 6. 10. having *n.* yet possessing all
1 Tim. 6. 7. we brought *n.* into world
NOUGHT, Gen. 29. 15. Deut. 13. 17.
Is. 41. 12. shall be as nothing and as a thing of *n.*
49. 4. I have spent my strength for *n.*
52. 3. sold yourselves for *n.,* Ps. 44. 12.
Amos 6. 13. rejoice in a thing of *n.*
Luke 23. 11. Herod . . . set him at *n.*
Acts 19. 27. in danger to be set at *n.*
Rom. 14. 10. why dost thou set at *n.* thy brother
NOVICE, not a, lest, 1 Tim. 3. 6.
NUMBER our days, Ps. 90. 12.
Is. 65. 12. I will *n.* you to the sword
Rev. 7. 9. multitude no man could *n.*
13. 17. the *n.* of his name, 18.
Is. 53. 12. *numbered* with transgressors
Hos. 1. 10. children of Israel as sand of the sea which cannot be . . . *n.,* Jer. 33. 22.
Job 14. 16. thou *numberest* my steps
Ps. 71. 15. I know not the *numbers*
NURSE, 1 Thes. 2. 7. Is. 49. 23.

O

OATH, Gen. 24. 8; 26. 3, 28.
1 Sam. 14. 26. people feared the *o.*
2 Sam. 21. 7. Lord's *o.,* that was between
2 Chr. 15. 15. all Judah rejoiced at *o.*
Eccl. 8. 2. in regard of *o.* of God
Ezek. 16. 59. despised the *o.,* 17. 18, 19.
Luke 1. 73. *o.* which he sware to our

Heb. 6. 16. *oath* for confirmation is . . . **end**
Jas. 5. 12. swear not by heaven, **neither by** earth, neither by any other *o.*
OBEY, Gen. 27. 8. Ex. 5. 2.
Deut. 11. 27, 28. blessing if ye *o.* . . . and a curse if ye will not *o.* commandments
13. 4. keep his commandments and *o.* his voice
Josh. 24. 24. his voice will we *o.*
1 Sam. 12. 14. serve him and *o.* his voice
15. 22. to *o.* is better than sacrifice
Jer. 7. 23. *o.* my voice, 11. 4, 7.
Acts 5. 29. ought to *o.* God rather than men
Rom. 2. 8. contentious, and do not *o.* truth
6. 16. servants ye are to whom ye *o.*
Eph. 6. 1. children, *o.* your parents in Lord,
Col. 3. 22. servants, *o.* in all things   [Col. 3. 20.
2 Thes. 1. 8. that *o.* not the gospel
3. 14. if any man *o.* not our word
Tit. 3. 1. in mind to . . . *o.* magistrates
Heb. 5. 9. salvation to all them that *o.*
13. 17. *o.* them that have rule over
1 Pet. 3. 1. if any *o.* not the word
Rom. 6. 17. *obeyed* from heart that
1 Pet. 3. 6. Sarah *o.* Abraham
Is. 50. 10. *obeyeth* voice, Jer. 11. 3.
1 Pet. 1. 22. purified your souls in *obeying* truth
Rom. 1. 5. received grace . . . for *obedience*
5. 19. by *o.* of one many made righteous
16. 19. your *o.* is come abroad
26. made known to all nations for *o.* of faith
1 Cor. 14. 34. (women) are commanded to be under *o.*
2 Cor. 7. 15. he remembereth the *o.* of you
10. 5. every thought to *o.* of Christ
6. when your *o.* is fulfilled
Heb. 5. 8. learned *o.* by things suffered
1 Pet. 1. 2. sanctification of Spirit to *o.* [*obedient*
Ex. 24. 7. all Lord said will we do, and be
Num. 27. 20. children of Israel may be *o.*
Deut. 4. 30. turn and be *o.* to his voice
8. 20. perish; because ye would not be *o.* to voice
2 Sam. 22. 45. strangers . . . shall be *o.*
Prov. 25. 12. so is wise reprover upon an *o.* ear
Is. 1. 19. if ye be . . . . *o.* ye shall eat the
42. 24. neither were they *o.* to his law
Acts 6. 7. priests were *o.* to the faith
Rom. 15. 18. to make Gentiles *o.* by word
2 Cor. 2. 9. whether ye be *o.* in all
Eph. 6. 5. servants, be *o.* to . . . masters
Phil. 2. 8. he became *o.* unto death
Tit. 2. 9. exhort servants to be *o.*
1 Pet. 1. 14. as *o.* children, not
OBSCURITY, Is. 29. 18; 58. 10.
OBSERVE, Ex. 12. 17; 34. 11.
Ps. 107. 43. who is wise and will *o.*
119. 34. *o.* it with my whole heart
Prov. 23. 26. let thine eyes *o.* my ways
Jonah 2. 8. that *o.* lying vanities
Mat. 28. 20. teaching them to *o.* all things
Gal. 4. 10. ye *o.* days and months
Luke 17. 20. not with *observation*
Ex. 12. 42. a night to be much *observed*
Mark 6. 20. Herod feared John and *o.*
10. 20. all these I *o.* from my youth
OBSTINATE, Deut. 2. 30. Is. 48. 4.
OBTAIN favour of Lord, Prov. 8. 35.
Is. 35. 10. *o.* joy and gladness, 51. 11.
Luke 20. 35. worthy to *o.* that world
1 Cor. 9. 24. so run, that ye may *o.*
Heb. 4. 16. may *o.* mercy and find
11. 35. might *o.* better resurrection
Jas. 4. 2. ye desire to have, and cannot *o.*
Hos. 2. 23. her that had not *obtained* mercy

Acts 26. 22. having *obtained* help of God
Rom. 11. 7. the election hath *o.* it
Eph. 1. 11. we have *o.* inheritance
1 Tim. 1. 13. I *o.* mercy, because, 16.
Heb. 1. 4. *o.* a more excellent name
6. 15. endured, he *o.* the promise
8. 6. *o.* a more excellent ministry
9. 12. *o.* eternal redemption for us
OCCASION, Gen. 43. 18. Judg. 14. 4.
2 Sam. 12. 14. given great *o.* to enemies
Jer. 2. 24. in her *o.* who can turn
Rom. 7. 8. *o.* by commandment, 11.
14. 13. *o.* to fall in brother's way
2 Cor. 11. 12. I may cut off *o.* . . . desire *o.*
Gal. 5. 13. use not liberty for *o.* to the flesh
1 Tim. 5. 14. give none *o.* to adversary
1 John 2. 10. none *o.* of stumbling
Job 33. 10. he findeth *occasions* against me
OCCUPY, Luke 19. 13. Heb. 13. 9.
ODOUR, Phil. 4. 18. Rev. 5. 8.
OFFENCE, 1 Sam. 25. 31. Is. 8. 14.
Mat. 16. 23. thou art an *o.* unto me
18. 7. woe . . . because of offences! for offences
    must come; woe . . . by whom the *o.* cometh
Acts 24. 16. conscience void of *o.*
Rom. 5. 15. not as *o.* so is free gift
17. by one man's *o.* death reigned
9. 33. rock of *o.*, 1 Pet. 2. 8. Is. 8. 14.
14. 20. for him that eateth with *o.*
2 Cor. 6. 3. giving no *o.* in any thing
11. 7. have I committed an *o.*
Gal. 5. 11. then is *o.* of cross ceased
Phil. 1. 10. without *o.* till day of Christ
Eccl. 10. 4. yielding pacifieth great *offences*
Rom. 4. 25. delivered for our *o.* and
16. 17. cause divisions and *o.*
OFFEND, not any more, Job 34. 31.
Ps. 73. 15. *o.* against generation
119. 165. nothing shall *o.* them
Jer. 2. 3. all that devour him shall *o.*
50. 7. we *o.* not because they have
Hos. 4. 15. harlot, yet let not Judah *o.*
Mat. 5. 29. if right eye *o.* thee, 30.
13. 41. gather out . . . all things that *o.*
17. 27. yet lest we should *o.* them, go
18. 6. whoso shall *o.* one of these little ones, 8, 9.
    if hand, foot, eye *o.*, Mark 9. 43–47.
Jas. 2. 10. *o.* in one point is guilty
3. 2. in many things we *o.* all
Prov. 18. 19. brother *offended* is harder to be won
Mat. 11. 6. blessed . . . not be *o.* in   [14. 27.
26. 33. though all be *o.* . . . . I never be *o.* Mark
Mark 4. 17. immediately they are *o.*
Rom. 14. 21. brother . . . . *o.* or is made weak
2 Cor. 11. 29. who is *o.* and I burn not
Is. 29. 21. make a man *offender* for
OFFER, Gen. 31. 54. Lev. 1. 3.
Mat. 5. 24. then come and *o.* thy gift
Heb. 13. 15. *o.* the sacrifice of praise
Rev. 8. 3. *o.* it with prayers of saints
Phil. 2. 17. *offered* upon the sacrifice and service
2 Tim. 4. 6. I am now ready to be *o.*
Heb. 9. 14. *o.* himself without spot
28. Christ was once *o.* to bear sins
11. 4. by faith Abel *o.* to God
17. Abraham . . . *o.* up Isaac
Ps. 50. 23. whoso *offereth* praise glorifieth
Eph. 5. 2. an *offering* to God for us
Heb. 10. 5. sacrifice and *o.* thou wouldest not
14. by one *o.* he hath perfected for ever
OFFSCOURING, Lam. 3. 45.
1 Cor. 4. 13. we are the *o.* of all things
OFFSPRING, Acts 17. 28. Rev. 22. 16.

OFTEN reproved hardeneth, Prov. 29. 1.
Mal. 3. 16. spake *o.* one to another
Mat. 23. 37. how *o.* would I have gathered
1 Cor. 11. 26. as *o.* as ye eat this bread
Phil. 3. 18. of whom I have told you *o.*
Heb. 9. 25. should offer himself *o.*
OIL, Gen. 28. 18. Ex. 25. 6.
Ps. 45. 7. with *o.* of gladness, Heb. 1. 9.
89. 20. with my holy *o.* I have
92. 10. be anointed with fresh *o.*, 23. 5.
104. 15. *o.* to make his face shine
141. 5. it shall be an excellent *o.*
Is. 61. 3. *o.* of joy for mourning
Mic. 6. 7. will Lord be pleased with . . . rivers of *o.*
Mat. 25. 3. foolish . . . took no *o.* with them
4. wise took *o.* in their vessels
8. give us of your *o.*; for our lamps
Luke 7. 46. head with *o.* didst not anoint
10. 34. pouring in *o.* and wine
OINTMENT, Ps. 133. 2. Prov. 27. 9, 16. Eccl.
    7. 1; 10. 1. Sol. 1. 3. Is. 1. 6. Amos 6. 6.
    Mat. 26. 7, 9, 12. Mark 14. 3. Luke 7. 37.
OLD, Gen. 5. 32; 18. 12, 13.   [John 12. 5.
Ps. 37. 25. been young, and now am *o.*
Prov. 22. 6. when he is *o.* he will not
Jer. 6. 16. ask for the *o.* paths
1 Cor. 5. 7. purge out the *o.* leaven
2 Cor. 5. 17. *o.* things are passed away
2 Pet. 1. 9. purged from his *o.* sins
Gen. 15. 15. *old age*, Judg. 8. 32. Job 30. 2. Ps.
    71. 9; 92. 14. Is. 46. 4.
Rom. 6. 6. *old man*, Eph. 4. 22. Col. 3. 9.
Prov. 17. 6. of *old men*, 20. 29.
OMEGA, Alpha and, Rev. 1. 8, 11; 21. 6.; 22. 13.
ONE, Gen. 2. 24. Mat. 19. 5.
Ps. 89. 19. help on *o.* that is mighty
Eccl. 4. 9, 12. two better than *o.*
Jer. 3. 14. *o.* of a city, and two of a
Mat. 19. 17. none good but *o.*, God
1 Cor. 8. 4. none other God but *o.*, 6.
10. 17. we being many are *o.* bread and *o.* body;
    . . . partakers of *o.* bread
Gal. 3. 20. not mediator of *o.*, but God is *o.*
1 John 5. 7. these three are *o.*
Ps. 27. 4. *one thing* have I desired of Lord
Mark 10. 21.—thou lackest, go . . . sell . . . and
Luke 10. 42. but—is needful   [give to poor
Phil. 3. 13. this—I do, forgetting
OPEN thou my lips, Ps. 51. 15.
Ps. 81. 10. *o.* thy mouth wide
119. 18. *o.* thou mine eyes, that I
Prov. 31. 8. *o.* thy mouth for dumb
Sol. 5. 2. *o.* to me, my sister, my
Is. 22. 22. shall *o.* and none shall shut
42. 7. to *o.* blind eyes, Ps. 146. 8.
Ezek. 16. 63. never *o.* thy mouth any
Mat. 25. 11. Lord, *o.* to us, Luke 13. 25.
Acts 26. 18. to *o.* their eyes, and
Col. 4. 3. *o.* to us door of utterance
Rev. 5. 2. worthy to *o.* book, 3, 9.
Gen. 3. 7. eyes of them both were *opened*
Is. 35. 5. eyes of the blind shall be *o.*
53. 7. he *o.* not his mouth
Mat. 7. 7. knock, and it shall be *o.*, Luke 11. 9.
Acts 14. 27. *o.* door of faith to Gentiles
16. 14. (Lydia,) whose heart Lord *o.*
1 Cor. 16. 9. great door and effectual is *o.*
2 Cor. 2. 12. door *o.* unto me of the Lord
Heb. 4. 13. naked and *o.* to eyes of
Ps. 104. 28. *openest* thy hand, 145. 16.
OPERATION, Ps. 28. 5. Is. 5. 12. Col. 2. 12.
    1 Cor. 12. 6.
OPINION, Job 32. 6, 10. 1 Ki. 18. 21.

OPPORTUNITY, Mat. 26. 16. Gal. 6. 10.
Phil. 4. 10. Heb. 11. 15.
OPPOSE, 2 Tim. 2. 25. 2 Thes. 2. 4.
OPPRESS, Ex. 3. 9. Judg. 10. 12.
Ex. 22. 21. neither vex a stranger nor *o.* him, 23. 9.
Lev. 25. 14. *o.* not one another, 17.
Job 10. 3. is it good . . . thou shouldest *o.*
Ps. 10. 18. that man . . . may no more *o.*
Prov. 22. 22. neither *o.* afflicted in the gate
Zech. 7. 10. *o.* not the widow, nor
Mal. 3. 5. witness against those that *o.*
Jas. 2. 6. do not rich men *o.* you?
Ps. 9. 9. Lord a refuge for *oppressed*
10. 18. judge the fatherless and *o.*
Eccl. 4. 1. tears of such as were *o.*
Is. 1. 17. relieve the *o.*, 58. 6.
Ezek. 18. 7. not *o.*, 16. hath *o.*, 12; 22. 29.
Acts 10. 38. healing all that were *o.* of devil
Prov. 22. 16. *oppresseth*, 14. 31; 28. 3.
Deut. 26. 7. Lord heard our voice, and looked on
our . . . *oppression*
2 Ki. 13. 4. the Lord saw the *o.*
Ps. 12. 5. for *o.* of poor
62. 10. trust not in *o.* and become
Eccl. 7. 7. *o.* maketh a wise man mad
Is. 5. 7. judgment, but behold *o.*
33. 15. he that despiseth gain of *oppressions*
Ps. 72. 4. *oppressor*, 54. 3; 119. 121. Prov. 3. 31;
28. 16. Eccl. 4. 1. Is. 3. 12; 14. 4; 51. 13.
ORACLES of God, Acts 7. 38. Rom. 3. 2. Heb.
5. 12. 1 Pet. 4. 11.
ORDAIN, Is. 26. 12. Tit. 1. 5.
Ps. 8. 2. hast thou *ordained* strength
132. 17. *o.* a lamp for mine anointed
Is. 30. 33. Tophet is *o.* of old, for
Jer. 1. 5. *o.* thee a prophet to nations
Hab. 1. 12. *o.* them for judgment
Acts 13. 48. as were *o.* to eternal life
14. 23. *o.* them elders in every church
17. 31. judge by that man whom he *o.*
Rom. 7. 10. commandment which was *o.*
13. 1. powers that be are *o.* of God
Gal. 3. 19. *o.* by angels in hand of
Eph. 2. 10. God before *o.* that we should
1 Tim. 2. 7. *o.* a preacher and an
Heb. 5. 1. *o.* for men in things pertaining to God
Jude 4. *o.* to this condemnation
ORDER, Gen. 22. 9. Job 33. 5.
Job 23. 4. *o.* cause before him, 13. 18.
Ps. 40. 5. be reckoned up in *o.*
50. 21. set them in *o.* before thine eyes
1 Cor. 14. 40. all things done . . . in *o.*
Col. 2. 5. joying and beholding your *o.*
Tit. 1. 5. set in *o.* things wanting
2 Sam. 23. 5. everlasting covenant, *ordered*
Ps. 37. 23. steps of a good man are *o.*
ORDINANCE of God, Is. 58. 2. Rom. 13. 2.
1 Pet. 2. 13. submit to every *o.* of man
Neh. 10. 32. made *ordinances* for us
Is. 58. 2. ask of me the *o.* of justice
Jer. 31. 35. *o.* of moon and of stars
Ezek. 11. 20. keep mine *o.*, Lev. 18. 4, 30; 22. 9.
1 Cor. 11. 2.
Luke 1. 6. walking in all . . . *o.* of Lord
Eph. 2. 15. law . . . contained in *o.*
Col. 2. 14. handwriting of *o.* against
Heb. 9. 1. had *o.* of divine service.
ORNAMENTS, Ex. 33. 5. Prov. 1. 9; 25. 12.
Is. 49. 18; 61. 10. Jer. 2. 32. Ezek. 16. 7, 11.
1 Pet. 3. 4.
OUGHT ye to do, Mat. 23. 23. Jas. 3. 10.
OURS, Gen. 26. 20. Num. 32. 32.   [20. 14.
Mark 12. 7. inheritance shall be *o.* Luke

1 Cor. 1. 2. Christ our Lord, both theirs and *ours*
Tit. 3. 14. let *o.* learn to maintain
OUTCASTS of Israel, Ps. 147. 2. Is. 11. 12;
56. 8.
Is. 16. 3. hide the *o.* 4. let mine *o.* dwell with
27. 13. *o.* in land of Egypt, Jer. 30. 17.
OUTER (UTTER), Ezek. 46. 21; 47. 2. Mat. 8. 12;
22. 13; 25. 30.
OUTGOINGS, Josh. 17. 9. Ps. 65. 8.
OUTRAGEOUS, Prov. 27. 4.
OUTSIDE, Ezek. 40. 5. Mat. 23. 25.   [27. 5.
OUTSTRETCHED arm, Deut. 26. 8. Jer. 21. 5;
OUTWARD, 1 Sam. 16. 7. Rom. 2. 28. 2 Cor.
4. 16; 10. 7. 1 Pet. 3. 3.
Mat. 23. 28. *outwardly*, Rom. 2. 28.
OVEN, Ps. 21. 9. Hos. 7. 4. Mal. 4. 1.
OVERCHARGE, Luke 21. 34. 2 Cor. 2. 5.
OVERCOME, Gen. 49. 19. Num. 13. 30.
Sol. 6. 5. thine eyes . . . have *o.* me
John 16. 33. I have *o.* the world
1 John 2. 13. ye have *o.* wicked one, 14.
4. 4. ye are of God . . . and have *o.*
Rev. 17. 14. Lamb shall *o.* them
1 John 5. 4. born of God *overcometh* the world
Rev. 2. 7. to him that *o.* I will give
11. he that *o.* shall not be hurt of
3. 5. he that *o.* shall be clothed
12. him that *o.* will I make a pillar
21. him that *o.* will I grant to sit
OVERMUCH, Eccl. 7. 16; 2 Cor. 2. 7.
OVERPAST, Ps. 57. 1. Is. 26. 20.
OVERSEER, Prov. 6. 7. Acts 20. 28.
OVERSIGHT, Gen. 43. 12. 1 Pet. 5. 2.
OVERTAKE, Ex. 15. 9. Amos 9. 13. Hos. 2. 7.
Gal. 6. 1. 1 Thes. 5. 4.
OVERTHROW, Deut. 12. 3; 29. 23. Job 12. 19.
Ps. 140. 4, 11. Prov. 13. 6; 21. 12. Amos
4. 11. Acts 5. 39. 2 Tim. 2. 18.
OVERTURN, Ezek. 21. 27. Job 9. 5; 12. 15;
28. 9; 34. 25.
OVERWHELMED, Ps. 55. 5; 61. 2; 77. 3; 124. 4;
142. 3; 143. 4.
OVER WISE, neither make thyself, Eccl. 7. 16.
OWE, Rom. 13. 8. Mat. 18. 24, 28.
OWL, Job 30. 29. Ps. 102. 6. Is. 13. 21; 34. 11,
15; 43. 20. Mic. 1. 8.
OWN, Deut. 24. 16. Judg. 7. 2.
John 1. 11. his *o.* . . . *o.* received him not
1 Cor. 6. 19. ye are not your *o.*
10. 24. let no man seek his *o.*
Phil. 2. 4. look not every man on his *o.* things
OX knoweth his owner, Is. 1. 3; 11. 7. Prov. 7. 22;
14. 4; 15. 17.
Ps. 144. 14. *oxen*, Is. 22. 13. Mat. 22. 4. Luke
14. 19. John 2. 14. 1 Cor. 9. 9.

P

PACIFY, Esth. 7. 10. Prov. 16. 14.
Prov. 21. 14. gift in secret *pacifieth*
Eccl. 10. 4. yielding *p.* great offences
PAIN, Is. 21. 3; 26. 18; 66. 7. Jer. 6. 24. Mic.
4. 10. Rev. 21. 4.
Ps. 55. 4. my heart is sore *pained*, Is. 23. 5. Jer.
4. 19. Joel 2. 6.
Rev. 12. 2. travailing in birth and *p.*
Ps. 73. 16. *painfulness*, 2 Cor. 11. 27.
116. 3. *pains* of hell gat hold on me
Acts 2. 24. loosed the *p.* of death   [23. 40.
PAINTED, 2 Ki. 9. 30. Jer. 4. 30; 22. 14. Ezek.
PALACE, 1 Chr. 29. 19. Ps. 45. 8, 15. Sol.
8. 9. Is. 25. 2. Phil. 1. 13.

PALM tree, Ps. 92. 12. Sol. 7. 7.
PANT, Amos 2. 7. Ps. 38. 10; 42. 1; 119. 131. Is.
21. 4.
PARABLE, Ps. 49. 4; 78. 2. Prov. 26. 7, 9.
Ezek. 20. 49. Mic. 2. 4. Mat. 13. 3. Luke
5. 36; 13. 6; 21. 29.
PARADISE, (Eden) Gen. 2. 15. (heaven) Luke
23. 43. 2 Cor. 12. 4. Rev. 2. 7.
PARCHMENTS, 2 Tim. 4. 13.
PARDON our iniquity, Ex. 34. 9.
Ex. 23. 21. he will not *p*. your transgressions
Num. 14. 19. *p*. iniquity of people
1 Sam. 15. 25. *p*. my sin, 2 Ki. 5. 18.
2 Ki. 24. 4. which the Lord would not *p*.
2 Chr. 30. 18. the good Lord *p*.
Neh. 9. 17. a God ready to *p*.   [sion
Job 7. 21. why dost thou not *p*. my transgres-
Ps. 25. 11. for name's sake . . . *p*. my iniquity
Is. 55. 7. God . . . will abundantly *p*.
Jer. 5. 7. how shall I *p*. thee for this
33. 8. I will *p*. all their iniquities
50. 20. I will *p*. them whom I reserve
Is. 40. 2. cry . . . that her iniquity is *pardoned*
Mic. 7. 18. God like thee that *pardoneth*
PARENTS, Luke 2. 27; 8. 56.   [Mark 13. 12.
Mat. 10. 21. children rise up against their *p*.,
Luke 18. 29. no man hath left house, or *p*.
21. 16. ye shall be betrayed both by *p*.
Rom. 1. 30. disobedient to *p*., 2 Tim. 3. 2.
2 Cor. 12. 14. children ought not to lay up for *p*.,
but *p*. for children
1 Tim. 5. 4. learn to requite their *p*.
PART, it shall be thy, Ex. 29. 26.
Num. 18. 20. thy *p*. and inheritance
Ps. 5. 9. inward *p*. is wickedness
118. 7. Lord taketh my *p*. with them
Luke 10. 42. Mary hath chosen that good *p*.
Acts 8. 21. neither *p*. nor lot in this
1 Cor. 13. 9. know in *p*. and prophesy in *p*., 10.
PARTAKER with adulterers, Ps. 50. 18.
1 Cor. 9. 10. should be *p*. of his hope
10. 30. if I by grace be a *p*. why am I
1 Tim. 5. 22. be not *p*. of other men's sins
1 Pet. 5. 1. a *p*. of the glory . . . revealed
2 John 11. is *p*. of his evil deeds
Rom. 15. 27. *partakers* of their spiritual
1 Cor. 9. 13. wait at altar *p*. with altar
10. 17. *p*. of that one bread
21. *p*. of Lord's table
Eph. 5. 7. be not *p*. with
Heb. 3. 14. for we are made *p*. of Christ
6. 4. and were made *p*. of the Holy Ghost
12. 10. might be *p*. of his holiness
PARTIAL, Mal. 2. 9. Jas. 2. 4.
1 Tim. 5. 21. *partiality*, Jas. 3. 17.
PASS, Ex. 33. 19. Ezek. 20. 37. Zeph. 2. 2.
Zech. 3. 4. 2 Pet. 3. 10.   [might *p*. from him
Mark 14. 35. Jesus prayed that . . . the hour
Luke 16. 17. easier for heaven and earth to *p*.
than one tittle of law to fail
John 5. 24. is *passed* from death to life
Is. 43. 2. when thou *passest* through the waters I
will be with thee   [of this heritage
Mic. 7. 18. *passeth* by transgression of remnant
1 Cor. 7. 31. fashion of this world *p*.
Phil. 4. 7. peace of God *p*. all understanding
1 John 2. 17. world *p*. away and lust
PASSION, Acts 1. 3; 14. 15.
PASSOVER, Ex. 12. 11. Deut. 16. 2. Josh. 5. 11.
2 Chr. 30. 15; 35. 1, 11. Heb. 11. 28.
1 Cor. 5. 7. Christ our *p*. is sacrificed
PASTORS, Jer. 3. 15; 17. 16.
Eph. 4. 11. and some, *p*. and teachers

PASTURE, Ps. 23. 2; 95. 7. Is. 30. 23; 49. 9.
Ezek. 34. 14, 18. John 10. 9.
Ps. 74. 1. sheep of thy *p*., 79. 13. his *p*., 100. 3.
PATH, Num. 22. 24. Job 28. 7.
Ps. 16. 11. wilt shew me *p*. of life
27. 11. lead me in a plain *p*.
119. 35. go in *p*. of thy commandments
139. 3. thou compassest my *p*.
Prov. 4. 18. *p*. of just is as shining light
26. ponder the *p*. of thy feet
5. 6. lest thou ponder the *p*. of life
Is. 26. 7. thou dost weigh *p*. of just
Ps. 17. 4. kept me from the *paths* of destroyer
5. hold up my goings in thy *p*.
25. 10. all *p*. of the Lord are mercy
65. 11. and thy *p*. drop fatness
Prov. 3. 17. all her *p*. are peace
Is. 59. 7. destruction are in their *p*.
8. they have made them crooked *p*.
Hos. 2. 6. shall not find her *p*.
Mat. 3. 3. make his *p*. straight, Is. 40. 3.
Heb. 12. 13. make straight *p*. for feet
PATIENCE with me, Mat. 18. 26, 29.
Luke 8. 15. bring forth fruit with *p*.
21. 19. in your *p*. possess ye your souls
Rom. 5. 3. tribulation worketh *p*.
15. 4. that we through *p*. . . . might have hope
5. God of *p*. . . . grant you to be likeminded
2. Cor. 12. 12. wrought among you in all *p*.
Col. 1. 11. strengthened . . . unto all *p*.
1 Thes. 1. 3. *p*. of hope in our Lord
2 Thes. 1. 4. for your *p*. and faith
1 Tim. 6. 11. follow after . . . *p*., meekness
2 Tim. 3. 10. faith, long suffering, charity, *p*.
Tit. 2. 2. sound in faith, charity, *p*.
Heb. 6. 12. though faith and *p*. inherit promises
10. 36. have need of *p*., that after
12. 1. run with *p*. race that is set before us
Jas. 1. 3. trying of your faith worketh *p*.
4. let *p*. have her perfect work
5. 10. prophets . . . for an example of . . . *p*.
11. ye have heard of the *p*. of Job
2 Pet. 1. 6. to temperance *p*.; to *p*.
Rev. 1. 9. brother in the . . . *p*. of Jesus
2. 2. I know thy . . . *p*. 3. hast *p*.
13. 10. here is *p*. of saints, 14. 12.   [the proud
Eccl. 7. 8. the *patient* in spirit better than
Rom. 2. 7. by *p*. continuance in well doing
12. 12. *p*. in tribulation, instant in
2 Thes. 3. 5. *p*. waiting for Christ
1 Tim. 3. 3. not greedy of filthy lucre, but *p*.
2 Tim. 2. 24. gentle . . . apt to teach, *p*.
Jas. 5. 7. *p*. . . . unto coming of Lord
Ps. 37. 7. wait *patiently* for (Lord), 40. 1.
Heb. 6. 15. after he had *p*. endured
1 Pet. 2. 20. ye be buffeted . . . take it *p*.
PATRIARCH, Acts 2. 29; 7. 8. Heb. 7. 4.
PATRIMONY, his, Deut. 18. 8.
PATTERN, 1 Tim. 1. 16. Tit. 2. 7. Ezek. 43. 10.
Heb. 8. 5; 9. 23.
PAVILION, Ps. 27. 5; 31. 20; 18. 11. 1 Ki.
20. 12, 16. Jer. 43. 10.
PAY, Mat. 18. 28. Ps. 37. 21.
PEACE, Lev. 26. 6. Num. 6. 26.
Job 22. 21. acquaint thyself . . . and be at *p*.
Ps. 34. 14. seek *p*. and pursue it
37. 37. the end of that man is *p*.
85. 8. he will speak *p*. unto his people
119. 165. great *p*. have they which love
120. 6. hateth *p*. 7. I am for *p*.
122. 6. pray for *p*. of Jerusalem
125. 5. *p*. shall be upon Israel, 128. 6.

Prov. 16. 7. his enemies to be at *peace*
Is. 9. 6. everlasting Father, Prince of *p.*
26. 3. keep him in perfect *p.*
27. 5. that he may make *p.* with me; and he shall make p. with me
45. 7. I make *p.* and create evil
48. 18. had thy *p.* been as a river
22. there is no *p.* . . . to the wicked, 57. 21.
57. 19. *p.*, *p.* to him that is far off
59. 8. way of *p.* they know not, Rom. 3. 17.
60. 17. will make thy officers *p.*
66. 12. extend *p.* to her like a river
Jer. 6. 14. saying *p.*, *p.*, when there is no *p.*, 8. 11.
Ezek. 13. 10. 2 Ki. 9. 18, 22.
8. 15. looked for *p.* but no good came
29. 7. seek *p.* of the city . . . for in the *p.* thereof shall ye have *p.*
11. thoughts of *p.* and not of evil
Mic. 5. 5. this man shall be the *p.*
Zech. 8. 19. love the truth and *p.*
Mat. 10. 34. I came not to send *p.*
Mark 9. 50. have *p.* one with another
Luke 2. 14. on earth *p.*, good will towards
29. lettest thou thy servant depart in *p.*
19. 42. things that belong to thy *p.*
John 14. 27. *p.* I leave with you; my *p.* I give
16. 33. in me ye might have *p.*
Rom. 5. 1. we have *p.* with God through Jesus Christ
8. 6. spiritually minded is life and *p.*
14. 17. kingdom of God is . . . righteousness, *p.*
1 Cor. 7. 15. God hath called us to *p.*
2 Cor. 13. 11. live in *p.*, and God of . . . *p.*
Gal. 5. 22. fruit of Spirit is love, joy, *p.*
Eph. 2. 14. he is our *p.* 15. making *p.*
Phil. 4. 7. the *p.* of God, Col. 3. 15.
1 Thes. 5. 13. at *p.* among yourselves
Heb. 12. 14. follow *p.* with all men
Jas. 3. 18. righteousness sown in *p.*
1 Pet. 3. 11. let him seek *p.* and ensue
2 Pet. 3. 14. found of him in *p.*
1 Tim. 2. 2. lead a quiet and *peaceable life*
Jas. 3. 17. is first pure, then *p.*
Rom. 12. 18. live *peaceably* with all
Mat. 5. 9. blessed are the *peacemakers*
PEARL of great price, Mat. 13. 46.
Mat. 7. 6. cast not *pearls* before swine
Rev. 21. 21. gates were twelve *p.*
PECULIAR treasure to me, Ex. 19. 5.
Ps. 135. 4. Israel for his *p.* treasure
Eccl. 2. 8. *p.* treasure of kings
Deut. 14. 2. chosen thee to be a *p.* people, 26. 18. Tit. 2. 14. 1 Pet. 2. 9.
PEN of iron, Job 19. 24. Jer. 17. 1.
Ps. 45. 1. the *p.* of a ready writer
PENURY, Prov. 14. 23. Luke 21. 4.
PEOPLE, Gen. 27. 29. Ex. 6. 7.
Ps. 144. 15. happy is that *p.* whose God
148. 14. Israel a *p.* near unto him
Is. 1. 4. a *p.* laden with iniquity
10. 6. against the *p.* of my wrath
27. 11. a *p.* of no understanding
34. 5. upon the *p.* of my curse
Hos. 4. 9. like *p.*, like priest
1 Pet. 2. 10. in time past were not *p.*
Ps. 100. 3. we are *his people* and sheep of his
Mat. 1. 21. Jesus shall save—from their sins
Rom. 11. 2. God hath not cast away—
Ps. 50. 7. hear, O *my people*, and
81. 11.—would not hearken, 8. 13.
Is. 19. 25. blessed be Egypt—, and Assyria
26. 20. come—enter thou into thy chambers
63. 8. they are—that will not lie

Jer. 30. 22. ye shall be *my people* and I will be
24. 7; 31. 33; 32. 38. Ezek. 11. 20; 36. 28; 37. 27. Zech. 2. 11; 8. 8; 13. 9. 2 Cor. 6. 16.
Hos. 1. 9. ye are not—, 10. it was said to them, ye are not—, ye are
Heb. 4. 9. *p.* of God, 11. 25. 1 Pet. 2. 10.
PERCEIVE, Deut. 29. 4. 1 John 3. 16.
PERDITION, John 17. 12. Phil. 1. 28. 2 Thes. 2. 3. 1 Tim. 6. 9. Heb. 10. 39. 2 Pet. 3. 7. Rev.
PERFECT, Deut. 25. 15. Ps. 18. 32. [17. 8, 11.
Gen. 6. 9. Noah was a just man and *p.*
17. 1. walk before me, and be *p.*
Deut. 18. 13. shalt be *p.* with . . . God
2 Sam. 22. 31. his way is *p.*, Ps. 18. 30.
Job 1. 1. man *p.* and upright, 8; 2. 3.
Ps. 19. 7. law of the Lord is *p.*
37. 37. mark the *p.* man, and behold
Mat. 5. 48. *p.* as your Father . . . is *p.*
19. 21. if . . . be *p.* go and sell
1 Cor. 2. 6. among them that are *p.*
2 Cor. 12. 9. strength made *p.* in weakness
13. 11. be *p.*, be of good comfort [Christ
Eph. 4. 13. a *p.* man, unto the measure of . . .
Phil. 3. 12. not as though . . . already *p.*
Col. 1. 28. present every man *p.* in Christ
4. 12. may stand *p.* and complete
2 Tim. 3. 17. man of God may be *p.*
Heb. 2. 10. captain of salvation *p.*
7. 19. the law made nothing *p.*
12. 23. spirits of just men made *p.*
13. 21. make you *p.* in every good work
Jas. 1. 4. let patience have her *p.* work, that ye may be
17. good gift and every *p.* gift is from above
1 John 4. 18. *p.* love casteth out fear
Rev. 3. 2. not found thy works *p.*
2 Cor. 7. 1. *perfecting* holiness in fear of God
Eph. 4. 12. for the *p.* of the saints
Job 11. 7. find out Almighty to *perfection*
Ps. 119. 96. have seen an end of all *p.*
Luke 8. 14. bring no fruit to *p.*
2 Cor. 13. 9. we wish, even your *p.*
Heb. 6. 1. let us go on unto *p.*
PERFORM, Gen. 26. 3. Ruth 3. 13.
Job 5. 12. hands cannot *p.* enterprise
Ps. 119. 106. have sworn and will *p.* it
112. inclined heart to *p.* statutes
Is. 9. 7. zeal of Lord of hosts will *p.*
44. 28. shall *p.* all my pleasure
Mic. 7. 20. thou wilt *p.* truth to Jacob
Rom. 4. 21. promised, was able to *p.*
7. 18. how to *p.* that which is good
Phil. 1. 6. it to day of Jesus Christ
Neh. 9. 8. hast *performed* thy words
Is. 10. 12. Lord *p.* his whole work
Jer. 51. 29. purpose of Lord shall be *p.*
Ps. 57. 2. God that *performeth* all things
Is. 44. 26. by *p.* counsel of messengers
PERILOUS times, 2 Tim. 3. 1.
PERISH, Gen. 41. 36. Lev. 26. 38.
Num. 17. 12. we die, we *p.*, we all *p.*
Esth. 4. 16. I will go in . . . if I *p.*, I *p.*
Ps. 2. 12. ye *p.* from the way, when
Prov. 29. 18. no vision, the people *p.*
Mat. 8. 25. Lord, save us, we *p.*, Luke 8. 24.
John 3. 15. believeth in him should not *p.*
16. should not *p.* but have everlasting life
10. 28. they shall never *p.*
1 Cor. 8. 11. the weak *p.* for whom Christ died
2 Pet. 3. 9. not willing that any *p.*
Ps. 119. 92. have *perished* in my affliction
PERMIT, if Lord, 1 Cor. 16. 7. Heb. 6. 3. 1 Cor.
7. 6. by *permission*, not

PERNICIOUS ways, 2 Pet. 2. 2.
PERPETUAL, Jer. 50. 5; 51. 39, 57.
PERPLEXED, 2 Cor. 4. 8. Is. 22. 5.
PERSECUTE me, Ps. 7. 1; 31. 15.
  Job 19. 22. why *p.* me as God, 28.
  Ps. 10. 2. wicked . . . doth *p.* the poor
  35. 6. let angel of the Lord *p.* them
  83. 15. *p.* them with thy tempest
  Mat. 5. 11. blessed are ye when men . . . *p.* you
  44. pray for them that . . . *p.* you
  10. 23. when they *p.* you in this city
  Rom. 12. 14. bless them which *p.*
  Ps. 109. 16. *persecuted* the poor
  119. 161. princes *p.* me without cause
  143. 3. the enemy hath *p.* my soul
  John 15. 20. if they *p.* me they will *p.* you
  Acts 22. 4. I *p.* this way to death, 7, 8.
  26. 11. I *p.* them to strange cities, 14.
  1 Cor. 4. 12. being *p.* we suffer it
  15. 9. because I *p.* the church of God
  2 Cor. 4. 9. *p.* but not forsaken, cast
  Gal. 1. 13. I *p.* the church of God
  4. 29. *p.* him born after the Spirit
  Acts 9. 4. why *persecutest* thou me? 22. 7.
  2 Tim. 3. 12. live godly . . . shall suffer *persecution*
  1 Tim. 1. 13. who was . . . a *persecutor*
PERSEVERANCE, watching, Eph. 6. 18.
PERSON, Lev. 19. 15.
  Mal. 1. 8. will he accept thy *p.*
  Mat. 22. 16. regardest not *p.* of men
  Heb. 1. 3. express image of his *p.*
  Acts 10. 34. God is no respecter of *persons,* Deut.
  10. 17. Gal. 2. 6. Eph. 6. 9. Col. 3. 25. 1 Pet.
  1. 17.
  2 Pet. 3. 11. what manner of *p.* ought
  Jude 16. men's *p.* in admiration
PERSUADE we men, 2 Cor. 5. 11.
  Gal. 1. 10. do I *p.* men, or God
  Acts 13. 43. *persuaded* to continue
  21. 14. when he would not be *p.*
  Rom. 8. 38. I am *p.* that neither death
  Heb. 6. 9. are *p.* better things of you
  11. 13. having seen them . . . were *p.*
  Gal. 5. 8. this *persuasion* cometh
PERTAIN, Lev. 7. 20. 1 Cor. 6. 3, 4. Rom. 9. 4.
  Heb. 2. 17; 5. 1; 9. 9. 2 Pet. 1. 3.
  Acts 1. 3. *pertaining* to kingdom of God
PERVERSE, Num. 22. 32. Deut. 32. 5. Job 6. 30.
  Prov. 4. 24; 12. 8; 14. 2; 17. 20. Is. 19. 14.
  Mat. 17. 17. Acts 20. 30. Phil. 2. 15. 1 Tim.
  6. 5.
PERVERT judgment, Deut. 24. 17; 16. 19.
  1 Sam. 8. 3. Job 8. 3; 34. 12. Prov. 17. 23;
  31. 5. Mic. 3. 9.
  Acts 13. 10. not cease to *p.* right
  Job 33. 27. *perverted* that which was right
  Jer. 3. 21. they have *p.* their way
  Luke 23. 2. this fellow *perverting* the nation
PESTILENCE, 2 Sam. 24. 15. 1 Ki. 8. 37.
  Ps. 78. 50; 91. 3. Jer. 14. 12. Ezek. 5. 12.
  Amos 4. 10. Hab. 3. 5. Mat. 24. 7.
  Acts 24. 5. this man a *pestilent* fellow
PETITION, 1 Sam. 1. 17. Esth. 5. 6.
  Ps. 20. 5. *petitions,* 1 John 5. 15.
PHILOSOPHY, Col. 2. 8.
PHYLACTERIES, Mat. 23. 5.
PHYSICIAN of no value, Job 13. 4.
  Jer. 8. 22. is there no *p.* there
  Mat. 9. 12. that be whole need not *p.*
  Luke 4. 23. say . . . *P.,* heal thyself
  Col. 4. 14. Luke the beloved *p.*
PIECE of bread, Prov. 6. 26; 28. 21.
  Mat. 9. 16. putteth *p.* of new cloth

Luke 14. 18. bought a *piece* of ground
PIERCE, Num. 24. 8. 2 Ki. 18. 21.
  Luke 2. 35. sword shall *p.* through thy
  Ps. 22. 16. they *pierced* my hands
  1 Tim. 6. 10. *p.* themselves through
  Rev. 1. 7. they also which *p.* him
  Heb. 4. 12. *piercing* even to dividing
PIETY at home, 1 Tim. 5. 4.
PILGRIMS, Heb. 11. 13. 1 Pet. 2. 11. *pilgrimage,*
  Gen. 47. 9. Ex. 6. 4. Ps. 119. 54.
PILLAR of salt, Gen. 19. 26.
  Ex. 13. 21. by day in *p.* of cloud . . . by night in *p.*
  of fire, Num. 12. 5; 14. 14. Deut. 31. 15.
  Neh. 9. 12. Ps. 99. 7.
  Is. 19. 19. *p.* at the border thereof
  Jer. 1. 18. I made thee an iron *p.*
  1 Tim. 3. 15. *p.* and ground of truth
  Rev. 3. 12. make a *p.* in temple
  Job 9. 6. *pillars* thereof tremble
  26. 11. the *p.* of heaven tremble
  Ps. 75. 3. I bear up the *p.* of it
  Prov. 9. 1. hath hewn out her seven *p.*
  Sol. 3. 6. *p.* of smoke
  5. 15. his legs are as *p.* of marble
  3. 10. made the *p.* thereof silver
PILLOW, Gen. 28. 11. Ezek. 13. 18.
PINE, Lev. 26. 39. Ezek. 24. 23.
PIPE, Zech. 4. 2, 12. Mat. 11. 17.
PIT, Gen. 14. 10; 37. 20.
  Ex. 21. 33. if a man dig a *p.,* 34.
  Job 33. 24. deliver him from. . . the *p.*
  Ps. 9. 15. sunk down in *p.* they had made
  28. 1. go down to the *p.* 30. 3; 88. 4; 143. 7.
  Prov. 1. 12. Is. 38. 18.
  40. 2. out of an horrible *p.*
  55. 23. *p.* of destruction
  Prov. 22. 14. strange women a deep *p.*
  23. 27. strange women is a narrow *p.*
  Is. 38. 17. from the *p.* of corruption
  51. 1. *p.* whence ye are digged
  Zech. 9. 11. sent prisoners out of *p.*
  Rev. 9. 1. key of bottomless *p.,* 20. 1.
  Ps. 119. 85. proud digged *pits* for me
  Jer. 14. 3. to *p.* and found no water
PITY, Deut. 7. 16; 13. 8; 19. 13.
  Job 6. 14. *p.* should be shewed
  19. 21. have *p.* on me, have *p.*
  Is. 63. 9. in his *p.* he redeemed
  Ezek. 36. 21. had *p.* for my holy name
  Mat. 18. 33. even as I had *p.* on thee
  Ps. 103. 13. as a father *pitieth* his children, so the
  Lord *p.* them that
  Jas. 5. 11. *pitiful,* 1 Pet. 3. 8.
PLACE, Ex. 3. 5. Deut. 12. 5, 14.
  Ps. 26. 8. *p.* where thine honour
  32. 7. art my hiding *p.,* 119. 114.
  90. 1. Lord, thou hast been our dwelling *p.*
  Prov. 15. 3. eyes of Lord are in every *p.*
  Is. 66. 1. where is the *p.* of my rest, 18. 4.
  Hos. 5. 15. will go and return to my *p.*
  John 8. 37. my word hath no *p.* in
  11. 48. take away both our *p.* and
  Rom. 12. 19. avenge not, but give *p.*
  1 Cor. 4. 11. no certain dwelling *p.*
  11. 20. ye come together into one *p.*
  Eph. 4. 27. neither give *p.* to devil
  Rev. 12. 6. hath *p.* prepared of God
  Job 7. 10. neither shall *his place* know him any
  Ps. 37. 10. diligently consider—and [more, 20. 9.
  Is. 26. 21. Lord cometh out of—
  Acts 1. 25. might go to—
  Ps. 16. 6. lines fallen unto me in pleasant *places*
  Is. 40. 4. rough *p.* plain

Eph. 1. 3. *heavenly places*, 20; 2. 6; 3. 10.
6. 12. *high p.*, Hab. 3. 19. Amos 4. 13. Hos. 10. 8.
Prov. 8. 2; 9. 14.
PLAGUE, 1 Ki. 8. 37, 38. Ps. 89. 23. *plagues*,
Hos. 13. 14. Rev. 16. 9; 18. 4, 8; 22. 18.
PLAIN man, Jacob was a, Gen. 25. 27.
Ps. 27. 11. lead me in a *p.* path
Prov. 8. 9. (words) are all *p.* to him
Zech. 4. 7. thou shalt become a *p.*
John 16. 29. now speakest thou *plainly*
2 Cor. 3. 12. we use great *plainness*
PLAISTER, Lev. 14. 42. Is. 38. 21.
PLAIT, Mat. 27. 29. 1 Pet. 3. 3.
PLANT, Gen. 2. 5. Job 14. 9.
Jer. 2. 21. turned into degenerate *p.* of a strange
18. 9. concerning a kingdom, to . . . *p.*
24. 6. *p.* them and not pluck, 42. 10.
Ezek. 34. 29. raise . . . a *p.* of renown
1. 3. a tree *planted* by rivers
92. 13. *p.* in the house of the Lord
Is. 40. 24. yea, they shall not be *p.*
Jer. 2. 21. I *p.* thee a noble vine
17. 8. as a tree *p.* by the waters
Mat. 15. 13. my heavenly Father hath not *p.*
21. 33. *p.* a vineyard and hedged it
Rom. 6. 5. we have been *p.* together
1 Cor. 3. 6. I have *p.*, Apollos watered
9. 7. who *planteth* a vineyard and eateth not
Is. 60. 21. the branch of my *planting*
61. 3. trees of righteousness, the *p.* of the Lord
Ps. 128. 3. children like olive *plants*, 144. 12.
PLAY, Ex. 32. 6. 2 Sam. 2. 14; 10. 12. Ezek.
33. 32. 1 Cor. 10. 7.
PLEAD for Baal, Judg. 6. 31.
Job 13. 19. who will *p.* with me, 9. 19.
16. 21. might *p.* for man with God
23. 6. will he *p.* against me with great power
Is. 1. 17. *p.* for the widow
43. 26. let us *p.* together
66. 16. by fire and sword will Lord *p.*
Jer. 2. 29. wherefore will ye *p.* with me
12. 1. righteous art thou, Lord, when I *p.*
25. 31. he will *p.* with all flesh
Hos. 2. 2. *p.* with your mother, *p.*
Joel 3. 2. I will *p.* for them there with my people
PLEASE, 2 Sam. 7. 29. Job 6. 9.
Ps. 69. 31. this also shall *p.* the Lord
Prov. 16. 7. when man's ways *p.* Lord
Is. 55. 11. accomplish that which I *p.*
56. 4. choose the things that *p.* me
Rom. 8. 8. that are in flesh cannot *p.* God
15. 1. bear . . . and not *p.* ourselves
2. let every one of us *p.* his neighbour
1 Cor. 7. 32. how he may *p.* the Lord
10. 33. I *p.* men in all things
Gal. 1. 10. do I seek to *p.* men
1 Thes. 4. 1. how . . . to walk, and to *p.* him
Heb. 11. 6. without faith it is impossible to *p.*
him
Ps. 115. 3. God hath done whatsoever he *pleased*,
Is. 42. 21. Lord is well *p.* for his   [135. 6.
53. 10. it *p.* the Lord to bruise him
Mic. 6. 7. will the Lord be *p.* with
Mat. 3. 17. . . . Son, in whom I am well *p.*,
17. 5.
Rom. 15. 3. Christ *p.* not himself
Col. 1. 19. *p.* the Father that in him
Heb. 11. 5. (Enoch) *p.* God
13. 16. with such sacrifices God is well *p.*
Eccl. 7. 26. whoso *pleaseth* God shall escape
8. 3. he doeth whatsoever *p.* him
Phil. 4. 18. a sacrifice well *pleasing*
Col. 1. 10. worthy of Lord unto all *p.*

1 Thes. 2. 4. not as *pleasing* men, but God, Eph.
6. 6. Col. 3. 22. (menpleasers)
Heb. 13. 21. working that is well *p.*
1 John 3. 22. do things *p.* in his sight
Gen. 2. 9. *pleasant*, 3. 6. Mic. 2. 9.
2 Sam. 1. 23. Saul and Jonathan were . . . *p.*
Ps. 16. 6. lines fallen to me in *p.* places
133. 1. how *p.* for brethren to dwell
Prov. 2. 10. knowledge is *p.* to soul
5. 19. as a loving hind and *p.* roe
9. 17. bread eaten in secret is *p.*
Eccl. 11. 7. *p.* for eyes to behold the sun
Sol. 1. 16. thou art fair, yea, *p.*
4. 13. *p.* fruits, 16; 7. 13.
7. 6. how *p.* art thou, O love, for delights
Jer. 31. 20. Ephraim . . . is he a *p.* child
Prov. 3. 17. ways of *pleasantness*
Gen. 18. 12. shall I have *pleasure*
1 Chr. 29. 17. *p.* in uprightness
Ps. 5. 4. not a God that hath *p.* in
35. 27. hath *p.* in prosperity of his
51. 18. do good in thy good *p.* unto Zion
102. 14. servants take *p.* in her stones
103. 21. ministers of his that do his *p.*
147. 11. Lord taketh *p.* in them
Prov. 21. 17. he that loveth *p.* shall be poor
Eccl. 5. 4. for he hath no *p.* in fools
12. 1. say, I have no *p.* in them
Is. 44. 28. shall perform all my *p.*
53. 10. *p.* of Lord shall prosper in
Jer. 22. 28. vessel wherein is no *p.*, Hos. 8. 8.
Ezek. 18. 32. no *p.* in death of, 33. 11.
Mal. 1. 10. I have no *p.* in you, saith the Lord
Luke 12. 32. it is your Father's good *p.*
2 Cor. 12. 10. I take *p.* in infirmities
Eph. 1. 5. according to the good *p.* of
Phil. 2. 13. and to do of his good *p.*
2 Thes. 1. 11. fulfil all good *p.* of
Heb. 10. 38. my soul shall have no *p.*
12. 10. chastened us after their own *p.*
Rev. 4. 11. for thy *p.* they . . . were created
Ps. 16. 11. at thy right hand *pleasures* for evermore
36. 8. drink of the river of thy *p.*
2 Tim. 3. 4. lovers of *p.* more than . . . God
Tit. 3. 3. serving divers lusts and *p.*
Heb. 11. 25. than to enjoy *p.* of sin
PLEDGE, Ex. 22. 26. Deut. 24. 6.
PLEIADES, Job 9. 9; 38. 31.
PLENTY, Job 37. 23. Prov. 3. 10.
Ps. 86. 5. *plenteous* in mercy, 103. 8.
130. 7. with him is *p.* redemption
Mat. 9. 37. harvest is *p.*, but labourers
PLOUGH, PLOW, Deut. 22. 10. Prov. 20. 4.
Luke 9. 62. having put his hand to the *plough*
Job 4. 8. they that *plow* iniquity, and
Is. 28. 24. doth plowman *p.* all day
Judg. 14. 18. *plowed* with my heifer
Ps. 129. 3. plowers *p.* on my back
Jer. 26. 18. Zion shall be *p.* like a field, Mic. 3. 12.
Hos. 10. 13. ye have *p.* wickedness
1 Cor. 9. 10. *ploweth* should *p.* in hope
Prov. 21. 4. *plowing* of wicked is sin
Amos 9. 13. *plowman*, Is. 61. 5.
Is. 2. 4. *plowshares*, Joel 3. 10. Mic. 4. 3.
PLUCK out, Ps. 25. 15; 52. 5; 74. 11. Amos 4. 11.
Zech. 3. 9. Mat. 5. 29; 18. 9. John 10. 28, 29.
Gal. 4. 15.
2 Chr. 7. 20. *pluck up*, Jer. 12. 17; 18. 7;
31. 28, 40. Dan. 11. 4. Jude 12.
Ezra 9. 3. *pluck off*, Job 29. 17. Is. 50. 6. Ezek.
23. 34. Mic. 3. 2.
POISON, Deut. 32. 24, 33. Job 6. 4; 20. 16. Ps.
58. 4; 140. 3. Rom. 3. 13. Jas. 3. 8.

POLLUTE, Num. 18. 32. Ezek. 7. 21. Mic. 2. 10.
Zeph. 3. 1. Mal. 1. 7, 12.
Acts 15. 20. *pollutions*, 2 Pet. 2. 20.
PONDER path of feet, Prov. 4. 26.
Luke 2. 19. *pondered* them in her heart
Prov. 21. 2. Lord *pondereth* the hearts, **24. 12.**
POOR may eat, Ex. 23. 11.
Ex. 30. 15. the *p*. shall not give less
Lev. 19. 15. not respect person of *p*.
Deut. 15. 11. for the *p*. shall never cease out
1 Sam. 2. 7. Lord maketh *p*. and
8. raiseth *p*. out of dust, Ps. 113. 7.
Job 5. 16. the *p*. hath hope
36. 15. deliver *p*. in affliction
Ps. 10. 14. *p*. committeth himself to thee
69. 33. the Lord heareth the *p*. and
72. 4. he shall judge the *p*., 2, 13.
132. 15. satisfy her *p*. with bread
140. 12. Lord will maintain . . . right of *p*.
Prov. 13. 7. there is that maketh himself *p*.
14. 20. *p*. is hated of his neighbour
31. oppresseth *p*. reproacheth his Maker: he that
honoureth him hath mercy on *p*.
19. 4. is separated from his neighbour
7. all brethren of the *p*. do hate him
22. 22. rob not *p*. because he is *p*., neither oppress
30. 9. lest I be *p*. and steal
Is. 14. 32. *p*. of his people shall trust
29. 19. *p*. among men shall rejoice
41. 17. when the *p*. and needy seek water
58. 7. bring *p*. that are cast out to thy house
66. 2. that is *p*. and of a contrite
Jer. 5. 4. surely these are *p*.
Amos. 2. 6. sold *p*. for pair of shoes, 8. 6.
Zeph. 3. 12. an afflicted and *p*. people
Zech. 11. 11. *p*. of flock waited on me
Mat. 5. 3. blessed are the *p*. in spirit
11. 5. *p*. have gospel preached to
26. 11. have *p*. always with you, John 12. 8.
Luke 6. 20. blessed be ye *p*.: for yours is the
2 Cor. 6. 10. as *p*., yet making many rich
8. 9. for your sakes he became *p*.
9. 9. he hath given to *p*., Ps. 112. 9.
Gal. 2. 10. we should remember the *p*.
Jas. 2. 5. God chosen *p*. of this world
Rev. 3. 17. knowest not thou art wretched,
and miserable and *p*.
PORTION, Deut. 21. 17; 33. 21.
Deut. 32. 9. Lord's *p*. is his people
2 Ki. 2. 9. double *p*. of thy spirit
Job 24. 18. their *p*. is cursed in earth
26. 11. how little a *p*. is heard
31. 2. what *p*. of God is from above
Ps. 16. 5. Lord is *p*. of my inheritance
17. 14. have their *p*. in this life
63. 10. shall be a *p*. for foxes
73. 26. God is my *p*. for ever, 119. 57.
142. 5. art my *p*. in land of living
Eccl. 11. 2. give *p*. to seven and to
Is. 53. 12. divide him a *p*. with the
61. 7. they shall rejoice in their *p*.
Jer. 10. 16. the *p*. of Jacob not like them, **51. 19.**
Hab. 1. 16. by them their *p*. is fat
Zech. 2. 12. Lord shall inherit Judah his *p*.
Neh. 8. 10. send *portions*, Esth. 9. 19, 22.
POSSESS, Gen. 22. 17. Judg. 11. 24.
Job 7. 3. made to *p*. months of vanity
13. 26. *p*. iniquities of my youth
Luke 21. 19. in patience *p*. your souls
1 Thes. 4. 4. know how to *p*. vessel
Ps. 139. 13. hast *possessed* my reins
Prov. 8. 22. Lord *p*. me in beginning
Is. 63. 18. people of thy holiness *p*. it a little

1 Cor. 7. 30. as though they *possessed* not
2 Cor. 6. 10. as having nothing yet *possessing* all
Eph. 1. 14. purchased *possession*
Gen. 14. 19. God, *possessor* of heaven
POSSIBLE, all things with God, Mat. 19. 26.
Mat. 24. 24. if *p*. shall deceive the very elect
Mark 9. 23. all things *p*. to him that
14. 36. Father, all things are *p*. to thee
Luke 18. 27. impossible with men *p*. with God
Rom. 12. 18. if *p*. . . . live peaceably
Heb. 10. 4. not *p*. that blood of bulls
POSTERITY, Gen. 45. 7. Ps. 49. 13.
POT, Ex. 16. 33. Ps. 68. 13; 81. 6. Jer. 1. 13. Zech.
14. 21.   [Is. 45. 9.
Job 2. 8. *potsherd*, Ps. 22. 15. Prov. 26. 23.
Is. 29. 16. *potter*, 64. 8. Jer. 18. 6. Lam. 4. 2.
Rom. 9. 21. Rev. 2. 27.
POTENTATE, blessed, 1 Tim. 6. 15.
POUND, Luke 19. 13. John 19. 39.
POUR, Job 36. 27. Lev. 14. 18, 41.
Ps. 62. 8. *p*. out your heart
79. 6. *p*. out thy wrath on heathen, 69. 24. Jer.
10. 25. Zeph. 3. 8.
Prov. 1. 23. I will *p*. out my Spirit
Is. 44. 3. *p*. water on him that is thirsty
Lam. 2. 19. *p*. thine heart like water
Rev. 16. 1, 17. *p*. vials of God's wrath
Job 10. 10. *poured* me out as milk
30. 16. my soul *p*. out in me, Ps. 42. 4.
Ps. 45. 2. grace is *p*. into thy lips
Sol. 1. 3. name is as ointment *p*.
Is. 32. 15. till Spirit be *p*. on us from high
53. 12. *p*. out his soul unto death
Jer. 7. 20. my fury shall be *p*. out, 42. 18; 44. 6.
Is. 42. 25. Ezek. 7. 8; 14. 19; 20. 8, 13, 21;
30. 15.
Job 12. 21. *poureth* contempt on princes, Ps.
16. 20. mine eye *p*. out tears   [107. 40.
POVERTY, Gen. 45. 11. Prov. 11. 24.
Prov. 6. 11. so shall *p*. come, 24. 34.
10. 15. destruction of the poor is their *p*.
20. 13. love not sleep lest thou come to *p*.
30. 8. give me neither *p*. nor riches
2 Cor. 8. 2. their deep *p*. abounded
9. ye through his *p*. might be rich
Rev. 2. 9. I know thy works . . . and *p*.
POWDER, Ex. 32. 20. Deut. 28. 24. 2 Ki. 23. 15.
Sol. 3. 6. Mat. 21. 44.
POWER, as a prince, Gen. 32. 28.
Gen. 49. 3. dignity and excellency of *p*.
Deut. 8. 18. giveth *p*. to get wealth
32. 36. when he seeth that their *p*. is gone
2 Sam. 22. 33. God is my strength and *p*.
1 Chr. 29. 11. thine is the *p*. and
Ezra 8. 22. *p*. and wrath is against
Job 26. 2. him that is without *p*.
14. thunder of his *p*. who can
Ps. 62. 11. *p*. belongeth unto God
Prov. 3. 27. when it is in *p*. of hand
18. 21. death and life in *p*. of tongue
Is. 40. 29. he giveth *p*. to the faint
Eccl. 8. 4. where word of king is, there is *p*.
8. 8. no man that hath *p*. over the spirit to
Jer. 10. 12. made earth by his *p*., 51. 15.
Hos. 12. 3. by strength he had *p*. with God
Mic. 3. 8. I am full of *p*. by the Spirit
Hab. 1. 11. imputing *p*. to his God
3. 4. there was the hiding of his *p*.
Zech. 4. 6. not by might, nor by *p*.
Mat. 9. 6. *p*. on earth to forgive sins
8. glorified God which had given such *p*.
22. 29. not knowing scriptures nor *p*. of God
28. 18. all *p*. is given unto me in heaven and

Mark 9. 1. kingdom of God come with *power*
Luke 1. 35. *p.* of the Highest shall
5. 17. *p.* of the Lord to heal them
22. 53. this is your hour and *p.* of
24. 49. till ye be endued with *p.*
John 1. 12. gave he *p.* to become
10. 18. *p.* to lay it down and *p.* to
17. 2. given him *p.* over all flesh
19. 10. *p.* to crucify, . . . *p.* to release
Acts 26. 18. turn them from the *p.* of
Rom. 1. 16. gospel is *p.* of God to
20. his eternal *p.* and Godhead, 4.
9. 22. to make his *p.* known
13. 1. there is no *p.* but of God
1 Cor. 1. 24. Christ the *p.* of God, 18.
2. 4. demonstration of Spirit and *p.*
4. 19. not speech of them . . . but the *p.*
5. 4. gathered together with the *p.* of our Lord
6. 12. not be brought under *p.* of
9. 4. have we not *p.* to eat and
2 Cor. 4. 7. excellency of *p.* may be
13. 10. according to the *p.* . . . Lord hath given
Eph. 1. 19. exceeding greatness of his *p.*
2. 2. prince of the *p.* of air
Phil. 3. 10. know *p.* of his resurrection
Col. 1. 11. according to his glorious *p.*
13. delivered from the *p.* of darkness
2 Thes. 1. 9. the glory of his *p.*
2 Tim. 1. 7. Spirit of *p.* and of love
3. 5. form of godliness, denying *p.*
Heb. 1. 3. upholding all things by word of his *p.*
2. 14. destroy him that had the *p.* of death
1 Pet. 1. 5. kept by *p.* of God through faith
2 Pet. 1. 3. his divine *p.* hath given
Rev. 2. 26. will give *p.* over nations
4. 11. worthy to receive . . . *p.*, 5. 13; 7. 12; 19. 1.
    1 Tim. 6. 16. Jude 25.
11. 3. *p.* to my two witnesses
17. taken to thee thy great *p.*
12. 10. now is come . . . *p.* of his Christ
16. 9. hath *p.* over these plagues
Ex. 15. 6. *in power*, Job 37. 23. Nah. 1. 3. 1 Cor.
    4. 20; 15. 43. Eph. 6. 10.
Ps. 63. 2. *thy power*, 110. 3; 145. 11.
29. 4. *powerful*, Heb. 4. 12.
Eph. 6. 12. principalities, *powers*, 1. 21. Col. 1. 16;
    2. 10, 15. 1 Pet. 3. 22.
Heb. 6. 5. tasted good word of God and *p.* of
PRAISE, Judg. 5. 3. Ps. 7. 17.
Deut. 10. 21. he is thy *p.* and thy God
Neh. 9. 5. above all blessing and *p.*
Ps. 22. 25. my *p.* shall be of thee
33. 1. *p.* is comely for upright, 147. 1.
65. 1. *p.* waiteth for thee, O God
109. 1. hold not peace, God of my *p.*
Prov. 27. 21. so is a man to his *p.*
Is. 60. 18. walls Salvation and thy gates *p.*
62. 7. Jerusalem a *p.* in the earth
Jer. 13. 11. for a *p.* and for a glory
17. 14. art my *p.* 26. sacrifices of *p.*
Hab. 3. 3. earth was full of his *p.*
John 12. 43. loved *p.* of men more than *p.* of God
Rom. 2. 29. whose *p.* is not of men
Eph. 1. 6. *p.* of glory of his grace, 12.
Phil. 4. 8. if there be any *p.*, think on
Heb. 13. 15. offer sacrifice of *p.*
1 Pet. 2. 14. *p.* of them that do well
Ex. 15. 11. *praises*, Ps. 22. 3; 78. 4; 149. 6. Is.
    60. 6; 63. 7. 1 Pet. 2. 9.
Ps. 30. 9. shall dust *praise* thee, 12.
42. 5. shall *p.* him for help, 11; 43. 5.
63. 3. my lips shall *p.* thee
88. 10. shall the dead arise and *p.*, 115. 17.

119. 164. seven times a day do I *praise*
145. 10. all thy works *p.* thee
Prov. 27. 2. let another *p.* thee, not
31. 31. her own works *p.* her in gates
Is. 38. 18. the grave cannot *p.* thee
19. the living shall *p.* thee as I do
Joel 2. 26. eat in plenty . . . and *p.* . . . . **Lord**
Ps. 9. 1. *I will praise thee*, 111. 1; 138. 1; 35. 18;
    52. 9; 56. 4; 118. 21; 119. 7; 139. 14. Is. 12. 1.
2 Sam. 22. 4. worthy to be *praised* [145. 3; 72. 15.
1 Chr. 16. 25. greatly to be *p.*, Ps. 48. 1; 96. 4;
2 Chr. 5. 13. *praising*, Ezra 3. 11. Ps. 84. 4.
Luke 2. 13, 20. Acts 2. 47.
PRATING, Prov. 10. 8, 10. 3 John 10.
PRAY for thee, and thou shalt live, Gen. 20. 7.
1 Sam. 7. 5. I will *p.* for you to Lord, 12. 19.
2 Sam. 7. 27. found in his heart to *p.* this
Job 21. 15. profit we have if we *p.*
42. 8. my servant Job shall *p.* for
Ps. 5. 2. my God: to thee will I *p.*
55. 17. morning and noon will I *p.*
122. 6. *p.* for the peace of Jerusalem
Jer. 7. 16. *p.* not for this people, 11. 14; 14. 11.
Mat. 5. 44. *p.* for them which despitefully
26. 41. watch and *p.* that ye enter not
Mark 11. 24. things ye desire when ye *p.*
Luke 11. 1. teach us to *p.*, as John
16. 27. I *p.* thee therefore, father
18. 1. men ought always to *p.*
21. 36. watch ye and *p.* always
John 16. 26. I will *p.* the Father for
17. 9. I *p.* for them: I *p.* not
20. neither *p.* I for these alone
Acts 8. 22. *p.* God, if perhaps, 24.
10. 9. Peter went on housetop to *p.*
Rom. 8. 26. know not what we should *p.* for
1 Cor. 14. 15. I will *p.* with spirit, 14.
2 Cor. 5. 20. *p.* you in Christ's stead
Col. 1. 9. do not cease to *p.* for you
1 Thes. 5. 17. *p.* without ceasing
25. *p.* for us, 2 Thes. 3. 1. Heb. 13. 18.
1 Tim. 2. 8. that men *p.* every where
Jas. 5. 13. any afflicted? let him *p.*
16. *p.* one for another, Eph. 6. 18.
Luke 22. 32. I have *prayed* for thee
44. in agony he *p.* more earnestly
Acts 10. 2. gave much alms to people and *p.* to God
20. 36. (Paul) *p.* with them all
Jas. 5. 17. (Elias) . . . . that it might not rain
Acts 9. 11. behold, he *prayeth*
Dan. 9. 20. *praying*, 1 Cor. 11. 4.
1 Thes. 3. 10. night and day *p.*
1 Ki. 8. 45. hear in heaven their *prayer*
28. respect to *p.* of servant
38. what *p.* and supplication
2 Sam. 7. 27. to pray this *p.* to thee
Neh. 1. 6. mayest hear *p.* of servant
4. 9. we made our *p.* to our God
Job 15. 4. restrainest *p.* before God
Ps. 65. 2. thou that hearest *p.*, to
102. 17. he will regard *p.* of destitute, and not
109. 4. I give myself to *p.*   [despise their *p.*
Prov. 15. 8. *p.* of the upright is his
29. Lord heareth *p.* of righteous
28. 9. his *p.* shall be abomination, Ps. 109. 7.
Is. 26. 16. poured out a *p.* when
56. 7. an house of *p.* for all people
Lam. 3. 44. our *p.* should not pass
Dan. 9. 3. by *p.* and supplications
Mat. 17. 21. goeth not out but by *p.*
23. 14. make long *p.*
Acts 3. 1. to temple at hour of *p.*
6. 4. give ourselves continually to *p.*

Acts 12. 5. *prayer* was made without ceasing
16. 13. *p.* was wont to be made
1 Cor. 7. 5. may give yourselves to *p.*
2 Cor. 1. 11. helping together by *p.*
Phil. 4. 6. in every thing by *p.* and
1 Tim. 4. 5. sanctified by word of God and *p.*
Jas. 5. 15. *p.* of faith shall save
16. effectual fervent *p.* of righteous
1 Pet. 4. 7. watch unto *p.*, Col. 4. 2.
Luke 6. 12. continued *in prayer*, Acts 1. 14.
Rom. 12. 12. Col. 4. 2.
Job 16. 17. *my prayer*, Ps. 5. 3; 6. 9; 17. 1;
35. 13; 66. 20; 88. 2. Lam. 3. 8. Jonah 2. 7.
Job 22. 27. *thy prayer*, Is. 37. 4. Luke 1. 13.
Acts 10. 31.
Ps. 72. 20. *prayers* of David . . . ended
Acts 10. 4. thy *p.* and thine alms are
1 Tim. 2. 1. first of all that supplications, *p.* and
1 Pet. 3. 7. your *p.* be not hindered
12. his ears are open to their *p.*
Rev. 5. 8. which are *p.* of saints, 8. 3.
PREACH at Jerusalem, Neh. 6. 7.
Jonah 3. 2. *p.* unto it the preaching that I bid
Mat. 4. 17. Jesus began to *p.* and, 10. 7.
10. 27. what ye hear in ear, *p.* on
Mark 1. 4. *p.* baptism of repentance
Luke 4. 18. *p.* deliverance to captives, 19.
9. 60. go and *p.* kingdom of God
Acts 10. 42. commanded us to *p.*
15. 21. in every city them that *p.* him
Rom. 10. 8. word of faith which we *p.*
15. how shall they *p.* except they
1 Cor. 1. 23. we *p.* Christ crucified
15. 11. so we *p.* and so ye believed
2 Cor. 4. 5. we *p.* not ourselves but
Phil. 1. 15. some *p.* Christ of envy
2 Tim. 4. 2. *p.* the word; be instant
Ps. 40. 9. I *preached* righteousness
Mark 2. 2. he *p.* the word unto them
6. 12. he *p.* that men should repent
16. 20. *p.* every where, the Lord
Luke 4. 44. *p.* in synagogues of Galilee
24. 47. remission of sins be *p.* in his
Acts 8. 5. Philip . . . *p.* Christ, 40.
9. 20. Saul *p.* Christ in synagogues
13. 38. through this man is *p.* to
1 Cor. 9. 27. when I have *p.* to others
15. 1. gospel which I *p.* unto you
2. keep in memory what I *p.*
12. if Christ be *p.* that he rose
Col. 1. 23. which was *p.* to every
1 Tim. 3. 16. God manifest in flesh . . . *p.* to
Heb. 4. 2. the word *p.* did not profit [Gentiles
1 Pet. 3. 19. *p.* to the spirits in prison
Eccl. 1. 1. *preacher*, 2, 12; 12. 8, 9.
1 Tim. 2. 7. ordained a *p.*, 2 Tim. 1. 11.
Gal. 1. 23. *preacheth* faith he once destroyed
Acts 10. 36. *preaching* peace by Jesus Christ
11. 19. *p.* word to none but Jews
1 Cor. 1. 18. *p.* of cross is to them
21. by foolishness of *p.* to save them
2. 4. my *p.* was not with enticing words
15. 14. then is our *p.* vain, and faith
PRECEPTS, Neh. 9. 14. Jer. 35. 18.
Ps. 119. 4. commanded us to keep *p.*
15. I will meditate in thy *p.*, 78.
27. way of thy *p.*, 40. longed after thy *p.*
45. I seek thy *p.*, 87. I forsook not thy *p.*
56. I kept thy *p.*, 63, 69, 100, 134.
94. I sought thy *p.*, 104. through thy *p.*
110. I erred not from thy *p.*
128. I esteem all thy *p.* to be right
141. I do not forget thy *p.*, 93.

159. I love thy *p.* 173. chosen thy *precepts*
Is. 28. 10. *p.* upon *p.*, *p.* upon *p.*
29. 13. fear is taught by *p.* of men
PRECIOUS things, Deut. 33. 13–16.
1 Sam. 3. 1. word of the Lord was *p.*
26. 21. my soul was *p.* in thine eyes
Ps. 49. 8. redemption of soul is *p.*
116. 15. *p.* in sight of the Lord
126. 6. goeth forth and weepeth, bearing *p.* seed
139. 17. how *p.* are thy thoughts
Eccl. 7. 1. better than *p.* ointment
Is. 13. 12. a man more *p.* than gold
28. 16. I lay in Zion a . . . *p.* corner stone
43. 4. since thou wast *p.* in my sight
Jer. 15. 19. if thou take *p.* from vile
Lam. 4. 2. *p.* sons of Zion are
Jas. 5. 7. husbandman waiteth for *p.* fruit
1 Pet. 1. 7. the trial of your faith more *p.* than
of gold
19. redeemed with the *p.* blood of Christ
2. 4. stone chosen of God and *p.*, 6.
2 Pet. 1. 1. obtained like *p.* faith
4. exceeding great and *p.* promises
PREDESTINATE, Rom. 8. 29, 30.
Eph. 1. 5. *predestinated*, 11.
PREEMINENCE, man hath no, Eccl. 3. 19.
Col. 1. 18. 3 John 9.
PREFER, Ps. 137. 6. John 1. 15, 27, 30.
Rom. 12. 10. *preferring*, 1 Tim. 5. 21.
PREMEDITATE not, Mark 13. 11.
PREPARE, Ex. 15. 2; 16. 5.
1 Sam. 7. 3. *p.* your hearts to Lord
1 Chr. 29. 18. *p.* their heart unto thee
2 Chr. 35. 6. *p.* your brethren
Job 11. 13. if thou *p.* thy heart and
Ps. 10. 17. thou wilt *p.* their heart
61. 7. O *p.* mercy and truth
Prov. 24. 27. *p.* thy work without
Is. 40. 3. *p.* ye the way of the Lord
Amos 4. 12. *p.* to meet thy God, O Israel
Mic. 3. 5. they *p.* war against him
Mat. 11. 10. shall *p.* thy way before
John 14. 2. I go to *p.* a place for you
Mark 15. 42. it was the *preparation*, the day
Prov. 16. 1. *preparations* of heart
2 Chr. 19. 3. hast *prepared* thine heart
27. 6. his ways before the Lord
29. 36. God had *p.* the people
Neh. 8. 10. for whom nothing is *p.*
Ps. 68. 10. *p.* of thy goodness for the poor
Is. 64. 4. what he hath *p.* for him, 1 Cor. 2. 9.
Hos. 6. 3. his going forth is *p.* as the
Mat. 20. 23. given to them for whom it is *p.*
22. 4. I have *p.* my dinner; my oxen
25. 34. inherit the kingdom *p.* for you
Luke 1. 17. ready a people *p.* for Lord
12. 47. knew his lord's will, and *p.* not
Rom. 9. 23. vessels of mercy *p.* to
2 Tim. 2. 21. *p.* to every good work
Heb. 10. 5. a body hast thou *p.* me
11. 16. God . . . hath *p.* for them a city
Rev. 12. 6. to wilderness, a place *p.* of God
21. 2. new Jerusalem . . . *p.* as a bride
Ps. 23. 5. thou *preparest* a table before
65. 9. thou *p.* them corn [God
2 Chr. 30. 19. that *prepareth* his heart to seek
Ps. 147. 8. who *p.* rain for the earth
PRESBYTERY, 1 Tim. 4. 14.
PRESENT help in trouble, Ps. 46. 1.
Acts 10. 33. all here *p.* before God
Rom. 7. 18. to will is *p.* 21. evil is *p.*
8. 38. nor things *p.* nor, 1 Cor. 3. 22.
1 Cor. 5. 3. absent in body, but *p.* in spirit

2 Cor. 5. 8. to be *present* with the Lord
Gal. 1. 4. deliver us from this *p.* evil world
2 Tim. 4. 10. having loved this *p.* world
2 Pet. 1. 12. established in *p.* truth
Rom. 12. 1. *p.* your bodies a living sacrifice
2 Cor. 11. 2. *p.* you as a chaste virgin
Col. 1. 22. to *p.* you holy and
28. *p.* every man perfect in Christ
Jude 24. *p.* you faultless before the
Gen. 3. 8. hide from *presence* of Lord
4. 16. Cain went from *p.* of Lord, Job 1. 12;
  2. 7. Ps. 114. 7. Jer. 4. 26. Jonah 1. 3, 10.
  Zech. 1. 7. Jude 24.
Job 23. 15. I am troubled at his *p.*
Ps. 16. 11. in thy *p.* is fulness of joy
31. 20. hide them in secret of thy *p.*
51. 11. cast me not away from thy *p.*
100. 2. come before his *p.* with singing
114. 7. tremble, thou earth, at *p.* of Lord
139. 7. whither shall I flee from thy *p.*
140. 13. upright shall dwell in thy *p.*
Is. 63. 9. angel of his *p.* saved them
Jer. 5. 22. will ye not tremble at my *p.*
1 Cor. 1. 29. no flesh glory in his *p.*
2 Cor. 10. 1. in *p.* am base, 10.
Rev. 14. 10. *p.* of holy angels and in *p.* of Lamb
PRESERVE, Gen. 45. 7. Ps. 12. 7.
Ps. 16. 1 *p.* me, O God, for in thee
25. 21. let integrity and uprightness *p.* me
32. 7. thou shalt *p.* me from trouble
41. 2. Lord will *p.* and keep him alive
61. 7. mercy and truth may *p.* him
64. 1. *p.* my life from fear of enemy
86. 2. *p.* my soul, for I am holy
121. 7. Lord shall *p.* thee from all evil
140. 1. *p.* me from the violent man
Prov. 2. 11. discretion shall *p.* thee
Luke 17. 33. shall lose his life shall *p.* it
2 Tim. 4. 18. *p.* me to his heavenly kingdom
2 Sam. 8. 6. the Lord *preserved* David
Job 10. 12. thy visitation *p.* my spirit
1 Thes. 5. 23. soul and body be *p.*
Jude 1. *p.* in Christ Jesus, and called
Job 7. 20. O thou *preserver* of men
Ps. 36. 6. Lord, thou *preservest* man
97. 10. he *preserveth* the souls of his saints
116. 6. Lord *p.* the simple
145. 20. Lord *p.* all them that love him
146. 9. Lord *p.* the stranger
Prov. 2. 8. he *p.* way of his saints
PRESS, Gen. 40. 11. Judg. 16. 16.
Phil. 3. 14. I *p.* towards the mark for
Amos 2. 13. *pressed* under you as a cart is *p.*
Luke 6. 38. good measure, *p.* down
Acts 18. 5. Paul was *p.* in spirit
2 Cor. 1. 8. were *p.* out of measure
Ps. 38. 2. thy hand *presseth* me sore
PRESUMPTUOUS, Ps. 19. 13. 2 Pet. 2. 10.
Num. 15. 30. Deut. 17. 12, 13.
PRETENCE, Mat. 23. 14. Phil. 1. 18.
PREVAIL, Gen. 7. 20. Judg. 16. 5.
1 Sam. 2. 9. by strength shall no man *p.*
Ps. 9. 19. arise, O Lord, let not man *p.*
65. 3. iniquities *p.* against me
Eccl. 4. 12. if one *p.* against him
Mat. 16. 18. gates of hell shall not *p.*
Gen. 32. 28. power with God and men, and hast
  prevailed
Ex. 17. 11. Moses held up his hand, Israel *p.*
Hos. 12. 4. power over angel, and *p.*
Acts 19. 20. grew word of God, and *p.*
Job 14. 20. thou *prevailest* for ever

PREVENT, Job 3. 12. Ps. 59. 10; 79. 8; 88. 13;
  119. 148. Amos 9. 10. 1 Thes. 4. 15.
2 Sam. 22. 6. *prevented,* 19. Job 30. 27; 41. 11.
  Ps. 18. 5, 18; 119. 147. Is. 21. 14. Mat. 17. 25.
  preventest, Ps. 21. 3.
PREY, Gen. 49. 9, 27. Esth. 9. 15, 16.
Is. 49. 24. *p.* be taken from mighty
59. 15. departeth from evil maketh himself a *p.*
Jer. 21. 9. life for a *p.* 38. 2; 39. 18; 45. 5.
Ps. 124. 6. not given us a *p.* to their teeth
PRICE, Lev. 25. 16. Deut. 23. 18.
Job 28. 13. man knoweth not the *p.*
Prov. 17. 16. a *p.* in hand of fool
Is. 55. 1. wine and milk without *p.*
Mat. 13. 46. pearl of great *p.*
Acts 5. 2. kept back part of the *p.*
1 Cor. 6. 20. bought with a *p.,* 7. 23.
1 Pet. 3. 4. in sight of God of great *p.*
PRICKS, kick against, Acts 9. 5; 26. 14.
Ps. 73. 21. *pricked,* Acts 2. 37.
PRIDE of heart, 2 Chr. 32. 26. Ps. 10. 4.
Job 33. 17. he may . . . hide *p.*
Ps. 10. 2. wicked in *p.* doth persecute
31. 20. hide them from *p.* of man
73. 6. *p.* compasseth them about
Prov. 8. 13. *p.* and arrogancy. . . I hate
11. 2. when *p.* cometh, then
13. 10. by *p.* cometh contention
16. 18. *p.* goeth before destruction
29. 23. man's *p.* shall bring him low
Jer. 13. 17. weep in secret for your *p.*
Ezek. 7. 10. rod hath blossomed, *p.* hath budded
16. 49. iniquity of Sodom, *p.,* fulness of bread
Dan. 4. 37. those that walk in *p.*
Hos. 5. 5. *p.* of Israel testify, 7. 10.
Obad. 3. *p.* of heart deceived thee
1 Tim. 3. 6. lifted up with *p.* he fall
1 John 2. 16. lust of the eyes, and the *p.* of life
PRIEST, Gen. 14. 18. Ex. 2. 16. Lev. 5. 6;
  6. 7, 22, 26; 12. 8.
Is. 24. 2. as with people, so with the *p.*
28. 7. *p.* and prophet have erred
Jer. 23. 11. prophet and *p.* are profane
Ezek. 7. 26. law shall perish from *p.*
Hos. 4. 4. they that strive with *p.*
9. and there shall be like people, like *p.*
Heb. 5. 6. a *p.* for ever, 7. 17, 21.
Lev. 21. 10. *high priest,* Heb. 2. 17; 3. 1;
  4. 14, 15; 5. 1, 10; 6. 20; 7. 26; 8. 1, 3;
  9. 11; 10. 21.
Ps. 132. 9. let thy *priests* be clothed
Is. 61. 6. ye be named *P.* of the Lord
Jer. 5. 31. *p.* bear rule by their means
31. 14. satiate soul of *p.* with fatness
Ezek. 22. 26. *p.* have violated my law
Joel 1. 9. *p.* Lord's ministers, 2. 17.
Mat. 12. 5. *p.* in the temple profane sabbath
Acts 6. 7. company of *p.* obedient
Rev. 1. 6. kings and *p.* to God, 5. 10; 20. 6.
Ex. 40. 15. everlasting *priesthood*
Heb. 7. 24. an unchangeable *p.*
1 Pet. 2. 5. ye are a holy *p.* 9. royal *p.*
PRINCE, Gen. 23. 6; 34. 2.
Gen. 32. 28. as a *p.* hast thou power with
Ex. 2. 14. who made thee a *p.* and judge over
2 Sam. 3. 38. *p.* and great man fallen . . . in Israel
Job 31. 37. as a *p.* would I go near
Is. 9. 6. everlasting Father, *P.* of peace
Ezek. 34. 24. my servant David, a *p.* among
  them, 37. 24, 25; 44. 3; 45. 7; 46. 10, 16. Dan.
Dan. 10. 21. Michael your *p.*   [9. 25.
12. 1. Michael . . . the great *p.*
Hos. 3. 4. many days without a *p.*

John 12. 31. now shall *prince* of this world
14. 30. *p.* of this world cometh and hath
16. 11. *p.* of this world judged
Acts 3. 15. ye killed the *P.* of life
5. 31. to be a *P.* and a Saviour
Eph. 2. 2. *p.* of the power of the air
Rev. 1. 5. Jesus . . . *p.* of kings of earth
Job 12. 19. leadeth *princes* away
21. poureth contempt on *p.*, Ps. 107. 40.
34. 19. that accepteth not persons of *p.*
Ps. 45. 16. thou mayest make *p.* in earth
76. 12. he shall cut off spirit of *p.*
82. 7. shall fall like one of the *p.*
118. 9. than to put confidence in *p.*
119. 23. *p.* did sit and speak against me
161. *p.* persecuted me without cause
Prov. 8. 15. *p.* decree justice, 16.
17. 26. not good, nor to strike *p.* for equity
28. 2. many are the *p.* thereof
31. 4. nor for *p.* strong drink
Is. 3. 4. give children to be their *p.*
Hos. 7. 5. *p.* made him sick with . . . wine
8. 4. made *p.* and I knew it not
Mat. 20. 25. *p.* of Gentiles exercise
1 Cor. 2. 6. not wisdom of . . . *p.* of this world
Prov. 4. 7. wisdom is the *principal* thing
principality(ies), Jer. 13. 18.—*and power(s)*,
Eph. 1. 21; 6. 12. Col. 2. 10, 15. Rom. 8.
38. Tit. 3. 1.
Heb. 5. 12. *principles*, 6. 1.
PRISON, Gen. 39. 20. Eccl. 4. 14.
Is. 42. 7. bring out prisoners from *p.*
53. 8. he was taken from *p.*
61. 1. opening of *p.* to them that are bound
Mat. 5. 25. and thou be cast into *p.*
18. 30. cast into *p.* till he should pay
25. 36. I was in *p.* and ye came, 43.
1 Pet. 3. 19. preached to spirits in *p.*
Rev. 2. 10. devil cast some of you into *p.*
Ps. 79. 11. sighing of *prisoner* come
102. 20. to hear the groaning of *p.*
Eph. 4. 1. I *p.* of Lord beseech you, 3. 1.
Ps. 69. 33. Lord despiseth not his *prisoners*
146. 7. the Lord looseth the *p.*
Zech. 9. 11. send forth thy *p.* out of
12. turn to stronghold, ye *p.* of hope
Luke 21. 12. *prisons*, 2 Cor. 11. 23.
PRIVATE, 2 Pet. 1. 20. Gal. 2. 2.
PRIVY, Deut. 23. 1. Acts 5. 2.
Ps. 10. 8. *privily*, 11. 2; 101. 5. Acts 16. 37.
Gal. 2. 4. 2 Pet. 2. 1.
PRIZE, 1 Cor. 9. 24. Phil. 3. 14.
PROCEED, 2 Sam. 7. 12. Jer. 30. 21.
Is. 29. 14. I will *p.* to do a marvellous work
51. 4. a law shall *p.* from me
Jer. 9. 3. they *p.* from evil to evil
Mat. 15. 19. out of heart *p.* evil thoughts
Eph. 4. 29. no corrupt communication *p.* out of
2 Tim. 3. 9. they shall *p.* no further
Luke 4. 22. the gracious words which *proceeded*
out of him
John 8. 42. I *p.* forth and came from God
Gen. 24. 50. thing *proceedeth* from Lord
Deut. 8. 3. by every word that *p.* out of the
mouth of God, Mat. 4. 4. Luke 4. 4.
1 Sam. 24. 13. wickedness *p.* from the wicked
Lam. 3. 38. of mouth of most High *p.* not evil
John 15. 26. Spirit of truth, which *p.*
Jas. 3. 10. out of mouth *p.* blessing
Rev. 11. 5. fire *p.* out of their mouth
PROCLAIM, Lev. 23. 2. Deut. 20. 10.
Ex. 33. 19. I will *p.* the name of the Lord
Prov. 20. 6. men *p.* every one his own goodness

Is. 61. 2. to *proclaim* the acceptable year of Lord
Ex. 34. 6. Lord passed . . . and *proclaimed*
Prov. 12. 23. the heart of fools *proclaimeth* fool-
PROCURED, Jer. 2. 17; 4. 18.   [ishness
PROFANE not name of Lord, Lev. 18. 21; 19. 12;
20. 3; 21. 6; 22. 9, 15.
Neh. 13. 17. *p.* sabbath, Mat. 12. 5.
Ezek. 22. 26. put not difference between holy and
1 Tim. 1. 9. law is for unholy and *p.*   [*p.*
4. 7. refuse *p.* and old wives' fables
6. 20. avoiding *p.* and vain babblings
Heb. 12. 16. fornicator or *p.* person
Ezek. 22. 8. thou . . . hast *profaned* my sabbaths
Mal. 1. 12. have *p.* it, in that ye say
2. 11. Judah *p.* holiness of the Lord
10. *profaning* covenant of our fathers
PROFESS, Deut. 26. 3. Tit. 1. 16.   [10. 23.
1 Tim. 6. 12. *profession*, 13. Heb. 3. 1; 4. 14;
PROFIT, Prov. 14. 23. Eccl. 7. 11. Jer. 16. 19.
2 Tim. 2. 14. Heb. 12. 10.
1 Sam. 12. 21. *not profit*, Job 33. 27; 34. 9.
Prov. 10. 2; 11. 4. Is. 30. 5; 44. 9, 10;
57. 12. Jer. 2. 8, 11; 7. 8; 23. 32. John 6. 63.
1 Cor. 13. 3. Gal. 5. 2. Heb. 4. 2. Jas. 2. 14.
Job 22. 2. *profitable*, Eccl. 10. 10. Acts 20. 20.
1 Tim. 4. 8. 2 Tim. 3. 16. Tit. 3. 8. Philem.
11.
1 Tim. 4. 15. thy *profiting* appear
PROLONG thy days, Deut. 4. 26, 40; 5. 16, 33;
6. 2; 11. 9; 17. 20; 22. 7; 30. 18; 32. 47.
Prov. 10. 27; 28. 16. Eccl. 8. 13. Is. 53. 10.
PROMISE, Num. 14. 34. Neh. 5. 12.
Ps. 77. 8. doth his *p.* fail for evermore
Luke 24. 49. the *p.* of my Father, Acts 1. 4.
Rom. 4. 16. *p.* might be sure to all
9. 8. children of *p.*, 9. Gal. 4. 28.
Eph. 1. 13. with that holy Spirit of *p.*
6. 2. the first commandment with *p.*
1 Tim. 4. 8. *p.* of the life, 2 Tim. 1. 1.
Heb. 4. 1. lest a *p.* being left us of
6. 17. willing to shew to heirs of *p.*, 11. 9.
9. 15. receive *p.* of eternal inheritance
2 Pet. 3. 4. where is the *p.* of his coming?
1 John 2. 25. the *p.* that he promised us, even
eternal life, Luke 1. 72. Rom. 1. 2; 4. 21.
Tit. 1. 2. Heb. 10. 23; 11. 11; 12. 26.
Rom. 9. 4. pertaineth the *promises*
15. 8. confirm *p.* made to fathers
2 Cor. 1. 20. all *p.* of God are yea
7. 1. having these *p.* . . . let us cleanse ourselves
Gal. 3. 21. is the law against the *p.*
Heb. 6. 12. inherit *p.* 8. 6. better *p.*
11. 17. he that had received *p.*
2 Pet. 1. 4. precious *p.*
PROMOTION, Ps. 75. 6. Prov. 3. 35.
PROOF, Acts 1. 3. 2 Cor. 2. 9; 8. 24.
PROPER, 1 Chr. 29. 3. Heb. 11. 23.
PROPHECY, 1 Cor. 12. 10. 1 Tim. 4. 14; 1. 18.
2 Pet. 1. 19, 20. Rev. 1. 3; 11. 6; 19. 10;
22. 7, 10, 18, 19.
1 Ki. 22. 8. not *prophesy* good, 18.
Is. 30. 10. *p.* not right things *p.* deceits
Joel 2. 28. thy sons and thy daughters shall *p.*
Amos 2. 12. *p.* not
3. 8. Lord spoken, who can but *p.*?
1 Cor. 13. 9. we *p.* in part
14. 1. but rather that ye may *p.*
31. for ye may all *p.* one by one
39. covet to *p.* and forbid not to
Rev. 10. 11. thou must *p.* again before many
Ezra 6. 14. *prophesying*, 1 Cor. 11. 4; 14. 6, 22.
1 Thes. 5. 20.
Num. 11. 25. *prophesied* and did not cease

Jer. 23. 21. I have not spoken to them, yet they
  prophesied
Mat. 7. 22. have we not *p.* in thy name
11. 13. the prophets . . . *p.* until John
John 11. 51. *p.* that Jesus should die
1 Pet. 1. 10. prophets *p.* of the grace
Jude 14. Enoch . . . also *p.* of these   [thee
PROPHET, Gen. 20. 7. he is a *p.* and shall pray for
Ex. 7. 1. and Aaron thy brother shall be thy *p.*
Deut. 18. 15. raise up unto thee a *p.*
18. raise them up a *p.* from among
2 Ki. 5. 13. if the *p.* had bid thee
Ezek. 33. 33. *p.* hath been among them
Hos. 9. 7. *p.* is a fool, the spiritual man
12. 13. by a *p.* was he preserved
Mat. 10. 41. he that receiveth a *p.* in the name
  of a *p.* shall receive a *p.*'s reward
13. 57. a *p.* is not without honour
Luke 7. 28. there is not a greater *p.*
13. 33. a *p.* perish out of Jerusalem
24. 19. *p.* mighty in deed and word
John 7. 40, this is the *P.*, 1. 21; 6. 14.
52. out of Galilee ariseth no *p.*
Acts 3. 22. a *p.* shall the Lord raise
23. will not hear *p.* shall be destroyed
Tit. 1. 12. a *p.* of their own, said
2 Pet. 2. 16. ass . . . forbade madness of *p.*
Num. 11. 29. all Lord's people *prophets*
Ps. 105. 15. do my *p.* no harm
Jer. 5. 13. the *p.* shall become wind
23. 26. are *p.* of the deceit of their
Lam. 2. 14. *p.* have seen vain and foolish things
Hos. 6. 5. I hewed them by the *p.*
Mic. 3. 11. *p.* divine for money
Zeph. 3. 4. her *p.* are light and treacherous
Mat. 5. 17. come to destroy the law, or *p.*
7. 12. this is the law and the *p.*
13. 17. many *p.* . . . have desired
22. 40. on these hang all the law and *p.*
23. 34. I send you *p.* and wise men
Luke 1. 70. spake by mouth of his holy *p.*, Acts
  3. 18. 2 Pet. 1. 20, 21.
6. 23. so did their fathers to *p.*
16. 29. they have Moses and the *p.*
31. if they hear not Moses and the *p.*
24. 25. to believe all that *p.* have spoken, 27.
Luke 24. 44. written in the . . . *p.* concerning me
John 8. 52. Abraham is dead, and the *p.*
Acts 3. 25. ye are children of the *p.*
10. 43. to him give all the *p.* witness
13. 27. knew him not nor yet voices of the *p.*
26. 27. believest thou the *p.?*
22. things which the *p.* and Moses
Rom. 1. 2. which he had promised afore by his
  p. in holy scriptures
3. 21. witnessed by the law and *p.*
1 Cor. 12. 28. secondarily *p.*, 29.
14. 32. spirits of *p.* are subject to *p.*
Eph. 2. 20. are built upon the foundation of the
  apostles and *p.*   [own *p.*
1 Thes. 2. 15. who killed Lord Jesus and their
Heb. 1. 1. God . . . spake to fathers by *p.*
Jas. 5. 10. take . . . *p.* . . . for example
Rev. 18. 20. rejoice, ye apostles and *p.*
22. 6. Lord God of holy *p.* sent his
  9. and of thy brethren the *p.*
PROPITIATION, Rom. 3. 25. 1 John 2. 2; 4. 10.
PROPORTION of faith, Rom. 12. 6.
PROSELYTE, Mat. 23. 15. Acts 2. 10; 6. 5;
PROSPER, Gen. 24. 40. Neh. 1. 11.   [13. 43.
Gen. 39. 3. Lord made all that he did to *p.*, 23.
Deut. 29. 9. *p.* in all ye do, Josh. 1. 7.
Job 12. 6. tabernacles of robbers *p.*

Ps. 1. 3. whatsoever he doeth shall *prosper*
122. 6. they shall *p.* that love thee
Is. 53. 10. pleasure of Lord shall *p.*
54. 17. no weapon against thee shall *p.*
55. 11. shall *p.* in the thing whereto
Jer. 12. 1. Wherefore doth the way of the
23. 5. a King shall reign and *p.*   [wicked *p.?*
1 Cor. 16. 2. God hath *prospered* him
3 John 2. *p.* . . . as thy soul *prospereth*
Job 36. 11. spend days in *prosperity*
1 Ki. 10. 7. thy wisdom and *p.*
Ps. 30. 6. in my *p.* I said I shall never
73. 3. when I saw *p.* of the wicked
118. 25. O Lord, I beseech thee, send now *p.*
122. 7. *p.* be in thy palaces, 35. 27.
Prov. 1. 32. *p.* of fools shall destroy them
Eccl. 7. 14. in day of *p.* be joyful
Jer. 22. 21. I spake to thee in thy *p.*
Gen. 24. 21. journey *prosperous*, Josh. 1. 8. Ps.
  45. 4. Rom. 1. 10.
PROTEST, Gen. 43. 3. 1 Sam. 8. 9. Jer. 11. 7.
  Zech. 3. 6. 1 Cor. 15. 31.
PROUD, Job 9. 13; 26. 12; 38. 11; 40. 11, 12.
Ps. 40. 4. respecteth not the *p.* nor   [Ps. 12. 3.
138. 6. the *p.* he knoweth afar off
Prov. 6. 17. *p.* look and lying tongue
21. 4. high look and *p.* heart, 28. 25.
Eccl. 7. 8. patient is better than *p.*
Mal. 3. 15. we call the *p.* happy
Luke 1. 51. the *p.* in imagination
Jas. 4. 6. God resisteth *p.* 1 Pet. 5. 5.
Ex. 18. 11. wherein they dealt *proudly*
1 Sam. 2. 3. talk no more so exceeding *p.*
Neh. 9. 10. knowest they dealt *p.*, 16.
Ps. 17. 10. they speak *p.*, 31. 18.
Is. 3. 5. child behave *p.* against ancient
PROVE them, Ex. 16. 4. Deut. 8. 16.
Ex. 20. 20. God is come to *p.* you
Deut. 33. 8. holy one . . . thou didst *p.* at
1 Ki. 10. 1. she came to *p.* him
Job 9. 20. mouth shall *p.* me perverse
Ps. 26. 2. examine me, O Lord, *p.* me
Mal. 3. 10. *p.* me now herewith
Rom. 12. 2. *p.* what is . . . will of God
2 Cor. 8. 8. to *p.* the sincerity of your love
13. 5. *p.* your own selves, know
Gal. 6. 4. let every man *p.* his work
1 Thes. 5. 21. *p.* all things; hold fast
Ps. 17. 3. thou hast *proved* mine heart
66. 10. thou, O God, hast *p.* us
95. 9. *p.* me, and saw, Heb. 3. 9.
Deut. 13. 3. the Lord *proveth* you, 8. 2, 16.
Acts 9. 22. *proving*, Eph. 5. 10.
PROVERB and a byword, Deut. 28. 37. 1 Ki.
  9. 7. Jer. 24. 9. Ezek. 14. 8.
Ps. 69. 11. I became a *p.* to them
Eccl. 12. 9. he set in order many *p.*, 1 Ki. 4. 32.
  Prov. 1. 1; 10. 1; 25. 1.
Is. 14. 4. thou shalt take up this *p.* against
John 16. 25. spoken in *p.* 29. no *p.*
2 Pet. 2. 22. according to true *p.*
PROVIDE, Ex. 18. 21. Acts 23. 24.
Gen. 22. 8. God will *p.* himself a lamb
Ps. 78. 20. can he *p.* flesh for people
Mat. 10. 9. *p.* neither gold nor silver
Luke 12. 33. *p.* bags which wax not old
Rom. 12. 17. *p.* things honest in sight
Job 38. 41. *provideth* raven his food
Prov. 6. 8. *p.* her meat in summer
1 Tim. 5. 8. if any *p.* not for his own
Ps. 132. 15. *provision*, Rom. 13. 14.
PROVOKE him not, Ex. 23. 21.
Num. 14. 11. how long will this people *p.* me

Deut. 31. 20. *provoke* me, and break my
Ps. 78. 40. how oft did they *p.* him
Is. 3. 8. to *p.* the eyes of his glory
Jer. 7. 19. do they *p.* me to anger . . . do they not *p.*
　themselves to
44. 8. ye *p.* me to wrath with your
Luke 11. 53. to *p.* him to speak of
Rom. 10. 19. *p.* to jealousy, 11. 11, 14.
1 Cor. 10. 22. do we *p.* Lord to jealousy
Heb. 3. 16. when they heard, did *p.*
10. 24. to *p.* unto love and good works
Num. 16. 30. these men have *provoked* the
　Lord
14. 23. neither any of them that *p.* me
Deut. 9. 8. ye *p.* Lord to wrath, 22.
1 Ki. 14. 22. *p.* him to jealousy
2 Ki. 23. 26. that Manasseh *p.* him
1 Chr. 21. 1. Satan . . . *p.* David
Ezra 5. 12. our fathers had *p.* God to
Ps. 78. 56. and *p.* the most high
106. 7. *p.* him . . . at the Red sea
33. because they *p.* his Spirit
43. they *p.* him with their counsel
Zech. 8. 14. when your fathers *p.* me
2 Cor. 9. 2. your zeal hath *p.* many
Is. 65. 3. a people that *provoketh* me to anger
Deut. 32. 19. *provoking*, 1 Ki. 14. 15; 16. 7.
　Ps. 78. 17. Gal. 5. 26.
PRUDENT in matters, 1 Sam. 16. 18.
Prov. 12. 16. a *p.* man covereth shame
23. *p.* man concealeth knowledge
13. 16. *p.* man dealeth with knowledge
14. 8. wisdom of *p.* is to understand
15. *p.* man looketh
18. *p.* are crowned with knowledge
15. 5. he that regardeth reproof is *p.*
16. 21. wise in heart shall be called *p.*
18. 15. heart of *p.* getteth knowledge
19. 14. a *p.* wife is from the Lord
22. 3. a *p.* man forseeth the evil, 27. 12.
Is. 5. 21. woe to them that are . . . *p.* in
Hos. 14. 9. who is *p.* and he shall
Mat. 11. 25. hid from wise and *p.*
1 Cor. 1. 19. I will bring to nothing the under-
　standing of the *p.*
2 Chr. 2. 12. endued with *prudence* and under-
　standing, Prov. 8. 12. Eph. 1. 8.
Is. 52. 13. my servant shall deal *prudently*
PSALM, 1 Chr. 16. 7. Ps. 81. 2; 98. 5. Acts
　13. 33. 1 Cor. 14. 26.
1 Chr. 16. 9. sing *psalms* to him, Ps. 105. 2.
Ps. 95. 2. joyful noise unto him with *p.*
Eph. 5. 19. speaking to yourselves in *p.*
Jas. 5. 13. merry? let him sing *p.*
PUBLICAN, Mat. 18. 17. Luke 18. 13.
Mat. 5. 46. do not even the *publicans* the same, 47.
11. 19. a friend of *p.* and sinners
21. 31. *p.* and harlots go into kingdom of God
32. *p.* and harlots believed him
Luke 3. 12. came also *p.* to be baptized
7. 29. the *p.* justified God
PUBLISH name of Lord, Deut. 32. 3.
2 Sam. 1. 20. *p.* it not in the streets
Ps. 26. 7. *p.* with voice of thanksgiving
Acts 13. 49. word of the Lord was *published*
Is. 52. 7. feet of him that . . . *publisheth* peace,
　that *p.* salvation
Jer. 4. 15. a voice . . . *p.* affliction
PUFFED up, 1 Cor. 4. 6, 19; 5. 2; 8. 1; 13. 4.
　Col. 2. 18.　　　　　　　　　[14. 5. Jude 23.
PULL out, Ps. 31. 4. Jer. 12. 3. Mat. 7. 4. Luke
　pull down, Is. 22. 19. Jer. 1. 10; 18. 7; 24. 6;
　42. 10. Luke 12. 18. 2 Cor. 10. 4.

Lam. 3. 11. *pull in pieces*, Acts 23. 10.
Ezek. 17. 9. *pull up*, Amos 9. 15.
Zech. 7. 11. *pulled* away shoulder
PULPIT of wood, Neh. 8. 4.
PUNISH, seven times, Lev. 26. 18, 24.
Is. 10. 12. *p.* fruit of the stout heart
13. 11. I will *p.* the world for their
Jer. 9. 25. *p.* all circumcised with
Hos. 4. 14. I will not *p.* daughters
12. 2. will *p.* Jacob according to
Ezra 9. 13. *p.* us less than we deserve
2 Thes. 1. 9. be *p.* with everlasting destruction
2 Pet. 2. 9. reserve unjust . . . to be *p.*
Gen. 4. 13. my *punishment* is greater
Lev. 26. 41. accept *p.* of their iniquity
Lam. 3. 39. complain . . . for *p.* of sins
Amos 1. 3. not turn away the *p.*, 13.
Mat. 25. 46. go into everlasting *p.*
2 Cor. 2. 6. sufficient to such a man is this *p.*
Heb. 10. 29. of how much sorer *p.*
1 Pet. 2. 14. sent by him, for the *p.* of
PURCHASED, Ps. 74. 2. Acts 8. 20; 20. 28.
　Eph. 1. 14. 1 Tim. 3. 13.
PURE, Ex. 27. 20; 30. 23, 34.
2 Sam. 22. 27. with the *p.* thou wilt shew thyself
　p., Ps. 18. 26.
Job 4. 17. man can be more *p.* than his Maker
25. 5. stars are not *p.* in his sight
Ps. 12. 6. words of the Lord are *p.*
19. 8. commandment of Lord is *p.*, 119. 140.
24. 4. clean hands and a *p.* heart
Prov. 15. 26. words of *p.* are pleasant
30. 5. every word of God is *p.*, Ps. 119. 140.
30. 12. generation *p.* in own eyes
Zeph. 3. 9. turn to people *p.* language
Acts 20. 26. I am *p.* from blood of all
Rom. 14. 20. all things indeed are *p.*
Phil. 4. 8. whatsoever things are *p.*
1 Tim. 3. 9. faith in a *p.* conscience
5. 22. keep thyself *p.*
Tit. 1. 15. to the *p.* all things are *p.*
Heb. 10. 22. washed with *p.* water
Jas. 1. 27. *p.* religion and undefiled
3. 17. wisdom from above is first *p.*
2 Pet. 3. 1. stir up your *p.* minds
Is. 1. 25. *purely* purge away dross
Job 22. 30. by *pureness*, 2 Cor. 6. 6.
Hab. 1. 13. of *purer* eyes than to
1 Tim. 4. 12. *purity*, 5. 2.
PURGE me with hyssop, Ps. 51. 7.
Ps. 65. 3. transgressions, thou shalt *p.*
79. 9. *p.* away our sins for thy name's
Mal. 3. 3. purify and *p.* them as gold
Mat. 3. 12. throughly *p.* his floor
1 Cor. 5. 7. *p.* the old leaven
2 Tim. 2. 21. if a man *p.* himself
Heb. 9. 14. *p.* your conscience from
Is. 6. 7. iniquity is taken, and sin *purged*
27. 9. shall the iniquity of Jacob be *p.*
Heb. 1. 3. had by himself *p.* our sins
2 Pet. 1. 9. he was *p.* from old sins
PURIFY sons of Levi, Mal. 3. 3.
Tit. 2. 14. *p.* unto himself a peculiar
Jas. 4. 8. *p.* your hearts, ye double
Ps. 12. 6. silver . . . *purified* seven times
Dan. 12. 10. many shall be *p.*
1 Pet. 1. 22. *p.* your souls in obeying
Mal. 3. 3. sit as a . . . *purifier* of silver
1 John 3. 3. *purifieth* himself, as he
Acts 15. 9. *purifying* their hearts by
Heb. 9. 13. sanctifieth to *p.* of flesh
PURPOSE, Jer. 6. 20; 49. 30.
Job 33. 17. withdraw man from his *p.*

Prov. 20. 18. every *purpose* is established
Eccl. 3. 17. a time for every *p*., 8. 6.
Is. 14. 26. the *p*. that is purposed
Jer. 51. 29. *p*. of Lord shall be performed
Acts 11. 23. with *p*. of heart cleave
Rom. 8. 28. called according to his *p*.
Eph. 1. 11. according to *p*. of him
3. 11. the eternal *p*. . . . in Christ
2 Tim. 1. 9. according to his own *p*.
1 John 3. 8. for this *p*. the Son of God
Eph. 1. 9. mystery . . . which he *p*. in himself, 3.
PURSE, Prov. 1. 14. Mat. 10. 9.   [11.
PURSUE, Gen. 35. 5. Deut. 28. 22.
Ex. 15. 9. the enemy said, I will *p*.
Job 13. 25. wilt thou *p*. dry stubble
Ps. 34. 14. seek peace and *p*. it
Prov. 11. 19. that *pursueth* evil, *p*. it
PUT, Gen. 2. 8; 3. 15, 22.   [7. 27. Rev. 17. 17.
Neh. 2. 12. what God *p*. in heart, 7. 5. Ezra
3. 5. nobles *p*. not their necks to the work of their
    Lord
Job 4. 18. he *p*. no trust in his servants
38. 36. hath *p*. wisdom in inward parts
Ps. 4. 7. hast *p*. gladness in my heart
8. 6. *p*. all things under his feet
9. 20. *p*. them in fear, that they may
Eccl. 10. 10. *p*. to more strength
Sol. 5. 3. *p*. off my coat, how shall I *p*. it on?
Is. 5. 20. woe to them that *p*. darkness for light,
    p. bitter for sweet
42. 1. I have *p*. my Spirit upon him
43. 26. *p*. me in remembrance
63. 11. who *p*. his Holy Spirit
Jer. 31. 33. *p*. my law in their inward parts
32. 40. I will *p*. my fear in hearts
Ezek. 11. 19. *p*. a new spirit within you
36. 27. I will *p*. my Spirit in you, 26.
Mic. 7. 5. *p*. not confidence in guide
Mat. 5. 15. *p*. it under a bushel
19. 6. let no man *p*. asunder
Luke 1. 52. *p*. down mighty from
Acts 1. 7. Father hath *p*. in his own power
15. 9. *p*. no difference between us
Eph. 4. 22. *p*. off . . . old man, Col. 3. 9.
2 Pet. 1. 14. *p*. off this tabernacle
Gen. 28. 20. God . . . give . . . raiment to *put on*
Job 29. 14. I—righteousness and it
Is. 51. 9. awake,—strength, arm of Lord
59. 17. for he—righteousness as a breastplate,—
    garments of
Mat. 6. 25. nor for body, what ye shall—
Rom. 13. 12.—armour of light
14.—Lord Jesus Christ
Gal. 3. 27. baptized into Christ have—Christ
Eph. 4. 24.—the new man, Col. 3. 10.
6. 11.—whole armour of God
Col. 3. 12.— . . . bowels of mercies
14. above all things—charity
1 Chr. 5. 20. *put trust* in, Ps. 4. 5; 7. 1; 9. 10;
56. 4; 146. 3. Prov. 28. 25; 29. 25. Is. 57. 13.
Jer. 39. 18. Heb. 2. 13.
Num. 22. 38. word that God *putteth* in my mouth
Job 15. 15. he *p*. no trust in saints
Ps. 15. 5. that *p*. not out his money,
75. 7. God *p*. down one, and setteth
Sol. 2. 13. *p*. forth green figs
Lam. 3. 29. he *p*. his mouth in dust
Mal. 2. 16. he hateth *putting* away
Eph. 4. 25. *p*. away lying, speak
Col. 2. 11. in *p*. off the body of sins
1 Thes. 5. 8. *p*. on breastplate of faith
1 Pet. 3. 3. wearing of gold or *p*. on of
21. not *p*. away of the filth of the flesh

Q

QUAILS, Ex. 16. 13. Num. 11. 31.
QUAKE, Ex. 19. 18. Mat. 27. 51.
Ezek. 12. 18. *quaking*, Dan. 10. 7.
QUARREL, Lev. 26. 25. Col. 3. 13.
QUEEN, 1 Ki. 10. 1; 15. 13. Ps. 45. 9. Sol. 6. 8.
Jer. 44. 17, 25. Rev. 18. 7.
Mat. 12. 42. *q*. of the south rise up
QUENCH my coal, 2 Sam. 14. 7.
2 Sam. 21. 17. that thou *q*. not light
Sol. 8. 7. many waters cannot *q*. love
Is. 42. 3. smoking flax shall he not *q*.
Eph. 6. 16. to *q*. fiery darts of wicked
1 Thes. 5. 19. *q*. not the Spirit   [46, 48.
Mark 9. 43. fire that never shall be *quenched*, 44,
QUESTION, Mark 12. 34. 1 Cor. 10. 25.
1 Ki. 10. 1. *questions*, Luke 2. 46. 1 Tim. 1. 4;
6. 4. 2 Tim. 2. 23.
QUICK, Num. 16. 30. Ps. 55. 15.
Is. 11. 3. of *q*. understanding in fear
Acts 10. 42. Judge of *q*. and dead
2 Tim. 4. 1. who shall judge *q*. and dead
Ps. 71. 20. *quicken* me again and
80. 18. *q*. us, and we will call on thy name
119. 25. *q*. thou me according to thy word
37. *q*. thou me in thy way
40. *q*. me in thy righteousness
149. *q*. me according to thy judgment
Rom. 8. 11. *q*. your mortal bodies
Ps. 119. 50. thy word hath *quickened* me
Col. 2. 13, *q*. together with him
1 Pet. 3. 18. but *q*. by the Spirit
John 5. 21. Son *quickeneth* whom he will
6. 63. it is the Spirit that *q*.   [spirit
1 Cor. 15. 45. last Adam was made a *quickening*
QUICKLY, Ex. 32. 8. Deut. 11. 17.
Eccl. 4. 12. threefold cord is not *q*. broken
Mat. 5. 25. agree with thine adversary *q*.
Rev. 3. 11. behold, I come *q*., 22. 7, 12, 20.
QUIET, Judg. 18. 27. Job 3. 13, 26.
Eccl. 4. 6. words of wise heard in *q*.
Is. 7. 4. take heed and be *q*., fear not
1 Thes. 4. 11. study to be *q*. and to
1 Tim. 2. 2. lead a *q*. and peaceable
1 Pet. 3. 4. ornament of a meek and *q*. spirit
1 Chr. 22. 9. *quietness*, Job 20. 20.
Job 34. 29. when he giveth *q*. who
Eccl. 4. 6. better is a handful with *q*.
Is. 30. 15. in *q*. and confidence shall be your
    strength
32. 17. effect of righteousness shall be *q*.
2 Thes. 3. 12. exhort that with *q*. they work
QUIT you like men, 1 Sam. 4. 9. 1 Cor. 16. 13.
QUIVER full of them, Ps. 127. 5.
Is. 49. 2. in his *q*. hath he hid me
Jer. 5. 16. *q*. is as an open sepulchre

R

RABBI, Mat. 23. 7, 8. *Rabboni*, John 20. 16.
RACE, Ps. 19. 5. Eccl. 9. 11. 1 Cor. 9. 24. Heb.
RAGE, 2 Ki. 5. 12. 2 Chr. 16. 10.   [12. 1.
2 Chr. 28. 9. ye have slain them in a *r*.
Prov. 6. 34. jealousy is *r*. of a man
29. 9. whether he *r*. or laugh is no
Ps. 46. 6. the heathen *raged*
Prov. 14. 16. the fool *rageth*
Ps. 89. 9. rulest the *raging* of sea
Prov. 20. 1. mocker, strong drink is *r*.
Jude 13. *r*. waves of sea, foaming
RAGS, Prov. 23. 21. Is. 64. 6.

RAILER, or drunkard, 1 Cor. 5. 11.
1 Pet. 3. 9. *railing,* 1 Tim. 6. 4.
2 Pet. 2. 11. *r.* accusation, Jude 9.
RAIMENT to put on, Gen. 28. 20.
Ex. 21. 10. *r.* not diminished
Deut. 8. 4. thy *r.* waxed not old upon
24. 17. not take widow's *r.* to
Zech. 3. 4. clothe thee with change of *r.*
Mat. 6. 25. body more than *r.,* 28.
11. 8. man clothed in soft *r.*
17. 2. his *r.* was white as the light
1 Tim. 6. 8. having food and *r.* let
Rev. 3. 5. clothed in white *r.,* 18; 4. 4.
RAIN in due season, Lev. 26. 4. Deut. 11. 14;
28. 12.
Deut. 32. 2. my doctrine drop as *r.*
2 Sam. 23. 4. clear shining after *r.*
1 Ki. 8. 35. no *r.* because they have sinned
2 Chr. 7. 13. that there be no *r.*
Job 5. 10. who giveth *r.* on the earth
28. 26. he made a decree for the *r.*
Ps. 68. 9. didst send a plentiful *r.*
72. 6. he shall come down like *r.*
147. 8. who prepareth *r.* for earth
Prov. 16. 15. his favour is as cloud of latter *r.*
Eccl. 12. 2. nor clouds return after *r.*
Sol. 2. 11. winter is past; *r.* is over
Is. 4. 6. covert from storm and *r.*
5. 6. clouds that they *r.* no *r.* upon
55. 10. as *r.* cometh down from
Jer. 5. 24. fear Lord our God, that giveth *r.*
Amos 4. 7. witholden *r.* from you
Zech. 10. 1. ask of the Lord *r.*
14. 17. upon them shall be no *r.*
Mat. 5. 45. sendeth *r.* on the just
Heb. 6. 7. earth which drinketh in *r.*
Jas. 5. 18. prayed again, heaven gave *r.*
Job 38. 26. cause it to *r.* on earth
Ps. 11. 6. on wicked he shall *r.* snares
Hos. 10. 12. till he *r.* righteousness
Ps. 78. 27. he *rained* flesh upon
Ezek. 22. 24. land not cleansed, nor *r.* upon
RAISE, Deut. 18. 15, 18. 2 Sam. 12. 11.
Is. 44. 26. *r.* up decayed places
58. 12. *r.* up foundations of many
Hos. 6. 2. third day he will *r.* us up
Amos 9. 11. I will *r.* up tabernacle of
John 6. 40. I will *r.* him dip at last day
Ex. 9. 16. *raised* thee up to shew . . . my power
Mat. 11. 5. deaf hear, dead are *r.*
Luke 1. 69. *r.* up an horn of salvation
Rom. 4. 25. *r.* again for our justification
6. 4. as Christ was *r.* from the dead, 8. 11.
1 Cor. 6. 14. God hath *r.* up the Lord
2 Cor. 4. 14. he which *r.* up the Lord Jesus, shall
raise us also by Jesus
Eph. 2. 6. hath *r.* us up together
Ps. 113. 7. he *raiseth* up poor out of dust
145. 14. *r.* up those that are bowed down
RANSOM of life, Ex. 21. 30.
Ex. 30. 12. give every man a *r.* for
Job 33. 24. I have found *r.*
36. 18. great *r.* cannot deliver thee
Ps. 49. 7. nor give to God a *r.* for
Prov. 6. 35. he will not regard any *r.*
13. 8. *r.* of man's life are his riches
21. 18. wicked shall be a *r.* for righteous
Is. 43. 3. I gave Egypt for thy *r.*
Mat. 20. 28. to give his life a *r.* for
1 Tim. 2. 6. gave himself a *r.* for all
Is. 35. 10. *ransomed,* 51. 10. Jer. 31. 11.
RASH, Eccl. 5. 2. Is. 32. 4.
RAVISHED, Prov. 5. 19. Sol. 4. 9.

REACH, Gen. 11. 4. John 20. 27.
Ps. 36. 5. faithfulness *reacheth* to clouds
Phil. 3. 13. *reaching* forth to those things
READ in audience, Ex. 24. 7.
Deut. 17. 19. *r.* therein all . . . his life
Neh. 13. 1. *r.* in the book of Moses
Acts 15. 21. *r.* in synagogues every
2 Cor. 3. 2. known and *r.* of all men
1 Thes. 5. 27. epistle be *r.,* Col. 4. 16.
Acts 8. 30. understandest thou what thou *readest?*
Rev. 1. 3. blessed is he that *readeth*
Neh. 8. 8. *reading,* 1 Tim. 4. 13.
READY to pardon, a God, Neh. 9. 17.
Ps. 45. 1. tongue is pen of *r.* writer
Eccl. 5. 1. more *r.* to hear, than
Mat. 24. 44. be ye also *r.,* Luke 12. 40.
Mark 14. 38. spirit is *r.* but the flesh
Acts 21. 13. *r.* not to be bound only
1 Tim. 6. 18. do good, *r.* to distribute
2 Tim. 4. 6. now *r.* to be offered
Tit. 3. 1. *r.* to every good work
Rev. 3. 2. strengthen things . . . *r.* to die
Acts 17. 11. *readiness,* 2 Cor. 10. 6.
REAP the harvest, Lev. 19. 9.
Hos. 10. 12. *r.* in mercy
Mat. 6. 26. sow not, neither do they *r.,* Luke
1 Cor. 9. 11. a great thing if we *r.*   [12. 24.
Gal. 6. 7. man soweth, that shall he also *r.*
8. soweth to flesh . . . *r.* corruption; . . . soweth
to Spirit . . . *r.* life everlasting
9. shall *r.* if we faint not   [iniquity
Hos. 10. 13. plowed wickedness, ye have *reaped*
Rev. 14. 16. the earth was *r.,* 15.
Mat. 13. 39. *reapers* are angels, Mat.
John 4. 36. he that *reapeth* receiveth
REASON, Prov. 26. 16. Dan. 4. 36.
1 Pet. 3. 15. asketh a *r.* of the hope
Rom. 12. 1. your *reasonable* service
Acts 24. 25. as he *reasoned* of righteousness
Is. 41. 21. bring forth your strong *reasons*
REBEL not against Lord, Num. 14. 9. Josh. 22. 19.
Job 24. 13. of those that *r.* against the light
Neh. 9. 26. *rebelled* against thee, Ps. 5. 10.
Is. 63. 10. *r.* and vexed his holy Spirit
1 Sam. 15. 23. *rebellion* as sin of witchcraft
Deut. 9. 7. been *rebellious* against Lord, 24.
Is. 30. 9. this is a *r.* people, lying
50. 5. I was not *r.* neither turned away
65. 2. spread my hands . . . to a *r.* people, 1. 23.
Jer. 4. 17. hath been *r.*
5. 23. this people hath a revolting and *r.* heart
Ezek. 2. 5, 8. *r. house,* 3. 9, 26; 12. 2, 3; 17. 12.
24. 3; 44. 6.
Num. 20. 10. hear now, ye *rebels*
Ezek. 20. 38. purge out from you the *r.*
REBUKE thy neighbour, Lev. 19. 17.
2 Ki. 19. 3. a day of trouble, *r.* and blasphemy
Ps. 6. 1. *r.* me not in thine anger, nor
Prov. 9. 8. *r.* a wise man, he will love
27. 5. open *r.* is better than secret love
Zech. 3. 2. Lord said to Satan, The Lord *r.* thee
Mat. 16. 22. Peter . . . began to *r.* him
Luke 17. 3. if thy brother trespass . . . *r.* him
Phil. 2. 15. sons of God, without *r.*
1 Tim. 5. 1. *r.* not an elder, entreat
20. them that sin *r.* before all
Tit. 1. 13. *r.* them sharply, 2. 15.
Heb. 12. 5. nor faint when *rebuked*
Ps. 39. 11. thou with *rebukes* dost correct
Amos 5. 10. hate him that *rebuketh* in gate
RECEIVE good and not evil, Job 2. 10.
Job 22. 22. *r.* I pray thee the law from his mouth
Ps. 6. 9. the Lord will *r.* my prayer

Ps. 49. 15. he shall *receive* me
73. 24. guide me . . . and afterward *r.* me
75. 2. when I shall *r.* congregation
Mat. 10. 41. *r.* a prophet's reward
18. 5. *r.* one such little child in my name
19. 11. all men cannot *r.* this saying
21. 22. ask, believing, ye shall *r.*
Mark 4. 16. heard the word, *r.* it with gladness
11. 24. believe that ye *r.* them
Luke 16. 9. may *r.* you into everlasting
John 3. 27. man can *r.* nothing except
5. 44. which *r.* honour one of
16. 24. ask, and ye shall *r.*, that your joy
Acts 2. 38. shall *r.* gift of Holy Ghost
7. 59. Lord Jesus, *r.* my spirit   [sins
10. 43. whosoever believeth shall *r.* remission of
20. 35. more blessed to give than to *r.*
26. 18. may *r.* forgiveness of sins
Rom. 14. 1. him that is weak in faith *r.* ye
1 Cor. 3. 8. every man *r.* his own reward
2 Cor. 5. 10. may *r.* things done in the body
6. 1. *r.* not grace of God in vain
Gal. 3. 14. *r.* promise of the Spirit
Eph. 6. 8. same shall he *r.* of the Lord
Col. 3. 24. *r.* reward of inheritance
Jas. 1. 21. *r.* with meekness the engrafted word
3. 1. *r.* greater condemnation
1 Pet. 5. 4. shall *r.* a crown of glory
1 John 3. 22. whatsoever we ask, we *r.*
2 John 8. we *r.* a full reward
Job 4. 12. mine ear *received* a little
Ps. 68. 18. thou hast *r.* gifts for men
Mat. 10. 8. freely ye have *r.*, freely give
Luke 6. 24. ye have *r.* your consolation
John 1. 11. own *r.* him not, 12.
Acts 8. 17. they *r.* the Holy Ghost
17. 11. *r.* the word with all readiness
20. 24. which I *r.* of Lord, 1 Cor. 11. 23.
Rom. 5. 11. by whom we have *r.* atonement
8. 15. have *r.* the spirit of adoption
14. 3. him that eateth, for God hath *r.* him
15. 7. receive ye one another, as Christ also *r.* us
1 Tim. 3. 16. *r.* into glory, Mark 16. 19.
4. 3. meats which God hath created to be *r.*
Heb. 11. 13. not having *r.* promises
Luke 16. 25. *receivedst* thy good things
Jer. 7. 28. nor *receiveth* correction
Mat. 7. 8. every one that asketh *r.*
10. 40. he that *r.* you *r.* me, and he that *r.* me *r.*
    him that sent me
John 3. 32. no man *r.* his testimony
12. 48. rejecteth me, and *r.* not my words
1 Cor. 2. 14. natural man *r.* not things
Phil. 4. 15. in giving and *receiving*
Heb. 12. 28. we *r.* a kingdom
1 Pet. 1. 9. *r.* the end of your faith
RECKON(ED), Ps. 40. 5. Is. 38. 13. Luke 22. 37.
    Rom. 4. 4, 9, 10; 6. 11; 8. 18.
RECOMPEN(C)SE, Prov. 12. 14. Is. 35. 4.
Deut. 32. 35. to me belongeth vengeance and *r.*
Job 15. 31. vanity shall be his *r.*
Jer. 25. 14. *r.* them . . . their deeds, Hos. 12. 2.
Luke 14. 14. they cannot *r.* thee
Rom. 12. 17. *r.* to no man evil for evil
Is. 66. 6. render *r.* to his enemies, 59. 18.
Hos. 9. 7. the days of *r.* are come
Luke 14. 12. lest a *r.* be made, 14.
Heb. 2. 2. disobedience received just *r.* of
    reward
10. 35. confidence, which hath great *r.* of
11. 26. he had respect unto *r.* of
2 Sam. 22. 21. according to cleanness of my
    hands hath he *recompensed* me

Prov. 11. 31. the righteous shall be *recompensed*
Jer. 18. 20. shall evil be *r.* for good
Rom. 11. 35. it shall be *r.* to him
Is. 34. 8. it is the year of *recompences* for Zion
Jer. 51. 56. the Lord God of *r.* shall
RECONCILE with blood, Lev. 6. 30.
Col. 1. 20. to *r.* all things to himself
Mat. 5. 24. be *reconciled* to thy brother
Rom. 5. 10. when we were enemies we were *r.*
2 Cor. 5. 18. God, who hath *r.* us to himself
20. we pray you . . . , be ye *r.* to God.
Lev. 8. 15. to make *reconciliation*, 2 Chr. 29. 24.
    Ezek. 45. 15, 17. Dan. 9. 24.
2 Cor. 5. 18. given to us ministry of *r.*
19. committed to us the word of *r.*
Heb. 2. 17. to make *r.* for sins of people
2 Cor. 5. 19. God was in Christ *reconciling* world
RECORD my name, Ex. 20. 24.
Deut. 30. 19. I call heaven and earth to *r.* this
    day, 31. 28.
Job 16. 19. my witness . . . and my *r.*
John 1. 32. bare *r.* 8. 13, 14; 12. 17; 19. 35. Rom.
    10. 2. Gal. 4. 15.
2 Cor. 1. 23. I call God for a *r.*, Phil. 1. 8.
1 John 5. 7. three bear *r.* in heaven
Rev. 1. 2. bare *r.* of the word of God
RECOVER strength, Ps. 39. 13.
Hos. 2. 9. I will *r.* my wool and flax
2 Tim. 2. 26. may *r.* themselves
Jer. 8. 22. is not . . . my people *recovered*
Luke 4. 18. *recovering* of sight to
RED, Ps. 75. 8. Is. 1. 18; 27. 2; 63. 2. Zech. 1. 8;
    6. 2. Rev. 6. 4; 12. 3.
REDEEM with a stretched out arm, Ex. 6. 6.
2 Sam. 7. 23. Israel whom God went to *r.*
Job 5. 20. in famine he shall *r.* thee
Ps. 49. 15. God will *r.* my soul from power
130. 8. *r.* Israel from all his iniquities
Hos. 13. 14. I will *r.* them from death
Tit. 2. 14. might *r.* us from all iniquity
Gen. 48. 16. angel which *redeemed* me
2 Sam. 4. 9. *r.* my soul out of adversity
Ps. 136. 24. *r.* us from our enemies, 31. 5.
Is. 1. 27. Zion shall be *r.* with judgment
52. 3. shall be *r.* without money, 63.
63. 9. in his love and in his pity he *r.* them, 4.
Luke 1. 68. visited and *r.* his people
24. 21. which should have *r.* Israel   [the law
Gal. 3. 13. Christ hath *r.* us from the curse of
1 Pet. 1. 18. nor *r.* with corruptible
Rev. 5. 9. hast *r.* us to God by thy blood
14. 4. these were *r.* from among men
Job 19. 25. I know that my *redeemer* liveth
Ps. 19. 14. my strength and my *r.*
Prov. 23. 11. their *r.* is mighty
Is. 63. 16. our father and *r.* 48. 17.
Jer. 50. 34. *R.* is strong, Is. 49. 26.
Ps. 34. 22. the Lord *redeemeth* the soul of his
    servants
103. 4. who *r.* thy life from destruction, 72. 14.
Eph. 5. 16. *redeeming* time, Col. 4. 5.
Lev. 25. 24. *redemption*, Num. 3. 49.
Ps. 49. 8. *r.* of their soul is precious
111. 9. he sent *r.* unto his people
Luke 2. 38. looked for *r.* in Jerusalem
21. 28. your *r.* draweth nigh
Rom. 3. 24. through *r.* that is in Christ Jesus
8. 23. waiting for the *r.* of our body
1 Cor. 1. 30. Christ . . . made unto us . . . *r.*
Eph. 1. 7. in whom we have *r.*, Col. 1. 14.
14. until *r.* of the purchased possession
4. 30. sealed unto the day of *r.*
Heb. 9. 12. obtained eternal *r.* for us

REFINE, Is. 25. 6; 48. 10. Zech. 13. 9. Mal 3. 2, 3.
REFORMATION, Heb. 9. 10.
REFRAIN, Prov. 1. 15. 1 Pet. 3. 10.
Prov. 10. 19. he that *refraineth* his lips is wise
REFRESHING, Is. 28. 12. Acts 3. 19.
REFUGE, Num. 35. 13. Josh. 20. 3.
Deut. 33. 27. eternal God is thy *r.*
Ps. 9. 9. the Lord also will be a *r.* for the oppressed, a *r.* in times of trouble, 14. 6.
Is. 4. 6; 25. 4.
46. 1. God is our *r.*, 7, 11; 62. 8.
57. 1. thy wings make my *r.*
59. 16. hast been my defence and *r.*
62. 7. and my *r.* is in God
Is. 28. 15. we have made lies our *r.*
Jer. 16. 19. Lord my strength . . . my *r.*
Heb. 6. 18. fled for *r.* to lay hold on
REFUSE, Lam. 3. 45. Amos 8. 6.
1 Tim. 4. 7. *r.* profane and old wives' fables
Heb. 12. 25. *r.* not him that speaketh
Neh. 9. 17. *refused* to obey, neither
Ps. 77. 2. my soul *r.* to be comforted
118. 22. the stone which builders *r.*
Jer. 5. 3. have *r.* to receive correction
8. 5. *r.* to return, 11. 10. *r.* to hear
31. 15. Rahel . . . *r.* to be comforted
1 Tim. 4. 4. nothing to be *r.*
Heb. 12. 25. *r.* him that spake on earth
Jer. 3. 3. *refusedst* to be ashamed
15. 18. *refuseth* to be healed
REGARD not works of Lord, Ps. 28. 5.
Ps. 66. 18. if I *r.* iniquity in my heart
102. 17. will *r.* prayer of destitute
Is. 5. 12. that *r.* not work of Lord
Ps. 106. 44. he *regarded* their affliction and
Luke 1. 48. *r.* low estate of his handmaiden
Heb. 8. 9. I *r.* them not saith the Lord
Mat. 22. 16. *regardest* not person
Deut. 10. 17. God . . . *regardeth* not persons
Job 34. 19. nor *r.* rich more than the
Prov. 12. 10. righteous *r.* life of beast
13. 18. he that *r.* reproof shall be
15. 5. he that *r.* reproof is prudent
Rom. 14. 6. he that *r.* the day *r.* it
REGENERATION, Mat. 19. 28. Tit. 3. 5.
REIGN, Gen. 37. 8. Lev. 26. 17.
Ex. 15. 18. Lord shall *r.* for ever, Ps. 146. 10.
Prov. 8. 15. by me kings *r.* and princes
Jer. 23. 5. a King shall *r.* and prosper
Luke 19. 14. not have this man to *r.* over us
Rom. 5. 17. *r.* in life by one, Jesus
1 Cor. 4. 8. would to God ye did *r.*
2 Tim. 2. 12. if we suffer, we shall *r.*
Rev. 5. 10. we shall *r.* on the earth
22. 5. they shall *r.* for ever and ever
Rom. 5. 14. nevertheless death *reigned* from Adam to Moses
21. that as sin *r.* unto death so
Rev. 20. 4. *r.* with Christ a thousand years
1 Chr. 29. 12. thou *reignest* over all
Ps. 93. 1. Lord *reigneth*, 97. 1; 99. 1.
Is. 52. 7. saith unto Zion, Thy God *r.*
Rev. 19. 6. Lord God omnipotent *r.*
REINS, Job 16. 13; 19. 27.
Ps. 7. 9. God trieth hearts and *r.*, 26. 2. Jer. 17. 10; 20. 12. Rev. 2. 23.
16. 7. my *r.* also instruct me in the night
73. 21. I was pricked in my *r.*
Prov. 23. 16. my *r.* shall rejoice
Jer. 12. 2. thou art . . . far from their *r.*
REJECT, Mark 6. 26. Gal. 4. 14.
Mark 7. 9. ye *r.* commandment of God
Tit. 3. 10. after . . . second admonition *r.*

1 Sam. 8. 7. have not *rejected* thee . . . *r.* me
Is. 53. 3. is despised and *r.* of men
Jer. 6. 19. nor to my law, but *r.* it
8. 9. *r.* word of the Lord
6. 30. Lord *r.* them, 7. 29; 14. 19. 2. Ki. 17. 15, 20. Lam. 5. 22.
Hos. 4. 6. hast *r.* knowledge, I will also reject thee
Luke 7. 30. *r.* the counsel of God
Heb. 12. 17. was *r.*, for he found no
John 12. 48. he that *rejecteth* me
REJOICE, Ex. 18. 9. Deut. 12. 7.
Deut. 28. 63. Lord will *r.* over you
1 Sam. 2. 1. because I *r.* in thy salvation
2 Chr. 6. 41. let thy saints *r.* in goodness
20. 27. the Lord made them to *r.*
Neh. 12. 43. God made them *r.* with
Ps. 2. 11. serve Lord . . . and *r.* with trembling
5. 11. let those that . . . trust in thee *r.*
9. 14. I will *r.* in thy salvation, 13. 5.
51. 8. bones which thou hast broken may *r.*
58. 10. righteous shall *r.* when he
65. 8. morning and evening to *r.*
68. 3. let them *r.* before God
85. 6. that thy people may *r.* in thee
86. 4. *r.* the soul of thy servant
104. 31. Lord shall *r.* in his works
105. 3. heart of them *r.*, 48. 11.
119. 162. I *r.* at thy word as one
Prov. 5. 18. *r.* with wife of thy youth
24. 17. *r.* not when thine enemy falleth
Is. 29. 19. poor among men shall *r.*
62. 5. shall thy God *r.* over thee
65. 13. my servants shall *r.*
Jer. 32. 41. I will *r.* over them to do
Zeph. 3. 17. *r.* over thee with joy
Luke 6. 23. *r.* ye in that day; leap
10. 20. rather *r.* because your names
John 5. 35. willing . . . to *r.* in his light
14. 28. if ye loved me ye would *r.*
Rom. 5. 2. *r.* in hope of glory of God
12. 15. *r.* with them that do *r.*
1 Cor. 7. 30. that *r.*, as though they rejoiced not
Phil. 3. 3. worship God . . . and *r.* in Christ Jesus
Col. 1. 24. *r.* in my sufferings for you
1 Thes. 5. 16. *r.* evermore
Jas. 1. 19. brother of low degree *r.*
1 Pet. 1. 8. *r.* with joy unspeakable
Ps. 33. 1. *rejoice in the Lord*, 97. 12. Is. 41. 16; 61. 10. Joel 2. 23. Hab. 3. 18. Zech. 10. 7. Phil. 3. 1; 4. 4.
119. 14. I have *rejoiced* in way
Luke 1. 47. my spirit *r.* in God my
10. 21. Jesus *r.* in spirit and said
John 8. 56. Abraham *r.* to see my day
1 Cor. 7. 30. as though they *r.* not
Ps. 28. 7. my heart greatly *rejoiceth*
Prov. 13. 9. the light of righteous *r.*
15. 30. light of the eyes *r.* the heart
Is. 62. 5. bridegroom *r.* over bride
64. 5. thou meetest him that *r.*
1 Cor. 13. 6. *r.* not in iniquity
Jas. 2. 13. mercy *r.* against judgment
Ps. 19. 8. statutes of Lord . . . *rejoicing* the heart
119. 111. *r.* of my heart
Prov. 8. 31. *r.* in the habitable part
Jer. 15. 16. thy word was *r.* of my heart
Acts 5. 41. *r.* that they were counted worthy
8. 39. (eunuch) went on his way *r.*
Rom. 5. 2. *r.* in hope, 12. 12.
2 Cor. 1. 12. our *r.* is this, the testimony
Gal. 6. 4. shall he have *r.* in himself
Heb. 3. 6. *r.* of hope firm unto the end

RELIEVE, Lev. 25. 35. Is. 1. 17. Ps. 146. 9. Acts
  11. 29. 1 Tim. 5. 16.
RELIGION, Acts 26. 5. Gal. 1. 13, 14.
  Jas. 1. 27. pure *r.* and undefiled, 26.
  Acts 13. 43. *religious,* Jas. 1. 26.
REMAIN, 1 Thes. 4. 15. Rev. 3. 2. Eccl. 2. 9.
  Lam. 5. 19. John 1. 33.
  Ps. 76. 10. *remainder* of wrath
  John 9. 41. your sin *remaineth*
  2 Cor. 9. 9. righteousness *r.* for ever
  Heb. 4. 9. *r.* a rest to people of God
  1 John 3. 9. his seed *r.* in him
REMEDY, 2 Chr. 36. 16. Prov. 6. 15; 29. 1.
REMEMBER, Gen. 40. 23. Neh. 1. 8.
  Gen. 9. 16. look upon it that I may *r.*
  Ex. 13. 3. *r.* this day . . . ye came out of Egypt
  Deut. 5. 15. *r.* thou wast a servant
  7. 18. shalt well *r.* what Lord . . . did
  8. 18. thou shalt *r.* Lord thy God
  9. 7. *r.* . . . how thou provokedst Lord
  2 Ki. 20. 3. *r.* how I walked before
  Ps. 20. 7. we will *r.* name of Lord
  25. 6. *r.* . . . mercies, 7. *r.* not sins
  74. 2. *r.* thy congregation, 18.
  79. 8. not against us former iniquities, Is. 64. 9.
    Jer. 14. 10. Hos. 8. 13.
  89. 47. *r.* how short my time is
  119. 49. *r.* word unto thy servant
  132. 1. *r.* David and all his afflictions
  Eccl. 12. 1. *r.* now thy Creator in days of
  Sol. 1. 4. we will *r.* thy love more
  Is. 43. 25. I will not *r.* thy sins
  46. 8. *r.* this, shew yourselves men
  Jer. 31. 20. I do earnestly *r.* him still
  Ezek. 16. 61. shalt *r.* thy ways
  36. 31. shall ye *r.* your own evil ways
  Mic. 6. 5. *r.* what Balak . . . consulted
  Hab. 3. 2. in wrath *r.* mercy
  Luke 1. 72. to *r.* his holy covenant
  17. 32. *r.* Lot's wife, Gen. 19. 26.
  Gal. 2. 10. that we should *r.* the poor
  Col. 4. 18. *r.* my bonds
  Heb. 8. 12. iniquities will I *r.* no more
  13. 3. *r.* them that are in bonds
  Neh. 13. 14. *r. me,* 22, 31. Ps. 25. 7; 106. 4.
    Luke 23. 42.
  Ps. 63. 6. *I remember,* 143. 5.
  Jer. 2. 2. for—thee, the kindness of thy youth
  Lev. 26. 42. *I will remember* my covenant, 45.
    Ezek. 16. 60.
  Ps. 77. 11.—the works of the Lord
  Jer. 31. 34.—their sin no more
  Gen. 8. 1. God *remembered* Noah
  19. 29. God *r.* Abraham and sent
  30. 22. God *r.* Rachel, 1 Sam. 1. 19.
  Ex. 2. 24. and God *r.* his covenant with Abraham,
    6. 5.
  Num. 10. 9. shall be *r.* before Lord
  Ps. 77. 3. I *r.* God and was troubled
  78. 39. he *r.* they were but flesh
  98. 3. hath *r.* his mercy and truth
  119. 52. I *r.* thy judgments of old
  55. I have *r.* thy name, O Lord, in the night
  136. 23. who *r.* us in our low estate
  137. 1. we wept when we *r.* Zion
  Mat. 26. 75. Peter *r.* word of Jesus
  Luke 24. 8. they *r.* his words, and
  John 2. 17. disciples *r.* it was written
  Rev. 18. 5. God hath *r.* her iniquities
  Lam. 1. 9. she *remembereth* not her last end
  3. 19. *remembering,* 1 Thes. 1. 3.
  1 Ki. 17. 18. call my sin to *remembrance*
  Ps. 6. 5. in death is no *r.* of

Is. 26. 8. and to the *remembrance* of thee
Lam. 3. 20. my soul hath them still in *r.*
Mal. 3. 16. a book of *r.* was written
Luke 1. 54. he hath holpen . . . Israel in *r.*
22. 19. this do in *r.,* 1 Cor. 11. 24, 25.
John 14. 26. bring all things to your *r.*
Acts 10. 31. thine alms are had in *r.*
2 Tim. 1. 6. put in *r.,* 2. 14. 2 Pet. 1. 12; 3. 1.
Rev. 16. 19. Babylon came in *r.*   [Jude 5.
REMIT sins, they shall, John 20. 23.
  Mat. 26. 28. *remission of sins,* Mark 1. 4. Luke
    1. 77; 3. 3; 24. 47. Acts 2. 38; 10. 43. Rom.
    3. 25. Heb. 9. 22; 10. 18.
REMNANT, Lev. 2. 3. Deut. 3. 11.
  2 Ki. 19. 4. lift up thy prayer for the *r.*
  Ezra 9. 8. leave us a *r.* to escape
  Is. 1. 9. left unto us a very small *r.*
  10. 21. a *r.* shall return, 22.
  Jer. 23. 3. I will gather *r.* of my flock
  Ezek. 6. 8. yet will I leave a *r.*
  Rom. 9. 27. a *r.* shall be saved, 11. 5.
REMOVE thy stroke, Ps. 39. 10.
  Ps. 119. 22. *r.* from me reproach and
  29. *r.* from me the way of lying
  Prov. 4. 27. *r.* thy foot from evil
  30. 8. *r.* far from me vanity and lies
  Eccl. 11. 10. *r.* sorrow from thy heart
  Mat. 17. 20. *r.* hence and it shall *r.*
  Luke 22. 42. if thou be willing *r.* this cup
  Rev. 2. 5. I will *r.* thy candlestick
  Ps. 103. 12. so far hath he *removed* our trans-
    gressions from us
  Prov. 10. 30. righteous shall never be *r.*
  Is. 30. 20. shall not thy teachers be *r.*
  Ezek. 36. 17. uncleanness of a *r.* woman
REND heavens and come, Is. 64. 1.
  Joel 2. 13. *r.* your heart and not your garments
  Jer. 4. 30. though thou *rentest* thy face
RENDER vengeance, Deut. 32. 41, 43.
  2 Chr. 6. 30. *r.* to every man according to his ways
  Job 33. 26. he will *r.* to man his righteousness
  34. 11. work of a man shall he *r.* to
  Ps. 116. 12. what shall I *r.* to Lord
  Prov. 26. 16. seven men that can *r.* a reason
  Hos. 14. 2. *r.* the calves of our lips
  Mat. 22. 21. *r.* to Cæsar the things
  Rom. 13. 7. *r.* to all their dues
  1 Thes. 5. 15. that none *r.* evil for evil, 3. 9.
RENEW right spirit in me, Ps. 51. 10.
  Is. 40. 31. they that wait up on Lord shall *r.* . . .
    strength
  Heb. 6. 6. *r.* them to repentance
  Ps. 103. 5. thy youth is *renewed* like
  2 Cor. 4. 16. inward man is *r.* day by day
  Eph. 4. 23. be *r.* in spirit of your mind
  Ps. 104. 30. *renewest* face of earth
  Rom. 12. 2. *renewing,* Tit. 3. 5.
RENOUNCED hidden things, 2 Cor. 4. 2.
RENOWN, Ezek. 34. 29; 39. 13.
  Is. 14. 20. *renowned,* Ezek. 23. 23.
REPAIRER of breaches, Is. 58. 12.
REPAY, Job 21. 31; 41. 11.
  Deut. 7. 10. he will *r.* him to his face
  Is. 59. 18. according to their deeds . . . he will *r.*
  Rom. 12. 19. I will *r.,* saith the Lord
  Prov. 13. 21. to righteous good shall be *repayed*
REPENT of this evil, Ex. 32. 12.
  Num. 23. 19. neither son of man . . . *r.*
  Deut. 32. 36. Lord shall . . . *r.* himself
  1 Ki. 8. 47. *r.* and make supplication
  Job 42. 6. I abhor myself and *r.* in dust
  Ps. 90. 13. let it *r.* thee concerning
  135. 14. will *r.* himself concerning

Jer. 18. 8. I will *repent* of evil I thought
Ezek. 14. 6. *r*. and turn yourselves, 18. 30.
Jonah 3. 9. if God will turn and *r*.
Mat. 3. 2. *r*. ye, for the kingdom of heaven is at
   hand, 4. 17.
Mark 1. 15. *r*. and believe gospel
6. 12. preached that men should *r*.
Luke 13. 3. except ye *r*. ye shall all likewise
   perish, 5.
16. 30. went unto them from dead, they will *r*.
17. 3. if he *r*. forgive him, 4.
Acts 2. 38. *r*. and be baptized everyone
3. 19. *r*. and be converted, that
8. 22. *r*. of this thy wickedness
17. 30. but now commandeth all men every
   where to *r*.
26. 20. should *r*. and turn to God
Rev. 2. 5. whence thou art fallen, and *r*.
16. *r*.; or I will come unto thee
3. 19. be zealous therefore, and *r*.
Hos. 13. 14. *repentance* hid from my
Mat. 3. 8. fruits meet for *r*., Luke 3. 8.
11. baptize you with water unto *r*.
Mat. 9. 13. not righteous but sinners to *r*.
Mark 1. 4. baptism of *r*., Luke 3.3.
Luke 15. 7. just persons which need no *r*.
24. 47. that *r*. and remission of sins be
Acts 5. 31. give *r*. to Israel and
11. 18. God also to Gentiles granted *r*.
13. 24. preached baptism of *r*. to all
Rom. 2. 4. goodness of God leadeth thee to *r*.
11. 29. gifts and calling of God are without *r*.
2 Cor. 7. 10. godly sorrow worketh *r*.
Heb. 6. 1. not laying again foundation of *r*.
12. 17. found no place of *r*.
2 Pet. 3. 9. that all should come to *r*.
Gen. 6. 6. *repented* the Lord, Ex. 32. 14. Judg.
   2. 18. 2. Sam. 24. 16. Joel 2. 13.
Jer. 8. 6. no man *r*. him of his wickedness
Mat. 21. 29. afterward *r*., and went
27. 3. (Judas) *r*. himself, and brought
Luke 15. 7. one sinner that *repenteth*
Jer. 15. 6. *repenting*, Hos. 11. 8.
REPETITIONS, vain, Mat. 6. 7.
REPLIEST against God, Rom. 9. 20.
REPORT, evil, Gen. 37. 2. Num. 13. 32; 14. 37.
   Neh. 6. 13.
Ex. 23. 1. shalt not raise a false *r*.
Is. 53. 1. who hath believed our *r*.? John 12. 38.
   Rom. 10. 16.
2 Cor. 6. 8. by evil *r*. and good *r*.
Heb. 11. 2. obtained a good *r*.
REPROACH, Josh. 5. 9. Neh. 1. 3. Ps. 69. 7.
   Prov. 18. 3. Is. 54. 4. Jer. 31. 19. Heb. 13. 13.
   Gen. 30. 23. Luke 1. 25.
Job. 27. 6. my heart shall not *r*. me
Ps. 15. 3. up a *r*. against his neighbour
69. 20. *r*. hath broken my heart, 119. 22.
Prov. 14. 34. sin is a *r*. to any people
Is. 51. 7. fear ye not the *r*. of men
Zeph. 3. 18. the *r*. of it was a burden
Heb. 11. 26. esteeming the *r*. of Christ greater
   riches than the treasures
1 Pet. 4. 14. if *reproached* for Christ
Ps. 69. 9. *reproaches* of them that reproached
2 Cor. 12. 10. pleasure in *r*.
Prov. 14. 31. *reproacheth* Maker, 17. 5.
REPROBATE, Jer. 6. 30. Rom. 1. 28. 2 Cor.
   13. 5, 6, 7. 2 Tim. 3. 8. Tit. 1. 16.
REPROOF, astonished at, Job 26. 11.
Prov. 1. 23. turn you at my *r*.
25. would none of my *r*., 30.
10. 17. he that refuseth *r*. erreth

12. 1. he that hateth *reproof* is brutish
13. 18. he that regardeth *r*. shall be honoured
15. 5. he that regardeth *r*. is prudent
31. heareth *r*. of life abideth among wise
32. heareth *r*. getteth understanding
17. 10. *r*. entereth more into a wise
29. 15. the rod and *r*. give wisdom
2 Tim. 3. 16. scripture . . . profitable for . . . *r*.
Ps. 38. 14. *reproofs*, Prov. 6. 23.
50. 21. I will *reprove* thee, and
141. 5. let him *r*. me, it shall be an excellent oil
Prov. 9. 8. *r*. not a scorner, lest he
Hos. 4. 4. let no man strive nor *r*.
John 16. 8. *r*. world of sin, righteousness
Ps. 105. 14. he *reproved* kings for their sakes,
   1 Chr. 16. 21.
Prov. 29. 1. he that being often *r*.
John 3. 20. lest his deeds should be *r*.
Eph. 5. 13. all things that are *r*. are
Prov. 25. 12. *reprover*, Ezek. 3. 26.
Is. 29. 21. that *reproveth* in gate
Prov. 9. 7. that *r*. a scorner getteth
15. 12. a scorner loveth not one that *r*. him
REPUTATION, Eccl. 10. 1. Acts 5. 34. Gal. 2. 2.
   Phil. 2. 7, 29.
REQUEST, Ps. 106. 15. Phil. 4. 6.
REQUIRE, Gen. 9. 5; 42. 22. Ezek. 3. 18, 20;
   33. 8.
Deut. 10. 12. what doth the Lord *r*., Mic.
   6. 8.
1 Ki. 8. 59. maintain as matter *r*.
Prov. 30. 7. two things have I *required*
Is. 1. 12. who *r*. this at your hand
Luke 12. 20. thy soul shall be *r*. of
48. of him shall much be *r*.
1 Cor. 4. 2. it is *r*. in stewards, that
REQUITE, Gen. 50. 15. 2 Sam. 16. 12.
Deut. 32. 6. do ye thus *r*. the Lord
1 Tim. 5. 4. learn . . . to *r*. their parents
2 Chr. 6. 23. by *requiting* wicked
REREWARD, Is. 52. 12; 58. 8.
RESERVE, Jer. 50. 20. 2 Pet. 2. 9.
Jer. 3. 5. will he *r*. his anger for ever
Job 21. 30. wicked is *reserved* to the
1 Pet. 1. 4. inheritance . . . *r*. in heaven
Jude 6. *r*. in everlasting chains
Nah. 1. 2. *reserveth* wrath for his enemies
RESIDUE, Zeph. 2. 9. Mal. 2. 15.
RESIST not evil, Mat. 5. 39.
Zech. 3. 1. Satan . . . at his right hand to *r*. him
Acts 7. 51. ye do always *r*. the Holy Ghost
2 Tim. 3. 8. so do these *r*. the truth
Jas. 4. 7. *r*. the devil, and he will
1 Pet. 5. 9. whom *r*. stedfast in the faith
Rom. 9. 19. who hath *resisted* his will?
Heb. 12. 4. have not yet *r*. to blood
Rom. 13. 2. that *resisteth* the power *r*.
Jas. 4. 6. God *r*. proud, 1 Pet. 5. 5.
RESPECT to Abel, Lord had, Gen. 4. 4. Ex.
   2. 25. Lev. 26. 9. 2 Ki. 13. 23.
2. Chr. 19. 7. nor *r*. of persons (with God).
   Rom. 2. 11. Eph. 6. 9. Col. 3. 25. Acts 10. 34.
Job 37. 24. 1 Pet. 1. 17.
119. 6. *r*. to all thy commandments
138. 6. yet hath he *r*. unto the lowly
Prov. 24. 23. not good to have *r*. of persons,
   28. 21. Lev. 19. 15. Jas. 2. 1, 3, 9.
Heb. 11. 26. he had *r*. to recompence
Ps. 40. 4. *respecteth* not the proud, nor such as turn
REST, Ex. 16. 23; 33. 14. Deut. 12. 9.
Ps. 95. 11. not enter into my *r*., Heb. 3. 11.
132. 14. this is my *r*. for ever: here will I
Is. 11. 10. his *r*. shall be glorious

Is. 30. 15. in returning and *rest* shall ye be saved
62. 7. him no *r.* till he establish
Jer. 6. 16. shall find *r.* for your souls
Mic. 2. 10. this is not your *r.*
Acts 9. 31. then had the churches *r.*
2 Thes. 1. 7. you who are troubled *r.*
Heb. 4. 9. a *r.* to the people of God
10. enter into his *r.* 11. entered into that *r.*
Rev. 14. 11. they have no *r.* day nor night
Ps. 16. 9. my flesh shall *r.* in hope
125. 3. rod of the wicked shall not *r.*
Is. 57. 2. he shall *r.* in their beds
20. like the troubled sea, when it cannot *r.*
Hab. 3. 16. I might *r.* in day of trouble
Rev. 14. 13. dead . . . in the Lord . . . *r.* from
Rom. 2. 17. art called a Jew, and *restest* in
Prov. 14. 33. wisdom *resteth*, Job 24. 23.
Eccl. 7. 9. anger *r.* in bosom of fools
1 Pet. 4. 14. spirit of . . . God *r.* upon you
Num. 10. 33. *resting place*, 2 Chr. 6. 41.
Prov. 24. 15. Is. 32. 18. Jer. 50. 6.
RESTORE, Ps. 51. 12; 23. 3; 69. 4. Is. 58. 12.
Luke 19. 8. Gal. 6. 1.
Ex. 22. 3. *restitution,* Acts 3. 21.
RESTRAIN, 1 Sam. 3. 13. Job 15. 4. Ps. 76. 10.
Is. 63. 15.
RESURRECTION, Mat. 22. 23, 28, 30. Acts
23. 8. 1 Cor. 15. 12. Heb. 6. 2.
Luke 20. 36. and are the children of God, being
children of the *r.*
John 5. 29. done good to *r.* of life . . . done evil
to *r.* of damnation
11. 25. I am the *r.* and the life
Acts 17. 18. preached unto them Jesus and the *r.*
24. 15. there shall be a *r.* of dead
Rom. 6. 5. in likeness of his *r.*
Phil. 3. 10. power of *r.* 11. attain *r.*
Heb. 11. 35. might obtain a better *r.*
Rev. 20. 5. this is the first *r.* 6.
RETAIN, Job 2. 9. John 20. 23. Prov. 3. 18;
11. 16. Eccl. 8. 8. Rom. 1. 28.
Mic. 7. 18. *retaineth* not his anger
RETURN, to the dust, Gen. 3. 19.
1 Ki. 8. 48. *r.* to thee with all their heart
Job 1. 21. naked shall I *r.* thither
Ps. 73. 10. his people *r.* hither
116. 7. *r.* unto thy rest, O my soul
Eccl. 12. 7. dust shall *r.* to the earth
Sol. 6. 13. *r., r.,* O Shulamite; *r., r.*
Is. 10. 21. remnant shall *r.* . . . to . . . God, 22.
35. 10. ransomed of Lord shall *r.*, 51. 11.
55. 11. (my word) shall not *r.* unto me void
Jer. 3. 12. *r.*, backsliding Israel, 14, 22.
4. 1. if thou wilt *r.* . . . *r.* unto me
5. 3. they refused to *r.*, 8. 5. Hos. 11. 5.
15. 19. if thou *r.* . . . let them *r.* . . . but *r.* not
thou
Hos. 2. 7. *r.* to my first husband
5. 15. I will go and *r.* to my place
7. 16. they *r.*, but not to Most High
11. 9. not *r.* to destroy Ephraim
Mal. 3. 7. *r.* to me, and I will *r.* to
18. then shall ye *r.* and
Ps. 35. 13. my prayer *returned* into my bosom
78. 34. they *r.* and inquired early after God
Amos 4. 6. have ye not *r.* to me, 8–11.
1 Pet. 2. 25. are *r.* unto Shepherd
Is. 30. 15. in *returning* find rest
Deut. 30. 2. *return to the Lord,* 1 Sam. 7. 3. Is.
55. 7. Hos. 6. 1; 3. 5; 7. 10; 14. 1, 7.
REVEAL, Prov. 11. 13. Dan. 2. 19.
Job 20. 27. heaven shall *r.* his iniquity
Gal. 1. 16. pleased God . . . to *r.* his Son

Deut. 29. 29. things which are *revealed*
Is. 22. 14. it was *r.* in mine ears
53. 1. to whom is arm of Lord *r.?*
Mat. 10. 26. covered that shall not be *r.*
11. 25. hid . . . from wise . . . , *r.* them to babes
16. 17. flesh and blood hath not *r.*
Rom. 1. 17. righteousness of God *r.*
8. 18. glory which shall be *r.* in us
1 Cor. 2. 10. God hath *r.* them to us
2 Thes. 1. 7. when Lord Jesus shall be *r.*
2. 3. falling away . . . man of sin be *r.*
Amos 3. 7. *revealeth* his secret to his servants
Rom. 2. 5. *revelation,* 16. 25. Gal. 1. 12. Eph.
1. 17; 3. 3. 1 Pet. 1. 13. 2 Cor. 12. 1. Rev. 1. 1.
REVELLINGS, Gal. 5. 21. 1 Pet. 4. 3.
REVENGE, Jer. 15. 15. 2 Cor. 7. 11; 10. 6. Nah.
1. 2.
Num. 35. 19. *revenger*, Rom. 13. 4.
Ps. 79. 10. by the *revenging* of the blood of
thy servants
REVERENCE my sanctuary, Lev. 19. 30.
Ps. 89. 7. to be had in *r.* of all them
Eph. 5. 33. wife see that she *r.* her
Heb. 12. 28. serve God acceptably with *r.*
Ps. 111. 9. and *reverend* is his name
REVILE, Ex. 22. 28. Mat. 5. 11.
1 Cor. 4. 12. being *reviled* we bless
1 Pet. 2. 23. when he was *r.*, *r.* not
1 Cor. 6. 10. nor *revilers* . . . inherit the
Is. 51. 7. *revilings*, Zeph. 2. 8.
REVIVE us again, Ps. 85. 6.
Is. 57. 15. to *r.* the spirit of the humble, to *r.*
heart of contrite
Hos. 6. 2. after two days will he *r.* us
14. 7. they shall *r.* as the corn, and
Rom. 7. 9. sin *revived* and I died
14. 9. Christ both died and rose, and *r.*
REVOLT more and more, Is. 1. 5.
Is. 31. 6. children of Israel have deeply *revolted*
Jer. 5. 23. this people hath a *revolting* and a
rebellious heart
6. 28. *revolters*, Hos. 5. 2.; 9. 15.
REWARD, exceeding great, Gen. 15. 1.
Deut. 10. 17. God . . . nor taketh *r.*, Ps. 15. 5.
Ps. 19. 11. in keeping them is great *r.*
58. 11. there is a *r.* for righteous
127. 3. fruit of the womb is his *r.*
Prov. 11. 18. righteousness shall be a sure *r.*
Is. 3. 11. *r.* of his hands shall be
Mic. 7. 3. the judge asketh for a *r.*
Mat. 5. 12. great is your *r.* in heaven
6. 2. verily . . . they have their *r.*
4. thy Father . . . shall *r.* thee openly
10. 41. shall receive a prophet's *r.*
Rom. 4. 4. is the *r.* not reckoned of
1 Cor. 3. 8. shall receive his own *r.*
Col. 2. 18. no man beguile you of your *r.*
3. 24. receive the *r.* of inheritance
1 Tim. 5. 18. labourer is worthy of his *r.*
2 Tim. 4. 14. Lord *r.* him according
Heb. 2. 2. just recompence of *r.*
2 John 8. we receive a full *r.*
Rev. 22. 12. I come quickly; and my *r.* is with
18. 6. *r.* her as she *rewarded* you
Ps. 103. 10. nor *r.* us according to our iniquities
Is. 3. 9. have *r.* evil to themselves
Heb. 11. 6. *rewarder* of them that
Ps. 31. 23. plentifully *rewardeth* proud
RICH, Gen. 13. 2; 14. 23. Ex. 30. 15.
Prov. 10. 4. hand of diligent maketh *r.*
22. blessing of the Lord, it maketh *r.*
14. 20. *r.* hath many friends
18. 11. *r.* man's wealth is his strong city, 10. 15.

Prov. 22. 2. *rich* and poor meet together
23. 4. labour not to be *r.*
28. 11. *r.* man wise in his own conceit
20. that maketh haste to be *r.* shall not
Eccl. 5. 12. abundance of *r.* will not suffer
10. 20. curse not *r.* in thy bedchamber
Jer. 9. 23. let not *r.* man glory in his
Mat. 19. 23. *r.* man shall hardly enter
Luke 1. 53. *r.* he hath sent empty away
6. 24. woe unto you that are *r.*
16. 1. certain *r.* man which had
18. 23. sorrowful: for he was very *r.*
2 Cor. 6. 10. as poor yet making many *r.*
8. 9. though he was *r.* yet . . . he became poor
Eph. 2. 4. God who is *r.* in mercy
1 Tim. 6. 9. they that will be *r.* fall
17. charge them that are *r.* in this
18. that they be *r.* in good works
Jas. 2. 5. poor of this world *r.* in faith
Rev. 2. 9. I know . . . thy poverty, (but thou art *r.*)
3. 17. because thou sayest, I am *r.*
1 Chr. 29. 12. *riches* and honour
Ps. 39. 6. he heapeth up *r.* and
49. 6. boast themselves in multitude of their *r.*
52. 7. trusted in abundance of his *r.*
62. 10. if *r.* increase, set not your heart
104. 24. the earth is full of thy *r.*
112. 3. wealth and *r.* shall be in his house
Prov. 3. 16. in her left hand *r.* and
11. 4. *r.* profit not in day of wrath
28. that trusteth in his *r.* shall fall
13. 8. ransom of man's life are his *r.*
14. 24. crown of the wise is their *r.*
23. 5. *r.* certainly make themselves wings
27. 24. *r.* are not for ever, nor the
30. 8. give me neither poverty nor *r.*
Jer. 17. 11. so he that getteth *r.* and
Mat. 13. 22. deceitfulness of *r.* choke
Luke 16. 11. to your trust the true *r.*
Rom. 2. 4. despisest thou the *r.*
11. 12. if fall of them be *r.* of world
2 Cor. 8. 2. unto *r.* of their liberality
Eph. 1. 7. according to the *r.* of his
2. 7. shew exceeding *r.* of grace
Phil. 4. 19. according to his *r.* in glory
Col. 1. 27. the *r.* of the glory of this mystery
2. 2. unto all *r.* of the full assurance
1 Tim. 6. 17. not trust in uncertain *r.*
Heb. 11. 20. reproach of Christ greater *r.* than
Jas. 5. 2. your *r.* are corrupted
Col. 3. 16. word of Christ dwell in you *richly*
1 Tim. 6. 17. giveth us *r.* all things
RIDE, Ps. 45. 4; 66. 12. Hab. 3. 8.
Deut. 33. 26. *rideth*, Ps. 68. 4, 33. Is. 19. 1.
RIGHT, Num. 27. 7. Deut. 21. 17.
Gen. 18. 25. Judge of all the earth do *r.*
Ezra 8. 21. seek of him a *r.* way for
Job 34. 23. not lay on man more than *r.*
Ps. 19. 8. statutes of Lord are *r.*, 33. 4.
51. 10. renew a *r.* spirit within me
119. 128. I esteem thy precepts . . . to be *r.*
Prov. 4. 11. I have led thee in *r.* paths
8. 9. *r.* to them that find knowledge
12. 5. thoughts of righteous are *r.*
14. 12. a way which seemeth *r.* to
21. 2. way of man is *r.* in his own eyes
Is. 30. 10. prophesy not unto us *r.* things
Ezek. 18. 5. do that which is lawful and *r.*
Hos. 14. 9. ways of the Lord are *r.*
Amos 3. 10. they know not to do *r.*
Mark 5. 15. and in his *r.* mind
Luke 12. 57. judge ye not what is *r.*
Acts 4. 19. whether it be *r.* in sight of God

Acts. 8. 21. thy heart is not *right* in sight of
13. 10. not cease to pervert *r.* ways
Eph. 6. 1. obey your parents . . . this is *r.*
2 Pet. 2. 15. forsaken *r.* way and are gone
Rev. 22. 14. have *r.* to tree of life
2 Tim. 2. 15. *rightly* dividing word
Gen. 7. 1. thee have I seen *righteous* before me
18. 23. wilt destroy *r.* with wicked, 20. 4.
Num. 23. 10. let me die death of *r.*
Deut. 25. 1. justify *r.* and condemn
Job 4. 7. where were the *r.* cut off?
17. 9. the *r.* shall hold on his way
Ps. 1. 6. Lord knoweth way of *r.*
5. 12. thou, Lord, wilt bless the *r.*; with favour
7. 11. God judgeth the *r.* and God is angry
32. 11. glad in the Lord and rejoice, ye *r.*, 33. 1.
34. 17. *r.* cry, and Lord heareth
19. many are afflictions of the *r.*
37. 25. have I not seen the *r.* forsaken
29. the *r.* shall inherit the land
55. 22. never suffer *r.* to be moved
58. 11. there is a reward for the *r.*
64. 10. *r.* shall be glad in the Lord
68. 3. let the *r.* be glad; let them rejoice
92. 12. the *r.* shall flourish like palm tree
97. 11. light is sown for the *r.*
112. 6. the *r.* shall be in everlasting
Ps. 125. 3. rod of wicked shall not rest on lot
        of *r.*
145. 17. Lord is *r.*, Lam. 1. 18. Dan. 9. 14.
146. 8. the Lord loveth the *r.*
Prov. 3. 32. his secret is with the *r.*
10. 3. not suffer soul of *r.* to famish
21. the lips of the *r.* feed many
24. desire of the *r.* shall be granted
25. *r.* is an everlasting foundation
38. the hope of *r.* shall be gladness
30. the *r.* shall never be removed
32. lips of *r.* know what is acceptable
11. 8. *r.* is delivered out of trouble
21. seed of *r.* shall be delivered
28. the *r.* shall flourish as a branch
30. fruit of the *r.* is a tree of life
31. the *r.* shall be recompensed in
12. 3. root of *r.* shall not be moved
5. the thoughts of the *r.* are *r.*
7. the house of the *r.* shall stand
10. a *r.* man regardeth life of his beast
12. root of *r.* yieldeth fruit
26. *r.* is more excellent than his neighbour
13. 9. the light of the *r.* rejoiceth
25. *r.* eateth to satisfying of his soul
14. 32. *r.* hath hope in his death
15. 6. in house of *r.* is much treasure
19. the way of the *r.* is made plain
29. he heareth the prayer of *r.*
28. 1. the *r.* are bold as a lion
Eccl. 7. 16. be not *r.* over much, nor
9. 2. one event to the *r.* and to the wicked
Is. 3. 10. say to *r.*, it shall be well
41. 2. raised up *r.* man from east
57. 1. the *r.* perisheth . . . *r.* is taken away
60. 21. thy people also shall be all *r.*
Ezek. 3. 20. when a *r.* man doth turn from his
        righteousness, 21; 18. 24, 26.
Mal. 3. 18. discern between *r.* and
Mat. 9. 13. not come to call *r.* but
10. 41. shall receive *r.* man's reward
25. 46. *r.* (shall go) into life eternal
Luke 1. 6. were both *r.* before God
18. 9. trusted . . . that they were *r.* and
Rom. 3. 10. there is none *r.*, no not
5. 7. scarcely for a *r.* man will one

2 Thes. 1. 5. a token of *righteous* judgment
1 Tim. 1. 9. law is not made for a *r.*
Jas. 5. 16. fervent prayer of *r.* man
1 Pet. 4. 18. the *r.* scarcely be saved
Rev. 22. 11. he that is *r.* let him be *r.*
Tit. 2. 12. live soberly, *righteously*
Deut. 6. 25. it shall be our *righteousness,* if
33. 19. offer sacrifices of *r.,* Ps. 4. 5.
Job 29. 14. I put on *r.* and it clothed
36. 3. and will ascribe *r.* to my Maker
Ps. 11. 7. righteous Lord loveth *r.,* 45. 7.
15. 2. walketh uprightly and worketh *r.*
85. 10. *r.* and peace have kissed
97. 2. *r.* and judgment are habitation
106. 3. he that doeth *r.* at all times
Prov. 10. 2. *r.* delivereth from death, 11. 4.
11. 5. *r.* of perfect shall direct his way
6. *r.* of upright shall deliver them
18. to him that soweth *r.* a sure
19. as *r.* tendeth to life; so he that
12. 28. in the way of *r.* is life
13. 6. *r.* keepeth him that is upright in way
14. 34. *r.* exalteth a nation: but sin
15. 9. he loveth him that followeth *r.*
16. 12. the throne is established by *r.*
31. if it be found in the way of *r.*
Is. 11. 5. *r.* shall be the girdle of his loins
26. 9. inhabitants of world will learn *r.*
28. 17. judgment . . . to line and *r.* to the plummet
32. 17. work of *r.* shall be peace
45. 24. in the Lord have I *r.* and
46. 12. that are far from *r.*
13. I bring near my *r.*; it shall not
54. 17. their *r.* is of me, saith Lord
61. 3. trees of *r.,* planting of Lord
10. covered me with robe of *r.*
64. 5. that rejoiceth and worketh *r.*
Jer. 23. 6. be called Lord our *R.,* 33. 16.
Dan. 4. 27. break off thy sins by *r.*
9. 7. O Lord, *r.* belongeth unto thee
24. to bring in everlasting *r.*
12. 3. they that turn many to *r.* (shall shine) as the stars
Zeph. 2. 3. seek *r.,* seek meekness
Mal. 4. 2. Sun of *r.* arise with healing
Mat. 3. 15. it becometh us to fulfil all *r.*
5. 6. which do hunger and thirst after *r.*
20. except your *r.* exceed the *r.* of
21. 32. John came . . . in the way of *r.*
Luke 1. 75. in holiness and *r.* before
John 16. 8. reprove world of sin, of *r.*
Acts 10. 35. he that . . . worketh *r.* is accepted
13. 10. thou enemy of all *r.*
Rom. 1. 17. therein is the *r.* of God revealed
3. 22. even *r.* of God which is by faith of
4. 6. man to whom God imputeth *r.*
5. 18. by *r.* of one the free gift came to all
21. grace reign through *r.* to eternal
6. 13. members as instruments of *r.*
19. servants to *r.* unto holiness, 18.
8. 4. that the *r.* of the law might
9. 30. have attained to *r.,* even *r.,* 31.
10. 3. ignorant of God's *r.* . . . . establish their own *r.,* have not submitted themselves unto the *r.* of God. 4. Christ is end of law for *r.* 6. *r.* which is of faith. 10. with heart man believeth to *r.*
14. 17. kingdom of God is . . . *r.,* peace
1 Cor. 1. 30. made unto us wisdom and *r.*
15. 34. awake to *r.* and sin not
2 Cor. 5. 21. the *r.* of God in him
6. 7. armour of *r.* on right hand
9. 10. increase the fruits of your *r.*
11. 15. ministers . . . transformed as ministers of *r.*

Gal. 2. 21. if *righteousness* come by the law, then
Eph. 6. 14. having on breastplate of *r.*
Phil. 1. 11. being filled with fruits of *r.*
3. 6. touching *r.* which is in the law blameless
9. not mine own *r.* but the *r.* which is of God
1 Tim. 6. 11. follow after *r.,* 2 Tim. 2. 22.
Heb. 12. 11. peaceable fruit of *r.*
Jas. 1. 20. man worketh not *r.* of God
3. 18. fruit of *r.* is sown in peace
1 Pet. 3. 14. if ye suffer for *r.*' sake happy
2 Pet. 1. 1. through the *r.* of God and our
3. 13. new earth, wherein dwelleth *r.*
1 John 2. 29. that doeth *r.* is born
Rev. 19. 8. fine linen is the *r.* of saints
Gen. 15. 6. counted it to him for *r.,* Ps. 106. 31. Rom. 4. 3, 5, 9, 22. Gal. 3. 6.
1 Ki. 8. 32. *his righteousness,* Job 33. 26. Ps. 50. 6. Ezek. 3. 20. Mat. 6. 33. Rom. 3. 25. 2 Cor. 9. 9.
Ps. 17. 15. *in righteousness,* Hos. 10. 12. Acts 17. 31. Eph. 4. 24. Rev. 19. 11. *with righteousness,* Ps. 96. 13; 98. 9.
Deut. 9. 5. *thy righteousness,* Job 35. 8. Ps. 35. 28; 40. 10; 51. 14; 89. 16; 119. 142. Is. 57. 12; 58. 8; 62. 2.
Is. 64. 6. *all our righteousnesses,* Ezek. 33. 13. Dan. 9. 18.
RIGOUR, Ex. 1. 13. Lev. 25. 43, 53.
RIOT, Tit. 1. 6. 1 Pet. 4. 4. 2 Pet. 2. 13.
Rom. 13. 13. *rioting*
Prov. 23. 20. *riotous,* 28. 7. Luke 15. 13.
RIPE fruit, Ex. 22. 29. Num. 18. 13. Mic. 7. 1. Jer. 24. 2. *r.* figs, Hos. 9. 10. Nah. 3. 12.
Gen. 40. 10. *ripe grapes,* Num. 13. 20. Is. 18. 5. Joel 3. 13.
Rev. 14. 15. harvest of the earth is *r.*
RISE, Sol. 3. 2. Is. 14. 21; 24. 20; 26. 14; 33. 10; 43. 17; 54. 17; 58. 10. 1 Thes. 4. 16.
Prov. 30. 31. *rising,* Luke 2. 34.
RIVER, Ex. 1. 22; 4. 9. Job 40. 23. Ps. 36. 8; 46. 4; 65. 9. Is. 48. 18; 66. 12. Rev. 22. 1, 2.
Job 20. 17. *rivers,* 29. 6. Ps. 119. 136. Prov. 5. 16; 21. 1. Is. 32. 2; 33. 21. Mic. 6. 7. John 7. 38.
ROAR, Is. 42. 13. Jer. 25. 30. Hos. 11. 10. Joel 3. 16. Amos 1. 2.
ROB, Lev. 19. 13. Prov. 22. 22.
Is. 42. 22. a people *robbed* and
2 Cor. 11. 8. I *r.* other churches
Job 5. 5. the *robber* swalloweth up, 18. 9.
John 10. 1. that climbeth up some other way is a thief and a *r.*   [3. 10. Phil. 2. 6.
Ps. 62. 10. *robbery,* Prov. 21. 7. Is. 61. 8. Amos
ROBE, Is. 61. 10. Rev. 7. 9, 13, 14.
ROCK, Ex. 17. 6. Num. 20. 8, 11. Deut. 32. 4; 13, 15, 18, 30, 31.
Ps. 18. 2. Lord is my *r.,* 92. 15.
31. 3. thou art my *r.* and my fortress, 2; 71. 3.
61. 2. lead me to the *r.* that is higher than
62. 2. he only is my *r.,* 6.
89. 26. my father . . . and *r.* of my salvation
94. 22. God is the *r.* of my refuge
Mat. 7. 24. wise man, which built his house on a *r.*
16. 18. on this *r.* I will build my church
1 Cor. 10. 4. that *R.* was Christ
Rev. 6. 16. said to . . . *rocks,* Fall on us
ROD, Ex. 4. 4, 20. Num. 17. 2, 8.
Ps. 23. 4. thy *r.* and staff they comfort
125. 3. *r.* of wicked shall not
Prov. 13. 24. spareth his *r.* hateth his son
23. 14. thou shalt beat him with *r.*
29. 15. *r.* and reproof give wisdom
Ezek. 20. 37. cause to pass under *r.,* Lev. 27. 32.

Mic. 6. 9. hear ye the *rod* and who hath
7. 14. feed thy people with thy *r.*
Rev. 2. 27. rule with *r.* of iron, 12. 5. 19. 15.
ROOM, Prov. 18. 16. Luke 14. 22.
ROOT, Job 5. 3; 31. 12. Ps. 52. 5.
Deut. 29. 18. a *r.* that beareth gall
Job 19. 28. seeing *r.* of the matter
Is. 11. 10. there shall be *r.* of Jesse
37. 31. take *r.* downwards, 27. 6.
Mat. 3. 10. axe is laid to *r.* of trees
13. 6. because they had no *r.*
Luke 17. 6. be thou plucked up by *r.*
Rom. 11. 16. if *r.* be holy, so are the
1 Tim. 6. 10. love of money is *r.* of
Mat. 15. 13. planted . . . shall be *rooted* up
Eph. 3. 17. being *r.* and grounded in love
Col. 2. 7. *r.* and built up in him
ROSE, Sol. 2. 1. Is. 35. 1.
ROYAL diadem in hand of thy God, Is. 62. 3.
Jas. 2. 8. if ye fulfil *r.* law
1 Pet. 2. 9. ye are . . . a *r.* priesthood
RUBIES, price of wisdom is above, Job 28. 18.
Prov. 3. 15; 8. 11; 31. 10.
RUDDY, Sol. 5. 10. Lam. 4. 7.
RUDIMENTS, Col. 2. 8, 20.
RULE, Esth. 9. 1. Prov. 17. 2; 19. 10.
Prov. 25. 28. no *r.* over his own spirit
Gal. 6. 16. walk according to this *r.*
Phil. 3. 16. let us walk by same *r.*
Heb. 13. 7. which have *r.* over you, 17.
Col. 3. 15. let the peace of God *r.* in
1 Tim. 3. 5. how to *r.* his own house
5. 17. elders that *r.* well be counted worthy
Rev. 12. 5. man child who was to *r.* all
Mic. 5. 2. is to be *ruler* in Israel
Mat. 25. 21. make thee *r.* over many
Rom. 13. 3. *rulers* are not a terror to
Eph. 6. 12. *r.* of darkness of this world
Ps. 103. 19. his kingdom *ruleth* over all
Prov. 16. 23. he that *r.* his spirit than
Hos. 11. 12. Judah yet *r.* with God
RUN, Gen. 49. 22. Lev. 15. 3. 1 Sam. 8. 11. Ps.
19. 5. Eccl. 1. 7. *forerunner,* Heb. 6. 20.
2 Chr. 16. 9. eyes of the Lord *r.*   [ments
Ps. 119. 32. I will *r.* way of thy command-
Sol. 1. 4. draw me, we will *r.* after
Is. 40. 31. shall *r.* and not be weary
Dan. 12. 4. many shall *r.* to and fro
Gal. 2. 2. *r.* in vain, 5. 7. did *r.* well
Heb. 12. 1. *r.* with patience the race
1 Pet. 4. 4. *r.* not with them to same excess of
Ps. 23. 5. my cup *runneth* over
Rom. 9. 16. nor of him that *r.,* but

S

SABBATH holy, Ex. 16. 23, 29; 20. 8–11; 31. 14.
Acts 13. 42; 18. 4.
Lev. 23. 3. seventh day is *s.* of rest
Neh. 9. 14. madest known . . . thy holy *s.*
13. 18. bring more wrath . . . by profaning *s.*
Is. 56. 2. keepeth *s.* from polluting it, 6.
58. 13. call *s.* a delight, holy of the Lord
Mat. 12. 5. priests in the temple profane *s.*
28. 1. end of *s.* as it began to dawn
Lev. 19. 3. *my sabbaths,* 30; 26. 2. Is. 56. 4.
Ezek. 20. 12, 13; 22. 8, 26; 23. 38; 44. 24; 46. 3.
Deut. 5. 12. *sabbath day,* Neh. 13. 22. Jer.
17. 21. Acts 15. 21. Col. 2. 16.
SACKCLOTH, Gen. 37. 34. Job 16. 15. Ps.
30. 11; 35. 13. Is. 22. 12. Rev. 11. 3.

SACRIFICE, Gen. 31. 54. Ex. 8. 25.
1 Sam. 2. 29. wherefore kick ye at my *s.*
3. 14. Eli's house shall not purged with *s.*
15. 22. to obey is better than *s.*
Ps. 50. 5. made covenant with me by *s.*
107. 22. *s.* the sacrifices of thanksgiving, 116. 17.
141. 2. lifting up of my hands as evening *s.*
Prov. 15. 8. *s.* of wicked is abomination
21. 3. justice . . . more acceptable to Lord than *s.*
Eccl. 5. 1. than to give *s.* of fools
Dan. 8. 11. daily *s.* was taken away
9. 27. cause *s.* and oblation to cease
11. 31. take away daily *s.,* 12. 11.
Hos. 6. 6. desired mercy and not *s.,* Mat. 9. 13;
Mark 9. 49. every *s.* be salted with   [12. 7.
Rom. 12. 1. present your bodies a living *s.*
Eph. 5. 2. *s.* to God for a sweetsmelling
Phil. 2. 17. offered on *s.* and service of your faith
4. 18. a *s.* acceptable, well pleasing to God
Heb. 9. 26. put away sin by *s.* of
1 Cor. 5. 7. Christ our passover is *sacrificed*
Ps. 4. 5. offer *sacrifices* of righteousness
51. 17. *s.* of God are a broken spirit
Heb. 13. 15. *s.* of praise, 16. with such *s.*
1 Pet. 2. 5. priesthood, to offer up *s.*
SACRILEGE, commit, Rom. 2. 22.
SAD, 1 Sam. 1. 18. Ezek. 13. 22. Mark. 10. 22.
Eccl. 7. 3. by *sadness* of countenance heart is
SAFE, Ps. 119. 117. Prov. 18. 10; 29. 25.
Job 5. 4. *safety,* 11. Ps. 4. 8; 12. 5; 33. 17. Prov.
11. 14; 21. 31.
SAINTS, Ps. 52. 9; 79. 2; 89. 5.
Ps. 106. 16. envied . . . Aaron *saint* of Lord
Deut. 33. 2. came with ten thousands of *saints,*
3. all his *s.* are in thy hand   [Jude 14.
1 Sam. 2. 9. he will keep feet of his *s.*
Job 15. 15. he putteth no trust in his *s.*
Ps. 16. 3. goodness extendeth . . . to *s.*
50. 5. gather my *s.* together unto me
97. 10. he preserveth souls of his *s.*
116. 15. in sight of Lord is death of his *s.*
Prov. 2. 8. preserveth way of his *s.*
Dan. 7. 18. *s.* of most High shall take kingdom, 27.
Hos. 11. 12. and is faithful with the *s.*
Zech. 14. 5. Lord shall come, and all *s.*
Rom. 1. 7. called to be *s.,* 1 Cor. 1. 2. 2 Cor. 1. 1.
Eph. 1. 1. Col. 1. 2, 4, 12, 26.
8. 27. intercession for *s.,* Eph. 6. 18.
12. 13. necessity of *s.,* 2 Cor. 9. 12.
15. 25. minister to *s.,* 26, 31. 1 Cor. 16. 1. 2 Cor.
8. 4; 9. 1. Heb. 6. 10.
1 Cor. 6. 2. *s.* shall judge the world
Eph. 3. 8. less than the least of all *s.*
1 Thes. 3. 13. coming of . . . Jesus . . . with all his *s.*
2 Thes. 1. 10. to be glorified in his *s.*
Rev. 5. 8. prayers of the *s.,* 8. 3, 4.
11. 18. reward to thy servants the prophets and
13. 7. to make war with the *s.*   [. . . *s.*
14. 12. here is the patience of the *s.*
15. 3. just and true are thy ways, thou King of *s.*
16. 6. blood of *s.,* 17. 6; 18. 24.
19. 8. fine linen is righteousness of *s.*
20. 9. compassed the camp of the *s.*
SALT, Gen. 19. 26. Lev. 2. 13. Mat. 5. 13.
Mark 9. 49, 50. Col. 4. 6.
SALVATION, Ps. 14. 7; 53. 6.
Ex. 14. 13. stand still and see *s.* of Lord, 2 Chr.
Ps. 3. 8. *s.* belongeth to Lord   [20. 17.
37. 39. *s.* of righteous is of Lord
50. 23. I will shew him *s.* of God, 96. 2.
68. 20. God is the God of *s.,* 65. 5.
85. 9. his *s.* is nigh them that fear him
119. 155. *s.* is far from the wicked

Ps. 132. 16. clothe her priests with *salvation*
149. 4. (Lord) will beautify meek with *s.*
Is. 25. 9. we will . . . rejoice in his *s.*, 12. 3.
26. 1. *s.* will God appoint for walls
33. 2. be our *s.* 6. strength of *s.*
45. 17. Israel shall be saved . . . with everlasting *s.*
46. 13. I will place *s.* in Zion for
52. 10. earth shall see *s.* of our God
59. 16. arm brought *s.* unto me, 63. 5.
17. for an helmet of *s.*, Eph. 6. 17.
60. 18. call thy walls *S.*, thy gates
61. 10. clothed me with garments of *s.*
62. 1. *s.* as a lamp
Jer. 3. 23. in vain is *s.* hoped for from hills . . .;
     God is *s.* of Israel
Lam. 3. 26. quietly wait for *s.* of Lord
Jonah 2. 9. *s.* is of the Lord
Hab. 3. 8. ride on . . . thy chariots of *s.*
Zech. 9. 9. he is just and having *s.*
Luke 19. 9. is *s.* come to this house
John 4. 22. *s.* is of the Jews
Acts 4. 12. neither is there *s.* in any
13. 26. word of *s.* sent, 47. be for *s.*
Rom. 1. 16. it is the power of God to *s.*
11. 11. through their fall *s.* is come
13. 11. now is our *s.* nearer than
2 Cor. 1 6. for your . . . *s.* 6. 2. day of *s.*
Phil. 2. 12. work out your own *s.* with
1 Thes. 5. 8. hope of *s.* 9. to obtain *s.*
2 Thes. 2. 13. hath chosen you to *s.*
2 Tim. 2. 10. to obtain *s.* which is in Christ
3. 15. scriptures . . . able to make thee wise unto *s.*
Tit. 2. 11. grace of God that bringeth *s.*
Heb. 1. 14. who shall be heirs of *s.*
2. 3. escape if we neglect so great *s.*
5. 9. became author of eternal *s.*
6. 9. things that accompany *s.*
9. 28. appear the second time without sin unto *s.*
1 Pet. 1. 5. kept . . . through faith to *s.*
Jude 3. write unto you of common *s.*
Rev. 7. 10. *S.* to our God, 12. 10; 19. 1.
Ex. 15. 2. (God) is become *my salvation*, Job
     13. 16. Ps. 18. 2; 25. 5; 27. 1.; 38. 22; 51. 14;
     62. 7; 88. 1; 118. 14. Is. 12. 2. Mic. 7. 7.
     Hab. 3. 18.
Ps. 89. 26. rock of—140. 7. strength of—
2 Sam. 23. 5. this is all—   [56. 1.
Is. 46. 13.—shall not tarry, 49. 6; 51. 5, 6, 8.
Gen. 49. 18. *thy salvation*, 1 Sam. 2. 1. Ps.
     9. 14; 13. 5; 20. 5; 18. 35; 21. 1, 5; 35. 3;
     40. 10, 16; 51. 12; 69. 13, 29; 70. 4; 71. 15;
     85. 7; 106. 4; 119. 41, 81, 123, 166, 174. Is.
     17. 10; 62. 11. Luke 2. 30.
SAME, Ps. 102. 27. Heb. 13. 8. Rom. 10. 12.
     1 Cor. 12. 4, 5, 6. Eph. 4. 10.
SANCTIFY, Ex. 13. 2; 19. 10.
Ex. 31. 13. I am the Lord that doth *s.*
Lev. 20. 7. *s.* yourselves therefore and be ye holy
Is. 8. 13. *s.* the Lord of hosts himself
Ezek. 38. 23. I magnify myself and *s.* myself
Joel 1. 14. *s.* a fast, 2. 15.
2. 16. *s.* the congregation
John 17. 17. *s.* them through thy truth
19. for their sakes I *s.* myself
1 Thes. 5. 23. God of peace *s.* you
Heb. 13. 12. that he might *s.* people
1 Pet. 3. 15. *s.* Lord God in your hearts
Gen. 2. 3. blessed seventh day and *sanctified* it
Lev. 10. 3. I will be *s.* in them that
Deut. 32. 51. ye *s.* me not in midst of
Job 1. 5. Job sent and *s.* them and
Is. 5. 16. God that is holy shall be *s.*
Jer. 1. 5. before thou camest . . . I *s.* thee

Ezek. 20. 41. be *sanctified* in you before the
     heathen, 28. 22, 25; 38. 16; 39. 27.
John 10. 36. him whom Father hath *s.*
Acts 20. 32. inheritance among all them which
     are *s.*, 26. 18.
Rom. 15. 16. offering of Gentiles . . . *s.*
1 Cor. 1. 2. *s.* in Christ Jesus
6. 11. ye are washed, but ye are *s.*
7. 14. unbelieving husband is *s.* by the wife
1 Tim. 4. 5. *s.* by word of God and prayer
Heb. 2. 11. they who are *s.* are all of one
10. 14. perfected for ever them that are *s.*
Mat. 23. 17. temple that *sanctifieth*
1 Cor. 1. 30. *sanctification,* 1 Thes. 4. 3, 4.
     2. Thes. 2. 13. 1 Pet. 1. 2.
SANCTUARY, Ps. 63. 2; 73. 17. Is. 8. 14.
     Ezek. 11. 16. Dan. 9. 17. Heb. 9. 2.
SAND, Gen. 22. 17; 32. 12. Job 6. 3; 29. 18. Is.
     10. 22. Mat. 7. 26.
SATAN provoked David, 1 Chr. 21. 1.
Job 1. 6. *S.* came also among, 2. 1.
Ps. 109. 6. let *S.* stand at his right
Mat. 4. 10. get thee hence, *S.*, 16. 23.
Luke 10. 18. I beheld *S.* as lightning
22. 3. entered *S.* into Judas
Acts 26. 18. turn from power of *S.*
Rom. 16. 20. God of peace shall bruise *S.*
1 Cor. 5. 5. deliver one to such a one to *S.*
7. 5. *S.* tempt you not for your incontinency
2 Cor. 2. 11. lest *S.* should get an advantage
11. 14. *S.* is transformed into angel
12. 7. messenger of *S.* to buffet me
1 Tim. 1. 20. I have delivered to *S.*
Rev. 2. 9. synagogue of *S.*
24. have not known the depths of *S.*
SATIATE, Jer. 31. 14, 25; 46. 10.
SATISFY, Job 38. 27. Prov. 6. 30.
Ps. 90. 14. O *s.* us early with thy mercy
91. 16. with long life will I *s.* him
103. 5. who *s.* thy mouth with good
107. 9. he *s.* the longing soul
132. 15. will *s.* her poor with bread
Prov. 5. 19. breasts *s.* thee at all times
Is. 55. 2. labour for that which *s.* not
Ps. 17. 15. *satisfied* with thy likeness
22. 26. meek shall eat and be *s.*
63. 5. soul shall be *s.* as with
65. 4. *s.* with goodness of thy house
Prov. 14. 14. good man shall be *s.* from himself
27. 20. eyes of man are never *s.*
30. 15. are three things never *s.*
Eccl. 5. 10. loveth silver shall not be *s.*
Is. 9. 20. eat . . . and they shall not be *s.*, Mic. 6. 14.
53. 11. see travail of his soul and be *s.*
66. 11. be *s.* with breasts of her consolations
Jer. 31. 14. people shall be *s.* with my goodness
Ezek. 16. 28. yet couldest not be *s.*
Hab. 2. 5. and cannot be *s.*
Num. 35. 31. shall take no *satisfaction* for life of
     a murderer, 32.
SAVE your lives, preserve, Gen. 45. 7.
Gen. 50. 20. people alive, to *s.* much
Job 22. 29. he shall *s.* the humble
Ps. 18. 27. wilt *s.* afflicted people
69. 35. God will *s.* Zion and build the
72. 4. he shall *s.* children of needy
13. and shall *s.* the souls of needy
86. 2. *s.* thy servant that trusteth
16. *s.* son of thine handmaid
109. 31. those that condemn to *s.* him from
118. 25. *s.* now; I beseech thee, O Lord
145. 19. hear their cry and will *s.* them
Prov. 20. 22. wait on Lord, he shall *s.* thee

Is. 35. 4. (God) will come and *save* you
45. 20. cannot *s.*, 59. 1. Jer. 14. 9.
Ezek. 18. 27. shall *s.* his soul, 3. 18.
36. 29. *s.* you from all your uncleanness, 37. 23.
Zeph. 3. 17. Lord . . . is mighty; he will *s.*
19. *s.* her that halteth
Zech. 8. 7. I will *s.* my people, 9. 16; 10. 6.
Mat. 1. 21. *s.* his people from their sins
16. 25. whosoever will *s.* his life shall lose
18. 11. Son of man is come to *s.* that which was
    lost, Luke 19. 10.
Mark 3. 4. is it lawful . . . to *s.* life or to
John 12. 47. not to judge world but to *s.* world
Acts 2. 40. *s.* yourselves from this . . . generation
1 Cor. 1. 21. by foolishness of preaching to *s.*
    them that believe
9. 22. that I might by all means *s.* some
1 Tim. 1. 15. to *s.* sinners, of
Heb. 7. 25. able to *s.* them to the uttermost
Jas. 1. 21. word which is able to *s.*
2. 14. can faith *s.* him?
5. 15. prayer of faith shall *s.* sick
20. converteth a sinner . . . shall *s.* soul
Jude 23. others *s.* with fear, pulling
Ps. 6. 4. *save me,* 55. 16; 57. 3; 119. 94. Jer.
    17. 14. John 12. 27.
Is. 25. 9. *save us,* 33. 22; 37. 20. Hos. 14. 3.
    Mat. 8. 25. 1 Pet. 3. 21.
Ps. 44. 7. thou hast *saved* us from our enemies
106. 8. *s.* them for his name's sake
Is. 45. 22. look unto me and be ye *s.*
Jer. 8. 20. we are not *s.*
Jer. 4. 14. that thou mayest be *s.*
Mat. 19. 25. who then can be *s.*? Luke 18. 26.
Luke 1. 71. be *s.* from our enemies
7. 50. thy faith hath *s.* thee, 18. 42.
23. 35. he *s.* others, let him save himself
John 3. 17. world through him might be *s.*
Acts 2. 47. Lord added . . . daily such as should
    be *s.*
4. 12. none other name whereby we must be *s.*
16. 30. what must I do to be *s.*?
Rom. 8. 24. we are *s.* by hope
10. 1. prayer . . . for Israel is that they might be *s.*
1 Cor. 1. 18. to us which are *s.* it is
5. 5. spirit may be *s.* in day of Lord
Eph. 2. 5. by grace ye are *s.*, 8.
Tit. 3. 5. according to his mercy he *s.* us
1 Pet. 4. 18. righteous scarcely be *s.*
Rev. 21. 24. nations which are *s.*
Ps. 80. 3. *shall be saved,* 7, 19. Is. 45. 17;
    64. 5. Jer. 23. 6; 30. 7. Mat. 10. 22; 24. 13.
    Mark 16. 16. Acts 16. 31. Rom. 5. 10; 11. 26.
    1 Tim. 2. 15.
2 Sam. 22. 3. God . . . my refuge, my *Saviour*
2 Ki. 13. 5. Lord gave Israel a *s.*, Neh. 9. 27.
Is. 43. 3. I am thy *S.*, 49. 26; 60. 16.
11. beside me there is no *S.*, Hos. 13. 4.
45. 15. God of Israel, the *S.*, Jer. 14. 8.
Obad. 21. *saviours* shall come up on . . . Zion
Luke 1. 47. spirit rejoiced in God my *S.*
2. 11. to you is born . . . a *S.* which is
Acts 5. 31. him God exalted . . . to be . . . *S.*
Eph. 5. 23. (Christ) is the *s.* of body
1 Tim. 4. 10. who is the *s.* of all men
1. 1. God our *S.*, Tit. 1. 4; 2. 10, 13; 3. 4, 6.
    2 Pet. 1, 11. Jude 25.
2 Pet. 2. 20. knowledge of the Lord and *S.*
SAVOUR, sweet, Gen. 8. 21. Ex. 29. 18. Lev.
    1. 9; 2. 9; 3. 16.
Sol. 1. 3. of *s.* of thy good ointments
2 Cor. 2. 14. the *s.* of his knowledge
15. are to God a sweet *s.* of Christ

Eph. 5. 2. sacrifice to God for a sweetsmelling
    savour
Mat. 16. 23. *savourest* not things, . . . of God
SAY, Mat. 3. 9; 5. 22, 28, 32, 34, 39, 44; 7. 22;
    23. 3. 1 Cor. 12. 3.
SCARCELY, Rom. 5. 7. 1 Pet. 4. 18.
SCATTER them in Israel, Gen. 49. 7.
Num. 10. 35. let thine enemies be *scattered*
Mat. 9. 36. *s.* abroad as sheep, Ezek. 34. 5.
Luke 1. 51. *s.* proud in imagination
Prov. 11. 24. that *scattereth* and yet
SCEPTRE not depart from Judah, Gen. 49. 10.
Num. 24. 17. *S.* shall rise out of Israel   [1. 8.
Ps. 45. 6. *s.* of thy kingdom is a right *s.* Heb.
Zech. 10. 11. *s.* of Egypt shall depart
SCHISM, 1 Cor. 1. 10; 12. 25.
SCHOLAR, 1 Chr. 25. 8. Mal. 2. 12.
Gal. 3. 24. law was our *schoolmaster*
SCOFFERS, Hab. 1. 10. 2 Pet. 3. 3.
SCORN, Job 16. 20. Ps. 44. 13.
Prov. 9. 8. reprove not a *scorner*
14. 6. a *s.* seeketh wisdom and
15. 12. *s.* loveth not one that reproveth
1. 22. *scorners* delight in scorning
19. 29. judgments are prepared for *s.*
9. 12. if thou *scornest* thou shalt bear it
Ps. 1. 1. *scornful*, Prov. 29. 8. Is. 28. 14.
SCORPIONS, 2 Chr. 10. 11. Ezek. 2. 6.
SCOURGE of the tongue, Job 5. 21.
Is. 28. 15. overflowing *s.*, 18.
Heb. 12. 6. Lord . . . *scourgeth* every son
SCRIPTURE of truth, Dan. 10. 21.
2 Tim. 3. 16. all *s.* is given by inspiration
2 Pet. 1. 20. no prophecy of *s.* is of
Mat. 22. 29. ye err, not knowing *scriptures*
John 5. 39. search *s.*, Acts 17. 11; 18. 24.
Rom. 15. 4. through comfort of *s.*
2 Tim. 3. 15. from a child known holy *s.*
2 Pet. 3. 16. wrest, as they do also other *s.*
SEA, Ps. 33. 7; 72. 8. Prov. 8. 29. Is. 48. 18;
    57. 20. Zech. 9. 10. Rev. 4. 6; 10. 2; 15. 2;
    21. 1.
SEAL upon thine heart, Sol. 8. 6.
John 3. 33. set to his *s.* that God is
Rom. 4. 11. *s.* of the righteousness
1 Cor. 9. 2. *s.* of my apostleship are ye
Rev. 7. 2. angel . . . having *s.* of living God
Job 14. 17. my transgression is *sealed* up
Sol. 4. 12. spring shut up, fountain *s.*
John 6. 27. hath God *sealed* for us
2 Cor. 1. 22. who hath *s.* us and
Eph. 1. 13. ye were *s.* with that Holy Spirit
Rev. 5. 1. a book *s.* with seven seals
7. 3. *s.* the servants of our God
4. were *s.* an hundred and forty and four
SEARCH out resting place, Num. 10. 33.
Ps. 139. 23. *s.* me, O God, and know
Prov. 25. 27. men to *s.* their own glory is
Jer. 17. 10. I the Lord *s.* the heart
29. 13. when ye shall *s.* for me with
Zeph. 1. 12. *s.* Jerusalem with candles
John 5. 39. *s.* scriptures
Acts 17. 11. these *searched* the scriptures daily
Job 10. 6. that *searchest* after my sin
Prov. 2. 4. *s.* for her as for hid treasure
1 Chr. 28. 9. the Lord *searcheth* all hearts
Prov. 18. 17. neighbour cometh and *s.*
1 Cor. 2. 10. Spirit *s.* . . . deep things of God
Rev. 2. 23. I am he which *s.* the reins
SEARED with hot iron, 1 Tim. 4. 2.
SEASON, Gen. 40. 4. Ex. 13. 10.
Ps. 1. 3. bringeth forth his fruit in his *s.*
Is. 50. 4. to speak a word in *s.*

Luke 4. 13. departed from him for a *season*
John 5. 35. willing for a *s.* to rejoice
2 Tim. 4. 2. instant in *s.*, out of *s.*
Heb. 11. 25. pleasures of sin for a *s.*
1 Pet. 1. 6. for a *s.* . . . ye are in heaviness
Col. 4. 6. let speech be *seasoned* with
Acts 1. 7. to know the times or *seasons*
14. 17. gave us rain . . . and fruitful *s.*
1 Thes. 5. 1. of times and *s.* brethren ye have
SECRET, Gen. 49. 6. Job 40. 13.
Job 29. 4. *s.* of God was on my tabernacle, **15. 8.**
Ps. 25. 14. *s.* of Lord is with them that
27. 5. in *s.* of his tabernacle he will
139. 15. when I was made in *s.*
Prov. 3. 32. his *s.* is with righteous
9. 17. bread eaten in *s.* is pleasant
Amos 3. 7. revealeth his *s.* to his servants
Mat. 6. 4. alms in *s.* . . . Father seeth
John 18. 20. in *s.* have I said nothing
19. 38. *secretly* for fear of Jews
Job 11. 6. shew thee *secrets* of wisdom
Ps. 44. 21. he knoweth the *s.* of heart
Prov. 11. 13. talebearer revealeth *s.*, 20. 19.
Dan. 2. 28. a God . . . that revealeth *s.*
Rom. 2. 16. God shall judge *s.*
SECT, Acts 24. 5; 26. 5; 28. 22.
SEDUCE, Ezek. 13. 10. Mark 13. 22.
2 Tim. 3. 13. *seducers—ing*, 1 Tim. 4. 1.
SEE, Ps. 34. 8. Mat. 5. 8. John 16. 22. 1 John 3. 2.
Rev. 1. 7; 22. 4.
Mat. 6. 1. before men to be *seen* of
13. 17. desired to see . . . and have not *s.*
23. 5. their works they do to be *s.* of men
John 1. 18. no man hath *s.* God at **any time**
14. 9. he that hath *s.* me hath *s.* the Father
20. 29. thou hast *s.* me . . . blessed are they that
have not *s.*, and yet have believed
2 Cor. 4. 18. look not at things . . . *s.* but
1 Tim. 6. 16. whom no man hath *s.*
Heb. 11. 1. evidence of things not *s.*
1 Pet. 1. 8. whom not having *s.* ye love
1 John 1. 1. that which we have *s.* and
4. 12. no man hath *s.* God at any time
John 12. 45. he that *seeth* me *s.* him that
14. 17. because it *s.* him not, 19.
SEED, Gen. 1. 11; 17. 7; 38. 9.
Ps. 126. 6. bearing precious *s.*
Eccl. 11. 6. in morning sow thy *s.*
Is. 55. 10. give *s.* to the sower
Mat. 13. 38. good *s.* are children of
Luke 8. 11. the *s.* is word of God
1 John 3. 9. his *s.* remaineth in him
Ps. 37. 28. *s.* of wicked shall be cut off
69. 36. *s.* of his servants shall inherit it
Prov. 11. 21. *s.* of righteous shall be
Is. 1. 4. sinful nation, . . . *s.* of evildoers
45. 25. all *s.* of Israel be justified
53. 10. see his *s.*, prolong his days
Mal. 2. 15. he might seek a godly *s.*
Rom. 9. 8. children of promise counted for *s.*
29. except Lord of Sabaoth had left us a *s.*
Gal. 3. 16. not to *seeds*, but to thy *s.*
SEEK, Ezra 8. 21. Job 5. 8. Ps. 10. 15.
Deut. 4. 29. if thou *s.* him with all thy heart,
1 Chr. 28. 9. 2 Chr. 15. 2. Jer. 29. 13.
Ezra 8. 22. on them for good that *s.*
Ps. 9. 10. not forsake them that *s.*
63. 1. my God, early will I *s.* thee
69. 32. heart shall live that *s.* God
119. 2. blessed are they that *s.* him
176. *s.* thy servant, for I do not forget
Prov. 8. 17. that *s.* me early shall find
Sol. 3. 2. *s.* him whom my soul loveth

Is. 26. 9. with my spirit . . . will I *seek* thee
45. 19. I said not. . . . *s.* me in vain
Jer. 29. 13. ye shall *s.* me and find
Amos. 5. 4. *s.* ye me, ye shall live, **6. 8.** [ness
Zeph. 2. 3. *s.* Lord, . . . *s.* righteousness, *s.* meek-
Mal. 2. 7. *s.* the law
15. that he might *s.* a godly seed
Mat. 6. 33. *s.* ye first the kingdom of God
7. 7. *s.* and ye shall find, 8. Deut. 4. 29.
Luke 13. 24. many will *s.* to enter in
19. 10. *s.* and to save that which was lost, Mat.
John 8. 21. ye shall *s.* me and [18. 11.
Rom. 2. 7. *s.* for glory, honour
1 Cor. 10. 24. let no man *s.* his own but
Phil. 2. 21. all *s.* their own, not . . . Jesus Christ's
Col. 3. 1. *s.* those things which are above
1 Pet. 3. 11. *s.* peace, and ensue it
John 4. 23. Father *seeketh* such to worship
1 Cor. 13. 5. charity *s.* not her own
1 Pet. 5. 8. *seeking* whom he may devour
SEEM, Gen. 27. 12. Deut. 25. 3.
1 Cor. 11. 16. if any man *s.* to be contentious
Heb. 4. 1. lest any of you *s.* to come short
Jas. 1. 26. if any . . . . *s.* to be religious
Luke 8. 18. even that which he *seemeth* to
1 Cor. 3. 18. if any man . . . . *s.* to be wise in
Heb. 12. 11. no chastening . . . *s.* to be joyous
SELL me thy birthright, Gen. 25. 31.
Prov. 23. 23. buy truth and *s.* it not
Mat. 19. 21. go, and *s.* that thou hast
13. 44. he . . . *selleth* all that he hath and buyeth
SENATORS, Ps. 105. 22.
SEND help from the sanctuary, Ps. 20. 2.
Ps. 43. 3. O *s.* out thy light and
57. 3. he shall *s.* from heaven and
Mat. 9. 38. *s.* forth labourers into
John 14. 26. whom the Father will *s.*
16. 7. if I depart I will *s.* him unto
2 Thes. 2. 11. *s.* them strong delusion
SENSE, Neh. 8. 8. Heb. 5. 14.
Jas. 3. 15. *sensual*, Jude 19.
SENTENCE, Deut. 17. 9. Dan. 5. 12.
Prov. 16. 10. a divine *s.* is in lips of
Eccl. 8. 11. because *s.* is not executed
2 Cor. 1. 9. we had *s.* of death in
SEPARATE, Gen. 13. 9. Ex. 33. 16. [33. 16.
Gen. 49. 26. was *s.* from his brethren, Deut.
Deut. 29. 21. Lord shall *s.* him
Acts 13. 2. *s.* me Barnabas and Saul
Rom. 8. 35. who shall *s.* us from love of Christ, 39.
2 Cor. 6. 17. be ye *s.*, saith the Lord
Heb. 7. 26. holy, harmless, . . . *s.* from sinners
Is. 59. 2. iniquities have *separated*
Acts 19. 9. departed from them and *s.* the disciples
Gal. 1. 15. who *s.* me from my mother's womb
SERAPHIMS, Is. 6. 2, 6.
SERPENT, Gen. 3. 1, 13; 49. 17.
Prov. 23. 32. at last it biteth like a *serpent*,
Mat. 7. 10. will he give him a *s.*?
John 3. 14. as Moses lifted up *s.* in
2 Cor. 11. 3. as the *s.* beguiled Eve
Rev. 12. 9. that old *s.*, called the Devil
Num. 21. 6. Lord sent fiery *serpents*, 8, 9.
Mat. 10. 16. be ye wise as *s.*, harmless as
SERVE Lord with all thy heart, Deut. 10. 12, 20;
11. 13. Josh. 22. 5. 1 Sam. 12. 20.
Deut. 13. 4. shall *s.* him, and cleave
Josh. 24. 14. fear the Lord, *s.* him
15. choose you this day whom ye will *s.* . . . . me
and my house, we will *s.* the Lord
1 Chr. 28. 9. *s.* him with a perfect
Job 21. 15. Almighty that we should *s.* **him**
Ps. 2. 11. *s.* Lord with fear, rejoice

Mat. 6. 24. no man can *serve* two masters; ye
  cannot *s.* God and mammon
Luke 1. 74. *s.* him without fear in
12. 37. will come forth and *s.* them
John 12. 26. if any man *s.* me let him
Acts 6. 2. leave word of God and *s.* tables
27. 23. whose I am, and whom I *s.*
Rom. 1. 9. whom I *s.* with my spirit
7. 6. *s.* in newness of spirit
25. with the mind I myself *s.* law of God
16. 18. they *s.* not Lord Jesus Christ
Col. 3. 24. ye *s.* Lord Christ
Gal. 5. 13. by love *s.* one another
1 Thes. 1. 9. to *s.* living God, Heb. 9. 14.
Heb. 12. 28. may *s.* God acceptably
Rev. 7. 15. *s.* him day and night in
Is. 24. 2. with *servant* so with his master
42. 1. behold my *s.*, 49. 3; 52. 13.
Mat. 20. 27. be chief . . . let him be your *s.*
25. 21. well done, good and faithful *s.*, 23.
John 8. 34. committeth sin is *s.* of sin
13. 16. *s.* not greater than lord, 15. 20.
1 Cor. 7. 21. art thou called, being *s.?*
9. 19. have I made myself *s.* to all
Gal. 1. 10. if I yet pleased men . . . not *s.* of Christ
Phil. 2. 7. took on him form of a *s.*
2 Tim. 2. 24. *s.* of Lord must not
Ezra 5. 11. *servants* of the God of heaven, Dan.
  3. 26. Acts 16. 17. 1 Pet. 2. 16. Rev. 7. 3.
Rom. 6. 16. yield yourselves *s.* to obey; his *s.* ye
  are to whom
17. ye were the *s.* of sin
18. ye became *s.* of righteousness
1 Cor. 7. 23. be not ye the *s.* of men
Phil. 1. 1. the *s.* of Jesus Christ
2 Pet. 2. 19. *s.* of corruption
Rev. 22. 3. his *s.* shall serve him
Rom. 12. 1. your reasonable *service*
Jer. 22. 13. useth neighbour's *s.*   [*serving*
Luke 10. 40. Martha cumbered about much
Acts 20. 19. *s.* Lord with all humility
26. 7. twelve tribes instantly *s.* God
Rom. 12. 11. fervent in spirit; *s.* Lord
Tit. 3. 3. *s.* divers lusts and pleasures
SET, Ps. 2. 6; 4. 3; 12. 5; 16. 8; 54. 3; 75. 7;
  113. 8. Prov. 1. 25. Sol. 8. 6. Rom. 3. 25.
  Col. 3. 2.
SETTLE, Luke 21. 14. 1 Pet. 5. 10.
Col. 1. 23. in faith grounded and *settled*
SEVERITY, goodness and, Rom. 11. 22.
SHADE, Lord is thy, Ps. 121. 5.
SHADOW, our days are as a, 1 Chr. 29. 15.
  Eccl. 8. 13; 6. 12. Job 8. 9. Ps. 107. 10;
  109. 23; 144. 4.
Ps. 17. 8. me under the *s.* of thy wings, 36. 7;
  57. 1 ; 63. 7.
Sol. 2. 3. I sat under his *s.*
Is. 4. 6. for a *s.* in day, 25. 4; 32. 2.
49. 2. in *s.* of his hand hath he hid
Acts 5. 15. *s.* of Peter might overshadow
Jas. 1. 17. no variableness, neither *s.* of
Jer. 6. 4. *shadows* of evening are stretched
SHAKE heaven and earth, Hag. 2. 6, 21.
Hag. 2. 7. I will *s.* all nations and
Mat. 10. 14. *s.* off the dust of your feet
11. 7. a reed *shaken* with the wind
Luke 6. 38. good measure, *s.* together
Heb. 12. 27. things which cannot be *s.*
Ps. 44. 14. *shaking*, Is. 17. 6; 24. 13; 30. 32.
  Ezek. 37. 7; 38. 19.
SHAME, 1 Sam. 20. 34. 2 Sam. 13. 13.
Ex. 32. 25. made them naked to their *s.*
Ps. 119. 31. put me not to *s.*, 69. 7.

Prov. 3. 35. *shame* shall be the promotion of fools,
  9. 7; 10. 5; 11. 2; 13. 5, 18; 14. 35; 17. 2;
  18. 13; 19. 26; 25. 8; 29. 15. Is. 22. 18.
Is. 50. 6. I hid not my face from *s.*
Hos. 4. 7. change their glory to *s.*, Ps. 4. 2.
Zeph. 3. 5. the unjust knoweth no *s.*
Acts 5. 41. worthy to suffer *s.* for his
Heb. 12. 2. endured cross, despising *s.*
Rev. 3. 18. *s.* of thy nakedness do not
16. 15. naked, and they see his *s.*
1 Tim. 2. 9. *shamefacedness*
SHAPE, Luke 3. 22. John 5. 37. Ps. 51. 5.
SHARP, Is. 41. 15; 49. 2. Rev. 1. 16.
Job 16. 9. *sharpeneth*, Prov. 27. 17.
Mic. 7. 4. *sharper* than, Heb. 4. 12.
Judg. 8. 1. *sharply*, Tit. 1. 13.
2 Cor. 13. 10. should use *sharpness*
SHED for many for remission Mat. 26. 28.
Rom. 5. 5. love of God is *s.* abroad
Tit. 3. 6. Holy Ghost which he *s.* on us
SHEEP, Ps. 49. 14; 74. 1; 78. 52.
Ps. 44. 22. *s.* for slaughter, Rom. 8. 36.
79. 13. *s.* of thy pasture, 95. 7; 100. 3.
119. 176. gone astray like lost *s.*
Is. 53. 6. like *s.* have gone astray
Zech. 13. 7. smite shepherd, and *s.* shall
Mat. 9. 36. as *s.* having no shepherd
10. 6. to lost *s.* of house of Israel, 15. 24.
18. 12. If a man have an hundred *s.*
25. 32. divideth his *s.* from goats, 33.
John 10. 2–16. the *s.* 27. my *s.*
21. 15. feed my lambs. 16–17. feed my *s.*
1 Pet. 2. 25. were as *s.* going astray
SHEPHERD, Gen. 46. 34; 49. 24. Ex. 2. 17, 19.
Num. 27. 17. as sheep that have no *s.* 1 Ki.
  22. 17. Mark 6. 34.
Ps. 23. 1. the Lord is my *s.*
80. 1. give ear, O *S.* of Israel
Ezek. 34. 5. were scattered because there is no *s.*
12. *s.* seeketh out his flock
23. set up one *s.* . . . even my servant David
37. 24. they all shall have one *s.*
Zech. 13. 7. awake, O sword, against my *s.*
John 10. 11. I am the good *s.*; the good *s.* giveth
  his life, 14.
Heb. 13. 20. Lord Jesus, that great *s.*
1 Pet. 2. 25. returned to *S.* of souls
5. 4. when the chief *S.* shall appear
Sol. 1. 8. feed kids before *shepherds'* tents
Ezek. 34. 2. prophesy against *s.* . . . woe to the *s.*
7. ye *s.*, hear the word of the Lord
Mic. 5. 5. raise against him seven *s.*
SHEW, Ps. 39. 6. Luke 20. 47. Col. 2. 23.
Ps. 4. 6. who will *s.* us any good?
16. 11. thou wilt *s.* me path of life
91. 16. I will *s.* him my salvation
92. 15. to *s.* that Lord is upright
1 Cor. 11. 26. *s.* Lord's death
1 Pet. 2. 9. *s.* forth the praises of him
Rev. 22. 6. sent his angel to *s.* to his servants
John 5. 20. loveth Son, and *sheweth*
Tit. 2. 7. *shewing* thyself a pattern of good works
SHIELD and great reward, Gen. 15. 1.
Deut. 33. 29. Lord the *s.* of thy help
Ps. 3. 3. thou, O Lord art a *s.* for me, 28. 7.
18. 35. the *s.* of thy salvation
33. 20. he is our help and our *s.*
59. 11. bring them down, O Lord our *s.*, 84. 9.
115. 9, 10, 11. their help and their *s.*
Eph. 6. 16. taking the *s.* of faith
SHINE, Job 22. 28; 36. 32; 37. 15.
Num. 6. 25. Lord make his face *s.*
Job 10. 3. *s.* on counsel of wicked

Ps. 31. 16. face to *shine* up on thy servant, 119. 135.
Eccl. 8. 1. man's wisdom maketh his face *s.*
Mat. 5. 16. let your light so *s.* before
13. 43. righteous *s.* forth as the sun
2 Cor. 4. 6. God, who commanded light to *s.*
Phil. 2. 15. among whom ye *s.* as
SHIPWRECK, 1 Tim. 1. 19.
2 Cor. 11. 25. thrice I suffered *s.*
SHORT, is Lord's hand waxed, Num. 11. 23.
Ps. 89. 47. remember how *s.* my time is
Rom. 3. 23. and come *s.* of glory of God
Ps. 102. 23. *shortened* my days, 89. 45.
Is. 50. 2. is my hand *s.*
Mat. 24. 22. except those days be *s.* Mark 13. 20. Prov. 10. 27.
SHOUT, Num. 23. 21. Is. 12. 6; 42. 11; 44. 23. Zeph. 3. 14. Zech. 9. 9.
Ps. 47. 5. God is gone up with a *s.*
1 Thes. 4. 16. Lord shall descend with a *s.*
SHRINES, Acts 19. 24.
SHUT up, or left, Deut. 32. 36.
1 Sam. 6. 10. *s.* up their calves at home
Mat. 23. 13. ye *s.* up the kingdom of
Gal. 3. 23. *s.* up unto the faith which
Rev. 3. 7. that openeth, and no man *shutteth,*
SICK of love, Sol. 2. 5; 5. 8.   [Is. 22. 22.
Is. 1. 5. whole head is *s.* and whole heart
John 11. 1. man was *s.* named Lazarus, 2, 3, 4, 6.
Jas. 5. 14. is any *s. . . . ?* let him call the elders
15. prayer of faith shall save the *s.*
1 Cor. 11. 30. are weak and *sickly*
Ex. 23. 25. I will take *sickness* away
Mat. 8. 17. bare our *sicknesses*
SIFT, Is. 30. 28. Amos 9. 9. Luke 22. 31.
SIGHT, Ex. 3. 3. 2 Cor. 5. 7.
SIGN (token), Gen. 9. 12, 13; 17. 11. **Ex.** 4. 17. Is. 8. 18. Rom. 15. 19.
Rom. 4. 11. received the *s.* of circumcision
Jer. 22. 24. *signet,* Hag. 2. 23.
SILENT in darkness, 1 Sam. 2. 9.
Ps. 28. 1. be not *s.* to me, 30. 12.
31. 18. *silence,* 32. 3; 35. 22; 50. 3, 21; 83. 1; 94. 17. Jer. 8. 14. Amos 5. 13.; 8. 3. 1 Cor. 14. 34. 1 Tim. 2. 11, 12. 1 Pet. 2. 15. Rev. 8. 1.
SILLY, Job 5. 2. 2 Tim. 3. 6.
SIMPLE, Prov. 1. 4, 22, 32; 7. 7; 8. 5; 9. 4, 13; 19. 25; 21. 11.
Ps. 19. 7. testimony . . . sure, making wise the *s.*
116. 6. Lord preserveth the *s.*
119. 130. understanding to the *s.*
Prov. 14. 15. *s.* believeth every word, **18.**
Rom. 16. 18. deceive the hearts of the *s.*
19. but *s.* concerning evil
SIN lieth at the door, Gen. 4. 7.
Job 10. 6. thou . . . searchest after my *s.*
Ps. 4. 4. stand in awe and *s.* not
32. 1. blessed is he . . . whose *s.* is covered
5. I acknowledged my *s.* unto thee
38. 18. I will be sorry for my *s.*
51. 3. my *s.* is ever before me
5. in *s.* did my mother conceive me
Prov. 14. 34. *s.* is a reproach to any
Is. 30. 1. that they may add *s.* to *s.*
53. 10. make his soul an offering for *s.*
12. and he bare the *s.* of many
John 1. 29. taketh away *s.* of the world
5. 14. *s.* no more lest a worse thing
Rom. 5. 12. by one man *s.* entered world, and death by *s.*
6. 14. *s.* shall not have dominion
7. 9. *s.* revived, and I died, 8. 10.
13. but *s.,* that it might appear *s.*

14. I am carnal, sold under *sin*
17. *s.* that dwelleth in me
25. with the flesh the law of *s.*
8. 2. made me free from the law of *s.*   [no *s.*
2 Cor. 5. 21. made him to be *s.* for us, who knew
Eph. 4. 26. be ye angry and *s.* not
Jas. 1. 15. lust bringeth forth *s.,* and *s.*
1 Pet. 2. 22. who did no *s.,* neither
1 John 1. 8. if we say we have no *s.*
2. 1. ye *s.* not; if any man *s.* we have
3. 9. he cannot *s.* because he is born of God
5. 16. there is *s.* unto death
Ps. 19. 13. keep . . . from presumptuous *sins*
Is. 43. 25. not remember thy *s.,* 44. 22.
Ezek. 33. 16. none of his *s. . . .* shall be mentioned
Dan. 9. 24. finish transgression make end of *s.*
1 Tim. 5. 22. neither . . . partaker of other men's *s.*
2 Tim. 3. 6. silly women laden with *s.*
1 John 2. 2. propitiation for our *s. . . .* also for *s.* of the whole world
Ps. 69. 5. *my sins,* 51. 9. Is. 38. 17.
79. 9. *our sins,* 90. 8; 103. 10. Is. 59. 12. Dan. 9. 16. Gal. 1. 4. 1 Cor. 15. 3. Heb. 1. 3. 1 Pet. 2. 24. Rev. 1. 5.
Mat. 1. 21. *their sins,* Rom. 11. 27. Heb. 8. 12; 10. 17. Num. 16. 26.
Is. 59. 2. *your sins,* Jer. 5. 25. John 8. 21. 1 Cor. 15. 17. Josh. 24. 19.
Ex. 32. 33. whosoever hath *sinned . . .* will I
Job 1. 22. in all this Job *s.* not
Lam. 1. 8. Jerusalem grievously *s.*
Rom. 2. 12. many as *s.* without law
3. 23. all have *s.* and come short
1 John 1. 10. if we say we have not *s.*
Ex. 9. 27. *I have sinned,* Num. 22. 34. Josh. 7. 20. 1 Sam. 15. 24, 30. 2 Sam. 12. 13; 24. 10. Job 7. 20; 33. 27. Ps. 41. 4; 51. 4. Mic. 7. 9. Mat. 27. 4. Luke 15. 18, 21.
Judg. 10. 10. *we have sinned,* 1 Sam. 7. 6. Ps. 106. 6. Is. 42. 24; 64. 5. Jer. 3. 25; 8. 14; 14. 7, 20. Lam. 5. 16. Dan. 9. 5, 8, 11, 15.
Prov. 8. 36. but he that *sinneth* against me wrongeth his own soul
Eccl. 7. 20. not just man . . . doeth good, *s.* not
Ezek. 18. 4. soul that *s.* it shall die
1 John 5. 18. is born of God *s.* not
Eccl. 7. 26. the *sinner* shall be taken
9. 18. one *s.* destroyeth much good
Luke 15. 7. joy in heaven over one *s.* that
18. 13. God be merciful to me a *s.*
Jas. 5. 20. convertteth the *s.* from
1 Pet. 4. 18. where shall *s.* appear
Gen. 13. 13. *sinners* before the Lord
Ps. 1. 1. nor standeth in way of *s.*
25. 8. therefore will he teach *s.* in the way
Is. 33. 14. the *s.* in Zion are afraid
Mat. 9. 13. I am not come to call righteous, but *s.*
Luke 13. 2. *s.* above all Galilæans, 4.
John 9. 31. God heareth not *s.*
Rom. 5. 8. while we were yet *s.* Christ died for us
19. by one man's disobedience many . . . *s.*
Gal. 2. 15. Jews . . . and not *s.* of the Gentiles
1 Tim. 1. 15. Jesus came into world to save *s.*
Heb. 7. 26. holy . . . separate from *s.*
Jas. 4. 8. cleanse your hands, ye *s.*
Jude 15. ungodly *s.* have spoken
Num. 32. 14. *sinful,* Is. 1. 4. Luke 5. 8. Rom. 7. 13; 8. 3.
SINCERE, Phil. 1. 10, 16. 1 Pet. 2. 2.
Josh. 24. 14. serve him in *sincerity*
1 Cor. 5. 8. unleavened bread of *s.*
2 Cor. 1. 12. in simplicity and godly *s.* we have
8. 8. to prove the *s.* of your love

Eph. 6. 24. that love Lord Jesus in *sincerity*
Tit. 2. 7. shewing uncorruptness, gravity, *s.*
SINEW, Is. 48. 4. Job 10. 11.
SING to the Lord, Ex. 15. 21. 1 Chr. 16. 23.
Ps. 30. 4; 68. 32; 81. 1; 95. 1; 96. 1, 2;
98. 1; 147. 7; 149. 1. Is. 12. 5; Eph. 5. 19.
Ex. 15. 1. *I will s.,* Judg. 5. 3. Ps. 13. 6; 57. 7,
9; 59. 16, 17; 101. 1; 104. 33; 144. 9. Is. 5. 1.
1 Cor. 14. 15.
Job 29. 13. *s. for joy,* Is. 65. 14.
Ps. 9. 11. *s. praise(s),* 18. 49; 27. 6; 30. 12; 47. 6, 7;
68. 4; 75. 9; 92. 1; 108. 1, 3; 135. 3; 146. 2;
147. 1; 149. 3.
Ps. 145. 7. *s.* of thy righteousness
Prov. 29. 6. the righteous doth *s.* and
Is. 35. 6. and the tongue of the dumb *s.*
1 Cor. 14. 15. I will *s.* with the spirit
Jas. 5. 13. is any merry? let him *s.*
SINGLE eye, Mat. 6. 22. Luke 11. 34.
Acts 2. 46. *singleness* of heart, Eph. 6. 5. Col. 3. 22.
SINK, Ps. 69. 2, 14. Luke 9. 44.
SISTER, Sol. 4. 9; 5. 1; 8. 8.
SITUATION, 2 Ki. 2. 19. Ps. 48. 2.
SKIN, Job 2. 4; 10. 11; 19. 26. Jer. 13. 23. sheeps.
and goats., Heb. 11. 37.
SKIP, Ps. 29. 6; 114. 4. Sol. 2. 8.
SLACK, Deut. 7. 10. Prov. 10. 4. Hab. 1. 4. Zeph.
3. 16. 2 Pet. 3. 9.
SLAY, Job 13. 15. Ps. 139. 19. Lev. 14. 13.
Eph. 2. 16. having *slain* the enmity
Rev. 5. 9. wast *s.* and hast redeemed
13. 8. Lamb *s.* from foundation of
SLEEP, deep, Gen. 2. 21; 15. 12. 1 Sam. 26. 12.
Job 4. 13. Ps. 76. 7. Prov. 19. 15. Is. 29. 10.
Ps. 90. 5. they are as a *s.:* in morning
127. 2. he giveth his beloved *s.*
132. 4. will not give *s.* to mine eyes
Prov. 3. 24. thy *s.* shall be sweet
6. 4. give not *s.* to thine eyes, nor
20. 13. love not *s.* lest thou come to poverty
Eccl. 5. 12. *s.* of labouring man is sweet . . . but
abundance of rich will not suffer him to *s.*
Jer. 31. 26. my *s.* was sweet to me
51. 39. *s.* a perpetual *s.,* 57.
Luke 9. 32. were heavy with *s.*
Rom. 13. 11. time to awake out of *s.*
Sol. 5. 2. I *s.* but my heart waketh
1 Cor. 11. 30. for this cause . . . many *s.*
15. 51. we shall not all *s.* but shall
1 Thes. 4. 14. them which *s.* in Jesus
5. 6. let us not *s.* as others; but
7. they that *s. s.* in the night
10. whether we wake or *s.* should
Eph. 5. 14. awake, thou that *sleepest*
Ps. 3. 5. laid me down and *slept,* 4. 8.
76. 5. they have *s.* their sleep
1 Cor. 15. 20. firstfruits of them that *s.*
SLIDE, Deut. 32. 35. Ps. 26. 1; 37. 31. Jer. 8. 5.
Hos. 4. 16.
SLIGHTLY, Jer. 6. 14; 8. 11.
SLING, 1 Sam. 25. 29. Jer. 10. 18.
SLIP, Ps. 17. 5; 18. 36; 38. 16; 94. 18. Heb. 2. 1.
slippery, Ps. 35. 6; 73. 18. Jer. 23. 12.
SLOTHFUL under tribute, Prov. 12. 24.
Prov. 12. 27. *s.* man roasteth not that which he
15. 19. way of *s.* man is as hedge of thorns
18. 9. *s.* is brother to . . . great waster
21. 25. desire of the *s.* killeth him
24. 30. I went by the field of the *s.*
26. 14. as door turneth on hinges, so doth *s.*
Heb. 6. 12. be not *s.* but followers of
Prov. 19. 15. *slothfulness* casteth into a deep sleep
SLOW to anger, Neh. 9. 17.

Luke 24. 25. fools, *slow* of heart to
Jas. 1. 19. swift to hear, *s.* to speak, *s.* to wrath,
Prov. 14. 29.
SLUGGARD, go to ant, Prov. 6. 6.
Prov. 6. 9. how long wilt sleep, O *s.*
13. 4. the soul of the *s.* desireth
20. 4. *s.* will not plow by reason
26. 16. *s.* is wiser in his own conceit
SLUMBER, Ps. 132. 4. Rom. 11. 8.
Mat. 25. 5. they all *slumbered* and
2 Pet. 2. 3. their damnation *slumbereth* not
SMITE, Lord shall, Deut. 28. 22.
Ps. 141. 5. let the righteous *s.* me
Jer. 18. 18. let us *s.* him with tongue
Mat. 5. 39. *s.* thee on thy right cheek
John 18. 23. why *smitest* thou me
Is. 53. 4. him *smitten* of God
Hos. 6. 1. hath *s.* and he will bind
SMOKE, Gen. 19. 28. Ex. 19. 18.
Deut. 29. 20. his jealousy shall *s.*
Ps. 74. 1. why doth thine anger *s.*
Rev. 14. 11. *s.* of their torment ascendeth
Is. 42. 3. *smoking* flax, Mat. 12. 20.
SMOOTH, Gen. 27. 11; 16. Is. 30. 10.
Ps. 55. 21. *smoother,* Prov. 5. 3.
SNARE, Ex. 23. 33. Judg. 2. 3.
Ps. 69. 22. let their table become a *s.,* Rom. 11. 9.
91. 3. deliver thee from the *s.* of
119. 110. wicked laid a *s.* for me
124. 7. *s.* is broken, and we are escaped
Prov. 29. 25. fear of man bringeth a *s.*
2 Tim. 2. 26. out of the *s.* of devil
Ps. 9. 16. *snared,* Prov. 6. 2; 12. 13. Eccl. 9. 12.
Is. 8. 15; 28. 13; 42. 22.
11. 6. on wicked he will rain *snares*
18. 5. *s.* of death prevented me
Prov. 13. 14. depart from *s.* of death
SNOW, as, Ps. 51. 7; 68. 14. Is. 1. 18. Dan. 7. 9.
Mat. 28. 3. Rev. 1. 14.
SNUFFED, Mal. 1. 13. Jer. 2. 24.
SOAP, Jer. 2. 22. Mal. 3. 2.
SOBER . . . for your cause, 2 Cor. 5. 13.
1 Thes. 5. 6. let us watch and be *s.,* 8.
1 Tim. 3. 2. bishop must be . . . vigilant, *s.*
11. wives be grave, not slanderers, *s.*
Tit. 1. 8. *s.,* just, holy, temperate
2. 2. aged men be *s.,* grave
4. teach young women to be *s.*
1 Pet. 1. 13. gird up loins of your mind, be *s.*
4. 7. be ye therefore *s.* and watch unto prayer
5. 8. be *s.,* be vigilant
Rom. 12. 3. but to think *soberly*
Tit. 2. 12. teaching us that we should live *s.*
Acts 26. 25. words of truth and *soberness*
1 Tim. 2. 9. *sobriety,* 15.
SOFT, God maketh my heart, Job 23. 16.
Prov. 15. 1. *s.* answer turneth away
25. 15. *s.* tongue breaketh the bone
Mat. 11. 8. man clothed in *s.* raiment
SOJOURN, Gen. 12. 10. Ps. 120. 5.
Lev. 25. 23. *sojourners* with me, 1 Chr. 29. 15.
Ps. 39. 12.
Ex. 12. 40. *sojourning,* 1 Pet. 1. 17.
SOLD thyself to work evil, 1 Ki. 21. 20.
2 Ki. 17. 17. *s.* themselves to do evil
Rom. 7. 14. I am carnal, *s.* under sin
SOLDIER of Jesus Christ, 2 Tim. 2. 3, 4.
SON, 2 Sam. 18. 33; 19. 4.
Ps. 2. 12. kiss the *S.* lest he be angry
Prov. 10. 1. a wise *s.* . . . a foolish *s.,* 15. 20.
Mal. 1. 3. as a man spareth his own *s.*
Mat. 11. 27. no man knoweth the *S.*
17. 5. this is my beloved *S.,* 3. 17.

Luke 10. 6. if *son* of peace be there
John 1. 18. only begotten *S*., 3. 16, 18, 35.
5. 21. *S*. quickeneth whom he will
23. men should honour the *S*.
8. 35. but the *S*. abideth ever
36. if the *S*. shall make you free
Rom. 8. 3. sending his own *S*. in, 32.
Gal. 4. 7. if *s*. then an heir of God
Heb. 5. 8. though he were a *S*. yet learned he
1 John 2. 22. antichrist that denieth . . . *S*., 23.
5. 11. eternal life, and this life is in his *S*.
12. hath *S*. hath life, hath not *S*. hath not life
Mat. 21. 37. *his Son*, Acts 3. 13. Rom. 1. 3, 9;
   5. 10; 8. 29, 32. 1 Cor. 1. 9. Gal. 1. 16; 4. 4, 6.
   1 Thes. 1. 10. Heb. 1. 2. 1 John 1. 7; 3. 23;
   4, 9, 10, 14; 5. 9, 10, 11, 20.
Luke 15. 19. *thy son*, John 17. 1; 19. 26.
Dan. 3. 25. *the Son of God*, Mat. 4. 3; 16. 16.
   and 41 other places
Num. 23. 19. *Son of man*, Job 25. 6. Ps. 8. 4;
   80. 17; 144. 3. Dan. 7. 13. Ezekiel is so called
   about 90, and Christ about 84 times
Ps. 144. 12. that our *sons* may be as plants
Sol. 2. 3. so is my beloved among *s*.
Mal. 3. 3. purify *s*. of Levi
Mark 3. 17. Boanerges, . . . *s*. of thunder
1 Cor. 4. 14. as my beloved *s*. I warn
Gal. 4. 6. because ye are *s*. God sent Spirit of his
Heb. 2. 10. bringing many *s*. to glory
12. 7. God dealeth with you as with *s*.
Gen. 6. 2. *sons of God*, Job 1. 6; 2. 1; 38. 7.
   Hos. 1. 10. John 1. 12. Rom. 8. 14, 19. Phil.
   2. 15. 1 John 3. 1, 2.
SONG to the Lord, Ex. 15. 1. Num. 21. 17.
Ex. 15. 2. Lord is my . . . *s*., Ps. 118. 14. Is. 12. 2.
Job 30. 9. I am their *s*., Ps. 69. 12.
Ezek. 33. 32. as a very lovely *s*.
Rev. 14. 3. no man could learn that *s*.
15. 3. sing *s*. of Moses . . . of Lamb
Ps. 33. 3. sing a *new song*, 40. 3; 96. 1; 144. 9;
   149. 1. Is. 42. 10. Rev. 5. 9.
Job 35. 10. giveth *songs* in the night, Ps. 42. 8;
   77. 6. Is. 30. 29.
Ps. 32. 7. compass . . . with *s*. of deliverance
119. 54. *s*. in house of my pilgrimage
Eph. 5. 19. speaking in . . . spiritual *s*.
SOON as they be born, Ps. 58. 3.
Prov. 14. 17. *s*. angry dealeth foolishly
Gal. 1. 6. so *s*. removed . . . to another gospel
2 Thes. 2. 2. not *s*. shaken
SORCERER, Acts 13. 6, 8; 8. 9, 11.
Jer. 27. 9. *sorcerers*, Mal. 3. 5. Rev. 21. 8.
SORE, 2 Chr. 6. 28. Job 5. 18.
Heb. 10. 29. much *sorer* punishment
Is. 1. 6. and putrifying *sores*
SORRY, Ps. 38. 18. 2 Cor. 2. 2; 7. 8.
Ps. 90. 10. labour and *sorrow*
Prov. 15. 13. by *s*. of heart spirit is broken
Eccl. 1. 18. increaseth knowledge increaseth *s*.
7. 3. *s*. is better than laughter
Is. 35. 10. *s*. and sighing shall flee away, 51. 11.
50. 11. ye shall lie down in *s*.
Lam. 1. 12. if there be any *s*. like unto my *s*.
John 16. 6. *s*. hath filled your heart
20. your *s*. shall be turned into joy
2 Cor. 2. 7. swallowed up with overmuch *s*.
7. 10. godly *s*. worketh repentance to salvation :
   but *s*. of world worketh death, 9.
Phil. 2. 27. should have *s*. upon *s*.
1 Thes. 4. 13. *s*. not, as others which have no hope
Rev. 21. 4. no more death, neither *s*.
2 Cor. 7. 9. *sorrowed*, Jer. 31. 12.
Job 6. 7. are as my *sorrowful* meat

Prov. 14. 13. in laughter heart is *sorrowful*
Jer. 31. 25. replenished *s*. soul, Ps. 69. 29
Zeph. 3. 18. gather them that are *s*.
Mat. 19. 22. young man . . . went way *s*.
26. 22, 38. my soul is exceeding *s*.
Luke 2. 48. *sorrowing*, Acts 20. 38.
Ps. 18. 4. *sorrows* of death compassed me, 116. 3.
5. the *s*. of hell compassed me
127. 2. it is vain . . . to eat bread of *s*.
Is. 53. 3. man of *s*. 4. carried our *s*.
Mat. 24. 8. beginning of *s*.
1 Tim. 6. 10. and pierced through with many *s*.
SORT, 2 Cor. 7. 11. 3 John 6.
SOUGHT the Lord, Ex. 33. 7. 2 Chr. 14. 7.
Ps. 34. 4. I *s*. Lord, and he heard
111. 2. *s*. out of all them that have
119. 10. with my whole heart have I *s*. thee
Eccl. 7. 29. *s*. out many inventions
Is. 62. 12. be called *S*. out, a city
65. 1. found of them that *s*. me not
Rom. 9. 32. *s*. it not by faith, but by
2 Chr. 16. 12. *s*. not to Lord, Zeph. 1. 6.
1 Chr. 15. 13. *sought him*, 2 Chr. 14. 7;
   15. 4. Ps. 78. 34. Sol. 3. 1, 2; 5. 6. Jer. 8. 2;
   26. 21.
SOUL abhor my judgments, Lev. 26. 15, 43.
Deut. 11. 13. serve him with . . . all *s*.
13. 3. love the Lord with all . . . your *s*., Josh.
   22. 5. 1 Ki. 2. 4. Mark 12. 33.
1 Sam. 18. 1. *s*. of Jonathan knit with *s*. of David
1 Ki. 8. 48. return with all their . . . *s*.
1 Chr. 22. 19. set your . . . *s*. to seek Lord
Ps. 19. 7. law of Lord is perfect, converting *s*.
34. 22. Lord redeemeth *s*. of his servants
49. 8. redemption of their *s*. is precious
74. 19. deliver not the *s*. of thy turtledove
107. 9. filleth the hungry *s*.
Prov. 10. 3. not suffer *s*. of righteous
19. 2. that *s*. be without knowledge it is not good
27. 7. full *s*. loatheth honeycomb
Is. 55. 2. let your *s*. delight in fatness
55. 3. hear and your *s*. shall live
58. 10. and satisfy the afflicted *s*.
Jer. 31. 25. I have satiated weary *s*., 12, 14.
38. 16. Lord liveth, that made us this *s*.
Mat. 10. 28. not able to kill *s*.
Rom. 13. 1. let every *s*. be subject to
1 Thes. 5. 23. *s*. and body be preserved
Heb. 4. 12. piercing even to dividing . . . of *s*.
10. 39. believe to saving of the *s*.
Ex. 30. 12. ransom for *his soul*
Judg. 10. 16.—was grieved for misery
2 Ki. 23. 25. turned to Lord . . . with all—
Job 27. 8. when God taketh away—
Hab. 2. 4.—lifted up is not upright
Mat. 16. 26. gain whole world, and lose—
Ps. 16. 10. not leave *my soul* in hell
31. 7. hast known—in adversities
35. 3. say to—I am thy salvation
9.—shall be joyful in the Lord
42. 5, 11. why cast down, O—, 43. 5.
62. 1.—waiteth upon God, 5.
63. 1.—thirsteth for thee, my flesh
8.—followeth hard after thee
Is. 26. 9. with—have I desired thee, 8.
61. 10.—shall be joyful in my God
Luke 1. 46.—doth magnify the Lord
John 12. 27.—troubled, Mat. 26. 38.
Ps. 33. 19. *our soul*, 44. 25; 66. 9; 123. 4; 124. 4.
   Is. 26. 8.
Deut. 13. 6. *own soul*, 1 Sam. 18. 1; 20. 17. Ps.
   22. 29. Prov. 8. 36; 11. 17; 15. 32; 19. 8, 16;
   6. 32; 20. 2; 29. 24. Mark 8. 36. Luke 2. 35.

Deut. 4. 9. *with all thy soul*, 6. 5; 10. 12; 30. 6.
  Mat. 22. 37.
Ezek. 3. 19. delivered *thy soul*, 21; 33. 9.
Luke 12. 20. this night—shall be
3 John 2. be in health even as—prospereth
Prov. 11. 30. that winneth *souls* is wise
Is. 57. 16. spirit fail . . . and *s.* which I
Ezek. 14. 14. should deliver but their own *s.*
1 Pet. 4. 19. commit keeping of their *s.* to him
2 Pet. 2. 14. beguiling unstable *s.*
Rev. 6. 9. *s.* of slain 20. 4. *s.* of beheaded
Luke 21. 19. *your souls*, Josh. 23. 14. Jer. 6. 16;
  26. 19. Mat. 11. 29. Heb. 13. 17. 1 Pet 1.
SOUND, dreadful, Job 15. 21.   [9, 22; 2. 25.
Ps. 47. 5. Lord with *s.* of a trumpet
89. 15. people that know joyful *s.*
119. 80. let my heart be *s.* in thy statutes
Prov. 2. 7. *s.* wisdom, 3. 21; 8. 14.
Eccl. 12. 4. *s.* of the grinding is low
Amos 6. 5. that chant to *s.* of viol
Rom. 10. 18. *s.* went into all the earth
1 Tim. 1. 10. contrary to *s.* doctrine, 2 Tim. 4. 3.
2 Tim. 1. 7. *s.* mind, 13. *s.* words
Tit. 1. 9; 2. 1, *s.* doctrine. 2. 2, *s.* in faith
Is. 63. 15. *sounding* of bowels, 16. 11.
Ps. 38. 3, 7. no *soundness*. Is. 1. 6.
SOW that was washed, 2 Pet. 2. 22.
SOW wickedness reap same, Job 4. 8.
Ps. 126. 5. *s.* in tears shall reap in joy
Eccl. 11. 4. observeth wind shall not *s.*
Jer. 4. 3. *s.* not among thorns
31. 27. I will *s.* the house of Israel
Hos. 10. 12. *s.* to yourselves in righteousness, reap
Mic. 6. 15. thou shalt *s.* but . . . not reap
Mat. 13. 3. sower went forth to *s.*
Luke 12. 24. the ravens; for they neither *s.* nor
19. 22. reaping that I did not *s.*
Is. 55. 10. seed to *sower*, 2 Cor. 9. 10.
Prov. 11. 18. *soweth* righteousness
22. 8. *s.* iniquity shall reap vanity
John 4. 37. one *s.*, another reapeth
2 Cor. 9. 6. *s.* sparingly . . . *s.* bountifully
Gal. 6. 7. whatsoever a man *s.*, that shall, 8.
Ps. 97. 11. light is *sown* for righteous
Hos. 8. 7. *s.* wind, they shall reap whirlwind
1 Cor. 9. 11. have *s.* to you spiritual things
15. 42. it is *s.* in corruption
43. *s.* in dishonour . . . *s.* in weakness
2 Cor. 9. 10. multiply your seed *s.*
Jas. 3. 18. fruit of righteousness *s.* in peace
SPARE all the place, Gen. 18. 26.
Neh. 13. 22. *s.* me according to . . . thy mercy
Ps. 39. 13. *s.* me that I may recover
Joel 2. 17. *s.* thy people O Lord and give not
Mal. 3. 17. I will *s.* them, as a man *spareth*
Rom. 8. 32. *spared* not his own Son
11. 21. if God *s.* not the natural
2 Pet. 2. 4. God *s.* not angels that sinned
Prov. 13. 24. he that *spareth* rod
SPARKS, Job 5. 7. Is. 50. 11.
SPARROW, Ps. 102. 7. Mat. 10. 29.
SPEAK against Moses, Num. 12. 8.
Gen. 18. 27. taken on me to *s.* to Lord
Ex. 4. 14. I know he (Aaron) can *s.* well
34. 35. went in to *s.* with him
1 Sam. 3. 9. *S.*, Lord, for thy servant heareth, 10.
Ps. 85. 8. he will *s.* peace to his people
Is. 50. 4. how to *s.* a word in season
Jer. 18. 7. at what instant I shall *s.*, 9.
Mat. 10. 19. how or what ye shall *s.*
Luke 6. 26. when all men *s.* well of
John 3. 11. we *s.* that we do know
Acts 4. 20. cannot but *s.* things we

1 Cor. 1. 10. ye all *speak* the same thing
Tit. 3. 2. to *s.* evil of no man
Jas. 1. 19. swift to hear, slow to *s.*
2 Pet. 2. 10. *s.* evil of dignities, Jude 8.
Jude 10. *s.* evil of things which they
Mat. 12. 32. *speaketh* a word against Son of man
34. out of abundance of heart mouth *s.*
Heb. 11. 4. he being dead yet *s.*
12. 24. *s.* better things than that of Abel
12. 25. refuse not him that *s.*
Is. 45. 19. *I speak*, 63. 1. John 4. 26; 7. 17;
  8. 26, 28, 38; 12. 50. Rom. 3. 5; 6. 19. 1 Tim.
                                            [2. 7.
58. 13. nor *speaking* thine own words
65. 24. while they are *s.* I will hear, 58. 9.
Dan. 9. 20. whiles I was *s.* and
Mat. 6. 7. shall be heard for their much *s.*
Eph. 4. 15. *s.* the truth in love
31. evil *s.* be put away, 1 Pet. 2. 1.
5. 19. *s.* to yourselves in psalms
1 Tim. 4. 2. *s.* lies in hypocrisy, Ps. 58. 3.
Rev. 13. 5. a mouth *s.* great things
Gen. 11. 1. earth was of one *speech*
Mat. 26. 73. thy *s.* bewrayeth thee
1 Cor. 2. 1. not with excellency of *s.*
2 Cor. 3. 12. use great plainness of *s.*
10. 10. his *s.* contemptible
Col. 4. 6. let your *s.* be always with grace
Tit. 2. 8. sound *s.*, that cannot be condemned
Jude 15. of all their hard *speeches*
Rom. 16. 18. by fair *s.* deceive hearts
Mat. 22. 12. he was *speechless*
SPECTACLE to angels, 1 Cor. 4. 9.
SPEED, Gen. 24. 12. 2 John 10, 11.
Ezra 7. 21. *speedily*, 26. Ps. 31. 2; 79. 8. Eccl.
  8. 11. Luke 18. 8.
SPEND their days in wealth, Job 21. 13.
Ps. 90. 9. *s.* our years as a tale that
Is. 55. 2. *s.* money for that which is
49. 4. have *spent* my strength for
Rom. 13. 12. night is far *s.*
2 Cor. 12. 15. spend and be *s.*
SPICES, Sol. 4. 10, 14, 16; 8. 14.
SPIDER, Prov. 30. 28. Job 8. 14. Is. 59. 5.
SPIKENARD, Sol. 1. 12; 4. 13, 14.
SPIRIT made willing, Ex. 35. 21.
Num. 11. 17. take of *s.* which is on
14. 24. Caleb had another *s.* with
2 Ki. 2. 9. double portion of thy *s.*
Ezra 1. 5. whose *s.* God raised
Neh. 9. 20. gavest also thy good *s.* to instruct
Job 26. 13. by his *s.* he garnished the
32. 18. the *s.* within constraineth me
Ps. 31. 5. to thine hand I commit my *s.*
32. 2. in whose *s.* there is no guile
34. 18. a contrite *s.*, Is. 57. 15; 66. 2.
51. 10. renew a right *s.* within me
11. take not thy holy *s.* from me
12. uphold me with thy free *s.*
17. a broken *s.*, Prov. 17. 22.
76. 12. he shall cut off *s.* of princes
78. 8. *s.* was not stedfast with God
139. 7. whither should I go from thy *s.*?
142. 3. my *s.* was overwhelmed, 143. 4.
143. 7. *s.* faileth. 10. thy *s.* is good
Prov. 14. 29. hasty of *s.* exalteth folly
15. 13. by sorrow of heart *s.* is broken
16. 18. a haughty *s.* before a fall
32. he that ruleth his *s.* (is better) than he
18. 14. a wounded *s.* who can bear?
20. 27. *s.* of man is candle of Lord
Eccl. 3. 21. who knoweth *s.* of man
8. 8. no power over *s.* to retain *s.*

12. 7. the *spirit* shall return to God
Is. 32. 15. until *s.* be poured upon us
34. 16. his *s.* it hath gathered them
57. 15. to revive the *s.* of the humble
16. for the *s.* fail before me
61. 3. garment of praise for *s.* of
Mic. 2. 11. walking in *s.* and falsehood
Zech. 12. 1. formeth *s.* of man within
12. 10. *s.* of grace and supplication
Mat. 22. 43. David in *s.* call him Lord
26. 41. *s.* is willing, but flesh weak
Luke 1. 80. (John) waxed strong in *s.*
2. 27. came by the *S.* into temple
8. 55. *s.* came again and she arose
9. 55. know not what manner of *s.* ye are
24. 39. *s.* hath not flesh and bones
John 3. 5. born of water and of *s.*
6. that which is born of the *S.* is *s.*
4. 24. God is a *S.* 23. worship Father in *s.*
6. 63. it is the *S.* that quickeneth; the words I
   speak . . . are *s.* and life
Acts 6. 10. not able to resist the . . . *s.*
16. 7. the *S.* suffered them not
17. 16. (Paul's) *s.* was stirred in him
18. 5. Paul was pressed in *s.* and
Rom. 8. 1. not after flesh, but after *S.*, 4.
2. *S.* of life in Christ Jesus made
9. if any have not *S.* of Christ, he
13. if ye through *S.* mortify deeds
15. *s.* of bondage, *S.* of adoption
16. *S.* beareth witness with our *s.*
1 Cor. 2. 10. *S.* searcheth all things
5. 3. present in *s.* 5. *s.* may be saved
6. 17. joined unto Lord is one *s.*
12. 13. by one *S.* . . . baptized . . . drink into
   one *S.*
2 Cor. 3. 3. written with *S.* of living God
6. not of letter but *s.* . . . . *s.* giveth life
17. *S.* of Lord is, there is liberty
7. 1. from filthiness of flesh and *s.*
Gal. 3. 3. begun in *S.* are ye now perfect
4. 6. sent forth *S.* of his Son into your hearts
5. 17. flesh lusteth against *S.* and *S.* against flesh
18. if led of *S.* ye are not under law
22. fruit of *S.* is love, joy, peace
25. if we live in *S.* let us walk in *S.*
6. 18. the grace of our Lord Jesus Christ be with
   your *s.*, 2 Tim. 4. 22.
Eph. 1. 13. with holy *S.* of promise
4. 4. there is one body and one *S.*
23. be renewed in *s.* of your mind
5. 9. fruit of *S.* is in all goodness
6. 18. praying always . . . in *S.*, Jude 20.
Col. 2. 5. am I with you in the *s.*
1 Thes. 5. 23. whole *s.* be preserved
Heb. 4. 12. diving asunder of soul and *s.*
9. 14. through eternal *s.* offered
Jas. 4. 5. *s.* that dwelleth in us
1 Pet. 3. 4. ornament of a meek and quiet *s.*
18. in flesh, but quickened by the *S.*
1 John 4. 1. believe not every *s.*
Jude 19. sensual, not having the *S.*
Rev. 1. 10. I was in the *S.* on Lord's day
11. 11. *S.* of life from God entered
14. 13. yea, saith the *S.*, that they
Gen. 6. 3. *my spirit*, Job 10. 12. Ps. 31. 5; 77. 6.
   Is. 38. 16. Ezek. 36. 27. Zech. 4. 6. Luke 1. 47;
   23. 46. Acts 7. 59. Rom. 1. 9. 1 Cor. 14. 14.
Gen. 1. 2. *Spirit of God*, Ex. 31. 3. 2 Chr. 15. 1.
   Job 33. 4. Ezek. 11. 24. Mat. 3. 16; 12. 28.
   Rom. 8. 9, 14; 15. 19. 1 Cor. 2. 11, 14; 3. 16;
   6. 11; 12. 3. 2 Cor. 3. 3. Eph. 4. 30. 1 Pet.
   4. 14. 1 John 4. 2.

Is. 11. 2. *spirit* of Lord, *s.* of wisdom, *s.* of counsel,
   s. of knowledge, Eph. 1. 17.
Zech. 13. 2. unclean *s.*, Mat. 12. 43.
Num. 16. 22. God of *spirits.* of all flesh, 27. 16.
Prov. 16. 2. Lord weigheth the *s.*
Mat. 10. 1. *unclean spirits*, Acts 5. 16; 8. 7. Rev.
   16. 13, 14.
Luke 10. 20. rejoice not that the *s.* are subject to
   you
1 Cor. 14. 32. *s.* of the prophets are subject
Heb. 12. 23. to *s.* of just men made
1 Pet. 3. 19. preached to *s.* in prison
1 John 4. 1. believe not every *spirit* but try *s.*
Hos. 9. 7. the *spiritual* man is mad
Rom. 1. 11. impart unto you some *s.* gift
7. 14. law is *s.*, but I am carnal
15. 27. partakers of their *s.* things
1 Cor. 2. 13. comparing *s.* things with *s.*
15. he that is *s.* judgeth all things
3. 1. not speak unto you as unto *s.*
9. 11. have sown to you *s.* things
10. 3. did all eat the same *s.* meat
4. same *s.* drink . . . *S.* rock that followed
15. 44. it is raised a *s.* body
Gal. 6. 1. ye which are *s.* restore
Eph. 1. 3. blessed us with all *s.* blessings
5. 19. speaking in . . . *s.* songs, Col. 3. 16.
6. 12. wrestle against . . . *s.* wickedness
1 Pet. 2. 5. built up *s.* house
Rom. 8. 6. to be *spiritually* minded
1 Cor. 2. 14. because they are *s.* discerned
Rev. 11. 8. which *s.* is called Sodom and Egypt
SPITE, Ps. 10. 14. Mat. 22. 6.
SPITTING, Is. 50. 6. Luke 18. 32.
SPOIL, Gen. 49. 27. Ps. 68. 12.
Is. 53. 12. divide *s.* with the strong
Mat. 12. 29. he will *s.* his house
Col. 2. 8. beware lest any man *s.* you
Ex. 12. 36. *spoiled* the Egyptians
Col. 2. 15. having *s.* principalities
Heb. 10. 34. took joyfully *spoiling* of
SPOT, without, Num. 19. 2; 28. 3, 9. Job 11. 15.
   1 Tim. 6. 14. Heb. 9. 14. 1 Pet. 1. 19. 2 Pet.
   3. 14.
Deut. 32. 5. *s.* is not *s.* of his children
Sol. 4. 7. there is no *s.* in thee
Jer. 13. 23. *spots*, Jude 12, 23.
SPREAD, Job 9. 8. Is. 25. 11; 37. 14. Jer. 43. 10.
   Lam. 1. 17. Ezek. 16. 8.
SPRING, Ps. 85. 11. Mat. 13. 5, 7.
   Ps. 65. 10. *springing*, John 4. 14. Heb. 12. 15.
SPRINKLE, Lev. 14. 7; 16. 14.
Is. 52. 15. shall he *s.* many nations
Ezek. 36. 25. will I *s.* clean water on
Heb. 10. 22. hearts *sprinkled* from an evil
12. 24. to blood of *sprinkling*
1 Pet. 1. 2. *s.* of the blood of Jesus Christ
SPUE thee out of my mouth, Rev. 3. 16. Hab.
   2. 16. Lev. 18. 28. Jer. 25. 27.
SPY, Num. 13. 16. Josh 2. 1. Gal. 2. 4.
STABILITY of times, Is. 33. 6.
STAFF, Gen. 32. 10. Zech. 11. 10.
   Ps. 23. 4. thy rod and thy *s.* they comfort me
   Is. 3. 1. stay and *s.* . . . of bread
   9. 4. broken . . . . *s.* of his shoulder, 14. 5.
   10. 5. *s.* in their hand is mine indignation
STAGGER, Ps. 107. 27. Rom. 4. 20.
STAIN, Is. 23. 9; 63. 3.
STAKES, Is. 33. 30; 54. 2.
STAMMER, Is. 28. 11; 33. 19; 32. 4.
STAND, Ezek. 29. 7. Ex. 9. 11.
Job 19. 25. *s.* at latter day up on earth
Ps. 76. 7. who may *s.* in thy sight

Ps. 130. 3. Lord who shall *stand*?
Prov. 19. 21. the counsel of the Lord, that shall *s*.
Is. 46. 10. my counsel shall *s*.
Mal. 3. 2. who shall *s*. when he appeareth?
Mat. 12. 25. house divided . . . shall not *s*.
Rom. 5. 2. this grace wherein we *s*.
2 Cor. 1. 24. by faith ye *s*., Rom. 11. 20.
1 Pet. 5. 12. grace of God wherein ye *s*.
Rev. 3. 20. I *s*. at the door and knock
Nah. 1. 6. *stand before*, 1 Sam. 6. 20. Luke 21. 36. Rom. 14. 10. Rev. 20. 12.
1 Cor. 16. 13. *stand fast* in the faith
Gal. 5. 1.—in liberty wherewith Christ hath made us free
Phil. 1. 27.—in one spirit
4. 1.—in the Lord, dearly beloved
1Thes. 3. 8. we live, if ye—in Lord
2 Thes. 2. 15.—and hold traditions
Ps. 1. 5. *stand in*, 4. 4; 24. 3.
Ex. 14. 13. *stand still*, see salvation, 2 Chr. 20. 17. Josh. 10. 12. Zech. 11. 16.
Ps. 1. 1. *standeth*, 26. 12; 33. 11. Prov. 8. 2. Sol. 2. 9. Is. 3. 13.
Rom. 14. 4. to his own master he *s*. or falleth
1 Cor. 10. 12. thinketh he *s*. take heed
2 Tim. 2. 19. foundation of God *s*.
Jas. 5. 9. the Judge *s*. before the door
STAR, Num. 24. 17. Mat. 2. 2.
Judg. 5. 20. the *stars* in their courses
Job 25. 5. *s*. are not pure in his sight
38. 7. the morning *s*. sang together
Dan. 12. 3. shall shine as *s*. for ever
Rev. 12. 1. on her head crown of twelve *s*.
STATURE, Mat. 6. 27. Eph. 4. 13.
STATUTES and laws, Neh. 9. 14.
Ps. 19. 8. *s*. of the Lord are right
Ezek. 20. 24. had despised my *s*., 25.
33. 15. walk in *s*. of life without . . . iniquity
Mic. 6. 16. the *s*. of Omri are kept
Ex. 15. 26. *his statutes*, Deut. 6. 17. 2 Ki. 17. 15. Ps. 18. 22; 105. 45.
1 Chr. 29. 19. *thy statutes*, Ps. 119. 12, 16, 23, 26, 33, 54, 64, 68, 71, 117.
STAY, Ps. 18. 18. Sol. 2. 5. Is. 10. 20; 26. 3; 27. 8; 48. 2; 50. 10.
STEAD, INSTEAD, Gen. 4. 25; 22. 13.
Gen. 30. 2. Jacob said, Am I in God's *s*.?
Prov. 11. 8. wicked cometh in his *s*.
2 Cor. 5. 20. pray you in Christ's *s*.
STEAL, Ex. 20. 15. Lev. 19. 11.
Prov. 6. 30. is he *s*. to satisfy his soul
Jer. 23. 30. I am against prophets, saith the Lord, that *s*. my words
Mat. 6. 19. thieves break through and *s*.
27. 64. lest his disciples . . . *s*. him away
Eph. 4. 28. that *stole* steal no more
Prov. 9. 17. *stolen* waters are sweet
STEDFAST, Job 11. 15. Dan. 6. 26.
Ps. 78. 8. spirit not *s*. with God, 37.
1 Cor. 15. 58. be ye *s*., unmoveable
Heb. 3. 14. hold . . . confidence *s*. to the end
1 Pet. 5. 9. whom resist *s*. in faith
Col. 2. 5. *stedfastness* of your faith
2 Pet. 3. 17. fall from your own *s*.
STEPS, Ex. 20. 26. Ps. 18. 36.
Ps. 37. 23. *s*. of good man are ordered
31. none of his *s*. shall slide
119. 133. order my *s*. in thy word
Prov. 16. 9. but Lord directeth his *s*.
Jer. 10. 23. not in man . . . to direct his *s*.
Rom. 4. 12. walk in *s*. of that faith
1 Pet. 2. 21. ye should follow his *s*.

STEWARD, Luke 12. 42; 16. 2. 1. Cor. 4. 1. Tit. 1. 7. 1 Pet. 4. 10.
STIFF neck, Deut. 31. 27. Jer. 17. 23.
2 Chr. 36. 13. he *stiffeneth* his neck
Ex. 32. 9. *stiffnecked* people, 33. 3, 5; 34. 9. Deut. 9. 6, 13; 10. 16.
Acts 7. 51.—and uncircumcised in heart
STILL, Ex. 15. 16. Ps. 8. 2; 139. 18.
Ps. 4. 4. be *s*., Jer. 47. 6. Mark 4. 39.
46. 10. be *s*. and know that I am God
83. 1. be not *s*., O God
Is. 30. 7. their strength is to sit *s*.
Ps. 65. 7. *stilleth* noise of seas, 89. 9.
STING, 1 Cor. 15. 55, 56. Rev. 9. 10.
Prov. 23. 32. *stingeth* like an adder
STINK, Ps. 38. 5. Is. 3. 24.
STIR up, Num. 24. 9. Job 17. 8.
Ps. 35. 23. *s*. up thyself, awake, 80. 2.
78. 38. did not *s*. up all his wrath
Sol. 2. 7. that ye *s*. not, 3. 5; 8. 4.
2 Tim. 1. 6. *s*. up gift of God that is
STONE of Israel, Gen. 49. 24.
Ps. 118. 22. *s*. which the builders refused
Is. 8. 14. *s*. of stumbling, Rom. 9. 32, 33.
28. 16. a *s*., a tried *s*., a precious corner *s*.
Dan. 2. 34. *s*. cut out without hands
Hab. 2. 11. *s*. shall cry out of wall
Zech. 3. 9. on one *s*. shall be seven eyes
Mat. 7. 9. ask bread, will he give him *s*.?
1 Pet. 2. 4. living *s*. 6. chief corner *s*.
Mat. 3. 9. God is able of these *stones* to raise up
Luke 19. 40. *s*. would immediately cry
Ezek. 11. 19. *stony*, Mat. 13. 5.
STOOP, Job 9. 13. Prov. 12. 25. Mark 1. 7.
STORE, 1 Cor. 16. 2. 1 Tim. 6. 19.
Luke 12. 24. *storehouse*, Ps. 33. 7.
STORM, Ps. 55. 8; 83. 15.
Ps. 107. 29. he maketh the *s*. a calm
Is. 4. 6. covert from the *s*. 25. 4. refuge from the *s*.
Nah. 1. 3. Lord hath his way in . . . the *s*.
Mark 4. 27. a great *s*., Luke 8. 23.
Ps. 148. 8. *stormy* wind fulfilling his word
STOUT hearted, Ps. 76. 5. Is. 46. 12.
Is. 10. 12. punish fruit of *s*. heart
Dan. 7. 20. whose look was more *s*.
Mal. 3. 13. words have been *s*. against me
Is. 9. 9. say in pride and *stoutness* of heart
STRAIGHT, Josh. 6. 5. Jer. 31. 9.
Ps. 5. 8. thy way *s*. before my face
Eccl. 1. 15. crooked cannot be made *s*.
7. 31. who can make that *s*.
Is. 40. 3. make *s*. in the desert a highway for our
4. crooked made *s*. 45. 2. Luke 3. 5.
Luke 3. 4. way of Lord, make his paths *s*.
Heb. 12. 13. make *s*. paths for your feet
STRAIN at a gnat, Mat. 23. 24.
STRAIT, 2 Sam. 24. 14. Job 20. 22; 36. 16. Is. 49. 20. Phil. 1. 23.
Mat. 7. 13. enter in at the *s*. gate, 14.
Mic. 2. 7. is the spirit of Lord *straitened*?
Luke 12. 50. how am I *s*. till it be
2 Cor. 6. 12. not *s*. in us, but ye are *s*. in
STRANGE, Ex. 21. 8; 30. 9. Lev. 10. 1. Ps. 81. 9. Jer. 2. 21. Luke 5. 26. Heb. 11. 9. 1 Pet. 4. 12. Jude 7.
Is. 28. 21. do his *s*. work . . . his *s*. act
Hos. 8. 12. they were counted as a *s*. thing
Zeph. 1. 8. clothed with *s*. apparel
Heb. 13. 9. about with divers and *s*. doctrines
1 Pet. 4. 4. think it *s*. that ye run not
Judg. 11. 2. *strange women*, Prov. 2. 16; 5. 3, 20; 6. 24; 20. 16; 23. 27; 27. 13. Ezra 10. 2, 11.

Gen. 23. 4. *stranger* and sojourner, Ps. 39. 12.;
119. 19. 1 Chr. 29. 15.
Jer. 14. 8. shouldest thou be as a *s.*
Mat. 25. 35. I was a *s.* and ye took
Luke 17. 18. not found . . . save this *s.*
John 10. 5. a *s.* will they not follow
Ps. 105. 12. very few and *strangers*
146. 9. the Lord preserveth the *s.*
Eph. 2. 19. are no more *s.* and foreigners
Heb. 11. 13. confessed they were *s.*
13. 2. be not forgetful to entertain *s.*, for thereby
1 Pet. 2. 11. beseech you as *s.* and
STRANGLED, Acts 15. 20, 29; 21. 25.
Job 7. 15. soul chooseth *strangling*
STREAM, Is. 30. 33; 66. 12. Dan. 7. 10. Amos
5. 24. Luke 6. 48.   [33. 21; 35. 6.
Ps. 46. 4. *streams*, 126. 4. Sol. 4. 15. Is. 30. 25;
STREET, Rev. 11. 8; 21. 21; 22. 2.
Prov. 1. 20. *streets*, Sol. 3. 2. Luke 14. 21.
STRENGTH, Gen. 49. 24. Ex. 13. 3.
Ex. 15. 2. the Lord is my *s.*, Ps. 18. 2; 28. 7;
118. 14. Is. 12. 2.
1 Sam. 2. 9. by *s.* shall no man prevail
15. 29. the *S.* of Israel will not lie
Job 9. 19. if I speak of *s.* lo, he is
12. 13. with him is wisdom and *s.*, 16.
Ps. 18. 32. girded me with *s.*, 39.
27. 1. the Lord is the *s.* of my life
29. 11. Lord will give *s.* to his people
33. 16. mighty man not delivered by much *s.*
39. 13. spare me that I recover *s.*
46. 1. God is our refuge and *s.*, 81. 1.
68. 35. God of Israel . . . giveth *s.* and power
73. 26. God is *s.* of my heart, 43. 2.
84. 5. blessed is the man whose *s.* is in thee
7. they go from *s.* to *s.*, every one
93. 1. the Lord is clothed with *s.*
96. 6. *s.* and beauty are in his sanctuary
138. 3. strengthenedst me with *s.* in my soul
140. 7. Lord, the *s.* of my salvation
Eccl. 9. 16. wisdom is better than *s.*
10. 10. if iron be blunt . . . put to more *s.*
Is. 25. 4. *s.* to poor, *s.* to needy
26. 4. in Lord Jehovah is everlasting *s.*
40. 29. have no might he increaseth *s.*
45. 24. in Lord have I righteousness and *s.*
Joel 3. 16. Lord is the *s.* of children of Israel
Luke 1. 51. shewed *s.* with his arm
Rom. 5. 6. when we were without *s.*
1 Cor. 15. 56. *s.* of sin is the law
Rev. 3. 8. thou hast a little *s.*
5. 12. worthy is Lamb . . . to receive . . . *s.*
12. 10. now is come salvation and *s.*
1 Chr. 16. 11. *his strength*, Ps. 33. 17. Is. 63. 1.
Hos. 7. 9; 12. 3.
Gen. 49. 24. *in strength*, Job 9. 4; 36. 5. Ps.
71. 16; 103. 20; 147. 10. Is. 33. 6.
Gen. 49. 3. *my strength*, Ex. 15. 2. 2 Sam.
22. 33. Job 6. 12. Ps. 18. 1, 2; 19. 14; 28. 7;
38. 10; 43. 2; 59. 17; 62. 7; 71. 9; 102. 23;
118. 14; 144. 1. Is. 12. 2; 27. 5; 49. 4, 5.
Jer. 16. 19. Hab. 3. 19. 2 Cor. 12. 9.
Ps. 37. 39. *their strength*, 89. 17. Prov. 20. 29.
Is. 30. 7; 40. 31.
Ps. 86. 16. *thy strength*, 110. 2. Prov. 24. 10;
31. 3. Is. 17. 10; 63. 15. Mark 12. 30. Deut.
33. 25.
Neh. 8. 10. *your strength*, Is. 23. 14; 30. 15.
Ezek. 24. 21. Lev. 26. 20.
Ps. 20. 2. *strengthen* thee out of Zion
27. 14. wait on Lord . . . he shall *s.* thine heart,
41. 3. *s.* him on bed of languishing   [31. 24.
Is. 35. 3. *s.* ye the weak hands

Is. 41. 10. I will *strengthen* thee, 54. 2. *s.* thy stakes
Dan. 11. 1. stood to confirm and *s.* him
Zech. 10. 12. I will *s.* them in Lord
Luke 22. 32. when . . . converted *s.* thy brethren
1 Pet. 5. 10. God of grace stablish, *s.*
Rev. 3. 2. *s.* the things which remain
1 Sam. 23. 16. *strengthened* his hand in God
Ezek. 34. 4. diseased have ye not *s.*
Eph. 3. 16. *s.* with might, Col. 1. 11.
2 Tim. 4. 17. Lord stood with me and *s.* me
Ps. 138. 3. *strengthenedst* me with strength.
104. 15. bread which *strengtheneth*
STRETCH thy hands, Job 11. 13.
Amos 6. 4. *s.* themselves on their couches
Mat. 12. 13. *s.* forth thy hand
John 21. 18. thou shalt *s.* forth thy hands
Gen. 22. 10. *stretched* hand, Is. 5. 25.
1 Ki. 17. 21. *s.* himself upon child
1 Chr. 21. 16. sword *s.* out over Jerusalem
Is. 5. 25. hand is *s.* out, 9. 12; 10. 4.
Rom. 10. 21. all day I have *s.* forth my hands
Job 15. 25. he *stretcheth* out his hand
Prov. 31. 20. she *s.* out her hand to poor
Is. 40. 22. *s.* out the heavens as a curtain, 42. 5;
44. 24; 45. 12; 51. 13. Jer. 10. 12; 51. 15.
Zech. 12. 1.
STRIFE between me and thee, Gen. 13. 8.
Ps. 80. 6. us a *s.* to our neighbours
Prov. 15. 18. wrathful man stirreth up *s.*
16. 28. froward man soweth *s.*
20. 3. honour for a man to cease from *s.*
28. 25. a proud heart stirreth up *s.*
29. 22. an angry man stirreth up *s.*
30. 33. forcing of wrath bringeth *s.*
Is. 58. 4. ye fast for *s.* and debate
Jer. 15. 10. hast borne me a man of *s.*
Luke 22. 24. was a *s.* among them
1 Cor. 3. 3. among you envying, *s.*
Gal. 5. 20. wrath, *s.*, seditions
Phil. 1. 15. preach Christ even of envy and *s.* and
2. 3. let nothing be done through *s.*
1 Tim. 6. 4. whereof cometh envy, *s.*
Jas. 3. 14. bitter envying and *s.*, 16.
Prov. 10. 12. hatred stirreth up *strifes*
2 Tim. 2. 23. gender *s.*, 2 Cor. 12. 20.
STRIKE hands, Job 17. 3. Prov. 6. 1.
Prov. 17. 26. to *s.* princes for equity
Is. 1. 5. why . . . be *stricken* any more? Jer. 5. 3.
1 Tim. 3. 3. bishop . . . no *striker*, Tit. 1. 7.
STRIPES, Is. 53. 5. 1 Pet. 2. 24. Prov. 17. 10;
20. 30. Luke 12. 47, 48.
STRIVE, Ex. 21. 18, 22. Job 33. 13.
Gen. 6. 3. Spirit shall not always *s.*
Prov. 3. 30. *s.* not with a man without cause
Mat. 12. 19. he shall not *s.* nor cry
Luke 13. 24. *s.* to enter in at strait gate
2 Tim. 2. 24. servant of Lord must not *s.*
Is. 45. 9. woe to him that *striveth* with his Maker
Phil. 1. 27. *striving* together for the faith
Heb. 12. 4. resisted unto blood, *s.* against sin
STRONG this day, Josh. 14. 11.
Ps. 24. 8. Lord *s.* and mighty . . . in battle
30. 7. made mountain to stand *s.*
31. 2. be thou my *s.* rock, for an house
71. 7. thou art my *s.* refuge, 3.
Prov. 10. 15. rich man's wealth is his *s.* city
14. 26. fear of Lord is *s.* confidence
18. 10. name of Lord is *s.* tower
24. 5. a wise man is *s.*; yea, a man of
Eccl. 9. 11. nor the battle to the *s.*
12. 3. and the *s.* men shall bow
Sol. 8. 6. love is *s.* as death
Is. 1. 31. *s.* shall be as tow and burn

Is. 26. 1. we have a *strong* city, 60. 22.
53. 12. shall divide the spoil with the *s.*
Jer. 50. 34. their Redeemer is *s.*
Joel 3. 10. let the weak say, I am *s.*
Luke 11. 21. *s.* man armed keepeth his palace, 22.
Rom. 4. 20. *s.* in faith
15. 1. we that are *s.* ought to bear the infirmities
2 Cor. 12. 10. when I am weak then am I *s.*
Heb. 11. 34. out of weakness made *s.*
Is. 35. 4. *be strong*, Hag. 2. 4. 1 Cor. 16. 13. Eph.
6. 10. 2 Tim. 2. 1.
1 Cor. 1. 25. *stronger* than men, 10. 22.
Job 17. 9. clean hands shall be *s.* and *s.*
Jer. 20. 7. thou art *s.* than I
STUBBLE, Job 13. 25; 21. 18. Ps. 83. 13. Is.
33. 11. Mal. 4. 1. 1 Cor. 3. 12.
STUBBORN, Deut. 21. 18. Ps. 78. 8.
1 Sam. 15. 23. *stubbornness*, Deut. 9. 27.
STUDY, Eccl. 12. 12. 1 Thes. 4. 11. 2 Tim. 2. 15.
Prov. 15. 28; 24. 2.
STUMBLE, foot shall not, Prov. 3. 23.
Prov. 4. 12. runnest, thou shalt not *s.*
19. they know not at what they *s.*
Is. 5. 27. none shall be weary nor *s.*
8. 15. many among them shall *s.* and fall and
28. 7. err in vision, *s.* in judgment
1 Pet. 2. 8. which *s.* at the word   [stone
Rom. 9. 32. they *stumbled* at that stumbling-
John 11. 9. walk in the day he *stumbleth* not
Rom. 14. 21. whereby thy brother *s.*
Is. 8. 14. *stumbling*, 1 John 2. 10. 1 Pet. 2. 8.
Rom. 9. 32.
Lev. 19. 14. *stumblingblock*, Is. 57. 14. Jer. 6. 21.
Ezek. 3. 20; 7. 19; 14. 3, 4, 7. Rom. 11. 9;
14. 13. 1 Cor. 1. 23; 8. 9. Rev. 2. 14.
stumblingstone, Rom. 9. 32, 33.
SUBDUE our iniquities, Mic. 7. 19.
Phil. 3. 21. able to *s.* all things
Heb. 11. 33. through faith *subdued*
SUBJECT, devils are, Luke 10. 17, 20.
Rom. 8. 7. not *s.* to law of God
20. creature made *s.* to vanity
13. 1. every soul be *s.* to higher powers, 5.
1 Cor. 14. 32. spirits of prophets *s.* to
15. 28. Son . . . shall be *s.* to him that
Eph. 5. 24. as church is *s.* to Christ
Heb. 2. 15. all lifetime *s.* to bondage
Jas. 5. 17. Elias was a man *s.* to like passions
1 Pet. 2. 18. servants be *s.* to your masters
5. 5. all of you be *s.* one to another
1 Cor. 9. 27. *subjection*, 1 Tim. 2. 11; 3. 4. Heb.
2. 5, 8; 12. 9. 1 Pet. 3. 1, 5.
SUBMIT, Gen. 16. 9. Ps. 18. 44; 66. 3; 68. 30;
81. 15.
1 Cor. 16. 16. *submit yourselves*, Eph. 5. 21, 22.
Col. 3. 18. Heb. 13. 17. Jas. 4. 7. 1 Pet. 2. 13;
5. 5.   [righteousness of God
Rom. 10. 3. have not *submitted* unto the
SUBSCRIBE, Is. 44. 5. Jer. 32. 44.
SUBSTANCE, Gen. 7. 4; 15. 14.
Deut. 33. 11. bless, Lord, his *s.*
Job 30. 22. and dissolvest my *s.*
Ps. 139. 15. my *s.* was not hid from thee, 16.
Prov. 3. 9. honour Lord with thy *s.*
Hos. 12. 8. I have found me out *s.*
Luke 8. 3. ministered to him of their *s.*
Heb. 10. 34. a better and an enduring *s.*
11. 1. faith is *s.* of things hoped for
SUBTIL, Gen. 3. 1. Prov. 7. 10.
Acts 13. 10. *subtilty*, 2 Cor. 11. 3. Prov. 1. 4.
SUBVERT, Lam. 3. 36. Tit. 1. 11; 3. 11.
Acts 15. 24. *subverting*, 2 Tim. 2. 14.
SUCK, Gen. 21. 7. Deut. 32. 13; 33. 19.

Job 20. 16. he shall *suck* poison of asps
Is. 60. 16. *s.* milk of Gentiles
Mat. 24. 19. woe to them . . . that give *s.*
Luke 23. 29. paps which never gave *s.*
11. 27. blessed are paps thou hast *sucked*
Is. 11. 8. *sucking* child, 49. 15. Lam. 4. 4.
Ps. 8. 2. *suckling*, Lam. 2. 11.
SUDDEN, Prov. 3. 25. 1 Thes. 5. 3.
SUFFER, Ex. 12. 23. Lev. 19. 17.
Ps. 55. 22. never *s.* righteous to be moved
89. 33. nor *s.* my faithfulness to fail
121. 3. not *s.* thy foot to be moved
Prov. 10. 3. not *s.* soul of righteous to famish
Mat. 16. 21. he must . . . *s.* many things
17. 17. how long shall I *s.* you?
19. 14. *s.* little children . . . to come to me
1 Cor. 4. 12. being persecuted, we *s.*
10. 13. God will not *s.* you to be tempted
Phil. 1. 29. but also to *s.* for his sake
2 Tim. 2. 12. if we *s.* we shall also reign
Heb. 11. 25. choosing rather to *s.* affliction
13. 22. *s.* the word of exhortation
1 Pet. 4. 15. none of you *s.* as a murderer
19. that *s.* according to will of God
Ps. 105. 14. he *suffered* no man to do them
wrong, 1 Chr. 16. 21.
Acts 14. 16. *s.* all nations to walk in their own
16. 7. the Spirit *s.* them not   [ways
Phil. 3. 8. for whom I *s.* loss of all
Heb. 5. 8. learned . . . by things which he *s.*
1 Pet. 2. 21. Christ *s.* for us, leaving
5. 10. after that ye have *s.* a while
Mat. 11. 12. *suffereth*, 1 Cor. 13. 4.
Rom. 8. 18. *sufferings*, 2 Cor. 1. 5, 6. Phil. 3. 10.
Col. 1. 24. Heb. 2. 10. 1 Pet. 1. 11; 4. 13; 5. 1.
SUFFICE, 1 Pet. 4. 3. John 14. 8.
Job 20. 22. *sufficiency*, 2 Cor. 3. 5; 9. 8.
Mat. 6. 34. *sufficient* to day is evil
2 Cor. 2. 16. who is *s.* for these things?
3. 5. not that we are *s.* of ourselves
12. 8. my grace is *s.* for thee
SUM, Ps. 139. 17. Ezek. 28. 12. Heb. 8. 1.
SUMMER and winter not cease, Gen. 8. 22.
Ps. 74. 17. hast made *s.* and winter
Prov. 6. 8. provideth her meat in *s.*
10. 5. that gathereth in *s.* is a wise son
Is. 18. 6. fowls shall *s.* upon them
Zech. 14. 8. in *s.* and in winter shall it be
SUMPTUOUSLY, fared, Luke 16. 19.
SUN, stand thou still, Josh. 10. 12.
Ps. 19. 4. he set a tabernacle for *s.*
74. 16. prepared the light and *s.*
104. 19. *s.* knoweth his going down
121. 6. *s.* shall not smite thee by day, Is. 49. 10.
136. 8. *s.* to rule day, Gen. 1. 16.
Sol. 1. 6. because *s.* looked on me
6. 10. fair as moon, clear as the *s.*
Is. 30. 26. light of the *s.* shall be sevenfold
60. 19. *s.* shall be no more thy light by day
20. thy *s.* shall no more go down
Jer. 31. 35. giveth *s.* for a light by day
Mal. 4. 2. *S.* of righteousness arise
Mat. 5. 45. his *s.* to rise on evil and
13. 43. shine forth as *s.* in the kingdom of
1 Cor. 15. 41. there is one glory of *s.*
Eph. 4. 26. let not *s.* go down upon
Rev. 10. 1. his face as *s.*, 1. 16. Mat. 17. 2.
7. 16. neither shall the *s.* light on them
21. 23. city had no need of the *s.*, 22. 5.
SUP, Luke 17. 8. Rev. 3. 20. Hab. 1. 9.
Luke 14. 16. made a great *supper*
1 Cor. 11. 20. the Lord's *s.*, Luke 22. 20.
Rev. 19. 9. to marriage *s.* of Lamb

SUPERFLUITY of naughtiness, Jas. 1. 21.
SUPERSTITION, Acts 25. 19; 17. 22.
SUPPLICATION, 1 Ki. 8. 28; 9. 3. Job 8. 5;
   9. 15. Ps. 6. 9; 30. 8; 55. 1; 142. 1; 119. 170.
   Dan. 6. 11; 9. 20. Hos. 12. 4. Zech. 12. 10.
   Eph. 6. 18. Phil. 4. 6. 1 Tim. 2. 1; 5. 5. Heb.
   5. 7.
SUPPLY of Spirit of Jesus, Phil. 1. 19.
   Phil. 4. 19. my God shall *s.* all your need
   2 Cor. 9. 12. *supplieth,* Eph. 4. 16.
SUPPORT the weak, Acts 20. 35. 1 Thes. 5. 14.
SUPREME, 1 Pet. 2. 13.
SURE, Gen. 23. 17. 1 Sam. 25. 28.
   2 Sam. 23. 5. covenant, ordered . . . and *s.*
   Ps. 19. 7. testimony of the Lord is *s.*
   93. 5. thy testimonies are very *s.*
   111. 7. all his commandments are *s.*
   Prov. 11. 15. that hateth suretiship is *s.*
   18. righteousness shall be *s.* reward
   Is. 22. 23, 25. fasten him as a nail in a *s.* place
   28. 16. I lay in Zion . . . a *s.* foundation
   33. 16. his waters shall be *s.*
   55. 3. *s.* mercies of David, Acts 13. 34.
   John 6. 69. we are *s.* thou art that Christ
   Rom. 4. 16. promise might be *s.* to all
   2 Tim. 2. 19. foundation of God standeth *s.*
   2 Pet. 1. 10. calling and election *s.*
   19. a more *s.* word of prophecy
SURETY for servant, Ps. 119. 122.
   Heb. 7. 22. Jesus made *s.* of better
SURFEITING, Luke 21. 34.
SURPRISED hypocrites, Is. 33. 14.
SUSTAIN, Ps. 55. 22. Prov. 18. 14.
   Ps. 3. 5. *sustained,* Is. 59. 16.
SWALLOW, Ps. 84. 3. Jer. 8. 7.
   Is. 25. 8. will *s.* up death in victory
   Mat. 23. 24. strain at a gnat, *s.* a camel
   Ex. 15. 12. earth *swallowed,* Num. 16. 32.
   2 Cor. 2. 7. be *s.* with overmuch sorrow
   5. 4. mortality be *s.* up of life
SWEAR, Num. 30. 2. Deut. 6. 13.
   Is. 45. 23. every tongue shall *s.*
   65. 16. shall *s.* by the God of truth
   Jer. 4. 2. shalt *s.,* The Lord liveth, 12. 16.
   Zeph. 1. 5. *s.* by Lord . . . *s.* by Malcham
   Mat. 5. 34. *s.* not at all, Jas. 5. 12.
   Mal. 3. 5. swift witness against . . . false *swearers*
   Ps. 15. 4. *sweareth* to his own hurt
   Eccl. 9. 2. that *s.* as he that feareth
   Zech. 5. 3. every one that *s.* shall be cut off
   Jer. 23. 10. because of *swearing* land mourneth
   Hos. 4. 2. by *s.* and lying . . . they break
   10. 4. *s.* falsely in making a covenant
SWEAT, Gen. 3. 19. Luke 22. 44.
SWEET, Job 20. 12. Ps. 55. 14.
   Ps. 104. 34. my meditation of him shall be *s.*
   119. 103. how *s.* are thy words unto my taste
   Prov. 3. 24. thy sleep shall be *s.,* Jer. 31. 26.
   9. 17. stolen waters are *s.,* 20. 17.
   27. 7. to hungry soul every bitter thing is *s.*
   Eccl. 5. 12. sleep of labouring man is *s.*
   Sol. 2. 3. his fruit was *s.* to my taste
   14. *s.* is thy voice and thy countenance
   5. 16. his mouth is most *s.*
   Is. 5. 20. put bitter for *s.* and *s.* for bitter
   Phil. 4. 18. odour of a *s.* smell
   Rev. 10. 9. in thy mouth *s.* as honey
   Ps. 19. 10. *sweeter* also than honey, 119. 103.
   Judg. 14. 14. *sweetness,* Prov. 16. 21; 27. 9.
SWELLING, Jer. 12. 5. 2 Pet. 2. 18.
SWIFT, Deut. 28. 49. Job 9. 26.
   Eccl. 9. 11. the race is not to the *s.*
   Rom. 3. 15. *s.* to shed blood, Prov. 6. 18.

Jas. 1. 19. *swift* to hear, slow to speak
2 Pet. 2. 1. bring on themselves *s.* destruction
Job 7. 6. days *swifter* than a shuttle, 9. 25.
Ps. 147. 15. *swiftly,* Joel 3. 4.
SWIM, 2 Ki. 6. 6. Ps. 6. 6. Ezek. 47. 5.
SWORD, Ex. 32. 27. Lev. 26. 6, 25.
   Gen. 3. 24. cherubims and a flaming *s.*
   Judg. 7. 20. *s.* of Lord and Gideon
   2 Sam. 12. 10. *s.* shall never depart
   Ps. 17. 13. from wicked which is thy *s.*
   Sol. 3. 8. every man hath his *s.* on
   Jer. 9. 16. I will send a *s.* after them
   15. 2. such as are for *s.* to the *s.,* 43. 11.
   Ezek. 21. 13. what if *s.* contemn even the rod
   Zech. 11. 17. *s.* shall be upon his arm
   Mat. 10. 34. not to send peace, but *s.*
   Luke 2. 35. a *s.* shall pierce through
   Rom. 13. 4. he beareth not *s.* in vain
   Eph. 6. 17. *s.* of Spirit which is word of God
   Heb. 4. 12. sharper than any twoedged *s.*
   Rev. 1. 16. sharp twoedged *s.,* 19. 15.
   Ps. 55. 21. *swords,* 59. 7. Prov. 30. 14. Is. 2. 4.
   Ezek. 32. 27. Joel 3. 10.
SWORN by myself, Gen. 22. 16.
   Ps. 24. 4. nor *s.* deceitfully
   119. 106. I have *s.* and I will perform
SYNAGOGUE, Ps. 74. 8. Mat. 6. 5; 23. 6.
   Luke 7. 5. John 9. 22; 18. 20. Acts 15. 21.
   Rev. 2. 9; 3. 9.

T

TABERNACLE, Ex. 26. 1; 29. 43.
   Job 5. 24. thy *t.* shall be in peace
   Ps. 15. 1. who shall abide in thy *t.?*
   Prov. 14. 11. *t.* of upright shall flourish
   Is. 33. 20. a *t.* that shall not be taken down
   Amos. 9. 11. raise *t.* of David, Acts 15. 16.
   2 Cor. 5. 1. if our earthly house of this *t.*
   4. we that are in this *t.* do groan
   Heb. 8. 2. minister of sanctuary and the true *t.*
   2 Pet. 1. 13. I am in this *t.*
   14. knowing I must put off this my *t.*
   Rev. 21. 3. the *t.* of God is with men
   Job 12. 6. *tabernacles* of robbers
   Ps. 84. 1. how amiable are thy *t.*
   118. 15. salvation is in the *t.* of the
   Heb. 11. 9. dwelling in *t.* with Isaac and
TABLE, Ex. 25. 23. Job 36. 16.
   Ps. 23. 5. preparest a *t.* before me
   69. 22. let their *t.* become a snare
   128. 3. olive plants round thy *t.*
   Prov. 3. write them on *t.* of heart
   Sol. 1. 12. while king sitteth at his *t.*
   Jer. 17. 1. sin . . . is graven on *t.* of their heart
   Mal. 1. 7. *t.* of Lord is contemptible
   Mat. 15. 27. crumbs . . . from their masters' *t.*
   1 Cor. 10. 21. partakers of Lord's *t.*
   Deut. 10. 4. *tables,* 5. Heb. 9. 4. 2 Chr. 4. 8, 19.
   Is. 28. 8. Ezek. 40. 41.
   Hab. 2. make it plain upon *t.*
   Acts 6. 2. leave word of God and serve *t.*
   2 Cor. 3. 3. not in *t.* of stone, but fleshy *t.*
TAKE you for a people, Ex. 6. 7.
   Ex. 20. 7. not *t.* name of the Lord in vain
   34. 9. *t.* us for thine inheritance
   Ps. 27. 10. the Lord will *t.* me up
   51. 11. *t.* not thy holy spirit from me
   116. 13. I will *t.* cup of salvation
   119. 43. *t.* not the word of truth out
   Hos. 14. 2. *t.* with you words . . . *t.* away all

Mat. 16. 24. *take* up his cross and follow
18. 16. *t.* with thee one or two more
23. would *t.* account of his servants
20. 14. *T.,* that is thine and go thy
26. 26. Jesus said *T.,* eat, 1 Cor. 11. 24.
Luke 12. 19. *t.* thine ease, eat, drink
John 10. 17. that I might *t.* it again, 18.
Eph. 6. 13. *t.* . . . whole armour of God, 17.
Rev. 3. 11. that no man *t.* thy crown
Ex. 23. 25. *take away,* Josh. 7. 13. 2 Sam.
24. 10. 1 Chr. 17. 13. Job 7. 21; 32. 22;
36. 18. Ps. 58. 9. Is. 58. 9. Jer. 15. 15. Hos.
1. 6; 4. 11; 14. 2. Amos. 4. 2. Mal. 2. 3.
Luke 17. 31. John 11. 39. 1 John 3. 5. Rev.
22. 19.
Deut. 4. 9. *take heed,* 11. 16; 27. 9. 2 Chr.
19. 6. Ps. 39. 1. Is. 7. 4. Mal. 2. 15. Mat. 6. 1;
16. 6; 18. 10; 24. 4. Mark 4. 24; 13. 33. Luke
8. 18; 12. 15. 1 Cor. 10. 12. Col. 4. 17. Heb.
3. 12. 2 Pet. 1. 19.   [56. 4; 64. 7. Zech. 1. 6.
Deut. 32. 41. *take hold,* Ps. 69. 24. Is. 27. 5;
Ps. 83. 3. *taken* crafty counsel
119. 111. thy testimonies have I *t.*
Is. 53. 8. he was *t.* from prison and
Lam. 4. 20. the anointed . . . was *t.* in their pits
Mat. 21. 43. kingdom of God *t.* from
24. 40. one shall be *t.,* the other left
Mark 4. 25. shall be *t.* even that which he hath
Acts 1. 9. he was *t.* up, 11. 22.
2 Tim. 2. 26. *t.* captive by him
Is. 6. 7. thy iniquity is *taken away*
16. 10. gladness is—and joy out of
57. 1. and merciful men are—
Luke 10. 42. good part not be—from
2 Cor. 3. 16. turneth to Lord, veil shall be—
Ps. 40. 12. my iniquities have *taken away*
119. 143. trouble and anguish have—of me
Prov. 1. 19. *taketh away,* John 1. 29; 15. 2.
John 16. 22. your joy no man *taketh from* you
Ps. 119. 9. by *taking* heed thereto
Mat. 6. 27. which of you by *t.* thought can
Rom. 7. 8, 11. sin *t.* occasion
Eph. 6. 16. above all *t.* shield of faith
TALE, Ps. 90. 9. Ezek. 22. 9. Luke 24. 11.
Lev. 19. 16. *talebearer,* Prov. 11. 13; 18. 8; 20. 19;
26. 20, 22.
TALENTS, Mat. 18. 24; 25. 15, 25.
TALK of them when thou, Deut. 6. 7.
1 Sam. 2. 3. *t.* no more so exceeding proudly
Job 13. 7. and *t.* deceitfully for him
Ps. 71. 24. my tongue shall *t.* righteousness
105. 2. *t.* ye of all his wondrous works
145. 11. speak of glory of thy kingdom and *t.* of thy
Jer. 12. 1. *t.* with thee of thy judgments
John 14. 30. I will not *t.* much with
Tit. 1. 10. unruly and vain *talkers*
Ps. 37. 30. his tongue *talketh* of judgment
Eph. 5. 4. foolish *talking*
TAME, Mark 5. 4. Jas. 3. 7, 8.
TARRY, 1 Chr. 19. 5. 2 Ki. 14. 10.
Ps. 101. 7. telleth lies shall not *t.* in my sight
Prov. 23. 30. that *t.* long at wine
Jer. 14. 8. turneth aside to *t.* for a night
Hab. 2. 3. though it *t.* wait for it
Mat. 26. 38. *t.* ye here and watch
John 21. 22. that he *t.* till I come
1 Cor. 11. 33. *t.* one for another
Ps. 68. 12. she that *tarried* at home
Mat. 25. 5. bridegroom *t.,* they all slumbered
Luke 2. 43. child Jesus *t.* behind in
Ps. 40. 17. make no *tarrying,* 70. 5.
TASTE, Ex. 16. 31. 1 Sam. 14. 43.
Job 6. 6. is there any *t.* in white of an egg?

Ps. 34. 8. O *taste* and see that the Lord is good
Sol. 2. 3. his fruit was sweet to my *t.*
Jer. 48. 11. his *t.* remained in him
Mat. 16. 28. shall not *t.* of death
Luke 14. 24. shall *t.* of my supper
John 8. 52. keep my saying shall never *t.* death
Col. 2. 21. touch not, *t.* not, handle not
Heb. 2. 9. *t.* death for every man
6. 4. have *tasted* of the heavenly gift
1 Pet. 2. 3. if ye have *t.* that Lord is gracious
TATTLERS, 1 Tim. 5. 13.
TEACH, Ex. 4. 12. Lev. 10. 11.
Deut. 4. 9. *t.* them thy sons, 6. 7; 11. 19.
33. 10. shall *t.* Jacob thy judgments
1 Sam. 12. 23. *t.* you good . . . way, 1 Ki. 8. 36.
2 Chr. 17. 7. to *t.* in cities of Judah
Job 21. 22. shall any *t.* God
Ps. 25. 8. *t.* sinners in the way
34. 11. *t.* you fear of Lord, 32. 8.
51. 13. *t.* transgressors thy ways
90. 12. so *t.* us to number our days
Is. 2. 3. *t.* us of his ways, Mic. 4. 2.
Jer. 31. 34. *t.* no more every man his neighbour
Mat. 28. 19. go ye therefore and *t.* all nations
John 9. 34. and dost thou *t.* us?
14. 26. (Holy Ghost) shall *t.* you all
1 Cor. 4. 17. as I *t.* every where in every church
1 Tim. 2. 12. I suffer not a woman to *t.*
3. 2. a bishop must be . . . given to hospitality, apt
2 Tim. 2. 2. faithful men . . . able to *t.*   [to *t.*
Heb. 5. 12. have need that one *t.* you
1 John 2. 27. need not that any man *t.* you
Job 34. 32. that which I see not *teach* thou *me*
teach me, Ps. 25. 5.—thy paths, 4.—thy way,
27. 11; 86. 11.—thy statutes, 119. 12, 26, 64, 68,
124, 135.—good judgment, 66.—thy judgments, 108.—to do thy will, 143. 10.
Hab. 2. 18. *teacher,* John 3. 2. Rom. 2. 20. 1 Tim.
2. 7. 2 Tim. 1. 11.
Ps. 119. 99. *teachers,* Is. 30. 20.
2 Tim. 4. 3. heap to themselves *t.*
Tit. 2. 3. be *t.* of good things
Heb. 5. 12. ought to be *t.* ye need
Ps. 94. 12. *teachest* him out of thy law
Mat. 22. 16. *t.* way of God in truth
Rom. 2. 21. *t.* another, *t.* thou not thyself
Job 36. 22. who *teacheth* like him
35. 11. who *t.* us more than beasts
Ps. 18. 34. *t.* my hands to war, 144. 1.
Is. 48. 17. Lord thy God which *t.* thee to profit
1 Cor. 2. 13. words which man's wisdom *t.* but
which the Holy Ghost *t.*
1 John 2. 27. same anointing *t.* you
2 Chr. 15. 3. a *teaching* priest
Mat. 15. 9. *t.* for doctrines the command-
ments
28. 20. *t.* them to observe all things
Col. 1. 28. *t.* every man in all wisdom
Tit. 2. 12. *t.* us that denying ungodliness
2 Chr. 30. 22. *taught* good knowledge
Ps. 71. 17. hast *t.* me from my youth
Eccl. 12. 9. he still *t.* people knowledge
Is. 54. 13. children shall be *t.* of Lord
John 6. 45. shall be all *t.* of God
Acts 20. 20. *t.* you publickly and from
Gal. 6. 6. let him that is *t.* in the word
1 Thes. 4. 9. yourselves are *t.* of God
TEAR, Ps. 50. 22. Hos. 5. 14. Job 16. 9.
TEARS, Job 16. 20. Ps. 6. 6. Is. 38. 5.
Ps. 56. 8. put thou my *t.* in thy bottle, 39. 12.
80. 5. feedest them with bread of *t.*
126. 5. they that sow in *t.* shall
Is. 25. 8. wipe away all *t.* from off

Jer. 9. 1. mine eyes were a fountain of *tears*
Luke 7. 38. to wash his feet with *t.*
Acts 20. 19. *t.* and temptations, 31.
2 Cor. 2. 4. I wrote unto you with many *t.*
2 Tim. 1. 4. being mindful of thy *t.*
Heb. 5. 7. with strong crying and *t.*
Rev. 7. 17. wipe all *t.* from their eyes, 21. 4.
TEATS, Is. 32. 12. Ezek. 23. 3, 21.
TEETH white with milk, Gen. 49. 12.
Job 4. 10. *t.* broken, Ps. 3. 7; 58. 6.
Sol. 4. 2. *t.* like a flock of sheep, 6. 6.
Jer. 31. 29. *t.* set on edge, Ezek. 18. 2.
Amos 4. 6. cleanness of *t.* in all cities
Mat. 8. 12. weeping and gnashing of *t.,* 22. 13;
24. 51; 25. 30. Ps. 112. 10.
TELL it not in Gath, 2 Sam. 1. 20.
Ps. 48. 13. *t.* it to the generation following
Prov. 30. 4. name, if thou canst *t.*
Mat. 8. 4. see thou *t.* no man, 16. 20.
18. 15. go and *t.* him his fault
John 3. 8. not *t.* whence it cometh
4. 25. when he is come he will *t.* us all
8. 14. ye cannot *t.* whence I come
2 Cor. 12. 2. in the body, I cannot *t.* . . . . out of
the body, I cannot *t.,* 3.
Gal. 4. 16. because I *t.* you the truth
Phil. 3. 18. now *t.* you even weeping   [1. 6.
TEMPERANCE, Acts 24. 25. Gal. 5. 23. 2 Pet.
1 Cor. 9. 25. *temperate,* Tit. 1. 8; 2. 2.
TEMPLE, 1 Sam. 1. 9. 1 Ki. 6. 5.
Ps. 29. 9. in his *t.* doth every one speak of
Jer. 7. 4. *t.* of the Lord, *t.* of Lord, *t.* of Lord
Mal. 3. 1. suddenly come to his *t.*
Mat. 12. 6. one greater than the *t.* is
John 2. 19. destroy this *t.* and in three days
21. he spake of the *t.* of his body
1 Cor. 3. 16. ye are the *t.* of God, 17.
6. 19. your body is *t.* of Holy Ghost
9. 13. live of the things of the *t.*
2 Cor. 6. 16. hath *t.* of God with idols
Rev. 7. 15. serve him day and night in his *t.*
11. 19. *t.* of God was opened in heaven
21. 22. saw no *t.* . . . . the Lord God and Lamb are
Sol. 4. 3. thy *temples,* 6. 7.   [the *t.*
Acts 7. 48. most High dwelleth not in *t.*
TEMPORAL, 2 Cor. 4. 18.
TEMPT Abraham, God did, Gen. 22. 1.
Deut. 6. 16. ye shall not *t.* the Lord
Is. 7. 12. not ask, neither will I *t.* Lord, *t.* of Lord
Mal. 3. 15. that *t.* God are delivered
Mat. 4. 7. thou shalt not *t.* the Lord
22. 18. why *t.* ye me. . . ? shew me a penny
Acts 5. 9. have agreed together to *t.*
15. 10. why *t.* ye God to put a yoke
1 Cor. 7. 5. that Satan *t.* you not for
Ex. 17. 7. because they *tempted* Lord
Num. 14. 22. *t.* me now these ten times
Ps. 78. 18. *t.* God in their heart, 106. 14.
56. *t.* and provoked most high God
95. 9. when your fathers *t.* me, Heb. 3. 9.
Mat. 4. 1. in wilderness, to be *t.* of devil
Luke 10. 25. lawyer . . . *t.* him, saying
1 Cor. 10. 13. not suffer you to be *t.*
Gal. 6. 1. lest thou also be *t.*
1 Thes. 3. 5. the tempter have *t.* you
Heb. 2. 18. being *t.* he is able to succour
4. 15. in all points *t.* as we are, yet
Jas. 1. 13. let no man say when he is *t.,* I am *t.* of
God; for God cannot be *t.*
14. every man is he *t.* when he is drawn
Mat. 16. 1. *tempting* him, 19. 3; 22. 35. Luke
11. 16. John 8. 6.
Ps. 95. 8. as in day of *temptation*

Mat. 6. 13. lead us not into *temptation,* Luke 11. 4.
Luke 4. 13. the devil had ended all *t.*
8. 13. in time of *t.* fall away
1 Cor. 10. 13. no *t.* taken you but such
Gal. 4. 14. my *t.* . . . . in my flesh ye despised not
Heb. 3. 8. in day of *t.* in wilderness
Jas. 1. 12. blessed is the man that endureth *t.*
Rev. 3. 10. keep thee from hour of *t.*
Deut. 4. 34. *temptations,* 7. 19. Luke 22. 28.
Acts 20. 19. Jas. 1. 2. 1 Pet. 1. 6. 2 Pet. 2. 9.
Mat. 4. 3. *tempter,* 1 Thes. 3. 5.
TENDER, thy heart was, 2 Ki. 22. 19.
Luke 1. 78. *t.* mercy, Jas. 5. 11.
Eph. 4. 32. *tenderhearted*
TENDETH, Prov. 10. 16; 11. 19, 24; 14. 23;
19. 23; 21. 5.
TENTS of Shem, dwell in, Gen. 9. 27.
Num. 24. 5. how goodly are thy *t.,* O Jacob
1 Ki. 12. 16. to your *t.,* O Israel, 2 Sam. 20. 1.
Ps. 84. 10. dwell in *t.* of wickedness
120. 5. I dwell in the *t.* of Kedar
Sol. 1. 8. kids beside shepherds' *t.*
TERRESTRIAL, 1 Cor. 15. 40.
TERRIBLE, Ex. 34. 10. Deut. 1. 19.
Deut. 7. 21. a mighty God and *t.,* 10. 17. Neh.
1. 5; 4. 14; 9. 32. Jer. 20. 11.
10. 21. done *t.* things, 2 Sam. 7. 23.
Job 37. 22. with God is *t.* majesty
Ps. 45. 4. hand shall teach thee *t.* things
47. 2. Lord most high is *t.,* 68. 35.
66. 3. how *t.* art thou in thy works
5. God is *t.* in his doing toward children of men
76. 12. he is *t.* to kings of the earth
99. 3. praise thy great and *t.* name
Sol. 6. 4. *t.* as an army with banners
Joel 2. 11. day of Lord . . . very *t.,* 31. Zeph. 2. 11.
Heb. 12. 21. so *t.* was sight that Moses
1 Chr. 17. 21. *terribleness,* Jer. 49. 16.
Job 7. 14. *terrifiest,* Phil. 1. 28.
TERROR, Gen. 35. 5. Deut. 32. 25.
Job 31. 23. destruction from God was a *t.*
Jer. 17. 17. be not a *t.* unto me
20. 4. a *t.* to thyself, and all, Ezek. 26. 21.
Rom. 13. 3. rulers are not a *t.* to good
2 Cor. 5. 1. knowing therefore *t.* of the Lord
Job 6. 4. *terrors,* 18. 11, 14; 27. 20. Ps. 55. 4;
73. 19; 88. 15, 16.
TESTAMENT, Mat. 26. 28. Luke 22. 20. 1 Cor.
11. 25. 2 Cor. 3. 6, 14. Gal. 3. 15. Heb. 7. 22;
9. 15, 16, 17, 18. Rev. 11. 19.
Heb. 9. 16. death of the *testator*
17. no strength at all while the *t.* liveth
TESTIFY, Deut. 8. 19; 32. 46. Neh. 9. 26, 34.
Ps. 50. 7; 81. 8.
Num. 35. 30. one witness shall not *t.*
Is. 59. 12. sins *t.* against us, Jer. 14. 7.
Hos. 5. 5. pride of Israel *t.* to his face, 7. 10.
John 3. 11. and *t.* that we have seen
Acts 20. 24. *t.* gospel of grace of God, 21.
1 John 4. 14. *t.* that the Father sent
2 Chr. 24. 19. *testified,* Neh. 13. 15. Acts 23. 11.
1 Tim. 2. 6. 1 John 5. 9.
Heb. 11. 4. *testifying,* 1 Pet. 5. 12.
2 Ki. 11. 12. gave him the *testimony*
Ps. 78. 5. established a *t.* in Jacob
Is. 8. 16. bind up the *t.,* seal the law
Mat. 10. 18. for a *t.* against them
John 3. 32. no man receiveth his *t.*
Acts 14. 3. *t.* to word of his grace
2 Cor. 1. 12. the *t.* of our conscience
Heb. 11. 5. before his translation he had this *t.*
Rev. 1. 9. *t.* of Jesus Christ, 12. 17; 19. 10.
11. 7. when they shall have finished their *t.*

Ps. 25. 10. keep his *testimonies*, 119. 2.
93. 5. *thy testimonies*, 119. 14, 24, 31, 46, 59,
95, 111, 129, 144.
THANK, 1 Chr. 16. 4; 29. 13. Mat. 11. 25.
Luke 6. 32, 33; 17. 9; 18. 11. John 11. 41.
Rom. 1. 8; 7. 25. 1 Cor. 1. 4. 2 Thes. 2. 13.
1 Tim. 1. 12.
Ps. 100. 4. be *thankful*, Col. 3. 15. Rom. 1. 21.
Dan. 6. 10. *gave thanks*, Mat. 26. 27. Mark 8. 6.
Luke 22. 17.
2 Cor. 9. 15. *t*. be to God for his unspeakable gift,
2. 14; 8. 16. 1 Cor. 15. 57.   [Heb. 13. 15.
Eph. 5. 4. *giving (of) thanks*, 20. 1 Tim. 2. 1.
1 Thes. 3. 9. what *t*. can we render to God
Lev. 7. 12. *thanksgiving*, Neh. 11. 17. Ps. 26. 7;
50. 14; 100. 4; 107. 22; 116. 17. Is. 51. 3.
Phil. 4. 6. 1 Tim. 4. 3. Rev. 7. 12.
1 Pet. 2. 19. this is *thankworthy*
THEATRE, Acts 19. 29.
THINE is the day and night, Ps. 74. 16.
Ps. 119. 94. I am *t*., save me
Mat. 20. 14. take that *t*. is and go
John 17. 6. *t*. they were, and thou
10. all mine are *t*., and *t*. are mine
THINK on me . . . for good, Neh. 5. 19.
Jer. 29. 11. I know thoughts that I *t*. toward you
Rom. 12. 3. not to *t*. of himself more highly than
he ought to *t*., but to *t*. soberly
1 Cor. 8. 2. if any man *t*. that he knoweth
Gal. 6. 3. if a man *t*. himself to be something
Eph. 3. 20. above all that we ask or *t*.
Phil. 4. 8. *t*. on these things
Gen. 50. 20. *thought* evil against me
Ps. 48. 9. we have *t*. of thy lovingkindness
119. 59. I *t*. on my ways and turned
Mal. 3. 16. and that *t*. on his name
Mark 14. 72. when he *t*. thereon he wept
1 Cor. 13. 11. I *t*. as a child, but when
Phil. 2. 6. being in the form of God, *t*. it not
robbery to be equal with God.
Ps. 139. 2. understandest my *t*. afar
Prov. 24. 9. the *t*. of foolishness is sin
Eccl. 10.20. curse not king, no not in thy *t*.
Mat. 6. 25. take no *t*. for your life, Luke 12. 22.
6. 34. take no *t*. for the morrow
Mark 13. 11. take no *t*. beforehand
2 Cor. 10. 5. bringing into captivity every *t*.
Ps. 50. 21. thou *thoughtest* that I was
Gen. 6. 5. imagination of *thoughts*
Judg. 5. 15. were great *t*. of heart
1 Chr. 28. 9. Lord understandeth . . . the *t*.
29. 18. keep this for ever in imagination of *t*.
Ps. 10. 4. God is not in all his *t*.
33. 11. the *t*. of his heart to all
40. 5. many are . . . thy *t*. which are to us-ward
94. 11. Lord knoweth the *t*. of man
19. in multitude of my *t*. within me
139. 17. how precious are thy *t*. to me
23. try me and know my *t*.
Prov. 12. 5. *t*. of righteous are right
15. 26. *t*. of wicked are abomination
Prov. 16. 3. thy *t*. shall be established
Is. 55. 7. the unrighteous man his *t*.
8. my *t*. are not your *t*.
59. 7. their *t*. are *t*. of iniquity
66. 18. I know their works and their *t*.
Jer. 4. 14. how long shall thy vain *t*.
Mic. 4. 12. know not *t*. of the Lord
Mat. 15. 19. out of heart proceed evil *t*.
Luke 2. 35. the *t*. of many hearts
Rom. 2. 15. their *t*. . . . else accusing or excusing
1 Cor. 3. 20. the Lord knoweth the *t*. of the wise
Heb. 4. 12. a discerner of the *t*. and

Jas. 2. 4. become judges of evil *thoughts*
THIRST, Deut. 28. 48; 29. 19.
Is. 49. 10. shall not hunger nor *t*.
Mat. 5. 6. blessed are they which do hunger and *t*.
after righteousness
John 4. 14. shall never *t*., 6. 35.
7. 37. if any man *t*., let him come unto me
Rom. 12. 20. if he *t*. give him drink
Rev. 7. 16. neither *t*. any more
Ps. 42. 2. my soul *thirsteth* for God
Is. 55. 1. Ho, every one that *t*.
THORNS in your sides, Num. 33. 55. Judg. 2. 3.
Gen. 3. 18.
Josh. 23. 13. and *t*. in your eyes
2 Sam. 23. 6. as *t*. thrust away
Jer. 4. 3. sow not among *t*.
12. 13. sown wheat, but shall reap *t*.
Mat. 7. 16. do men gather grapes of *t*.?
13. 7. some fell among *t*., 22.
THREATENING, Eph. 6. 9. Acts 4. 29; 9. 1.
1 Pet. 2. 23.
THREE, 2 Sam. 24. 12. Prov. 30. 15, 18, 21,
29. Amos 1. 3, 13; 2. 1. 1 Cor. 14. 27.
1 John 5. 7, 8. Rev. 16. 13.
THRESH, Is. 21. 10; 41. 15. Jer. 51. 33. Mic.
4. 13. Hab. 3. 12. 1 Cor. 9. 10.
Lev. 26. 5. and your *threshing* shall reach unto
the vintage
2 Sam. 24. 18. *threshingfloor*, 21, 24.
THROAT an open sepulchre, Ps. 5. 9.
Ps. 69. 3. weary of my crying, my *t*. is dried
Prov. 23. 2. put a knife to thy *t*.
THRONE, Lord's is in heaven, Ps. 11. 4.
Ps. 94. 20. *t*. of iniquity have fellowship
Prov. 25. 5. *t*. shall be established in righteousness
Jer. 14. 21. do not disgrace *t*. of thy glory
Lam. 5. 19. thy *t*. from generation to
Dan. 7. 9. his *t*. was like fiery flame
Mat. 19. 28. shall sit in *t*. of his glory, ye shall sit
on twelve thrones
25. 31. shall sit on *t*. of his glory
Heb. 4. 16. boldly to the *t*. of grace
Rev. 3. 21. sit with me in my *t*. . . . with my Father
20. 11. a great white *t*.   [in his *t*.
22. 3. *t*. of God and Lamb shall be in it
Job 26. 9. *his throne*, Ps. 89. 29, 44; 97. 2;
103. 19. Prov. 20. 28; 25. 5. Dan. 7. 9. Zech.
6. 13.
Is. 22. 23. *glorious throne*, Jer. 17. 12.
Ps. 45. 6. *thy throne*, 89. 4, 14. Heb. 1. 8.
THRUST, Ex. 11. 1. Job 32. 13. Luke 13. 28.
John 20. 25. Acts 16. 37.
THUNDER, Job 26. 14; 40. 9. Ps. 29. 3; 81. 7.
Mark 3. 17.
Rev. 4. 5. *thunderings*, 8. 5; 10. 3; 11. 19;
16. 18; 19. 6.
TIDINGS, evil, Ex. 33. 4. Ps. 112. 7.
Luke 1. 19. shew thee glad *t*., 8. 1. Acts 13. 32.
Rom. 10. 15.
TIME when thou mayest be found, Ps. 32. 6.
Ps. 37. 19. evil *t*. 41. 1. *t*. of trouble
69. 13. acceptable *t*., Is. 49. 8. 2 Cor. 6. 2.
Ps. 89. 47. remember how short my *t*. is
Eccl. 3. 1–8. *a t*. to every purpose—to be born—
to die—to plant—to pluck up—to kill—to
heal—to break down—to build up—to weep
—to laugh—to mourn—to dance—to cast
away—to gather—to embrace—to refrain—
to get—to lose—to keep—to cast away—to
rend—to sew—to keep silence—to speak—
to love—to hate—of war—of peace
9. 11. *t*. and chance happeneth to them all
Ezek. 16. 8. thy *t*. was the *t*. of love

Dan. 7. 25. till a *time* and times
12. 7. for a *t.*, times, and a half, Rev. 12. 14.
Amos 5. 13. evil *t.*, Mic. 2. 3.
Luke 19. 44. knewest not *t.* of thy visitation
John 7. 6. my *t.* is not yet come: your *t.*
Acts 17. 21. spent their *t.* in nothing else
Rom. 13. 11. high *t.* to awake out of
2 Cor. 6. 2. now is the accepted *t.*
Eph. 5. 16. redeeming the *t.*, Col. 4. 5.
1 Pet. 1. 17. pass *t.* of your sojourning
Rev. 10. 6. there should be *t.* no longer
Ps. 31. 15. my *times* are in thy hand
Luke 21. 24. till *t.* of the Gentiles
Acts 1. 7. not for you to know the *t.*
3. 19. *t.* of refreshing shall come, 21.
17. 26. determined *t.* before appointed
1 Tim. 4. 1. in latter *t.* some shall
2 Tim. 3. 1. in last days perilous *t.*
Ps. 34. 1. bless the Lord *at all times*
62. 8. trust in him—
106. 3. that doeth righteousness—
119. 20. longing . . . unto thy judgments—
Prov. 5. 19. let her breasts satisfy thee—
17. 17. a friend loveth—
TIN, Num. 31. 22. Is. 1. 25. Ezek. 22. 18.
TITHES, Gen. 14. 20. Mal. 3. 8. Amos 4. 4.
Mat. 23. 23. Luke 18. 12.
TITTLE pass from the law, Mat. 5. 18.
TOGETHER, Ps. 2. 2. Prov. 22. 2.
Rom. 8. 28. all things work *t.* for good
1 Cor. 3. 9. labourers *t.* with God
2 Cor. 6. 1. as workers *t.* with him
Eph. 2. 5. quickened us *t.* with Christ
6. raised us up *t.* and made us sit *t.* in Christ
TOKEN of covenant, Gen. 9. 12, 13; 17. 11.
Ps. 86. 17. shew me *t.* for good
Phil. 1. 28. evident *t.* of perdition
2 Thes. 1. 5. *t.* of righteous judgment
Ps. 65. 8. they . . . are afraid at thy *tokens*
135. 9. who sent *t.* and wonders
TONGUE, Ex. 11. 7. Josh. 10. 21.
Job 5. 21. be hid from scourge of *t.*
20. 12. hide it under his *t.*
Ps. 34. 13. keep thy *t.* from evil
Prov. 10. 20. *t.* of just is as choice silver
12. 18. *t.* of wise is health, 31. 26.
15. 4. wholesome *t.* is a tree of life
18. 21. death and life are in power of *t.*
21. 6. getting of treasures by a lying *t.*
23. keepeth his *t.* keepeth his soul
25. 15. a soft *t.* breaketh the bone
Is. 30. 27. his *t.* as a devouring fire
50. 4. the Lord hath given me *t.* of learned
Jer. 9. 5. taught their *t.* to speak lies
Jas. 1. 26. and bridleth not his *t.*
3. 5. *t.* is a little member
8. the *t.* can no man tame
1 Pet. 3. 10. refrain his *t.* from evil
Ps. 35. 28. *my tongue*, 39. 1; 45. 1; 51. 14;
71. 24; 119. 172; 137. 6; 139. 4. Acts 2. 26.
Ps. 31. 20. *tongues*, 55. 9. Mark 16. 17. Acts
19. 6. 1 Cor. 12. 10, 28.
1 Cor. 14. 23. and all speak with *t.*
TOOK me out of the womb, Ps. 22. 9.
Phil. 2. 7. *t.* on him form of servant
Heb. 10. 34. *t.* joyfully the spoiling of
TOPHET, Is. 30. 33. Jer. 7. 31, 32.
TORCH, Zech. 12. 6. Nah. 2. 3, 4.
TORMENT us before time, Mat. 8. 29.
Luke 16. 28. come to this place of *t.*
Rev. 18. 7. so much *t.* and sorrow
14. 11. smoke of their *t.* ascendeth
Luke 16. 24. I am *tormented* in this

Heb. 11. 37. destitute, afflicted, *tormented*
TORN, Hos. 6. 1. Mal. 1. 13. Mark 1. 26.
TOSS, Is. 22. 18. Jer. 5. 22. Jas. 1. 6.
Ps. 109. 23. I am *tossed* up and down
Eph. 4. 14. children *t.* to and fro
TOUCH not mine anointed, Ps. 105. 15.
Job 5. 19. in seven there shall no evil *t.*
Is. 52. 11. *t.* no unclean thing
Mat. 9. 21. may but *t.* his garment
14. 36. only *t.* hem of his garment
Mark 10. 13. children . . . that he should *t.*
Luke 11. 46. *t.* not the burdens with
John 20. 17. *t.* me not, for I am not
1 Cor. 7. 1. good for a man not to *t.* a woman
2 Cor. 6. 17. *t.* not the unclean thing
Col. 2. 21. *t.* not, taste not, handle not
1 Sam. 10. 26. there went with him a band of
men whose hearts God had *touched*
Job 19. 21. hand of God hath *t.* me
Zech. 2. 8. he that *toucheth* you *t.* apple of his eye
1 John 5. 18. wicked one *t.* him not
TOWER, God is a high, Ps. 144. 2.
Ps. 61. 3. strong *t.*, Prov. 18. 10.
Sol. 4. 4. thy neck like the *t.* of David
7. 4. *t.* of ivory . . . *t.* of Lebanon
Is. 5. 2. built a *t.*, Mat. 21. 33.
TRADITION, Mat. 15. 3. Gal. 1. 14.
Col. 2. 8. 2 Thes. 2. 15; 3. 6. 1 Pet. 1. 18.
TRAIN, Prov. 22. 6. Is. 6. 1.
TRAITOR, Luke 6. 16. 2 Tim. 3. 4.
TRAMPLE, Is. 63. 3. Mat. 7. 6.
TRANCE, Num. 24. 4. Acts 10. 10; 11. 5;
22. 17. *See* 2 Cor. 12. 2, 3, 4.
TRANQUILLITY, Dan. 4. 27.
TRANSFIGURED, Mat. 17. 2. Mark 9. 2.
TRANSFORMED, Rom. 12. 2. 2 Cor. 11. 14, 15.
TRANSGRESS the commandment of the Lord,
Num. 14. 41.
1 Sam. 2. 24. make the Lord's people to *t.*
2 Chr. 24. 20. why *t.* ye the commandments of
the Lord?
Neh. 1. 8. if ye *t.* I will scatter you
Ps. 17. 3. my mouth shall not *t.*
25. 3. be ashamed which *t.* without
Prov. 28. 21. for . . . bread that man will *t.*
Amos 4. 4. come to Bethel and *t.*
Mat. 15. 2. why do thy disciples *t.?*
Rom. 2. 27. and circumcision dost *t.* law
Deut. 26. 13. not *transgressed* thy command-
ments
Josh. 7. 11. hath *t.* my covenant, Judg. 2. 20.
Is. 43. 27. teachers have *t.* against
Jer. 2. 8. pastors also *t.* against me
Lam. 3. 42. we have *t.* and rebelled
Ezek. 2. 3. they and their fath∘rs have *t.*
Dan. 9. 11. all Israel have *t.* thy law
Hos. 6. 7. there have *t.* the covenant
Hab. 2. 5. he *transgresseth* by wine
1 John 3. 4. whosoever committeth sin *t.*
Ps. 59. 13. in *transgressing* and lying against Lord
Ex. 34. 7. forgiving iniquity, *transgression*, and
Num. 14. 18. forgiving iniquity and *t.*　　　[sin
1 Chr. 10. 13. Saul died for his *t.*
Job 13. 23. make me to know my *t.*
Ps. 19. 13. innocent from the great *t.*
32. 1. blessed he whose *t.* is forgiven
89. 32. I will visit their *t.* with rod
107. 17. fools because of *t.* are afflicted
Prov. 17. 9. that covereth a *t.* seeketh love
Is. 53. 8. for the *t.* of my people was he stricken
58. 1. shew my people their *t.*
20. them that turn from *t.* in Jacob
Dan. 9. 24. to finish *t.* and make an end

Amos 4. 4. at Gilgal multiply *transgression*
Mic. 3. 8. to declare to Jacob his *t.*
6. 7. shall I give my firstborn for my *t.*
Rom. 4. 15. where no law is, there is no *t.*
1 John 3. 4. sin is the *t.* of the law
Ex. 23. 21. not pardon your *transgressions*
Lev. 16. 21. all their *t.* in all their sins
Josh. 24. 19. will not forgive your *t.*
Job 31. 33. I covered my *t.* as Adam
Ps. 25. 7. remember not . . . nor my *t.*
32. 5. I said, I will confess my *t.*
39. 8. deliver me from all my *t.*
51. 1 blot out my *t.*
3. I acknowledge my *t.* and my sin is ever before me
103. 12. so far hath he removed our *t.*
Is. 43. 25. I am he that blotteth out thy *t.*
44. 22. blotted out as a thick cloud thy *t.*
53. 5. he was wounded for our *t.*
59. 12. our *t.* are multiplied before thee
Ezek. 18. 31. cast away from you all your *t.*
Heb. 9. 15. for the redemption of *t.*
Is. 48. 8. called a *transgressor* from the womb
Jas. 2. 11. if thou kill, thou art become a *t.* of the law
Ps. 51. 13. teach *transgressors* thy ways
59. 5. be not merciful to any wicked *t.*
119. 158. I beheld *t.* and was grieved
Prov. 13. 15. the way of *t.* is hard
Is. 53. 12. he was numbered with *t.* . . . . made intercession for *t.*, Mark 15. 28.
Hos. 14. 9. the *t.* shall fall therein
Jas. 2. 9. convinced of the law as *t.*
TRAVAIL, Is. 53. 11. Gal. 4. 19, 27. Eccl. 1. 13; 2. 23, 26; 4. 4, 6, 8; 5. 14. 2 Thes. 3. 8.
Is. 66. 7. before she *travailed,* 8.
Job 15. 20. wicked man *travaileth* with pain
42. 14. *travailing* woman, Hos. 13. 13. Is. 13. 8; 21. 3. Jer. 31. 8. Rev. 12. 2.
TRAVEL, Num. 20. 14. Acts 19. 29. 2 Cor. 8. 19.
Prov. 6. 11. *travelleth,* 24. 34.
Is. 21. 13. *travelling,* 63. 1.
TREACHEROUS, Is. 21. 2; 24. 16.
Jer. 9. 2. an assembly of *t.* men
Is. 21. 2. *treacherously,* 24. 16; 33. 1.
Jer. 3. 20. as wife *t.* departeth from her husband, so have ye dealt *t.*
Hos. 5. 7. dealt *t.* against Lord, 6. 7.
Mal. 2. 15. none deal *t.* against wife
TREAD down wicked, Job 40. 12.
Ps. 7. 5. let him *t.* down my life
44. 5. through thy name will we *t.* them under
Is. 1. 12. required . . . to *t.* my courts?
63. 3. I will *t.* them in mine anger, 6.
Rev. 11. 2. holy city shall they *t.*
Deut. 25. 4. not muzzle ox that *treadeth* out corn, 1 Cor. 9. 9. 1 Tim. 5. 18.
Is. 22. 5. *treading,* Amos 5. 11.
TREASURE, Prov. 15. 6, 16; 21. 20.
Deut. 28. 12. Lord shall open to thee his good *t.*
Ex. 19. 5. peculiar *t.* unto me
Ps. 135. 4. and Israel for his peculiar *t.*
Is. 33. 6. fear of Lord is his *t.*
Mat. 6. 21. where your *t.* is, there will
12. 35. good man out of good *t.*
13. 52. bringeth forth out of his *t.*
19. 21. thou shalt have *t.* in heaven
Luke 12. 21. layeth up *t.* for himself
2 Cor. 4. 7. this *t.* in earthen vessels
Deut. 32. 34. sealed up among my *treasures*
Prov. 2. 4. searchest for her as for hid *t.*
10. 2. *t.* of wickedness profit nothing
21. 6. getting *t.* by lying tongue

Mat. 6. 19. lay not up . . . *treasures* on earth
20. lay up for yourselves *t.* in heaven
Col. 2. 3. hid all the *t.* of wisdom
Heb. 11. 26. greater riches than *t.* in
Rom. 2. 5. *treasurest* up unto thyself
TREE, Gen. 2. 16, 17; 3. 22.
Ps. 1. 3. like a *t.* planted by rivers
37. 35. spreading himself like a bay *t.*
52. 8. I am like a green olive *t.*
Prov. 3. 18. she is a *t.* of life to them
11. 30. fruit of the righteous is *t.* of
Is. 6. 13. shall be eaten: as a teil *t.*
Jer. 17. 8. a *t.* planted by the waters
Mat. 3. 10. *t.* that bringeth not forth
7. 17. good *t.* bringeth forth good
12. 33. make the *t.* good . . . else make the *t.* corrupt . . . the *t.* is known by his fruit
1 Pet. 2. 24. in his own body on *t.*
Rev. 2. 7. will I give to eat of *t.* of life
22. 2. in midst of street was *t.* of life
14. may have right to the *t.* of life
Ps. 104. 16. *trees* of Lord full of sap
Is. 61. 3. called *t.* of righteousness
Ezek. 47. 12. grow all *t.* for meat
Mark 8. 24. I see men as *t.* walking
Jude 12. *t.* whose fruit withereth
TREMBLE at the commandment of our God, Ezra 10. 3.
Eccl. 12. 3. keepers of house shall *t.*
Is. 66. 5. ye that *t.* at his word, 2.
Jer. 5. 22. will ye not *t.* at my presence?
10. 10. at his wrath earth shall *t.*
Dan. 6. 26. men *t.* . . . before God of Daniel
Jas. 2. 19. devils also believe and *t.*
1 Sam. 4. 13. heart *trembled* for ark
Ezra 9. 4. every one that *t.* at the words of God of Israel
Acts 24. 25. as he reasoned Felix *t.*
Job 37. 1. *trembleth,* Ps. 119. 120. Is. 66. 2.
1 Sam. 13. 7. all the people followed him *trembling*
Deut. 28. 65. give thee there a *t.* heart
Ezra 10. 9. people sat *t.* because of
Ps. 2. 11. and rejoice with *t.*
Ezek. 12. 18. drink thy water with *t.*
26. 16. clothe themselves with *t.*
Hos. 13. 1. when Ephraim spake *t.*
Zech. 12. 2. make Jerusalem a cup of *t.*
1 Cor. 2. 3. in fear and in much *t.*
Phil. 2. 12. your own salvation with fear and *t.*
TRESPASS, Lev. 26. 40. Ezra 9. 6. 1 Ki. 8. 31. Mat. 18. 15. Luke 17. 3.
Ezra 9. 15. *trespasses,* Ezek. 39. 26.
Mat. 6. 14. if ye forgive men their *t.*
6. 15. if ye forgive not men their *t.* neither will your Father forgive your *t.*, 18. 35.
2 Cor. 5. 19. not imputing their *t.* to
Eph. 2. 1. dead in *t.* and sins
Col. 2. 13. having forgiven you all *t.*
TRIAL, Job 9. 23. Ezek. 21. 13. 2 Cor. 8. 2. Heb. 11. 36. 1 Pet. 1. 7; 4. 12.
TRIBES, Num. 24. 2.
Ps. 105. 37. not one feeble person among their *t.*
122. 4. whither *t.* go up, *t.* of Lord
Mat. 24. 30. shall all the *t.* of earth
Acts 26. 7. promise our twelve *t.* hope
TRIBULATION, art in, Deut. 4. 30.
Judg. 10. 14. let them deliver you in . . . *t.*
1 Sam. 26. 24. deliver me out of all *t.*
Mat. 13. 21. when *t.* or persecution
24. 29. immediately after *t.*, Mark 13. 24.
John 16. 33. in world ye shall have *t.*
Acts 14. 22. we must through much *t.*

Rom. 2. 9. *tribulation* and anguish upon every soul
5. 3. knowing *t.* worketh patience
8. 35. who shall separate us from the love of Christ? shall *t.*
12. 12. rejoicing in hope, patient in *t.*
2 Cor. 1. 4. comforteth us in all our *t.*
7. 4. exceeding joyful in all our *t.*
2 Thes. 1. 6. to recompense *t.* to
Rev. 1. 9. brother and companion in *t.*
2. 9. I know thy works and *t.*
10. ye shall have *t.* ten days
22. into great *t.* except they repent
7. 14. which came out of great *t.*
Rom. 5. 3. glory in *tribulations* also
1 Sam. 10. 19. saved you out of all . . . *t.*
Eph. 3. 13. faint not at my *t.* for you
2 Thes. 1. 4. patience in all . . . *t.*
TRIBUTE, Gen. 49. 15. Num. 31. 28.
Prov. 12. 24. slothful . . . be under *t.*
Mat. 17. 24. doth not master pay *t.?* 25.
22. 17. is it lawful to give *t.* to Caesar? 19.
Rom. 13. 7. *t.* to whom *t.* is due
TRIMMED, Jer. 2. 33. Mat. 25. 7.
TRIUMPH, 2 Sam. 1. 20. Ps. 25. 2.
Ps. 92. 4. *t.* in works of thy hands
2 Cor. 2. 14. always causeth us to *t.*
Ex. 15. 1. *triumphed* gloriously, 21.
Job 20. 5. *triumphing*, Col. 2. 15.
TRODDEN down strength, Judg. 5. 21.
Ps. 119. 118. *t.* down all them that err
Is. 63. 3. I have *t.* winepress alone
Luke 21. 24. Jerusalem shall be *t.*
Heb. 10. 29. *t.* under foot Son of God
TROUBLE, 2 Chr. 15. 4. Neh. 9. 32.
Job 5. 6. neither doth *t.* spring out
7. man is born to *t.* as sparks fly
14. 1. man . . . is of few days and full of *t.*
Ps. 9. 9. a refuge in times of *t.*
27. 5. in time of *t.* he shall hide me
37. 39. their strength in time of *t.*
46. 1. a very present help in *t.*
60. 11. give us help from *t.*
91. 15. I will be with him in *t.*
119. 143. *t.* and anguish have taken
143. 11. bring my soul out of *t.*
Prov. 11. 8. righteous delivered out of *t.*
Is. 26. 16. Lord, in *t.* have they visited
33. 2. our salvation also in time of *t.*
Jer. 8. 15. time of health, and behold *t.*
14. 8. saviour thereof in time of *t.*
19. for time of healing, and behold *t.*
Dan. 12. 1. there shall be a time of *t.*
1 Cor. 7. 28. shall have *t.* in the flesh
Ex. 14. 24. Lord *troubled* the host of Egypt
Ps. 30. 7. hide thy face, and I was *t.*
77. 3. I remembered God, and was *t.*
Is. 57. 20. wicked are like the *t.* sea
John 5. 4. an angel . . . *t.* the water
12. 27. now is my soul *t.*
14. 1. let not your heart be *t.*, 27.
2 Thes. 1. 7. to you who are *t.* rest
Ps. 25. 17. *troubles* of my heart are enlarged
34. 17. deliver them out of all their *t.*
71. 20. shewed me great and sore *t.*
88. 3. my soul is full of *t.*
Job 23. 16. Almighty *troubleth* me
1 Ki. 18. 17. thou he that *t.* Israel
Prov. 11. 17. cruel *t.* his own flesh
29. he that *t.* his own house
Luke 18. 5. because this widow *t.* me
Gal. 5. 10. he that *t.* you shall bear
Job 3. 17. the wicked cease from *troubling*
John 5. 4. after *t.* of the water

TRUCE breakers, 2 Tim. 3. 3.
TRUE, Gen. 42. 11. 2 Sam. 7. 28.
Ps. 19. 9. judgments of Lord are *t.*
119. 160. thy word is *t.* from beginning
Prov. 14. 25. *t.* witness delivereth souls
Ezek. 18. 8. *t.* judgment, Zech. 7. 9.
Mat. 22. 16. we know thou art *t.*
Luke 16. 11. commit to your trust *t.* riches
John 1. 9. that was the *t.* light
4. 23. *t.* worshippers worship the Father in spirit
6. 32. giveth you *t.* bread from heaven
7. 28. but he that sent me is *t.*
15. 1. I am the *t.* vine, and my Father
2 Cor. 1. 18. as God is *t.* our word to
6. 8. as deceivers and yet *t.*
Phil. 4. 8. whatsoever things are *t.*
1 John 5. 20. may know him that is *t.*
Rev. 3. 7. saith he that is *t.*
14. the faithful and *t.* witness
19. 11. was called Faithful and *T.*
TRUMP, 1 Cor. 15. 52. 1 Thes. 4. 16.
TRUMPET, Ex. 19. 16. Ps. 81. 3.
Is. 27. 13. great *t.* shall be blown
58. 1 lift up thy voice like a *t.*
Mat. 6. 2. do not sound a *t.* before thee
Num. 10. 2. *trumpets*, Josh. 6. 4. Ps. 98. 6.
TRUST in him, 1 Chr. 5. 20. [Rev. 8. 6.
Job 4. 18. put no *t.* in his servants, 15. 15.
8. 14. whose *t.* shall be a spider's web
Ps. 4. 5. put your *t.* in the Lord
9. 10. that know thy name will put their *t.*
40. 3. blessed . . . that maketh the Lord his *t.*
71. 5. thou art my *t.* from my youth
Prov. 22. 19. thy *t.* may be in Lord
Job 13. 15. though he slay me, yet will I *t.*
Ps. 37. 3. *t.* in Lord, and do good
5. *t.* also in him; he shall bring it to pass
40. he shall . . . save them because they *t.*
55. 23. but I will *t.* in thee
62. 8. *t.* in him at all times, ye
115. 9, 10, 11. *t.* in the Lord
118. 8. it is better to *t.* in Lord, 9.
119. 42. for I *t.* in thy word
125. 1. they that *t.* in Lord shall
Is. 26. 4. *t.* ye in the Lord for ever
50. 10. *t.* in the name of the Lord
Jer. 7. 4. *t.* ye not in lying words
9. 4. and *t.* ye not in any brother
Mic. 7. 5. *t.* ye not in a friend
Mark 10. 24. hard for them that *t.* in riches
2 Cor. 1. 9. should not *t.* in ourselves
Phil. 3. 4. he might *t.* in flesh
Ps. 22. 4. our fathers *trusted* in thee
28. 7. my heart *t.* in him, and I am
52. 7. *t.* in abundance of his riches
Luke 18. 9. which *t.* in themselves
Ps. 32. 10. that *trusteth* in Lord, mercy
34. 8. blessed is man that *t.* in him
57. 1. be merciful . . . for my soul *t.* in thee
84. 12. blessed is man that *t.* in thee
86. 2. save thy servant that *t.* in thee
Jer. 17. 5. cursed be man that *t.* in man
7. blessed is man that *t.* in Lord
1 Tim. 5. 5. widow indeed and desolate *t.* in God
Ps. 112. 7. his heart is fixed, *trusting*
TRUTH, Gen. 24. 27. Ex. 18. 21.
Ex. 34. 6. abundant in goodness and *t.*
Deut. 32. 4. a God of *t.* and without
Ps. 15. 2. speaketh *t.* in his heart
25. 10. paths of Lord are mercy and *t.*
51. 6. desirest *t.* in inward parts
91. 4. his *t.* shall be thy shield
117. 2. *t.* of Lord endureth for ever

Ps. 119. 30. I have chosen the way of *truth*
142. righteousness, and thy law is *t.*
151. all thy commandments are *t.*
Prov. 12. 19. lip of *t.* shall be established
16. 6. by mercy and *t.* iniquity is purged
23. 23. buy the *t.* and sell it not
Is. 59. 14. *t.* is fallen in the street
Jer. 4. 2. swear, The Lord liveth, in *t.*
Dan. 4. 37. all whose works are *t.*
Zech. 8. 16. speak every man *t.* to his
John 1. 14. full of grace and *t.*, 17.
8. 32. know the *t.*, and the *t.* shall
14. 6. I am the way, the *t.*, and life
17. Spirit of *t.* 16. 13. guide you into all *t.*
17. 17. thy word is *t.*
19. sanctified through the *t.*
18. 37. bear witness to *t.* 38. what is *t.?*
Acts 26. 25. words of *t.* and soberness
Rom. 1. 18. hold *t.* in unrighteousness
25. changed the *t.* of God into a lie
2. 2. judgment of God is according to *t.*
1 Cor. 5. 8. bread of sincerity and *t.*
2 Cor. 13. 8. do nothing against *t.*
Gal. 3. 1. should not obey the *t.*, 5. 7.
Eph. 4. 15. speaking *t.* in love, 25.
21. taught by him, as *t.* is in Jesus
5. 9. fruit of the Spirit is in all . . . *t.*
6. 14. having your loins girt about with *t.*
2 Thes. 2. 10. received not love of *t.*
1 Tim. 3. 15. pillar and ground of *t.*
6. 5. destitute of the *t.*
2 Tim. 2. 18. who concerning the *t.* have erred
25. to the acknowledging of the *t.*
3. 7. never able to come to knowledge of the *t.*
8. do these also resist the *t.*
4. 4. turn away their ears from *t.*
Jas. 3. 14. lie not against the *t.*
1 Pet. 1. 22. purified your souls in obeying *t.*
2 Pet. 1. 12. established in present *t.*
1 John 1. 8. and the *t.* is not in us
5. 6. because the Spirit is *t.*
Josh. 24. 14. *in truth*, 1 Sam. 12. 24. Ps. 145. 18.
    Jer. 4. 2. John 4. 24. 1. Thes. 2. 13. 1 John
    3. 18. 2 John 4.
Ps. 25. 5. *thy truth*, 26. 3; 43. 3; 108. 4. John
    17. 17.
TRY, Judg. 7. 4. Job 12. 11. Jer. 6. 27.
2 Chr. 32. 31. God left him, to *t.* him
Job 7. 18. visit him . . . and *t.* him every moment
Ps. 11. 4. his eyelids *t.* children of men
139. 23. *t.* me, and know my thoughts
Jer. 9. 7. will melt them, and *t.* them
Lam. 3. 40. search and *t.* our ways
Dan. 11. 35. some . . . shall fall, to *t.* them
Zech. 13. 9. will *t.* them as gold is tried
1 Cor. 3. 13. fire shall *t.* every man's work
1 Pet. 4. 12. fiery trial which is to *t.*
1 John 4. 1. *t.* the spirits whether
Rev. 3. 10. to *t.* them which dwell on the earth
2 Sam. 22. 31. word of Lord is *tried*, Ps. 18. 30.
Ps. 12. 6. words of Lord are pure . . . as silver *t.* in
17. 3. *t.* me, 66. 10. *t.* us as silver is *t.*
105. 19. word of the Lord *t.* him
Dan. 12. 10. many shall be purified . . . and *t.*
Heb. 11. 17. Abraham, when he was *t.*
Jas. 1. 12. when he is *t.* he shall receive the
    crown of life
1 Pet. 1. 7. though it be *t.* with fire
Rev. 2. 2. hast *t.* them which say they are apostles
10. into prison, that ye may be *t.*
3. 18. buy of me gold *t.* in the fire
1 Chr. 29. 17. I know . . . thou *triest*
Jer. 11. 20. that *t.* the reins and heart

Ps. 7. 9. the righteous God *trieth* the heart,
11. 5. Lord *t.* the righteous   [Prov. 17. 3.
1 Thes. 2. 4. pleasing . . . God, which *t.* hearts
Jas. 1. 3. *trying* of your faith
TUMULT, Ps. 65. 7. 2 Cor. 12. 20.
TURN from their sin, 1 Ki. 8. 35.
2 Ki. 17. 13. *t.* ye from your evil ways
Prov. 1. 23. *t.* you at my reproof
Sol. 2. 17. *t.*, my beloved, be thou
Is. 31. 6. *t.* ye not unto him from
Jer. 18. 8. if that nation . . . *t.* from their evil
31. 18. *t.* thou me and I shall be turned
Lam. 5. 21. *t.* us unto thee, O Lord, and we shall
    be turned
Ezek. 3. 19. *t.* not from his wickedness
18. 32. *t.* yourselves and live, 33. 9, 11; 14. 6.
    Hos. 12. 6. Joel 2. 12. Zech. 9. 12.
Zech. 1. 3. *t.* to me, . . . and I will *t.* to you
Acts 26. 18. *t.* them from darkness
20. should repent, and *t.* to God
2 Pet. 2. 21. to *t.* from holy commandment
2 Chr. 30. 6. *turn again*, Ps. 60. 1; 80. 3, 7, 19;
    85. 8. Lam. 3. 40. Mic. 7. 19. Zech. 10. 9.
    Gal. 4. 9.
1 Sam. 12. 20. *turn aside*, Ps. 40. 4. Is. 30. 11.
    Lam. 3. 35. Amos 2. 7; 5. 12.
Ps. 119. 37. *turn away*, 39. Sol. 6. 5. Is. 58. 13.
    2 Tim. 3. 5. Heb. 12. 25.
Deut. 4. 30. *turn (un)to Lord*, 30. 10. 2 Chr. **15.** 4.
    Ps. 22. 27. Lam. 3. 40. Hos. 14. 2. Joel
    2. 13. Luke 1. 16. 2 Cor. 3. 16.
Ps. 9. 17. wicked be *turned* into hell
30. 11. *t.* for me my mourning into dancing
119. 59. *t.* my feet to thy testimonies
Is. 53. 6. *t.* every one to his own way
Jer. 2. 27. *t.* their back to me, 32. 33.
8. 6. every one *t.* to his course
Hos. 7. 8. Ephraim is a cake not *t.*
John 16. 20. sorrow shall be *t.* to joy
1 Thes. 1. 9. *t.* to God from idols
Jas. 4. 9. laughter be *t.* to mourning
2 Pet. 2. 22. dog is *t.* to his own vomit
Deut. 9. 12. *turned aside*, Ps. 78. 57. Is. 44. 20.
    1 Tim. 1. 6; 5. 15.
1 Ki. 11. 3. *turned away*, Ps. 78. 38. Jer. 5. 25.
    turned not away, Ps. 66. 20. Is. 5. 25; 9. 12;
    10. 4.   [Jer. 4. 8. Zeph. 1. 6.
Ps. 44. 18. *turned back*, 78. 9, 41. Is. 42. 17.
Job 15. 13. *turnest*, Ps. 90. 3.
Ps. 146. 9. way of wicked he *turneth* upside down
Prov. 15. 1. soft answer *t.* away wrath
Is. 9. 13. the people *t.* not unto him
Jer. 14. 8. *t.* aside to tarry for a night
Jas. 1. 17. neither shadow of *turning*
Jude 4. *t.* grace of God into lasciviousness
TURTLE(DOVES), Lev. 1. 14; 5. 7, 11; 12. 6.
    Ps. 74. 19. Sol. 2. 12. Jer. 8. 7.
TUTORS, Gal. 4. 2.
TWAIN, Mat. 5. 41; 19. 5. Eph. 2. 15.
TWICE, Gen. 41. 32. Ex. 16. 22. Num. 20. 11.
    1 Ki. 11. 9. Job 33. 14; 40. 5. Ps. 62. 11.
    Mark 14. 30.
Luke 18. 12. I fast *t.* in the week
TWINKLING, 1 Cor. 15. 52.

U

UNACCUSTOMED, Jer. 31. 18.
UNADVISEDLY, Ps. 106. 33.
UNAWARES, Deut. 4. 42. Ps. 35. 8. Luke
    21. 34. Heb. 13. 2. Jude 4.

UNBELIEF, did not many mighty works there because of, Mat. 13. 58.
Mark 6. 6. marvelled because of their *u.*
9. 24. I believe; help thou mine *u.*
16. 14. upbraided them with their *u.*
Rom. 4. 20. staggered not . . . through *u.*
11. 20. because of *u.* they were broken off
32. hath concluded them all in *u.*
1 Tim. 1. 13. I did it ignorantly in *u.*
Heb. 3. 12. in any of you an evil heart of *u.*
UNBELIEVERS, Luke 12. 46. 1 Cor. 6. 6; 14. 23. 2 Cor. 6. 14.
UNBELIEVING, Acts 14. 2. 1 Cor. 7. 14, 15. Tit. 1. 15. Rev. 21. 8.
UNBLAMEABLE, Col. 1. 22. 1 Thes. 3. 13. 1 Thes. 2. 10. *unblameably* we behaved
UNCERTAIN, 1 Cor. 14. 8. 1 Tim. 6. 17.
UNCIRCUMCISED, Ex. 6. 12, 30. Jer. 6. 10; 9. 25, 26. Acts 7. 51.
UNCIRCUMCISION, Rom. 2. 25, 26, 27; 3. 30; 4. 10. 1 Cor. 7. 18, 19. Gal. 2. 7; 5. 6; 6. 15. Col. 2. 13; 3. 11.
UNCLEAN, Lev. 5. 2; 11. 4, 26; 13. 15. Num. 19. 19.
Lev. 10. 10. difference between *u.* and clean,
Is. 6. 5. I am a man of *u.* lips   [Ezek. 22. 26.
Lam. 4. 15. depart ye; it is *u.*
Ezek. 44. 23. discern between *u.* and clean
Hag. 2. 13. if one . . . *u.* by a dead body touch . . . these, shall it be *u.?*
Rom. 14. 14. is nothing *u.* of itself
1 Cor. 7. 14. else were your children *u.*
Eph. 5. 5. no *u.* person hath . . . inheritance
Num. 5. 19. *uncleanness,* Ezra 9. 11.
Mat. 23. 27. are within full of . . . all *u.*
Rom. 6. 19. members servants to *u.*
Eph. 4. 19. all *u.* with greediness
5. 3. all *u.* let it not once be named
1 Thes. 4. 7. hath not called us to *u.*
Ezek. 36. 29. save you from all . . . *uncleannesses*
UNCLOTHED, 2 Cor. 5. 4.
UNCOMELY, 1 Cor. 7. 36; 12. 23.
UNCONDEMNED, Acts 16. 37; 22. 25.
UNCORRUPTNESS, Tit. 2. 7.
UNCOVER, Lev. 18. 18. 1 Cor. 11. 5, 13.
UNCTION, 1 John 2. 20.
UNDEFILED in the way, Ps. 119. 1.
Sol. 5. 2. my dove, my *u.,* 6. 9.
Heb. 7. 26. holy, harmless, *u.*
13. 4. marriage honourable in all, and bed *u.*
Jas. 1. 27. pure religion and *u.*
1 Pet. 1. 4. inheritance incorruptible, *u.*
UNDER their God, Hos. 4. 12.
Rom. 3. 9. all *u.* sin, 7. 14. Gal. 3. 22. *u.* law,
Rom. 6. 15. 1 Cor. 9. 20. Gal. 3. 23; 4. 4.
1 Cor. 9. 27. I keep *u.* my body
UNDERSTAND not, Gen. 11. 7.
Neh. 8. 7. caused people to *u.* law, 13.
Ps. 19. 12. who can *u.* his errors?
107. 43. shalt *u.* lovingkindness of Lord
119. 100. I *u.* more than ancients
Prov. 2. 5. shalt thou *u.* fear of Lord, 9.
8. 5. *u.* wisdom. 14. 8; 20. 24. *u.* way,
19. 25, *u.* knowledge. 28. 5, *u.* all things
Is. 32. 4. heart also of the rash shall *u.*
1 Cor. 13. 2. to *u.* all mysteries
Ps. 139. 2. *understandest* my thought
Acts 8. 30. *u.* thou what thou readest?
1 Chr. 28. 9. *understandeth* all imaginations
Prov. 8. 9. plain to him that *u.,* 14. 6.
Jer. 9. 24. glory in this, that he *u.* . . . me
Mat. 13. 19. heareth word . . . and *u.* it not, 23.
Rom. 3. 11. none that *u.,* none that seeketh

Ex. 31. 3. wisdom and in *understanding*
Deut. 4. 6. is your wisdom and your *u.*
1 Ki. 3. 11. asked for thyself *u.*
4. 29. gave Solomon wisdom and *u.*
7. 14. filled with wisdom and *u.*
1 Chr. 12. 32. men that had *u.* of
2 Chr. 26. 5. who had *u.* in visions of God
Job 12. 13. he hath counsel and *u.*
20. he taketh away the *u.* of aged
17. 4. hast hid their heart from *u.*
28. 28. to depart from evil is *u.*
32. 8. the Almighty giveth them *u.*
38. 36. who hath given *u.* to heart
39. 17. neither imparted to her *u.*
Ps. 47. 7. sing ye praises with *u.*
49. 3. meditation of my heart be of *u.*
119. 34. give me *u.* and I shall keep
99. have more *u.* than all my teachers
104. through thy precepts I get *u.*
130. it giveth *u.* unto the simple
147. 5. great power; his *u.* is infinite
Prov. 2. 2. apply thine heart to *u.*
11. *u.* shall keep thee
3. 5. lean not to thine own *u.*
13. happy is the man that getteth *u.*
4. 5. get wisdom, get *u.,* 7.
8. 1. *u.* put forth her voice. 14. I am *u.*
5. ye fools, be ye of an *u.* heart
9. 6. and go in the way of *u.*
10. knowledge of the holy is *u.*
14. 29. slow to wrath is of great *u.*
16. 22. *u.* is a wellspring of life
19. 8. keepeth *u.* shall find good
21. 30. nor *u.* nor counsel against the Lord
23. 23. buy truth . . . wisdom . . . and *u.*
30. 2. I have not the *u.* of a man
Eccl. 9. 11. nor yet riches to men of *u.*
Is. 11. 2. spirit of wisdom and *u.*
3. make him of quick *u.* in the fear of Lord
27. 11. it is a people of no *u.*
40. 28. is no searching of his *u.*
Jer. 51. 15. stretched out heaven by his *u.*
Mark 12. 33. love him with all the heart and with all the *u.*
Luke 2. 47. astonished at his *u.*
24. 45. then opened he their *u.*
1 Cor. 1. 19. bring to nothing *u.* of the prudent
14. 14. spirit prayeth, but *understanding* is unfruitful
14. 15. pray with *u.* . . . sing with *u.*
20. not children in *u.* . . . in *u.* be men
Eph. 1. 18. eyes of your *u.* being enlightened
4. 18. having the *u.* darkened
Phil. 4. 7. peace of God which passeth all *u.*
Col. 1. 9. in all wisdom and spiritual *u.*
2. 2. riches of full assurance of *u.*
2 Tim. 2. 7. give thee *u.* in all things
Ps. 111. 10. *good understanding,* Prov. 3. 4; 13. 15.
Prov. 1. 5. *a man of understanding,* 10. 23; 11. 12; 15. 21; 17. 27.
Deut. 32. 29. O that . . . they *understood* this
Ps. 73. 17. then *u.* I their end
Mat. 13. 51. have ye *u.* all these
John 12. 16. *u.* not his disciples
1 Cor. 13. 11. when . . . a child I . . . *u.* as a child
2 Pet. 3. 16. things hard to be *u.*
UNDERTAKE for me, Is. 38. 14.
UNDONE, Is. 6. 5. Mat. 23. 23.
UNEQUAL, your ways, Ezek. 18. 25.
2 Cor. 6. 14. not *unequally* yoked
UNFAITHFUL, Prov. 25. 19. Ps. 78. 57.
UNFEIGNED, 2 Cor. 6. 6. 1 Tim. 1. 5. 2 Tim. 1. 5. 1 Pet. 1. 22.

UNFRUITFUL, Mat. 13. 22. 1 Cor. 14. 14. Eph.
　5. 11. Tit. 3. 14. 2 Pet. 1. 8.
UNGODLY men, 2 Sam. 22. 5.
　2 Chr. 19. 2. shouldest help the *u.*
　Job 16. 11. God hath delivered me to *u.*
　Ps. 1. 1. walketh not in counsel of *u.*
　4. the *u.* are not so, but are like
　5. *u.* shall not stand in the judgment
　6. way of *u.* shall perish
　3. 7. hast broken the teeth of *u.*
　43. 1. plead cause against an *u.* nation
　Prov. 16. 27. *u.* man diggeth up evil
　19. 28. an *u.* witness scorneth judgment
　Rom. 4. 5. him that justifieth the *u.*
　5. 6. in due time Christ died for *u.*
　1 Tim. 1. 9. law (made) . . . for the *u.*
　1 Pet. 4. 18. where shall *u.* . . . . appear
　2 Pet. 2. 5. bringing in flood on world of *u.*
　6. those that after should live *u.*
　3. 7. day of judgment and perdition of *u.* men
　Jude 4. *u.* men, turning grace of God
　15. convince . . . *u.* . . . of all their *u.* deeds
　18. walk after their own *u.* lusts
　Rom. 1. 18. wrath . . . against all *ungodliness*
　11. 26. turn away *u.* from Jacob
　Tit. 2. 12. denying *u.* and wordly lusts
UNHOLY, Lev. 10. 10. 1 Tim. 1. 9. 2 Tim. 3. 2.
　Heb. 10. 29.
UNITE, Ps. 86. 11. Gen. 49. 6.
　Ps. 133. 1. brethren to dwell together in *unity*
　Eph. 4. 3. endeavour to keep *u.* of Spirit
　13. till we all come in *u.* of faith
UNJUST, deliver from, Ps. 43. 1.
　Prov. 11. 7. hope of *u.* men perisheth
　28. 8. by usury and *u.* gain
　29. 27. *u.* man is abomination to
　Zeph. 3. 5. the *u.* knoweth no shame
　Mat. 5. 45. rain on the just and *u.*
　Luke 16. 8. lord commended *u.* steward
　18. 6. hear what the *u.* judge saith
　11. I am not as other men are, . . . *u.*
　Acts 24. 15. resurrection of . . . just and *u.*
　1 Pet. 3. 18. once suffered for sins, just for *u.*
　2 Pet. 2. 9. reserve the *u.* to day of
　Rev. 22. 11. that is *u.* let him be *u.*
　Ps. 82. 2. will ye judge *unjustly*
　Is. 26. 10. in land of uprightness will he deal *u.*
UNKNOWN God, Acts 17. 23. Gal. 1. 22.
　1 Cor. 14. 2. speaketh in *u.* tongue, 4, 27.
　2 Cor. 6. 9. as *u.* and yet well known
UNLAWFUL, Acts 10. 28. 2 Pet. 2. 8.
UNLEARNED, Acts 4. 13. 1 Cor. 14. 16, 23, 24.
　2 Tim. 2. 23. 2 Pet. 3. 16.
UNLEAVENED, Ex. 12. 39. 1 Cor. 5. 7.
UNMERCIFUL, Rom. 1. 31.
UNMINDFUL, Deut. 32. 18.
UNMOVEABLE, 1 Cor. 15. 58.
UNPERFECT, Ps. 139. 16.
UNPREPARED, 2 Cor. 9. 4.
UNPROFITABLE talk, Job 15. 3.
　Mat. 25. 30. cast ye *u.* servant to outer darkness
　Luke 17. 10. we are *u.* servants
　Rom. 3. 12. they are together become *u.*
　Tit. 3. 9. they are *u.* and vain
　Heb. 13. 17. for that is *u.* for you
UNPUNISHED, Prov. 11. 21; 16. 5; 17. 5;
　19. 5, 9. Jer. 25. 29; 30. 11; 46. 28; 49. 12.
UNQUENCHABLE, Mat. 3. 12. Luke 3. 17.
UNREASONABLE, Acts 25. 27. 2 Thes. 3. 2.
UNREBUKEABLE, 1 Tim. 6. 14.
UNREPROVEABLE, Col. 1. 22.
UNRIGHTEOUS decrees, Is. 10. 1.
　Luke 16. 11. not been faithful in *u.* mammon

Rom. 3. 5. is God *unrighteous* who taketh
　vengeance?
1 Cor. 6. 9. *u.* shall not inherit the kingdom
Heb. 6. 10. God is not *u.* to forget
Lev. 19. 15. do no *unrighteousness*
Jer. 22. 13. woe to him that buildeth his house
　by *u.*
Luke 16. 9. friends of mammon of *u.*
John 7. 18. is true, and no *u.* in him
Rom. 1. 18. who hold the truth in *u.*
6. 13. members instruments of *u.*
9. 14. is there *u.* with God? God forbid
2 Cor. 6. 14. what fellowship hath righteousness
　with *u.*
2 Thes. 2. 10. all deceivableness of *u.*
12. believed not truth, but had pleasure in *u.*
Heb. 8. 12. will be merciful to their *u.*
2 Pet. 2. 15. Balaam . . . who loved wages of *u.*
1 John 1. 9. to cleanse us from all *u.*
5. 17. all *u.* is sin
UNRULY, 1 Thes. 5. 14. Tit. 1. 6, 10. Jas. 3. 8.
UNSAVOURY, Job 6. 6. Jer. 23. 13.
UNSEARCHABLE things, Job 5. 9.
　Ps. 145. 3. his greatness is *u.*
　Prov. 25. 3. heart of kings is *u.*
　Eph. 3. 8. preach . . . *u.* riches of Christ
UNSEEMLY, Rom. 1. 27. 1 Cor. 13. 5.
UNSKILFUL in word, Heb. 5. 13.
UNSPEAKABLE, 2 Cor. 9. 15; 12. 4. 1 Pet. 1. 8.
UNSPOTTED, Jas. 1. 27.
UNSTABLE, Gen. 49. 4. Jas. 1. 8.
　2 Pet. 2. 14. beguiling *u.* souls
　3. 16. unlearned and *u.* wrest
UNTHANKFUL, Luke 6. 35. 2 Tim. 3. 2.
UNTOWARD, Acts 2. 40.
UNWASHEN, Mat. 15. 20. Mark 7. 2, 5.
UNWISE, Deut. 32. 6. Hos. 13. 13. Rom. 1. 14.
　Eph. 5. 17.
UNWORTHY, Acts 13. 46. 1 Cor. 6. 2.
　1 Cor. 11. 27. drinketh *unworthily*　　[Jas. 1. 5.
UPBRAID, Judg. 8. 15. Mat. 11. 20. Mark 16. 14.
UPHOLD me with thy Spirit, Ps. 51. 12.
　Ps. 119. 116. *u.* me according to
　Prov. 29. 23. honour shall *u.* humble
　Is. 41. 10. I will *u.* thee with the right hand of my
　righteousness
　Ps. 41. 12. thou *upholdest* me in my integrity
　37. 17. Lord *upholdeth* righteous
　63. 8. thy right hand *u.* me
　145. 14. Lord *u.* all that fall
　Heb. 1. 3. *upholding* all things by word of
　Is. 63. 5. my fury it *upheld* me
UPRIGHT in heart, Ps. 7. 10.
　Ps. 11. 7. his countenance doth behold *u.*
　18. 23. I was also *u.* before him
　25. with *u.* man thou wilt shew thyself *u.*
　25. 8. good and *u.* is the Lord
　37. 37. mark perfect man, and behold the *u.*
　64. 10. all *u.* in heart shall glory
　112. 2. generation of *u.* shall be blessed
　4. to *u.* there ariseth light in darkness
　140. 13. *u.* shall dwell in thy presence
　Prov. 2. 21. *u.* shall dwell in the land
　10. 29. way of Lord is strength to *u.*
　11. 3. integrity of *u.* shall guide
　6. righteousness of *u.* shall deliver
　12. 6. mouth of *u.* shall deliver
　13. 6. righteousness keepeth him that is *u.*
　14. 11. tabernacle of *u.* shall flourish
　28. 10. *u.* shall have good things
　Eccl. 7. 29. God hath made man *u.*
　Sol. 1. 4. the *u.* love thee
　Hab. 2. 4. his soul . . . is not *u.* in him

Ps. 15. 2. that walketh *uprightly*, 84. 11. Prov.
2. 7; 10. 9; 15. 21; 28. 28. Mic. 2. 7. Gal. 2. 14.
58. 1. do ye judge *u*., 75. 2.
Is. 33. 15. he that . . . speaketh *u*., Amos 5. 10.
Deut. 9. 5. *uprightness* of thine heart
1 Chr. 29. 17. hast pleasure in *u*.
Job 33. 23. to shew unto man his *u*.
Ps. 25. 21. let integrity and *u*. preserve me
143. 10. lead me into land of *u*.
Is. 26. 7. the way of the just is *u*.
URIM and Thummim, Ex. 28. 30. Lev. 8. 8.
Num. 27. 21. Deut. 33. 8. 1 Sam. 28. 6.
Ezra 2. 63. Neh. 7. 65.
US, Gen. 1. 26; 3. 22; 11. 7. Is. 6. 8; 9. 6. Rom.
4. 24. 2 Cor. 5. 21. Gal. 3. 13. 1 Thes. 5. 10.
Heb. 6. 20. 1 Pet. 2. 21; 4. 1. 1 John 5. 11.
USE, Rom. 1. 26. Eph. 4. 29. Heb. 5. 14.
1 Cor. 7. 31. *u*. world as not abusing
Gal. 5. 13. *u*. not liberty for occasion
1 Tim. 1. 8. if a man *u*. it lawfully
Tit. 3. 14. good works for necessary *uses*
Ps. 119. 132. as thou *usest* to do
Jer. 22. 13. *useth* his neighbour's service
Col. 2. 22. *using*, 1 Pet. 2. 16.
USURP, 1 Tim. 2. 12.
USURY, Ex. 22. 25. Lev. 25. 36, 37. Deut.
23. 19, 20. Neh. 5. 7, 10. Ps. 15. 5. Prov.
28. 8. Is. 24. 2. Jer. 15. 10. Ezek. 18. 8, 13, 17;
22. 12. Mat. 25. 27. Luke 19. 23.
UTTER, Ps. 78. 2; 94. 4.
2 Cor. 12. 4. words not lawful for a man to *u*.
Acts 2. 4. as Spirit gave them *utterance*
Eph. 6. 19. that *u*. may be given me
Col. 4. 3. God would open unto us a door of *u*.
Rom. 8. 26. groanings which cannot be *uttered*
Heb. 5. 11. things to say and hard to be *u*.
Ps. 19. 2. day to day *uttereth*
Deut. 7. 2. *utterly*, Ps. 89. 33; 119. 8, 43. Sol.
8. 7. Jer. 14. 19.
1 Thes. 2. 16. *uttermost*, Heb. 7. 25.

V

VAIN, Ex. 5. 9; 20. 7.
Deut. 32. 47. it is not a *v*. thing for
1 Sam. 12. 21. should ye go after *v*. things
Ps. 39. 6. every man walketh in a *v*. shew, they
are disquieted in *v*.
Job 11. 12. *v*. man would be wise
Ps. 60. 11. *v*. is help of man, 108. 12.
119. 113. I hate *v*. thoughts, but
127. 2. it is *v*. for you to rise up early
Jer. 4. 14. how long shall thy *v*. thoughts
Mat. 6. 7. use not *v*. repetitions
Rom. 1. 21. they glorified him not as God, but
became *v*. in their imaginations
1 Cor. 3. 20. thoughts of wise are *v*.
Eph. 5. 6. deceive you with *v*. words
Jas. 1. 26. this man's religion is *v*.
1 Pet. 1. 18. from your *v*. conversation
Ps. 73. 13. cleansed my heart *in vain*
89. 47. why hast thou made all men—
127. 1. labour— . . . waketh but—
Is. 45. 19. seek ye me—
Jer. 3. 23.—is salvation hoped for from hills
Mat. 15. 9.—do they worship me
Rom. 13. 4. beareth not the sword—
1 Cor. 15. 58. your labour is not—
2 Cor. 6. 1. receive not grace of God—
Phil. 2. 16. not run—neither laboured—
2 Ki. 17. 15. they followed *vanity*
Job 7. 3. made to possess months of *v*.

Job 7. 16. for my days are *vanity*
Ps. 12. 2. speak *v*. every one
24. 4. hath not lifted up his soul to *v*.
39. 5. his best state is altogether *v*.
11. surely every man is *v*.
62. 9. men of low degree are *v*.
94. 11. thoughts of man that they are *v*.
119. 37. turn away mine eyes from beholding *v*.
144. 4. man is like to *v*.
8. whose mouth speaketh *v*., 11.
Prov. 22. 8. soweth iniquity shall reap *v*.
Eccl. 1. 2. *v*. of vanities, all is *v*., 14; 2. 1; 3. 19;
4. 8; 12. 8.
11. 10. childhood and youth are *v*.
Is. 5. 18. draw iniquity with cords of *v*.
40. 17. less than nothing and *v*.
Hab. 2. 13. weary themselves for very *v*.
Rom. 8. 20. creature subject to *v*.
Eph. 4. 17. walk in *v*. of their mind
2 Pet. 2. 18. great swelling worlds of *v*.
Ps. 31. 6. that regard lying *vanities*
Jer. 10. 8. the stock is a doctrine of *v*.
Jonah 2. 8. that observe lying *v*.
Acts 14. 15. turn from these *v*. unto
VALIANT, Sol. 3. 7. Is. 10. 13.
Jer. 9. 3. not *v*. for the truth
Heb. 11. 34. through faith waxed *v*.
Ps. 60. 12. *valiantly*, 108. 13; 118. 15, 16. Num.
VALUE, Job 13. 4. Mat. 10. 31.   [24. 18.
VAPOUR, Jer. 10. 13. Jas. 4. 14.
VARIABLENESS, Jas. 1. 17.
VARIANCE, Mat. 10. 35. Gal. 5. 20.
VAUNT, Judg. 7. 2. 1 Cor. 13. 4.
VEHEMENT, Sol. 8. 6. 2 Cor. 7. 11.
VEIL, Gen. 24. 65. Sol. 5. 7.
Is. 25. 7. destroy . . . the *v*. spread over
Mat. 27. 51. *v*. of the temple was rent
2 Cor. 3. 13. Moses put a *v*. over his
Heb. 6. 19. entereth into that within *v*.
10. 20. through *v*., that is to say, his flesh
VENGEANCE taken, Gen. 4. 15.
Deut. 32. 35. to me belongeth *v*., 41, 43, Ps.
94. 1. Rom. 12. 19. Heb. 10. 30.
Ps. 58. 10. rejoice when he seeth *v*.
Is. 34. 8. the day of the Lord's *v*.
Jer. 11. 20. let me see thy *v*., 20. 12.
51. 6. time of the Lord's *v*., 11.
Luke 21. 22. these be days of *v*., Is. 63. 4.
2 Thes. 1. 8. in flaming fire taking *v*.
Jude 7. suffering *v*. of eternal fire
VERILY, Gen. 42. 21. Jer. 15. 11. It is often used
by Christ, as well as *verily, verily*, John 1. 51;
3. 3, 5, 11; 5. 19, 24, 25; 6. 26, &c.
VERITY, Ps. 111. 7. 1 Tim. 2. 7.
VERY, Prov. 17. 9. Mat. 24. 24. John 7. 26;
14. 11. 1 Thes. 5. 23.
VESSEL, Ps. 2. 9; 31. 12. Jer. 18. 4.
Jer. 22. 28. is he a *v*. wherein is no pleasure,
48. 11. not been emptied from *v*. to *v*. [Hos. 8. 8.
Acts 9. 15. he is a chosen *v*. unto me
Rom. 9. 21. one *v*. to honour
1 Thes. 4. 4. possess his *v*. in sanctification
2 Tim. 2. 21. be a *v*. unto honour
1 Pet. 3. 7. honour to wife as unto weaker *v*.
Rom. 9. 22. *vessels* of wrath fitted
2 Cor. 4. 7. treasure in earthen *v*.
VEXED, Job 27. 2. Ps. 6. 2, 3, 10.
Is. 63. 10. and *v*. his holy spirit
2 Pet. 2. 7. Lot *v*. with filthy conversation, 8.
VIAL, Rev. 5. 8; 16. 1; 21. 9.
VICTORY is thine, O Lord, 1 Chr. 29. 11.
Ps. 98. 1. his holy arm hath gotten him *v*.
Is. 25. 8. swallow up death in *v*.

1 Cor. 15. 54. death is swallowed up in *victory*
55. O grave, where is thy *v.?*
57. thanks to God, who giveth us *v.*
1 John 5. 4. the *v.* that overcometh
VIGILANT, 1 Tim. 3. 2. 1 Pet. 5. 8.
VILE, thy brother seem, Deut. 25. 3.
1 Sam. 3. 13. sons made themselves *v.*
2 Sam. 6. 22. I will yet be more *v.*
Ps. 15. 4. a *v.* person is contemned
Is. 32. 6. *v.* person will speak villany
Jer. 15. 19. take forth the precious from the *v.*
Rom. 1. 26 gave them up to *v.* affections
Phil. 3. 21. shall change our *v.* body
VINE, 1 Ki. 4. 25. Mic. 4. 4.
Deut. 32. 32. *v.* is the *v.* of Sodom
Ps. 128. 3. wife shall be as fruitful *v.*
Jer. 2. 21. I planted thee a noble *v.*
Hos. 10. 1. Israel is an empty *v.*
Mat. 26. 29. not drink of this fruit of the *v.*
John 15. 1. I am the true *v.* and my
5. I am the *v.*, ye are the branches
Ps. 80. 15. *vineyard*, Prov. 24. 30. Sol. 1. 6. Is.
5. 1, 7. Mat. 20. 1; 21. 33. Luke 13. 6. 1 Cor.
9. 7. Sol. 8. 11, 12.
VIOLENCE, Lev. 6. 2. 2 Sam. 22. 3.
Gen. 6. 11. earth was filled with *v.*, 13.
Ps. 72. 14. redeem their soul from . . . *v.*
73. 6. *v.* covereth them as a garment
Hab. 1. 2. cry out unto thee of *v.*
Mat. 11. 12. kingdom of heaven suffereth *v.*
Luke 3. 14. do *v.* to no man, and be
Heb. 11. 34. quenched the *v.* of fire
VIRGIN, Is. 7. 14. 2 Cor. 11. 2.
Sol. 1. 3. *virgins*, Rev. 14. 4.
VIRTUE, Mark 5. 30. Luke 6. 19.
2 Pet. 1. 3. called us to glory and *v.*
Phil. 4. 8. if there be any *v.*, think
Prov. 12. 4. *virtuous* woman, 31. 10.
VISAGE, Is. 52. 14. Lam. 4. 8.
VISIBLE and invisible, Col. 1. 16.
VISION, 1 Sam. 3. 1. Ps. 89. 19. Mat. 17. 9. Acts
10. 19; 16. 9.
Prov. 29. 18. where there is no *v.* the people
Hab. 2. 2. write the *v.*   [perish
3. the *v.* is yet for an appointed time
Ezek. 13. 16. see *visions* of peace
Hos. 12. 10. have multiplied *v.*
Joel 2. 28. young men shall see *v.*, Acts 2. 17.
VISIT you, Gen. 50. 24, 25. Ex. 13. 19.
Job 7. 18. thou shouldest *v.* him every
Ps. 106. 4. *v.* me with thy salvation
Jer. 5. 9. shall I not *v.* for these things? 9. 9.
Lam. 4. 22. he will *v.* thine iniquity, Jer. 14. 10.;
23. 2. Hos. 2. 13; 8. 13.
Acts 7. 23. *v.* his brethren, 15. 36.
15. 14. God . . . did *v.* the Gentiles
Jas. 1. 27. to *v.* the fatherless and
Ps. 17. 3. thou hast *visited* me in the night
Mat. 25. 36. I was sick and ye *v.*
Luke 1. 68. *v.* and redeemed his people
78. dayspring from on high hath *v.* us
Ps. 8. 4. *visitest*, 65. 9. Heb. 2. 6.
Ex. 20. 5. *visiting* the iniquity of the fathers upon
the children, 34. 7. Num. 14. 18. Deut. 5. 9.
VOCATION, worthy of, Eph. 4. 1.
VOICE is Jacob's *v.*, Gen. 27. 22.
Gen. 4. 10. *v.* of thy brother's blood
Ex. 5. 2. who is Lord that I should obey his *v.?*
Ps. 5. 3. my *v.* shalt thou hear in the morning
18. 13. the Highest gave his *v.*
42. 4. to house of God with *v.* of joy and praise
95. 7. to day, if ye will hear his *v.*
103. 20. hearkening to *v.* of his word

Sol. 2. 14. let me hear thy *voice*, 8. 13.
Is. 30. 19. gracious unto thee at *v.* of thy cry
50. 10. obeyeth *v.* of his servant
Ezek. 33. 32. that hath a pleasant *v.*
John 5. 25. dead shall hear the *v.* of
10. 3. sheep hear his *v.* 4, 16, 27.
Gal. 4. 20. I desire . . . to change my *v.*
1 Thes. 4. 16. with *v.* of archangel
Rev. 3. 20. if any man hear my *v.*
Acts 13. 27. *voices*, Rev. 4. 5; 11. 19.
VOID of counsel, Deut. 32. 28.
Ps. 89. 39. made *v.* covenant of thy servant
119. 126. have made *v.* thy law
Is. 55. 11. it shall not return to me *v.*
Acts 24. 16. conscience *v.* of offence
1 Cor. 9. 15. make my glorying *v.*
VOLUME, Ps. 40. 7. Heb. 10. 7.
VOMIT, Job 20. 15. Prov. 23. 8; 26. 11.
Is. 19. 14. 2 Pet. 2. 22.
VOW, Jacob vowed a, Gen. 28. 20; 31. 13. Num.
6. 2; 21. 2; 30. 2. 1 Sam. 1. 11. 2 Sam.
15. 7, 8.
Deut. 23. 21. when thou shalt *v.* a *v.*, 22.
Ps. 65. 1. unto thee shall the *v.* be performed
76. 11. *v.*, and pay unto the Lord
Eccl. 5. 4. a *v.* defer not to pay, 5.
Is. 19. 21. shall *v.* a *v.* to Lord, Ps. 132. 2.
Jonah 2. 9. I will pay that that I have *vowed*
Job 22. 27. thou shalt pay thy *vows*
Ps. 50. 14. pay thy *v.* to most High
56. 12. thy *v.* are upon me, O God
61. 5. heard my *v.* 8. perform my *v.*
Prov. 20. 25. after *v.* to make inquiry
31. 2. son of my *v.* 1 Sam. 1. 11.
Jonah 1. 15. offered sacrifice . . . and made *v.*

W

WAGES, Lev. 19. 13. Ezek. 29. 18.
Hag. 1. 6. earneth *w.* to put it into bag
Mal. 3. 5. oppress hireling in his *w.*
Luke 3. 14. be content with your *w.*
Rom. 6. 23. the *w.* of sin is death
WAIT till my change come, Job 14. 14.
Ps. 25. 5. on thee do I *w.* all the day
27. 14. *w.* on the Lord . . . *w.*, I say
37. 34. *w.* on the Lord and keep his way
62. 5. *w.* thou only upon God
104. 27. these *w.* all upon thee
130. 5. I *w.* for Lord, my soul doth *w.*
145. 15. eyes of all *w.* upon thee
Prov. 20. 22. *w.* on the Lord and he
Is. 8. 17. I will *w.* upon the Lord
30. 18. with the Lord *w.* . . . . blessed are all they
that *w.* for him
40. 31. that *w.* on Lord shall renew
Lam. 3. 25. good to them that *w.* for
26. quietly *w.* for salvation of Lord
Hos. 12. 6. *w.* on thy God continually
Mic. 7. 7. *w.* for God of my salvation
Hab. 2. 3. *w.* for it, because it will surely
Zeph. 3. 8. *w.* ye on me . . . saith the Lord
Luke 12. 36. men that *w.* for their lord
1 Thes. 1. 10. *w.* for his Son from
Gen. 49. 18. *waited* for thy salvation
Ps. 40. 1. I *w.* patiently for the Lord
Is. 25. 9. our God, we have *w.* for
26. 8. in way of thy judgments have we *w.*
33. 2. O Lord, we have *w.* for thee
Zech. 11. 11. poor of flock that *w.* on
Mark 15. 43. *w.* for kingdom of God
1 Pet. 3. 20. longsuffering of God *w.*

Ps. 33. 20. our soul *waiteth* for Lord, 40. 1.
130. 6. my soul *w.* for the Lord more
Is. 64. 4. prepared for him that *w.*
Prov. 8. 34. *waiting* at the posts of
Luke 2. 25. *w.* for consolation of Israel
Rom. 8. 23. *w.* for the adoption
1 Cor. 1. 7. *w.* for coming of our Lord
2 Thes. 3. 5. into the patient *w.* for Christ
WAKETH, Ps. 127. 1. Sol. 5. 2.
Is. 50. 4. *wakeneth*, Joel 3. 12.
WALK in my law, Ex. 16. 4.
Gen. 24. 40. Lord before whom I *w.*
17. 1. *w.* before me and be thou perfect
Lev. 26. 12. I will *w.* among you
21. if ye *w.* contrary unto me
23. but will *w.* contrary unto me
24. will I also *w.* contrary unto you
Deut. 5. 33. *w.* in all the ways which Lord, 8. 6.;
10. 12; 11. 22; 13. 5; 28. 9.
13. 4. ye shall *w.* after the Lord
Ps. 23. 4. though I *w.* through valley
84. 11. no good . . . withhold from them that *w.*
116. 9. I will *w.* before Lord   [uprightly
119. 3. do no iniquity, they *w.* in
Eccl. 11. 9. *w.* in ways of thine heart
Is. 2. 3. will *w.* in his paths
5. let us *w.* in the light of the Lord
30. 21. this is the way, *w.* ye in it
40. 31. shall *w.* and not faint
Jer. 23. 14. commit adultery and *w.*
Dan. 4. 37. those that *w.* in pride he is able
Hos. 14. 9. just shall *w.* in them
Mic. 6. 8. *w.* humbly with thy God
Amos 3. 3. can two *w.* together except they
Zech. 10. 12. *w.* up and down in his name
John 8. 12. not *w.* in darkness
11. 9. *w.* in day he stumbleth not
12. 35. *w.* while ye have light
Rom. 4. 12. *w.* in steps of that faith
6. 4. should *w.* in newness of life
8. 1 *w.* not after the flesh, 4.
13. 13. let us *w.* honestly as in
2 Cor. 5. 7. we *w.* by faith, not by sight
10. 3. though we *w.* in the flesh, we do not war
Gal. 5. 16. *w.* in the Spirit, and not fulfil the
25. if we live in the Spirit, let us *w.* in
6. 16. as many as *w.* according
Eph. 2. 10. ordained that we should *w.* in
4. 1. *w.* worthy of the vocation
5. 2. *w.* in love, as Christ also hath loved
8. *w.* as children of light
15. *w.* circumspectly, not as
Phil. 3. 16. let us *w.* by the same rule
Col. 1. 10. that ye might *w.* worthy
2. 6. received Christ . . . so *w.* ye in him
4. 5. *w.* in wisdom . . . redeeming the time
1 Thes. 2. 12. ye would *w.* worthy of
4. 1. how ye ought to *w.* and to please
1 John 1. 7. if we *w.* in the light
2. 6. ought himself also so to *w.* as he walked
3 John 4. my children *w.* in truth, 3.
Rev. 3. 4. shall *w.* with me in white
16. 15. lest he *w.* naked and they see his
21. 24. nations . . . shall *w.* in light of
Ps. 55. 14. we *walked* unto house of God
81. 12. *w.* in their own counsels
13. O that Israel had *w.* in my
Is. 9. 2. people that *w.* in darkness
2 Cor. 10. 2. *w.* according to flesh
12. 18. *w.* we not in same spirit
Gal. 2. 14. saw they *w.* not uprightly
Eph. 2. 2. in time past ye *w.*, Col. 3. 7.
1 Pet. 4. 3. we *w.* in lasciviousness

Rom. 14. 15. *walkest* thou not charitably
Ps. 15. 2. he that *walketh* uprightly
39. 6. every man *w.* in a vain shew
Mic. 2. 7. do good to him that *w.* uprightly
2 Thes. 3. 6. brother that *w.* disorderly
1 Pet. 5. 8. devil . . . *w.* about seeking
Rev. 2. 1. *w.* in midst of seven golden
Gen. 3. 8. voice of Lord God *walking* in
Is. 57. 2. *w.* in his uprightness
Jer. 6. 28. revolters *w.* with slanders
Mic. 2. 11. if man *w.* in spirit and falsehood
Luke 1. 6. *w.* in all commandments
Acts 9. 31. *w.* in the fear of the Lord
2 Cor. 4. 2. not *w.* in craftiness
2 Pet. 3. 3. *w.* after their own lusts, Jude 16.
2 John 4. thy children *w.* in truth
WALL, Ps. 62. 3. Prov. 18. 11. Sol. 2. 9; 8. 9, 10.
Is. 26. 1; 60. 18.
WANDER, Num. 14. 33. Ps. 119. 10.
Lam. 4. 14. *wandered*, Heb. 11. 37.
Prov. 21. 16. *wandereth*, 27. 8.
1 Tim. 5. 13. *wandering*, Jude 13.
Ps. 56. 8. tellest my *wanderings*
WANT, Deut. 28. 48. Job 31. 19.
Ps. 23. 1. the Lord . . . I shall not *w.*
34. 9. no *w.* to them that fear him, 10.
2 Cor. 8. 14. a supply for your *w.*
Phil. 4. 11. not that I speak in respect of *w.*
WANTONNESS, Rom. 13. 13. 2 Pet. 2. 18.
WAR, Ex. 13. 17; 17. 16. Ps. 27. 3.
Job 10. 17. changes and *w.* are against
Ps. 18. 34. teacheth my hands to *w.*, 144. 1.
120. 7. I am for peace . . . they are for *w.*
Prov. 20. 18. with good advice make *w.*
Eccl. 8. 8. is no discharge in that *w.*
Is. 2. 4. neither . . . learn *w.* any more, Mic. 4. 3.
Mic. 3. 5. prepare *w.* against
2 Cor. 10. 3. we do not *w.* after flesh
1 Tim. 1. 18. *w.* a good warfare
1 Pet. 2. 11. fleshly lusts which *w.*
Rev. 11. 7. beast . . . shall make *w.*
12. 7. there was *w.* in heaven
17. 14. these shall make *w.* with the Lamb
19. 11. in righteousness doth he . . . make *w.*
Num. 21. 14. in book of *wars* of Lord
Ps. 46. 9. he maketh *w.* to cease
Mat. 24. 6. hear of *w.* and rumours of *w.*
Jas. 4. 1. from whence come *w.* and
2 Tim. 2. 4. no man that *warreth*
Is. 37. 8. *warring*, Rom. 7. 23.
WARFARE, Is. 40. 2. 1 Cor. 9. 7. 2 Cor. 10. 4.
1 Tim. 1. 18.
WARN, 2 Chr. 19. 10. Acts 10. 22.
Ezek. 3. 19. if thou *w.* the wicked
33. 3. blow trumpet, *w.* people, 9.
Acts 20. 31. I ceased not to *w.*
1 Cor. 4. 14. my beloved sons I *w.* you
1 Thes. 5. 14. *w.* them that are unruly
Ps. 19. 11. by them is thy servant *warned*
Mat. 3. 7. who hath *w.* you to flee
Heb. 11. 7. Noah being *w.* of God
Jer. 6. 10. to whom I give *warning*
Col. 1. 28. Christ . . . *w.* we preach, *w.*
WASH, Lev. 6. 27; 14. 9; 15. 16.
Job 9. 30. if I *w.* myself with snow water
Ps. 26. 6. *w.* my hands in innocency
51. 2. *w.* me throughly from mine iniquity
7. *w.* me and I shall be whiter than
58. 10. he shall *w.* his feet in blood
Is. 1. 16. *w.* you, make you clean
Jer. 2. 22. thou *w.* thee with nitre
4. 14. *w.* thy heart from wickedness
Luke 7. 38. to *w.* his feet with tears

John 13. 5. began to *wash* disciples' feet
8. I *w*. thee not, thou hast no part
14. ought to *w*. one another's feet
Acts 22. 16. be baptized and *w*. away
Job 29. 6. when I *washed* my steps
Sol. 5. 3. I have *w*. my feet
Is. 4. 4. *w*. away filth of daughters
Ezek. 16. 4. neither wast thou *w*. in
Heb. 10. 22. *w*. with pure water
Rev. 1. 5. *w*. us from our sins in his own blood
7. 14. *w*. their robes, and made them white in
Eph. 5. 26. *washing*, Tit. 3. 5.
WASTE, Ps. 80. 13. Mat. 26. 8.
Luke 15. 13. *wasted*, 16. 1. Gal. 1. 13.
Prov. 18. 9. *waster*, Is. 54. 16.
Job 14. 10. *wasteth*, Prov. 19. 26.
Is. 59. 7. *wasting* and destruction, 60. 18.
WATCH, Neh. 4. 9. Job 7. 12.
Job 14. 16. dost thou not *w*. over my sin?
Ps. 102. 7. I *w*. and am as a sparrow
130. 6. they that *w*. for morning
141. 3. set a *w*., O Lord, before my mouth
Jer. 44. 27. *w*. over them for evil
Mat. 24. 42. *w*. therefore, for ye know not, 25. 13.
Mark 13. 33. take ye heed, *w*. and pray, 37.
1 Cor. 16. 13. *w*. ye, stand fast in the
Col. 4. 2. *w*. in the same with thanksgiving
1 Thes. 5. 6. let us *w*. and be sober
2 Tim. 4. 5. *w*. thou in all things
Heb. 13. 17. they *w*. for your souls
1 Pet. 4. 7. be sober, *w*. unto prayer
Rev. 3. 3. if therefore thou shalt not *w*. I will
Jer. 31. 28. like as I have *watched* over them
20. 10. familiars *w*. for my halting
Mat. 24. 43. he would have *w*.
Ps. 63. 6. *watches*, 119. 148. Lam. 2. 19.
37. 32. the wicked *watcheth* the
Ezek. 7. 6. the end is come; it *w*. for
Rev. 16. 15. blessed is he that *w*. and
3. 2. be *watchful* and strengthen
Prov. 8. 34. *watching* daily at my gates
Eph. 6. 18. *w*. with all perseverance
2 Cor. 6. 5. in *watchings*, 11. 27.
Is. 21. 11. *watchman*, Ezek. 3. 17; 33. 7.
Sol. 3. 3. *watchmen*, 5. 7. Is. 52. 8; 56. 10; 62. 6.
Jer. 31. 6.
WATER, Gen. 49. 4. Ex. 12. 9; 17. 6.
2 Sam. 14. 14. we are as *w*. spilt
Job 15. 16. drinketh iniquity like *w*.
Ps. 22. 14. I am poured out like *w*.
Is. 12. 3. draw *w*. out of wells of salvation
27. 3. I will *w*. it every moment
30. 20. give you . . . *w*. of affliction
41. 17. when poor and needy seek *w*. and there
44. 3. pour *w*. on him that is thirsty
58. 11. shalt be like . . . a spring of *w*.
Lam. 1. 16. eye runneth down with *w*., 3. 48.
Ezek. 36. 25. sprinkle clean *w*.
Amos 8. 11. nor a thirst for *w*.
Mat. 3. 11. I indeed baptize you with *w*.
10. 42. cup of cold *w*. only in name of a
Luke 16. 24. dip tip of his finger in *w*.
John 3. 5. except a man be born of *w*.
23. baptized because there was much *w*.
4. 14. shall be in him a well of *w*.
John 7. 38. flow rivers of living *w*.
19. 34. came there out blood and *w*.
Acts 8. 38. went down both into *w*.
10. 47. can any man forbid *w*. that these
Eph. 5. 26. cleanse it with washing of *w*.
1 John 5. 6. he that came by *w*.
8. three bear witness in earth, spirit, *w*., and
Jude 12. clouds they are without *w*.

Rev. 21. 6. fountain of *water* of life, 22. 1.
22. 17. take the *w*. of life freely
Is. 58. 11. like a *watered* garden, Jer. 31. 12.
1 Cor. 3. 6. I have planted, Apollos *w*., 7.
Ps. 23. 2. leadeth me beside still *waters*
124. 4. *w*. had overwhelmed us, 5.
Prov. 5. 15. drink *w*. out of thine own cistern,
and running *w*. out of thine own well
9. 17. stolen *w*. are sweet
Eccl. 11. 1. cast thy bread upon *w*.
Sol. 4. 15. a well of living *w*.
Is. 32. 20. blessed are ye that sow beside all *w*.
33. 16. bread . . . given him; his *w*. shall be sure
35. 6. in wilderness shall *w*. break forth
43. 20. I give *w*. in the wilderness
54. 9. this is as *w*. of Noah unto me
58. 11. a spring of water, whose *w*. fail not
Jer. 2. 13. fountain of living *w*., 17. 13.
9. 1. O that my head were *w*.
Hab. 2. 14. as *w*. cover the sea, Is. 11. 9.
Zech. 14. 8. living *w*. shall go out from Jerusalem,
Ezek. 47. 1.   [*w*., 14. 2; 19. 6.
Rev. 1. 15. sound of many
7. 17. lead them unto living fountains of *w*.
Ps. 42. 7. noise of thy *waterspouts*
WAVERING, Heb. 10. 23. Jas. 1. 6.
WAX, Ex. 32. 10, 11, 22. Ps. 22. 14; 68. 2; 97. 5.
Mat. 24. 12. Luke 12. 33. 1 Tim. 5. 11.
WAY, Ex. 13. 21; 23. 20; 32. 8.   [2 Tim. 3. 13.
1 Sam. 12. 23. teach you good and right *w*.
1 Ki. 2. 2. I go *w*. of all the earth
Ezra 8. 21. seek of him a right *w*.
Ps. 1. 6. *w*. of righteous . . . *w*. of ungodly
2. 12. and ye perish from the *w*.
49. 13. this their *w*. is their folly
67. 2. that thy *w*. may be known
78. 50. made a *w*. to his anger
119. 30. I have chosen *w*. of truth
32. run *w*. of thy commandments
Prov. 2. 8. Lord preserveth the *w*. of his saints
10. 29. *w*. of the Lord is strength
14. 12. a *w*. which seemeth right
15. 9. *w*. of wicked is abomination
24. *w*. of life is above to the wise
Eccl. 11. 5. knowest not what is *w*. of spirit
Is. 26. 7. *w*. of just is uprightness, 8.
30. 21. this is the *w*. walk ye in it
35. 8. a *w*. . . . called The *w*. of holiness
43. 19. make a *w*. in wilderness, 16.
59. 8. *w*. of peace they know not
Jer. 6. 16. where is the good *w*. and
10. 23. *w*. of man is not in himself
21. 8. the *w*. of life and *w*. of death
32. 39. give them one heart and one *w*.
50. 5. shall ask the *w*. to Zion
Mat. 7. 13. broad is *w*. . . . to destruction
John 1. 23. straight the *w*. of Lord
14. 4. *w*. ye know. 6. I am the *w*.
Acts 16. 17. shew unto us *w*. of salvation
18. 25. instructed in *w*. of Lord, 26.
1 Cor. 10. 13. make a *w*. to escape
12. 31. shew I unto you a more excellent *w*.
2 Pet. 2. 2. *w*. of truth shall be evil spoken of
1 Ki. 8. 32. bring *his way* on his head
Job 17. 9. righteous shall hold on—
Ps. 18. 30. as for God—is perfect
37. 23. delighteth in—34. and keep—
119. 9. shall a young man cleanse—
Prov. 14. 8. prudent is to understand—
16. 9. man's heart deviseth—
Is. 55. 7. let the wicked forsake—
Ps. 25. 8. teach sinners *in the way*
119. 14. I rejoiced—of thy testimonies

Ps. 139. 24. lead me *in the way* everlasting
Is. 26. 8.—of thy judgments . . . we waited
Mat. 5. 25. whiles thou art—with him
21. 32. John came—of righteousness
Luke 1. 79. guide our feet—of peace
Job 40. 19. he is chief of *ways* of God
Ps. 84. 5. in whose heart are *w.* of
Prov. 3. 17. Her *w.* are *w.* of pleasantness
5. 21. *w.* of man are before eyes of the Lord
16. 2. *w.* of man are clean in his
7. when a man's *w.* please Lord
Jer. 7. 3. amend your *w.* and your doings
Lam. 1. 4. the *w.* of Zion do mourn
3. 40. let us search and try our *w.*
Deut. 32. 4. *his ways*, Ps. 145. 17. Is. 2. 3. Mic.
4. 2. Rom. 11. 33.
Ps. 119. 5. *my ways*, 26, 59, 168; 139. 3; 39. 1.
Prov. 23. 26. Is. 55. 8. *highways*, 49. 11.
Prov. 14. 14. *own way(s)*, Is. 53. 6; 58. 13; 66. 3.
Ezek. 36. 31, 32.
Job 21. 14. *thy ways*, Ps. 25. 4; 91. 11; 119. 15.
Prov. 4. 26. Is. 63. 17. Ezek. 16. 61. Dan. 5. 23.
Rev. 15. 3.
Is. 35. 8. *wayfaring*, Jer. 14. 8.
WEAK, 2 Chr. 15. 7. Job 4. 3. Ps. 6. 2.
Is. 35. 3. strengthen ye the *w.* hands
Ezek. 16. 30. how *w.* is thy heart
Mat. 26. 41. the flesh is *w.*, Mark 14. 38.
Rom. 4. 19. and being not *w.* in faith
14. 1. him that is *w.* in the faith receive
1 Cor. 4. 10. we are *w.* but ye are strong
9. 22. to the *w.* became I as *w.*
11. 30. for this cause many are *w.* and sickly
12. 10. I am *w.* then am I strong
1 Thes. 5. 14. support the *w.*
Is. 14. 12. *weaken*, Ps. 102. 23. Job 12. 21.
2 Sam. 3. 1. *weaker*, 1 Pet. 3. 7.
1 Cor. 1. 25. *weakness*, 2. 3; 15. 43. 2 Cor. 12. 9;
13. 4. Heb. 11. 34.
WEALTH, Gen. 34. 29. Deut. 8. 17.
Deut. 8. 18. giveth thee power to get *w.*
Job 21. 13. spend their days in *w.*
Ps. 49. 6. that trust in their *w.*
10. and leave their *w.* to others
112. 3. *w.* and riches shall be in his
Prov. 10. 15. rich man's *w.* is his strong city,
13. 11. *w.* gotten by vanity shall be   [18. 11.
22. *w.* of the sinner is laid up for
19. 4. *w.* maketh many friends
1 Cor. 10. 24. but every man another's *w.*
WEANED, Ps. 131. 2. Is. 11. 8; 28. 9.
WEAPON, Deut. 23. 13. Neh. 4. 17. Job 20. 24.
Is. 13. 5; 54. 17. 2 Cor. 10. 4.
WEARY of my life, Gen. 27. 46.
Job 3. 17. there the *w.* be at rest
10. 1. soul is *w.* of life, Jer. 4. 31.
Prov. 3. 11. nor be *w.* of his correction
Is. 7. 13. *w.* men, will ye *w.* mv God
40. 28. Lord . . . fainteth not, neither is *w.*
31. shall run and not be *w.*
50. 4. speak a word in season to him that is *w.*
Jer. 6. 11. *w.* with holding in
9. 5. *w.* themselves to commit
20. 9. I was *w.* with forbearing
31. 25. I have satiated the *w.* soul
Gal. 6. 9. not be *w.* in welldoing, 2 Thes. 3. 13.
Is. 43. 24. *wearied*, 57. 10. Jer. 12. 5. Ezek.
24. 12. Mic. 6. 3. Mal. 2. 17. John 4. 6. Heb.
12. 3.
Eccl. 12. 12. *weariness*, Mal. 1. 13.
Job 7. 3. *wearisome* nights
WEB, Job 8. 14. Is. 59. 5, 6.
WEDDING, Mat. 22. 3, 8, 11. Luke 14. 8.

WEEK, Dan. 9. 27. Mat. 28. 1. Luke 18. 12. Acts
20. 7. 1 Cor. 16. 2.
Jer. 5. 24. *weeks*, Dan. 9. 24–26; 10. 2.
WEEP, Job 30. 25. Is. 30. 19; 33. 7. Jer. 9. 1;
13. 17. Joel 2. 17.
Luke 6. 21. blessed are ye that *w.*
23. 28. *w.* not for me, but *w.* for
Rom. 12. 15. *w.* with them that *w.*
1 Cor. 7. 30. that *w.* as though they wept not
Jas. 5. 1. rich men, *w.* and howl
1 Sam. 1. 8. why *weepest* thou, John 20. 13, 15.
Ps. 126. 6. he that goeth forth and *weepeth*
Lam. 1. 2. she *w.* sore in the night
Ps. 30. 5. *weeping* may endure for a night
Is. 22. 12. Lord God of hosts call to *w.* and
Joel 2. 12. turn ye even to me with . . . *w.*
Mal. 2. 13. covering altar of Lord with *w.*
Mat. 8. 12. *w.* and gnashing of teeth, 22. 13;
24. 51; 25. 30.
WEIGH the path of the just, Is. 26. 7.
Job 31. 6. let me be *weighed* in an even balance
Dan. 5. 27. art *w.* in the balances
Prov. 16. 2. Lord *weigheth* spirits
11. 1. just *weight* is his delight
16. 11. just *w.* and balance are the Lord's
2 Cor. 4. 17. eternal *w.* of glory
Heb. 12. 1. let us lay aside every *w.*
Mat. 23. 23. omitted *weightier* matters
Lev. 19. 36. just *weights*
Deut. 25. 13. divers *w.*, Prov. 20. 10, 23.
WELL, Ps. 84. 6. Prov. 5. 15; 10. 11. Sol. 4. 15.
Is. 12. 3. John 4. 14. 2 Pet. 2. 17.
Gen. 4. 7. if thou doest *well*, shalt
Ex. 1. 20. God dealt *w.* with midwives
Ps. 119. 65. hast dealt *w.* with thy servant
128. 2. it shall be *w.* with thee
Eccl. 8. 12. it shall be *w.* with them
Is. 3. 10. shall be *w.* with them
Rom. 2. 7. *well doing*, Gal. 6. 9. 2 Thes. 3. 13.
1 Pet. 2. 15; 3. 17; 4. 19.
WENT, Ps. 42. 4; 119. 67. Mat. 21. 30.
WEPT, Neh. 1. 4. Ps. 69. 10. Hos. 12. 4. Mat.
26. 75. Luke 19. 41. John 11. 35.
WHEAT, Ps. 81. 16. Prov. 27. 22. Sol. 7. 2.
Jer. 12. 13. they have sown *w.*
Amos 8. 5. we may set forth *w.*
Mat. 3. 12. gather his *w.* into the garner
Luke 22. 31. may sift you as *w.*
John 12. 24. except a corn of *w.* fall
WHEEL, Ps. 83. 13. Prov. 20. 26.
Ezek. 1. 16. *w.* in midddle of *w.* 10. 10.
10. 13. it was cried unto them, O *w.*
Ex. 14. 25. *wheels*, Judg. 5. 28. Ezek. 1. 16;
10. 9, 12, 13. Dan. 7. 9. Nah. 3. 2.
WHET, Deut. 32. 41. Ps. 7. 12; 64. 3.
WHISPERER, Prov. 16. 28.
WHIT, 1 Sam. 3. 18. John 7. 23. 2 Cor. 11. 5.
WHITE, Lev. 13. 3, 4. Num. 12. 10.
Job 6. 6. any taste in *w.* of an egg
Ps. 68. 14. *w.* as snow, Dan. 7. 9.
Eccl. 9. 8. thy garments be always *w.*
Sol. 5. 10. my beloved is *w.* and
Is. 1. 18. sins . . . shall be *w.* as snow
Dan. 11. 35. to purge and to make them *w.*
12. 10. many shall be purified and made *w.*
Mat. 17. 2. his raiment was *w.*, 28. 3.
Rev. 2. 17. give him a *w.* stone
3. 4. walk with me in *w.* (raiment), 5, 18; 4. 4;
7. 9, 13; 16. 9; 19. 8, 14.
Mat. 23. 27. *whited*, Acts 23. 3.
Ps. 51. 7. *whiter* than snow, Lam. 4. 7.
WHOLE, Ps. 9. 1; 119. 10. Is. 54. 5. Mic. 4. 13.
Zec. 4. 14. Mat. 9. 21. 1 John 2. 2; 5. 19.

Job 5. 18. he woundeth and his hands make *whole*
Mark 5. 34. thy faith hath made thee *w.*, 10. 52.
John 5. 4. *w.* of whatsoever disease
6. wilt thou be made *w.* 14. thou art made *w.*
Acts 9. 34. Christ maketh thee *w.*
Prov. 15. 4. *wholesome*, 1 Tim. 6. 3.
Num. 32. 11. *wholly*, Deut. 1. 36. Jer. 46. 28.
1 Thes. 5. 23. 1 Tim. 4. 15.
WHORE, Lev. 19. 29; 21. 7, 9. Deut. 22. 21;
23. 17, 18. Prov. 23. 27. Ezek. 16. 28. Rev.
17. 1, 16.
Jer. 3. 9. *whoredom*, Ezek. 16. 26. Hos. 2. 2, 4;
4. 11, 12; 5. 3, 4.
Eph. 5. 5. *whoremonger*, 1 Tim. 1. 10. Heb. 13. 4.
Rev. 21. 8; 22. 15.
WICKED, Ex. 23. 7. Deut. 15. 9; 25. 1.
Gen. 18. 25. slay the righteous with *w.*
1 Sam. 2. 9. the *w.* shall be silent in
Job 21. 30. *w.* is reserved to the day
Ps. 7. 11. God is angry with the *w.*
9. 17. *w.* shall be turned into hell
11. 6. on *w.* he shall rain snares
58. 3. *w.* are estranged from womb
119. 155. salvation is far from the *w.*
145. 20. all *w.* will he destroy, 147. 6.
Prov. 11. 5. *w.* shall fall by his own
21. 12. God overthroweth the *w.*
28. 1. *w.* flee when no man pursueth
Eccl. 7. 17. be not overmuch *w.*
Is. 55. 7. let the *w.* forsake his way
Jer. 17. 9. heart is deceitful and desperately *w.*
25. 31. he will give . . . *w.* to the sword
Ezek. 3. 18. warn the *w.*, 33. 8, 9, 11.
Dan. 12. 10. *w.* shall do *wickedly*
Gen. 19. 7. do not so *w.*, Neh. 9. 33.
1 Sam. 12. 25. if ye shall still do *w.*
Job 13. 7. will ye speak *w.* for God?
Ps. 18. 21. have not *w.* departed
Gen. 6. 5. God saw that the *wickedness*
39. 9. how can I do this great *w.*
1 Sam. 24. 13. *w.* proceedeth from the wicked
Job 4. 8. and sow *w.* shall reap same
Ps. 7. 9. *w.* of wicked come to an end
45. 7. righteousness, and hatest *w.*
Prov. 8. 7. *w.* is an abomination to my lips
10. 2. treasures of *w.* profit nothing
Eccl. 8. 8. neither shall *w.* deliver
Is. 9. 18. *w.* burneth as the fire
Jer. 2. 19. thine own *w.* shall correct
4. 14. O Jerusalem, wash thy heart from *w.*
14. 20. we acknowledge, O Lord, our *w.*
Hos. 10. 13. ye have plowed *w.*
Acts 8. 22. repent therefore of this thy *w.*
1 John 4. 19. whole world lieth in *w.*
WIDE, Deut. 15. 8, 11. Ps. 35. 21; 81. 10. Prov.
13. 3. Mat. 7. 13.
WIDOW, Mark 12. 42. 1 Tim. 5. 5. Deut. 10. 18.
Ps. 146. 9. Luke 18. 3, 5.
Ps. 68. 5. *widows*, Jer. 49. 11. Mat. 23. 14.
1 Tim. 5. 3. Jas. 1. 27.
WIFE, Ex. 20. 17. Lev. 21. 13.
Prov. 5. 18. rejoice with *w.* of youth
18. 22. findeth a *w.* findeth a good
19. 14. a prudent *w.* is from Lord
Eccl. 9. 9. live joyfully with the *w.*
Mal. 2. 15. against *w.* of his youth
Luke 17. 32. remember Lot's *w.*
Eph. 5. 33. every one . . . love his *w.* even as
Rev. 19. 7. his *w.* hath made herself ready
21. 9. the bride, the Lamb's *w.*
1 Cor. 7. 29. *wives*, Eph. 5. 25, 28. Col. 3. 18, 19.
1 Tim. 3. 11. 1 Pet. 3. 1.

WILDERNESS, Deut. 32. 10. Prov. 21. 19.
Sol. 3. 6; 8. 5. Is. 35. 1, 6; 41. 18, 19; 42. 11;
43. 19, 20. Rev. 12. 6.
WILES, Num. 25. 18. Eph. 6. 11.
WILL, Lev. 1. 3; 19. 5; 22. 19.
Deut. 33. 16. the good *w.* of him that
Mat. 7. 21. doeth *w.* of my Father, 12. 50.
John 1. 13. *w.* of flesh, nor of *w.* of man
4. 34. my meat is to do *w.* of him that
6. 40. this is the *w.* of him that sent
Acts 21. 14. the *w.* of the Lord be done
22. 14. *his will*, John 7. 17. Rom. 2. 18. Eph.
1. 5, 9. Col. 1. 9. 2 Tim. 2. 26. Heb. 13. 21.
1 John 5. 14. Rev. 17. 17.
Luke 22. 42. *my will*, Acts 13. 22.
John 5. 30. *own will*, 6. 38. Eph. 1. 11. Heb. 2. 4.
Jas. 1. 18. [Heb. 10. 7, 9.
Ps. 40. 8. *thy will*, 143. 10. Mat. 6. 10; 26. 42.
Ezra 7. 18. *will of God*, Mark 3. 35. Rom. 1. 10;
8. 27; 12. 2. 1 Cor. 1. 1. 2 Cor. 8. 5. Gal. 1. 4.
Eph. 1. 1; 6. 6. Col. 1. 1; 4. 12. 1 Thes.
4. 3. Heb. 10. 36. 1 Pet. 4. 2, 19. 1 John
2. 17.
John 15. 7. ask what ye *w.* and it
17. 24. I *w.* that they also, whom thou hast
Rom. 7. 18. to *w.* is present with me
9. 18. on whom he *w.* have mercy
Phil. 2. 13. worketh both to *w.* and to do
Rev. 22. 17. whosoever *w.* let him
Heb. 10. 26. if we sin *wilfully*
Rom. 9. 16. not of him that *willeth*
Ex. 35. 5. whosoever is of a *willing* heart
22. as many as were *w.* hearted.
1 Chr. 28. 9. serve him with a perfect heart and
with a *w.* mind
Ps. 110. 3. thy people shall be *w.*
Mat. 26. 41. spirit is indeed *w.* but the flesh
Luke 22. 42. if thou be *w.*, remove this cup
John 5. 35. *w.* for a season to rejoice
2 Cor. 5. 8. *w.* rather to be absent
1 Tim. 6. 18. *w.* to communicate
Heb. 13. 18. in all things *w.* to live
2 Pet. 3. 9. not *w.* that any should perish
Judg. 5. 2. *willingly* offered, 9.
Lam. 3. 33. he doth not afflict *w.*
Hos. 5. 11. he *w.* walked after
1 Pet. 5. 2. not by constraint, but *w.*
Col. 2. 23. wisdom in *will worship*
WILLOWS, Lev. 23. 40. Is. 44. 4.
WIN, that I may, Phil. 3. 8.
Prov. 11. 30. *winneth* souls is wise
WIND, Job 7. 7; 30. 15. Ps. 103. 16.
Ps. 135. 7. he bringeth the *w.* out of
Prov. 11. 29. inherit *w.* 27. 16. hideth *w.*
Eccl. 11. 4. he that observeth the *w.*
Is. 26. 18. have . . . brought forth *w.*
27. 8. he stayeth his rough *w.* in
Jer. 5. 13. prophets shall become *w.*
10. 13. *w.* out of his treasures, 51. 16.
Hos. 8. 7. sown *w.* 12. 1. feedeth on *w.*
John 3. 8. *w.* bloweth where it listeth
Eph. 4. 14. about with every *w.* of
2 Ki. 2. 11. *whirlwind*, Prov. 1. 27; 10. 25.
Is. 66. 15. Hos. 8. 7; 13. 3. Nah. 1. 3. Hab.
3. 14. Zech. 7. 14; 9. 14.
Ezek. 37. 9. *winds*, Mat. 8. 26. Luke 8. 25.
WINDOWS, Gen. 7. 11. Eccl. 12. 3. Sol. 2. 9.
Is. 60. 8. Jer. 9. 21.
WINE that maketh glad the heart, Ps. 104. 15.
Prov. 20. 1. *w.* is a mocker
21. 17. loveth *w.* shall not be rich
23. 31. look not thou upon the *w.* when it is red
31. 6. and *w.* to those that be of heavy heart

Sol. 1. 2. love is better than *wine*, 4.
Is. 5. 11. till *w.* inflame them
12. pipe and *w.* are in their feasts
28. 7. they have erred through *w.*
55. 1. buy *w.* and milk, Sol. 5. 1.
Hos. 2. 9. and my *w.* in the season
3. 1. look to other gods, and love flagons of *w.*
Hab. 2. 5. he transgresseth by *w.*
Eph. 5. 18. be not drunk with *w.*
1 Tim. 3. 3. not given to *w.*, 8. Tit. 1. 7.
5. 23. use a little *w.* for thy stomach's sake
Prov. 23. 20. *winebibber*, Mat. 11. 19.
Is. 25. 6. *wines* on the lees well refined
WINGS of the God of Israel, Ruth 2. 12.
Ps. 17. 8. hide me under shadow of thy *w.*,
    36. 7; 57. 1; 61. 4; 91. 4.
18. 10. on *w.* of wind, 2 Sam. 22. 11.
Prov. 23. 5. riches certainly make themselves *w.*
Is. 6. 2. seraphims, each one had six *w.*
Mal. 4. 2. with healing in his *w.*
WINK, Job 15. 12. Ps. 35. 19. Prov. 6. 13; 10. 10.
    Acts 17. 30.
WINTER, Sol. 2. 11. Zech. 14. 8.
WISE, Gen. 41. 39. Ex. 23. 8. Deut. 16. 19.
Job 11. 12. vain man would be *w.*
32. 9. great men are not always *w.*
Ps. 2. 10. be *w.* . . . ., O ye kings; be instructed
19. 7. making *w.* the simple
107. 43. whoso is *w.* and will observe
Prov. 3. 7. be not *w.* in thine own eyes
3. 35. the *w.* shall inherit glory
13. 20. walketh with *w.* men shall be *w.*
26. 12. a man *w.* in his own conceit
Eccl. 7. 4. heart of *w.* is in house of
9. 1. the *w.* and their work are in hand of God
Is. 5. 21. are *w.* in their own eyes
Jer. 4. 22. they are *w.* to do evil
Dan. 12. 3. *w.* shall shine as brightness
Hos. 14. 9. who is *w.* and he shall
Mat. 10. 16. be ye therefore *w.* as serpents
11. 25. hid these things from the *w.*
Rom. 1. 22. professing themselves to be *w.*
16. 19. be *w.* to that which is good
1 Cor. 3. 18. seemeth to be *w.* in this world
4. 10. but ye are *w.* in Christ
Eph. 5. 15. not as fools but as *w.*
Mat. 10. 42. *in no wise* lose his reward
Luke 18. 17. shall—enter therein
John 6. 37. cometh to me I will—cast out
Rev. 21. 27. shall—enter into it
Deut. 4. 6. this is your *wisdom*
1 Ki. 4. 29. God gave Solomon *w.*, 5. 12.
Job 28. 28. fear of Lord, that is *w.*
Prov. 4. 5. get *w.*, get understanding
7. *w.* is the principal thing, ch. 8.
16. 16. better is it to get *w.* than gold
19. 8. he that getteth *w.* loveth his own soul
23. 4. cease from thine own *w.*
23. buy truth . . . also *w.*, and instruction
Eccl. 1. 18. in much *w.* is much grief
8. 1. a man's *w.* maketh his face
Mat. 11. 19. *w.* is justified of her
1 Cor. 1. 17. not with *w.* of words
24. Christ the . . . *w.* of God, Luke 11. 49.
30. who of God is made unto us *w.*
2. 6. we speak *w.* among them that are perfect
3. 19. *w.* of this world is foolishness
2 Cor. 1. 12. not with fleshly *w.*
Col. 1. 9. in all *w.* and spiritual understanding
Jas. 1. 5. if any of you lack *w.* let him ask of God
3. 17. *w.* from above is first pure, then peaceable
Rev. 5. 12. worthy is the Lamb to receive *w.*
13. 18. here is *w.*, 17. 9.

Ps. 111. 10. *of wisdom*, Prov. 9. 10; 10. 21. Mic.
    6. 9. Col. 2. 3. Jas. 3. 13.
64. 9. *wisely*, 101. 2. Eccl. 7. 10.
1 Ki. 4. 31. *wiser*, Job 35. 11. Ps. 119. 98.
    Luke 16. 8. 1 Cor. 1. 25.
WITCH, Ex. 22. 18. Deut. 18. 10.
1 Sam. 15. 23. *witchcraft*, Gal. 5. 20.
WITHDRAW, Job. 9. 13; 33. 17. Prov. 25. 17.
    Sol. 5. 6. 2 Thes. 3. 6. 1 Tim. 6. 5.
WITHHOLD not thy mercies, Ps. 40. 11.
Ps. 84. 11. no good thing will he *w.*
Prov. 3. 27. *w.* no good from them
23. 13. *w.* not correction from child
Job 42. 2. *withholden*, Jer. 5. 25.
Prov. 11. 24, 26. *withholdeth*, 2 Thes. 2. 6.
Gen. 20. 6. *withheld*, 22. 12. Job 31. 16.
WITHIN, Ps. 40. 8; 45. 13. Mat. 3. 9; 23. 26.
    Mark 7. 21. 2 Cor. 7. 5. Rev. 5. 1.
WITHOUT, Prov. 1. 20; 24. 27. 1 Cor. 5. 12.
    2 Cor. 7. 5. Col. 4. 5. Rev. 22. 15.
WITHSTAND, Eccl. 4. 12. Eph. 6. 13.
Acts 11. 17. that I could *w.* God
Gal. 2. 11. *withstood*, 2 Tim. 4. 15.
WITNESS, Gen. 31. 44, 48. Lev. 5. 1.
Num. 35. 30. one *w.* shall not testify, Deut.
    17. 6; 19. 15. 2 Cor. 13. 1.
Judg. 11. 10. Lord be *w.*, 1 Sam. 12. 5. Jer.
    42. 5; 29. 23. Mic. 1. 2. Mal. 2. 14.
Job 16. 19. my *w.* is in heaven
Ps. 89. 37. as a faithful *w.* in heaven
Is. 55. 4. him for a *w.* to the people
Mal. 3. 4. I will be a swift *w.* against
John 3. 11. ye receive not our *w.* 5. 36. greater *w.*
5. 37. Father . . . borne *w.* of me
Acts 14. 17. left not himself without *w.*
1 John 5. 10. that believeth on Son of God hath *w.*
Rev. 1. 5. Christ, who is the faithful *w.*, 3. 14.
20. 4. beheaded for *w.* of Jesus
Deut. 17. 6. two or three *witnesses*, 19. 15. 2 Cor.
    13. 1. Mat. 18. 16. Heb. 10. 28. 1 Tim. 5. 19.
    Num. 35. 30.
Josh. 24. 22. *w.* against yourselves
Is. 43. 10. my *w.*, saith the Lord, 12; 44. 8.
1 Thes. 2. 10. ye are *w.* and God also
1 Tim. 6. 12. a good profession before many *w.*
Heb. 12. 1. so great a cloud of *w.*
Rev. 11. 3. power to my two *w.*
WIZARDS, Lev. 19. 31; 20. 6. Is. 8. 19.
WOLF, Is. 11. 6; 65. 25. Jer. 5. 6.
Ezek. 22. 27. *wolves*, Hab. 1. 8. Zeph. 3. 3. Mat.
    7. 15; 10. 16. Acts 20. 29.
WOMAN, Gen. 2. 23; 3. 15. Lev. 18. 22, 23;
    20. 13. Num. 30. 3.
Prov. 11. 16. gracious *w.* retaineth honour
Ps. 48. 6. pain as of a *w.* in travail, Is. 13. 8;
    21. 3; 26. 17; 42. 14. Jer. 4. 31; 6. 24; 13. 21;
    22. 23; 30. 6; 31. 8; 48. 41; 49. 22, 24;
    50. 43.
Prov. 12. 4. a virtuous *w.* is a crown
14. 1. every wise *w.* buildeth her house
31. 10. who can find a virtuous *w.*?
30. *w.* that feareth Lord, she shall be praised
Eccl. 7. 26. *w.* whose heart is snares
28. among all have I not found
Is. 49. 15. can *w.* forget her sucking child
54. 6. called thee as a *w.* forsaken
Jer. 31. 22. *w.* shall compass a man
Mat. 5. 28. looketh on a *w.* to lust
John 2. 4. *w.*, what have I to do with
8. 3. brought unto him a *w.* taken in adultery
19. 26. *w.*, behold thy son
Rom. 1. 27. the natural use of *w.*
1 Cor. 11. 7. *w.* is the glory of man

Gal. 4. 4. sent forth his Son, made of a *woman*
1 Tim. 2. 11. let *w.* learn in silence with
12. I suffer not *w.* to teach
Rev. 12. 1. *w.* clothed with sun, 6, 16.
17. 18. *w.* which thou sawest is that great city
Judg. 5. 24. blessed above *women* shall Jael
Prov. 31. 3. give not thy strength to *w.*
Sol. 1. 8. fairest among *w.*, 5. 9; 6. 1.
Is. 3. 12. *w.* rule over them
32. 11. tremble, ye *w.* that are at ease
Jer. 9. 17. call for the mourning *w.*
Lam. 4. 10. *w.* have sodden their own children
Mat. 11. 11. among them that are born of *w.*
Luke 1. 28. blessed art thou among *w.*
Rom. 1. 26. *w.* did change the natural use
1 Cor. 14. 34. let *w.* keep silence
1 Tim. 2. 9. *w.* adorn themselves in modest apparel
5. 14. that the younger *w.* marry
2 Tim. 3. 6. lead captive silly *w.*
1 Pet. 3. 5. in the old time holy *w.*
Rev. 14. 4. were not defiled with *w.*
WOMB, Gen. 25. 23; 29. 31.
Gen. 49. 25. blessings . . . of the *w.*
Ps. 22. 9. took me out of the *w.*
10. I was cast upon thee from *w.*
127. 3. fruit of the *w.* is his reward
Ps. 139. 13. covered me in my mother's *w.*
Eccl. 11. 5. how the bones do grow in the *w.*
Is. 44. 2. (Lord) formed thee from *w.*
66. 9. to bring forth, and shut *w.*
Hos. 9. 14. give them a miscarrying *w.*
Luke 1. 42. blessed is fruit of thy *w.*
11. 27. blessed is *w.* that bare thee
23. 29. blessed are *wombs* that never
WONDER, Deut. 13. 1; 28. 46. Ps. 71. 7. Is. 29. 14.
Rev. 12. 1.
Acts 13. 41. *w.* and perish, Hab. 1. 5.
Zech. 3. 8. they are men *wondered* at
Is. 59. 16. *w.* was no intercessor
Luke 4. 22. *w.* at the gracious words
Deut. 28. 59. thy plagues *wonderful*
Job 42. 3. things too *w.* for me
Ps. 119. 129. thy testimonies are *w.*
139. 6. such knowledge is too *w.*
Prov. 30. 18. three things which are too *w.* for
Is. 9. 6. his name shall be called *W.*
25. 1. thou hast done *w.* things
Jer. 5. 30. a *w.* and horrible thing is committed
Ps. 139. 14. *wonderfully,* Lam. 1. 9.
Ex. 3. 20. *wonders,* 7. 3; 15. 11.
Job 9. 10. God doeth *w.,* Ps. 77. 11, 14.
Ps. 78. 11. forgat . . . his *w.,* Neh. 9. 17.
88. 10. wilt thou shew *w.* to the dead?
136. 4. who alone doeth great *w.*
Dan. 12. 6. how long . . . to end of these *w.?*
Joel. 2. 30. shew *w.* in heavens, Acts 2. 19.
John 4. 48. except ye see signs and *w.*
Acts 2. 43. many *w.* and signs were done, 6. 8.
Rom. 15. 19. mighty signs and *w.*
Rev. 13. 13. he doeth great *w.*
Job 37. 14. *wondrous* works, Ps. 26. 7; 71. 17;
75. 1; 78. 32; 105. 2; 106. 22; 119. 27; 145. 5.
Ps. 72. 18. *w.* things, 86. 10; 119. 18.
Judg. 13. 19. *wondrously,* Joel 2. 26.
WOOD, hay, stubble, 1 Cor. 3. 12.
2 Tim. 2. 20. also of *w.* and of earth
WORD, Num. 23. 5. Deut. 4. 2.
Deut. 8. 3. every *w.* . . . . of God, Mat. 4. 4.
30. 14. *w.* is very nigh, Rom. 10. 8.
Ps. 68. 11. the Lord gave the *w.*
119. 49. remember the *w.* to thy servant
Prov. 15. 23. *w.* spoken in due season
25. 11. a *w.* fitly spoken is like apples

Is. 29. 21. an offender for a *word*
30. 21. shall hear a *w.* behind thee
44. 26. confirmeth *w.* of his servant
50. 4. how to speak a *w.* in season
Jer. 5. 13. the *w.* is not in them
Mat. 8. 8. speak the *w.* only and my
12. 36. every idle *w.* that men
Luke 4. 36. what a *w.* is this
John 1. 1. in beginning was the *W.*
14. the *W.* was made flesh
15. 3. ye are clean through the *w.*
Acts 13. 15. any *w.* of exhortation
26. to you is *w.* of this salvation sent
17. 11. the *w.* with all readiness
20. 32. and to the *w.* of his grace
1 Cor. 4. 20. kingdom of God is not in *w.*
Gal. 6. 6. taught in *w.* communicate
Eph. 5. 26. washing of water by *w.*
Col. 3. 16. let *w.* of Christ dwell in
17. whatsoever ye do in *w.* or deed
2 Thes. 2. 17. stablish you in every good *w.*
3. 14. if any obey not our *w.*
1 Tim. 5. 17. labour in *w.* and doctrine
Tit. 1. 9. holding fast the faithful *w.*
Heb. 4. 2. the *w.* preached did not
5. 13. is unskilful in *w.* of righteousness
13. 22. suffer the *w.* of exhortation
Jas. 1. 21. receive with meekness the engrafted *w.*
3. 2. if any man offend not in *w.*
1 Pet. 3. 1. if any obey not the *w.*
2 Pet. 1. 19. sure *w.* of prophecy
1 John 1. 1. hands have handled of the *W.*
Rev. 3. 10. kept *w.* of my patience
12. 11. overcame by *w.* of their testimony
Ps. 130. 5. in *his word* do I hope, 119. 81.
147. 19. sheweth—unto Jacob
Jer. 20. 9.—was in mine heart as fire
John 5. 38. have not—abiding in you
Acts 2. 41. that gladly received—
John 8. 31. *my word,* 43. Rev. 3. 8.
Is. 8. 20. *this word,* Rom. 9. 9.
Ps. 119. 11. *thy word* have I hid in mine heart
50. for—hath quickened me
105.—is a lamp unto my feet
140.—is very pure. 160.—is true
138. 2. magnified—above all thy
Jer. 15. 16.—was unto me joy and
John 17. 6. they have kept—17.—is truth
Prov. 30. 5. *word of God,* Is. 40. 8. Mark 7. 13.
Rom. 10. 17. 1 Thes. 2. 13. Heb. 4. 12; 6. 5.
1 Pet. 1. 23. Rev. 19. 13.
2 Ki. 20. 19. *word of the Lord,* Ps. 18. 30; 33. 4.
2 Thes. 3. 1. 1 Pet. 1. 25.
Ps. 119. 43. *word of truth,* 2 Cor. 6. 7. Eph. 1. 13.
Col. 1. 5. 2 Tim. 2. 15. Jas. 1. 18.
Job 23. 12. esteemed *words* of his mouth
Prov. 15. 26. *w.* of the pure are pleasant *w.*
19. 7. he pursueth them with *w.*
22. 17. bow down thine ear, hear *w.*
Eccl. 10. 12. the *w.* of a wise man's mouth
12. 10. to find out acceptable *w.*
11. *w.* of the wise are as goads
Jer. 7. 4. trust ye not in lying *w.*
44. 28. know whose *w.* shall stand
Dan. 7. 25. speak great *w.* against most High
Jos. 6. 5. slain them by *w.* of my mouth
14. 2. take with you *w.*
Zech. 1. 13. good *w.* and comfortable *w.*
Mat. 26. 44. prayed third time, saying same *w.*
Luke 4. 22. the gracious *w.* which proceeded out
of his mouth
Acts 7. 22. (Moses) . . . mighty in *w.* and
15. 24. troubled you with *w.,* 18. 15.

20. 35. remember the *words* of Lord
26. 25. speak forth the *w.* of truth and soberness
1 Cor. 2. 4. not with enticing *w.* of
2 Tim. 1. 13. hold fast form of sound *w.*
2. 14. strive not about *w.* to no profit
Rev. 1. 3. hear *w.* of this prophecy, 22. 18.
Ps. 50. 17. *my words*, Is. 51. 16; 59. 21. Jer.
5. 14. Mic. 2. 7. Mark 8. 38; 13. 31. John
5. 47; 15. 7.
1 Thes. 4. 18. *these words*, Rev. 21. 5.
Ps. 119. 103. *thy words*, 130, 139. Prov. 23. 8.
Eccl. 5. 2. Ezek. 33. 31. Mat. 12. 37.
WORK, Gen. 2. 3. Ex. 20. 10; 31. 14.
Deut. 33. 11. accept *w.* of his hands
Job 1. 10. blessed the *w.* of his hands
10. 3. despise the *w.* of thine hands
14. 15. a desire to *w.* of thine hands
36. 9. he sheweth them their *w.*
Ps. 8. 3. heavens, *w.* of thy fingers
9. 16. wicked is snared in *w.*
101. 3. I hate the *w.* of them that
143. 5. muse on *w.* of thy hands
Eccl. 8. 14. according to *w.* of the wicked
8. 17. I beheld all the *w.* of God
12. 14. God shall bring every *w.* into judgment
Is. 10. 12. performed his whole *w.*
28. 21. do his *w.*, his strange *w.*
29. 16. shall *w.* say of him that
45. 11. concerning *w.* of my hands
49. 4. my *w.* with my God
64. 8. we all are the *w.* of thy hand
Jer. 10. 15. vanity and *w.* of errors
18. 3. potter wrought a *w.* on the
John 17. 4. finished *w.* which thou gavest
Acts 5. 38. if this *w.* be of men
13. 2. for the *w.* whereto I have called
Rom. 2. 15. shew *w.* of law written
11. 6. otherwise *w.* is no more *w.*
1 Cor. 3. 13. every man's *w.* shall be made
9. 1. are not ye my *w.* in the Lord?
Eph. 4. 12. for *w.* of the ministry
2 Thes. 1. 11. *w.* of faith with power
2. 17. stablish you in every good *w.*
2 Tim. 4. 5. do *w.* of an evangelist
Jas. 1. 4. let patience have her perfect *w.*
25. doer of the *w.* this man shall be blessed
1 Pet. 1. 17. judgeth according to every man's *w.*
Ps. 104. 23. *his work*, 62. 12; 111. 3. Prov. 24. 29.
Is. 40. 10. Job 36. 24.
90. 16. *thy work*, 92. 4. Prov. 24. 27. Jer. 31. 16.
Hab. 3. 2.
Ex. 32. 16. *work of God*, Ps. 64. 9. Eccl. 7. 13;
8. 17. John 6. 29. Rom. 14. 20.
Ps. 28. 5. *work of the Lord*, Is. 5. 12. Jer. 48. 10.
1 Cor. 15. 58; 16. 10.
17. 4. concerning *works* of men
92. 4. triumph in *w.* of thy hands
111. 7. *w.* of his hands are verity
138. 8. forsake not *w.* of thine own hands
Prov. 31. 31. let her own *w.* praise
Is. 26. 12. wrought all our *w.* in us
Dan. 4. 37. all whose *w.* are truth
John 5. 20. shew him greater *w.*
10. 32. of those *w.* do ye stone me?
38. believe the *w.*
14. 11. believe me for the very *w.* sake
12. greater *w.* than these shall he do
Acts 26. 20. *w.* meet for repentance
Rom. 3. 27. by what law? of *w.*? nay: but by the
law of faith
4. 6. God imputeth righteousness without *w.*
9. 11. not of *w.* but of him that calleth
32. but as it were by *w.* of the law

Rom. 11. 6. then is it no more of *works*
Gal. 2. 16. by *w.* of law no flesh be
3. 10. as many as are of the *w.* of the law
5. 19. *w.* of the flesh are manifest
Eph. 2. 9. not of *w.* 10. to good *w.*
5. 11. unfruitful *w.* of darkness
Col. 1. 21. enemies in your mind by wicked *w.*
1 Thes. 5. 13. esteem them . . . for their *w's.* sake
2 Tim. 1. 9. not according to our *w.*
Tit. 1. 16. in *w.* they deny him
3. 5. not by *w.* or righteousness which
Heb. 6. 1. repentance from dead *w.*
9. 14. conscience from dead *w.*
Jas. 2. 14. and have not *w.*
21. justified by *w.*, 24, 25.
22. by *w.* was faith made perfect
1 John 3. 8. he might destroy *w.* of
Rev. 9. 20. repented not of the *w.* of
18. 6. according to her *w.*, 20. 12, 13.
Ps. 33. 4. *his works*, 78. 11; 103. 22; 104. 31;
107. 15, 22; 145. 9, 17. Dan. 9. 14. Acts 15. 18.
Heb. 4. 10.
Ps. 106. 35. *their works*, Is. 66. 18. Jonah 3. 10.
Mat. 23. 3, 5. 2 Cor. 11. 15. Rev. 14. 13;
20. 12, 13.
Deut. 15. 10. *thy works*, Ps. 66. 3; 73. 28; 92. 5;
104. 24; 143. 5. Prov. 16. 3. Eccl. 9. 7. Rev.
2. 13.
Ps. 40. 5. *wonderful works*, 78. 4; 107. 8; 111. 4.
Mat. 7. 22. Acts 2. 11.
Job 37. 14. *works of God*, Ps. 66. 5; 78. 7. Eccl.
11. 5. John 6. 28; 9. 3.
Ps. 46. 8. *w.* of the Lord, 111. 2.
1 Sam. 14. 6. the Lord will *work* for us
Ps. 119. 126. time for thee, O Lord, to *w.*
Is. 43. 13. I will *w.* and who shall
John 6. 28. might *w.* works of God
9. 4. I must *w.* the works of him
1 Thes. 4. 11. to *w.* with your hands
2 Thes. 2. 7. iniquity doth already *w.*
3. 10. if any would not *w.*, neither should he eat
Prov. 11. 18. wicked *worketh* a deceitful *w.*
Is. 64. 5. meetest him that . . . *w.* righteousness
John 5. 17. my Father *w.* hitherto, and I *w.*
Acts 10. 35. that *w.* righteousness is
Rom. 4. 4. to him that *w.* is reward
1 Cor. 12. 6. same God which *w.* all
2 Cor. 4. 17. *w.* for us a far more
Gal. 5. 6. faith which *w.* by love
Eph. 1. 11. *w.* all things according
Phil. 2. 13. it is God which *w.* in you
1 Thes. 2. 13. effectually *w.* also in you
Is. 28. 29. excellent in *working*
Rom. 7. 13. sin *w.* death in me
Eph. 1. 19. according to *w.* of his mighty
3. 7. by effectual *w.* of his power
4. 28. *w.* with his hands the thing
Phil. 3. 21. according to *w.* whereby
2 Thes. 3. 11. *w.* not at all, but are
Heb. 13. 21. *w.* in you that which is well pleasing
2 Cor. 6. 1. *workers*, 11. 13. Phil. 3. 2.
Job 31. 3. *workers of iniquity*, 34. 8, 22. Ps. 5. 5;
6. 8; 28. 3; 125. 5; 141. 9. Prov. 10. 29; 21. 15.
Mat. 10. 10. *workman*, 2 Tim. 2. 15.
Ex. 31. 3. *workmanship*, Eph. 2. 10.
WORLD, 1 Sam. 2. 8. 1 Chr. 16. 30.
Ps. 17. 14. from men of this *world*
24. I *w.* and they that dwell therein, 9. 8. Nah. 1. 5.
50. 12. *w.* is mine and the fulness
Eccl. 3. 11. hath set *w.* in their heart
Is. 26. 9. inhabitants of *w.* will learn
Jer. 10. 12. established the *w.* by his wisdom,
51. 15. Ps. 93. 1; 96. 10.

Mat. 16. 26. what is a man profited if he shall gain the whole *world* and lose his own soul? Mark 8. 36.
18. 7. woe to *w*. because of offences
24. 3. what shall be . . . the end of *w*.
Mark 16. 15. go ye into all the *w*. and
Luke 20. 35. worthy to obtain that *w*.
John 1. 29. Lamb of God which taketh away sin of *w*.
3. 16. God so loved the *w*. that he gave
17. *w*. through him might be saved
7. 7. the *w*. cannot hate you, but
12. 47. not to judge *w*. but to save *w*.
14. 17. whom *w*. cannot receive
19. *w*. seeth me no more; but ye
31. *w*. may know that I love the Father
15. 18. if the *w*. hate you, ye know that it hated
19. chosen you out of the *w*., therefore the *w*.
16. 28. I leave *w*. and go to the Father
17. 9. I pray not for the *w*.
11. I am no more in the *w*., but these
John 17. 16. not of *w*., even as I am not of *w*.
17. 18. thou hast sent me into the *w*.
23. *w*. may know that thou hast sent
Rom. 3. 19. all the *w*. may become guilty
1 Cor. 1. 21. *w*. by wisdom knew not
Gal. 6. 14. *w*. is crucified unto me
Col. 1. 6. as it is in all *w*.; and bringeth
Tit. 1. 2. promised before *w*. began
Heb. 2. 5. *w*. to come, 6. 5.
11. 38. the *w*. was not worthy
1 John 2. 2. propitiation . . . for sins of the *w*.
17. *w*. passeth away and the lust
3. 1. the *w*. knoweth us not
4. 5. they are of the *w*. therefore speak they of the *w*. and the *w*. heareth them
5. 19. whole *w*. lieth in wickedness
Rev. 3. 10. temptation shall come on all *w*.
13. 3. all *w*. wondered after beast
Mat. 12. 32. *this world*, John 8. 23; 13. 1. Rom. 12. 2. 1 Tim. 6. 7.
Heb. 1. 2. he made the *worlds*
11. 3. the *w*. were framed by him
WORM, Ex. 16. 20. Is. 51. 8.
Job 25. 6. man that is a *w*.
Ps. 22. 6. I am a *w*. and no man   [Israel
Is. 41. 14. fear not, thou *w*. Jacob, and ye men of
66. 24. their *w*. shall not die, Mark 9. 44, 48.
Job 19. 26. *worms* destroy body, Acts 12. 23.
WORMWOOD, Deut. 29. 18. Prov. 5. 4. Lam. 3. 15, 19. Amos 5. 7. Rev. 8. 11.
WORSE, Gen. 19. 9. Jer. 7. 26. Mat. 12. 45. John 5. 14. 1 Cor. 8. 8; 11. 17. 2 Tim. 3. 13. 2 Pet. 2. 20.
WORSHIP the Lord in beauty of holiness, 1 Chr. 16. 29. Ps. 29. 2; 66. 4; 96. 9; 45. 11; 95. 6; 99. 5. Mat. 4. 10.
Mat. 15. 9. in vain do they *w*. me
John 4. 24. *w*. him must *w*. him in spirit
Acts 17. 23. whom therefore ye ignorantly *w*.
24. 14. so *w*. I the God of my fathers
Rev. 3. 9. *w*. before thy feet
13. 12. causeth earth . . . to *w*. first beast
19. 10. to *w*. God, 22. 9.
Ex. 4. 31. *worshipped*, 32. 8. Jer. 1. 16. 1 Chr. 29. 20. Rom. 1. 25. 2 Thes. 2. 4. Rev. 5. 14; 7. 11; 11. 16; 13. 4.
WORTH, Job 24. 25. Prov. 10. 20.
Gen. 32. 10. I am not *worthy* of least
Mat. 8. 8. I am not *w*. . . . under my roof
10. 10. workman is *w*. of his meat
13. if house be *w*. let your peace
22. 8. which were bidden were not *w*.

Luke 3. 8. fruits *worthy* of repentance
7. 4. *w*. for whom he should do this
10. 7. labourer is *w*. of his hire
15. 19. no more *w*. to be called thy son, 21.
20. 35. counted *w*. to obtain
21. 36. *w*. to escape all these things
Acts 5. 41. counted *w*. to suffer shame
Rom. 8. 18. not *w*. to be compared
Eph. 4. 1. walk *w*. of the vocation
1 Thes. 2. 12. walk *w*. of God, who
2 Thes. 1. 5. *w*. of the kingdom of God
11. God would count you *w*. of this calling
1 Tim. 1. 15. *w*. of all acceptation, 4. 9.
5. 18. labourer is *w*. of his reward
6. 1. count their masters *w*. of all honour
Heb. 3. 3. *w*. of more glory than Moses
10. 29. of how much sorer punishment shall he be thought *w*.   [*worthy*
Rev. 3. 4. in white, for they are
5. 12. *w*. is the Lamb that was slain
16. 6. blood to drink; for they are *w*.
WOULD God, Ex. 16. 3. Num. 11. 29. Acts 26. 29. 1 Cor. 4. 8. 2 Cor. 11. 1.
Ps. 81. 11. Israel *w*. none of me
Prov. 1. 25. *w*. none of my reproof
30. they *w*. none of my counsel
Mat. 7. 12. whatsoever ye *w*. that men should do
Rom. 7. 15. what I *w*., that I do not, 19.
Gal. 5. 17. cannot do the things ye *w*.
Rev. 3. 15. I *w*. thou wert cold or hot
Neh. 9. 30. *would not*, Is. 30. 15. Mat. 18. 30; 23. 30, 37. Rom. 11. 25.
WOUND, Ex. 21. 25. Prov. 6. 33. Jer. 10. 19; 15. 18; 30. 12, 14. Mic. 1. 9.
Deut. 32. 39. I *wound* and I heal
1 Cor. 8. 12. *w*. their weak conscience
Rev. 13. 3. his deadly *w*. healed, 14.
Ps. 69. 26. *wounded*, 109. 22. Sol. 5. 7.
Prov. 18. 14. a *w*. spirit who can bear?
Is. 53. 5. *w*. for our transgressions
Job 5. 18. he *woundeth* and his hands
Prov. 27. 6. *wounds*, Is. 1. 6. Jer. 30. 17.
WRATH, Gen. 49. 7. Ex. 32. 10, 11.
Num. 16. 46. *w*. gone out from Lord
Deut. 32. 27. feared *w*. of the enemy
Neh. 13. 18. bring more *w*. on Israel
Job 5. 2. *w*. killeth the foolish man
Ps. 76. 10. *w*. of man shall praise thee
Is. 54. 8. in a little *w*. I hid my face
Hab. 3. 2. in *w*. remember mercy
Mat. 3. 7. flee from *w*. to come
Rom. 2. 5. treasurest up . . . *w*. against day of *w*.
5. 9. saved from *w*. through him
12. 19. give place unto *w*.
13. 5. not only for *w*. but also for conscience
Eph. 2. 3. by nature children of *w*.
4. 26. let not sun go down on your *w*.
1 Thes. 1. 10. delivered us from *w*. to come
5. 9. not appointed us to *w*.
1 Tim. 2. 8. holy hands without *w*.
Heb. 11. 27. not fearing *w*. of king
Jas. 1. 19. slow to speak, slow to *w*.
20. *w*. of man worketh not righteousness of God
Rev. 6. 16. from *w*. of Lamb
14. 8. wine of *w*. of her fornication, 18. 3.
Ezra 8. 22. *his wrath*, Ps. 2. 5, 12; 78. 38. Jer. 7. 29; 10. 10. Rev. 6. 17.
Num. 25. 11. *my wrath*, Ps. 95. 11. Is. 10. 6; 60. 10. Ezek. 7. 14. Hos. 5. 10.
Ps. 38. 1. *thy wrath*, 85. 3; 88. 7, 16; 89. 46; 90. 9, 11; 102. 10.
89. 38. *wroth*, Is. 54. 9; 57. 17.
WREST, Ex. 23. 2. 2 Pet. 3. 16.

WRESTLE, Gen. 32. 24, 25. Eph. 6. 12.
WRETCHED, Rom. 7. 24. Rev. 3. 17.
WRINKLE, Job 16. 8. Eph. 5. 27.
WRITE, Ex. 34. 1, 27. Deut. 27. 3. Is. 8. 1. Jer.
    30. 2. Hab. 2. 2.
    Deut. 6. 9. *w*. them upon the posts
    Prov. 3. 3. *w*. them on table of thine heart, 7. 3.
    1 John 2. 1. little children, these things *w*. I unto
       you that ye sin not, 12.
    7. I *w*. no new commandment unto you
    8. a new commandment I *w*. unto you
    13. I *w*. unto you, fathers . . . I *w*. to you, young
       men . . . I *w*. to you, little children
    Ps. 69. 28. not be *written* with the
    102. 18. be *w*. for the generation
    Prov. 22. 20. have not I *w*. to thee
    Eccl. 12. 10. that which was *w*.
    1 Cor. 10. 11. *w*. for our admonition
    2 Cor. 3. 2. epistle *w*. in our hearts
    3 *w*. not with ink but with the Spirit
    Heb. 12. 23. are *w*. in heaven, Luke 10. 20.
    1 John 2. 14. I have *w*. to you, fathers . . . I have
       w. to you, young men
    21. I have not *w*. unto you because ye
    26. these things have I *w*. unto you
WRONG, Ps. 105. 14. Jer. 22. 3, 13.
    1 Cor. 6. 7. why do ye not rather take *w*., 8.
    Col. 3. 25. he that doeth *w*. shall receive
    2 Cor. 7. 2. *wronged*, Philem. 18.
    Prov. 8. 36. *wrongeth* his own soul
WROUGHT, 1 Sam. 6. 6; 14. 45.
    Ps. 139. 15. curiously *w*.
    Is. 26. 12. *w*. all our works in us
    Ezek. 20. 9. I *w*. for my name's sake, 22.
    John 3. 21. that they are *w*. in God
    Rom. 7. 8. *w*. in me all manner of concupiscence
    2 Cor. 5. 5. that hath *w*. us for selfsame thing is
       God
    1 Pet. 4. 3. have *w*. will of Gentiles

Y

YEA, yea, nay, nay, Mat. 5. 37.
    2 Cor. 1. 18. *y*. and nay, 20. *y*. and in him amen
YEAR, acceptable, Is. 61. 2. Luke 4. 19.
    Is. 63. 4. *y*. of my redeemed is come
    Jer. 11. 23. *y*. of their visitation, 23. 12; 48. 44.
    Job 10. 5. thy *years* as man's days
    Ps. 90. 4. a thousand *y*. in thy sight
    2 Pet. 3. 8. a thousand *y*. as one day
    Rev. 20. 2. bound him a thousand *y*., 3.
YESTERDAY, Job 8. 9. Heb. 13. 8.
YIELD yourselves, 2 Chr. 30. 8.
    Ps. 67. 6. earth *y*. her increase, 85. 12.
    Rom. 6. 13. neither *y*. ye your members as
       instruments . . . but *y*. yourselves

    Rom. 6. 16. whom ye *yield* yourselves
    19. *yielded* members servants
    Heb. 12. 11. *yieldeth* peaceable fruit
YOKE, Deut. 28. 48. 1 Ki. 12. 4.
    Is. 9. 4. broken the *y*. of his burden
    10. 27. the *y*. shall be destroyed
    Lam. 1. 14. *y*. of my transgressions
    Mat. 11. 29. take my *y*. upon you
    11. 30. my *y*. is easy and my burden is light
    Gal. 5. 1. *y*. of bondage, Acts 15. 10.
    2 Cor. 6. 14. be ye not unequally *yoked*
YOU only have I known, Amos 3. 2.
    Luke 10. 16. despiseth *y*. despiseth me
    13. 28. and *y*. yourselves thrust out
    2 Cor. 12. 14. I seek not yours but *y*.
    Eph. 2. 1. *y*. hath he quickened
    Col. 1. 21. *y*. that were sometime alienated and
       enemies in your mind
    Luke 6. 20. *yours* is the kingdom of God
YOUNG, I have been, Ps. 37. 25.
    Is. 40. 11. gently lead those that are with *y*.
    1 Tim. 5. 1. and the *younger* men
    14. I will therefore that *y*. women marry
    1 Pet. 5. 5. ye *y*. submit yourselves to elder
    Gen. 8. 21. the imagination of man is evil from
       his *youth*
    1 Ki. 18. 12. fear the Lord from my *y*.
    Job 13. 26. possess iniquities of my *y*.
    Ps. 25. 7. sins of my *y*.
    Eccl. 11. 9. Rejoice, O young man, in thy *y*.
    10. childhood and *y*. are vanity
    Jer. 2. 2. the kindness of thy *y*.
    1 Tim. 4. 12. let no man despise thy *y*.
    2 Tim. 2. 22. flee *youthful* lusts
    Prov. 7. 7. *youths*, Is. 40. 30.

Z

ZEAL for Lord, 2 Ki. 10. 16.
    Ps. 69. 9. the *z*. of thine house hath
    119. 139. my *z*. hath consumed me
    Is. 9. 7. *z*. of the Lord of hosts will perform
    59. 17. and was clad with *z*. as a cloak
    63. 15. where is thy *z*. and thy strength
    Rom. 10. 2. they have a *z*. of God
    Phil. 3. 6. concerning *z*., persecuting
    Num. 25. 13. was *zealous* for his God
    Acts 22. 3. and was *z*. toward God as
    Tit. 2. 14. people *z*. of good works
    Rev. 3. 19. be *z*. therefore and repent
    Gal. 4. 18. *zealously* affected always in a
ZION, 2 Sam. 5. 7. 1 Ki. 8. 1. for Jerusalem,
    temple, or church, 2 Ki. 19. 31. Ps. 2. 6;
    9. 11; 14. 7; 48. 2, 11, 12; 146. 10; 147. 12.
    Is. 1. 27; 2. 3; 60. 14; 62. 1, and in about
    seventy other places